The
World
Factbook

The
World
Factbook
1991-92

**Central
Intelligence
Agency**

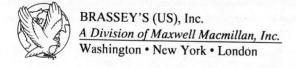

BRASSEY'S (US), Inc.
A Division of Maxwell Macmillan, Inc.
Washington • New York • London

First Brassey's Edition 1992

Brassey's (US), Inc.

Editorial Offices
Brassey's (US), Inc.
8000 Westpark Drive
First Floor
McLean, Virginia 22102

Order Department
Brassey's Book Orders
c/o Macmillan Publishing Co.
100 Front Street, Box 500
Riverside, New Jersey 08075

Brassey's (US), Inc. books are available at special discounts for bulk purchases for sales promotions, premiums, fund-raising, or educational use through the Special Sales Director, Macmillan Publishing Company, 866 Third Avenue, New York, New York 10022.

ISSN 0277-1527

ISBN 0-02-881033-3

The World Factbook is produced annually by the Central Intelligence Agency for the use of U.S. government officials; and the style, format, coverage, and content are designed to meet their specific requirements. Information was provided by the Bureau of the Census, CIA, Defense Intelligence Agency, Defense Nuclear Agency, Department of State, Foreign Broadcast Information Service, Maritime Administration, National Science Foundation (Polar Information Program), Navy Operational Intelligence Center, Office of Territorial and International Affairs, U.S. Board of Geographic Names, U.S. Coast Guard, and others.

Printed in the United States of America

Publisher's Note

Brassey's (US), Inc. has commercially published *The World Factbook* to extend the limited audience recently reached through publication by the U.S. Central Intelligence Agency. We are pleased to contribute to a wider dissemination of this excellent volume by using the worldwide sales and distribution system of our parent New York company, Macmillan Publishing.

Contents

Notes, Definitions, and Abbreviations

There have been some significant changes in this edition. The Literacy entry now includes rates for males, females, and both sexes. Appendix C: International Organizations and Groups is new and includes date established, aim, and list of members.

Abbreviations: (see Appendix B for international organizations and groups)

avdp.	avoirdupois
c.i.f.	cost, insurance, and freight
CY	calendar year
DWT	deadweight ton
est.	estimate
Ex-Im	Export-Import Bank of the United States
f.o.b.	free on board
FRG	Federal Republic of Germany (West Germany); used for information dated before 3 October 1990 or CY91
FY	fiscal year
GDP	gross domestic product
GDR	German Democratic Republic (East Germany); used for information dated before 3 October 1990 or CY91
GNP	gross national product
GRT	gross register ton
km	kilometer
km²	square kilometer
kW	kilowatt
kWh	kilowatt-hour
m	meter
NA	not available
NEGL	negligible
nm	nautical mile
NZ	New Zealand
ODA	official development assistance
OOF	other official flows
PDRY	People's Democratic Republic of Yemen [Yemen (Aden) or South Yemen]; used for information dated before 22 May 1990 or CY91
UAE	United Arab Emirates
UK	United Kingdom
US	United States
USSR	Union of Soviet Socialist Republics (Soviet Union)
YAR	Yemen Arab Republic [Yemen (Sanaa) or North Yemen]; used for information dated before 22 May 1990 or CY91

Administrative divisions: The numbers, designatory terms, and first-order administrative divisions are generally those approved by the United States Board on Geographic Names (BGN). Changes that have been reported but not yet acted upon by BGN are noted.

Area: Total area is the sum of all land and water areas delimited by international boundaries and/or coastlines. Land area is the aggregate of all surfaces delimited by international boundaries and/or coastlines, excluding inland water bodies (lakes, reservoirs, rivers).

Comparative areas are based on total area equivalents. Most entities are compared with the entire US or one of the 50 states. The smaller entities are compared with Washington, DC (178 km², 69 miles²) or The Mall in Washington, DC (0.59 km², 0.23 miles², 146 acres).

Birth rate: The average annual number of births during a year per 1,000 population at midyear. Also known as crude birth rate.

Dates of information: In general, information available as of 1 January 1991 was used in the preparation of this edition. Population figures are estimates for 1 July 1991, with population growth rates estimated for mid-1991 through mid-1992. Major political events have been updated through 30 June 1991. Military age figures are average annual estimates for 1991-95.

Death rate: The average annual number of deaths during a year per 1,000 population at midyear. Also known as crude death rate.

Diplomatic representation: The US Government has diplomatic relations with 162 nations. There are only 144 US embassies, since some nations have US ambassadors accredited to them, but no physical US mission exists. The US has diplomatic relations with 151 of the 159 UN members—the exceptions are Angola, Belorussia (Byelorussia; constituent republic of the Soviet Union), Cambodia, Cuba, Iran, Vietnam, Ukraine (constituent republic of the Soviet Union), and, obviously, the US itself. In addition, the US has diplomatic relations with 12 nations that are not in the UN—Andorra, Federated States of Micronesia, Kiribati, Marshall Islands, Monaco, Nauru, San Marino, South Korea, Switzerland, Tonga, Tuvalu, and the Vatican City. North Korea is not in the UN and the US does not have diplomatic relations with that nation. The US has not recognized the incorporation of Estonia, Latvia, and Lithuania into the Soviet Union and continues to accredit the diplomatic representatives of their last free governments.

Disputes: This category includes a wide variety of situations that range from traditional bilateral boundary disputes to unilateral claims of one sort or another. Every international land boundary dispute in the "Guide to International Boundaries," a map published by the Department of State, is included. References to other situations may also be included that are border- or frontier-relevant, such as maritime disputes, geopolitical questions, or irredentist issues. However, inclusion does not necessarily constitute official acceptance or recognition by the US Government.

Economic Aid: This entry refers to bilateral commitments of:
Official Development Assistance (ODA), which is defined as government grants that (a) are administered with the promotion of economic development and welfare of LDCs as their main objective and (b) are concessional in character and contain a grant element of at least 25%; and
Other Official Flows (OOF) or transactions by the official sector whose main objective is other than development-motivated or whose grant element is below the 25% threshold for ODA. OOF transactions include official export credits (such as Eximbank credits), official equity and portfolio investment, and debt reorganization by the official sector that does not meet concessional terms.

Aid is considered to have been committed when agreements are initialed by the parties involved and constitute a formal declaration of intent.

Entities: Some of the nations, dependent areas, areas of special sovereignty, and governments included in this publication are not independent, and others are not officially recognized by the US Government. Nation refers to a people politically organized into a sovereign state with a definite territory. Dependent area refers to a broad category of political entities that are associated in some way with a nation. Names used for page headings are usually the short-form names as approved by the US Board on Geographic Names. The long-form name is included in the Government section and an entry of "none" indicates a long-form name does not exist. In some instances, no short-form name exists—then the long-form name must serve for all usages.
There are 247 entities in the Factbook that may be categorized as follows:

NATIONS
157 UN members (There are 159 members in the UN, but only 157 are included in *The World Factbook* because Belorussia (Byelorussia) and Ukraine are constituent republics of the Soviet Union.)
 13 nations that are not members of the UN—Andorra, Federated States of Micronesia, Kiribati, Marshall Islands, Monaco, Nauru, North Korea, San Marino, South Korea, Switzerland, Tonga, Tuvalu, Vatican City

OTHER
 1 Taiwan

DEPENDENT AREAS
 6 Australia—Ashmore and Cartier Islands, Christmas Island, Cocos (Keeling) Islands, Coral Sea Islands, Heard Island and McDonald Islands, Norfolk Island
 2 Denmark—Faroe Islands, Greenland
 16 France—Bassas da India, Clipperton Island, Europa Island, French Guiana, French Polynesia, French Southern and Antarctic Lands, Glorioso Islands, Guadeloupe, Juan de Nova Island, Martinique, Mayotte, New Caledonia, Reunion, Saint Pierre and Miquelon, Tromelin Island, Wallis and Futuna
 2 Netherlands—Aruba, Netherlands Antilles
 3 New Zealand—Cook Islands, Niue, Tokelau
 3 Norway—Bouvet Island, Jan Mayen, Svalbard
 1 Portugal—Macau
 16 United Kingdom—Anguilla, Bermuda, British Indian Ocean Territory, British Virgin Islands, Cayman Islands, Falkland Islands, Gibraltar, Guernsey, Hong Kong, Isle of Man, Jersey, Montserrat, Pitcairn Islands, Saint Helena, South Georgia and the South Sandwich Islands, Turks and Caicos Islands
 15 United States—American Samoa, Baker Island, Guam, Howland Island, Jarvis Island, Johnston Atoll, Kingman Reef, Midway Islands, Navassa Island, Northern Mariana Islands, Palmyra Atoll, Puerto Rico, Trust Territory of the Pacific Islands (Palau), Virgin Islands, Wake Island

MISCELLANEOUS
 7 Antarctica, Gaza Strip, Iraq-Saudi Arabia Neutral Zone, Paracel Islands, Spratly Islands, West Bank, Western Sahara

OTHER ENTITIES
   4 oceans—Arctic Ocean, Atlantic Ocean, Indian Ocean, Pacific
   Ocean

   1 World
   —
 247 total

Notes: The US Government has not recognized the incorporation of
Estonia, Latvia, and Lithuania into the Soviet Union as constituent
republics during World War II. Those Baltic states are not members
of the UN and are not included in the list of nations. The US
Government does not recognize the four so-called "independent"
homelands of Bophuthatswana, Ciskei, Transkei, and Venda in South
Africa.

Gross domestic product (GDP): The value of all goods and services
produced domestically.

Gross national product (GNP): The value of all goods and services
produced domestically, plus income earned abroad, minus income
earned by foreigners from domestic production.

GNP/GDP methodology: In the Economy section, GNP/GDP dollar
estimates for the OECD countries, the USSR, and the East European
countries are derived from *purchasing power parity (PPP)* calcula-
tions rather than from conversions at official currency exchange
rates. The PPP method normally involves the use of international
dollar price weights, which are applied to the quantities of goods and
services produced in a given economy. In addition to the lack of
reliable data from the majority of countries, the statistician faces a
major difficulty in specifying, identifying, and allowing for the
quality of goods and services. The division of a PPP GNP/GDP
estimate in dollars by the corresponding estimate in the local
currency gives *the PPP conversion rate.* One thousand dollars will
buy the same market basket of goods in the US as one thousand
dollars, converted to the local currency at the PPP conversion rate,
will buy in the other country. GNP/GDP estimates for the LDCs, on
the other hand, are based on the conversion of GNP/GDP estimates
in local currencies to dollars at the official currency exchange rates.
One caution: the proportion of, say, defense expenditures as a percent
of GNP/GDP in local currency accounts may differ substantially
from the proportion when GNP/GDP accounts are expressed in PPP
terms, as, for example, when an observer estimates the dollar level of
Soviet or Japanese military expenditures; similar problems exist when
components are expressed in dollars under currency exchange rate
procedures. Finally, as academic research moves forward on the PPP
method, we hope to convert all GNP/GDP estimates to this method
in future editions of the Factbook.

Growth rate (population): The annual percent change in the population, resulting from a surplus (or deficit) of births over deaths and the
balance of migrants entering and leaving a country. The rate may be
positive or negative.

Illicit drugs: There are five categories of illicit drugs—narcotics, stimulants, depressants (sedatives), hallucinogens, and cannabis. These categories include many drugs legally produced and prescribed by doctors as well as those illegally produced and sold outside medical channels.

Cannabis (Cannabis sativa) is the common hemp plant, provides hallucinogens with some sedative properties, and includes marijuana (pot, Acapulco gold, grass, reefer), tetrahydrocannabinol (THC, Marinol), hashish (hash), and hashish oil (hash oil).

Coca (Erythroxylon coca) is a bush and the leaves contain the stimulant cocaine. Coca is not to be confused with cocoa which comes from cacao seeds and is used in making chocolate, cocoa, and cocoa butter.

Cocaine is a stimulant derived from the leaves of the coca bush.

Depressants (sedatives) are drugs that reduce tension and anxiety and include chloral hydrate, barbiturates (Amytal, Nembutal, Seconal, phenobarbital), benzodiazepines (Librium, Valium), methaqualone (Quaalude), glutethimide (Doriden), and others (Equanil, Placidyl, Valmid).

Drugs are any chemical substances that effect a physical, mental, emotional, or behavioral change in an individual.

Drug abuse is the use of any licit or illicit chemical substance that results in physical, mental, emotional, or behavioral impairment in an individual.

Hallucinogens are drugs that affect sensation, thinking, self-awareness, and emotion. Hallucinogens include LSD (acid, microdot), mescaline and peyote (mexc, buttons, cactus), amphetamine variants (PMA, STP, DOB), phencyclidine (PCP, angel dust, hog), phencyclidine analogues (PCE, PCPy, TCP), and others (psilocybin, psilocyn).

Hashish is the resinous exudate of the cannabis or hemp plant (Cannabis sativa).

Heroin is a semisynthetic derivative of morphine.

Marijuana is the dried leaves of the cannabis or hemp plant (Cannabis sativa).

Narcotics are drugs that relieve pain, often induce sleep, and refer to opium, opium derivatives, and synthetic substitutes. Natural narcotics include opium (paregoric, parepectolin), morphine (MS-Contin, Roxanol), codeine (Tylenol w/codeine, Empirin w/codeine, Robitussan A-C), and thebaine. Semisynthetic narcotics include heroin (horse, smack) and hydromorphone (Dilaudid). Synthetic narcotics include meperidine or Pethidine (Demerol, Mepergan), methadone (Dolophine, Methadose), and others (Darvon, Lomotil).

Opium is the milky exudate of the incised, unripe seedpod of the opium poppy.

Opium poppy (Papaver somniferum) is the source for many natural and semisynthetic narcotics.

Poppy straw concentrate is the alkaloid derived from the mature dried opium poppy.

Qat (kat, khat) is a stimulant from the buds or leaves of Catha edulis and is chewed or drunk as tea.

Stimulants are drugs that relieve mild depression, increase energy and activity, and include cocaine (coke, snow, crack), amphetamines (Desoxyn, Dexedrine), phenmetrazine (Preludin), methylphenidate (Ritalin), and others (Cylert, Sanorex, Tenuate).

Infant mortality rate: The number of deaths to infants under one year of age in a given year per 1,000 live births occurring in the same year.

Land use: Human use of the land surface is categorized as *arable land*—land cultivated for crops that are replanted after each harvest (wheat, maize, rice); *permanent crops*—land cultivated for crops that are not replanted after each harvest (citrus, coffee, rubber); *meadows and pastures*—land permanently used for herbaceous forage crops; *forest and woodland*—land under dense or open stands of trees; and *other*—any land type not specifically mentioned above (urban areas, roads, desert). The percentage figure for irrigated refers to the portion of the entire amount of land area that is artificially supplied with water.

Leaders: The chief of state is the titular leader of the country who represents the state at official and ceremonial functions but is not involved with the day-to-day activities of the government. The head of government is the administrative leader who manages the day-to-day activities of the government. In the UK, the monarch is the chief of state and the prime minister is the head of government. In the US, the President is both the chief of state and the head of government.

Life expectancy at birth: The average number of years to be lived by a group of people all born in the same year, if mortality at each age remains constant in the future.

Literacy: There are no universal definitions and standards of literacy. Unless otherwise noted, all rates are based on the most common definition—the ability to read and write at a specified age. Detailing the standards that individual countries use to assess the ability to read and write is beyond the scope of this publication.

Maritime claims: The proximity of neighboring states may prevent some national claims from being fully extended.

Merchant marine: All ships engaged in the carriage of goods. All commercial vessels (as opposed to all nonmilitary ships), which excludes tugs, fishing vessels, offshore oil rigs, etc. Also, a grouping of merchant ships by nationality or register.

Captive register—A register of ships maintained by a territory, possession, or colony primarily or exclusively for the use of ships owned in the parent country. Also referred to as an offshore register, the offshore equivalent of an internal register. Ships on a captive register will fly the same flag as the parent country, or a local variant of it, but will be subject to the maritime laws and taxation rules of the offshore territory. Although the nature of a captive register makes it especially desirable for ships owned in the parent country, just as in the internal register, the ships may also be owned abroad. The captive register then acts as a flag of convenience register, except that it is not the register of an independent state.

Flag of convenience register—A national register offering registration to a merchant ship not owned in the flag state. The major flags of convenience (FOC) attract ships to their register by virtue of low fees, low or nonexistent taxation of profits, and liberal manning requirements. True FOC registers are characterized by having relatively few of the ships registered actually owned in the flag state. Thus, while virtually any flag can be used for ships under a given set of circumstances, an FOC register is one where the majority of the merchant fleet is owned abroad. It is also referred to as an open register.

Flag state—The nation in which a ship is registered and which holds legal jurisdiction over operation of the ship, whether at home or abroad. Differences in flag state maritime legislation determine how a ship is manned and taxed and whether a foreign-owned ship may be placed on the register.

Internal register—A register of ships maintained as a subset of a national register. Ships on the internal register fly the national flag and have that nationality but are subject to a separate set of maritime rules from those on the main national register. These differences usually include lower taxation of profits, manning by foreign nationals, and, usually, ownership outside the flag state (when it functions as an FOC register). The Norwegian International Ship Register and Danish International Ship Register are the most notable examples of an internal register. Both have been instrumental in stemming flight from the national flag to flags of convenience and in attracting foreign-owned ships to the Norwegian and Danish flags.

Merchant ship—A vessel that carries goods against payment of freight. Commonly used to denote any nonmilitary ship but accurately restricted to commercial vessels only.

Register—The record of a ship's ownership and nationality as listed with the maritime authorities of a country. Also, the compendium of such individual ships' registrations. Registration of a ship provides it with a nationality and makes it subject to the laws of the country in which registered (the flag state) regardless of the nationality of the ship's ultimate owner.

Money figures: All are expressed in contemporaneous US dollars unless otherwise indicated.

Net migration rate: The balance between the number of persons entering and leaving a country during the year per 1,000 persons (based on midyear population). An excess of persons entering the country is referred to as net immigration (3.56 migrants/1,000 population); an excess of persons leaving the country as net emigration (−9.26 migrants/1,000 population).

Population: Figures are estimates from the Bureau of the Census based on statistics from population censuses, vital registration systems, or sample surveys pertaining to the recent past, and on assumptions about future trends.

Total fertility rate: The average number of children that would be born per woman if all women lived to the end of their childbearing years and bore children according to a given fertility rate at each age.

Years: All year references are for the calendar year (CY) unless indicated as fiscal year (FY).

Notes, Definitions,
and Abbreviations *(continued)*

Note: Information for the US and US dependencies was compiled from material in the public domain and does not represent Intelligence Community estimates. The *Handbook of Economic Statistics,* published annually in September by the Central Intelligence Agency, contains detailed economic information for the Organization for Economic Cooperation and Development (OECD) countries, Eastern Europe, the USSR, and selected other countries. The Handbook can be obtained wherever *The World Factbook* is available.

Afghanistan

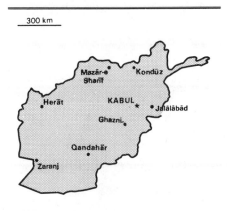

300 km

Geography

Total area: 647,500 km²; land area: 647,500 km²

Comparative area: slightly smaller than Texas

Land boundaries: 5,826 km total; China 76 km, Iran 936 km, Pakistan 2,430 km, USSR 2,384 km

Coastline: none—landlocked

Maritime claims: none—landlocked

Disputes: Pashtun question with Pakistan; Baloch question with Iran and Pakistan; periodic disputes with Iran over Helmand water rights; insurgency with Iranian and Pakistani involvement; traditional tribal rivalries

Climate: arid to semiarid; cold winters and hot summers

Terrain: mostly rugged mountains; plains in north and southwest

Natural resources: natural gas, crude oil, coal, copper, talc, barites, sulphur, lead, zinc, iron ore, salt, precious and semiprecious stones

Land use: arable land 12%; permanent crops NEGL%; meadows and pastures 46%; forest and woodland 3%; other 39%; includes irrigated NEGL%

Environment: damaging earthquakes occur in Hindu Kush mountains; soil degradation, desertification, overgrazing, deforestation, pollution

Note: landlocked

People

Population: US Bureau of the Census— 16,450,304 (July 1991), growth rate 5.2% (1991) and excludes 3,750,796 refugees in Pakistan and 1,607,281 refugees in Iran; note—another report indicates a July 1990 population of 16,904,904, including 3,271,580 refugees in Pakistan and 1,277,700 refugees in Iran

Birth rate: 44 births/1,000 population (1991)

Death rate: 20 deaths/1,000 population (1991)

Net migration rate: 28 migrants/1,000 population (1991); note—there are flows across the border in both directions, but data are fragmentary and unreliable

Infant mortality rate: 164 deaths/1,000 live births (1991)

Life expectancy at birth: 44 years male, 43 years female (1991)

Total fertility rate: 6.3 children born/woman (1991)

Nationality: noun—Afghan(s); adjective— Afghan

Ethnic divisions: Pashtun 50%, Tajik 25%, Uzbek 9%, Hazara 12-15%; minor ethnic groups include Chahar Aimaks, Turkmen, Baloch, and other

Religion: Sunni Muslim 84%, Shi'a Muslim 15%, other 1%

Language: Pashtu 50%, Afghan Persian (Dari) 35%, Turkic languages (primarily Uzbek and Turkmen) 11%, 30 minor languages (primarily Balochi and Pashai) 4%; much bilingualism

Literacy: 29% (male 44%, female 14%) age 15 and over can read and write (1990 est.)

Labor force: 4,980,000; agriculture and animal husbandry 67.8%, industry 10.2%, construction 6.3%, commerce 5.0%, services and other 10.7% (1980 est.)

Organized labor: some small government-controlled unions

Government

Long-form name: Republic of Afghanistan

Type: authoritarian

Capital: Kabul

Administrative divisions: 30 provinces (velayat, singular—velāyat); Badakhshān, Bādghīs, Baghlān, Balkh, Bāmiān, Farāh, Fāryāb, Ghaznī, Ghowr, Helmand, Herāt, Jowzjān, Kābol, Kandahār, Kāpīsā, Konar, Kondoz, Laghmān, Lowgar, Nangarhār, Nīmrūz, Orūzgān, Paktīā, Paktīkā, Parvān, Samangān, Sar-e Pol, Takhār, Vardak, Zābol; note—there may be a new province of Nūrestān (Nuristan)

Independence: 19 August 1919 (from UK)

Constitution: adopted 30 November 1987, revised May 1990

Legal system: has not accepted compulsory ICJ jurisdiction

National holiday: Anniversary of the Saur Revolution, 27 April (1978)

Executive branch: president, four vice presidents, prime minister, deputy prime minister, Council of Ministers (cabinet)

Legislative branch: bicameral National Assembly (Meli Shura) consists of an upper house or Council of Elders (Sena) and a lower house or Council of Representatives (Wolosi Jirga)

Judicial branch: Supreme Court

Leaders:

Chief of State and Head of Government— President (Mohammad) NAJIBULLAH (Ahmadzai) (since 30 November 1987); First Vice President Abdul Wahed SORABI (since 7 January 1991); Prime Minister Fazil Haq KHALIQYAR (since 21 May 1990)

Political parties and leaders: main party— Hizbi Watan Homeland Party (formerly known as the People's Democratic Party of Afghanistan or PDPA); there are other, much smaller political parties recognized by the government

Suffrage: universal, male ages 15-50

Elections:

Senate—last held NA April 1988 (next to be held April 1991); results—Hizbi Watan was the only party; seats—(192 total, 128 elected) Hizbi Watan 128;

House of Representatives—last held NA April 1988 (next to be held April 1993); results—Hizbi Watan was the only party; seats—(234 total) Hizbi Watan 184, opposition 50; note—members may or may not be affiliated with a political party

Communists: Hizbi Watan Homeland Party (formerly the People's Democratic Party of Afghanistan or PDPA) claims 200,000 members and no longer considers itself a Communist party

Other political or pressure groups: the military and other branches of internal security have been rebuilt by the USSR; insurgency continues throughout the country; widespread antiregime sentiment and opposition on religious and political grounds

Member of: AsDB, CP, ESCAP, FAO, G-77, IAEA, IBRD, ICAO, IDA, IDB, IFAD, IFC, ILO, IMF, INTELSAT, IOC, ITU, LORCS, NAM, OIC, UN, UNCTAD, UNESCO, UNIDO, UPU, WFTU, WHO, WMO, WTO; note—Afghanistan was suspended from the OIC in January 1980, but in March 1989 the self-proclaimed Mujaheddin Government of Afghanistan was given membership

Diplomatic representation: Minister-Counselor, Chargé d'Affaires Abdul Ghafur JOUSHAN; Chancery at 2341 Wyoming Avenue NW, Washington DC 20008; telephone (202) 234-3770 or 3771;

US—Chargé d'Affaires (vacant); Embassy at Ansari Wat, Wazir Akbar Khan Mina, Kabul; telephone 62230 through 62235 or 62436; note—US Embassy in Kabul was closed in January 1989

Flag: three equal horizontal bands of black (top), red, and green with the national coat of arms superimposed on the hoist side of the black and red bands; similar to the flag of Malawi which is shorter and bears a radiant, rising red sun centered in the black band

Afghanistan *(continued)*

Economy

Overview: Fundamentally, Afghanistan is an extremely poor, landlocked country, highly dependent on farming (wheat especially) and livestock raising (sheep and goats). Economic considerations, however, have played second fiddle to political and military upheavals, including the nine-year Soviet military occupation (ended 15 February 1989) and the continuing bloody civil war. Over the past decade, one-third of the population has fled the country, with Pakistan sheltering about 3.3 million refugees and Iran about 1.3 million. Another 1 million have probably moved into and around urban areas within Afghanistan. Large numbers of bridges, buildings, and factories have been destroyed or damaged by military action or sabotage. Government claims to the contrary, gross domestic product almost certainly is lower than 10 years ago because of the loss of labor and capital and the disruption of trade and transport. Official claims indicate that agriculture grew by 0.7% and industry by 3.5% in 1988.
GDP: $3 billion, per capita $200; real growth rate 0% (1989 est.)
Inflation rate (consumer prices): over 92% (1990 est.)
Unemployment rate: NA%
Budget: revenues $962 million; expenditures $3.2 billion, including capital expenditures of $296 million (FY90 est.)
Exports: $433 million (f.o.b., FY89); *commodities*—natural gas 55%, fruits and nuts 24%, handwoven carpets, wool, cotton, hides, and pelts; *partners*—mostly USSR and Eastern Europe
Imports: $900 million (c.i.f., FY89); *commodities*—food and petroleum products; *partners*—mostly USSR and Eastern Europe
External debt: $1.8 billion (December 1989 est.)
Industrial production: growth rate 6.2% (FY89 plan); accounts for about 25% of GDP
Electricity: 480,000 kW capacity; 1,470 million kWh produced, 100 kWh per capita (1989)
Industries: small-scale production of textiles, soap, furniture, shoes, fertilizer, and cement; handwoven carpets; natural gas, oil, coal, copper
Agriculture: largely subsistence farming and nomadic animal husbandry; cash products—wheat, fruits, nuts, karakul pelts, wool, mutton
Illicit drugs: an illicit producer of opium poppy and cannabis for the international drug trade; world's second-largest opium producer (after Burma) and a major source of hashish

Economic aid: US commitments, including Ex-Im (FY70-89), $322 million; Western (non-US) countries, ODA and OOF bilateral commitments (1970-88), $465 million; OPEC bilateral aid (1979-89), $57 million; Communist countries (1970-89), $4.1 billion
Currency: afghani (plural—afghanis); 1 afghani (Af) = 100 puls
Exchange rates: afghanis (Af) per US$1—586 (March 1991)
Fiscal year: 21 March-20 March

Communications

Railroads: 9.6 km (single track) 1.524-meter gauge from Kushka (USSR) to Towraghondī and 15.0 km from Termez (USSR) to Kheyrābād transshipment point on south bank of Amu Darya
Highways: 21,000 km total (1984); 2,800 km hard surface, 1,650 km bituminous-treated gravel and improved earth, 16,550 km unimproved earth and tracks
Inland waterways: total navigability 1,200 km; chiefly Amu Darya, which handles steamers up to about 500 metric tons
Pipelines: petroleum, oil, and lubricants pipelines—USSR to Bagrām and USSR to Shīndand; natural gas, 180 km
Ports: Shīr Khān and Kheyrābād (river ports)
Civil air: 2 TU-154, 2 Boeing 727, 4 Yak-40, assorted smaller transports
Airports: 40 total, 36 usable; 9 with permanent-surface runways; none with runways over 3,659 m; 10 with runways 2,440-3,659 m; 17 with runways 1,220-2,439 m
Telecommunications: limited telephone, telegraph, and radiobroadcast services; television introduced in 1980; 31,200 telephones; stations—5 AM, no FM, 1 TV; 1 satellite earth station

Defense Forces

Branches: Armed Forces, Air and Air Defense Forces, Special Guard/National Guard, Border Guard Forces, National Police Force (Sarandoi), Ministry of State Security (WAD), Tribal Militia
Manpower availability: males 15-49, 4,049,092; 2,171,757 fit for military service; 166,135 reach military age (22) annually
Defense expenditures: $450 million, 15% of GDP (1990)

Albania

Geography

Total area: 28,750 km²; land area: 27,400 km²
Comparative area: slightly larger than Maryland
Land boundaries: 768 km total; Greece 282 km, Yugoslavia 486 km
Coastline: 362 km
Maritime claims:
Continental shelf: not specified;
Territorial sea: 12 nm
Disputes: Kosovo question with Yugoslavia; Northern Epirus question with Greece
Climate: mild temperate; cool, cloudy, wet winters; hot, clear, dry summers; interior is cooler and wetter
Terrain: mostly mountains and hills; small plains along coast
Natural resources: crude oil, natural gas, coal, chromium, copper, timber, nickel
Land use: arable land 21%; permanent crops 4%; meadows and pastures 15%; forest and woodland 38%; other 22%; includes irrigated 1%
Environment: subject to destructive earthquakes; tsunami occur along southwestern coast; deforestation seems to be slowing
Note: strategic location along Strait of Otranto (links Adriatic Sea to Ionian Sea and Mediterranean Sea)

People

Population: 3,335,044 (July 1991), growth rate 1.8% (1991)
Birth rate: 24 births/1,000 population (1991)
Death rate: 5 deaths/1,000 population (1991)
Net migration rate: 0 migrants/1,000 population (1991)
Infant mortality rate: 50 deaths/1,000 live births (1991)
Life expectancy at birth: 72 years male, 79 years female (1991)

Total fertility rate: 2.9 children born/woman (1991)
Nationality: noun—Albanian(s); adjective—Albanian
Ethnic divisions: Albanian 90%, Greeks 8%, other 2% (Vlachs, Gypsies, Serbs, and Bulgarians) (1989 est.)
Religion: all mosques and churches were closed in 1967 and religious observances prohibited; in November 1990 Albania began allowing private religious practice and was considering the repeal of the constitutional amendment banning religious activities; estimates of religious affiliation—Muslim 70%, Greek Orthodox 20%, Roman Catholic 10%
Language: Albanian (Tosk is official dialect), Greek
Literacy: 72% (male 80%, female 63%) age 9 and over can read and write (1955)
Labor force: 1,500,000 (1987); agriculture about 60%, industry and commerce 40% (1986)
Organized labor: Central Council of Albanian Trade Unions, 610,000 members

Government

Long-form name: People's Socialist Republic of Albania; may be changed to Republic of Albania
Type: nascent democracy with strong Communist party influence; basic law has dropped all references to socialism
Capital: Tiranë
Administrative divisions: 26 districts (rrethe, singular—rreth); Berat, Dibrë, Durrës, Elbasan, Fier, Gjirokastër, Gramsh, Kolonjë, Korçë, Krujë, Kukës, Lezhë, Librazhd, Lushnjë, Mat, Mirditë, Përmet, Pogradec, Pukë, Sarandë, Shkodër, Skrapar, Tepelenë, Tiranë, Tropojë, Vlorë
Independence: 28 November 1912 (from Ottoman Empire); People's Socialist Republic of Albania declared 11 January 1946
Constitution: an interim basic law was approved by the People's Assembly on 29 April 1991; a new constitution is to be drafted for adoption in four to six months
Legal system: has not accepted compulsory ICJ jurisdiction
National holiday: Liberation Day, 29 November (1944)
Executive branch: president, prime minister of the Council of Ministers, one deputy prime minister of the Council of Ministers
Legislative branch: unicameral People's Assembly (Kuvëndi Popullor)
Judicial branch: Supreme Court
Leaders:
Chief of State—President of the Republic Ramiz ALIA (since 22 November 1982);
Head of Government—Prime Minister of the Council of Ministers Fatos Thanas NANO (since 22 February 1991); Deputy Prime Minister Shkelqim Islam CANI

Political parties and leaders: Albanian Workers Party (AWP), Ramiz ALIA, first secretary; Democratic Party (DP), Sali BERISHA, chairman and cofounder with Gramoz PASHKO; Albanian Republican Party, Sabri GODO; Ecology Party, Namik HOTI; Omonia (Greek minority party), leader NA; Agrarian Party, leader NA; note—in December 1990 President ALIA allowed new political parties to be formed in addition to the AWP for the first time since 1944
Suffrage: universal and compulsory at age 18
Elections:
President—last held 30 April 1991 (next to be held NA 1995); results—President Ramiz ALIA was reelected with token opposition;
People's Assembly—last held 31 March 1991 (next to be held March 1995); results—AWP 68%, DP 25%; seats—(250 total) preliminary results AWP 168, DP 75, Omonia 5, Veterans Association 1, other 1; note—the AWP's votes came mostly from the countryside while the DP won majorities in the six-largest cities
Communists: 147,000 party members (November 1986); note—in March 1991 the Albanian Workers' Party announced that it considered itself no longer Communist but socialist
Member of: ECE, FAO, IAEA, IOC, ISO, ITU, LORCS, UN, UNCTAD, UNESCO, UNIDO, UPU, WFTU, WHO, WMO
Diplomatic representation: the Governments of the United States and Albania agreed to reestablish diplomatic relations to be effective from 15 March 1991 and to exchange diplomatic missions at the level of ambassador
Flag: red with a black two-headed eagle in the center below a red five-pointed star outlined in yellow

Economy

Overview: As the poorest country in Europe, Albania's development lags behind even the least favored areas of the Yugoslav economy. For over 40 years, the Stalinist-type economy has operated on the principles of central planning and state ownership of the means of production. In recent years Albania has implemented limited economic reforms to stimulate its lagging economy, provide incentives, and decentralize decisionmaking. In an effort to expand international ties, Tiranë has reestablished diplomatic relations with the Soviet Union and the US. The Albanians have also passed legislation allowing foreign investment. Albania possesses considerable mineral resources and, until 1990, was largely self-sufficient in food; several years of drought have hindered agricultural development. Numerical estimates of Albanian economic

activity are subject to an especially wide margin of error because the government until recently did not release economic information.
GNP: $4.1 billion, per capita $1,250; real growth rate NA% (1990 est.)
Inflation rate (consumer prices): NA%
Unemployment rate: NA%
Budget: revenues $2.3 billion; expenditures $2.3 billion, including capital expenditures of NA (1989)
Exports: $378 million (f.o.b., 1987 est.); *commodities*—asphalt, bitumen, petroleum products, metals and metallic ores, electricity, oil, vegetables, fruits, tobacco; *partners*—Italy, Yugoslavia, FRG, Greece, Czechoslovakia, Poland, Romania, Bulgaria, Hungary
Imports: $255 million (f.o.b., 1987 est.); *commodities*—machinery, machine tools, iron and steel products, textiles, chemicals, pharmaceuticals; *partners*—Italy, Yugoslavia, FRG, Czechoslovakia, Romania, Poland, Hungary, Bulgaria, GDR
External debt: $NA
Industrial production: growth rate NA
Electricity: 1,690,000 kW capacity; 5,000 million kWh produced, 1,530 kWh per capita (1990)
Industries: food processing, textiles and clothing, lumber, oil, cement, chemicals, basic metals, hydropower
Agriculture: arable land per capita among lowest in Europe; one-half of work force engaged in farming; produces wide range of temperate-zone crops and livestock; claims self-sufficiency in grain output
Economic aid: Western (non-US) countries, ODA (1988) $5.8 million
Currency: lek (plural—lekë); 1 lek (L) = 100 qintars
Exchange rates: lekë (L) per US$1—8.00 (noncommercial fixed rate since 1986), 4.14 (commercial fixed rate since 1987)
Fiscal year: calendar year

Communications

Railroads: 543 km total; 509 1.435-meter standard gauge, single track and 34 km narrow gauge, single track (1990); line connecting Titograd (Yugoslavia) and Shkodër (Albania) completed August 1986
Highways: 16,700 km total; 6,700 km highway and roads, 10,000 km forest and agricultural (1990)
Inland waterways: 43 km plus Albanian sections of Lake Scutari, Lake Ohrid, and Lake Prespa (1990)
Pipelines: crude oil, 145 km; refined products, 55 km; natural gas, 64 km (1988)
Ports: Durrës, Sarandë, Vlorë
Merchant marine: 11 cargo ships (1,000 GRT or over) totaling 52,886 GRT/75,993 DWT

Albania (continued)

Airports: 12 total, 10 usable; more than 5 with permanent-surface runways; more than 5 with runways 2,440-3,659 m; 5 with runways 1,220-2,439 m
Telecommunications: stations—17 AM, 1 FM, 9 TV; 246,000 TVs (1990); 210,000 radios

Defense Forces

Branches: Albanian People's Army, Albanian Coastal Defense Command, Air and Air Defense Force, Frontier Troops, Interior Troops
Manpower availability: males 15-49, 900,723; 743,594 fit for military service; 33,497 reach military age (19) annually
Defense expenditures: 1.0 billion leks, NA% of GDP (FY90); note—conversion of defense expenditures into US dollars using the official administratively set exchange rate would produce misleading results

Algeria

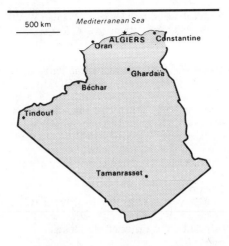

Geography

Total area: 2,381,740 km²; land area: 2,381,740 km²
Comparative area: slightly less than 3.5 times the size of Texas
Land boundaries: 6,343 km total; Libya 982 km, Mali 1,376 km, Mauritania 463 km, Morocco 1,559 km, Niger 956 km, Tunisia 965 km, Western Sahara 42 km
Coastline: 998 km
Maritime claims:
Territorial sea: 12 nm
Disputes: Libya claims about 19,400 km² in southeastern Algeria
Climate: arid to semiarid; mild, wet winters with hot, dry summers along coast; drier with cold winters and hot summers on high plateau; sirocco is a hot, dust/sand-laden wind especially common in summer
Terrain: mostly high plateau and desert; some mountains; narrow, discontinuous coastal plain
Natural resources: crude oil, natural gas, iron ore, phosphates, uranium, lead, zinc
Land use: arable land 3%; permanent crops NEGL%; meadows and pastures 13%; forest and woodland 2%; other 82%; includes irrigated NEGL%
Environment: mountainous areas subject to severe earthquakes; desertification
Note: second-largest country in Africa (after Sudan)

People

Population: 26,022,188 (July 1991), growth rate 2.5% (1991)
Birth rate: 32 births/1,000 population (1991)
Death rate: 7 deaths/1,000 population (1991)
Net migration rate: 0 migrants/1,000 population (1991)
Infant mortality rate: 57 deaths/1,000 live births (1991)
Life expectancy at birth: 66 years male, 68 years female (1991)

Total fertility rate: 4.2 children born/woman (1991)
Nationality: noun—Algerian(s); adjective—Algerian
Ethnic divisions: Arab-Berber 99%, European less than 1%
Religion: Sunni Muslim (state religion) 99%, Christian and Jewish 1%
Language: Arabic (official), French, Berber dialects
Literacy: 50% (male 63%, female 36%) age 15 and over can read and write (1987)
Labor force: 3,700,000; industry and commerce 40%, agriculture 24%, government 17%, services 10% (1984)
Organized labor: 16-19% of labor force claimed; General Union of Algerian Workers (UGTA) is the only labor organization and is subordinate to the National Liberation Front

Government

Long-form name: Democratic and Popular Republic of Algeria
Type: republic
Capital: Algiers
Administrative divisions: 48 provinces (wilayat, singular—wilaya); Adrar, Aïn Defla, Aïn Temouchent, Alger, Annaba, Batna, Béchar, Bejaïa, Biskra, Blida, Bordj Bou Arréridj, Bouira, Boumerdes, Chlef, Constantine, Djelfa, El Bayadh, El Oued, El Tarf, Ghardaïa, Guelma, Illizi, Jijel, Khenchela, Laghouat, Mascara, Médéa, Mila, Mostaganem, M'sila, Naama, Oran, Ouargla, Oum el Bouaghi, Relizane, Saïda, Setif, Sidi Bel Abbès, Skikda, Souk Ahras, Tamanghasset, Tébessa, Tiaret, Tindouf, Tipaza, Tissemsilt, Tizi Ouzou, Tlemcen
Independence: 5 July 1962 (from France)
Constitution: 19 November 1976, effective 22 November 1976
Legal system: socialist, based on French and Islamic law; judicial review of legislative acts in ad hoc Constitutional Council composed of various public officials, including several Supreme Court justices; has not accepted compulsory ICJ jurisdiction
National holiday: Anniversary of the Revolution, 1 November (1954)
Executive branch: president, prime minister, Council of Ministers (cabinet)
Legislative branch: unicameral National People's Assembly (Al-Majlis Ech-Chaabi Al-Watani)
Judicial branch: Supreme Court (Cour Suprême)
Leaders:
Chief of State—President Chadli BENDJEDID (since 7 February 1979);
Head of Government—Prime Minister Sid Ahmed GHOZALI (since 6 June 1991)
Political parties and leaders: National Liberation Front (FLN), Chadli BENDJEDID,

president; Islamic Salvation Front (FIS), Abassi MADANI; the government established a multiparty system in September 1989 and as of 31 December 1990 over 30 legal parties existed

Suffrage: universal at age 18

Elections:

President—last held on 22 December 1988 (next to be held December 1993); results—President BENDJEDID was reelected without opposition;

National People's Assembly—last held on 26 February 1987 (next were to be held 27 June 1991 but postponed indefinitely because of civil unrest); results—FLN was the only party; seats—(281 total) FLN 281; note—the government held multiparty elections (municipal and wilaya) in June 1990, the first in Algerian history; results—FIS 55%, FLN 27.5%, other 17.5%, with 65% of the voters participating

Communists: 400 (est.); Communist party banned 1962

Member of: ABEDA, AfDB, AFESD, AL, AMF, AMU, CCC, ECA, FAO, G-19, G-24, G-77, IAEA, IBRD, ICAO, IDA, IDB, IFAD, ILO, IMF, IMO, INMARSAT, INTELSAT, INTERPOL, IOC, ISO, ITU, LORCS, NAM, OAPEC, OAS (observer), OAU, OIC, OPEC, UN, UNAVEM, UNCTAD, UNESCO, UNHCR, UNIDO, UPU, WCL, WHO, WIPO, WMO, WTO

Diplomatic representation: Ambassador Abderrahmane BENSID; Chancery at 2118 Kalorama Road NW, Washington DC 20008; telephone (202) 328-5300; *US*—Ambassador Christopher W. S. ROSS; Embassy at 4 Chemin Cheich Bachir El-Ibrahimi, Algiers (mailing address is B. P. Box 549, Alger-Gare, 16000 Algiers); telephone [213] (2) 601-425 or 255, 186; there is a US Consulate in Oran

Flag: two equal vertical bands of green (hoist side) and white with a red five-pointed star within a red crescent; the crescent, star, and color green are traditional symbols of Islam (the state religion)

Economy

Overview: The exploitation of oil and natural gas products forms the backbone of the economy. Algeria depends on hydrocarbons for nearly all of its export receipts, about 30% of government revenues, and nearly 25% of GDP. In 1973-74 the sharp increase in oil prices led to a booming economy and helped to finance an ambitious program of industrialization. Plunging oil and gas prices, combined with the mismanagement of Algeria's highly centralized economy, have brought the nation to its most serious social and economic crisis since independence. The government has promised far-reaching reforms, including giving public-sector companies more autonomy,

encouraging private-sector activity, boosting gas and nonhydrocarbon exports, and proposing a major overhaul of the banking and financial systems, but to date has made little progress.

GDP: $54 billion, per capita $2,130; real growth rate 2.5% (1990 est.)

Inflation rate (consumer prices): 20% (1990 est.)

Unemployment rate: 26% (1990 est.)

Budget: revenues $16.7 billion; expenditures $17.3 billion, including capital expenditures of $6.6 billion (1990 est.)

Exports: $10.2 billion (f.o.b., 1990 est.); *commodities*—petroleum and natural gas 98%; *partners*—Netherlands, Czechoslovakia, Romania, Italy, France, US

Imports: $9.2 billion (f.o.b., 1990 est.); *commodities*—capital goods 35%, consumer goods 36%, food 20%; *partners*—France 25%, Italy 8%, FRG 8%, US 6-7%

External debt: $26.6 billion (December 1990)

Industrial production: growth rate 0.9% (1988 est.)

Electricity: 5,156,000 kW capacity; 14,900 million kWh produced, 580 kWh per capita (1990)

Industries: petroleum, light industries, natural gas, mining, electrical, petrochemical, food processing

Agriculture: accounts for 8% of GDP and employs 24% of labor force; net importer of food—grain, vegetable oil, and sugar; farm production includes wheat, barley, oats, grapes, olives, citrus, fruits, sheep, and cattle

Economic aid: US commitments, including Ex-Im (FY70-85), $1.4 billion; Western (non-US) countries, ODA and OOF bilateral commitments (1970-88), $8.5 billion; OPEC bilateral aid (1979-89), $1.8 billion; Communist countries (1970-89), $2.7 billion

Currency: Algerian dinar (plural—dinars); 1 Algerian dinar (DA) = 100 centimes

Exchange rates: Algerian dinars (DA) per US$1—13.581 (January 1991), 8.958 (1990), 7.6086 (1989), 5.9148 (1988), 4.8497 (1987), 4.7023 (1986), 5.0278 (1985)

Fiscal year: calendar year

Communications

Railroads: 4,146 km total; 2,632 km standard gauge (1.435 m), 1,258 km 1.055-meter gauge, 256 km 1.000-meter gauge; 300 km electrified; 215 km double track

Highways: 80,000 km total; 60,000 km concrete or bituminous, 20,000 km gravel, crushed stone, unimproved earth

Pipelines: crude oil, 6,612 km; refined products, 298 km; natural gas, 2,948 km

Ports: Algiers, Annaba, Arzew, Bejaia, Jijel, Mers el Kebir, Mostaganem, Oran, Skikda

Merchant marine: 75 ships (1,000 GRT or over) totaling 903,179 GRT/1,063,994 DWT; includes 5 short-sea passenger, 27 cargo, 2 vehicle carrier, 10 roll-on/roll-off cargo, 5 petroleum, oils, and lubricants (POL) tanker, 9 liquefied gas, 7 chemical tanker, 9 bulk, 1 specialized tanker

Civil air: 42 major transport aircraft

Airports: 145 total, 134 usable; 53 with permanent-surface runways; 3 with runways over 3,659 m; 30 with runways 2,440-3,659 m; 66 with runways 1,220-2,439 m

Telecommunications: excellent domestic and international service in the north, sparse in the south; 693,000 telephones; stations—26 AM, no FM, 113 TV; 1,550,000 TV sets; 3,500,000 receiver sets; 6 submarine cables; coaxial cable or radio relay to Italy, France, Spain, Morocco, and Tunisia; satellite earth stations—1 Atlantic Ocean INTELSAT, 1 Indian Ocean INTELSAT, 1 Intersputnik, 1 ARABSAT, and 15 domestic

---

Defense Forces

Branches: Army, Navy, Air Force, Territorial Air Defense, National Gendarmerie

Manpower availability: males 15-49, 6,142,818; 3,780,873 fit for military service; 293,175 reach military age (19) annually

Defense expenditures: $857 million, 1.8% of GDP (1991)

American Samoa
(territory of the US)

South Pacific Ocean

Swains Island   80 km

Tutuila   Ofu   Olosega
PAGO PAGO   Ta'u   Rose Island

Geography

Total area: 199 km²; land area: 199 km²
Comparative area: slightly larger than Washington, DC
Land boundaries: none
Coastline: 116 km
Maritime claims:
Contiguous zone: 12 nm;
Continental shelf: 200 m (depth);
Exclusive economic zone: 200 nm;
Territorial sea: 12 nm
Climate: tropical marine, moderated by southeast trade winds; annual rainfall averages 124 inches; rainy season from November to April, dry season from May to October; little seasonal temperature variation
Terrain: five volcanic islands with rugged peaks and limited coastal plains, two coral atolls
Natural resources: pumice and pumicite
Land use: arable land 10%; permanent crops 5%; meadows and pastures 0%; forest and woodland 75%; other 10%
Environment: typhoons common from December to March
Note: Pago Pago has one of the best natural deepwater harbors in the South Pacific Ocean, sheltered by shape from rough seas and protected by peripheral mountains from high winds; strategic location about 3,700 km south-southwest of Honolulu in the South Pacific Ocean about halfway between Hawaii and New Zealand

People

Population: 43,052 (July 1991), growth rate 2.9% (1991)
Birth rate: 41 births/1,000 population (1991)
Death rate: 4 deaths/1,000 population (1991)
Net migration rate: −8 immigrants/1,000 population (1991)
Infant mortality rate: 11 deaths/1,000 live births (1991)

Life expectancy at birth: 69 years male, 74 years female (1991)
Total fertility rate: 5.4 children born/woman (1991)
Nationality: noun—American Samoan(s); adjective—American Samoan
Ethnic divisions: Samoan (Polynesian) 90%, Caucasian 2%, Tongan 2%, other 6%
Religion: Christian Congregationalist 50%, Roman Catholic 20%, Protestant denominations and other 30%
Language: Samoan (closely related to Hawaiian and other Polynesian languages) and English; most people are bilingual
Literacy: 97% (male 97%, female 97%) age 15 and over can read and write (1980)
Labor force: 11,145; government 48%, tuna canneries 33%, other 19% (1986 est.)
Organized labor: NA
Note: about 65,000 American Samoans live in the States of California and Washington and 20,000 in Hawaii

Government

Long-form name: Territory of American Samoa
Type: unincorporated and unorganized territory of the US
Capital: Pago Pago
Administrative divisions: none (territory of the US)
Independence: none (territory of the US)
Constitution: ratified 1966, in effect 1967
National holiday: Flag Day, 17 April (1900)
Executive branch: President of the US, governor, lieutenant governor
Legislative branch: bicameral Legislative Assembly (Fono) consists of an upper house or Senate and a lower house or House of Representatives
Judicial branch: High Court
Leaders:
Chief of State—President George BUSH (since 20 January 1989); Vice President Dan QUAYLE (since 20 January 1989);
Head of Government—Governor Peter Tali COLEMAN (since 20 January 1989); Lieutenant Governor Galea'i POUMELE (since NA 1989)
Suffrage: universal at age 18; indigenous inhabitants are US nationals, not US citizens
Elections:
Governor—last held 7 November 1988 (next to be held November 1992); results—Peter T. COLEMAN was elected (percent of vote NA);
Senate—last held 7 November 1988 (next to be held November 1992); results—senators elected by county councils from 12 senate districts; seats—(18 total) number of seats by party NA;
House of Representatives—last held NA November 1990 (next to be held November 1992); results—representatives popularly

elected from 17 house districts; seats—(21 total, 20 elected and 1 nonvoting delegate from Swain's Island);
US House of Representatives—last held 19 November 1990 (next to be held November 1992); results—Eni R. F. H. FALEOMAVAEGA reelected as a nonvoting delegate
Communists: none
Member of: IOC, SPC
Diplomatic representation: none (territory of the US)
Flag: blue with a white triangle edged in red that is based on the fly side and extends to the hoist side; a brown and white American bald eagle flying toward the hoist side is carrying two traditional Samoan symbols of authority, a staff and a war club
Note: administered by the US Department of Interior, Office of Territorial and International Affairs; indigenous inhabitants are US nationals, not citizens of the US

Economy

Overview: Economic development is strongly linked to the US, with which American Samoa does 90% of its foreign trade. Tuna fishing and tuna processing plants are the backbone of the private-sector economy, with canned tuna the primary export. The tuna canneries are the second-largest employer, exceeded only by the government. Other economic activities include meat canning, handicrafts, dairy farming, and a slowly developing tourist industry.
GNP: $190 million, per capita $5,210; real growth rate NA% (1985)
Inflation rate (consumer prices): 4.3% (1989)
Unemployment rate: 13.4% (1986)
Budget: revenues $51.2 million; expenditures $59.9 million, including capital expenditures of $NA million (1990)
Exports: $288 million (f.o.b., 1987);
commodities—canned tuna 93%;
partners—US 99.6%
Imports: $346 million (c.i.f., 1987);
commodities—building materials 18%, food 17%, petroleum products 14%;
partners—US 72%, Japan 7%, NZ 7%, Australia 5%, other 9%
External debt: $NA
Industrial production: growth rate NA%
Electricity: 42,000 kW capacity; 85 million kWh produced, 2,020 kWh per capita (1990)
Industries: tuna canneries (largely dependent on foreign supplies of raw tuna)
Agriculture: bananas, coconuts, vegetables, taro, breadfruit, yams, copra, pineapples, papayas
Economic aid: $21,042,650 million in operational funds and $5,948,931 million in construction funds for capital improvement projects from the US Department of Interior (1991)
Currency: US currency is used

Andorra

Exchange rates: US currency is used
Fiscal year: 1 October-30 September

Communications

Railroads: none
Highways: 350 km total; 150 km paved, 200 km unpaved
Ports: Pago Pago, Ta'u
Airports: 4 total, 4 usable; 2 with permanent-surface runways; none with runways over 3,659 m; 1 with runways 2,440 to 3,659 m (international airport at Tafuna, near Pago Pago); small airstrips on Ta'u and Ofu
Telecommunications: 6,500 telephones; stations—1 AM, 2 FM, 1 TV; good telex, telegraph, and facsimile services; 1 Pacific Ocean INTELSAT earth station, 1 COMSAT earth station

Defense Forces

Note: defense is the responsibility of the US

Geography

Total area: 450 km²; land area: 450 km²
Comparative area: slightly more than 2.5 times the size of Washington, DC
Land boundaries: 125 km total; France 60 km, Spain 65 km
Coastline: none—landlocked
Maritime claims: none—landlocked
Climate: temperate; snowy, cold winters and cool, dry summers
Terrain: rugged mountains dissected by narrow valleys
Natural resources: hydropower, mineral water, timber, iron ore, lead
Land use: arable land 2%; permanent crops 0%; meadows and pastures 56%; forest and woodland 22%; other 20%
Environment: deforestation, overgrazing
Note: landlocked

People

Population: 53,197 (July 1991), growth rate 2.4% (1991)
Birth rate: 11 births/1,000 population (1991)
Death rate: 4 deaths/1,000 population (1991)
Net migration rate: 16 migrants/1,000 population (1991)
Infant mortality rate: 7 deaths/1,000 live births (1991)
Life expectancy at birth: 74 years male, 81 years female (1991)
Total fertility rate: 1.3 children born/woman (1991)
Nationality: noun—Andorran(s); adjective—Andorran
Ethnic divisions: Catalan stock; Spanish 61%, Andorran 30%, French 6%, other 3%
Religion: virtually all Roman Catholic
Language: Catalan (official); many also speak some French and Castilian
Literacy: NA% (male NA%, female NA%)
Labor force: NA
Organized labor: none

Government

Long-form name: Principality of Andorra
Type: unique coprincipality under formal sovereignty of president of France and Spanish bishop of Seo de Urgel, who are represented locally by officials called verguers
Capital: Andorra la Vella
Administrative divisions: 7 parishes (parròquies, singular—parròquia); Andorra, Canillo, Encamp, La Massana, Les Escaldes, Ordino, Sant Julià de Lòria
Independence: 1278
Constitution: none; some pareatges and decrees, mostly custom and usage
Legal system: based on French and Spanish civil codes; no judicial review of legislative acts; has not accepted compulsory ICJ jurisdiction
National holiday: Mare de Deu de Meritxell, 8 September
Executive branch: two co-princes (president of France, bishop of Seo de Urgel in Spain), two designated representatives (French veguer, Episcopal veguer), two permanent delegates (French prefect for the department of Pyrénées-Orientales, Spanish vicar general for the Seo de Urgel diocese), president of government, Executive Council
Legislative branch: unicameral General Council of the Valleys (Consell General de las Valls)
Judicial branch: civil cases—Supreme Court of Andorra at Perpignan (France) or the Ecclesiastical Court of the bishop of Seo de Urgel (Spain); criminal cases—Tribunal of the Courts (Tribunal des Cortes)
Leaders:
Chiefs of State—French Co-Prince François MITTERRAND (since 21 May 1981), represented by Veguer de França Jean Pierre COURTOIS; Spanish Episcopal Co-Prince Mgr. Joan MARTÍ y Alanís (since 31 January 1971), represented by Veguer Episcopal Francesc BADIA Batalla;
Head of Government—Oscar RIBAS Reig (since NA January 1990)
Political parties and leaders: political parties not yet legally recognized; traditionally no political parties but partisans for particular independent candidates for the General Council on the basis of competence, personality, and orientation toward Spain or France; various small pressure groups developed in 1972; first formal political party, Andorran Democratic Association, was formed in 1976 and reorganized in 1979 as Andorran Democratic Party
Suffrage: universal at age 18
Elections:
General Council of the Valleys—last held 11 December 1989 (next to be held December 1993); results—percent of vote NA; seats—(28 total) number of seats by party NA

Andorra *(continued)*

Communists: negligible
Member of: CSCE, INTERPOL, IOC
Diplomatic representation: Andorra has no mission in the US;
US—includes Andorra within the Barcelona (Spain) Consular District and the US Consul General visits Andorra periodically; Consul General Ruth A. DAVIS; Consulate General at Via Layetana 33, Barcelona 3, Spain (mailing address APO NY 09286); telephone [34] (3) 319-9550
Flag: three equal vertical bands of blue (hoist side), yellow, and red with the national coat of arms centered in the yellow band; the coat of arms features a quartered shield; similar to the flag of Chad which does not have a national coat of arms in the center; also similar to the flag of Romania which has a national coat of arms featuring a mountain landscape below a red five-pointed star and the words *REPUBLICA SOCIALISTA ROMANIA* at the bottom

Economy

Overview: The mainstay of Andorra's economy is tourism. An estimated 12 million tourists visit annually, attracted by Andorra's duty-free status and by its summer and winter resorts. Agricultural production is limited by a scarcity of arable land, and most food has to be imported. The principal livestock activity is sheep raising. Manufacturing consists mainly of cigarettes, cigars, and furniture. The rapid pace of European economic integration is a potential threat to Andorra's advantages from its duty-free status.
GDP: $727 million, per capita $14,000; real growth rate NA% (1990 est.)
Inflation rate (consumer prices): NA%
Unemployment rate: none
Budget: revenues $NA; expenditures $NA, including capital expenditures of $NA
Exports: $0.017 million (f.o.b., 1986);
commodities—electricity;
partners—France, Spain
Imports: $531 million (f.o.b., 1986);
commodities—consumer goods, food;
partners—France, Spain
External debt: $NA
Industrial production: growth rate NA%
Electricity: 35,000 kW capacity; 140 million kWh produced, 2,800 kWh per capita (1989)
Industries: tourism (particularly skiing), sheep, timber, tobacco, smuggling, banking
Agriculture: sheep raising; small quantities of tobacco, rye, wheat, barley, oats, and some vegetables
Economic aid: none
Currency: French franc (plural—francs) and Spanish peseta (plural—pesetas); 1 French franc (F) = 100 centimes and 1 Spanish peseta (Pta) = 100 céntimos

Exchange rates: French francs (F) per US$1—5.1307 (January 1991), 5.4453 (1990), 6.3801 (1989), 5.9569 (1988), 6.0107 (1987), 6.9261 (1986), 8.9852 (1985); Spanish pesetas (Ptas) per US$1—95.20 (January 1991), 101.93 (1990), 118.38 (1989), 116.49 (1988), 123.48 (1987), 140.05 (1986), 170.04 (1985)
Fiscal year: calendar year

Communications

Highways: 96 km
Telecommunications: international digital microwave network; international landline circuits to France and Spain; stations—1 AM, no FM, no TV; 17,700 telephones

Defense Forces

Note: defense is the responsibility of France and Spain

Angola

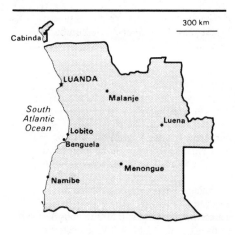

Geography

Total area: 1,246,700 km²; land area: 1,246,700 km²
Comparative area: slightly less than twice the size of Texas
Land boundaries: 5,198 km total; Congo 201 km, Namibia 1,376 km, Zaire 2,511 km, Zambia 1,110 km
Coastline: 1,600 km
Maritime claims:
Exclusive fishing zone: 200 nm;
Territorial sea: 20 nm
Disputes: civil war since independence on 11 November 1975; on 31 May 1991 Angolan President José Eduardo dos SANTOS and Jonas SAVIMBI, leader of the National Union for the Total Independence of Angola (UNITA), signed a peace treaty that calls for multiparty elections between September and November 1992, an internationally monitored cease-fire, and termination of outside military assistance
Climate: semiarid in south and along coast to Luanda; north has cool, dry season (May to October) and hot, rainy season (November to April)
Terrain: narrow coastal plain rises abruptly to vast interior plateau
Natural resources: petroleum, diamonds, iron ore, phosphates, copper, feldspar, gold, bauxite, uranium
Land use: arable land 2%; permanent crops NEGL%; meadows and pastures 23%; forest and woodland 43%; other 32%
Environment: locally heavy rainfall causes periodic flooding on plateau; desertification
Note: Cabinda is separated from rest of country by Zaire

People

Population: 8,668,281 (July 1991), growth rate 2.7% (1991)
Birth rate: 47 births/1,000 population (1991)

Death rate: 20 deaths/1,000 population (1991)

Net migration rate: NEGL migrants/1,000 population (1991)

Infant mortality rate: 151 deaths/1,000 live births (1991)

Life expectancy at birth: 42 years male, 46 years female (1991)

Total fertility rate: 6.7 children born/woman (1991)

Nationality: noun—Angolan(s); adjective—Angolan

Ethnic divisions: Ovimbundu 37%, Kimbundu 25%, Bakongo 13%, Mestiço 2%, European 1%, other 22%

Religion: indigenous beliefs 47%, Roman Catholic 38%, Protestant 15% (est.)

Language: Portuguese (official); various Bantu dialects

Literacy: 42% (male 56%, female 28%) age 15 and over can read and write (1990 est.)

Labor force: 2,783,000 economically active; agriculture 85%, industry 15% (1985 est.)

Organized labor: about 450,695 (1980)

Government

Long-form name: People's Republic of Angola

Type: in transition from a one-party Marxist state to a multiparty democracy with a strong presidential system

Capital: Luanda

Administrative divisions: 18 provinces (províncias, singular—província); Bengo, Benguela, Bié, Cabinda, Cuando Cubango, Cuanza Norte, Cuanza Sul, Cunene, Huambo, Huíla, Luanda, Lunda Norte, Lunda Sul, Malanje, Moxico, Namibe, Uíge, Zaire

Independence: 11 November 1975 (from Portugal)

Constitution: 11 November 1975; revised 7 January 1978, 11 August 1980, and 6 March 1991

Legal system: based on Portuguese civil law system and customary law; recently modified to accommodate multipartyism and increased use of free markets

National holiday: Independence Day, 11 November (1975)

Executive branch: president, chairman of the Council of Ministers, Council of Ministers (cabinet)

Legislative branch: unicameral People's Assembly (Assembleia do Povo)

Judicial branch: Supreme Court (Tribunal da Relacao)

Leaders:
Chief of State and Head of Government— President José Eduardo dos SANTOS (since 21 September 1979)

Political parties and leaders: only one party exists—the Popular Movement for the Liberation of Angola-Labor Party (MPLA), José Eduardo dos SANTOS—although others are expected to form as legalization of a

multiparty system proceeds; National Union for the Total Independence of Angola (UNITA) lost to the MPLA and Cuban military support forces in the immediate postindependence struggle, but is to receive recognition as a legal party

Suffrage: universal at age 18

Elections: first nationwide, multiparty elections to be held between September and November 1992

Member of: ACP, AfDB, CEEAC (observer), ECA, FAO, FLS, G-77, ICAO, IFAD, ILO, IMF, IMO, INTELSAT, INTERPOL, IOC, ITU, LORCS, NAM, OAU, SADCC, UN, UNCTAD, UNESCO, UNIDO, UPU, WCL, WFTU, WHO, WIPO, WMO, WTO

Diplomatic representation: none

Flag: two equal horizontal bands of red (top) and black with a centered yellow emblem consisting of a five-pointed star within half a cogwheel crossed by a machete (in the style of a hammer and sickle)

Economy

Overview: Subsistence agriculture provides the main livelihood for 80 to 90% of the population, but accounts for less than 15% of GDP. Oil production is the most lucrative sector of the economy, contributing about 50% to GDP. In recent years, however, the impact of fighting an internal war has severely affected the nonoil economy, and food has to be imported.

GDP: $7.9 billion, per capita $925; real growth rate 2.0% (1990 est.)

Inflation rate (consumer prices): 23.2% (1988)

Unemployment rate: NA%

Budget: revenues $2.6 billion; expenditures $4.4 billion, including capital expenditures of $963 million (1990 est.)

Exports: $3.8 billion (f.o.b., 1990 est.); *commodities*—oil, diamonds, coffee, sisal, fish and fish products, timber, cotton; *partners*—US, USSR, Cuba, Portugal, Brazil, France

Imports: $1.5 billion (f.o.b., 1990 est.); *commodities*—capital equipment (machinery and electrical equipment), food, vehicles and spare parts, textiles and clothing, medicines; substantial military deliveries; *partners*—US, USSR, Cuba, Portugal, Brazil

External debt: $7.0 billion (1990)

Industrial production: growth rate NA%; accounts for about 60% of GDP, including petroleum output

Electricity: 506,000 kW capacity; 770 million kWh produced, 90 kWh per capita (1989)

Industries: petroleum, mining (phosphate rock, diamonds), fish processing, brewing, tobacco, sugar, textiles, cement, food processing, building construction

Agriculture: cash crops—coffee, sisal, corn, cotton, sugar, manioc, tobacco; food crops—cassava, corn, vegetables, plantains, bananas; livestock production accounts for 20%, fishing 4%, forestry 2% of total agricultural output; disruptions caused by civil war and marketing deficiencies require food imports

Economic aid: US commitments, including Ex-Im (FY70-89), $265 million; Western (non-US) countries, ODA and OOF bilateral commitments (1970-88), $1,005 million; Communist countries (1970-89), $1.3 billion

Currency: kwanza (plural—kwanza); 1 kwanza (Kz) = 100 lwei

Exchange rates: kwanza (Kz) per US$1—29.62 (fixed rate since 1976)

Fiscal year: calendar year

Communications

Railroads: 3,189 km total; 2,879 km 1.067-meter gauge, 310 km 0.600-meter gauge; limited trackage in use because of insurgent attacks; sections of the Benguela Railroad closed because of insurgency

Highways: 73,828 km total; 8,577 km bituminous-surface treatment, 29,350 km crushed stone, gravel, or improved earth, remainder unimproved earth

Inland waterways: 1,295 km navigable

Pipelines: crude oil, 179 km

Ports: Luanda, Lobito, Namibe, Cabinda

Merchant marine: 12 ships (1,000 GRT or over) totaling 66,348 GRT/102,825 DWT; includes 11 cargo, 1 petroleum, oils, and lubricants (POL) tanker

Civil air: 27 major transport aircraft

Airports: 315 total, 183 usable; 28 with permanent-surface runways; 1 with runways over 3,659 m; 13 with runways 2,440-3,659 m; 58 with runways 1,220-2,439 m

Telecommunications: fair system of wire, radio relay, and troposcatter routes; high frequency used extensively for military/Cuban links; 40,300 telephones; stations—17 AM, 13 FM, 2 TV; 2 Atlantic Ocean INTELSAT earth stations

Defense Forces

Branches: Army, Navy, Air Force/Air Defense; People's Defense Organization and Territorial Troops, Frontier Guard

Manpower availability: males 15-49, 2,080,837; 1,047,500 fit for military service; 92,430 reach military age (18) annually

Defense expenditures: $NA, NA% of GDP

Anguilla
(dependent territory of the UK)

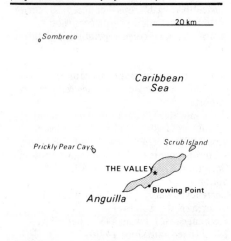

Geography

Total area: 91 km²; land area: 91 km²
Comparative area: about half the size of Washington, DC
Land boundaries: none
Coastline: 61 km
Maritime claims:
Exclusive fishing zone: 200 nm;
Territorial sea: 3 nm
Climate: tropical; moderated by northeast trade winds
Terrain: flat and low-lying island of coral and limestone
Natural resources: negligible; salt, fish, lobster
Land use: arable land NA%; permanent crops NA%; meadows and pastures NA%; forest and woodland NA%; other NA%; mostly rock with sparse scrub oak, few trees, some commercial salt ponds
Environment: frequent hurricanes, other tropical storms (July to October)
Note: located 270 km east of Puerto Rico

People

Population: 6,922 (July 1991), growth rate 0.6% (1991)
Birth rate: 24 births/1,000 population (1991)
Death rate: 9 deaths/1,000 population (1991)
Net migration rate: −10 migrants/1,000 population (1991)
Infant mortality rate: 18 deaths/1,000 live births (1991)
Life expectancy at birth: 71 years male, 77 years female (1991)
Total fertility rate: 3.1 children born/woman (1991)
Nationality: noun—Anguillan(s); adjective—Anguillan
Ethnic divisions: mainly of black African descent
Religion: Anglican 40%, Methodist 33%, Seventh-Day Adventist 7%, Baptist 5%, Roman Catholic 3%, other 12%

Language: English (official)
Literacy: 95% (male 95%, female 95%) age 12 and over can read and write (1984)
Labor force: 2,780 (1984)
Organized labor: NA

Government

Long-form name: none
Type: dependent territory of the UK
Capital: The Valley
Administrative divisions: none (dependent territory of the UK)
Independence: none (dependent territory of the UK)
Constitution: 1 April 1982
Legal system: based on English common law
National holiday: Anguilla Day, 30 May
Executive branch: British monarch, governor, chief minister, Executive Council (cabinet)
Legislative branch: unicameral House of Assembly
Judicial branch: High Court
Leaders:
Chief of State—Queen ELIZABETH II (since 6 February 1952), represented by Governor Brian G. J. CANTY (since NA 1989);
Head of Government—Chief Minister Emile GUMBS (since NA March 1984, served previously from February 1977 to May 1980)
Political parties and leaders: Anguilla National Alliance (ANA), Emile GUMBS; Anguilla United Party (AUP), Ronald WEBSTER; Anguilla Democratic Party (ADP), Victor BANKS
Suffrage: universal at age 18
Elections:
House of Assembly—last held 27 February 1989 (next to be held February 1994); results—percent of vote by party NA; seats—(11 total, 7 elected) ANA 3, AUP 2, ADP 1, independent 1
Communists: none
Member of: CARICOM (observer), CDB
Diplomatic representation: none (dependent territory of the UK)
Flag: two horizontal bands of white (top, almost triple width) and light blue with three orange dolphins in an interlocking circular design centered in the white band; a new flag may have been in use since 30 May 1990

Economy

Overview: Anguilla has few natural resources, and the economy depends heavily on lobster fishing, offshore banking, tourism, and remittances from emigrants. In recent years the economy has benefited from a boom in tourism. Development is

planned to improve the infrastructure, particularly transport and tourist facilities, and also light industry. Improvement in the economy has reduced unemployment from 40% in 1984 to about 5% in 1988.
GDP: $23 million, per capita $3,300; real growth rate 8.2% (1988 est.)
Inflation rate (consumer prices): 4.5% (1988 est.)
Unemployment rate: 5.0% (1988 est.)
Budget: revenues $10.4 million; expenditures $11.0 million, including capital expenditures of $1.1 million (1989 est.)
Exports: $NA;
commodities—lobster and salt;
partners—NA
Imports: $NA;
commodities—NA;
partners—NA
External debt: $NA
Industrial production: growth rate NA%
Electricity: 2,000 kW capacity; 6 million kWh produced, 870 kWh per capita (1990)
Industries: tourism, boat building, salt, fishing (including lobster)
Agriculture: pigeon peas, corn, sweet potatoes, sheep, goats, pigs, cattle, poultry
Economic aid: Western (non-US) countries, ODA and OOF bilateral commitments (1970-89), $38 million
Currency: East Caribbean dollar (plural—dollars); 1 EC dollar (EC$) = 100 cents
Exchange rates: East Caribbean dollars (EC$) per US$1—2.70 (fixed rate since 1976)
Fiscal year: NA

Communications

Highways: 60 km surfaced
Ports: Road Bay, Blowing Point
Civil air: no major transport aircraft
Airports: 3 total, 3 usable; 1 with permanent-surface runways of 1,100 m (Wallblake Airport)
Telecommunications: modern internal telephone system; 890 telephones; stations—3 AM, 1 FM, no TV; radio relay link to island of Saint Martin

Defense Forces

Note: defense is the responsibility of the UK

Antarctica

1000 km

South Atlantic Ocean
South Orkney Islands
Graham Land
ice shelf
South Pole
ice shelf
South Pacific Ocean
Indian Ocean
Victoria Land
Wilkes Land
Indian Ocean

Geography

Total area: about 14,000,000 km²; land area: about 14,000,000 km²
Comparative area: slightly less than 1.5 times the size of the US; second-smallest continent (after Australia)
Land boundaries: see entry on **Disputes**
Coastline: 17,968 km
Maritime claims: see entry on **Disputes**
Disputes: Antarctic Treaty defers claims (see Antarctic Treaty Summary below); sections (some overlapping) claimed by Argentina, Australia, Chile, France (Adélie Land), New Zealand (Ross Dependency), Norway (Queen Maud Land), and UK; Brazil has noted possible Latin claims; the US and USSR do not recognize the territorial claims of other nations and have made no claims themselves (but reserve the right to do so); no formal claims have been made in the sector between 90° west and 150° west
Climate: severe low temperatures vary with latitude, elevation, and distance from the ocean; East Antarctica colder than West Antarctica because of its higher elevation; Antarctic Peninsula has most moderate climate; warmest temperatures occur in January along the coast and average slightly below freezing
Terrain: about 98% thick continental ice sheet, with average elevations between 2,000 and 4,000 meters; mountain ranges up to 4,897 meters high; ice-free coastal areas include parts of southern Victoria Land, Wilkes Land, the Antarctic Peninsula area, and Ross Island on McMurdo Sound; glaciers form ice shelves along about half of coastline and floating ice shelves constitute 11% of the area of the continent
Natural resources: none presently exploited; coal and iron ore; chromium, copper, gold, nickel, platinum, and hydrocarbons have been found in small uncommercial quantities
Land use: arable land 0%; permanent crops 0%; pastures 0%; meadows and forest and woodland 0%; other 100% (ice 98%, barren rock 2%)
Environment: mostly uninhabitable; katabatic (gravity) winds blow coastward from the high interior; frequent blizzards form near the foot of the plateau; cyclonic storms form over the ocean and move clockwise around the coast, as does a circumpolar ocean current; during summer more solar radiation reaches the surface at the South Pole than is received at the Equator in an equivalent period; in April 1991 it was reported that the ozone shield, which protects the Earth's surface from harmful ultraviolet radiation, had dwindled to its lowest level ever over Antarctica; subject to active volcanism (Deception Island and isolated areas of West Antarctica); other seismic activity rare and weak
Note: the coldest, windiest, highest, and driest continent

People

Population: no indigenous inhabitants; staffing of research stations varies seasonally;
Summer (January) population—4,120; Argentina 207, Australia 268, Belgium 13, Brazil 80, Chile 256, China NA, Ecuador NA, Finland 16, France 78, Germany 32, Greenpeace 12, India 60, Italy 210, Japan 59, South Korea 14, Netherlands 10, NZ 264, Norway 23, Peru 39, Poland NA, South Africa 79, Spain 43, Sweden 10, UK 116, Uruguay NA, US 1,666, USSR 565 (1989-90);
Winter (July) population—1,066 total; Argentina 150, Australia 71, Brazil 12, Chile 73, China NA, France 33, Germany 19, Greenpeace 5, India 21, Japan 38, South Korea 14, NZ 11, Poland NA, South Africa 12, UK 69, Uruguay NA, US 225, USSR 313 (1989-90);
Year-round stations—42 total; Argentina 6, Australia 3, Brazil 1, Chile 3, China 2, France 1, Germany 2, Greenpeace 1, India 2, Japan 2, South Korea 1, NZ 1, Poland 1, South Africa 1, UK 5, Uruguay 1, US 3, USSR 6 (1990-91);
Summer only stations—34 total; Argentina 1, Australia 3, Chile 5, Finland 1, Germany 4, India 1, Italy 1, Japan 1, NZ 2, Norway 1, Peru 1, South Africa 1, Spain 1, Sweden 2, UK 1, US 3, USSR 5 (1989-90)

Government

Long-form name: none
Type: The Antarctic Treaty, signed on 1 December 1959 and entered into force on 23 June 1961, established for at least 30 years a legal framework for peaceful use, scientific research, and deferral of legal questions regarding territorial claims. Administration is carried out through consultative member meetings—the last meeting was held in Madrid (Spain) in April 1991.

Consultative (voting) members include seven nations that claim portions of Antarctica as national territory (some claims overlap) and nonclaimant nations. The US and other nations have made no claims, but have reserved the right to claim territory. The US does not recognize the claims of others. The year in parentheses indicates when an acceding nation was voted to full consultative (voting) status, while no date indicates an original 1959 treaty signatory. Claimant nations are—Argentina, Australia, Chile, France, New Zealand, Norway, and the UK. Nonclaimant consultative nations are—Belgium, Brazil (1983), China (1985), Ecuador (1990), Finland (1989), Germany (1981), India (1983), Italy (1987), Japan, South Korea (1989), Netherlands (1990), Peru (1989), Poland (1977), South Africa, Spain (1988), Sweden (1988), Uruguay (1985), the US, and the USSR.

Acceding (nonvoting) members, with year of accession in parenthesis, are—Austria (1987), Bulgaria (1978), Canada (1988), Colombia (1988), Cuba (1984), Czechoslovakia (1962), Denmark (1965), Greece (1987), Hungary (1984), North Korea (1987), Papua New Guinea (1981), Romania (1971), and Switzerland (1990).

Antarctic Treaty Summary:
Article 1—area to be used for peaceful purposes only; military activity, such as weapons testing, is prohibited, but military personnel and equipment may be used for peaceful scientific and logistics purposes;
Article 2—freedom of scientific investigation and cooperation shall continue;
Article 3—free exchange of information and personnel in cooperation with the UN and other international agencies;
Article 4—does not recognize, dispute, or establish territorial claims and no new claims shall be asserted while the treaty is in force;
Article 5—prohibits nuclear explosions or disposal of radioactive wastes;
Article 6—includes under the treaty all land and ice shelves south of 60° 00Ł south, but that the water areas be covered by international law;
Article 7—treaty-state observers have free access, including aerial observation, to any area and may inspect all stations, installations, and equipment; advance notice of all activities and the introduction of military personnel must be given;
Article 8—allows for jurisdiction over observers and scientists by their own states;
Article 9—frequent consultative meetings take place among member nations;
Article 10—treaty states will discourage activities by any country in Antarctica that are contrary to the treaty;

Antarctica (continued)

Article 11—disputes to be settled peacefully by the parties concerned or, ultimately, by the ICJ;
Articles 12, 13, 14—deal with upholding, interpreting, and amending the treaty among involved nations.

Other agreements: more than 150 recommendations adopted at treaty consultative meetings and ratified by governments include—Agreed Measures for the Conservation of Antarctic Fauna and Flora (1964); Convention for the Conservation of Antarctic Seals (1972); Convention on the Conservation of Antarctic Marine Living Resources (1980); a mineral resources agreement was signed in 1988 but was subsequently rejected by some signatories and is likely to be replaced in 1991 by a comprehensive environmental protection agreement that defers minerals development for a long period.

Economy

Overview: No economic activity at present except for fishing off the coast and small-scale tourism, both based abroad. Exploitation of mineral resources is unlikely because of technical difficulties, high costs, and objections by environmentalists.

Communications

Airports: 37 total; 27 usable; none with permanent hard-surface runways; 2 with runways over 3,659 m; 5 with runways 2,440-3,659 m; 4 with runways 1,220-2,439 m
Ports: none; offshore anchorage only

Defense Forces

Note: none; Article 7 of the Antarctic Treaty states that advance notice of all activities and the introduction of military personnel must be given

Antigua and Barbuda

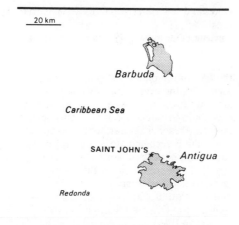

Geography

Total area: 440 km²; land area: 440 km²; includes Redonda
Comparative area: slightly less than 2.5 times the size of Washington, DC
Land boundaries: none
Coastline: 153 km
Maritime claims:
Contiguous zone: 24 nm;
Exclusive economic zone: 200 nm;
Territorial sea: 12 nm
Climate: tropical marine; little seasonal temperature variation
Terrain: mostly low-lying limestone and coral islands with some higher volcanic areas
Natural resources: negligible; pleasant climate fosters tourism
Land use: arable land 18%; permanent crops 0%; meadows and pastures 7%; forest and woodland 16%; other 59%
Environment: subject to hurricanes and tropical storms (July to October); insufficient freshwater resources; deeply indented coastline provides many natural harbors
Note: 420 km east-southeast of Puerto Rico

People

Population: 63,917 (July 1991), growth rate 0.4% (1991)
Birth rate: 18 births/1,000 population (1991)
Death rate: 6 deaths/1,000 population (1991)
Net migration rate: −9 migrants/1,000 population (1991)
Infant mortality rate: 22 deaths/1,000 live births (1991)
Life expectancy at birth: 70 years male, 74 years female (1991)
Total fertility rate: 1.7 children born/woman (1991)
Nationality: noun—Antiguan(s); adjective—Antiguan

Ethnic divisions: almost entirely of black African origin; some of British, Portuguese, Lebanese, and Syrian origin
Religion: Anglican (predominant), other Protestant sects, some Roman Catholic
Language: English (official), local dialects
Literacy: 89% (male 90%, female 88%) age 15 and over having completed 5 or more years of schooling (1960)
Labor force: 30,000; commerce and services 82%, agriculture 11%, industry 7% (1983)
Organized labor: Antigua and Barbuda Public Service Association (ABPSA), membership 500; Antigua Trades and Labor Union (ATLU), 10,000 members; Antigua Workers Union (AWU), 10,000 members (1986 est.)

Government

Long-form name: none
Type: parliamentary democracy
Capital: Saint John's
Administrative divisions: 6 parishes and 2 dependencies*; Barbuda*, Redonda*, Saint George, Saint John, Saint Mary, Saint Paul, Saint Peter, Saint Philip
Independence: 1 November 1981 (from UK)
Constitution: 1 November 1981
Legal system: based on English common law
National holiday: Independence Day, 1 November (1981)
Executive branch: British monarch, governor general, prime minister, deputy prime minister, Cabinet
Legislative branch: bicameral Parliament consists of an upper house or Senate and a lower house or House of Representatives
Judicial branch: Eastern Caribbean Supreme Court
Leaders:
Chief of State—Queen ELIZABETH II (since 6 February 1952), represented by Governor General Sir Wilfred Ebenezer JACOBS (since 1 November 1981, previously Governor since 1976);
Head of Government—Prime Minister Vere Cornwall BIRD, Sr. (since NA 1976)
Political parties and leaders: Antigua Labor Party (ALP), Vere C. BIRD, Sr., Lester BIRD; United National Democratic Party (UNDP), Dr. Ivor HEATH
Suffrage: universal at age 18
Elections:
House of Representatives—last held 9 March 1989 (next to be held 1994); results—percentage of vote by party NA; seats—(17 total) ALP 15, UNDP 1, independent 1
Communists: negligible
Other political or pressure groups: Antigua Caribbean Liberation Movement (ACLM),

12

a small leftist nationalist group led by Leonard (Tim) HECTOR; Antigua Trades and Labor Union (ATLU), headed by Noel THOMAS

Member of: ACP, C, CARICOM, CDB, ECLAC, FAO, G-77, GATT, IBRD, ICAO, ICFTU, IFAD, IFC, ILO, IMF, IMO, INTERPOL, IOC, ITU, NAM (observer), OAS, OECS, OPANAL, UN, UNCTAD, UNESCO, WCL, WHO, WMO

Diplomatic representation: Ambassador Edmund Hawkins LAKE; Chancery at Suite 2H, 3400 International Drive NW, Washington DC 20008; telephone (202) 362-5211 or 5166, 5122, 5225; there is an Antiguan Consulate in Miami;
US—the US Ambassador to Barbados is accredited to Antigua and Barbuda, and in his absence, the Embassy is headed by Chargé d'Affaires Bryant SALTER; Embassy at Queen Elizabeth Highway, Saint John's (mailing address is FPO Miami 34054); telephone (809) 462-3505 or 3506

Flag: red with an inverted isosceles triangle based on the top edge of the flag; the triangle contains three horizontal bands of black (top), light blue, and white with a yellow rising sun in the black band

Economy

Overview: The economy is primarily service oriented, with tourism the most important determinant of economic performance. During the period 1983-89, real GDP expanded at an annual average rate of about 7%. Tourism's contribution to GDP, as measured by value added tax in hotels and restaurants, rose from about 14% in 1983 to 16% in 1989, and stimulated growth in other sectors—particularly in construction, communications, and public utilities. Antigua and Barbuda is one of the few areas in the Caribbean experiencing a labor shortage in some sectors of the economy.

GDP: $350 million, per capita $5,470; real growth rate 6.2% (1989 est.)

Inflation rate (consumer prices): 3.6% (1989 est.)

Unemployment rate: 5.0% (1988 est.)

Budget: revenues $92.8 million; expenditures $101 million, including capital expenditures of $NA (1990 est.)

Exports: $31.6 million (f.o.b., 1989 est.);
commodities—petroleum products 48%, manufactures 23%, food and live animals 4%, machinery and transport equipment 17%;
partners—OECS 26%, Barbados 15%, Guyana 4%, Trinidad and Tobago 2%, US 0.3%

Imports: $347.8 million (c.i.f., 1989 est.);
commodities—food and live animals, machinery and transport equipment, manufactures, chemicals, oil;
partners—US 27%, UK 16%, Canada 4%, OECS 3%, other 50%

External debt: $250 million (1990 est.)

Industrial production: growth rate 3% (1989 est.); accounts for 10% of GDP

Electricity: 52,000 kW capacity; 95 million kWh produced, 1,490 kWh per capita (1990)

Industries: tourism, construction, light manufacturing (clothing, alcohol, household appliances)

Agriculture: accounts for 4% of GDP; expanding output of cotton, fruits, vegetables, and livestock sector; other crops—bananas, coconuts, cucumbers, mangoes, sugarcane; not self-sufficient in food

Economic aid: US commitments, $10 million (1985-88); Western (non-US) countries, ODA and OOF bilateral commitments (1970-88), $45 million

Currency: East Caribbean dollar (plural—dollars); 1 EC dollar (EC$) = 100 cents

Exchange rates: East Caribbean dollars (EC$) per US$1—2.70 (fixed rate since 1976)

Fiscal year: 1 April-31 March

Communications

Railroads: 64 km 0.760-meter narrow gauge and 13 km 0.610-meter gauge used almost exclusively for handling sugarcane

Highways: 240 km

Ports: Saint John's

Merchant marine: 86 ships (1,000 GRT or over) totaling 319,477 GRT/497,194 DWT; includes 61 cargo, 5 refrigerated cargo, 6 container, 4 roll-on/roll-off cargo, 1 multifunction large load carrier, 3 petroleum, oils, and lubricants (POL) tanker, 6 chemical tanker; note—a flag of convenience registry

Civil air: 10 major transport aircraft

Airports: 3 total, 3 usable; 2 with permanent-surface runways; 1 with runways 2,440-3,659 m; 2 with runways less than 1,220 m

Telecommunications: good automatic telephone system; 6,700 telephones; tropospheric scatter links with Saba and Guadeloupe; stations—4 AM, 2 FM, 2 TV, 2 shortwave; 1 coaxial submarine cable; 1 Atlantic Ocean INTELSAT earth station

Defense Forces

Branches: Royal Antigua and Barbuda Defense Force, Royal Antigua and Barbuda Police Force (includes the Coast Guard)

Manpower availability: NA

Defense expenditures: $1.4 million, less than 1% of GDP (FY91)

Arctic Ocean

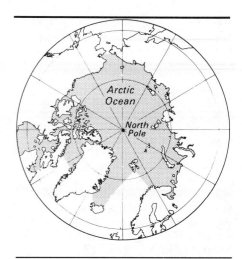

Geography

Total area: 14,056,000 km²; includes Baffin Bay, Barents Sea, Beaufort Sea, Chukchi Sea, East Siberian Sea, Greenland Sea, Hudson Bay, Hudson Strait, Kara Sea, Laptev Sea, and other tributary water bodies

Comparative area: slightly more than 1.5 times the size of the US; smallest of the world's four oceans (after Pacific Ocean, Atlantic Ocean, and Indian Ocean)

Coastline: 45,389 km

Climate: persistent cold and relatively narrow annual temperature ranges; winters characterized by continuous darkness, cold and stable weather conditions, and clear skies; summers characterized by continuous daylight, damp and foggy weather, and weak cyclones with rain or snow

Terrain: central surface covered by a perennial drifting polar icepack which averages about 3 meters in thickness, although pressure ridges may be three times that size; clockwise drift pattern in the Beaufort Gyral Stream, but nearly straight line movement from the New Siberian Islands (USSR) to Denmark Strait (between Greenland and Iceland); the ice pack is surrounded by open seas during the summer, but more than doubles in size during the winter and extends to the encircling land masses; the ocean floor is about 50% continental shelf (highest percentage of any ocean) with the remainder a central basin interrupted by three submarine ridges (Alpha Cordillera, Nansen Cordillera, and Lomonsov Ridge); maximum depth is 4,665 meters in the Fram Basin

Natural resources: sand and gravel aggregates, placer deposits, polymetallic nodules, oil and gas fields, fish, marine mammals (seals, whales)

Environment: endangered marine species include walruses and whales; ice islands occasionally break away from northern Ellesmere

Arctic Ocean *(continued)*

Island; icebergs calved from western Greenland and extreme northeastern Canada; maximum snow cover in March or April about 20 to 50 centimeters over the frozen ocean and lasts about 10 months; permafrost in islands; virtually icelocked from October to June; fragile ecosystem slow to change and slow to recover from disruptions or damage
Note: major chokepoint is the southern Chukchi Sea (northern access to the Pacific Ocean via the Bering Strait); ships subject to superstructure icing from October to May; strategic location between North America and the USSR; shortest marine link between the extremes of eastern and western USSR; floating research stations operated by the US and USSR

Economy

Overview: Economic activity is limited to the exploitation of natural resources, including crude oil, natural gas, fishing, and sealing.

Communications

Ports: Churchill (Canada), Murmansk (USSR), Prudhoe Bay (US)
Telecommunications: no submarine cables
Note: sparse network of air, ocean, river, and land routes; the Northwest Passage (North America) and Northern Sea Route (Asia) are important waterways

Argentina

Boundary representation is not necessarily authoritative.

Geography

Total area: 2,766,890 km²; land area: 2,736,690 km²
Comparative area: slightly more than four times the size of Texas
Land boundaries: 9,665 km total; Bolivia 832 km, Brazil 1,224 km, Chile 5,150 km, Paraguay 1,880 km, Uruguay 579 km
Coastline: 4,989 km
Maritime claims:
Continental shelf: 200 m (depth) or to depth of exploitation;
Territorial sea: 200 nm (overflight and navigation permitted beyond 12 nm)
Disputes: short section of the boundary with Uruguay is in dispute; short section of the boundary with Chile is indefinite; claims British-administered Falkland Islands (Islas Malvinas); claims British-administered South Georgia and the South Sandwich Islands; territorial claim in Antarctica
Climate: mostly temperate; arid in southeast; subantarctic in southwest
Terrain: rich plains of the Pampas in northern half, flat to rolling plateau of Patagonia in south, rugged Andes along western border
Natural resources: fertile plains of the pampas, lead, zinc, tin, copper, iron ore, manganese, crude oil, uranium
Land use: arable land 9%; permanent crops 4%; meadows and pastures 52%; forest and woodland 22%; other 13%; includes irrigated 1%
Environment: Tucumán and Mendoza areas in Andes subject to earthquakes; pamperos are violent windstorms that can strike Pampas and northeast; irrigated soil degradation; desertification; air and water pollution in Buenos Aires
Note: second-largest country in South America (after Brazil); strategic location relative to sea lanes between South Atlantic and South Pacific Oceans (Strait of Magellan, Beagle Channel, Drake Passage)

People

Population: 32,663,983 (July 1991), growth rate 1.1% (1991)
Birth rate: 20 births/1,000 population (1991)
Death rate: 9 deaths/1,000 population (1991)
Net migration rate: NEGL migrants/1,000 population (1991)
Infant mortality rate: 31 deaths/1,000 live births (1991)
Life expectancy at birth: 68 years male, 74 years female (1991)
Total fertility rate: 2.7 children born/woman (1991)
Nationality: noun—Argentine(s); adjective—Argentine
Ethnic divisions: white 85%; mestizo, Indian, or other nonwhite groups 15%
Religion: nominally Roman Catholic 90% (less than 20% practicing), Protestant 2%, Jewish 2%, other 6%
Language: Spanish (official), English, Italian, German, French
Literacy: 95% (male 96%, female 95%) age 15 and over can read and write (1990 est.)
Labor force: 10,900,000; agriculture 12%, industry 31%, services 57% (1985 est.)
Organized labor: 3,000,000; 28% of labor force

Government

Long-form name: Argentine Republic
Type: republic
Capital: Buenos Aires (tentative plans to move to Viedma by 1990 indefinitely postponed)
Administrative divisions: 22 provinces (provincias, singular—provincia), 1 national territory* (territorio nacional), and 1 district** (distrito); Buenos Aires, Catamarca, Chaco, Chubut, Córdoba, Corrientes, Distrito Federal**, Entre Ríos, Formosa, Jujuy, La Pampa, La Rioja, Mendoza, Misiones, Neuquén, Río Negro, Salta, San Juan, San Luis, Santa Cruz, Santa Fe, Santiago del Estero, Tierra del Fuego, Antártida e Islas del Atlántico Sur*, Tucumán; note—the national territory is in the process of becoming a province; the US does not recognize claims to Antarctica
Independence: 9 July 1816 (from Spain)
Constitution: 1 May 1853
Legal system: mixture of US and West European legal systems; has not accepted compulsory ICJ jurisdiction
National holiday: Revolution Day, 25 May (1810)
Executive branch: president, vice president, Cabinet
Legislative branch: bicameral National Congress (Congreso Nacional) consists of

an upper chamber or Senate (Senado) and a lower chamber or Chamber of Deputies (Cámara de Diputados)

Judicial branch: Supreme Court (Corte Suprema)

Leaders:
Chief of State and Head of Government—President Carlos Saúl MENEM (since 8 July 1989); Vice President Eduardo DUHALDE (since 8 July 1989)

Political parties and leaders: Justicialist Party (JP), Carlos Saúl MENEM, Peronist umbrella political organization; Radical Civic Union (UCR), Raúl ALFONSÍN, moderately left of center; Union of the Democratic Center (UCD), Alvaro ALSOGARAY, conservative party; Intransigent Party (PI), Dr. Oscar ALENDE, leftist party; several provincial parties

Suffrage: universal at age 18

Elections:
President—last held 14 May 1989 (next to be held May 1995); results—Carlos Saúl MENEM was elected;
Chamber of Deputies—last held 14 May 1989 (next to be held October 1991); results—JP 47%, UCR 30%, UCD 7%, other 16%; seats—(254 total); JP 122, UCR 93, UCD 11, other 28

Communists: some 70,000 members in various party organizations, including a small nucleus of activists

Other political or pressure groups: Peronist-dominated labor movement, General Confederation of Labor (Peronist-leaning umbrella labor organization), Argentine Industrial Union (manufacturers' association), Argentine Rural Society (large landowners' association), business organizations, students, the Roman Catholic Church, the Armed Forces

Member of: AfDB, AG (observer), CCC, ECLAC, FAO, G-6, G-11, G-19, G-24, G-77, GATT, IADB, IAEA, IBRD, ICAO, ICC, ICFTU, IDA, IFAD, IFC, ILO, IMF, IMO, INMARSAT, INTELSAT, INTERPOL, IOC, IOM, ISO, ITU, LAES, LAIA, LORCS, NAM, OAS, PCA, RG, UN, UNAVEM, UNCTAD, UNESCO, UNHCR, UNIDO, UNIIMOG, UNTSO, UPU, WCL, WFTU, WHO, WIPO, WMO, WTO

Diplomatic representation: Ambassador Ortiz de ROZAS; Chancery at 1600 New Hampshire Avenue NW, Washington DC 20009; telephone (202) 939-6400 through 6403; there are Argentine Consulates General in Houston, Miami, New Orleans, New York, San Francisco, and San Juan (Puerto Rico), and Consulates in Baltimore, Chicago, and Los Angeles;
US—Ambassador Terence A. TODMAN; Embassy at 4300 Colombia, 1425 Buenos Aires (mailing address is APO Miami 34034); telephone [54] (1) 774-7611 or 8811, 9911

Flag: three equal horizontal bands of light blue (top), white, and light blue; centered in the white band is a radiant yellow sun with a human face known as the Sun of May

---

Economy

Overview: Argentina is rich in natural resources and has a highly literate population, an export-oriented agricultural sector, and a diversified industrial base. Nevertheless, following decades of mismanagement and statist policies, the economy has encountered major problems in recent years, leading to escalating inflation and a recession in 1988-90. A widening public-sector deficit and a multidigit inflation rate have dominated the economy over the past three years; retail prices rose nearly 5,000% in 1989 and another 1,345% in 1990. Since 1978, Argentina's external debt has nearly doubled to $60 billion, creating severe debt-servicing difficulties and hurting the country's creditworthiness with international lenders.

GNP: $82.7 billion, per capita $2,560; real growth rate −3.5% (1990 est.)

Inflation rate (consumer prices): 1,345% (1990)

Unemployment rate: 8.6% (May 1990)

Budget: revenues $12.2 billion; expenditures $17.3 billion, including capital expenditures of $2.8 billion (1989)

Exports: $12.1 billion (f.o.b., 1990);
commodities—meat, wheat, corn, oilseed, hides, wool;
partners—US 12%, USSR, Italy, Brazil, Japan, Netherlands

Imports: $3.8 billion (c.i.f., 1990);
commodities—machinery and equipment, chemicals, metals, fuels and lubricants, agricultural products;
partners—US 22%, Brazil, FRG, Bolivia, Japan, Italy, Netherlands

External debt: $60 billion (December 1990)

Industrial production: growth rate −6% (1990 est.); accounts for 30% of GDP

Electricity: 16,749,000 kW capacity; 45,580 million kWh produced, 1,410 kWh per capita (1990)

Industries: food processing (especially meat packing), motor vehicles, consumer durables, textiles, chemicals and petrochemicals, printing, metallurgy, steel

Agriculture: accounts for 15% of GNP (including fishing); produces abundant food for both domestic consumption and exports; among world's top five exporters of grain and beef; principal crops—wheat, corn, sorghum, soybeans, sugar beets; 1987 fish catch estimated at 500,000 tons

Economic aid: US commitments, including Ex-Im (FY70-89), $1.0 billion; Western (non-US) countries, ODA and OOF bilateral commitments (1970-88), $4.0 billion; Communist countries (1970-89), $718 million

Currency: austral (plural—australes); 1 austral (₳) = 100 centavos

Exchange rates: australes (₳) per US$1—9,900 (April 1991), 4,707 (1990), 423 (1989), 8.7526 (1988), 2.1443 (1987), 0.9430 (1986), 0.6018 (1985)

Fiscal year: calendar year

Communications

Railroads: 34,172 km total (includes 169 km electrified); includes a mixture of 1.435-meter standard gauge, 1.676-meter broad gauge, 1.000-meter gauge, and 0.750-meter gauge

Highways: 208,350 km total; 47,550 km paved, 39,500 km gravel, 101,000 km improved earth, 20,300 km unimproved earth

Inland waterways: 11,000 km navigable

Pipelines: 4,090 km crude oil; 2,900 km refined products; 9,918 km natural gas

Ports: Bahia Blanca, Buenos Aires, Necochea, Rio Gallegos, Rosario, Santa Fe

Merchant marine: 129 ships (1,000 GRT or over) totaling 1,663,884 GRT/2,689,645 DWT; includes 42 cargo, 7 refrigerated cargo, 6 container, 1 railcar carrier, 47 petroleum, oils, and lubricants (POL) tanker, 4 chemical tanker, 4 liquefied gas, 18 bulk; additionally, 2 naval tankers and 1 military transport are sometimes used commercially

Civil air: 54 major transport aircraft

Airports: 1,763 total, 1,575 usable; 135 with permanent-surface runways; 1 with runways over 3,659 m; 31 with runways 2,440-3,659 m; 336 with runways 1,220-2,439 m

Telecommunications: extensive modern system; 2,650,000 telephones (12,000 public telephones); radio relay widely used; stations—171 AM, no FM, 231 TV, 13 shortwave; 2 Atlantic Ocean INTELSAT earth stations; domestic satellite network has 40 stations

---

Defense Forces

Branches: Argentine Army, Navy of the Argentine Republic, Argentine Air Force, National Gendarmerie, Argentine Naval Prefecture (Coast Guard only), National Aeronautical Police Force

Manpower availability: males 15-49, 7,992,140; 6,478,730 fit for military service; 285,047 reach military age (20) annually

Defense expenditures: $700 million, 1% of GNP (1990)

Aruba
(part of the Dutch realm)

Geography

Total area: 193 km²; land area: 193 km²
Comparative area: slightly larger than Washington, DC
Land boundaries: none
Coastline: 68.5 km
Maritime claims:
Exclusive fishing zone: 12 nm;
Territorial sea: 12 nm
Climate: tropical marine; little seasonal temperature variation
Terrain: flat with a few hills; scant vegetation
Natural resources: negligible; white sandy beaches
Land use: arable land 0%; permanent crops 0%; meadows and pastures 0%; forest and woodland 0%; other 100%
Environment: lies outside the Caribbean hurricane belt
Note: 28 km north of Venezuela

People

Population: 64,052 (July 1991), growth rate 0.6% (1991)
Birth rate: 15 births/1,000 population (1991)
Death rate: 6 deaths/1,000 population (1991)
Net migration rate: −4 migrants/1,000 population (1991)
Infant mortality rate: 8 deaths/1,000 live births (1991)
Life expectancy at birth: 72 years male, 80 years female (1991)
Total fertility rate: 1.8 children born/woman (1991)
Nationality: noun—Aruban(s); adjective—Aruban
Ethnic divisions: mixed European/Caribbean Indian 80%
Religion: Roman Catholic 82%, Protestant 8%, also small Hindu, Muslim, Confucian, and Jewish minority

Language: Dutch (official), Papiamento (a Spanish, Portuguese, Dutch, English dialect), English (widely spoken), Spanish
Literacy: NA% (male NA%, female NA%)
Labor force: NA, but most employment is in the tourist industry (1986)
Organized labor: Aruban Workers' Federation (FTA)

Government

Long-form name: none
Type: part of the Dutch realm—full autonomy in internal affairs obtained in 1986 upon separation from the Netherlands Antilles
Capital: Oranjestad
Administrative divisions: none (self-governing part of the Netherlands)
Independence: none (part of the Dutch realm); note—in 1990 Aruba requested and received from the Netherlands cancellation of the agreement to automatically give independence to the island in 1996
Constitution: 1 January 1986
Legal system: based on Dutch civil law system, with some English common law influence
National holiday: Flag Day, 18 March
Executive branch: Dutch monarch, governor, prime minister, Council of Ministers (cabinet)
Legislative branch: unicameral legislature (Staten)
Judicial branch: Joint High Court of Justice
Leaders:
Chief of State—Queen BEATRIX Wilhelmina Armgard (since 30 April 1980), represented by Governor General Felipe B. TROMP (since 1 January 1986);
Head of Government—Prime Minister Nelson ODUBER (since NA February 1989)
Political parties and leaders: Electoral Movement Party (MEP), Nelson ODUBER; Aruban People's Party (AVP), Henny EMAN; National Democratic Action (ADN), Pedro Charro KELLY; New Patriotic Party (PPN), Eddy WERLEMEN; Aruban Patriotic Party (PPA), Leo CHANCE; Aruban Democratic Party (PDA), Leo BERLINSKI; Democratic Action 86 (AD'86), Arturo ODUBER; governing coalition includes the MEP, PPA, and ADN
Suffrage: universal at age 18
Elections:
Legislature—last held 6 January 1989 (next to be held by January 1993); results—percent of vote by party NA; seats—(21 total) MEP 10, AVP 8, ADN 1, PPN 1, PPA 1
Member of: ECLAC (associate), INTERPOL, IOC, UNESCO (associate), WCL, WTO (associate)
Diplomatic representation: none (self-governing part of the Netherlands)
Flag: blue with two narrow horizontal yellow stripes across the lower portion and a

red, four-pointed star outlined in white in the upper hoist-side corner

Economy

Overview: Tourism is the mainstay of the economy, although offshore banking and oil refining and storage are also important. Hotel capacity expanded rapidly between 1985 and 1989 and nearly doubled in 1990 alone. Unemployment has steadily declined from about 20% in 1986 to about 2% in 1990. The reopening of the local oil refinery, once a major source of employment and foreign exchange earnings, promises to give the economy an additional boost.
GDP: $730 million, per capita $11,600; real growth rate 8.8% (1989 est.)
Inflation rate (consumer prices): 5.8% (1990 est.)
Unemployment rate: 1.6% (1990 est.)
Budget: revenues $145 million; expenditures $185 million, including capital expenditures of $42 million (1988)
Exports: $131.6 million (f.o.b., 1990 est.); *commodities*—mostly petroleum products; *partners*—US 64%, EC
Imports: $496 million (f.o.b., 1990 est.); *commodities*—food, consumer goods, manufactures; *partners*—US 8%, EC
External debt: $81 million (1987)
Industrial production: growth rate NA
Electricity: 310,000 kW capacity; 945 million kWh produced, 15,000 kWh per capita (1990)
Industries: tourism, transshipment facilities, oil refining
Agriculture: poor quality soils and low rainfall limit agricultural activity to the cultivation of aloes, some livestock, and fishing
Economic aid: Western (non-US) countries ODA and OOF bilateral commitments (1980-1988), $200 million
Currency: Aruban florin (plural—florins); 1 Aruban florin (Af.) = 100 cents
Exchange rates: Aruban florins (Af.) per US$1—1.7900 (fixed rate since 1986)
Fiscal year: calendar year

Communications

Ports: Oranjestad, Sint Nicolaas
Airfield: government-owned airport east of Oranjestad
Telecommunications: generally adequate; extensive interisland radio relay links; 72,168 telephones; stations—4 AM, 4 FM, 1 TV; 1 sea cable to Sint Maarten

Defense Forces

Note: defense is the responsibility of the Netherlands

Ashmore and Cartier Islands

(territory of Australia)

Geography

Total area: 5 km²; land area: 5 km²; includes Ashmore Reef (West, Middle, and East Islets) and Cartier Island
Comparative area: about 8.5 times the size of The Mall in Washington, DC
Land boundaries: none
Coastline: 74.1 km
Maritime claims:
Contiguous zone: 12 nm;
Continental shelf: 200 m (depth) or to depth of exploration;
Exclusive fishing zone: 200 nm;
Territorial sea: 3 nm
Climate: tropical
Terrain: low with sand and coral
Natural resources: fish
Land use: arable land 0%; permanent crops 0%; meadows and pastures 0%; forest and woodland 0%; other—grass and sand 100%
Environment: surrounded by shoals and reefs; Ashmore Reef National Nature Reserve established in August 1983
Note: located in extreme eastern Indian Ocean between Australia and Indonesia 320 km off the northwest coast of Australia

People

Population: no permanent inhabitants; seasonal caretakers

Government

Long-form name: Territory of Ashmore and Cartier Islands
Type: territory of Australia administered by the Australian Ministry for Territories and Local Government
Administrative divisions: none (territory of Australia)
Legal system: relevant laws of the Northern Territory of Australia
Note: administered by the Australian Minister for Arts, Sports, the Environment, Tourism, and Territories Roslyn KELLY
Diplomatic representation: none (territory of Australia)

Economy

Overview: no economic activity

Communications

Ports: none; offshore anchorage only

Defense Forces

Note: defense is the responsibility of Australia; periodic visits by the Royal Australian Navy and Royal Australian Air Force

Atlantic Ocean

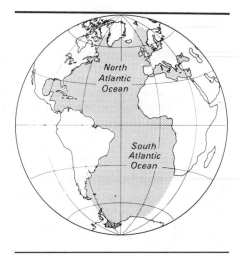

Geography

Total area: 82,217,000 km²; includes Baltic Sea, Black Sea, Caribbean Sea, Davis Strait, Denmark Strait, Drake Passage, Gulf of Mexico, Mediterranean Sea, North Sea, Norwegian Sea, Weddell Sea, and other tributary water bodies
Comparative area: slightly less than nine times the size of the US; second-largest of the world's four oceans (after the Pacific Ocean, but larger than Indian Ocean or Arctic Ocean)
Coastline: 111,866 km
Climate: tropical cyclones (hurricanes) develop off the coast of Africa near Cape Verde and move westward into the Caribbean Sea; hurricanes can occur from May to December, but are most frequent from August to November
Terrain: surface usually covered with sea ice in Labrador Sea, Denmark Strait, and Baltic Sea from October to June; clockwise warm water gyre (broad, circular system of currents) in the north Atlantic, counterclockwise warm water gyre in the south Atlantic; the ocean floor is dominated by the Mid-Atlantic Ridge, a rugged north-south centerline for the entire Atlantic basin; maximum depth is 8,605 meters in the Puerto Rico Trench
Natural resources: oil and gas fields, fish, marine mammals (seals and whales), sand and gravel aggregates, placer deposits, polymetallic nodules, precious stones
Environment: endangered marine species include the manatee, seals, sea lions, turtles, and whales; municipal sludge pollution off eastern US, southern Brazil, and eastern Argentina; oil pollution in Caribbean Sea, Gulf of Mexico, Lake Maracaibo, Mediterranean Sea, and North Sea; industrial waste and municipal sewage pollution in Baltic Sea, North Sea, and Mediterranean Sea; icebergs common in Davis Strait, Denmark

Atlantic Ocean (continued)

Strait, and the northwestern Atlantic from February to August and have been spotted as far south as Bermuda and the Madeira Islands; icebergs from Antarctica occur in the extreme southern Atlantic
Note: ships subject to superstructure icing in extreme north Atlantic from October to May and extreme south Atlantic from May to October; persistent fog can be a hazard to shipping from May to September; major choke points include the Dardanelles, Strait of Gibraltar, access to the Panama and Suez Canals; strategic straits include the Dover Strait, Straits of Florida, Mona Passage, The Sound (øCresund), and Windward Passage; north Atlantic shipping lanes subject to icebergs from February to August; the Equator divides the Atlantic Ocean into the North Atlantic Ocean and South Atlantic Ocean

Economy

Overview: Economic activity is limited to exploitation of natural resources, especially fish, dredging aragonite sands (The Bahamas), and crude oil and natural gas production (Caribbean Sea and North Sea).

Communications

Ports: Alexandria (Egypt), Algiers (Algeria), Antwerp (Belgium), Barcelona (Spain), Buenos Aires (Argentina), Casablanca (Morocco), Colon (Panama), Copenhagen (Denmark), Dakar (Senegal), Gdansk (Poland), Hamburg (Germany), Helsinki (Finland), Las Palmas (Canary Islands, Spain), Le Havre (France), Leningrad (USSR), Lisbon (Portugal), London (UK), Marseille (France), Montevideo (Uruguay), Montreal (Canada), Naples (Italy), New Orleans (US), New York (US), Oran (Algeria), Oslo (Norway), Piraeus (Greece), Rio de Janeiro (Brazil), Rotterdam (Netherlands), Stockholm (Sweden)
Telecommunications: numerous submarine cables with most between continental Europe and the UK, North America and the UK, and in the Mediterranean; numerous direct links across Atlantic via INTELSAT satellite network
Note: Kiel Canal and Saint Lawrence Seaway are two important waterways

Australia

Geography

Total area: 7,686,850 km²; land area: 7,617,930 km²; includes Macquarie Island
Comparative area: slightly smaller than the US
Land boundaries: none
Coastline: 25,760 km
Maritime claims:
Contiguous zone: 12 nm;
Continental shelf: 200 m (depth) or to depth of exploitation;
Exclusive fishing zone: 200 nm;
Territorial sea: 3 nm
Disputes: territorial claim in Antarctica (Australian Antarctic Territory)
Climate: generally arid to semiarid; temperate in south and east; tropical in north
Terrain: mostly low plateau with deserts; fertile plain in southeast
Natural resources: bauxite, coal, iron ore, copper, tin, silver, uranium, nickel, tungsten, mineral sands, lead, zinc, diamonds, natural gas, crude oil
Land use: arable land 6%; permanent crops NEGL%; meadows and pastures 58%; forest and woodland 14%; other 22%; includes irrigated NEGL%
Environment: subject to severe droughts and floods; cyclones along coast; limited freshwater availability; irrigated soil degradation; regular, tropical, invigorating, sea breeze known as the doctor occurs along west coast in summer; desertification
Note: world's smallest continent but sixth-largest country

People

Population: 17,288,044 (July 1991), growth rate 1.5% (1991)
Birth rate: 15 births/1,000 population (1991)
Death rate: 7 deaths/1,000 population (1991)
Net migration rate: 7 migrants/1,000 population (1991)

Infant mortality rate: 8 deaths/1,000 live births (1991)
Life expectancy at birth: 74 years male, 80 years female (1991)
Total fertility rate: 1.8 children born/woman (1991)
Nationality: noun—Australian(s); adjective—Australian
Ethnic divisions: Caucasian 95%, Asian 4%, Aboriginal and other 1%
Religion: Anglican 26.1%, Roman Catholic 26.0%, other Christian 24.3%
Language: English, native languages
Literacy: 100% (male 100%, female 100%) age 15 and over can read and write (1980 est.)
Labor force: 7,700,000; finance and services 33.8%, public and community services 22.3%, wholesale and retail trade 20.1%, manufacturing and industry 16.2%, agriculture 6.1% (1987)
Organized labor: 42% of labor force (1988)

Government

Long-form name: Commonwealth of Australia
Type: federal parliamentary state
Capital: Canberra
Administrative divisions: 6 states and 2 territories*; Australian Capital Territory*, New South Wales, Northern Territory*, Queensland, South Australia, Tasmania, Victoria, Western Australia
Dependent areas: Ashmore and Cartier Islands, Christmas Island, Cocos (Keeling) Islands, Coral Sea Islands, Heard Island and McDonald Islands, Norfolk Island
Independence: 1 January 1901 (federation of UK colonies)
Constitution: 9 July 1900, effective 1 January 1901
Legal system: based on English common law; accepts compulsory ICJ jurisdiction, with reservations
National holiday: Australia Day (last Monday in January), 29 January 1990
Executive branch: British monarch, governor general, prime minister, deputy prime minister, Cabinet
Legislative branch: bicameral Federal Parliament consists of an upper house or Senate and a lower house or House of Representatives
Judicial branch: High Court
Leaders:
Chief of State—Queen ELIZABETH II (since February 1952), represented by Governor General William George HAYDEN (since NA February 1989);
Head of Government—Prime Minister Robert James Lee HAWKE (since 11 March 1983); Deputy Prime Minister Paul KEATING (since 3 April 1990)

Political parties and leaders:
government—Australian Labor Party, Robert James Lee HAWKE;
opposition—Liberal Party, John HEWSON; National Party, Timothy FISCHER; Australian Democratic Party, Janet POWELL
Suffrage: universal and compulsory at age 18
Elections:
Senate—last held 11 July 1987 (next to be held by July 1993); results—Labor 43%, Liberal-National 42%, Australian Democrats 8%, independents 2%; seats—(76 total) Labor 32, Liberal-National 34, Australian Democrats 7, independents 3;
House of Representatives—last held 24 March 1990 (next to be held by November 1993); results—Labor 39.7%, Liberal-National 43%, Australian Democrats and independents 11.1%; seats—(148 total) Labor 78, Liberal-National 69, independent 1
Communists: 4,000 members (est.)
Other political or pressure groups: Australian Democratic Labor Party (anti-Communist Labor Party splinter group); Peace and Nuclear Disarmament Action (Nuclear Disarmament Party splinter group)
Member of: AfDB, AG (observer), ANZUS, APEC, AsDB, BIS, C, CCC, CP, EBRD, ESCAP, FAO, GATT, G-8, IAEA, IBRD, ICAO, ICC, ICFTU, IDA, IEA, IFAD, IFC, ILO, IMF, IMO, INMARSAT, INTELSAT, INTERPOL, IOC, IOM, ISO, ITU, LORCS, NAM (guest), NEA, OECD, PCA, SPC, SPF, UN, UNCTAD, UNESCO, UNFICYP, UNHCR, UNIIMOG, UNTAG, UNTSO, UPU, WHO, WIPO, WMO, WTO
Diplomatic representation: Ambassador Michael J. COOK; Chancery at 1601 Massachusetts Avenue NW, Washington DC 20036; telephone (202) 797-3000; there are Australian Consulates General in Chicago, Honolulu, Houston, Los Angeles, New York, Pago Pago (American Samoa), and San Francisco;
US—Ambassador Melvin F. SEMBLER; Moonah Place, Yarralumla, Canberra, Australian Capital Territory 2600 (mailing address is APO San Francisco 96404); telephone [61] (6) 270-5000; there are US Consulates General in Melbourne, Perth, and Sydney, and a Consulate in Brisbane
Flag: blue with the flag of the UK in the upper hoist-side quadrant and a large seven-pointed star in the lower hoist-side quadrant; the remaining half is a representation of the Southern Cross constellation in white with one small five-pointed star and four, larger, seven-pointed stars

Economy

Overview: Australia has a prosperous Western-style capitalist economy, with a per capita GNP comparable to levels in industrialized West European countries. Rich in natural resources, Australia is a major exporter of agricultural products, minerals, metals, and fossil fuels. Of the top 25 exports, 21 are primary products, so that, as happened during 1983-84, a downturn in world commodity prices can have a big impact on the economy. The government is pushing for increased exports of manufactured goods but competition in international markets will be severe.
GDP: $254.4 billion, per capita $14,900; real growth rate 1.6% (1990)
Inflation rate (consumer prices): 6.9% (December 1990)
Unemployment rate: 9.2% (March 1991)
Budget: revenues $74.2 billion; expenditures $67.9 billion, including capital expenditures of NA (FY90)
Exports: $37.3 billion (f.o.b., FY90);
commodities—wheat, barley, beef, lamb, dairy products, wool, coal, iron ore;
partners—Japan 26%, US 11%, NZ 6%, South Korea 4%, Singapore 4%, USSR 3%
Imports: $39.8 billion (f.o.b., FY90);
commodities—manufactured raw materials, capital equipment, consumer goods;
partners—US 22%, Japan 22%, UK 7%, FRG 6%, NZ 4% (1984)
External debt: $123.7 billion (September 1990)
Industrial production: growth rate 5.6% (FY88); accounts for 32% of GDP
Electricity: 38,000,000 kW capacity; 150,000 million kWh produced, 8,860 kWh per capita (1990)
Industries: mining, industrial and transportation equipment, food processing, chemicals, steel, motor vehicles
Agriculture: accounts for 5% of GNP and 37% of export revenues; world's largest exporter of beef and wool, second-largest for mutton, and among top wheat exporters; major crops—wheat, barley, sugarcane, fruit; livestock—cattle, sheep, poultry
Economic aid: donor—ODA and OOF commitments (1970-87), $8.8 billion
Currency: Australian dollar (plural—dollars); 1 Australian dollar ($A) = 100 cents
Exchange rates: Australian dollars ($A) per US$1—1.2834 (January 1991), 1.2799 (1990), 1.2618 (1989), 1.2752 (1988), 1.4267 (1987), 1.4905 (1986), 1.4269 (1985)
Fiscal year: 1 July-30 June

Communications

Railroads: 40,478 km total; 7,970 km 1.600-meter gauge, 16,201 km 1.435-meter standard gauge, 16,307 km 1.067-meter gauge; 183 km dual gauge; 1,130 km electrified; government owned (except for a few hundred kilometers of privately owned track) (1985)
Highways: 837,872 km total; 243,750 km paved, 228,396 km gravel, crushed stone, or stabilized soil surface, 365,726 km unimproved earth
Inland waterways: 8,368 km; mainly by small, shallow-draft craft
Pipelines: crude oil, 2,500 km; refined products, 500 km; natural gas, 5,600 km
Ports: Adelaide, Brisbane, Cairns, Darwin, Devonport, Fremantle, Geelong, Hobart, Launceston, Mackay, Melbourne, Sydney, Townsville
Merchant marine: 77 ships (1,000 GRT or over) totaling 2,249,926 GRT/3,391,323 DWT; includes 2 short-sea passenger, 6 cargo, 6 container, 10 roll-on/roll-off cargo, 1 vehicle carrier, 16 petroleum, oils, and lubricants (POL) tanker, 1 chemical tanker, 4 liquefied gas, 1 combination ore/oil, 30 bulk
Civil air: around 150 major transport aircraft
Airports: 747 total, 524 usable; 270 with permanent-surface runways, 1 with runways over 3,659 m; 17 with runways 2,440-3,659 m; 401 with runways 1,220-2,439 m
Telecommunications: good international and domestic service; 8.7 million telephones; stations—258 AM, 67 FM, 134 TV; submarine cables to New Zealand, Papua New Guinea, and Indonesia; domestic satellite service; satellite stations—4 Indian Ocean INTELSAT, 6 Pacific Ocean INTELSAT earth stations

Defense Forces

Branches: Australian Army, Royal Australian Navy, Royal Australian Air Force
Manpower availability: males 15-49, 4,689,559; 4,090,921 fit for military service; 135,435 reach military age (17) annually
Defense expenditures: $6.6 billion, 2.2% of GDP (FY90)

Austria

150 km

Geography

Total area: 83,850 km²; land area: 82,730 km²
Comparative area: slightly smaller than Maine
Land boundaries: 2,640 km total; Czechoslovakia 548 km, Germany 784 km, Hungary 366 km, Italy 430 km, Liechtenstein 37 km, Switzerland 164 km, Yugoslavia 311 km
Coastline: none—landlocked
Maritime claims: none—landlocked
Climate: temperate; continental, cloudy; cold winters with frequent rain in lowlands and snow in mountains; cool summers with occasional showers
Terrain: mostly mountains with Alps in west and south; mostly flat, with gentle slopes along eastern and northern margins
Natural resources: iron ore, crude oil, timber, magnesite, aluminum, lead, coal, lignite, copper, hydropower
Land use: arable land 17%; permanent crops 1%; meadows and pastures 24%; forest and woodland 39%; other 19%; includes irrigated NEGL%
Environment: because of steep slopes, poor soils, and cold temperatures, population is concentrated on eastern lowlands
Note: landlocked; strategic location at the crossroads of central Europe with many easily traversable Alpine passes and valleys; major river is the Danube

People

Population: 7,665,804 (July 1991), growth rate 0.3% (1991)
Birth rate: 12 births/1,000 population (1991)
Death rate: 11 deaths/1,000 population (1991)
Net migration rate: 2 migrants/1,000 population (1991)
Infant mortality rate: 5 deaths/1,000 live births (1991)

Life expectancy at birth: 74 years male, 81 years female (1991)
Total fertility rate: 1.5 children born/woman (1991)
Nationality: noun—Austrian(s); adjective—Austrian
Ethnic divisions: German 99.4%, Croatian 0.3%, Slovene 0.2%, other 0.1%
Religion: Roman Catholic 85%, Protestant 6%, other 9%
Language: German
Literacy: 99% (male NA%, female NA%) age 15 and over can read and write (1974 est.)
Labor force: 3,470,000 (1989); services 56.4%, industry and crafts 35.4%, agriculture and forestry 8.1%; an estimated 200,000 Austrians are employed in other European countries; foreign laborers in Austria number 177,840, about 6% of labor force (1988)
Organized labor: 60.1% of work force; the Austrian Trade Union Federation has 1,644,408 members (1989)

Government

Long-form name: Republic of Austria
Type: federal republic
Capital: Vienna
Administrative divisions: 9 states (bundesländer, singular—bundesland); Burgenland, Kärnten, Niederösterreich, Oberösterreich, Salzburg, Steiermark, Tirol, Vorarlberg, Wien
Independence: 12 November 1918 (from Austro-Hungarian Empire)
Constitution: 1920, revised 1929 (reinstated 1945)
Legal system: civil law system with Roman law origin; judicial review of legislative acts by a Constitutional Court; separate administrative and civil/penal supreme courts; has not accepted compulsory ICJ jurisdiction
National holiday: National Day, 26 October (1955)
Executive branch: president, chancellor, vice chancellor, Council of Ministers (cabinet)
Legislative branch: bicameral Federal Assembly (Bundesversammlung) consists of an upper council or Federal Council (Bundesrat) and a lower council or National Council (Nationalrat)
Judicial branch: Supreme Judicial Court (Oberster Gerichtshof) for civil and criminal cases, Administrative Court (Verwaltungsgerichtshof) for bureaucratic cases, Constitutional Court (Verfassungsgerichtshof) for constitutional cases
Leaders:
Chief of State—President Kurt WALDHEIM (since 8 July 1986);
Head of Government—Chancellor Franz VRANITZKY (since 16 June 1986); Vice Chancellor Josef RIEGLER (since 19 May 1989)

Political parties and leaders: Socialist Party of Austria (SPÖ), Franz VRANITZKY, chairman; Austrian People's Party (ÖVP), Josef RIEGLER, chairman; Freedom Party of Austria (FPÖ), Jörg HAIDER, chairman; Communist Party (KPÖ), Franz MUHRI, chairman; Green Alternative List (GAL), Andreas WABL, chairman
Suffrage: universal at age 19; compulsory for presidential elections
Elections:
President—last held 8 June 1986 (next to be held May 1992); results of Second Ballot—Dr. Kurt WALDHEIM 53.89%, Dr. Kurt STEYRER 46.11%;
National Council—last held 7 October 1990 (next to be held October 1994); results—SPÖ 43%, ÖVP 32.1%, FPÖ 16.6%, GAL 4.5%, KPÖ 0.7%, other 0.32%; seats—(183 total) SPÖ 80, ÖVP 60, FPÖ 33, GAL 10
Communists: membership 15,000 est.; activists 7,000-8,000
Other political or pressure groups: Federal Chamber of Commerce and Industry; Austrian Trade Union Federation (primarily Socialist); three composite leagues of the Austrian People's Party (ÖVP) representing business, labor, and farmers; ÖVP-oriented League of Austrian Industrialists; Roman Catholic Church, including its chief lay organization, Catholic Action
Member of: AfDB, AG (observer), AsDB, BIS, CCC, CE, CERN, CSCE, EBRD, ECE, EFTA, ESA, FAO, G-9, GATT, IADB, IAEA, IBRD, ICAO, ICC, ICFTU, IDA, IEA, IFAD, IFC, ILO, IMF, IMO, INTELSAT, INTERPOL, IOC, IOM, ISO, ITU, LORCS, NAM (guest), NEA, OAS (observer), OECD, PCA, UN, UNCTAD, UNESCO, UNDOF, UNFICYP, UNHCR, UNIDO, UNIIMOG, UNTSO, UPU, WCL, WFTU, WHO, WIPO, WMO, WTO
Diplomatic representation: Ambassador Friedrich HOESS; Embassy at 2343 Massachusetts Avenue NW, Washington DC 20008; telephone (202) 483-4474; there are Austrian Consulates General in Chicago, Los Angeles, and New York;
US—Ambassador Roy Michael HUFFINGTON; Embassy at Boltzmanngasse 16, A-1091, Vienna (mailing address is APO New York 09108-0001); telephone [43] (222) 31-55-11; there is a US Consulate General in Salzburg
Flag: three equal horizontal bands of red (top), white, and red

Economy

Overview: Austria boasts a prosperous and stable capitalist economy with a sizable proportion of nationalized industry and extensive welfare benefits. Thanks to an excellent raw material endowment, a technically skilled labor force, and strong links to West German industrial firms, Austria has successfully occupied specialized niches in European industry and services (tourism, banking) and produces almost enough food to feed itself with only 8% of the labor force in agriculture. Improved export prospects from German unification and the opening of Eastern Europe will also boost the economy during the next few years. Living standards are roughly comparable with the large industrial countries of Western Europe. Problems for the 1990s include an aging population, the high level of subsidies, and the struggle to keep welfare benefits within budget capabilities. Austria, which has applied for EC membership, is currently involved in EC and European Free Trade Association negotiations for a European Economic Area and will have to adapt its economy to achieve freer movement of goods, services, capital, and labor with the EC.

GDP: $111.0 billion, per capita $14,500; real growth rate 4.5% (1990)

Inflation rate (consumer prices): 3.3% (1990)

Unemployment: 5.4% (1990)

Budget: revenues $44.1 billion; expenditures $49.6 billion, including capital expenditures of $NA (1990)

Exports: $40.9 billion (f.o.b., 1990);
commodities—machinery and equipment, iron and steel, lumber, textiles, paper products, chemicals;
partners—EC 64.8%, EFTA 10.3%, CEMA 7.7%, US 3.2%, Japan 1.5%

Imports: $46.6 billion (c.i.f., 1990);
commodities—petroleum, foodstuffs, machinery and equipment, vehicles, chemicals, textiles and clothing, pharmaceuticals;
partners—EC 68.4%, EFTA 7%, CEMA 5.7%, Japan 4.6%, US 3.6%

External debt: $11.8 billion (1990 est.)

Industrial production: real growth rate 8.5% (1990)

Electricity: 17,562,000 kW capacity; 49,290 million kWh produced, 6,500 kWh per capita (1989)

Industries: foods, iron and steel, machines, textiles, chemicals, electrical, paper and pulp, tourism, mining

Agriculture: accounts for 3.2% of GDP (including forestry); principal crops and animals—grains, fruit, potatoes, sugar beets, sawn wood, cattle, pigs poultry; 80-90% self-sufficient in food

Economic aid: donor—ODA and OOF commitments (1970-88), $1.8 billion

Currency: Austrian schilling (plural—schillings); 1 Austrian schilling (S) = 100 groschen

Exchange rates: Austrian schillings (S) per US$1—10.627 (January 1991), 11.370 (1990), 13.231 (1989), 12.348 (1988), 12.643 (1987), 15.267 (1986), 20.690 (1985)

Fiscal year: calendar year

Communications

Railroads: 6,028 km total; 5,388 km government owned and 640 km privately owned (1.435- and 1.000-meter gauge); 5,403 km 1.435-meter standard gauge of which 3,051 km is electrified and 1,520 km is double tracked; 363 km 0.760-meter narrow gauge of which 91 km is electrified

Highways: 95,412 km total; 34,612 are the primary network (including 1,012 km of autobahn, 10,400 km of federal, and 23,200 km of provincial roads); of this number, 21,812 km are paved and 12,800 km are unpaved; in addition, there are 60,800 km of communal roads (mostly gravel, crushed stone, earth)

Inland waterways: 446 km

Ports: Vienna, Linz (river ports)

Merchant marine: 32 ships (1,000 GRT or over) totaling 150,735 GRT/252,237 DWT; includes 26 cargo, 1 container, 1 chemical tanker, 4 bulk

Pipelines: 554 km crude oil; 2,611 km natural gas; 171 km refined products

Civil air: 25 major transport aircraft

Airports: 55 total, 54 usable; 20 with permanent-surface runways; none with runways over 3,659 m; 5 with runways 2,440-3,659 m; 4 with runways 1,220-2,439 m

Telecommunications: highly developed and efficient; 4,014,000 telephones; extensive TV and radiobroadcast systems; stations—6 AM, 21 (545 repeaters) FM, 47 (870 repeaters) TV; satellite stations operating in INTELSAT 1 Atlantic Ocean earth station and 1 Indian Ocean earth station and EUTELSAT systems

Defense Forces

Branches: Army, Flying Division, Gendarmerie

Manpower availability: males 15-49, 1,957,414; 1,646,179 fit for military service; 48,038 reach military age (19) annually

Defense expenditures: $1.4 billion, 1% of GDP (1990)

The Bahamas

Geography

Total area: 13,940 km²; land area: 10,070 km²

Comparative area: slightly larger than Connecticut

Land boundaries: none

Coastline: 3,542 km

Maritime claims:
Continental shelf: 200 m (depth) or to depth of exploitation;
Exclusive fishing zone: 200 nm;
Territorial sea: 3 nm

Climate: tropical marine; moderated by warm waters of Gulf Stream

Terrain: long, flat coral formations with some low rounded hills

Natural resources: salt, aragonite, timber

Land use: arable land 1%; permanent crops NEGL%; meadows and pastures NEGL%; forest and woodland 32%; other 67%

Environment: subject to hurricanes and other tropical storms that cause extensive flood damage

Note: strategic location adjacent to US and Cuba; extensive island chain

People

Population: 252,110 (July 1991), growth rate 1.4% (1991)

Birth rate: 19 births/1,000 population (1991)

Death rate: 5 deaths/1,000 population (1991)

Net migration rate: 0 migrants/1,000 population (1991)

Infant mortality rate: 18 deaths/1,000 live births (1991)

Life expectancy at birth: 69 years male, 76 years female (1991)

Total fertility rate: 2.2 children born/woman (1991)

Nationality: noun—Bahamian(s); adjective—Bahamian

Ethnic divisions: black 85%, white 15%

The Bahamas *(continued)*

Religion: Baptist 32%, Anglican 20%, Roman Catholic 19%, Methodist 6%, Church of God 6%, other Protestant 12%, none or unknown 3%, other 2% (1980)
Language: English; some Creole among Haitian immigrants
Literacy: 90% (male 90%, female 89%) age 15 and over but definition of literacy not available (1963 est.)
Labor force: 132,600; government 30%, hotels and restaurants 25%, business services 10%, agriculture 5% (1986)
Organized labor: 25% of labor force

Government

Long-form name: The Commonwealth of The Bahamas
Type: commonwealth
Capital: Nassau
Administrative divisions: 21 districts; Abaco, Acklins Island, Andros Island, Berry Islands, Biminis, Cat Island, Cay Lobos, Crooked Island, Eleuthera, Exuma, Grand Bahama, Harbour Island, Inagua, Long Cay, Long Island, Mayaguana, New Providence, Ragged Island, Rum Cay, San Salvador, Spanish Wells
Independence: 10 July 1973 (from UK)
Constitution: 10 July 1973
Legal system: based on English common law
National holiday: Independence Day, 10 July (1973)
Executive branch: British monarch, governor general, prime minister, deputy prime minister, Cabinet
Legislative branch: bicameral Parliament consists of an upper house or Senate and a lower house or House of Assembly
Judicial branch: Supreme Court
Leaders:
Chief of State—Queen ELIZABETH II (since 6 February 1952), represented by Acting Governor General Sir Henry TAYLOR (since 26 June 1988);
Head of Government—Prime Minister Sir Lynden Oscar PINDLING (since 16 January 1967)
Political parties and leaders: Progressive Liberal Party (PLP), Sir Lynden O. PINDLING; Free National Movement (FNM), Hubert Alexander INGRAHAM
Suffrage: universal at age 18
Elections:
House of Assembly—last held 19 June 1987 (next to be held by June 1992); results—percent of vote by party NA; seats—(49 total) PLP 32, FNM 17
Communists: none known
Other political or pressure groups: Vanguard Nationalist and Socialist Party (VNSP), a small leftist party headed by Lionel CAREY; Trade Union Congress (TUC), headed by Arlington MILLER
Member of: ACP, C, CCC, CARICOM, CDB, ECLAC, FAO, G-77, IADB, IBRD, ICAO, ICFTU, IFC, ILO, IMF, IMO, INTELSAT, INTERPOL, IOC, ITU, LORCS, NAM, OAS, OPANAL, UN, UNCTAD, UNESCO, UNIDO, UPU, WHO, WIPO, WMO
Diplomatic representation: Ambassador Margaret E. McDONALD; Chancery at Suite 865, 600 New Hampshire Avenue NW, Washington DC 20037; telephone (202) 944-3390; there are Bahamian Consulates General in Miami and New York; *US*—Ambassador Chic HECHT; Embassy at Mosmar Building, Queen Street, Nassau (mailing address is P. O. Box N-8197, Nassau); telephone (809) 322-1181 or 328-2206
Flag: three equal horizontal bands of aquamarine (top), gold, and aquamarine with a black equilateral triangle based on the hoist side

---

Economy

Overview: The Bahamas is a stable, middle-income developing nation whose economy is based primarily on tourism and offshore banking. Tourism alone provides about 50% of GDP and directly or indirectly employs about 50,000 people or 40% of the local work force. The economy has slackened in recent years, as the annual increase in the number of tourists slowed. Nonetheless, the per capita GDP of $9,800 is one of the highest in the region.
GDP: $2.4 billion, per capita $9,800; real growth rate 2.0% (1989 est.)
Inflation rate (consumer prices): 5.4% (1989)
Unemployment: 11% (1988)
Budget: revenues $1.03 billion; expenditures $1.1 billion, including capital expenditures of $275 million (1990)
Exports: $259 million (f.o.b., 1989);
commodities—pharmaceuticals, cement, rum, crawfish;
partners—US 41%, Norway 30%, Denmark 4%
Imports: $1.15 billion (f.o.b., 1989);
commodities—foodstuffs, manufactured goods, mineral fuels;
partners—US 35%, Nigeria 21%, Japan 13%, Angola 11%
External debt: $1.2 billion (December 1990)
Industrial production: growth rate NA%; accounts for 15% of GDP
Electricity: 368,000 kW capacity; 857 million kWh produced, 3,480 kWh per capita (1990)
Industries: banking, tourism, cement, oil refining and transshipment, salt production, rum, aragonite, pharmaceuticals, spiral weld, steel pipe
Agriculture: accounts for less than 5% of GDP; dominated by small-scale producers; principal products—citrus fruit, vegetables, poultry; large net importer of food
Illicit drugs: transshipment point for cocaine

Economic aid: US commitments, including Ex-Im (FY85-88), $1.0 million; Western (non-US) countries, ODA and OOF bilateral commitments (1970-88), $345 million
Currency: Bahamian dollar (plural—dollars); 1 Bahamian dollar (B$) = 100 cents
Exchange rates: Bahamian dollar (B$) per US$1—1.00 (fixed rate)
Fiscal year: calendar year

Communications

Highways: 2,400 km total; 1,350 km paved, 1,050 km gravel
Ports: Freeport, Nassau
Merchant marine: 636 ships (1,000 GRT or over) totaling 14,266,066 GRT/23,585,465 DWT; includes 42 passenger, 16 short-sea passenger, 190 cargo, 41 roll-on/roll-off cargo, 23 container, 5 car carrier, 1 railroad carrier, 141 petroleum, oils, and lubricants (POL) tanker, 8 liquefied gas, 15 combination ore/oil, 33 chemical tanker, 1 specialized tanker, 112 bulk, 8 combination bulk; note—a flag of convenience registry
Civil air: 9 major transport aircraft
Airports: 59 total, 57 usable; 31 with permanent-surface runways; none with runways over 3,659 m; 3 with runways 2,440-3,659 m; 25 with runways 1,220-2,439 m
Telecommunications: highly developed; 99,000 telephones in totally automatic system; tropospheric scatter and submarine cable links to Florida; stations—3 AM, 2 FM, 1 TV; 3 coaxial submarine cables; 1 Atlantic Ocean INTELSAT earth station

---

Defense Forces

Branches: Royal Bahamas Defense Force (a coast guard element only), Royal Bahamas Police Force
Manpower availability: males 15-49, 68,020; NA fit for military service
Defense expenditures: $65 million, 2.7% of GDP (1990)

Bahrain

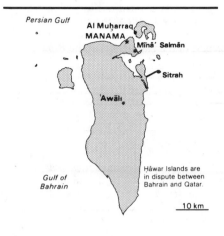

Persian Gulf

Al Muḥarraq
MANAMA
Mīnā' Salmān

Sitrah

'Awālī

Gulf of
Bahrain

Ḥāwar Islands are
in dispute between
Bahrain and Qatar.

10 km

Geography

Total area: 620 km²; land area: 620 km²
Comparative area: slightly less than 3.5 times the size of Washington, DC
Land boundaries: none
Coastline: 161 km
Maritime claims:
Continental shelf: not specific;
Territorial sea: 3 nm
Disputes: territorial dispute with Qatar over the Ḥawār Islands
Climate: arid; mild, pleasant winters; very hot, humid summers
Terrain: mostly low desert plain rising gently to low central escarpment
Natural resources: oil, associated and non-associated natural gas, fish
Land use: arable land 2%; permanent crops 2%; meadows and pastures 6%; forest and woodland 0%; other 90%, includes irrigated NEGL%
Environment: subsurface water sources being rapidly depleted (requires development of desalination facilities); dust storms; desertification
Note: close to primary Middle Eastern crude oil sources; strategic location in Persian Gulf through which much of Western world's crude oil must transit to reach open ocean

People

Population: 536,974 (July 1991), growth rate 3.2% (1991)
Birth rate: 27 births/1,000 population (1991)
Death rate: 3 deaths/1,000 population (1991)
Net migration rate: 7 migrants/1,000 population (1991)
Infant mortality rate: 17 deaths/1,000 live births (1991)
Life expectancy at birth: 71 years male, 76 years female (1991)

Total fertility rate: 4.0 children born/woman (1991)
Nationality: noun—Bahraini(s); adjective—Bahraini
Ethnic divisions: Bahraini 63%, Asian 13%, other Arab 10%, Iranian 8%, other 6%
Religion: Muslim (Shi'a 70%, Sunni 30%)
Language: Arabic (official); English also widely spoken; Farsi, Urdu
Literacy: 77% (male 82%, female 69%) age 15 and over can read and write (1990 est.)
Labor force: 140,000; 42% of labor force is Bahraini; industry and commerce 85%, agriculture 5%, services 5%, government 3% (1982)
Organized labor: General Committee for Bahrain Workers exists in only eight major designated companies

Government

Long-form name: State of Bahrain
Type: traditional monarchy
Capital: Manama
Administrative divisions: 12 municipalities (baladīyat, singular—baladīyah); Al Ḥadd, Al Manāmah, Al Minṭaqah al Gharbīyah, Al Minṭaqah al Wusṭá, Al Minṭaqah ash Shamālīyah, Al Muḥarraq, Ar Rifā' wa al Minṭaqah al Janūbīyah, Jidd Ḥafṣ, Madīnat Ḥamad, Madīnat 'Isá, Minṭaqat Juzur Ḥawār, Sitrah
Independence: 15 August 1971 (from UK)
Constitution: 26 May 1973, effective 6 December 1973
Legal system: based on Islamic law and English common law
National holiday: National Day, 16 December
Executive branch: amir, crown prince and heir apparent, prime minister, Cabinet
Legislative branch: unicameral National Assembly was dissolved 26 August 1975 and legislative powers were assumed by the Cabinet
Judicial branch: High Civil Appeals Court
Leaders:
Chief of State—Amir 'Isa bin Salman Al KHALIFA (since 2 November 1961); Heir Apparent Hamad bin 'Isa Al KHALIFA (son of Amir; born 28 January 1950);
Head of Government—Prime Minister Khalifa bin Salman Al KHALIFA, (since 19 January 1970)
Political parties and pressure groups: political parties prohibited; several small, clandestine leftist and Shi'a fundamentalist groups are active
Suffrage: none
Elections: none
Communists: negligible
Member of: ABEDA, AFESD, AL, AMF, ESCWA, FAO, G-77, GCC, IBRD, ICAO, IDB, ILO, IMF, IMO, INMARSAT, INTERPOL, IOC, ISO (correspondent), ITU, LORCS, NAM, OAPEC, OIC,

UN, UNCTAD, UNESCO, UNIDO, UPU, WFTU, WHO, WMO
Diplomatic representation: Ambassador Ghazi Muhammad AL-QUSAYBI; Chancery at 3502 International Drive NW, Washington DC 20008; telephone (202) 342-0741 or 342-0742; there is a Bahraini Consulate General in New York;
US—Ambassador Dr. Charles W. HOSTLER; Embassy at Building No. 979, Road No. 3119, Block/Area 331, Manama ZINJ (mailing address is P. O. 26431, Manama, or FPO New York 09526-6210); telephone [973] 273-300 or 275-126
Flag: red with a white serrated band (eight white points) on the hoist side

Economy

Overview: Petroleum production and processing account for about 85% of export receipts, 60% of government revenues, and 20% of GDP. In 1986 soft oil-market conditions led to a 5% drop in GDP, in sharp contrast with the 5% average annual growth rate during the early 1980s. The slowdown in economic activity, however, has helped to check the inflation of the 1970s. The government's past economic diversification efforts have moderated the severity of the downturn but failed to offset oil and gas revenue losses.
GDP: $3.4 billion, per capita $7,000 (1989 est.); real growth rate 0% (1988)
Inflation rate (consumer prices): 1.5% (1989)
Unemployment: 8-10% (1989)
Budget: revenues $1.2 billion; expenditures $1.32 billion, including capital expenditures of $NA (1989)
Exports: $2.7 billion (f.o.b., 1989 est.);
commodities—petroleum 80%, aluminum 7%, other 13%;
partners—UAE, Japan, US, India
Imports: $3.0 billion (f.o.b., 1989);
commodities—nonoil 59%, crude oil 41%;
partners—Saudi Arabia, Japan, US, UK
External debt: $1.1 billion (December 1989 est.)
Industrial production: growth rate 3.8% (1988); accounts for 43% of GDP
Electricity: 1,652,000 kW capacity; 6,000 million kWh produced, 12,080 kWh per capita (1989)
Industries: petroleum processing and refining, aluminum smelting, offshore banking, ship repairing
Agriculture: including fishing, accounts for less than 2% of GDP; not self-sufficient in food production; heavily subsidized sector produces fruit, vegetables, poultry, dairy products, shrimp, and fish; fish catch 9,000 metric tons in 1987
Economic aid: US commitments, including Ex-Im (FY70-79), $24 million; Western (non-US) countries, ODA and OOF bilateral commitments (1970-88), $35 million; OPEC bilateral aid (1979-89), $9.8 billion

Bahrain *(continued)*

Currency: Bahraini dinar (plural—dinars); 1 Bahraini dinar (BD) = 1,000 fils
Exchange rates: Bahraini dinars (BD) per US$1—0.3760 (fixed rate)
Fiscal year: calendar year

Communications

Highways: 200 km bituminous surfaced, including 25 km bridge-causeway to Saudi Arabia opened in November 1986; NA km natural surface tracks
Ports: Mīnā' Salmān, Manamah, Sitrah
Merchant marine: 4 cargo and 2 container (1,000 GRT or over) totaling 114,733 GRT/155,065 DWT
Pipelines: crude oil, 56 km; refined products, 16 km; natural gas, 32 km
Civil air: 24 major transport aircraft
Airports: 3 total, 3 usable; 2 with permanent-surface runways; 2 with runways over 3,659 m; 1 with runways 1,220-2,439 m
Telecommunications: excellent international telecommunications; adequate domestic services; 98,000 telephones; stations—2 AM, 1 FM, 2 TV; satellite earth stations—1 Atlantic Ocean INTELSAT, 1 Indian Ocean INTELSAT, 1 ARABSAT; tropospheric scatter and microwave to Qatar, UAE, Saudi Arabia; submarine cable to Qatar and UAE

Defense Forces

Branches: Army (Defense Force), Navy, Air Force, Air Defense, Police Force
Manpower availability: males 15-49, 187,606; 104,285 fit for military service
Defense expenditures: $194 million, 6% of GDP (1990)

Baker Island
(territory of the US)

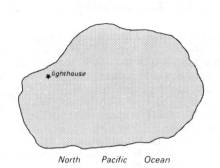

300 m

North   Pacific   Ocean

Geography

Total area: 1.4 km²; land area: 1.4 km²
Comparative area: about 2.3 times the size of The Mall in Washington, DC
Land boundaries: none
Coastline: 4.8 km
Maritime claims:
Contiguous zone: 12 nm;
Continental shelf: 200 m (depth);
Exclusive economic zone: 200 nm;
Territorial sea: 12 nm
Climate: equatorial; scant rainfall, constant wind, burning sun
Terrain: low, nearly level coral island surrounded by a narrow fringing reef
Natural resources: guano (deposits worked until 1891)
Land use: arable land 0%; permanent crops 0%; meadows and pastures 0%; forest and woodland 0%; other 100%
Environment: treeless, sparse and scattered vegetation consisting of grasses, prostrate vines, and low growing shrubs; lacks fresh water; primarily a nesting, roosting, and foraging habitat for seabirds, shorebirds, and marine wildlife
Note: remote location 2,575 km southwest of Honolulu in the North Pacific Ocean, just north of the Equator, about halfway between Hawaii and Australia

People

Population: uninhabited
Note: American civilians evacuated in 1942 after Japanese air and naval attacks during World War II; occupied by US military during World War II, but abandoned after the war; public entry is by special-use permit only and generally restricted to scientists and educators; a cemetery and cemetery ruins located near the middle of the west coast

Government

Long-form name: none

Type: unincorporated territory of the US administered by the Fish and Wildlife Service of the US Department of the Interior as part of the National Wildlife Refuge system

Economy

Overview: no economic activity

Communications

Ports: none; offshore anchorage only, one boat landing area along the middle of the west coast

Defense Forces

Note: defense is the responsibility of the US; visited annually by the US Coast Guard

Bangladesh

Boundary representation is not necessarily authoritative.

Bay of Bengal

Geography

Total area: 144,000 km²; land area: 133,910 km²

Comparative area: slightly smaller than Wisconsin

Land boundaries: 4,246 km total; Burma 193 km, India 4,053 km

Coastline: 580 km

Maritime claims:

Contiguous zone: 18 nm;

Continental shelf: up to outer limits of continental margin;

Exclusive economic zone: 200 nm;

Territorial sea: 12 nm

Disputes: a portion of the boundary with India is in dispute; water sharing problems with upstream riparian India over the Ganges

Climate: tropical; cool, dry winter (October to March); hot, humid summer (March to June); cool, rainy monsoon (June to October)

Terrain: mostly flat alluvial plain; hilly in southeast

Natural resources: natural gas, uranium, arable land, timber

Land use: arable land 67%; permanent crops 2%; meadows and pastures 4%; forest and woodland 16%; other 11%; includes irrigated 14%

Environment: vulnerable to droughts; much of country routinely flooded during summer monsoon season; overpopulation; deforestation

Note: almost completely surrounded by India

People

Population: 116,601,424 (July 1991), growth rate 2.3% (1991)

Birth rate: 36 births/1,000 population (1991)

Death rate: 13 deaths/1,000 population (1991)

Net migration rate: 0 migrants/1,000 population (1991)

Infant mortality rate: 118 deaths/1,000 live births (1991)

Life expectancy at birth: 54 years male, 52 years female (1991)

Total fertility rate: 4.7 children born/woman (1991)

Nationality: noun—Bangladeshi(s); adjective—Bangladesh

Ethnic divisions: Bengali 98%, Biharis 250,000, and tribals less than 1 million

Religion: Muslim 83%, Hindu 16%, Buddhist, Christian, and other less than 1%

Language: Bangla (official), English widely used

Literacy: 35% (male 47%, female 22%) age 15 and over can read and write (1990 est.)

Labor force: 35,100,000; agriculture 74%, services 15%, industry and commerce 11% (FY86); extensive export of labor to Saudi Arabia, UAE, and Oman (1991)

Organized labor: 3% of labor force belongs to 2,614 registered unions (1986 est.)

Government

Long-form name: People's Republic of Bangladesh

Type: republic

Capital: Dhaka

Administrative divisions: 64 districts (zillagulo, singular—zilla); Bāgerhāt, Bāndarban, Barguna, Barisāl, Bhola, Bogra, Brāhmanbāria, Chāndpur, Chapai Nawābganj, Chattagram, Chuādānga, Comilla, Cox's Bāzār, Dhaka, Dinājpur, Farīdpur, Feni, Gaibandha, Gāzipur, Gopālganj, Habiganj, Jaipurhāt, Jamālpur, Jessore, Jhālakāti, Jhenaidah, Khagrāchari, Khulna, Kishorganj, Kurīgrām, Kushtia, Laksmipur, Lālmonirhāt, Mādārīpur, Māgura, Mānikganj, Meherpur, Moulavibāzār, Munshiganj, Mymensingh, Naogaon, Narail, Nārāyanganj, Narsingdi, Nator, Netrakona, Nilphāmāri, Noākhāli, Pābna, Panchāgar, Parbattya Chattagram, Patuākhāli, Pirojpur, Rājbāri, Rājshāhi, Rangpur, Sātkhira, Shariyatpur, Sherpur, Sirājganj, Sunāmganj, Sylhet, Tangail, Thākurgaon

Independence: 16 December 1971 (from Pakistan; formerly East Pakistan)

Constitution: 4 November 1972, effective 16 December 1972, suspended following coup of 24 March 1982, restored 10 November 1986, amended NA March 1991

Legal system: based on English common law

National holiday: Independence Day, 26 March (1971)

Executive branch: president, vice president, prime minister, three deputy prime ministers, Council of Ministers (cabinet)

Legislative branch: unicameral National Parliament (Jatiya Sangsad)

Judicial branch: Supreme Court

Leaders:

Chief of State—Acting President Shahabuddin AHMED (since 6 December 1990); Vice President (vacant); note—Acting President AHMED stepped in after the resignation of former President Hussain Mohammed ERSHAD, who left office under a storm of popular protest;

Head of Government—Prime Minister Begum Khaleda ZIA (since 20 March 1991)

Political parties and leaders: Bangladesh Nationalist Party, Begum Khaleda ZIA; Awami League, Sheikh Hasina WAZED; Jatiyo Party, Hussain Mohammad ERSHAD; Jamaat-E-Islami, Ali KHAN; Bangladesh Communist Party (pro-Soviet), Saifuddin Ahmed MANIK; Bangladesh Peasant/Workers League (BAKSAL), Abdur RAZZAK; Muslim League, Khan A. SABUR; Jatiyo Samajtantrik Dal (National Socialist Party—SIRAJ), M. A. JALIL; Democratic League, Khondakar MUSHTAQUE Ahmed; National Awami Party (Muzaffar); United People's Party, Kazi ZAFAR Ahmed

Suffrage: universal at age 18

Elections:

President—last held 15 October 1986 (next to be held first half of 1991); results—President Hussain Mohammad ERSHAD received 83.5% of vote; note—President ERSHAD resigned in December 1990;

National Parliament—last held 27 February 1991 (next to be held February 1996); results—percent of vote by party NA; seats—(330 total, 300 elected and 30 seats reserved for women) BNP 140, AL 84, JP 35, JI 18, CBP 5, BAKSAL 4, SIRAJ 1, DP 1, Islamic Coalition 1, National Awami Party (Muzaffar) 1, Workers Party 1, independents 3, other 6

Communists: 5,000 members (1987 est.)

Member of: AsDB, C, CCC, CP, ESCAP, FAO, G-77, GATT, IAEA, IBRD, ICAO, ICFTU, IDA, IDB, IFAD, IFC, ILO, IMF, IMO, INTELSAT, INTERPOL, IOC, ISO, ITU, LORCS, NAM, OIC, SAARC, UN, UNCTAD, UNESCO, UNIDO, UNIIMOG, UPU, WHO, WFTU, WIPO, WCL, WMO, WTO

Diplomatic representation: Ambassador A. H. S. Ataul KARIM; Chancery at 2201 Wisconsin Avenue NW, Washington DC 20007; telephone (202) 342-8372 through 8376; there is a Bangladesh Consulate General in New York;

US—Ambassador William B. MILAM; Embassy at Diplomatic Enclave, Madani Avenue, Baridhara, Dhaka (mailing address is G. P. O. Box 323, Dhaka 1212); telephone [880] (2) 884700-22

Flag: green with a large red disk slightly to the hoist side of center; green is the traditional color of Islam

Bangladesh (continued)

Economy

Overview: Bangladesh is one of the poorest nations in the world. The economy is based on the output of a narrow range of agricultural products, such as jute, which is the main cash crop and major source of export earnings. Bangladesh is hampered by a relative lack of natural resources, population growth of more than 2% a year, large-scale unemployment, and a limited infrastructure; furthermore, it is highly vulnerable to natural disasters. Despite these constraints, real GDP growth averaged about 3.5% annually during 1985-89. A strong agricultural performance in FY90 pushed the growth rate up to 5.5%. Alleviation of poverty remains the cornerstone of the government's development strategy.

GDP: $20.4 billion, per capita $180; real growth rate 4.0% (1990 est.)

Inflation rate (consumer prices): 10% (FY90 est.)

Unemployment rate: 30% (FY90 est.)

Budget: revenues $2.2 billion; expenditures $3.9 billion, including capital expenditures of $1.6 billion (FY90)

Exports: $1.5 billion (FY90 est.); *commodities*—jute, tea, leather, shrimp, textiles; *partners*—US 25%, Western Europe 22%, Middle East 9%, Japan 8%, Eastern Europe 7%

Imports: $3.6 billion (FY90 est.); *commodities*—food, petroleum and other energy, nonfood consumer goods, semiprocessed goods, and capital equipment; *partners*—Western Europe 18%, Japan 14%, Middle East 9%, US 8%

External debt: $10.9 billion (FY90 est.)

Industrial production: growth rate 4.1% (FY90 est.); accounts for 10% of GDP

Electricity: 1,990,000 kW capacity; 5,700 million kWh produced, 50 kWh per capita (1990)

Industries: jute manufacturing, food processing, cotton textiles, petroleum, urea fertilizer

Agriculture: accounts for about 40% of GDP, 60% of employment, and one third of exports; imports 10% of food grain requirements; world's largest exporter of jute; commercial products—jute, rice, wheat, tea, sugarcane, potatoes, beef, milk, poultry; shortages include wheat, vegetable oils and cotton; fish catch 778,000 metric tons in 1986

Economic aid: US commitments, including Ex-Im (FY70-89), $3.4 billion; Western (non-US) countries, ODA and OOF bilateral commitments (1980-88), $10.6 billion; OPEC bilateral aid (1979-89), $652 million; Communist countries (1970-89), $1.5 billion

Currency: taka (plural—taka); 1 taka (Tk) = 100 paise

Exchange rates: taka (Tk) per US$1—35.790 (January 1991), 34.567 (1990), 32.270 (1989), 31.733 (1988), 30.950 (1987), 30.407 (1986), 27.995 (1985)

Fiscal year: 1 July-30 June

Communications

Railroads: 2,892 km total (1986); 1,914 km 1.000 meter gauge, 978 km 1.676 meter broad gauge

Highways: 7,240 km total (1985); 3,840 km paved, 3,400 km unpaved

Inland waterways: 5,150-8,046 km navigable waterways (includes 2,575-3,058 km main cargo routes)

Ports: Chittagong, Chalna

Merchant marine: 47 ships (1,000 GRT or over) totaling 339,081 GRT/500,008 DWT; includes 38 cargo, 2 petroleum, oils, and lubricants (POL) tanker, 3 refrigerated cargo, 1 roll-on/roll-off, 3 bulk

Pipelines: 1,220 km natural gas

Civil air: 15 major transport aircraft

Airports: 16 total, 12 usable; 12 with permanent-surface runways; none with runways over 3,659 m; 4 with runways 2,440-3,659 m; 6 with runways 1,220-2,439 m

Telecommunications: adequate international radio communications and landline service; fair domestic wire and microwave service; fair broadcast service; 241,250 telephones; stations—9 AM, 6 FM, 11 TV; 2 Indian Ocean INTELSAT satellite earth stations

Defense Forces

Branches: Army, Navy, Air Force; paramilitary forces—Bangladesh Rifles, Bangladesh Ansars, Armed Police Reserve, Coastal Police

Manpower availability: males 15-49, 28,896,632; 17,154,593 fit for military service

Defense expenditures: $319 million, 1.5% of GDP (FY91)

Barbados

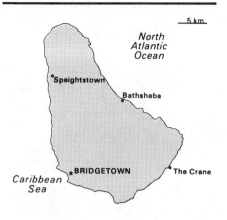

Geography

Total area: 430 km²; land area: 430 km²

Comparative area: slightly less than 2.5 times the size of Washington, DC

Land boundaries: none

Coastline: 97 km

Maritime claims:

Exclusive economic zone: 200 nm;

Territorial sea: 12 nm

Climate: tropical; rainy season (June to October)

Terrain: relatively flat; rises gently to central highland region

Natural resources: crude oil, fishing, natural gas

Land use: arable land 77%; permanent crops 0%; meadows and pastures 9%; forest and woodland 0%; other 14%

Environment: subject to hurricanes (especially June to October)

Note: easternmost Caribbean island

People

Population: 254,626 (July 1991), growth rate 0.1% (1991)

Birth rate: 16 births/1,000 population (1991)

Death rate: 9 deaths/1,000 population (1991)

Net migration rate: −6 migrants/1,000 population (1991)

Infant mortality rate: 23 deaths/1,000 live births (1991)

Life expectancy at birth: 70 years male, 76 years female (1991)

Total fertility rate: 1.8 children born/woman (1991)

Nationality: noun—Barbadian(s); adjective—Barbadian

Ethnic divisions: African 80%, mixed 16%, European 4%

Religion: Protestant 67% (Anglican 40%, Pentecostal 8%, Methodist 7%, other 12%), Roman Catholic 4%; none 17%, unknown 3%, other 9% (1980)

Language: English
Literacy: 99% (male 99%, female 99%) age 15 and over having ever attended school (1970)
Labor force: 112,300; services and government 37%; commerce 22%; manufacturing and construction 22%; transportation, storage, communications, and financial institutions 9%; agriculture 8%; utilities 2% (1985 est.)
Organized labor: 32% of labor force

Government

Long-form name: none
Type: parliamentary democracy
Capital: Bridgetown
Administrative divisions: 11 parishes; Christ Church, Saint Andrew, Saint George, Saint James, Saint John, Saint Joseph, Saint Lucy, Saint Michael, Saint Peter, Saint Philip, Saint Thomas; note—there may be a new city of Bridgetown
Independence: 30 November 1966 (from UK)
Constitution: 30 November 1966
Legal system: English common law; no judicial review of legislative acts
National holiday: Independence Day, 30 November (1966)
Executive branch: British monarch, governor general, prime minister, deputy prime minister, Cabinet
Legislative branch: bicameral Parliament consists of an upper house or Senate and a lower house or House of Assembly
Judicial branch: Supreme Court of Judicature
Leaders:
Chief of State—Queen ELIZABETH II (since 6 February 1952), represented by Governor General Sir Hugh SPRINGER (since 24 February 1984);
Head of Government—Prime Minister Lloyd Erskine SANDIFORD (since 2 June 1987)
Political parties and leaders: Democratic Labor Party (DLP), Erskine SANDIFORD; Barbados Labor Party (BLP), Henry FORDE; National Democratic Party (NDP), Richie HAYNES
Suffrage: universal at age 18
Elections:
House of Assembly—last held 22 January 1991 (next to be held by January 1996); results—DLP 49.8%; seats—(28 total) DLP 18, BLP 10
Communists: negligible
Other political or pressure groups: Industrial and General Workers Union, Sir Frank WALCOTT; People's Progressive Movement, Eric SEALY; Workers' Party of Barbados, Dr. George BELLE
Member of: ACP, C, CARICOM, CDB, ECLAC, FAO, G-77, GATT, IADB, IBRD, ICAO, ICFTU, IFAD, IFC, ILO, IMF,

IMO, INTELSAT, INTERPOL, IOC, ISO (correspondent), ITU, LAES, LORCS, NAM, OAS, OPANAL, UN, UNCTAD, UNESCO, UNIDO, UPU, WHO, WIPO, WMO
Diplomatic representation: Ambassador Sir William DOUGLAS; Chancery at 2144 Wyoming Avenue NW, Washington DC 20008; telephone (202) 939-9200 through 9202; there is a Barbadian Consulate General in New York and a Consulate in Los Angeles;
US—Ambassador G. Philip HUGHES; Embassy at Canadian Imperial Bank of Commerce Building, Broad Street, Bridgetown (mailing address is P. O. Box 302, Bridgetown or FPO Miami 34054); telephone (809) 436-4950 through 4957
Flag: three equal vertical bands of blue (hoist side), yellow, and blue with the head of a black trident centered on the gold band; the trident head represents independence and a break with the past (the colonial coat of arms contained a complete trident)

Economy

Overview: A per capita income of $6,500 gives Barbados one of the highest standards of living of all the small island states of the eastern Caribbean. Historically, the economy was based on the cultivation of sugarcane and related activities. In recent years, however, the economy has diversified into manufacturing and tourism. The tourist industry is now a major employer of the labor force and a primary source of foreign exchange. An unemployment rate of 18% remains one of the most serious economic problems facing the country.
GDP: $1.7 billion, per capita $6,500; real growth rate 3.6% (1989 est.)
Inflation rate (consumer prices): 6.2% (1989)
Unemployment: 18% (1990)
Budget: revenues $501 million; expenditures $484 million, including capital expenditures of $113 million (FY91)
Exports: $186 million (f.o.b., 1989);
commodities—sugar and molasses, electrical components, clothing, rum, machinery and transport equipment;
partners: CARICOM 30%, US 20%, UK 20%
Imports: $673 million (c.i.f., 1989);
commodities—foodstuffs, consumer durables, raw materials, crude oil;
partners—US 35%, CARICOM 13%, UK 12%, Japan 6%, Canada 8%, Venezuela 4%
External debt: $550 million (June 1990 est.)
Industrial production: growth rate −1.5% (1989); accounts for almost 10% of GDP
Electricity: 132,000 kW capacity; 494 million kWh produced, 1,880 kWh per capita (1990)
Industries: tourism, sugar, light manufacturing, component assembly for export

Agriculture: accounts for 10% of GDP; major cash crop is sugarcane; other crops—vegetables and cotton; not self-sufficient in food
Economic aid: US commitments, including Ex-Im (FY70-89), $15 million; Western (non-US) countries, ODA and OOF bilateral commitments (1970-88), $169 million
Currency: Barbadian dollars (plural—dollars); 1 Barbadian dollar (Bds$) = 100 cents
Exchange rates: Barbadian dollars (Bds$) per US$1—2.0113 (fixed rate)
Fiscal year: 1 April-31 March

Communications

Highways: 1,570 km total; 1,475 km paved, 95 km gravel and earth
Ports: Bridgetown
Merchant marine: 2 cargo ships (1,000 GRT or over) totaling 3,200 GRT/7,338 DWT
Civil air: 2 major transport aircraft
Airports: 1 with permanent-surface runways 2,440-3,659 m
Telecommunications: islandwide automatic telephone system with 89,000 telephones; tropospheric scatter link to Trinidad and Saint Lucia; stations—3 AM, 2 FM, 2 (1 is pay) TV; 1 Atlantic Ocean INTELSAT earth station

---

Defense Forces

Branches: Royal Barbados Defense Force, Coast Guard, Royal Barbados Police Force
Manpower availability: males 15-49, 69,038; 48,455 fit for military service, no conscription
Defense expenditures: $10 million, 0.7% of GDP (1989)

Bassas da India
(French possession)

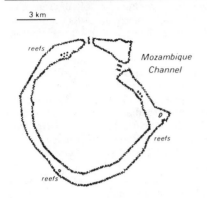

3 km

reefs

Mozambique Channel

reefs

reefs

Geography

Total area: undetermined
Comparative area: undetermined
Land boundaries: none
Coastline: 35.2 km
Maritime claims:
Contiguous zone: 12 nm;
Continental shelf: 200 m (depth) or to depth of exploitation;
Exclusive economic zone: 200 nm;
Territorial sea: 12 nm
Disputes: claimed by Madagascar
Climate: tropical
Terrain: a volcanic rock 2.4 m high
Natural resources: none
Land use: arable land 0%; permanent crops 0%; meadows and pastures 0%; forest and woodland 0%; other (rock) 100%
Environment: surrounded by reefs; subject to periodic cyclones
Note: navigational hazard since it is usually under water during high tide; located in southern Mozambique Channel about half-way between Africa and Madagascar

People

Population: uninhabited

Government

Long-form name: none
Type: French possession administered by Commissioner of the Republic Daniel CONSTANTIN, resident in Reunion

Economy

Overview: no economic activity

Communications

Ports: none; offshore anchorage only

Defense Forces

Note: defense is the responsibility of France

Belgium

North Sea

50 km

Oostende   Antwerp

Kortrijk   BRUSSELS

Mons   Liège

Charleroi

Bastogne

Geography

Total area: 30,510 km²; land area: 30,230 km²
Comparative area: slightly larger than Maryland
Land boundaries: 1,385 km total; France 620 km, Germany 167 km, Luxembourg 148 km, Netherlands 450 km
Coastline: 64 km
Maritime claims:
Continental shelf: not specific;
Exclusive fishing zone: equidistant line with neighbors (extends about 68 km from coast);
Territorial sea: 12 nm
Climate: temperate; mild winters, cool summers; rainy, humid, cloudy
Terrain: flat coastal plains in northwest, central rolling hills, rugged mountains of Ardennes Forest in southeast
Natural resources: coal, natural gas
Land use: arable land 24%; permanent crops 1%; meadows and pastures 20%; forest and woodland 21%; other 34%, includes irrigated NEGL%
Environment: air and water pollution
Note: majority of West European capitals within 1,000 km of Brussels; crossroads of Western Europe; Brussels is the seat of the EC

People

Population: 9,921,910 (July 1991), growth rate 0.1% (1991)
Birth rate: 12 births/1,000 population (1991)
Death rate: 11 deaths/1,000 population (1991)
Net migration rate: 0 migrants/1,000 population (1991)
Infant mortality rate: 6 deaths/1,000 live births (1991)
Life expectancy at birth: 74 years male, 81 years female (1991)
Total fertility rate: 1.6 children born/woman (1991)

Nationality: noun—Belgian(s); adjective—Belgian
Ethnic divisions: Fleming 55%, Walloon 33%, mixed or other 12%
Religion: Roman Catholic 75%, remainder Protestant or other
Language: Flemish (Dutch) 56%, French 32%, German 1%; legally bilingual 11%; divided along ethnic lines
Literacy: 99% (male NA%, female NA%) age 15 and over can read and write (1980 est.)
Labor force: 4,200,000; services 69%, industry 28%, agriculture 3% (1988)
Organized labor: 70% of labor force

Government

Long-form name: Kingdom of Belgium
Type: constitutional monarchy
Capital: Brussels
Administrative divisions: 9 provinces (French—provinces, singular—province; Flemish—provinciën, singular—provincie); Antwerpen, Brabant, Hainaut, Liège, Limburg, Luxembourg, Namur, Oost-Vlaanderen, West-Vlaanderen
Independence: 4 October 1830 (from the Netherlands)
Constitution: 7 February 1831, last revised 8-9 August 1980; the government is in the process of revising the Constitution, with the aim of federalizing the Belgian state
Legal system: civil law system influenced by English constitutional theory; judicial review of legislative acts; accepts compulsory ICJ jurisdiction, with reservations
National holiday: National Day, 21 July (ascension of King Leopold to the throne in 1831)
Executive branch: monarch, prime minister, five deputy prime ministers, Cabinet
Legislative branch: bicameral Parliament consists of an upper chamber or Senate (Flemish—Senaat, French—Sénat) and a lower chamber or Chamber of Representatives (Flemish—Kamer van Volksvertegenwoordigers, French—Chambre des Représentants)
Judicial branch: Supreme Court of Justice (Flemish—Hof van Cassatie, French—Cour de Cassation)
Leaders:
Chief of State—King BAUDOUIN I (since 17 July 1951); Heir Apparent Prince ALBERT of Liège (brother of the King; born 6 June 1934);
Head of Government—Prime Minister Wilfried MARTENS, (since April 1979, with a 10-month interruption in 1981)
Political parties and leaders: Flemish Social Christian (CVP), Herman van ROMPUY, president; Walloon Social Christian (PSC), Gérard DEPREZ, president; Flemish Socialist (SP), Frank VANDENBROUCKE, president; Walloon Socialist (PS), Guy SPITAELS, president; Flemish Liberal (PVV),

Guy VERHOFSTADT, president; Walloon Liberal (PRL), Antoine DUQUESNE, president; Francophone Democratic Front (FDF), Georges CLERFAYT, president; Volksunie (VU), Jaak GABRIELS, president; Communist Party (PCB), Louis van GEYT, president; Vlaams Blok (VB), Karel DILLEN; other minor parties

Suffrage: universal and compulsory at age 18

Elections:
Senate—last held 13 December 1987 (next to be held by January 1992); results—CVP 19.2%, PS 15.7%, SP 14.7%, PVV 11.3%, PRL 9.3%, VU 8.1%, PSC 7.8%, ECOLO-AGALEV 7.7%, VB 2.0%, VDF 1.3%, other 1.96%; seats—(106 total) CVP 22, PS 20, SP 17, PRL 12, PVV 11, PSC 9, VU 8, ECOLO-AGALEV 5, VB 1, FDF 1;
Chamber of Representatives—last held 13 December 1987 (next to be held by January 1992); results—CVP 19.45%, PS 15.66%, SP 14.88%, PVV 11.55%, PRL 9.41%, PSC 8.01%, VU 8.05%, ECOLO-AGALEV 7.05%, VB 1.90%, FDF 1.16%, other 2.88%; seats—(212 total) CVP 43, PS 40, SP 32, PVV 25, PRL 23, PSC 19, VU 16, ECOLO-AGALEV 9, FDF 3, VB 2

Communists: under 5,000 members (December 1985 est.)

Other political or pressure groups: Christian and Socialist Trade Unions; Federation of Belgian Industries; numerous other associations representing bankers, manufacturers, middle-class artisans, and the legal and medical professions; various organizations represent the cultural interests of Flanders and Wallonia; various peace groups such as the Flemish Action Committee Against Nuclear Weapons and Pax Christi

Member of: ACCT, AfDB, AG (observer), AsDB, Benelux, BIS, CCC, CE, CERN, CO-COM, CSCE, EBRD, EC, ECE, EIB, ESA, FAO, G-9, G-10, GATT, IADB, IAEA, IBRD, ICAO, ICC, ICFTU, IDA, IEA, IFAD, IFC, ILO, IMF, IMO, INMARSAT, INTELSAT, INTERPOL, IOC, IOM, ISO, ITU, LORCS, NATO, NEA, OAS (observer), OECD, PCA, UN, UNCTAD, UNESCO, UNHCR, UNIDO, UNMOGIP, UNRWA, UPU, WCL, WEU, WHO, WIPO, WMO, WTO

Diplomatic representation: Ambassador Juan CASSIERS; Chancery at 3330 Garfield Street NW, Washington DC 20008; telephone (202) 333-6900; there are Belgian Consulates General in Atlanta, Chicago, Houston, Los Angeles, and New York; *US*—Ambassador Maynard W. GLITMAN; Embassy at 27 Boulevard du Regent, B-1000 Brussels (mailing address is APO New York 09667-1000); telephone [32] (2) 513-3830; there is a US Consulate General in Antwerp

Flag: three equal vertical bands of black (hoist side), yellow, and red; the design was based on the flag of France

Economy

Overview: This small private-enterprise economy has capitalized on its central geographic location, highly developed transport network, and diversified industrial and commercial base. Industry is concentrated mainly in the populous Flemish area in the north, although the government is encouraging reinvestment in the southern region of Walloon. With few natural resources Belgium must import essential raw materials, making its economy closely dependent on the state of world markets. Over 70% of trade is with other EC countries. During the period 1988-90 Belgium's economic performance was marked by buoyant output growth, moderate inflation, and a substantial external surplus. Real GDP grew by an average of 3.9% in 1988-90. However, the economy is likely to slow in 1991-92 to below 3% GDP growth.

GDP: $144.8 billion, per capita $14,600; real growth rate 3.3% (1990)

Inflation rate (consumer prices): 3.3% (1990)

Unemployment rate: 8.5% est. (1990 est.)

Budget: revenues $45.0 billion; expenditures $55.3 billion, including capital expenditures of NA (1989)

Exports: $106 billion (f.o.b., 1990 est.) Belgium-Luxembourg Economic Union; *commodities*—iron and steel, transportation equipment, tractors, diamonds, petroleum products; *partners*—EC 74%, US 5%, Communist countries 2% (1989)

Imports: $108 billion (c.i.f., 1989) Belgium-Luxembourg Economic Union; *commodities*—fuels, grains, chemicals, foodstuffs; *partners*—EC 73%, US 4%, oil-exporting less developed countries 4%, Communist countries 3% (1989)

External debt: $28.8 billion (1990 est.)

Industrial production: growth rate 2.3% (1990 est.); accounts for almost 30% of GDP

Electricity: 17,325,000 kW capacity; 62,780 million kWh produced, 6,350 kWh per capita (1989)

Industries: engineering and metal products, processed food and beverages, chemicals, basic metals, textiles, glass, petroleum, coal

Agriculture: accounts for 2% of GDP; emphasis on livestock production—beef, veal, pork, milk; major crops are sugar beets, fresh vegetables, fruits, grain, and tobacco; net importer of farm products

Economic aid: donor—ODA and OOF commitments (1970-88), $5.0 billion

Currency: Belgian franc (plural—francs); 1 Belgian franc (BF) = 100 centimes

Exchange rates: Belgian francs (BF) per US$1—31.102 (January 1991), 33.418 (1990), 39.404 (1989), 36.768 (1988), 37.334 (1987), 44.672 (1986), 59.378 (1985)

Fiscal year: calendar year

Communications

Railroads: Belgian National Railways (SNCB) operates 3,667 km 1.435-meter standard gauge, government owned; 2,563 km double track; 1,978 km electrified; 191 km 1.000-meter gauge, government owned and operated

Highways: 103,396 km total; 1,317 km limited access, divided autoroute; 11,717 km national highway; 1,362 km provincial road; about 38,000 km paved and 51,000 km unpaved rural roads

Inland waterways: 2,043 km (1,528 km in regular commercial use)

Ports: Antwerp, Brugge, Gent, Oostende, Zeebrugge

Merchant marine: 69 ships (1,000 GRT or over) totaling 1,785,066 GRT/2,927,618 DWT; includes 12 cargo, 6 roll-on/roll-off, 6 container, 7 petroleum, oils, and lubricants (POL) tanker, 9 liquefied gas, 3 combination ore/oil, 9 chemical tanker, 11 bulk, 6 combination bulk

Pipelines: refined products 1,167 km; crude 161 km; natural gas 3,300 km

Civil air: 47 major transport aircraft

Airports: 42 total, 42 usable; 24 with permanent-surface runways; none with runways over 3,659 m; 14 with runways 2,440-3,659 m; 3 with runways 1,220-2,439 m

Telecommunications: excellent domestic and international telephone and telegraph facilities; 4,720,000 telephones; stations—8 AM, 19 FM (42 relays), 25 TV (10 relays); 5 submarine cables; satellite earth stations operating in INTELSAT 3 Atlantic Ocean and EUTELSAT systems

Defense Forces

Branches: Army, Navy, Air Force, National Gendarmerie

Manpower availability: males 15-49, 2,521,178; 2,115,935 fit for military service; 64,634 reach military age (19) annually

Defense expenditures: $4.8 billion, 2.5% of GDP (1990)

Belize

Geography

Total area: 22,960 km²; land area: 22,800 km²
Comparative area: slightly larger than Massachusetts
Land boundaries: 516 km total; Guatemala 266 km, Mexico 250 km
Coastline: 386 km
Maritime claims:
Territorial sea: 3 nm
Disputes: claimed by Guatemala, but boundary negotiations to resolve dispute are nearing completion
Climate: tropical; very hot and humid; rainy season (May to February)
Terrain: flat, swampy coastal plain; low mountains in south
Natural resources: arable land potential, timber, fish
Land use: arable land 2%; permanent crops NEGL%; meadows and pastures 2%; forest and woodland 44%; other 52%, includes irrigated NEGL%
Environment: frequent devastating hurricanes (September to December) and coastal flooding (especially in south); deforestation
Note: national capital moved 80 km inland from Belize City to Belmopan because of hurricanes; only country in Central America without a coastline on the North Pacific Ocean

People

Population: 228,069 (July 1991), growth rate 3.6% (1991)
Birth rate: 38 births/1,000 population (1991)
Death rate: 5 deaths/1,000 population (1991)
Net migration rate: 4 migrants/1,000 population (1991)
Infant mortality rate: 35 deaths/1,000 live births (1991)

Life expectancy at birth: male 67 years, female 72 years (1991)
Total fertility rate: 4.7 children born/woman (1991)
Nationality: noun—Belizean(s); adjective—Belizean
Ethnic divisions: Creole 39.7%, Mestizo 33.1%, Maya 9.5%, Garifuna 7.6%, East Indian 2.1%, other 8.0%
Religion: Roman Catholic 62%, Protestant 30% (Anglican 12%, Methodist 6%, Mennonite 4%, Seventh-Day Adventist 3%, Pentecostal 2%, Jehovah's Witnesses 1%, other 2%), none 2%, unknown 3%, other 3% (1980)
Language: English (official), Spanish, Maya, Garifuna (Carib)
Literacy: 91% (male 91%, female 91%) age 15 and over having ever attended school (1970)
Labor force: 51,500; agriculture 30.0%, services 16.0%, government 15.4%, commerce 11.2%, manufacturing 10.3%; shortage of skilled labor and all types of technical personnel (1985)
Organized labor: 12% of labor force; 7 unions currently active

Government

Long-form name: none
Type: parliamentary democracy
Capital: Belmopan
Administrative divisions: 6 districts; Belize, Cayo, Corozal, Orange Walk, Stann Creek, Toledo
Independence: 21 September 1981 (from UK; formerly British Honduras)
Constitution: 21 September 1981
Legal system: English law
National holiday: Independence Day, 21 September
Executive branch: British monarch, governor general, prime minister, deputy prime minister, Cabinet
Legislative branch: bicameral National Assembly consists of an upper house or Senate and a lower house or House of Representatives
Judicial branch: Supreme Court
Leaders:
Chief of State—Queen ELIZABETH II (since 6 February 1952), represented by Governor General Dame Elmira Minita GORDON (since 21 September 1981);
Head of Government—Prime Minister George Cadle PRICE (since 4 September 1989)
Political parties and leaders: People's United Party (PUP), George PRICE, Florencio MARIN, Said MUSA; United Democratic Party (UDP), Manuel ESQUIVEL, Dean LINDO, Dean BARROW; Belize Popular Party (BPP), Louis SYLVESTRE
Suffrage: universal at age 18
Elections:

National Assembly—last held 4 September 1989 (next to be held September 1994); results—percent of vote by party NA; seats—(28 total) PUP 15 seats, UDP 13 seats; note—in January 1990 one member expelled from UDP joined PUP, making the seat count 16 PUP, UDP 12
Communists: negligible
Other political or pressure groups: Society for the Promotion of Education and Research (SPEAR) headed by former PUP minister; United Workers Front
Member of: ACP, C, CARICOM, CDB, ECLAC, FAO, G-77, GATT, IBRD, IDA, IFAD, IFC, ILO, IMF, INTERPOL, IOC, IOM, (observer), ITU, LORCS, NAM, OAS, UN, UNCTAD, UNESCO, UNIDO, UPU, WCL, WMO
Diplomatic representation: Ambassador James V. HYDE; Chancery at Suite 2J, 3400 International Drive NW, Washington DC 20008; telephone (202) 363-4505; *US*—Ambassador Eugene L. SCASSA; Embassy at Gabourel Lane and Hutson Street, Belize City (mailing address is P. O. Box 286, Belize City); telephone [501] 77161 through 77163
Flag: blue with a narrow red stripe along the top and the bottom edges; centered is a large white disk bearing the coat of arms; the coat of arms features a shield flanked by two workers in front of a mahogany tree with the related motto *SUB UMBRA FLOREO* (I Flourish in the Shade) on a scroll at the bottom, all encircled by a green garland

Economy

Overview: The economy is based primarily on agriculture and merchandising. Agriculture accounts for more than 30% of GDP and provides 75% of export earnings, while sugar, the chief crop, accounts for almost 40% of hard currency earnings. The US, Belize's main trading partner, is assisting in efforts to reduce dependency on sugar with an agricultural diversification program.
GDP: $290 million, per capita $1,320; real growth rate 9% (1990 est.)
Inflation rate (consumer prices): 1.8% (1990 est.)
Unemployment rate: 12% (1988)
Budget: revenues $87.4 million; expenditures $130.5 million, including capital expenditures of $53.5 million (FY90 est.)
Exports: $108 million (f.o.b., 1990 est.); *commodities*—sugar, clothing, seafood, molasses, citrus, wood and wood products; *partners*—US 47%, UK, Trinidad and Tobago, Canada (1987)
Imports: $204 million (c.i.f., 1990 est.); *commodities*—machinery and transportation equipment, food, manufactured goods, fuels, chemicals, pharmaceuticals; *partners*—US 55%, UK, Netherlands Antilles, Mexico (1987)

Benin

External debt: $169 million (December 1990)

Industrial production: growth rate 9.7% (1989); accounts for 16% of GDP

Electricity: 34,700 kW capacity; 90 million kWh produced, 410 kWh per capita (1990)

Industries: sugar refining, clothing, timber and forest products, furniture, rum, soap, beverages, cigarettes, tourism

Agriculture: accounts for 30% of GDP (including fish and forestry); commercial crops include sugarcane, bananas, coca, citrus fruits; expanding output of lumber and cultured shrimp; net importer of basic foods

Illicit drugs: an illicit producer of cannabis for the international drug trade; eradication program cut marijuana production from 200 metric tons in 1987 to 66 metric tons in 1989; transshipment point for cocaine

Economic aid: US commitments, including Ex-Im (FY70-89), $104 million; Western (non-US) countries, ODA and OOF bilateral commitments (1970-88), $199 million

Currency: Belizean dollar (plural—dollars); 1 Belizean dollar (Bz$) = 100 cents

Exchange rates: Belizean dollars (Bz$) per US$1—2.00 (fixed rate)

Fiscal year: 1 April-31 March

Communications

Highways: 2,710 km total; 500 km paved, 1,600 km gravel, 300 km improved earth, and 310 km unimproved earth

Inland waterways: 825 km river network used by shallow-draft craft; seasonally navigable

Ports: Belize City; additional ports for shallow draught craft include Corozol, Punta Gorda, Big Creek

Civil air: no major transport aircraft

Airports: 42 total, 32 usable; 3 with permanent-surface runways; none with runways over 2,439 m; 2 with runways 1,220-2,439 m

Telecommunications: 8,650 telephones; above-average system based on radio relay; stations—6 AM, 5 FM, 1 TV, 1 shortwave; 1 Atlantic Ocean INTELSAT earth station

Defense Forces

Branches: British Forces Belize, Belize Defense Force (including Army, Navy, Air Force, and Volunteer Guard), Belize National Police

Manpower availability: males 15-49, 53,184; 31,790 fit for military service; 2,545 reach military age (18) annually

Defense expenditures: $4.8 million, 1.8% of GDP (1990 est.)

Bight of Benin

Geography

Total area: 112,620 km²; land area: 110,620 km²

Comparative area: slightly smaller than Pennsylvania

Land boundaries: 1,989 km total; Burkina 306 km, Niger 266 km, Nigeria 773 km, Togo 644 km

Coastline: 121 km

Maritime claims:
Territorial sea: 200 nm

Climate: tropical; hot, humid in south; semiarid in north

Terrain: mostly flat to undulating plain; some hills and low mountains

Natural resources: small offshore oil deposits, limestone, marble, timber

Land use: arable land 12%; permanent crops 4%; meadows and pastures 4%; forest and woodland 35%; other 45%, includes irrigated NEGL%

Environment: hot, dry, dusty harmattan wind may affect north in winter; deforestation; desertification

Note: recent droughts have severely affected marginal agriculture in north; no natural harbors

People

Population: 4,831,823 (July 1991), growth rate 3.3% (1991)

Birth rate: 49 births/1,000 population (1991)

Death rate: 16 deaths/1,000 population (1991)

Net migration rate: 0 migrants/1,000 population (1991)

Infant mortality rate: 119 deaths/1,000 live births (1991)

Life expectancy at birth: 49 years male, 52 years female (1991)

Total fertility rate: 7.0 children born/woman (1991)

Nationality: noun—Beninese (sing., pl.); adjective—Beninese

Ethnic divisions: African 99% (42 ethnic groups, most important being Fon, Adja, Yoruba, Bariba); Europeans 5,500

Religion: indigenous beliefs 70%, Muslim 15%, Christian 15%

Language: French (official); Fon and Yoruba most common vernaculars in south; at least six major tribal languages in north

Literacy: 23% (male 32%, female 16%) age 15 and over can read and write (1990 est.)

Labor force: 1,900,000 (1987); agriculture 60%, transport, commerce, and public services 38%, industry less than 2%; 49% of population of working age (1985)

Organized labor: about 75% of wage earners

Government

Long-form name: Republic of Benin

Type: dropped Marxism-Leninism December 1989; democratic reforms adopted February 1990; transition to multiparty system completed 4 April 1991

Capital: Porto-Novo (official), Cotonou (de facto)

Administrative divisions: 6 provinces; Atakora, Atlantique, Borgou, Mono, Ouémé, Zou

Independence: 1 August 1960 (from France; formerly Dahomey)

Constitution: 2 December 1990

Legal system: based on French civil law and customary law; has not accepted compulsory ICJ jurisdiction

National holiday: National Day, 1 August (1990)

Executive branch: president, cabinet

Legislative branch: unicameral National Assembly (Assemblée Nationale)

Judicial branch: Supreme Court (Cour Supreme)

Leaders:
Chief of State and Head of Government—President Nicephore SOGLO (since 4 April 1991)

Political parties and leaders: the People's Revolutionary Party of Benin (PRPB) headed by President Mathieu KÉRÉKOU, chairman of the Central Committee, was dissolved 30 April 1990; Alliance of the Democratic Union for the Forces of Progress (UDFP), Timothee ADANLIN; Movement for Democracy and Social Progress (MDPS), Jean-Roger AHOYO; and the Union for Liberty and Development (ULD), Marcellin DEGBE;
Alliance of the National Party for Democracy and Development (PNDD) and the Democratic Renewal Party (PRD), Pascal Chabi KAO;
Alliance of the Social Democratic Party (PSD) and the National Union for Solidarity and Progress (UNSP), Bruno AMOUSSOU;

Benin (continued)

Our Common Cause (NCC), Albert TE-VEODJRE; National Rally for Democracy (RND), Joseph KEKE;
Alliance of the National Movement for Democracy and Development (MNDD); Movement for Solidarity, Union, and Progress (MSUP); and Union for Democracy and National Reconstruction (UDRN), Bertin BORNA;
Union for Democracy and National Solidarity (UDS), Mama Amadou N'DIAYE;
Assembly of Liberal Democrats for National Reconstruction (RDL), Severin ADJOVI;
Alliance of the Alliance for Social Democracy (ASD) and Bloc for Social Democracy (BSD), Robert DOSSOU;
Alliance of the Alliance for Democracy and Progress (ADP) and Democratic Union for Social Renewal (UDRS), Bio Gado Seko N'GOYE; National Union for Democracy and Progress (UNDP), Robert TAGNON; numerous other small parties
Suffrage: universal at age 18
Elections:
President—last held 10 and 24 March 1991 (next to be held March 1996); results—Nicephore SOGLO 68%, Mathieu KÉRÉ-KOU 32%;
National Assembly—last held 10 and 24 March 1991 (next to be held March 1996); results—NA percent of the vote; seats—(64 total) UDFP-MDPS-ULD 12, PNDD/PRD 9, PSD/UNSP 8, NCC 7, RND 7, MNDD/MSUP/UDRN 6, UDS 5, RDL 4, ASD/BSD 3, ADP/UDRS 2, UNDP 1
Communists: Communist Party of Dahomey (PCD) remains active
Member of: ACCT, ACP, AfDB, CEAO, ECA, ECOWAS, Entente, FAO, FZ, G-77, GATT, IBRD, ICAO, IDA, IDB, IFAD, IFC, ILO, IMF, IMO, INTELSAT, INTERPOL, IOC, ITU, LORCS, NAM, OAU, OIC, UN, UNCTAD, UNESCO, UNIDO, UPU, WADB, WCL, WFTU, WHO, WIPO, WMO, WTO
Diplomatic representation: Ambassador Candide AHOUANSOU; Charge d'Affaires Corneille MEHISSOU; Chancery at 2737 Cathedral Avenue NW, Washington DC 20008; telephone (202) 232-6656;
US—Ambassador Harriet ISOM; Embassy at Rue Caporal Anani Bernard, Cotonou (mailing address is B. P. 2012, Cotonou); telephone [229] 30-06-50
Flag: two equal horizontal bands of yellow (top) and red with a vertical green band on the hoist side

Economy

Overview: Benin is one of the least developed countries in the world because of limited natural resources and a poorly developed infrastructure. Agriculture accounts for almost 40% of GDP, employs about 60% of the labor force, and generates a major share of foreign exchange earnings. The industrial sector contributes only about 15% to GDP and employs 2% of the work force. Persistently low prices in recent years have limited hard currency earnings from Benin's major exports of agricultural products and crude oil.
GDP: $1.8 billion, per capita $400; real growth rate 1.8% (1989 est.)
Inflation rate (consumer prices): 4.3% (1988)
Unemployment: NA%
Budget: revenues $168 million; expenditures $317 million, including capital expenditures of $97 million (1989)
Exports: $250 million (f.o.b., 1989 est.);
commodities—crude oil, cotton, palm products, cocoa;
partners—FRG 36%, France 16%, Spain 14%, Italy 8%, UK 4%
Imports: $442 million (f.o.b., 1990 est.);
commodities—foodstuffs, beverages, tobacco, petroleum products, intermediate goods, capital goods, light consumer goods;
partners—France 34%, Netherlands 10%, Japan 7%, Italy 6%, US 4%
External debt: $1.0 billion (December 1990 est.)
Industrial production: growth rate –0.7% (1988); accounts for 13% of GDP
Electricity: 28,000 kW capacity; 24 million kWh produced, 5 kWh per capita (1989)
Industries: palm oil and palm kernel oil processing, textiles, beverages, petroleum
Agriculture: small farms produce 90% of agricultural output; production is dominated by food crops—corn, sorghum, cassava, beans, and rice; cash crops include cotton, palm oil, and peanuts; poultry and livestock output has not kept up with consumption
Economic aid: US commitments, including Ex-Im (FY70-89), $46 million; Western (non-US) countries, ODA and OOF bilateral commitments (1970-88), $1.1 billion; OPEC bilateral aid (1979-89), $19 million; Communist countries (1970-89), $101 million
Currency: Communauté Financière Africaine franc (plural—francs); 1 CFA franc (CFAF) = 100 centimes
Exchange rates: Communauté Financière Africaine francs (CFAF) per US$1—256.54 (January 1991), 272.26 (1990), 319.01 (1989), 297.85 (1988), 300.54 (1987), 346.30 (1986), 449.26 (1985)
Fiscal year: calendar year

Communications

Railroads: 578 km, all 1.000-meter gauge, single track
Highways: 5,050 km total; 920 km paved, 2,600 laterite, 1,530 km improved earth
Inland waterways: navigable along small sections, important only locally
Ports: Cotonou
Civil air: 3 major transport aircraft
Airports: 6 total, 4 usable; 1 with permanent-surface runways; none with runways over 2,439 m; 4 with runways 1,220-2,439 m
Telecommunications: fair system of open wire, submarine cable, and radio relay; 16,200 telephones; stations—2 AM, 2 FM, 1 TV; 1 Atlantic Ocean INTELSAT satellite earth station

Defense Forces

Branches: Peoples Armed Forces (including Army, Navy, Air Force), National Gendarmerie, People's Militia, Presidential Guard
Manpower availability: eligible 15-49, 2,089,646; of the 991,278 males 15-49, 507,482 are fit for military service; of the 1,098,368 females 15-49, 554,454 are fit for military service; about 57,106 males and 55,297 females reach military age (18) annually; both sexes are liable for military service
Defense expenditures: $38 million, 2.3% of GDP (1988)

Bermuda
(dependent territory of the UK)

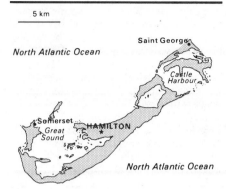

Geography

Total area: 50 km²; land area: 50 km²
Comparative area: about 0.3 times the size of Washington, DC
Land boundaries: none
Coastline: 103 km
Maritime claims:
Exclusive fishing zone: 200 nm;
Territorial sea: 12 nm
Climate: subtropical; mild, humid; gales, strong winds common in winter
Terrain: low hills separated by fertile depressions
Natural resources: limestone, pleasant climate fostering tourism
Land use: arable land 0%; permanent crops 0%; meadows and pastures 0%; forest and woodland 20%; other 80%
Environment: ample rainfall, but no rivers or freshwater lakes; consists of about 360 small coral islands
Note: 1,050 km east of North Carolina; some reclaimed land leased by US Government

People

Population: 58,433 (July 1991), growth rate 1.5% (1991)
Birth rate: 15 births/1,000 population (1991)
Death rate: 7 deaths/1,000 population (1991)
Net migration rate: 7 migrants/1,000 population (1991)
Infant mortality rate: 12 deaths/1,000 live births (1991)
Life expectancy at birth: 72 years male, 78 years female (1991)
Total fertility rate: 1.7 children born/woman (1991)
Nationality: noun—Bermudian(s); adjective—Bermudian
Ethnic divisions: black 61%, white and other 39%
Religion: Anglican 37%, Roman Catholic 14%, African Methodist Episcopal (Zion)

10%, Methodist 6%, Seventh-Day Adventist 5%, other 28%
Language: English
Literacy: 98% (male 98%, female 99%) age 15 and over can read and write (1970)
Labor force: 32,000; clerical 25%, services 22%, laborers 21%, professional and technical 13%, administrative and managerial 10%, sales 7%, agriculture and fishing 2% (1984)
Organized labor: 8,573 members (1985); largest union is Bermuda Industrial Union

Government

Long-form name: none
Type: dependent territory of the UK
Capital: Hamilton
Administrative divisions: 9 parishes and 2 municipalities*; Devonshire, Hamilton, Hamilton*, Paget, Pembroke, Saint George*, Saint George's, Sandys, Smiths, Southampton, Warwick
Independence: none (dependent territory of the UK)
Constitution: 8 June 1968
Legal system: English law
National holiday: Bermuda Day, 22 May
Executive branch: British monarch, governor, deputy governor, premier, deputy premier, Executive Council (cabinet)
Legislative branch: bicameral Parliament consists of an upper house or Senate and a lower house or House of Assembly
Judicial branch: Supreme Court
Leaders:
Chief of State—Queen ELIZABETH II (since 6 February 1952), represented by Governor Sir Desmond LANGLEY (since NA October 1988);
Head of Government—Premier John William David SWAN (since NA January 1982)
Political parties and leaders: United Bermuda Party (UBP), John W. D. SWAN; Progressive Labor Party (PLP), Frederick WADE; National Liberal Party (NLP), Gilbert DARRELL
Suffrage: universal at age 21
Elections:
House of Assembly—last held 9 February 1989 (next to be held by February 1994); results—percent of vote by party NA; seats—(40 total) UBP 23, PLP 15, NLP 1, other 1
Communists: negligible
Other political or pressure groups: Bermuda Industrial Union (BIU), headed by Ottiwell SIMMONS
Member of: CARICOM (observer), ICFTU, IOC
Diplomatic representation: as a dependent territory of the UK, Bermuda's interests in the US are represented by the UK;

US—Consul General L. Ebersole GAINES; Consulate General at Crown Hill, 16 Middle Road, Devonshire, Hamilton (mailing address is P. O. Box HM325, Hamilton HMBX, or FPO New York 09560-5300); telephone (809) 295-1342
Flag: red with the flag of the UK in the upper hoist-side quadrant and the Bermudian coat of arms (white and blue shield with a red lion holding a scrolled shield showing the sinking of the ship Sea Venture off Bermuda in 1609) centered on the outer half of the flag

Economy

Overview: Bermuda enjoys one of the highest per capita incomes in the world, having successfully exploited its location by providing luxury tourist facilities and financial services. The tourist industry attracts more than 90% of its business from North America. The industrial sector is small, and agriculture is severely limited by a lack of suitable land. About 80% of food needs are imported.
GDP: $1.3 billion, per capita $22,400; real growth rate 2.0% (1989 est.)
Inflation rate (consumer prices): 5.8% (June 1989)
Unemployment: 2.0% (1988)
Budget: revenues $307 million; expenditures $275 million, including capital expenditures of $31 million (FY90 est.)
Exports: $30 million (f.o.b., FY88); *commodities*—semitropical produce, light manufactures; *partners*—US 25%, Italy 25%, UK 14%, Canada 5%, other 31%
Imports: $420 million (c.i.f., FY88); *commodities*—fuel, foodstuffs, machinery; *partners*—US 58%, Netherlands Antilles 9%, UK 8%, Canada 6%, Japan 5%, other 14%
External debt: NA
Industrial production: growth rate NA%
Electricity: 154,000 kW capacity; 504 million kWh produced, 8,640 kWh per capita (1990)
Industries: tourism, finance, structural concrete products, paints, pharmaceuticals, ship repairing
Agriculture: accounts for less than 1% of GDP; most basic foods must be imported; produces bananas, vegetables, citrus fruits, flowers, dairy products
Economic aid: US commitments, including Ex-Im (FY70-81), $34 million; Western (non-US) countries, ODA and OOF bilateral commitments (1970-88), $267 million
Currency: Bermudian dollar (plural—dollars); 1 Bermudian dollar (Bd$) = 100 cents
Exchange rates: Bermudian dollar (Bd$) per US$1—1.0000 (fixed rate)
Fiscal year: 1 April-31 March

Bermuda *(continued)*

Communications

Highways: 210 km public roads, all paved (about 400 km of private roads)
Ports: Freeport, Hamilton, Saint George
Merchant marine: 84 ships (1,000 GRT or over) totaling 3,826,756 GRT/6,932,981 DWT; includes 3 short-sea passenger, 8 cargo, 7 refrigerated cargo, 4 container, 8 roll-on/roll-off, 26 petroleum, oils, and lubricants (POL) tanker, 11 liquefied gas, 17 bulk; note—a flag of convenience registry
Civil air: 16 major transport aircraft
Airports: 1 with permanent-surface runways 2,440-3,659 m
Telecommunications: modern with fully automatic telephone system; 52,670 telephones; stations—5 AM, 3 FM, 2 TV; 3 submarine cables; 2 Atlantic Ocean INTELSAT earth stations

Defense Forces

Branches: Bermuda Regiment, Bermuda Police Force, Reserve Constabulary
Note: defense is the responsibility of the UK

Bhutan

Geography

Total area: 47,000 km²; land area: 47,000 km²
Comparative area: slightly more than half the size of Indiana
Land boundaries: 1,075 km total; China 470 km, India 605 km
Coastline: none—landlocked
Maritime claims: none—landlocked
Climate: varies; tropical in southern plains; cool winters and hot summers in central valleys; severe winters and cool summers in Himalayas
Terrain: mostly mountainous with some fertile valleys and savanna
Natural resources: timber, hydropower, gypsum, calcium carbide, tourism potential
Land use: arable land 2%; permanent crops NEGL%; meadows and pastures 5%; forest and woodland 70%; other 23%
Environment: violent storms coming down from the Himalayas were the source of the country name which translates as Land of the Thunder Dragon
Note: landlocked; strategic location between China and India; controls several key Himalayan mountain passes

People

Population: 1,598,216 (July 1991), growth rate 2.0% (1991)
Birth rate: 37 births/1,000 population (1991)
Death rate: 17 deaths/1,000 population (1991)
Net migration rate: 0 migrants/1,000 population (1991)
Infant mortality rate: 135 deaths/1,000 live births (1991)
Life expectancy at birth: 50 years male, 48 years female (1991)
Total fertility rate: 4.9 children born/woman (1991)
Nationality: noun—Bhutanese (sing., pl.); adjective—Bhutanese

Ethnic divisions: Bhote 60%, ethnic Nepalese 25%, indigenous or migrant tribes 15%
Religion: Lamaistic Buddhism 75%, Indian- and Nepalese-influenced Hinduism 25%
Language: Bhotes speak various Tibetan dialects—most widely spoken dialect is Dzongkha (official); Nepalese speak various Nepalese dialects
Literacy: NA% (male NA%, female NA%)
Labor force: NA; agriculture 93%, services 5%, industry and commerce 2%; massive lack of skilled labor
Organized labor: not permitted

Government

Long-form name: Kingdom of Bhutan
Type: monarchy; special treaty relationship with India
Capital: Thimphu
Administrative divisions: 18 districts (dzongkhag, singular and plural); Bumthang, Chhukha, Chirang, Daga, Geylegphug, Ha, Lhuntshi, Mongar, Paro, Pemagatsel, Punakha, Samchi, Samdrup Jongkhar, Shemgang, Tashigang, Thimphu, Tongsa, Wangdi Phodrang
Independence: 8 August 1949 (from India)
Constitution: no written constitution or bill of rights
Legal system: based on Indian law and English common law; has not accepted compulsory ICJ jurisdiction
National holiday: National Day (Ugyen Wangchuck became first hereditary king), 17 December (1907)
Executive branch: monarch, chairman of the Royal Advisory Council, Royal Advisory Council (Lodoi Tsokde), chairman of the Council of Ministers, Council of Ministers (Lhengye Shungtsog)
Legislative branch: unicameral National Assembly (Tshogdu)
Judicial branch: High Court
Leaders:
Chief of State and Head of Government—King Jigme Singye WANGCHUCK (since 24 July 1972)
Political parties: no legal parties
Suffrage: each family has one vote in village-level elections
Elections: no national elections
Communists: no overt Communist presence
Other political or pressure groups: Buddhist clergy, Indian merchant community; ethnic Nepalese organizations leading militant antigovernment campaign
Member of: AsDB, CP, ESCAP, FAO, G-77, IBRD, ICAO, IDA, IFAD, IMF, IOC, ITU, NAM, SAARC, UN, UNCTAD, UNESCO, UNIDO, UPU, WHO
Diplomatic representation: no formal diplomatic relations, although informal contact

is maintained between the Bhutanese and US Embassies in New Delhi (India); the Bhutanese mission to the UN in New York has consular jurisdiction in the US

Flag: divided diagonally from the lower hoist side corner; the upper triangle is orange and the lower triangle is red; centered along the dividing line is a large black and white dragon facing away from the hoist side

Economy

Overview: The economy, one of the world's least developed, is based on agriculture and forestry, which provide the main livelihood for 90% of the population and account for about 50% of GDP. Rugged mountains dominate the terrain and make the building of roads and other infrastructure difficult and expensive. The economy is closely aligned with that of India through strong trade and monetary links. Low wages in industry lead most Bhutanese to stay in agriculture. Most development projects, such as road construction, rely on Indian migrant labor. Bhutan's hydropower potential and its attraction for tourists are its most important natural resources.

GDP: $273 million, per capita $199; real growth rate 6.3% (1988 est.)

Inflation rate (consumer prices): 10% (1989 est.)

Unemployment: NA

Budget: revenues $99 million; expenditures $128 million, including capital expenditures of $65 million (FY89 est.)

Exports: $70.9 million (f.o.b., FY89); *commodities*—cardamon, gypsum, timber, handicrafts, cement, fruit; *partners*—India 93%

Imports: $138.3 million (c.i.f., FY89 est.); *commodities*—fuel and lubricants, grain, machinery and parts, vehicles, fabrics; *partners*—India 67%

External debt: $70.1 million (FY89 est.)

Industrial production: growth rate −12.4% (1988 est.); accounts for 8% of GDP

Electricity: 353,000 kW capacity; 2,000 million kWh produced, 1,280 kWh per capita (1990)

Industries: cement, chemical products, mining, distilling, food processing, handicrafts

Agriculture: accounts for 50% of GDP; based on subsistence farming and animal husbandry; self-sufficient in food except for foodgrains; other production—rice, corn, root crops, citrus fruit, dairy, and eggs

Economic aid: Western (non-US) countries, ODA and OOF bilateral commitments (1970-88), $86.0 million; OPEC bilateral aid (1979-89), $11 million

Currency: ngultrum (plural—ngultrum); 1 ngultrum (Nu) = 100 chetrum; note—Indian currency is also legal tender

Exchange rates: ngultrum (Nu) per US$1— 18.329 (January 1991), 17.504 (1990), 16.226 (1989), 13.917 (1988), 12.962 (1987), 12.611 (1986), 12.369 (1985); note—the Bhutanese ngultrum is at par with the Indian rupee

Fiscal year: 1 July-30 June

Communications

Highways: 1,304 km total; 418 km surfaced, 515 km improved, 371 km unimproved earth

Civil air: 1 jet, 2 prop

Airports: 2 total, 2 usable; 1 with permanent-surface runways; none with runways over 2,439 m; 2 with runways 1,220-2,439 m

Telecommunications: inadequate; 1,990 telephones (1988); 22,000 radios (1990 est.); 85 TVs (1985); stations—1 AM, 1 FM, no TV (1990)

Defense Forces

Branches: Royal Bhutan Army, Palace Guard, Militia

Manpower availability: males 15-49, 398,263; 213,083 fit for military service; 17,321 reach military age (18) annually

Defense expenditures: $NA, NA% of GDP

Bolivia

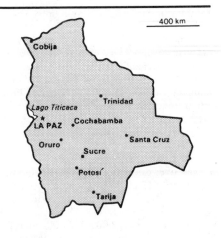

Geography

Total area: 1,098,580 km²; land area: 1,084,390 km²

Comparative area: slightly less than three times the size of Montana

Land boundaries: 6,743 km total; Argentina 832 km, Brazil 3,400 km, Chile 861 km, Paraguay 750 km, Peru 900 km

Coastline: none—landlocked

Maritime claims: none—landlocked

Disputes: has wanted a sovereign corridor to the South Pacific Ocean since the Atacama area was lost to Chile in 1884; dispute with Chile over Río Lauca water rights

Climate: varies with altitude; humid and tropical to cold and semiarid

Terrain: high plateau, hills, lowland plains

Natural resources: tin, natural gas, crude oil, zinc, tungsten, antimony, silver, iron ore, lead, gold, timber

Land use: arable land 3%; permanent crops NEGL%; meadows and pastures 25%; forest and woodland 52%; other 20%; includes irrigated NEGL%

Environment: cold, thin air of high plateau is obstacle to efficient fuel combustion; overgrazing; soil erosion; desertification

Note: landlocked; shares control of Lago Titicaca, world's highest navigable lake, with Peru

People

Population: 7,156,591 (July 1991), growth rate 2.4% (1991)

Birth rate: 34 births/1,000 population (1991)

Death rate: 9 deaths/1,000 population (1991)

Net migration rate: −1 migrant/1,000 population (1991)

Infant mortality rate: 83 deaths/1,000 live births (1991)

Life expectancy at birth: 59 years male, 64 years female (1991)

Bolivia (continued)

Total fertility rate: 4.6 children born/woman (1991)
Nationality: noun—Bolivian(s); adjective Bolivian
Ethnic divisions: Quechua 30%, Aymara 25%, mixed 25-30%, European 5-15%
Religion: Roman Catholic 95%; active Protestant minority, especially Evangelical Methodist
Language: Spanish, Quechua, and Aymara (all official)
Literacy: 78% (male 85%, female 71%) age 15 and over can read and write (1990 est.)
Labor force: 1,700,000; agriculture 50%, services and utilities 26%, manufacturing 10%, mining 4%, other 10% (1983)
Organized labor: 150,000-200,000, concentrated in mining, industry, construction, and transportation; mostly organized under Bolivian Workers' Central (COB) labor federation

---

Government

Long-form name: Republic of Bolivia
Type: republic
Capital: La Paz (seat of government); Sucre (legal capital and seat of judiciary)
Administrative divisions: 9 departments (departamentos, singular—departamento); Chuquisaca, Cochabamba, El Beni, La Paz, Oruro, Pando, Potosí, Santa Cruz, Tarija
Independence: 6 August 1825 (from Spain)
Constitution: 2 February 1967
Legal system: based on Spanish law and Code Napoleon; has not accepted compulsory ICJ jurisdiction
National holiday: Independence Day, 6 August (1825)
Executive branch: president, vice president, Cabinet
Legislative branch: bicameral National Congress (Congreso Nacional) consists of an upper chamber or Chamber of Senators (Cámara de Senadores) and a lower chamber or Chamber of Deputies (Cámara de Diputados)
Judicial branch: Supreme Court (Corte Suprema)
Leaders:
Chief of State and Head of Government—President Jaime PAZ Zamora (since 6 August 1989); Vice President Luis OSSIO Sanjines (since 6 August 1989)
Political parties and leaders: Movement of the Revolutionary Left (MIR), Jaime PAZ Zamora; Nationalist Democratic Action (ADN), Hugo BANZER Suárez; Nationalist Revolutionary Movement (MNR), Gonzalo SÁNCHEZ de Lozada; Christian Democratic Party (PDC), Jorge AGREDO; Free Bolivia Movement (MBL), led by Antonio ARANIBAR; United Left (IU), a coalition of leftist parties which includes Patriotic National Convergency Axis (EJE-P) led by

Walter DELGADILLO, and Bolivian Communist Party (PCB) led by Humberto RAMIREZ; Conscience of the Fatherland (CONDEPA), Carlos PALENQUE Avilés; Revolutionary Vanguard-9th of April (VR-9), Carlos SERRATE Reich; Civic Union Solidarity (UCS), Max FERNANDEZ
Suffrage: universal and compulsory at age 18 (married) or 21 (single)
Elections:
President—last held 7 May 1989 (next to be held May 1993); results—Gonzalo SÁNCHEZ de Lozada (MNR) 23%, Hugo BANZER Suárez (ADN) 22%, Jaime PAZ Zamora (MIR) 19%; no candidate received a majority of the popular vote; Jaime PAZ Zamora (MIR) formed a coalition with Hugo BANZER (ADN); with ADN support PAZ Zamora won the congressional runoff election on 4 August and was inaugurated on 6 August 1989;
Senate—last held 7 May 1989 (next to be held May 1993); results—percent of vote NA; seats (27 total) MNR 9, ADN 7, MIR 8, CONDEPA 2, PDC 1;
Chamber of Deputies—last held 7 May 1989 (next to be held May 1993); results—percent of vote by party NA; seats (130 total) MNR 40, ADN 35, MIR 33, IU 10, CONDEPA 9, PDC 3
Member of: AG, ECLAC, FAO, G-11, G-77, GATT, IADB, IAEA, IBRD, ICAO, IDA, IFAD, IFC, ILO, IMF, IMO, INTELSAT, INTERPOL, IOC, IOM, ITU, LAES, LAIA, LORCS, NAM, OAS, OPANAL, PCA, RG, UN, UNCTAD, UNESCO, UNIDO, UPU, WCL, WFTU, WHO, WMO, WTO
Diplomatic representation: Ambassador Jorge CRESPO; Chancery at 3014 Massachusetts Avenue NW, Washington DC 20008; telephone (202) 483-4410 through 4412; there are Bolivian Consulates General in Houston, Los Angeles, Miami, New Orleans, New York, and San Francisco;
US—Ambassador Robert S. GELBARD; Embassy at Banco Popular del Peru Building, corner of Calles Mercado y Colon, La Paz (mailing address is P. O. Box 425, La Paz, or APO Miami 34032); telephone [591] (2) 350251 or 350120
Flag: three equal horizontal bands of red (top), yellow, and green with the coat of arms centered on the yellow band; similar to the flag of Ghana, which has a large black five-pointed star centered in the yellow band

---

Economy

Overview: The Bolivian economy steadily deteriorated between 1980 and 1985 as La Paz financed growing budget deficits by expanding the money supply and inflation spiraled—peaking at 11,700%. An austere orthodox economic program adopted by

newly elected President Paz Estenssoro in 1985, however, succeeded in reducing inflation to between 10% and 20% annually since 1987, eventually restarting economic growth. President Paz Zamora retained the economic policies of the previous government, keeping inflation down and continuing the moderate growth begun under his predecessor. Nevertheless, Bolivia continues to be one of the poorest countries in Latin America, and it remains vulnerable to price fluctuations for its limited exports—agricultural products, minerals, and natural gas. Moreover, for many farmers, who constitute half of the country's work force, the main cash crop is coca, which is sold for cocaine processing.
GDP: $4.85 billion, per capita $690; real growth rate 2.7% (1990)
Inflation rate (consumer prices): 18% (1990)
Unemployment rate: 21.5% (1990 est.)
Budget: revenues $2.5 billion; expenditures $2.8 billion, including capital expenditures of $850 million (1990 est.)
Exports: $805 million (f.o.b., 1990);
commodities—metals 45%, natural gas 30%, other 25% (coffee, soybeans, sugar, cotton, timber);
partners—US 15%, Argentina
Imports: $690 million (c.i.f., 1990);
commodities—food, petroleum, consumer goods, capital goods;
partners—US 22%
External debt: $3.7 billion (December 1990)
Industrial production: growth rate 5% (1990); accounts for 25% of GDP
Electricity: 833,000 kW capacity; 1,763 million kWh produced, 260 kWh per capita (1990)
Industries: mining, smelting, petroleum, food and beverage, tobacco, handicrafts, clothing; illicit drug industry reportedly produces significant revenues
Agriculture: accounts for about 20% of GDP (including forestry and fisheries); principal commodities—coffee, coca, cotton, corn, sugarcane, rice, potatoes, timber; self-sufficient in food
Illicit drugs: world's second-largest producer of coca (after Peru) with an estimated 51,900 hectares under cultivation; government considers all but 12,000 hectares illicit; intermediate coca products and cocaine exported to or through Colombia and Brazil to the US and other international drug markets
Economic aid: US commitments, including Ex-Im (FY70-89), $990 million; Western (non-US) countries, ODA and OOF bilateral commitments (1970-88), $1.7 billion; Communist countries (1970-89), $340 million
Currency: boliviano (plural—bolivianos); 1 boliviano ($B) = 100 centavos
Exchange rates: bolivianos ($B) per US$1—3.3732 (December 1990), 3.1727 (1990),

Botswana

2.6917 (1989), 2.3502 (1988), 2.0549 (1987), 1.9220 (1986), 0.4400 (1985)
Fiscal year: calendar year

Communications

Railroads: 3,675 km total; 3,643 km 1.000-meter gauge and 32 km 0.760-meter gauge, all government owned, single track
Highways: 38,836 km total; 1,300 km paved, 6,700 km gravel, 30,836 km improved and unimproved earth
Inland waterways: 10,000 km of commercially navigable waterways
Pipelines: crude oil 1,800 km; refined products 580 km; natural gas 1,495 km
Ports: none; maritime outlets are Arica and Antofagasta in Chile and Matarani in Peru
Merchant marine: 2 cargo ships (1,000 GRT or over) totaling 14,051 GRT/22,155 DWT
Civil air: 56 major transport aircraft
Airports: 807 total, 659 usable; 9 with permanent-surface runways; 1 with runways over 3,659 m; 8 with runways 2,440-3,659 m; 120 with runways 1,220-2,439 m
Telecommunications: radio relay system being expanded; improved international services; 144,300 telephones; stations—129 AM, no FM, 43 TV, 68 shortwave; 1 Atlantic Ocean INTELSAT earth station

Defense Forces

Branches: Bolivian Army, Bolivian Navy (including Marines), Bolivian Air Force, National Police Force
Manpower availability: males 15-49, 1,679,352; 1,091,368 fit for military service; 72,979 reach military age (19) annually
Defense expenditures: $162 million, 4% of GNP (1988 est.)

Geography

Total area: 600,370 km²; land area: 585,370 km²
Comparative area: slightly smaller than Texas
Land boundaries: 4,013 km total; Namibia 1,360 km, South Africa 1,840 km, Zimbabwe 813 km
Coastline: none—landlocked
Maritime claims: none—landlocked
Disputes: short section of the boundary with Namibia is indefinite; quadripoint with Namibia, Zambia, and Zimbabwe is in disagreement
Climate: semiarid; warm winters and hot summers
Terrain: predominately flat to gently rolling tableland; Kalahari Desert in southwest
Natural resources: diamonds, copper, nickel, salt, soda ash, potash, coal, iron ore, silver, natural gas
Land use: arable land 2%; permanent crops 0%; meadows and pastures 75%; forest and woodland 2%; other 21%; includes irrigated NEGL%
Environment: rains in early 1988 broke six years of drought that had severely affected the important cattle industry; overgrazing; desertification
Note: landlocked

People

Population: 1,258,392 (July 1991), growth rate 2.7% (1991)
Birth rate: 36 births/1,000 population (1991)
Death rate: 9 deaths/1,000 population (1991)
Net migration rate: 0 migrants/1,000 population (1991)
Infant mortality rate: 43 deaths/1,000 live births (1991)
Life expectancy at birth: 59 years male, 65 years female (1991)
Total fertility rate: 4.6 children born/woman (1991)

Nationality: noun and adjective—Motswana (singular), Batswana (plural)
Ethnic divisions: Batswana 95%; Kalanga, Basarwa, and Kgalagadi about 4%; white about 1%
Religion: indigenous beliefs 50%, Christian 50%
Language: English (official), Setswana
Literacy: 23% (male 32%, female 16%) age 15 and over can read and write (1990 est.)
Labor force: 400,000; 182,200 formal sector employees, most others are engaged in cattle raising and subsistence agriculture (1988 est.); 19,000 are employed in various mines in South Africa (1988)
Organized labor: 19 trade unions

Government

Long-form name: Republic of Botswana
Type: parliamentary republic
Capital: Gaborone
Administrative divisions: 10 districts; Central, Chobe, Ghanzi, Kgalagadi, Kgatleng, Kweneng, Ngamiland, North-East, South-East, Southern; note—in addition, there may now be 4 town councils named Francistown, Gaborone, Lobaste, Selebi-Pikwe
Independence: 30 September 1966 (from UK; formerly Bechuanaland)
Constitution: March 1965, effective 30 September 1966
Legal system: based on Roman-Dutch law and local customary law; judicial review limited to matters of interpretation; has not accepted compulsory ICJ jurisdiction
National holiday: Botswana Day, 30 September (1966)
Executive branch: president, vice president, Cabinet
Legislative branch: bicameral National Assembly consists of an upper house or House of Chiefs and a lower house or National Assembly
Judicial branch: High Court, Court of Appeal
Leaders:
Chief of State and Head of Government—President Quett K. J. MASIRE (since 13 July 1980); Vice President Peter S. MMUSI (since 3 January 1983)
Political parties and leaders: Botswana Democratic Party (BDP), Quett MASIRE; Botswana National Front (BNF), Kenneth KOMA; Botswana People's Party (BPP), Knight MARIPE; Botswana Independence Party (BIP), Motsamai MPHO
Suffrage: universal at age 21
Elections:
President—last held 7 October 1989 (next to be held October 1994); results—President Quett K. J. MASIRE was reelected by the National Assembly;
National Assembly—last held 7 October 1989 (next to be held October 1994); results—percent of vote by party NA;

Botswana (continued)

seats—(38 total, 34 elected) BDP 35, BNF 3
Communists: no known Communist organization; Kenneth Koma of BNF has long history of Communist contacts
Member of: ACP, AfDB, C, CCC, ECA, FAO, FLS, G-77, GATT, IBRD, ICAO, ICFTU, IDA, IFAD, IFC, ILO, IMF, INTERPOL, IOC, ITU, LORCS, NAM, OAU, SACU, SADCC, UN, UNCTAD, UNESCO, UNIDO, UPU, WCL, WHO, WMO
Diplomatic representation: Ambassador Botsweletse Kingsley SEBELE; Chancery at Suite 404, 4301 Connecticut Avenue NW, Washington DC 20008; telephone (202) 244-4990 or 4991;
US—Ambassador David PASSAGE; Embassy at Botswana Road, Gaborone (mailing address is P. O. Box 90, Gaborone); telephone [267] 353-982 through 353-984
Flag: light blue with a horizontal white-edged black stripe in the center

Economy

Overview: The economy has historically been based on cattle raising and crops. Agriculture today provides a livelihood for over 80% of the population, but produces only about 50% of food needs and contributes a small 3% to GDP. The driving force behind the rapid economic growth of the 1970s and 1980s has been the mining industry. This sector, mostly on the strength of diamonds, has gone from generating 25% of GDP in 1980 to over 50% in 1989. No other sector has experienced such growth, especially not agriculture, which is plagued by erratic rainfall and poor soils. The unemployment rate remains a problem at 25%.
GDP: $3.1 billion, per capita $2,500; real growth rate 6.3% (1990)
Inflation rate (consumer prices): 12.0% (1990)
Unemployment rate: 25% (1989)
Budget: revenues $1,719 million; expenditures $1,792 million, including capital expenditures of $NA (FY92 est.)
Exports: $1.8 billion (f.o.b., 1990 est.); *commodities*—diamonds 77%, copper and nickel 12%, meat 4%, cattle, animal products; *partners*—Switzerland, UK, US, SACU (Southern African Customs Union)
Imports: $1.7 billion (c.i.f., 1990 est.); *commodities*—foodstuffs, vehicles and transport equipment, textiles, petroleum products; *partners*—Switzerland, SACU (Southern African Customs Union), UK, US
External debt: $780 million (December 1990 est.)
Industrial production: growth rate 16.8% (FY86); accounts for about 50% of GDP, including mining

Electricity: 217,000 kW capacity; 630 million kWh produced, 510 kWh per capita (1989)
Industries: livestock processing; mining of diamonds, copper, nickel, coal, salt, soda ash, potash; tourism
Agriculture: accounts for only 3% of GDP; subsistence farming predominates; cattle raising supports 50% of the population; must import large share of food needs
Economic aid: US commitments, including Ex-Im (FY70-89), $257 million; Western (non-US) countries, ODA and OOF bilateral commitments (1970-88), $1.8 billion; OPEC bilateral aid (1979-89), $43 million; Communist countries (1970-89), $29 million
Currency: pula (plural—pula); 1 pula (P) = 100 thebe
Exchange rates: pula (P) per US$1—1.8720 (January 1991), 1.8601 (1990), 2.0125 (1989), 1.8159 (1988), 1.6779 (1987), 1.8678 (1986), 1.8882 (1985)
Fiscal year: 1 April-31 March

Communications

Railroads: 712 km 1.0 67-meter gauge
Highways: 11,514 km total; 1,600 km paved; 1,700 km crushed stone or gravel, 5,177 km improved earth, 3,037 km unimproved earth
Civil air: 6 major transport aircraft
Airports: 100 total, 87 usable; 8 with permanent-surface runways; none with runways over 3,659 m; 2 with runways 2,440-3,659 m; 26 with runways 1,220-2,439 m
Telecommunications: the small system is a combination of open-wire lines, radio relay links, and a few radiocommunication stations; 17,900 telephones; stations—2 AM, 3 FM, no TV; 1 Indian Ocean INTELSAT earth station

Defense Forces

Branches: Botswana Defense Force (including Army and Air Wing), Botswana National Police
Manpower availability: males 15-49, 260,290; 137,038 fit for military service; 14,767 reach military age (18) annually
Defense expenditures: $99 million, 8.2% of GNP (1989)

Bouvet Island
(territory of Norway)

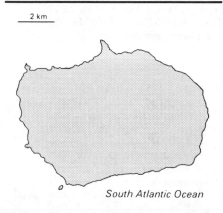

South Atlantic Ocean

Geography

Total area: 58 km²; land area: 58 km²
Comparative area: about 0.3 times the size of Washington, DC
Land boundaries: none
Coastline: 29.6 km
Maritime claims:
Territorial sea: 4 nm
Climate: antarctic
Terrain: volcanic; maximum elevation about 800 meters; coast is mostly inacessible
Natural resources: none
Land use: arable land 0%; permanent crops 0%; meadows and pastures 0%; forest and woodland 0%; other 100% (ice)
Environment: covered by glacial ice
Note: located in the South Atlantic Ocean 2,575 km south-southwest of the Cape of Good Hope, South Africa

People

Population: uninhabited

Government

Long-form name: none
Type: territory of Norway

Economy

Overview: no economic activity

Communications

Ports: none; offshore anchorage only
Telecommunications: automatic meteorological station

Defense Forces

Note: defense is the responsibility of Norway

Brazil

Boundary representation is not necessarily authoritative

1000 km

Geography

Total area: 8,511,965 km²; land area: 8,456,510 km²; includes Arquipélago de Fernando de Noronha, Atol das Rocas, Ilha da Trindade, Ilhas Martin Vaz, and Penedos de São Pedro e São Paulo
Comparative area: slightly smaller than the US
Land boundaries: 14,691 km total; Argentina 1,224 km, Bolivia 3,400 km, Colombia 1,643 km, French Guiana 673 km, Guyana 1,119 km, Paraguay 1,290 km, Peru 1,560 km, Suriname 597 km, Uruguay 985 km, Venezuela 2,200 km
Coastline: 7,491 km
Maritime claims:
Continental shelf: 200 m (depth) or to depth of exploitation;
Exclusive fishing zone: 200 nm;
Territorial sea: 200 nm
Disputes: short section of the boundary with Paraguay (just west of Guaíra Falls on the Rio Paraná) is in dispute; two short sections of boundary with Uruguay are in dispute (Arroyo de la Invernada area of the Rio Quarai and the islands at the confluence of the Rio Quarai and the Uruguay); has noted possible Latin claims in Antarctica
Climate: mostly tropical, but temperate in south
Terrain: mostly flat to rolling lowlands in north; some plains, hills, mountains, and narrow coastal belt
Natural resources: iron ore, manganese, bauxite, nickel, uranium, phosphates, tin, hydropower, gold, platinum, crude oil, timber
Land use: arable land 7%; permanent crops 1%; meadows and pastures 19%; forest and woodland 67%; other 6%; includes irrigated NEGL%
Environment: recurrent droughts in northeast; floods and frost in south; deforestation in Amazon basin; air and water pollution in Rio de Janeiro and São Paulo

Note: largest country in South America; shares common boundaries with every South American country except Chile and Ecuador

People

Population: 155,356,073 (July 1991), growth rate 1.8% (1991)
Birth rate: 26 births/1,000 population (1991)
Death rate: 7 deaths/1,000 population (1991)
Net migration rate: 0 migrants/1,000 population (1991)
Infant mortality rate: 68 deaths/1,000 live births (1991)
Life expectancy at birth: 62 years male, 68 years female (1991)
Total fertility rate: 3.1 children born/woman (1991)
Nationality: noun—Brazilian(s); adjective—Brazilian
Ethnic divisions: Portuguese, Italian, German, Japanese, black, Amerindian; white 55%, mixed 38%, black 6%, other 1%
Religion: Roman Catholic (nominal) 90%
Language: Portuguese (official), Spanish, English, French
Literacy: 81% (male 82%, female 80%) age 15 and over can read and write (1990 est.)
Labor force: 57,000,000 (1989 est.); services 42%, agriculture 31%, industry 27%
Organized labor: 13,000,000 dues paying members (1989 est.)

Government

Long-form name: Federative Republic of Brazil
Type: federal republic
Capital: Brasília
Administrative divisions: 26 states (estados, singular—estado) and 1 federal district* (distrito federal); Acre, Alagoas, Amapá, Amazonas, Bahia, Ceará, Distrito Federal*, Espírito Santo, Goiás, Maranhão, Mato Grosso, Mato Grosso do Sul, Minas Gerais, Pará, Paraíba, Paraná, Pernambuco, Piauí, Rio de Janeiro, Rio Grande do Norte, Rio Grande do Sul, Rondônia, Roraima, Santa Catarina, São Paulo, Sergipe, Tocantins; note—the former territories of Amapá and Roraima became states in January 1991
Independence: 7 September 1822 (from Portugal)
Constitution: 5 October 1988
Legal system: based on Latin codes; has not accepted compulsory ICJ jurisdiction
National holiday: Independence Day, 7 September (1822)
Executive branch: president, vice president, Cabinet
Legislative branch: bicameral National Congress (Congresso Nacional) consists of

an upper chamber or Federal Senate (Senado Federal) and a lower chamber or Chamber of Deputies (Cámara dos Deputados)
Judicial branch: Supreme Federal Tribunal
Leaders:
Chief of State and Head of Government— President Fernando Affonso COLLOR de Mello (since 15 March 1990); Vice President Itamar FRANCO (since 15 March 1990)
Political parties and leaders: National Reconstruction Party (PRN), Daniel TOURINHO, president; Brazilian Democratic Movement Party (PMDB), Orestes QUÉRCIA, president; Liberal Front Party (PFL), Hugo NAPOLEÃO, president; Workers' Party (PT), Luis Ignácio (Lula) da SILVA, president; Brazilian Labor Party (PTB), Luiz GONZAGA de Paiva Muniz, president; Democratic Labor Party (PDT), Leonel BRIZOLA, president; Democratic Social Party (PDS), Amaral NETTO, president; Brazilian Social Democracy Party (PSDB), Mário COVAS, president; Brazilian Communist Party (PCB), Salomão MALINA, secretary general; Communist Party of Brazil (PCdoB), João AMAZONAS, president; Christian Democratic Party (PDC), Eduardo CAMPOS, president
Suffrage: voluntary at age 16; compulsory between ages 18 and 70; voluntary at age 70
Elections:
President—last held 15 November 1989, with runoff on 17 December 1989 (next to be held November 1994); results—Fernando COLLOR de Mello 53%, Luis Inácio da SILVA 47%; note—first free, direct presidential election since 1960;
Senate—last held 3 October 1990 (next to be held November 1994); results—percent of vote by party NA; seats—(81 total as of 3 February 1991) PMDB 27, PFL 15, PSDB 10, PTB 8, PDT 5, other 16;
Chamber of Deputies—last held 3 October 1990 (next to be held November 1994); results—PMDB 21%, PFL 17%, PDT 9%, PDS 8%, PRN 7.9%, PTB 7%, PT 7%, other 23.1%; seats—(503 total as of 3 February 1991) PMDB 108, PFL 87, PDT 46, PDS 43, PRN 40, PTB 35, PT 35, other 109;
Communists: about 30,000
Other political or pressure groups: left wing of the Catholic Church and labor unions allied to leftist Worker's Party are critical of government's social and economic policies
Member of: AfDB, AG (observer), CCC, ECLAC, FAO, G-11, G-19, G-24, G-77, GATT, IADB, IAEA, IBRD, ICAO, ICC, ICFTU, IDA, IFAD, IFC, ILO, IMF, IMO, INMARSAT, INTELSAT, INTERPOL, IOC, IOM (observer), ISO, ITU, LAES, LAIA, LORCS, NAM (observer), OAS, OPANAL, PCA, RG, UN, UNAVEM, UNCTAD, UNESCO, UNHCR, UNIDO, UPU, WCL, WHO, WIPO, WMO, WTO

Brazil (continued)

Diplomatic representation: Ambassador Marcilio Marques MOREIRA; Chancery at 3006 Massachusetts Avenue NW, Washington DC 20008; telephone (202) 745-2700; there are Brazilian Consulates General in Atlanta, Chicago, Los Angeles, Miami, New Orleans, and New York, and Consulates in Dallas, Houston, and San Francisco; *US*—Ambassador Richard MELTON; Embassy at Avenida das Nocoes, Lote 3, Brasilia, Distrito Federal (mailing address is APO Miami 34030); telephone [55] (6) 321-7272; there are US Consulates General in Rio de Janeiro and São Paulo, and Consulates in Pôrto Alegre and Recife

Flag: green with a large yellow diamond in the center bearing a blue celestial globe with 23 white five-pointed stars (one for each state) arranged in the same pattern as the night sky over Brazil; the globe has a white equatorial band with the motto *ORDEM E PROGRESSO* (Order and Progress)

Economy

Overview: The economy, with large agrarian, mining, and manufacturing sectors, entered the 1990s with declining real growth, runaway inflation, an unserviceable foreign debt of $122 billion, and a lack of policy direction. In addition, the economy remained highly regulated, inward-looking, and protected by substantial trade and investment barriers. Ownership of major industrial and mining facilities is divided among private interests—including several multinationals—and the government. Most large agricultural holdings are private, with the government channeling financing to this sector. Conflicts between large landholders and landless peasants have produced intermittent violence. The government is seeking an IMF standby loan despite several failed agreements over the past decade. Relations with foreign commercial banks remain strained because of mounting interest arrears on Brazil's long-term debt. The Collor government, which assumed office in March 1990, is embarked on an ambitious reform program that seeks to modernize and reinvigorate the economy by stabilizing prices, deregulating the economy, and opening it to increased foreign competition. A major long-run strength is Brazil's vast natural resources.

GDP: $388 billion, per capita $2,540; real growth rate −4.6% (1990)

Inflation rate (consumer prices): 1,795% (December 1990)

Unemployment rate: 4.4% (1990)

Budget: revenues $36.5 billion; expenditures $48.2 billion, including capital expenditures of $4.6 billion (1988)

Exports: $31.4 billion (1990); *commodities*—coffee, metallurgical products, chemical products, foodstuffs, iron ore, automobiles and parts; *partners*—EC 29%, US 23%, Latin America 10%, Japan 7% (1989)

Imports: $20.4 billion (1990); *commodities*—crude oil, capital goods, chemical products, foodstuffs, coal; *partners*—US 21%, Middle East and Africa 20%, EC 20%, Latin America 18%, Japan 7% (1989)

External debt: $122 billion (December 1990)

Industrial production: growth rate −8.9% (1990); accounts for 35% of GDP

Electricity: 55,773,000 kW capacity; 214,116 million kWh produced, 1,400 kWh per capita (1990)

Industries: textiles and other consumer goods, shoes, chemicals, cement, lumber, iron ore, steel, motor vehicles and auto parts, metalworking, capital goods, tin

Agriculture: accounts for 12% of GDP; world's largest producer and exporter of coffee and orange juice concentrate and second-largest exporter of soybeans; other products—rice, corn, sugarcane, cocoa, beef; self-sufficient in food, except for wheat

Illicit drugs: illicit producer of cannabis and coca, mostly for domestic consumption; government has a modest eradication program to control cannabis and coca cultivation

Economic aid: US commitments, including Ex-Im (FY70-89), $2.5 billion; Western (non-US) countries, ODA and OOF bilateral commitments (1970-88) $9.9 billion; OPEC bilateral aid (1979-89), $284 million; Communist countries (1970-89), $1.3 billion

Currency: cruzeiro (plural—cruzeiros); 1 cruzeiro (Cr$) = 100 centavos

Exchange rates: cruzeiros (Cr$) per US$1—193.189 (January 1991), 68.300 (1990), 2.834 (1989), 0.26238 (1988), 0.03923 (1987), 0.01366 (1986), 0.00620 (1985)

Fiscal year: calendar year

Communications

Railroads: 29,694 km total; 25,268 km 1.000-meter gauge, 4,339 km 1.600-meter gauge, 74 km mixed 1.600-1.000-meter gauge, 13 km 0.760-meter gauge; 2,308 km electrified

Highways: 1,448,000 km total; 48,000 km paved, 1,400,000 km gravel or earth

Inland waterways: 50,000 km navigable

Pipelines: crude oil, 2,000 km; refined products, 3,804 km; natural gas, 1,095 km

Ports: Belém, Fortaleza, Ilhéus, Manaus, Paranagua, Pôrto Alegre, Recife, Rio de Janeiro, Rio Grande, Salvador, Santos

Merchant marine: 263 ships (1,000 GRT or over) totaling 5,898,838 GRT/9,975,272 DWT; includes 2 passenger-cargo, 59 cargo, 1 refrigerated cargo, 13 container, 7 roll-on/roll-off, 60 petroleum, oils, and lubricants (POL) tanker, 15 chemical tanker, 11 liquefied gas, 14 combination ore/oil, 79 bulk, 2 combination bulk; additionally, 2 naval tanker and 4 military transport are sometimes used commercially

Civil air: 176 major transport aircraft

Airports: 3,751 total, 3,078 usable; 401 with permanent-surface runways; 2 with runways over 3,659 m; 22 with runways 2,240-3,659 m; 533 with runways 1,220-2,439 m

Telecommunications: good system; extensive radio relay facilities; 9.86 million telephones; stations—1,223 AM, no FM, 112 TV, 151 shortwave; 3 coaxial submarine cables 3 Atlantic Ocean INTELSAT earth stations with total of 3 antennas; 64 domestic satellite stations

Defense Forces

Branches: Brazilian Army, Navy of Brazil (including Marines), Brazilian Air Force, Federal Police Force

Manpower availability: males 15-49, 40,559,052; 27,364,392 fit for military service; 1,637,434 reach military age (18) annually

Defense expenditures: $1.1 billion, 2.6% of GDP (1990)

British Indian Ocean Territory

(dependent territory of the UK)

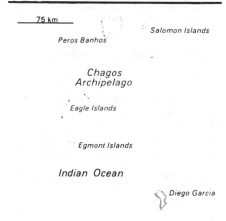

Geography

Total area: 60 km²; land area: 60 km²
Comparative area: about 0.3 times the size of Washington, DC
Land boundaries: none
Coastline: 698 km
Maritime claims:
Territorial sea: 3 nm
Disputes: the entire Chagos Archipelago is claimed by Mauritius
Climate: tropical marine; hot, humid, moderated by trade winds
Terrain: flat and low (up to 4 meters in elevation)
Natural resources: coconuts, fish
Land use: arable land 0%; permanent crops 0%; meadows and pastures 0%; forest and woodland 0%; other 100%
Environment: archipelago of 2,300 islands
Note: Diego Garcia, largest and southernmost island, occupies strategic location in central Indian Ocean

People

Population: no permanent civilian population; formerly about 3,000 islanders
Ethnic divisions: civilian inhabitants, known as the Ilois, evacuated to Mauritius before construction of UK and US defense facilities

Government

Long-form name: British Indian Ocean Territory (no short-form name); abbreviated BIOT
Type: dependent territory of the UK
Capital: none
Leaders:
Chief of State—Queen ELIZABETH II (since 6 February 1952);
Head of Government—Commissioner and Administrator R. EDIS (since NA 1988); note—resides in the UK
Diplomatic representation: none (dependent territory of the UK)

Flag: white with the flag of the UK in the upper hoist-side quadrant and six blue wavy horizontal stripes bearing a palm tree and yellow crown centered on the outer half of the flag

Economy

Overview: All economic activity is concentrated on the largest island of Diego Garcia, where joint UK-US defense facilities are located. Construction projects and various services needed to support the military installations are done by military and contract employees from the UK and the US. There are no industrial or agricultural activities on the islands.
Electricity: provided by the US military

Communications

Highways: short stretch of paved road between port and airfield on Diego Garcia
Ports: Diego Garcia
Airports: 1 with permanent-surface runways over 3,659 m on Diego Garcia
Telecommunications: minimal facilities; stations (operated by the US Navy)—1 AM, 1 FM, 1 TV; 1 Atlantic Ocean INTELSAT earth station

Defense Forces

Note: defense is the responsibility of the UK

British Virgin Islands

(dependent territory of the UK)

Geography

Total area: 150 km²; land area: 150 km²
Comparative area: about 0.8 times the size of Washington, DC
Coastline: 80 km
Maritime claims:
Exclusive fishing zone: 200 nm;
Territorial sea: 3 nm
Climate: subtropical; humid; temperatures moderated by trade winds
Terrain: coral islands relatively flat; volcanic islands steep, hilly
Natural resources: negligible
Land use: arable land 20%; permanent crops 7%; meadows and pastures 33%; forest and woodland 7%; other 33%
Environment: subject to hurricanes and tropical storms from July to October
Note: strong ties to nearby US Virgin Islands and Puerto Rico

People

Population: 12,396 (July 1991), growth rate 1.1% (1991)
Birth rate: 19 births/1,000 population (1991)
Death rate: 5 deaths/1,000 population (1991)
Net migration rate: −3 migrants/1,000 population (1991)
Infant mortality rate: 14 deaths/1,000 live births (1991)
Life expectancy at birth: 72 years male, 77 years female (1991)
Total fertility rate: 2.1 children born/woman (1991)
Nationality: noun—British Virgin Islander(s); adjective—British Virgin Islander
Ethnic divisions: black over 90%, remainder of white and Asian origin
Religion: Protestant 86% (Methodist 45%, Anglican 21%, Church of God 7%, Seventh-Day Adventist 5%, Baptist 4%, Jehovah's Witnesses 2%, other 2%), Roman Catholic 6%, none 2%, other 6% (1981)
Language: English (official)

British Virgin Islands *(continued)*

Literacy: 98% (male 98%, female 98%) age 15 and over can read and write (1970)
Labor force: 4,911 (1980)
Organized labor: NA% of labor force

Government

Long-form name: none
Type: dependent territory of the UK
Capital: Road Town
Administrative divisions: none (dependent territory of the UK)
Independence: none (dependent territory of the UK)
Constitution: 1 June 1977
Legal system: English law
National holiday: Territory Day, 1 July
Executive branch: British monarch, governor, chief minister, Executive Council (cabinet)
Legislative branch: unicameral Legislative Council
Judicial branch: Eastern Caribbean Supreme Court
Leaders:
Chief of State—Queen ELIZABETH II (since 6 February 1952), represented by Governor John Mark Ambrose HERDMAN (since NA 1986);
Head of Government—Chief Minister H. Lavity STOUTT (since NA 1986)
Political parties and leaders: United Party (UP), Conrad MADURO; Virgin Islands Party (VIP), H. Lavity STOUTT; Independent People's Movement (IPM), Cyril B. ROMNEY
Suffrage: universal at age 18
Elections:
Legislative Council—last held 12 November 1990 (next to be held by November 1995); results—percent of vote by party NA; seats—(9 total) VIP 6, IPM 1, independent 2
Communists: probably none
Member of: CARICOM (observer), CDB, ECLAC (associate), IOC, OECS (associate), UNESCO (associate)
Diplomatic representation: none (dependent territory of the UK)
Flag: blue with the flag of the UK in the upper hoist-side quadrant and the Virgin Islander coat of arms centered in the outer half of the flag; the coat of arms depicts a woman flanked on either side by a vertical column of six oil lamps above a scroll bearing the Latin word *VIGILATE* (Be Watchful)

Economy

Overview: The economy is highly dependent on the tourist industry, which generates about 21% of the national income. In 1985 the government offered offshore registration to companies wishing to incorporate in the islands, and, in consequence, incorporation fees generated about $2 million in 1987. Livestock raising is the most significant agricultural activity. The islands' crops, limited by poor soils, are unable to meet food requirements.
GDP: $106.7 million, per capita $8,900; real growth rate 2.5% (1987)
Inflation rate (consumer prices): 1.0% (1987)
Unemployment rate: NEGL%
Budget: revenues $32.8 million; expenditures $32.4 million, including capital expenditures of $6.3 million (FY90)
Exports: $2.7 million (f.o.b., 1988);
commodities—rum, fresh fish, gravel, sand, fruits, animals;
partners—Virgin Islands (US), Puerto Rico, US
Imports: $11.5 million (c.i.f., 1988);
commodities—building materials, automobiles, foodstuffs, machinery;
partners—Virgin Islands (US), Puerto Rico, US
External debt: $4.5 million (1985)
Industrial production: growth rate −4.0% (1985)
Electricity: 10,500 kW capacity; 43 million kWh produced, 3,510 kWh per capita (1990)
Industries: tourism, light industry, construction, rum, concrete block, offshore financial center
Agriculture: livestock (including poultry), fish, fruit, vegetables
Economic aid: NA
Currency: US currency is used
Exchange rates: US currency is used
Fiscal year: 1 April-31 March

Communications

Highways: 106 km motorable roads (1983)
Ports: Road Town
Airports: 3 total, 3 usable; 2 with permanent-surface runways less than 1,220 m
Telecommunications: 3,000 telephones; worldwide external telephone service; submarine cable communication links to Bermuda; stations—1 AM, no FM, 1 TV

Defense Forces

Note: defense is the responsibility of the UK

Brunei

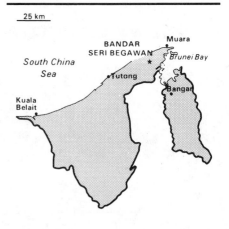

Geography

Total area: 5,770 km²; land area: 5,270 km²
Comparative area: slightly larger than Delaware
Land boundary: 381 km with Malaysia
Coastline: 161 km
Maritime claims:
Exclusive fishing zone: 200 nm;
Territorial sea: 12 nm
Disputes: may wish to purchase the Malaysian salient that divides the country
Climate: tropical; hot, humid, rainy
Terrain: flat coastal plain rises to mountains in east; hilly lowland in west
Natural resources: crude oil, natural gas, timber
Land use: arable land 1%; permanent crops 1%; meadows and pastures 1%; forest and woodland 79%; other 18%; includes irrigated NEGL%
Environment: typhoons, earthquakes, and severe flooding are rare
Note: close to vital sea lanes through South China Sea linking Indian and Pacific Oceans; two parts physically separated by Malaysia; almost an enclave of Malaysia

People

Population: 397,777 (July 1991), growth rate 6.3% (1991)
Birth rate: 22 births/1,000 population (1991)
Death rate: 4 deaths/1,000 population (1991)
Net migration rate: 45 migrants/1,000 population (1991)
Infant mortality rate: 10 deaths/1,000 live births (1991)
Life expectancy at birth: 74 years male, 77 years female (1991)
Total fertility rate: 2.9 children born/woman (1991)
Nationality: noun—Bruneian(s); adjective—Bruneian

Ethnic divisions: Malay 64%, Chinese 20%, other 16%

Religion: Muslim (official) 63%, Buddhism 14%, Christian 8%, indigenous beliefs and other 15% (1981)

Language: Malay (official), English, and Chinese

Literacy: 77% (male 85%, female 69%) age 15 and over can read and write (1981)

Labor force: 89,000 (includes members of the Army); 33% of labor force is foreign (1988); government 47.5%; production of oil, natural gas, services, and construction 41.9%; agriculture, forestry, and fishing 3.8% (1986)

Organized labor: 2% of labor force

Government

Long-form name: Negara Brunei Darussalam

Type: constitutional sultanate

Capital: Bandar Seri Begawan

Administrative divisions: 4 districts (daerah-daerah, singular—daerah); Belait, Brunei and Muara, Temburong, Tutong

Independence: 1 January 1984 (from UK)

Constitution: 29 September 1959 (some provisions suspended under a State of Emergency since December 1962, others since independence on 1 January 1984)

Legal system: based on Islamic law

National holiday: National Day, 23 February (1984)

Executive branch: sultan, prime minister, Council of Cabinet Ministers

Legislative branch: unicameral Legislative Council (Majlis Masyuarat Megeri)

Judicial branch: Supreme Court

Leaders:
Chief of State and Head of Government—Sultan and Prime Minister Sir Muda HASSANAL BOLKIAH Mu'izzaddin Waddaulah (since 5 October 1967)

Political parties and leaders: Brunei United National Party (inactive), Anak HASANUDDIN, chairman; Brunei National Democratic Party (the first legal political party and now banned), leader NA

Suffrage: none

Elections:
Legislative Council—last held in March 1962; in 1970 the Council was changed to an appointive body by decree of the sultan and no elections are planned

Communists: probably none

Member of: APEC, ASEAN, C, ESCAP, ICAO, IDB, IMO, INTERPOL, IOC, ISO (correspondent), ITU, OIC, UN, UNCTAD, UPU, WHO, WMO

Diplomatic representation: Ambassador Dato Paduka Haji Mohamed SUNI bin Haji Idris; Chancery at 2600 Virginia Avenue NW, Washington DC 20037; telephone (202) 342-0159;

US—Ambassador Christopher H. PHILLIPS; Embassy at Third Floor, Teck Guan Plaza, Jalan Sultan, Bandar Seri Begawan (mailing address is P. O. Box 2991, Bandar Seri Begawan and Box B, APO San Francisco, 96528); telephone [673] (2) 229-670

Flag: yellow with two diagonal bands of white (top, almost double width) and black starting from the upper hoist side; the national emblem in red is superimposed at the center; the emblem includes a swallow-tailed flag on top of a winged column within an upturned crescent above a scroll and flanked by two upraised hands

Economy

Overview: The economy is a mixture of foreign and domestic entrepreneurship, government regulation and welfare measures, and village tradition. It is almost totally supported by exports of crude oil and natural gas, with revenues from the petroleum sector accounting for more than 50% of GDP. Per capita GDP of $9,600 is among the highest in the Third World, and substantial income from overseas investment supplements domestic production. The government provides for all medical services and subsidizes food and housing.

GDP: $3.3 billion, per capita $9,600; real growth rate 2.7% (1989 est.)

Inflation rate (consumer prices): 1.3% (1989 est.)

Unemployment: 2.5%, shortage of skilled labor (1989 est.)

Budget: revenues $1.2 billion; expenditures $1.4 billion, including capital expenditures of $230 million (1988 est.)

Exports: $1.9 billion (f.o.b., 1989);
commodities—crude oil, liquefied natural gas, petroleum products;
partners—Japan 60%, Thailand 10%, Singapore 4% (1988)

Imports: $1.2 billion (c.i.f., 1989);
commodities—machinery and transport equipment, manufactured goods, food, chemicals;
partners—Singapore 36%, UK 26%, Switzerland 7%, US 7%, Japan 6% (1988)

External debt: none

Industrial production: growth rate 12.9% (1987); accounts for 52.4% of GDP

Electricity: 310,000 kW capacity; 890 million kWh produced, 2,400 kWh per capita (1990)

Industries: petroleum, liquefied natural gas, construction

Agriculture: imports about 80% of its food needs; principal crops and livestock include rice, cassava, bananas, buffaloes, and pigs

Economic aid: US commitments, including Ex-Im (FY70-87), $20.6 million; Western (non-US) countries, ODA and OOF bilateral commitments (1970-87), $143.7 million

Currency: Bruneian dollar (plural—dollars); 1 Bruneian dollar (B$) = 100 cents

Exchange rates: Bruneian dollars (B$) per US$1—1.7454 (January 1991), 1.8125 (1990), 1.9503 (1989), 2.0124 (1988), 2.1060 (1987), 2.1774 (1986), 2.2002 (1985); note—the Bruneian dollar is at par with the Singapore dollar

Fiscal year: calendar year

Communications

Railroads: 13 km 0.610-meter narrow-gauge private line

Highways: 1,090 km total; 370 km paved (bituminous treated) and another 52 km under construction, 720 km gravel or unimproved

Inland waterways: 209 km; navigable by craft drawing less than 1.2 meters

Ports: Kuala Belait, Muara

Merchant marine: 7 liquefied gas carriers (1,000 GRT or over) totaling 348,476 GRT/340,635 DWT

Pipelines: crude oil, 135 km; refined products, 418 km; natural gas, 920 km

Civil air: 4 major transport aircraft (3 Boeing 757-200, 1 Boeing 737-200)

Airports: 2 total, 2 usable; 1 with permanent-surface runways; 1 with runway over 3,659 m; 1 with runway 1,406 m

Telecommunications: service throughout country is adequate for present needs; international service good to adjacent Malaysia; radiobroadcast coverage good; 33,000 telephones (1987); stations—4 AM/FM, 1 TV; 74,000 radio receivers (1987); satellite earth stations—1 Indian Ocean INTELSAT and 1 Pacific Ocean INTELSAT

Defense Forces

Branches: Royal Brunei Armed Forces (including Ground Forces, Flotilla, and Air Wing), Royal Brunei Police

Manpower availability: males 15-49, 110,727; 63,730 fit for military service; 3,199 reach military age (18) annually

Defense expenditures: $233.1 million, 7.1% of GDP (1988)

Bulgaria

125 km

Geography

Total area: 110,910 km²; land area: 110,550 km²

Comparative area: slightly larger than Tennessee

Land boundaries: 1,881 km total; Greece 494 km, Romania 608 km, Turkey 240 km, Yugoslavia 539 km

Coastline: 354 km

Maritime claims:
Contiguous zone: 24 nm;
Exclusive economic zone: 200 nm;
Territorial sea: 12 nm

Disputes: Macedonia question with Greece and Yugoslavia

Climate: temperate; cold, damp winters; hot, dry summers

Terrain: mostly mountains with lowlands in north and south

Natural resources: bauxite, copper, lead, zinc, coal, timber, arable land

Land use: arable land 34%; permanent crops 3%; meadows and pastures 18%; forest and woodland 35%; other 10%; includes irrigated 11%

Environment: subject to earthquakes, landslides; deforestation; air pollution

Note: strategic location near Turkish Straits; controls key land routes from Europe to Middle East and Asia

People

Population: 8,910,622 (July 1991), growth rate −0.2% (1991)

Birth rate: 13 births/1,000 population (1991)

Death rate: 12 deaths/1,000 population (1991)

Net migration rate: −3 migrants/1,000 population (1991)

Infant mortality rate: 13 deaths/1,000 live births (1991)

Life expectancy at birth: 69 years male, 76 years female (1991)

Total fertility rate: 1.9 children born/woman (1991)

Nationality: noun—Bulgarian(s); adjective—Bulgarian

Ethnic divisions: Bulgarian 85.3%, Turk 8.5%, Gypsy 2.6%, Macedonian 2.5%, Armenian 0.3%, Russian 0.2%, other 0.6%

Religion: Bulgarian Orthodox 85%; Muslim 13%; Jewish 0.8%; Roman Catholic 0.5%; Uniate Catholic 0.2%; Protestant, Gregorian-Armenian, and other 0.5%

Language: Bulgarian; secondary languages closely correspond to ethnic breakdown

Literacy: 93% (male NA%, female NA%) age 15 and over can read and write (1970 est.)

Labor force: 4,300,000; industry 33%, agriculture 20%, other 47% (1987)

Organized labor: Confederation of Independent Trade Unions of Bulgaria (KNSB); Edinstvo (Unity) People's Trade Union (splinter confederation from KNSB); Podkrepa (Support) Labor Confederation, legally registered in January 1990

Government

Long-form name: Republic of Bulgaria

Type: emerging democracy, continuing significant Communist party influence

Capital: Sofia

Administrative divisions: 9 provinces (oblasti, singular—oblast); Burgas, Grad Sofiya, Khaskovo, Lovech, Mikhaylovgrad, Plovdiv, Razgrad, Sofiya, Varna

Independence: 22 September 1908 (from Ottoman Empire)

Constitution: 16 May 1971, effective 18 May 1971; a new constitution is likely to be adopted in 1991

Legal system: based on civil law system, with Soviet law influence; judicial review of legislative acts in the State Council; has accepted compulsory ICJ jurisdiction

National holiday: Liberation of Bulgaria from the Ottoman Empire, 3 March (1878)

Executive branch: president, chairman of the Council of Ministers (premier), three deputy chairmen of the Council of Ministers, Council of Ministers

Legislative branch: unicameral National Assembly (Narodno Sobranie)

Judicial branch: Supreme Court

Leaders:
Chief of State—President Zhelyu ZHELEV (since 1 August 1990);
Head of Government—Chairman of the Council of Ministers (Premier) Dimitur POPOV (since 19 December 1990); Deputy Chairman of the Council of Ministers Aleksandur TOMOV (since 19 December 1990); Deputy Chairman of the Council of Ministers Viktor VULKOV (since 19 December 1990); Deputy Chairman of the Council of Ministers Dimitur LUDZHEV (since 19 December 1990);

Political parties and leaders: *government*—Bulgarian Socialist Party (BSP), formerly Bulgarian Communist Party (BCP), Aleksandur LILOV, chairman;
opposition—Union of Democratic Forces (UDF), Filip DIMITROV, chairman, consisting of Nikola Petkov Bulgarian Agrarian National Union, Milan DRENCHEV, secretary of Permanent Board; Bulgarian Social Democratic Party, Petur DERTLIEV; Green Party; Christian Democrats; Radical Democratic Party; Rights and Freedoms Movement (pro-Muslim party), Ahmed DOGAN; Bulgarian Agrarian National Union (BZNS), Viktor VULKOV

Suffrage: universal and compulsory at age 18

Elections:
Chairman of the State Council—last held 1 August 1990 (next to be held May 1991); results—Zhelyo ZHELEV was elected by the National Assembly;
National Assembly—last held 10 and 17 June 1990 (next to be held in autumn 1991); results—BSP 48%, UDF 32%; seats—(400 total) BSP 211, UDF 144, Rights and Freedoms Movement 23, Agrarian Party 16, Nationalist parties 3, independents and other 3

Communists: Bulgarian Socialist Party (BSP), formerly Bulgarian Communist Party (BCP), 501,793 members

Other political or pressure groups: Ecoglasnost; Podkrepa (Support) Labor Confederation; Fatherland Union; Bulgarian Democratic Youth (formerly Communist Youth Union); Confederation of Independent Trade Unions of Bulgaria (KNSB); Committee for Defense of National Interests; Peasant Youth League; National Coalition of Extraparliamentary Political Forces; numerous regional, ethnic, and national interest groups with various agendas

Member of: BIS, CCC, CSCE, ECE, FAO, G-9, IAEA, IBEC, ICAO, IIB, ILO, IMO, INMARSAT, IOC, ISO, ITU, LORCS, PCA, UN, UNCTAD, UNESCO, UNIDO, UPU, WFTU, WHO, WIPO, WMO, WTO

Diplomatic representation: Ambassador Ognyan PISHEV; Chancery at 1621 22nd Street NW, Washington DC 20008; telephone (202) 387-7969;
US—Ambassador H. Kenneth HILL; Embassy at 1 Alexander Stamboliski Boulevard, Sofia (mailing address is APO New York 09213-5740); telephone [359] (2) 88-48-01 through 05

Flag: three equal horizontal bands of white (top), green, and red; the national emblem formerly on the hoist side of the white stripe has been removed—it contained a rampant lion within a wreath of wheat ears below a red five-pointed star and above a ribbon bearing the dates 681 (first Bulgarian state established) and 1944 (liberation from Nazi control)

Economy

Overview: Growth in the lackluster Bulgarian economy fell to the 2% annual level in the 1980s. By 1990 Sofia's foreign debt had skyrocketed to over $10 billion—giving a debt service ratio of more than 40% of hard currency earnings and leading the regime to declare a moratorium on its hard currency payments. The post-Zhivkov regime faces major problems of renovating an aging industrial plant; coping with worsening energy, food, and consumer goods shortages; keeping abreast of rapidly unfolding technological developments; investing in additional energy capacity (the portion of electric power from nuclear energy reached over one-third in 1990); and motivating workers, in part by giving them a share in the earnings of their enterprises. A major decree of January 1989 summarized and extended the government's economic restructuring efforts, which include a partial decentralization of controls over production decisions and foreign trade. In October 1990 the Lukanov government proposed an economic reform program based on a US Chamber of Commerce study. It was never instituted because of a political stalemate between the BSP and the UDF. The new Popov government launched a similar reform program in January 1991, but full implementation has been slowed by continuing political disputes.
GNP: $47.3 billion, per capita $5,300; real growth rate −6.0% (1990)
Inflation rate (consumer prices): 100% (1990 est.)
Unemployment rate: 2% (1990 est.)
Budget: revenues $26 billion; expenditures $28 billion, including capital expenditures of $NA billion (1988)
Exports: $16.0 billion (f.o.b., 1989); *commodities*—machinery and equipment 60.5%; agricultural products 14.7%; manufactured consumer goods 10.6%; fuels, minerals, raw materials, and metals 8.5%; other 5.7%; *partners*—Communist countries 82.5% (USSR 61%, GDR 5.5%, Czechoslovakia 4.9%); developed countries 6.8% (FRG 1.2%, Greece 1.0%); less developed countries 10.7% (Libya 3.5%, Iraq 2.9%)
Imports: $15.0 billion (f.o.b., 1989); *commodities*—fuels, minerals, and raw materials 45.2%; machinery and equipment 39.8%; manufactured consumer goods 4.6%; agricultural products 3.8%; other 6.6%; *partners*—Communist countries 80.5% (USSR 57.5%, GDR 5.7%), developed countries 15.1% (FRG 4.8%, Austria 1.6%); less developed countries 4.4% (Libya 1.0%, Brazil 0.9%)
External debt: $10 billion (1990)

Industrial production: growth rate −10.7% (1990)
Electricity: 11,500,000 kW capacity; 45,000 million kWh produced, 5,040 kWh per capita (1990)
Industries: food processing, machine and metal building, electronics, chemicals
Agriculture: accounts for 15% of GNP; climate and soil conditions support livestock raising and the growing of various grain crops, oilseeds, vegetables, fruits and tobacco; more than one-third of the arable land devoted to grain; world's fourth-largest tobacco exporter; surplus food producer
Economic aid: donor—$1.6 billion in bilateral aid to non-Communist less developed countries (1956-89)
Currency: lev (plural—leva); 1 lev (Lv) = 100 stotinki
Exchange rates: leva (Lv) per US$1—16.13 (March 1991), 0.7446 (November 1990), 0.84 (1989), 0.82 (1988), 0.90 (1987), 0.95 (1986), 1.03 (1985); note—floating exchange rate since February 1990
Fiscal year: calendar year

Communications

Railroads: 4,300 km total, all government owned (1987); 4,055 km 1.435-meter standard gauge, 245 km narrow gauge; 917 km double track; 2,510 km electrified
Highways: 36,908 km total; 33,535 km hard surface (including 242 km superhighways); 3,373 km earth roads (1987)
Inland waterways: 470 km (1987)
Pipelines: crude, 193 km; refined product, 418 km; natural gas, 1,400 km (1986)
Ports: Burgas, Varna, Varna West; river ports are Ruse, Vidin, and Lom on the Danube
Merchant marine: 112 ships (1,000 GRT and over) totaling 1,227,817 GRT/1,860,294 DWT; includes 2 short-sea passenger, 33 cargo, 2 container, 1 passenger-cargo training, 6 roll-on/roll-off, 18 petroleum, oils, and lubricants (POL) tanker, 1 chemical carrier, 2 railcar carrier, 47 bulk; Bulgaria owns 3 ships (1,000 GRT or over) totaling 51,035 DWT operating under Liberian registry
Civil air: 86 major transport aircraft
Airports: 380 total, 380 usable; about 120 with permanent-surface runways; 20 with runways 2,440-3,659 m; 20 with runways 1,220-2,439 m
Telecommunications: 2.5 million telephones; direct dialing to 36 countries; phone density is 25 phones per 100 persons; 67% of Sofia households now have a phone (November 1988); stations—21 AM, 16 FM, and 19 TV, with 1 Soviet TV relay in Sofia; 2.1 million TV sets (1990); 92% of country receives No. 1 television program (May 1990)

Defense Forces

Branches: Bulgarian People's Army, Bulgarian Navy, Air and Air Defense Forces, Frontier Troops, Civil Defense
Manpower availability: males 15-49, 2,183,539; 1,826,992 fit for military service; 67,836 reach military age (19) annually
Defense expenditures: 1.615 billion leva, NA% of GDP (1990); note—conversion of defense expenditures into US dollars using the current exchange rate would produce misleading results

Burkina

200 km

Boundary representation is not necessarily authoritative.

Geography

Total area: 274,200 km²; land area: 273,800 km²
Comparative area: slightly larger than Colorado
Land boundaries: 3,192 km total; Benin 306 km, Ghana 548 km, Ivory Coast 584 km, Mali 1,000 km, Niger 628 km, Togo 126 km
Coastline: none—landlocked
Maritime claims: none—landlocked
Disputes: the disputed international boundary between Burkina and Mali was submitted to the International Court of Justice (ICJ) in October 1983 and the ICJ issued its final ruling in December 1986, which both sides agreed to accept; Burkina and Mali are proceeding with boundary demarcation, including the tripoint with Niger
Climate: tropical; warm, dry winters; hot, wet summers
Terrain: mostly flat to dissected, undulating plains; hills in west and southeast
Natural resources: manganese, limestone, marble; small deposits of gold, antimony, copper, nickel, bauxite, lead, phosphates, zinc, silver
Land use: arable land 10%; permanent crops NEGL%; meadows and pastures 37%; forest and woodland 26%; other 27%, includes irrigated NEGL%
Environment: recent droughts and desertification severely affecting marginal agricultural activities, population distribution, economy; overgrazing; deforestation
Note: landlocked

People

Population: 9,359,889 (July 1991), growth rate 3.1% (1991)
Birth rate: 50 births/1,000 population (1991)
Death rate: 16 deaths/1,000 population (1991)
Net migration rate: −3 migrants/1,000 population (1991)

Infant mortality rate: 119 deaths/1,000 live births (1991)
Life expectancy at birth: 52 years male, 53 years female (1991)
Total fertility rate: 7.1 children born/woman (1991)
Nationality: noun—Burkinabe; adjective—Burkinabe
Ethnic divisions: more than 50 tribes; principal tribe is Mossi (about 2.5 million); other important groups are Gurunsi, Senufo, Lobi, Bobo, Mande, and Fulani
Religion: indigenous beliefs about 65%, Muslim 25%, Christian (mainly Roman Catholic) 10%
Language: French (official); tribal languages belong to Sudanic family, spoken by 90% of the population
Literacy: 18% (male 28%, female 9%) age 15 and over can read and write (1990 est.)
Labor force: 3,300,000 residents; 30,000 are wage earners; agriculture 82%, industry 13%, commerce, services, and government 5%; 20% of male labor force migrates annually to neighboring countries for seasonal employment (1984); 44% of population of working age (1985)
Organized labor: four principal trade union groups represent less than 1% of population

Government

Long-form name: Burkina Faso
Type: military; established by coup on 4 August 1983
Capital: Ouagadougou
Administrative divisions: 30 provinces; Bam, Bazéga, Bougouriba, Boulgou, Boulkiemdé, Ganzourgou, Gnagna, Gourma, Houet, Kadiogo, Kénédougou, Komoé, Kossi, Kouritenga, Mouhoun, Namentenga, Naouri, Oubritenga, Oudalan, Passore, Poni, Sanguié, Sanmatenga, Séno, Sissili, Soum, Sourou, Tapoa, Yatenga, Zoundwéogo
Independence: 5 August 1960 (from France; formerly Upper Volta)
Constitution: none; constitution of 27 November 1977 was abolished following coup of 25 November 1980; constitutional referendum scheduled for June 1991
Legal system: based on French civil law system and customary law
National holiday: Anniversary of the Revolution, 4 August (1983)
Executive branch: chairman of the Popular Front, Council of Ministers
Legislative branch: unicameral National Assembly (Assemblée Nationale) was dissolved on 25 November 1980
Judicial branch: Appeals Court
Leaders:
Chief of State and Head of Government—Chairman of the Popular Front Captain Blaise COMPAORÉ (since 15 October 1987)

Political parties and leaders: all political parties banned following November 1980 coup
Suffrage: none
Elections: the National Assembly was dissolved 25 November 1980; presidential elections are scheduled for 3 November 1991 and legislative elections for 8 December 1991
Communists: small Communist party front group; some sympathizers
Other political or pressure groups: committees for the defense of the revolution, watchdog/political action groups throughout the country in both organizations and communities
Member of: ACCT, ACP, AfDB, CCC, CEAO, ECA, ECOWAS, Entente, FAO, FZ, G-77, GATT, IBRD, ICAO, ICC, ICFTU, IDA, IDB, IFAD, IFC, ILO, IMF, INTELSAT, INTERPOL, IOC, ITU, LORCS, NAM, OAU, OIC, PCA, UN, UNCTAD, UNESCO, UNIDO, UPU, WADB, WCL, WFTU, WHO, WIPO, WMO, WTO
Diplomatic representation: Ambassador Paul Désiré KABORÉ; Chancery at 2340 Massachusetts Avenue NW, Washington DC 20008; telephone (202) 332-5577 or 6895;
US—Ambassador Edward P. BRYNN; Embassy at Avenue Raoul Follereau, Ouagadougou (mailing address is 01 B. P. 35, Ouagadougou); telephone [226] 30-67-23 through 25 and [226] 33-34-22
Flag: two equal horizontal bands of red (top) and green with a yellow five-pointed star in the center; uses the popular pan-African colors of Ethiopia

Economy

Overview: One of the poorest countries in the world, Burkina has a high population density, few natural resources, and relatively infertile soil. Economic development is hindered by a poor communications network within a landlocked country. Agriculture provides about 40% of GDP and is entirely of a subsistence nature. Industry, dominated by unprofitable government-controlled corporations, accounted for 13% of GDP in 1988.
GDP: $1.75 billion, per capita $205 (1988); real growth rate 3% (1989)
Inflation rate (consumer prices): −0.5% (1989)
Unemployment rate: NA%
Budget: revenues $275 million; expenditures $287 million, including capital expenditures of $NA (1989)
Exports: $262 million (f.o.b., 1989); *commodities*—oilseeds, cotton, live animals, gold; *partners*—EC 42% (France 30%, other 12%), Taiwan 17%, Ivory Coast 15% (1985)

Burma

Imports: $619 million (f.o.b., 1989); *commodities*—grain, dairy products, petroleum, machinery; *partners*—EC 37% (France 23%, other 14%), Africa 31%, US 15% (1985)

External debt: $962 million (December 1990 est.)

Industrial production: growth rate NA%, accounts for about 13% of GDP (1988)

Electricity: 121,000 kW capacity; 320 million kWh produced, 37 kWh per capita (1989)

Industries: agricultural processing plants; brewery, cement, and brick plants; a few other small consumer goods enterprises

Agriculture: accounts for about 40% of GDP; cash crops—peanuts, shea nuts, sesame, cotton; food crops—sorghum, millet, corn, rice; livestock; not self-sufficient in food grains

Economic aid: US commitments, including Ex-Im (FY70-89), $294 million; Western (non-US) countries, ODA and OOF bilateral commitments (1970-88), $2.7 billion; Communist countries (1970-89), $113 million

Currency: Communauté Financière Africaine franc (plural—francs); 1 CFA franc (CFAF) = 100 centimes

Exchange rates: CFA francs (CFAF) per US$1—256.54 (January 1991), 272.26 (1990), 319.01 (1989), 297.85 (1988), 300.54 (1987), 346.30 (1986), 449.26 (1985)

Fiscal year: calendar year

Communications

Railroads: 620 km total; 520 km Ouagadougou to Ivory Coast border and 100 km Ouagadougou to Kaya; all 1.00-meter gauge and single track

Highways: 16,500 km total; 1,300 km paved, 7,400 km improved, 7,800 km unimproved (1985)

Civil air: 2 major transport aircraft

Airports: 50 total, 43 usable; 2 with permanent-surface runways; none with runways over 3,659 m; 2 with runways 2,440-3,659 m; 7 with runways 1,220-2,439 m

Telecommunications: all services only fair; radio relay, wire, and radio communication stations in use; 13,900 telephones; stations—2 AM, 2 FM, 2 TV; 1 Atlantic Ocean INTELSAT earth station

Defense Forces

Branches: Army, Air Force, National Gendarmerie, National Police

Manpower availability: males 15-49, 1,838,000; 937,304 fit for military service; no conscription

Defense expenditures: $55 million, 2.7% of GDP (1988)

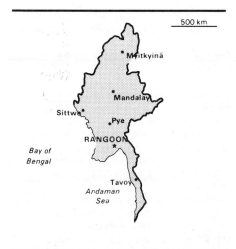

Geography

Total area: 678,500 km²; land area: 657,740 km²

Comparative area: slightly smaller than Texas

Land boundaries: 5,876 km total; Bangladesh 193 km, China 2,185 km, India 1,463 km, Laos 235 km, Thailand 1,800 km

Coastline: 1,930 km

Maritime claims:
Contiguous zone: 24 nm;
Continental shelf: edge of continental margin or 200 nm;
Exclusive economic zone: 200 nm;
Territorial sea: 12 nm

Climate: tropical monsoon; cloudy, rainy, hot, humid summers (southwest monsoon, June to September); less cloudy, scant rainfall, mild temperatures, lower humidity during winter (northeast monsoon, December to April)

Terrain: central lowlands ringed by steep, rugged highlands

Natural resources: crude oil, timber, tin, antimony, zinc, copper, tungsten, lead, coal, some marble, limestone, precious stones, natural gas

Land use: arable land 15%; permanent crops 1%; meadows and pastures 1%; forest and woodland 49%; other 34%; includes irrigated 2%

Environment: subject to destructive earthquakes and cyclones; flooding and landslides common during rainy season (June to September); deforestation

Note: strategic location near major Indian Ocean shipping lanes

People

Population: 42,112,082 (July 1991), growth rate 2.0% (1991)

Birth rate: 32 births/1,000 population (1991)

Death rate: 13 deaths/1,000 population (1991)

Net migration rate: 0 migrants/1,000 population (1991)

Infant mortality rate: 95 deaths/1,000 live births (1991)

Life expectancy at birth: 53 years male, 56 years female (1991)

Total fertility rate: 4.1 children born/woman (1991)

Nationality: noun—Burmese; adjective—Burmese

Ethnic divisions: Burman 68%, Shan 9%, Karen 7%, Rakhine 4%, Chinese 3%, Mon 2%, Indian 2%, other 5%

Religion: Buddhist 89%, Christian 4% (Baptist 3%, Roman Catholic 1%), Muslim 4%, animist beliefs 1%, other 2%

Language: Burmese; minority ethnic groups have their own languages

Literacy: 81% (male 89%, female 72%) age 15 and over can read and write (1990 est.)

Labor force: 16,036,000; agriculture 65.2%, industry 14.3%, trade 10.1%, government 6.3%, other 4.1% (FY89 est.)

Organized labor: Workers' Asiayone (association), 1,800,000 members; Peasants' Asiayone, 7,600,000 members

Government

Long-form name: Union of Burma; note—the local official name is Pyidaungzu Myanma Naingngandaw which has been translated by the US Government as Union of Myanma and by the Burmese as Union of Myanmar

Type: military regime

Capital: Rangoon (sometimes translated as Yangon)

Administrative divisions: 7 divisions* (yinmya, singular—yin) and 7 states (pyinemya, singular—pyine); Chin State, Irrawaddy*, Kachin State, Karan State, Kayah State, Magwe*, Mandalay*, Mon State, Pegu*, Rakhine State, Rangoon*, Sagaing*, Shan State, Tenasserim*

Independence: 4 January 1948 (from UK)

Constitution: 3 January 1974 (suspended since 18 September 1988)

Legal system: martial law in effect throughout most of the country; has not accepted compulsory ICJ jurisdiction

National holiday: Independence Day, 4 January (1948)

Executive branch: chairman of the State Law and Order Restoration Council, State Law and Order Restoration Council

Legislative branch: unicameral People's Assembly (Pyithu Hluttaw) was dissolved after the coup of 18 September 1988

Judicial branch: Council of People's Justices was abolished after the coup of 18 September 1988

Leaders:
Chief of State and Head of Government—Chairman of the State Law and Order Restoration Council Gen. SAW MAUNG (since 18 September 1988)

Political parties and leaders: National Unity Party (NUP; proregime), THA KYAW; National League for Democracy (NLD), U TIN OO and AUNG SAN SUU KYI; League for Democracy and Peace, U NU
Suffrage: universal at age 18
Elections:
People's Assembly—last held 27 May 1990, but Assembly never convened; results—NLD 80%; seats—(485 total) NLD 396, the regime-favored NUP 10, other 79
Communists: several hundred (est.) in Burma Communist Party (BCP)
Other political or pressure groups: Kachin Independence Army (KIA), United Wa State Army (UWSA), Karen National Union (KNU), several Shan factions, including the Shan United Army (SUA) (all ethnically-based insurgent groups)
Member of: AsDB, CP, ESCAP, FAO, G-77, GATT, IAEA, IBRD, ICAO, IDA, IFAD, IFC, ILO, IMF, IMO, INTERPOL, IOC, ITU, LORCS, UN, UNCTAD, UNESCO, UNIDO, UPU, WHO, WMO
Diplomatic representation: Ambassador U MYO AUNG; Chancery at 2300 S Street NW, Washington DC 20008; telephone (202) 332-9044 through 9046; there is a Burmese Consulate General in New York; *US*—Ambassador (vacant); Deputy Chief of Mission Franklin P. HUDDLE, Jr.; Embassy at 581 Merchant Street, Rangoon (mailing address is G. P. O. Box 521, Rangoon or Box B, APO San Francisco 96346); telephone 82055 or 82181
Flag: red with a blue rectangle in the upper hoist-side corner bearing, all in white, 14 five-pointed stars encircling a cogwheel containing a stalk of rice; the 14 stars represent the 14 administrative divisions

---

Economy

Overview: Burma is a poor Asian country, with a per capita GDP of about $400. The nation has been unable to achieve any substantial improvement in export earnings because of falling prices for many of its major commodity exports. For rice, traditionally the most important export, the drop in world prices has been accompanied by shrinking markets and a smaller volume of sales. In 1985 teak replaced rice as the largest export and continues to hold this position. The economy is heavily dependent on the agricultural sector, which generates about half of GDP and provides employment for 66% of the work force.
GDP: $16.8 billion, per capita $408; real growth rate NEGL% (FY90 est.)
Inflation rate (consumer prices): 22.6% (FY89 est.)
Unemployment rate: 9.6% in urban areas (FY89 est.)

Budget: revenues $4.9 billion; expenditures $5.0 billion, including capital expenditures of $0.7 billion (FY89 est.)
Exports: $228 million (f.o.b., FY89)
commodities—teak, rice, oilseed, metals, rubber, gems;
partners—Southeast Asia, India, China, EC, Africa
Imports: $540 million (c.i.f., FY89)
commodities—machinery, transport equipment, chemicals, food products;
partners—Japan, EC, China, Southeast Asia
External debt: $5.5 billion (December 1990 est.)
Industrial production: growth rate 2.6% (FY90 est.); accounts for 10% of GDP
Electricity: 950,000 kW capacity; 2,900 million kWh produced, 70 kWh per capita (1990)
Industries: agricultural processing; textiles and footwear; wood and wood products; petroleum refining; mining of copper, tin, tungsten, iron; construction materials; pharmaceuticals; fertilizer
Agriculture: accounts for 51% of GDP (including fish and forestry); self-sufficient in food; principal crops—paddy rice, corn, oilseed, sugarcane, pulses; world's largest stand of hardwood trees; rice and teak account for 55% of export revenues; fish catch of 732,000 metric tons (FY90)
Illicit drugs: world's largest illicit producer of opium poppy and minor producer of cannabis for the international drug trade; opium production is on the increase as growers respond to the collapse of Rangoon's antinarcotic programs
Economic aid: US commitments, including Ex-Im (FY70-89), $158 million; Western (non-US) countries, ODA and OOF bilateral commitments (1970-88), $3.9 billion; Communist countries (1970-88), $424 million
Currency: kyat (plural—kyats); 1 kyat (K) = 100 pyas
Exchange rates: kyats (K) per US$1—6.0476 (January 1991), 6.3386 (1990), 6.7049 (1989), 6.3945 (1988), 6.6535 (1987), 7.3304 (1986), 8.4749 (1985)
Fiscal year: 1 April-31 March

Communications

Railroads: 3,991 km total, all government owned; 3,878 km 1.000-meter gauge, 113 km narrow-gauge industrial lines; 362 km double track
Highways: 27,000 km total; 3,200 km bituminous, 17,700 km improved earth or gravel, 6,100 km unimproved earth
Inland waterways: 12,800 km; 3,200 km navigable by large commercial vessels
Pipelines: crude, 1,343 km; natural gas, 330 km
Ports: Rangoon, Moulmein, Bassein

Merchant marine: 60 ships (1,000 GRT or over) totaling 968,226 GRT/1,433,584 DWT; includes 3 passenger-cargo, 19 cargo, 2 refrigerated cargo, 3 vehicle carrier, 2 container, 3 petroleum, oils, and lubricants (POL) tanker, 2 chemical, 1 combination ore/oil, 24 bulk, 1 combination bulk
Civil air: 17 major transport aircraft (including 3 helicopters)
Airports: 86 total, 79 usable; 29 with permanent-surface runways; none with runways over 3,659 m; 3 with runways 2,440-3,659 m; 37 with runways 1,220-2,439 m
Telecommunications: meets minimum requirements for local and intercity service; international service is good; radiobroadcast coverage is limited to the most populous areas; 53,000 telephones (1986); stations—2 AM, 1 FM, 1 TV (1985); 1 Indian Ocean INTELSAT earth station

---

Defense Forces

Branches: Army, Navy, Air Force
Manpower availability: eligible 15-49, 20,766,975; of the 10,378,743 males 15-49, 5,566,247 are fit for military service; of the 10,388,232 females 15-49, 5,558,007 are fit for military service; 442,200 males and 431,407 females reach military age (18) annually; both sexes are liable for military service
Defense expenditures: $315.0 million, 3% of GDP (FY88)

Burundi

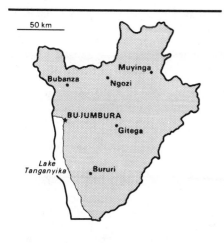

Geography

Total area: 27,830 km²; land area: 25,650 km²

Comparative area: slightly larger than Maryland

Land boundaries: 974 km total; Rwanda 290 km, Tanzania 451 km, Zaire 233 km

Coastline: none—landlocked

Maritime claims: none—landlocked

Climate: temperate; warm; occasional frost in uplands

Terrain: mostly rolling to hilly highland; some plains

Natural resources: nickel, uranium, rare earth oxide, peat, cobalt, copper, platinum (not yet exploited), vanadium

Land use: arable land 43%; permanent crops 8%; meadows and pastures 35%; forest and woodland 2%; other 12%; includes irrigated NEGL%

Environment: soil exhaustion; soil erosion; deforestation

Note: landlocked; straddles crest of the Nile-Congo watershed

People

Population: 5,831,233 (July 1991), growth rate 3.2% (1991)

Birth rate: 47 births/1,000 population (1991)

Death rate: 15 deaths/1,000 population (1991)

Net migration rate: 0 migrants/1,000 population (1991)

Infant mortality rate: 109 deaths/1,000 live births (1991)

Life expectancy at birth: 50 years male, 54 years female (1991)

Total fertility rate: 6.9 children born/woman (1991)

Nationality: noun—Burundian(s); adjective—Burundi

Ethnic divisions: Africans—Hutu (Bantu) 85%, Tutsi (Hamitic) 14%, Twa (Pygmy) 1%; other Africans include about 70,000 refugees, mostly Rwandans and Zairians; non-Africans include about 3,000 Europeans and 2,000 South Asians

Religion: Christian about 67% (Roman Catholic 62%, Protestant 5%). indigenous beliefs 32%, Muslim 1%

Language: Kirundi and French (official); Swahili (along Lake Tanganyika and in the Bujumbura area)

Literacy: 50% (male 61%, female 40%) age 15 and over can read and write (1990 est.)

Labor force: 1,900,000 (1983 est.); agriculture 93.0%, government 4.0%, industry and commerce 1.5%, services 1.5; 52% of population of working age (1985)

Organized labor: sole group is the Union of Burundi Workers (UTB); by charter, membership is extended to all Burundi workers (informally); active membership figures NA

Government

Long-form name: Republic of Burundi

Type: republic

Capital: Bujumbura

Administrative divisions: 15 provinces; Bubanza, Bujumbura, Bururi, Cankuzo, Cibitoke, Gitega, Karuzi, Kayanza, Kirundo, Makamba, Muramvya, Muyinga, Ngozi, Rutana, Ruyigi

Independence: 1 July 1962 (from UN trusteeship under Belgian administration)

Constitution: 20 November 1981; suspended following the coup of 3 September 1987; referendum for a new constitution scheduled for March 1992

Legal system: based on German and Belgian civil codes and customary law; has not accepted compulsory ICJ jurisdiction

National holiday: Independence Day, 1 July (1962)

Executive branch: president; chairman of the Central Committee of the National Party of Unity and Progress (UPRONA), prime minister

Legislative branch: unicameral National Assembly (Assemblée Nationale) was dissolved following the coup of 3 September 1987; at an extraordinary party congress held from 27 to 29 December 1990, the Central Committee of the National Party of Unity and Progress (UPRONA) replaced the Military Committee for National Salvation, and became the supreme governing body during the transition to constitutional government

Judicial branch: Supreme Court (Cour Suprême)

Leaders:

Chief of State—President Pierre BUYOYA (since 9 September 1987);

Head of Government Prime Minister Adrien SIBOMANA (since 26 October 1988)

Political parties and leaders: only party—National Party of Unity and Progress (UPRONA), President Pierre BUYOYA, chairman, and Nicolas MAYUGI, secretary general

Suffrage: universal adult at age NA

Elections:

National Assembly—dissolved after the coup of 3 September 1987;

note—The National Unity Charter outlining the principles for constitutional government was adopted by a national referendum on 5 February 1991

Communists: no Communist party

Member of: ACCT, ACP, AfDB, CCC, CEEAC, CEPGL, ECA, FAO, G-77, GATT, IBRD, ICAO, IDA, IFAD, IFC, ILO, IMF, INTERPOL, ITU, LORCS, NAM, OAU, UN, UNCTAD, UNESCO, UNIDO, UPU, WHO, WIPO, WMO, WTO

Diplomatic representation: Ambassador Julien KAVAKURE; Chancery at Suite 212, 2233 Wisconsin Avenue NW, Washington DC 20007; telephone (202) 342-2574; *US*—Ambassador Cynthia Shepherd PERRY; Embassy at Avenue du Zaire, Bujumbura (mailing address is B. P. 1720, Avenue des Etats-Unis, Bujumbura); telephone 234-54 through 56

Flag: divided by a white diagonal cross into red panels (top and bottom) and green panels (hoist side and outer side) with a white disk superimposed at the center bearing three red six-pointed stars outlined in green arranged in a triangular design (one star above, two stars below)

Economy

Overview: A landlocked, resource-poor country in an early stage of economic development, Burundi is predominately agricultural with only a few basic industries. Its economic health depends on the coffee crop, which accounts for an average 90% of foreign exchange earnings each year. The ability to pay for imports therefore continues to rest largely on the vagaries of the climate and the international coffee market.

GDP: $1.1 billion, per capita $200; real growth rate 1.5% (1989)

Inflation rate (consumer prices): 11.7% (1989)

Unemployment rate: NA%

Budget: revenues $158 million; expenditures $204 million, including capital expenditures of $131 million (1989 est.)

Exports: $81 million (f.o.b., 1989); *commodities*—coffee 88%, tea, hides, and skins; *partners*—EC 83%, US 5%, Asia 2%

Imports: $197 million (c.i.f., 1989); *commodities*—capital goods 31%, petroleum products 15%, foodstuffs, consumer goods; *partners*—EC 57%, Asia 23%, US 3%

External debt: $957 million (December 1990 est.)

Burundi (continued)

Industrial production: real growth rate 5.1% (1986); accounts for about 10% of GDP
Electricity: 51,000 kW capacity; 105 million kWh produced, 19 kWh per capita (1989)
Industries: light consumer goods such as blankets, shoes, soap; assembly of imports; public works construction; food processing
Agriculture: accounts for 60% of GDP; 90% of population dependent on subsistence farming; marginally self-sufficient in food production; cash crops—coffee, cotton, tea; food crops—corn, sorghum, sweet potatoes, bananas, manioc; livestock—meat, milk, hides, and skins
Economic aid: US commitments, including Ex-Im (FY70-89), $71 million; Western (non-US) countries, ODA and OOF bilateral commitments (1970-88), $10.1 billion; OPEC bilateral aid (1979-89), $32 million; Communist countries (1970-89), $175 million
Currency: Burundi franc (plural—francs); 1 Burundi franc (FBu) = 100 centimes
Exchange rates: Burundi francs (FBu) per US$1—163.29 (January 1991), 171.26 (1990), 158.67 (1989), 140.40 (1988), 123.56 (1987), 114.17 (1986), 120.69 (1985)
Fiscal year: calendar year

Communications

Highways: 5,900 km total; 400 km paved, 2,500 km gravel or laterite, 3,000 km improved or unimproved earth
Inland waterways: Lake Tanganyika
Ports: Bujumbura (lake port) connects to transportation systems of Tanzania and Zaire
Civil air: 1 major transport aircraft
Airports: 8 total, 7 usable; 1 with permanent-surface runways; none with runways over 3,659 m; 1 with runways 2,440-3,659 m; none with runways 1,220 to 2,439 m
Telecommunications: sparse system of wire, radiocommunications, and low-capacity radio relay links; 8,000 telephones; stations—2 AM, 2 FM, 1 TV; 1 Indian Ocean INTELSAT earth station

Defense Forces

Branches: Army (includes naval and air units); paramilitary Gendarmerie
Manpower availability: males 15-49, 1,268,342; 661,888 fit for military service; 64,538 reach military age (16) annually
Defense expenditures: $33 million, 3.1% of GDP (1988)

Cambodia

125 km

Boundary representation is not necessarily authoritative.

Geography

Total area: 181,040 km²; land area: 176,520 km²
Comparative area: slightly smaller than Oklahoma
Land boundaries: 2,572 km total; Laos 541 km, Thailand 803 km, Vietnam 1,228 km
Coastline: 443 km
Maritime claims:
Contiguous zone: 24 nm;
Continental shelf: 200 nm;
Exclusive economic zone: 200 nm;
Territorial sea: 12 nm
Disputes: offshore islands and three sections of the boundary with Vietnam are in dispute; maritime boundary with Vietnam not defined; occupied by Vietnam on 25 December 1978
Climate: tropical; rainy, monsoon season (May to October); dry season (December to March); little seasonal temperature variation
Terrain: mostly low, flat plains; mountains in southwest and north
Natural resources: timber, gemstones, some iron ore, manganese, phosphates, hydropower potential
Land use: arable land 16%; permanent crops 1%; meadows and pastures 3%; forest and woodland 76%; other 4%; includes irrigated 1%
Environment: a land of paddies and forests dominated by Mekong River and Tonle Sap
Note: buffer between Thailand and Vietnam

People

Population: 7,146,386 (July 1991), growth rate 2.2% (1991)
Birth rate: 38 births/1,000 population (1991)
Death rate: 16 deaths/1,000 population (1991)
Net migration rate: 0 migrants/1,000 population (1991)

Infant mortality rate: 125 deaths/1,000 live births (1991)
Life expectancy at birth: 48 years male, 51 years female (1991)
Total fertility rate: 4.5 children born/woman (1991)
Nationality: noun—Cambodian(s); adjective—Cambodian
Ethnic divisions: Khmer 90%, Chinese 5%, other 5%
Religion: Theravada Buddhism 95%, other 5%
Language: Khmer (official), French
Literacy: 35% (male 48%, female 22%) age 15 and over can read and write (1990 est.)
Labor force: 2.5-3.0 million; agriculture 80% (1988 est.)
Organized labor: Kampuchea Federation of Trade Unions (FSC); under government control

Government

Long-form name: none
Type: disputed between the National Government of Cambodia (NGC) led by Prince NORODOM SIHANOUK, and the State of Cambodia (SOC) led by HENG SAMRIN
Capital: Phnom Penh
Administrative divisions: NGC—18 provinces (khêt, singular and plural) and 1 capital city* (rottatheanei); Bătdâmbâng, Kâmpóng Cham, Kâmpóng Chhnăng, Kâmpóng Spoe, Kâmpóng Thum, Kâmpôt, Kândal, Kaôh Kŏng, Krâchéh, Môndól Kiri, Phnum Pénh*, Poŭthĭsăt, Preăh Vihéar, Prey Vêng, Rôtânôkiri, Siĕmréab-Ŏtdâr Méanchey, Stŏeng Trêng, Svay Riĕng, Takêv; note—the SOC adds a province of Banteay Méanchey and an autonomous municipality of Kâmpóng Saôm to the NGC administrative structure
Independence: 9 November 1953 (from France)
Constitution: SOC—27 June 1981
National holidays: NGC—Independence Day, 17 April (1975); SOC—Liberation Day, 7 January (1979)
Executive branch: NGC—president, prime minister; SOC—chairman of the Council of State, Council of State, chairman of the Council of Ministers, Council of Ministers
Legislative branch: NGC—none; SOC—unicameral National Assembly
Judicial branch: NGC—none; SOC—Supreme People's Court
Leaders:
Chief of State—NGC—President Prince NORODOM SIHANOUK (since NA July 1982); SOC—Chairman of the Council of State HENG SAMRIN (since 27 June 1981);
Head of Government—NGC—Prime Minister SON SANN (since NA July 1982); SOC—Chairman of the Council of Ministers HUN SEN (since 14 January 1985)

Political parties and leaders: NGC—three resistance groups including: Democratic Kampuchea (DK, also known as the Khmer Rouge) under KHIEU SAMPHAN; Khmer People's National Liberation Front (KPNLF) under SON SANN; and National United Front for an Independent, Neutral, Peaceful, and Cooperative Cambodia (FUNCINPEC) under Prince NORODOM RANNARIDH; SOC—Kampuchean People's Revolutionary Party (KPRP) led by HENG SAMRIN

Suffrage: NGC—none; SOC—universal at age 18

Elections:
NGC—none;
SOC—*National Assembly*—last held 1 May 1981; in February 1986 the Assembly voted to extend its term for five years; results—KPRP is the only party; seats—(123 total) KPRP 123

Member of: AsDB, CP, ESCAP, FAO, G-77, IAEA, IBRD, ICAO, IDA, ILO, IMF, IMO, INTERPOL, ITU, LORCS, NAM, PCA, UN, UNCTAD, UNESCO, UPU, WFTU, WHO, WMO, WTO

Diplomatic representation: none

Flag: NGC—three horizontal bands of blue (top), red (double width), and blue with a white stylized three-towered temple representing Angkor Wat centered on the red band;
SOC—two equal horizontal bands of red (top) and blue with a gold stylized five-towered temple representing Angkor Wat in the center

---

Economy

Overview: Cambodia is a desperately poor country whose economic development has been stymied by deadly political infighting. The economy is based on agriculture and related industries. Over the past decade Cambodia has been slowly recovering from its near destruction by war and political upheaval. It still remains, however, one of the world's poorest countries, with an estimated per capita GDP of about $130. The food situation is precarious; during the 1980s famine has been averted only through international relief. In 1986 the production level of rice, the staple food crop, was able to meet only 80% of domestic needs. The biggest success of the nation's recovery program has been in new rubber plantings and in fishing. Industry, other than rice processing, is almost nonexistent. Foreign trade is primarily with the USSR and Vietnam. Statistical data on the economy continues to be sparse and unreliable. Foreign aid from the USSR and Eastern Europe almost certainly is being slashed.
GDP: $890 million, per capita $130; real growth rate 0% (1989 est.)
Unemployment rate: NA%

Budget: revenues $NA; expenditures $NA, including capital expenditures of $NA
Inflation rate (consumer prices): 50% (first half 1990)
Exports: $32 million (f.o.b., 1988); *commodities*—natural rubber, rice, pepper, wood;
partners—Vietnam, USSR, Eastern Europe, Japan, India
Imports: $147 million (c.i.f., 1988); *commodities*—international food aid; fuels, consumer goods, machinery;
partners—Vietnam, USSR, Eastern Europe, Japan, India
External debt: $600 million (1989)
Industrial production: growth rate NA%
Electricity: 126,000 kW capacity; 150 million kWh produced, 20 kWh per capita (1990)
Industries: rice milling, fishing, wood and wood products, rubber, cement, gem mining
Agriculture: mainly subsistence farming except for rubber plantations; main crops—rice, rubber, corn; food shortages—rice, meat, vegetables, dairy products, sugar, flour
Economic aid: US commitments, including Ex-Im (FY70-88), $719 million; Western (non-US) countries (1970-88), $285 million; Communist countries (1970-89), $1,800 million
Currency: riel (plural—riels); 1 riel (CR) = 100 sen
Exchange rates: riels (CR) per US$1—560 (November 1990), 159.00 (1988), 100.00 (1987), 30.00 (1986), 7.00 (1985)
Fiscal year: calendar year

Communications

Railroads: 612 km 1.000-meter gauge, government owned
Highways: 13,351 km total; 2,622 km bituminous; 7,105 km crushed stone, gravel, or improved earth; 3,624 km unimproved earth; some roads in disrepair
Inland waterways: 3,700 km navigable all year to craft drawing 0.6 meters; 282 km navigable to craft drawing 1.8 meters
Ports: Kâmpóng Saôm, Phnom Penh
Airports: 22 total, 9 usable; 6 with permanent-surface runways; none with runways over 3,659 m; 2 with runways 2,440-3,659 m; 4 with runways 1,220-2,439 m
Telecommunications: service barely adequate for government requirements and virtually nonexistent for general public; international service limited to Vietnam and other adjacent countries; stations—1 AM, no FM, 1 TV

Defense Forces

Branches: SOC—Cambodian People's Armed Forces (CPAF); Communist resistance forces—National Army of Democratic Kampuchea (Khmer Rouge); non-Communist resistance forces—Armeé National Kampuchea Independent (ANKI) which is sometimes anglicized as National Army of Independent Cambodia (NAIC) and Khmer People's National Liberation Armed Forces (KPNLAF)
Manpower availability: males 15-49, 1,869,880; 1,030,356 fit for military service; 57,288 reach military age (18) annually
Defense expenditures: $NA, NA% of GDP

Cameroon

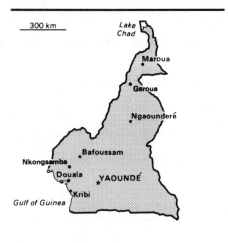

Geography

Total area: 475,440 km²; land area: 469,440 km²

Comparative area: slightly larger than California

Land boundaries: 4,591 km total; Central African Republic 797 km, Chad 1,094 km, Congo 523 km, Equatorial Guinea 189 km, Gabon 298 km, Nigeria 1,690 km

Coastline: 402 km

Maritime claims:

Territorial sea: 50 nm

Disputes: demarcation of international boundaries in Lake Chad, the lack of which has led to border incidents in the past, is completed and awaiting ratification by Cameroon, Chad, Niger, and Nigeria; Nigerian proposals to reopen maritime boundary negotiations and redemarcate the entire land boundary have been rejected by Cameroon

Climate: varies with terrain from tropical along coast to semiarid and hot in north

Terrain: diverse with coastal plain in southwest, dissected plateau in center, mountains in west, plains in north

Natural resources: crude oil, bauxite, iron ore, timber, hydropower potential

Land use: arable land 13%; permanent crops 2%; meadows and pastures 18%; forest and woodland 54%; other 13%; includes irrigated NEGL%

Environment: recent volcanic activity with release of poisonous gases; deforestation; overgrazing; desertification

Note: sometimes referred to as the hinge of Africa

People

Population: 11,390,374 (July 1991), growth rate 2.7% (1991)

Birth rate: 41 births/1,000 population (1991)

Death rate: 15 deaths/1,000 population (1991)

Net migration rate: 0 migrants/1,000 population (1991)

Infant mortality rate: 118 deaths/1,000 live births (1991)

Life expectancy at birth: 49 years male, 53 years female (1991)

Total fertility rate: 5.6 children born/woman (1991)

Nationality: noun—Cameroonian(s); adjective—Cameroonian

Ethnic divisions: over 200 tribes of widely differing background; Cameroon Highlanders 31%, Equatorial Bantu 19%, Kirdi 11%, Fulani 10%, Northwestern Bantu 8%, Eastern Nigritic 7%, other African 13%, non-African less than 1%

Religion: indigenous beliefs 51%, Christian 33%, Muslim 16%

Language: English and French (official), 24 major African language groups

Literacy: 54% (male 66%, female 43%) age 15 and over can read and write (1990 est.)

Labor force: NA; agriculture 74.4%, industry and transport 11.4%, other services 14.2% (1983); 50% of population of working age (15-64 years) (1985)

Organized labor: under 45% of wage labor force

Government

Long-form name: Republic of Cameroon

Type: unitary republic; multiparty presidential regime (opposition parties legalized 1990)

Capital: Yaoundé

Administrative divisions: 10 provinces; Adamaoua, Centre, Est, Extrême-Nord, Littoral, Nord, Nord-Ouest, Ouest, Sud, Sud-Ouest

Independence: 1 January 1960 (from UN trusteeship under French administration; formerly French Cameroon)

Constitution: 20 May 1972

Legal system: based on French civil law system, with common law influence; has not accepted compulsory ICJ jurisdiction

National holiday: National Day, 20 May (1972)

Executive branch: president, Cabinet

Legislative branch: unicameral National Assembly (Assemblée Nationale)

Judicial branch: Supreme Court

Leaders:

Chief of State President Paul BIYA (since 6 November 1982);

Head of Government interim Prime Minister Sadou HAYATOU (since 25 April 1991)

Political parties and leaders: Cameroon People's Democratic Movement (RDPC), Paul BIYA, president, is government-controlled and was formerly the only party; 17 parties formed by 1 May 1991

Suffrage: universal at age 21

Elections:

President—last held 24 April 1988 (next to be held April 1993); results—President Paul BIYA reelected without opposition;

National Assembly—last held 24 April 1988 (next to be held by the end of 1992); results—RDPC was the only party; seats—(180 total) RDPC 180

Communists: no Communist party or significant number of sympathizers

Other political or pressure groups: NA

Member of: ACCT (associate), ACP, AfDB, BDEAC, CCC, CEEAC, ECA, FAO, FZ, G-19, G-77, GATT, IAEA, IBRD, ICAO, ICC, IDA, IDB, IFAD, IFC, ILO, IMF, IMO, INTELSAT, INTERPOL, IOC, ITU, LORCS, NAM, OAU, OIC, PCA, UDEAC, UN, UNCTAD, UNESCO, UNIDO, UPU, WCL, WHO, WIPO, WMO, WTO

Diplomatic representation: Ambassador Paul PONDI; Chancery at 2349 Massachusetts Avenue NW, Washington DC 20008; telephone (202) 265-8790 through 8794; *US*—Ambassador Frances D. COOK; Embassy at Rue Nachtigal, Yaounde (mailing address is B. P. 817, Yaounde); telephone [237] 234014; there is a US Consulate General in Douala

Flag: three equal vertical bands of green (hoist side), red, and yellow with a yellow five-pointed star centered in the red band; uses the popular pan-African colors of Ethiopia

Economy

Overview: Over the past decade the economy has registered a remarkable performance because of the development of an offshore oil industry. Real GDP growth annually averaged 10% from 1978 to 1985. In 1986 Cameroon had one of the highest levels of income per capita in tropical Africa, with oil revenues picking up the slack as growth in other sectors softened. Because of the sharp drop in oil prices, however, the economy experienced serious budgetary difficulties and balance-of-payments disequilibrium. Despite the recent upsurge in oil prices, Cameroon's economic outlook is troubled. Oil reserves currently being exploited will be depleted in the early 1990s, so ways must be found to boost agricultural and industrial exports in the medium term. The Sixth Cameroon Development Plan (1986-91) stresses balanced development and designates agriculture as the basis of the country's economic future.

GDP: $11.5 billion, per capita $1,040; real growth rate 0.7% (1990 est.)

Inflation rate (consumer prices): 8.6% (FY88)

Unemployment rate: 15-20% (1989 est.)

Budget: revenues $1.7 billion; expenditures $2.2 billion, including capital expenditures of $NA million (FY89)

Exports: $2.1 billion (f.o.b., 1990 est.); *commodities*—petroleum products 56%, coffee, cocoa, timber, manufactures; *partners*—EC (particularly the Netherlands) about 50%, US 3%
Imports: $2.1 billion (c.i.f., 1990 est.); *commodities*—machines and electrical equipment, transport equipment, chemical products, consumer goods; *partners*—France 42%, Japan 7%, US 4%
External debt: $4.9 billion (December 1989 est.)
Industrial production: growth rate −6.4% (FY87); accounts for 30% of GDP
Electricity: 752,000 kW capacity; 2,940 million kWh produced, 270 kWh per capita (1989)
Industries: crude oil products, small aluminum plant, food processing, light consumer goods industries, sawmills
Agriculture: the agriculture and forestry sectors provide employment for the majority of the population, contributing nearly 25% to GDP and providing a high degree of self-sufficiency in staple foods; commercial and food crops include coffee, cocoa, timber, cotton, rubber, bananas, oilseed, grains, livestock, root starches
Economic aid: US commitments, including Ex-Im (FY70-89), $440 million; Western (non-US) countries, ODA and OOF bilateral commitments (1970-88), $4.2 billion; OPEC bilateral aid (1979-89), $29 million; Communist countries (1970-89), $125 million
Currency: Communauté Financière Africaine franc (plural—francs); 1 CFA franc (CFAF) = 100 centimes
Exchange rates: Communauté Financière Africaine francs (CFAF) per US$1—256.54 (January 1991), 272.26 (1990), 319.01 (1989), 297.85 (1988), 300.54 (1987), 346.30 (1986), 449.26 (1985)
Fiscal year: 1 July-30 June

Communications

Railroads: 1,003 km total; 858 km 1.000-meter gauge, 145 km 0.600-meter gauge
Highways: about 65,000 km total; includes 2,682 km bituminous, 30,000 km unimproved earth, 32,318 km gravel, earth, and improved earth
Inland waterways: 2,090 km; of decreasing importance
Ports: Douala
Merchant marine: 2 cargo ships (1,000 GRT or over) totaling 24,122 GRT/33,509 DWT
Civil air: 5 major transport aircraft
Airports: 60 total, 52 usable; 10 with permanent-surface runways; 1 with runways over 3,659 m; 5 with runways 2,440-3,659 m; 21 with runways 1,220-2,439 m
Telecommunications: good system of open wire, cable, troposcatter, and radio relay; 26,000 telephones; stations—10 AM, 1 FM, 1 TV; 2 Atlantic Ocean INTELSAT earth stations

Defense Forces

Branches: Army, Navy (including Marines), Air Force; paramilitary Gendarmerie
Manpower availability: males 15-49, 2,628,909; 1,324,899 fit for military service; 125,421 reach military age (18) annually
Defense expenditures: $219 million, 1.7% of GDP (1990 est.)

Canada

Geography

Total area: 9,976,140 km²; land area: 9,220,970 km²
Comparative area: slightly larger than US
Land boundaries: 8,893 km with US (includes 2,477 km with Alaska)
Coastline: 243,791 km
Maritime claims:
Continental shelf: 200 m (depth) or to depth of exploitation;
Exclusive fishing zone: 200 nm;
Territorial sea: 12 nm
Disputes: maritime boundary disputes with France (Saint Pierre and Miquelon) and US
Climate: varies from temperate in south to subarctic and arctic in north
Terrain: mostly plains with mountains in west and lowlands in southeast
Natural resources: nickel, zinc, copper, gold, lead, molybdenum, potash, silver, fish, timber, wildlife, coal, crude oil, natural gas
Land use: arable land 5%; permanent crops NEGL%; meadows and pastures 3%; forest and woodland 35%; other 57%; includes NEGL% irrigated
Environment: 80% of population concentrated within 160 km of US border; continuous permafrost in north a serious obstacle to development
Note: second-largest country in world (after USSR); strategic location between USSR and US via north polar route

People

Population: 26,835,036 (July 1991), growth rate 1.1% (1991)
Birth rate: 14 births/1,000 population (1991)
Death rate: 7 deaths/1,000 population (1991)
Net migration rate: 5 migrants/1,000 population (1991)
Infant mortality rate: 7 deaths/1,000 live births (1991)

Canada *(continued)*

Life expectancy at birth: 74 years male, 81 years female (1991)
Total fertility rate: 1.7 children born/woman (1991)
Nationality: noun—Canadian(s); adjective—Canadian
Ethnic divisions: British Isles origin 40%, French origin 27%, other European 20%, indigenous Indian and Eskimo 1.5%
Religion: Roman Catholic 46%, United Church 16%, Anglican 10%
Language: English and French (both official)
Literacy: 99% (male NA%, female NA%) age 15 and over can read and write (1981 est.)
Labor force: 13,380,000; services 75%, manufacturing 14%, agriculture 4%, construction 3%, other 4% (1988)
Organized labor: 30.6% of labor force; 39.6% of nonagricultural paid workers

Government

Long-form name: none
Type: confederation with parliamentary democracy
Capital: Ottawa
Administrative divisions: 10 provinces and 2 territories*; Alberta, British Columbia, Manitoba, New Brunswick, Newfoundland, Northwest Territories*, Nova Scotia, Ontario, Prince Edward Island, Quebec, Saskatchewan, Yukon Territory*
Independence: 1 July 1867 (from UK)
Constitution: amended British North America Act 1867 patriated to Canada 17 April 1982; charter of rights and unwritten customs
Legal system: based on English common law, except in Quebec, where civil law system based on French law prevails; accepts compulsory ICJ jurisdiction, with reservations
National holiday: Canada Day, 1 July (1867)
Executive branch: British monarch, governor general, prime minister, deputy prime minister, Cabinet
Legislative branch: bicameral Parliament (Parlement) consists of an upper house or Senate (Senat) and a lower house or House of Commons (Chambre des Communes)
Judicial branch: Supreme Court
Leaders:
Chief of State—Queen ELIZABETH II (since 6 February 1952), represented by Governor General Raymond John HNATSHYN (since 29 January 1990);
Head of Government—Prime Minister (Martin) Brian MULRONEY (since 4 September 1984); Deputy Prime Minister Donald Frank MAZANKOWSKI (since NA June 1986)
Political parties and leaders: Progressive Conservative, Brian MULRONEY; Liberal, Jean CHRETIEN; New Democratic, Audrey McLAUGHLIN

Suffrage: universal at age 18
Elections:
House of Commons—last held 21 November 1988 (next to be held by November 1993); results—Progressive Conservative 43.0%, Liberal 32%, New Democratic Party 20%, other 5%; seats—(295 total) Progressive Conservative 159, Liberal 80, New Democratic Party 44, independent 12
Communists: 3,000
Member of: ACCT, AfDB, AG (observer), APEC, AsDB, BIS, C, CCC, CDB, COCOM, CP, CSCE, EBRD, ECE, ECLAC, FAO, G-7, G-8, G-10, GATT, IADB, IAEA, IBRD, ICAO, ICC, ICFTU, IDA, IEA, IFAD, IFC, ILO, IMF, IMO, INMARSAT, INTELSAT, INTERPOL, IOC, IOM (observer), ISO, ITU, LORCS, NATO, NEA, OAS, OECD, PCA, UN, UNCTAD, UNDOF, UNESCO, UNFICYP, UNHCR, UNIDO, UNIIMOG, UNTSO, UPU, WCL, WHO, WIPO, WMO, WTO
Diplomatic representation: Ambassador Derek BURNEY; Chancery at 1746 Massachusetts Avenue NW, Washington DC 20036; telephone (202) 785-1400; there are Canadian Consulates General in Atlanta, Boston, Buffalo, Chicago, Cleveland, Dallas, Detroit, Los Angeles, Minneapolis, New York, Philadelphia, San Francisco, and Seattle;
US—Ambassador Edward N. NEY; Embassy at 100 Wellington Street, K1P 5T1, Ottawa (mailing address is P. O. Box 5000, Ogdensburg, NY 13669-0430); telephone (613) 248-25256, 25106, 25271, and 25170; there are US Consulates General in Calgary, Halifax, Montreal, Quebec, Toronto, and Vancouver
Flag: three vertical bands of red (hoist side), white (double width, square), and red with a red maple leaf centered in the white band

Economy

Overview: As an affluent, high-tech industrial society, Canada today closely resembles the US in per capita output, market-oriented economic system, and pattern of production. Since World War II the impressive growth of the manufacturing, mining, and service sectors has transformed the nation from a largely rural economy into one primarily industrial and urban. In the 1980s Canada registered one of the highest rates of real growth among the OECD nations, averaging about 3.2%. With its great natural resources, skilled labor force, and modern capital plant, Canada has excellent economic prospects. In mid-1990, however, the long-simmering problems between English- and French-speaking areas became so acute that observers spoke openly of a possible split in the confederation; foreign investors were becoming edgy.

GDP: $516.7 billion, per capita $19,500; real growth rate 0.9% (1990)
Inflation rate (consumer prices): 4.8% (1990)
Unemployment rate: 8.1% (1990)
Budget: revenues $105.8 billion; expenditures $131.6 billion, including capital expenditures of $NA (FY90 est.)
Exports: $126.7 billion (f.o.b., 1990);
commodities—newsprint, wood pulp, timber, grain, crude petroleum, machinery, natural gas, ferrous and nonferrous ores, motor vehicles and parts;
partners—US, Japan, UK, FRG, other EC, USSR
Imports: $116.3 billion (c.i.f., 1990);
commodities—processed foods, beverages, crude petroleum, chemicals, industrial machinery, motor vehicles and parts, durable consumer goods, electronic computers;
partners—US, Japan, UK, FRG, other EC, Taiwan, South Korea, Mexico
External debt: $247 billion (1987)
Industrial production: growth rate −2.7% (1990); accounts for 24% of GDP
Electricity: 105,000,000 kW capacity; 500,000 million kWh produced, 18,840 kWh per capita (1990)
Industries: processed and unprocessed minerals, food products, wood and paper products, transportation equipment, chemicals, fish products, petroleum and natural gas
Agriculture: accounts for about 3% of GDP; one of the world's major producers and exporters of grain (wheat and barley); key source of US agricultural imports; large forest resources cover 35% of total land area; commercial fisheries provide annual catch of 1.5 million metric tons, of which 75% is exported
Illicit drugs: illicit producer of cannabis for the domestic drug market; use of hydroponics technology permits growers to plant large quantities of high-quality marijuana indoors
Economic aid: donor—ODA and OOF commitments (1987-88), $4.1 billion
Currency: Canadian dollar (plural—dollars); 1 Canadian dollar (Can$) = 100 cents
Exchange rates: Canadian dollars (Can$) per US$1—1.1559 (January 1991), 1.1668 (1990), 1.1840 (1989), 1.2307 (1988), 1.3260 (1987), 1.3895 (1986), 1.3655 (1985)
Fiscal year: 1 April-31 March

Communications

Railroads: 93,544 km total; two major transcontinental freight railway systems—Canadian National (government owned) and Canadian Pacific Railway; passenger service—VIA (government operated)
Highways: 884,272 km total; 712,936 km surfaced (250,023 km paved), 171,336 km earth

Cape Verde

Inland waterways: 3,000 km, including Saint Lawrence Seaway

Pipelines: oil, 23,564 km total crude and refined; natural gas, 74,980 km

Ports: Halifax, Montreal, Quebec, Saint John (New Brunswick), Saint John's (Newfoundland), Toronto, Vancouver

Merchant marine: 75 ships (1,000 GRT or over) totaling 532,062 GRT/727,118 DWT; includes 1 passenger, 5 short-sea passenger, 2 passenger-cargo, 13 cargo, 2 railcar carrier, 1 refrigerated cargo, 8 roll-on/roll-off, 1 container, 27 petroleum, oils, and lubricants (POL) tanker, 6 chemical tanker, 1 specialized tanker, 8 bulk; note—does not include ships used exclusively in the Great Lakes

Civil air: 636 major transport aircraft; Air Canada is the major carrier

Airports: 1,397 total, 1,154 usable; 443 with permanent-surface runways; 4 with runways over 3,659 m; 30 with runways 2,440-3,659 m; 328 with runways 1,220-2,439 m

Telecommunications: excellent service provided by modern media; 18.0 million telephones; stations—900 AM, 29 FM, 53 (1,400 repeaters) TV; 5 coaxial submarine cables; over 300 earth stations operating in INTELSAT (including 4 Atlantic Ocean and 1 Pacific Ocean) and domestic systems

Defense Forces

Branches: Canadian Armed Forces (including Mobile Command, Maritime Command, Air Command, Communications Command, Canadian Forces Europe, Training Commands), Royal Canadian Mounted Police (RCMP)

Manpower availability: males 15-49, 7,243,909; 6,297,520 fit for military service; 188,996 reach military age (17) annually

Defense expenditures: $11.3 billion, 2% of GDP (FY90)

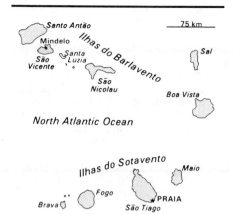

Geography

Total area: 4,030 km²; land area: 4,030 km²

Comparative area: slightly larger than Rhode Island

Land boundaries: none

Coastline: 965 km

Maritime claims: (measured from claimed archipelagic baselines);

Exclusive economic zone: 200 nm;

Territorial sea: 12 nm

Climate: temperate; warm, dry, summer precipitation very erratic

Terrain: steep, rugged, rocky, volcanic

Natural resources: salt, basalt rock, pozzolana, limestone, kaolin, fish

Land use: arable land 9%; permanent crops NEGL%; meadows and pastures 6%; forest and woodland NEGL%; other 85%; includes irrigated 1%

Environment: subject to prolonged droughts; harmattan wind can obscure visibility; volcanically and seismically active; deforestation; overgrazing

Note: strategic location 500 km from African coast near major north-south sea routes; important communications station; important sea and air refueling site

People

Population: 386,501 (July 1991), growth rate 3.0% (1991)

Birth rate: 48 births/1,000 population (1991)

Death rate: 10 deaths/1,000 population (1991)

Net migration rate: −8 migrants/1,000 population (1991)

Infant mortality rate: 63 deaths/1,000 live births (1991)

Life expectancy at birth: 60 years male, 63 years female (1991)

Total fertility rate: 6.6 children born/woman (1991)

Nationality: noun—Cape Verdean(s); adjective—Cape Verdean

Ethnic divisions: Creole (mulatto) about 71%, African 28%, European 1%

Religion: Roman Catholicism fused with indigenous beliefs

Language: Portuguese and Crioulo, a blend of Portuguese and West African words

Literacy: 66% (male NA%, female NA%) age 15 and over can read and write (1989 est.)

Labor force: 102,000 (1985 est.); agriculture (mostly subsistence) 57%, services 29%, industry 14% (1981); 51% of population of working age (1985)

Organized labor: Trade Unions of Cape Verde Unity Center (UNTC-CS)

Government

Long-form name: Republic of Cape Verde

Type: republic

Capital: Praia

Administrative divisions: 14 districts (concelhos, singular—concelho); Boa Vista, Brava, Fogo, Maio, Paul, Praia, Porto Novo, Ribeira Grande, Sal, Santa Catarina, Santa Cruz, São Nicolau, São Vicente, Tarrafal

Independence: 5 July 1975 (from Portugal)

Constitution: 7 September 1980; amended 12 February 1981, NA December 1988, and 28 September 1990 (legalized opposition parties)

National holiday: Independence Day, 5 July (1975)

Executive branch: president, prime minister, deputy minister, secretaries of state, Council of Ministers (cabinet)

Legislative branch: unicameral People's National Assembly (Assembléia Nacional Popular)

Judicial branch: Supreme Tribunal of Justice (Supremo Tribunal de Justia)

Leaders:

Chief of State—President Antonio Mascarenhas MONTEIRO (since 22 March 1991);

Head of Government—Prime Minister Carlos VEIGA (since 13 January 1991)

Political parties and leaders: Movement for Democracy (MPD), Prime Minister Carlos VEIGA, founder and chairman; African Party for Independence of Cape Verde (PAICV), Pedro Verona Rodrigues PIRES, chairman

Suffrage: universal at age 18

Elections:

President—last held 17 February 1991 (next to be held February 1996); results—Antonio Mascarenhas MONTEIRO (MPD) received 72.6% of vote;

People's National Assembly—last held 13 January 1991 (next to be held January 1996); results—percent of vote by party NA; seats—(79 total) MPD 56, PAICV 23; note—this multiparty Assembly election ended 15 years of single-party rule

Communists: no Communist party

Member of: ACP, AfDB, ECA, ECOWAS, FAO, G-77, IBRD, ICAO, IDA, IFAD,

Cape Verde *(continued)*

ILO, IMF, IMO, INTERPOL, IOM (observer), ITU, LORCS, NAM, OAU, UN, UNCTAD, UNESCO, UNIDO, UPU, WCL, WHO, WMO
Diplomatic representation: Ambassador Luis de Matos Monteiro da FONSECA; Chancery at 3415 Massachusetts Avenue NW, Washington DC 20007; telephone (202) 965-6820; there is a Cape Verdean Consulate General in Boston;
US—Ambassador Francis T. (Terry) Mc-NAMARA; Embassy at Rua Hojl Ya Yenna 81, Praia (mailing address is C. P. 201, Praia); telephone [238] 614-363 or 614-253
Flag: two equal horizontal bands of yellow (top) and green with a vertical red band on the hoist side; in the upper portion of the red band is a black five-pointed star framed by two corn stalks and a yellow clam shell; uses the popular pan-African colors of Ethiopia; similar to the flag of Guinea-Bissau which is longer and has an unadorned black star centered in the red band

Economy

Overview: Cape Verde's low per capita GDP reflects a poor natural resource base, a 17-year drought, and a high birthrate. The economy is service oriented, with commerce, transport, and public services accounting for 65% of GDP during the period 1985-88. Although nearly 70% of the population lives in rural areas, agriculture's share of GDP is only 16%; the fishing sector accounts for 4%. About 90% of food must be imported. The fishing potential, mostly lobster and tuna, is not fully exploited. In 1988 fishing represented only 3.5% of GDP. Cape Verde annually runs a high trade deficit, financed by remittances from emigrants and foreign aid.
GDP: $262 million, per capita $740; real growth rate 3.2% (1988 est.)
Inflation rate (consumer prices): 8.2% (1988 est.)
Unemployment rate: 25% (1988)
Budget: revenues $98.3 million; expenditures $138.4 million, including capital expenditures of $NA (1988 est.)
Exports: $10.9 million (f.o.b., 1989 est.);
commodities—fish, bananas, salt;
partners—Portugal, Angola, Algeria, France, Italy
Imports: $107.8 million (c.i.f., 1989);
commodities—petroleum, foodstuffs, consumer goods, industrial products;
partners—Portugal, Netherlands, Spain, France, Brazil, FRG
External debt: $150 million (December 1990 est.)
Industrial production: growth rate 18% (1988 est.); accounts for 7% of GDP
Electricity: 13,000 kW capacity; 15 million kWh produced, 40 kWh per capita (1990)

Industry: fish processing, salt mining, clothing factories, ship repair
Agriculture: accounts for 16% of GDP; largely subsistence farming; bananas are the only export crop; other crops—corn, beans, sweet potatoes, coffee; growth potential of agricultural sector limited by poor soils and limited rainfall; annual food imports required; fish catch provides for both domestic consumption and small exports
Economic aid: US commitments, including Ex-Im (FY75-89), $88 million; Western (non-US) countries, ODA and OOF bilateral commitments (1970-88), $590 million; OPEC bilateral aid (1979-89), $12 million; Communist countries (1970-88), $36 million
Currency: Cape Verdean escudo (plural—escudos); 1 Cape Verdean escudo (CVEsc) = 100 centavos
Exchange rates: Cape Verdean escudos (CVEsc) per US$1—64.10 (November 1990), 74.86 (December 1989), 72.01 (1988), 72.5 (1987), 76.56 (1986), 85.38 (1985)
Fiscal year: calendar year

Communications

Ports: Mindelo and Praia
Merchant marine: 7 cargo ships (1,000 GRT or over) totaling 11,708 GRT/19,000 DWT
Civil air: 5 major transport aircraft (4 owned, 1 leased)
Airports: 6 total, 6 usable; 6 with permanent-surface runways; none with runways over 3,659 m; 1 with runways 2,440-3,659 m; 1 with runways 1,220-2,439 m
Telecommunications: interisland radio relay system, high-frequency radio to mainland Portugal and Guinea-Bissau; 1,740 telephones; stations—5 AM, 1 FM, 1 TV; 2 coaxial submarine cables; 1 Atlantic Ocean INTELSAT earth station

Defense Forces

Branches: People's Revolutionary Armed Forces (FARP)—Army and Navy are separate components of FARP; Militia, Security Service
Manpower availability: males 15-49, 70,771; 41,844 fit for military service
Defense expenditures: $15 million, 11% of GDP (1981)

Cayman Islands
(dependent territory of the UK)

Geography

Total area: 260 km²; land area: 260 km²
Comparative area: slightly less than 1.5 times the size of Washington, DC
Land boundaries: none
Coastline: 160 km
Maritime claims:
Exclusive fishing zone: 200 nm;
Territorial sea: 3 nm
Climate: tropical marine; warm, rainy summers (May to October) and cool, relatively dry winters (November to April)
Terrain: low-lying limestone base surrounded by coral reefs
Natural resources: fish, climate and beaches that foster tourism
Land use: arable land 0%; permanent crops 0%; meadows and pastures 8%; forest and woodland 23%; other 69%
Environment: within the Caribbean hurricane belt
Note: important location between Cuba and Central America

People

Population: 27,489 (July 1991), growth rate 4.2% (1991)
Birth rate: 13 births/1,000 population (1991)
Death rate: 5 deaths/1,000 population (1991)
Net migration rate: 33 migrants/1,000 population (1991)
Infant mortality rate: 10 deaths/1,000 live births (1991)
Life expectancy at birth: 74 years male, 80 years female (1991)
Total fertility rate: 1.4 children born/woman (1991)
Nationality: noun—Caymanian(s); adjective—Caymanian
Ethnic divisions: 40% mixed, 20% white, 20% black, 20% expatriates of various ethnic groups

Religion: United Church (Presbyterian and Congregational), Anglican, Baptist, Roman Catholic, Church of God, other Protestant denominations

Language: English

Literacy: 98% (male 98%, female 98%) age 15 and over having ever attended school (1970)

Labor force: 8,061; service workers 18.7%, clerical 18.6%, construction 12.5%, finance and investment 6.7%, directors and business managers 5.9% (1979)

Organized labor: Global Seaman's Union; Cayman All Trade Union

Government

Long-form name: none

Type: dependent territory of the UK

Capital: George Town

Administrative divisions: 8 districts; Creek, Eastern, Midland, South Town, Spot Bay, Stake Bay, West End, Western

Independence: none (dependent territory of the UK)

Legal system: British common law and local statutes

Constitution: 1959, revised 1972

National holiday: Constitution Day (first Monday in July), 1 July 1991

Executive branch: British monarch, governor, Executive Council (cabinet)

Legislative branch: unicameral Legislative Assembly

Judicial branch: Grand Court, Cayman Islands Court of Appeal

Leaders:
Chief of State—Queen ELIZABETH II (since 6 February 1952), represented by Governor Alan James SCOTT (since NA 1987);
Head of Government—Governor and President of the Executive Council Alan James SCOTT (since NA 1987)

Political parties and leaders: no formal political parties

Suffrage: universal at age 18

Elections:
Legislative Assembly—last held NA November 1988 (next to be held November 1992); results—percent of vote NA; seats—(15 total, 12 elected)

Communists: none

Member of: CDB, IOC

Diplomatic representation: as a dependent territory of the UK, Caymanian interests in the US are represented by the UK;
US—none

Flag: blue with the flag of the UK in the upper hoist-side quadrant and the Caymanian coat of arms on a white disk centered on the outer half of the flag; the coat of arms includes a pineapple and turtle above a shield with three stars (representing the three islands) and a scroll at the bottom bearing the motto *HE HATH FOUNDED IT UPON THE SEAS*

Economy

Overview: The economy depends heavily on tourism (70% of GDP and 75% of export earnings) and offshore financial services, with the tourist industry aimed at the luxury market and catering mainly to visitors from North America. About 90% of the islands' food and consumer goods needs must be imported. The Caymanians enjoy one of the highest standards of living in the region.

GDP: $342 million, per capita $13,670 (1989); real growth rate 15% (1988)

Inflation rate (consumer prices): 5.2% (1988)

Unemployment rate: NA%

Budget: revenues $76 million; expenditures $56 million, including capital expenditures of $NA (1988)

Exports: $1.5 million (f.o.b., 1987 est.);
commodities—turtle products, manufactured consumer goods;
partners—mostly US

Imports: $136 million (c.i.f., 1987 est.);
commodities—foodstuffs, manufactured goods;
partners—US, Trinidad and Tobago, UK, Netherlands Antilles, Japan

External debt: $15 million (1986)

Industrial production: growth rate NA%

Electricity: 74,000 kW capacity; 256 million kWh produced, 9,710 kWh per capita (1990)

Industries: tourism, banking, insurance and finance, real estate and construction

Agriculture: minor production of vegetables, fruit, livestock; turtle farming

Economic aid: US commitments, including Ex-Im (FY70-87), $26.7 million; Western (non-US) countries, ODA and OOF bilateral commitments (1970-88), $35.0 million

Currency: Caymanian dollar (plural—dollars); 1 Caymanian dollar (CI$) = 100 cents

Exchange rates: Caymanian dollars (CI$) per US$1—1.20 (fixed rate)

Fiscal year: 1 April-31 March

Communications

Highways: 160 km of main roads

Ports: George Town, Cayman Brac

Merchant marine: 33 ships (1,000 GRT or over) totaling 372,732 GRT/604,395 DWT; includes 1 passenger-cargo, 6 cargo, 7 roll-on/roll-off cargo, 6 petroleum, oils, and lubricants (POL) tanker, 1 chemical tanker, 2 specialized tanker, 1 liquefied gas carrier, 9 bulk; note—a flag of convenience registry

Airports: 3 total; 3 usable; 2 with permanent-surface runways; none with runways over 2,439 m; 2 with runways 1,220-2,439 m

Telecommunications: 35,000 telephones; telephone system uses 1 submarine coaxial cable and 1 Atlantic Ocean INTELSAT earth station to link islands and access international services; stations—2 AM, 1 FM, no TV

Defense Forces

Branches: Royal Cayman Islands Police Force (RCIPF)

Note: defense is the responsibility of the UK

Central African Republic

400 km

Geography

Total area: 622,980 km²; land area: 622,980 km²

Comparative area: slightly smaller than Texas

Land boundaries: 5,203 km total; Cameroon 797 km, Chad 1,197 km, Congo 467 km, Sudan 1,165 km, Zaire 1,577 km

Coastline: none—landlocked

Maritime claims: none—landlocked

Climate: tropical; hot, dry winters; mild to hot, wet summers

Terrain: vast, flat to rolling, monotonous plateau; scattered hills in northeast and southwest

Natural resources: diamonds, uranium, timber, gold, oil

Land use: arable land 3%; permanent crops NEGL%; meadows and pastures 5%; forest and woodland 64%; other 28%

Environment: hot, dry, dusty harmattan winds affect northern areas; poaching has diminished reputation as one of last great wildlife refuges; desertification

Note: landlocked; almost the precise center of Africa

People

Population: 2,952,382 (July 1991), growth rate 2.6% (1991)

Birth rate: 44 births/1,000 population (1991)

Death rate: 18 deaths/1,000 population (1991)

Net migration rate: 0 migrants/1,000 population (1991)

Infant mortality rate: 138 deaths/1,000 live births (1991)

Life expectancy at birth: 45 years male, 49 years female (1991)

Total fertility rate: 5.6 children born/woman (1991)

Nationality: noun—Central African(s); adjective—Central African

Ethnic divisions: about 80 ethnic groups, the majority of which have related ethnic and linguistic characteristics; Baya 34%, Banda 27%, Sara 10%, Mandjia 21%, Mboum 4%, M'Baka 4%; 6,500 Europeans, of whom 3,600 are French

Religion: indigenous beliefs 24%, Protestant 25%, Roman Catholic 25%, Muslim 15%, other 11%; animistic beliefs and practices strongly influence the Christian majority

Language: French (official); Sangho (lingua franca and national language); Arabic, Hunsa, Swahili

Literacy: 27% (male 33%, female 15%) age 15 and over can read and write (1990 est.)

Labor force: 775,413 (1986 est.); agriculture 85%, commerce and services 9%, industry 3%, government 3%; about 64,000 salaried workers; 55% of population of working age (1985)

Organized labor: 1% of labor force

Government

Long-form name: Central African Republic (no short-form name); abbreviated CAR

Type: republic, one-party presidential regime since 1986

Capital: Bangui

Administrative divisions: 14 prefectures (préfectures, singular—préfecture) and 2 economic prefectures* (préfectures économiques, singular—préfecture économique); Bamingui-Bangoran, Basse-Kotto, Gribingui*, Haute-Kotto, Haute-Sangha, Haut-Mbomou, Kémo-Gribingui, Lobaye, Mbomou, Nana-Mambéré, Ombella-Mpoko, Ouaka, Ouham, Ouham-Pendé, Sangha*, Vakaga; note—there may be a new autonomous commune of Bangui

Independence: 13 August 1960 (from France; formerly Central African Empire)

Constitution: 21 November 1986

Legal system: based on French law

National holiday: National Day (proclamation of the republic), 1 December (1958)

Executive branch: president, Council of Ministers (cabinet)

Legislative branch: unicameral National Assembly (Assemblée Nationale) advised by the Economic and Regional Council (Conseil Économique et Régional); when they sit together this is known as the Congress (Congrès)

Judicial branch: Supreme Court (Cour Suprême)

Leaders:
Chief of State and Head of Government—President André-Dieudonné KOLINGBA (since 1 September 1981)

Political parties and leaders: only party—Centrafrican Democrtic Rally Party (RDC), André-Dieudonné KOLINGBA

Suffrage: universal at age 21

Elections:
President—last held 21 November 1986 (next to be held November 1993); results—President KOLINGBA was reelected without opposition;
National Assembly—last held 31 July 1987 (next to be held July 1992); results—RDC is the only party; seats—(52 total) RDC 52

Communists: small number of Communist sympathizers

Member of: ACCT, ACP, AfDB, BDEAC, CCC, CEEAC, ECA, FAO, FZ, G-77, GATT, IBRD, ICAO, ICFTU, IDA, IFAD, ILO, IMF, INTELSAT, INTERPOL, IOC, ITU, LORCS, NAM, OAU, UDEAC, UN, UNCTAD, UNESCO, UNIDO, UPU, WCL, WHO, WIPO, WMO

Diplomatic representation: Ambassador Jean-Pierre SOHAHONG-KOMBET; Chancery at 1618 22nd Street NW, Washington DC 20008; telephone (202) 483-7800 or 7801;
US—Ambassador Daniel H. SIMPSON; Embassy at Avenue du President David Dacko, Bangui (mailing address is B. P. 924, Bangui); telephone 61-02-00 or 61-25-78, 61-43-33

Flag: four equal horizontal bands of blue (top), white, green, and yellow with a vertical red band in center; there is a yellow five-pointed star on the hoist side of the blue band

Economy

Overview: The Central African Republic (CAR) had a per capita income of roughly $440 in 1990. Subsistence agriculture, including forestry, is the backbone of the economy, with over 70% of the population living in the countryside. In 1988 the agricultural sector generated about 40% of GDP. Agricultural products accounted for about 60% of export earnings and the diamond industry for 30%. Important constraints to economic development include the CAR's landlocked position, a poor transportation infrastructure, and a weak human resource base. Multilateral and bilateral development assistance plays a major role in providing capital for new investment.

GDP: $1.3 billion, per capita $440; real growth rate 2.0% (1990 est.)

Inflation rate (consumer prices): −4.2% (1988 est.)

Unemployment rate: 30% in Bangui (1988 est.)

Budget: revenues $132 million; current expenditures $305 million, including capital expenditures of $NA million (1989 est.)

Exports: $148 million (f.o.b., 1989 est.);
commodities—diamonds, cotton, coffee, timber, tobacco;
partners—France, Belgium, Italy, Japan, US

Chad

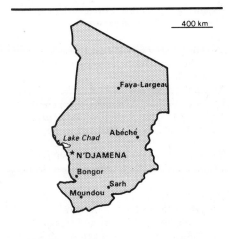

400 km

Imports: $239 million (c.i.f., 1989 est.);
commodities—food, textiles, petroleum
products, machinery, electrical equipment,
motor vehicles, chemicals, pharmaceuticals,
consumer goods, industrial products;
partners—France, other EC, Japan, Algeria,
Yugoslavia
External debt: $671 million (December
1989)
Industrial production: 0.8% (1988); accounts
for 12% of GDP
Electricity: 35,000 kW capacity; 84 million
kWh produced, 30 kWh per capita (1989)
Industries: sawmills, breweries, diamond
mining, textiles, footwear, assembly of bicy-
cles and motorcycles
Agriculture: accounts for 40% of GDP; self-
sufficient in food production except for
grain; commercial crops—cotton, coffee, to-
bacco, timber; food crops—manioc, yams,
millet, corn, bananas
Economic aid: US commitments, including
Ex-Im (FY70-89), $49 million; Western
(non-US) countries, ODA and OOF bilateral commitments (1970-88), $1.4 billion;
OPEC bilateral aid (1979-89), $6 million;
Communist countries (1970-88), $38
million
Currency: Communauté Financière Afri-
caine franc (plural—francs); 1 CFA franc
(CFAF) = 100 centimes
Exchange rates: Communauté Financière
Africaine francs (CFAF) per US$1—256.54
(January 1991), 272.26 (1990), 319.01
(1989), 297.85 (1988), 300.54 (1987),
346.30 (1986), 449.26 (1985)
Fiscal year: calendar year

Communications

Highways: 22,000 km total; 458 km bituminous, 10,542 km improved earth, 11,000
unimproved earth
Inland waterways: 800 km; traditional trade
carried on by means of shallow-draft dug-
outs; Oubangui is the most important river
Civil air: 2 major transport aircraft
Airports: 66 total, 49 usable; 4 with permanent-surface runways; none with runways
over 3,659 m; 2 with runways 2,440-3,659
m; 22 with runways 1,220-2,439 m
Telecommunications: fair system; network
relies primarily on radio relay links, with
low-capacity, low-powered radiocommunication also used; 6,000 telephones; stations—1 AM, 1 FM, 1 TV; 1 Atlantic Ocean
INTELSAT earth station

Defense Forces

Branches: Central African Armed Forces,
Air Force, National Gendarmerie, Police
Force
Manpower availability: males 15-49,
659,802; 345,049 fit for military service
Defense expenditures: $23 million, 1.8% of
GDP (1989 est.)

Geography

Total area: 1,284,000 km²; land area:
1,259,200 km²
Comparative area: slightly more than three
times the size of California
Land boundaries: 5,968 km total; Cameroon
1,094 km, Central African Republic 1,197
km, Libya 1,055 km, Niger 1,175 km, Nigeria 87 km, Sudan 1,360 km
Coastline: none—landlocked
Maritime claims: none—landlocked
Disputes: Libya claims and occupies the
100,000 km² Aozou Strip in the far north;
demarcation of international boundaries in
Lake Chad, the lack of which has led to
border incidents in the past, is completed
and awaiting ratification by Cameroon,
Chad, Niger, and Nigeria
Climate: tropical in south, desert in north
Terrain: broad, arid plains in center, desert
in north, mountains in northwest, lowlands
in south
Natural resources: crude oil (unexploited
but exploration beginning), uranium, natron, kaolin, fish (Lake Chad)
Land use: arable land 2%; permanent crops
NEGL%; meadows and pastures 36%; forest
and woodland 11%; other 51%; includes
irrigated NEGL%
Environment: hot, dry, dusty harmattan
winds occur in north; drought and desertification adversely affecting south; subject to
plagues of locusts
Note: landlocked; Lake Chad is the most
significant water body in the Sahel

People

Population: 5,122,467 (July 1991), growth
rate 2.1% (1991)
Birth rate: 42 births/1,000 population
(1991)
Death rate: 22 deaths/1,000 population
(1991)
Net migration rate: NEGL migrants/1,000
population (1991)

Infant mortality rate: 134 deaths/1,000 live
births (1991)
Life expectancy at birth: 39 years male, 41
years female (1991)
Total fertility rate: 5.3 children born/wo-
man (1991)
Nationality: noun—Chadian(s); adjective—
Chadian
Ethnic divisions: some 200 distinct ethnic
groups, most of whom are Muslims (Arabs,
Toubou, Hadjerai, Fulbe, Kotoko, Kanem-
bou, Baguirmi, Boulala, Zaghawa, and
Maba) in the north and center and non-
Muslims (Sara, Ngambaye, Mbaye, Gou-
laye, Moundang, Moussei, Massa) in the
south; some 150,000 nonindigenous, of
whom 1,000 are French
Religion: Muslim 44%, Christian 33%, in-
digenous beliefs, animism 23%
Language: French and Arabic (official);
Sara and Sango in south; more than 100
different languages and dialects are spoken
Literacy: 30% (male 42%, female 18%) age
15 and over can read and write French or
Arabic (1990 est.)
Labor force: NA; agriculture (engaged in
unpaid subsistence farming, herding, and
fishing) 85%
Organized labor: about 20% of wage labor
force

Government

Long-form name: Republic of Chad
Type: republic
Capital: N'Djamena
Administrative divisions: 14 prefectures
(préfectures, singular—préfecture); Batha,
Biltine, Borkou-Ennedi-Tibesti, Chari-Ba-
guirmi, Guéra, Kanem, Lac, Logone Occi-
dental, Logone Oriental, Mayo-Kébbi,
Moyen-Chari, Ouaddaï, Salamat, Tandjilé
Independence: 11 August 1960 (from
France)
Constitution: 22 December 1989, suspended
3 December 1990; Provisional National
Charter 1 March 1991
Legal system: based on French civil law
system and Chadian customary law; has not
accepted compulsory ICJ jurisdiction
National holiday: NA
Executive branch: president, Council of
State (cabinet)
Legislative branch: the National Consulta-
tive Council (Conseil National Consultatif)
was disbanded 3 December 1990 and re-
placed by the Provisional Council of the
Republic; 30 members appointed by Presi-
dent DÉBY on 8 March 1991
Judicial branch: Court of Appeal
Leaders:
Chief of State—Col. Idriss DÉBY (since 4
December 1990);
Head of Government—Prime Minister Jean
LINGUE Bawoyeu (since 8 March 1991)

Chad *(continued)*

Political parties and leaders: Patriotic Salvation Movement (MPS; former dissident group), Idriss DÉBY, chairman; President DÉBY has promised political pluralism, a new constitution, and free elections by September 1993; numerous dissident groups
Suffrage: universal at age NA
Elections:
President—last held 10 December 1989 (next to be held NA); results—President Hissein HABRÉ was elected without opposition; note—the government of then President HABRÉ fell on 1 December 1990 and Idriss DÉBY seized power on 3 December 1990;
National Consultative Council—last held 8 July 1990; disbanded 3 December 1990
Communists: no front organizations or underground party; probably a few Communists and some sympathizers
Other political or pressure groups: NA
Member of: ACCT, ACP, AfDB, BDEAC, CEEAC, ECA, FAO, FZ, G-77, GATT, IBRD, ICAO, ICFTU, IDA, IDB, IFAD, ILO, IMF, INTELSAT, INTERPOL, IOC, ITU, LORCS, NAM, OAU, OIC, UDEAC, UN, UNCTAD, UNESCO, UPU, WCL, WHO, WIPO, WMO, WTO
Diplomatic representation: Ambassador Mahamat Ali ADOUM; Chancery at 2002 R Steet NW, Washington DC 20009; telephone (202) 462-4009;
US—Ambassador Richard W. BOGOSIAN; Embassy at Avenue Felix Eboue, N'Djamena (mailing address is B. P. 413, N'Djamena); telephone [235] (51) 62-18, 40-09
Flag: three equal vertical bands of blue (hoist side), yellow, and red; similar to the flag of Andorra which has a national coat of arms featuring a quartered shield centered in the yellow band; also similar to the flag of Romania which has a national coat of arms featuring a mountain landscape centered in the yellow band; design was based on the flag of France

Economy

Overview: The climate, geographic location, and lack of infrastructure and natural resources potential make Chad one of the most underdeveloped countries in the world. Its economy is burdened by the ravages of civil war, conflict with Libya, drought, and food shortages. In 1986 real GDP returned to its 1977 level, with cotton, the major cash crop, accounting for 48% of exports. Over 80% of the work force is employed in subsistence farming and fishing. Industry is based almost entirely on the processing of agricultural products, including cotton, sugarcane, and cattle. Chad is highly dependent on foreign aid, with its economy in trouble and many regions suffering from shortages. Oil companies are

exploring areas north of Lake Chad and in the Doba basin in the south.
GDP: $1,015 million, per capita $205; real growth rate 0.9% (1989 est.)
Inflation rate (consumer prices): −4.9% (1989)
Unemployment rate: NA
Budget: revenues $78 million; expenditures $127 million, not including capital expenditures that are mostly financed by foreign aid donors (1989 est.)
Exports: $174 million (f.o.b., 1990 est.); *commodities*—cotton 48%, cattle 35%, textiles 5%, fish;
partners—France, Nigeria, Cameroon
Imports: $264 million (c.i.f., 1990 est.); *commodities*—machinery and transportation equipment 39%, industrial goods 20%, petroleum products 13%, foodstuffs 9%; note—excludes military equipment;
partners—US, France, Nigeria, Cameroon
External debt: $530 million (December 1990 est.)
Industrial production: growth rate 12.9% (1989 est.); accounts for nearly 15% of GDP
Electricity: 38,000 kW capacity; 70 million kWh produced, 14 kWh per capita (1989)
Industries: cotton textile mills, slaughterhouses, brewery, natron (sodium carbonate)
Agriculture: accounts for about 45% of GDP; largely subsistence farming; cotton most important cash crop; food crops include sorghum, millet, peanuts, rice, potatoes, manioc; livestock—cattle, sheep, goats, camels; self-sufficient in food in years of adequate rainfall
Economic aid: US commitments, including Ex-Im (FY70-89), $198 million; Western (non-US) countries, ODA and OOF bilateral commitments (1970-88), $1.3 billion; OPEC bilateral aid (1979-89), $28 million; Communist countries (1970-89), $80 million
Currency: Communauté Financière Africaine franc (plural—francs); 1 CFA franc (CFAF) = 100 centimes
Exchange rates: Communauté Financière Africaine francs (CFAF) per US$1—256.54 (January 1991), 272.26 (1990), 319.01 (1989), 297.85 (1988), 300.54 (1987), 346.30 (1986), 449.26 (1985)
Fiscal year: calendar year

Communications

Highways: 31,322 km total; 32 km bituminous; 7,300 km gravel and laterite; remainder unimproved
Inland waterways: 2,000 km navigable
Civil air: 3 major transport aircraft
Airports: 70 total, 54 usable; 4 with permanent-surface runways; none with runways over 3,659 m; 3 with runways 2,440-3,659 m; 23 with runways 1,220-2,439 m
Telecommunications: fair system of radiocommunication stations for intercity links;

5,000 telephones; stations—3 AM, 1 FM, limited TV service; many facilities are inoperative; 1 Atlantic Ocean INTELSAT earth station

Defense Forces

Branches: Patriotic Salvation Force (FPS; Army, Air Force), paramilitary Gendarmerie, National Police
Manpower availability: males 15-49, 1,188,222; 616,932 fit for military service; 51,713 reach military age (20) annually
Defense expenditures: $39 million, 4.3% of GDP (1988)

Chile

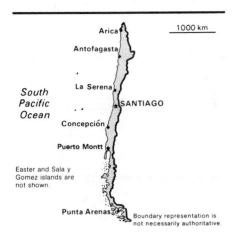

South Pacific Ocean

Arica
Antofagasta
La Serena
SANTIAGO
Concepción
Puerto Montt
Punta Arenas

1000 km

Easter and Sala y Gomez islands are not shown.

Boundary representation is not necessarily authoritative.

Geography

Total area: 756,950 km²; land area: 748,800 km²; includes Isla de Pascua (Easter Island) and Isla Sala y Gómez
Comparative area: slightly smaller than twice the size of Montana
Land boundaries: 6,171 km total; Argentina 5,150 km, Bolivia 861 km, Peru 160 km
Coastline: 6,435 km
Maritime claims:
Contiguous zone: 24 nm;
Continental shelf: 200 nm;
Exclusive economic zone: 200 nm;
Territorial sea: 12 nm
Disputes: short section of the southern boundary with Argentina is indefinite; Bolivia has wanted a sovereign corridor to the South Pacific Ocean since the Atacama area was lost to Chile in 1884; dispute with Bolivia over Río Lauca water rights; territorial claim in Antarctica (Chilean Antarctic Territory) partially overlaps Argentine claim
Climate: temperate; desert in north; cool and damp in south
Terrain: low coastal mountains; fertile central valley; rugged Andes in east
Natural resources: copper, timber, iron ore, nitrates, precious metals, molybdenum
Land use: arable land 7%; permanent crops NEGL%; meadows and pastures 16%; forest and woodland 21%; other 56%; includes irrigated 2%
Environment: subject to severe earthquakes, active volcanism, tsunami; Atacama Desert one of world's driest regions; desertification
Note: strategic location relative to sea lanes between Atlantic and Pacific Oceans (Strait of Magellan, Beagle Channel, Drake Passage)

People

Population: 13,286,620 (July 1991), growth rate 1.5% (1991)

Birth rate: 21 births/1,000 population (1991)
Death rate: 6 deaths/1,000 population (1991)
Net migration rate: 0 migrants/1,000 population (1991)
Infant mortality rate: 18 deaths/1,000 live births (1991)
Life expectancy at birth: 70 years male, 77 years female (1991)
Total fertility rate: 2.5 children born/woman (1991)
Nationality: noun—Chilean(s); adjective—Chilean
Ethnic divisions: European and European-Indian 95%, Indian 3%, other 2%
Religion: Roman Catholic 89%, Protestant 11%, and small Jewish population
Language: Spanish
Literacy: 93% (male 94%, female 93%) age 15 and over can read and write (1990 est.)
Labor force: 3,840,000; services 38.6% (includes government 12%) 38.6%; industry and commerce 31.3%; agriculture, forestry, and fishing 15.9%; mining 8.7%; construction 4.4% (1985)
Organized labor: 11% of labor force (1990)

Government

Long-form name: Republic of Chile
Type: republic
Capital: Santiago
Administrative divisions: 13 regions (regiones, singular—región); Aisén del General Carlos Ibáñez del Campo, Antofagasta, Araucanía, Atacama, Bío-Bío, Coquimbo, Libertador General Bernardo O'Higgins, Los Lagos, Magallanes y de la Antártica Chilena, Maule, Región Metropolitana, Tarapacá, Valparaíso; note—the US does not recognize claims to Antarctica
Independence: 18 September 1810 (from Spain)
Constitution: 11 September 1980, effective 11 March 1981; amended 30 July 1989
Legal system: based on Code of 1857 derived from Spanish law and subsequent codes influenced by French and Austrian law; judicial review of legislative acts in the Supreme Court; has not accepted compulsory ICJ jurisdiction
National holiday: Independence Day, 18 September (1810)
Executive branch: president, Cabinet
Legislative branch: bicameral National Congress (Congreso Nacional) consisting of an upper house or Senate (Senado) and a lower house or Chamber of Deputies (Cámara de Diputados)
Judicial branch: Supreme Court (Corte Suprema)
Leaders:
Chief of State and Head of Government—President Patricio AYLWIN (since 11 March 1990)

Political parties and leaders: Concertation of Parties for Democracy now consists mainly of six parties—Christian Democratic Party (PDC), Andrés ZALDIVAR; Party for Democracy (PPD), Erich SCHNAKE; Radical Party (PR), Mario ASTORGA; Democratic Socialist Radical Party (PRSD), Jorge IBANEZ; Social Democratic Party (PSD), Rene ABELIUK; and Socialist Party, Jorge ARRATE; National Renovation (RN), Andrés ALLAMAND; Independent Democratic Union (UDI), Joaquin LAVIN; Communist Party of Chile (PCCh), Volodia TEITELBOIM; Movement of Revolutionary Left (MIR) is splintered, no single leader
Suffrage: universal and compulsory at age 18
Elections:
President—last held 14 December 1989 (next to be held December 1993 or January 1994); results—Patricio AYLWIN (PDC) 55.2%, Hernan BÜCHI 29.4%, other 15.4%;
Senate—last held 14 December 1989 (next to be held December 1993 or January 1994); seats—(46 total, 38 elected) Concertation of Parties for Democracy 22 (PDC 13, PPD 5, PR 2, PSD 1, PRSD 1), RN 6, UDI 2, independents 8;
Chamber of Deputies—last held 14 December 1989 (next to be held December 1993 or January 1994); seats—(120 total) Concertation of Parties for Democracy 72 (PDC 38, PPD 17, PR 5, other 12), RN 29, UDI 11, right-wing independents 8
Communists: The PCCh is currently in the process of regaining legal party status and has less than 60,000 members
Other political or pressure groups: revitalized university student federations at all major universities dominated by opposition political groups; labor—United Labor Central (CUT) includes trade unionists from the country's five-largest labor confederations; Roman Catholic Church
Member of: CCC, ECLAC, FAO, G-11, G-77, GATT, IADB, IAEA, IBRD, ICAO, ICFTU, IDA, IFAD, IFC, ILO, IMF, IMO, INMARSAT, INTELSAT, INTERPOL, IOC, IOM, ISO, ITU, LAES, LAIA, LORCS, OAS, OPANAL, PCA, RG, UN, UNCTAD, UNESCO, UNIDO, UNMOGIP, UNTSO, UPU, WCL, WHO, WIPO, WMO, WTO
Diplomatic representation: Ambassador Patricio SILVA Echenique; Chancery at 1732 Massachusetts Avenue NW, Washington DC 20036; telephone (202) 785-1746; there are Chilean Consulates General in Chicago, Houston, Los Angeles, Miami, New York, and San Francisco;
US—Ambassador Charles A. GILLESPIE, Jr.; Embassy at Codina Building, 1343 Agustinas, Santiago (mailing address is APO Miami 34033); telephone [56] (2) 710133 or 710190, 710326, 710375

Chile *(continued)*

Flag: two equal horizontal bands of white (top) and red; there is a blue square the same height as the white band at the hoist-side end of the white band; the square bears a white five-pointed star in the center; design was based on the US flag

Economy

Overview: In 1990 economic growth slowed from an average of 6.2% for the previous six years to about 1.5% as a result of tight monetary policy aimed at reducing inflation. Monetary policy was not successful at slowing price increases until the end of the year, however, and inflation, exacerbated by higher world oil prices, increased to 27.3% in 1990 from 21.4% in 1989. Copper prices held strong in 1990, helping to maintain a balance-of-payments surplus and increase international reserves. Most observers expect that inflationary pressures have run their course and price increases will slow during 1991, contributing to growth of 4-5%.

GDP: $27.8 billion, per capita $2,130; real growth rate 1.8% (1990 est.)

Inflation rate (consumer prices): 27.3% (1990)

Unemployment rate: 6.0% (1990 est.)

Budget: revenues $6.6 billion; expenditures $7.1 billion, including capital expenditures of $575 million (1990 est.)

Exports: $8.6 billion (f.o.b., 1990 est.); *commodities*—copper 48%, industrial products 33%, molybdenum, iron ore, wood pulp, fishmeal, fruits; *partners*—EC 34%, US 22%, Japan 10%, Brazil 7%

Imports: $7.2 billion (f.o.b., 1990 est.); *commodities*—petroleum, wheat, capital goods, spare parts, raw materials; *partners*—EC 23%, US 20%, Japan 10%, Brazil 9%

External debt: $16.4 billion (December 1990)

Industrial production: growth rate 1.0% (1990 est.); accounts for almost 25% of GDP

Electricity: 4,138,000 kW capacity; 17,784 million kWh produced, 1,360 kWh per capita (1990)

Industries: copper, other minerals, foodstuffs, fish processing, iron and steel, wood and wood products

Agriculture: accounts for about 8% of GDP (including fishing and forestry); major exporter of fruit, fish, and timber products; major crops—wheat, corn, grapes, beans, sugar beets, potatoes, deciduous fruit; livestock products—beef, poultry, wool; self-sufficient in most foods; 1986 fish catch of 5.6 million metric tons net agricultural importer

Economic aid: US commitments, including Ex-Im (FY70-89), $521 million; Western (non-US) countries, ODA and OOF bilateral commitments (1970-88), $1.4 billion; Communist countries (1970-88), $386 million

Currency: Chilean peso (plural—pesos); 1 Chilean peso (Ch$) = 100 centavos

Exchange rates: Chilean pesos (Ch$) per US$1—337.24 (January 1991), 305.06 (1990), 267.16 (1989), 245.05 (1988), 219.54 (1987), 193.02 (1986), 161.08 (1985)

Fiscal year: calendar year

Communications

Railroads: 8,613 km total; 4,257 km 1.676-meter gauge, 135 km 1.435-meter standard gauge, 4,221 km 1.000-meter gauge; electrification, 1,865 km 1.676-meter gauge, 80 km 1.000-meter gauge

Highways: 79,025 km total; 9,913 km paved, 33,140 km gravel, 35,972 km improved and unimproved earth (1984)

Inland waterways: 725 km

Pipelines: crude oil, 755 km; refined products, 785 km; natural gas, 320 km

Ports: Antofagasta, Iquique, Puerto Montt, Punta Arenas, Valparaiso, San Antonio, Talcahuano, Arica

Merchant marine: 35 ships (1,000 GRT or over) totaling 485,935 GRT/800,969 DWT; includes 14 cargo, 1 refrigerated cargo, 3 roll-on/roll-off cargo, 2 petroleum, oils, and lubricants (POL) tanker, 1 chemical tanker, 2 liquefied gas, 3 combination ore/oil, 9 bulk; note—in addition, 2 naval tanker and 2 military transport are sometimes used commercially

Civil air: 22 major transport aircraft

Airports: 392 total, 353 usable; 50 with permanent-surface runways; none with runways over 3,659 m; 12 with runways 2,440-3,659 m; 55 with runways 1,220-2,439 m

Telecommunications: modern telephone system based on extensive radio relay facilities; 768,000 telephones; stations—159 AM, no FM, 131 TV, 11 shortwave; satellite stations—2 Atlantic Ocean INTELSAT and 3 domestic

Defense Forces

Branches: Army of the Nation, National Navy (including Naval Air and Marines), Air Force of the Nation, Carabineros of Chile (National Police)

Manpower availability: males 15-49, 3,544,962; 2,647,148 fit for military service; 119,511 reach military age (19) annually

Defense expenditures: $737 million, 3% of GNP (1991 est.)

China
(also see separate Taiwan entry)

Geography

Total area: 9,596,960 km²; land area: 9,326,410 km²

Comparative area: slightly larger than the US

Land boundaries: 23,213.34 km total; Afghanistan 76 km, Bhutan 470 km, Burma 2,185 km, Hong Kong 30 km, India 3,380 km, North Korea 1,416 km, Laos 423 km, Macau 0.34 km, Mongolia 4,673 km, Nepal 1,236 km, Pakistan 523 km, USSR 7,520 km, Vietnam 1,281 km

Coastline: 14,500 km

Maritime claims:

Continental shelf: claim to shallow areas of East China Sea and Yellow Sea

Territorial sea: 12 nm

Disputes: boundary with India; bilateral negotiations are under way to resolve disputed sections of the boundary with the USSR; a short section of the boundary with North Korea is indefinite; sporadic border clashes with Vietnam; involved in a complex dispute over the Spratly Islands with Malaysia, Philippines, Taiwan, and Vietnam; maritime boundary dispute with Vietnam in the Gulf of Tonkin; Paracel Islands occupied by China, but claimed by Vietnam and Taiwan; claims Japanese-administered Senkaku-shotō (Senkaku Islands)

Climate: extremely diverse; tropical in south to subarctic in north

Terrain: mostly mountains, high plateaus, deserts in west; plains, deltas, and hills in east

Natural resources: coal, iron ore, crude oil, mercury, tin, tungsten, antimony, manganese, molybdenum, vanadium, magnetite, aluminum, lead, zinc, uranium, world's largest hydropower potential

Land use: arable land 10%; permanent crops NEGL%; meadows and pastures 31%; forest and woodland 14%; other 45%; includes irrigated 5%

Environment: frequent typhoons (about five times per year along southern and eastern coasts), damaging floods, tsunamis, earthquakes; deforestation; soil erosion;

industrial pollution; water pollution; air pollution; desertification
Note: world's third-largest country (after USSR and Canada)

People

Population: 1,151,486,981 (July 1991), growth rate 1.6% (1991)
Birth rate: 22 births/1,000 population (1991)
Death rate: 7 deaths/1,000 population (1991)
Net migration rate: 0 migrants/1,000 population (1991)
Infant mortality rate: 33 deaths/1,000 live births (1991)
Life expectancy at birth: 68 years male, 72 years female (1991)
Total fertility rate: 2.3 children born/woman (1991)
Nationality: noun—Chinese (sing., pl.); adjective—Chinese
Ethnic divisions: Han Chinese 93.3%; Zhuang, Uygur, Hui, Yi, Tibetan, Miao, Manchu, Mongol, Buyi, Korean, and other nationalities 6.7%
Religion: officially atheist, but traditionally pragmatic and eclectic; most important elements of religion are Confucianism, Taoism, and Buddhism; Muslim 2-3%, Christian 1% (est.)
Language: Standard Chinese (Putonghua) or Mandarin (based on the Beijing dialect); also Yue (Cantonese), Wu (Shanghainese), Minbei (Fuzhou), Minnan (Hokkien-Taiwanese), Xiang, Gan, Hakka dialects, and minority languages (see ethnic divisions)
Literacy: 73% (male 84%, female 62%) age 15 and over can read and write (1990 est.)
Labor force: 553,000,000; agriculture and forestry 60%, industry and commerce 25%, construction and mining 5%, social services 5%, other 5% (1989 est.)
Organized labor: All-China Federation of Trade Unions (ACFTU) follows the leadership of the Chinese Communist Party; membership over 80 million or about 65% of the urban work force (1985)

Government

Long-form name: People's Republic of China; abbreviated PRC
Type: Communist Party-led state
Capital: Beijing
Administrative divisions: 23 provinces (sheng, singular and plural), 5 autonomous regions* (zizhiqu, singular and plural), and 3 municipalities** (shi, singular and plural); Anhui, Beijing**, Fujian, Gansu, Guangdong, Guangxi*, Guizhou, Hainan, Hebei, Heilongjiang, Henan, Hubei, Hunan, Jiangsu, Jiangxi, Jilin, Liaoning, Nei Mongol*, Ningxia*, Qinghai, Shaanxi, Shandong, Shanghai**, Shanxi, Sichuan, Tianjin**, Xinjiang*, Xizang*, Yunnan, Zhejiang; note—China considers Taiwan its 23rd province

Independence: unification under the Qin (Ch'in) Dynasty 221 BC, Qing (Ch'ing or Manchu) Dynasty replaced by the Republic on 12 February 1912, People's Republic established 1 October 1949
Constitution: 4 December 1982
Legal system: a complex amalgam of custom and statute, largely criminal law; rudimentary civil code in effect since 1 January 1987; new legal codes in effect since 1 January 1980; continuing efforts are being made to improve civil, administrative, criminal, and commercial law
National holiday: National Day, 1 October (1949)
Executive branch: president, vice president, premier, five vice premiers, State Council
Legislative branch: unicameral National People's Congress (Quanguo Renmin Daibiao Dahui)
Judicial branch: Supreme People's Court
Leaders:
Chief of State and Head of Government (de facto)—DENG Xiaoping (since mid-1977);
Chief of State—President YANG Shangkun (since 8 April 1988); Vice President WANG Zhen (since 8 April 1988);
Head of Government—Premier LI Peng (Acting Premier since 24 November 1987, Premier since 9 April 1988); Vice Premier YAO Yilin (since 2 July 1979); Vice Premier TIAN Jiyun (since 20 June 1983); Vice Premier WU Xueqian (since 12 April 1988); Vice Premier ZOU Jiahua (since 8 April 1991); Vice Premier ZHU Rongji (since 8 April 1991)
Political parties and leaders: only party—Chinese Communist Party (CCP), JIANG Zemin, general secretary of the Central Committee (since NA June 1989)
Suffrage: universal at age 18
Elections:
President—last held 8 April 1988 (next to be held March 1993); YANG Shangkun was nominally elected by the Seventh National People's Congress;
National People's Congress—last held NA March 1988 (next to be held March 1993); results—CCP is the only party but there are also independents; seats—(2,976 total) CCP and independents 2,976 (indirectly elected at county or xian level)
Communists: 49,000,000 party members (1990 est.)
Other political or pressure groups: such meaningful opposition as exists consists of loose coalitions, usually within the party and government organization, that vary by issue
Member of: AfDB, AsDB, CCC, ESCAP, FAO, IAEA, IBRD, ICAO, IDA, IFAD, IFC, ILO, IMF, IMO, INMARSAT, INTELSAT, INTERPOL, IOC, ISO, ITU, LORCS, PCA, UN, UNCTAD, UNESCO, UNHCR, UNIDO, UN Security Council, UN Trusteeship Council, UPU, WFTU, WHO, WIPO, WMO, WTO

Diplomatic representation: Ambassador ZHU Qizhen; Chancery at 2300 Connecticut Avenue NW, Washington DC 20008; telephone (202) 328-2500 through 2502; there are Chinese Consulates General in Chicago, Houston, Los Angeles, New York, and San Francisco;
US—Ambassador James R. LILLEY; Embassy at Xiu Shui Bei Jie 3, Beijing (mailing address is 100600, PRC Box 50, Beijing or FPO San Francisco 96655-0001); telephone [86] (1) 532-3831; there are US Consulates General in Chengdu, Guangzhou, Shanghai, and Shenyang
Flag: red with a large yellow five-pointed star and four smaller yellow five-pointed stars (arranged in a vertical arc toward the middle of the flag) in the upper hoist-side corner

Economy

Overview: Beginning in late 1978 the Chinese leadership has been trying to move the economy from the sluggish Soviet-style centrally planned economy to a more productive and flexible economy with market elements—but still within the framework of monolithic Communist control. To this end the authorities have switched to a system of household responsibility in agriculture in place of the old collectivization, increased the authority of local officials and plant managers in industry, permitted a wide variety of small-scale enterprise in services and light manufacturing, and opened the foreign economic sector to increased trade and joint ventures. The most gratifying result has been a strong spurt in production, particularly in agriculture in the early 1980s. Otherwise, the leadership has often experienced in its hybrid system the worst results of socialism (bureaucracy, lassitude, corruption) and of capitalism (windfall gains and stepped-up inflation). Beijing thus has periodically backtracked, retightening central controls at intervals and thereby undermining the credibility of the reform process. Popular resistance and changes in central policy have weakened China's population control program, which is essential to the nation's long-term economic viability.
GNP: $413 billion (1989 est.), per capita $370 (World Bank est.); real growth rate 5% (1990)
Inflation rate (consumer prices): 2.1% (1990)
Unemployment rate: 2.6% in urban areas (1990)
Budget: revenues $NA; expenditures $NA, including capital expenditures of $NA
Exports: $62.1 billion (f.o.b., 1990); *commodities*—textiles, garments, telecommunications and recording equipment, petroleum, minerals; *partners*—Hong Kong, US, Japan, USSR, Singapore, FRG (1989)
Imports: $53.4 billion (c.i.f., 1990);

China (continued)

commodities—specialized industrial machinery, chemicals, manufactured goods, steel, textile yarn, fertilizer;
partners—Hong Kong, Japan, US, FRG, USSR (1989)
External debt: $51 billion (1990 est.)
Industrial production: growth rate 7.6% (1990); accounts for almost 40% of GNP
Electricity: 117,580,000 kW capacity; 585,000 million kWh produced, 520 kWh per capita (1990)
Industries: iron, steel, coal, machine building, armaments, textiles, petroleum
Agriculture: accounts for 26% of GNP; among the world's largest producers of rice, potatoes, sorghum, peanuts, tea, millet, barley, and pork; commercial crops include cotton, other fibers, and oilseeds; produces variety of livestock products; basically self-sufficient in food; fish catch of 8 million metric tons in 1986
Economic aid: donor—to less developed countries (1970-89) $7.0 billion; US commitments, including Ex-Im (FY70-87), $220.7 million; Western (non-US) countries, ODA and OOF bilateral commitments (1970-87), $13.5 billion
Currency: yuan (plural—yuan); 1 yuan (¥) = 10 jiao
Exchange rates: yuan (¥) per US$1—5.31 (April 1991), 4.7832 (1990), 3.7651 (1989), 3.7221 (1988), 3.7221 (1987), 3.4528 (1986), 2.9367 (1985)
Fiscal year: calendar year

Communications

Railroads: total about 54,000 km common carrier lines; 53,400 km 1.435-meter standard gauge; 600 km 1.000-meter gauge; all single track except 11,200 km double track on standard-gauge lines; 6,500 km electrified; 10,000 km industrial lines (gauges range from 0.762 to 1.067 meters)
Highways: about 980,000 km all types roads; 162,000 km paved roads, 617,200 km gravel/improved earth roads, 200,800 km unimproved natural earth roads and tracks
Inland waterways: 138,600 km; about 109,800 km navigable
Pipelines: crude, 6,500 km; refined products, 1,100 km; natural gas, 6,200 km
Ports: Dalian, Guangzhou, Huangpu, Qingdao, Qinhuangdao, Shanghai, Xingang, Zhanjiang, Ningbo, Xiamen, Tanggu, Shantou
Merchant marine: 1,421 ships (1,000 GRT or over) totaling 14,010,317 GRT/21,223,170 DWT; includes 24 passenger, 42 short-sea passenger, 19 passenger-cargo, 7 cargo/training, 776 cargo, 11 refrigerated cargo, 70 container, 17 roll-on/roll-off cargo, 2 multifunction barge carrier, 181 petroleum, oils, and lubricants (POL) tanker, 9 chemical tanker, 250 bulk, 2 liquefied gas, 2 vehicle carrier, 9 combination bulk;

note—China beneficially owns an additional 183 ships (1,000 GRT or over) totaling approximately 5,921,000 DWT that operate under Maltese and Liberian registry
Airports: 330 total, 330 usable; 260 with permanent-surface runways; fewer than 10 with runways over 3,500 m; 90 with runways 2,440-3,659 m; 200 with runways 1,220-2,439 m
Telecommunications: domestic and international services are increasingly available for private use; unevenly distributed internal system serves principal cities, industrial centers, and most townships; 11,000,000 telephones (December 1989); stations—274 AM, unknown FM, 202 (2,050 relays) TV; more than 215 million radio receivers; 75 million TVs; satellite earth stations—4 Pacific Ocean INTELSAT, 1 Indian Ocean INTELSAT, 1 INMARSAT, and 55 domestic

---

Defense Forces

Branches: Chinese People's Liberation Army (CPLA), CPLA Navy (including Marines), CPLA Air Force, Chinese People's Armed Police
Manpower availability: males 15-49, 335,382,062; 187,046,680 fit for military service; 10,967,622 reach military age (18) annually
Defense expenditures: $NA, NA% of GNP

Christmas Island
(territory of Australia)

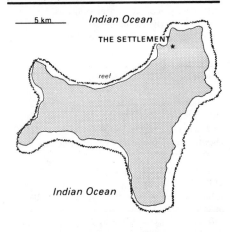

Geography

Total area: 135 km²; land area: 135 km²
Comparative area: about 0.8 times the size of Washington, DC
Land boundaries: none
Coastline: 138.9 km
Maritime claims:
Contiguous zone: 12 nm;
Exclusive fishing zone: 200 nm;
Territorial sea: 3 nm
Climate: tropical; heat and humidity moderated by trade winds
Terrain: steep cliffs along coast rise abruptly to central plateau
Natural resources: phosphate
Land use: arable land 0%; permanent crops 0%; meadows and pastures 0%; forest and woodland 0%; other 100%
Environment: almost completely surrounded by a reef
Note: located along major sea lanes of Indian Ocean

People

Population: 2,278 (July 1991), growth rate NA% (1991)
Birth rate: NA births/1,000 population (1991)
Death rate: NA deaths/1,000 population (1991)
Net migration rate: NA migrants/1,000 population (1991)
Infant mortality rate: NA deaths/1,000 live births (1991)
Life expectancy at birth: NA years male, NA years female (1991)
Total fertility rate: NA children born/woman (1991)
Nationality: noun—Christmas Islander(s), adjective—Christmas Island
Ethnic divisions: Chinese 61%, Malay 25%, European 11%, other 3%; no indigenous population
Religion: Buddhist 36.1%, Muslim 25.4%, Christian 17.7% (Roman Catholic 8.2%,

Church of England 3.2%, Presbyterian 0.9%, Uniting Church 0.4%, Methodist 0.2%, Baptist 0.1%, and other 4.7%), none 12.7%, unknown 4.6%, other 3.5% (1981)
Language: English
Literacy: NA% (male NA%, female NA%)
Labor force: NA; all workers are employees of the Phosphate Mining Company of Christmas Island, Ltd.
Organized labor: NA

Government

Long-form name: Territory of Christmas Island
Type: territory of Australia
Capital: The Settlement
Administrative divisions: none (territory of Australia)
Independence: none (territory of Australia)
Constitution: Christmas Island Act of 1958
Legal system: under the authority of the governor general of Australia
National holiday: NA
Executive branch: British monarch, governor general of Australia, administrator, Advisory Council (cabinet)
Legislative branch: none
Judicial branch: none
Leaders:
Chief of State—Queen ELIZABETH II (since 6 February 1952);
Head of Government—Administrator A. D. TAYLOR (since NA)
Communists: none
Member of: none
Diplomatic representation: none (territory of Australia)
Flag: the flag of Australia is used

Economy

Overview: Phosphate mining had been the only significant economic activity, but in December 1987 the Australian Government closed the mine as no longer economically viable. Plans have been under way to re-open the mine and also to build a casino and hotel to develop tourism, with a possible opening date during the first half of 1992.
GDP: $NA, per capita $NA; real growth rate NA%
Inflation rate (consumer prices): NA%
Unemployment rate: 0%
Budget: revenues $NA; expenditures $NA, including capital expenditures of $NA
Exports: $NA;
commodities—phosphate;
partners—Australia, NZ
Imports: $NA;
commodities—NA;
partners—NA
External debt: $NA
Industrial production: growth rate NA%

Electricity: 11,000 kW capacity; 30 million kWh produced, 13,170 kWh per capita (1990)
Industries: phosphate extraction (near depletion)
Agriculture: NA
Economic aid: none
Currency: Australian dollar (plural—dollars); 1 Australian dollar ($A) = 100 cents
Exchange rates: Australian dollars ($A) per US$1—1.2834 (January 1991), 1.2799 (1990), 1.2618 (1989), 1.2752 (1988), 1.4267 (1987), 1.4905 (1986), 1.4269 (1985)
Fiscal year: 1 July-30 June

Communications

Ports: Flying Fish Cove
Airports: 1 usable with permanent-surface runway 1,220-2,439 m
Telecommunications: 4,000 radios (1982)

Defense Forces

Note: defense is the responsibility of Australia

Clipperton Island
(French possession)

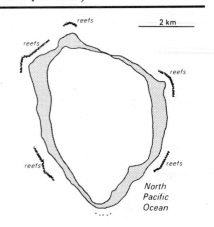

Geography

Total area: 7 km²
Comparative area: about 12 times the size of The Mall in Washington, DC
Land boundaries: none
Coastline: 11.1 km
Maritime claims:
Exclusive economic zone: 200 nm;
Territorial sea: 12 nm
Disputes: claimed by Mexico
Climate: tropical
Terrain: coral atoll
Natural resources: none
Land use: arable land 0%; permanent crops 0%; meadows and pastures 0%; forest and woodland 0%; other (coral) 100%
Environment: reef about 8 km in circumference
Note: located 1,120 km southwest of Mexico in the North Pacific Ocean; also called Île de la Passion

People

Population: uninhabited

Government

Long-form name: none
Type: French possession administered from French Polynesia by High Commissioner of the Republic Jean MONTPEZAT; note—may have become a dependency of French Polynesia

Economy

Overview: only economic activity is a tuna fishing station

Communications

Ports: none; offshore anchorage only

Defense Forces

Note: defense is the responsibility of France

Cocos (Keeling) Islands
(territory of Australia)

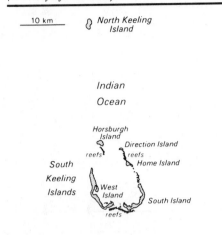

Geography

Total area: 14 km²; land area: 14 km²; main islands are West Island and Home Island
Comparative area: about 24 times the size of The Mall in Washington, DC
Land boundaries: none
Coastline: 42.6 km
Maritime claims:
Exclusive fishing zone: 200 nm;
Territorial sea: 3 nm
Climate: pleasant, modified by the southeast trade winds for about nine months of the year; moderate rainfall
Terrain: flat, low-lying coral atolls
Natural resources: fish
Land use: arable land 0%; permanent crops 0%; meadows and pastures 0%; forest and woodland 0%; other 100%
Environment: two coral atolls thickly covered with coconut palms and other vegetation
Note: located 1,070 km southwest of Sumatra (Indonesia) in the Indian Ocean about halfway between Australia and Sri Lanka

People

Population: 684 (July 1991), growth rate NEGL% (1991)
Birth rate: NA births/1,000 population (1991)
Death rate: NA deaths/1,000 population (1991)
Net migration rate: NA migrants/1,000 population (1991)
Infant mortality rate: NA deaths/1,000 live births (1991)
Life expectancy at birth: NA years male, NA years female (1991)
Total fertility rate: NA children born/woman (1991)
Nationality: noun—Cocos Islander(s); adjective—Cocos Islander(s)
Ethnic divisions: mostly Europeans on West Island and Cocos Malays on Home Island
Religion: almost all Sunni Muslims

Language: English
Literacy: NA% (male NA%, female NA%)
Labor force: NA
Organized labor: none

Government

Long-form name: Territory of Cocos (Keeling) Islands
Type: territory of Australia
Capital: West Island
Administrative divisions: none (territory of Australia)
Independence: none (territory of Australia)
Constitution: Cocos (Keeling) Islands Act of 1955
Legal system: based upon the laws of Australia and local laws
National holiday: NA
Executive branch: British monarch, governor general of Australia, administrator, chairman of the Islands Council
Legislative branch: unicameral Islands Council
Judicial branch: Supreme Court
Leaders:
Chief of State—Queen ELIZABETH II (since 6 February 1952);
Head of Government—Administrator D. LAWRIE (since NA 1989); Chairman of the Islands Council Parson Bin YAPAT (since NA)
Suffrage: NA
Elections: NA
Member of: none
Diplomatic representation: none (territory of Australia)
Flag: the flag of Australia is used

Economy

Overview: Grown throughout the islands, coconuts are the sole cash crop. Copra and fresh coconuts are the major export earners. Small local gardens and fishing contribute to the food supply, but additional food and most other necessities must be imported from Australia.
GDP: $NA, per capita $NA; real growth rate NA%
Inflation rate (consumer prices): NA%
Unemployment: NA
Budget: revenues $NA; expenditures $NA, including capital expenditures of $NA
Exports: $NA;
commodities—copra;
partners—Australia
Imports: $NA;
commodities—foodstuffs;
partners—Australia
External debt: $NA
Industrial production: growth rate NA%
Electricity: 1,000 kW capacity; 2 million kWh produced, 2,980 kWh per capita (1990)
Industries: copra products

Agriculture: gardens provide vegetables, bananas, pawpaws, coconuts
Economic aid: none
Currency: Australian dollar (plural—dollars); 1 Australian dollar ($A) = 100 cents
Exchange rates: Australian dollars ($A) per US$1—1.2834 (January 1991), 1.2799 (1990), 1.2618 (1989), 1.2752 (1988), 1.4267 (1987), 1.4905 (1986), 1.4269 (1985)
Fiscal year: 1 July-30 June

Communications

Ports: none; lagoon anchorage only
Airports: 1 airfield with permanent-surface runway, 1,220-2,439 m; airport on West Island is a link in service between Australia and South Africa
Telecommunications: 250 radios (1985); linked by telephone, telex, and facsimile communications via satellite with Australia; stations—1 AM, no FM, no TV

Defense Forces

Note: defense is the responsibility of Australia

Colombia

Providencia, Malpelo, and San Andrés islands are not shown.

Geography

Total area: 1,138,910 km²; land area: 1,038,700 km²; includes Isla de Malpelo, Roncador Cay, Serrana Bank, and Serranilla Bank
Comparative area: slightly less than three times the size of Montana
Land boundaries: 7,408 km total; Brazil 1,643 km, Ecuador 590 km, Panama 225 km, Peru 2,900, Venezuela 2,050 km
Coastline: 3,208 km total (1,448 km North Pacific Ocean; 1,760 Caribbean Sea)
Maritime claims:
Continental shelf: not specified;
Exclusive economic zone: 200 nm;
Territorial sea: 12 nm
Disputes: maritime boundary dispute with Venezuela in the Gulf of Venezuela; territorial dispute with Nicaragua over Archipelago de San Andrés y Providencia and Quita Sueño Bank
Climate: tropical along coast and eastern plains; cooler in highlands
Terrain: mixture of flat coastal lowlands, plains in east, central highlands, some high mountains
Natural resources: crude oil, natural gas, coal, iron ore, nickel, gold, copper, emeralds
Land use: arable land 4%; permanent crops 2%; meadows and pastures 29%; forest and woodland 49%; other 16%; includes irrigated NEGL%
Environment: highlands subject to volcanic eruptions; deforestation; soil damage from overuse of pesticides; periodic droughts
Note: only South American country with coastlines on both North Pacific Ocean and Caribbean Sea

People

Population: 33,777,550 (July 1991), growth rate 2.1% (1991)
Birth rate: 26 births/1,000 population (1991)
Death rate: 5 deaths/1,000 population (1991)
Net migration rate: NEGL migrants/1,000 population (1991)
Infant mortality rate: 37 deaths/1,000 live births (1991)
Life expectancy at birth: 68 years male, 74 years female (1991)
Total fertility rate: 2.8 children born/woman (1991)
Nationality: noun—Colombian(s); adjective—Colombian
Ethnic divisions: mestizo 58%, white 20%, mulatto 14%, black 4%, mixed black-Indian 3%, Indian 1%
Religion: Roman Catholic 95%
Language: Spanish
Literacy: 87% (male 88%, female 86%) age 15 and over can read and write (1990 est.)
Labor force: 11,000,000 (1986); services 53%, agriculture 26%, industry 21% (1981)
Organized labor: 1,400,000 members (1987), about 12% of labor force; the Communist-backed Unitary Workers Central or CUT is the largest labor organization, with about 725,000 members (including all affiliate unions)

Government

Long-form name: Republic of Colombia
Type: republic; executive branch dominates government structure
Capital: Bogotá
Administrative divisions: 23 departments (départamentos, singular—départamento), 5 commissariats* (comisarías, singular—comisaría), and 4 intendancies** (intendencias, singular—intendencia); Amazonas*, Antioquia, Arauca**, Atlántico, Bolívar, Boyacá, Caldas, Caquetá, Casanare**, Cauca, Cesar, Chocó, Córdoba, Cundinamarca, Guainía*, Guaviare*, Huila, La Guajira, Magdalena, Meta, Nariño, Norte de Santander, Putumayo**, Quindío, Risaralda, San Andrés y Providencia**, Santander, Sucre, Tolima, Valle del Cauca, Vaupés*, Vichada*; note—there may be a new special district (distrito especial) named Bogotá; the Constitution of 5 July 1991 states that the commissariats and intendancies are to become full departments and a capital district (distrito capital) of Santa Fe de Bogotá is to be established by 1997
Independence: 20 July 1810 (from Spain)
Constitution: 5 July 1991
Legal system: based on Spanish law; judicial review of legislative acts in the Supreme Court; accepts compulsory ICJ jurisdiction, with reservations
National holiday: Independence Day, 20 July (1810)
Executive branch: president, presidential designate, Cabinet
Legislative branch: bicameral Congress (Congreso) consists of a nationally elected upper chamber or Senate (Senado) and a regionally elected lower chamber or Chamber of Representatives (Cámara de Representantes)
Judicial branch: Supreme Court of Justice (Corte Suprema de Justica)
Leaders:
*Chief of State and Head of Government—*President César GAVIRIA Trujillo (since 7 August 1990)
Political parties and leaders: Liberal Party (PL), César GAVIRIA Trujillo, president, and Alfonso LÓPEZ Michelsen, party head; Social Conservative Party (PCS), Misael PASTRANA Borrero; National Salvation Movement (MSN), Álvaro GÓMEZ Hurtado; Democratic Alliance (AD) is headed by 19th of April Movement (M-19) leader Antonio NAVARRO Wolf, coalition of small leftist parties and dissident liberals and conservatives; Patriotic Union (UP), is a legal political party formed by Revolutionary Armed Forces of Colombia (FARC) and Colombian Communist Party (PCC), Carlos ROMERO
Suffrage: universal at age 18
Elections:
President—last held 27 May 1990 (next to be held May 1994); results—César GAVIRIA Trujillo (Liberal) 47%, Alvaro GOMEZ Hurtado (National Salvation Movement) 24%, Antonio NAVARRO Wolff (M-19) 13%, Rodrigo LLOREDA (Conservative) 12%;
Senate—last held 11 March 1990 (next to be held 27 October 1991); results—percent of vote by party NA; seats—(114 total) Liberal 72, Conservative 40, UP 1, vacant 1;
Chamber of Representatives last held 11 March 1990 (next to be held 27 October 1991); results—percent of vote by party NA; seats—(199 total) Liberal 122, Conservative 68, UP 3, M-19 1, other 5; note—on 5 July 1991 the new Constitution dissolved Congress and replaced it with a multiparty 36-member legislative commission until a new congress, to be elected on 27 October 1991, takes office on 1 December 1991
Communists: 18,000 members (est.), including Communist Party Youth Organization (JUCO)
Other political or pressure groups: three insurgent groups are active in Colombia—Revolutionary Armed Forces of Colombia (FARC), led by Manuel MARULANDA and Alfonso CANO; National Liberation Army (ELN), led by Manuel PEREZ; and dissidents of the recently demobilized People's Liberation Army (EPL) led by Francisco CARABALLO
Member of: AG, CDB, CG, ECLAC, FAO, G-3, G-11, G-24, G-77, GATT, IADB, IAEA, IBRD, ICAO, ICC, ICFTU, IDA, IFAD, IFC, ILO, IMF, IMO, INMARSAT, INTELSAT, INTERPOL, IOC, IOM, ISO, ITU, LAES, LAIA, LORCS, NAM, OAS, OPANAL, PCA, RG, UN, UNCTAD, UNESCO, UNHCR, UNIDO, UPU, WCL, WHO, WIPO, WMO, WTO
Diplomatic representation: Ambassador Jaime GARCIA Parra; Chancery at 2118 Leroy Place NW, Washington DC 20008; telephone (202) 387-8338; there are

Colombia (continued)

Colombian Consulates General in Chicago, Houston, Miami, New Orleans, New York, San Francisco, and San Juan (Puerto Rico), and Consulates in Atlanta, Boston, Detroit, Ft. Lauderdale, Los Angeles, San Diego, and Tampa;
US—Ambassador-designate Morris D. BUSBY; Embassy at Calle 38, No.8-61, Bogotá (mailing address is P. O. Box A. A. 3831, Bogotá or APO Miami 34038); telephone [57] (1) 285-1300 or 1688; there is a US Consulate in Barranquilla
Flag: three horizontal bands of yellow (top, double-width), blue, and red; similar to the flag of Ecuador which is longer and bears the Ecuadorian coat of arms superimposed in the center

Economy

Overview: Economic development has slowed gradually since 1986, but growth rates remain high by Latin American standards. Conservative economic policies have kept inflation and unemployment near 30% and 10%, respectively. The rapid development of oil, coal, and other nontraditional industries over the past four years has helped to offset the decline in coffee prices—Colombia's major export. The collapse of the International Coffee Agreement in the summer of 1989, a troublesome rural insurgency, and drug-related violence dampen prospects for future growth.
GDP: $43.0 billion, per capita $1,300; real growth rate 3.7% (1990 est.)
Inflation rate (consumer prices): 32.4% (1990)
Unemployment rate: 10.4% (1990)
Budget: revenues $4.39 billion; current expenditures $3.93 billion, capital expenditures $1.03 billion (1989 est.)
Exports: $6.9 billion (f.o.b., 1990);
commodities—coffee 24%, petroleum, coal, bananas, fresh cut flowers;
partners—US 36%, EC 21%, Japan 5%, Netherlands 4%, Sweden 3%
Imports: $5.0 billion (c.i.f., 1990);
commodities—industrial equipment, transportation equipment, foodstuffs, chemicals, paper products;
partners—US 34%, EC 16%, Brazil 4%, Venezuela 3%, Japan 3%
External debt: $16.7 billion (1990)
Industrial production: growth rate 5.0% (1990 est.); accounts for 25% of GDP
Electricity: 9,435,000 kW capacity; 36,071 million kWh produced, 1,090 kWh per capita (1990)
Industries: textiles, food processing, oil, clothing and footwear, beverages, chemicals, metal products, cement; mining—gold, coal, emeralds, iron, nickel, silver, salt
Agriculture: growth rate 4.9% (1990); accounts for 22% of GDP; crops make up two-thirds and livestock one-third of agricultural output; climate and soils permit a wide variety of crops, such as coffee, rice, tobacco, corn, sugarcane, cocoa beans, oilseeds, vegetables; forest products and shrimp farming are becoming more important
Illicit drugs: major illicit producer of cannabis and coca; key supplier of marijuana and cocaine to the US and other international drug markets; drug production and trafficking accounts for an estimated 4% of GDP and 28% of foreign exchange earnings
Economic aid: US commitments, including Ex-Im (FY70-89), $1.6 billion; Western (non-US) countries, ODA and OOF bilateral commitments (1970-88), $3.1 billion; Communist countries (1970-89), $399 million
Currency: Colombian peso (plural—pesos); 1 Colombian peso (Col$) = 100 centavos
Exchange rates: Colombian pesos (Col$) per US$1—574.09 (January 1991), 502.24 (1990), 382.57 (1989), 299.17 (1988), 242.61 (1987), 194.26 (1986), 142.31 (1985)
Fiscal year: calendar year

Communications

Railroads: 3,386 km; 3,236 km 0.914-meter gauge, single track (2,611 km in use), 150 km 1.435-meter gauge
Highways: 75,450 km total; 9,350 km paved, 66,100 km earth and gravel surfaces
Inland waterways: 14,300 km, navigable by river boats
Pipelines: crude oil, 3,585 km; refined products, 1,350 km; natural gas, 830 km; natural gas liquids, 125 km
Ports: Barranquilla, Buenaventura, Cartagena, Covenas, San Andres, Santa Marta, Tumaco
Merchant marine: 35 ships (1,000 GRT or over) totaling 330,316 GRT/484,351 DWT; includes 23 cargo, 1 chemical tanker, 3 petroleum, oils, and lubricants (POL) tanker, 8 bulk; note—2 naval tankers are sometimes used commercially
Civil air: 106 major transport aircraft
Airports: 1,165 total, 1,045 usable; 69 with permanent-surface runways; 1 with runways over 3,659 m; 8 with runways 2,440-3,659 m; 192 with runways 1,220-2,439 m
Telecommunications: nationwide radio relay system; 1,890,000 telephones; stations—413 AM, no FM, 33 TV, 28 shortwave 2 Atlantic Ocean INTELSAT earth stations with 2 antennas and 11 domestic satellite stations

Defense Forces

Branches: Army (Ejercito Nacional), Navy (Armada Nacional), Air Force (Fuerza Aerea de Colombia), National Police (Policia Nacional)

Manpower availability: males 15-49, 8,998,759; 6,102,745 fit for military service; 353,122 reach military age (18) annually
Defense expenditures: $892 million, 2.2% of GDP (1990)

Comoros

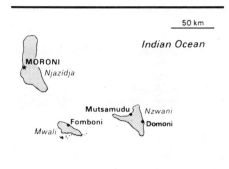

Indian Ocean

MORONI • Njazidja

Mutsamudu • Nzwani
Fomboni • Domoni
Mwali

Mozambique
Channel

Geography

Total area: 2,170 km²; land area: 2,170 km²
Comparative area: slightly more than 12 times the size of Washington, DC
Land boundaries: none
Coastline: 340 km
Maritime claims:
Exclusive economic zone: 200 nm;
Territorial sea: 12 nm
Disputes: claims French-administered Mayotte
Climate: tropical marine; rainy season (November to May)
Terrain: volcanic islands, interiors vary from steep mountains to low hills
Natural resources: negligible
Land use: arable land 35%; permanent crops 8%; meadows and pastures 7%; forest and woodland 16%; other 34%
Environment: soil degradation and erosion; deforestation; cyclones possible during rainy season
Note: important location at northern end of Mozambique Channel

People

Population: 476,678 (July 1991), growth rate 3.5% (1991)
Birth rate: 47 births/1,000 population (1991)
Death rate: 12 deaths/1,000 population (1991)
Net migration rate: 0 migrants/1,000 population (1991)
Infant mortality rate: 87 deaths/1,000 live births (1991)
Life expectancy at birth: 54 years male, 59 years female (1991)
Total fertility rate: 7.0 children born/woman (1991)
Nationality: noun—Comoran(s); adjective—Comoran
Ethnic divisions: Antalote, Cafre, Makoa, Oimatsaha, Sakalava

Religion: Sunni Muslim 86%, Roman Catholic 14%
Language: Shaafi Islam (a Swahili dialect), Malagasy, French
Literacy: 48% (male 56%, female 40%) age 15 and over can read and write (1980)
Labor force: 140,000 (1982); agriculture 80%, government 3%; 51% of population of working age (1985)
Organized labor: NA

Government

Long-form name: Federal Islamic Republic of the Comoros
Type: independent republic
Capital: Moroni
Administrative divisions: 3 islands; Anjouan, Grande Comore, Mohéli; note—there may also be 4 municipalities named Domoni, Fomboni, Moroni, and Mutsamudu
Independence: 6 July 1975 (from France)
Constitution: 1 October 1978, amended October 1982 and January 1985
Legal system: French and Muslim law in a new consolidated code
National holiday: Independence Day, 6 July (1975)
Executive branch: president, Council of Ministers (cabinet)
Legislative branch: unicameral Federal Assembly (Assemblée Fédérale)
Judicial branch: Supreme Court (Cour Suprême)
Leaders:
*Chief of State and Head of Government—*President Said Mohamed DJOHAR (since 11 March 1990)
Political parties: Comoran Union for Progress (Udzima), Said Mohamed DJOHAR, president; National Union for Democracy (UNDC), Mohamed TAKI
Suffrage: universal at age 18
Elections:
*President—*last held 11 March 1990 (next to be held March 1996); results—Said Mohamed DJOHAR (Udzima) 55%; Mohamed TAKI Abdulkarim (UNDC) 45%;
*Federal Assembly—*last held 22 March 1987 (next to be held March 1992); results—percent of vote by party NA; seats—(42 total) Udzima 42
Member of: ACCT, ACP, AfDB, ECA, FAO, FZ, G-77, IBRD, ICAO, IDA, IDB, IFAD, ILO, IMF, ITU, NAM, OAU, OIC, UN, UNCTAD, UNESCO, UNIDO, UPU, WHO, WMO
Diplomatic representation: Ambassador Amini Ali MOUMIN; Chancery (temporary) at the Comoran Permanent Mission to the UN, 336 East 45th Street, 2nd Floor, New York, NY 10017; telephone (212) 972-8010;
*US—*Ambassador Kenneth N. PELTIER; Embassy at address NA, Moroni (mailing

address B. P. 1318, Moroni); telephone 73-22-03, 73-29-22
Flag: green with a white crescent placed diagonally (closed side of the crescent points to the upper hoist-side corner of the flag); there are four white five-pointed stars placed in a line between the points of the crescent; the crescent, stars, and color green are traditional symbols of Islam; the four stars represent the four main islands of the archipelago—Mwali, Njazidja, Nzwani, and Mayotte (which is a territorial collectivity of France, but claimed by the Comoros)

Economy

Overview: One of the world's poorest countries, Comoros is made up of several islands that have poor transportation links, a young and rapidly increasing population, and few natural resources. The low educational level of the labor force contributes to a low level of economic activity, high unemployment, and a heavy dependence on foreign grants and technical assistance. Agriculture, including fishing and forestry, is the leading sector of the economy. It contributes about 40% to GDP, employs 80% of the labor force, and provides most of the exports. The country is not self-sufficient in food production, and rice, the main staple, accounts for 90% of imports. During the period 1982-86 the industrial sector grew at an annual average rate of 5.3%, but its contribution to GDP was only 5% in 1988. Despite major investment in the tourist industry, which accounts for about 25% of GDP, growth has stagnated since 1983. A sluggish growth rate of 1.5% during 1985-90 has led to large budget deficits, declining incomes, and balance-of-payments difficulties.
GDP: $245 million, per capita $530; real growth rate 1.5% (1990 est.)
Inflation rate (consumer prices): 2.9% (1989)
Unemployment rate: over 16% (1988 est.)
Budget: revenues $88 million; expenditures $92 million, including capital expenditures of $13 million (1990 est.)
Exports: $16 million (f.o.b., 1990 est.);
commodities—vanilla, cloves, perfume oil, copra;
partners—US 53%, France 41%, Africa 4%, FRG 2% (1988)
Imports: $41 million (f.o.b., 1990 est.);
commodities—rice and other foodstuffs, cement, petroleum products, consumer goods;
partners—Europe 62% (France 22%, other 40%), Africa 5%, Pakistan, China (1988)
External debt: $223 million (December 1990 est.)
Industrial production: growth rate 3.4% (1988 est.); accounts for 5% of GDP
Electricity: 16,000 kW capacity; 24 million kWh produced, 55 kWh per capita (1989)
Industries: perfume distillation

Comoros *(continued)*

Agriculture: accounts for 40% of GDP; most of population works in subsistence agriculture and fishing; plantations produce cash crops for export—vanilla, cloves, perfume essences, and copra; principal food crops—coconuts, bananas, cassava; world's leading producer of essence of ylang-ylang (for perfumes) and second-largest producer of vanilla; large net food importer

Economic aid: US commitments, including Ex-Im (FY80-89), $10 million; Western (non-US) countries, ODA and OOF bilateral commitments (1970-88), $406 million; OPEC bilateral aid (1979-89), $22 million; Communist countries (1970-89), $18 million

Currency: Comoran franc (plural—francs); 1 Comoran franc (CF) = 100 centimes

Exchange rates: Comoran francs (CF) per US$1—256.54 (January 1991), 272.26 (1990), 319.01 (1989), 297.85 (1988), 300.54 (1987), 346.30 (1986), 449.26 (1985); note—linked to the French franc at 50 to 1 French franc

Fiscal year: calendar year

Communications

Highways: 750 km total; about 210 km bituminous, remainder crushed stone or gravel

Ports: Mutsamudu, Moroni

Civil air: 4 major transport aircraft

Airports: 4 total, 4 usable; 4 with permanent-surface runways; none with runways over 3,659 m; 1 with runways 2,440-3,659 m; 3 with runways 1,220-2,439 m

Telecommunications: sparse system of radio relay and high-frequency radio communication stations for interisland and external communications to Madagascar and Reunion; over 1,800 telephones; stations—2 AM, 1 FM, 1 TV

Defense Forces

Branches: Comoran Defense Force (FCD), Federal Gendarmerie (GFC)

Manpower availability: males 15-49, 101,332; 60,592 fit for military service

Defense expenditures: $NA, 3% of GDP (1981)

Congo

Geography

Total area: 342,000 km²; land area: 341,500 km²

Comparative area: slightly smaller than Montana

Land boundaries: 5,504 km total; Angola 201 km, Cameroon 523 km, Central African Republic 467 km, Gabon 1,903 km, Zaire 2,410 km

Coastline: 169 km

Maritime claims:

Territorial sea: 200 nm

Disputes: long section with Zaire along the Congo River is indefinite (no division of the river or its islands has been made)

Climate: tropical; rainy season (March to June); dry season (June to October); constantly high temperatures and humidity; particularly enervating climate astride the Equator

Terrain: coastal plain, southern basin, central plateau, northern basin

Natural resources: petroleum, timber, potash, lead, zinc, uranium, copper, phosphates, natural gas

Land use: arable land 2%; permanent crops NEGL%; meadows and pastures 29%; forest and woodland 62%; other 7%

Environment: deforestation; about 70% of the population lives in Brazzaville, Pointe Noire, or along the railroad between them

People

Population: 2,309,444 (July 1991), growth rate 3.0% (1991)

Birth rate: 43 births/1,000 population (1991)

Death rate: 13 deaths/1,000 population (1991)

Net migration rate: 0 migrants/1,000 population (1991)

Infant mortality rate: 108 deaths/1,000 live births (1991)

Life expectancy at birth: 52 years male, 56 years female (1991)

Total fertility rate: 5.7 children born/woman (1991)

Nationality: noun—Congolese (sing., pl.); adjective—Congolese or Congo

Ethnic divisions: about 15 ethnic groups divided into some 75 tribes, almost all Bantu; most important ethnic groups are Kongo (48%) in the south, Sangha (20%) and M'Bochi (12%) in the north, Teke (17%) in the center; about 8,500 Europeans, mostly French

Religion: Christian 50%, animist 48%, Muslim 2%

Language: French (official); many African languages with Lingala and Kikongo most widely used

Literacy: 57% (male 70%, female 44%) age 15 and over can read and write (1990 est.)

Labor force: 79,100 wage earners; agriculture 75%, commerce, industry, and government 25%; 51% of population of working age; 40% of population economically active (1985)

Organized labor: 20% of labor force (1979 est.)

Government

Long-form name: Republic of the Congo

Type: republic

Capital: Brazzaville

Administrative divisions: 9 regions (régions, singular—région); Bouenza, Cuvette, Kouilou, Lékoumou, Likouala, Niari, Plateaux, Pool, Sangha; note—there may be a new capital district of Brazzaville

Independence: 15 August 1960 (from France; formerly Congo/Brazzaville)

Constitution: 8 July 1979, currently being modified

Legal system: based on French civil law system and customary law

National holiday: National Day, 15 August (1960)

Executive branch: president, prime minister, Council of Ministers (cabinet)

Legislative branch: unicameral National People's Assembly (Assemblée Nationale Populaire)

Judicial branch: Supreme Court (Cour Suprême)

Leaders:

Chief of State—President Denis SASSOU-NGUESSO (since 8 February 1979);

Head of Government—Prime Minister Brig. Gen. Louis-Sylvain GOMA (since 9 January 1991)

Political parties and leaders: Congolese Labor Party (PCT), President Denis SASSOU-NGUESSO, leader; note—multiparty system legalized, with over 50 parties established

Suffrage: universal at age 18

Elections:
President—last held 26-31 July 1989 (next to be held July 1994); results—President SASSOU-NGUESSO unanimously reelected leader of the PCT by the Party Congress, which automatically made him president; *People's National Assembly*—last held 24 September 1989 (next to be held NA 1994); results—PCT was the only party; seats—(153 total) single list of candidates nominated by the PCT

Communists: unknown number of Communists and sympathizers

Other political or pressure groups: Union of Congolese Socialist Youth (UJSC), Congolese Trade Union Congress (CSC), Revolutionary Union of Congolese Women (URFC), General Union of Congolese Pupils and Students (UGEEC)

Member of: ACCT, ACP, AfDB, BDEAC, CCC, CEEAC, ECA, FAO, FZ, G-77, GATT, IBRD, ICAO, IDA, IFAD, IFC, ILO, IMF, IMO, INTELSAT, INTERPOL, IOC, ITU, LORCS, NAM, OAU, UDEAC, UN, UNAVEM, UNCTAD, UNESCO, UNIDO, UPU, WFTU, WHO, WIPO, WMO, WTO

Diplomatic representation: Ambassador Roger ISSOMBO; Chancery at 4891 Colorado Avenue NW, Washington DC 20011; telephone (202) 726-5500; *US*—Ambassador James Daniel PHILLIPS; Embassy at Avenue Amilcar Cabral, Brazzaville (mailing address is B. P. 1015, Brazzaville, or Box C, APO New York 09662-0006); telephone (242) 83-20-70 or 83-26-24

Flag: red with the national emblem in the upper hoist-side corner; the emblem includes a yellow five-pointed star above a crossed hoe and hammer (like the hammer and sickle design) in yellow, flanked by two curved green palm branches; uses the popular pan-African colors of Ethiopia

Economy

Overview: Oil has supplanted forestry as the mainstay of the economy, providing about two-thirds of government revenues and exports. In the early 1980s rapidly rising oil revenues enabled Congo to finance large-scale development projects with growth averaging 5% annually, one of the highest rates in Africa. The world decline in oil prices, however, has forced the government to launch an austerity program to cope with declining receipts and mounting foreign debts.

GDP: $2.26 billion, per capita $1,050; real growth rate 0.6% (1989 est.)

Inflation rate (consumer prices): 4.6% (1989 est.)

Unemployment rate: NA%

Budget: revenues $522 million; expenditures $767 million, including capital expenditures of $141 million (1989)

Exports: $751 million (f.o.b., 1988); *commodities*—crude petroleum 72%, lumber, plywood, coffee, cocoa, sugar, diamonds; *partners*—US, France, other EC

Imports: $564 million (c.i.f., 1988); *commodities*—foodstuffs, consumer goods, intermediate manufactures, capital equipment; *partners*—France, Italy, other EC, US, FRG, Spain, Japan, Brazil

External debt: $4.5 billion (December 1988)

Industrial production: growth rate 1.2% (1989); accounts for 14% of GDP

Electricity: 133,000 kW capacity; 300 million kWh produced, 130 kWh per capita (1989)

Industries: crude oil, cement, sawmills, brewery, sugar mill, palm oil, soap, cigarettes

Agriculture: accounts for 10% of GDP (including fishing and forestry); cassava accounts for 90% of food output; other crops—rice, corn, peanuts, vegetables; cash crops include coffee and cocoa; forest products important export earner; imports over 90% of food needs

Economic aid: US commitments, including Ex-Im (FY70-89), $60 million; Western (non-US) countries, ODA and OOF bilateral commitments (1970-88), $2.2 billion; OPEC bilateral aid (1979-89), $15 million; Communist countries (1970-89), $338 million

Currency: Communauté Financière Africaine franc (plural—francs); 1 CFA franc (CFAF) = 100 centimes

Exchange rates: Communauté Financière Africaine francs (CFAF) per US$1—256.54 (January 1991), 272.26 (1990), 319.01 (1989), 297.85 (1988), 300.54 (1987), 346.30 (1986), 449.26 (1985)

Fiscal year: calendar year

Communications

Railroads: 797 km, 1.067-meter gauge, single track (includes 285 km that are privately owned)

Highways: 12,000 km total; 560 km bituminous surface treated; 850 km gravel, laterite; 5,350 km improved earth; 5,240 km unimproved roads

Inland waterways: the Congo and Ubangi (Oubangui) Rivers provide 1,120 km of commercially navigable water transport; the rest are used for local traffic only

Pipelines: crude oil 25 km

Ports: Pointe-Noire (ocean port), Brazzaville (river port)

Civil air: 4 major transport aircraft

Airports: 50 total, 45 usable; 5 with permanent-surface runways; none with runways over 3,659 m; 1 with runways 2,440-3,659 m; 18 with runways 1,220-2,439 m

Telecommunications: services adequate for government use; primary network is composed of radio relay routes and coaxial cables; key centers are Brazzaville, Pointe-Noire, and Loubomo; 18,100 telephones; stations—3 AM, 1 FM, 4 TV; 1 Atlantic Ocean satellite station

Defense Forces

Branches: Army, Navy (including Marines), Air Force, paramilitary National People's Militia, National Police

Manpower availability: males 15-49, 509,040; 258,861 fit for military service; 24,068 reach military age (20) annually

Defense expenditures: $99 million, 4.6% of GDP (1987 est.)

Cook Islands
(free association with New Zealand)

Rakahanga
Penrhyn
Pukapuka
Manihiki
Nassau Island
Suwarrow

South Pacific Ocean

Palmerston
Aitutaki
Manuae
Takutea
Mitiaro
Mauke
Rarotonga
★AVARUA
Mangaia

400 km

Geography

Total area: 240 km²; land area: 240 km²
Comparative area: slightly less than 1.3 times the size of Washington, DC
Land boundaries: none
Coastline: 120 km
Maritime claims:
Continental shelf: edge of continental margin or minimum of 200 nm;
Exclusive economic zone: 200 nm;
Territorial sea: 12 nm
Climate: tropical; moderated by trade winds
Terrain: low coral atolls in north; volcanic, hilly islands in south
Natural resources: negligible
Land use: arable land 4%; permanent crops 22%; meadows and pastures 0%; forest and woodland 0%; other 74%
Environment: subject to typhoons from November to March
Note: located 4,500 km south of Hawaii in the South Pacific Ocean

People

Population: 17,882 (July 1991), growth rate 0.5% (1991)
Birth rate: 22 births/1,000 population (1991)
Death rate: 7 deaths/1,000 population (1991)
Net migration rate: −10 migrants/1,000 population (1991)
Infant mortality rate: 24 deaths/1,000 live births (1991)
Life expectancy at birth: 67 years male, 72 years female (1991)
Total fertility rate: 3.5 children born/woman (1991)
Nationality: noun—Cook Islander(s); adjective—Cook Islander
Ethnic divisions: Polynesian (full blood) 81.3%, Polynesian and European 7.7%, Polynesian and other 7.7%, European 2.4%, other 0.9%
Religion: Christian, majority of populace members of Cook Islands Christian Church

Language: English
Literacy: NA% (male NA%, female NA%)
Labor force: 5,810; agriculture 29%, government 27%, services 25%, industry 15%, and other 4% (1981)
Organized labor: NA

Government

Long-form name: none
Type: self-governing in free association with New Zealand; Cook Islands fully responsible for internal affairs; New Zealand retains responsibility for external affairs, in consultation with the Cook Islands
Capital: Avarua
Administrative divisions: none
Independence: became self-governing in free association with New Zealand on 4 August 1965 and has the right at any time to move to full independence by unilateral action
Constitution: 4 August 1965
National holiday: NA
Executive branch: British monarch, representative of the UK, representative of New Zealand, prime minister, deputy prime minister, Cabinet
Legislative branch: unicameral Parliament; note—the House of Arikis (chiefs) advises on traditional matters, but has no legislative powers
Judicial branch: High Court
Leaders:
Chief of State—Queen ELIZABETH II (since 6 February 1952); Representative of the UK Sir Tangaroa TANGAROA (since NA); Representative of New Zealand Adrian SINCOCK (since NA);
Head of Government—Prime Minister Geoffrey HENRY (since NA February 1989); Deputy Prime Minister Inatio AKARURU (since NA February 1989)
Political parties and leaders: Cook Islands Party, Geoffrey HENRY; Democratic Tumu Party, Vincent INGRAM; Democratic Party, Dr. Vincent Pupuke ROBATI; Cook Islands Labor Party, Rena JONASSEN; Cook Islands People's Party, Sadaraka SADARAKA
Suffrage: universal adult at age NA
Elections:
Parliament—last held 19 January 1989 (next to be held by January 1994); results—percent of vote by party NA; seats—(24 total) Cook Islands Party 12, Democratic Tumu Party 2, opposition coalition (including Democratic Party) 9, independent 1
Member of: AsDB, ESCAP (associate), FAO, ICAO, IOC, SPC, SPF, UNESCO, WHO
Diplomatic representation: none (self-governing in free association with New Zealand)
Flag: blue with the flag of the UK in the upper hoist-side quadrant and a large circle

of 15 white five-pointed stars (one for every island) centered in the outer half of the flag

Economy

Overview: Agriculture provides the economic base. The major export earners are fruit, copra, and clothing. Manufacturing activities are limited to a fruit-processing plant and several clothing factories. Economic development is hindered by the isolation of the islands from foreign markets and a lack of natural resources and good transportation links. A large trade deficit is annually made up for by remittances from emigrants and from foreign aid. Current economic development plans call for exploiting the tourism potential and expanding the fishing industry.
GDP: $40.0 million, per capita $2,200 (1988 est.); real growth rate 5.3% (1986-88 est.)
Inflation rate (consumer prices): 8.0% (1988)
Unemployment rate: NA%
Budget: revenues $33.8 million; expenditures $34.4 million, including capital expenditures of $NA (1990 est.)
Exports: $4.0 million (f.o.b., 1988);
commodities—copra, fresh and canned fruit, clothing;
partners—NZ 80%, Japan
Imports: $38.7 million (c.i.f., 1988);
commodities—foodstuffs, textiles, fuels, timber;
partners—NZ 49%, Japan, Australia, US
External debt: $NA
Industrial production: growth rate NA%
Electricity: 14,000 kW capacity; 21 million kWh produced, 1,170 kWh per capita (1990)
Industries: fruit processing, tourism
Agriculture: export crops—copra, citrus fruits, pineapples, tomatoes, bananas; subsistence crops—yams, taro
Economic aid: Western (non-US) countries, ODA and OOF bilateral commitments (1970-89), $128 million
Currency: New Zealand dollar (plural—dollars); 1 New Zealand dollar (NZ$) = 100 cents
Exchange rates: New Zealand dollars (NZ$) per US$1—1.6798 (January 1991), 1.6750 (1990), 1.6711 (1989), 1.5244 (1988), 1.6886 (1987), 1.9088 (1986), 2.0064 (1985)
Fiscal year: 1 April-31 March

Communications

Highways: 187 km total (1980); 35 km paved, 35 km gravel, 84 km improved earth, 33 km unimproved earth
Ports: Avatiu
Civil air: no major transport aircraft

Airports: 7 total, 6 usable; 1 with permanent-surface runways; none with runways over 2,439 m; 3 with runways 1,220-2,439 m

Telecommunications: stations—2 AM, no FM, no TV; 10,000 radio receivers; 2,052 telephones; 1 Pacific Ocean INTELSAT earth station

Defense Forces

Note: defense is the responsibility of New Zealand

Coral Sea Islands
(territory of Australia)

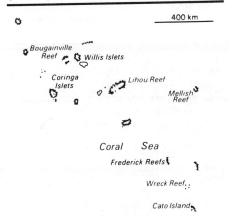

Communications

Ports: none; offshore anchorages only

Defense Forces

Note: defense is the responsibility of Australia; visited regularly by the Royal Australian Navy; Australia has control over the activities of visitors

Geography

Total area: undetermined; includes numerous small islands and reefs scattered over a sea area of about 1 million km², with Willis Islets the most important

Comparative area: undetermined

Land boundaries: none

Coastline: 3,095 km

Maritime claims:

Exclusive fishing zone: 200 nm;

Territorial sea: 3 nm

Climate: tropical

Terrain: sand and coral reefs and islands (or cays)

Natural resources: negligible

Land use: arable land 0%; permanent crops 0%; meadows and pastures 0%; forest and woodland 0%; other, mostly grass or scrub cover 100%; Lihou Reef Reserve and Coringa-Herald Reserve were declared National Nature Reserves on 3 August 1982

Environment: subject to occasional tropical cyclones; no permanent fresh water; important nesting area for birds and turtles

Note: the islands are located just off the northeast coast of Australia in the Coral Sea

People

Population: 3 meteorologists (1991)

Government

Long-form name: Coral Sea Islands Territory

Type: territory of Australia administered by the Minister for Arts, Sport, the Environment, Tourism, and Territories Roslyn KELLY

Flag: the flag of Australia is used

Economy

Overview: no economic activity

Costa Rica

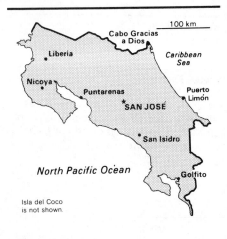

100 km

Cabo Gracias
a Dios

Liberia

Caribbean
Sea

Nicoya

Puntarenas

Puerto
Limón

SAN JOSÉ

San Isidro

North Pacific Ocean

Golfito

Isla del Coco
is not shown.

Geography

Total area: 51,100 km²; land area: 50,660
km²; includes Isla del Coco
Comparative area: slightly smaller than
West Virginia
Land boundaries: 639 km total; Nicaragua
309 km, Panama 330 km
Coastline: 1,290 km
Maritime claims:
Continental shelf: 200 nm;
Exclusive economic zone: 200 nm;
Territorial sea: 12 nm
Climate: tropical; dry season (December to
April); rainy season (May to November)
Terrain: coastal plains separated by rugged
mountains
Natural resources: hydropower potential
Land use: arable land 6%; permanent crops
7%; meadows and pastures 45%; forest and
woodland 34%; other 8%; includes irrigated
1%
Environment: subject to occasional earth-
quakes, hurricanes along Atlantic coast; frequent flooding of lowlands at onset of rainy
season; active volcanoes; deforestation; soil
erosion

People

Population: 3,111,403 (July 1991), growth
rate 2.5% (1991)
Birth rate: 27 births/1,000 population
(1991)
Death rate: 4 deaths/1,000 population
(1991)
Net migration rate: 2 migrants/1,000 population (1991)
Infant mortality rate: 15 deaths/1,000 live
births (1991)
Life expectancy at birth: 75 years male, 79
years female (1991)
Total fertility rate: 3.2 children born/wo-
man (1991)
Nationality: noun—Costa Rican(s); adjective—Costa Rican

Ethnic divisions: white (including mestizo)
96%, black 2%, Indian 1%, Chinese 1%
Religion: Roman Catholic 95%
Language: Spanish (official), English spoken
around Puerto Limón
Literacy: 93% (male 93%, female 93%) age
15 and over can read and write (1990 est.)
Labor force: 868,300; industry and commerce 35.1%, government and services
33%, agriculture 27%, other 4.9% (1985
est.)
Organized labor: 15.1% of labor force

Government

Long-form name: Republic of Costa Rica
Type: democratic republic
Capital: San José
Administrative divisions: 7 provinces (pro-
vincias, singular—provincia); Alajuela, Car-
tago, Guanacaste, Heredia, Limón, Puntar-
enas, San José
Independence: 15 September 1821 (from
Spain)
Constitution: 9 November 1949
Legal system: based on Spanish civil law
system; judicial review of legislative acts in
the Supreme Court; has not accepted com-
pulsory ICJ jurisdiction
National holiday: Independence Day, 15
September (1821)
Executive branch: president, two vice presi-
dents, Cabinet
Legislative branch: unicameral Legislative
Assembly (Asamblea Legislativa)
Judicial branch: Supreme Court (Corte
Suprema)
Leaders:
Chief of State and Head of Government—
President Rafael Angel CALDERÓN Four-
nier (since 8 May 1990); First Vice Presi-
dent German SERRANO Pinto (since 8
May 1990); Second Vice President Arnoldo
LOPEZ Echandi (since 8 May 1990)
Political parties and leaders: National Lib-
eration Party (PLN), Rolando ARAYA
Monge; Social Christian Unity Party
(PUSC), Rafael Angel CALDERÓN Four-
nier; Marxist Popular Vanguard Party
(PVP), Humberto VARGAS Carbonell;
New Republic Movement (MNR), Sergio
Erick ARDÓN Ramirez; Progressive Party
(PP), Isaac Felipe AZOFEIFA Bolaños;
People's Party of Costa Rica (PPC), Lenin
ChACON Vargas; Radical Democratic Par-
ty (PRD), Juan José ECHEVERRÍA
Brealey
Suffrage: universal and compulsory at age
18
Elections:
President—last held 4 February 1990 (next
to be held February 1994); results—Rafael
Angel CALDERÓN Fournier 51%, Carlos
Manuel CASTILLO 47%;
Legislative Assembly—last held 4 February
1990 (next to be held February 1994);

results—percent of vote by party NA;
seats—(57 total) PUSC 29, PLN 25,
PVP/PPC 1, regional parties 2
Communists: 7,500 members and
sympathizers
Other political or pressure groups: Costa
Rican Confederation of Democratic Work-
ers (CCTD; Liberation Party affiliate), Con-
federated Union of Workers (CUT; Com-
munist Party affiliate), Authentic
Confederation of Democratic Workers
(CATD; Communist Party affiliate), Cham-
ber of Coffee Growers, National Associa-
tion for Economic Development (ANFE),
Free Costa Rica Movement (MCRL;
rightwing militants), National Association
of Educators (ANDE)
Member of: AG (observer), BCIE, CACM,
ECLAC, FAO, G-77, GATT, IADB, IAEA,
IBRD, ICAO, ICFTU, IDA, IFAD, IFC,
ILO, IMF, IMO, INTELSAT, INTERPOL,
IOC, IOM, ITU, LAES, LAIA (observer),
LORCS, NAM (observer), OAS, OPANAL,
UN, UNCTAD, UNESCO, UNIDO, UPU,
WCL, WFTU, WHO, WIPO, WMO
Diplomatic representation: Ambassador
Gonzalo FACIO Segreda; Chancery at Suite
211, 1825 Connecticut Avenue NW, Wash-
ington DC 20009; telephone (202) 234-
2945 through 2947; there are Costa Rican
Consulates General at Albuquerque, Bos-
ton, Houston, Los Angeles, Miami, New
Orleans, New York, San Antonio, San Diego, San Francisco, San Juan (Puerto Rico),
and Tampa, and Consulates in Austin, Buffalo, Honolulu, and Raleigh;
US—Ambassador (vacant); Chargé d'Affaires Robert O. HOMME; Embassy at Pa-
vas Road, San Jose (mailing address is APO
Miami 34020); telephone [506] 20-39-39
Flag: five horizontal bands of blue (top),
white, red (double width), white, and blue
with the coat of arms in a white disk on the
hoist side of the red band

Economy

Overview: In 1990 the economy grew at an
estimated 3.5% rate, a decrease from the
strong 5.0% gain of the previous year. Gains
in agricultural production (on the strength
of good coffee and banana crops) and in
construction, were partially offset by lower
rates of growth for industry. In 1990 consumer prices rose by about 25% and the
trade deficit widened. Unemployment is
officially reported at 6%, but much underemployment remains. External debt, on a
per capita basis, is among the world's
highest.
GDP: $5.5 billion, per capita $1,810; real
growth rate 3.5% (1990 est.)
Inflation rate (consumer prices): 25% (1990
est.)
Unemployment rate: 6% (1990)

Budget: revenues $782 million; expenditures $917 million, including capital expenditures of $NA (1988)
Exports: $1.4 billion (f.o.b., 1990); *commodities*—coffee, bananas, textiles, sugar; *partners*—US 75%, FRG, Guatemala, Netherlands, UK, Japan
Imports: $1.8 billion (c.i.f., 1990); *commodities*—petroleum, machinery, consumer durables, chemicals, fertilizer, foodstuffs; *partners*—US 35%, Japan, Guatemala, FRG
External debt: $4.5 billion (1989)
Industrial production: growth rate 4.4% (1989); accounts for 25% of GDP
Electricity: 927,000 kW capacity; 2,987 million kWh produced, 980 kWh per capita (1990)
Industries: food processing, textiles and clothing, construction materials, fertilizer
Agriculture: accounts for 20-25% of GDP and 70% of exports; cash commodities—coffee, beef, bananas, sugar; other food crops include corn, rice, beans, potatoes; normally self-sufficient in food except for grain; depletion of forest resources resulting in lower timber output
Illicit drugs: illicit production of cannabis on small scattered plots; transshipment country for cocaine from South America
Economic aid: US commitments, including Ex-Im (FY70-89), $1.4 billion; Western (non-US) countries, ODA and OOF bilateral commitments (1970-88), $781 million; Communist countries (1971-88), $27 million
Currency: Costa Rican colón (plural—colones); 1 Costa Rican colón (C) = 100 céntimos
Exchange rates: Costa Rican colones (C) per US$1—105.82 (January 1991), 91.58 (1990), 81.504 (1989), 75.805 (1988), 62.776 (1987), 55.986 (1986), 50.453 (1985)
Fiscal year: calendar year

Communications

Railroads: 950 km total, all 1.067-meter gauge; 260 km electrified
Highways: 15,400 km total; 7,030 km paved, 7,010 km gravel, 1,360 km unimproved earth
Inland waterways: about 730 km, seasonally navigable
Pipelines: refined products, 176 km
Ports: Puerto Limon, Caldera, Golfito, Moin, Puntarenas
Merchant marine: 12 cargo ships (1,000 GRT or over) totaling 2,831 GRT/4,506 DWT
Civil air: 9 major transport aircraft

Airports: 173 total, 159 usable; 26 with permanent-surface runways; none with runways over 3,659 m; 1 with runways 2,440-3,659 m; 11 with runways 1,220-2,439 m
Telecommunications: very good domestic telephone service; 292,000 telephones; connection into Central American Microwave System; stations—71 AM, no FM, 18 TV, 13 shortwave; 1 Atlantic Ocean INTELSAT earth station

Defense Forces

Branches: Civil Guard, Rural Assistance Guard; note—Constitution prohibits armed forces
Manpower availability: males 15-49, 807,853; 545,541 fit for military service; 32,149 reach military age (18) annually
Defense expenditures: $20 million, 0.4% of GDP (1988)

Cuba

Geography

Total area: 110,860 km²; land area: 110,860 km²
Comparative area: slightly smaller than Pennsylvania
Land boundary: 29.1 km with US Naval Base at Guantánamo; note—Guantánamo is leased and as such remains part of Cuba
Coastline: 3,735 km
Maritime claims:
Exclusive economic zone: 200 nm;
Territorial sea: 12 nm
Disputes: US Naval Base at Guantánamo is leased to US and only mutual agreement or US abandonment of the area can terminate the lease
Climate: tropical; moderated by trade winds; dry season (November to April); rainy season (May to October)
Terrain: mostly flat to rolling plains with rugged hills and mountains in the southeast
Natural resources: cobalt, nickel, iron ore, copper, manganese, salt, timber, silica
Land use: arable land 23%; permanent crops 6%; meadows and pastures 23%; forest and woodland 17%; other 31%; includes irrigated 10%
Environment: averages one hurricane every other year
Note: largest country in Caribbean; 145 km south of Florida

People

Population: 10,732,037 (July 1991), growth rate 1.0% (1991)
Birth rate: 18 births/1,000 population (1991)
Death rate: 7 deaths/1,000 population (1991)
Net migration rate: −1 migrant/1,000 population (1991)
Infant mortality rate: 12 deaths/1,000 live births (1991)
Life expectancy at birth: 73 years male, 78 years female (1991)

Cuba (continued)

Total fertility rate: 1.9 children born/woman (1991)
Nationality: noun—Cuban(s); adjective—Cuban
Ethnic divisions: mulatto 51%, white 37%, black 11%, Chinese 1%
Religion: 85% nominally Roman Catholic before Castro assumed power
Language: Spanish
Literacy: 94% (male 95%, female 93%) age 15 and over can read and write (1990 est.)
Labor force: 3,578,800 in state sector; services and government 30%, industry 22%, agriculture 20%, commerce 11%, construction 10%, transportation and communications 7% (June 1990); economically active population 4,620,800 (1988)
Organized labor: Workers Central Union of Cuba (CTC), only labor federation approved by government; 2,910,000 members; the CTC is an umbrella organization composed of 17 member unions

Government

Long-form name: Republic of Cuba
Type: Communist state
Capital: Havana
Administrative divisions: 14 provinces (provincias, singular—provincia) and 1 special municipality* (municipio especial); Camagüey, Ciego de Ávila, Cienfuegos, Ciudad de La Habana, Granma, Guantánamo, Holguín, Isla de la Juventud*, La Habana, Las Tunas, Matanzas, Pinar del Río, Sancti Spíritus, Santiago de Cuba, Villa Clara
Independence: 20 May 1902 (from Spain 10 December 1898; administered by the US from 1898 to 1902)
Constitution: 24 February 1976
Legal system: based on Spanish and American law, with large elements of Communist legal theory; does not accept compulsory ICJ jurisdiction
National holiday: Revolution Day, 1 January (1959)
Executive branch: president of the Council of State, first vice president of the Council of State, Council of State, president of the Council of Ministers, first vice president of the Council of Ministers, Council of Ministers
Legislative branch: unicameral National Assembly of the People's Power (Asamblea Nacional del Poder Popular)
Judicial branch: People's Supreme Court
Leaders:
Chief of State and Head of Government—President of the Council of State and President of the Council of Ministers Fidel CASTRO Ruz (became Prime Minister in February 1959 and President since 2 December 1976); First Vice President of the Council of State and First Vice President of the Council of Ministers Gen. Raúl CASTRO Ruz (since 2 December 1976)

Political parties and leaders: only party—Cuban Communist Party (PCC), Fidel CASTRO Ruz, first secretary
Suffrage: universal at age 16
Elections:
National Assembly of the People's Power—last held NA December 1986 (next to be held December 1991); results—PCC is the only party; seats—(510 total) PCC 510 (indirectly elected)
Communists: about 600,000 full and candidate members
Member of: CCC, ECLAC, FAO, G-77, GATT, IAEA, IBEC, ICAO, IFAD, IIB, ILO, IMO, INTERPOL, IOC, ISO, ITU, LAES, LAIA (observer), LORCS, NAM, OAS (excluded from formal participation since 1962), OPANAL (observer), PCA, UN, UNCTAD, UNESCO, UNIDO, UPU, WCL, WFTU, WHO, WIPO, WMO, WTO
Diplomatic representation: none; protecting power in the US is Switzerland—Cuban Interests Section; Counselor José Antonio ARBESU Fraga; 2630 and 2639 16th Street NW, Washington DC 20009; telephone (202) 797-8518 or 8519, 8520, 8609, 8610; *US*—protecting power in Cuba is Switzerland—US Interests Section; Principal Officer Alan H. FLANIGAN; Calzada entre L y M, Vedado Seccion, Havana (mailing address is USINT, c/o International Purchasing Group, 2052 NW 93rd Avenue, Miami, FL 33172); telephone 329-700
Flag: five equal horizontal bands of blue (top and bottom) alternating with white; a red equilateral triangle based on the hoist side bears a white five-pointed star in the center

Economy

Overview: The economy, centrally planned and largely state owned, is highly dependent on the agricultural sector and foreign trade. Sugar provides about 75% of export revenues and over half is exported to the USSR. The economy has stagnated since 1985 under policies that have deemphasized material incentives in the workplace, abolished farmers' informal produce markets, and raised prices of government-supplied goods and services. In 1990 the economy probably fell 3%, largely as a result of declining trade with the Soviet Union and Eastern Europe. Recently the government has been trying to increase trade with Latin America and China. Cuba has had difficulty servicing its foreign debt since 1982. The government currently is encouraging foreign investment in tourist facilities. Other investment priorities include sugar, basic foods, and nickel. The annual $4 billion Soviet subsidy, a main prop to Cuba's threadbare economy, is likely to show a substantial decline over the next few years in view of the USSR's mounting economic problems. Instead of

highly subsidized trade, Cuba will be shifting to trade at market prices in convertible currencies. In early 1991, the shortages of fuels, spare parts, and industrial products in general had become so severe as to amount to a deindustrialization process in the eyes of some observers.
GNP: $20.9 billion, per capita $2,000; real growth rate −3% (1990 est.)
Inflation rate (consumer prices): NA%
Unemployment: 6% overall, 10% for women (1989)
Budget: revenues $12.46 billion; expenditures $14.45 billion, including capital expenditures of $NA (1990 est.)
Exports: $5.4 billion (f.o.b., 1989); *commodities*—sugar, nickel, shellfish, citrus, tobacco, coffee; *partners*—USSR 67%, GDR 6%, China 4% (1988)
Imports: $8.1 billion (c.i.f., 1989); *commodities*—capital goods, industrial raw materials, food, petroleum; *partners*—USSR 71%, other Communist countries 15% (1988)
External debt: $6.8 billion (convertible currency, July 1989)
Industrial production: 3% (1988); accounts for 45% of GDP
Electricity: 3,890,000 kW capacity; 16,267 million kWh produced, 1,530 kWh per capita (1990)
Industries: sugar milling, petroleum refining, food and tobacco processing, textiles, chemicals, paper and wood products, metals (particularly nickel), cement, fertilizers, consumer goods, agricultural machinery
Agriculture: accounts for 11% of GNP (including fishing and forestry); key commercial crops—sugarcane, tobacco, and citrus fruits; other products—coffee, rice, potatoes, meat, beans; world's largest sugar exporter; not self-sufficient in food (excluding sugar)
Economic aid: Western (non-US) countries, ODA and OOF bilateral commitments (1970-88), $695 million; Communist countries (1970-89), $18.5 billion
Currency: Cuban peso (plural—pesos); 1 Cuban peso (Cu$) = 100 centavos
Exchange rates: Cuban pesos (Cu$) per US$1—1.0000 (linked to the US dollar)
Fiscal year: calendar year

Communications

Railroads: 14,925 km total; Cuban National Railways operates 5,295 km of 1.435-meter gauge track; 199 km electrified; 9,630 km of sugar plantation lines of 0.914-1.435-meter gauge
Highways: 26,477 km total; 14,477 km paved, 12,000 km gravel and earth surfaced (1989 est.)
Inland waterways: 240 km

Cyprus

Ports: Cienfuegos, Havana, Mariel, Matanzas, Santiago de Cuba; 7 secondary, 35 minor

Merchant marine: 87 ships (1,000 GRT or over) totaling 638,462 GRT/925,380 DWT; includes 54 cargo, 9 refrigerated cargo, 2 cargo/training, 12 petroleum, oils, and lubricants (POL) tanker, 1 chemical tanker, 3 liquefied gas, 6 bulk; note—Cuba beneficially owns an additional 37 ships (1,000 GRT and over) totaling 512,346 DWT under the registry of Panama, Cyprus, and Malta

Civil air: 59 major transport aircraft

Airports: 205 total, 176 usable; 75 with permanent-surface runways; 3 with runways over 3,659 m; 12 with runways 2,440-3,659 m; 25 with runways 1,220-2,439 m

Telecommunications: stations—150 AM, 5 FM, 58 TV; 1,530,000 TVs; 2,140,000 radios; 229,000 telephones; 1 Atlantic Ocean INTELSAT earth station

Defense Forces

Branches: Revolutionary Armed Forces (including Ground Forces, Revolutionary Navy, Air and Air Defense Force), Ministry of Interior Special Troops, Border Guard Troops, Territorial Militia Troops, Youth Labor Army, Civil Defense, National Revolutionary Police

Manpower availability: eligible 15-49, 6,087,253; of the 3,054,158 males 15-49, 1,914,080 are fit for military service; of the 3,033,095 females 15-49, 1,896,449 are fit for military service; 89,194 males and 85,968 females reach military age (17) annually

Defense expenditures: $1.2-$1.4 billion, 6% of GNP (1989 est.)

Geography

Total area: 9,250 km²; land area: 9,240 km²

Comparative area: about 0.7 times the size of Connecticut

Land boundaries: none

Coastline: 648 km

Maritime claims:

Continental shelf: 200 m (depth) or to depth of exploitation;

Territorial sea: 12 nm

Disputes: 1974 hostilities divided the island into two de facto autonomous areas—a Greek area controlled by the Cypriot Government (60% of the island's land area) and a Turkish-Cypriot area (35% of the island) that are separated by a narrow UN buffer zone; in addition, there are two UK sovereign base areas (about 5% of the island's land area)

Climate: temperate, Mediterranean with hot, dry summers and cool, wet winters

Terrain: central plain with mountains to north and south

Natural resources: copper, pyrites, asbestos, gypsum, timber, salt, marble, clay earth pigment

Land use: arable land 40%; permanent crops 7%; meadows and pastures 10%; forest and woodland 18%; other 25%; includes irrigated 10% (most irrigated lands are in the Turkish-Cypriot area of the island)

Environment: moderate earthquake activity; water resource problems (no natural reservoir catchments, seasonal disparity in rainfall, and most potable resources concentrated in the Turkish-Cypriot area)

People

Population: 709,343 (July 1991), growth rate 1.0% (1991)

Birth rate: 18 births/1,000 population (1991)

Death rate: 8 deaths/1,000 population (1991)

Net migration rate: 0 migrants/1,000 population (1991)

Infant mortality rate: 10 deaths/1,000 live births (1991)

Life expectancy at birth: 73 years male, 78 years female (1991)

Total fertility rate: 2.4 children born/woman (1991)

Nationality: noun—Cypriot(s); adjective—Cypriot

Ethnic divisions: Greek 78%; Turkish 18%; other 4%

Religion: Greek Orthodox 78%, Muslim 18%, Maronite, Armenian, Apostolic, and other 4%

Language: Greek, Turkish, English

Literacy: 90% (male 96%, female 85%) age 10 and over can read and write (1976)

Labor force: Greek area—246,100; services 42%, industry 33%, agriculture 22%; Turkish area—NA (1989)

Organized labor: 156,000 (1985 est.)

Government

Long-form name: Republic of Cyprus

Type: republic; a disaggregation of the two ethnic communities inhabiting the island began after the outbreak of communal strife in 1963; this separation was further solidified following the Turkish invasion of the island in July 1974, which gave the Turkish Cypriots de facto control in the north; Greek Cypriots control the only internationally recognized government; on 15 November 1983 Turkish Cypriot President Rauf Denktash declared independence and the formation of a Turkish Republic of Northern Cyprus, which has been recognized only by Turkey; both sides publicly call for the resolution of intercommunal differences and creation of a new federal system of government

Capital: Nicosia

Administrative divisions: 6 districts; Famagusta, Kyrenia, Larnaca, Limassol, Nicosia, Paphos

Independence: 16 August 1960 (from UK)

Constitution: 16 August 1960; negotiations to create the basis for a new or revised constitution to govern the island and to better relations between Greek and Turkish Cypriots have been held intermittently; in 1975 Turkish Cypriots created their own Constitution and governing bodies within the Turkish Federated State of Cyprus, which was renamed the Turkish Republic of Northern Cyprus in 1983; a new Constitution for the Turkish area passed by referendum in May 1985

Legal system: based on common law, with civil law modifications

National holiday: Independence Day, 1 October

Cyprus (continued)

Executive branch: president, Council of Ministers (cabinet); note—there is a president, prime minister, and Council of Ministers (cabinet) in the Turkish area
Legislative branch: unicameral House of Representatives (Vouli Antiprosópon); note—there is a unicameral Assembly of the Republic (Cumhuriyet Meclisi) in the Turkish area
Judicial branch: Supreme Court; note—there is also a Supreme Court in the Turkish area
Leaders:
Chief of State and Head of Government—President George VASSILIOU (since February 1988); note—Rauf R. DENKTAŞH has been president of the Turkish area since 13 February 1975
Political parties and leaders: *Greek Cypriot*—Progressive Party of the Working People (AKEL; Communist Party), Dimitrios CHRISTOFIAS, Democratic Rally (DESY), Glafcos CLERIDES; Democratic Party (DEKO), Spyros KYPRIANOU; United Democratic Union of the Center (EDEK), Vassos LYSSARIDES; Socialist Democratic Renewal Movement (ADESOK), Pavlos DINGLIS, chairman; Liberal Party, Nikos ROLANDIS;
Turkish area—National Unity Party (UBP), Dervis EROĞLU; Communal Liberation Party (TKP), Mustafa AKINCI; Republican Turkish Party (CTP), Özker ÖZGÜR; New Cyprus Party (NKP), Alpay DURDURAN; New Dawn Party (YDP), Ali Ozkan AL-TINISHIK; Free Democratic Party, Ismet KOTAK; note—CTP, TKP, and YDP joined in the coalition Democratic Struggle Party (DMP) for the 22 April 1990 legislative election
Suffrage: universal at age 18
Elections:
President—last held 14 February and 21 February 1988 (next to be held February 1993); results—George VASSILIOU 52%, Glafcos CLERIDES 48%;
House of Representatives—last held 8 December 1985 (next to be held 19 May 1991); results—DESY 33.56%, DEKO 27.65%, AKEL (Communist) 27.43%, EDEK 11.07%; seats—(56 total) DESY 19, DEKO 16, AKEL (Communist) 15, EDEK 6;
Turkish Area: President—last held 22 April 1990 (next to be held April 1995); results—Rauf R. DENKTAŞH 66%, Ismail BOZKURT 32.05%;
Turkish Area: Assembly of the Republic—last held 6 May 1990 (next to be held May 1995); results—UBP (conservative) about 55%, DMP NA%; seats—(50 total) UBP (conservative) 34, CTP (Communist) 7, TKP (center-right) 7, New Dawn Party 2
Communists: about 12,000

Other political or pressure groups: United Democratic Youth Organization (EDON; Communist controlled); Union of Cyprus Farmers (EKA; Communist controlled); Cyprus Farmers Union (PEK; pro-West); Pan-Cyprian Labor Federation (PEO; Communist controlled); Confederation of Cypriot Workers (SEK; pro-West); Federation of Turkish Cypriot Labor Unions (Turk-Sen); Confederation of Revolutionary Labor Unions (Dev-Is)
Member of: C, CCC, CE, CSCE, EBRD, ECE, FAO, G-77, GATT, IAEA, IBRD, ICAO, ICC, ICFTU, IDA, IFAD, IFC, ILO, IMF, IMO, INTELSAT, INTERPOL, IOC, IOM, ISO, ITU, NAM, OAS (observer), UN, UNCTAD, UNESCO, UNIDO, UPU, WCL, WFTU, WHO, WIPO, WMO, WTO
Diplomatic representation: Ambassador Michael E. SHERIFIS; Chancery at 2211 R Street NW, Washington DC 20008; telephone (202) 462-5772; there is a Cypriot Consulate General in New York;
US—Ambassador Robert E. LAMB; Embassy at the corner of Therissos Street and Dositheos Street, Nicosia (mailing address is FPO New York 09530); telephone [357] (2) 4651511
Flag: white with a copper-colored silhouette of the island (the name Cyprus is derived from the Greek word for copper) above two green crossed olive branches in the center of the flag; the branches symbolize the hope for peace and reconciliation between the Greek and Turkish communities

---

Economy

Overview: These data are for the area controlled by the Republic of Cyprus (information on the northern Turkish-Cypriot area is sparse). The economy is small, diversified, and prosperous. Industry contributes about 25% to GDP and employs 35% of the labor force, while the service sector contributes about 55% to GDP and employs 40% of the labor force. Rapid growth in exports of agricultural and manufactured products and in tourism have played important roles in the average 6% rise in GDP in recent years.
GDP: $5.3 billion, per capita $7,585; real growth rate 5.0% (1990)
Inflation rate (consumer prices): 5.0% (1990)
Unemployment rate: 2.3% (1989)
Budget: revenues $1.2 billion; expenditures $1.4 billion, including capital expenditures of $178 million (1989 est.)
Exports: $770 million (f.o.b., 1990);
commodities—citrus, potatoes, grapes, wine, cement, clothing and shoes;
partners—UK 23%, Greece 10%, Lebanon 9%, Saudi Arabia 4%
Imports: $2.5 billion (f.o.b., 1990);

commodities—consumer goods, petroleum and lubricants, food and feed grains, machinery;
partners—France 12%, UK 11%, Japan 11%, Italy 10%
External debt: $2.2 billion (1990)
Industrial production: growth rate 6.5% (1988); accounts for 25% of GDP
Electricity: 620,000 kW capacity; 1,770 million kWh produced, 2,530 kWh per capita (1989)
Industries: mining (iron pyrites, gypsum, asbestos); manufactured products—beverages, footwear, clothing, and cement—are principally for local consumption
Agriculture: accounts for 7% of GDP and employs 22% of labor force; major crops—potatoes, vegetables, barley, grapes, olives, and citrus fruits; vegetables and fruit provide 25% of export revenues
Economic aid: US commitments, including Ex-Im (FY70-89), $292 million; Western (non-US) countries, ODA and OOF bilateral commitments (1970-87), $230 million; OPEC bilateral aid (1979-89), $62 million; Communist countries (1970-89), $24 million
Currency: Cypriot pound (plural—pounds) and in Turkish area, Turkish lira (plural—liras); 1 Cypriot pound (£C) = 100 cents and 1 Turkish lira (TL) = 100 kuruş
Exchange rates: Cypriot pounds (£C) per US$1—0.4325 (December 1990), 0.4572 (1990), 0.4933 (1989), 0.4663 (1988), 0.4807 (1987), 0.5167 (1986), 0.6095 (1985); in Turkish area, Turkish liras (TL) per US$1—2,873.9 (December 1990), 2,608.6 (1990), 2,121.7 (1989), 1,422.3 (1988), 857.2 (1987), 674.5 (1986), 522.0 (1985)
Fiscal year: calendar year

Communications

Highways: 10,780 km total; 5,170 km bituminous surface treated; 5,610 km gravel, crushed stone, and earth
Ports: Famagusta, Kyrenia, Larnaca, Limassol, Paphos
Merchant marine: 1,169 ships (1,000 GRT or over) totaling 19,310,063 GRT/34,338,028 DWT; 10 short-sea passenger, 2 passenger-cargo, 435 cargo, 76 refrigerated cargo, 20 roll-on/roll-off cargo, 48 container, 4 multifunction large load carrier, 111 petroleum, oils, and lubricants (POL) tanker, 2 specialized tanker, 8 liquefied gas, 17 chemical tanker, 30 combination ore/oil, 360 bulk, 2 vehicle carrier, 44 combination bulk; note—a flag of convenience registry; Cuba owns at least 25 of these ships, USSR owns 52, and Yugoslavia owns 1
Civil air: 11 major transport aircraft

Czechoslovakia

Airports: 13 total, 13 usable; 10 with permanent-surface runways; none with runways over 3,659 m; 7 with runways 2,440-3,659 m; 2 with runways 1,220-2,439 m

Telecommunications: excellent in the area controlled by the Cypriot Government (Greek area), moderately good in the Turkish-Cypriot administered area; 210,000 telephones; stations—14 AM, 7 (7 repeaters) FM, 2 (40 repeaters) TV; tropospheric scatter circuits to Greece and Turkey; 3 submarine coaxial cables; satellite earth stations—INTELSAT, 1 Atlantic Ocean and 1 Indian Ocean, and EUTELSAT systems

Defense Forces

Branches: Greek area—Greek Cypriot National Guard (GCNG; includes air and naval elements), Greek Cypriot Police; Turkish area—Turkish Cypriot Security Force

Manpower availability: males 15-49, 182,426; 125,839 fit for military service; 5,169 reach military age (18) annually

Defense expenditures: $209 million, 5% of GDP (1990 est.)

200 km

Geography

Total area: 127,870 km²; land area: 125,460 km²

Comparative area: slightly larger than New York State

Land boundaries: 3,446 km total; Austria 548 km, Germany 815 km, Hungary 676 km, Poland 1,309 km, USSR 98 km

Coastline: none—landlocked

Maritime claims: none—landlocked

Disputes: Nagymaros Dam dispute with Hungary

Climate: temperate; cool summers; cold, cloudy, humid winters

Terrain: mixture of hills and mountains separated by plains and basins

Natural resources: coal, timber, lignite, uranium, magnesite, iron ore, copper, zinc

Land use: arable land 40%; permanent crops 1%; meadows and pastures 13%; forest and woodland 37%; other 9%; includes irrigated 1%

Environment: infrequent earthquakes; acid rain; water pollution; air pollution

Note: landlocked; strategically located astride some of oldest and most significant land routes in Europe; Moravian Gate is a traditional military corridor between the North European Plain and the Danube in central Europe

People

Population: 15,724,940 (July 1991), growth rate 0.3% (1991)

Birth rate: 14 births/1,000 population (1991)

Death rate: 11 deaths/1,000 population (1991)

Net migration rate: NEGL migrants/1,000 population (1991)

Infant mortality rate: 11 deaths/1,000 live births (1991)

Life expectancy at birth: 69 years male, 77 years female (1991)

Total fertility rate: 1.9 children born/woman (1991)

Nationality: noun—Czechoslovak(s); adjective—Czechoslovak

Ethnic divisions: Czech 62.9%, Slovak 31.8%, Hungarian 3.8%, Polish 0.5%, German 0.3%, Ukrainian 0.3%, Russian 0.1%, other 0.3%

Religion: Roman Catholic 50%, Protestant 20%, Orthodox 2%, other 28%

Language: Czech and Slovak (official), Hungarian

Literacy: 99% (male NA%, female NA%) age 15 and over can read and write (1970 est.)

Labor force: 8,200,000 (1987); industry 36.9%, agriculture 12.3%, construction, communications, and other 50.8% (1982)

Organized labor: Czech and Slovak Confederation of Trade Unions (CSKOS); new independent trade unions forming

Government

Long-form name: Czech and Slovak Federal Republic; note—on 23 March 1990 the Czechoslovak Socialist Republic was renamed the Czechoslovak Federative Republic; Slovak concerns about their status in the federation prompted the Federal Assembly to approve the name Czech and Slovak Federative Republic on 20 April 1990; on 23 April 1990 the name was modified to Czech and Slovak Federal Republic

Type: federal republic in transition to a confederative republic

Capital: Prague

Administrative divisions: 2 republics (republiky, singular—republika); Czech Republic (Česká Republika), Slovak Republic (Slovenská Republika)

Independence: 28 October 1918 (from Austro-Hungarian Empire)

Constitution: 11 July 1960; amended in 1968 and 1970; new Czech, Slovak, and federal constitutions to be drafted in 1991-92

Legal system: civil law system based on Austro-Hungarian codes, modified by Communist legal theory; no judicial review of legislative acts; has not accepted compulsory ICJ jurisdiction; legal code in process of modification to bring it in line with Conference on Security and Cooperation in Europe (CSCE) obligations and to expunge Marxist-Leninist legal theory

National holiday: National Liberation Day, 9 May (1945) and Founding of the Republic, 28 October (1918)

Executive branch: president, prime minister, Cabinet

Czechoslovakia *(continued)*

Legislative branch: bicameral Federal Assembly (Federální Shromáždění) consists of an upper house or Chamber of Nations (Sněmovna Národů) and a lower house or Chamber of the People (Sněmovna Lidu)
Judicial branch: Supreme Court
Leaders:
Chief of State—President Václav HAVEL; (interim president from 29 December 1989 and president since 5 July 1990);
Head of Government—Premier Marián ČALFA (since 10 December 1989); Deputy Premier Václav VALEŠ (since 28 June 1990); Deputy Premier Jiří DIENSTBIER (since 28 June 1990); Deputy Premier Jozef MIKLOŠKO (since 28 June 1990); Deputy Premier Pavel RYCHETSKÝ (since 28 June 1990)
Political parties and leaders: Civic Forum, Václav KLAUS, chairman; Public Against Violence, Fedor GAL, chairman; Christian and Democratic Union, Václav BENDA; Christian Democratic Movement, Jan CARNOGURSKY; Communist Party of Czechoslovakia (KSČ), Pavol KANIS, chairman; KSČ toppled from power in November 1989 by massive antiregime demonstrations, minority role in coalition government since 10 December 1989
Suffrage: universal at age 18
Elections:
President—last held 5 July 1990 (next to be held July 1992); results—Václav HAVEL elected by the Federal Assembly;
Federal Assembly—last held 8-9 June 1990 (next to be held June 1992); results—Civic Forum/Public Against Violence coalition 46%, KSČ 13.6%; seats—(300 total) Civic Forum/Public Against Violence coalition 170, KSČ 47, Christian and Democratic Union/Christian Democratic Movement 40, Czech, Slovak, Moravian, and Hungarian groups 43
Communists: 760,000 party members (September 1990); about 1,000,000 members lost since November 1989
Other political or pressure groups: Czechoslovak Socialist Party, Czechoslovak People's Party, Czechoslovak Social Democracy, Slovak Nationalist Party, Slovak Revival Party, Christian Democratic Party; over 80 registered political groups fielded candidates in the 8-9 June 1990 legislative election
Member of: BIS, CCC, CSCE, ECE, FAO, GATT, IAEA, IBEC, ICAO, IIB, ILO, IMF, IMO, INMARSAT, IOC, ISO, ITU, LORCS, PCA, UN, UNAVEM, UNCTAD, UNESCO, UNIDO, UPU, WFTU, WHO, WIPO, WMO, WTO
Diplomatic representation: Ambassador Rita KLIMOVA; Chancery at 3900 Linnean Avenue NW, Washington DC 20008; telephone (202) 363-6315 or 6316;

US—Ambassador Shirley Temple BLACK; Embassy at Trziste 15, 125 48, Prague 1 (mailing address is AMEM, Box 5630, APO New York 09213-5630); telephone [42] (2) 536641 through 536649
Flag: two equal horizontal bands of white (top) and red with a blue isosceles triangle based on the hoist side

---

Economy

Overview: Czechoslovakia is highly industrialized and has a well-educated and skilled labor force. Its industry, transport, energy sources, banking, and most other means of production are state owned. The country is deficient, however, in energy and in many raw materials. Moreover, its aging capital plant lags well behind West European standards. Industry contributes over 50% to GNP and construction contributes 10%. About 95% of agricultural land is in collectives or state farms. The centrally planned economy has been tightly linked in trade (80%) to the USSR and Eastern Europe. Growth has been sluggish, averaging less than 2% in the period 1982-89. GNP per capita is the highest in Eastern Europe. As in the rest of Eastern Europe, the sweeping political changes of 1989-90 have been disrupting normal channels of supply and compounding the government's economic problems. Having eased restrictions on private enterprise in 1990 and having adjusted some key prices, Czechoslovakia is now implementing a broad two-year program to make the difficult transition from a command to a market economy. Inflation and unemployment are beginning to rise, albeit from comparatively low levels.
GNP: $120.3 billion, per capita $7,700; real growth rate −2.9% (1990 est.)
Inflation rate (consumer prices): 9% (1990 est.)
Unemployment rate: officially 0.8% (1990)
Budget: revenues $17.1 billion; expenditures $16.8 billion, including capital expenditures of $1.5 billion (1991)
Exports: $14.4 billion (f.o.b., 1989); *commodities*—machinery and equipment 42.7%; fuels, minerals, and metals 16.4%; agricultural and forestry products 12.5%, other 28.4%; *partners*—USSR, GDR, Poland, Hungary, FRG, Yugoslavia, Austria, Bulgaria, Romania, US
Imports: $14.3 billion (f.o.b., 1989); *commodities*—machinery and equipment 38.6%; fuels, minerals, and metals 24.1%; agricultural and forestry products 16.4%, other 20.9%; *partners*—USSR, GDR, Poland, Hungary, FRG, Yugoslavia, Austria, Bulgaria, Romania, US
External debt: $7.6 billion, hard currency indebtedness (September 1990)

Industrial production: growth rate −3.3% (1990 est.)
Electricity: 23,000,000 kW capacity; 90,000 million kWh produced, 5,740 kWh per capita (1990)
Industries: iron and steel, machinery and equipment, cement, sheet glass, motor vehicles, armaments, chemicals, ceramics, wood, paper products, footwear
Agriculture: accounts for 7% of GNP (includes forestry); largely self-sufficient in food production; diversified crop and livestock production, including grains, potatoes, sugar beets, hops, fruit, hogs, cattle, and poultry; exporter of forest products
Economic aid: donor—$4.2 billion in bilateral aid to non-Communist less developed countries (1954-89)
Currency: koruna (plural—koruny); 1 koruna (Kč) = 100 haléřu
Exchange rates: koruny (Kčs) per US$1— 27.65 (January 1991), 17.95 (1990), 15.05 (1989), 14.36 (1988), 13.69 (1987), 14.99 (1986), 17.14 (1985)
Fiscal year: calendar year

Communications

Railroads: 13,103 km total; 12,855 km 1.435-meter standard gauge, 102 km 1.520-meter broad gauge, 146 km 0.750- and 0.760-meter narrow gauge; 2,861 km double track; 3,798 km electrified; government owned (1988)
Highways: 73,540 km total; including 517 km superhighway (1988)
Inland waterways: 475 km (1988); the Elbe (Labe) is the principal river
Pipelines: crude oil, 1,448 km; refined products, 1,500 km; natural gas, 8,100 km
Ports: maritime outlets are in Poland (Gdynia, Gdansk, Szczecin), Yugoslavia (Rijeka, Koper), Germany (Hamburg, Rostock); principal river ports are Prague on the Vltava, Děčín on the Elbe (Labe), Komárno on the Danube, Bratislava on the Danube
Merchant marine: 24 ships (1,000 GRT or over) totaling 363,002 GRT/ 565,813 DWT; includes 15 cargo, 6 bulk
Civil air: 47 major transport aircraft
Airports: 158 total, 158 usable; 40 with permanent-surface runways; 19 with runways 2,440-3,659 m; 37 with runways 1,220-2,439 m
Telecommunications: 4 million telephones; 25% of households have a telephone; stations—60 AM, 16 FM, 39 TV (11 Soviet TV relays); 4.4 million TVs (1990)

Defense Forces

Branches: Czechoslovak People's Army, Air and Air Defense Forces, Civil Defense, Border Guard

Denmark

Manpower availability: males 15-49, 4,066,419; 3,110,958 fit for military service; 140,620 reach military age (18) annually

Defense expenditures: 26.9 billion koruny, NA% of GDP (1991); note—conversion of defense expenditures into US dollars using the official administratively set exchange rate would produce misleading results

Geography

Total area: 43,070 km²; land area: 42,370 km²; includes the island of Bornholm in the Baltic Sea and the rest of metropolitan Denmark, but excludes the Faroe Islands and Greenland

Comparative area: slightly more than twice the size of Massachusetts

Land boundaries: 68 km with Germany

Coastline: 3,379 km

Maritime claims:

Contiguous zone: 4 nm;

Continental shelf: 200 m (depth) or to depth of exploitation;

Exclusive fishing zone: 200 nm;

Territorial sea: 3 nm

Disputes: Rockall continental shelf dispute involving Iceland, Ireland, and the UK (Ireland and the UK have signed a boundary agreement in the Rockall area); Denmark has challenged Norway's maritime claims between Greenland and Jan Mayen

Climate: temperate; humid and overcast; mild, windy winters and cool summers

Terrain: low and flat to gently rolling plains

Natural resources: crude oil, natural gas, fish, salt, limestone

Land use: arable land 61%; permanent crops NEGL%; meadows and pastures 6%; forest and woodland 12%; other 21%; includes irrigated 9%

Environment: air and water pollution

Note: controls Danish Straits linking Baltic and North Seas

People

Population: 5,132,626 (July 1991), growth rate NEGL% (1991)

Birth rate: 12 births/1,000 population (1991)

Death rate: 11 deaths/1,000 population (1991)

Net migration rate: NEGL migrants/1,000 population (1991)

Infant mortality rate: 6 deaths/1,000 live births (1991)

Life expectancy at birth: 73 years male, 79 years female (1991)

Total fertility rate: 1.6 children born/woman (1991)

Nationality: noun—Dane(s); adjective—Danish

Ethnic divisions: Scandinavian, Eskimo, Faroese, German

Religion: Evangelical Lutheran 91%, other Protestant and Roman Catholic 2%, other 7% (1988)

Language: Danish, Faroese, Greenlandic (an Eskimo dialect); small German-speaking minority

Literacy: 99% (male NA%, female NA%) age 15 and over can read and write (1980 est.)

Labor force: 2,581,400; private services 36.4%; government services 30.2%; manufacturing and mining 20%; construction 6.8%; agriculture, forestry, and fishing 5.9%; electricity/gas/water 0.7% (1990)

Organized labor: 65% of labor force

Government

Long-form name: Kingdom of Denmark

Type: constitutional monarchy

Capital: Copenhagen

Administrative divisions: metropolitan Denmark—14 counties (amter, singular—amt) and 1 city* (stad); Århus, Bornholm, Frederiksborg, Fyn, København, Nordjylland, Ribe, Ringkøbing, Roskilde, Sønderjylland, Staden København*, Storstrøm, Vejle, Vestsjaelland, Viborg; note—see separate entries for the Faroe Islands and Greenland which are part of the Danish realm and self-governing administrative divisions

Independence: became a constitutional monarchy in 1849

Constitution: 5 June 1953

Legal system: civil law system; judicial review of legislative acts; accepts compulsory ICJ jurisdiction, with reservations

National holiday: Birthday of the Queen, 16 April (1940)

Executive branch: monarch, heir apparent, prime minister, Cabinet

Legislative branch: unicameral Parliament (Folketing)

Judicial branch: Supreme Court

Leaders:

Chief of State—Queen MARGRETHE II (since January 1972); Heir Apparent Crown Prince FREDERIK, elder son of the Queen (born 26 May 1968);

Head of Government—Prime Minister Poul SCHLÜTER (since 10 September 1982)

Denmark (continued)

Political parties and leaders: Social Democratic, Svend AUKEN; Conservative, Poul SCHLÜTER; Liberal, Uffe ELLEMANN-JENSEN; Socialist People's, Holger K. NIELSEN; Progress Party, Pia KJAERSGAARD; Center Democratic, Mimi Stilling JAKOBSEN; Radical Liberal, Marianne JELVED; Christian People's, Flemming KOTOED-SVENDSEN; Left Socialist, Elizabeth BRUN-OLESEN; Justice, Poul Gerhard KRISTIANSEN; Socialist Workers Party, leader NA; Communist Workers' Party (KAP), leader NA; Common Course, Preben Møller HANSEN; Green Party, Inger BORLEHMANN
Suffrage: universal at age 21
Elections:
Parliament—last held 12 December 1990 (next to be held by December 1994); results—Social Democratic 37.4%, Conservative 16.0%, Liberal 15.8%, Socialist People's 8.3%, Progress Party 6.4%, Center Democratic 5.1%, Radical Liberal 3.5%, Christian People's 2.3%, other 5.2%; seats—(175 total; includes 2 from Greenland and 2 from the Faroe Islands) Social Democratic 69, Conservative 30, Liberal 29, Socialist People's 15, Progress Party 12, Center Democratic 9, Radical Liberal 7, Christian People's 4
Member of: AfDB, AG (observer), AsDB, BIS, CCC, CE, CERN, COCOM, CSCE, EBRD, EC, ECE, EIB, ESA, FAO, G-9, GATT, IADB, IAEA, IBRD, ICAO, ICC, ICFTU, IDA, IEA, IFAD, IFC, ILO, IMF, IMO, INMARSAT, INTELSAT, INTERPOL, IOC, IOM, ISO, ITU, LORCS, NATO, NC, NEA, NIB, OECD, PCA, UN, UNCTAD, UNESCO, UNFICYP, UNHCR, UNIDO, UNIIMOG, UNMOGIP, UNTSO, UPU, WHO, WIPO, WMO
Diplomatic representation: Ambassador Peter Pedersen DYVIG; Chancery at 3200 Whitehaven Street NW, Washington DC 20008; telephone (202) 234-4300; there are Danish Consulates General at Chicago, Houston, Los Angeles, and New York; *US*—Ambassador Keith L. BROWN; Embassy at Dag Hammarskjolds Alle 24, 2100 Copenhagen O (mailing address is APO New York 09170); telephone [45] (31) 42 31 44
Flag: red with a white cross that extends to the edges of the flag; the vertical part of the cross is shifted to the hoist side and that design element of the *Dannebrog* (Danish flag) was subsequently adopted by the other Nordic countries of Finland, Iceland, Norway, and Sweden

Economy

Overview: This modern economy features high-tech agriculture, up-to-date small-scale and corporate industry, extensive government welfare measures, comfortable living standards, and high dependence on foreign trade. The Danish economy is likely to maintain its slow but steady improvement in 1991. GDP grew by 1.3% in 1990 and probably will grow by about 1.25% in 1991; unemployment is running close to 10%. In 1990 Denmark had the lowest inflation rate in the EC, a record trade surplus, and the first balance-of-payments surplus in 26 years. As the government prepares for the economic integration of Europe during 1992, growth, investment, and competitiveness are expected to improve, reducing unemployment, inflation, and debt.
GDP: $78.0 billion, per capita $15,200; real growth rate 1.3% (1990)
Inflation rate (consumer prices): 2.7% (1990)
Unemployment rate: 9.5% (1990)
Budget: revenues $62.5 billion; expenditures $60 billion, including capital expenditures of $NA billion (1989)
Exports: $34.8 billion (f.o.b., 1990); *commodities*—meat and meat products, dairy products, transport equipment, fish, chemicals, industrial machinery; *partners*—EC 52.2% (Germany 19.5%, UK 10.9%, France 6.1%), Sweden 12.5%, Norway 5.8%, US 5.0%, Japan 4.3% (1990)
Imports: $31.6 billion (c.i.f., 1990); *commodities*—petroleum, machinery and equipment, chemicals, grain and foodstuffs, textiles, paper; *partners*—EC 57% (Germany 25.6%, UK 8.4%), Sweden 12.7%, US 6.7% (1990)
External debt: $45 billion (1990)
Industrial production: growth rate 2.1% (1989)
Electricity: 11,215,000 kW capacity; 30,910 million kWh produced, 6,030 kWh per capita (1989)
Industries: food processing, machinery and equipment, textiles and clothing, chemical products, electronics, construction, furniture, and other wood products
Agriculture: accounts for 5% of GNP and employs 6% of labor force (includes fishing and forestry); farm products account for nearly 15% of export revenues; principal products—meat, dairy, grain, potatoes, rape, sugar beets, fish; self-sufficient in food production
Economic aid: donor—ODA and OOF commitments (1970-87) $5.6 billion
Currency: Danish krone (plural—kroner); 1 Danish krone (DKr) = 100 øre

Exchange rates: Danish kroner (DKr) per US$1—5.817 (January (1991), 6.189 (1990), 7.310 (1989), 6.732 (1988), 6.840 (1987), 8.091 (1986), 10.596 (1985)
Fiscal year: calendar year

Communications

Railroads: 2,675 km 1.435-meter standard gauge; Danish State Railways (DSB) operate 2,025 km (1,999 km rail line and 121 km rail ferry services); 188 km electrified, 730 km double tracked; 650 km of standard-gauge lines are privately owned and operated
Highways: 66,482 km total; 64,551 km concrete, bitumen, or stone block; 1,931 km gravel, crushed stone, improved earth
Inland waterways: 417 km
Pipelines: crude oil, 110 km; refined products, 578 km; natural gas, 700 km
Ports: Ålborg, Århus, Copenhagen, Esbjerg, Fredericia; numerous secondary and minor ports
Merchant marine: 281 ships (1,000 GRT or over) totaling 4,888,064 GRT/7,131,949 DWT; includes 13 short-sea passenger, 85 cargo, 15 refrigerated cargo, 35 container, 40 roll-on/roll-off cargo, 1 railcar carrier, 37 petroleum, oils, and lubricants (POL) tanker, 14 chemical tanker, 22 liquefied gas, 4 livestock carrier, 14 bulk, 1 combination bulk; note—Denmark has created its own internal register, called the Danish International Ship Register (DIS); DIS ships do not have to meet Danish manning regulations, and they amount to a flag of convenience within the Danish register; by the end of 1990, 258 of the Danish-flag ships belonged to the DIS
Civil air: 69 major transport aircraft
Airports: 129 total, 112 usable; 27 with permanent-surface runways; none with runways over 3,659 m; 9 with runways 2,440-3,659 m; 7 with runways 1,220-2,439 m
Telecommunications: excellent telephone, telegraph, and broadcast services; 4,509,000 telephones; stations—2 AM, 15 (39 repeaters) FM, 27 (25 repeaters) TV; 7 submarine coaxial cables; 1 earth station operating in INTELSAT, 4 Atlantic Ocean, EUTELSAT, and domestic systems

Defense Forces

Branches: Royal Danish Army, Royal Danish Navy, Royal Danish Air Force
Manpower availability: males 15-49, 1,369,684; 1,179,991 fit for military service; 36,991 reach military age (20) annually
Defense expenditures: $2.4 billion, 2% of GDP (1990)

Djibouti

Geography

Total area: 22,000 km²; land area: 21,980 km²

Comparative area: slightly larger than Massachusetts

Land boundaries: 517 km total; Ethiopia 459 km, Somalia 58 km

Coastline: 314 km

Maritime claims:

Contiguous zone: 24 nm;

Exclusive economic zone: 200 nm;

Territorial sea: 12 nm

Disputes: possible claim by Somalia based on unification of ethnic Somalis

Climate: desert; torrid, dry

Terrain: coastal plain and plateau separated by central mountains

Natural resources: geothermal areas

Land use: arable land 0%; permanent crops 0%; meadows and pastures 9%; forest and woodland NEGL%; other 91%

Environment: vast wasteland

Note: strategic location near world's busiest shipping lanes and close to Arabian oilfields; terminus of rail traffic into Ethiopia

People

Population: 346,311 (July 1991), growth rate 2.6% (1991)

Birth rate: 43 births/1,000 population (1991)

Death rate: 16 deaths/1,000 population (1991)

Net migration rate: 0 migrants/1,000 population (1991)

Infant mortality rate: 117 deaths/1,000 live births (1991)

Life expectancy at birth: 46 years male, 50 years female (1991)

Total fertility rate: 6.4 children born/woman (1991)

Nationality: noun—Djiboutian(s); adjective—Djiboutian

Ethnic divisions: Somali (Issa) 60%, Afar 35%, French, Arab, Ethiopian, and Italian 5%

Religion: Muslim 94%, Christian 6%

Language: French and Arabic (both official); Somali and Afar widely used

Literacy: 48% (male 63%, female 34%) age 15 and over can read and write (1990 est.)

Labor force: NA, but a small number of semiskilled laborers at the port and 3,000 railway workers; 52% of population of working age (1983)

Organized labor: 3,000 railway workers

Government

Long-form name: Republic of Djibouti

Type: republic

Capital: Djibouti

Administrative divisions: 5 districts (cercles, singular—cercle); 'Ali Sabîh, Dikhil, Djibouti, Obock, Tadjoura

Independence: 27 June 1977 (from France; formerly French Territory of the Afars and Issas)

Constitution: partial constitution ratified January 1981 by the National Assembly

Legal system: based on French civil law system, traditional practices, and Islamic law

National holiday: Independence Day, 27 June (1977)

Executive branch: president, prime minister, Council of Ministers

Legislative branch: National Assembly (Assemblée Nationale)

Judicial branch: Supreme Court (Cour Suprême)

Leaders:

Chief of State—President Hassan GOULED Aptidon (since 24 June 1977);

Head of Government—Prime Minister BARKAT Gourad Hamadou (since 30 September 1978)

Political parties and leaders: only party—People's Progress Assembly (RPP), Hassan GOULED Aptidon

Suffrage: universal adult at age NA

Elections:

President—last held 24 April 1987 (next to be held April 1993); results—President Hassan GOULED Aptidon was reelected without opposition;

National Assembly—last held 24 April 1987 (next to be held April 1992); results—RPP is the only party; seats—(65 total) RPP 65

Communists: NA

Member of: ACCT, ACP, AfDB, AFESD, AL, ECA, FAO, G-77, IBRD, ICAO, IDA, IDB, IFAD, IFC, IGADD, ILO, IMF, IMO, INTERPOL, IOC, ITU, LORCS, NAM, OAU, OIC, UN, UNESCO, UNCTAD, UPU, WHO, WMO

Diplomatic representation: Ambassador Roble OLHAYE; Chancery (temporary) at the Djiboutian Permanent Mission to the UN; 866 United Nations Plaza, Suite 4011, New York, NY 10017; telephone (212) 753-3163;

US—Ambassador Robert S. BARRETT IV; Embassy at Villa Plateau du Serpent, Boulevard Marechal Joffre, Djibouti (mailing address is B. P. 185, Djibouti); telephone [253] 35-39-95

Flag: two equal horizontal bands of light blue (top) and light green with a white isosceles triangle based on the hoist side bearing a red five-pointed star in the center

Economy

Overview: The economy is based on service activities connected with the country's strategic location and status as a free trade zone in northeast Africa. Djibouti provides services as both a transit port for the region and an international transshipment and refueling center. It has few natural resources and little industry. The nation is, therefore, heavily dependent on foreign assistance to help support its balance of payments and to finance development projects. An unemployment rate of over 40% continues to be a major problem. Per capita consumption dropped an estimated 35% over the last five years with a population growth rate of 6% (including immigrants and refugees) and a recession.

GDP: $340 million, $1,030 per capita; real growth rate -1.0% (1989 est.)

Inflation rate (consumer prices): 3.7% (1989)

Unemployment rate: over 40% (1989)

Budget: revenues $131 million; expenditures $154 million, including capital expenditures of $25 million (1990 est.)

Exports: $190 million (f.o.b., 1990 est.);

commodities—hides and skins, coffee (in transit);

partners—Middle East 50%, Africa 43%, Western Europe 7%

Imports: $311 million (f.o.b., 1990 est.);

commodities—foods, beverages, transport equipment, chemicals, petroleum products;

partners—EC 36%, Africa 21%, Asia 12%, US 2%

External debt: $355 million (December 1990)

Industrial production: growth rate 0.1% (1989); manufacturing accounts for 4% of GDP

Electricity: 110,000 kW capacity; 190 million kWh produced, 580 kWh per capita (1989)

Industries: limited to a few small-scale enterprises, such as dairy products and mineral-water bottling

Djibouti (continued)

Agriculture: accounts for only 5% of GDP; scanty rainfall limits crop production to mostly fruit and vegetables; half of population pastoral nomads herding goats, sheep, and camels; imports bulk of food needs
Economic aid: US commitments, including Ex-Im (FY78-89), $39 million; Western (non-US) countries, including ODA and OOF bilateral commitments (1970-88), $1,035 million; OPEC bilateral aid (1979-89), $149 million; Communist countries (1970-89), $35 million
Currency: Djiboutian franc (plural—francs); 1 Djiboutian franc (DF) = 100 centimes
Exchange rates: Djiboutian francs (DF) per US$1—177.721 (fixed rate since 1973)
Fiscal year: calendar year

Communications

Railroads: the Ethiopian-Djibouti railroad extends for 97 km through Djibouti
Highways: 2,900 km total; 280 km bituminous surface, 2,620 km improved or unimproved earth (1982)
Ports: Djibouti
Civil air: 2 major transport aircraft
Airports: 13 total, 10 usable; 2 with permanent-surface runways; none with runways over 3,659 m; 2 with runways 2,440-3,659 m; 4 with runways 1,220-2,439 m
Telecommunications: fair system of urban facilities in Djibouti and radio relay stations at outlying places; 7,300 telephones; stations—2 AM, 1 FM, 2 TV; 1 Indian Ocean INTELSAT earth station and 1 ARABSAT; 1 submarine cable to Saudi Arabia

Defense Forces

Branches: Army, (including Navy and Air Force), paramilitary National Security Force, National Police Force
Manpower availability: males 15-49, 89,519; 52,093 fit for military service
Defense expenditures: $29.9 million, NA% of GDP (1986)

Dominica

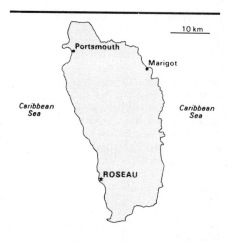

Geography

Total area: 750 km²; land area: 750 km²
Comparative area: slightly more than four times the size of Washington, DC
Land boundaries: none
Coastline: 148 km
Maritime claims:
Contiguous zone: 24 nm;
Exclusive economic zone: 200 nm;
Territorial sea: 12 nm
Climate: tropical; moderated by northeast trade winds; heavy rainfall
Terrain: rugged mountains of volcanic origin
Natural resources: timber
Land use: arable land 9%; permanent crops 13%; meadows and pastures 3%; forest and woodland 41%; other 34%
Environment: flash floods a constant hazard; occasional hurricanes
Note: located 550 km southeast of Puerto Rico in the Caribbean Sea

People

Population: 86,285 (July 1991), growth rate 1.7% (1991)
Birth rate: 26 births/1,000 population (1991)
Death rate: 5 deaths/1,000 population (1991)
Net migration rate: –3 migrants/1,000 population (1991)
Infant mortality rate: 13 deaths/1,000 live births (1991)
Life expectancy at birth: 73 years male, 79 years female (1991)
Total fertility rate: 2.6 children born/woman (1991)
Nationality: noun—Dominican(s); adjective—Dominican
Ethnic divisions: mostly black; some Carib indians
Religion: Roman Catholic 77%, Protestant 15% (Methodist 5%, Pentecostal 3%, Seventh-Day Adventist 3%, Baptist 2%, other 2%), none 2%, unknown 1%, other 5%

Language: English (official); French patois widely spoken
Literacy: 94% (male 94%, female 94%) age 15 and over having ever attended school (1970)
Labor force: 25,000; agriculture 40%, industry and commerce 32%, services 28% (1984) and over having ever %, industry an Commonwealth of Dominica
Organized labor: 25% of labor force

Government

Long-form name: Commonwealth of Dominica
Type: parliamentary democracy
Capital: Roseau
Administrative divisions: 10 parishes; Saint Andrew, Saint David, Saint George, Saint John, Saint Joseph, Saint Luke, Saint Mark, Saint Patrick, Saint Paul, Saint Peter
Independence: 3 November 1978 (from UK)
Constitution: 3 November 1978
Legal system: based on English common law
National holiday: Independence Day, 3 November (1978)
Executive branch: president, prime minister, Cabinet
Legislative branch: unicameral House of Assembly
Judicial branch: Eastern Caribbean Supreme Court
Leaders:
Chief of State—President Sir Clarence Augustus SEIGNORET (since 19 December 1983);
Head of Government—Prime Minister (Mary) Eugenia CHARLES (since 21 July 1980, elected for a third term 28 May 1990)
Political parties and leaders: Dominica Freedom Party (DFP), (Mary) Eugenia CHARLES; Dominica Labor Party (DLP), Michael DOUGLAS; United Workers Party (UWP), Edison JAMES
Suffrage: universal at age 18
Elections:
President—last held 20 December 1988 (next to be held December 1993); the president is elected by the House of Assembly;
House of Assembly—last held 28 May 1990 (next to be held May 1995); results—percent of vote by party NA; seats—(30 total; 9 appointed senators and 21 elected representatives) DFP 11, UWP 6, DLP 4
Communists: negligible
Other political or pressure groups: Dominica Liberation Movement (DLM), a small leftist group
Member of: ACCT, ACP, C, CARICOM, CDB, ECLAC, FAO, G-77, IBRD, ICFTU, IDA, IFAD, IFC, ILO, IMF, IMO, INTERPOL, LORCS, NAM (observer), OAS, OECS, UN, UNCTAD, UNESCO, UNIDO, UPU, WCL, WHO, WMO
Diplomatic representation: there is no Chancery in the US;

US—no official presence since the Ambassador resides in Bridgetown (Barbados), but travels frequently to Dominica

Flag: green with a centered cross of three equal bands—the vertical part is yellow (hoist side), black, and white—the horizontal part is yellow (top), black, and white; superimposed in the center of the cross is a red disk bearing a sisserou parrot encircled by 10 green five-pointed stars edged in yellow; the 10 stars represent the 10 administrative divisions (parishes)

Economy

Overview: The economy is dependent on agriculture and thus is highly vulnerable to climatic conditions. Agriculture accounts for about 30% of GDP and employs 40% of the labor force. Principal products include bananas, citrus, mangoes, root crops, and coconuts. In 1988 the economy achieved a 5.6% growth in real GDP on the strength of a boost in construction, higher agricultural production, and growth of the small manufacturing sector based on the soap and garment industries. In 1989, however, Hurricane Hugo wiped out 70% of the banana crop and affected other economic activity. The tourist industry remains undeveloped because of a rugged coastline and the lack of an international-class airport.

GDP: $153 million, per capita $1,840; real growth rate −1.7% (1989 est.)

Inflation rate (consumer prices): 6.3% (1989)

Unemployment rate: 10% (1989 est.)

Budget: revenues $48 million; expenditures $85 million, including capital expenditures of $41 million (FY90)

Exports: $59 million (f.o.b., 1990);
commodities—bananas, coconuts, grapefruit, soap, galvanized sheets;
partners—UK 72%, Jamaica 10%, OECS 6%, US 3%, other 9%

Imports: $115 million (c.i.f., 1990);
commodities—food, oils and fats, chemicals, fuels and lubricants, manufactured goods, machinery and equipment;
partners—US 23%, UK 18%, CARICOM 15%, OECS 15%, Japan 5%, Canada 3%, other 21%

External debt: $73 million (1990 est.)

Industrial production: growth rate 4.5% in manufacturing (1988 est.); accounts for 11% of GDP

Electricity: 7,000 kW capacity; 16 million kWh produced, 190 kWh per capita (1990)

Industries: agricultural processing, tourism, soap and other coconut-based products, cigars, pumice mining

Agriculture: accounts for 30% of GDP; principal crops—bananas, citrus, mangoes, root crops, and coconuts; bananas provide the bulk of export earnings; forestry and fisheries potential not exploited

Economic aid: Western (non-US) countries, ODA and OOF bilateral commitments (1970-88), $115 million

Currency: East Caribbean dollar (plural—dollars); 1 EC dollar (EC$) = 100 cents

Exchange rates: East Caribbean dollars (EC$) per US$1—2.70 (fixed rate since 1976)

Fiscal year: 1 July-30 June

Communications

Highways: 750 km total; 370 km paved, 380 km gravel and earth

Ports: Roseau, Portsmouth

Civil air: NA

Airports: 2 total, 2 usable; 2 with permanent-surface runways; none with runways over 2,439 m; 1 with runways 1,220-2,439 m

Telecommunications: 4,600 telephones in fully automatic network; VHF and UHF link to Saint Lucia; new SHF links to Martinique and Guadeloupe; stations—3 AM, 2 FM, 1 cable TV

Defense Forces

Branches: Commonwealth of Dominica Police Force

Manpower availability: NA

Defense expenditures: $NA, NA% of GDP

Dominican Republic

Geography

Total area: 48,730 km²; land area: 48,380 km²

Comparative area: slightly more than twice the size of New Hampshire

Land boundary 275 km with Haiti

Coastline: 1,288 km

Maritime claims:
Contiguous zone: 24 nm;
Continental shelf: outer edge of continental margin or 200 m;
Exclusive economic zone: 200 nm;
Territorial sea: 6 nm

Climate: tropical maritime; little seasonal temperature variation

Terrain: rugged highlands and mountains with fertile valleys interspersed

Natural resources: nickel, bauxite, gold, silver

Land use: arable land 23%; permanent crops 7%; meadows and pastures 43%; forest and woodland 13%; other 14%; includes irrigated 4%

Environment: subject to occasional hurricanes (July to October); deforestation

Note: shares island of Hispaniola with Haiti (western one-third is Haiti, eastern two-thirds is the Dominican Republic)

People

Population: 7,384,837 (July 1991), growth rate 2.0% (1991)

Birth rate: 27 births/1,000 population (1991)

Death rate: 7 deaths/1,000 population (1991)

Net migration rate: −1 migrant/1,000 population (1991)

Infant mortality rate: 60 deaths/1,000 live births (1991)

Life expectancy at birth: 65 years male, 69 years female (1991)

Total fertility rate: 3.1 children born/woman (1991)

Nationality: noun—Dominican(s); adjective—Dominican

Dominican Republic *(continued)*

Ethnic divisions: mixed 73%, white 16%, black 11%
Religion: Roman Catholic 95%
Language: Spanish
Literacy: 83% (male 85%, female 82%) age 15 and over can read and write (1990 est.)
Labor force: 2,300,000-2,600,000; agriculture 49%, services 33%, industry 18% (1986)
Organized labor: 12% of labor force (1989 est.)

Government

Long-form name: Dominican Republic (no short-form name)
Type: republic
Capital: Santo Domingo
Administrative divisions: 29 provinces (provincias, singular—provincia) and 1 district* (distrito); Azua, Baoruco, Barahona, Dajabón, Distrito Nacional*, Duarte, Elías Piña, El Seíbo, Espaillat, Hato Mayor, Independencia, La Altagracia, La Romana, La Vega, María Trinidad Sánchez, Monseñor Nouel, Monte Cristi, Monte Plata, Pedernales, Peravia, Puerto Plata, Salcedo, Samaná, Sánchez Ramírez, San Cristóbal, San Juan, San Pedro De Macorís, Santiago, Santiago Rodríguez, Valverde
Independence: 27 February 1844 (from Haiti)
Constitution: 28 November 1966
Legal system: based on French civil codes
National holiday: Independence Day, 27 February (1844)
Executive branch: president, vice president, Cabinet
Legislative branch: bicameral National Congress (Congreso Nacional) consists of an upper chamber or Senate (Senado) and lower chamber or Chamber of Deputies (Cámara de Diputados)
Judicial branch: Supreme Court (Corte Suprema)
Leaders:
Chief of State and Head of Government— President Joaquín BALAGUER Ricardo (since 16 August 1986, fifth elected term began 16 August 1990); Vice President Carlos A. MORALES Troncoso (since 16 August 1986)
Political parties and leaders:
Major parties— Social Christian Reformist Party (PRSC), Joaquín BALAGUER Ricardo; Dominican Revolutionary Party (PRD), José Francisco PEÑA Gómez; Dominican Liberation Party (PLD), Juan BOSCH Gaviño; Independent Revolutionary Party (PRI), Jacobo MAJLUTA;
Minor parties— National Veterans and Civilian Party (PNVC), Juan Rene BEAUCHAMPS Javier; Liberal Party of the Dominican Republic (PLRD), Andres Van Der HORST; Democratic Quisqueyan Party

(PQD), Elías WESSÍN Chavez; Constitutional Action Party (PAC), Luis ARZENO Rodríguez; National Progressive Force (FNP), Marino VINICIO Castillo; Popular Christian Party (PPC), Rogelio DELGADO Bogaert; Dominican Communist Party (PCD), Narciso ISA Conde; Anti-Imperialist Patriotic Union (UPA), Iván RODRÍGUEZ;
note—in 1983 several leftist parties, including the PCD, joined to form the Dominican Leftist Front (FID); however, they still retain individual party structures
Suffrage: universal and compulsory at age 18 or if married; members of the armed forces and police cannot vote
Elections:
*President—*last held 16 May 1990 (next to be held May 1994); results—Joaquín BALAGUER (PRSC) 35.7%, Juan BOSCH Gaviño (PLD) 34.4%;
*Senate—*last held 16 May 1990 (next to be held May 1994); results—percent of vote by party NA; seats—(30 total) PRSC 16, PLD 12, PRD 2;
*Chamber of Deputies—*last held 16 May 1990 (next to be held May 1994); results—percent of vote by party NA; seats—(120 total) PLD 44, PRSC 41, PRD 33, PRI 2
Communists: an estimated 8,000 to 10,000 members in several legal and illegal factions; effectiveness limited by ideological differences, organizational inadequacies, and severe funding shortages
Member of: CARICOM (observer), ECLAC, FAO, G-11, G-77, GATT, IADB, IAEA, IBRD, ICAO, ICFTU, IDA, IFAD, IFC, ILO, IMF, IMO, INTELSAT, INTERPOL, IOC, IOM, ITU, LAES, LAIA (observer), LORCS, NAM (guest), OAS, OPANAL, PCA, UN, UNCTAD, UNESCO, UNIDO, UPU, WCL, WFTU, WHO, WMO, WTO
Diplomatic representation: Ambassador Carlos A. MORALES Troncoso (serves concurrently as Vice President); Chancery at 1715 22nd Street NW, Washington DC 20008; telephone (202) 332-6280; there are Dominican Consulates General in Boston, Chicago, Los Angeles, Mayaguez (Puerto Rico), Miami, New Orleans, New York, Philadelphia, San Juan (Puerto Rico), and Consulates in Charlotte Amalie (Virgin Islands), Detroit, Houston, Jacksonville, Minneapolis, Mobile, Ponce (Puerto Rico), and San Francisco;
*US—*Ambassador Paul D. TAYLOR; Embassy at the corner of Calle César Nicolás Penson and Calle Leopoldo Navarro, Santo Domingo (mailing address is APO Miami 34041-0008); telephone [809] 541-2171
Flag: a centered white cross that extends to the edges, divides the flag into four rectangles—the top ones are blue (hoist side) and red, the bottom ones are red (hoist side) and blue; a small coat of arms is at the center of the cross

---

Economy

Overview: The economy is largely dependent on trade; imported components average 60% of the value of goods consumed in the domestic market. Rapid growth of free trade zones has established a significant expansion of manufacturing for export, especially wearing apparel. Over the past decade tourism has also increased in importance and is a major earner of foreign exchange and a source of new jobs. Agriculture remains a key sector of the economy. The principal commercial crop is sugarcane, followed by coffee, cotton, cocoa, and tobacco. Domestic industry is based on the processing of agricultural products, durable consumer goods, minerals, and chemicals. Unemployment is officially reported at about 30%, but there is considerable underemployment. An increasing foreign debt burden and galloping inflation are the economy's greatest weaknesses.
GDP: $6.68 billion, per capita $940; real growth rate 4.2% (1989)
Inflation rate (consumer prices): 70% (1990 est.)
Unemployment rate: 29% (1990 est.)
Budget: revenues $413 million; expenditures $522 million, including capital expenditures of $218 million (1988)
Exports: $922 million (f.o.b., 1990 est.);
commodities—sugar, coffee, cocoa, gold, ferronickel;
partners—US 63%
Imports: $1.9 billion (c.i.f., 1990 est.);
commodities—foodstuffs, petroleum, cotton and fabrics, chemicals and pharmaceuticals;
partners—US 50%
External debt: $4.2 billion (1990 est.)
Industrial production: growth rate 2.3% (1989 est.); accounts for 22% of GDP
Electricity: 1,445,000 kW capacity; 4,200 million kWh produced, 580 kWh per capita (1990)
Industries: tourism, sugar processing, ferronickel and gold mining, textiles, cement, tobacco
Agriculture: accounts for 15% of GDP and employs 49% of labor force; sugarcane most important commercial crop, followed by coffee, cotton, cocoa, and tobacco; food crops—rice, beans, potatoes, corn, bananas; animal output—cattle, hogs, dairy products, meat, eggs; not self-sufficient in food
Economic aid: US commitments, including Ex-Im (FY85-89), $576.5 million; Western (non-US) countries, ODA and OOF bilateral commitments (1970-88), $569 million
Currency: Dominican peso (plural—pesos); 1 Dominican peso (RD$) = 100 centavos

Ecuador

Exchange rates: Dominican pesos per US$1—11.850 (January 1991), 8.290 (1990), 6.3400 (1989), 6.1125 (1988), 3.8448 (1987), 2.9043 (1986), 3.1126 (1985)
Fiscal year: calendar year

Communications

Railroads: 1,655 km total in numerous segments; 4 different gauges from 0.558 m to 1.435 m
Highways: 12,000 km total; 5,800 km paved, 5,600 km gravel and improved earth, 600 km unimproved
Pipelines: crude oil, 96 km; refined products, 8 km
Ports: Santo Domingo, Haina, San Pedro de Macoris, Puerto Plata
Merchant marine: 4 cargo ships (1,000 GRT or over) totaling 23,326 GRT/38,661 DWT
Civil air: 14 major transport aircraft
Airports: 44 total, 30 usable; 14 with permanent-surface runways; none with runways over 3,659 m; 3 with runways 2,440-3,659 m; 9 with runways 1,220-2,439 m
Telecommunications: relatively efficient domestic system based on islandwide radio relay network; 190,000 telephones; stations—120 AM, no FM, 18 TV, 6 shortwave; 1 coaxial submarine cable; 1 Atlantic Ocean INTELSAT earth station

Defense Forces

Branches: Army, Navy, Air Force, National Police
Manpower availability: males 15-49, 1,963,260; 1,241,370 fit for military service; 81,083 reach military age (18) annually
Defense expenditures: $70 million, 1% of GDP (1990)

Galapagos Islands

Geography

Total area: 283,560 km²; land area: 276,840 km²; includes Galapagos Islands
Comparative area: slightly smaller than Nevada
Land boundaries: 2,010 km total; Colombia 590 km, Peru 1,420 km
Coastline: 2,237 km
Maritime claims:
Continental shelf: claims continental shelf between mainland and Galapagos Islands;
Territorial sea: 200 nm
Disputes: two sections of the boundary with Peru are in dispute
Climate: tropical along coast becoming cooler inland
Terrain: coastal plain (Costa), inter-Andean central highlands (Sierra), and flat to rolling eastern jungle (Oriente)
Natural resources: petroleum, fish, timber
Land use: arable land 6%; permanent crops 3%; meadows and pastures 17%; forest and woodland 51%; other 23% ; includes irrigated 2%
Environment: subject to frequent earthquakes, landslides, volcanic activity; deforestation; desertification; soil erosion; periodic droughts
Note: Cotopaxi in Andes is highest active volcano in world

People

Population: 10,751,648 (July 1991), growth rate 2.3% (1991)
Birth rate: 30 births/1,000 population (1991)
Death rate: 7 deaths/1,000 population (1991)
Net migration rate: 0 migrants/1,000 population (1991)
Infant mortality rate: 60 deaths/1,000 live births (1991)
Life expectancy at birth: 64 years male, 68 years female (1991)

Total fertility rate: 3.7 children born/woman (1991)
Nationality: noun—Ecuadorian(s); adjective—Ecuadorian
Ethnic divisions: mestizo (mixed Indian and Spanish) 55%, Indian 25%, Spanish 10%, black 10%
Religion: Roman Catholic 95%
Language: Spanish (official); Indian languages, especially Quechua
Literacy: 86% (male 88%, female 84%) age 15 and over can read and write (1990 est.)
Labor force: 2,800,000; agriculture 35%, manufacturing 21%, commerce 16%, services and other activities 28% (1982)
Organized labor: less than 15% of labor force

Government

Long-form name: Republic of Ecuador
Type: republic
Capital: Quito
Administrative divisions: 21 provinces (provincias, singular—provincia); Azuay, Bolívar, Cañar, Carchi, Chimborazo, Cotopaxi, El Oro, Esmeraldas, Galápagos, Guayas, Imbabura, Loja, Los Ríos, Manabí, Morona-Santiago, Napo, Pastaza, Pichincha, Sucumbíos, Tungurahua, Zamora-Chinchipe
Independence: 24 May 1822 (from Spain; Battle of Pichincha)
Constitution: 10 August 1979
Legal system: based on civil law system; has not accepted compulsory ICJ jurisdiction
National holiday: Independence Day, 10 August (1809, independence of Quito)
Executive branch: president, vice president, Cabinet
Legislative branch: unicameral National Congress (Congreso Nacional)
Judicial branch: Supreme Court (Corte Suprema)
Leaders:
Chief of State and Head of Government—President Rodrigo BORJA Cevallos (since 10 August 1988); Vice President Luis PARODÍ Valverde (since 10 August 1988)
Political parties and leaders:
Right to center parties— Social Christian Party (PSC), former President Leon FEBRES Cordero Rivadeneira; Conservative Party (PC), Alberto DAHIK, leader; Radical Liberal Party (PLR), Blasco Manuel PEÑAHERRERA Padilla, director;
Centrist parties— Concentration of Popular Forces (CFP), Averroes BUCARAM Saxida, director; Radical Alfarist Front (FRA), Cecilia CALDERÓN de Castro, leader; People, Change, and Democracy (PCD), Aquiles RIGAÍL Santistéván, director; Revolutionary Nationalist Party (PNR), Carlos Julio AROSEMENA Monroy, leader;

Center-left parties— Democratic Left (ID), President Rodrigo BORJA Cevallos, leader; Roldosist Party of Ecuador (PRE), Abdalá BUCARAM Ortiz, director; Popular Democracy (DP), Vladimiro ALVAREZ, president; Christian Democratic (CD), Julio César TRUJILLO; Democratic Party (PD), Francisco HUERTA Montalvo, leader; *Far-left parties*— Broad Leftist Front (FADI), René MAUGÉ Mosquera, director; Socialist Party (PSE), Víctor GRANDA Aguilar, secretary general; Democratic Popular Movement (MPD), Jaime HURTADO González, leader; Ecuadorian National Liberation (LN), Alfredo CASTILLO, president; Popular Revolutionary Action Party (APRE), Lt. Gen. Frank VARGAS Pazzos, leader
Suffrage: universal at age 18; compulsory for literate persons ages 18-65, optional for other eligible voters
Elections:
President—first round held 31 January 1988 and second round on 8 May 1988 (next first round to be held May 1992 and second round June 1992); results—Rodrigo BORJA Cevallos (ID) 54%, Abdalá BUCARAM Ortiz (PRE) 46%;
Chamber of Representatives—last held 17 June 1990 (next to be held June 1992); results—percent of vote by party NA; seats—(72 total) PSC 16, ID 14, PRE 13, PSE 8, DP 7, CFP 3, PC 3, PLR 3, FADI 2, FRA 2, MPD 1
Communists: Communist Party of Ecuador (PCE, pro-Moscow), René Maugé Mosquera, secretary general, 5,000 members; Communist Party of Ecuador/Marxist Leninist (PCMLE, Maoist), 3,000 members; Socialist Party of Ecuador (PSE, pro-Cuba), 5,000 members (est.); National Liberation Party (PLN, Communist), 5,000 members (est.)
Member of: AG, ECLAC, FAO, G-11, G-77, IADB, IAEA, IBRD, ICAO, ICC, ICFTU, IDA, IFAD, IFC, ILO, IMF, IMO, INTELSAT, INTERPOL, IOC, IOM, ITU, LAES, LAIA, LORCS, NAM, OAS, OPANAL, OPEC, PCA, RG, UN, UNCTAD, UNESCO, UNIDO, UPU, WCL, WFTU, WHO, WIPO, WMO, WTO
Diplomatic representation: Ambassador Jaime MONCAYO; Chancery at 2535 15th Street NW, Washington DC 20009; telephone (202) 234-7200; there are Ecuadorian Consulates General in Chicago, Houston, Los Angeles, Miami, New Orleans, New York, and San Francisco, and a Consulate in San Diego;
US—Ambassador Paul C. LAMBERT; Embassy at Avenida Patria 120, on the corner of Avenida 12 de Octubre, Quito (mailing address is P. O. Box 538, Quito, or APO Miami 34039); telephone [593] (2) 562-890; there is a US Consulate General in Guayaquil
Flag: three horizontal bands of yellow (top, double width), blue, and red with the coat of arms superimposed at the center of the flag; similar to the flag of Colombia which is shorter and does not bear a coat of arms

Economy

Overview: Ecuador continues to recover from a 1986 drop in international oil prices and a major earthquake in 1987 that interrupted oil exports for six months and forced Ecuador to suspend foreign debt payments. In 1988-89 oil exports recovered—accounting for nearly half of Ecuador's total export revenues—and Quito resumed full interest payments on its official debt and partial payments on its commercial debt. The Borja administration has pursued austere economic policies that have helped reduce inflation and restore international reserves. Ecuador was granted an IMF standby agreement worth $135 million in 1989, and Quito will seek to reschedule its foreign commercial debt in 1991.
GDP: $9.7 billion, per capita $920; real growth rate 0.2% (1990)
Inflation rate (consumer prices): 45% (1990)
Unemployment rate: 7.0% (1990)
Budget: revenues $2.2 billion; expenditures $2.2 billion, including capital expenditures of $375 million (1991)
Exports: $2.7 billion (f.o.b., 1990); *commodities*—petroleum 47%, coffee, bananas, cocoa products, shrimp, fish products; *partners*—US 60%, Latin America, Caribbean, EC countries
Imports: $1.9 billion (f.o.b., 1990); *commodities*—transport equipment, vehicles, machinery, chemicals; *partners*—US 34%, Latin America, Caribbean, EC, Japan
External debt: $11.8 billion (December 1990)
Industrial production: growth rate 0.7% (1988); accounts for 31% of GDP
Electricity: 1,983,000 kW capacity; 6,011 million kWh produced, 570 kWh per capita (1990)
Industries: food processing, textiles, chemicals, fishing, timber, petroleum
Agriculture: accounts for 18% of GDP and 35% of labor force (including fishing and forestry); leading producer and exporter of bananas and balsawood; other exports—coffee, cocoa, fish, shrimp; crop production—rice, potatoes, manioc, plantains, sugarcane; livestock sector—cattle, sheep, hogs, beef, pork, dairy products; net importer of foodgrains, dairy products, and sugar

Illicit drugs: relatively small producer of coca following the successful eradication campaign of 1985-87; significant transit country, however, for derivatives of coca originating in Colombia, Bolivia, and Peru
Economic aid: US commitments, including Ex-Im (FY70-89), $498 million; Western (non-US) countries, ODA and OOF bilateral commitments (1970-88), $1.7 billion; Communist countries (1970-89), $64 million
Currency: sucre (plural—sucres); 1 sucre (S/) = 100 centavos
Exchange rates: sucres (S/) per US$1— 869.54 (December 1990), 767.75 (1990), 526.35 (1989), 301.61 (1988), 170.46 (1987), 122.78 (1986), 69.56 (1985)
Fiscal year: calendar year

Communications

Railroads: 965 km total; all 1.067-meter-gauge single track
Highways: 28,000 km total; 3,600 km paved, 17,400 km gravel and improved earth, 7,000 km unimproved earth
Inland waterways: 1,500 km
Pipelines: crude oil, 800 km; refined products, 1,358 km
Ports: Guayaquil, Manta, Puerto Bolivar, Esmeraldas
Merchant marine: 47 ships (1,000 GRT or over) totaling 342,411 GRT/495,482 DWT; includes 1 passenger, 8 cargo, 17 refrigerated cargo, 2 container, 1 roll-on/roll-off cargo, 16 petroleum, oils, and lubricants (POL) tanker, 1 liquefied gas, 1 bulk
Civil air: 44 major transport aircraft
Airports: 153 total, 151 usable; 46 with permanent-surface runways; 1 with runways over 3,659 m; 6 with runways 2,440-3,659 m; 23 with runways 1,220-2,439 m
Telecommunications: domestic facilities generally adequate; 318,000 telephones; stations—272 AM, no FM, 33 TV, 39 shortwave; 1 Atlantic Ocean INTELSAT earth station

Defense Forces

Branches: Army (Ejercito Ecuatoriano), Navy (Armada Ecuatoriana), Air Force (Fuerza Aerea Ecuatoriana), National Police
Manpower availability: males 15-49, 2,716,919; 1,840,296 fit for military service; 117,113 reach military age (20) annually
Defense expenditures: $176 million, 1.6% of GDP (1990 est.)

Egypt

Boundary representation is not necessarily authoritative

Geography

Total area: 1,001,450 km²; land area: 995,450 km²
Comparative area: slightly more than three times the size of New Mexico
Land boundaries: 2,689 km total; Gaza Strip 11 km, Israel 255 km, Libya 1,150 km, Sudan 1,273 km
Coastline: 2,450 km
Maritime claims:
Contiguous zone: 24 nm;
Continental shelf: 200 m (depth) or to depth of exploitation;
Exclusive economic zone: undefined;
Territorial sea: 12 nm
Disputes: Administrative boundary with Sudan does not coincide with international boundary
Climate: desert; hot, dry summers with moderate winters
Terrain: vast desert plateau interrupted by Nile valley and delta
Natural resources: crude oil, natural gas, iron ore, phosphates, manganese, limestone, gypsum, talc, asbestos, lead, zinc
Land use: arable land 3%; permanent crops 2%; meadows and pastures 0%; forest and woodland NEGL%; other 95%; includes irrigated 5%
Environment: Nile is only perennial water source; increasing soil salinization below Aswan High Dam; hot, driving windstorm called khamsin occurs in spring; water pollution; desertification
Note: controls Sinai Peninsula, only land bridge between Africa and remainder of Eastern Hemisphere; controls Suez Canal, shortest sea link between Indian Ocean and Mediterranean; size and juxtaposition to Israel establish its major role in Middle Eastern geopolitics

People

Population: 54,451,588 (July 1991), growth rate 2.3% (1991)

Birth rate: 33 births/1,000 population (1991)
Death rate: 10 deaths/1,000 population (1991)
Net migration rate: NEGL migrants/1,000 population (1991)
Infant mortality rate: 82 deaths/1,000 live births (1991)
Life expectancy at birth: 60 years male, 61 years female (1991)
Total fertility rate: 4.5 children born/woman (1991)
Nationality: noun—Egyptian(s); adjective—Egyptian
Ethnic divisions: Eastern Hamitic stock 90%; Greek, Italian, Syro-Lebanese 10%
Religion: (official estimate) Muslim (mostly Sunni) 94%; Coptic Christian and other 6%
Language: Arabic (official); English and French widely understood by educated classes
Literacy: 48% (male 63%, female 34%) age 15 and over can read and write (1990 est.)
Labor force: 15,000,000 (1989 est.); government, public sector enterprises, and armed forces 36%; agriculture 34%; privately owned service and manufacturing enterprises 20% (1984); shortage of skilled labor; 2,500,000 Egyptians work abroad, mostly in Iraq and the Gulf Arab states (1988 est.)
Organized labor: 2,500,000 (est.)

Government

Long-form name: Arab Republic of Egypt
Type: republic
Capital: Cairo
Administrative divisions: 24 governorates (muḥāfaẓat, singular—muḥāfaẓah); Ad Daqahlīyah, Al Baḥr al Aḥmar, Al Buḥayrah, Al Fayyūm, Al Gharbīyah, Al Iskandarīyah, Al Ismāʻīlīyah, Al Jīzah, Al Minūfīyah, Al Minyā, Al Qāhirah, Al Qalyūbīyah, Al Wādī al Jadīd, Ash Sharqīyah, As Suways, Aswān, Asyūṭ, Banī Suwayf, Būr Saʻīd, Dumyāṭ, Janūb Sīnāʼ, Maṭrūḥ, Shamāl Sīnāʼ, Sūhāj
Independence: 28 February 1922 (from UK); formerly United Arab Republic
Constitution: 11 September 1971
Legal system: based on English common law, Islamic law, and Napoleonic codes; judicial review by Supreme Court and Council of State (oversees validity of administrative decisions); accepts compulsory ICJ jurisdiction, with reservations
National holiday: Anniversary of the Revolution, 23 July (1952)
Executive branch: president, prime minister, Cabinet
Legislative branch: unicameral People's Assembly (Majlis al-Chaʼab); note—there is an Advisory Council (Majlis al-Shura) that functions in a consultative role
Judicial branch: Supreme Constitutional Court

Leaders:
Chief of State—President Mohammed Hosni MUBARAK (was made acting President on 6 October 1981 upon the assassination of President Sadat and sworn in as President on 14 October 1981);
Head of Government—Prime Minister Atef Mohammed Najib SEDKY (since 12 November 1986)
Political parties and leaders: formation of political parties must be approved by government; National Democratic Party (NDP), President Mohammed Hosni MUBARAK, leader, is the dominant party; legal opposition parties are Socialist Liberal Party (SLP), Kamal MURAD; Socialist Labor Party, Ibrahim SHUKRI; National Progressive Unionist Grouping (NPUG), Khalid MUHYI-AL-DIN; Umma Party, Ahmad al-SABAHI; New Wafd Party (NWP), Fuʼad SIRAJ AL-DIN; Misr al-Fatah Party (Young Egypt Party), Ali al-Din SALIH; Democratic Unionist Party, Muhammad ʻAbd al-Munʼim TURK; The Greens Party, Hasan RAJAB
Suffrage: universal and compulsory at age 18
Elections:
President—last held 5 October 1987 (next to be held October 1993); results—President Hosni MUBAREK was reelected;
People's Assembly—last held 29 November 1990 (next to be held November 1995); results—NDP 78.4%, NPUG 1.4%, independents 18.7%; seats—(454 total, 444 elected)—including NDP 348, NPUG 6, independents 83; note—most opposition parties boycotted;
Advisory Council—last held 8 June 1989 (next to be held June 1995); results—NDP 100%; seats—(258 total, 172 elected) NDP 172
Communists: about 500 party members
Other political or pressure groups: Islamic groups are illegal, but the largest one, the Muslim Brotherhood, is tolerated by the government; trade unions and professional associations are officially sanctioned
Member of: ABEDA, ACC, ACCT (associate), AfDB, AFESD, AG (observer), AL, AMF, CAEU, CCC, EBRD, ECA, ESCWA, FAO, G-19, G-24, G-77, GATT, IAEA, IBRD, ICAO, ICC, IDA, IDB, IFAD, IFC, ILO, IMF, IMO, INMARSAT, INTELSAT, INTERPOL, IOC, IOM (observer), ISO, ITU, LORCS, NAM, OAPEC, OAS (observer), OAU, OIC, PCA, UN, UNCTAD, UNESCO, UNIDO, UNRWA, UPU, WHO, WIPO, WMO, WTO
Diplomatic representation: Ambassador El Sayed Abdel Raouf EL REEDY; Chancery at 2310 Decatur Place NW, Washington DC 20008; telephone (202) 232-5400; there are Egyptian Consulates General in Chicago, Houston, New York, and San Francisco;

Egypt (continued)

US—Ambassador Frank G. WISNER; Embassy at Lazougi Street, Garden City, Cairo (mailing address is APO New York 09674-0006); telephone [20] (2) 355-7371; there is a US Consulate General in Alexandria

Flag: three equal horizontal bands of red (top), white, and black with the national emblem (a shield superimposed on a golden eagle facing the hoist side above a scroll bearing the name of the country in Arabic) centered in the white band; similar to the flag of Yemen which has a plain white band; also similar to the flag of Syria which has two green stars and of Iraq which has three green stars (plus an Arabic inscription) in a horizontal line centered in the white band

Economy

Overview: Egypt has one of the largest public sectors of all the Third World economies, most industrial plants being owned by the government. Overregulation holds back technical modernization and foreign investment. Even so, the economy grew rapidly during the late 1970s and early 1980s, but in 1986 the collapse of world oil prices and an increasingly heavy burden of debt servicing led Egypt to begin negotiations with the IMF for balance-of-payments support. As part of the 1987 agreement with the IMF, the government agreed to institute a reform program to reduce inflation, promote economic growth, and improve its external position. The reforms have been slow in coming, however, and the economy has been largely stagnant for the past three years. The addition of 1 million people every seven months to Egypt's population exerts enormous pressure on the 5% of the total land area available for agriculture.

GDP: $37.0 billion, per capita $700; real growth rate 1.0% (1990 est.)

Inflation rate (consumer prices): 26% (FY90)

Unemployment rate: 15% (1989 est.)

Budget: revenues $7 billion; expenditures $11.5 billion, including capital expenditures of $4 billion (FY89 est.)

Exports: $3.8 billion (f.o.b., 1989); *commodities*—crude and refined petroleum, raw cotton, cotton yarn, textiles, metal products; *partners*—US, EC, Japan, Eastern Europe

Imports: $11.4 billion (f.o.b., 1989); *commodities*—foods, machinery and equipment, fertilizers, wood products, durable consumer goods, capital goods; *partners*—US, EC, Japan, Eastern Europe

External debt: $52 billion (December 1990 est.)

Industrial production: growth rate 2-4% (1989 est.); accounts for 24% of GDP

Electricity: 11,273,000 kW capacity; 42,500 million kWh produced, 780 kWh per capita (1989)

Industries: textiles, food processing, tourism, chemicals, petroleum, construction, cement, metals

Agriculture: accounts for 20% of GNP and employs more than one-third of labor force; dependent on irrigation water from the Nile; world's sixth-largest cotton exporter; other crops produced include rice, corn, wheat, beans, fruit, vegetables; not self-sufficient in food; livestock—cattle, water buffalo, sheep, and goats; annual fish catch about 140,000 metric tons

Economic aid: US commitments, including Ex-Im (FY70-89), $15.7 billion; Western (non-US) countries, ODA and OOF bilateral commitments (1970-88), $9.3 billion; OPEC bilateral aid (1979-89), $2.9 billion; Communist countries (1970-89), $2.4 billion

Currency: Egyptian pound (plural—pounds); 1 Egyptian pound (£E) = 100 piasters

Exchange rates: Egyptian pounds (£E) per US$1—2.9030 (January 1991), 2.7072 (1990), 2.5171 (1989), 2.2233 (1988), 1.5183 (1987), 1.3503 (1986), 1.3010 (1985)

Fiscal year: 1 July-30 June

Communications

Railroads: 5,110 km total; 4,763 km 1,435-meter standard gauge, 347 km 0.750-meter gauge; 951 km double track; 25 km electrified

Highways: 51,925 km total; 17,900 km paved, 2,500 km gravel, 13,500 km improved earth, 18,025 km unimproved earth

Inland waterways: 3,500 km (including the Nile, Lake Nasser, Alexandria-Cairo Waterway, and numerous smaller canals in the delta); Suez Canal, 193.5 km long (including approaches), used by oceangoing vessels drawing up to 16.1 meters of water

Pipelines: crude oil, 1,171 km; refined products, 596 km; natural gas, 460 km

Ports: Alexandria, Port Said, Suez, Bur Safajah, Damietta

Merchant marine: 144 ships (1,000 GRT or over) totaling 1,121,534 GRT/1,725,369 DWT; includes 5 passenger, 7 short-sea passenger, 2 passenger-cargo, 85 cargo, 3 refrigerated cargo, 13 roll-on/roll-off cargo, 14 petroleum, oils, and lubricants (POL) tanker, 15 bulk

Civil air: 43 major transport aircraft

Airports: 91 total, 82 usable; 66 with permanent-surface runways; 2 with runways over 3,659 m; 44 with runways 2,440-3,659 m; 22 with runways 1,220-2,439 m

Telecommunications: system is large but still inadequate for needs; principal centers are Alexandria, Cairo, Al Manṣūrah, Ismailia, and Ṭanṭā; intercity connections by coaxial cable and microwave; extensive upgrading in progress; 600,000 telephones (est.); stations—25 AM, 5 FM, 47 TV; satellite earth stations—1 Atlantic Ocean INTELSAT, 1 Indian Ocean INTELSAT, 1 INMARSAT, 1 ARABSAT; 4 submarine coaxial cables; tropospheric scatter to Sudan; radio relay to Libya (may not be operational); radio relay to Jordan

Defense Forces

Branches: Army, Navy, Air Force, Air Defense Command

Manpower availability: males 15-49, 13,333,285; 8,665,260 fit for military service; 584,780 reach military age (20) annually

Defense expenditures: $2.8 billion, 7.3% of GDP (1991)

El Salvador

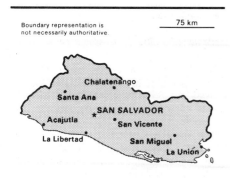

Boundary representation is not necessarily authoritative.

75 km

North Pacific Ocean

Geography

Total area: 21,040 km²; land area: 20,720 km²

Comparative area: slightly smaller than Massachusetts

Land boundaries: 545 km total; Guatemala 203 km, Honduras 342 km

Coastline: 307 km

Maritime claims:

Territorial sea: 200 nm (overflight and navigation permitted beyond 12 nm)

Disputes: dispute with Honduras over several sections of the land boundary; dispute over Golfo de Fonseca maritime boundary because of disputed sovereignty of islands

Climate: tropical; rainy season (May to October); dry season (November to April)

Terrain: mostly mountains with narrow coastal belt and central plateau

Natural resources: hydropower, geothermal power, crude oil

Land use: arable land 27%; permanent crops 8%; meadows and pastures 29%; forest and woodland 6%; other 30%; includes irrigated 5%

Environment: The Land of Volcanoes; subject to frequent and sometimes very destructive earthquakes; deforestation; soil erosion; water pollution

Note: smallest Central American country and only one without a coastline on Caribbean Sea

People

Population: 5,418,736 (July 1991), growth rate 2.0% (1991)

Birth rate: 34 births/1,000 population (1991)

Death rate: 7 deaths/1,000 population (1991)

Net migration rate: −6 migrants/1,000 population (1991)

Infant mortality rate: 47 deaths/1,000 live births (1991)

Life expectancy at birth: 63 years male, 68 years female (1991)

Total fertility rate: 4.1 children born/woman (1991)

Nationality: noun—Salvadoran(s); adjective—Salvadoran

Ethnic divisions: mestizo 89%, Indian 10%, white 1%

Religion: Roman Catholic about 75%, with extensive activity by Protestant groups throughout the country (more than 1 million Protestant evangelicals in El Salvador at the end of 1990)

Language: Spanish, Nahua (among some Indians)

Literacy: 73% (male 76%, female 70%) age 15 and over can read and write (1990 est.)

Labor force: 1,700,000 (1982 est.); agriculture 40%, commerce 16%, manufacturing 15%, government 13%, financial services 9%, transportation 6%, other 1%; shortage of skilled labor and a large pool of unskilled labor, but manpower training programs improving situation (1984 est.)

Organized labor: total labor force 15%; agricultural labor force 10%; urban labor force 7% (1987 est.)

Government

Long-form name: Republic of El Salvador

Type: republic

Capital: San Salvador

Administrative divisions: 14 departments (departamentos, singular—departamento); Ahuachapán, Cabañas, Chalatenango, Cuscatlán, La Libertad, La Paz, La Unión, Morazán, San Miguel, San Salvador, Santa Ana, San Vicente, Sonsonate, Usulután

Independence: 15 September 1821 (from Spain)

Constitution: 20 December 1983

Legal system: based on civil and Roman law, with traces of common law; judicial review of legislative acts in the Supreme Court; accepts compulsory ICJ jurisdiction, with reservations

National holiday: Independence Day, 15 September (1821)

Executive branch: president, vice president, Council of Ministers (cabinet)

Legislative branch: unicameral Legislative Assembly (Asamblea Legislativa)

Judicial branch: Supreme Court (Corte Suprema)

Leaders:

Chief of State and Head of Government—President Alfredo CRISTIANI (since 1 June 1989); Vice President José Francisco MERINO (since 1 June 1989)

Political parties and leaders: National Republican Alliance (ARENA), Armando CALDERON Sol; Christian Democratic Party (PDC), Fidel CHAVEZ Mena; National Conciliation Party (PCN), Ciro CRUZ Zepeda; National Democratic Union (UDN), Mario AGUINADA Carranza; the Democratic Convergence (CD) is a coalition of three parties—the Social Democratic Party (PSD), Wilfredo BARILLAS; the National Revolutionary Movement (MNR), Rene FLORES; and the Popular Social Christian Movement (MPSC), Ruben ZAMORA; Authentic Christian Movement (MAC), Julio REY PRENDES; Democratic Action (AD), Ricardo GONZÁLEZ Camacho

Suffrage: universal at age 18

Elections:

President—last held 19 March 1989 (next to be held March 1994); results—Alfredo CRISTIANI (ARENA) 53.8%, Fidel CHAVEZ Mena (PDC) 36.6%, other 9.6%;

Legislative Assembly—last held 10 March 1991 (next to be held March 1994); results—ARENA 44.3%, PDC 27.96%, CD 12.16%, PCN 8.99%, MAC 3.23%, UDN 2.68%; seats—(84 total) ARENA 39, PDC 26, PCN 9, CD 8, UDN 1, MAC 1

Other political or pressure groups:

Leftist revolutionary movement—Farabundo Martí National Liberation Front (FMLN), leadership body of the insurgency, four factions—Popular Liberation Forces (FPL), Armed Forces of National Resistance (FARN), People's Revolutionary Army (ERP), Salvadoran Communist Party/Armed Forces of Liberation (PCES/FAL), and Central American Workers' Revolutionary Party (PRTC)/Popular Liberation Revolutionary Armed Forces (FARLP);

Leftist political parties—National Democratic Union (UDN), National Revolutionary Movement (MNR), and Popular Social Movement (MPSC);

FMLN front organizations:

Labor fronts—National Union of Salvadoran Workers (UNTS), leftist umbrella front group, leads FMLN front network; National Federation of Salvadoran Workers (FENASTRAS), best organized of front groups and controlled by FMLN's National Resistance (RN); Social Security Institute Workers Union (STISSS), one of the most militant fronts, is controlled by FMLN'S Armed Forces of National Resistance (FARN) and RN; Association of Telecommunications Workers (ASTTEL); Centralized Union Federation of El Salvador (FUSS); Treasury Ministry Employees (AGEMHA);

Nonlabor fronts include—Committee of Mothers and Families of Political Prisoners, Disappeared Persons, and Assassinated of El Salvador (COMADRES); Nongovernmental Human Rights Commission (CDHES); Committee of Dismissed and Unemployed of El Salvador (CODYDES); General Association of Salvadoran University Students (AGEUS); National Association of Salvadoran Educators (ANDES-21 DE JUNIO); Salvadoran Revolutionary Student Front (FERS), associated with the

El Salvador (continued)

Popular Forces of Liberation (FPL); Association of National University Educators (ADUES); Salvadoran University Students Front (FEUS); Christian Committee for the Displaced of El Salvador (CRIPDES), an FPL front; The Association for Communal Development in El Salvador (PADECOES), controlled by the People's Revolutionary Army (ERP); Confederation of Cooperative Associations of El Salvador (COACES); *Labor organizations*—Federation of Construction and Transport Workers Unions (FESINCONSTRANS), independent; Salvadoran Communal Union (UCS), peasant association; Unitary Federation of Salvadoran Unions (FUSS), leftist; National Federation of Salvadoran Workers (FENASTRAS), leftist; Democratic Workers Central (CTD), moderate; General Confederation of Workers (CGT), moderate; National Unity of Salvadoran Workers (UNTS), leftist; National Union of Workers and Peasants (UNOC), moderate labor coalition of democratic labor organizations; United Workers Front (FUT); *Business organizations*—National Association of Private Enterprise (ANEP), conservative; Productive Alliance (AP), conservative; National Federation of Salvadoran Small Businessmen (FENAPES), conservative

Member of: BCIE, CACM, ECLAC, FAO, G-77, IADB, IAEA, IBRD, ICAO, ICFTU, IDA, IFAD, IFC, ILO, IMF, IMO, INTELSAT, IOC, IOM, ITU, LAES, LORCS, NAM (observer), OAS, OPANAL, PCA, UN, UNCTAD, UNESCO, UNIDO, UPU, WCL, WFTU, WHO, WIPO, WMO

Diplomatic representation: Ambassador Miguel Angel SALAVERRIA; Chancery at 2308 California Street NW, Washington DC 20008; telephone (202) 265-3480 through 3482; there are Salvadoran Consulates General in Houston, Los Angeles, Miami, New Orleans, New York, and San Francisco;

US—Ambassador William G. WALKER; Embassy at 25 Avenida Norte No. 1230, San Salvador (mailing address is APO Miami 34023); telephone [503] 26-7100

Flag: three equal horizontal bands of blue (top), white, and blue with the national coat of arms centered in the white band; the coat of arms features a round emblem encircled by the words *REPUBLICA DE EL SALVADOR EN LA AMERICA CENTRAL*; similar to the flag of Nicaragua which has a different coat of arms centered in the white band—it features a triangle encircled by the words *REPUBLICA DE NICARAGUA* on top and *AMERICA CENTRAL* on the bottom; also similar to the flag of Honduras which has five blue stars arranged in an *X* pattern centered in the white band

Economy

Overview: The agricultural sector accounts for 25% of GDP, employs about 40% of the labor force, and contributes about 66% to total exports. Coffee is the major commercial crop, accounting for 45% of export earnings. The manufacturing sector, based largely on food and beverage processing, accounts for 18% of GDP and 15% of employment. Economic losses because of guerrilla sabotage total more than $2.0 billion since 1979. The costs of maintaining a large military seriously constrain the government's efforts to provide essential social services. Nevertheless, growth in national output last year exceeded growth in population for the first time since 1987.

GDP: $5.1 billion, per capita $940; real growth rate 3.4% (1990 est.)

Inflation rate (consumer prices): 20% (1990)

Unemployment rate: 10% (1989)

Budget: revenues $751 million; expenditures $790 million, including capital expenditures of $NA (1990 est.)

Exports: $571 million (f.o.b., 1990 est.); *commodities*—coffee 45%, sugar, cotton, shrimp; *partners*—US 49%, FRG 24%, Guatemala 7%, Costa Rica 4%, Japan 4%

Imports: $1.2 billion (c.i.f., 1990 est.); *commodities*—petroleum products, consumer goods, foodstuffs, machinery, construction materials, fertilizer; *partners*—US 40%, Guatemala 12%, Venezuela 7%, Mexico 7%, FRG 5%, Japan 4%

External debt: $2.1 billion (December 1990 est.)

Industrial production: growth rate 2.4% (1990); accounts for 18% of GDP

Electricity: 682,000 kW capacity; 1,849 million kWh produced, 350 kWh per capita (1990)

Industries: food processing, textiles, clothing, petroleum products, cement

Agriculture: accounts for 25% of GDP and 40% of labor force (including fishing and forestry); coffee most important commercial crop; other products—sugarcane, corn, rice, beans, oilseeds, beef, dairy products, shrimp; not self-sufficient in food

Economic aid: US commitments, including Ex-Im (FY70-90), $2.95 billion; Western (non-US) countries, ODA and OOF bilateral commitments (1970-88), $455 million

Currency: Salvadoran colón (plural—colones); 1 Salvadoran colón (C) = 100 centavos

Exchange rates: Salvadoran colones (C) per US$1—8.0 (April 1991, floating rate since mid-1990); 5.0000 (fixed rate 1986 to mid-1990)

Fiscal year: calendar year

Communications

Railroads: 602 km 0.914-meter gauge, single track

Highways: 10,000 km total; 1,500 km paved, 4,100 km gravel, 4,400 km improved and unimproved earth

Inland waterways: Río Lempa partially navigable

Ports: Acajutla, Cutuco

Civil air: 7 major transport aircraft

Airports: 116 total, 82 usable; 6 with permanent-surface runways; none with runways over 3,659 m; 1 with runways 2,440-3,659 m; 5 with runways 1,220-2,439 m

Telecommunications: nationwide trunk radio relay system; connection into Central American Microwave System; 116,000 telephones; stations—77 AM, no FM, 5 TV, 2 shortwave; 1 Atlantic Ocean INTELSAT earth station

Defense Forces

Branches: Army, Navy, Air Force, National Guard, National Police, Treasury Police

Manpower availability: males 15-49, 1,220,088; 780,108 fit for military service; 71,709 reach military age (18) annually

Defense expenditures: $220 million, 3.6% of GDP (1990)

Equatorial Guinea

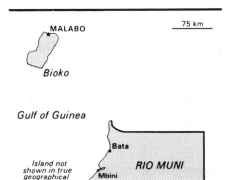

Geography

Total area: 28,050 km²; land area: 28,050 km²

Comparative area: slightly larger than Maryland

Land boundaries: 539 km total; Cameroon 189 km, Gabon 350 km

Coastline: 296 km

Maritime claims:

Exclusive economic zone: 200 nm;

Territorial sea: 12 nm

Disputes: maritime boundary dispute with Gabon because of disputed sovereignty over islands in Corisco Bay

Climate: tropical; always hot, humid

Terrain: coastal plains rise to interior hills; islands are volcanic

Natural resources: timber, crude oil, small unexploited deposits of gold, manganese, uranium

Land use: arable land 8%; permanent crops 4%; meadows and pastures 4%; forest and woodland 51%; other 33%

Environment: subject to violent windstorms

Note: insular and continental regions rather widely separated

People

Population: 378,729 (July 1991), growth rate 2.6% (1991)

Birth rate: 42 births/1,000 population (1991)

Death rate: 16 deaths/1,000 population (1991)

Net migration rate: 0 migrants/1,000 population (1991)

Infant mortality rate: 116 deaths/1,000 live births (1991)

Life expectancy at birth: 49 years male, 53 years female (1991)

Total fertility rate: 5.4 children born/woman (1991)

Nationality: noun—Equatorial Guinean(s) or Equatoguinean(s); adjective—Equatorial Guinean or Equatoguinean

Ethnic divisions: indigenous population of Bioko, primarily Bubi, some Fernandinos; Rio Muni, primarily Fang; less than 1,000 Europeans, mostly Spanish

Religion: natives all nominally Christian and predominantly Roman Catholic; some pagan practices retained

Language: Spanish (official), pidgin English, Fang, Bubi, Ibo

Literacy: 50% (male 64%, female 37%) age 15 and over can read and write (1990 est.)

Labor force: 172,000 (1986 est.); agriculture 66%, services 23%, industry 11% (1980); labor shortages on plantations; 58% of population of working age (1985)

Organized labor: no formal trade unions

Government

Long-form name: Republic of Equatorial Guinea

Type: republic

Capital: Malabo

Administrative divisions: 2 provinces (provincias, singular—provincia); Bioko, Rio Muni; note—there may now be 6 provinces named Bioko Norte, Bioko Sur, Centro Sur, Kié-Ntem, Litoral, Wele Nzas

Independence: 12 October 1968 (from Spain; formerly Spanish Guinea)

Constitution: 15 August 1982

Legal system: in transition; partly based on Spanish civil law and tribal custom

National holiday: Independence Day, 12 October (1968)

Executive branch: president, prime minister, deputy prime minister, Council of Ministers (cabinet)

Legislative branch: unicameral House of Representatives of the People (Cámara de Representantes del Pueblo)

Judicial branch: Supreme Tribunal

Leaders:

Chief of State—President Brig. Gen. (Ret.) Teodoro OBIANG NGUEMA MBASOGO (since 3 August 1979);

Head of Government—Prime Minister Cristino SERICHE BIOKO MALABO (since 15 August 1982); Deputy Prime Minister Isidoro Eyi MONSUY ANDEME (since 15 August 1989)

Political parties and leaders: only party—Democratic Party for Equatorial Guinea (PDGE), President Brig. Gen. (Ret.) Teodoro OBIANG NGUEMA MBASOGO, party leader

Suffrage: universal adult at age NA

Elections:

President—last held 25 June 1989 (next to be held 25 June 1996); results—President Brig. Gen. (Ret.) Teodoro OBIANG NGUEMA MBASOGO was reelected without opposition;

Chamber of People's Representatives—last held 10 July 1988 (next to be held 10 July 1993); results—PDGE is the only party; seats—(41 total) PDGE 41

Communists: no significant number

Member of: ACP, AfDB, BDEAC, CEEAC, ECA, FAO, FZ, G-77, IBRD, ICAO, IDA, IFAD, ILO, IMF, IMO, INTERPOL, IOC, ITU, LORCS (associate), NAM, OAS (observer), OAU, UDEAC, UN, UNCTAD, UNESCO, UNIDO, UPU, WHO

Diplomatic representation: Ambassador Damaso OBIANG NDONG; Chancery at 801 Second Avenue, Suite 1403, New York, NY 10017; telephone (212) 599-1523;

US—Ambassador (vacant); Chargé d'Affaires William MITHOEFER; Embassy at Calle de Los Ministros, Malabo (mailing address is P. O. Box 597, Malabo; telephone [240] (9) 2185, 2406, 2507

Flag: three equal horizontal bands of green (top), white, and red with a blue isosceles triangle based on the hoist side and the coat of arms centered in the white band; the coat of arms has six yellow six-pointed stars (representing the mainland and five offshore islands) above a gray shield bearing a silk-cotton tree and below which is a scroll with the motto *UNIDAD, PAZ, JUSTICIA* (Unity, Peace, Justice)

Economy

Overview: The economy, destroyed during the regime of former President Macías Nguema, is now based on agriculture, forestry, and fishing, which account for about 60% of GNP and nearly all exports. Subsistence agriculture predominates, with cocoa, coffee, and wood products providing income, foreign exchange, and government revenues. There is little industry. Commerce accounts for about 10% of GNP, and the construction, public works, and service sectors for about 34%. Undeveloped natural resources include titanium, iron ore, manganese, uranium, and alluvial gold. Oil exploration, taking place under concessions offered to US, French, and Spanish firms, has been moderately successful, and some revenues from oil exports will begin rolling in by mid-1991.

GDP: $144 million, per capita $411; real growth rate 2.9% (1988 est.)

Inflation rate (consumer prices): 5.9% (1989 est.)

Unemployment rate: NA%

Budget: revenues $23 million; expenditures $31 million, including capital expenditures of NA (1988)

Exports: $41 million (f.o.b., 1989 est.); *commodities*—coffee, timber, cocoa beans; *partners*—Spain 44%, FRG 19%, Italy 12%, Netherlands 11% (1987)

Imports: $57.1 million (c.i.f., 1988); *commodities*—petroleum, food, beverages, clothing, machinery; *partners*—Spain 34%, Italy 16%, France 14%, Netherlands 8% (1987)

External debt: $195 million (1989)

Equatorial Guinea *(continued)*

Industrial production: growth rate –2.7% (1987); accounts for about 10% of GDP
Electricity: 23,000 kW capacity; 60 million kWh produced, 170 kWh per capita (1989)
Industries: fishing, sawmilling
Agriculture: cash crops—timber and coffee from Rio Muni, cocoa from Bioko; food crops—rice, yams, cassava, bananas, oil palm nuts, manioc, livestock
Economic aid: US commitments, including Ex-Im (FY81-89), $14 million; Western (non-US) countries, ODA and OOF bilateral commitments (1970-88), $112 million; Communist countries (1970-89), $55 million
Currency: Communauté Financière Africaine franc (plural—francs); 1 CFA franc (CFAF) = 100 centimes
Exchange rates: Communauté Financière Africaine francs (CFAF) per US$1—256.54 (January 1991), 272.26 (1990), 319.01 (1989), 297.85 (1988), 300.54 (1987), 346.30 (1986), 449.26 (1985)
Fiscal year: 1 April-31 March

Communications

Highways: Rio Muni—1,024 km; Bioko—216 km
Ports: Malabo, Bata
Merchant marine: 2 ships (1,000 GRT or over) totaling 6,413 GRT/6,699 DWT; includes 1 cargo and 1 passenger-cargo
Civil air: 1 major transport aircraft
Airports: 4 total, 3 usable; 2 with permanent-surface runways; none with runways over 3,659 m; 1 with runways 2,440-3,659 m; 1 with runways 1,220-2,439 m
Telecommunications: poor system with adequate government services; international communications from Bata and Malabo to African and European countries; 2,000 telephones; stations—2 AM, no FM, 1 TV; 1 Indian Ocean INTELSAT earth station

Defense Forces

Branches: Army, Navy, Air Force, National Guard, National Police
Manpower availability: males 15-49, 79,641; 40,369 fit for military service
Defense expenditures: $NA, 11% of GNP (FY81 est.)

Ethiopia

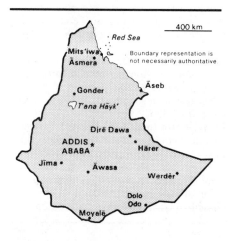

Geography

Total area: 1,221,900 km²; land area: 1,101,000 km²
Comparative area: slightly less than twice the size of Texas
Land boundaries: 5,141 km total; Djibouti 459 km, Kenya 861 km, Somalia 1,600 km, Sudan 2,221 km
Coastline: 1,094 km
Maritime claims:
Territorial sea: 12 nm
Disputes: southern half of the boundary with Somalia is a Provisional Administrative Line; possible claim by Somalia based on unification of ethnic Somalis; territorial dispute with Somalia over the Ogaden; separatist movement in Eritrea; antigovernment insurgencies in Tigray and other areas
Climate: tropical monsoon with wide topographic-induced variation; some areas prone to extended droughts
Terrain: high plateau with central mountain range divided by Great Rift Valley
Natural resources: small reserves of gold, platinum, copper, potash
Land use: arable land 12%; permanent crops 1%; meadows and pastures 41%; forest and woodland 24%; other 22%; includes irrigated NEGL%
Environment: geologically active Great Rift Valley susceptible to earthquakes, volcanic eruptions; deforestation; overgrazing; soil erosion; desertification; frequent droughts; famine
Note: strategic geopolitical position along world's busiest shipping lanes and close to Arabian oilfields; major resettlement project—that was ongoing in rural areas and would have significantly altered population distribution and settlement patterns over the next several decades—has been derailed because of ongoing civil wars

People

Population: 53,191,127 (July 1991), growth rate 3.1% (1991)

Birth rate: 45 births/1,000 population (1991)
Death rate: 15 deaths/1,000 population (1991)
Net migration rate: NEGL migrants/1,000 population (1991)
Infant mortality rate: 114 deaths/1,000 live births (1991)
Life expectancy at birth: 50 years male, 53 years female (1991)
Total fertility rate: 7.0 children born/woman (1991)
Nationality: noun—Ethiopian(s); adjective—Ethiopian
Ethnic divisions: Oromo 40%, Amhara and Tigrean 32%, Sidamo 9%, Shankella 6%, Somali 6%, Afar 4%, Gurage 2%, other 1%
Religion: Muslim 40-45%, Ethiopian Orthodox 35-40%, animist 15-20%, other 5%
Language: Amharic (official), Tigrinya, Orominga, Guaraginga, Somali, Arabic, English (major foreign language taught in schools)
Literacy: 62% (male NA%, female NA%) age 10 and over can read and write (1983 est.)
Labor force: 18,000,000; agriculture and animal husbandry 80%, government and services 12%, industry and construction 8% (1985)
Organized labor: All Ethiopian Trade Union formed by the government in January 1977 to represent 273,000 registered trade union members

Government

Long-form name: People's Democratic Republic of Ethiopia
Type: on 28 May 1991 the Ethiopian People's Revolutionary Democratic Front (EPRDF) took control in Addis Ababa; on 29 May 1991 Issayas AFEWORKE, secretary general of the Eritrean People's Liberation Front (EPLF), announced the formation of a provisional government in Eritrea, in preparation for an eventual referendum on independence for the province
Capital: Addis Ababa
Administrative divisions: 25 administrative regions (āstedader ākababīwach, singular—āstedader ākababī) and 5 autonomous regions* (rasgez ākababīwach, singular—rasgez ākababī); Āddīs Ābeba (Addis Ababa), Ārsī, Āseb*, Āsosa, Balē, Borena, Debub Gonder, Debub Shewa, Debub Welo, Dirē Dawa*, Ērtra (Eritrea)*, Gambēla, Gamo Gofa, Īlubabor, Kefa, Metekel, Mirab Gojam, Mirab Hārergē, Mirab Shewa, Misrak Gojam, Misrak Hārergē, Nazarēt, Ogadēn*, Omo, Semēn Gonder, Semēn Shewa, Semēn Welo, Sīdamo, Tigray*, Welega

Constitution: 12 September 1987
Legal system: complex structure with civil, Islamic, common, and customary law influences; has not accepted compulsory ICJ jurisdiction
National holiday: National Revolution Day, 12 September (1974)
Executive branch: president, vice president, Council of State prime minister, five deputy prime ministers, Council of Ministers
Legislative branch: unicameral National Assembly (Shengo)
Judicial branch: Supreme Court
Leaders:
Chief of State—Interim President Meles ZENAWI (since 1 June 1991);
Head of Government—Acting Prime Minister Tamrat LAYNE (since 6 June 1991)
Political parties and leaders: only party—Workers' Party of Ethiopia (WPE)
Suffrage: universal at age 18
Elections:
President—last held 10 September 1987 (next to be held September 1992); results—MENGISTU Haile-Mariam elected by the National Assembly, but resigned and left Ethiopia on 21 May 1991;
National Assembly—last held 14 June 1987 (next to be held NA); results—WPE was the only party; seats—(835 total) WPE 835
Other political or pressure groups: Oromo Liberation Front; Ethiopian People's Revolutionary Party (EPRP)
Member of: ACP, AfDB, CCC, ECA, FAO, G-24, G-77, IAEA, IBRD, ICAO, IDA, IFAD, IFC, IGADD, ILO, IMF, IMO, INTELSAT, INTERPOL, IOC, ISO, ITU, LORCS, NAM, OAU, UN, UNCTAD, UNESCO, UNIDO, UPU, WFTU, WHO, WMO, WTO
Diplomatic representation: Counselor, Chargé d'Affaires ad interim GIRMA Amare; Chancery at 2134 Kalorama Road NW, Washington DC 20008; telephone (202) 234-2281 or 2282;
US—Chargé d'Affaires Robert G. HOUDEK; Embassy at Entoto Street, Addis Ababa (mailing address is P.O. Box 1014, Addis Ababa); telephone [251] (01) 550666
Flag: three equal horizontal bands of green (top), yellow, and red; Ethiopia is the oldest independent country in Africa and the colors of her flag were so often adopted by other African countries upon independence that they became known as the pan-African colors

Economy

Overview: Ethiopia is one of the poorest and least developed countries in Africa. Its economy is based on subsistence agriculture, which accounts for about 45% of GDP, 90% of exports, and 80% of total employment; coffee generates 60% of export earnings. The manufacturing sector is heavily dependent on inputs from the agricultural sector. Over 90% of large-scale industry, but less then 10% of agriculture, is state run. Favorable agricultural weather largely explains the 4.5% growth in output in FY89.
GDP: $6.6 billion, per capita $130, real growth rate 4.5% (FY89 est.)
Inflation rate (consumer prices): 7.8% (1989)
Unemployment rate: NA
Budget: revenues $1.8 billion; expenditures $1.7 billion, including capital expenditures of $842 million (FY88)
Exports: $429 million (f.o.b., FY88); *commodities*—coffee 60%, hides; *partners*—US, FRG, Djibouti, Japan, PDRY, France, Italy, Saudi Arabia
Imports: $1.1 billion (c.i.f., FY88); *commodities*—food, fuels, capital goods; *partners*—USSR, Italy, FRG, Japan, UK, US, France
External debt: $2.6 billion (1988)
Industrial production: growth rate 2.3% (FY89 est.); accounts for 12% of GDP
Electricity: 330,000 kW capacity; 700 million kWh produced, 14 kWh per capita (1989)
Industries: cement, textiles, food processing, oil refinery
Agriculture: accounts for 45% of GDP and is the most important sector of the economy even though frequent droughts and poor cultivation practices keep farm output low; famines not uncommon; export crops of coffee and oilseeds grown partly on state farms; estimated 50% of agricultural production at subsistence level; principal crops and livestock—cereals, pulses, coffee, oilseeds, sugarcane, potatoes and other vegetables, hides and skins, cattle, sheep, goats
Economic aid: US commitments, including Ex-Im (FY70-89), $504 million; Western (non-US) countries, ODA and OOF bilateral commitments (1970-88), $3.1 billion; OPEC bilateral aid (1979-89), $8 million; Communist countries (1970-89), $2.0 billion
Currency: birr (plural—birr); 1 birr (Br) = 100 cents
Exchange rates: birr (Br) per US$1—2.0700 (fixed rate)
Fiscal year: 8 July-7 July

Communications

Railroads: 988 km total; 681 km 1.000-meter gauge; 307 km 0.950-meter gauge (nonoperational)
Highways: 44,300 km total; 3,650 km bituminous, 9,650 km gravel, 3,000 km improved earth, 28,000 km unimproved earth
Ports: Aseb, Mitsiwa
Merchant marine: 13 ships (1,000 GRT or over) totaling 69,398 GRT/89,457 DWT; includes 9 cargo, 1 roll-on/roll off cargo, 1 livestock carrier, 2 petroleum, oils, and lubricants (POL) tanker
Civil air: 21 major transport aircraft
Airports: 153 total, 111 usable; 9 with permanent-surface runways; 2 with runways over 3,659 m; 13 with runways 2,440-3,659 m; 49 with runways 1,220-2,439 m
Telecommunications: open-wire and radio relay system adequate for government use; open-wire to Sudan and Djibouti; radio relay to Kenya and Djibouti; stations—4 AM, no FM, 1 TV; 45,000 TV sets; 3,300,000 radios; 1 Atlantic Ocean INTELSAT earth station

Defense Forces

Branches: Army, Navy, Air Force, Air Defense, Police Force
Manpower availability: males 15-49, 11,717,614; 6,072,112 fit for military service; 609,346 reach military age (18) annually
Defense expenditures: $NA, 8.5% of GDP (1988)

Europa Island
(French possession)

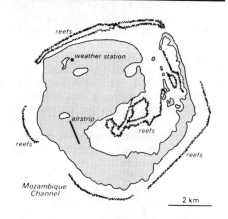

Geography

Total area: 28 km²; land area: 28 km²
Comparative area: about 0.2 times the size of Washington, DC
Land boundaries: none
Coastline: 22.2 km
Maritime claims:
Exclusive economic zone: 200 nm;
Territorial sea: 12 nm
Disputes: claimed by Madagascar
Climate: tropical
Terrain: NA
Natural resources: negligible
Land use: arable land NA%; permanent crops NA%; meadows and pastures NA%; forest and woodland NA%; other NA%; heavily wooded
Environment: wildlife sanctuary
Note: located in the Mozambique Channel 340 km west of Madagascar

People

Population: uninhabited

Government

Long-form name: none
Type: French possession administered by Commissioner of the Republic Daniel CONSTANTIN, resident in Reunion

Economy

Overview: no economic activity

Communications

Airports: 1 with runway 1,220 to 2,439 m
Ports: none; offshore anchorage only
Telecommunications: 1 meteorological station

Defense Forces

Note: defense is the responsibility of France

Falkland Islands
(Islas Malvinas)
(dependent territory of the UK)

Geography

Total area: 12,170 km²; land area: 12,170 km²; includes the two main islands of East and West Falkland and about 200 small islands
Comparative area: slightly smaller than Connecticut
Land boundaries: none
Coastline: 1,288 km
Maritime claims:
Continental shelf: 100 meter depth;
Exclusive fishing zone: 150 nm;
Territorial sea: 12 nm
Disputes: administered by the UK, claimed by Argentina
Climate: cold marine; strong westerly winds, cloudy, humid; rain occurs on more than half of days in year; occasional snow all year, except in January and February, but does not accumulate
Terrain: rocky, hilly, mountainous with some boggy, undulating plains
Natural resources: fish and wildlife
Land use: arable land 0%; permanent crops 0%; meadows and pastures 99%; forest and woodland 0%; other 1%
Environment: poor soil fertility and a short growing season
Note: deeply indented coast provides good natural harbors

People

Population: 1,968 (July 1991), growth rate NEGL% (1991)
Birth rate: NA births/1,000 population (1991)
Death rate: NA deaths/1,000 population (1991)
Net migration rate: NA migrants/1,000 population (1991)
Infant mortality rate: NA deaths/1,000 live births (1991)
Life expectancy at birth: NA years male, NA years female (1991)

Total fertility rate: NA children born/woman (1991)
Nationality: noun—Falkland Islander(s); adjective—Falkland Island
Ethnic divisions: almost totally British
Religion: primarily Anglican, Roman Catholic, and United Free Church; Evangelist Church, Jehovah's Witnesses, Lutheran, Seventh-Day Adventist
Language: English
Literacy: NA% (male NA%, female NA%) but compulsory education age 5 to 15 (1988)
Labor force: 1,100 (est.); agriculture, mostly sheepherding about 95%
Organized labor: Falkland Islands General Employees Union, 400 members

Government

Long-form name: Colony of the Falkland Islands
Type: dependent territory of the UK
Capital: Stanley
Administrative divisions: none (dependent territory of the UK)
Independence: none (dependent territory of the UK)
Constitution: 3 October 1985
Legal system: English common law
National holiday: Liberation Day, 14 June (1982)
Executive branch: British monarch, governor, Executive Council
Legislative branch: unicameral Legislative Council
Judicial branch: Supreme Court
Leaders:
Chief of State—Queen ELIZABETH II (since 6 February 1952);
Head of Government—Governor William Hugh FULLERTON (since NA 1988)
Political parties: NA
Suffrage: universal at age 18
Elections:
Legislative Council—last held 11 October 1989 (next to be held October 1994); results—percent of vote by party NA; seats—(10 total, 8 elected) number of seats by party NA
Member of: ICFTU
Diplomatic representation: none (dependent territory of the UK)
Flag: blue with the flag of the UK in the upper hoist-side quadrant and the Falkland Island coat of arms in a white disk centered on the outer half of the flag; the coat of arms contains a white ram (sheep raising is the major economic activity) above the sailing ship Desire (whose crew discovered the islands) with a scroll at the bottom bearing the motto *DESIRE THE RIGHT*

Economy

Overview: The economy is based on sheep farming, which directly or indirectly

employs most of the work force. A few dairy herds are kept to meet domestic consumption of milk and milk products, and crops grown are primarily those for providing winter fodder. Exports feature shipments of high-grade wool to the UK and the sale of postage stamps and coins. Rich stocks of fish in the surrounding waters are not presently exploited by the islanders. So far efforts to establish a domestic fishing industry have been unsuccessful. In 1987 the government began selling fishing licenses to foreign trawlers operating within the Falklands exclusive fishing zone. These license fees amount to more than $40 million per year and are a primary source of income for the government. To encourage tourism, the Falkland Islands Development Corporation has built three lodges for visitors attracted by the abundant wildlife and trout fishing.
GDP: $NA, per capita $NA; real growth rate NA%
Inflation rate (consumer prices): 7.4% (1980-87 average)
Unemployment rate: NA%; labor shortage
Budget: revenues $62.7 million; expenditures $41.8 million, excluding capital expenditures of $NA (FY90)
Exports: at least $14.7 million;
commodities—wool, hides and skins, and other;
partners—UK, Netherlands, Japan (1987 est.)
Imports: at least $13.9 million;
commodities—food, clothing, fuels, and machinery;
partners—UK, Netherlands Antilles (Curaçao), Japan (1987 est.)
External debt: $NA
Industrial production: growth rate NA%
Electricity: 9,200 kW capacity; 17 million kWh produced, 8,680 kWh per capita (1990)
Industries: wool and fish processing
Agriculture: predominantly sheep farming; small dairy herds; some fodder and vegetable crops
Economic aid: Western (non-US) countries, ODA and OOF bilateral commitments (1970-88), $109 million
Currency: Falkland pound (plural—pounds); 1 Falkland pound (£F) = 100 pence
Exchange rates: Falkland pound (£F) per US$1—0.5171 (January 1991), 0.5603 (1990), 0.6099 (1989), 0.5614 (1988), 0.6102 (1987), 0.6817 (1986), 0.7714 (1985); note—the Falkland pound is at par with the British pound
Fiscal year: 1 April-31 March

Communications

Highways: 510 km total; 30 km paved, 80 km gravel, and 400 km unimproved earth
Ports: Port Stanley

Civil air: no major transport aircraft
Airports: 5 total, 5 usable; 2 with permanent-surface runways; none with runways over 3,659 m; 1 with runways 2,440-3,659 m; none with runways 1,220 to 2,439 m
Telecommunications: government-operated radiotelephone and private VHF/CB radio networks provide effective service to almost all points on both islands; 590 telephones; stations—2 AM, 3 FM, no TV; 1 Atlantic Ocean INTELSAT earth station with links through London to other countries

Defense Forces

Branches: British Forces Falkland Islands (including Army, Royal Air Force, Royal Navy, and Royal Marines); Police Force
Note: defense is the responsibility of the UK

Faroe Islands
(part of the Danish realm)

Geography

Total area: 1,400 km²; land area: 1,400 km²
Comparative area: slightly less than eight times the size of Washington, DC
Land boundaries: none
Coastline: 764 km
Maritime claims:
Exclusive fishing zone: 200 nm;
Territorial sea: 3 nm
Climate: mild winters, cool summers; usually overcast; foggy, windy
Terrain: rugged, rocky, some low peaks; cliffs along most of coast
Natural resources: fish
Land use: arable land 2%; permanent crops 0%; meadows and pastures 0%; forest and woodland 0%; other 98%
Environment: precipitous terrain limits habitation to small coastal lowlands; archipelago of 18 inhabited islands and a few uninhabited islets
Note: strategically located along important sea lanes in northeastern Atlantic about midway between Iceland and Shetland Islands

People

Population: 48,151 (July 1991), growth rate 0.9% (1991)
Birth rate: 17 births/1,000 population (1991)
Death rate: 8 deaths/1,000 population (1991)
Net migration rate: 0 migrants/1,000 population (1991)
Infant mortality rate: 9 deaths/1,000 live births (1991)
Life expectancy at birth: 75 years male, 81 years female (1991)
Total fertility rate: 2.2 children born/woman (1991)
Nationality: noun—Faroese (sing., pl.); adjective—Faroese
Life expectancy at birth: 61 years male, 66 years female (1991)

Faroe Islands *(continued)*

Ethnic divisions: homogeneous Scandinavian population
Religion: Evangelical Lutheran
Language: Faroese (derived from Old Norse), Danish
Literacy: NA% (male NA%, female NA%)
Labor force: 17,585; largely engaged in fishing, manufacturing, transportation, and commerce
Organized labor: NA

Government

Long-form name: none
Type: part of the Danish realm; self-governing overseas administrative division of Denmark
Capital: Tórshavn
Administrative divisions: none (self-governing overseas administrative division of Denmark)
Independence: part of the Danish realm; self-governing overseas administrative division of Denmark
Constitution: Danish
Legal system: Danish
National holiday: Birthday of the Queen, 16 April (1940)
Executive branch: Danish monarch, high commissioner, prime minister, deputy prime minister, Cabinet (Landsstýri)
Legislative branch: unicameral Parliament (Løgting)
Judicial branch: none
Leaders:
Chief of State—Queen MARGRETHE II (since 14 January 1972), represented by High Commissioner Bent KLINTE (since NA);
Head of Government—Prime Minister Atli P. DAM (since 15 January 1991)
Political parties and leaders: *two-party ruling coalition*—Social Democratic Party, Atli P. DAM; People's Party, Jógvan SUNDSTEIN;
opposition—Cooperation Coalition Party, Pauli ELLEFSEN; Republican Party, Signer HANSEN; Progressive and Fishing Industry Party-Christian People's Party (PFIP-CPP), leader NA; Progress Party, leader NA; Home Rule Party, Hilmar KASS
Suffrage: universal at age 20
Elections:
Faroese Parliament—last held 17 November 1990 (next to be held November 1994); results—Social Democratic 27.4%, People's Party 21.9%, Cooperation Coalition Party 18.9%, Republican Party 14.7%, Home Rule 8.8%, PFIP-CPP 5.9%, other 2.4%; seats—(32 total) two-party coalition 17 (Social Democratic 10, People's Party 7), Cooperation Coalition Party 6, Republican Party 4, Home Rule 3, PFIP-CPP 2;
Danish Parliament—last held on 12 December 1990 (next to be held by December 1994); results—percent of vote by party

NA; seats—(2 total) Social Democratic 1, People's Party 1; note—the Faroe Islands elects two representatives to the Danish Parliament
Communists: insignificant number
Member of: none
Diplomatic representation: none (self-governing overseas administrative division of Denmark)
Flag: white with a red cross outlined in blue that extends to the edges of the flag; the vertical part of the cross is shifted to the hoist side in the style of the *Dannebrog* (Danish flag)

Economy

Overview: The Faroese, who have long been enjoying the affluent living standards of the Danes and other Scandinavians, now must cope with the decline of the all-important fishing industry and with an external debt twice the size of annual income. When the nations of the world extended their fishing zones to 200 nautical miles in the early 1970s, the Faroese no longer could continue their traditional long-distance fishing and subsequently depleted their own nearby fishing areas; one estimate foresaw a 25% drop in fish catch in 1990 alone. Half the fishing fleet is for sale, and the 22 fish-processing plants work at only half capacity. The government no longer can maintain its high level of spending on roads and tunnels, hospitals, sports facilities, and other social welfare programs.
GDP: $662 million, per capita $14,000; real growth rate 3% (1989 est.)
Inflation rate (consumer prices): 2.0% (1988)
Unemployment rate: NA%, but increasing
Budget: revenues $442 million; expenditures $442 million, including capital expenditures of NA (1989)
Exports: $343 million (f.o.b., 1989 est.);
commodities—fish and fish products 88%, animal feedstuffs, transport equipment;
partners—Denmark 16%, UK 14%, FRG 13.4%, US 10%, France 9%, Japan 5%
Imports: $344 million (c.i.f., 1989 est.);
commodities—machinery and transport equipment 30%, manufactures 16%, food and livestock 15%, chemicals 6%, fuels 4%;
partners: Denmark 44%, Norway 16%, FRG 6%, Sweden 6%, US 3%
External debt: $1.3 billion (1989)
Industrial production: growth rate NA%
Electricity: 80,000 kW capacity; 280 million kWh produced, 5,910 kWh per capita (1989)
Industries: fishing, shipbuilding, handicrafts
Agriculture: accounts for 27% of GDP and employs 27% of labor force; principal crops—potatoes and vegetables; livestock—sheep; annual fish catch about 360,000 metric tons

Economic aid: none
Currency: Danish krone (plural—kroner); 1 Danish krone (DKr) = 100 øre
Exchange rates: Danish kroner (DKr) per US$1—5.817 (January 1991), 6.189 (1990), 7.310 (1989), 6.732 (1988), 6.840 (1987), 8.091 (1986), 10.596 (1985)
Fiscal year: 1 April-31 March

Communications

Highways: 200 km
Ports: Torshavn, Tvoroyri
Merchant marine: 7 ships (1,000 GRT or over) totaling 17,249 GRT/11,887 DWT; includes 1 short-sea passenger, 2 cargo, 2 roll-on/roll-off cargo, 2 refrigerated cargo; note—a subset of the Danish register
Airports: 1 with permanent surface runway 1,220-2,439 m
Telecommunications: good international communications; fair domestic facilities; 27,900 telephones; stations—1 AM, 3 (10 repeaters) FM, 3 (29 repeaters) TV; 3 coaxial submarine cables

Defense Forces

Branches: no organized native military forces; only a small Police Force is maintained
Note: defense is the responsibility of Denmark

Fiji

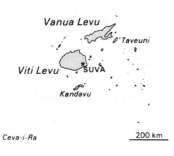

Geography

Total area: 18,270 km²; land area: 18,270 km²

Comparative area: slightly smaller than New Jersey

Land boundaries: none

Coastline: 1,129 km

Maritime claims: (measured from claimed archipelagic baselines)

Continental shelf: 200 m (depth) or to depth of exploitation; rectilinear shelf claim added;

Exclusive economic zone: 200 nm;

Territorial sea: 12 nm

Climate: tropical marine; only slight seasonal temperature variation

Terrain: mostly mountains of volcanic origin

Natural resources: timber, fish, gold, copper; offshore oil potential

Land use: arable land 8%; permanent crops 5%; meadows and pastures 3%; forest and woodland 65%; other 19%; includes irrigated NEGL%

Environment: subject to hurricanes from November to January; includes 332 islands of which approximately 110 are inhabited

Note: located 2,500 km north of New Zealand in the South Pacific Ocean

People

Population: 744,006 (July 1991), growth rate 0.8% (1991)

Birth rate: 26 births/1,000 population (1991)

Death rate: 7 deaths/1,000 population (1991)

Net migration rate: −12 migrants/1,000 population (1991)

Infant mortality rate: 19 deaths/1,000 live births (1991)

Life expectancy at birth: 62 years male, 67 years female (1991)

Total fertility rate: 3.1 children born/woman (1991)

Nationality: noun—Fijian(s); adjective—Fijian

Ethnic divisions: Indian 49%, Fijian 46%, European, other Pacific Islanders, overseas Chinese, and other 5%

Religion: Christian 52% (Methodist 37%, Roman Catholic 9%), Hindu 38%, Muslim 8%, other 2%; note—Fijians are mainly Christian, Indians are Hindu, and there is a Muslim minority (1986)

Language: English (official); Fijian; Hindustani

Literacy: 86% (male 90%, female 81%) age 15 and over can read and write (1985 est.)

Labor force: 235,000; subsistence agriculture 67%, wage earners 18%, salary earners 15% (1987)

Organized labor: about 45,000 employees belong to some 46 trade unions, which are organized along lines of work and ethnic origin (1983)

Government

Long-form name: Republic of Fiji

Type: military coup leader Major General Sitiveni Rabuka formally declared Fiji a republic on 6 October 1987

Capital: Suva

Administrative divisions: 4 divisions and 1 dependency*; Central, Eastern, Northern, Rotuma*, Western

Independence: 10 October 1970 (from UK)

Constitution: 10 October 1970 (suspended 1 October 1987); a new Constitution was proposed on 23 September 1988 and promulgated on 25 July 1990

Legal system: based on British system

National holiday: Independence Day, 10 October (1970)

Executive branch: president, prime minister, Cabinet

Legislative branch: the bicameral Parliament, consisting of an upper house or Senate and a lower house or House of Representatives, was dissolved following the coup of 14 May 1987; the Constitution of 23 September 1988 provides for a bicameral Parliament

Judicial branch: Supreme Court

Leaders:

Chief of State—President Ratu Sir Penaia Kanatabatu GANILAU (since 5 December 1987);

Head of Government—Prime Minister Ratu Sir Kamisese MARA (since 5 December 1987); Deputy Prime Minister Josefata KAMIKAMICA (since NA October 1989); note—Ratu MARA served as prime minister from 10 October 1970 until the 5-11 April 1987 election; after a second coup led by Maj. Gen. Sitiveni RABUKA on 25 September 1987, Ratu MARA was reappointed as prime minister

Political parties and leaders: Fijian Political Party (primarily Fijian), leader NA; National Federation (primarily Indian), Siddiq KOYA;

Western United Front (Fijian), Ratu Osea GAVIDI; Fiji Labor Party, Adi Kuini BAVADRA

Suffrage: none

Elections:

House of Representatives—last held 14 May 1987 (next to be held July 1992); results—percent of vote by party NA; seats—(70 total, with ethnic Fijians allocated 37 seats, ethnic Indians 27 seats, and independents and other 6 seats) number of seats by party NA

Communists: some

Member of: ACP, AsDB, CP, ESCAP, FAO, G-77, IBRD, ICAO, ICFTU, IDA, IFAD, IFC, ILO, IMF, IMO, INTELSAT, INTERPOL, IOC, ITU, LORCS, PCA, SPC, SPF, UN, UNCTAD, UNESCO, UNIDO, UNIFIL, UPU, WHO, WIPO, WMO

Diplomatic representation: Chargé d'Affaires Ratu Finau MARA; Chancery at Suite 240, 2233 Wisconsin Avenue NW, Washington, DC 20007; telephone (202) 337-8320; there is a Fijian Consulate in New York;

US—Ambassador Evelyn I. H. TEEGEN; Embassy at 31 Loftus Street, Suva (mailing address is P. O. Box 218, Suva); telephone [679] 314-466 or 314-069

Flag: light blue with the flag of the UK in the upper hoist-side quadrant and the Fijian shield centered on the outer half of the flag; the shield depicts a yellow lion above a white field quartered by the cross of Saint George featuring stalks of sugarcane, a palm tree, bananas, and a white dove

Economy

Overview: Fiji's economy is primarily agricultural, with a large subsistence sector. Sugar exports are a major source of foreign exchange and sugar processing accounts for one-third of industrial output. Industry, including sugar milling, contributes 13% to GDP. Fiji traditionally had earned considerable sums of hard currency from the 250,000 tourists who visited each year. In 1987, however, after two military coups, the economy went into decline. GDP dropped by 7.8% in 1987 and by another 2.5% in 1988; political uncertainty created a drop in tourism, and the worst drought of the century caused sugar production to fall sharply. In contrast, sugar and tourism turned in strong performances in 1989, and the economy rebounded vigorously. In 1990 the economy received a setback from cyclone Sina which cut sugar output by an estimated 21%.

GDP: $1.36 billion, per capita $1,840; real growth rate 4.7% (1990 est.)

Inflation rate (consumer prices): 8.2% (1990)

Unemployment rate: 11% (1988)

Budget: revenues $314 million; expenditures $355 million, including capital expenditures of $81 million (1990 est.)

Fiji (continued)

Exports: $435 million (f.o.b., 1990); *commodities*—sugar 40%, gold, clothing, copra, processed fish, lumber; *partners*—EC 31%, Australia 21%, Japan 8%, US 6%

Imports: $738 million (c.i.f., 1990); *commodities*—machinery and transport 32%, food 15%, petroleum products, consumer goods, chemicals; *partners*—Australia 30%, NZ 17%, Japan 13%, EC 6%, US 6%

External debt: $428 million (December 1990 est.)

Industrial production: growth rate 5% (1990 est.); accounts for 13% of GDP

Electricity: 215,000 kW capacity; 330 million kWh produced, 430 kWh per capita (1990)

Industries: sugar, copra, tourism, gold, silver, fishing, clothing, lumber, small cottage industries

Agriculture: accounts for 23% of GDP; principal cash crop is sugarcane; coconuts, cassava, rice, sweet potatoes, and bananas; small livestock sector includes cattle, pigs, horses, and goats

Economic aid: Western (non-US) countries, ODA and OOF bilateral commitments (1980-87), $732 million

Currency: Fijian dollar (plural—dollars); 1 Fijian dollar (F$) = 100 cents

Exchange rates: Fijian dollars (F$) per US$1—1.4476 (January 1991), 1.4809 (1990), 1.4833 (1989), 1.4303 (1988), 1.2439 (1987), 1.1329 (1986), 1.1536 (1985)

Fiscal year: calendar year

Communications

Railroads: 644 km 0.610-meter narrow gauge, belonging to the government-owned Fiji Sugar Corporation

Highways: 3,300 km total (1984)—390 km paved; 1,200 km bituminous-surface treatment; 1,290 km gravel, crushed stone, or stabilized soil surface; 420 unimproved earth

Inland waterways: 203 km; 122 km navigable by motorized craft and 200-metric-ton barges

Ports: Lambasa, Lautoka, Savusavu, Suva

Merchant marine: 6 ships (1,000 GRT or over) totaling 34,214 GRT/37,161 DWT; includes 2 roll-on/roll-off cargo, 2 container, 1 petroleum, oils, and lubricants (POL) tanker, 1 chemical tanker

Civil air: 1 DC-3 and 1 light aircraft

Airports: 26 total, 24 usable; 2 with permanent-surface runways; none with runways over 3,659 m; 1 with runways 2,440-3,659 m; 2 with runways 1,220-2,439 m

Telecommunications: modern local, interisland, and international (wire/radio integrated) public and special-purpose telephone, telegraph, and teleprinter facilities; regional radio center; important COMPAC cable link between US-Canada and New Zealand-Australia; 53,228 telephones; stations—7 AM, 1 FM, no TV; 1 Pacific Ocean INTELSAT earth station

Defense Forces

Branches: Fiji Military Force (FMF; Army, Navy, Police)

Manpower availability: males 15-49, 190,120; 104,861 fit for military service; 7,879 reach military age (18) annually

Defense expenditures: $25.8 million, 2.5% of GDP (1988)

Finland

Geography

Total area: 337,030 km²; land area: 305,470 km²

Comparative area: slightly smaller than Montana

Land boundaries: 2,628 km total; Norway 729 km, Sweden 586 km, USSR 1,313 km

Coastline: 1,126 km excluding islands and coastal indentations

Maritime claims:
Contiguous zone: 6 nm;
Continental shelf: 200 m (depth) or to depth of exploitation;
Exclusive fishing zone: 12 nm;
Territorial sea: 4 nm

Climate: cold temperate; potentially subarctic, but comparatively mild because of moderating influence of the North Atlantic Current, Baltic Sea, and more than 60,000 lakes

Terrain: mostly low, flat to rolling plains interspersed with lakes and low hills

Natural resources: timber, copper, zinc, iron ore, silver

Land use: arable land 8%; permanent crops 0%; meadows and pastures NEGL%; forest and woodland 76%; other 16%; includes irrigated NEGL%

Environment: permanently wet ground covers about 30% of land; population concentrated on small southwestern coastal plain

Note: long boundary with USSR; Helsinki is northernmost national capital on European continent

People

Population: 4,991,131 (July 1991), growth rate 0.3% (1991)

Birth rate: 12 births/1,000 population (1991)

Death rate: 10 deaths/1,000 population (1991)

Net migration rate: NEGL migrants/1,000 population (1991)

Infant mortality rate: 6 deaths/1,000 live births (1991)

Life expectancy at birth: 71 years male, 80 years female (1991)
Total fertility rate: 1.7 children born/woman (1991)
Nationality: noun—Finn(s); adjective—Finnish
Ethnic divisions: Finn, Swede, Lapp, Gypsy, Tatar
Religion: Evangelical Lutheran 89%, Greek Orthodox 1%, none 9%, other 1%
Language: Finnish 93.5%, Swedish (both official) 6.3%; small Lapp- and Russian-speaking minorities
Literacy: 100% (male NA%, female NA%) age 15 and over can read and write (1980 est.)
Labor force: 2,470,000; services 38.2%, mining and manufacturing 22.7%, commerce 14.9%, agriculture, forestry, and fishing 8.8%, construction 8.0%, transportation and communications 7.2% (1989)
Organized labor: 80% of labor force

Government

Long-form name: Republic of Finland
Type: republic
Capital: Helsinki
Administrative divisions: 12 provinces (läänit, singular—lääni); Ahvenanmaa, Häme, Keski-Suomi, Kuopio, Kymi, Lappi, Mikkeli, Oulu, Pohjois-Karjala, Turku ja Pori, Uusimaa, Vaasa
Independence: 6 December 1917 (from Soviet Union)
Constitution: 17 July 1919
Legal system: civil law system based on Swedish law; Supreme Court may request legislation interpreting or modifying laws; accepts compulsory ICJ jurisdiction, with reservations
National holiday: Independence Day, 6 December (1917)
Executive branch: president, prime minister, deputy prime minister, Council of State (Valtioneuvosto)
Legislative branch: unicameral Eduskunta
Judicial branch: Supreme Court (Korkein Oikeus)
Leaders:
Chief of State—President Mauno KOIVISTO (since 27 January 1982);
Head of Government—Prime Minister Esko AHO (since 26 April 1991); Deputy Prime Minister Ilkka KANERVA (since 26 April 1991)
Political parties and leaders:
government coalition—Center Party, Esko AHO; National Coalition (Conservative) Party, Ilkka SUOMINEN; and Swedish People's Party, (Johan) Ole NORRBACK; *other parties*—Social Democratic Party, Pertti PAASIO; Leftist Alliance (Communist) consisting of People's Democratic League and Democratic Alternative, Claes

ANDERSSON; Green League, Heidi HAUTALA; Rural Party, Heikki RIIHIJAERVI; Finnish Christian League, Esko ALMGREN; Liberal People's Party, Kyösti LALLUKKA
Suffrage: universal at age 18
Elections:
President—last held 31 January-1 February and 15 February 1988 (next to be held January 1994); results—Mauno KOIVISTO 48%, Paavo VÄYRYNEN 20%, Harri HOLKERI 18%;
Eduskunta—last held 17 March 1991 (next to be held March 1995); results—Center Party 24.8%, Social Democratic Party 22.1%, National Coalition (Conservative) Party 19.3%, Leftist Alliance (Communist) 10.1%, Green League 6.8%, Swedish People's Party 5.5%, Rural 4.8%, Finnish Christian League 3.1%, Liberal People's Party 0.8%; seats—(200 total) Center Party 55, Social Democratic Party 48, National Coalition (Conservative) Party 40, Leftist Alliance (Communist) 19, Swedish People's Party 12, Green League 10, Finnish Christian League 8, Rural 7, Liberal People's Party 1
Communists: 28,000 registered members; an additional 45,000 persons belong to People's Democratic League
Other political or pressure groups: Finnish Communist Party-Unity, Esko-Juhani TENNILA; Constitutional Rightist Party; Finnish Pensioners Party; Communist Workers Party, Timo LAHDENMAKI
Member of: AfDB, AG (observer), AsDB, BIS, CCC, CE, CSCE, EBRD, ECE, EFTA, ESA (associate), FAO, G-9, GATT, IADB, IAEA, IBRD, ICAO, ICC, ICFTU, IDA, IFAD, IFC, ILO, IMF, IMO, INMARSAT, INTELSAT, INTERPOL, IOC, IOM (observer), ISO, ITU, LORCS, NAM (guest), NC, NEA, NIB, OAS (observer), OECD, PCA, UN, UNCTAD, UNDOF, UNESCO, UNFICYP, UNHCR, UNIDO, UNIFIL, UNIIMOG, UNMOGIP, UNTSO, UPU, WHO, WIPO, WMO, WTO
Diplomatic representation: Ambassador Jukka VALTASAARI; Chancery at 3216 New Mexico Avenue NW, Washington DC 20016; telephone (202) 363-2430; there are Finnish Consulates General in Los Angeles and New York, and Consulates in Chicago and Houston;
US—Ambassador John G. WEINMANN; Embassy at Itainen Puistotie 14A, SF-00140, Helsinki (mailing address is APO New York 09664); telephone [358] (0) 171931
Flag: white with a blue cross that extends to the edges of the flag; the vertical part of the cross is shifted to the hoist side in the style of the *Dannebrog* (Danish flag)

Economy

Overview: Finland has a highly industrialized, largely free market economy, with per capita output nearly three-fourths the US figure. Its main economic force is the manufacturing sector—principally the wood, metals, and engineering industries. Trade is important, with the export of goods representing about 30% of GDP. Except for timber and several minerals, Finland depends on imported raw materials, energy, and some components of manufactured goods. Because of the climate, agricultural development is limited to maintaining self-sufficiency in basic commodities. The economy, which experienced an average of 4.9% annual growth between 1987 and 1989, leveled off in 1990 and is now in a recession facing negative growth in 1991. The clearing account system between Finland and the Soviet Union in the postwar period—mainly Soviet oil and gas for Finnish manufactured goods—had kept Finland isolated from world recessions; the system, however, was dismantled on 1 January 1991 in favor of hard currency trade. As a result, Finland must increase its competitiveness in certain sectors, for example, textiles, foodstuffs, paper, and metals, and has already begun to shift trade westward. Finland, as a member of EFTA, is negotiating a European Economic Area arrangement with the EC which would allow for free movement of capital, goods, services, and labor within the organization.
GDP: $77.3 billion, per capita $15,500; real growth rate -0.1% (1990)
Inflation rate (consumer prices): 6.1% (1990)
Unemployment rate: 3.4% (1990)
Budget: revenues $35.1 billion; expenditures $33.1 billion, including capital expenditures of $1.4 billion (1990)
Exports: $23.3 billion (f.o.b., 1989);
commodities—timber, paper and pulp, ships, machinery, clothing and footwear;
partners—EC 44.0% (UK 12.0%, FRG 10.8%), USSR 14.5%, Sweden 14.3%, US 6.4%
Imports: $24.4 billion (c.i.f., 1989);
commodities—foodstuffs, petroleum and petroleum products, chemicals, transport equipment, iron and steel, machinery, textile yarn and fabrics, fodder grains;
partners—EC 44.5% (FRG 17.3%, UK 6.6%), Sweden 13.6%, USSR 11.5%, US 6.3%
External debt: $5.3 billion (1989)
Industrial production: growth rate -2.0% (1990 est.); accounts for 28% of GDP
Electricity: 13,324,000 kW capacity; 49,330 million kWh produced, 9,940 kWh per capita (1989)

Finland (continued)

Industries: metal manufacturing and ship-building, forestry and wood processing (pulp, paper), copper refining, foodstuffs, textiles, clothing

Agriculture: accounts for 8% of GNP (including forestry); livestock production, especially dairy cattle, predominates; forestry is an important export earner and a secondary occupation for the rural population; main crops—cereals, sugar beets, potatoes; 85% self-sufficient, but short of food and fodder grains; annual fish catch about 160,000 metric tons

Economic aid: donor—ODA and OOF commitments (1970-88), $2.1 billion

Currency: markka (plural—markkaa); 1 markka (FMk) or Finmark = 100 penniä

Exchange rates: markkaa (FMk) per US$1—3.6421 (January 1991), 3.8235 (1990), 4.2912 (1989), 4.1828 (1988), 4.3956 (1987), 5.0695 (1986), 6.1979 (1985)

Fiscal year: calendar year

Communications

Railroads: 5,924 km total; Finnish State Railways (VR) operate a total of 5,863 km 1.524-meter gauge, of which 480 km are multiple track and 1,445 km are electrified

Highways: about 103,000 km total, including 35,000 km paved (bituminous, concrete, bituminous-treated surface) and 38,000 km unpaved (stabilized gravel, gravel, earth); additional 30,000 km of private (state-subsidized) roads

Inland waterways: 6,675 km total (including Saimaa Canal); 3,700 km suitable for steamers

Pipelines: natural gas, 580 km

Ports: Helsinki, Oulu, Pori, Rauma, Turku; 6 secondary, numerous minor ports

Merchant marine: 83 ships (1,000 GRT or over) totaling 807,020 GRT/831,774 DWT; includes 3 passenger, 10 short-sea passenger, 16 cargo, 1 refrigerated cargo, 23 roll-on/roll-off cargo, 14 petroleum, oils, and lubricants (POL) tanker, 6 chemical tanker, 2 liquefied gas, 8 bulk

Civil air: 42 major transport

Airports: 160 total, 157 usable; 57 with permanent-surface runways; none with runways over 3,659 m; 23 with runways 2,440-3,659 m; 22 with runways 1,220-2,439 m

Telecommunications: good service from cable and radio relay network; 3,140,000 telephones; stations—4 AM, 42 (101 relays) FM, 79 (197 relays) TV; 2 submarine cables; satellite service via Swedish earth stations; earth stations—2 Atlantic Ocean INTELSAT and 1 EUTELSAT

Defense Forces

Branches: Army, Navy, Air Force, Frontier Guard (including Sea Guard)

Manpower availability: males 15-49, 1,313,346; 1,089,217 fit for military service; 32,866 reach military age (17) annually

Defense expenditures: $1.1 billion, 1.5% of GDP (1989 est.)

France

Geography

Total area: 547,030 km²; land area: 545,630 km²; includes Corsica and the rest of metropolitan France, but excludes the overseas administrative divisions

Comparative area: slightly more than twice the size of Colorado

Land boundaries: 2,892.4 km total; Andorra 60 km, Belgium 620 km, Germany 451 km, Italy 488 km, Luxembourg 73 km, Monaco 4.4 km, Spain 623 km, Switzerland 573 km

Coastline: 3,427 km (includes Corsica, 644 km)

Maritime claims:
Contiguous zone: 12-24 nm;
Exclusive economic zone: 200 nm;
Territorial sea: 12 nm

Disputes: maritime boundary dispute with Canada (Saint Pierre and Miquelon); Madagascar claims Bassas da India, Europa Island, Glorioso Islands, Juan de Nova Island, and Tromelin Island; Comoros claims Mayotte; Mauritius claims Tromelin Island; Seychelles claims Tromelin Island; Suriname claims part of French Guiana; Mexico claims Clipperton Island; territorial claim in Antarctica (Adélie Land)

Climate: generally cool winters and mild summers, but mild winters and hot summers along the Mediterranean

Terrain: mostly flat plains or gently rolling hills in north and west; remainder is mountainous, especially Pyrenees in south, Alps in east

Natural resources: coal, iron ore, bauxite, fish, timber, zinc, potash

Land use: arable land 32%; permanent crops 2%; meadows and pastures 23%; forest and woodland 27%; other 16%; includes irrigated 2%

Environment: most of large urban areas and industrial centers in Rhône, Garonne, Seine, or Loire River basins; occasional warm tropical wind known as mistral

Note: largest West European nation

People

Population: 56,595,587 (July 1991), growth rate 0.4% (1991)
Birth rate: 14 births/1,000 population (1991)
Death rate: 9 deaths/1,000 population (1991)
Net migration rate: 0 migrants/1,000 population (1991)
Infant mortality rate: 6 deaths/1,000 live births (1991)
Life expectancy at birth: 74 years male, 82 years female (1991)
Total fertility rate: 1.8 children born/woman (1991)
Nationality: noun—Frenchman(men), Frenchwoman(women); adjective—French
Ethnic divisions: Celtic and Latin with Teutonic, Slavic, North African, Indochinese, and Basque minorities
Religion: Roman Catholic 90%, Protestant 2%, Jewish 1%, Muslim (North African workers) 1%, unaffiliated 6%
Language: French (100% of population); rapidly declining regional dialects (Provençal, Breton, Alsatian, Corsican, Catalan, Basque, Flemish)
Literacy: 99% (male NA%, female NA%) age 15 and over can read and write (1980 est.)
Labor force: 24,170,000; services 61.5%, industry 31.3%, agriculture 7.3% (1987)
Organized labor: 20% of labor force (est.)

Government

Long-form name: French Republic
Type: republic
Capital: Paris
Administrative divisions: metropolitan France—22 regions (régions, singular—région); Alsace, Aquitaine, Auvergne, Basse-Normandie, Bourgogne, Bretagne, Centre, Champagne-Ardenne, Corse, Franche-Comté, Haute-Normandie, Île-de-France, Languedoc-Roussillon, Limousin, Lorraine, Midi-Pyrénées, Nord-Pas-de-Calais, Pays de la Loire, Picardie, Poitou-Charentes, Provence-Alpes-Côte d'Azur, Rhône-Alpes; note—the 22 regions are subdivided into 96 departments; see separate entries for the overseas departments (French Guiana, Guadeloupe, Martinique, Reunion) and the territorial collectivities (Mayotte, Saint Pierre and Miquelon)
Dependent areas: Bassas da India, Clipperton Island, Europa Island, French Polynesia, French Southern and Antarctic Lands, Glorioso Islands, Juan de Nova Island, New Caledonia, Tromelin Island, Wallis and Futuna; note—the US does not recognize claims to Antarctica
Independence: unified by Clovis in 486, First Republic proclaimed in 1792

Constitution: 28 September 1958, amended concerning election of president in 1962
Legal system: civil law system with indigenous concepts; review of administrative but not legislative acts
National holiday: Taking of the Bastille, 14 July (1789)
Executive branch: president, prime minister, Council of Ministers (cabinet)
Legislative branch: bicameral Parliament (Parlement) consists of an upper house or Senate (Sénat) and a lower house or National Assembly (Assemblée Nationale)
Judicial branch: Court of Cassation (Cour de Cassation)
Leaders:
Chief of State—President François MITTERRAND (since 21 May 1981);
Head of Government—Prime Minister Edith CRESSON (since 15 May 1991)
Political parties and leaders: Rally for the Republic (RPR, formerly UDR), Jacques CHIRAC; Union for French Democracy (UDF, federation of PR, CDS, and RAD), Valéry Giscard d'ESTAING; Republican Party (PR), Gerard LONGUET; Center for Social Democrats (CDS), Pierre MÉHAIGNERIE; Radical (RAD), Yves GALLARD; Socialist Party (PS), Pierre MAUROY; Left Radical Movement (MRG), Yves COLLIN; Communist Party (PCF), Georges MARCHAIS; National Front (FN), Jean-Marie LE PEN
Suffrage: universal at age 18
Elections:
President—last held 8 May 1988 (next to be held May 1995); results—Second Ballot François MITTERRAND 54%, Jacques CHIRAC 46%;
Senate—last held 24 September 1989 (next to be held September 1992); results—percent of vote by party NA; seats—(321 total; 296 metropolitan France, 13 for overseas departments and territories, and 12 for French nationals abroad) RPR 93, UDF 143 (PR 53, CDS 65, RAD 25), PS 64, PCF 16, independents 2, unknown 3;
National Assembly—last held 5 and 12 June 1988 (next to be held June 1993); results—Second Ballot PS-MRG 48.7%, RPR 23.1%, UDF 21%, PCF 3.4%, other 3.8%; seats—(577 total) PS 275, RPR 132, UDF 90, UDC 40, PCF 25, independents 15
Communists: 700,000 claimed but probably closer to 150,000; Communist voters, 2.8 million in 1988 election
Other political or pressure groups: Communist-controlled labor union (Confédération Générale du Travail) nearly 2.4 million members (claimed); Socialist-leaning labor union (Confédération Française Démocratique du Travail or CFDT) about 800,000 members est.; independent labor union (Force Ouvrière) 1 million members (est.); independent white-collar union (Confédération Générale des Cadres) 340,000

members (claimed); National Council of French Employers (Conseil National du Patronat Français—CNPF or Patronat)
Member of: ACCT, AfDB, AG (observer), AsDB, BDEAC, BIS, CCC, CDB, CE, CERN, COCOM, CSCE, EBRD, EC, ECA (associate), ECE, ECLAC, EIB, ESA, ESCAP, FAO, FZ, GATT, G-5, G-7, G-10, IABD, IAEA, IBRD, ICAO, ICC, ICFTU, IDA, IFAD, IFC, ILO, IMF, IMO, INMARSAT, INTELSAT, INTERPOL, IOC, IOM (observer), ISO, ITU, LORCS, NATO, NEA, OAS (observer), OECD, PCA, SPC, UN, UNCTAD, UNESCO, UNHCR, UNIDO, UNIFIL, UNRWA, UN Security Council, UN Trusteeship Council, UNTSO, UPU, WCL, WEU, WFTU, WHO, WIPO, WMO, WTO
Diplomatic representation: Ambassador Jacques ANDREANI; Chancery at 4101 Reservoir Road NW, Washington DC 20007; telephone (202) 944-6000; there are French Consulates General in Boston, Chicago, Detroit, Houston, Los Angeles, New Orleans, Miami, New York, San Francisco, and San Juan (Puerto Rico);
US—Ambassador Walter J. P. CURLEY; Embassy at 2 Avenue Gabriel, 75382 Paris Cedex 08 (mailing address is APO New York 09777); telephone [33] (1) 42-96-12-02 or 42-61-80-75; there are US Consulates General in Bordeaux, Lyon, Marseille, and Strasbourg
Flag: three equal vertical bands of blue (hoist side), white, and red; known as the French *Tricouleur* (Tricolor); the design and colors have been the basis for a number of other flags, including those of Belgium, Chad, Ireland, Ivory Coast, and Luxembourg; the official flag for all French dependent areas

Economy

Overview: One of the world's most developed economies, France has substantial agricultural resources and a highly diversified modern industrial sector. Large tracts of fertile land, the application of modern technology, and subsidies have combined to make it the leading agricultural producer in Western Europe. France is largely self-sufficient in agricultural products and is a major exporter of wheat and dairy products. The industrial sector generates about one-quarter of GDP, and the growing services sector has become crucial to the economy. After sluggish growth during the period 1982-87, the economy expanded at a rapid 3.8% pace in 1988-89. The economy slowed down in 1990, with growth of 2.0% expected in 1991. The economy has had difficulty generating enough jobs for new entrants into the labor force, resulting in a high unemployment rate, which probably will rise to around 10% during the slowdown. The

France *(continued)*

steadily advancing economic integration within the European Community is a major force affecting the fortunes of the various economic sectors.

GDP: $873.5 billion, per capita $15,500; real growth rate 2.8% (1990 est.)

Inflation rate (consumer prices): 3.7% (1990 est.)

Unemployment rate: 9% (1990)

Budget: revenues $207.6 billion; expenditures $224.2 billion, including capital expenditures of $34 billion (1990 est.)

Exports: $181.2 billion (f.o.b., 1990); *commodities*—machinery and transportation equipment, chemicals, foodstuffs, agricultural products, iron and steel products, textiles and clothing; *partners*—FRG 16%, Italy 12.1%, UK 9.5%, Spain 9.5%, Netherlands 9.2%, Belgium-Luxembourg 8.9%, US 6.6%, Japan 1.9%, USSR 1.0% (1989 est.)

Imports: $201.6 billion (c.i.f., 1989); *commodities*—crude oil, machinery and equipment, agricultural products, chemicals, iron and steel products; *partners*—FRG 19.4%, Italy 11.6%, Belgium-Luxembourg 9.2%, Netherlands 8.6%, US 7.6%, Spain 7.4%, UK 7.1%, Japan 4.1%, USSR 1.4% (1989 est.)

External debt: $59.3 billion (December 1987)

Industrial production: growth rate 3.7% (1989); accounts for 26% of GDP

Electricity: 109,972,000 kW capacity; 403,570 million kWh produced, 7,210 kWh per capita (1989)

Industries: steel, machinery, chemicals, automobiles, metallurgy, aircraft, electronics, mining, textiles, food processing, and tourism

Agriculture: accounts for 4% of GNP (including fishing and forestry); one of the world's top five wheat producers; other principal products—beef, dairy products, cereals, sugar beets, potatoes, wine grapes; self-sufficient for most temperate-zone foods; shortages include fats and oils and tropical produce, but overall net exporter of farm products; fish catch of 850,000 metric tons ranks among world's top 20 countries and is all used domestically

Economic aid: donor—ODA and OOF commitments (1970-88), $67.1 billion

Currency: French franc (plural—francs); 1 French franc (F) = 100 centimes

Exchange rates: French francs (F) per US$1—5.8 (May 1991), 5.4453 (1990), 6.3801 (1989), 5.9569 (1988), 6.0107 (1987), 6.9261 (1986), 8.9852 (1985)

Fiscal year: calendar year

Communications

Railroads: French National Railways (SNCF) operates 34,568 km 1.435-meter standard gauge; 11,674 km electrified, 15,132 km double or multiple track; 2,138 km of various gauges (1.000-meter to 1.440-meter), privately owned and operated

Highways: 1,551,400 km total; 33,400 km national highway; 347,000 km departmental highway; 421,000 km community roads; 750,000 km rural roads; 5,401 km of controlled-access divided autoroutes; about 803,000 km paved

Inland waterways: 14,932 km; 6,969 km heavily traveled

Pipelines: crude oil, 3,059 km; refined products, 4,487 km; natural gas, 24,746 km

Ports: maritime—Bordeaux, Boulogne, Brest, Cherbourg, Dunkerque, Fos-Sur-Mer, Le Havre, Marseille, Nantes, Rouen, Sète, Toulon; inland—42

Merchant marine: 133 ships (1,000 GRT or over) totaling 3,141,276 GRT/5,006,695 DWT; includes 8 short-sea passenger, 15 cargo, 18 container, 2 multifunction large-load carrier, 29 roll-on/roll-off cargo, 34 petroleum, oils, and lubricants (POL) tanker, 8 chemical tanker, 6 liquefied gas, 2 specialized tanker, 11 bulk; note—France also maintains a captive register for French-owned ships in the Kerguelen Islands (French Southern and Antarctic Lands) and French Polynesia

Civil air: 195 (1989 est.)

Airports: 470 total, 460 usable; 246 with permanent-surface runways; 3 with runways over 3,659 m; 34 with runways 2,440-3,659 m; 136 with runways 1,220-2,439 m

Telecommunications: highly developed system provides satisfactory telephone, telegraph, radio and TV broadcast services; 39,200,000 telephones; stations—40 AM, 138 (777 relays) FM, 216 (8,902 relays) TV; 25 submarine coaxial cables; communication satellite earth stations operating in INTELSAT, 3 Atlantic Ocean and 2 Indian Ocean, EUTELSAT, MARISAT, and domestic systems

Defense Forces

Branches: Army, Navy (including Naval Air), Air Force, National Gendarmerie

Manpower availability: males 15-49, 14,366,492; 12,077,706 fit for military service; 395,128 reach military age (18) annually

Defense expenditures: $29.7 billion, 3.6% of GDP (1990)

French Guiana
(overseas department of France)

Boundary representation is not necessarily authoritative

Geography

Total area: 91,000 km²; land area: 89,150 km²

Comparative area: slightly smaller than Indiana

Land boundaries: 1,183 km total; Brazil 673 km, Suriname 510 km

Coastline: 378 km

Maritime claims:
Exclusive economic zone: 200 nm;
Territorial sea: 12 nm

Disputes: Suriname claims area between Rivière Litani and Rivière Marouini (both headwaters of the Lawa)

Climate: tropical; hot, humid; little seasonal temperature variation

Terrain: low-lying coastal plains rising to hills and small mountains

Natural resources: bauxite, timber, gold (widely scattered), cinnabar, kaolin, fish

Land use: arable land NEGL%; permanent crops NEGL%; meadows and pastures NEGL%; forest and woodland 82%; other 18%

Environment: mostly an unsettled wilderness

People

Population: 101,603 (July 1991), growth rate 3.3% (1991)

Birth rate: 28 births/1,000 population (1991)

Death rate: 5 deaths/1,000 population (1991)

Net migration rate: 10 migrants/1,000 population (1991)

Infant mortality rate: 18 deaths/1,000 live births (1991)

Life expectancy at birth: 69 years male, 76 years female (1991)

Total fertility rate: 3.7 children born/woman (1991)

Nationality: noun—French Guianese (sing., pl.); adjective—French Guiana

Ethnic divisions: black or mulatto 66%; Caucasian 12%; East Indian, Chinese, Amerindian 12%; other 10%

Religion: predominantly Roman Catholic
Language: French
Literacy: 82% (male 81%, female 83%) age 15 and over can read and write (1982)
Labor force: 23,265; services, government, and commerce 60.6%, industry 21.2%, agriculture 18.2% (1980)
Organized labor: 7% of labor force

Government

Long-form name: Department of Guiana
Type: overseas department of France
Capital: Cayenne
Administrative divisions: none (overseas department of France)
Independence: none (overseas department of France)
Constitution: 28 September 1958 (French Constitution)
Legal system: French legal system
National holiday: Taking of the Bastille, 14 July (1789)
Executive branch: French president, commissioner of the republic
Legislative branch: unicameral General Council and a unicameral Regional Council
Judicial branch: highest local court is the Court of Appeals based in Martinique with jurisdiction over Martinique, Guadeloupe, and French Guiana
Leaders:
Chief of State—President François MITTERRAND (since 21 May 1981);
Head of Government—Commissioner of the Republic Jean-François DI CHIARA (since NA 1990)
Political parties and leaders: Guianese Socialist Party (PSG), Gérard HOLDER; Rally for the Republic (RPR), Paulin BRUNÉ; Guyanese Democratic Action (ADG), André Lecante; Union for French Democracy (UDF), Claude Ho A CHUCK; National Front (FN), Guy MALON; Popular and National Party of Guiana (PNPG), Claude ROBO; National Anti-Colonist Guianese Party (PANGA), Michel KAPEL
Suffrage: universal at age 18
Elections:
Regional Council—last held 16 March 1986 (next to be held NA 1991); results—PSG 43%, RPR 27.7%, ADG 12.2%, UDF 8.9%, FN 3.7%, PNPG 1.4%, other 3.1%; seats—(31 total) PSG 15, RPR 9, ADG 4, UDF 3;
French Senate—last held 24 September 1989 (next to be held September 1992); results—percent of vote by party NA; seats—(1 total) PSG 1;
French National Assembly—last held 24 September 1989 (next to be held September 1992); results—percent of vote by party NA; seats—(2 total) PSG 1, RPR 1
Communists: Communist party membership negligible
Member of: FZ, WCL, WFTU

Diplomatic representation: as an overseas department of France the interests of French Guiana are represented in the US by France
Flag: the flag of France is used

Economy

Overview: The economy is tied closely to that of France through subsidies and imports. Besides the French space center at Kourou, fishing and forestry are the most important economic activities, with exports of fish and fish products (mostly shrimp) accounting for more than 60% of total revenue in 1987. The large reserves of tropical hardwoods, not fully exploited, support an expanding sawmill industry that provides sawn logs for export. Cultivation of crops—rice, cassava, bananas, and sugarcane—are limited to the coastal area, where the population is largely concentrated. French Guiana is heavily dependent on imports of food and energy. Unemployment is a serious problem, particularly among younger workers.
GDP: $186 million, per capita $2,240; real growth rate NA% (1985)
Inflation rate (consumer prices): 4.1% (1987)
Unemployment rate: 15% (1987)
Budget: revenues $735 million; expenditures $735 million, including capital expenditures of NA (1987)
Exports: $54.0 million (f.o.b., 1987); *commodities*—shrimp, timber, rum, rosewood essence; *partners*—France 31%, US 22%, Japan 10% (1987)
Imports: $394.0 million (c.i.f., 1987); *commodities*—food (grains, processed meat), other consumer goods, producer goods, petroleum; *partners*—France 62%, Trinidad and Tobago 9%, US 4%, FRG 3% (1987)
External debt: $1.2 billion (1988)
Industrial production: growth rate NA%
Electricity: 92,000 kW capacity; 185 million kWh produced, 1,890 kWh per capita (1990)
Industries: construction, shrimp processing, forestry products, rum, gold mining
Agriculture: some vegetables for local consumption; rice, corn, manioc, cocoa, bananas, sugar; livestock—cattle, pigs, poultry
Economic aid: Western (non-US) countries, ODA and OOF bilateral commitments (1970-87), $1.25 billion
Currency: French franc (plural—francs); 1 French franc (F) = 100 centimes
Exchange rates: French francs (F) per US$1—5.1307 (January 1991), 5.4453 (1990), 6.3801 (1989), 5.9569 (1988), 6.0107 (1987), 6.9261 (1986), 8.9852 (1985)
Fiscal year: calendar year

Communications

Highways: 680 km total; 510 km paved, 170 km improved and unimproved earth
Inland waterways: 460 km, navigable by small oceangoing vessels and river and coastal steamers; 3,300 km possibly navigable by native craft
Ports: Cayenne
Civil air: no major transport aircraft
Airports: 10 total, 10 usable; 5 with permanent-surface runways; none with runways over 3,659 m; 1 with runways 2,440-3,659 m; 1 with runways 1,220-2,439 m
Telecommunications: fair open wire and radio relay system; 18,100 telephones; stations—5 AM, 7 FM, 9 TV; 1 Atlantic Ocean INTELSAT earth station

Defense Forces

Branches: French Forces, Gendarmerie
Manpower availability: males 15-49 28,650; 18,903 fit for military service
Note: defense is the responsibility of France

French Polynesia
(overseas territory of France)

Geography

Total area: 3,941 km²; land area: 3,660 km²
Comparative area: slightly less than one-third the size of Connecticut
Land boundaries: none
Coastline: 2,525 km
Maritime claims:
Exclusive economic zone: 200 nm;
Territorial sea: 12 nm
Climate: tropical, but moderate
Terrain: mixture of rugged high islands and low islands with reefs
Natural resources: timber, fish, cobalt
Land use: arable land 1%; permanent crops 19%; meadows and pastures 5%; forest and woodland 31%; other 44%
Environment: occasional cyclonic storm in January; includes five archipelagoes
Note: Makatea in French Polynesia is one of the three great phosphate rock islands in the Pacific Ocean—the others are Banaba (Ocean Island) in Kiribati and Nauru

People

Population: 195,046 (July 1991), growth rate 2.5% (1991)
Birth rate: 31 births/1,000 population (1991)
Death rate: 6 deaths/1,000 population (1991)
Net migration rate: 0 migrants/1,000 population (1991)
Infant mortality rate: 22 deaths/1,000 live births (1991)
Life expectancy at birth: 66 years male, 71 years female (1991)
Total fertility rate: 3.9 children born/woman (1991)
Nationality: noun—French Polynesian(s); adjective—French Polynesian
Ethnic divisions: Polynesian 78%, Chinese 12%, local French 6%, metropolitan French 4%
Religion: mainly Christian; Protestant 54%, Roman Catholic 30%, other 16%
Language: French (official), Tahitian

Literacy: 98% (male 98%, female 98%) age 14 and over but definition of literacy not available (1977)
Labor force: 76,630 employed (1988)
Organized labor: NA

Government

Long-form name: Territory of French Polynesia
Type: overseas territory of France since 1946
Capital: Papeete
Administrative divisions: none (overseas territory of France); there are no first-order administrative divisions as defined by the US Government, but there are 5 archipelagic divisions named Archipel des Marquises, Archipel des Tuamotu, Archipel des Tubuai, Îles du Vent, and Îles Sous-le-Vent; note—Clipperton Island is administered from French Polynesia and may have become a dependency of French Polynesia
Independence: none (overseas territory of France)
Constitution: 28 September 1958 (French Constitution)
Legal system: based on French system
National holiday: Taking of the Bastille, 14 July (1789)
Executive branch: French president, high commissioner of the republic, president of the Council of Ministers, vice president of the Council of Ministers, Council of Ministers
Legislative branch: unicameral Territorial Assembly
Judicial branch: Court of Appeal
Leaders:
Chief of State—President François MITTERRAND (since 21 May 1981); High Commissioner of the Republic Jean MONTPEZAT (since NA November 1987);
Head of Government—President of the Council of Ministers Gaston FLOSSE (since 10 May 1991); Vice President of the Council of Ministers NA
Political parties and leaders: People's Rally (Tahoeraa Huiraatira; Gaullist), Gaston FLOSSE; Polynesian Union Party (Te Tiarama; centrist), Alexandre LÉONTIEFF; New Fatherland Party (Ai'a Api), Emile VERNAUDON; Polynesian Liberation Front (Tavini Huiraatira), Oscar TEMARU; other small parties
Suffrage: universal at age 18
Elections:
Territorial Assembly—last held 17 March 1991 (next to be held March 1996); results—percent of vote by party NA; seats—(41 total) People's Rally (Gaullist) 18, Polynesian Union Party 14, New Fatherland Party 5, other 4;
French Senate—last held 24 September 1989 (next to be held September 1992);

results—percent of vote by party NA; seats—(1 total) party NA;
French National Assembly last held 5 and 12 June 1988 (next to be held June 1993); results—percent of vote by party NA; seats—(2 total) People's Rally (Gaullist) 1, New Fatherland Party 1
Member of: FZ, SPC, WMO
Diplomatic representation: as an overseas territory of France, French Polynesian interests are represented in the US by France
Flag: the flag of France is used

Economy

Overview: Since 1962, when France stationed military personnel in the region, French Polynesia has changed from a subsistence economy to one in which a high proportion of the work force is either employed by the military or supports the tourist industry. Tourism accounts for about 20% of GDP and is a primary source of hard currency earnings.
GDP: $1.2 billion, per capita $6,300; real growth rate NA% (1990 est.)
Inflation rate (consumer prices): 1.3% (1989 est.)
Unemployment rate: 8% (1986 est.)
Budget: revenues $614 million; expenditures $957 million, including capital expenditures of $NA (1988)
Exports: $75 million (f.o.b., 1988);
commodities—coconut products 79%, mother-of-pearl 14%, vanilla, shark meat;
partners—France 54%, US 17%, Japan 17%
Imports: $806 million (c.i.f., 1988);
commodities—fuels, foodstuffs, equipment;
partners—France 53%, US 11%, Australia 6%, NZ 5%
External debt: $NA
Industrial production: growth rate NA%
Electricity: 72,000 kW capacity; 265 million kWh produced, 1,390 kWh per capita (1990)
Industries: tourism, pearls, agricultural processing, handicrafts
Agriculture: coconut and vanilla plantations; vegetables and fruit; poultry, beef, dairy products
Economic aid: Western (non-US) countries, ODA and OOF bilateral commitments (1970-88), $3.95 billion
Currency: Comptoirs Français du Pacifique franc (plural—francs); 1 CFP franc (CFPF) = 100 centimes
Exchange rates: Comptoirs Français du Pacifique francs (CFPF) per US$1—93.28 (January 1991), 99.00 (1990), 115.99 (1989), 108.30 (1988), 109.27 (1987), 125.92 (1986), 163.35 (1985); note—linked at the rate of 18.18 to the French franc
Fiscal year: calendar year

French Southern and Antarctic Lands

(overseas territory of France)

Communications

Highways: 600 km (1982)
Ports: Papeete, Bora-bora
Merchant marine: 3 ships (1,000 GRT or over) totaling 4,128 GRT/6,710 DWT; includes 1 passenger-cargo, 1 cargo, 1 refrigerated cargo; note—a captive subset of the French register
Civil air: about 6 major transport aircraft
Airports: 43 total, 41 usable; 23 with permanent-surface runways; none with runways over 3,659 m; 2 with runways 2,440-3,659 m; 12 with runways 1,220-2,439 m
Telecommunications: 33,200 telephones; 84,000 radio receivers; 26,400 TV sets; stations—5 AM, 2 FM, 6 TV; 1 Pacific Ocean INTELSAT earth station

Defense Forces

Manpower availability: males 15-49, 50,844; NA fit for military service
Note: defense is responsibility of France

700 km

Indian Ocean

Île Amsterdam
Île Saint-Paul

Îles Crozet

Îles Kerguelen

Geography

Total area: 7,781 km²; land area: 7,781 km²; includes Île Amsterdam, Île Saint-Paul, Îles Kerguelen, and Îles Crozet; excludes Terre Adélie claim of about 500,000 km² in Antarctica that is not recognized by the US
Comparative area: slightly less than 1.5 times the size of Delaware
Land boundaries: none
Coastline: 1,232 km
Maritime claims:
Exclusive economic zone: 200 nm (Îles Kerguelen only);
Territorial sea: 12 nm
Disputes: Terre Adélie claim in Antarctica is not recognized by the US
Climate: antarctic
Terrain: volcanic
Natural resources: fish, crayfish
Land use: arable land 0%; permanent crops 0%; meadows and pastures 0%; forest and woodland 0%; other 100%
Environment: Île Amsterdam and Île Saint-Paul are extinct volcanoes
Note: located in the southern Indian Ocean about equidistant between Africa, Antarctica, and Australia

People

Population: summer (January 1991)—180, winter (July 1991)—150, growth rate 0.0% (1991); note—mostly researchers

Government

Long-form name: Territory of the French Southern and Antarctic Lands
Type: overseas territory of France since 1955; governed by High Administrator Bernard de GOUTTES (since NA May 1990), who is assisted by a 7-member Consultative Council and a 12-member Scientific Council
Administrative divisions: none (overseas territory of France); there are no first-order administrative divisions as defined by the US Government, but there are 3 districts named Île Crozet, Îles Kerguelen, and Îles Saint-Paul et Amsterdam; excludes Terre Adélie claim in Antarctica that is not recognized by the US
Flag: the flag of France is used

Economy

Overview: Economic activity is limited to servicing meteorological and geophysical research stations and French and other fishing fleets. The fishing catches landed on Îles Kerguelen by foreign ships are exported to France and Reunion.
Budget: $33.6 million (1990)

Communications

Ports: none; offshore anchorage only
Merchant marine: 12 ships (1,000 GRT or over) totaling 220,392 GRT/350,131 DWT; includes 2 cargo, 3 refrigerated cargo, 2 roll-on/roll-off cargo, 1 petroleum, oils, and lubricants (POL) tanker, 2 liquefied gas, 2 bulk; note—a captive subset of the French register
Telecommunications: NA

Defense Forces

Branches: French Forces (including Army, Navy, Air Force)
Note: defense is the responsibility of France

Gabon

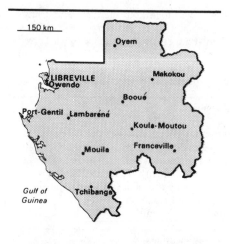

Geography

Total area: 267,670 km²; land area: 257,670 km²
Comparative area: slightly smaller than Colorado
Land boundaries: 2,551 km total; Cameroon 298 km, Congo 1,903 km, Equatorial Guinea 350 km
Coastline: 885 km
Maritime claims:
Contiguous zone: 24 nm;
Exclusive economic zone: 200 nm;
Territorial sea: 12 nm
Disputes: maritime boundary dispute with Equatorial Guinea because of disputed sovereignty over islands in Corisco Bay
Climate: tropical; always hot, humid
Terrain: narrow coastal plain; hilly interior; savanna in east and south
Natural resources: crude oil, manganese, uranium, gold, timber, iron ore
Land use: arable land 1%; permanent crops 1%; meadows and pastures 18%; forest and woodland 78%; other 2%
Environment: deforestation

People

Population: 1,079,980 (July 1991), growth rate 1.4% (1991)
Birth rate: 28 births/1,000 population (1991)
Death rate: 14 deaths/1,000 population (1991)
Net migration rate: 0 migrants/1,000 population (1991)
Infant mortality rate: 104 deaths/1,000 live births (1991)
Life expectancy at birth: 51 years male, 56 years female (1991)
Total fertility rate: 4.0 children born/woman (1991)
Nationality: noun—Gabonese (sing., pl.); adjective—Gabonese
Ethnic divisions: about 40 Bantu tribes, including four major tribal groupings (Fang,

Eshira, Bapounou, Bateke); about 100,000 expatriate Africans and Europeans, including 27,000 French
Religion: Christian 55-75%, Muslim less than 1%, remainder animist
Language: French (official), Fang, Myene, Bateke, Bapounou/Eschira, Bandjabi
Literacy: 61% (male 74%, female 48%) age 15 and over can read and write (1990 est.)
Labor force: 120,000 salaried; agriculture 65.0%, industry and commerce 30.0%, services 2.5%, government 2.5%; 58% of population of working age (1983)
Organized labor: there are 38,000 members of the national trade union, the Gabonese Trade Union Confederation (COSYGA)

Government

Long-form name: Gabonese Republic
Type: republic; multiparty presidential regime (opposition parties legalized 1990)
Capital: Libreville
Administrative divisions: 9 provinces; Estuaire, Haut-Ogooué, Moyen-Ogooué, Ngounié, Nyanga, Ogooué-Ivindo, Ogooué-Lolo, Ogooué-Maritime, Woleu-Ntem
Independence: 17 August 1960 (from France)
Constitution: 21 February 1961, revised 15 April 1975
Legal system: based on French civil law system and customary law; judicial review of legislative acts in Constitutional Chamber of the Supreme Court; compulsory ICJ jurisdiction not accepted
National holiday: Renovation Day (Gabonese Democratic Party established), 12 March (1968)
Executive branch: president, prime minister, Cabinet
Legislative branch: unicameral National Assembly (Assemblée Nationale)
Judicial branch: Supreme Court (Cour Suprême)
Leaders:
Chief of State—President El Hadj Omar BONGO (since 2 December 1967);
Head of Government—Prime Minister Casimir OYÉ-MBA (since 3 May 1990)
Political parties and leaders: Gabonese Democratic Party (PDG, former sole party), El Hadj Omar BONGO, president; National Recovery Movement-Lumberjacks (Morena-Bucherons); Gabonese Party for Progress (PGP); National Recovery Movement (Morena-Original); Association for Socialism in Gabon (APSG); Gabonese Socialist Union (USG); Circle for Renewal and Progress (CRP); Union for Democracy and Development (UDD)
Suffrage: universal at age 21
Elections:
President—last held on 9 November 1986 (next to be held November 1993); results—President Omar BONGO was reelected without opposition;

National Assembly—last held on 28 October 1990 (next to be held by February 1992); results—percent of vote NA; seats—(120 total, 111 elected) PDG 62, National Recovery Movement-Lumberjacks (Morena-Bucherons) 19, PGP 18, National Recovery Movement (Morena-Original) 7, ASPG 6, USG 4, CRP 1, independent 3
Communists: no organized party; probably some Communist sympathizers
Member of: ACCT, ACP, AfDB, BDEAC, CCC, CEEAC, ECA, FAO, FZ, G-24, G-77, GATT, IAEA, IBRD, ICAO, ICC, IDA, IDB, IFAD, IFC, ILO, IMF, IMO, INMARSAT, INTELSAT, INTERPOL, IOC, ITU, LORCS (associate), NAM, OAU, OIC, OPEC, UDEAC, UN, UNCTAD, UNESCO, UNIDO, UPU, WCL, WHO, WIPO, WMO, WTO
Diplomatic representation: Ambassador-designate Alexandre SAMBAT; Chancery at 2034 20th Street NW, Washington DC 20009; telephone (202) 797-1000; *US*—Ambassador Keith L. WAUCHOPE; Embassy at Boulevard de la Mer, Libreville (mailing address is B. P. 4000, Libreville); telephone 762003 or 762004, 743492
Flag: three equal horizontal bands of green (top), yellow, and blue

Economy

Overview: The economy, dependent on timber and manganese until the early 1970s, is now dominated by the oil sector. During the period 1981-85 oil accounted for about 46% of GDP, 83% of export earnings, and 65% of government revenues on average. The high oil prices of the early 1980s contributed to a substantial increase in per capita income, stimulated domestic demand, reinforced migration from rural to urban areas, and raised the level of real wages to among the highest in Sub-Saharan Africa. The three-year slide of Gabon's economy, which began with falling oil prices in 1985, was reversed in 1989 because of a near doubling of oil prices over their 1988 lows. In 1990 the economy continued to grow, but debt servicing problems are hindering economic advancement. The agricultural and industrial sectors are relatively underdeveloped, except for oil.
GDP: $3.3 billion, per capita $3,090; real growth rate 13% (1990 est.)
Inflation rate (consumer prices): 3% (1989 est.)
Unemployment rate: NA%
Budget: revenues $1.1 billion; expenditures $1.5 billion, including capital expenditures of $277 million (1990 est.)
Exports: $1.16 billion (f.o.b., 1989); *commodities*—crude oil 70%, manganese 11%, wood 12%, uranium 6%; *partners*—France 53%, US 22%, FRG, Japan

Imports: $0.78 billion (c.i.f., 1989); *commodities*—foodstuffs, chemical products, petroleum products, construction materials, manufactures, machinery; *partners*—France 48%, US 2.6%, FRG, Japan, UK
External debt: $3.4 billion (December 1990 est.)
Industrial production: growth rate −10% (1988 est.)
Electricity: 310,000 kW capacity; 980 million kWh produced, 920 kWh per capita (1989)
Industries: sawmills, petroleum, food and beverages; mining of increasing importance (especially manganese and uranium)
Agriculture: accounts for 10% of GDP (including fishing and forestry); cash crops—cocoa, coffee, palm oil; livestock not developed; importer of food; small fishing operations provide a catch of about 20,000 metric tons; okoume (a tropical softwood) is the most important timber product
Economic aid: US commitments, including Ex-Im (FY70-89), $66 million; Western (non-US) countries, ODA and OOF bilateral commitments (1970-88), $1.9 billion; Communist countries (1970-89), $27 million
Currency: Communauté Financière Africaine franc (plural—francs); 1 CFA franc (CFAF) = 100 centimes
Exchange rates: Communauté Financière Africaine francs (CFAF) per US$1—253.32 (December 1990), 171.26 (1990), 319.01 (1989), 297.85 (1988), 300.54 (1987), 346.30 (1986), 449.26 (1985)
Fiscal year: calendar year

Communications

Railroads: 649 km 1.437-meter standard-gauge single track (Transgabonese Railroad)
Highways: 7,500 km total; 560 km paved, 960 km laterite, 5,980 km earth
Inland waterways: 1,600 km perennially navigable
Pipelines: crude oil, 270 km; refined products, 14 km
Ports: Owendo, Port-Gentil, Libreville
Merchant marine: 2 cargo ships (1,000 GRT or over) totaling 18,563 GRT/25,330 DWT
Civil air: 11 major transport aircraft
Airports: 73 total, 61 usable; 10 with permanent-surface runways; none with runways over 3,659 m; 2 with runways 2,440-3,659 m; 22 with runways 1,220-2,439 m
Telecommunications: adequate system of open-wire, radio relay, tropospheric scatter links and radiocommunication stations; 13,800 telephones; stations—6 AM, 6 FM, 8 TV; satellite earth stations—2 Atlantic Ocean INTELSAT and 12 domestic satellite

Defense Forces

Branches: Army, Navy, Air Force, Presidential Guard, paramilitary Gendarmerie, National Police
Manpower availability: males 15-49, 266,472; 133,648 fit for military service; 9,634 reach military age (20) annually
Defense expenditures: $102 million, 3.2% of GDP (1990 est.)

The Gambia

Boundary representation is not necessarily authoritative.

Geography

Total area: 11,300 km²; land area: 10,000 km²
Comparative area: slightly more than twice the size of Delaware
Land boundary: 740 km with Senegal
Coastline: 80 km
Maritime claims:
Contiguous zone: 18 nm;
Continental shelf: not specific;
Exclusive fishing zone: 200 nm;
Territorial sea: 12 nm
Disputes: short section of boundary with Senegal is indefinite
Climate: tropical; hot, rainy season (June to November); cooler, dry season (November to May)
Terrain: flood plain of the Gambia River flanked by some low hills
Natural resources: fish
Land use: arable land 16%; permanent crops 0%; meadows and pastures 9%; forest and woodland 20%; other 55%; includes irrigated 3%
Environment: deforestation
Note: almost an enclave of Senegal; smallest country on the continent of Africa

---

People

Population: 874,553 (July 1991), growth rate 3.1% (1991)
Birth rate: 48 births/1,000 population (1991)
Death rate: 17 deaths/1,000 population (1991)
Net migration rate: 0 migrants/1,000 population (1991)
Infant mortality rate: 138 deaths/1,000 live births (1991)
Life expectancy at birth: 47 years male, 51 years female (1991)
Total fertility rate: 6.5 children born/woman (1991)
Nationality: noun—Gambian(s); adjective—Gambian

The Gambia *(continued)*

Ethnic divisions: African 99% (Mandinka 42%, Fula 18%, Wolof 16%, Jola 10%, Serahuli 9%, other 4%); non-Gambian 1%
Religion: Muslim 90%, Christian 9%, indigenous beliefs 1%
Language: English (official); Mandinka, Wolof, Fula, other indigenous vernaculars
Literacy: 27% (male 39%, female 16%) age 15 and over can read and write (1990 est.)
Labor force: 400,000 (1986 est.); agriculture 75.0%, industry, commerce, and services 18.9%, government 6.1%; 55% population of working age (1983)
Organized labor: 25-30% of wage labor force

Government

Long-form name: Republic of The Gambia
Type: republic
Capital: Banjul
Administrative divisions: 5 divisions and 1 city*; Banjul*, Lower River, MacCarthy Island, North Bank, Upper River, Western
Independence: 18 February 1965 (from UK); The Gambia and Senegal signed an agreement on 12 December 1981 (effective 1 February 1982) that called for the creation of a loose confederation to be known as Senegambia, but the agreement was dissolved on 30 September 1989
Constitution: 24 April 1970
Legal system: based on a composite of English common law, Koranic law, and customary law; accepts compulsory ICJ jurisdiction, with reservations
National holiday: Independence Day, 18 February (1965)
Executive branch: president, vice president, Cabinet
Legislative branch: unicameral House of Representatives
Judicial branch: Supreme Court
Leaders:
Chief of State and Head of Government—President Alhaji Sir Dawda Kairaba JAWARA (since 24 April 1970); Vice President Bakary Bunja DARBO (since 12 May 1982)
Political parties and leaders: People's Progressive Party (PPP), Dawda K. JAWARA, secretary general; National Convention Party (NCP), Sheriff DIBBA; Gambian People's Party (GPP), Assan Musa CAMARA; United Party (UP); People's Democratic Organization of Independence and Socialism (PDOIS)
Suffrage: universal at age 21
Elections:
President—last held on 11 March 1987 (next to be held March 1992); results—Sir Dawda JAWARA (PPP) 61.1%, Sherif Mustapha DIBBA (NCP) 25.2%, Assan Musa CAMARA (GPP) 13.7%;
House of Representatives—last held on 11 March 1987 (next to be held by March 1992); results—PPP 56.6%, NCP 27.6%,

GPP 14.7%, PDOIS 1%; seats—(43 total, 36 elected) PPP 31, NCP 5
Communists: no Communist party
Member of: ACP, AfDB, C, CCC, ECA, ECOWAS, FAO, G-77, GATT, IBRD, ICAO, ICFTU, IDA, IDB, IFAD, IFC, IMF, IMO, INTERPOL, IOC, ITU, LORCS, NAM, OAU, OIC, UN, UNCTAD, UNESCO, UNIDO, UPU, WCL, WFTU, WHO, WIPO, WMO, WTO
Diplomatic representation: Ambassador Ousman A. SALLAH; Chancery at Suite 720, 1030 15th Street NW, Washington DC 20005; telephone (202) 842-1356 or 842-1359;
US—Ambassador Arlene RENDER; Embassy at Pipeline Road (Kairaba Avenue), Fajara, Banjul (mailing address is P. M. B. No. 19, Banjul); telephone Serrekunda [220] 92856 or 92858, 91970, 91971
Flag: three equal horizontal bands of red (top), blue with white edges, and green

Economy

Overview: The Gambia has no important mineral or other natural resources and has a limited agricultural base. It is one of the world's poorest countries with a per capita income of about $230. About 75% of the population is engaged in crop production and livestock raising, which contributes 30% to GDP. Small-scale manufacturing activity—processing peanuts, fish, and hides—accounts for less than 10% of GDP. Tourism is a growing industry. The Gambia imports one-third of its food, all fuel, and most manufactured goods. Exports are concentrated on peanut products (about 75% of total value).
GDP: $195 million, per capita $230; real growth rate 6.0% (FY90 est.)
Inflation rate (consumer prices): 10.1% (FY90)
Unemployment rate: NA%
Budget: revenues $69.3 million; expenditures $95.5 million, including capital expenditures of $21 million (FY89)
Exports: $122.2 million (f.o.b., FY90 est.);
commodities—peanuts and peanut products, fish, cotton lint, palm kernels;
partners—Japan 60%, Europe 29%, Africa 5%, US 1% other 5% (1989)
Imports: $155.2 million (f.o.b., FY90 est.);
commodities—foodstuffs, manufactures, raw materials, fuel, machinery and transport equipment;
partners—Europe 57%, Asia 25%, USSR/EE 9%, US 6%, other 3% (1989)
External debt: $336 million (December 1990 est.)
Industrial production: growth rate 6.7%; accounts for 5.8% of GDP (FY90)
Electricity: 29,000 kW capacity; 64 million kWh produced, 80 kWh per capita (1989)

Industries: peanut processing, tourism, beverages, agricultural machinery assembly, woodworking, metalworking, clothing
Agriculture: accounts for 30% of GDP and employs about 75% of the population; imports one-third of food requirements; major export crop is peanuts; the principal crops—millet, sorghum, rice, corn, cassava, palm kernels; livestock—cattle, sheep, and goats; forestry and fishing resources not fully exploited
Economic aid: US commitments, including Ex-Im (FY70-89), $93 million; Western (non-US) countries, ODA and OOF bilateral commitments (1970-88), $492 million; Communist countries (1970-88), $39 million
Currency: dalasi (plural—dalasi); 1 dalasi (D) = 100 bututs
Exchange rates: dalasi (D) per US$1—7.610 (January 1991), 7.883 (1990), 7.5846 (1989), 6.7086 (1988), 7.0744 (1987), 6.9380 (1986), 3.8939 (1985)
Fiscal year: 1 July-30 June

Communications

Highways: 3,083 km total; 431 km paved, 501 km gravel/laterite, and 2,151 km unimproved earth
Inland waterways: 400 km
Ports: Banjul
Civil air: 2 major transport aircraft
Airports: 1 with permanent-surface runway 2,440-3,659 m
Telecommunications: adequate network of radio relay and wire; 3,500 telephones; stations—3 AM, 2 FM, 1 TV; 1 Atlantic Ocean INTELSAT earth station

Defense Forces

Branches: Army, Navy, paramilitary Gendarmerie, National Police
Manpower availability: males 15-49, 188,393; 95,133 fit for military service
Defense expenditures: $NA, 0.7% of GDP (1988)

Gaza Strip

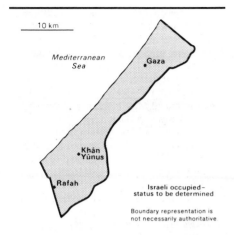

10 km

Mediterranean Sea

Gaza

Khân Yûnus

Rafah

Israeli occupied–
status to be determined

Boundary representation is
not necessarily authoritative

Note: The war between Israel and the Arab states in June 1967 ended with Israel in control of the West Bank and the Gaza Strip, the Sinai, and the Golan Heights. As stated in the 1978 Camp David Accords and reaffirmed by President Reagan's 1 September 1982 peace initiative, the final status of the West Bank and the Gaza Strip, their relationship with their neighbors, and a peace treaty between Israel and Jordan are to be negotiated among the concerned parties. Camp David further specifies that these negotiations will resolve the respective boundaries. Pending the completion of this process, it is US policy that the final status of the West Bank and the Gaza Strip has yet to be determined. In the view of the US, the term West Bank describes all of the area west of the Jordan under Jordanian administration before the 1967 Arab-Israeli war. With respect to negotiations envisaged in the framework agreement, however, it is US policy that a distinction must be made between Jerusalem and the rest of the West Bank because of the city's special status and circumstances. Therefore, a negotiated solution for the final status of Jerusalem could be different in character from that of the rest of the West Bank.

Geography

Total area: 380km²; land area: 380 km²
Comparative area: slightly more than twice the size of Washington, DC
Land boundaries: 62 km total; Egypt 11 km, Israel 51 km
Coastline: 40 km
Maritime claims: Israeli occupied with status to be determined
Disputes: Israeli occupied with status to be determined
Climate: temperate, mild winters, dry and warm to hot summers
Terrain: flat to rolling, sand and dune covered coastal plain
Natural resources: negligible

Land use: arable land 13%, permanent crops 32%, meadows and pastures 0%, forest and woodland 0%, other 55%
Environment: desertification
Note: there are 18 Jewish settlements in the Gaza Strip

People

Population: 642,253 (July 1991), growth rate 3.2% (1991); in addition, there are 2,500 Jewish settlers in the Gaza Strip (1990 est.)
Birth rate: 43 births/1,000 population (1991)
Death rate: 6 deaths/1,000 population (1991)
Net migration rate: −5 migrants/1,000 population (1991)
Infant mortality rate: 41 deaths/1,000 live births (1991)
Life expectancy at birth: 65 years male, 67 years female (1991)
Total fertility rate: 6.9 children born/woman (1991)
Nationality: NA
Ethnic divisions: Palestinian Arab and other 99.8%, Jewish 0.2%
Religion: Muslim (predominantly Sunni) 99%, Christian 0.7%, Jewish 0.3%
Language: Arabic, Israeli settlers speak Hebrew, English widely understood
Literacy: NA% (male NA%, female NA%)
Labor force: (excluding Israeli Jewish settlers) small industry, commerce and business 32.0%, construction 24.4%, service and other 25.5%, and agriculture 18.1% (1984)
Organized labor: NA

Government

Long-form name: none
Note: The Gaza Strip is currently governed by Israeli military authorities and Israeli civil administration. It is US policy that the final status of the Gaza Strip will be determined by negotiations among the concerned parties. These negotiations will determine how this area is to be governed.

Economy

Overview: Nearly half the labor force of the Gaza Strip is employed across the border by Israeli industrial, construction, and agricultural enterprises, with worker transfer funds accounting for 46% of GNP in 1990. The once dominant agricultural sector now contributes only 13% to GNP, about the same as that of the construction sector, and industry accounts for 7%. Gaza depends upon Israel for 90% of its imports and as a market for 80% of its exports. Unrest in the territory in 1988-91 (*intifadah*) has raised unemployment and substantially lowered the incomes of the population. Furthermore, the Persian Gulf crisis dealt a severe blow to the Gaza Strip in 1990 and on into 1991. Worker remittances from the Gulf states have plunged, unemployment has increased, and export revenues have fallen dramatically. The risk of malnutrition is a real possibility in 1991.
GNP: $270 million, per capita $430; real growth rate −25% (1990 est.)
Inflation rate (consumer prices): NA%
Unemployment rate: NA%
Budget: revenues $36.6 million; expenditures $32.0 million, including capital expenditures of NA (1986)
Exports: $88 million;
commodities—citrus;
partners—Israel, Egypt (1989 est.)
Imports: $260 million;
commodities—food, consumer goods, construction materials;
partners—Israel, Egypt (1989 est.)
External debt: $NA
Industrial production: growth rate NA%
Electricity: power supplied by Israel
Industries: generally small family businesses that produce cement, textiles, soap, olive-wood carvings, and mother-of-pearl souvenirs; the Israelis have established some small-scale modern industries in an industrial center
Agriculture: olives, citrus and other fruits, vegetables, beef, dairy products
Economic aid: none
Currency: new Israeli shekel (plural—shekels); 1 new Israeli shekel (NIS) = 100 new agorot
Exchange rates: new Israeli shekels (NIS) per US$1—2.0120 (January 1991), 2.0162 (1990), 1.9164 (1989), 1.5989 (1988), 1.5946 (1987), 1.4878 (1986), 1.1788 (1985)
Fiscal year: 1 April-March 31

Communications

Railroads: one line, abandoned and in disrepair, but trackage remains
Highways: small, poorly developed indigenous road network
Ports: facilities for small boats to service Gaza
Airports: 1 with permanent-surface runway less than 1,220 m
Telecommunications: stations—no AM, no FM, no TV

Defense Forces

Branches: NA
manpower availability: males 15-49, 136,311; NA fit for military service
Defense expenditures: $NA, NA% of GDP

111

Germany

Geography

Total area: 356,910 km²; land area: 349,520 km²; comprises the formerly separate Federal Republic of Germany, the German Democratic Republic, and Berlin following formal unification on 3 October 1990
Comparative area: slightly smaller than Montana
Land boundaries: 3,790 km total; Austria 784 km, Belgium 167 km, Czechoslovakia 815 km, Denmark 68 km, France 451 km, Luxembourg 138 km, Netherlands 577 km, Poland 456 km, Switzerland 334 km
Coastline: 2,389 km
Maritime claims:
Continental shelf: 200 m (depth) or to depth of exploitation;
Exclusive fishing zone: 200 nm;
Territorial sea: North Sea and Schleswig-Holstein coast of Baltic Sea—3 nm (extends, at one point, to 16 nm in the Helgoländer Bucht); remainder of Baltic Sea—12 nm
Disputes: the boundaries of Germany were set by the Treaty on the Final Settlement With Respect to Germany signed 12 September 1990 in Moscow by the Federal Republic of Germany, the German Democratic Republic, France, the United Kingdom, the United States, and the Soviet Union; this treaty entered into force on 15 March 1991; a subsequent treaty between Germany and Poland, reaffirming the German-Polish boundary, was signed on 14 November 1990 and is set to be ratified in 1991; the US Government is seeking to settle the property claims of US nationals against the former GDR
Climate: temperate and marine; cool, cloudy, wet winters and summers; occasional warm, tropical foehn wind; high relative humidity
Terrain: lowlands in north, uplands in center, Bavarian Alps in south
Natural resources: iron ore, coal, potash, timber, lignite, uranium, copper, natural gas, salt, nickel

Land use: arable land 34%; permanent crops 1%; meadows and pastures 16%; forest and woodland 30%; other 19%; includes irrigated 1%
Environment: air and water pollution; ground water, lakes, and air quality in eastern Germany are especially bad; significant deforestation in the eastern mountains caused by air pollution and acid rain
Note: strategic location on North European Plain and along the entrance to the Baltic Sea

People

Population: 79,548,498 (July 1991), growth rate 0.4% (1991)
Birth rate: 11 births/1,000 population (1991)
Death rate: 11 deaths/1,000 population (1991)
Net migration rate: 4 migrants/1,000 population (1991)
Infant mortality rate: 7 deaths/1,000 live births (1991)
Life expectancy at birth: 73 years male, 79 years female (1991)
Total fertility rate: 1.4 children born/woman (1991)
Nationality: noun—German(s); adjective—German
Ethnic divisions: primarily German; small Danish and Slavic minorities
Religion: Protestant 45%, Roman Catholic 37%, unaffiliated or other 18%
Language: German
Literacy: 99% (male NA%, female NA%) age 15 and over can read and write (1970 est.)
Labor force: 36,750,000; industry 41%, agriculture 6%, other 53% (1987)
Organized labor: 47% of labor force (1986 est.)

Government

Long-form name: Federal Republic of Germany
Type: federal republic
Capital: Berlin; note—the shift from Bonn to Berlin will take place over a period of years with Bonn retaining many administrative functions
Administrative divisions: 16 states (länder, singular—land); Baden-Württemberg, Bayern, Berlin, Brandenburg, Bremen, Hamburg, Hessen, Mecklenburg-Vorpommern, Niedersachsen, Nordrhein-Westfalen, Rheinland-Pfalz, Saarland, Sachsen, Sachsen-Anhalt, Schleswig-Holstein, Thüringen
Independence: 18 January 1871 (German Empire unification); divided into four zones of occupation (UK, US, USSR, and later, France) in 1945 following World War II; Federal Republic of Germany (FRG or West Germany) proclaimed 23 May 1949 and included the former UK, US, and

French zones; German Democratic Republic (GDR or East Germany) proclaimed 7 October 1949 and included the former USSR zone; unification of West Germany and East Germany took place 3 October 1990; all four power rights formally relinquished 15 March 1991
Constitution: 23 May 1949, provisional constitution known as Basic Law
Legal system: civil law system with indigenous concepts; judicial review of legislative acts in the Federal Constitutional Court; has not accepted compulsory ICJ jurisdiction
National holiday: 3 October 1990, German Unity Day
Executive branch: president, chancellor, Cabinet
Legislative branch: bicameral parliament (no official name for the two chambers as a whole) consists of an upper chamber or Federal Council (Bundesrat) and a lower chamber or Federal Diet (Bundestag)
Judicial branch: Federal Constitutional Court (Bundesverfassungsgericht)
Leaders: *Chief of State*—President Dr. Richard von WEIZSÄCKER (since 1 July 1984);
Head of Government—Chancellor Dr. Helmut KOHL (since 4 October 1982)
Political parties and leaders: Christian Democratic Union (CDU), Helmut KOHL, chairman; Christian Social Union (CSU), Theo WAIGEL; Free Democratic Party (FDP), Otto Count LAMBSDORFF, chairman; Social Democratic Party (SPD), Bjoern ENGHOLM, chairman; Green Party—Volmer LUDGER, Christine WEISKE, co-chairmen (after the 2 December 1990 election the East and West German Green Parties united); Alliance 90 includes three parties—New Forum, Jens REICH, Sebastian PFLUGBEIL, spokespersons; Democracy Now, Konrad WEISS, spokesperson; and Initiative, Peace, and Human Rights Party, Gerd POPPE; Party of Democratic Socialism (PDS, formerly the East German Communist Party), Gregor GYSI, chairman; Republikaner, Franz SCHÖN-HUBER; National Democratic Party (NPD), Martin MUSSGNUG; Communist Party (DKP), Herbert MIES
Suffrage: universal at age 18
Elections: *Federal Diet*—last held 2 December 1990 (next to be held by December 1994); results—CDU 36.7%, SPD 33.5%, FDP 11.0%, CSU 7.1%, Green Party (West Germany) 3.9%, PDS 2.4%, Republikaner 2.1%, Alliance 90/Green Party (East Germany) 1.2%, other 2.1%; seats—(662 total, 656 statutory with special rules to allow for slight expansion) CDU 268, SPD 239, FDP 79, CSU 51, PDS 17, Alliance 90/Green Party (East Germany) 8; note—special rules for this election allowed former East German parties to win seats if they received at least 5% of vote in eastern Germany

Communists: West—about 40,000 members and supporters; East—284,000 party members (December 1990)

Other political or pressure groups: expellee, refugee, and veterans groups

Member of: AfDB, AG (observer), AsDB, BDEAC, BIS, CCC, CE, CERN, COCOM, CSCE, EBRD, EC, ECE, EIB, ESA, FAO, G-5, G-7, G-10, GATT, IADB, IAEA, IBRD, ICAO, ICC, ICFTU, IDA, IEA, IFAD, IFC, ILO, IMF, IMO, INMARSAT, INTELSAT, INTERPOL, IOC, IOM, ISO, ITU, LORCS, NATO, NEA, OAS (observer), OECD, PCA, UN, UNCTAD, UNESCO, UNIDO, UNHCR, UPU, WEU, WFTU, WHO, WIPO, WMO, WTO

Diplomatic representation:
Ambassador Jeurgen RUHFUS; Chancery at 4645 Reservoir Road NW, Washington DC 20007; telephone (202) 298-4000; there are German Consulates General in Atlanta, Boston, Chicago, Detroit, Houston, Los Angeles, San Francisco, Seattle, and New York, and Consulates in Miami and New Orleans;
US—Ambassador-designate Robert M. KIMMITT; Embassy at Deichmanns Avenue, 5300 Bonn 2 (mailing address is APO New York 09080); telephone [49] (228) 3391; there is a US Branch Office in Berlin and US Consulates General in Frankfurt, Hamburg, Leipzig, Munich, and Stuttgart

Flag: three equal horizontal bands of black (top), red, and yellow

---

Economy

Overview: The newly unified German economy presents a starkly contrasting picture. Western Germany has an advanced market economy and is a leading exporter. It experienced faster-than-projected real growth largely because of demand in eastern Germany for western German goods. Western Germany has a highly urbanized and skilled population which enjoys excellent living standards, abundant leisure time, and comprehensive social welfare benefits. Western Germany is relatively poor in natural resources, coal being the most important mineral. Western Germany's world-class companies manufacture technologically advanced goods. The region's economy is mature: manufacturing and service industries account for the dominant share of economic activity, and raw materials and semimanufactured products constitute a large proportion of imports. In 1989 manufacturing accounted for 31% of GDP, with other sectors contributing lesser amounts. In recent years, gross fixed investment has accounted for about 21% of GDP. In 1990 GDP in the western region was an estimated $16,300 per capita.

In contrast, eastern Germany's obsolete command economy, once dominated by smokestack heavy industries, has been undergoing a wrenching change to a market economy. Industrial production in early 1991 is down 50% from the same period last year, due largely to the slump in domestic demand for eastern German-made goods and the ongoing economic restructuring. The FRG's legal, social welfare, and economic systems have been extended to the east, but economic restructuring—privatizing industry, establishing clear property rights, clarifying responsibility for environmental clean-up, and removing Communist-era holdovers from management—is proceeding slowly so far, deterring outside investors. The region is one of the world's largest producers of low-grade lignite coal, but has few other resources. The quality of statistics from eastern Germany remains poor; Bonn is still trying to bring statistics for the region in line with West German practices.

The most challenging economic problem of a united Germany is the reconstruction of eastern Germany's economy—specifically, finding the right mix of fiscal, regulatory, monetary, and tax policies that will spur investment in the east without derailing western Germany's healthy economy or damaging relations with Western partners. The biggest danger is that soaring unemployment in eastern Germany, which could climb to the 30 to 40% range, could touch off labor disputes or renewed mass relocation to western Germany and erode investor confidence in eastern Germany. Overall economic activity grew an estimated 4.6% in western Germany in 1990, while dropping roughly 15% in eastern Germany. Per capita GDP in the eastern region was approximately $8,700 in 1990.

GDP: $1,157.2 billion, per capita $14,600; real growth rate 1.7% (1990)

Inflation rate (consumer prices): West—3.0% (1989); East—0.8% (1989)

Unemployment rate: West—7.1% (1990); East—1% (1989); 3% (first half, 1990)

Budget: West—revenues $539 billion; expenditures $563 billion, including capital expenditures of $11.5 billion (1988); East—revenues $147.0 billion; expenditures $153.4 billion, including capital expenditures of $NA (1988)

Exports:
West—$324.3 billion (f.o.b., 1989);
commodities—manufactures 86.6% (including machines and machine tools, chemicals, motor vehicles, iron and steel products), agricultural products 4.9%, raw materials 2.3%, fuels 1.3%;
partners—EC 52.7% (France 12%, Netherlands 9%, Italy 9%, UK 9%, Belgium-Luxembourg 7%), other West Europe 18%, US 10%, Eastern Europe 4%, OPEC 3% (1987);

East—$32.4 billion (f.o.b., 1989);
commodities—machinery and transport equipment 47%, fuels and metals 16%, consumer goods 16%, chemical products and building materials 13%, semimanufactured goods and processed foodstuffs 8%;
partners—USSR, Czechoslovakia, Poland, FRG, Hungary, Bulgaria, Switzerland, Romania, EC, US (1989)

Imports:
West—$247.7 billion (f.o.b., 1989);
commodities—manufactures 68.5%, agricultural products 12.0%, fuels 9.7%, raw materials 7.1%;
partners—EC 52.7% (France 12%, Netherlands 11%, Italy 10%, UK 7%, Belgium-Luxembourg 7%), other West Europe 15%, US 6%, Japan 6%, Eastern Europe 5%, OPEC 3% (1987);
East—$30.0 billion (f.o.b., 1989);
commodities—fuels and metals 40%, machinery and transport equipment 29%, chemical products and building materials 9%;
partners—USSR and Eastern Europe 65%, FRG 12.7%, EC 6.0%, US 0.3% (1989)

External debt: West—$500 million (June 1988); East—$20.6 billion (1989)

Industrial production: growth rates, West—3.3% (1988); East—2.7% (1989 est.)

Electricity: 133,000,000 kW capacity; 580,000 million kWh produced, 7,390 kWh per capita (1990)

Industries: West—among world's largest producers of iron, steel, coal, cement, chemicals, machinery, vehicles, machine tools, electronics; food and beverages; East—metal fabrication, chemicals, brown coal, shipbuilding, machine building, food and beverages, textiles, petroleum

Agriculture: West—accounts for about 2% of GDP (including fishing and forestry); diversified crop and livestock farming; principal crops and livestock include potatoes, wheat, barley, sugar beets, fruit, cabbage, cattle, pigs, poultry; net importer of food; fish catch of 202,000 metric tons in 1987; East—accounts for about 10% of GNP (including fishing and forestry); principal crops—wheat, rye, barley, potatoes, sugar beets, fruit; livestock products include pork, beef, chicken, milk, hides and skins; net importer of food; fish catch of 193,600 metric tons in 1987

Economic aid: West—donor—ODA and OOF commitments (1970-89), $75.5 billion; East—donor—$4.0 billion extended bilaterally to non-Communist less developed countries (1956-88)

Currency: deutsche mark (plural—marks); 1 deutsche mark (DM) = 100 pfennige

Exchange rates: deutsche marks (DM) per US$1—1.5100 (January 1991), 1.6157 (1990), 1.8800 (1989), 1.7562 (1988), 1.7974 (1987), 2.1715 (1986), 2.9440 (1985)

Fiscal year: calendar year

Germany (continued)

Communications

Railroads: West—31,443 km total; 27,421 km government owned, 1.435-meter standard gauge (12,491 km double track, 11,501 km electrified); 4,022 km nongovernment owned, including 3,598 km 1.435-meter standard gauge (214 km electrified) and 424 km 1.000-meter gauge (186 km electrified); East—14,025 km total; 13,750 km 1.435-meter standard gauge, 275 km 1.000-meter or other narrow gauge; 3,830 (est.) km 1.435-meter double-track standard gauge; 3,475 km overhead electrified (1988)
Highways: West—466,305 km total; 169,568 km primary, includes 6,435 km autobahn, 32,460 km national highways (Bundesstrassen), 65,425 km state highways (Landesstrassen), 65,248 km county roads (Kreisstrassen); 296,737 km of secondary communal roads (Gemeindestrassen); East—124,604 km total; 47,203 km concrete, asphalt, stone block, of which 1,855 km are autobahn and limited access roads, 11,326 are trunk roads, and 34,022 are regional roads; 77,401 municipal roads (1988)
Inland waterways: West—5,222 km, of which almost 70% are usable by craft of 1,000-metric ton capacity or larger; major rivers include the Rhine and Elbe; Kiel Canal is an important connection between the Baltic Sea and North Sea; East—2,319 km (1988)
Pipelines: crude oil 3,644 km, refined products 3,946 km, natural gas 97,564 km (1988)
Ports: maritime—Bremerhaven, Brünsbuttel, Cuxhaven, Emden, Bremen, Hamburg, Kiel, Lübeck, Wilhelmshaven, Rostock, Wismar, Stralsund, Sassnitz; inland—31 major
Merchant marine: 598 ships (1,000 GRT or over) totaling 5,029,615 GRT/6,391,875 DWT; includes 3 passenger, 5 short-sea passenger, 315 cargo, 11 refrigerated cargo, 126 container, 1 multifunction large-load carrier, 33 roll-on/roll-off cargo, 5 railcar carrier, 6 barge carrier, 11 petroleum, oils, and lubricants (POL) tanker, 27 chemical tanker, 21 liquefied gas tanker, 5 combination ore/oil, 14 combination bulk, 15 bulk; note—the German register includes ships of the former East Germany and West Germany; during 1991 the fleet is expected to undergo major restructuring as now-surplus ships are sold off
Civil air: 239 major transport aircraft
Airports: 655 total, 647 usable; 312 with permanent-surface runways; 4 with runways over 3,659 m; 86 with runways 2,440-3,659 m; 95 with runways 1,220-2,439 m
Telecommunications: West—highly developed, modern telecommunication service to all parts of the country; fully adequate in all respects; 41,740,000 telephones; stations—70 AM, 205 (370 relays) FM, 300 (6,422 relays) TV; 6 submarine coaxial cables; earth stations operating in INTELSAT (12 Atlantic Ocean, 2 Indian Ocean), EUTELSAT, and domestic systems; East—3,970,000 telephones; stations—23 AM, 17 FM, 21 TV (15 Soviet TV relays); 6,181,860 TVs; 6,700,000 radios; at least 1 earth station

Defense Forces

Branches: Army, Navy, Air Force, Federal Border Police
Manpower availability:—males 15-49, 20,219,289; 17,557,807 fit for military service; 415,108 reach military age (18) annually
Defense expenditures: $47.1 billion, 4.7% of GDP (1990)

Ghana

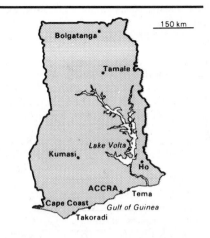

Geography

Total area: 238,540 km²; land area: 230,020 km²
Comparative area: slightly smaller than Oregon
Land boundaries: 2,093 km total; Burkina 548 km, Ivory Coast 668 km, Togo 877 km
Coastline: 539 km
Maritime claims:
Contiguous zone: 24 nm;
Continental shelf: 200 nm;
Exclusive economic zone: 200 nm;
Territorial sea: 12 nm
Climate: tropical; warm and comparatively dry along southeast coast; hot and humid in southwest; hot and dry in north
Terrain: mostly low plains with dissected plateau in south-central area
Natural resources: gold, timber, industrial diamonds, bauxite, manganese, fish, rubber
Land use: arable land 5%; permanent crops 7%; meadows and pastures 15%; forest and woodland 37%; other 36%; includes irrigated NEGL%
Environment: recent drought in north severely affecting marginal agricultural activities; deforestation; overgrazing; soil erosion; dry, northeasterly harmattan wind (January to March)
Note: Lake Volta is world's largest artificial lake

People

Population: 15,616,934 (July 1991), growth rate 3.2% (1991)
Birth rate: 46 births/1,000 population (1991)
Death rate: 13 deaths/1,000 population (1991)
Net migration rate: -1 migrant/1,000 population (1991)
Infant mortality rate: 86 deaths/1,000 live births (1991)
Life expectancy at birth: 53 years male, 56 years female (1991)

Total fertility rate: 6.3 children born/woman (1991)

Nationality: noun—Ghanaian(s); adjective—Ghanaian

Ethnic divisions: black African 99.8% (major tribes—Akan 44%, Moshi-Dagomba 16%, Ewe 13%, Ga 8%), European and other 0.2%

Religion: indigenous beliefs 38%, Muslim 30%, Christian 24%, other 8%

Language: English (official); African languages include Akan, Moshi-Dagomba, Ewe, and Ga

Literacy: 60% (male 70%, female 51%) age 15 and over can read and write (1990 est.)

Labor force: 3,700,000; agriculture and fishing 54.7%, industry 18.7%, sales and clerical 15.2%, services, transportation, and communications 7.7%, professional 3.7%; 48% of population of working age (1983)

Organized labor: 467,000 (about 13% of labor force)

Government

Long-form name: Republic of Ghana

Type: military

Capital: Accra

Administrative divisions: 10 regions; Ashanti, Brong-Ahafo, Central, Eastern, Greater Accra, Northern, Upper East, Upper West, Volta, Western

Independence: 6 March 1957 (from UK, formerly Gold Coast)

Constitution: 24 September 1979; suspended 31 December 1981

Legal system: based on English common law and customary law; has not accepted compulsory ICJ jurisdiction

National holiday: Independence Day, 6 March (1957)

Executive branch: chairman of the Provisional National Defense Council (PNDC), PNDC, Cabinet

Legislative branch: unicameral National Assembly dissolved after 31 December 1981 coup, and legislative powers were assumed by the Provisional National Defense Council

Judicial branch: Supreme Court

Leaders:

Chief of State and Head of Government— Chairman of the Provisional National Defense Council Flt. Lt. (Ret.) Jerry John RAWLINGS (since 31 December 1981)

Political parties and leaders: none; political parties outlawed after 31 December 1981 coup

Suffrage: none

Elections: none

Communists: a small number of Communists and sympathizers

Member of: ACP, AfDB, C, CCC, ECA, ECOWAS, FAO, G-24, G-77, GATT, IAEA, IBRD, ICAO, IDA, IFAD, IFC, ILO, IMF, IMO, INTELSAT, INTERPOL, IOC, IOM (observer), ISO, ITU, LORCS, NAM, OAU, UN, UNCTAD, UNESCO, UNIDO, UNIFIL, UNIIMOG, UPU, WCL, WHO, WIPO, WMO, WTO

Diplomatic representation: Ambassador Dr. Joseph ABBEY; Chancery at 2460 16th Street NW, Washington DC 20009; telephone (202) 462-0761; there is a Ghanaian Consulate General in New York; US—Ambassador Raymond C. EWING; Embassy at Ring Road East, East of Danquah Circle, Accra (mailing address is P. O. Box 194, Accra); telephone [233] (21) 775347 through 775349

Flag: three equal horizontal bands of red (top), yellow, and green with a large black five-pointed star centered in the gold band; uses the popular pan-African colors of Ethiopia; similar to the flag of Bolivia which has a coat of arms centered in the yellow band

Economy

Overview: Supported by substantial international assistance, Ghana has been implementing a steady economic rebuilding program since 1983, including moves toward privatization and relaxation of government controls. Heavily dependent on cocoa, gold, and timber exports, economic growth is threatened by a poor cocoa harvest and higher oil prices in 1991. Rising inflation—unofficially estimated at 50%—could undermine Ghana's relationships with multilateral lenders. Civil service wage increases and the cost of peacekeeping forces sent to Liberia are boosting government expenditures and undercutting structural adjustment reforms. Ghana opened a stock exchange in 1990.

GNP: $5.8 billion, per capita $380; real growth rate 2.7% (1990 est.)

Inflation rate (consumer prices): 50% (1990 est.)

Unemployment rate: 1.9% (1989)

Budget: revenues $821 million; expenditures $782 million, including capital expenditures of $151 million (1990 est.)

Exports: $826 million (f.o.b., 1990 est.); *commodities*—cocoa 45%, gold, timber, tuna, bauxite, and aluminum; *partners*—US 23%, UK, other EC

Imports: $1.2 billion (c.i.f., 1990 est.); *commodities*—petroleum 16%, consumer goods, foods, intermediate goods, capital equipment; *partners*—US 10%, UK, FRG, France, Japan, South Korea, GDR

External debt: $3.1 billion (1990 est.)

Industrial production: growth rate 7.4% in manufacturing (1989); accounts for almost 1.5% of GDP

Electricity: 1,172,000 kW capacity; 4,110 million kWh produced, 280 kWh per capita (1989)

Industries: mining, lumbering, light manufacturing, fishing, aluminum, food processing

Agriculture: accounts for more than 50% of GDP (including fishing and forestry); the major cash crop is cocoa; other principal crops—rice, coffee, cassava, peanuts, corn, shea nuts, timber; normally self-sufficient in food

Illicit drugs: illicit producer of cannabis for the international drug trade

Economic aid: US commitments, including Ex-Im (FY70-89), $455 million; Western (non-US) countries, ODA and OOF bilateral commitments (1970-88), $2.3 billion; OPEC bilateral aid (1979-89), $78 million; Communist countries (1970-89), $106 million

Currency: cedi (plural—cedis); 1 cedi (C) = 100 pesewas

Exchange rates: cedis (C) per US$1— 342.91 (November 1990), 270.00 (1989), 202.35 (1988), 153.73 (1987), 89.20 (1986), 54.37 (1985)

Fiscal year: calendar year

Communications

Railroads: 953 km, all 1.067-meter gauge; 32 km double track; railroads undergoing major renovation

Highways: 28,300 km total; 6,000 km concrete or bituminous surface, 22,300 km gravel, laterite, and improved earth surfaces

Inland waterways: Volta, Ankobra, and Tano Rivers provide 155 km of perennial navigation for launches and lighters; Lake Volta provides 1,125 km of arterial and feeder waterways

Pipelines: none

Ports: Tema, Takoradi

Merchant marine: 4 cargo ships (1,000 GRT or over) totaling 52,016 GRT/66,627 DWT

Civil air: 6 major transport aircraft

Airports: 10 total, 9 usable; 5 with permanent-surface runways; none with runways over 3,659 m; 1 with runways 2,440-3,659 m; 7 with runways 1,220-2,439 m

Telecommunications: poor to fair system of open-wire and cable, radio relay links; 38,000 telephones; stations—6 AM, no FM, 9 TV; 1 Atlantic Ocean INTELSAT earth station

Defense Forces

Branches: Army, Navy, Air Force, Police Force, paramilitary Palace Guard, National Civil Defense Organization

Manpower availability: males 15-49, 3,538,503; 1,983,493 fit for military service; 169,698 reach military age (18) annually

Defense expenditures: $23 million, 0.5% of GNP (1988)

Gibraltar
(dependent territory of the UK)

Geography

Total area: 6.5 km²; land area: 6.5 km²
Comparative area: about 11 times the size of The Mall in Washington, DC
Land boundaries: 1.2 km with Spain
Coastline: 12 km
Maritime claims:
Exclusive fishing zone: 3 nm;
Territorial sea: 3 nm
Disputes: source of occasional friction between Spain and the UK
Climate: Mediterranean with mild winters and warm summers
Terrain: a narrow coastal lowland borders The Rock
Natural resources: negligible
Land use: arable land 0%; permanent crops 0%; meadows and pastures 0%; forest and woodland 0%; other 100%
Environment: natural freshwater sources are meager so large water catchments (concrete or natural rock) collect rain water
Note: strategic location on Strait of Gibraltar that links the North Atlantic Ocean and Mediterranean Sea

People

Population: 29,613 (July 1991), growth rate 0.1% (1991)
Birth rate: 18 births/1,000 population (1991)
Death rate: 8 deaths/1,000 population (1991)
Net migration rate: −9 migrants/1,000 population (1991)
Infant mortality rate: 6 deaths/1,000 live births (1991)
Life expectancy at birth: 72 years male, 78 years female (1991)
Total fertility rate: 2.4 children born/woman (1991)
Nationality: noun—Gibraltarian; adjective—Gibraltar
Ethnic divisions: mostly Italian, English, Maltese, Portuguese, and Spanish descent

Religion: Roman Catholic 74%, Protestant 11% (Church of England 8%, other 3%), Moslem 8%, Jewish 2%, none or other 5% (1981)
Language: English and Spanish are primary languages; Italian, Portuguese, and Russian also spoken; English used in the schools and for official purposes
Literacy: NA% (male NA%, female NA%)
Labor force: about 14,800 (including non-Gibraltar laborers); UK military establishments and civil government employ nearly 50% of the labor force
Organized labor: over 6,000

Government

Long-form name: none
Type: dependent territory of the UK
Capital: Gibraltar
Administrative divisions: none (dependent territory of the UK)
Independence: none (dependent territory of the UK)
Constitution: 30 May 1969
Legal system: English law
National holiday: Commonwealth Day (second Monday of March), 12 March 1990
Executive branch: British monarch, governor, chief minister, Gibraltar Council, Council of Ministers (cabinet)
Legislative branch: unicameral House of Assembly
Judicial branch: Supreme Court, Court of Appeal
Leaders:
Chief of State—Queen ELIZABETH II (since 6 February 1952), represented by Governor and Commander in Chief Adm. Sir Derek REFFELL (since NA 1989);
Head of Government—Chief Minister Joe BOSSANO (since 25 March 1988)
Political parties and leaders: Socialist Labor Party (SL), Joe BOSSANO; Gibraltar Labor Party/Association for the Advancement of Civil Rights (GCL/AACR), Adolfo CANEPA; Independent Democratic Party, Joe PITALUGA
Suffrage: universal at age 18, plus other UK subjects resident six months or more
Elections:
House of Assembly: last held on 24 March 1988 (next to be held March 1992); results—percent of vote by party NA; seats—(18 total, 15 elected) SL 8, GCL/AACR 7
Communists: negligible
Other political or pressure groups: Housewives Association, Chamber of Commerce, Gibraltar Representatives Organization
Diplomatic representation: none (dependent territory of the UK)
Flag: two horizontal bands of white (top, double-width) and red with a three-towered red castle in the center of the white band; hanging from the castle gate is a gold key centered in the red band

Economy

Overview: The economy depends heavily on British defense expenditures, revenue from tourists, fees for services to shipping, and revenues from banking and finance activities. Because more than 70% of the economy is in the public sector, changes in government spending have a major impact on the level of employment. Construction workers are particularly affected when government expenditures are cut.
GNP: $182 million, per capita $4,600; real growth rate 5% (FY87)
Inflation rate (consumer prices): 4.4% (1986)
Unemployment rate: NA%
Budget: revenues $136 million; expenditures $139 million, including capital expenditures of NA (FY88)
Exports: $82 million (1988);
commodities—(principally reexports) petroleum 51%, manufactured goods 41%, other 8%;
partners—UK, Morocco, Portugal, Netherlands, Spain, US, FRG
Imports: $258 million (1988);
commodities—fuels, manufactured goods, and foodstuffs;
partners—UK, Spain, Japan, Netherlands
External debt: $NA
Industrial production: growth rate NA%
Electricity: 47,000 kW capacity; 200 million kWh produced, 6,670 kWh per capita (1990)
Industries: tourism, banking and finance, construction, commerce; support to large UK naval and air bases; transit trade and supply depot in the port; light manufacturing of tobacco, roasted coffee, ice, mineral waters, candy, beer, and canned fish
Agriculture: NA
Economic aid: US commitments, including Ex-Im (FY70-88), $0.8 million; Western (non-US) countries, ODA and OOF bilateral commitments (1970-88), $187 million
Currency: Gibraltar pound (plural—pounds); 1 Gibraltar pound (£G) = 100 pence
Exchange rates: Gibraltar pounds (£G) per US$1—0.5171 (January 1991), 0.5603 (1990), 0.6099 (1989), 0.5614 (1988), 0.6102 (1987), 0.6817 (1986), 0.7714 (1985); note—the Gibraltar pound is at par with the British pound
Fiscal year: 1 July-30 June

Communications

Railroads: 1.000-meter-gauge system in dockyard area only
Highways: 50 km, mostly good bitumen and concrete
Ports: Gibraltar
Merchant marine: 30 ships (1,000 GRT or over) totaling 1,399,594 GRT/2,667,656

DWT; includes 6 cargo, 2 refrigerated cargo, 1 container, 10 petroleum, oils, and lubricants (POL) tanker, 1 chemical tanker, 1 combination oil/ore, 9 bulk; note—a flag of convenience registry
Civil air: 1 major transport aircraft
Airports: 1 with permanent-surface runway 1,220-2,439 m
Telecommunications: adequate international radiocommunication facilities; automatic telephone system with 14,000 telephones; stations—1 AM, 6 FM, 4 TV; 1 Atlantic Ocean INTELSAT earth station

Defense Forces

Branches: British Army, Royal Navy, Royal Air Force
Note: defense is the responsibility of the UK

Glorioso Islands
(French possession)

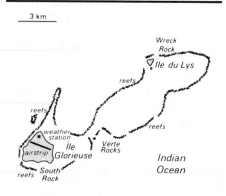

Geography

Total area: 5 km²; land area: 5 km²; includes Île Glorieuse, Île du Lys, Verte Rocks, Wreck Rock, and South Rock
Comparative area: about 8.5 times the size of The Mall in Washington, DC
Land boundaries: none
Coastline: 35.2 km
Maritime claims:
Contiguous zone: 12 nm;
Exclusive economic zone: 200 nm;
Territorial sea: 12 nm
Disputes: claimed by Madagascar
Climate: tropical
Terrain: undetermined
Natural resources: guano, coconuts
Land use: arable land 0%; permanent crops 0%; meadows and pastures 0%; forest and woodland 0%; other—lush vegetation and coconut palms 100%
Environment: subject to periodic cyclones
Note: located in the Indian Ocean just north of the Mozambique Channel between Africa and Madagascar

People

Population: uninhabited

Government

Long-form name: none
Type: French possession administered by Commissioner of the Republic Daniel CONSTANTIN, resident in Reunion

Economy

Overview: no economic activity

Communications

Airports: 1 with runway 1,220-2,439 m
Ports: none; offshore anchorage only

Defense Forces

Note: defense is the responsibility of France

Greece

Geography

Total area: 131,940 km²; land area: 130,800 km²
Comparative area: slightly smaller than Alabama
Land boundaries: 1,228 km total; Albania 282 km, Bulgaria 494 km, Turkey 206 km, Yugoslavia 246 km
Coastline: 13,676 km
Maritime claims:
Continental shelf: 200 m (depth) or to depth of exploitation;
Territorial sea: 6 nm
Disputes: complex maritime and air (but not territorial) disputes with Turkey in Aegean Sea; Cyprus question; Macedonia question with Bulgaria and Yugoslavia; Northern Epirus question with Albania
Climate: temperate; mild, wet winters; hot, dry summers
Terrain: mostly mountains with ranges extending into sea as peninsulas or chains of islands
Natural resources: bauxite, lignite, magnesite, crude oil, marble
Land use: arable land 23%; permanent crops 8%; meadows and pastures 40%; forest and woodland 20%; other 9%; includes irrigated 7%
Environment: subject to severe earthquakes; air pollution; archipelago of 2,000 islands
Note: strategic location dominating the Aegean Sea and southern approach to Turkish Straits

People

Population: 10,042,956 (July 1991), growth rate 0.2% (1991)
Birth rate: 11 births/1,000 population (1991)
Death rate: 9 deaths/1,000 population (1991)
Net migration rate: 0 migrants/1,000 population (1991)

Infant mortality rate: 10 deaths/1,000 live births (1991)
Life expectancy at birth: 75 years male, 80 years female (1991)
Total fertility rate: 1.5 children born/woman (1991)
Nationality: noun—Greek(s); adjective—Greek
Ethnic divisions: Greek 98%, other 2%; note—the Greek Government states there are no ethnic divisions in Greece
Religion: Greek Orthodox 98%, Muslim 1.3%, other 0.7%
Language: Greek (official); English and French widely understood
Literacy: 93% (male 98%, female 89%) age 15 and over can read and write (1990 est.)
Labor force: 3,860,000; services 43%, agriculture 27%, manufacturing and mining 20%, construction 7% (1985)
Organized labor: 10-15% of total labor force, 20-25% of urban labor force

---

Government

Long-form name: Hellenic Republic
Type: presidential parliamentary government; monarchy rejected by referendum 8 December 1974
Capital: Athens
Administrative divisions: 51 departments (nomoi, singular—nomós); Aitolía kai Akarnanía, Akhaïa, Argolís, Arkadhía, Árta, Attikí, Dhodhekánisos, Dráma, Evritanía, Évros, Évvoia, Flórina, Fokís, Fthiótis, Grevená, Ilía, Imathía, Ioánnina, Iráklion, Kardhítsa, Kastoría, Kavála, Kefallinía, Kérkira, Khalkidhikí, Khaniá, Khíos, Kikládhes, Kilkís, Korinthía, Kozáni, Lakonía, Lárisa, Lasíthi, Lésvos, Levkás, Magnisía, Messinía, Pélla, Piería, Préveza, Rethímni, Rodhópi, Sámos, Sérrai, Thesprotía, Thessaloníki, Tríkala, Voiotía, Xánthi, Zákinthos
Independence: 1827 (from the Ottoman Empire)
Constitution: 11 June 1975
Legal system: NA
National holiday: Independence Day (proclamation of the war of independence), 25 March (1821)
Executive branch: president, prime minister, Cabinet
Legislative branch: unicameral Greek Chamber of Deputies (Vouli ton Ellinon)
Judicial branch: Supreme Court
Leaders:
Chief of State—President Constantinos KARAMANLIS (since 5 May 1990);
Head of Government—Prime Minister Constantinos MITSOTAKIS (since 11 April 1990)
Political parties and leaders: New Democracy (ND; conservative), Constantinos MITSOTAKIS; Panhellenic Socialist Movement

(PASOK), Andreas PAPANDREOU; Democratic Renewal (DIANA), Constantine STEFANOPOULOS; Communist Party (KKE), Aleka PAPARIGA; Greek Left Party (EAR), Leonidas KYRKOS—KKE and EAR have joined in the Left Alliance, Maria DAMANAKI, president; Ecologist-Alternative List, leader NA; note—KKE and EAR have joined in the Left Alliance, Maria DAMANAKI, president
Suffrage: universal and compulsory at age 18
Elections:
President—last held 4 May 1990 (next to be held May 1995); results—Constantinos KARAMANLIS was elected by Parliament;
Parliament—last held on 8 April 1990 (next to be held April 1994); results—ND 46.89%, PASOK 38.62%, Left Alliance 10.27%, PASOK/Left Alliance 1.02%, Ecologist-Alternative List 0.77%, DIANA 0.67%, Muslim independents 0.5%; seats—(300 total) ND 150, PASOK 123, Left Alliance 19, PASOK/Left Alliance 4, Muslim independents 2, DIANA 1, Ecologist-Alternative List 1; note—one DIANA deputy joined ND in July, giving ND 151 seats; in November a special electoral court ruled in favor of ND on a contested seat, giving ND 152 seats and taking one from PASOK (now 122)
Communists: an estimated 60,000 members and sympathizers
Member of: BIS, CCC, CE, CERN, COCOM, CSCE, EBRD, EC, ECE, EIB, FAO, G-6, GATT, IAEA, IBRD, ICAO, ICC, ICFTU, IDA, IEA, IFAD, IFC, ILO, IMF, IMO, INMARSAT, INTELSAT, INTERPOL, IOC, IOM, ISO, ITU, LORCS, NAM (guest), NATO, NEA, OAS (observer), OECD, PCA, UN, UNCTAD, UNESCO, UNHCR, UNIDO, UPU, WHO, WIPO, WMO, WTO
Diplomatic representation: Ambassador Christos ZACHARAKIS; Chancery at 2221 Massachusetts Avenue NW, Washington DC 20008; telephone (202) 667-3168; there are Greek Consulates General in Atlanta, Boston, Chicago, Los Angeles, New York, and San Francisco, and a Consulate in New Orleans;
US—Ambassador Michael G. SOTIRHOS; Embassy at 91 Vasilissis Sophias Boulevard, 10160 Athens (mailing address is APO New York 09255-0006); telephone [30](1) 721-2951 or 721-8401; there is a US Consulate General in Thessaloniki
Flag: nine equal horizontal stripes of blue (top and bottom) alternating with white; there is a blue square in the upper hoist-side corner bearing a white cross; the cross symbolizes Christianity, the established religion of the country

---

Economy

Overview: Greece has a mixed capitalistic economy with the basic entrepreneurial system overlaid in 1981-89 by a socialist

government that enlarged the public sector from 55% of GDP in 1981 to about 70% when Prime Minister Mitsotakis took office. Mitsotakis inherited several severe economic problems from the preceding socialist and caretaker governments, which neglected the runaway budget deficit, a ballooning current account deficit, and accelerating inflation. With only a two-seat majority in the Chamber of Deputies, Mitsotakis has concentrated on cutting the public-sector payroll, cautiously expanding the tax base, and adopting guidelines for privatizing Greece's loss-ridden state-owned enterprises. Once the political situation is sorted out, Greece will have to face the challenges posed by the steadily increasing integration of the European Community, including the progressive lowering of trade and investment barriers. Tourism continues as a major industry, providing a vital offset to the sizable commodity trade deficit.
GDP: $76.7 billion, per capita $7,650; real growth rate 0.9% (1990 est.)
Inflation rate (consumer prices): 19.0% (1990)
Unemployment rate: 9.0% (1989)
Budget: revenues $20.9 billion; expenditures $34.1 billion, including capital expenditures of $NA (1990)
Exports: $9.0 billion (f.o.b., 1990);
commodities—manufactured goods, food and live animals, fuels and lubricants, raw materials;
partners—FRG 20%, Italy 17%, France 8%, UK 7%, US 6%
Imports: $20.2 billion (c.i.f., 1990);
commodities—machinery and transport equipment, light manufactures, fuels and lubricants, foodstuffs, chemicals;
partners—FRG 21%, Italy 16%, France 8%, Netherlands 7%, UK 6%
External debt: $18.7 billion (1989)
Industrial production: growth rate −1.0% (1990 est.); accounts for 22% of GDP
Electricity: 10,500,000 kW capacity; 36,420 million kWh produced, 3,630 kWh per capita (1989)
Industries: food and tobacco processing, textiles, chemicals, metal products, tourism, mining, petroleum
Agriculture: including fishing and forestry, accounts for 13% of GNP and 27% of the labor force; principal products—wheat, corn, barley, sugar beets, olives, tomatoes, wine, tobacco, potatoes, beef, mutton, pork, dairy products; self-sufficient in food; fish catch of 135,000 metric tons in 1987
Economic aid: US commitments, including Ex-Im (FY70-81), $525 million; Western (non-US) countries, ODA and OOF bilateral commitments (1970-88), $1.35 billion
Currency: drachma (plural—drachmas); 1 drachma (Dr) = 100 lepta
Exchange rates: drachma (Dr) per US$1—159.87 (January 1991), 158.51 (1990),

162.42 (1989), 141.86 (1988), 135.43 (1987), 139.98 (1986), 138.12 (1985)
Fiscal year: calendar year

Communications

Railroads: 2,479 km total; 1,565 km 1.435-meter standard gauge, of which 36 km electrified and 100 km double track, 892 km 1.000-meter gauge; 22 km 0.750-meter narrow gauge; all government owned
Highways: 38,938 km total; 16,090 km paved, 13,676 km crushed stone and gravel, 5,632 km improved earth, 3,540 km unimproved earth
Inland waterways: 80 km; system consists of three coastal canals and three unconnected rivers
Pipelines: crude oil, 26 km; refined products, 547 km
Ports: Piraeus, Thessaloniki
Merchant marine: 958 ships (1,000 GRT or over) totaling 21,585,048 GRT/39,011,361 DWT; includes 13 passenger, 63 short-sea passenger, 2 passenger-cargo, 152 cargo, 21 container, 17 roll-on/roll-off cargo, 23 refrigerated cargo, 1 vehicle carrier, 185 petroleum, oils, and lubricants (POL) tanker, 15 chemical tanker, 10 liquefied gas, 25 combination ore/oil, 5 specialized tanker, 407 bulk, 19 combination bulk; note—ethnic Greeks also own large numbers of ships under the registry of Liberia, Panama, Cyprus, and Lebanon
Civil air: 35 major transport aircraft
Airports: 81 total, 79 usable; 60 with permanent-surface runways; none with runways over 3,659 m; 20 with runways 2,440-3,659 m; 22 with runways 1,220-2,439 m
Telecommunications: adequate, modern networks reach all areas; 4,122,317 telephones; stations—30 AM, 17 (20 repeaters) FM, 39 (560 repeaters) TV; 8 submarine cables; satellite earth stations operating in INTELSAT (1 Atlantic Ocean and 1 Indian Ocean), EUTELSAT, and MARISAT systems

Defense Forces

Branches: Hellenic Army, Hellenic Navy, Hellenic Air Force, Police
Manpower availability: males 15-49, 2,434,762; 1,870,699 fit for military service; 72,707 reach military age (21) annually
Defense expenditures: $3.7 billion, 5.5% of GDP (1990)

Greenland
(part of the Danish realm)

Geography

Total area: 2,175,600 km²; land area: 341,700 km² (ice free)
Comparative area: slightly more than three times the size of Texas
Land boundaries: none
Coastline: 44,087 km
Maritime claims:
Exclusive fishing zone: 200 nm;
Territorial sea: 3 nm
Disputes: Denmark has challenged Norway's maritime claims between Greenland and Jan Mayen
Climate: arctic to subarctic; cool summers, cold winters
Terrain: flat to gradually sloping icecap covers all but a narrow, mountainous, barren, rocky coast
Natural resources: zinc, lead, iron ore, coal, molybdenum, cryolite, uranium, fish
Land use: arable land 0%; permanent crops 0%; meadows and pastures 1%; forest and woodland NEGL%; other 99%
Environment: sparse population confined to small settlements along coast; continuous permafrost over northern two-thirds of the island
Note: dominates North Atlantic Ocean between North America and Europe

People

Population: 56,752 (July 1991), growth rate 1.2% (1991)
Birth rate: 20 births/1,000 population (1991)
Death rate: 8 deaths/1,000 population (1991)
Net migration rate: 0 migrants/1,000 population (1991)
Infant mortality rate: 28 deaths/1,000 live births (1991)
Life expectancy at birth: 63 years male, 69 years female (1991)
Total fertility rate: 2.2 children born/woman (1991)

Nationality: noun—Greenlander(s); adjective—Greenlandic
Ethnic divisions: Greenlander (Eskimos and Greenland-born Caucasians) 86%, Danish 14%
Religion: Evangelical Lutheran
Language: Eskimo dialects, Danish
Literacy: NA% (male NA%, female NA%)
Labor force: 22,800; largely engaged in fishing, hunting, sheep breeding
Organized labor: NA

Government

Long-form name: none
Type: part of the Danish realm; self-governing overseas administrative division
Capital: Nuuk (Godthåb)
Administrative divisions: 3 municipalities (kommuner, singular—kommun); Nordgrønland, Østgrønland, Vestgrønland
Independence: part of the Danish realm; self-governing overseas administrative division
Constitution: Danish
Legal system: Danish
National holiday: Birthday of the Queen, 16 April (1940)
Executive branch: Danish monarch, high commissioner, home rule chairman, prime minister, Cabinet (Landsstyre)
Legislative branch: unicameral Landsting
Judicial branch: High Court (Landsret)
Leaders:
Chief of State—Queen MARGRETHE II (since 14 January 1972), represented by High Commissioner Bent KLINTE (since NA);
Head of Government—Home Rule Chairman Lars Emil JOHANSEN (since 15 March 1991)
Political parties and leaders: two-party ruling coalition—Siumut (a moderate socialist party that advocates more distinct Greenlandic identity and greater autonomy from Denmark), Lars Emil JOHANSEN, chairman; and Inuit Ataqatiigit (IA; a Marxist-Leninist party that favors complete independence from Denmark rather than home rule); Atassut Party (a more conservative party that favors continuing close relations with Denmark), leader NA; Polar Party (conservative-Greenland nationalist), leader NA; Center Party (a new nonsocialist protest party), leader NA
Suffrage: universal at age 18
Elections:
Landsting—last held on 5 March 1991 (next to be held 5 March 1995); results—percent of vote by party NA; seats—(27 total) Siumut 11, Atassut Party 8, Inuit Ataqatiigit 5, Center Party 2, Polar Party 1;
Danish Folketing—last held on 12 December 1990 (next to be held by December 1994); Greenland elects two representatives to the Folketing; results—percent of vote by party NA; seats—(2 total) Siumut 1, Atassut 1

Greenland (continued)

Member of: NC
Diplomatic representation: none (self-governing overseas administrative division of Denmark)
Flag: two equal horizontal bands of white (top) and red with a large disk slightly to the hoist side of center—the top half of the disk is red, the bottom half is white

Economy

Overview: Over the past 25 years, the economy has changed from one based on subsistence whaling, hunting, and fishing to one dependent on foreign trade. Fishing is still the most important industry, accounting for over 75% of exports and about 25% of the population's income. Maintenance of a social welfare system similar to Denmark's has given the public sector a dominant role in the economy. In 1990, the economy became critically dependent on shrimp exports and an annual subsidy (now about $355 million) from the Danish Government because cod exports had fallen, the zinc and lead mine closed, and a large promising platinum and gold mine was not yet operational. Greenland has signed a contract for its largest construction project, a power plant to supply the capital. To avoid a decline in the economy, Denmark has agreed to pay 75% of the costs of running Sondrestrom Airbase and Kulusuk Airfield as civilian bases after the US withdraws in 1992.
GNP: $500 million, per capita $9,000; real growth rate 5% (1988)
Inflation rate (consumer prices): 4.4% (1989)
Unemployment rate: 9% (1990 est.)
Budget: revenues $381 million; expenditures $381 million, including capital expenditures of $36 million (1989)
Exports: $417 million (f.o.b., 1989 est.); *commodities*—fish and fish products 78%, metallic ores and concentrates 19%; *partners*—Denmark 74%, FRG 11%, Sweden 6%
Imports: $394 million (c.i.f., 1989 est.); *commodities*—manufactured goods 36%, machinery and transport equipment 26%, food products 13%, petroleum and petroleum products 10%; *partners*—Denmark 69%, Norway, FRG, Japan, US, Sweden
External debt: $480 million (1990 est.)
Industrial production: growth rate NA%
Electricity: 84,000 kW capacity; 176 million kWh produced, 3,180 kWh per capita (1989)
Industries: fish processing (mainly shrimp), potential for platinum and gold mining, handicrafts, shipyards
Agriculture: sector dominated by fishing and sheep raising; crops limited to forage and small garden vegetables; 1988 fish catch of 133,500 metric tons

Economic aid: none
Currency: Danish krone (plural—kroner); 1 Danish krone (DKr) = 100 øre
Exchange rates: Danish kroner (DKr) per US$1—5.817 (January 1991), 6.189 (1990), 7.310 (1989), 6.732 (1988), 6.840 (1987), 8.091 (1986), 10.596 (1985)
Fiscal year: calendar year

Communications

Highways: 80 km
Ports: Kangerluarsoruseq (Faeringehavn), Paamiut (Frederikshaab), Nuuk (Godthaab), Sisimiut (Holsteinsborg), Julianehaab, Maarmorilik, North Star Bay
Merchant marine: 1 refrigerated cargo (1,000 GRT or over) totaling 1,021 GRT/1,778 DWT; note—operates under the registry of Denmark
Civil air: 2 major transport aircraft
Airports: 11 total, 8 usable; 5 with permanent-surface runways; none with runways over 3,659 m; 2 with runways 2,440-3,659 m; 2 with runways 1,220-2,439 m
Telecommunications: adequate domestic and international service provided by cables and radio relay; 17,900 telephones; stations—5 AM, 7 (35 relays) FM, 4 (9 relays) TV; 2 coaxial submarine cables; 1 Atlantic Ocean INTELSAT earth station

Defense Forces

Note: defense is responsibility of Denmark

Grenada

Geography

Total area: 340 km²; land area: 340 km²
Comparative area: slightly less than twice the size of Washington, DC
Land boundaries: none
Coastline: 121 km
Maritime claims:
Exclusive economic zone: 200 nm;
Territorial sea: 12 nm
Climate: tropical; tempered by northeast trade winds
Terrain: volcanic in origin with central mountains
Natural resources: timber, tropical fruit, deepwater harbors
Land use: arable land 15%; permanent crops 26%; meadows and pastures 3%; forest and woodland 9%; other 47%
Environment: lies on edge of hurricane belt; hurricane season lasts from June to November
Note: islands of the Grenadines group are divided politically with Saint Vincent and the Grenadines

People

Population: 83,812 (July 1991), growth rate −0.4% (1991)
Birth rate: 35 births/1,000 population (1991)
Death rate: 7 deaths/1,000 population (1991)
Net migration rate: −32 migrants/1,000 population (1991)
Infant mortality rate: 29 deaths/1,000 live births (1991)
Life expectancy at birth: 69 years male, 74 years female (1991)
Total fertility rate: 4.7 children born/woman (1991)
Nationality: noun—Grenadian(s); adjective—Grenadian
Ethnic divisions: mainly of black African descent

Religion: largely Roman Catholic; Anglican; other Protestant sects

Language: English (official); some French patois

Literacy: 98% (male 98%, female 98%) age 15 and over having ever attended school (1970)

Labor force: 36,000; services 31%, agriculture 24%, construction 8%, manufacturing 5%, other 32% (1985)

Organized labor: 20% of labor force

Government

Long-form name: none

Type: parliamentary democracy

Capital: Saint George's

Administrative divisions: 6 parishes and 1 dependency*; Carriacou and Little Martinique*, Saint Andrew, Saint David, Saint George, Saint John, Saint Mark, Saint Patrick

Independence: 7 February 1974 (from UK)

Constitution: 19 December 1973

Legal system: based on English common law

National holiday: Independence Day, 7 February (1974)

Executive branch: British monarch, governor general, prime minister, Ministers of Government (cabinet)

Legislative branch: bicameral Parliament consists of an upper house or Senate and a lower house or House of Representatives

Judicial branch: Supreme Court

Leaders:
Chief of State—Queen ELIZABETH II (since 6 February 1952), represented by Governor General Sir Paul SCOON (since 30 September 1978);

Head of Government—Prime Minister Nicholas BRATHWAITE (since 13 March 1990)

Political parties and leaders: National Democratic Congress (NDC), Nicholas BRATHWAITE; Grenada United Labor Party (GULP), Sir Eric GAIRY; The National Party (TNP), Ben JONES; New National Party (NNP), Keith MITCHELL; Maurice Bishop Patriotic Movement (MBPM), Terrence MERRYSHOW; New Jewel Movement (NJM), Bernard COARD

Suffrage: universal at age 18

Elections:
House of Representatives—last held on 13 March 1990 (next to be held by March 1996); results—percent of vote by party NA; seats—(15 total) NDC 8, GULP 3, TNP 2, NNP 2

Communists: about 450 members of the New Jewel Movement (pro-Soviet) and the Maurice Bishop Patriotic Movement (pro-Cuban)

Member of: ACP, C, CARICOM, CDB, ECLAC, FAO, G-77, IBRD, ICAO, ICFTU, IDA, IFAD, IFC, ILO, IMF, INTERPOL, IOC, ITU, LAES, LORCS, NAM, OAS, OECS, OPANAL, UN, UNCTAD, UNESCO, UNIDO, UPU, WCL, WHO, WTO

Diplomatic representation: Ambassador Denneth MODESTE; Chancery at 1701 New Hampshire Avenue NW, Washington DC 20009; telephone (202) 265-2561; there is a Grenadian Consulate General in New York;

US—Chargé d'Affaires Annette VELER; Embassy at Ross Point Inn, Saint George's (mailing address is P. O. Box 54, Saint George's); telephone (809) 444-1173 through 1178

Flag: a rectangle divided diagonally into yellow triangles (top and bottom) and green triangles (hoist side and outer side) with a red border around the flag; there are seven yellow five-pointed stars with three centered in the top red border, three centered in the bottom red border, and one on a red disk superimposed at the center of the flag; there is also a symbolic nutmeg pod on the hoist-side triangle (Grenada is the world's second-largest producer of nutmeg, after Indonesia); the seven stars represent the seven administrative divisions

---

Economy

Overview: The economy is essentially agricultural and centers on the traditional production of spices and tropical plants. Agriculture accounts for about 16% of GDP and 80% of exports and employs 24% of the labor force. Tourism is the leading foreign exchange earner, followed by agricultural exports. Manufacturing remains relatively undeveloped, but is expected to grow, given a more favorable private investment climate since 1983. Despite an impressive average annual growth rate for the economy of 5.6% during the period 1986-90, unemployment remains high at about 25%.

GDP: $200.7 million, per capita $2,390 (1989); real growth rate 5.4% (1990)

Inflation rate (consumer prices): 7.0% (1990)

Unemployment rate: 25% (1990 est.)

Budget: revenues $54.9 million; expenditures $77.6 million, including capital expenditures of $16.6 million (1990 est.)

Exports: $27.9 million (f.o.b., 1989 est.);
commodities—nutmeg 36%, cocoa beans 9%, bananas 14%, mace 8%, textiles 5;
partners—US 12%, UK, FRG, Netherlands, Trinidad and Tobago (1989)

Imports: $115.6 million (c.i.f., 1989 est.);
commodities—food 25%, manufactured goods 22%, machinery 20%, chemicals 10%, fuel 6% (1989);
partners—US 29%, UK, Trinidad and Tobago, Japan, Canada (1989)

External debt: $90 million (1990 est.)

Industrial production: growth rate 5.8% (1989 est.); accounts for 6% of GDP

Electricity: 12,500 kW capacity; 26 million kWh produced, 310 kWh per capita (1990)

Industries: food and beverage, textile, light assembly operations, tourism, construction

Agriculture: accounts for 16% of GDP and 80% of exports; bananas, cocoa, nutmeg, and mace account for two-thirds of total crop production; world's second-largest producer and fourth-largest exporter of nutmeg and mace; small-size farms predominate, growing a variety of citrus fruits, avocados, root crops, sugarcane, corn, and vegetables

Economic aid: US commitments, including Ex-Im (FY84-89), $60 million; Western (non-US) countries, ODA and OOF bilateral commitments (1970-88), $67 million; Communist countries (1970-89), $32 million

Currency: East Caribbean dollar (plural—dollars); 1 EC dollar (EC$) = 100 cents

Exchange rates: East Caribbean dollars (EC$) per US$1—2.70 (fixed rate since 1976)

Fiscal year: calendar year

Communications

Highways: 1,000 km total; 600 km paved, 300 km otherwise improved; 100 km unimproved

Ports: Saint George's

Civil air: no major transport aircraft

Airports: 3 total, 3 usable; 2 with permanent-surface runways; none with runways over 3,659 m; 1 with runways 2,440-3,659 m; 1 with runways 1,220-2,439 m

Telecommunications: automatic, islandwide telephone system with 5,650 telephones; new SHF links to Trinidad and Tobago and Saint Vincent; VHF and UHF links to Trinidad and Carriacou; stations—1 AM, no FM, 1 TV

Defense Forces

Branches: Royal Grenada Police Force, Coast Guard

Manpower availability: NA

Defense expenditures: $NA, NA% of GDP

Guadeloupe
(overseas department of France)

Marie-Galante

St. Martin and St. Barthélemy are not shown.

Geography

Total area: 1,780 km²; land area: 1,760 km²
Comparative area: 10 times the size of Washington, DC
Land boundaries: none
Coastline: 306 km
Maritime claims:
Continental shelf: 200 m (depth) or to depth of exploitation;
Exclusive economic zone: 200 nm;
Territorial sea: 12 nm
Climate: subtropical tempered by trade winds; relatively high humidity
Terrain: Basse-Terre is volcanic in origin with interior mountains; Grand-Terre is low limestone formation
Natural resources: cultivable land, beaches, and climate that foster tourism
Land use: arable land 18%; permanent crops 5%; meadows and pastures 13%; forest and woodland 40%; other 24%; includes irrigated 1%
Environment: subject to hurricanes (June to October); La Soufrière is an active volcano
Note: located 500 km southeast of Puerto Rico in the Caribbean Sea

People

Population: 344,897 (July 1991), growth rate 0.8% (1991)
Birth rate: 20 births/1,000 population (1991)
Death rate: 6 deaths/1,000 population (1991)
Net migration rate: −5 migrants/1,000 population (1991)
Infant mortality rate: 17 deaths/1,000 live births (1991)
Life expectancy at birth: 70 years male, 77 years female (1991)
Total fertility rate: 2.0 children born/woman (1991)
Nationality: noun—Guadeloupian(s); adjective—Guadeloupe

Ethnic divisions: black or mulatto 90%; white 5%; East Indian, Lebanese, Chinese less than 5%
Religion: Roman Catholic 95%, Hindu and pagan African 5%
Language: French, creole patois
Literacy: 90% (male 90%, female 91%) age 15 and over can read and write (1982)
Labor force: 120,000; 53.0% services, government, and commerce, 25.8% industry, 21.2% agriculture
Organized labor: 11% of labor force

Government

Long-form name: Department of Guadeloupe
Type: overseas department of France
Capital: Basse-Terre
Administrative divisions: none (overseas department of France)
Independence: none (overseas department of France)
Constitution: 28 September 1958 (French Constitution)
Legal system: French legal system
National holiday: Taking of the Bastille, 14 July (1789)
Executive branch: government commissioner
Legislative branch: unicameral General Council and unicameral Regional Council
Judicial branch: Court of Appeal (Cour d'Appel) with jurisdiction over Guadeloupe, French Guiana, and Martinique
Leaders:
Chief of State—President François MITTERRAND (since 21 May 1981);
Head of Government—Commissioner of the Republic Jean-Paul PROUST (since November 1989)
Political parties and leaders: Rally for the Republic (RPR), Marlène CAPTANT; Communist Party of Guadeloupe (PCG), Christian Medard CELESTE; Socialist Party (PSG), Dominique LARIFLA; Independent Republicans; Union for French Democracy (UDF); Union for a New Majority (UNM)
Suffrage: universal at age 18
Elections:
General Council—last held NA 1986 (next to be held by NA 1992); results—percent of vote by party NA; seats—(42 total) number of seats by party NA;
Regional Council—last held on 16 March 1986 (next to be held by 16 March 1992); results—RPR 33.1%, PS 28.7%, PCG 23.8%, UDF 10.7%, other 3.7%; seats—(41 total) RPR 15, PS 12, PCG 10, UDF 4;
French Senate—last held on 5 and 12 June 1988 (next to be held June 1994); Guadeloupe elects two representatives; results—percent of vote by party NA; seats—(2 total) PCG 1, PS 1;

French National Assembly—last held on 5 and 12 June 1988 (next to be held June 1994); Guadeloupe elects four representatives; results—percent of vote by party NA; seats—(4 total) PS 2 seats, RPR 1 seat, PCG 1 seat
Communists: 3,000 est.
Other political or pressure groups: Popular Union for the Liberation of Guadeloupe (UPLG); Popular Movement for Independent Guadeloupe (MPGI); General Union of Guadeloupe Workers (UGTG); General Federation of Guadeloupe Workers (CGT-G); Christian Movement for the Liberation of Guadeloupe (KLPG)
Member of: FZ, WCL, WFTU
Diplomatic representation: as an overseas department of France, the interests of Guadeloupe are represented in the US by France
Flag: the flag of France is used

Economy

Overview: The economy depends on agriculture, tourism, light industry, and services. It is also dependent upon France for large subsidies and imports. Tourism is a key industry, with most tourists from the US. In addition, an increasingly large number of cruise ships visit the islands. The traditionally important sugarcane crop is slowly being replaced by other crops, such as bananas (which now supply about 50% of export earnings), eggplant, and flowers. Other vegetables and root crops are cultivated for local consumption, although Guadeloupe is still dependent on imported food, which comes mainly from France. Light industry consists mostly of sugar and rum production. Most manufactured goods and fuel are imported. Unemployment is especially high among the young.
GDP: $1.1 billion, per capita $3,300; real growth rate NA% (1987)
Inflation rate (consumer prices): 2.3% (1988)
Unemployment rate: 38% (1987)
Budget: revenues $254 million; expenditures $254 million, including capital expenditures of NA (1989)
Exports: $153 million (f.o.b., 1988);
commodities—bananas, sugar, rum;
partners—France 68%, Martinique 22% (1987)
Imports: $1.2 billion (c.i.f., 1988);
commodities—vehicles, foodstuffs, clothing and other consumer goods, construction materials, petroleum products;
partners—France 64%, Italy, FRG, US (1987)
External debt: $NA
Industrial production: growth rate NA%
Electricity: 171,500 kW capacity; 441 million kWh produced, 1,290 kWh per capita (1990)

Guam
(territory of the US)

Industries: construction, cement, rum, sugar, tourism

Agriculture: cash crops—bananas and sugarcane; other products include tropical fruits and vegetables; livestock—cattle, pigs, and goats; not self-sufficient in food

Economic aid: US commitments, including Ex-Im (FY70-88), $4 million; Western (non-US) countries, ODA and OOF bilateral commitments (1970-88), $7.9 billion

Currency: French franc (plural—francs); 1 French franc (F) = 100 centimes

Exchange rates: French francs (F) per US$1—5.1307 (January 1991), 5.4453 (1990), 6.3801 (1989), 5.9569 (1988), 6.0107 (1987), 6.9261 (1986), 8.9852 (1985)

Fiscal year: calendar year

Communications

Railroads: privately owned, narrow-gauge plantation lines

Highways: 1,940 km total; 1,600 km paved, 340 km gravel and earth

Ports: Pointe-a-Pitre, Basse-Terre

Civil air: 2 major transport aircraft

Airports: 9 total, 9 usable, 8 with permanent-surface runways; none with runways over 3,659 m; 1 with runways 2,440-3,659 m; 1 with runways 1,220-2,439 m

Telecommunications: domestic facilities inadequate; 57,300 telephones; interisland radio relay to Antigua and Barbuda, Dominica, and Martinique; stations—2 AM, 8 FM (30 private stations licensed to broadcast FM), 9 TV; 1 Atlantic Ocean INTELSAT ground station

Defense Forces

Branches: French Forces, Gendarmerie

Manpower availability: males 15-49, 98,069; NA fit for military service

Note: defense is responsibility of France

Geography

Total area: 541 km²; land area: 541 km²

Comparative area: slightly more than three times the size of Washington, DC

Land boundaries: none

Coastline: 125.5 km

Maritime claims:

Contiguous zone: 12 nm;

Continental shelf: 200 m (depth);

Exclusive economic zone: 200 nm;

Territorial sea: 12 nm

Climate: tropical marine; generally warm and humid, moderated by northeast trade winds; dry season from January to June, rainy season from July to December; little seasonal temperature variation

Terrain: volcanic origin, surrounded by coral reefs; relatively flat coraline limestone plateau (source of most fresh water) with steep coastal cliffs and narrow coastal plains in north, low-rising hills in center, mountains in south

Natural resources: fishing (largely undeveloped), tourism (especially from Japan)

Land use: arable land 11%; permanent crops 11%; meadows and pastures 15%; forest and woodland 18%; other 45%

Environment: frequent squalls during rainy season; subject to relatively rare, but potentially very destructive typhoons (especially in August)

Note: largest and southernmost island in the Mariana Islands archipelago; strategic location in western North Pacific Ocean 5,955 km west-southwest of Honolulu about three-quarters of the way between Hawaii and the Philippines

People

Population: 144,928 (July 1991), growth rate 2.8% (1991)

Birth rate: 26 births/1,000 population (1991)

Death rate: 4 deaths/1,000 population (1991)

Net migration rate: 5 migrants/1,000 population (1991)

Infant mortality rate: 12 deaths/1,000 live births (1991)

Life expectancy at birth: 70 years male, 75 years female (1991)

Total fertility rate: 3.0 children born/woman (1991)

Nationality: noun—Guamanian(s); adjective—Guamanian

Ethnic divisions: Chamorro 47%, Filipino 25%, Caucasian 10%, Chinese, Japanese, Korean, and other 18%

Religion: Roman Catholic 98%, other 2%

Language: English and Chamorro, most residents bilingual; Japanese also widely spoken

Literacy: 96% (male 96%, female 96%) age 15 and over can read and write (1980)

Labor force: 54,000; government 42%, private 58% (1988)

Organized labor: 13% of labor force

Government

Long-form name: Territory of Guam

Type: organized, unincorporated territory of the US

Capital: Agana

Administrative divisions: none (territory of the US)

Independence: none (territory of the US)

Constitution: Organic Act of 1 August 1950

Legal system: NA

National holiday: Guam Discovery Day (first Monday in March), 6 March 1989

Executive branch: President of the US, governor, lieutenant governor, Cabinet

Legislative branch: unicameral Legislature

Judicial branch: Superior Court of Guam (Federal District Court)

Leaders:

Chief of State—President George BUSH (since 20 January 1989);

Head of Government—Governor Joseph A. ADA (since NA November 1986); Lieutenant Governor Frank F. BLAS

Political parties and leaders: Democratic Party (controls the legislature); Republican Party (party of the Governor)

Suffrage: universal at age 18; US citizens, but do not vote in US presidential elections

Elections:

Governor—last held on 6 November 1990 (next to be held November 1994);

Legislature—last held on 6 November 1990 (next to be held November 1994); results—percent of vote by party NA; seats—(21 total) Democratic 11, Republican 10;

US House of Representatives—last held 6 November 1990 (next to be held November 1992); Guam elects one nonvoting delegate; results—percent of vote by party NA; seats—(1 total) Republican 1

Communists: none

Guam *(continued)*

Note: relations between Guam and the US are under the jurisdiction of the Office of Territorial and International Affairs, US Department of the Interior
Member of: ESCAP (associate), IOC, SPC
Diplomatic representation: none (territory of the US)
Flag: dark blue with a narrow red border on all four sides; centered is a red-bordered, pointed, vertical ellipse containing a beach scene, outrigger canoe with sail, and a palm tree with the word *GUAM* superimposed in bold red letters

Economy

Overview: The economy is based on US military spending and on revenues from tourism. Over the past 20 years the tourist industry has grown rapidly, creating a construction boom for new hotels and the expansion of older ones. Visitors numbered about 900,000 in 1990. The small manufacturing sector includes textile and clothing, beverage, food, and watch production. About 60% of the labor force works for the private sector and the rest for government. Most food and industrial goods are imported, with about 75% from the US. In 1990 the unemployment rate was about 2%, down from 10% in 1983.
GNP: $1.0 billion, per capita $7,000; real growth rate 18% (1990 est.)
Inflation rate (consumer prices): 10% (1990)
Unemployment rate: 2% (1990 est.)
Budget: revenues $300 million; expenditures $290 million, including capital expenditures of $25 million (1990 est.)
Exports: $39 million (f.o.b., 1983);
commodities—mostly transshipments of refined petroleum products, construction materials, fish, food and beverage products;
partners—US 25%, other 75%
Imports: $611 million (c.i.f., 1983);
commodities—petroleum and petroleum products, food, manufactured goods;
partners—US 77%, other 23%
External debt: $NA
Industrial production: growth rate NA%
Electricity: 500,000 kW capacity; 2,300 million kWh produced, 16,300 kWh per capita (1990)
Industries: US military, tourism, construction, transshipment, concrete products, printing and publishing, food processing, textiles
Agriculture: relatively undeveloped with most food imported; fruits, vegetables, eggs, pork, poultry, beef, copra
Economic aid: NA
Currency: US currency is used
Exchange rates: US currency is used
Fiscal year: 1 October-30 September

Communications

Highways: 674 km all-weather roads

Ports: Apra Harbor
Airports: 5 total, 4 usable; 3 with permanent-surface runways; none with runways over 3,659 m; 3 with runways 2,440-3,659 m; none with runways 1,220-2,439 m
Telecommunications: 26,317 telephones (1989); stations—3 AM, 3 FM, 3 TV; 2 Pacific Ocean INTELSAT ground stations

Defense Forces

Note: defense is the responsibility of the US

Guatemala

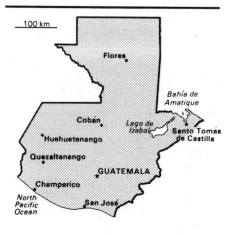

Geography

Total area: 108,890 km²; land area: 108,430 km²
Comparative area: slightly smaller than Tennessee
Land boundaries: 1,687 km total; Belize 266 km, El Salvador 203 km, Honduras 256 km, Mexico 962 km
Coastline: 400 km
Maritime claims:
Continental shelf: not specific;
Exclusive economic zone: 200 nm;
Territorial sea: 12 nm
Disputes: claims Belize, but boundary negotiations to resolve the dispute are underway
Climate: tropical; hot, humid in lowlands; cooler in highlands
Terrain: mostly mountains with narrow coastal plains and rolling limestone plateau (Petén)
Natural resources: crude oil, nickel, rare woods, fish, chicle
Land use: arable land 12%; permanent crops 4%; meadows and pastures 12%; forest and woodland 40%; other 32%; includes irrigated 1%
Environment: numerous volcanoes in mountains, with frequent violent earthquakes; Caribbean coast subject to hurricanes and other tropical storms; deforestation; soil erosion; water pollution
Note: no natural harbors on west coast

People

Population: 9,266,018 (July 1991), growth rate 2.5% (1991)
Birth rate: 35 births/1,000 population (1991)
Death rate: 8 deaths/1,000 population (1991)
Net migration rate: −2 migrants/1,000 population (1991)
Infant mortality rate: 58 deaths/1,000 live births (1991)

Total fertility rate: 4.8 children born/woman (1991)

Nationality: noun—Guatemalan(s); adjective—Guatemalan

Ethnic divisions: Ladino (mestizo—mixed Indian and European ancestry) 56%, Indian 44%

Religion: predominantly Roman Catholic; also Protestant, traditional Mayan

Language: Spanish, but over 40% of the population speaks an Indian language as a primary tongue (18 Indian dialects, including Quiche, Cakchiquel, Kekchi)

Literacy: 55% (male 63%, female 47%) age 15 and over can read and write (1990 est.)

Labor force: 2,500,000; agriculture 60%, services 13%, manufacturing 12%, commerce 7%, construction 4%, transport 3%, utilities 0.8%, mining 0.4% (1985)

Organized labor: 8% of labor force (1988 est.)

Government

Long-form name: Republic of Guatemala

Type: republic

Capital: Guatemala

Administrative divisions: 22 departments (departamentos, singular—departamento); Alta Verapaz, Baja Verapaz, Chimaltenango, Chiquimula, El Progreso, Escuintla, Guatemala, Huehuetenango, Izabal, Jalapa, Jutiapa, Petén, Quetzaltenango, Quiché, Retalhuleu, Sacatepéquez, San Marcos, Santa Rosa, Sololá, Suchitepéquez, Totonicapán, Zacapa

Independence: 15 September 1821 (from Spain)

Constitution: 31 May 1985, effective 14 January 1986

Legal system: civil law system; judicial review of legislative acts; has not accepted compulsory ICJ jurisdiction

National holiday: Independence Day, 15 September (1821)

Executive branch: president, vice president, Council of Ministers (cabinet)

Legislative branch: unicameral Congress of the Republic (Congreso de la Republica)

Judicial branch: Supreme Court of Justice (Corte Suprema de Justicia)

Leaders:
Chief of State and Head of Government—President Jorge SERRANO Elías (since 14 January 1991); Vice President Gustavo ESPINA Salguero (since 14 January 1991)

Political parties and leaders: National Centrist Union (UCN), Jorge CARPIO Nicolle; Solidarity Action Movement (MAS), Jorge SERRANO Elías; Christian Democratic Party (DCG), Alfonso CABRERA Hidalgo; National Advancement Party (PAN), Alvaro ARZÚ Irigoyen; National Liberation Movement (MLN), Mario SANDOVAL Alarcón; Social Democratic Party (PSD), Mario SOLARZANO Martínez; Popular

Alliance 5 (AP-5), Max ORLANDO Molina; Revolutionary Party (PR), Carlos CHAVARRIA; National Authentic Center (CAN), Hector MAYORA Dawe; Alliance for 90 led by Rios MONTT, consisting of three parties—Democratic Institutional Party (PID), Oscar RIVAS; Nationalist United Front (FUN), Gabriel GIRON; Guatemalan Republican Front (FRG), Berna ROLANDO Mendez

Suffrage: universal at age 18

Elections:
President—runoff held on 11 January 1991 (next to be held 11 November 1995); results—Jorge SERRANO Elías (MAS) 68.1%, Jorge CARPIO Nicolle (UCN) 31.9%;
Congress—last held on 11 November 1990 (next to be held 11 November 1995); results—UCN 25.6%, MAS 24.3%, DCG 17.5%, PAN 17.3%, MLN 4.8%, PSD/AP-5 3.6%, PR 2.1%; seats—(116 total) UCN 41, DCG 28, MAS 18, PAN 12, Alliance for 90 11, MLN 4, PR 1, PSD/AP-5 1

Communists: Guatemalan Labor Party (PGT); main radical left guerrilla groups—Guerrilla Army of the Poor (EGP), Revolutionary Organization of the People in Arms (ORPA), Rebel Armed Forces (FAR), and PGT dissidents

Other political or pressure groups: Federated Chambers of Commerce and Industry (CACIF), Mutual Support Group (GAM), Unity for Popular and Labor Action (UASP), Agrarian Owners Group (UNAGRO), Committee for Campesino Unity (CUC)

Member of: BCIE, CACM, CCC, ECLAC, FAO, G-24, G-77, IADB, IAEA, IBRD, ICAO, ICFTU, IDA, IFAD, IFC, ILO, IMF, IMO, INTELSAT, INTERPOL, IOC, IOM, ITU, LAES, LAIA (observer), LORCS, OAS, OPANAL, PCA, UN, UNCTAD, UNESCO, UNIDO, UPU, WCL, WFTU, WHO, WIPO, WMO

Diplomatic representation: Ambassador Juan José CASO Fanjul; Chancery at 2220 R Street NW, Washington DC 20008; telephone (202) 745-4952 through 4954; there are Guatemalan Consulates General in Chicago, Houston, Los Angeles, Miami, New Orleans, New York, and San Francisco;
US—Ambassador Thomas F. STROOCK; Embassy at 7-01 Avenida de la Reforma, Zone 10, Guatemala City (mailing address is APO Miami 34024); telephone [502] (2) 31-15-41

Flag: three equal vertical bands of light blue (hoist side), white, and light blue with the coat of arms centered in the white band; the coat of arms includes a green and red quetzal (the national bird) and a scroll bearing the inscription *LIBERTAD 15 DE SEPTIEMBRE DE 1821* (the original date of independence from Spain) all superimposed

on a pair of crossed rifles and a pair of crossed swords and framed by a wreath

Economy

Overview: The economy is based on agriculture, which accounts for 26% of GDP, employs about 60% of the labor force, and supplies two-thirds of exports. Manufacturing accounts for about 15% of GDP and 12% of the labor force. In 1990 the economy grew by 3.5%, the fourth consecutive year of mild growth. Government economic policies, however, were erratic in 1990—an election year—and inflation shot up to 60%, the highest level in modern times.

GDP: $11.1 billion, per capita $1,180; real growth rate 3.5% (1990 est.)

Inflation rate (consumer prices): 60% (1990 est.)

Unemployment rate: 13%, with 30-40% underemployment (1989 est.)

Budget: revenues $1.05 billion; expenditures $1.3 billion, including capital expenditures of $270 million (1989 est.)

Exports: $1.24 billion (f.o.b., 1990);
commodities—coffee 24%, sugar 9%, bananas 8%, beef 4%;
partners—US 28%, El Salvador, FRG, Costa Rica, Italy

Imports: $1.77 billion (c.i.f., 1990);
commodities—fuel and petroleum products, machinery, grain, fertilizers, motor vehicles;
partners—US 37%, Mexico, FRG, Japan, El Salvador

External debt: $2.8 billion (December 1990 est.)

Industrial production: growth rate 4.0% (1988); accounts for 15% of GDP

Electricity: 819,000 kW capacity; 2,594 million kWh produced, 280 kWh per capita (1990)

Industries: sugar, textiles and clothing, furniture, chemicals, petroleum, metals, rubber, tourism

Agriculture: accounts for 26% of GDP; most important sector of economy and contributes two-thirds to export earnings; principal crops—sugarcane, corn, bananas, coffee, beans, cardamom; livestock—cattle, sheep, pigs, chickens; food importer

Illicit drugs: illicit producer of opium poppy and cannabis for the international drug trade; the government has engaged in aerial eradication of opium poppy; transit country for cocaine shipments

Economic aid: US commitments, including Ex-Im (FY70-90), $1.1 billion; Western (non-US) countries, ODA and OOF bilateral commitments (1970-88), $7.8 billion

Currency: quetzal (plural—quetzales); 1 quetzal (Q) = 100 centavos

Exchange rates: free market quetzales (Q) per US$1—5.4 (April 1991), 4.4858 (1990), 2.8161 (1989), 2.6196 (1988), 2.500 (1987),

Guatemala *(continued)*

1.875 (1986), 1.000 (1985); note—black-market rate 2.800 (May 1989)
Fiscal year: calendar year

Communications

Railroads: 870 km 0.914-meter gauge, single track; 780 km government owned, 90 km privately owned
Highways: 26,429 km total; 2,868 km paved, 11,421 km gravel, and 12,140 unimproved
Inland waterways: 260 km navigable year round; additional 730 km navigable during high-water season
Pipelines: crude oil, 275 km
Ports: Puerto Barrios, Puerto Quetzal, Santo Tomas de Castilla
Merchant marine: 1 cargo ship (1,000 GRT or over) totaling 4,129 GRT/6,450 DWT
Civil air: 10 major transport aircraft
Airports: 430 total, 381 usable; 11 with permanent-surface runways; none with runways over 3,659 m; 3 with runways 2,440-3,659 m; 19 with runways 1,220-2,439 m
Telecommunications: fairly modern network centered in Guatemala [city]; 97,670 telephones; stations—91 AM, no FM, 25 TV, 15 shortwave; connection into Central American Microwave System; 1 Atlantic Ocean INTELSAT earth station

Defense Forces

Branches: Army, Navy, Air Force
Manpower availability: males 15-49, 2,097,234; 1,372,623 fit for military service; 110,949 reach military age (18) annually
Defense expenditures: $113 million, 1% of GDP (1990)

Guernsey
(British crown dependency)

Geography

Total area: 194 km²; land area: 194 km²; includes Alderney, Guernsey, Herm, Sark, and some other smaller islands
Comparative area: slightly larger than Washington, DC
Land boundaries: none
Coastline: 50 km
Maritime claims:
Exclusive fishing zone: 200 nm;
Territorial sea: 3 nm
Climate: temperate with mild winters and cool summers; about 50% of days are overcast
Terrain: mostly level with low hills in southwest
Natural resources: cropland
Land use: arable land NA%; permanent crops NA%; meadows and pastures NA%; forest and woodland NA%; other NA%; cultivated about 50%
Environment: large, deepwater harbor at Saint Peter Port
Note: 52 km west of France

People

Population: 57,596 (July 1991), growth rate 0.6% (1991)
Birth rate: 12 births/1,000 population (1991)
Death rate: 11 deaths/1,000 population (1991)
Net migration rate: 5 migrants/1,000 population (1991)
Infant mortality rate: 6 deaths/1,000 live births (1991)
Life expectancy at birth: 72 years male, 78 years female (1991)
Total fertility rate: 1.6 children born/woman (1991)
Nationality: noun—Channel Islander(s); adjective—Channel Islander
Ethnic divisions: UK and Norman-French descent

Religion: Anglican, Roman Catholic, Presbyterian, Baptist, Congregational, Methodist
Language: English, French; Norman-French dialect spoken in country districts
Literacy: NA% (male NA%, female NA%) but compulsory education age 5 to 16
Labor force: NA
Organized labor: NA

Government

Long-form name: Bailiwick of Guernsey
Type: British crown dependency
Capital: Saint Peter Port
Administrative divisions: none (British crown dependency)
Independence: none (British crown dependency)
Constitution: unwritten; partly statutes, partly common law and practice
Legal system: English law and local statute; justice is administered by the Royal Court
National holiday: Liberation Day, 9 May (1945)
Executive branch: British monarch, lieutenant governor, bailiff, deputy bailiff
Legislative branch: unicameral Assembly of the States
Judicial branch: Royal Court
Leaders:
Chief of State—Queen ELIZABETH II (since 6 February 1952);
Head of Government—Lieutenant Governor Lt. Gen. Sir Michael WILKINS (since 1990); Bailiff Sir Charles FROSSARD (since 1982)
Political parties and leaders: none; all independents
Suffrage: universal at age 18
Elections:
Assembly of the States—last held NA (next to be held NA); results—percent of vote NA; seats—(60 total, 33 elected), all independents
Communists: none
Member of: none
Diplomatic representation: none (British crown dependency)
Flag: white with the red cross of Saint George (patron saint of England) extending to the edges of the flag

Economy

Overview: Tourism is a major source of revenue. Other economic activity includes financial services, breeding the world-famous Guernsey cattle, and growing tomatoes and flowers for export.
GDP: $NA, per capita $NA; real growth rate 9% (1987)
Inflation rate (consumer prices): 7% (1988)
Unemployment rate: NA%

Guinea

Budget: revenues $208.9 million; expenditures $173.9 million, including capital expenditures of NA (1988)
Exports: $NA;
commodities—tomatoes, flowers and ferns, sweet peppers, eggplant, other vegetables; *partners*—UK (regarded as internal trade)
Imports: $NA;
commodities—coal, gasoline and oil; *partners*—UK (regarded as internal trade)
External debt: $NA
Industrial production: growth rate NA%
Electricity: 173,000 kW capacity; 525 million kWh produced, 9,340 kWh per capita (1989)
Industries: tourism, banking
Agriculture: tomatoes, flowers (mostly grown in greenhouses), sweet peppers, eggplant, other vegetables and fruit; Guernsey cattle
Economic aid: none
Currency: Guernsey pound (plural—pounds); 1 Guernsey (£G) pound = 100 pence
Exchange rates: Guernsey pounds (£G) per US$1—0.5171 (January 1991), 0.5603 (1990), 0.6099 (1989), 0.5614 (1988), 0.6102 (1987), 0.6817 (1986), 0.7714 (1985); note—the Guernsey pound is at par with the British pound
Fiscal year: calendar year

Communications

Ports: Saint Peter Port, Saint Sampson
Airport: 1 with permanent-surface runway 1,220-2,439 m (La Villiaze)
Telecommunications: stations—1 AM, no FM, 1 TV; 41,900 telephones; 1 submarine cable

Defense Forces

Note: defense is the responsibility of the UK

200 km

North Atlantic Ocean

Geography

Total area: 245,860 km²; land area: 245,860 km²
Comparative area: slightly smaller than Oregon
Land boundaries: 3,399 km total; Guinea-Bissau 386 km, Ivory Coast 610 km, Liberia 563 km, Mali 858 km, Senegal 330 km, Sierra Leone 652 km
Coastline: 320 km
Maritime claims:
Exclusive economic zone: 200 nm;
Territorial sea: 12 nm
Climate: generally hot and humid; monsoonal-type rainy season (June to November) with southwesterly winds; dry season (December to May) with northeasterly harmattan winds
Terrain: generally flat coastal plain, hilly to mountainous interior
Natural resources: bauxite, iron ore, diamonds, gold, uranium, hydropower, fish
Land use: arable land 6%; permanent crops NEGL%; meadows and pastures 12%; forest and woodland 42%; other 40%; includes irrigated NEGL%
Environment: hot, dry, dusty harmattan haze may reduce visibility during dry season; deforestation

People

Population: 7,455,850 (July 1991), growth rate 2.5% (1991)
Birth rate: 47 births/1,000 population (1991)
Death rate: 21 deaths/1,000 population (1991)
Net migration rate: 0 migrants/1,000 population (1991)
Infant mortality rate: 144 deaths/1,000 live births (1991)
Life expectancy at birth: 41 years male, 45 years female (1991)
Total fertility rate: 6.0 children born/woman (1991)

Nationality: noun—Guinean(s); adjective—Guinean
Ethnic divisions: Fulani 35%, Malinke 30%, Soussou 20%, small indigenous tribes 15%
Religion: Muslim 85%, Christian 8%, indigenous beliefs 7%
Language: French (official); each tribe has its own language
Literacy: 24% (male 35%, female 13%) age 15 and over can read and write (1990 est.)
Labor force: 2,400,000 (1983); agriculture 82.0%, industry and commerce 11.0%, services 5.4%; 88,112 civil servants (1987); 52% of population of working age (1985)
Organized labor: virtually 100% of wage earners loosely affiliated with the National Confederation of Guinean Workers

Government

Long-form name: Republic of Guinea
Type: republic
Capital: Conakry
Administrative divisions: 29 administrative regions (régions administratives, singular—région administrative); Beyla, Boffa, Boké, Conakry, Dabola, Dalaba, Dinguiraye, Dubréka, Faranah, Forécariah, Fria, Gaoual, Guéckédou, Kankan, Kérouane, Kindia, Kissidougou, Koundara, Kouroussa, Labé, Macenta, Mali, Mamou, Nzérékoré, Pita, Siguiri, Télimélé, Tougué, Yomou
Independence: 2 October 1958 (from France; formerly French Guinea)
Constitution: 23 December 1990 (Loi Fundamentale)
Legal system: based on French civil law system, customary law, and decree; legal codes currently being revised; has not accepted compulsory ICJ jurisdiction
National holiday: Anniversary of the Second Republic, 3 April (1984)
Executive branch: president, Transitional Committee for National Recovery (Comite Transitionale de Redressement National or CTRN) replaced the Military Committee for National Recovery (Comité Militaire de Redressement National or CMRN); Council of Ministers (cabinet)
Legislative branch: People's National Assembly (Assemblée Nationale Populaire) was dissolved after the 3 April 1984 coup
Judicial branch: Court of Appeal (Cour d'Appel)
Leaders:
Chief of State and Head of Government— Gen. Lansana CONTÉ (since 5 April 1984)
Political parties and leaders: none; following the 3 April 1984 coup all political activity was banned
Suffrage: none
Elections: none
Communists: no Communist party, although there are some sympathizers
Member of: ACCT, ACP, AfDB, CEAO (observer), ECA, ECOWAS, FAO, FZ,

Guinea (continued)

G-77, IBRD, ICAO, IDA, IDB, IFAD, IFC, ILO, IMF, IMO, INTELSAT, INTERPOL, IOC, ISO (correspondent), ITU, LORCS, NAM, OAU, OIC, UN, UNCTAD, UNESCO, UNIDO, UPU, WCL, WHO, WIPO, WMO, WTO

Diplomatic representation: Ambassador (vacant); Chancery at 2112 Leroy Place NW, Washington DC 20008; telephone (202) 483-9420;
US—Ambassador Dane F. SMITH, Jr.; Embassy at 2nd Boulevard and 9th Avenue, Conakry (mailing address is B. P. 603, Conakry); telephone (224) 44-15-20 through 24
Flag: three equal vertical bands of red (hoist side), yellow, and green; uses the popular pan-African colors of Ethiopia; similar to the flag of Rwanda which has a large black letter *R* centered in the yellow band

Economy

Overview: Although possessing many natural resources and considerable potential for agricultural development, Guinea is one of the poorest countries in the world. The agricultural sector contributes about 40% to GDP and employs more than 80% of the work force, while industry accounts for almost 30% of GDP. Guinea possesses over 25% of the world's bauxite reserves; exports of bauxite and alumina accounted for about 70% of total exports in 1989.
GDP: $2.7 billion, per capita $380; real growth rate 4.4% (1989 est.)
Inflation rate (consumer prices): 28.2% (1989 est.)
Unemployment rate: NA%
Budget: revenues $394 million; expenditures $548 million, including capital expenditures of $254 million (1989 est.)
Exports: $645 million (f.o.b., 1989 est.); *commodities*—alumina, bauxite, diamonds, coffee, pineapples, bananas, palm kernels; *partners*—US 33%, EC 33%, USSR and Eastern Europe 20%, Canada
Imports: $551 million (c.i.f., 1989 est.); *commodities*—petroleum products, metals, machinery, transport equipment, foodstuffs, textiles and other grain; *partners*—US 16%, France, Brazil
External debt: $2.6 billion (1990 est.)
Industrial production: growth rate NA%; accounts for almost 30% of GDP
Electricity: 113,000 kW capacity; 300 million kWh produced, 40 kWh per capita (1989)
Industries: bauxite mining, alumina, diamond mining, light manufacturing and agricultural processing industries
Agriculture: accounts for 40% of GDP (includes fishing and forestry); mostly subsistence farming; principal products—rice, coffee, pineapples, palm kernels, cassava, bananas, sweet potatoes, timber; livestock—cattle, sheep and goats; not self-sufficient in food grains
Economic aid: US commitments, including Ex-Im (FY70-89), $227 million; Western (non-US) countries, ODA and OOF bilateral commitments (1970-87), $1,075 million; OPEC bilateral aid (1979-89), $120 million; Communist countries (1970-88), $446 million
Currency: Guinean franc (plural—francs); 1 Guinean franc (FG) = 100 centimes
Exchange rates: Guinean francs (FG) per US$1—24.39 (1989), 19.23 (1988), 17.54 (1987), 14.29 (1986), NA (1985)
Fiscal year: calendar year

Communications

Railroads: 1,045 km; 806 km 1.000-meter gauge, 239 km 1.435-meter standard gauge
Highways: 30,100 km total; 1,145 km paved, 12,955 km gravel or laterite (of which barely 4,500 km are currently all-weather roads), 16,000 km unimproved earth (1987)
Inland waterways: 1,295 km navigable by shallow-draft native craft
Ports: Conakry, Kamsar
Civil air: 2 major transport aircraft
Airports: 16 total, 16 usable; 5 with permanent-surface runways; none with runways over 3,659 m; 2 with runways 2,440-3,659 m; 10 with runways 1,220-2,439 m
Telecommunications: fair system of open-wire lines, small radiocommunication stations, and new radio relay system; 10,000 telephones; stations—3 AM, 1 FM, 1 TV; 12,000 TV sets; 125,000 radio receivers; 1 Atlantic Ocean INTELSAT earth station

Defense Forces

Branches: Army, Navy (acts primarily as a coast guard), Air Force, Republican Guard, paramilitary National Gendarmerie, Sûreté Nationale
Manpower availability: males 15-49, 1,695,832; 853,593 fit for military service
Defense expenditures: $27 million, 1.2% of GDP (1988)

Guinea-Bissau

North Atlantic Ocean

Geography

Total area: 36,120 km²; land area: 28,000 km²
Comparative area: slightly less than three times the size of Connecticut
Land boundaries: 724 km total; Guinea 386, Senegal 338 km
Coastline: 350 km
Maritime claims:
Exclusive economic zone: 200 nm;
Territorial sea: 12 nm
Disputes: the International Court of Justice (ICJ) has rendered its decision on the Guinea-Bissau/Senegal maritime boundary (in favor of Senegal)—that decision has been rejected by Guinea-Bissau
Climate: tropical; generally hot and humid; monsoon-type rainy season (June to November) with southwesterly winds; dry season (December to May) with northeasterly harmattan winds
Terrain: mostly low coastal plain rising to savanna in east
Natural resources: unexploited deposits of petroleum, bauxite, phosphates; fish, timber
Land use: arable land 11%; permanent crops 1%; meadows and pastures 43%; forest and woodland 38%; other 7%
Environment: hot, dry, dusty harmattan haze may reduce visibility during dry season

People

Population: 1,023,544 (July 1991), growth rate 2.4% (1991)
Birth rate: 42 births/1,000 population (1991)
Death rate: 18 deaths/1,000 population (1991)
Net migration rate: 0 migrants/1,000 population (1991)
Infant mortality rate: 125 deaths/1,000 live births (1991)

Life expectancy at birth: 45 years male, 48 years female (1991)

Total fertility rate: 5.8 children born/woman (1991)

Nationality: noun—Guinea-Bissauan(s); adjective—Guinea-Bissauan

Ethnic divisions: African about 99% (Balanta 30%, Fula 20%, Manjaca 14%, Mandinga 13%, Papel 7%); European and mulatto less than 1%

Religion: indigenous beliefs 65%, Muslim 30%, Christian 5%

Language: Portuguese (official); Criolo and numerous African languages

Literacy: 36% (male 50%, female 24%) age 15 and over can read and write (1990 est.)

Labor force: 403,000 (est.); agriculture 90%, industry, services, and commerce 5%, government 5%; population of working age 53% (1983)

Organized labor: only one trade union—the National Union of Workers of Guinea-Bissau (UNTG)

Government

Long-form name: Republic of Guinea-Bissau

Type: republic; highly centralized one-party regime since September 1974; the African Party for the Independence of Guinea-Bissau and Cape Verde (PAIGC) held an extraordinary party congress in December 1990 and established a two-year transition program during which the constitution will be revised, allowing for multiple political parties and a presidential election in 1993

Capital: Bissau

Administrative divisions: 9 regions (regiões, singular—região); Bafatá, Biombo, Bissau, Bolama, Cacheu, Gabú, Oio, Quinara, Tombali

Independence: 24 September 1973 (from Portugal; formerly Portuguese Guinea)

Constitution: 16 May 1984

Legal system: NA

National holiday: Independence Day, 24 September (1973)

Executive branch: president of the Council of State, vice presidents of the Council of State, Council of State, Council of Ministers (cabinet)

Legislative branch: unicameral National People's Assembly (Assembléia Nacional Popular)

Judicial branch: none; there is a Ministry of Justice in the Council of Ministers

Leaders:
Chief of State and Head of Government—President of the Council of State Brig. Gen. João Bernardo VIEIRA (assumed power 14 November 1980 and elected President of Council of State on 16 May 1984); First Vice President Col. Iafai CAMARA (since 7 November 1985); Second Vice President Vasco CABRAL (since 21 June 1989)

Political parties and leaders: only party—African Party for the Independence of Guinea-Bissau and Cape Verde (PAIGC), President João Bernardo VIEIRA, leader; the party decided to retain the binational title despite its formal break with Cape Verde

Suffrage: universal at age 15

Elections:
President of Council of State—last held 19 June 1989 (next to be held NA 1993); results—Brig. Gen. João Bernardo VIEIRA was reelected without opposition by the National People's Assembly;
National People's Assembly—last held 15 June 1989 (next to be held 15 June 1994); results—PAIGC is the only party; seats—(150 total) PAIGC 150, appointed by Regional Councils

Communists: a few Communists, some sympathizers

Member of: ACCT (associate), ACP, AfDB, ECA, ECOWAS, FAO, G-77, IBRD, ICAO, IDA, IDB, IFAD, IFC, ILO, IMF, IMO, IOM (observer), ITU, LORCS, NAM, OAU, OIC, UN, UNCTAD, UNESCO, UNIDO, UPU, WFTU, WHO, WIPO, WMO

Diplomatic representation: Ambassador Alfredo Lopes CABRAL; Chancery (temporary) at the Guinea-Bissauan Permanent Mission to the UN, Suite 604, 211 East 43rd Street, New York, NY 10017; telephone (212) 661-3977;
US—Ambassador William L. JACOBSEN, Jr.; Embassy at 17 Avenida Domingos Ramos, Bissau (mailing address is 1067 Bissau Codex, Bissau, Guinea-Bissau); telephone [245] 20-1139, 20-1145, 20-1113

Flag: two equal horizontal bands of yellow (top) and green with a vertical red band on the hoist side; there is a black five-pointed star centered in the red band; uses the popular pan-African colors of Ethiopia; similar to the flag of Cape Verde which has the black star raised above the center of the red band and is framed by two corn stalks and a yellow clam shell

---

Economy

Overview: Guinea-Bissau ranks among the poorest countries in the world, with a per capita GDP below $200. Agriculture and fishing are the main economic activities, with cashew nuts, peanuts, and palm kernels the primary exports. Exploitation of known mineral deposits is unlikely at present because of a weak infrastructure and the high cost of development. The government's four-year plan (1988-91) has targeted agricultural development as the top priority.

GDP: $154 million, per capita $160; real growth rate 5.0% (1989)

Inflation rate (consumer prices): 25% (1990 est.)

Unemployment rate: NA%

Budget: revenues $22.7 million; expenditures $30.8 million, including capital expenditures of $18.0 million (1989 est.)

Exports: $14.2 million (f.o.b., 1989 est.);
commodities—cashews, fish, peanuts, palm kernels;
partners—Portugal, Spain, Switzerland, Cape Verde, China

Imports: $68.9 million (f.o.b., 1989 est.);
commodities—capital equipment, consumer goods, semiprocessed goods, foods, petroleum;
partners—Portugal, USSR, EC countries, other Europe, Senegal, US

External debt: $462 million (December 1990 est.)

Industrial production: growth rate -1.7% (1986 est.)

Electricity: 22,000 kW capacity; 28 million kWh produced, 30 kWh per capita (1989)

Industries: agricultural processing, beer, soft drinks

Agriculture: accounts for over 50% of GDP, nearly 100% of exports, and 90% of employment; rice is the staple food; other crops include corn, beans, cassava, cashew nuts, peanuts, palm kernels, and cotton; not self-sufficient in food; fishing and forestry potential not fully exploited

Economic aid: US commitments, including Ex-Im (FY70-89), $49 million; Western (non-US) countries, ODA and OOF bilateral commitments (1970-88), $561 million; OPEC bilateral aid (1979-89), $41 million; Communist countries (1970-89), $68 million

Currency: Guinea-Bissauan peso (plural—pesos); 1 Guinea-Bissauan peso (PG) = 100 centavos

Exchange rates: Guinea-Bissauan pesos (PG) per US$1—1987.2 (1989), 1363.6 (1988), 851.65 (1987), 238.98 (1986), 173.61 (1985)

Fiscal year: calendar year

Communications

Highways: 3,218 km; 2,698 km bituminous, remainder earth

Inland waterways: scattered stretches are important to coastal commerce

Ports: Bissau

Civil air: 2 major transport aircraft

Airports: 37 total, 18 usable; 5 with permanent-surface runways; none with runways over 3,659 m; 1 with runways 2,440-3,659 m; 5 with runways 1,220-2,439 m

Telecommunications: poor system of radio relay, open-wire lines, and radiocommunications; 3,000 telephones; stations—1 AM, 2 FM, 1 TV; 1 Atlantic Ocean INTELSAT earth station

129

Guinea-Bissau *(continued)*

Defense Forces

Branches: People's Revolutionary Armed Force (FARP; including Army, Navy, Air Force), paramilitary force
Manpower availability: males 15-49, 222,371; 126,797 fit for military service
Defense expenditures: $5 million, 3.2% of GDP (1987)

Guyana

Geography

Total area: 214,970 km²; land area: 196,850 km²
Comparative area: slightly smaller than Idaho
Land boundaries: 2,462 km total; Brazil 1,119 km, Suriname 600 km, Venezuela 743 km
Coastline: 459 km
Maritime claims:
Continental shelf: outer edge of continental margin or 200 nm;
Exclusive fishing zone: 200 nm;
Territorial sea: 12 nm
Disputes: all of the area west of the Essequibo river claimed by Venezuela; Suriname claims area between New (Upper Courantyne) and Courantyne/Kutari Rivers (all headwaters of the Courantyne)
Climate: tropical; hot, humid, moderated by northeast trade winds; two rainy seasons (May to mid-August, mid-November to mid-January)
Terrain: mostly rolling highlands; low coastal plain; savanna in south
Natural resources: bauxite, gold, diamonds, hardwood timber, shrimp, fish
Land use: arable land 3%; permanent crops NEGL%; meadows and pastures 6%; forest and woodland 83%; other 8%; includes irrigated 1%
Environment: flash floods a constant threat during rainy seasons; water pollution

People

Population: 749,508 (July 1991), growth rate −0.4% (1991)
Birth rate: 23 births/1,000 population (1991)
Death rate: 7 deaths/1,000 population (1991)
Net migration rate: −20 migrants/1,000 population (1991)
Infant mortality rate: 51 deaths/1,000 live births (1991)

Life expectancy at birth: 61 years male, 68 years female (1991)
Total fertility rate: 2.6 children born/woman (1991)
Nationality: noun—Guyanese (sing., pl.); adjective—Guyanese
Ethnic divisions: East Indian 51%, black and mixed 43%, Amerindian 4%, European and Chinese 2%
Religion: Christian 57%, Hindu 33%, Muslim 9%, other 1%
Language: English, Amerindian dialects
Literacy: 95% (male 98%, female 96%) age 15 and over having ever attended school (1990 est.)
Labor force: 268,000; industry and commerce 44.5%, agriculture 33.8%, services 21.7%; public-sector employment amounts to 60-80% of the total labor force (1985)
Organized labor: 34% of labor force

Government

Long-form name: Co-operative Republic of Guyana
Type: republic
Capital: Georgetown
Administrative divisions: 10 regions; Barima-Waini, Cuyuni-Mazaruni, Demerara-Mahaica, East Berbice-Corentyne, Essequibo Islands-West Demerara, Mahaica-Berbice, Pomeroon-Supenaam, Potaro-Siparuni, Upper Demerara-Berbice, Upper Takutu-Upper Essequibo
Independence: 26 May 1966 (from UK; formerly British Guiana)
Constitution: 6 October 1980
Legal system: based on English common law with certain admixtures of Roman-Dutch law; has not accepted compulsory ICJ jurisdiction
National holiday: Republic Day, 23 February (1970)
Executive branch: executive president, first vice president, prime minister, first deputy prime minister, Cabinet
Legislative branch: unicameral National Assembly
Judicial branch: Supreme Court of Judicature
Leaders:
Chief of State—Executive President Hugh Desmond HOYTE (since 6 August 1985); First Vice President Hamilton GREEN (since 6 August 1985);
Head of Government—Prime Minister Hamilton GREEN (since NA August 1985)
Political parties and leaders: People's National Congress (PNC), Hugh Desmond HOYTE; People's Progressive Party (PPP), Cheddi JAGAN; Working People's Alliance (WPA), Eusi KWAYANA, Rupert ROOPNARINE, Moses BHAGWAN; Democratic Labor Movement (DLM), Paul TENNASSEE; People's Democratic Movement

(PDM), Llewellyn JOHN; National Democratic Front (NDF), Joseph BACCHUS; United Force (UF), Marcellus Feilden SINGH; United Republican Party (URP), Leslie RAMSAMMY; National Republican Party (NRP), Robert GANGADEEN

Suffrage: universal at age 18

Elections:

Executive President—last held on 9 December 1985 (next to be held mid-1991); Hugh Desmond HOYTE was elected president (the leader of the party with the most votes in the National Assembly elections);

National Assembly—last held on 9 December 1985 (next to be held mid-1991); results—PNC 78%, PPP 16%, UF 4%, WPA 2%; seats—(65 total, 53 elected) PNC 42, PPP 8, UF 2, WPA 1

Communists: 100 (est.) hardcore within PPP; top echelons of PPP and PYO (Progressive Youth Organization, militant wing of the PPP) include many Communists; small but unknown number of orthodox Marxist-Leninists within PNC, some of whom formerly belonged to the PPP

Other political or pressure groups: Trades Union Congress (TUC); Guyanese Action for Reform and Democracy (GUARD) includes various labor groups as well as several of the smaller parties; Guyana Council of Indian Organizations (GCIO); Civil Liberties Action Committee (CLAC); the latter two organizations are small and active but not well organized; Guyanese Action for Reform and Democracy (GUARD) includes various labor groups, as well as several of the smaller political parties

Member of: ACP, C, CARICOM, CCC, CDB, ECLAC, FAO, G-77, GATT, IADB, IBRD, ICAO, ICFTU, IDA, IFAD, IFC, ILO, IMF, IMO, INTERPOL, IOC, ITU, LAES, LORCS, NAM, OAS, UN, UNCTAD, UNESCO, UNIDO, UPU, WCL, WFTU, WHO, WMO

Diplomatic representation: Ambassador Dr. Cedric Hilburn GRANT; Chancery at 2490 Tracy Place NW, Washington DC 20008; telephone (202) 265-6900; there is a Guyanese Consulate General in New York; *US*—Ambassador George JONES; Embassy at 31 Main Street, Georgetown; telephone [592] (02) 54900 through 54909

Flag: green with a red isosceles triangle (based on the hoist side) superimposed on a long yellow arrowhead; there is a narrow black border between the red and yellow, and a narrow white border between the yellow and the green

Economy

Overview: After growing on average at less than 1% a year in 1986-87, GDP dropped by 3% a year in 1988-89. The decline resulted from bad weather, labor trouble in the canefields, and flooding and equipment problems in the bauxite industry. Consumer prices rose about 35% in 1988 and by over 100% in 1989, and the current account deficit widened substantially as sugar and bauxite exports fell. Moreover, electric power is in short supply and constitutes a major barrier to future gains in national output. The government, in association with international financial agencies, seeks to reduce its payment arrears and to raise new funds. The government's stabilization program—aimed at establishing realistic exchange rates, reasonable price stability, and a resumption of growth—requires considerable public administrative abilities and continued patience by consumers during a long incubation period.

GDP: $287.2 million, per capita $380; real growth rate −3.3% (1989)

Inflation rate (consumer prices): 105% (1989)

Unemployment rate: NA%

Budget: revenues $65 million; expenditures $129 million, including capital expenditures of $6 million (1989 est.)

Exports: $224 million (f.o.b., 1989 est.); *commodities*—bauxite, sugar, rice, shrimp, gold, molasses, timber, rum; *partners*—UK 31%, US 23%, CARICOM 7%, Canada 6% (1988)

Imports: $257 million (c.i.f., 1989 est.); *commodities*—manufactures machinery, food, petroleum; *partners*—US 33%, CARICOM 10%, UK 9%, Canada 2% (1989)

External debt: $1.7 billion, including arrears (December 1990 est.)

Industrial production: growth rate −10.0% (1989 est.); accounts for more than 20% of GDP

Electricity: 250,000 kW capacity; 635 million kWh produced, 830 kWh per capita (1990)

Industries: bauxite mining, sugar, rice milling, timber, fishing (shrimp), textiles, gold mining

Agriculture: most important sector, accounting for 27% of GDP and about 50% of exports; sugar and rice are key crops; development potential exists for fishing and forestry; not self-sufficient in food, especially wheat, vegetable oils, and animal products

Economic aid: US commitments, including Ex-Im (FY70-89), $116 million; Western (non-US) countries, ODA and OOF bilateral commitments (1970-88), $244 million; Communist countries 1970-89, $242 million

Currency: Guyanese dollar (plural—dollars); 1 Guyanese dollar (G$) = 100 cents

Exchange rates: Guyanese dollars (G$) per US$1—45.00 (since June 1990), 39.533 (1990), 27.159 (1989), 10.000 (1988), 9.756 (1987), 4.272 (1986), 4.252 (1985)

Fiscal year: calendar year

Communications

Railroads: 187 km total, all single track 0.914-meter gauge

Highways: 7,665 km total; 550 km paved, 5,000 km gravel, 1,525 km earth, 590 km unimproved

Inland waterways: 6,000 km total of navigable waterways; Berbice, Demerara, and Essequibo Rivers are navigable by oceangoing vessels for 150 km, 100 km, and 80 km, respectively

Ports: Georgetown

Civil air: 5 major transport aircraft

Airports: 58 total, 55 usable; 5 with permanent-surface runways; none with runways over 3,659 m; none with runways 2,440-3,659 m; 14 with runways 1,220-2,439 m

Telecommunications: fair system with radio relay network; over 27,000 telephones; tropospheric scatter link to Trinidad; stations—4 AM, 3 FM, no TV, 1 shortwave; 1 Atlantic Ocean INTELSAT earth station

Defense Forces

Branches: Guyana Defense Force (GDF; includes Coast Guard and Air Corps), Guyana Police Force (GPF), Guyana People's Militia (GPM), Guyana National Service (GNS)

Manpower availability: males 15-49, 195,142; 148,477 fit for military service

Defense expenditures: $5.5 million, 6% of GDP (1989 est.)

Haiti

Geography

Total area: 27,750 km²; land area: 27,560 km²

Comparative area: slightly larger than Maryland

Land boundary: 275 km with the Dominican Republic

Coastline: 1,771 km

Maritime claims:

Contiguous zone: 24 nm;

Continental shelf: to depth of exploitation;

Exclusive economic zone: 200 nm;

Territorial sea: 12 nm

Disputes: claims US-administered Navassa Island

Climate: tropical; semiarid where mountains in east cut off trade winds

Terrain: mostly rough and mountainous

Natural resources: bauxite

Land use: arable land 20%; permanent crops 13%; meadows and pastures 18%; forest and woodland 4%; other 45%; includes irrigated 3%

Environment: lies in the middle of the hurricane belt and subject to severe storms from June to October; occasional flooding and earthquakes; deforestation; soil erosion

Note: shares island of Hispaniola with Dominican Republic

People

Population: 6,286,511 (July 1991), growth rate 2.3% (1991)

Birth rate: 43 births/1,000 population (1991)

Death rate: 15 deaths/1,000 population (1991)

Net migration rate: −5 migrants/1,000 population (1991)

Infant mortality rate: 106 deaths/1,000 live births (1991)

Life expectancy at birth: 52 years male, 55 years female (1991)

Total fertility rate: 6.3 children born/woman (1991)

Nationality: noun—Haitian(s); adjective—Haitian

Ethnic divisions: black 95%, mulatto and European 5%

Religion: Roman Catholic is the official religion; Roman Catholic 80% (of which an overwhelming majority also practice Voodoo), Protestant 16% (Baptist 10%, Pentecostal 4%, Adventist 1%, other 1%), none 1%, other 3% (1982)

Language: French (official) spoken by only 10% of population; all speak Creole

Literacy: 53% (male 59%, female 47%) age 15 and over can read and write (1990 est.)

Labor force: 2,300,000; agriculture 66%, services 25%, industry 9%; shortage of skilled labor, unskilled labor abundant (1982)

Organized labor: NA

Government

Long-form name: Republic of Haiti

Type: republic

Capital: Port-au-Prince

Administrative divisions: 9 departments, (départements, singular—département); Artibonite, Centre, Grand'Anse, Nord, Nord-Est, Nord-Ouest, Ouest, Sud, Sud-Est

Independence: 1 January 1804 (from France)

Constitution: 27 August 1983, suspended February 1986; draft constitution approved March 1987, suspended June 1988; most articles reinstated March 1989; March 1987 Constitution fully observed by government installed on 7 February 1991

Legal system: based on Roman civil law system; accepts compulsory ICJ jurisdiction

National holiday: Independence Day, 1 January (1804)

Executive branch: president, Council of Ministers (cabinet)

Legislative branch: bicameral National Assembly (Assemblée Nationale) consisting of an upper house or Senate and a lower house or House of Deputies

Judicial branch: Court of Appeal (Cour de Cassation)

Leaders:

Chief of State—President Jean-Bertrand ARISTIDE (since 7 February 1991);

Head of Government—Prime Minister René PREVAL (since 13 February 1991)

Political parties and leaders: National Front for Change and Democracy (FNCD) led by Jean-Bertrand ARISTIDE, including Congress of Democratic Movements (CONACOM), Victor BENOIT; National Konbite Movement (MKN), Volvick Remy JOSEPH; National Alliance for Democracy and Progress (ANDP), a coalition consisting of Movement for the Installation of Democracy in Haiti (MIDH), Marc BAZIN; National Progressive Revolutionary Party (PANPRA), Serge GILLES; and National Patriotic Movement of November 28

(MNP-28), Dejean BELIZAIRE; National Agricultural and Industrial Party (PAIN), Louis DEJOIE; Movement for National Reconstruction (MRN), René THÉODORE; Haitian Christian Democratic Party (PDCH), Sylvio CLAUDE; Assembly of Progressive National Democrats (RDNP), Leslie MANIGAT; National Party of Labor (PNT), Thomas DESULME; Mobilization for National Development (MDN), Hubert DE RONCERAY; Democratic Movement for the Liberation of Haiti (MODELH), François LATORTUE; Haitian Social Christian Party (PSCH), Grégoire EUGÉNE; Movement for the Organization of the Country (MOP), Gesner COMEAU

Suffrage: universal at age 18

Elections:

President—last held 16 December 1990 (next election to be held by December 1995); results—Rev. Jean-Bertrand ARISTIDE 67.5%, Marc BAZIN 14.2%, Louis DEJOIE 4.9%;

Senate—last held 16 December 1990, with runoff held 20 January 1991 (next to be held by December 1992); results—percent of vote NA; seats—(27) FNCD 13, ANDP 6, PAIN 2, MRN 2, PDCH 1, RDNP 1, PNT 1, independent 1;

Chamber of Deputies—last held 16 December 1990, with runoff held 20 January 1991 (next to be held by December 1994); results—percent of vote NA; seats—(83) FNCD 27, ANDP 17, PDCH 7, PAIN 6, RDNP 6, MDN 5, PNT 3, MKN 2, MODELH 2, MRN 1, independent 5, other 2

Communists: United Party of Haitian Communists (PUCH), René THÉODORE (roughly 2,000 members)

Other political or pressure groups: Democratic Unity Confederation (KID), Roman Catholic Church, Confederation of Haitian Workers (CTH), Federation of Workers Trade Unions (FOS), Autonomous Haitian Workers (CATH), National Popular Assembly (APN)

Member of: ACCT, CARICOM (observer), CCC, ECLAC, FAO, G-77, GATT, IADB, IAEA, IBRD, ICAO, IDA, IFAD, IFC, ILO, IMF, IMO, INTELSAT, INTERPOL, IOC, ITU, LAES, LORCS, OAS, OPANAL, PCA, UN, UNCTAD, UNESCO, UNIDO, UPU, WCL, WFTU, WHO, WIPO, WMO, WTO

Diplomatic representation: Ambassador (vacant), Chargé d'Affaires Raymond Alcide JOSEPH; Chancery at 2311 Massachusetts Avenue NW, Washington DC 20008; telephone (202) 332-4090 through 4092; there are Haitian Consulates General in Boston, Chicago, Miami, New York, and San Juan (Puerto Rico);

US—Ambassador Alvin P. ADAMS, Jr.; Embassy at Harry Truman Boulevard, Port-au-Prince (mailing address is P. O. Box 1761, Port-au-Prince), telephone [509] (1) 20-354 or 20-368, 20-200, 20-612

Flag: two equal horizontal bands of blue (top) and red with a centered white rectangle bearing the coat of arms which contains a palm tree flanked by flags and two cannons above a scroll bearing the motto *L'UNION FAIT LA FORCE* (Union Makes Strength)

Economy

Overview: About 85% of the population live in abject poverty. Agriculture is mainly small-scale subsistence farming and employs two-thirds of the work force. The majority of the population does not have ready access to safe drinking water, adequate medical care, or sufficient food. Few social assistance programs exist, and the lack of employment opportunities remains one of the most critical problems facing the economy, along with soil erosion and political instability.

GDP: $2.7 billion, per capita $440; real growth rate −3.0% (1990 est.)

Inflation rate (consumer prices): 20% (1990 est.)

Unemployment rate: 25-50% (1990 est.)

Budget: revenues $300 million; expenditures $416 million, including capital expenditures of $145 million (1990 est.)

Exports: $169 million (f.o.b., 1990 est.); *commodities*—light manufactures 65%, coffee 19%, other agriculture 8%, other 8%; *partners*—US 84%, Italy 4%, France 3%, other industrial 6%, less developed countries 3% (1987)

Imports: $348 million (c.i.f., 1990 est.); *commodities*—machines and manufactures 34%, food and beverages 22%, petroleum products 14%, chemicals 10%, fats and oils 9%; *partners*—US 64%, Netherlands Antilles 5%, Japan 5%, France 4%, FRG 3%, Canada 3%, Asia 3% (1987)

External debt: $838 million (December 1990)

Industrial production: growth rate 0.3% (FY88); accounts for 15% of GDP

Electricity: 230,000 kW capacity; 264 million kWh produced, 43 kWh per capita (1990)

Industries: sugar refining, textiles, flour milling, cement manufacturing, tourism, light assembly industries based on imported parts

Agriculture: accounts for 33% of GDP and employs 66% of work force; mostly small-scale subsistence farms; commercial crops—coffee, mangoes, sugarcane and wood; staple crops—rice, corn, sorghum; shortage of wheat flour

Illicit drugs: transshipment point for cocaine

Economic aid: US commitments, including Ex-Im (FY70-89), $700 million; Western (non-US) countries, ODA and OOF bilateral commitments (1970-88), $682 million

Currency: gourde (plural—gourdes); 1 gourde (G) = 100 centimes

Exchange rates: gourdes (G) per US$1—5.0 (fixed rate)

Fiscal year: 1 October-30 September

Communications

Railroads: 40 km 0.760-meter narrow gauge, single-track, privately owned industrial line

Highways: 4,000 km total; 950 km paved, 900 km otherwise improved, 2,150 km unimproved

Inland waterways: negligible; less than 100 km navigable

Ports: Port-au-Prince, Cap-Haitien

Civil air: 4 major transport aircraft

Airports: 15 total, 10 usable; 3 with permanent-surface runways; none with runways over 3,659 m; 1 with runways 2,440-3,659 m; 4 with runways 1,220-2,439 m

Telecommunications: domestic facilities barely adequate, international facilities slightly better; 36,000 telephones; stations—33 AM, no FM, 4 TV, 2 shortwave; 1 Atlantic Ocean earth station

Defense Forces

Branches: Army (including Police), Navy, Air Corps

Manpower availability: males 15-49, 1,287,179; 691,926 fit for military service; 61,265 reach military age (18) annually

Defense expenditures: $34 million, 1.5% of GDP (1988 est.)

Heard Island and McDonald Islands
(territory of Australia)

Geography

Total area: 412 km²; land area: 412 km²

Comparative area: slightly less than 2.5 times the size of Washington, DC

Land boundaries: none

Coastline: 101.9 km

Maritime claims:
Exclusive fishing zone: 200 nm;
Territorial sea: 3 nm

Climate: antarctic

Terrain: Heard Island—bleak and mountainous, with an extinct volcano; McDonald Islands—small and rocky

Land use: arable land 0%; permanent crops 0%; meadows and pastures 0%; forest and woodland 0%; other 100%

Environment: primarily used as research stations

Note: located 4,100 km southwest of Australia in the southern Indian Ocean

People

Population: uninhabited

Government

Long-form name: Territory of Heard Island and McDonald Islands

Type: territory of Australia administered by the Antarctic Division of the Department of Science in Canberra (Australia)

Economy

Overview: no economic activity

Communications

Ports: none; offshore anchorage only

Defense Forces

Note: defense is the responsibility of Australia

133

Honduras

150 km

Caribbean Sea

Swan Islands

Islas de la Bahía

Puerto Cortés

San Pedro Sula

Puerto Lempira

Santa Rosa de Copán

Juticalpa

TEGUCIGALPA

Choluteca

Golfo de Fonseca

Boundary representation is not necessarily authoritative.

Geography

Total area: 112,090 km²; land area: 111,890 km²
Comparative area: slightly larger than Tennessee
Land boundaries: 1,520 km total; Guatemala 256 km, El Salvador 342 km, Nicaragua 922 km
Coastline: 820 km
Maritime claims:
Contiguous zone: 24 nm;
Continental shelf: 200 m (depth) or to depth of exploitation;
Exclusive economic zone: 200 nm;
Territorial sea: 12 nm
Disputes: dispute with El Salvador over several sections of the land boundary; dispute over Golfo de Fonseca maritime boundary because of disputed sovereignty of islands; unresolved maritime boundary with Nicaragua
Climate: subtropical in lowlands, temperate in mountains
Terrain: mostly mountains in interior, narrow coastal plains
Natural resources: timber, gold, silver, copper, lead, zinc, iron ore, antimony, coal, fish
Land use: arable land 14%; permanent crops 2%; meadows and pastures 30%; forest and woodland 34%; other 20%; includes irrigated 1%
Environment: subject to frequent, but generally mild, earthquakes; damaging hurricanes and floods along Caribbean coast; deforestation; soil erosion

People

Population: 4,949,275 (July 1991), growth rate 2.9% (1991)
Birth rate: 38 births/1,000 population (1991)
Death rate: 7 deaths/1,000 population (1991)
Net migration rate: −2 migrants/1,000 population (1991)

Infant mortality rate: 56 deaths/1,000 live births (1991)
Life expectancy at birth: 64 years male, 68 years female (1991)
Total fertility rate: 5.0 children born/woman (1991)
Nationality: noun—Honduran(s); adjective—Honduran
Ethnic divisions: mestizo (mixed Indian and European) 90%, Indian 7%, black 2%, white 1%
Religion: Roman Catholic about 97%; small Protestant minority
Language: Spanish, Indian dialects
Literacy: 73% (male 76%, female 71%) age 15 and over can read and write (1990 est.)
Labor force: 1,300,000; agriculture 62%, services 20%, manufacturing 9%, construction 3%, other 6% (1985)
Organized labor: 40% of urban labor force, 20% of rural work force (1985)

Government

Long-form name: Republic of Honduras
Type: republic
Capital: Tegucigalpa
Administrative divisions: 18 departments (departamentos, singular—departamento); Atlántida, Choluteca, Colón, Comayagua, Copán, Cortés, El Paraíso, Francisco Morazán, Gracias a Dios, Intibucá, Islas de la Bahía, La Paz, Lempira, Ocotepeque, Olancho, Santa Bárbara, Valle, Yoro
Independence: 15 September 1821 (from Spain)
Constitution: 11 January 1982, effective 20 January 1982
Legal system: rooted in Roman and Spanish civil law; some influence of English common law; accepts ICJ jurisdiction, with reservations
National holiday: Independence Day, 15 September (1821)
Executive branch: president, Council of Ministers (cabinet)
Legislative branch: unicameral National Congress (Congreso Nacional)
Judicial branch: Supreme Court of Justice (Corte Suprema de Justica)
Leaders:
Chief of State and Head of Government—Rafael Leonardo CALLEJAS Romero (since 26 January 1990)
Political parties and leaders: Liberal Party (PLH)—faction leaders, Carlos FLORES Facussé (leader of Florista Liberal Movement), Carlos MONTOYA (Azconista subfaction), Ramon VILLEDA Bermudez and Jorge Arturo REINA (M-Líder faction); National Party (PNH), José Celin DISCUA, party president; PNH faction leaders—Oswaldo RAMOS Soto and Rafael Leonardo CALLEJAS (Monarca faction); National Innovation and Unity Party-Social Democrats (PINU-SD), Enrique AGUILAR

Cerrato Paz; Christian Democratic Party (PDCH), Jorge ILLESCAS; Democratic Action (AD), Walter LOPEZ Reyes
Suffrage: universal and compulsory at age 18
Elections:
President—last held on 26 November 1989 (next to be held November 1993); results—Rafael Leonardo CALLEJAS (PNH) 51%, Carlos FLORES Facussé (PLH) 43.3%, other 5.7%;
National Congress—last held on 26 November 1989 (next to be held November 1993); results—PNH 51%, PLH 43%, PDCH 1.9%, PINU 1.5%, other 2.6%; seats—(128 total) PNH 71, PLH 55, PINU 2
Communists: up to 1,500; Honduran leftist groups—Communist Party of Honduras (PCH), Party for the Transformation of Honduras (PTH), Morazanist Front for the Liberation of Honduras (FMLH), People's Revolutionary Union/Popular Liberation Movement (URP/MPL), Popular Revolutionary Forces-Lorenzo Zelaya (FPR/LZ), Socialist Party of Honduras Central American Workers Revolutionary Party (PASO/PRTC)
Other political or pressure groups: National Association of Honduran Campesinos (ANACH), Honduran Council of Private Enterprise (COHEP), Confederation of Honduran Workers (CTH), National Union of Campesinos (UNC), General Workers Confederation (CGT), United Federation of Honduran Workers (FUTH), Committee for the Defense of Human Rights in Honduras (CODEH), Coordinating Committee of Popular Organizations (CCOP)
Member of: BCIE, CACM, ECLAC, FAO, G-77, IADB, IBRD, ICAO, ICFTU, IDA, IFAD, IFC, ILO, IMF, IMO, INTELSAT, INTERPOL, IOC, IOM, ITU, LAES, LAIA (observer), LORCS, OAS, OPANAL, PCA, UN, UNCTAD, UNESCO, UNIDO, UPU, WCL, WFTU, WHO, WIPO, WMO
Diplomatic representation: Ambassador Jorge Ramon HERNANDEZ Alcerro; Chancery at Suite 100, 4301 Connecticut Avenue NW, Washington DC 20008; telephone (202) 966-7700 through 7702; there are Honduran Consulates General in Chicago, Los Angeles, Miami, New Orleans, New York, and San Francisco, and Consulates in Baton Rouge, Boston, Detroit, Houston, and Jacksonville;
US—Ambassador S. Crescencio ARCOS; Embassy at Avenida La Paz, Tegucigalpa (mailing address is APO Miami 34022); telephone [504] 32-3120
Flag: three equal horizontal bands of blue (top), white, and blue with five blue five-pointed stars arranged in an X pattern centered in the white band; the stars represent the members of the former Federal Republic of Central America—Costa Rica, El Salvador, Guatemala, Honduras, and Nicaragua;

similar to the flag of El Salvador which features a round emblem encircled by the words *REPUBLICA DE EL SALVADOR EN LA AMERICA CENTRAL* centered in the white band; also similar to the flag of Nicaragua which features a triangle encircled by the words *REPUBLICA DE NICARAGUA* on top and *AMERICA CENTRAL* on the bottom, centered in the white band

Economy

Overview: Honduras is one of the poorest countries in the Western Hemisphere. Agriculture is the most important sector of the economy, accounting for nearly 30% of GDP, employing 62% of the labor force, and producing two-thirds of exports. Productivity remains low, however, leaving considerable room for improvement. Although industry is still in its early stages, it employs nearly 9% of the labor force, accounts for 15% of GDP, and generates 20% of exports. The service sectors, including public administration, account for 48% of GDP and employ nearly 20% of the labor force. Basic problems facing the economy include a high population growth rate, a high unemployment rate, a lack of basic services, a large and inefficient public sector, and an export sector dependent mostly on coffee and bananas, which are subject to sharp price fluctuations.
GDP: $4.9 billion, per capita $960; real growth rate 0% (1990 est.)
Inflation rate (consumer prices): 30% (1990 est.)
Unemployment rate: 15% unemployed, 30-40% underemployed (1989)
Budget: revenues $1,053 million; expenditures $949 million, including capital expenditures of $159 million (1989)
Exports: $940 million (f.o.b., 1989); *commodities*—bananas, coffee, shrimp, lobster, minerals, lumber; *partners*—US 52%, FRG 11%, Japan, Italy, Belgium
Imports: $981 million (c.i.f. 1989); *commodities*—machinery and transport equipment, chemical products, manufactured goods, fuel and oil, foodstuffs; *partners*—US 39%, Japan 9%, CACM, Venezuela, Mexico
External debt: $4.0 billion (December 1989)
Industrial production: growth rate 2.9% (1989); accounts for 15% of GDP
Electricity: 668,000 kW capacity; 2,023 million kWh produced, 380 kWh per capita (1990)
Industries: agricultural processing (sugar and coffee), textiles, clothing, wood products
Agriculture: most important sector, accounting for nearly 30% of GDP, over 60% of the labor force, and two-thirds of exports; principal products include bananas, coffee, timber, beef, citrus fruit, shrimp; importer of wheat
Illicit drugs: illicit producer of cannabis, cultivated on small plots and used principally for local consumption; transshipment point for cocaine
Economic aid: US commitments, including Ex-Im (FY70-89), $1.4 billion; Western (non-US) countries, ODA and OOF bilateral commitments (1970-88), $1,027 million
Currency: lempira (plural—lempiras); 1 lempira (L) = 100 centavos
Exchange rates: lempiras (L) per US$1— 5.30 (fixed rate); 5.70 parallel black-market rate (November 1990)
Fiscal year: calendar year

Communications

Railroads: 785 km total; 508 km 1.067-meter gauge, 277 km 0.914-meter gauge
Highways: 8,950 km total; 1,700 km paved, 5,000 km otherwise improved, 2,250 km unimproved earth
Inland waterways: 465 km navigable by small craft
Ports: Puerto Castilla, Puerto Cortes, San Lorenzo
Merchant marine: 173 ships (1,000 GRT or over) totaling 527,481 GRT/812,095 DWT; includes 2 passenger-cargo, 107 cargo, 12 refrigerated cargo, 9 container, 1 roll-on/roll-off cargo, 20 petroleum, oils, and lubricants (POL) tanker, 1 chemical tanker, 2 specialized tanker, 1 vehicle carrier, 18 bulk; note—a flag of convenience registry; the USSR owns one ship under the Honduran flag
Civil air: 9 major transport aircraft
Airports: 175 total, 134 usable; 8 with permanent-surface runways; none with runways over 3,659 m; 4 with runways 2,440-3,659 m; 13 with runways 1,220-2,439 m
Telecommunications: improved, but still inadequate; connection into Central American Microwave System; 35,100 telephones; stations—176 AM, no FM, 28 TV, 7 shortwave; 2 Atlantic Ocean INTELSAT earth stations

Defense Forces

Branches: Army, Navy (including Marines), Air Force, Public Security Forces (FUSEP)
Manpower availability: males 15-49, 1,106,630; 659,520 fit for military service; 58,953 reach military age (18) annually
Defense expenditures: $82.5 million, 1.9% of GDP (1990 est.)

Hong Kong
(dependent territory of the UK)

15 km

Lema Channel

Geography

Total area: 1,040 km²; land area: 990 km²
Comparative area: slightly less than six times the size of Washington, DC
Land boundary: 30 km with China
Coastline: 733 km
Maritime claims:
Exclusive fishing zone: 3 nm;
Territorial sea: 3 nm
Climate: tropical monsoon; cool and humid in winter, hot and rainy from spring through summer, warm and sunny in fall
Terrain: hilly to mountainous with steep slopes; lowlands in north
Natural resources: outstanding deepwater harbor, feldspar
Land use: arable land 7%; permanent crops 1%; meadows and pastures 1%; forest and woodland 12%; other 79%; includes irrigated 3%
Environment: more than 200 islands; occasional typhoons

People

Population: 5,855,800 (July 1991), growth rate 0.6% (1991)
Birth rate: 13 births/1,000 population (1991)
Death rate: 5 deaths/1,000 population (1991)
Net migration rate: −2 migrants/1,000 population (1991)
Infant mortality rate: 7 deaths/1,000 live births (1991)
Life expectancy at birth: 77 years male, 84 years female (1991)
Total fertility rate: 1.4 children born/woman (1991)
Nationality: adjective—Hong Kong
Ethnic divisions: Chinese 98%, other 2%
Religion: eclectic mixture of local religions 90%, Christian 10%
Language: Chinese (Cantonese), English
Literacy: 77% (male 90%, female 64%) age 15 and over having ever attended school (1971)

135

Hong Kong *(continued)*

Labor force: 2,800,000 (1990); manufacturing 28.5%, wholesale and retail trade, restaurants, and hotels 27.9%, services 17.7%, financing, insurance, and real estate 9.2%, transport and communications 4.5%, construction 2.5%, other 9.7% (1989)
Organized labor: 16% of labor force (1990)

Government

Long-form name: none; abbreviated HK
Type: dependent territory of the UK; scheduled to revert to China in 1997
Capital: Victoria
Administrative divisions: none (dependent territory of the UK)
Independence: none (dependent territory of the UK); the UK signed an agreement with China on 19 December 1984 to return Hong Kong to China on 1 July 1997; in the joint declaration, China promises to respect Hong Kong's existing social and economic systems and lifestyle for 50 years after transition
Constitution: unwritten; partly statutes, partly common law and practice; new Basic Law approved in March 1990 in preparation for 1997
Legal system: based on English common law
National holiday: Liberation Day, 29 August (1945)
Executive branch: British monarch, governor, chief secretary of the Executive Council
Legislative branch: Legislative Council
Judicial branch: Supreme Court
Leaders:
Chief of State—Queen ELIZABETH II (since 6 February 1952);
Head of Government—Governor Sir David Clive WILSON (since 9 April 1987); Chief Secretary Sir David Robert FORD (since NA February 1987)
Political parties: United Democrats of Hong Kong (UDHK), Martin LEE, president; Liberal Democratic Federation (LDF), HU Fa-kuang; Hong Kong Democratic Federation (HKDF), LEONG Che-hung, chairman; Association for Democracy and People's Livelihood (ADPL), Frederick FUNG Kin-kee; Progressive Hong Kong Society (PHKS), Maria TAM, chairperson
Suffrage: limited to about 100,000 professionals of electoral college and functional constituencies
Elections:
Legislative Council—indirect elections last held 26 September 1985 (next to be held in September 1991); results—percent of vote NA; seats—(60 total; 18 elected, 21 indirectly elected by functional constituencies, 21 appointed by governor)
Communists: 5,000 (est.) cadres affiliated with Communist Party of China

Other political or pressure groups: Federation of Trade Unions (Communist controlled), Hong Kong and Kowloon Trade Union Council (Nationalist Chinese dominated), Hong Kong General Chamber of Commerce, Chinese General Chamber of Commerce (Communist controlled), Federation of Hong Kong Industries, Chinese Manufacturers' Association of Hong Kong, Hong Kong Professional Teachers' Union, Hong Kong Alliance in Support of the Patriotic Democratic Movement in China
Member of: AsDB, CCC, ESCAP (associate), GATT, ICFTU, IMO (associate), IOC, ISO (correspondent), WCL, WMO
Diplomatic representation: as a dependent territory of the UK, the interests of Hong Kong in the US are represented by the UK; *US*—Consul General Richard L. WILLIAMS; Consulate General at 26 Garden Road, Hong Kong (mailing address is Box 30, Hong Kong, or FPO San Francisco 96659-0002); telephone [852] (5) 845-1598
Flag: blue with the flag of the UK in the upper hoist-side quadrant with the Hong Kong coat of arms on a white disk centered on the outer half of the flag; the coat of arms contains a shield (bearing two junks below a crown) held by a lion (representing the UK) and a dragon (representing China) with another lion above the shield and a banner bearing the words *HONG KONG* below the shield

---

Economy

Overview: Hong Kong has a free market economy with few tariffs or nontariff barriers. Natural resources are limited, and food and raw materials must be imported. Manufacturing accounts for about 18% of GDP, employs 28% of the labor force, and export about 90% of its output. Real GDP growth averaged a remarkable 8% in 1987-88, then slowed to 2.5-3.0% in 1989-90. Unemployment, which has been declining since the mid-1980s, is now less than 2%. A shortage of labor continues to put upward pressure on prices and the cost of living. Short-term prospects remain solid so long as major trading partners continue to be prosperous. The crackdown in China in 1989-90 casts a long shadow over the longer term economic outlook.
GDP: $64 billion, per capita $11,000; real growth rate 2.5% (1990)
Inflation rate (consumer prices): 9.8% (1990)
Unemployment rate: 1.8% (1990)
Budget: $8.8 billion (FY90)
Exports: $80.3 billion (f.o.b., 1990), including reexports of $51.2 billion;
commodities—clothing, textile yarn and fabric, footwear, electrical appliances, watches and clocks, toys;
partners—US 32%, China 19%, FRG 7%, UK 6%, Japan 6% (1989)

Imports: $79.5 billion (c.i.f., 1990); *commodities*—foodstuffs, transport equipment, raw materials, semimanufactures, petroleum;
partners—China 35%, Japan 17%, Taiwan 9%, US 8% (1989)
External debt: $9.5 billion (December 1990 est.)
Industrial production: growth rate 1.7% (1989)
Electricity: 8,485,000 kW capacity; 25,000 million kWh produced, 4,340 kWh per capita (1990)
Industries: textiles, clothing, tourism, electronics, plastics, toys, watches, clocks
Agriculture: minor role in the economy; rice, vegetables, dairy products; less than 20% self-sufficient; shortages of rice, wheat, water
Illicit drugs: a hub for Southeast Asian heroin trade; transshipment and major financial and money-laundering center
Economic aid: US commitments, including Ex-Im (FY70-87), $152 million; Western (non-US) countries, ODA and OOF bilateral commitments (1970-88), $910 million
Currency: Hong Kong dollar (plural—dollars); 1 Hong Kong dollar (HK$) = 100 cents
Exchange rates: Hong Kong dollars (HK$) per US$—7.800 (March 1989), 7.810 (1988), 7.760 (1987), 7.795 (1986), 7.811 (1985); note—linked to the US dollar at the rate of about 7.8 HK$ per 1 US$ since 1985
Fiscal year: 1 April-31 March

Communications

Railroads: 35 km 1.435-meter standard gauge, government owned
Highways: 1,484 km total; 794 km paved, 306 km gravel, crushed stone, or earth
Ports: Hong Kong
Merchant marine: 134 ships (1,000 GRT or over), totaling 4,690,770 GRT/8,091,177 DWT; includes 1 passenger, 1 short-sea passenger, 16 cargo, 5 refrigerated cargo, 16 container, 1 roll-on/roll-off cargo, 9 petroleum, oils, and lubricants (POL) tanker, 2 chemical tanker, 6 combination ore/oil, 6 liquefied gas, 71 bulk; note—a flag of convenience registry; ships registered in Hong Kong fly the UK flag and an estimated 500 Hong Kong-owned ships are registered elsewhere
Civil air: 16 major transport aircraft
Airports: 2 total; 2 usable; 2 with permanent-surface runways; none with runways over 3,659 m; 1 with runways 2,440-3,659 m; none with runways 1,220-2,439 m
Telecommunications: modern facilities provide excellent domestic and international services; 3,000,000 telephones; microwave transmission links and extensive optical fiber transmission network; stations—6 AM,

6 FM, 4 TV; 1 British Broadcasting Corporation (BBC) relay station and 1 British Forces Broadcasting Service relay station; 2,500,000 radio receivers; 1,312,000 TV sets (1,224,000 color TV sets); satellite earth stations—1 Pacific Ocean INTELSAT and 2 Indian Ocean INTELSAT; coaxial cable to Guangzhou, China; links to 5 international submarine cables providing access to ASEAN member nations, Japan, Taiwan, Australia, Middle East, and Western Europe

Defense Forces

Branches: Headquarters of British Forces, Royal Navy, Royal Air Force, Royal Hong Kong Auxiliary Air Force, Gurkha Brigade, Royal Hong Kong Police Force
Manpower availability: males 15-49, 1,718,112; 1,328,230 fit for military service; 45,437 reach military age (18) annually
Defense expenditures: $300 million, 0.5% of GDP (1989 est.); this represents one-fourth of the total cost of defending itself, the remainder being paid by the UK
Note: defense is the responsibility of the UK

Howland Island
(territory of the US)

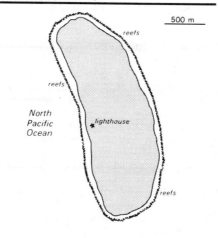

Geography

Total area: 1.6 km²; land area: 1.6 km²
Comparative area: about 2.7 times the size of The Mall in Washington, DC
Land boundaries: none
Coastline: 6.4 km
Maritime claims:
Contiguous zone: 12 nm;
Continental shelf: 200 m (depth);
Exclusive economic zone: 200 nm;
Territorial sea: 12 nm
Climate: equatorial; scant rainfall, constant wind, burning sun
Terrain: low-lying, nearly level, sandy, coral island surrounded by a narrow fringing reef; depressed central area
Natural resources: guano (deposits worked until late 1800s)
Land use: arable land 0%; permanent crops 0%; meadows and pastures 0%; forest and woodland 5%; other 95%
Environment: almost totally covered with grasses, prostrate vines, and low-growing shrubs; small area of trees in the center; lacks fresh water; primarily a nesting, roosting, and foraging habitat for seabirds, shorebirds, and marine wildlife; feral cats
Note: remote location 2,575 km southwest of Honolulu in the North Pacific Ocean, just north of the Equator, about halfway between Hawaii and Australia

People

Population: uninhabited
Note: American civilians evacuated in 1942 after Japanese air and naval attacks during World War II; occupied by US military during World War II, but abandoned after the war; public entry is by special-use permit only and generally restricted to scientists and educators

Government

Long-form name: none

Type: unincorporated territory of the US administered by the Fish and Wildlife Service of the US Department of the Interior as part of the National Wildlife Refuge System

Economy

Overview: no economic activity

Communications

Airports: airstrip constructed in 1937 for scheduled refueling stop on the round-the-world flight of Amelia Earhart and Fred Noonan—they left Lae, New Guinea, for Howland Island, but were never seen again; the airstrip is no longer serviceable
Ports: none; offshore anchorage only, one boat landing area along the middle of the west coast
Note: Earhart Light is a day beacon near the middle of the west coast that was partially destroyed during World War II, but has since been rebuilt in memory of famed aviatrix Amelia Earhart

Defense Forces

Note: defense is the responsibility of the US; visited annually by the US Coast Guard

Hungary

125 km

Geography

Total area: 93,030 km²; land area: 92,340 km²

Comparative area: slightly smaller than Indiana

Land boundaries: 2,251 km total; Austria 366 km, Czechoslovakia 676 km, Romania 443 km, USSR 135 km, Yugoslavia 631 km

Coastline: none—landlocked

Maritime claims: none—landlocked

Disputes: Nagymaros Dam dispute with Czechoslovakia

Climate: temperate; cold, cloudy, humid winters; warm summers

Terrain: mostly flat to rolling plains

Natural resources: bauxite, coal, natural gas, fertile soils

Land use: arable land 54%; permanent crops 3%; meadows and pastures 14%; forest and woodland 18%; other 11%; includes irrigated 2%

Environment: levees are common along many streams, but flooding occurs almost every year

Note: landlocked; strategic location astride main land routes between Western Europe and Balkan Peninsula as well as between USSR and Mediterranean basin

People

Population: 10,558,001 (July 1991), growth rate −0.1% (1991)

Birth rate: 12 births/1,000 population (1991)

Death rate: 13 deaths/1,000 population (1991)

Net migration rate: 0 migrants/1,000 population (1991)

Infant mortality rate: 14 deaths/1,000 live births (1991)

Life expectancy at birth: 68 years male, 76 years female (1991)

Total fertility rate: 1.8 children born/woman (1991)

Nationality: noun—Hungarian(s); adjective—Hungarian

Ethnic divisions: Hungarian 96.6%, German 1.6%, Slovak 1.1%, Southern Slav 0.3%, Romanian 0.2%

Religion: Roman Catholic 67.5%, Calvinist 20.0%, Lutheran 5.0%, atheist and other 7.5%

Language: Hungarian 98.2%, other 1.8%

Literacy: 99% (male 99%, female 98%) age 15 and over can read and write (1980)

Labor force: 4,860,000; services, trade, government, and other 43.2%, industry 30.9%, agriculture 18.8%, construction 7.1% (1988)

Organized labor: 96.5% of labor force; Central Council of Hungarian Trade Unions (SZOT) includes 19 affiliated unions, all controlled by the government; independent unions legal; may be as many as 12 small independent unions in operation

Government

Long-form name: Republic of Hungary

Type: republic

Capital: Budapest

Administrative divisions: 19 counties (megyék, singular—megye) and 1 capital city* (fováros); Bács-Kiskun, Baranya, Békés, Borsod-Abaúj-Zemplén, Budapest*, Csongrád, Fejér, Györ-Moson-Sopron, Hajdú-Bihar, Heves, Jász-Nagykun-Szolnok, Komárom-Esztergom, Nógrád, Pest, Somogy, Szabolcs-Szatmár-Bereg, Tolna, Vas, Veszprém, Zala

Independence: 1001, unification by King Stephen I

Constitution: 18 August 1949, effective 20 August 1949, revised 19 April 1972; 18 October 1989 revision ensures legal rights for individuals and constitutional checks on the authority of the prime minister and established the principle of parliamentary oversight

Legal system: in process of revision, moving toward rule of law based on Western model

National holiday: October 23 (1956); commemorates the Hungarian uprising

Executive branch: president, prime minister

Legislative branch: unicameral National Assembly (Országgyülés)

Judicial branch: Supreme Court, may be restructured as part of ongoing government overhaul

Leaders:
Chief of State—President Arpad GONCZ (since 3 August 1990; previously interim President from 2 May 1990);

Head of Government—Prime Minister Jozsef ANTALL (since 23 May 1990)

Political parties and leaders: Democratic Forum, Jozsef ANTALL, chairman; Free Democrats, Janos KIS, chairman; Independent Smallholders, Ferenc Jozsef NAGY, president; Hungarian Socialist Party (MSP), Gyula HORN, chairman; Young Democrats, Gabor FODOR, head; Christian Democrats, Dr. Lazlo SURJAN, president; note—the Hungarian Socialist (Communist) Workers' Party (MSZMP) renounced Communism and became the Hungarian Socialist Party (MSP) in October 1989

Suffrage: universal at age 18

Elections:
President last held 3 August 1990 (next to be held August 1995); elected by the National Assembly with a total of 294 votes out of 304; President GONCZ was elected by the National Assembly as interim President from 2 May 1990 until elected President;

National Assembly—last held on 25 March 1990 (first round, with the second round held 8 April 1990); results—percent of vote by party NA; seats—(394 total) Democratic Forum 165, Free Democrats 92, Independent Smallholders 43, Hungarian Socialist Party (MSP) 33, Young Democrats 21, Christian Democrats 21, independent candidates or jointly sponsored candidates 19

Communists: fewer than 100,000 (December 1989)

Member of: BIS, CCC, CE, CSCE, ECE, FAO, G-9, GATT, IAEA, IBEC, IBRD, ICAO, IDA, IFC, IIB, ILO, IMF, IMO, INTERPOL, IOC, ISO, ITU, LORCS, PCA, UN, UNCTAD, UNESCO, UNIDO, UNIIMOG, UPU, WFTU, WHO, WIPO, WMO, WTO

Diplomatic representation: Ambassador (vacant); Chancery at 3910 Shoemaker Street NW, Washington DC 20008; telephone (202) 362-6730; there is a Hungarian Consulate General in New York;

US—Ambassador Charles THOMAS; Embassy at V. Szabadsag Ter 12, Budapest (mailing address is APO New York 09213); telephone [36] (1) 112-6450

Flag: three equal horizontal bands of red (top), white, and green

Economy

Overview: Agriculture is an important sector, providing sizable export earnings and meeting domestic food needs. Industry accounts for about 40% of GNP and 30% of employment. About 40% of Hungary's foreign trade is with the USSR and Eastern Europe and a third is with the EC. Low rates of growth reflect the inability of the Soviet-style economy to modernize capital plant and motivate workers. GNP declined by 1% in 1989 and by an estimated 6% in 1990. Since 1985 external debt has more than doubled, to over $20 billion. In recent years Hungary has experimented widely with decentralized and market-oriented enterprises. The newly democratic government has renounced the Soviet economic growth model and plans to open the economy to wider market forces and to much closer economic relations with Western Europe. Prime Minister Antall has declared his intention to move foward on privatization of state enterprises, provision for bankruptcy, land reform, and marketization of international trade, but concerns over acceptable levels of unemployment and inflation may slow the reform process.

GNP: $60.9 billion, per capita $5,800; real growth rate −5.7% (1990 est.)

Inflation rate (consumer prices): 30% (1990 est.)

Unemployment rate: 1.7% (1990)

Budget: revenues $18.2 billion; expenditures $18.3 billion, including capital expenditures of $805 million (1989)

Exports: $10.2 billion (f.o.b. 1989); *commodities*—capital goods 33%, foods 25%, consumer goods 16%, fuels 1.5%, other 24.5%; *partners* USSR and Eastern Europe 42%, developed countries 37.4%, less developed countries 20.6% (1989)

Imports: $10.1 billion (c.i.f., 1989); *commodities*—capital goods 15%, fuels 20%, manufactured consumer goods 12.4%, agriculture 5%, other 47.6%; *partners*—USSR and Eastern Europe 34.9%, developed countries 45.5%, less developed countries 16.6%, US 3%

External debt: $20.7 billion (1989)

Industrial production: growth rate −7.9% (1990 est.)

Electricity: 7,800,000 kW capacity; 30,400 million kWh produced, 2,870 kWh per capita (1990)

Industries: mining, metallurgy, engineering industries, processed foods, textiles, chemicals (especially pharmaceuticals)

Agriculture: including forestry, accounts for about 15% of GNP and 19% of employment; highly diversified crop-livestock farming; principal crops—wheat, corn, sunflowers, potatoes, sugar beets; livestock—hogs, cattle, poultry, dairy products; self-sufficient in food output

Economic aid: donor—$2.0 billion in bilateral aid to non-Communist less developed countries (1962-89)

Currency: forint (plural—forints); 1 forint (Ft) = 100 fillér

Exchange rates: forints (Ft) per US$1—60.95 (December 1990), 63.21 (1990), 59.07 (1989), 50.41 (1988), 46.97 (1987), 45.83 (1986), 50.12 (1985)

Fiscal year: calendar year

Communications

Railroads: 7,765 km total; 7,508 km 1.435-meter standard gauge, 222 km narrow gauge (mostly 0.760-meter), 35 km 1.520-meter broad gauge; 1,147 km double track, 2,161 km electrified; all government owned (1988)

Highways: 130,014 km total; 29,715 km national highway system—26,834 km asphalt and bitumen, 142 km concrete, 51 km stone and road brick, 2,276 km macadam, 412 km unpaved; 58,495 km country roads (66% unpaved), and 41,804 km (est.) other roads (70% unpaved) (1988)

Inland waterways: 1,622 km (1988)

Pipelines: crude oil, 1,204 km; refined products, 630 km; natural gas, 3,895 km (1986)

Ports: Budapest and Dunaujvaros are river ports on the Danube; maritime outlets are Rostock (Germany), Gdansk (Poland), Gdynia (Poland), Szczecin (Poland), Galati (Romania), and Braila (Romania)

Merchant marine: 16 cargo ships (1,000 GRT or over) and 1 bulk totaling 94,393 GRT/131,946 DWT

Civil air: 28 major transport aircraft

Airports: 90 total, 90 usable; 20 with permanent-surface runways; 2 with runways over 3,659 m; 10 with runways 2,440-3,659 m; 15 with runways 1,220-2,439 m

Telecommunications: telephone density is at 17 per 100 inhabitants; 49% of all phones are in Budapest; 12-15 year wait for a phone; 16,000 telex lines (June 1990); stations—13 AM, 12 FM, 21 TV (8 Soviet TV relays); 4.2 TVs (1990)

Defense Forces

Branches: Ground Forces, Air and Air Defense Forces, Frontier Guard, Civil Defense

Manpower availability: males 15-49, 2,667,234; 2,130,749 fit for military service; 88,851 reach military age (18) annually

Defense expenditures: 43.7 billion forints, NA% of GDP (1989); note—conversion of defense expenditures into US dollars using the official administratively set exchange rate would produce misleading results

Iceland

Greenland Sea

North Atlantic Ocean

Geography

Total area: 103,000 km²; land area: 100,250 km²

Comparative area: slightly smaller than Kentucky

Land boundaries: none

Coastline: 4,988 km

Maritime claims:

Continental shelf: edge of continental margin or 200 nm;

Exclusive economic zone: 200 nm;

Territorial sea: 12 nm

Disputes: Rockall continental shelf dispute involving Denmark, Ireland, and the UK (Ireland and the UK have signed a boundary agreement in the Rockall area)

Climate: temperate; moderated by North Atlantic Current; mild, windy winters; damp, cool summers

Terrain: mostly plateau interspersed with mountain peaks, icefields; coast deeply indented by bays and fiords

Natural resources: fish, hydroelectric and geothermal power, diatomite

Land use: arable land NEGL%; permanent crops 0%; meadows and pastures 23%; forest and woodland 1%; other 76%

Environment: subject to earthquakes and volcanic activity

Note: strategic location between Greenland and Europe; westernmost European country

People

Population: 259,742 (July 1991), growth rate 1.0% (1991)

Birth rate: 17 births/1,000 population (1991)

Death rate: 7 deaths/1,000 population (1991)

Net migration rate: 0 migrants/1,000 population (1991)

Infant mortality rate: 7 deaths/1,000 live births (1991)

Life expectancy at birth: 75 years male, 80 years female (1991)

Iceland (continued)

Total fertility rate: 2.2 children born/woman (1991)
Nationality: noun—Icelander(s); adjective—Icelandic
Ethnic divisions: homogeneous mixture of descendants of Norwegians and Celts
Religion: Evangelical Lutheran 96%, other Protestant and Roman Catholic 3%, none 1% (1988)
Language: Icelandic
Literacy: 100% (male NA%, female NA%) age 15 and over can read and write (1976 est.)
Labor force: 134,429; commerce, finance, and services 55.4%, other manufacturing 14.3%., agriculture 5.8%, fish processing 7.9%, fishing 5.0% (1986)
Organized labor: 60% of labor force

Government

Long-form name: Republic of Iceland
Type: republic
Capital: Reykjavík
Administrative divisions: 23 counties (sýslar, singular—sýsla) and 14 independent towns* (kaupstadhir, singular—kaupstadhur); Akranes*, Akureyri*, Árnessýsla, Austur-Bardhastrandarsýsla, Austur-Húnavatnssýsla, Austur-Skaftafellssýsla, Borgarfjardharsýsla, Dalasýsla, Eyjafjardharsýsla, Gullbringusýsla, Hafnarfjördhur*, Húsavík*, Ísafjördhur*, Keflavík*, Kjósarsýsla, Kópavogur*, Mýrasýsla, Neskaupstadhur*, Nordhur-Ísafjardharsýsla, Nordhur-Múlasýsla, Nordhur-Thingeyjarsýsla, Ólafsfjördhur*, Rangárvallasýsla, Reykjavík*, Saudhárkrókur*, Seydhisfjördhur*, Siglufjördhur*, Skagafjardharsýsla, Snaefellsnes-og Hnappadalssýsla, Strandasýsla, Sudhur-Múlasýsla, Sudhur-Thingeyjarsýsla, Vestmannaeyjar*, Vestur-Bardhastrandarsýsla, Vestur-Húnavatnssýsla, Vestur-Ísafjardharsýsla, Vestur-Skaftafellssýsla
Independence: 17 June 1944 (from Denmark)
Constitution: 16 June 1944, effective 17 June 1944
Legal system: civil law system based on Danish law; does not accept compulsory ICJ jurisdiction
National holiday: Anniversary of the Establishment of the Republic, 17 June (1944)
Executive branch: president, prime minister, Cabinet
Legislative branch: bicameral Althingi with an Upper House (Efri Deild) and a Lower House (Nedri Deild)
Judicial branch: Supreme Court (Haestiréttur)
Leaders:
Chief of State—President Vigdís FINNBOGADÓTTIR (since 1 August 1980);
Head of Government—Prime Minister David ODDSSON (since 30 April 1991)

Political parties and leaders: Independence (conservative), David ODDSSON; Progressive, Steingrímur HERMANNSSON; Social Democratic, Jon Baldvin HANNIBALSSON; People's Alliance (left socialist), Olafur Ragnar GRIMSSON; Citizens Party (conservative nationalist), Julius SOLNES; Women's List
Suffrage: universal at age 20
Elections:
President—last held on 29 June 1980 (next scheduled for June 1992); results—there were no elections in 1984 and 1988 as President Vigdís FINNBOGADÓTTIR was unopposed;
Althing—last held on 20 April 1991 (next to be held by April 1995); results—Independence 38.6%, Progressive 18.9%, Social Democratic 15.5%, People's Alliance 14.4%, Womens List 8.13%, Liberals 1.2%, other 3.27% seats—(63 total) Independence 26, Progressive 13, Social Democratic 10, People's Alliance 9, Womens List 5
Communists: less than 100 (est.), some of whom participate in the People's Alliance
Member of: BIS, CCC, CE, CSCE, EBRD, ECE, EFTA, FAO, GATT, IAEA, IBRD, ICAO, ICC, ICFTU, IDA, IFC, ILO, IMF, IMO, INTELSAT, INTERPOL, IOC, ISO (correspondent), ITU, LORCS, NATO, NC, NEA, NIB, OECD, PCA, UN, UNCTAD, UNESCO, UPU, WHO, WIPO, WMO
Diplomatic representation: Ambassador Tomas A. TOMASSON; Chancery at 2022 Connecticut Avenue NW, Washington DC 20008; telephone (202) 265-6653 through 6655; there is an Icelandic Consulate General in New York;
US—Ambassador Charles E. COBB, Jr.; Embassy at Laufasvegur 21, Box 40, Reykjavik (mailing address is FPO New York 09571-0001); telephone [354] (1) 29100
Flag: blue with a red cross outlined in white that extends to the edges of the flag; the vertical part of the cross is shifted to the hoist side in the style of the *Dannebrog* (Danish flag)

Economy

Overview: Iceland's prosperous Scandinavian-type economy is basically capitalistic, but with extensive welfare measures, low unemployment, and comparatively even distribution of income. The economy is heavily dependent on the fishing industry, which provides nearly 75% of export earnings. In the absence of other natural resources, Iceland's economy is vulnerable to changing world fish prices. As a result of climbing fish prices in 1990 and a noninflationary labor agreement, Iceland is pulling out of a recession, which began in mid-1988 with a sharp decline in fish prices and an imposition of quotas on fish catches to conserve stocks. Inflation was down sharply from 20% in 1989 to 8% in 1990.

GDP: $4.2 billion, per capita $16,300; real growth rate 0% (1990)
Inflation rate (consumer prices): 7.8% (1990)
Unemployment rate: 1.8% (1990)
Budget: revenues $1.6 billion; expenditures $1.66 billion, including capital expenditures of $NA million (1990)
Exports: $1.6 billion (f.o.b., 1990);
commodities—fish and fish products, animal products, aluminum, diatomite;
partners—EC 67.7% (UK 25.3%, FRG 12.7%), US 9.9%, Japan 5%
Imports: $1.7 billion (c.i.f., 1990);
commodities—machinery and transportation equipment, petroleum, foodstuffs, textiles;
partners—EC 49.8% (FRG 12.4%, Denmark 8.6%, UK 8.1%), US 14.4%, Japan 5.6%
External debt: $3 billion (1990)
Industrial production: growth rate –0.8% (1988 est.); accounts for 22% of GDP
Electricity: 1,063,000 kW capacity; 5,165 million kWh produced, 20,780 kWh per capita (1989)
Industries: fish processing, aluminum smelting, ferro-silicon production, hydropower
Agriculture: accounts for about 25% of GDP (including fishing); fishing is most important economic activity, contributing nearly 75% to export earnings; principal crops—potatoes and turnips; livestock—cattle, sheep; self-sufficient in crops; fish catch of about 1.4 million metric tons in 1989
Economic aid: US commitments, including Ex-Im (FY70-81), $19.1 million
Currency: króna (plural—krónur); 1 Icelandic króna (IKr) = 100 aurar
Exchange rates: Icelandic krónur (IKr) per US$1—55.216 (January 1991), 58.284 (1990), 57.042 (1989), 43.014 (1988), 38.677 (1987), 41.104 (1986), 41.508 (1985)
Fiscal year: calendar year

Communications

Highways: 12,343 km total; 166 km bitumen and concrete; 1,284 km bituminous treated and gravel; 10,893 km earth
Ports: Reykjavik, Akureyri, Hafnarfjördhur, Keflavik, Seydhisfjördhur, Siglufjördhur, Vestmannaeyjar; numerous minor ports
Merchant marine: 16 ships (1,000 GRT or over) totaling 53,409 GRT/73,279 DWT; includes 8 cargo, 2 refrigerated cargo, 1 container, 2 roll-on/roll-off cargo, 1 petroleum, oils, and lubricants (POL) tanker, 1 chemical tanker, 1 bulk
Civil air: 20 major transport aircraft
Airports: 99 total, 92 usable; 4 with permanent-surface runways; none with runways over 3,659 m; 1 with runways 2,440-3,659 m; 14 with runways 1,220-2,439 m

India

Telecommunications: adequate domestic service, wire and radio communication system; 135,000 telephones; stations—10 AM, 17 (43 relays) FM, 14 (132 relays) TV; 2 submarine cables; 1 Atlantic Ocean INTELSAT earth station

Defense Forces

Branches: no armed forces; State Criminal Police, Coast Guard; Iceland's defense is provided by the US-manned Icelandic Defense Force (IDF) headquartered at Keflavik
Manpower availability: males 15-49, 69,644; 62,248 fit for military service; no conscription or compulsory military service
Defense expenditures: none

Geography

Total area: 3,287,590 km²; land area: 2,973,190 km²
Comparative area: slightly more than one-third the size of the US
Land boundaries: 14,103 km total; Bangladesh 4,053 km, Bhutan 605 km, Burma 1,463 km, China 3,380, Nepal 1,690 km, Pakistan 2,912 km
Coastline: 7,000 km
Maritime claims:
Contiguous zone: 24 nm;
Continental shelf: edge of continental margin or 200 nm;
Exclusive economic zone: 200 nm;
Territorial sea: 12 nm
Disputes: boundaries with Bangladesh, China, and Pakistan; water sharing problems with downstream riparians, Bangladesh over the Ganges and Pakistan over the Indus
Climate: varies from tropical monsoon in south to temperate in north
Terrain: upland plain (Deccan Plateau) in south, flat to rolling plain along the Ganges, deserts in west, Himalayas in north
Natural resources: coal (fourth-largest reserves in the world), iron ore, manganese, mica, bauxite, titanium ore, chromite, natural gas, diamonds, crude oil, limestone
Land use: arable land 55%; permanent crops 1%; meadows and pastures 4%; forest and woodland 23%; other 17%; includes irrigated 13%
Environment: droughts, flash floods, severe thunderstorms common; deforestation; soil erosion; overgrazing; air and water pollution; desertification
Note: dominates South Asian subcontinent; near important Indian Ocean trade routes

People

Population: 866,351,738 (July 1991), growth rate 1.9% (1991)

Birth rate: 29 births/1,000 population (1991)
Death rate: 10 deaths/1,000 population (1991)
Net migration rate: 0 migrants/1,000 population (1991)
Infant mortality rate: 87 deaths/1,000 live births (1991)
Life expectancy at birth: 57 years male, 59 years female (1991)
Total fertility rate: 3.7 children born/woman (1991)
Nationality: noun—Indian(s); adjective—Indian
Ethnic divisions: Indo-Aryan 72%, Dravidian 25%, Mongoloid and other 3%
Religion: Hindu 82.6%, Muslim 11.4%, Christian 2.4%, Sikh 2.0%, Buddhist 0.7%, Jains 0.5%, other 0.4%
Language: Hindi, English, and 14 other official languages—Bengali, Telugu, Marathi, Tamil, Urdu, Gujarati, Malayalam, Kannada, Oriya, Punjabi, Assamese, Kashmiri, Sindhi, and Sanskrit; 24 languages spoken by a million or more persons each; numerous other languages and dialects, for the most part mutually unintelligible; Hindi is the national language and primary tongue of 30% of the people; English enjoys associate status but is the most important language for national, political, and commercial communication; Hindustani, a popular variant of Hindi/Urdu, is spoken widely throughout northern India
Literacy: 48% (male 62%, female 34%) age 15 and over can read and write (1990 est.)
Labor force: 284,400,000; 67% agriculture (FY85)
Organized labor: less than 5% of the labor force

Government

Long-form name: Republic of India
Type: federal republic
Capital: New Delhi
Administrative divisions: 25 states and 7 union territories*; Andaman and Nicobar Islands*, Andhra Pradesh, Arunāchal Pradesh, Assam, Bihār, Chandīgarh*, Dādra and Nagar Haveli*, Damān and Diu*, Delhi*, Goa, Gujarāt, Haryāna, Himāchal Pradesh, Jammu and Kashmīr, Karnātaka, Kerala, Lakshadweep*, Madhya Pradesh, Mahārāshtra, Manipur, Meghālaya, Mizoram, Nāgāland, Orissa, Pondicherry*, Punjab, Rājasthān, Sikkim, Tamil Nādu, Tripura, Uttar Pradesh, West Bengal
Independence: 15 August 1947 (from UK)
Constitution: 26 January 1950
Legal system: based on English common law; limited judicial review of legislative acts; accepts compulsory ICJ jurisdiction, with reservations
National holiday: Anniversary of the Proclamation of the Republic, 26 January (1950)

India (continued)

Executive branch: president, vice president, prime minister, Council of Ministers
Legislative branch: bicameral Parliament (Sansad) consists of an upper house or Council of States (Rajya Sabha) and a lower house or House of the People (Lok Sabha)
Judicial branch: Supreme Court
Leaders:
Chief of State—President Ramaswamy Iyer VENKATARAMAN (since 25 July 1987); Vice President Dr. Shankar Dayal SHARMA (since 3 September 1987);
Head of Government—Prime Minister P. V. Narasimha RAO (since 21 June 1991)
Political parties and leaders: Congress (I) Party, P. V. Narasimha RAO, president; Bharatiya Janata Party, L. K. ADVANI; Janata Dal Party, V. P. SINGH; Communist Party of India/Marxist (CPI/M), E. M. S. NAMBOODIRIPAD; Communist Party of India (CPI), C. Rajeswara RAO; Telugu Desam (a regional party in Andhra Pradesh), N. T. Rama RAO; All-India Anna Dravida Munnetra Kazagham (AIADMK; a regional party in Tamil Nadu), JAYALA-LITHA; Samajwadi Janata Party, CHAN-DRA SHEKHAR; Shiv Sena, Bal THACK-ERAY; Revolutionary Socialist Party (RSP), Tridip CHOWDHURY; Bahujana Samaj Party (BSP), Kanshi RAM; Congress (S) Party, leader NA; Communist Party of India/Marxist-Leninist (CPI/ML), Satyanarayan SINGH; Dravida Munnetra Kazagham (a regional party in Tamil Nadu), M. KARUNANIDHI; Akali Dal factions representing Sikh religious community in the Punjab; National Conference (NC; a regional party in Jammu and Kashmir), Farooq ABDULLAH; Asom Gana Parishad (a regional party in Assam), Prafulla MAHANTA
Suffrage: universal at age 18
Elections:
People's Assembly—last held 21 May, 12 and 15 June 1991 (next to be held by November 1996); results—percent of vote by party NA; seats—(545 total; 509 elected) Congress (I) Party 225, Bharatiya Janata Party 117, Janata Dal Party 55, Communist Party of India (Marxist) 35, Communist Party of India 13, Telugu Desam 12, AIADMK 11, Samajwadi Janata Party 5, Shiv Sena 4, RSP 4, BSP 1, Congress (S) Party 1, other 26; note—second and third rounds of voting were delayed because of the assassination of Congress President Rajiv GANDHI on 21 May 1991
Communists: 466,000 members claimed by CPI, 361,000 members claimed by CPI/M; Communist extremist groups, about 15,000 members
Other political or pressure groups: various separatist groups seeking greater communal autonomy; numerous religious or militant/chauvinistic organizations, including

Adam Sena, Anand Marg, Vishwa Hindu Parishad, and Rashtriya Swayamsevak Sangh
Member of: AfDB, AG (observer), AsDB, C, CCC, CP, ESCAP, FAO, G-6, G-19, G-24, G-77, GATT, IAEA, IBRD, ICAO, ICC, ICFTU, IDA, IFAD, IFC, ILO, IMF, IMO, INMARSAT, INTELSAT, INTERPOL, IOC, ISO, ITU, LORCS, NAM, PCA, SAARC, UN, UNAVEM, UNCTAD, UNESCO, UNIDO, UNIIMOG, UPU, WFTU, WHO, WIPO, WMO, WTO
Diplomatic representation: Ambassador Abid HUSSEIN; Chancery at 2107 Massachusetts Avenue NW, Washington DC 20008; telephone (202) 939-7000; there are Indian Consulates General in Chicago, New York, and San Francisco;
US—Ambassador William CLARK, Jr.; Embassy at Shanti Path, Chanakyapuri 110021, New Delhi; telephone [91] (11) 600651; there are US Consulates General in Bombay, Calcutta, and Madras
Flag: three equal horizontal bands of orange (top), white, and green with a blue *chakra* (24-spoked wheel) centered in the white band; similar to the flag of Niger which has a small orange disk centered in the white band

---

Economy

Overview: India's economy is a mixture of traditional village farming and handicrafts, modern agriculture, old and new branches of industry, and a multitude of support services. It presents both the entrepreneurial skills and drives of the capitalist system and widespread government intervention of the socialist mold. Growth of 4% to 5% annually in the 1980s has softened the impact of population growth on unemployment, social tranquility, and the environment. Agricultural output has continued to expand, reflecting the greater use of modern farming techniques and improved seed that have helped to make India self-sufficient in food grains and a net agricultural exporter. However, tens of millions of villagers, particularly in the south, have not benefited from the green revolution and live in abject poverty. Industry has benefited from a partial liberalization of controls. The growth rate of the service sector has also been strong. India, however, has been challenged more recently by much lower foreign exchange reserves, higher inflation, and a large debt service burden.
GNP: $254 billion, per capita $300; real growth rate 4.5% (1990 est.)
Inflation rate (consumer prices): 10.0% (1990)
Unemployment rate: 20% (1990 est.)
Budget: revenues $34 billion; expenditures $54 billion, including capital expenditures of $13.3 billion (FY91)

Exports: $17.0 billion (f.o.b., FY90); *commodities*—gems and jewelry, engineering goods, clothing, textiles, chemicals, tea, coffee, fish products; *partners*—EC 25%, US 19%, USSR and Eastern Europe 17%, Japan 10%
Imports: $24.8 billion (c.i.f., FY90); *commodities*—petroleum, capital goods, uncut gems and jewelry, chemicals, iron and steel, edible oils; *partners*—EC 33%, Middle East 19%, Japan 10%, US 9%, USSR and Eastern Europe 8%
External debt: $69.8 billion (1990 est.)
Industrial production: growth rate 5.0% (1990 est.); accounts for about 25% of GDP
Electricity: 70,000,000 kW capacity; 245,000 million kWh produced, 290 kWh per capita (1990)
Industries: textiles, food processing, steel, machinery, transportation equipment, cement, jute manufactures, mining, petroleum, power, chemicals, pharmaceuticals, electronics
Agriculture: accounts for about 30% of GNP and employs 67% of labor force; self-sufficient in food grains; principal crops—rice, wheat, oilseeds, cotton, jute, tea, sugarcane, potatoes; livestock—cattle, buffaloes, sheep, goats and poultry; fish catch of about 3 million metric tons ranks among the world's top 10 fishing nations
Illicit drugs: licit producer of opium poppy for the pharmaceutical trade, but some opium is diverted to illicit international drug markets; major transit country for illicit narcotics produced in neighboring countries
Economic aid: US commitments, including Ex-Im (FY70-89), $4.4 billion; Western (non-US) countries, ODA and OOF bilateral commitments (1980-88), $20.1 billion; OPEC bilateral aid (1979-89), $315 million; USSR (1970-89), $11.6 billion; Eastern Europe (1970-89), $105 million
Currency: Indian rupee (plural—rupees); 1 Indian rupee (Re) = 100 paise
Exchange rates: Indian rupees (Rs) per US$1—18.329 (January 1990), 17.504 (1990), 16.226 (1989), 13.917 (1988), 12.962 (1987), 12.611 (1986), 12.369 (1985)
Fiscal year: 1 April-31 March

Communications

Railroads: 61,850 km total (1986); 33,553 km 1.676-meter broad gauge, 24,051 km 1.000-meter gauge, 4,246 km narrow gauge (0.762 meter and 0.610 meter); 12,617 km is double track; 6,500 km is electrified
Highways: 1,633,300 km total (1986); 515,300 km secondary and 1,118,000 km gravel, crushed stone, or earth
Inland waterways: 16,180 km; 3,631 km navigable by large vessels

Indian Ocean

Pipelines: crude oil, 3,497 km; refined products, 1,703 km; natural gas, 902 km (1989)
Ports: Bombay, Calcutta, Cochin, Kandla, Madras, New Mangalore, Port Blair (Andaman Islands)
Merchant marine: 308 ships (1,000 GRT or over) totaling 6,087,451 GRT/10,150,460 DWT; includes 1 short-sea passenger, 8 passenger-cargo, 100 cargo, 1 roll-on/roll-off cargo, 8 container, 54 petroleum, oils, and lubricants (POL) tanker, 10 chemical tanker, 9 combination ore/oil, 115 bulk, 2 combination bulk
Civil air: 93 major transport aircraft
Airports: 345 total, 288 usable; 198 with permanent-surface runways; 2 with runways over 3,659 m; 57 with runways 2,440-3,659 m; 88 with runways 1,220-2,439 m
Telecommunications: poor domestic telephone service, international radio communications adequate; 4,700,000 telephones; stations—96 AM, 4 FM, 274 TV (government controlled); domestic satellite system for communications and TV; 3 Indian Ocean INTELSAT earth stations; submarine cables to Malaysia and United Arab Emirates

Defense Forces

Branches: Army, Navy, Air Force, Police Force, Border Security Forces, Coast Guard, Assam Rifles
Manpower availability: males 15-49, 232,793,714; 137,259,444 fit for military service; about 9,431,908 reach military age (17) annually
Defense expenditures: $9.2 billion, 3.5% of GNP (FY91)

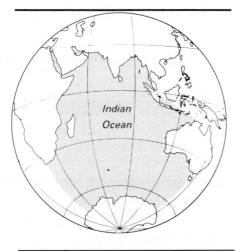

Geography

Total area: 73,600,000 km²; Arabian Sea, Bass Strait, Bay of Bengal, Java Sea, Persian Gulf, Red Sea, Strait of Malacca, Timor Sea, and other tributary water bodies
Comparative area: slightly less than eight times the size of the US; third-largest ocean (after the Pacific Ocean and Atlantic Ocean, but larger than the Arctic Ocean)
Coastline: 66,526 km
Climate: northeast monsoon (December to April), southwest monsoon (June to October); tropical cyclones occur during May-/June and October/November in the north Indian Ocean and January/February in the south Indian Ocean
Terrain: surface dominated by counter-clockwise gyre (broad, circular system of currents) in the south Indian Ocean; unique reversal of surface currents in the north Indian Ocean—low pressure over southwest Asia from hot, rising, summer air results in the southwest monsoon and southwest-to-northeast winds and currents, while high pressure over northern Asia from cold, falling, winter air results in the northeast monsoon and northeast-to-southwest winds and currents; ocean floor is dominated by the Mid-Indian Ocean Ridge and subdivided by the Southeast Indian Ocean Ridge, Southwest Indian Ocean Ridge, and Ninety East Ridge; maximum depth is 7,258 meters in the Java Trench
Natural resources: oil and gas fields, fish, shrimp, sand and gravel aggregates, placer deposits, polymetallic nodules
Environment: endangered marine species include the dugong, seals, turtles, and whales; oil pollution in the Arabian Sea, Persian Gulf, and Red Sea
Note: major choke points include Bab el Mandeb, Strait of Hormuz, Strait of Malacca, southern access to the Suez Canal, and the Lombok Strait; ships subject to superstructure icing in extreme south near Antarctica from May to October

Economy

Overview: The Indian Ocean provides a major transportation highway for the movement of petroleum products from the Middle East to Europe and North and South American countries. Fish from the ocean are of growing economic importance to many of the bordering countries as a source of both food and exports. Fishing fleets from the USSR, Japan, Korea, and Taiwan also exploit the Indian Ocean for mostly shrimp and tuna. Large reserves of hydrocarbons are being tapped in the offshore areas of Saudi Arabia, Iran, India, and Western Australia. An estimated 40% of the world's offshore oil production comes from the Indian Ocean. Beach sands rich in heavy minerals and offshore placer deposits are actively exploited by bordering countries, particularly India, South Africa, Indonesia, Sri Lanka, and Thailand.
Industries: based on exploitation of natural resources, particularly marine life, minerals, oil and gas production, fishing, sand and gravel aggregates, placer deposits

Communications

Ports: Bombay (India), Calcutta (India), Madras (India), Colombo (Sri Lanka), Durban (South Africa), Fremantle (Australia), Jakarta (Indonesia), Melbourne (Australia), Richard's Bay (South Africa)
Telecommunications: no submarine cables

Indonesia

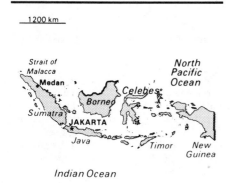

1200 km

Strait of Malacca
Medan
Sumatra
JAKARTA
Java
Borneo
Celebes
North Pacific Ocean
Timor
New Guinea

Indian Ocean

Geography

Total area: 1,919,440 km²; land area: 1,826,440 km²
Comparative area: slightly less than three times the size of Texas
Land boundaries: 2,602 km total; Malaysia 1,782 km, Papua New Guinea 820 km
Coastline: 54,716 km
Maritime claims: (measured from claimed archipelagic baselines);
Exclusive economic zone: 200 nm;
Territorial sea: 12 nm
Disputes: sovereignty over Timor Timur (East Timor Province) disputed with Portugal
Climate: tropical; hot, humid; more moderate in highlands
Terrain: mostly coastal lowlands; larger islands have interior mountains
Natural resources: crude oil, tin, natural gas liquids, nickel, timber, bauxite, copper, fertile soils, coal, gold, silver
Land use: arable land 8%; permanent crops 3%; meadows and pastures 7%; forest and woodland 67%; other 15%; includes irrigated 3%
Environment: archipelago of 13,500 islands (6,000 inhabited); occasional floods, severe droughts, and tsunamis; deforestation
Note: straddles Equator; strategic location astride or along major sea lanes from Indian Ocean to Pacific Ocean

People

Population: 193,560,494 (July 1991), growth rate 1.8% (1991)
Birth rate: 26 births/1,000 population (1991)
Death rate: 8 deaths/1,000 population (1991)
Net migration rate: 0 migrants/1,000 population (1991)
Infant mortality rate: 73 deaths/1,000 live births (1991)

Life expectancy at birth: 59 years male, 63 years female (1991)
Total fertility rate: 3.0 children born/woman (1991)
Nationality: noun—Indonesian(s); adjective—Indonesian
Ethnic divisions: majority of Malay stock comprising Javanese 45.0%, Sundanese 14.0%, Madurese 7.5%, coastal Malays 7.5%, other 26.0%
Religion: Muslim 87%, Protestant 6%, Roman Catholic 3%, Hindu 2%, Buddhist 1%, other 1% (1985)
Language: Bahasa Indonesia (modified form of Malay; official); English and Dutch leading foreign languages; local dialects, the most widely spoken of which is Javanese
Literacy: 77% (male 84%, female 68%) age 15 and over can read and write (1990 est.)
Labor force: 67,000,000; agriculture 55%, manufacturing 10%, construction 4%, transport and communications 3% (1985 est.)
Organized labor: 3,000,000 members (claimed); about 5% of labor force

Government

Long-form name: Republic of Indonesia
Type: republic
Capital: Jakarta
Administrative divisions: 24 provinces (propinsi-propinsi, singular—propinsi), 2 special regions* (daerah-daerah istimewa, singular—daerah istimewa), and 1 special capital city district** (daerah khusus ibukota); Aceh*, Bali, Bengkulu, Irian Jaya, Jakarta Raya**, Jambi, Jawa Barat, Jawa Tengah, Jawa Timur, Kalimantan Barat, Kalimantan Selatan, Kalimantan Tengah, Kalimantan Timur, Lampung, Maluku, Nusa Tenggara Barat, Nusa Tenggara Timur, Riau, Sulawesi Selatan, Sulawesi Tengah, Sulawesi Tenggara, Sulawesi Utara, Sumatera Barat, Sumatera Selatan, Sumatera Utara, Timor Timur, Yogyakarta*
Independence: 17 August 1945 (from Netherlands; formerly Netherlands or Dutch East Indies)
Constitution: August 1945, abrogated by Federal Constitution of 1949 and Provisional Constitution of 1950, restored 5 July 1959
Legal system: based on Roman-Dutch law, substantially modified by indigenous concepts and by new criminal procedures code; has not accepted compulsory ICJ jurisdiction
National holiday: Independence Day, 17 August (1945)
Executive branch: president, vice president, Cabinet
Legislative branch: unicameral House of Representatives (Dewan Perwakilan Rakyat or DPR); note—the People's Consultative Assembly (Majelis Permusyawaratan Rakyat or MPR) includes the DPR plus 500

indirectly elected members who meet every five years to elect the president and vice president and, theoretically, to determine national policy
Judicial branch: Supreme Court (Mahkamah Agung)
Leaders:
Chief of State and Head of Government—President Gen. (Ret.) SOEHARTO (since 27 March 1968); Vice President Lt. Gen. (Ret.) SUDHARMONO (since 11 March 1983)
Political parties and leaders: GOLKAR (quasi-official party based on functional groups), Lt. Gen. (Ret.) WAHONO, general chairman; Indonesia Democracy Party (PDI—federation of former Nationalist and Christian Parties), SOERYADI, chairman; Development Unity Party (PPP, federation of former Islamic parties), Ismail Hasan METAREUM, chairman
Suffrage: universal at age 17 and married persons regardless of age
Elections:
House of Representatives—last held on 23 April 1987 (next to be held 23 April 1992); results—Golkar 73%, UDP 16%, PDI 11%; seats—(500 total—400 elected, 100 appointed) Golkar 299, UDP 61, PDI 40
Communists: Communist Party (PKI) was officially banned in March 1966; current strength about 1,000-3,000, with less than 10% engaged in organized activity; pre-October 1965 hardcore membership about 1.5 million
Member of: APEC, AsDB, ASEAN, CCC, CP, ESCAP, FAO, G-19, G-77, GATT, IAEA, IBRD, ICAO, ICC, ICFTU, IDA, IDB, IFAD, IFC, ILO, IMF, IMO, INMARSAT, INTELSAT, INTERPOL, IOC, ISO, ITU, LORCS, NAM, OIC, OPEC, UN, UNCTAD, UNESCO, UNIDO, UNIIMOG, UPU, WCL, WFTU, WHO, WIPO, WMO, WTO
Diplomatic representation: Ambassador Abdul Rachman RAMLY; Chancery at 2020 Massachusetts Avenue NW, Washington DC 20036; telephone (202) 775-5200; there are Indonesian Consulates General in Houston, New York, and Los Angeles, and Consulates in Chicago and San Francisco; *US*—Ambassador John C. MONJO; Embassy at Medan Merdeka Selatan 5, Jakarta (mailing address is APO San Francisco 96356); telephone [62] (21) 360-360; there are US Consulates in Medan and Surabaya
Flag: two equal horizontal bands of red (top) and white; similar to the flag of Monaco which is shorter; also similar to the flag of Poland which is white (top) and red

Economy

Overview: Indonesia is a mixed economy with many socialist institutions and central planning but with a recent emphasis on deregulation and private enterprise. Indonesia has extensive natural wealth yet, with a large and rapidly increasing population, it remains a poor country. GDP growth in 1985-89 averaged about 4%, somewhat short of the more than 5% rate needed to absorb the 2.3 million workers annually entering the labor force. Agriculture, including forestry and fishing, is an important sector, accounting for 21% of GDP and over 50% of the labor force. The staple crop is rice. Once the world's largest rice importer, Indonesia is now nearly self-sufficient. Plantation crops—rubber and palm oil—and textiles and plywood are being encouraged for both export and job generation. Industrial output now accounts for 30% of GDP based on a supply of diverse natural resources, including crude oil, natural gas, timber, metals, and coal. Of these, the oil sector dominates the external economy, generating more than 20% of the government's revenues and 40% of export earnings in 1989. However, the economy's growth is very dependent on the continuing expansion of nonoil exports. Japan is Indonesia's most important customer and supplier of aid.

GDP: $94 billion, per capita $490; real growth rate 6.0% (1990 est.)

Inflation rate (consumer prices): 10.8% (1990)

Unemployment rate: 3%; underemployment 44% (1989 est.)

Budget: revenues $17.2 billion; expenditures $23.4 billion, including capital expenditures of $8.9 billion (FY91)

Exports: $23.5 billion (f.o.b., 1989 est.); *commodities*—petroleum and liquefied natural gas 40%, timber 15%, textiles 7%, rubber 5%, coffee 3%; *partners*—Japan 43%, US 16%, Singapore, EC

Imports: $17.1 billion (f.o.b., 1989 est.); *commodities*—machinery 39%, chemical products 19%, manufactured goods 16%; *partners*—Japan 23%, US 13%, EC, Singapore

External debt: $58.5 billion (1990 est.)

Industrial production: growth rate 11.6% (1989 est.); accounts for 30% of GDP

Electricity: 11,600,000 kW capacity; 38,000 million kWh produced, 200 kWh per capita (1990)

Industries: petroleum, textiles, mining, cement, chemical fertilizers, plywood, food, rubber

Agriculture: subsistence food production; small-holder and plantation production for export; rice, cassava, peanuts, rubber, cocoa, coffee, oil palm, copra, other tropical products; livestock products—poultry meat, beef, pork, eggs

Illicit drugs: illicit producer of cannabis for the international drug trade, but not a major player; government actively eradicating plantings and prosecuting traffickers

Economic aid: US commitments, including Ex-Im (FY70-89), $4.4 billion; Western (non-US) countries, ODA and OOF bilateral commitments (1970-88), $22.8 billion; OPEC bilateral aid (1979-89), $213 million; Communist countries (1970-89), $175 million

Currency: Indonesian rupiah (plural—rupiahs); 1 Indonesian rupiah (Rp) = 100 sen (sen no longer used)

Exchange rates: Indonesian rupiahs (Rp) per US$1—1,907.5 (January 1991), 1,842.8 (1990), 1,770.1 (1989), 1,685.7 (1988), 1,643.8 (1987), 1,282.6 (1986), 1,110.6 (1985)

Fiscal year: 1 April-31 March

Communications

Railroads: 6,964 km total; 6,389 km 1.067-meter gauge, 497 km 0.750-meter gauge, 78 km 0.600-meter gauge; 211 km double track; 101 km electrified; all government owned

Highways: 119,500 km total; 11,812 km state, 34,180 km provincial, and 73,508 km district roads

Inland waterways: 21,579 km total; Sumatra 5,471 km, Java and Madura 820 km, Kalimantan 10,460 km, Celebes 241 km, Irian Jaya 4,587 km

Pipelines: crude oil, 2,505 km; refined products, 456 km; natural gas, 1,703 km (1989)

Ports: Cilacap, Cirebon, Jakarta, Kupang, Palembang, Ujungpandang, Semarang, Surabaya

Merchant marine: 365 ships (1,000 GRT or over) totaling 1,647,632 GRT/2,481,432 DWT; includes 5 short-sea passenger, 13 passenger-cargo, 215 cargo, 7 container, 3 roll-on/roll-off cargo, 2 vehicle carrier, 80 petroleum, oils, and lubricants (POL) tanker, 3 chemical tanker, 5 liquefied gas, 6 specialized tanker, 1 livestock carrier, 25 bulk

Civil air: about 216 commercial transport aircraft

Airports: 470 total, 436 usable; 111 with permanent-surface runways; 1 with runways over 3,659 m; 12 with runways 2,440-3,659 m; 63 with runways 1,220-2,439 m

Telecommunications: interisland microwave system and HF police net; domestic service fair, international service good; radiobroadcast coverage good; 763,000 telephones (1986); stations—618 AM, 38 FM, 9 TV; satellite earth stations—1 Indian Ocean INTELSAT earth station and 1 Pacific Ocean INTELSAT earth station; and 1 domestic satellite communications system

Defense Forces

Branches: Army, Navy, Air Force, National Police

Manpower availability: males 15-49, 50,572,652; 29,893,127 fit for military service; 2,149,673 reach military age (18) annually

Defense expenditures: $1.4 billion, 1.8% of GNP (1988)

145

Iran

Geography

Total area: 1,648,000 km²; land area: 1,636,000 km²
Comparative area: slightly larger than Alaska
Land boundaries: 5,492 km total; Afghanistan 936 km, Iraq 1,458 km, Pakistan 909 km, Turkey 499 km, USSR 1,690 km
Coastline: 3,180 km
Maritime claims:
Continental shelf: not specific;
Exclusive fishing zone: 50 nm in the Sea of Oman; continental shelf limit, continental shelf boundaries, or median lines in the Persian Gulf;
Territorial sea: 12 nm
Disputes: Iran and Iraq restored diplomatic relations on 14 October 1990 following the end of the war that began on 22 September 1980; progress had been made on the major issues of contention—troop withdrawal, prisoner-of-war exchanges, demarcation of the border, freedom of navigation, and sovereignty over the the Shatt al Arab waterway—but written agreements had yet to be drawn up when frictions reemerged in March 1991 in the wake of Shi'a and Kurdish revolts in Iraq that Baghdad accused Tehrān of supporting; Kurdish question among Iran, Iraq, Syria, Turkey, and the USSR; occupies three islands in the Persian Gulf claimed by UAE (Jazīreh-ye Abū Mūsá or Abū Mūsá, Jazīreh-ye Tonb-e Bozorg or Greater Tunb, and Jazīreh-ye Tonb-e Kūchek or Lesser Tunb); periodic disputes with Afghanistan over Helmand water rights; Boluch question with Afghanistan and Pakistan
Climate: mostly arid or semiarid, subtropical along Caspian coast
Terrain: rugged, mountainous rim; high, central basin with deserts, mountains; small, discontinuous plains along both coasts
Natural resources: petroleum, natural gas, coal, chromium, copper, iron ore, lead, manganese, zinc, sulfur

Land use: arable land 8%; permanent crops NEGL%; meadows and pastures 27%; forest and woodland 11%; other 54%; includes irrigated 2%
Environment: deforestation; overgrazing; desertification

People

Population: 59,051,082 (July 1991), growth rate 3.6% (1991)
Birth rate: 44 births/1,000 population (1991)
Death rate: 9 deaths/1,000 population (1991)
Net migration rate: 0 migrants/1,000 population (1991)
Infant mortality rate: 66 deaths/1,000 live births (1991)
Life expectancy at birth: 64 years male, 65 years female (1991)
Total fertility rate: 6.6 children born/woman (1991)
Nationality: noun—Iranian(s); adjective—Iranian
Ethnic divisions: Persian 51%, Azerbaijani 25%, Kurd 9%, Gilaki and Mazandarani 8%, Lur 2%, Baloch 1%, Arab 1%, other 3%
Religion: Shi'a Muslim 95%, Sunni Muslim 4%, Zoroastrian, Jewish, Christian, and Baha'i 1%
Language: 58% Persian and Persian dialects, 26% Turkic and Turkic dialects, 9% Kurdish, 2% Luri, 1% Baloch, 1% Arabic, 1% Turkish, 2% other
Literacy: 54% (male 64%, female 43%) age 15 and over can read and write (1990 est.)
Labor force: 15,400,000; agriculture 33%, manufacturing 21%; shortage of skilled labor (1988 est.)
Organized labor: none

Government

Long-form name: Islamic Republic of Iran
Type: theocratic republic
Capital: Tehrān
Administrative divisions: 24 provinces (ostānha, singular—ostān); Āžarbāyjān-e Bākhtarī, Āžarbāyjān-e Khāvarī, Bākhtarān, Bushēhr, Chahār Maḥāll va Bakhtīārī, Eṣfahān, Fārs, Gīlān, Hamadān, Hormozgān, Īlām, Kermān, Khorāsān, Khūzestān, Kohkīlūyeh va Būyer Aḥmadī, Kordestān, Lorestān, Markazī, Māzandarān, Semnān, Sīstān va Balūchestān, Tehrān, Yazd, Zanjān
Independence: 1 April 1979, Islamic Republic of Iran proclaimed
Constitution: 2-3 December 1979; revised 1989 to expand powers of the presidency and eliminate the prime ministership
Legal system: the new Constitution codifies Islamic principles of government
National holiday: Islamic Republic Day, 1 April (1979)

Executive branch: cleric (faqih), president, Council of Ministers
Legislative branch: unicameral Islamic Consultative Assembly (Majles-e-Shura-ye-Eslami)
Judicial branch: Supreme Court
Leaders:
Cleric and functional Chief of State—Leader of the Islamic Revolution Ayatollah Ali Hoseini-KHAMENEI (since 4 June 1989);
Head of Government—President Ali Akbar HASHEMI-RAFSANJANI (since 3 August 1989);
Political parties and leaders: there are at least 14 licensed parties; the three most important are—Tehrān Militant Clergy Association, Mohammad Reza MAHDAVI-KANI; Militant Clerics Association, Mehdi MAHDAVI-KARUBI and Mohammad Asqar MUSAVI-KHOINIHA; Fedaiyin Islam Organization, Sadeq KHALKHALI
Suffrage: universal at age 15
Elections:
President—last held NA July 1989 (next to be held April 1993); results—Ali Akbar HASHEMI-RAFSANJANI was elected with only token opposition;
Islamic Consultative Assembly—last held 8 April 1988 (next to be held June 1992); results—percent of vote by party NA; seats—(270 seats total) number of seats by party NA
Communists: 1,000 to 2,000 est. hardcore; 15,000 to 20,000 est. sympathizers; crackdown in 1983 crippled the party; trials of captured leaders began in late 1983 and remain incomplete
Other political or pressure groups: groups that generally support the Islamic Republic include Hizballah, Hojjatiyeh Society, Mojahedin of the Islamic Revolution, Muslim Students Following the Line of the Imam; armed political groups that have been almost completely repressed by the government include Mojahedin Khalq Organization (MKO), People's Fedayeen, and Kurdish Democratic Party; the Society for the Defense of Freedom is a group of liberal nationalists that has been repressed by the government for accusing it of corruption
Member of: CCC, CP, ESCAP, FAO, G-19, G-24, G-77, IAEA, IBRD, ICAO, ICC, IDA, IDB, IFAD, IFC, ILO, IMF, IMO, INMARSAT, INTELSAT, INTERPOL, IOC, ISO, ITU, LORCS, NAM, OIC, OPEC, PCA, UN, UNCTAD, UNESCO, UNHCR, UNIDO, UPU, WFTU, WHO, WMO, WTO
Diplomatic representation: none; protecting power in the US is Algeria—Iranian Interests Section, 2209 Wisconsin Avenue NW, Washington DC 20007; telephone (202) 965-4990;
US—protecting power in Iran is Switzerland

Flag: three equal horizontal bands of green (top), white, and red; the national emblem (a stylized representation of the word Allah) in red is centered in the white band; *Allah Akbar* (God is Great) in white Arabic script is repeated 11 times along the bottom edge of the green band and 11 times along the top edge of the red band

Economy

Overview: Since the 1979 revolution, the banks, petroleum industry, transportation, utilities, and mining have been nationalized, but the new five-year plan—the first since the revolution—passed in January 1990, calls for the transfer of many government-controlled enterprises to the private sector. Disruptions from the bitter war with Iraq, massive corruption, mismanagement, demographic pressures, and ideological rigidities have kept economic growth at depressed levels. Oil accounts for over 90% of export revenues. A combination of war damage and low oil prices brought a 2% drop in GNP in 1988. GNP probably rose slightly in 1989, considerably short of the 3.2% population growth rate in 1989. Heating oil and gasoline are rationed. Agriculture has suffered from the war, land reform, and shortages of equipment and materials. The five-year plan seeks to reinvigorate the economy by increasing the role of the private sector, boosting nonoil income, and securing foreign loans. The plan is overly ambitious but probably will generate some short-term relief.
GNP: $80.0 billion, per capita $1,400; real growth rate 0.5% (1990 est.)
Inflation rate (consumer prices): 30-50% (1989 est.)
Unemployment rate: 30% (1989)
Budget: revenues $63 billion; expenditures $80 billion, including capital expenditures of $23 billion (FY90 est.)
Exports: $12.3 billion (f.o.b., 1989); *commodities*—petroleum 90%, carpets, fruits, nuts, hides; *partners*—Japan, Turkey, Italy, Netherlands, Spain, France, FRG
Imports: $11.6 billion (c.i.f., 1989); *commodities*—machinery, military supplies, metal works, foodstuffs, pharmaceuticals, technical services, refined oil products; *partners*—FRG, Japan, Turkey, UK, Italy
External debt: $4-5 billion (1989)
Industrial production: growth rate NA%
Electricity: 14,579,000 kW capacity; 40,000 million kWh produced, 740 kWh per capita (1989)
Industries: petroleum, petrochemicals, textiles, cement and other building materials, food processing (particularly sugar refining and vegetable oil production), metal fabricating (steel and copper)

Agriculture: principal products—wheat, rice, other grains, sugar beets, fruits, nuts, cotton, dairy products, wool, caviar; not self-sufficient in food
Illicit drugs: illicit producer of opium poppy for the domestic and international drug trade
Economic aid: US commitments, including Ex-Im (FY70-80), $1.0 billion; Western (non-US) countries, ODA and OOF bilateral commitments (1970-88), $1.6 billion; Communist countries (1970-89), $976 million; note—aid fell sharply following the 1979 revolution
Currency: Iranian rial (plural—rials); 1 Iranian rial (IR) = 100 dinars; note—domestic figures are generally referred to in terms of the toman (plural—tomans), which equals 10 rials
Exchange rates: Iranian rials (IR) per US$1—64.941 (January 1991), 68.096 (1990), 72.015 (1989), 68.683 (1988), 71.460 (1987), 78.760 (1986), 91.052 (1985) at the official rate; black market rate 1,400 (January 1991)
Fiscal year: 21 March-20 March

Communications

Railroads: 4,601 km total; 4,509 km 1.432-meter gauge, 92 km 1.676-meter gauge; 730 km under construction from Bafq to Bandar Abbas
Highways: 140,072 km total; 46,866 km gravel and crushed stone; 49,440 km improved earth; 42,566 km bituminous and bituminous-treated surfaces; 1,200 km (est.) rural road network
Inland waterways: 904 km; the Shatt al Arab is usually navigable by maritime traffic for about 130 km, but closed since September 1980 because of Iran-Iraq war
Pipelines: crude oil, 5,900 km; refined products, 3,900 km; natural gas, 3,300 km
Ports: Abadan (largely destroyed in fighting during 1980-88 war), Bandar Beheshtī, Bandar-e Abbas, Bandar-e Būshehr, Bandar-e Khomeyni, Bandar-e Shahīd Rāja'ī, Khorramshahr (largely destroyed in fighting during 1980-88 war)
Merchant marine: 133 ships (1,000 GRT or over) totaling 4,634,204 GRT/8,671,769 DWT; includes 36 cargo, 6 roll-on/roll-off cargo, 33 petroleum, oils, and lubricants (POL) tanker, 4 chemical tanker, 3 refrigerated cargo, 49 bulk, 2 combination bulk
Civil air: 42 major transport aircraft
Airports: 214 total, 186 usable; 80 with permanent-surface runways; 17 with runways over 3,659 m; 16 with runways 2,440-3,659 m; 70 with runways 1,220-2,439 m
Telecommunications: radio relay extends throughout country; system centered in Tehrān; 2,143,000 telephones; stations—62 AM, 30 FM, 250 TV; satellite earth stations—2 Atlantic Ocean INTELSAT and 1

Indian Ocean INTELSAT; HF and microwave to Turkey, Pakistan, Syria, Kuwait, and USSR

Defense Forces

Branches: Islamic Republic of Iran Ground Forces, Navy, Air Force, Air Defense, and Revolutionary Guard Corps (includes Basij militia and own ground, air, and naval forces); a merger of the Komiteh, Police, and Gendarmerie has produced a new Security Forces of the Islamic Republic of Iran
Manpower availability: males 15-49, 12,750,593; 7,588,711 fit for military service; 576,321 reach military age (21) annually
Defense expenditures: $13 billion, 13.3% of GNP (1991 est.)

147

Iraq

200 km

Mosul · Irbīl
Karkūk ·
Sāmarrā ·
BAGHDĀD ★
Ar Ruṭbah · Karbalā · · Al Kūt
An Nāṣirīyah ·
Al Baṣrah ·

Persian Gulf

Geography

Total area: 434,920 km²; land area: 433,970 km²
Comparative area: slightly more than twice the size of Idaho
Land boundaries: 3,454 km total; Iran 1,458 km, Iraq –Saudi Arabia Neutral Zone 191 km, Jordan 134 km, Kuwait 240 km, Saudi Arabia 495 km, Syria 605 km, Turkey 331 km
Coastline: 58 km
Maritime claims:
Continental shelf: not specific;
Territorial sea: 12 nm
Disputes: Iran and Iraq restored diplomatic relations on 14 October 1990 following the end of the war that began on 22 September 1980; progress had been made on the major issues of contention—troop withdrawal, prisoner-of-war exchanges, demarcation of the border, freedom of navigation, and sovereignty over the Shatt al Arab waterway— but written agreements had yet to be drawn up when frictions reemerged in March 1991 in the wake of Shi'a and Kurdish revolts in Iraq that Baghdād accused Tehrān of supporting; Kurdish question among Iran, Iraq, Syria, Turkey, and the USSR; shares Neutral Zone with Saudi Arabia—in December 1981, Iraq and Saudi Arabia signed a boundary agreement that divides the zone between them, but the agreement must be ratified before it becomes effective; Iraqi forces invaded and occupied Kuwait from 2 August 1990 until 27 February 1991; in April 1991 official Iraqi acceptance of UN Security Council Resolution 687, which demands that Iraq accept its internationally recognized border with Kuwait, ended earlier claims to Būbiyān and Warbah Islands or to all of Kuwait; periodic disputes with upstream riparian Syria over Euphrates water rights; potential dispute over water development plans by Turkey for the Tigris and Euphrates Rivers

Climate: desert; mild to cool winters with dry, hot, cloudless summers
Terrain: mostly broad plains; reedy marshes in southeast; mountains along borders with Iran and Turkey
Natural resources: crude oil, natural gas, phosphates, sulfur
Land use: arable land 12%; permanent crops 1%; meadows and pastures 9%; forest and woodland 3%; other 75%; includes irrigated 4%
Environment: development of Tigris-Euphrates river systems contingent upon agreements with upstream riparians (Syria, Turkey); air and water pollution; soil degradation (salinization) and erosion; desertification

People

Population: 19,524,718 (July 1991), growth rate 3.9% (1991)
Birth rate: 46 births/1,000 population (1991)
Death rate: 7 deaths/1,000 population (1991)
Net migration rate: 0 migrants/1,000 population (1991)
Infant mortality rate: 66 deaths/1,000 live births (1991)
Life expectancy at birth: 66 years male, 68 years female (1991)
Total fertility rate: 7.2 children born/woman (1991)
Nationality: noun—Iraqi(s); adjective— Iraqi
Ethnic divisions: Arab 75-80%, Kurdish 15-20%, Turkoman, Assyrian or other 5%
Religion: Muslim 97% (Shi'a 60-65%, Sunni 32-37%), Christian or other 3%
Language: Arabic (official), Kurdish (official in Kurdish regions), Assyrian, Armenian
Literacy: 60% (male 70%, female 49%) age 15 and over can read and write (1990 est.)
Labor force: 4,400,000 (1989); services 48%, agriculture 30%, industry 22%, severe labor shortage; expatriate labor force about 1,600,000 (July 1990)
Organized labor: less than 10% of the labor force

Government

Long-form name: Republic of Iraq
Type: republic
Capital: Baghdād
Administrative divisions: 18 provinces (muḥāfaẕat, singular—muḥāfaẕah); Al Anbār, Al Baṣrah, Al Muthanná, Al Qādisīyah, An Najaf, Arbīl, As Sulaymānīyah, At Ta'mīm, Bābil, Baghdād, Dahūk, Dhī Qār, Diyālá, Karbalā', Maysān, Nīnawá, Ṣalāḥ ad Dīn, Wāsiṭ

Independence: 3 October 1932 (from League of Nations mandate under British administration)
Constitution: 22 September 1968, effective 16 July 1970 (interim Constitution); new constitution drafted in 1990 but not adopted
Legal system: based on Islamic law in special religious courts, civil law system elsewhere; has not accepted compulsory ICJ jurisdiction
National holiday: Anniversary of the Revolution, 17 July (1968)
Executive branch: president, vice president, chairman of the Revolutionary Command Council, vice chairman of the Revolutionary Command Council, prime minister, first deputy prime minister, Council of Ministers
Legislative branch: unicameral National Assembly (Majlis Watani)
Judicial branch: Court of Cassation
Leaders:
Chief of State—President Saddam HUSAYN (since 16 July 1979); Vice President Taha Muhyi al-Din MA'RUF (since 21 April 1974); Vice President Taha Yasin RAMADAN (since 23 March 1991);
Head of Government—Prime Minister Sa-d'un HAMMADI (since 27 March 1991); Deputy Prime Minister Tariq 'AZIZ (since NA 1979); Deputy Prime Minister Muhammad Hamza al-ZUBAYDI (since 27 March 1991)
Political parties: National Progressive Front is a coalition of the Arab Ba'th Socialist Party, Kurdistan Democratic Party, and Kurdistan Revolutionary Party
Suffrage: universal adult at age 18
Elections:
National Assembly—last held on 1 April 1989 (next to be held NA); results—Sunni Arabs 53%, Shi'a Arabs 30%, Kurds 15%, Christians 2% est.; seats—(250 total) number of seats by party NA
Communists: about 1,500 hardcore members
Other political or pressure groups: political parties and activity severely restricted; possibly some opposition to regime from disaffected members of the regime, Army officers, and religious and ethnic dissidents
Member of: ABEDA, ACC, AFESD, AL, AMF, CAEU, ESCWA, FAO, G-19, G-77, IAEA, IBRD, ICAO, IDA, IDB, IFAD, IFC, ILO, IMF, IMO, INMARSAT, INTELSAT, INTERPOL, IOC, ISO, ITU, LORCS, NAM, OAPEC, OIC, OPEC, PCA, UN, UNCTAD, UNESCO, UNIDO, UPU, WFTU, WHO, WIPO, WMO, WTO
Diplomatic representation: no Iraqi representative in Washington; Chancery at 1801 P Street NW, Washington DC 20036; telephone (202) 483-7500;

US—no US representative in Baghdad since mid-January 1991; Embassy in Masbah Quarter (opposite the Foreign Ministry Club), Baghdad (mailing address is P. O. Box 2447 Alwiyah, Baghdad); telephone [964] (1) 719-6138 or 719-6139, 718-1840, 719-3791

Flag: three equal horizontal bands of red (top), white, and black with three green five-pointed stars in a horizontal line centered in the white band; the phrase Allahu Akbar (God is Great) in green Arabic script—Allahu to the right of the middle star and Akbar to the left of the middle star—was added in January 1991 during the Persian Gulf crisis; similar to the flag of Syria that has two stars but no script and the flag of Yemen that has a plain white band; also similar to the flag of Egypt that has a symbolic eagle centered in the white band

Economy

Overview: The Ba'thist regime engages in extensive central planning and management of industrial production and foreign trade while leaving some small-scale industry and services and most agriculture to private enterprise. The economy has been dominated by the oil sector, which has provided about 95% of foreign exchange earnings. In the 1980s financial problems, caused by massive expenditures in the eight-year war with Iran and damage to oil export facilities by Iran, led the government to implement austerity measures and to borrow heavily and later reschedule foreign debt payments. After the end of hostilities in 1988, oil exports gradually increased with the construction of new pipelines and restoration of damaged facilities. Agricultural development remained hampered by labor shortages, salinization, and dislocations caused by previous land reform and collectivization programs. The industrial sector, although accorded high priority by the government, also was under financial constraints. Iraq's seizure of Kuwait in August 1990, subsequent international economic embargoes, and military actions by an international coalition beginning in January 1991 drastically changed the economic picture. Oil exports were cut to near zero, and industrial and transportation facilities severely damaged.

GNP: $35 billion, per capita $1,940; real growth rate 5% (1989 est.)

Inflation rate (consumer prices): 30-40% (1989 est.)

Unemployment rate: less than 5% (1989 est.)

Budget: revenues $NA billion; expenditures $35 billion, including capital expenditures of NA (1989)

Exports: $12.1 billion (f.o.b., 1989);

commodities—crude oil and refined products, fertilizer, sulfur;
partners—US, Brazil, Turkey, Japan, France, Italy, USSR (1989)

Imports: $10.3 billion (c.i.f., 1989);
commodities—manufactures, food;
partners—US, FRG, Turkey, UK, Romania, Japan, France (1989)

External debt: $40 billion (1989 est.), excluding debt to Arab Gulf states

Industrial production: NA%; manufacturing accounts for 10% of GDP (1987)

Electricity: 9,902,000 kW capacity; 20,000 million kWh produced, 1,110 kWh per capita (1989)

Industries: petroleum, chemicals, textiles, construction materials, food processing

Agriculture: accounts for 11% of GNP but 30% of labor force; principal products—wheat, barley, rice, vegetables, dates, other fruit, cotton, wool; livestock—cattle, sheep; not self-sufficient in food output

Economic aid: US commitments, including Ex-Im (FY70-80), $3 million; Western (non-US) countries, ODA and OOF bilateral commitments (1970-88), $627 million; OPEC bilateral aid (1980-90), more than $30 billion; Communist countries (1970-89), $3.9 billion

Currency: Iraqi dinar (plural—dinars); 1 Iraqi dinar (ID) = 1,000 fils

Exchange rates: Iraqi dinars (ID) per US$1—0.3109 (fixed rate since 1982)

Fiscal year: calendar year

Communications

Railroads: 2,962 km total; 2,457 km 1.435-meter standard gauge, 505 km 1.000-meter gauge

Highways: 25,479 km total; 8,290 km paved, 5,534 km improved earth, 11,655 km unimproved earth

Inland waterways: 1,015 km; Shatt al Arab usually navigable by maritime traffic for about 130 km, but closed since September 1980 because of Iran-Iraq war; Tigris and Euphrates navigable by shallow-draft steamers (of little importance); Shatt al Başrah canal navigable in sections by shallow-draft vessels

Ports: Umm Qasr, Khawr az Zubayr, Al Başrah

Merchant marine: 43 ships (1,000 GRT or over) totaling 944,253 GRT/1,691,368 DWT; includes 1 passenger, 1 passenger-cargo, 17 cargo, 1 refrigerated cargo, 3 roll-on/roll-off cargo, 19 petroleum, oils, and lubricants (POL) tanker, 1 chemical tanker; note—since the 2 August 1990 invasion of Kuwait by Iraqi forces, Iraq has sought to register at least part of its merchant fleet under convenience flags; none of the Iraqi flag merchant fleet was trading internationally as of 1 January 1991

Pipelines: crude oil, 4,350 km; 725 km refined products; 1,360 km natural gas

Civil air: 64 major transport aircraft (including 30 IL-76s used by the Iraq Air Force)

Airports: 111 total, 102 usable; 73 with permanent-surface runways; 9 with runways over 3,659 m; 52 with runways 2,440-3,659 m; 15 with runways 1,220-2,439 m

Telecommunications: good network consists of coaxial cables, radio relay links, and radiocommunication stations; 632,000 telephones; stations—9 AM, 1 FM, 81 TV; satellite earth stations—1 Atlantic Ocean INTELSAT, 1 Indian Ocean INTELSAT, 1 GORIZONT Atlantic Ocean in the Intersputnik system; coaxial cable and radio relay to Kuwait, Jordan, Syria, and Turkey

Defense Forces

Branches: Army and Republican Guard, Navy, Air Force, Border Guard Force, Internal Security Forces

Manpower availability: males 15-49, 4,270,592; 2,380,439 fit for military service; 228,277 reach military age (18) annually

Defense expenditures: $NA, NA% of GDP

Iraq–Saudi Arabia Neutral Zone

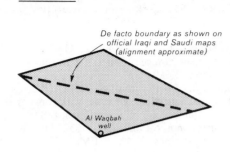

50 km

De facto boundary as shown on official Iraqi and Saudi maps (alignment approximate)

Al Waqbah well

Geography

Total area: 3,520 km²; land area: 3,520 km²
Comparative area: slightly larger than Rhode Island
Land boundaries: 389 km total; 191 km Iraq, 198 km Saudi Arabia
Coastline: none—landlocked
Maritime claims: none—landlocked
Climate: harsh, dry desert
Terrain: sandy desert
Natural resources: none
Land use: arable land 0%; permanent crops 0%; meadows and pastures 0%; forest and woodland 0%; other (sandy desert) 100%
Environment: harsh, inhospitable
Note: landlocked; located west of quadripoint with Iraq, Kuwait, and Saudi Arabia

People

Population: uninhabited

Government

Long-form name: none
Type: joint administration by Iraq and Saudi Arabia; in December 1981, Iraq and Saudi Arabia signed a boundary agreement that divides the zone between them, but the agreement must be ratified before it becomes effective

Economy

Overview: no economic activity

Communications

Highways: none; some secondary roads

Defense Forces

Note: defense is the joint responsibility of Iraq and Saudi Arabia

Ireland

100 km

Lifford
Sligo
Monaghan
Castlebar
Irish Sea
Galway
DUBLIN
Tullamore
Wicklow
North Atlantic Ocean
Limerick
Waterford
Killarney
Cork

Geography

Total area: 70,280 km²; land area: 68,890 km²
Comparative area: slightly larger than West Virginia
Land boundary: 360 km with UK
Coastline: 1,448 km
Maritime claims:
Continental shelf: no precise definition;
Exclusive fishing zone: 200 nm;
Territorial sea: 12 nm
Disputes: Northern Ireland question with the UK; Rockall continental shelf dispute involving Denmark, Iceland, and the UK (Ireland and the UK have signed a boundary agreement in the Rockall area)
Climate: temperate maritime; modified by North Atlantic Current; mild winters, cool summers; consistently humid; overcast about half the time
Terrain: mostly level to rolling interior plain surrounded by rugged hills and low mountains; sea cliffs on west coast
Natural resources: zinc, lead, natural gas, crude oil, barite, copper, gypsum, limestone, dolomite, peat, silver
Land use: arable land 14%; permanent crops NEGL%; meadows and pastures 71%; forest and woodland 5%; other 10%
Environment: deforestation

People

Population: 3,489,165 (July 1991), growth rate −0.3% (1991)
Birth rate: 15 births/1,000 population (1991)
Death rate: 9 deaths/1,000 population (1991)
Net migration rate: −9 migrants/1,000 population (1991)
Infant mortality rate: 6 deaths/1,000 live births (1991)
Life expectancy at birth: 73 years male, 79 years female (1991)
Total fertility rate: 2.1 children born/woman (1991)
Nationality: noun—Irishman(men), Irish (collective pl.); adjective—Irish
Ethnic divisions: Celtic, with English minority
Religion: Roman Catholic 93%, Anglican 3%, none 1%, unknown 2%, other 1% (1981)
Language: Irish (Gaelic) and English; English is the language generally used, with Gaelic spoken in a few areas, mostly along the western seaboard
Literacy: 98% (male NA%, female NA%) age 15 and over can read and write (1981 est.)
Labor force: 1,293,000; services 57.0%, manufacturing and construction 26.1%, agriculture, forestry, and fishing 15.0%, energy and mining 1.9% (1988)
Organized labor: 36% of labor force

Government

Long-form name: none
Type: republic
Capital: Dublin
Administrative divisions: 26 counties; Carlow, Cavan, Clare, Cork, Donegal, Dublin, Galway, Kerry, Kildare, Kilkenny, Laois, Leitrim, Limerick, Longford, Louth, Mayo, Meath, Monaghan, Offaly, Roscommon, Sligo, Tipperary, Waterford, Westmeath, Wexford, Wicklow
Independence: 6 December 1921 (from UK)
Constitution: 29 December 1937; adopted 1937
Legal system: based on English common law, substantially modified by indigenous concepts; judicial review of legislative acts in Supreme Court; has not accepted compulsory ICJ jurisdiction
National holiday: Saint Patrick's Day, 17 March
Executive branch: president, prime minister, deputy prime minister, Cabinet
Legislative branch: bicameral Parliament (Oireachtas) consists of an upper house or Senate (Seanad Éireann) and a lower house or House of Representatives (Dáil Éireann)
Judicial branch: Supreme Court
Leaders:
Chief of State—President Mary Bourke ROBINSON (since 9 November 1990);
Head of Government—Prime Minister Charles J. HAUGHEY (since 12 July 1989, the fourth time elected as Prime Minister)
Political parties and leaders: Fianna Fail, Charles HAUGHEY; Labor Party, Richard SPRING; Fine Gael, John BRUTON; Communist Party of Ireland, Michael O'RIORDAN; Workers' Party, Proinsias DEROSSA; Sinn Fein, Gerry ADAMS; Progressive Democrats, Desmond O'MALLEY; note—Prime Minister HAUGHEY heads a coalition consisting of the Fianna Fail and the Progressive Democrats
Suffrage: universal at age 18

President—last held 9 November 1990 (next to be held November 1997); results—Mary Bourke ROBINSON 52.8%, Brian LENIHAN 47.2%;

Senate—last held on 17 February 1987 (next to be held February 1992); results—percent of vote by party NA; seats—(60 total, 49 elected) Fianna Fail 30, Fine Gael 16, Labor 3, Independents 11;

House of Representatives—last held on 12 July 1989 (next to be held NA June 1994); results—Fianna Fail 44.0%, Fine Gael 29.4%, Labor Party 9.3%, Progressive Democrats 5.4%, Workers' Party 4.9%, Sinn Fein 1.1%, independents 5.9%; seats—(166 total) Fianna Fail 77, Fine Gael 55, Labor Party 15, Workers' Party 7, Progressive Democrats 6, independents 6

Communists: under 500

Member of: BIS, CCC, CE, CSCE, EBRD, EC, ECE, EIB, ESA, FAO, GATT, IAEA, IBRD, ICAO, ICC, IDA, IEA, IFAD, IFC, ILO, IMF, IMO, INTELSAT, INTERPOL, IOC, ISO, ITU, LORCS, NEA, OECD, UN, UNCTAD, UNESCO, UNFICYP, UNIDO, UNIFIL, UNIIMOG, UNTSO, UPU, WHO, WIPO, WMO

Diplomatic representation: Ambassador Padraic N. MACKERNAN; Chancery at 2234 Massachusetts Avenue NW, Washington DC 20008; telephone (202) 462-3939; there are Irish Consulates General in Boston, Chicago, New York, and San Francisco; *US*—Ambassador Richard A. MOORE; Embassy at 42 Elgin Road, Ballsbridge, Dublin; telephone [353] (1) 688777

Flag: three equal vertical bands of green (hoist side), white, and orange; similar to the flag of the Ivory Coast which is shorter and has the colors reversed—orange (hoist side), white, and green; also similar to the flag of Italy which is shorter and has colors of green (hoist side), white, and red

---

Economy

Overview: The economy is small, open, and trade dependent. Agriculture, once the most important sector, is now dwarfed by industry, which accounts for 37% of GDP and about 80% of exports and employs 26% of the labor force. The government has successfully reduced the rate of inflation from double-digit figures in the late 1970s to 3.3% in 1990. In 1987, after years of deficits, the balance of payments was brought into the black. Unemployment, however, is a serious problem. A 1990 unemployment rate of 16.6% placed Ireland along with Spain as the countries with the worst jobless records in Western Europe.

GDP: $33.9 billion, per capita $9,690; real growth rate 4.1% (1990)

Inflation rate (consumer prices): 3.3% (1990)

Unemployment rate: 16.6% (1990)

Budget: revenues $11.3 billion; expenditures $11.7 billion, including capital expenditures of $1.6 billion (1990)

Exports: $24.6 billion (f.o.b., 1990); *commodities*—chemicals, data processing equipment, industrial machinery, live animals, animal products; *partners*—EC 74% (UK 34%, FRG 11%, France 10%), US 8%

Imports: $20.7 billion (c.i.f., 1990); *commodities*—food, animal feed, chemicals, petroleum and petroleum products, machinery, textiles, clothing; *partners*—EC 66% (UK 41%, FRG 9%, France 4%), US 16%

External debt: $16.0 billion (1990)

Industrial production: growth rate 4.7% (1990); accounts for 37% of GDP

Electricity: 4,957,000 kW capacity; 14,480 million kWh produced, 4,080 kWh per capita (1989)

Industries: food products, brewing, textiles, clothing, chemicals, pharmaceuticals, machinery, transportation equipment, glass and crystal

Agriculture: accounts for 10% of GNP and 15% of the labor force; principal crops—turnips, barley, potatoes, sugar beets, wheat; livestock—meat and dairy products; 85% self-sufficient in food; food shortages include bread grain, fruits, vegetables

Economic aid: donor—ODA commitments (1980-89), $90 million

Currency: Irish pound (plural—pounds); 1 Irish pound (£Ir) = 100 pence

Exchange rates: Irish pounds (£Ir) per US$1—0.5656 (January 1991), 0.6030 (1990), 0.7472 (1989), 0.6553 (1988), 0.6720 (1987), 0.7454 (1986), 0.9384 (1985)

Fiscal year: calendar year

Communications

Railroads: Irish National Railways (CIE) operates 1,947 km 1.602-meter gauge, government owned; 485 km double track; 38 km electrified

Highways: 92,294 km total; 87,422 km surfaced, 4,872 km gravel or crushed stone

Inland waterways: limited for commercial traffic

Pipelines: natural gas, 225 km

Ports: Cork, Dublin, Shannon Estuary, Waterford

Merchant marine: 53 ships (1,000 GRT or over) totaling 138,967 GRT/164,628 DWT; includes 4 short-sea passenger, 31 cargo, 2 refrigerated cargo, 3 container, 2 petroleum, oils, and lubricants (POL) tanker, 3 specialized tanker, 2 chemical tanker, 6 bulk

Civil air: 23 major transport aircraft

Airports: 40 total, 37 usable; 18 with permanent-surface runways; none with runways over 3,659 m; 2 with runways 2,440-3,659 m; 6 with runways 1,220-2,439 m

Telecommunications: small, modern system using cable and radio relay circuits; 900,000 telephones; stations—45 AM, 16 (29 relays) FM, 18 (68 relays) TV; 5 coaxial submarine cables; 2 Atlantic Ocean INTELSAT earth stations

---

Defense Forces

Branches: Army (including Naval Service and Air Corps), National Police (GARDA)

Manpower availability: males 15-49, 871,578; 705,642 fit for military service; 33,175 reach military age (17) annually

Defense expenditures: $458 million, 1.6% of GDP (1990 est.)

Israel *(also see separate Gaza Strip and West Bank entries)*

100 km

Haifa
Nazareth
Lake Tiberias
Mediterranean Sea
Tel Aviv-Yafo
Ashdod
Jerusalem
Dead Sea
Beersheba
Elat

Boundary representation is not necessarily authoritative

Note: The Arab territories occupied by Israel since the 1967 war are not included in the data below. As stated in the 1978 Camp David Accords and reaffirmed by President Reagan's 1 September 1982 peace initiative, the final status of the West Bank and Gaza Strip, their relationship with their neighbors, and a peace treaty between Israel and Jordan are to be negotiated among the concerned parties. The Camp David Accords further specify that these negotiations will resolve the location of the respective boundaries. Pending the completion of this process, it is US policy that the final status of the West Bank and Gaza Strip has yet to be determined (see West Bank and Gaza Strip entries). On 25 April 1982 Israel relinquished control of the Sinai to Egypt. Statistics for the Israeli-occupied Golan Heights are included in the Syria entry.

Geography

Total area: 20,770 km²; land area: 20,330 km²
Comparative area: slightly larger than New Jersey
Land boundaries: 1,006 km total; Egypt 255 km, Jordan 238 km, Lebanon 79 km, Syria 76 km, West Bank 307 km, Gaza Strip 51 km
Coastline: 273 km
Maritime claims:
Continental shelf: to depth of exploitation;
Territorial sea: 6 nm
Disputes: separated from Lebanon, Syria, and the West Bank by the 1949 Armistice Line; differences with Jordan over the location of the 1949 Armistice Line which separates the two countries; West Bank and Gaza Strip are Israeli occupied with status to be determined; Golan Heights is Israeli occupied; Israeli troops in southern Lebanon since June 1982; water-sharing issues with Jordan
Climate: temperate; hot and dry in desert areas
Terrain: Negev desert in the south; low coastal plain; central mountains; Jordan Rift Valley

Natural resources: copper, phosphates, bromide, potash, clay, sand, sulfur, asphalt, manganese, small amounts of natural gas and crude oil
Land use: arable land 17%; permanent crops 5%; meadows and pastures 40%; forest and woodland 6%; other 32%; includes irrigated 11%
Environment: sandstorms may occur during spring and summer; limited arable land and natural water resources pose serious constraints; deforestation
Note: there are 175 Jewish settlements in the West Bank, 38 in the Israeli-occupied Golan Heights, 18 in the Gaza Strip, and 14 Israeli-built Jewish neighborhoods in East Jerusalem

People

Population: 4,477,105 (July 1991), growth rate 1.5% (1991); includes 90,000 Jewish settlers in the West Bank, 13,000 in the Israeli-occupied Golan Heights, 2,500 in the Gaza Strip, and 120,000 in East Jerusalem (1990 est.)
Birth rate: 21 births/1,000 population (1991)
Death rate: 6 deaths/1,000 population (1991)
Net migration rate: 0 migrants/1,000 population (1991)
Infant mortality rate: 9 deaths/1,000 live births (1991)
Life expectancy at birth: 76 years male, 79 years female (1991)
Total fertility rate: 2.9 children born/woman (1991)
Nationality: noun—Israeli(s); adjective—Israeli
Ethnic divisions: Jewish 83%, non-Jewish (mostly Arab) 17%
Religion: Judaism 82%, Islam (mostly Sunni Muslim) 14%, Christian 2%, Druze and other 2%
Language: Hebrew (official); Arabic used officially for Arab minority; English most commonly used foreign language
Literacy: 92% (male 95%, female 89%) age 15 and over can read and write (1983)
Labor force: 1,400,000 (1984 est.); public services 29.3%; industry, mining, and manufacturing 22.8%; commerce 12.8%; finance and business 9.5%; transport, storage, and communications 6.8%; construction and public works 6.5%; personal and other services 5.8%; agriculture, forestry, and fishing 5.5%; electricity and water 1.0% (1983)
Organized labor: 90% of labor force

Government

Long-form name: State of Israel
Type: republic
Capital: Israel proclaimed Jerusalem its capital in 1950, but the US, like nearly all

other countries, maintains its Embassy in Tel Aviv
Administrative divisions: 6 districts (mehozot, singular—mehoz); Central, Haifa, Jerusalem, Northern, Southern, Tel Aviv
Independence: 14 May 1948 (from League of Nations mandate under British administration)
Constitution: no formal constitution; some of the functions of a constitution are filled by the Declaration of Establishment (1948), the basic laws of the parliament (Knesset), and the Israeli citizenship law
Legal system: mixture of English common law, British Mandate regulations, and, in personal matters, Jewish, Christian, and Muslim legal systems; in December 1985 Israel informed the UN Secretariat that it would no longer accept compulsory ICJ jurisdiction
National holiday: Independence Day, 10 May 1989; Israel declared independence on 14 May 1948, but the Jewish calendar is lunar and the holiday may occur in April or May
Executive branch: president, prime minister, vice prime minister, Cabinet
Legislative branch: unicameral parliament (Knesset)
Judicial branch: Supreme Court
Leaders:
Chief of State—President Chaim HERZOG (since 5 May 1983);
Head of Government—Prime Minister Yitzhak SHAMIR (since 20 October 1986)
Political parties and leaders: Israel currently has a coalition government comprising eleven parties that hold 66 of the Knesset's 120 seats;
Members of the government—Likud bloc, Prime Minister Yitzhak SHAMIR; Sephardic Torah Guardians (SHAS), Minister of Interior Arieh DER'I; National Religious Party, Minister of Education Zevulun HAMMER; Agudat Yisrael, Moshe Zeev FELDMAN; Degel HaTorah, Avraham RAVITZ; Moriya, Minister of Immigrant Absorption, Yitzhak PERETZ; Ge'vlat Yisrael, Elizer MIZRAHI; Party for the Advancement of Zionist Ideology (PAZI), Minister of Finance Yitzhak MODAI; Tehiya Party, Minister of Science, Technology, Energy, and Infrastructure Yuval NE'EMAN; Tzomet Party, Minister of Agriculture Rafael EITAN; Unity for Peace and Aliyah, Efrayim GUR; Moledet Party, Rehavam ZE'EVI;
Opposition parties—Labor Party, Shimon PERES; Citizens' Rights Movement, Shulamit ALONI; United Workers' Party (MAPAM), Yair TZABAN; Center Movement-Shinui, Amnon RUBENSTEIN; New Israeli Communist Party (MAKI), Meir WILNER; Progressive List for Peace, Muhammad MI'ARI; Arab Democratic Party, 'Abd Al Wahab DARAWSHAH; Black Panthers, Charlie BITON

152

Suffrage: universal at age 18
Elections:
President—last held 23 February 1988 (next to be held February 1994); results—Chaim HERZOG reelected by Knesset;
Knesset—last held 1 November 1988 (next to be held by November 1992); seats—(120 total) Labor Party 38, Likud bloc 37, SHAS 5, National Religious Party 5, Citizens' Rights Movement 5, Agudat Yisrael 4, PAZI 3, MAKI 3, Tehiya Party 3, MAPAM 3, Tzomet Party 2, Moledet Party 2, Degel HaTorah 2, Center Movement-Shinui 2, Progressive List for Peace 1, Arab Democratic Party 1; Black Panthers 1, Moriya 1, Ge'ulat Yisrael 1, Unity for Peace and Aliyah 1
Communists: Hadash (predominantly Arab but with Jews in its leadership) has some 1,500 members
Other political or pressure groups: Gush Emunim, Jewish nationalists advocating Jewish settlement on the West Bank and Gaza Strip; Peace Now, critical of government's West Bank/Gaza Strip and Lebanon policies
Member of: AG (observer), CCC, EBRD, FAO, GATT, IADB, IAEA, IBRD, ICAO, ICC, ICFTU, IDA, IFAD, IFC, ILO, IMF, IMO, INMARSAT, INTELSAT, INTERPOL, IOC, IOM, ISO, ITU, OAS (observer), PCA, UN, UNCTAD, UNESCO, UNHCR, UNIDO, UPU, WHO, WIPO, WMO, WTO
Diplomatic representation: Ambassador Zalman SHOVAL; Chancery at 3514 International Drive NW, Washington DC 20008; telephone (202) 364-5500; there are Israeli Consulates General in Atlanta, Boston, Chicago, Houston, Los Angeles, Miami, New York, Philadelphia, and San Francisco;
US—Ambassador William A. BROWN; Embassy at 71 Hayarkon Street, Tel Aviv (mailing address is APO New York 09672); telephone [972] (3) 654338; there is a US Consulate General in Jerusalem
Flag: white with a blue hexagram (six-pointed linear star) known as the Magen David (Shield of David) centered between two equal horizontal blue bands near the top and bottom edges of the flag

Economy

Overview: Israel has a market economy with substantial government participation. It depends on imports for crude oil, food, grains, raw materials, and military equipment. Despite limited natural resources, Israel has developed its agricultural and industrial sectors on an intensive scale over the past 20 years. Industry accounts for about 23% of the labor force, agriculture for 5%, and services for most of the balance. Diamonds, high-technology machinery, and agricultural products (fruits and vegetables) are the biggest export earners. The balance of payments has traditionally been negative, but is offset by large transfer payments and foreign loans. About half of Israel's $18 billion external government debt is owed to the US, which is its major source for economic and military aid. To earn needed foreign exchange, Israel must continue to exploit high-technology niches in the international market, such as medical scanning equipment. Iraq's invasion of Kuwait on 2 August dealt a blow to Israel's economy in 1990. Higher world oil prices added an estimated $300 million to Israel's 1990 oil import bill, and helped keep the inflation rate at 18% for the year. Regional tensions and continuing acts of the Palestinian uprising (*intifadah*)-related violence contributed to a sharp dropoff in tourism—a key source of foreign exchange—to the lowest level since the 1973 Arab-Israeli war. In 1991, the influx of up to 400,000 Soviet immigrants will increase unemployment, intensify the country's housing crisis, and contribute to a widening budget deficit.
GNP: $46.5 billion, per capita $10,500; real growth rate 3.5% (1990 est.)
Inflation rate (consumer prices): 18% (1990)
Unemployment rate: 9.8% (March 1991)
Budget: revenues $28.7 billion; expenditures $33.0 billion, including capital expenditures of $NA (FY91)
Exports: $10.7 billion (f.o.b., 1989);
commodities—polished diamonds, citrus and other fruits, textiles and clothing, processed foods, fertilizer and chemical products, military hardware, electronics;
partners—US, UK, FRG, France, Belgium, Luxembourg, Italy
Imports: $14.2 billion (c.i.f., 1989 est.);
commodities—military equipment, rough diamonds, oil, chemicals, machinery, iron and steel, cereals, textiles, vehicles, ships, aircraft;
partners—US, FRG, UK, Switzerland, Italy, Belgium, Luxembourg
External debt: $24.5 billion, of which government debt is $18 billion (December 1990)
Industrial production: growth rate −1.5% (1989); accounts for about 40% of GDP
Electricity: 4,392,000 kW capacity; 17,500 million kWh produced, 4,000 kWh per capita (1989)
Industries: food processing, diamond cutting and polishing, textiles, clothing, chemicals, metal products, military equipment, transport equipment, electrical equipment, miscellaneous machinery, potash mining, high-technology electronics, tourism
Agriculture: accounts for 5% of GNP; largely self-sufficient in food production, except for bread grains; principal products—citrus and other fruits, vegetables, cotton; livestock products—beef, dairy, and poultry

Economic aid: US commitments, including Ex-Im (FY70-90), $18.2 billion; Western (non-US) countries, ODA and OOF bilateral commitments (1970-88), $2.5 billion
Currency: new Israeli shekel (plural—shekels); 1 new Israeli shekel (NIS) = 100 new agorot
Exchange rates: new Israeli shekels (NIS) per US$1—2.35 (May 1991), 2.0162 (1990), 1.9164 (1989), 1.5989 (1988), 1.5946 (1987), 1.4878 (1986), 1.1788 (1985)
Fiscal year: 1 April-31 March; changing to calender year basis starting January 1992

Communications

Railroads: 594 km 1.435-meter gauge, single track; diesel operated
Highways: 4,500 km; majority is bituminous surfaced
Pipelines: crude oil, 708 km; refined products, 290 km; natural gas, 89 km
Ports: Ashdod, Haifa, Elat
Merchant marine: 30 ships (1,000 GRT or over) totaling 516,714 GRT/611,795 DWT; includes 7 cargo, 21 container, 2 refrigerated cargo; note—Israel also maintains a significant flag of convenience fleet, which is normally at least as large as the Israeli flag fleet; the Israeli flag of convenience fleet typically includes all of its POL tankers
Civil air: 27 major transport aircraft
Airports: 51 total, 44 usable; 26 with permanent-surface runways; none with runways over 3,659 m; 6 with runways 2,440-3,659 m; 12 with runways 1,220-2,439 m
Telecommunications: most highly developed in the Middle East though not the largest; good system of coaxial cable and radio relay; 1,800,000 telephones; stations—11 AM, 24 FM, 54 TV; 2 submarine cables; satellite earth stations—2 Atlantic Ocean INTELSAT and 1 Indian Ocean INTELSAT

Defense Forces

Branches: Israel Defense Forces includes ground, naval, and air components; historically there have been no separate Israeli military services; Nahal or Pioneer Fighting Youth, Frontier Guard, Chen
Manpower availability: eligible 15-49, 2,213,808; of the 1,117,733 males 15-49, 920,449 are fit for military service; of the 1,096,075 females 15-49, 899,022 are fit for military service; 44,429 males and 42,249 females reach military age (18) annually; both sexes are liable for military service; Nahal or Pioneer Fighting Youth, Frontier Guard, Chen
Defense expenditures: $5.3 billion, 13.9% of GNP (1991); note—includes an estimated $1.8 billion in US military aid

Italy

Geography

Total area: 301,230 km²; land area: 294,020 km²; includes Sardinia and Sicily
Comparative area: slightly larger than Arizona
Land boundaries: 1,902.2 km total; Austria 430 km, France 488 km, San Marino 39 km, Switzerland 740 km, Vatican City 3.2 km, Yugoslavia 202 km
Coastline: 4,996 km
Maritime claims:
Continental shelf: 200 m (depth) or to depth of exploitation;
Territorial sea: 12 nm
Climate: predominantly Mediterranean; Alpine in far north; hot, dry in south
Terrain: mostly rugged and mountainous; some plains, coastal lowlands
Natural resources: mercury, potash, marble, sulfur, dwindling natural gas and crude oil reserves, fish, coal
Land use: arable land 32%; permanent crops 10%; meadows and pastures 17%; forest and woodland 22%; other 19%; includes irrigated 10%
Environment: regional risks include landslides, mudflows, snowslides, earthquakes, volcanic eruptions, flooding, pollution; land sinkage in Venice
Note: strategic location dominating central Mediterranean as well as southern sea and air approaches to Western Europe

People

Population: 57,772,375 (July 1991), growth rate 0.2% (1991)
Birth rate: 11 births/1,000 population (1991)
Death rate: 10 deaths/1,000 population (1991)
Net migration rate: 1 migrant/1,000 population (1991)
Infant mortality rate: 6 deaths/1,000 live births (1991)

Life expectancy at birth: 75 years male, 82 years female (1991)
Total fertility rate: 1.4 children born/woman (1991)
Nationality: noun—Italian(s); adjective—Italian
Ethnic divisions: primarily Italian but population includes small clusters of German-, French-, and Slovene-Italians in the north and Albanian-Italians and Greek-Italians in the south; Sicilians; Sardinians
Religion: nominally Roman Catholic almost 100%
Language: Italian; parts of Trentino-Alto Adige region are predominantly German speaking; significant French-speaking minority in Valle d'Aosta region; Slovene-speaking minority in the Trieste-Gorizia area
Literacy: 97% (male 98%, female 96%) age 15 and over can read and write (1990 est.)
Labor force: 23,988,000; services 58%, industry 32.2%, agriculture 9.8% (1988)
Organized labor: 40-45% of labor force (est.)

Government

Long-form name: Italian Republic
Type: republic
Capital: Rome
Administrative divisions: 20 regions (regioni, singular—regione); Abruzzi, Basilicata, Calabria, Campania, Emilia-Romagna, Friuli-Venezia Giulia, Lazio, Liguria, Lombardia, Marche, Molise, Piemonte, Puglia, Sardegna, Sicilia, Toscana, Trentino-Alto Adige, Umbria, Valle d'Aosta, Veneto
Independence: 17 March 1861, Kingdom of Italy proclaimed
Constitution: 1 January 1948
Legal system: based on civil law system, with ecclesiastical law influence; appeals treated as trials de novo; judicial review under certain conditions in Constitutional Court; has not accepted compulsory ICJ jurisdiction
National holiday: Anniversary of the Republic, 2 June (1946)
Executive branch: president, prime minister (president of the Council of Ministers)
Legislative branch: bicameral Parliament (Parlamento) consists of an upper chamber or Senate of the Republic (Senato della Repubblica) and a lower chamber or Chamber of Deputies (Camera dei Deputati)
Judicial branch: Constitutional Court (Corte Costituzionale)
Leaders:
Chief of State—President Francesco COSSIGA (since 3 July 1985);
Head of Government—Prime Minister Giulio ANDREOTTI (since 22 July 1989, heads the government for the seventh time); Deputy Prime Minister Claudio MARTELLI (since 23 July 1989)

Political parties and leaders: Christian Democratic Party (DC), Arnaldo FORLANI (general secretary), Ciriaco De MITA (president); Socialist Party (PSI), Bettino CRAXI (party secretary); Social Democratic Party (PSDI), Antonio CARIGLIA (party secretary); Liberal Party (PLI), Renato ALTISSIMO (secretary general); Democratic Party of the Left (PDS—was Communist Party, or PCI, until January 1991), Achille OCCHETTO (secretary general); Italian Social Movement (MSI), Giuseppe (Pino) RAUTI (national secretary); Republican Party (PRI), Giorgio La MALFA (political secretary); Lega Nord, Umberto BOSSI, president; Italy's 50th postwar government was formed on 13 April 1991, with Prime Minister ANDREOTTI, a Christian Democrat, presiding over a four-party coalition consisting of the Christian Democrats, Socialists, Social Democrats, and Liberals
Suffrage: universal at age 18 (except in senatorial elections, where minimum age is 25)
Elections:
Senate—last held 14-15 June 1987 (next to be held by June 1992); results—DC 33.9%, PCI 28.3%, PSI 10.7%, other 27.1%; seats—(320 total, 315 elected) DC 125, PCI 100, PSI 36, other 54;
Chamber of Deputies—last held 14-15 June 1987 (next to be held by June 1992); results—DC 34.3%, PCI 26.6%, PSI 14.3%, MSI 5.9%, PRI 3.7%, PSDI 3.0%, Radicals 2.6%, Greens 2.5%, PLI 2.1%, Proletarian Democrats 1.7%, other 3.3%; seats—(630 total) DC 234, PCI 177, PSI 94, MSI 35, PRI 21, PSDI 17, Radicals 13, Greens 13, PLI 11, Proletarian Democrats 8, other 7
Communists: 1.3 million (1990)
Other political or pressure groups: the Roman Catholic Church; three major trade union confederations (CGIL—Communist dominated, CISL—Christian Democratic, and UIL—Social Democratic, Socialist, and Republican); Italian manufacturers association (Confindustria); organized farm groups (Confcoltivatori, Confagricoltura)
Member of: AfDB, AG (observer), AsDB, BIS, CCC, CE, CERN, COCOM, CSCE, EBRD, EC, ECE, EIB, ESA, FAO, G-7, G-10, GATT, IADB, IAEA, IBRD, ICAO, ICC, ICFTU, IDA, IFAD, IEA, IFC, ILO, IMF, IMO, INMARSAT, INTELSAT, INTERPOL, IOC, IOM, ISO, ITU, LORCS, NATO, NEA, OAS (observer), OECD, PCA, UN, UNCTAD, UNESCO, UNHCR, UNIDO, UNIFIL, UNIIMOG, UNMOGIP, UNTSO, UPU, WCL, WEU, WHO, WIPO, WMO, WTO
Diplomatic representation: Ambassador Rinaldo PETRIGNANI; Chancery at 1601 Fuller Street NW, Washington DC 20009; telephone (202) 328-5500; there are Italian Consulates General in Boston, Chicago,

Houston, New Orleans, Los Angeles, Philadelphia, San Francisco, and Consulates in Detroit and Newark (New Jersey); *US*—Ambassador Peter F. SECCHIA; Embassy at Via Veneto 119/A, 00187-Rome (mailing address is APO New York 09794); telephone [39] (6) 46741; there are US Consulates General in Florence, Genoa, Milan, Naples, and Palermo (Sicily)

Flag: three equal vertical bands of green (hoist side), white, and red; similar to the flag of Ireland which is longer and is green (hoist side), white, and orange; also similar to the flag of the Ivory Coast which has the colors reversed—orange (hoist side), white, and green

---

Economy

Overview: Since World War II the economy has changed from one based on agriculture into a ranking industrial economy, with approximately the same total and per capita output as France and the UK. The country is still divided into a developed industrial north, dominated by small private companies, and an undeveloped agricultural south, dominated by large public enterprises. Services account for 48% of GDP, industry 34%, agriculture 4%, and public administration 13%. Most raw materials needed by industry and over 75% of energy requirements must be imported. The economic recovery that began in mid-1983 has continued through 1990, with the economy growing at an annual average rate of 3%. For the 1990s, Italy faces the problems of refurbishing a tottering communications system, curbing pollution in major industrial centers, and adjusting to the new competitive forces accompanying the ongoing economic integration of the European Community.

GDP: $844.7 billion, per capita $14,600; real growth rate 2.0% (1990)

Inflation rate (consumer prices): 6% (1990)

Unemployment rate: 11.0% (1990 est.)

Budget: revenues $355 billion; expenditures $448 billion, including capital expenditures of $NA (1989)

Exports: $170.4 billion (f.o.b., 1990); *commodities*—textiles, wearing apparel, metals, transportation equipment, chemicals; *partners*—EC 57%, US 8%, OPEC 4%

Imports: $182.0 billion (c.i.f., 1990); *commodities*—petroleum, industrial machinery, chemicals, metals, food, agricultural products; *partners*—EC 58%, OPEC 6%, US 5%

External debt: NA

Industrial production: growth rate –0.1% (1990); accounts for almost 35% of GDP

Electricity: 56,800,000 kW capacity; 225,000 million kWh produced, 3,900 kWh per capita (1990)

Industries: machinery, iron and steel, chemicals, food processing, textiles, motor vehicles, clothing, footwear, ceramics

Agriculture: accounts for about 4% of GDP and 10% of the work force; self-sufficient in foods other than meat and dairy products; principal crops—fruits, vegetables, grapes, potatoes, sugar beets, soybeans, grain, olives; fish catch of 388,200 metric tons in 1988

Economic aid: donor—ODA and OOF commitments (1970-89), $25.9 billion

Currency: Italian lira (plural—lire); 1 Italian lira (Lit) = 100 centesimi

Exchange rates: Italian lire (Lit) per US$1—1,134.4 (January 1991), 1,198.1 (1990), 1,372.1 (1989), 1,301.6 (1988), 1,296.1 (1987), 1,490.8 (1986), 1,909.4 (1985)

Fiscal year: calendar year

Communications

Railroads: 20,011 km total; 16,066 km 1.435-meter government-owned standard gauge (8,999 km electrified); 3,945 km privately owned—2,100 km 1.435-meter standard gauge (1,155 km electrified) and 1,845 km 0.950-meter narrow gauge (380 km electrified)

Highways: 294,410 km total; autostrada 5,900 km, state highways 45,170 km, provincial highways 101,680 km, communal highways 141,660 km; 260,500 km concrete, bituminous, or stone block, 26,900 km gravel and crushed stone, 7,010 km earth

Inland waterways: 2,400 km for various types of commercial traffic, although of limited overall value

Pipelines: crude oil, 1,703 km; refined products, 2,148 km; natural gas, 19,400 km

Ports: Cagliari (Sardinia), Genoa, La Spezia, Livorno, Naples, Palermo (Sicily), Taranto, Trieste, Venice

Merchant marine: 575 ships (1,000 GRT or over) totaling 7,462,744 GRT/11,593,730 DWT; includes 11 passenger, 44 short-sea passenger, 103 cargo, 5 refrigerated cargo, 23 container, 67 roll-on/roll-off cargo, 7 vehicle carrier, 1 multifunction large-load carrier, 2 livestock carrier, 151 petroleum, oils, and lubricants (POL) tanker, 37 chemical tanker, 38 liquefied gas, 10 specialized tanker, 14 combination ore/oil, 60 bulk, 2 combination bulk

Civil air: 125 major transport aircraft

Airports: 138 total, 135 usable; 90 with permanent-surface runways; 2 with runways over 3,659 m; 36 with runways 2,440-3,659 m; 38 with runways 1,220-2,439 m

Telecommunications: well engineered, constructed, and operated; 28,000,000 telephones; stations—144 AM, 54 (over 1,800 repeaters) FM, 450 (over 1,300 repeaters) TV; 22 submarine cables; communication

satellite earth stations operating in INTELSAT 3 Atlantic Ocean and 2 Indian Ocean, INMARSAT, and EUTELSAT systems

---

Defense Forces

Branches: Army, Navy, Air Force, Carabinieri

Manpower availability: males 15-49, 14,747,224; 12,877,803 fit for military service; 418,043 reach military age (18) annually

Defense expenditures: $19.2 billion, 2.2% of GDP (1990)

Ivory Coast
(also known as Côte d'Ivoire)

Geography

Total area: 322,460 km²; land area: 318,000 km²

Comparative area: slightly larger than New Mexico

Land boundaries: 3,110 km total; Burkina 584 km, Ghana 668 km, Guinea 610 km, Liberia 716 km, Mali 532 km

Coastline: 515 km

Maritime claims:
Continental shelf: 200 m (depth);
Exclusive economic zone: 200 nm;
Territorial sea: 12 nm

Climate: tropical along coast, semiarid in far north; three seasons—warm and dry (November to March), hot and dry (March to May), hot and wet (June to October)

Terrain: mostly flat to undulating plains; mountains in northwest

Natural resources: crude oil, diamonds, manganese, iron ore, cobalt, bauxite, copper

Land use: arable land 9%; permanent crops 4%; meadows and pastures 9%; forest and woodland 26%; other 52%; includes irrigated NEGL%

Environment: coast has heavy surf and no natural harbors; severe deforestation

People

Population: 12,977,909 (July 1991), growth rate 3.9% (1991)

Birth rate: 48 births/1,000 population (1991)

Death rate: 12 deaths/1,000 population (1991)

Net migration rate: 4 migrants/1,000 population (1991)

Infant mortality rate: 97 deaths/1,000 live births (1991)

Life expectancy at birth: 52 years male, 56 years female (1991)

Total fertility rate: 6.8 children born/woman (1991)

Nationality: noun—Ivorian(s); adjective—Ivorian

Ethnic divisions: over 60 ethnic groups; most important are the Baoule 23%, Bete 18%, Senoufou 15%, Malinke 11%, and Agni; foreign Africans, mostly Burkinabe about 2 million; non-Africans about 130,000 to 330,000 (French 30,000 and Lebanese 100,000 to 300,000)

Religion: indigenous 63%, Muslim 25%, Christian 12%,

Language: French (official), over 60 native dialects; Dioula most widely spoken

Literacy: 54% (male 67%, female 40%) age 15 and over can read and write (1990 est.)

Labor force: 5,718,000; over 85% of population engaged in agriculture, forestry, livestock raising; about 11% of labor force are wage earners, nearly half in agriculture and the remainder in government, industry, commerce, and professions; 54% of population of working age (1985)

Organized labor: 20% of wage labor force

Government

Long-form name: Republic of the Ivory Coast; note—the local official name is République de Côte d'Ivoire

Type: republic; multiparty presidential regime established 1960

Capital: Abidjan (capital city changed to Yamoussoukro in March 1983 but not recognized by US)

Administrative divisions: 49 departments (départements, singular—département); Abengourou, Abidjan, Aboisso, Adzopé, Agboville, Bangolo, Béoumi, Biankouma, Bondoukou, Bongouanou, Bouaflé, Bouaké, Bouna, Boundiali, Dabakala, Daloa, Danané, Daoukro, Dimbokro, Divo, Duékoué, Ferkessédougou, Gagnoa, Grand-Lahou, Guiglo, Issia, Katiola, Korhogo, Lakota, Man, Mankono, Mbahiakro, Odienné, Oumé, Sakassou, San-Pédro, Sassandra, Séguéla, Sinfra, Soubré, Tabou, Tanda, Tengréla, Tiassalé, Touba, Toumodi, Vavoua, Yamoussoukro, Zuénoula

Independence: 7 August 1960 (from France)

Constitution: 3 November 1960

Legal system: based on French civil law system and customary law; judicial review in the Constitutional Chamber of the Supreme Court; has not accepted compulsory ICJ jurisdiction

National holiday: National Day, 7 December

Executive branch: president, Council of Ministers (cabinet)

Legislative branch: unicameral National Assembly (Assemblée Nationale)

Judicial branch: Supreme Court (Cour Suprême)

Leaders:
Chief of State and Head of Government— President Dr. Félix HOUPHOUËT-BOIGNY (since 27 November 1960); Prime Minister Allassane OUATTARE (since 7 November 1990)

Political parties and leaders: Democratic Party of the Ivory Coast (PDCI), Dr. Félix HOUPHOUËT-BOIGNY; Ivorian Popular Front (FPI), Laurent GBAGBO; Ivorian Worker's Party (PIT), Francis WODIE; Ivorian Socialist Party (PSI), Morifere BAMBA; over 20 smaller parties

Suffrage: universal at age 21

Elections:
President—last held 28 October 1990 (next to be held October 1995); results—President Félix HOUPHOUËT-BOIGNY received 81% of the vote in his first contested election; he is currently serving his seventh consecutive five-year term;
National Assembly—last held 25 November 1990 (next to be held November 1995); results—percent of vote by party NA; seats—(175 total) PDCI 163, FPI 9, PIT 1, independents 2

Communists: no Communist party; possibly some sympathizers

Member of: ACCT, ACP, AfDB, CCC, CEAO, ECA, ECOWAS, Entente, FAO, FZ, G-24, G-77, GATT, IAEA, IBRD, ICAO, ICC, IDA, IFAD, IFC, ILO, IMF, IMO, INTELSAT, INTERPOL, IOC, ISO, ITU, LORCS, NAM, OAU, UN, UNCTAD, UNESCO, UNIDO, UPU, WADB, WCL, WHO, WIPO, WMO, WTO

Diplomatic representation: Ambassador Charles GOMIS; Chancery at 2424 Massachusetts Avenue NW, Washington DC 20008; telephone (202) 797-0300;
US—Ambassador Kenneth L. BROWN; Embassy at 5 Rue Jesse Owens, Abidjan (mailing address is 01 B. P. 1712, Abidjan); telephone [225] 21-09-79 or 21-46-72

Flag: three equal vertical bands of orange (hoist side), white, and green; similar to the flag of Ireland which is longer and has the colors reversed—green (hoist side), white, and orange; also similar to the flag of Italy which is green (hoist side), white, and red; design was based on the flag of France

Economy

Overview: Ivory Coast is among the world's largest producers and exporters of coffee, cocoa beans, and palm-kernel oil. Consequently, the economy is highly sensitive to fluctuations in international prices for coffee and cocoa and to weather conditions. Despite attempts by the government to diversify, the economy is still largely dependent on agriculture and related industries. The agricultural sector accounts for over one-third of GDP and about 80% of export earnings and employs about 85% of the labor force. A collapse of world cocoa and coffee prices in 1986 threw the economy into a recession, from which the country had not recovered by 1990.

GDP: $9.5 billion, per capita $820; real growth rate −1.2% (1989)
Inflation rate (consumer prices): 1.5% (1989)
Unemployment rate: 14% (1985)
Budget: revenues $2.8 billion (1989 est.); expenditures $4.1 billion, including capital expenditures of $NA (1989 est.)
Exports: $2.5 billion (f.o.b., 1989); *commodities*—cocoa 30%, coffee 20%, tropical woods 11%, cotton, bananas, pineapples, palm oil, cotton; *partners*—France, FRG, Netherlands, US, Belgium, Spain (1985)
Imports: $1.4 billion (f.o.b., 1989); *commodities*—manufactured goods and semifinished products 50%, consumer goods 40%, raw materials and fuels 10%; *partners*—France, other EC, Nigeria, US, Japan (1985)
External debt: $15.0 billion (1990 est.)
Industrial production: growth rate −6% (1989); accounts for 17% of GDP
Electricity: 1,081,000 kW capacity; 2,440 million kWh produced, 210 kWh per capita (1989)
Industries: foodstuffs, wood processing, oil refinery, automobile assembly, textiles, fertilizer, beverage
Agriculture: most important sector, contributing one-third to GDP and 80% to exports; cash crops include coffee, cocoa beans, timber, bananas, palm kernels, rubber; food crops—corn, rice, manioc, sweet potatoes; not self-sufficient in bread grain and dairy products
Illicit drugs: illicit producer of cannabis on a small scale for the international drug trade
Economic aid: US commitments, including Ex-Im (FY70-89), $356 million; Western (non-US) countries, ODA and OOF bilateral commitments (1970-88), $4.9 billion
Currency: Communauté Financière Africaine franc (plural—francs); 1 CFA franc (CFAF) = 100 centimes
Exchange rates: Communauté Financière Africaine francs (CFAF) per US$1—256.54 (January 1991), 272.26 (1990), 319.01 (1989), 297.85 (1988), 300.54 (1987), 346.30 (1986), 449.26 (1985)
Fiscal year: calendar year

Communications

Railroads: 660 km (Burkina border to Abidjan, 1.00-meter gauge, single track, except 25 km Abidjan-Anyama section is double track)
Highways: 46,600 km total; 3,600 km bituminous and bituminous-treated surface; 32,000 km gravel, crushed stone, laterite, and improved earth; 11,000 km unimproved

Inland waterways: 980 km navigable rivers, canals, and numerous coastal lagoons
Ports: Abidjan, San-Pedro
Merchant marine: 7 ships (1,000 GRT or over) totaling 71,945 GRT/ 90,684 DWT; includes 5 cargo, 1 petroleum, oils, and lubricants (POL) tanker, 1 chemical tanker
Civil air: 12 major transport aircraft, including multinationally owned Air Afrique fleet
Airports: 48 total, 41 usable; 7 with permanent-surface runways; none with runways over 3,659 m; 3 with runways 2,440-3,659 m; 16 with runways 1,220-2,439 m
Telecommunications: system above African average; consists of open-wire lines and radio relay links; 87,700 telephones; stations—3 AM, 17 FM, 11 TV; 2 Atlantic Ocean INTELSAT earth stations; 2 coaxial submarine cables

Defense Forces

Branches: Army, Navy, Air Force, paramilitary Gendarmerie, Presidential Guard
Manpower availability: males 15-49, 2,981,269; 1,543,412 fit for military service; 145,693 males reach military age (18) annually
Defense expenditures: $199 million, 2.3% of GDP (1988)

Jamaica

Geography

Total area: 10,990 km²; land area: 10,830 km²
Comparative area: slightly smaller than Connecticut
Land boundaries: none
Coastline: 1,022 km
Maritime claims:
Territorial sea: 12 nm
Climate: tropical; hot, humid; temperate interior
Terrain: mostly mountains with narrow, discontinuous coastal plain
Natural resources: bauxite, gypsum, limestone
Land use: arable land 19%; permanent crops 6%; meadows and pastures 18%; forest and woodland 28%; other 29%; includes irrigated 3%
Environment: subject to hurricanes (especially July to November); deforestation; water pollution
Note: strategic location between Cayman Trench and Jamaica Channel, the main sea lanes for Panama Canal

People

Population: 2,489,353 (July 1991), growth rate 0.9% (1991)
Birth rate: 24 births/1,000 population (1991)
Death rate: 6 deaths/1,000 population (1991)
Net migration rate: −9 migrants/1,000 population (1991)
Infant mortality rate: 18 deaths/1,000 live births (1991)
Life expectancy at birth: 72 years male, 76 years female (1991)
Total fertility rate: 2.6 children born/woman (1991)
Nationality: noun—Jamaican(s); adjective—Jamaican
Ethnic divisions: African 76.3%, Afro-European 15.1%, East Indian and Afro-East Indian 3.0%, white 3.2%, Chinese and Afro-Chinese 1.2%, other 1.2%

157

Jamaica *(continued)*

Religion: predominantly Protestant 55.9% (Church of God 18.4%, Baptist 10%, Anglican 7.1%, Seven-Day Adventist 6.9%, Pentecostal 5.2%, Methodist 3.1%, United Church 2.7%, other 2.5%), Roman Catholic 5%, other 39.1%, including some spiritualist cults (1982)
Language: English, Creole
Literacy: 98% (male 98%, female 99%) age 15 and over having ever attended school (1990 est.)
Labor force: 1,062,100; services 41%, agriculture 22.5%, industry 19%; unemployed 17.5% (1989)
Organized labor: 24% of labor force (1989)

Government

Long-form name: none
Type: parliamentary democracy
Capital: Kingston
Administrative divisions: 14 parishes; Clarendon, Hanover, Kingston, Manchester, Portland, Saint Andrew, Saint Ann, Saint Catherine, Saint Elizabeth, Saint James, Saint Mary, Saint Thomas, Trelawny, Westmoreland
Independence: 6 August 1962 (from UK)
Constitution: 6 August 1962
Legal system: based on English common law; has not accepted compulsory ICJ jurisdiction
National holiday: Independence Day (first Monday in August), 6 August 1990
Executive branch: British monarch, governor general, prime minister, Cabinet
Legislative branch: bicameral Parliament consists of an upper house or Senate and a lower house or House of Representatives
Judicial branch: Supreme Court
Leaders:
Chief of State—Queen ELIZABETH II (since 6 February 1952), represented by Governor General Sir Florizel A. GLASSPOLE (since 2 March 1973);
Head of Government—Prime Minister Michael MANLEY (since 13 February 1989)
Political parties and leaders: People's National Party (PNP), Michael MANLEY; Jamaica Labor Party (JLP), Edward SEAGA; Workers' Party of Jamaica (WPJ), Trevor MUNROE
Suffrage: universal at age 18
Elections:
House of Representatives—last held 9 February 1989 (next to be held by February 1994); results—PNP 57%, JLP 43%; seats—(60 total) PNP 45, JLP 15
Communists: Workers' Party of Jamaica (Marxist-Leninist)
Other political or pressure groups: Rastafarians (black religious/racial cultists, panAfricanists)
Member of: ACP, C, CARICOM, CCC, CDB, ECLAC, FAO, G-19, G-77, GATT, IADB, IAEA, IBRD, ICAO, ICFTU, IFAD, IFC, ILO, IMF, IMO, INTELSAT, INTERPOL, IOC, ISO, ITU, LAES, LORCS, NAM, OAS, OPANAL, UN, UNCTAD, UNESCO, UNIDO, UPU, WCL, WFTU, WHO, WIPO, WMO, WTO
Diplomatic representation: Ambassador Richard BERNAL; Chancery at Suite 355, 1850 K Street NW, Washington DC 20006; telephone (202) 452-0660; there are Jamaican Consulates General in Miami and New York;
US—Ambassador Glen A. HOLDEN; Embassy at 3rd Floor, Jamaica Mutual Life Center, 2 Oxford Road, Kingston; telephone (809) 929-4850
Flag: diagonal yellow cross divides the flag into four triangles—green (top and bottom) and black (hoist side and fly side)

Economy

Overview: The economy is based on sugar, bauxite, and tourism. In 1985 it suffered a setback with the closure of some facilities in the bauxite and alumina industry, a major source of hard currency earnings. Since 1986 an economic recovery has been under way. In 1987 conditions began to improve for the bauxite and alumina industry because of increases in world metal prices. The recovery has also been supported by growth in the manufacturing and tourism sectors. In September 1988, Hurricane Gilbert inflicted severe damage on crops and the electric power system, a sharp but temporary setback to the economy. By October 1989 the economic recovery from the hurricane was largely complete and real growth was up about 3% for 1989. In 1990, 3.5% economic growth was led by mining and tourism.
GDP: $3.9 billion, per capita $1,580; real growth rate 3.5% (1990)
Inflation rate (consumer prices): 16.0% (1990)
Unemployment rate: 18.2% (1990)
Budget: revenues $1.0 billion; expenditures $1.1 billion, including capital expenditures of $197 million (FY90 est.)
Exports: $1.02 billion (f.o.b., 1990);
commodities—bauxite, alumina, sugar, bananas;
partners—US 36%, UK, Canada, Norway, Trinidad and Tobago
Imports: $1.83 billion (c.i.f., 1990);
commodities—petroleum, machinery, food, consumer goods, construction goods;
partners—US 48%, UK, Venezuela, Canada, Japan, Trinidad and Tobago
External debt: $4.1 billion (1990 est.)
Industrial production: growth rate 3% (1989 est.); accounts for 22% of GDP
Electricity: 1,122,000 kW capacity; 2,508 million kWh produced, 1,030 kWh per capita (1990)
Industries: tourism, bauxite mining, textiles, food processing, light manufactures

Agriculture: accounts for about 9% of GDP, 22% of work force, and 17% of exports; commercial crops—sugarcane, bananas, coffee, citrus, potatoes, and vegetables; livestock and livestock products include poultry, goats, milk; not self-sufficient in grain, meat, and dairy products
Illicit drugs: illicit cultivation of cannabis; transshipment point for ships carrying cocaine and cannabis from central and South America to North America
Economic aid: US commitments, including Ex-Im (FY70-89), $1.2 billion; Western (non-US) countries, ODA and OOF bilateral commitments (1970-88), $1.45 billion; OPEC bilateral aid (1979-89), $27 million; Communist countries (1974-89), $349 million
Currency: Jamaican dollar (plural—dollars); 1 Jamaican dollar (J$) = 100 cents
Exchange rates: Jamaican dollars (J$) per US$1—8.106 (January 1991), 7.184 (1990), 5.7446 (1989), 5.4886 (1988), 5.4867 (1987), 5.4778 (1986), 5.5586 (1985)
Fiscal year: 1 April-31 March

Communications

Railroads: 370 km, all 1.435-meter standard gauge, single track
Highways: 18,200 km total; 12,600 km paved, 3,200 km gravel, 2,400 km improved earth
Pipelines: refined products, 10 km
Ports: Kingston, Montego Bay
Merchant marine: 5 ships (1,000 GRT or over) totaling 13,048 GRT/21,412 DWT; includes 1 cargo, 1 container, 1 roll-on/roll-off cargo, 1 petroleum, oils, and lubricants (POL) tanker, 1 bulk
Civil air: 6 major transport aircraft
Airports: 41 total, 25 usable; 14 with permanent-surface runways; none with runways over 3,659 m; 2 with runways 2,440-3,659 m; 2 with runways 1,220-2,439 m
Telecommunications: fully automatic domestic telephone network; 127,000 telephones; stations—10 AM, 17 FM, 8 TV; 2 Atlantic Ocean INTELSAT earth stations; 3 coaxial submarine cables

Defense Forces

Branches: Jamaica Defense Force (includes Coast Guard and Air Wing), Jamaica Constabulary Force
Manpower availability: males 15-49, 628,225; 446,229 fit for military service; no conscription; 26,442 reach minimum volunteer age (18) annually
Defense expenditures: $20 million, less than 1% of GDP (FY91)

Jan Mayen

(territory of Norway)

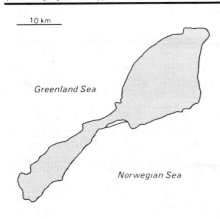

Geography

Total area: 373 km²; land area: 373 km²
Comparative area: slightly more than twice the size of Washington, DC
Land boundaries: none
Coastline: 124.1 km
Maritime claims:
Contiguous zone: 10 nm;
Continental shelf: 200 m (depth) or to depth of exploitation;
Exclusive fishing zone: 200 nm;
Territorial sea: 4 nm
Disputes: Denmark has challenged Norway's maritime claims beween Greenland and Jan Mayen
Climate: arctic maritime with frequent storms and persistent fog
Terrain: volcanic island, partly covered by glaciers; Beerenberg is the highest peak, with an elevation of 2,277 meters
Natural resources: none
Land use: arable land 0%; permanent crops 0%; meadows and pastures 0%; forest and woodland 0%; other 100%
Environment: barren volcanic island with some moss and grass; volcanic activity resumed in 1970
Note: located north of the Arctic Circle about 590 km north-northeast of Iceland between the Greenland Sea and the Norwegian Sea

People

Population: no permanent inhabitants

Government

Long-form name: none
Type: territory of Norway
Note: administered by a governor (sysselmann) resident in Longyearbyen (Svalbard)

Economy

Overview: Jan Mayen is a volcanic island with no exploitable natural resources.

Economic activity is limited to providing services for employees of Norway's radio and meteorological stations located on the island.
Electricity: 15,000 kW capacity; 40 million kWh produced, NA kWh per capita (1989)

Communications

Airports: 1 with runway 1,220 to 2,439 m
Ports: none; offshore anchorage only
Telecommunications: radio and meteorological station

Defense Forces

Note: defense is the responsibility of Norway

Japan

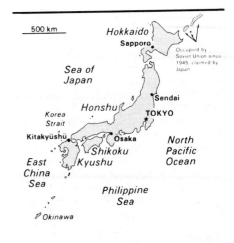

Geography

Total area: 377,835 km²; land area: 374,744 km²; includes Bonin Islands (Ogasawaragunto), Daitō-shotō, Minami-jima, Okinotori-shima, Ryukyu Islands (Nansei-shotō), and Volcano Islands (Kazan-rettō)
Comparative area: slightly smaller than California
Land boundaries: none
Coastline: 29,751 km
Maritime claims:
Exclusive fishing zone: 200 nm;
Territorial sea: 12 nm (3 nm in international straits—La Perouse or Soya, Tsugaru, Osumi, and Eastern and Western channels of the Korea or Tsushima Strait)
Disputes: Etorofu, Kunashiri, and Shikotan Islands and the Habomai island group occupied by Soviet Union since 1945, claimed by Japan; Liancourt Rocks disputed with South Korea; Senkaku-shotō (Senkaku Islands) claimed by China and Taiwan
Climate: varies from tropical in south to cool temperate in north
Terrain: mostly rugged and mountainous
Natural resources: negligible mineral resources, fish
Land use: arable land 13%; permanent crops 1%; meadows and pastures 1%; forest and woodland 67%; other 18%; includes irrigated 9%
Environment: many dormant and some active volcanoes; about 1,500 seismic occurrences (mostly tremors) every year; subject to tsunamis
Note: strategic location in northeast Asia

People

Population: 124,017,137 (July 1991), growth rate 0.4% (1991)
Birth rate: 10 births/1,000 population (1991)
Death rate: 7 deaths/1,000 population (1991)

Japan (continued)

Net migration rate: 0 migrants/1,000 population (1991)

Infant mortality rate: 4 deaths/1,000 live births (1991)

Life expectancy at birth: 76 years male, 82 years female (1991)

Total fertility rate: 1.6 children born/woman (1991)

Nationality: noun—Japanese (sing., pl.); adjective—Japanese

Ethnic divisions: Japanese 99.4%, other (mostly Korean) 0.6%

Religion: most Japanese observe both Shinto and Buddhist rites so the percentages add to more than 100%—Shinto 95.8%, Buddhist 76.3%, Christian 1.4%, other 12% (1985)

Language: Japanese

Literacy: 99% (male NA%, female NA%) age 15 and over can read and write (1970 est.)

Labor force: 63,330,000; trade and services 54%; manufacturing, mining, and construction 33%; agriculture, forestry, and fishing 7%; government 3% (1988)

Organized labor: about 29% of employed workers; public service 76.4%, transportation and telecommunications 57.9%, mining 48.7%, manufacturing 33.7%, services 18.2%, wholesale, retail, and restaurant 9.3%

Government

Long-form name: none

Type: constitutional monarchy

Capital: Tokyo

Administrative divisions: 47 prefectures (fuken, singular and plural); Aichi, Akita, Aomori, Chiba, Ehime, Fukui, Fukuoka, Fukushima, Gifu, Gumma, Hiroshima, Hokkaidō, Hyōgo, Ibaraki, Ishikawa, Iwate, Kagawa, Kagoshima, Kanagawa, Kōchi, Kumamoto, Kyōto, Mie, Miyagi, Miyazaki, Nagano, Nagasaki, Nara, Niigata, Ōita, Okayama, Okinawa, Ōsaka, Saga, Saitama, Shiga, Shimane, Shizuoka, Tochigi, Tokushima, Tōkyō, Tottori, Toyama, Wakayama, Yamagata, Yamaguchi, Yamanashi

Independence: 660 BC, traditional founding by Emperor Jimmu

Constitution: 3 May 1947

Legal system: civil law system with English-American influence; judicial review of legislative acts in the Supreme Court; accepts compulsory ICJ jurisdiction, with reservations

National holiday: Birthday of the Emperor, 23 December (1933)

Executive branch: emperor, prime minister, Cabinet

Legislative branch: bicameral Diet (Kokkai) consists of an upper house or House of Councillors (Sangi-in) and a lower house or House of Representatives (Shūgi-in)

Judicial branch: Supreme Court

Leaders:

Chief of State—Emperor AKIHITO (since 7 January 1989);

Head of Government—Prime Minister Toshiki KAIFU (since 9 August 1989)

Political parties and leaders: Liberal Democratic Party (LDP), Toshiki KAIFU, president; Keizo OBUCHI, secretary general; Japan Socialist Party (JSP), T. DOI, chairman; Democratic Socialist Party (DSP), Keigo OUCHI, chairman; Japan Communist Party (JCP), K. MIYAMOTO, Presidium chairman; Komeito (Clean Government Party, CGP), Koshiro ISHIDA, chairman

Suffrage: universal at age 20

Elections:

House of Councillors—last held on 23 July 1989 (next to be held 23 July 1992); results—percent of vote by party NA; seats—(252 total, 100 elected) LDP 109, JSP 67, CGP 21, JCP 14, other 41;

House of Representatives—last held on 18 February 1990 (next to be held by February 1993); results—percent of vote by party NA; seats—(512 total) LDP 275, JSP 136, CGP 45, JCP 16, DSP 14, other parties 5, independents 21; note—9 independents are expected to join the LDP, 5 the JSP

Communists: about 490,000 registered Communist party members

Member of: AfDB, AG (observer), APEC, AsDB, BIS, CCC, COCOM, CP, EBRD, ESCAP, FAO, G-2, G-5, G-7, G-8, G-10, GATT, IADB, IAEA, IBRD, ICAO, ICC, ICFTU, IDA, IEA, IFAD, IFC, ILO, IMF, IMO, INMARSAT, INTELSAT, INTERPOL, IOC, IOM (observer), ISO, ITU, LORCS, NEA, OAS (observer), OECD, PCA, UN, UNCTAD, UNESCO, UNHCR, UNIDO, UNRWA, UPU, WHO, WIPO, WMO, WTO

Diplomatic representation: Ambassador Ryohei MURATA; Chancery at 2520 Massachusetts Avenue NW, Washington DC 20008; telephone (202) 939-6700; there are Japanese Consulates General in Agana (Guam), Anchorage, Atlanta, Boston, Chicago, Honolulu, Houston, Kansas City (Missouri), Los Angeles, New Orleans, New York, San Francisco, Seattle, and Portland (Oregon), and a Consulate in Saipan (Northern Mariana Islands);

US—Ambassador Michael H. ARMACOST; Embassy at 10-1, Akasaka 1-chome, Minato-ku (107), Tokyo (mailing address is APO San Francisco 96503); telephone [81] (3) 3224-5000; there are US Consulates General in Naha (Okinawa), Osaka-Kobe, and Sapporo and a Consulate in Fukuoka

Flag: white with a large red disk (representing the sun without rays) in the center

Economy

Overview: Although Japan has few natural resources, since 1971 it has become the world's third-largest economy, ranking behind only the US and the USSR. Government-industry cooperation, a strong work ethic, and a comparatively small defense allocation have helped Japan advance rapidly, notably in high-technology fields. Industry, the most important sector of the economy, is heavily dependent on imported raw materials and fuels. Self-sufficent in rice, Japan must import 50% of its requirements for other grain and fodder crops. Japan maintains one of the world's largest fishing fleets and accounts for nearly 15% of the global catch. Overall economic growth has been spectacular: a 10% average in the 1960s, a 5% average in the 1970s and 1980s. In 1990 strong investment and consumption spending helped maintain growth at 5.6%. Inflation remains low at 3.1% despite higher oil prices and rising wages because of a tight labor market. Japan continues to run a huge trade surplus, $52 billion in 1990, which supports extensive investment in foreign properties.

GNP: $2,115.2 billion, per capita $17,100; real growth rate 5.6% (1990)

Inflation rate (consumer prices): 3.1% (1990)

Unemployment rate: 2.1% (1990)

Budget: revenues $499 billion; expenditures $532 billion, including capital expenditures (public works only) of $52 billion (FY90)

Exports: $286.5 billion (f.o.b., 1990); *commodities*—manufactures 97% (including machinery 38%, motor vehicles 17%, consumer electronics 10%); *partners*—US 31%, Southeast Asia 29%, Western Europe 21%, Communist countries 3%, Middle East 3%

Imports: $234.7 billion (c.i.f., 1990); *commodities*—manufactures 50%, fossil fuels 24%, foodstuffs and raw materials 26%; *partners*—Southeast Asia 23%, US 23%, Western Europe 18%, Middle East 13%, Communist countries 7%

External debt: $NA

Industrial production: growth rate 4.6% (1990 est.); accounts for 30% of GDP (mining and manufacturing)

Electricity: 191,000,000 kW capacity; 790,000 million kWh produced, 6,390 kWh per capita (1989)

Industries: metallurgy, engineering, electrical and electronic, textiles, chemicals, automobiles, fishing, telecommunications

Agriculture: accounts for only 2% of GNP; highly subsidized and protected sector, with crop yields among highest in world; principal crops—rice, sugar beets, vegetables, fruit; animal products include pork, poultry, dairy and eggs; about 50% self-sufficient in food production; shortages of wheat, corn, soybeans; world's largest fish catch of 11.9 million metric tons in 1988

Economic aid: donor—ODA and OOF commitments (1970-89), $83.2 billion; ODA outlay of $7.9 billion in 1989

Currency: yen (plural—yen); 1 yen (¥) = 100 sen
Exchange rates: yen (¥) per US$1—133.88 (January 1991), 144.79 (1990), 137.96 (1989), 128.15 (1988), 144.64 (1987), 168.52 (1986), 238.54 (1985)
Fiscal year: 1 April-31 March

Communications

Railroads: 27,327 km total; 2,012 km 1.435-meter standard gauge and 25,315 km predominantly 1.067-meter narrow gauge; 5,724 km doubletrack and multitrack sections, 9,038 km 1.067-meter narrow-gauge electrified, 2,012 km 1.435-meter standard-gauge electrified (1987)
Highways: 1,098,900 km total; 718,700 km paved, 380,200 km gravel, crushed stone, or unpaved; 3,900 km national expressways, 46,544 km national highways, 43,907 km principal local roads, 86,930 km prefectural roads, and 917,619 other (1987)
Inland waterways: about 1,770 km; seagoing craft ply all coastal inland seas
Pipelines: crude oil, 84 km; refined products, 322 km; natural gas, 1,800 km
Ports: Chiba, Muroran, Kitakyushu, Kobe, Tomakomai, Nagoya, Osaka, Tokyo, Yokkaichi, Yokohama, Kawasaki, Niigata, Fushiki-Toyama, Shimizu, Himeji, Wakayama-Shimozu, Shimonoseki, Tokuyama-Shimomatsu
Merchant marine: 1,019 ships (1,000 GRT or over) totaling 22,396,958 GRT/34,683,035 DWT; includes 9 passenger, 55 short-sea passenger, 4 passenger cargo, 95 cargo, 40 container, 33 roll-on-/roll-off cargo, 125 refrigerated cargo, 99 vehicle carrier, 231 petroleum, oils, and lubricants (POL) tanker, 14 chemical tanker, 41 liquefied gas, 11 combination ore/oil, 3 specialized tanker, 257 bulk, 2 combination bulk; note—Japan also owns a large flag of convenience fleet, including up to 40% of the total number of ships under Panamanian flag
Civil air: 360 major transport aircraft
Airports: 165 total, 157 usable; 129 with permanent-surface runways; 2 with runways over 3,659 m; 29 with runways 2,440-3,659 m; 56 with runways 1,220-2,439 m
Telecommunications: excellent domestic and international service; 64,000,000 telephones; stations—318 AM, 58 FM, 12,350 TV (196 major—1 kw or greater); satellite earth stations—4 Pacific Ocean INTELSAT and 1 Indian Ocean INTELSAT; submarine cables to US (via Guam), Philippines, China, and USSR

Defense Forces

Branches: Japan Ground Self-Defense Force (Army), Japan Maritime Self-Defense Force (Navy), Japan Air Self-Defense Force (Air Force), Maritime Safety Agency (Coast Guard)
Manpower availability: males 15-49, 32,256,893; 27,771,374 fit for military service; 992,255 reach military age (18) annually
Defense expenditures: $NA, 1.0% of GNP (1990 est.)

Jarvis Island
(territory of the US)

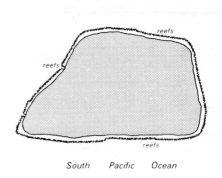

South Pacific Ocean

Geography

Total area: 4.5 km²; land area: 4.5 km²
Comparative area: about 7.5 times the size of The Mall in Washington, DC
Land boundaries: none
Coastline: 8 km
Maritime claims:
Contiguous zone: 12 nm;
Continental shelf: 200 m (depth);
Exclusive economic zone: 200 nm;
Territorial sea: 12 nm
Climate: tropical; scant rainfall, constant wind, burning sun
Terrain: sandy, coral island surrounded by a narrow fringing reef
Natural resources: guano (deposits worked until late 1800s)
Land use: arable land 0%; permanent crops 0%; meadows and pastures 0%; forest and woodland 0%; other 100%
Environment: sparse bunch grass, prostrate vines, and low-growing shrubs; lacks fresh water; primarily a nesting, roosting, and foraging habitat for seabirds, shorebirds, and marine wildlife; feral cats
Note: 2,090 km south of Honolulu in the South Pacific Ocean, just south of the Equator, about halfway between Hawaii and the Cook Islands

---

People

Population: uninhabited
Note: Millersville settlement on western side of island occasionally used as a weather station from 1935 until World War II, when it was abandoned; reoccupied in 1957 during the International Geophysical Year by scientists who left in 1958; public entry is by special-use permit only and generally restricted to scientists and educators

---

Government

Long-form name: none (territory of the US)

Jarvis Island (continued)

Type: unincorporated territory of the US administered by the Fish and Wildlife Service of the US Department of the Interior as part of the National Wildlife Refuge System

Economy

Overview: no economic activity

Communications

Ports: none; offshore anchorage only—one boat landing area in the middle of the west coast and another near the southwest corner of the island
Note: there is a day beacon near the middle of the west coast

Defense Forces

Note: defense is the responsibility of the US; visited annually by the US Coast Guard

Jersey
(British crown dependency)

Geography

Total area: 117 km²; land area: 117 km²
Comparative area: about 0.7 times the size of Washington, DC
Land boundaries: none
Coastline: 70 km
Maritime claims:
Exclusive fishing zone: 200 nm;
Territorial sea: 3 nm
Climate: temperate; mild winters and cool summers
Terrain: gently rolling plain with low, rugged hills along north coast
Natural resources: agricultural land
Land use: arable land NA%; permanent crops NA%; meadows and pastures NA%; forest and woodland NA%; other NA%; about 58% of land under cultivation
Environment: about 30% of population concentrated in Saint Helier
Note: largest and southernmost of Channel Islands; 27 km from France

People

Population: 84,331 (July 1991), growth rate 0.8% (1991)
Birth rate: 12 births/1,000 population (1991)
Death rate: 10 deaths/1,000 population (1991)
Net migration rate: 6 migrants/1,000 population (1991)
Infant mortality rate: 6 deaths/1,000 live births (1991)
Life expectancy at birth: 72 years male, 78 years female (1991)
Total fertility rate: 1.3 children born/woman (1991)
Nationality: noun—Channel Islander(s); adjective—Channel Islander
Ethnic divisions: UK and Norman-French descent
Religion: Anglican, Roman Catholic, Baptist, Congregational New Church, Methodist, Presbyterian

Language: English and French (official), with the Norman-French dialect spoken in country districts
Literacy: NA% (male NA%, female NA%) but compulsory education age 5 to 16
Labor force: NA
Organized labor: none

Government

Long-form name: Bailiwick of Jersey
Type: British crown dependency
Capital: Saint Helier
Administrative divisions: none (British crown dependency)
Independence: none (British crown dependency)
Constitution: unwritten; partly statutes, partly common law and practice
Legal system: English law and local statute
National holiday: Liberation Day, 9 May (1945)
Executive branch: British monarch, lieutenant governor, bailiff
Legislative branch: unicameral Assembly of the States
Judicial branch: Royal Court
Leaders:
Chief of State—Queen ELIZABETH II (since 6 February 1952);
Head of Government—Lieutenant Governor and Commander in Chief Air Marshal Sir John SUTTON (since NA 1990); Bailiff Peter CRILL (since NA)
Political parties and leaders: none; all independents
Suffrage: universal adult at age NA
Elections:
Assembly of the States—last held NA (next to be held NA); results—percent of vote NA; seats—(56 total, 52 elected) 52 independents
Communists: probably none
Member of: none
Diplomatic representation: none (British crown dependency)
Flag: white with the diagonal red cross of Saint Patrick (patron saint of Ireland) extending to the corners of the flag

Economy

Overview: The economy is based largely on financial services, agriculture, and tourism. Potatoes, cauliflower, tomatoes, and especially flowers are important export crops, shipped mostly to the UK. The Jersey breed of dairy cattle is known worldwide and represents an important export earner. Milk products go to the UK and other EC countries. In 1986 the finance sector overtook tourism as the main contributor to GDP, accounting for 40% of the island's output. In recent years the government has encouraged light industry to locate in Jersey, with the result that an electronics industry has developed alongside the traditional manufacturing of knitwear. All raw material and energy requirements are imported, as well as a large share of Jersey's food needs.

GDP: $NA, per capita $NA; real growth rate 8% (1987 est.)

Inflation rate (consumer prices): 8% (1988 est.)

Unemployment rate: NA%

Budget: revenues $308.0 million; expenditures $284.4 million, including capital expenditures of NA (1985)

Exports: $NA;
commodities—light industrial and electrical goods, foodstuffs, textiles;
partners—UK

Imports: $NA;
commodities—machinery and transport equipment, manufactured goods, foodstuffs, mineral fuels, chemicals;
partners—UK

External debt: $NA

Industrial production: growth rate NA%

Electricity: 50,000 kW standby capacity (1990); power supplied by France

Industries: tourism, banking and finance, dairy

Agriculture: potatoes, cauliflowers, tomatoes; dairy and cattle farming

Economic aid: none

Currency: Jersey pound (plural—pounds); 1 Jersey pound (£J) = 100 pence

Exchange rates: Jersey pounds (£J) per US$1—0.5171 (January 1991), 0.5603 (1990), 0.6099 (1989), 0.5614 (1988), 0.6102 (1987), 0.6817 (1986), 0.7714 (1985); the Jersey pound is at par with the British pound

Fiscal year: 1 April-31 March

Communications

Ports: Saint Helier, Gorey, Saint Aubin

Airports: 1 with permanent-surface runway 1,220-2,439 m (Saint Peter)

Telecommunications: 63,700 telephones; stations—1 AM, no FM, 1 TV; 3 submarine cables

---

Defense Forces

Note: defense is the responsibility of the UK

Johnston Atoll
(territory of the US)

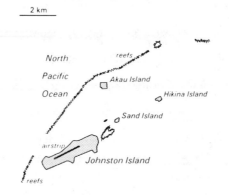

2 km

North Pacific Ocean

reefs

Akau Island

Hikina Island

Sand Island

airstrip

Johnston Island

reefs

Geography

Total area: 2.8 km²; land area: 2.8 km²

Comparative area: about 4.7 times the size of The Mall in Washington, DC

Land boundaries: none

Coastline: 10 km

Maritime claims:
Contiguous zone: 12 nm;
Continental shelf: 200 m (depth);
Exclusive economic zone: 200 nm;
Territorial sea: 12 nm

Climate: tropical, but generally dry; consistent northeast trade winds with little seasonal temperature variation

Terrain: mostly flat with a maximum elevation of 4 meters

Natural resources: guano (deposits worked until about 1890)

Land use: arable land 0%; permanent crops 0%; meadows and pastures 0%; forest and woodland 0%; other 100%

Environment: some low-growing vegetation

Note: strategic location 1,328 km west-southwest of Honolulu in the North Pacific Ocean, about one-third of the way between Hawaii and the Marshall Islands; Johnston Island and Sand Island are natural islands; North Island (Akau) and East Island (Hikina) are manmade islands formed from coral dredging; closed to the public; former nuclear weapons test site; site of Johnston Atoll Chemical Agent Disposal System (JACADS)

People

Population: 1,325 (December 1990); all US government personnel and contractors

---

Government

Long-form name: none (territory of the US)

Type: unincorporated territory of the US administered by the US Defense Nuclear Agency (DNA) and managed cooperatively by DNA and the Fish and Wildlife Service

of the US Department of the Interior as part of the National Wildlife Refuge system

Diplomatic representation: none (territory of the US)

Flag: the flag of the US is used

Economy

Overview: Economic activity is limited to providing services to US military personnel and contractors located on the island. All food and manufactured goods must be imported.

Electricity: supplied by the United States Military

Communications

Ports: Johnston Island

Airports: 1 with permanent-surface runway 2,743 m

Telecommunications: excellent system including 60-channel submarine cable, Autodin/SRT terminal, digital telephone switch, Military Affiliated Radio System (MARS station), commercial satellite television system (receive only), and UHF/VHF air-ground radio, marine VHF/FM Channel 16

Note: US Coast Guard operates a LORAN transmitting station

Defense Forces

Note: defense is the responsibility of the US

Jordan

(see separate West Bank entry)

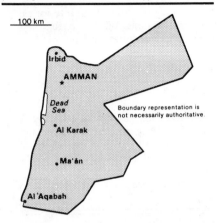

100 km

Irbid
AMMAN
Dead Sea
Al Karak
Ma'ān
Al 'Aqabah

Boundary representation is not necessarily authoritative.

Note: The war between Israel and the Arab states in June 1967 ended with Israel in control of the West Bank. As stated in the 1978 Camp David Accords and reaffirmed by President Reagan's 1 September 1982 peace initiative, the final status of the West Bank and Gaza Strip, their relationship with their neighbors, and a peace treaty between Israel and Jordan are to be negotiated among the concerned parties. The Camp David Accords further specify that these negotiations will resolve the location of the respective boundaries. Pending the completion of this process, it is US policy that the final status of the West Bank and Gaza Strip has yet to be determined.

Geography

Total area: 91,880 km²; land area: 91,540 km²
Comparative area: slightly smaller than Indiana
Land boundaries: 1,586 km total; Iraq 134 km, Israel 238 km, Saudi Arabia 742 km, Syria 375 km, West Bank 97 km
Coastline: 26 km
Maritime claims:
Territorial sea: 3 nm
Disputes: differences with Israel over the location of the 1949 Armistice Line which separates the two countries
Climate: mostly arid desert; rainy season in west (November to April)
Terrain: mostly desert plateau in east, highland area in west; Great Rift Valley separates East and West Banks of the Jordan River
Natural resources: phosphates, potash, shale oil
Land use: arable land 4%; permanent crops 0.5%; meadows and pastures 1%; forest and woodland 0.5%; other 94%; includes irrigated 0.5%
Environment: lack of natural water resources; deforestation; overgrazing; soil erosion; desertification

People

Population: 3,412,553 (July 1991), growth rate 4.2% (1991)
Birth rate: 46 births/1,000 population (1991)
Death rate: 5 deaths/1,000 population (1991)
Net migration rate: 1 migrants/1,000 population (1991)
Infant mortality rate: 38 deaths/1,000 live births (1991)
Life expectancy at birth: 70 years male, 73 years female (1991)
Total fertility rate: 7.1 children born/woman (1991)
Nationality: noun—Jordanian(s); adjective—Jordanian
Ethnic divisions: Arab 98%, Circassian 1%, Armenian 1%
Religion: Sunni Muslim 92%, Christian 8%
Language: Arabic (official); English widely understood among upper and middle classes
Literacy: 80% (male 89%, female 70%) age 15 and over can read and write (1990 est.)
Labor force: 572,000 (1988); agriculture 20%, manufacturing and mining 20% (1987 est.)
Organized labor: about 10% of labor force
Note: 1.5-1.7 million Palestinians live on the East Bank (55-60% of the population), most are Jordanian citizens

Government

Long-form name: Hashemite Kingdom of Jordan
Type: constitutional monarchy
Capital: Amman
Administrative divisions: 8 governorates (muḥāfaẓat, singular—muḥāfaẓah); Al Balqā', Al Karak, Al Mafraq, 'Ammān, Aṭ Ṭafīlah, Az Zarqā', Irbid, Ma'ān
Independence: 25 May 1946 (from League of Nations mandate under British administration; formerly Trans-Jordan)
Constitution: 8 January 1952
Legal system: based on Islamic law and French codes; judicial review of legislative acts in a specially provided High Tribunal; has not accepted compulsory ICJ jurisdiction
National holiday: Independence Day, 25 May (1946)
Executive branch: monarch, prime minister, deputy prime minister, Cabinet
Legislative branch: bicameral National Assembly (Majlis al-'Umma) consists of an upper house or House of Notables (Majlis al-A'ayan) and a lower house or House of Deputies (Majlis al-Nuwaab); note—the House of Deputies was dissolved by King Hussein on 30 July 1988 as part of Jordanian disengagement from the West Bank and

in November 1989 the first parliamentary elections in 22 years were held, with no seats going to Palestinians on the West Bank
Judicial branch: Court of Cassation
Leaders:
Chief of State—King HUSSEIN Ibn Talal I (since 11 August 1952);
Head of Government—Prime Minister Tahir al-MASRI (since 17 June 1991)
Political parties and leaders: none; after the 1989 parliamentary elections, King Hussein promised to allow the formation of political parties; a national charter that sets forth the ground rules for democracy in Jordan—including the creation of political parties—has been completed but not yet approved
Suffrage: universal at age 20
Elections:
House of Representatives—last held 8 November 1989 (next to be held November 1993); results—percent of vote by party NA; seats—(80 total) Muslim Brotherhood 22, Independent Islamic bloc 10, Democratic bloc (mostly leftist) 15, Liberal bloc (traditionalist) 7, Nationalist bloc (traditionalist) 14, independent 12
Communists: party actively repressed, membership less than 500 (est.)
Member of: ABEDA, ACC, AFESD, AL, AMF, CAEU, CCC, ESCWA, FAO, G-77, IAEA, IBRD, ICAO, ICC, IDA, IDB, IFAD, IFC, ILO, IMF, IMO, INTELSAT, INTERPOL, IOC, ISO (correspondent), ITU, LORCS, NAM, OIC, UN, UNAVEM, UNCTAD, UNESCO, UNIDO, UNRWA, UPU, WFTU, WHO, WIPO, WMO, WTO
Diplomatic representation: Ambassador Hussein A. HAMMAMI; Chancery at 3504 International Drive NW, Washington DC 20008; telephone (202) 966-2664;
US—Ambassador Roger Gram HARRISON; Embassy on Jebel Amman, Amman (mailing address is P. O. Box 354, Amman, or APO New York 09892); telephone [962] (6) 644-371
Flag: three equal horizontal bands of black (top), white, and green with a red isosceles triangle based on the hoist side bearing a small white seven-pointed star; the seven points on the star represent the seven fundamental laws of the Koran

Economy

Overview: Jordan was a secondary beneficiary of the oil boom of the late 1970s and early 1980s, when its annual GNP growth averaged 10-12%. Recent years, however, have witnessed a sharp reduction in grant aid from Arab oil-producing countries and a dropoff in worker remittances, with national growth averaging 1-2%. Imports—mainly oil, capital goods, consumer durables, and foodstuffs—have been outstripping exports by roughly $2 billion annually, the difference being made up by aid, remittances, and borrowing. In mid-1989, the Jordanian Government agreed to implement an IMF austerity program designed to tackle the country's serious economic problems. The program sought to gradually reduce the government's budget deficit over the next several years and implement badly needed structural reforms in the economy. In return for agreeing to the IMF program, Jordan was granted IMF standby loans of over $100 million. Recognizing that it would be unable to cover its debt obligations, the government also began debt rescheduling negotiations with creditors in mid-1989. The onset of the Gulf crisis in August 1990 forced the government to shelve the IMF program and suspend most debt payments and rescheduling negotiations. Economic prospects for 1991 are especially gloomy, given the unsettled conditions in the Middle East.

GNP: $4.6 billion, per capita $1,400; real growth rate −15% (1990 est.)
Inflation rate (consumer prices): 15% (1990 est.)
Unemployment rate: 30% (January 1991 est.)
Budget: revenues $1.05 billion; expenditures $1.6 billion, including capital expenditures of $NA (1991 est.)
Exports: $0.9 billion (f.o.b., 1990 est.); *commodities*—fruits and vegetables, phosphates, fertilizers; *partners*—Iraq, Saudi Arabia, India, Kuwait, Japan, China, Yugoslavia, Indonesia
Imports: $2.1 billion (c.i.f., 1990 est.); *commodities*—crude oil, textiles, capital goods, motor vehicles, foodstuffs; *partners*—EC, US, Saudi Arabia, Japan, Turkey, Romania, China, Taiwan
External debt: $8 billion (December 1990 est.)
Industrial production: growth rate −15% (1990 est.); accounts for 20% of GDP
Electricity: 981,000 kW capacity; 3,500 million kWh produced, 1,180 kWh per capita (1989)
Industries: phosphate mining, petroleum refining, cement, potash, light manufacturing
Agriculture: accounts for only 5% of GDP; principal products are wheat, barley, citrus fruit, tomatoes, melons, olives; livestock—sheep, goats, poultry; large net importer of food
Economic aid: US commitments, including Ex-Im (FY70-89), $1.7 billion; Western (non-US) countries, ODA and OOF bilateral commitments (1970-88), $1.3 billion; OPEC bilateral aid (1979-89), $9.5 billion; Communist countries (1970-89), $44 million
Currency: Jordanian dinar (plural—dinars); 1 Jordanian dinar (JD) = 1,000 fils
Exchange rates: Jordanian dinars (JD) per US$1—0.6670 (January 1991), 0.6636

(1990), 0.5704 (1989), 0.3709 (1988), 0.3387 (1987), 0.3499 (1986), 0.3940 (1985)
Fiscal year: calendar year

Communications

Railroads: 619 km 1.050-meter gauge, single track
Highways: 7,500 km; 5,500 km asphalt, 2,000 km gravel and crushed stone
Pipelines: crude oil, 209 km
Ports: Al Aqabah
Merchant marine: 2 ships (1,000 GRT or over) totaling 22,870 GRT/38,187 DWT; includes 1 bulk, 1 cargo
Civil air: 19 major transport aircraft
Airports: 19 total, 16 usable; 14 with permanent-surface runways; 1 with runways over 3,659 m; 13 with runways 2,440-3,659 m; none with runways 1,220-2,439 m
Telecommunications: adequate system of radio relay, cable, and radio; 81,500 telephones; stations—4 AM, 3 FM, 24 TV; satellite earth stations—1 Atlantic Ocean INTELSAT, 1 Indian Ocean INTELSAT, 1 ARABSAT, 1 domestic TV receive-only; coaxial cable and radio relay to Iraq, Saudi Arabia, and Syria; radio relay to Lebanon is inactive; a microwave network linking Syria, Egypt, Libya, Tunisia, Algeria, Morocco and Jordan

Defense Forces

Branches: Jordan Arab Army, Royal Jordanian Air Force, Royal Jordanian Coast Guard, Public Security Force
Manpower availability: males 15-49, 778,353; 555,144 fit for military service; 39,879 reach military age (18) annually
Defense expenditures: $377 million, 12.4% of GNP (1990)

Juan de Nova Island
(French possession)

Geography

Total area: 4.4 km²; land area: 4.4 km²
Comparative area: about 7.5 times the size of The Mall in Washington, DC
Land boundaries: none
Coastline: 24.1 km
Maritime claims:
Contiguous zone: 12 nm;
Continental shelf: 200 m (depth) or to depth of exploitation;
Exclusive economic zone: 200 nm;
Territorial sea: 12 nm
Disputes: claimed by Madagascar
Climate: tropical
Terrain: undetermined
Natural resources: guano deposits and other fertilizers
Land use: arable land 0%; permanent crops 0%; meadows and pastures 0%; forest and woodland 90%; other 10%
Environment: subject to periodic cyclones; wildlife sanctuary
Note: located in the central Mozambique Channel about halfway between Africa and Madagascar

People

Population: uninhabited

Government

Long-form name: none
Type: French possession administered by Commissioner of the Republic Daniel CONSTANTIN, resident in Reunion

Economy

Overview: no economic activity

Communications

Railroads: short line going to a jetty
Airports: 1 with nonpermanent-surface runway 1,220-2,439 m

Juan de Nova Island *(continued)*

Ports: none; offshore anchorage only

Defense Forces

Note: defense is the responsibility of France

Kenya

Geography

Total area: 582,650 km²; land area: 569,250 km²

Comparative area: slightly more than twice the size of Nevada

Land boundaries: 3,477 km total; Ethiopia 861 km, Somalia 682 km, Sudan 232 km, Tanzania 769 km, Uganda 933 km

Coastline: 536 km

Maritime claims:

Exclusive economic zone: 200 nm;

Territorial sea: 12 nm

Disputes: administrative boundary with Sudan does not coincide with international boundary; possible claim by Somalia based on unification of ethnic Somalis

Climate: varies from tropical along coast to arid in interior

Terrain: low plains rise to central highlands bisected by Great Rift Valley; fertile plateau in west

Natural resources: gold, limestone, soda ash, salt barytes, rubies, fluorspar, garnets, wildlife

Land use: arable land 3%; permanent crops 1%; meadows and pastures 7%; forest and woodland 4%; other 85%; includes irrigated NEGL%

Environment: unique physiography supports abundant and varied wildlife of scientific and economic value; deforestation; soil erosion; desertification; glaciers on Mt. Kenya

Note: Kenyan Highlands one of the most successful agricultural production regions in Africa

People

Population: 25,241,978 (July 1991), growth rate 3.6% (1991)

Birth rate: 45 births/1,000 population (1991)

Death rate: 8 deaths/1,000 population (1991)

Net migration rate: 0 migrants/1,000 population (1991)

Infant mortality rate: 69 deaths/1,000 live births (1991)

Life expectancy at birth: 60 years male, 64 years female (1991)

Total fertility rate: 6.4 children born/woman (1991)

Nationality: noun—Kenyan(s); adjective—Kenyan

Ethnic divisions: Kikuyu 21%, Luhya 14%, Luo 13%, Kalenjin 11%, Kamba 11%, Kisii 6%, Meru 6%, Asian, European, and Arab 1%

Religion: Protestant 38%, Roman Catholic 28%, indigenous beliefs 26%, Muslim 6%

Language: English and Swahili (official); numerous indigenous languages

Literacy: 69% (male 80%, female 58%) age 15 and over can read and write (1990 est.)

Labor force: 9,003,000; agriculture 78%, nonagriculture 22% (1987 est.)

Organized labor: 390,000 (est.)

Government

Long-form name: Republic of Kenya

Type: republic

Capital: Nairobi

Administrative divisions: 7 provinces and 1 area*; Central, Coast, Eastern, Nairobi Area*, North-Eastern, Nyanza, Rift Valley, Western

Independence: 12 December 1963 (from UK; formerly British East Africa)

Constitution: 12 December 1963, amended as a republic 1964; reissued with amendments 1979, 1983, 1986, and 1988

Legal system: based on English common law, tribal law, and Islamic law; judicial review in High Court; accepts compulsory ICJ jurisdiction, with reservations; constitutional amendment in 1982 made Kenya a de jure one-party state

National holiday: Independence Day, 12 December (1963)

Executive branch: president, vice president, Cabinet

Legislative branch: unicameral National Assembly (Bunge)

Judicial branch: Court of Appeal, High Court

Leaders:

Chief of State and Head of Government—President Daniel Teroitich arap MOI (since 14 October 1978); Vice President George SAITOTI (since 10 May 1989)

Political parties and leaders: only party—Kenya African National Union (KANU), Daniel T. arap MOI, president

Suffrage: universal at age 18

Elections:

President—last held on 21 March 1988 (next to be held by March 1993); results—President Daniel T. arap MOI was reelected;

National Assembly—last held on 21 March 1988 (next to be held by March 1993); results—KANU is the only party; seats—(202 total, 188 elected) KANU 200
Communists: may be a few Communists and sympathizers
Other political or pressure groups: labor unions; exile opposition—Mwakenya and other groups
Member of: ACP, AfDB, C, CCC, EADB, ECA, FAO, G-77, GATT, IAEA, IBRD, ICAO, IDA, IFAD, IFC, IGADD, ILO, IMF, IMO, INTELSAT, INTERPOL, IOC, IOM, ISO, ITU, LORCS, NAM, OAU, UN, UNCTAD, UNESCO, UNIDO, UNII-MOG, UPU, WCL, WHO, WIPO, WMO, WTO
Diplomatic representation: Ambassador Denis Daudi AFANDE; Chancery at 2249 R Street NW, Washington DC 20008; telephone (202) 387-6101; there are Kenyan Consulates General in Los Angeles and New York;
US—Ambassador Smith HEMPSTONE, Jr.; Embassy at the corner of Moi Avenue and Haile Selassie Avenue, Nairobi (mailing address is P. O. Box 30137, Nairobi or APO New York 09675); telephone [254] (2) 334141; there is a US Consulate in Mombasa
Flag: three equal horizontal bands of black (top), red, and green; the red band is edged in white; a large warrior's shield covering crossed spears is superimposed at the center

Economy

Overview: A serious underlying economic problem is Kenya's 3.6% annual population growth rate—one of the highest in the world. In the meantime, GDP growth in the near term has kept slightly ahead of population—annually averaging 4.9% in the 1986-90 period. Undependable weather conditions and a shortage of arable land hamper long-term growth in agriculture, the leading economic sector.
GDP: $8.5 billion, per capita $360; real growth rate 4% (1990 est.)
Inflation rate (consumer prices): 10.9% (1990 est.)
Unemployment rate: NA%, but there is a high level of unemployment and underemployment
Budget: revenues $2.0 billion; expenditures $2.3 billion, including capital expenditures of $NA billion (FY89)
Exports: $1.1 billion (f.o.b., 1990 est.); *commodities*—tea 25%, coffee 21%, petroleum products 7% (1989); *partners*—EC 44%, Africa 25%, Asia 5%, US 5%, Middle East 4% (1988)
Imports: $2.4 billion (c.i.f., 1990 est.); *commodities*—machinery and transportation equipment 29%, petroleum and petroleum products 15%, iron and steel 7%, raw

materials, food and consumer goods (1989 est.); *partners*—EC 45%, Asia 11%, Middle East 12%, US 5% (1988)
External debt: $5.8 billion (December 1990 est.)
Industrial production: growth rate 5.4% (1989 est.); accounts for 17% of GDP
Electricity: 730,000 kW capacity; 2,700 million kWh produced, 110 kWh per capita (1990)
Industries: small-scale consumer goods (plastic, furniture, batteries, textiles, soap, cigarettes, flour), agricultural processing, oil refining, cement, tourism
Agriculture: most important sector, accounting for 29% of GDP, about 80% of the work force, and over 50% of exports; cash crops—coffee, tea, sisal, pineapple; food products—corn, wheat, sugarcane, fruit, vegetables, dairy products; food output not keeping pace with population growth
Illicit drugs: illicit producer of cannabis used mostly for domestic consumption; widespread cultivation of cannabis and qat on small plots; transit country for heroin and methaqualone en route from Southwest Asia to West Africa, Western Europe, and the US
Economic aid: US commitments, including Ex-Im (FY70-89), $839 million; Western (non-US) countries, ODA and OOF bilateral commitments (1970-88), $6.7 billion; OPEC bilateral aid (1979-89), $74 million; Communist countries (1970-89), $83 million
Currency: Kenyan shilling (plural—shillings); 1 Kenyan shilling (KSh) = 100 cents
Exchange rates: Kenyan shillings (KSh) per US$1—24.427 (January 1991), 22.915 (1990), 20.572 (1989), 17.747 (1988), 16.454 (1987), 16.226 (1986), 16.432 (1985)
Fiscal year: 1 July-30 June

Communications

Railroads: 2,040 km 1.000-meter gauge
Highways: 64,590 km total; 7,000 km paved, 4,150 km gravel, remainder improved earth
Inland waterways: part of Lake Victoria system is within boundaries of Kenya; principal inland port is at Kisumu
Pipelines: refined products, 483 km
Ports: Mombasa, Lamu
Civil air: 14 major transport aircraft
Airports: 249 total, 213 usable; 22 with permanent-surface runways; 2 with runways over 3,659 m; 2 with runways 2,440-3,659 m; 47 with runways 1,220-2,439 m
Telecommunications: in top group of African systems; consists of radio relay links, open-wire lines, and radiocommunication stations; 260,000 telephones; stations—11 AM, 4 FM, 4 TV; satellite earth stations—1 Atlantic Ocean INTELSAT and 1 Indian Ocean INTLESAT

Defense Forces

Branches: Kenya Army, Kenya Navy, Air Force, paramilitary General Service Unit of the Police
Manpower availability: males 15-49, 5,444,247; 3,362,290 fit for military service; no conscription
Defense expenditures: $100 million, 1.0% of GDP (1989 est.)

Kingman Reef

(territory of the US)

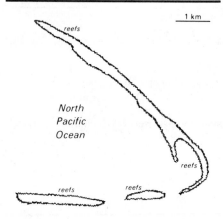

Geography

Total area: 1 km²; land area: 1 km²
Comparative area: about 1.7 times the size of The Mall in Washington, DC
Land boundaries: none
Coastline: 3 km
Maritime claims:
Contiguous zone: 12 nm;
Continental shelf: 200 m (depth);
Exclusive economic zone: 200 nm;
Territorial sea: 12 nm
Climate: tropical, but moderated by prevailing winds
Terrain: low and nearly level with a maximum elevation of about 1 meter
Natural resources: none
Land use: arable land 0%; permanent crops 0%; meadows and pastures 0%; forest and woodland 0%; other 100%
Environment: barren coral atoll with deep interior lagoon; wet or awash most of the time
Note: located 1,600 km south-southwest of Honolulu in the North Pacific Ocean, about halfway between Hawaii and American Samoa; maximum elevation of about 1 meter makes this a navigational hazard; closed to the public

People

Population: uninhabited

Government

Long-form name: none
Type: unincorporated territory of the US administered by the US Navy

Economy

Overview: no economic activity

Communications

Airports: lagoon was used as a halfway station between Hawaii and American Samoa by Pan American Airways for flying boats in 1937 and 1938
Ports: none; offshore anchorage only

Defense Forces

Note: defense is the responsibility of the US

Kiribati

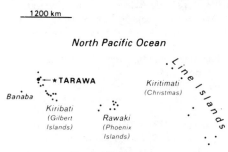

Geography

Total area: 717 km²; land area: 717 km²; includes three island groups—Gilbert Islands, Line Islands, Phoenix Islands
Comparative area: slightly more than four times the size of Washington, DC
Land boundaries: none
Coastline: 1,143 km
Maritime claims:
Exclusive economic zone: 200 nm;
Territorial sea: 12 nm
Climate: tropical; marine, hot and humid, moderated by trade winds
Terrain: mostly low-lying coral atolls surrounded by extensive reefs
Natural resources: phosphate (production discontinued in 1979)
Land use: arable land NEGL%; permanent crops 51%; meadows and pastures 0%; forest and woodland 3%; other 46%
Environment: typhoons can occur any time, but usually November to March; 20 of the 33 islands are inhabited
Note: Banaba (Ocean Island) in Kiribati is one of the three great phosphate rock islands in the Pacific Ocean—the others are Makatea in French Polynesia and Nauru

People

Population: 71,137 (July 1991), growth rate 1.6% (1991)
Birth rate: 33 births/1,000 population (1991)
Death rate: 12 deaths/1,000 population (1991)
Net migration rate: −5 migrants/1,000 population (1991)
Infant mortality rate: 63 deaths/1,000 live births (1991)
Life expectancy at birth: 52 years male, 58 years female (1991)
Total fertility rate: 4.2 children born/woman (1991)
Nationality: noun—I-Kiribati (sing., pl.); adjective—I-Kiribati
Ethnic divisions: Micronesian

Religion: Roman Catholic 52.6%, Protestant (Congregational) 40.9%, Seventh-Day Adventist, Baha'i, Church of God, Mormon 6% (1985)
Language: English (official), Gilbertese
Literacy: NA% (male NA%, female NA%)
Labor force: 7,870 economically active (1985 est.)
Organized labor: Kiribati Trades Union Congress—2,500 members

Government

Long-form name: Republic of Kiribati; note—pronounced Kiribas
Type: republic
Capital: Tarawa
Administrative divisions: 3 units; Gilbert Islands, Line Islands, Phoenix Islands; note—a new administrative structure of 6 districts (Banaba, Central Gilberts, Line Islands, Northern Gilberts, Southern Gilberts, Tarawa) may have been changed to 20 island councils (one for each of the inhabited islands) named Abaiang, Abemama, Aranuka, Arorae, Banaba, Beru, Butaritari, Kiritimati, Kuria, Maiana, Makin, Marakei, Nikunau, Nonouti, Onotoa, Tabiteuea, Tabuaeran, Tamana, Tarawa, Teraina
Independence: 12 July 1979 (from UK; formerly Gilbert Islands)
Constitution: 12 July 1979
National holiday: Independence Day, 12 July (1979)
Executive branch: president, vice president, Cabinet
Legislative branch: unicameral House of Assembly (Maneaba Ni Maungatabu)
Judicial branch: Court of Appeal, High Court
Leaders:
Chief of State and Head of Government—President Ieremia TABAI (since 12 July 1979); Vice President Teatao TEANNAKI (since 20 July 1979)
Political parties and leaders: Gilbertese National Party; Christian Democratic Party, Teburoro TITO, secretary; essentially not organized on the basis of political parties
Suffrage: universal at age 18
Elections:
President—last held on 12 May 1987 (next to be held May 1991); results—Ieremia TABAI 50.1%, Teburoro TITO 42.7%, Tetao TEANNAKI 7.2%;
House of Assembly—last held on 19 March 1987 (next to be held May 1991); results—percent of vote by party NA; seats—(40 total; 39 elected) percent of seats by party NA
Member of: ACP, AsDB, C, ESCAP (associate), IBRD, ICAO, ICFTU, IDA, IFC, IMF, INTERPOL, ITU, SPC, SPF, UNESCO, UPU, WHO

Diplomatic representation: Ambassador (vacant) lives in Tarawa (Kiribati); *US*—none
Flag: the upper half is red with a yellow frigate bird flying over a yellow rising sun and the lower half is blue with three horizontal wavy white stripes to represent the ocean

Economy

Overview: The country has few national resources. Commercially viable phosphate deposits were exhausted at the time of independence in 1979. Copra and fish now represent the bulk of production and exports. The economy has fluctuated widely in recent years. Real GDP declined about 8% in 1987, as the fish catch fell sharply to only one-fourth the level of 1986 and copra production was hampered by repeated rains. Output rebounded strongly in 1988, with real GDP growing by 17%. The upturn in economic growth came from an increase in copra production and a good fish catch. Following the strong surge in output in 1988, GNP increased 1% in 1989 and again in 1990.
GDP: $36.8 million, per capita $525; real growth rate 1.0% (1990 est.)
Inflation rate (consumer prices): 4.0% (1990 est.)
Unemployment rate: 2% (1985); considerable underemployment
Budget: revenues $29.9 million; expenditures $16.3 million, including capital expenditures of $14.0 million (1990 est.)
Exports: $5.8 million (f.o.b., 1990 est.); *commodities*—fish 55%, copra 42%; *partners*—EC 20%, Marshall Islands 12%, US 8%, American Samoa 4% (1985)
Imports: $26.7 million (c.i.f., 1990 est.); *commodities*—foodstuffs, fuel, transportation equipment; *partners*—Australia 39%, Japan 21%, NZ 6%, UK 6%, US 3% (1985)
External debt: $2.0 million (December 1989 est.)
Industrial production: growth rate 0.0% (1988 est.); accounts for less than 4% of GDP
Electricity: 5,000 kW capacity; 13 million kWh produced, 190 kWh per capita (1990)
Industries: fishing, handicrafts
Agriculture: accounts for 30% of GDP (including fishing); copra and fish contribute about 95% to exports; subsistence farming predominates; food crops—taro, breadfruit, sweet potatoes, vegetables; not self-sufficient in food
Economic aid: Western (non-US) countries, ODA and OOF bilateral commitments (1970-88), $258 million
Currency: Australian dollar (plural—dollars); 1 Australian dollar ($A) = 100 cents

Exchange rates: Australian dollars ($A) per US$1—1.2834 (January 1991), 1.2799 (1990), 1.2618 (1989), 1.2752 (1988), 1.4267 (1987), 1.4905 (1986), 1.4269 (1985)
Fiscal year: NA

Communications

Highways: 640 km of motorable roads
Inland waterways: small network of canals, totaling 5 km, in Line Islands
Ports: Banaba and Betio (Tarawa)
Civil air: 2 Trislanders; no major transport aircraft
Airports: 22 total; 21 usable; 4 with permanent-surface runways; none with runways over 2,439 m; 5 with runways 1,220-2,439 m
Telecommunications: 1,400 telephones; stations—1 AM, no FM, no TV; 1 Pacific Ocean INTELSAT earth station

Defense Forces

Branches: no military force maintained; the Police Force carries out law enforcement functions and paramilitary duties; there are small posts on all islands
Manpower availability: NA
Defense expenditures: $NA, NA% of GDP

Korea, North

150 km

Boundary representation is not necessarily authoritative

Geography

Total area: 120,540 km²; land area: 120,410 km²

Comparative area: slightly smaller than Mississippi

Land boundaries: 1,671 km total; China 1,416 km, South Korea 238 km, USSR 17 km

Coastline: 2,495 km

Maritime claims:

Exclusive economic zone: 200 nm;

Territorial sea: 12 nm;

Military boundary line: 50 nm in the Sea of Japan and the exclusive economic zone limit in the Yellow Sea (all foreign vessels and aircraft without permission are banned)

Disputes: short section of boundary with China is indefinite; Demarcation Line with South Korea

Climate: temperate with rainfall concentrated in summer

Terrain: mostly hills and mountains separated by deep, narrow valleys; coastal plains wide in west, discontinuous in east

Natural resources: coal, lead, tungsten, zinc, graphite, magnesite, iron ore, copper, gold, pyrites, salt, fluorspar, hydropower

Land use: arable land 18%; permanent crops 1%; meadows and pastures NEGL%; forest and woodland 74%; other 7%; includes irrigated 9%

Environment: mountainous interior is isolated, nearly inaccessible, and sparsely populated; late spring droughts often followed by severe flooding

Note: strategic location bordering China, South Korea, and USSR

People

Population: 21,814,656 (July 1991), growth rate 1.9% (1991)

Birth rate: 24 births/1,000 population (1991)

Death rate: 6 deaths/1,000 population (1991)

Net migration rate: 0 migrants/1,000 population (1991)

Infant mortality rate: 30 deaths/1,000 live births (1991)

Life expectancy at birth: 66 years male, 72 years female (1991)

Total fertility rate: 2.5 children born/woman (1991)

Nationality: noun—Korean(s); adjective—Korean

Ethnic divisions: racially homogeneous

Religion: Buddhism and Confucianism; religious activities now almost nonexistent

Language: Korean

Literacy: NA% (male NA%, female NA%)

Labor force: 9,615,000; agricultural 36%, nonagricultural 64%; shortage of skilled and unskilled labor (mid-1987 est.)

Organized labor: 1,600,000 members; single-trade union system coordinated by the General Federation of Trade Unions of Korea under the Central Committee

Government

Long-form name: Democratic People's Republic of Korea; abbreviated DPRK

Type: Communist state; dictatorship

Capital: P'yŏngyang

Administrative divisions: 9 provinces (do, singular and plural) and 3 special cities* (jikhalsi, singular and plural); Chagang-do, Hamgyŏng-namdo, Hamgyŏng-bukto, Hwanghae-namdo, Hwanghae-bukto, Kaesŏng-si*, Kangwŏn-do, Namp'o-si*, P'yŏngan-bukto, P'yŏngan-namdo, P'yŏngyang-si*, Yanggang-do

Independence: 9 September 1948

Constitution: adopted 1948, revised 27 December 1972

Legal system: based on German civil law system with Japanese influences and Communist legal theory; no judicial review of legislative acts; has not accepted compulsory ICJ jurisdiction

National holiday: Independence Day, 9 September (1948)

Executive branch: president, two vice presidents, premier, eleven vice premiers, State Administration Council (cabinet)

Legislative branch: unicameral Supreme People's Assembly (Ch'oego Inmin Hoeui)

Judicial branch: Central Court

Leaders:

Chief of State—President KIM Il-sŏng (since 28 December 1972); Designated Successor KIM Chong-il (son of President, born 16 February 1942);

Head of Government—Premier YON Hyong-muk (since NA December 1988)

Political parties and leaders: major party—Korean Workers' Party (KWP), KIM Il-sŏng, general secretary, and his son, KIM Chong-il, secretary, Central Committee; Korean Social Democratic Party, YI Kye-paek, chairman; Chondoist Chongu Party, CHONG Sin-hyok, chairman

Suffrage: universal at age 17

Elections:

President—last held 24 May 1990 (next to be held 1994); results—President KIM Il-sŏng was reelected without opposition;

Supreme People's Assembly—last held on 24 May 1990 (next to be held 1994); results—percent of vote by party NA; seats—(687 total) the KWP approves a single list of candidates who are elected without opposition; minor parties hold a few seats

Communists: KWP claims membership of about 3 million

Member of: FAO, G-77, IAEA, ICAO, IFAD, IMF (observer), IMO, IOC, ISO, ITU, LORCS, NAM, UN (observer), UNCTAD, UNESCO, UNIDO, UPU, WFTU, WHO, WIPO, WMO, WTO

Diplomatic representation: none

Flag: three horizontal bands of blue (top), red (triple width), and blue; the red band is edged in white; on the hoist side of the red band is a white disk with a red five-pointed star

Economy

Overview: More than 90% of this command economy is socialized; agricultural land is collectivized; and state-owned industry produces 95% of manufactured goods. State control of economic affairs is unusually tight even for a Communist country because of the small size and homogeneity of the society and the strict one-man rule of Kim. Economic growth during the period 1984-90 averaged approximately 3%. Abundant natural resources and hydropower form the basis of industrial development. Output of the extractive industries includes coal, iron ore, magnesite, graphite, copper, zinc, lead, and precious metals. Manufacturing emphasis is centered on heavy industry, with light industry lagging far behind. Despite the use of high-yielding seed varieties, expansion of irrigation, and the heavy use of fertilizers, North Korea has not yet become self-sufficient in food production. Four consecutive years of poor harvests, coupled with distribution problems, have led to chronic food shortages. North Korea remains far behind South Korea in economic development and living standards.

GNP: $29.7 billion, per capita $1,390; real growth rate 2% (1990 est.)

Inflation rate (consumer prices): NA%

Unemployment rate: officially none

Budget: revenues $15.6 billion; expenditures $15.6 billion, including capital expenditures of $NA (1989)

Exports: $1.95 billion (f.o.b., 1989); *commodities*—minerals, metallurgical products, agricultural products, manufactures; *partners*—USSR, China, Japan, Hong Kong, FRG, Singapore

Imports: $2.85 billion (f.o.b., 1989);

commodities—petroleum, machinery and equipment, coking coal, grain;
partners—USSR, Japan, China, Hong Kong, FRG, Singapore
External debt: $7 billion (1991)
Industrial production: growth rate NA%
Electricity: 6,700,000 kW capacity; 33,000 million kWh produced, 1,500 kWh per capita (1990)
Industries: machine building, military products, electric power, chemicals, mining, metallurgy, textiles, food processing
Agriculture: accounts for about 25% of GNP and 36% of work force; principal crops—rice, corn, potatoes, soybeans, pulses; livestock and livestock products—cattle, hogs, pork, eggs; not self-sufficient in grain; fish catch estimated at 1.7 million metric tons in 1987
Economic aid: Communist countries, $1.4 billion a year in the 1980s
Currency: North Korean won (plural—won); 1 North Korean won (Wn) = 100 chŏn
Exchange rates: North Korean won (Wn) per US$1—2.2 (March 1991), 2.1 (January 1990), 2.3 (December 1989), 2.13 (December 1988), 0.94 (March 1987), NA (1986), NA (1985)
Fiscal year: calendar year

Communications

Railroads: 4,535 km total; 3,870 km 1.435-meter standard gauge, 665 km 0.762-meter narrow gauge; 159 km double track; 3,175 km electrified; government owned (1989)
Highways: about 30,000 km (1989); 98.5% gravel, crushed stone, or earth surface; 1.5% concrete or bituminous
Inland waterways: 2,253 km; mostly navigable by small craft only
Pipelines: crude oil, 37 km
Ports: Ch'ŏngjin, Haeju, Hungnam, Namp'o, Wonsan, Songnim, Najin, Sonbong
Merchant marine: 68 ships (1,000 GRT and over) totaling 465,801 GRT/709,442 DWT; includes 1 passenger, 1 short-sea passenger, 1 passenger-cargo, 58 cargo, 2 petroleum, oils, and lubricants (POL) tanker, 4 bulk, 1 combination bulk
Airports: 55 total, 55 usable (est.); about 30 with permanent-surface runways; fewer than 5 with runways over 3,659 m; 20 with runways 2,440-3,659 m; 30 with runways 1,220-2,439 m
Telecommunications: stations—18 AM, no FM, 11 TV; 200,000 TV sets; 3,500,000 radio receivers; 1 Indian Ocean INTELSAT earth station

Defense Forces

Branches: Korean People's Army (includes Army, Navy, Air Force), Civil Security Forces
Manpower availability: males 15-49, 6,381,859; 3,899,606 fit for military service; 214,690 reach military age (18) annually
Defense expenditures: $NA, 20-25% of GNP (1991 est.); note—the officially announced but suspect figure is $1.7 billion, 6% of GNP (1991 est.)

Korea, South

Boundary representation is not necessarily authoritative.

Geography

Total area: 98,480 km²; land area: 98,190 km²
Comparative area: slightly larger than Indiana
Land boundary: 238 km with North Korea
Coastline: 2,413 km
Maritime claims:
Continental shelf: not specific
Territorial sea: 12 nm (3 nm in the Korea Strait)
Disputes: Demarcation Line with North Korea; Liancourt Rocks claimed by Japan
Climate: temperate, with rainfall heavier in summer than winter
Terrain: mostly hills and mountains; wide coastal plains in west and south
Natural resources: coal, tungsten, graphite, molybdenum, lead, hydropower
Land use: arable land 21%; permanent crops 1%; meadows and pastures 1%; forest and woodland 67%; other 10%; includes irrigated 12%
Environment: occasional typhoons bring high winds and floods; earthquakes in southwest; air pollution in large cities
Notes: strategic location along the Korea Strait, Sea of Japan, and Yellow Sea

People

Population: 43,134,386 (July 1991), growth rate 0.8% (1991)
Birth rate: 15 births/1,000 population (1991)
Death rate: 6 deaths/1,000 population (1991)
Net migration rate: −1 migrant/1,000 population (1991)
Infant mortality rate: 23 deaths/1,000 live births (1991)
Life expectancy at birth: 67 years male, 73 years female (1991)
Total fertility rate: 1.6 children born/woman (1991)

Korea, South (continued)

Nationality: noun—Korean(s); adjective—Korean

Ethnic divisions: homogeneous; small Chinese minority (about 20,000)

Religion: strong Confucian tradition; vigorous Christian minority (28% of the total population); Buddhism; pervasive folk religion (Shamanism); Chondokyo (religion of the heavenly way), eclectic religion with nationalist overtones founded in 19th century, claims about 1.5 million adherents

Language: Korean; English widely taught in high school

Literacy: 96% (male 99%, female 94%) age 15 and over can read and write (1990 est.)

Labor force: 16,900,000; 52% services and other; 27% mining and manufacturing; 21% agriculture, fishing, forestry (1987)

Organized labor: about 10% of nonagricultural labor force in government-sanctioned unions

---

Government

Long-form name: Republic of Korea; abbreviated ROK

Type: republic

Capital: Seoul

Administrative divisions: 9 provinces (do, singular and plural) and 6 special cities* (jikhalsi, singular and plural); Cheju-do, Chŏlla-bukto, Chŏlla-namdo, Ch'ungch'ŏng-bukto, Ch'ungch'ŏng-namdo, Inch'ŏn-jikhalsi*, Kangwŏn-do, Kwangju-jikhalsi*, Kyŏnggi-do, Kyŏngsang-bukto, Kyŏngsang-namdo, Pusan-jikhalsi*, Sŏul-t'ŭkpyŏlsi*, Taegu-jikhalsi*, Taejŏn-jikhalsi*

Independence: 15 August 1948

Constitution: 25 February 1988

Legal system: combines elements of continental European civil law systems, Anglo-American law, and Chinese classical thought; has not accepted compulsory ICJ jurisdiction

National holiday: Independence Day, 15 August (1948)

Executive branch: president, prime minister, deputy prime minister, State Council (cabinet)

Legislative branch: unicameral National Assembly (Kuk Hoe)

Judicial branch: Supreme Court

Leaders:
Chief of State—President ROH Tae Woo (since 25 February 1988);
Head of Government—Prime Minister CHUNG Won Shik (since 24 May 1991); Deputy Prime Minister CHOI Kak Kyu (since 19 February 1991)

Political parties and leaders:
ruling party—Democratic Liberal Party (DLP), ROH Tae Woo, president, KIM Young Sam, chairman; note—the DLP resulted from a merger of the Democratic Justice Party (DJP), Reunification Democratic Party (RDP), and New Democratic Republican Party (NDRP) on 9 February 1990;

opposition—New Democratic Party (NDP, formerly Party for Peace and Democracy or PPD), KIM Dae Jung, president; Democratic Party (DP), YI Ki Taek; several smaller parties

Suffrage: universal at age 20

Elections:
President—last held on 16 December 1987 (next to be held December 1992); results—ROH Tae Woo (DJP) 35.9%, KIM Young Sam (RDP) 27.5%, KIM Dae Jung (PPD) 26.5%, other 10.1%;

National Assembly—last held on 26 April 1988 (next to be held April 1992); results—DJP 34%, RDP 24%, PPD 19%, NDRP 15%, other 8%; seats—(299 total) DJP 125, PPD 70, RDP 59, NDRP 35, other 10; note—on 9 February 1990 the DJP, RDP, and NDRP merged to form the DLP; also the PPD became the NDP; as a result the distribution of seats changed to DLP 218, NDP 70, other 11 (June 1990)

Communists: Communist party activity banned by government

Other political or pressure groups: Korean National Council of Churches; National Democratic Alliance of Korea; National Council of College Student Representatives; National Federation of Farmers' Associations; National Council of Labor Unions; Federation of Korean Trade Unions; Korean Veterans' Association; Federation of Korean Industries; Korean Traders Association

Member of: AfDB, APEC, AsDB, CCC, CP, EBRD, ESCAP, FAO, G-77, GATT, IAEA, IBRD, ICAO, ICC, ICFTU, IDA, IFAD, IFC, IMF, IMO, INMARSAT, INTELSAT, INTERPOL, IOC, IOM, ISO, ITU, LORCS, UN (observer), UNCTAD, UNESCO, UNIDO, UPU, WHO, WIPO, WMO, WTO

Diplomatic representation: Ambassador HYUN Hong Joo; Chancery at 2320 Massachusetts Avenue NW, Washington DC 20008; telephone (202) 939-5600; there are Korean Consulates General in Agana (Guam), Anchorage, Atlanta, Chicago, Honolulu, Houston, Los Angeles, New York, San Francisco, and Seattle;

US—Ambassador Donald P. GREGG; Embassy at 82 Sejong-Ro, Chongro-ku, Seoul (mailing address is APO San Francisco 96301); telephone [82] (2) 732-2601 through 2618; there is a US Consulate in Pusan

Flag: white with a red (top) and blue yin-yang symbol in the center; there is a different black trigram from the ancient *I Ching* (Book of Changes) in each corner of the white field

---

Economy

Overview: The driving force behind the economy's dynamic growth has been the planned development of an export-oriented economy in a vigorously entrepreneurial society. Real GNP—which grew by 6.7% in 1989 after an average annual growth of over 12% between 1986-88—grew about 9% in 1990. Labor unrest—which led to substantial wage hikes in 1987-88—was noticeably calmer in 1990, unemployment averaged a low 2.5%, and investment was strong. Inflation rates, however, are beginning to challenge South Korea's strong economic performance. Consumer prices rose 8.6%, the highest rate in nine years. Policymakers are concerned higher prices could lead to a resurgence of labor unrest.

GNP: $238 billion, per capita $5,600; real growth rate 9% (1990 est.)

Inflation rate (consumer prices): 8.6% (1990)

Unemployment rate: 2.5% (1990)

Budget: revenues $38 billion; expenditures $38 billion, including capital expenditures of $NA (1991)

Exports: $65 billion (f.o.b., 1990); *commodities*—textiles, clothing, electronic and electrical equipment, footwear, machinery, steel, automobiles, ships, fish; *partners*—US 30%, Japan 19%

Imports: $70 billion (c.i.f., 1990); *commodities*—machinery, electronics and electronic equipment, oil, steel, transport equipment, textiles, organic chemicals, grains; *partners*—Japan 27%, US 24% (1990)

External debt: $31.7 billion (1990)

Industrial production: growth rate 8.6% (1990 est.); accounts for about 45% of GDP

Electricity: 21,000,000 kW capacity; 85,000 million kWh produced, 1,970 kWh per capita (1990)

Industries: textiles, clothing, footwear, food processing, chemicals, steel, electronics, automobile production, ship building

Agriculture: accounts for 11% of GNP and employs 21% of work force (including fishing and forestry); principal crops—rice, root crops, barley, vegetables, fruit; livestock and livestock products—cattle, hogs, chickens, milk, eggs; self-sufficient in food, except for wheat; fish catch of 2.9 million metric tons, seventh-largest in world

Economic aid: US commitments, including Ex-Im (FY70-89), $3.9 billion; non-US countries (1970-89), $3.0 billion

Currency: South Korean won (plural—won); 1 South Korean won (W) = 100 chŏn (theoretical)

Exchange rates: South Korean won (W) per US$1—718.14 (January 1991), 707.76 (1990), 671.46 (1989), 731.47 (1988), 822.57 (1987), 881.45 (1986), 870.02 (1985)

Fiscal year: calendar year

Kuwait

Communications

Railroads: 3,106 km operating in 1983; 3,059 km 1.435-meter standard gauge, 47 km 0.610-meter narrow gauge, 712 km double track, 418 km electrified; government owned

Highways: 62,936 km total (1982); 13,476 km national highway, 49,460 km provincial and local roads

Inland waterways: 1,609 km; use restricted to small native craft

Pipelines: 455 km refined products

Ports: Pusan, Inchon, Kunsan, Mokpo, Ulsan

Merchant marine: 439 ships (1,000 GRT or over) totaling 7,182,519 GRT/11,906,897 DWT; includes 2 short-sea passenger, 138 cargo, 45 container, 11 refrigerated cargo, 11 vehicle carrier, 48 petroleum, oils, and lubricants (POL) tanker, 10 chemical tanker, 13 liquefied gas, 7 combination ore/oil, 146 bulk, 7 combination bulk, 1 multifunction large-load carrier

Civil air: 93 major transport aircraft

Airports: 110 total, 102 usable; 60 with permanent-surface runways; none with runways over 3,659 m; 21 with runways 2,440-3,659 m; 17 with runways 1,220-2,439 m

Telecommunications: adequate domestic and international services; 4,800,000 telephones; stations—79 AM, 46 FM, 256 TV (57 of 1 kW or greater); satellite earth stations—2 Pacific Ocean INTELSAT and 1 Indian Ocean INTELSAT

Defense Forces

Branches: Army, Navy (including Marines), Air Force

Manpower availability: males 15-49, 12,859,511; 8,294,624 fit for military service; 429,088 reach military age (18) annually

Defense expenditures: $10.4 billion, 4.5% of GNP (1991)

Geography

Total area: 17,820 km²; land area: 17,820 km²

Comparative area: slightly smaller than New Jersey

Land boundaries: 462 km total; Iraq 240 km, Saudi Arabia 222 km

Coastline: 499 km

Maritime claims:

Continental shelf: not specific;

Territorial sea: 12 nm

Disputes: Iraqi forces invaded and occupied Kuwait from 2 August 1990 until 27 February 1991; in April 1991 official Iraqi acceptance of UN Security Council Resolution 687, which demands that Iraq accept its internationally recognized border with Kuwait, ended earlier claims to Būbiyān and Warbah Islands or to all of Kuwait; ownership of Qārūh and Umm al Marādim Islands disputed by Saudi Arabia

Climate: dry desert; intensely hot summers; short, cool winters

Terrain: flat to slightly undulating desert plain

Natural resources: petroleum, fish, shrimp, natural gas

Land use: arable land NEGL%; permanent crops 0%; meadows and pastures 8%; forest and woodland NEGL%; other 92%; includes irrigated NEGL%

Environment: some of world's largest and most sophisticated desalination facilities provide most of water; air and water pollution; desertification

Note: strategic location at head of Persian Gulf

People

Population: 2,204,400 (July 1991), growth rate 3.6% (1991)

Birth rate: 29 births/1,000 population (1991)

Death rate: 2 deaths/1,000 population (1991)

Net migration rate: 10 migrants/1,000 population (1991)

Infant mortality rate: 15 deaths/1,000 live births (1991)

Life expectancy at birth: 72 years male, 76 years female (1991)

Total fertility rate: 3.7 children born/woman (1991)

Nationality: noun—Kuwaiti(s); adjective—Kuwaiti

Ethnic divisions: Kuwaiti 27.9%, other Arab 39%, South Asian 9%, Iranian 4%, other 20.1%

Religion: Muslim 85% (Shi'a 30%, Sunni 45%, other 10%), Christian, Hindu, Parsi, and other 15%

Language: Arabic (official); English widely spoken

Literacy: 74% (male 78%, female 69%) age 15 and over can read and write (1985)

Labor force: 566,000 (1986); services 45.0%, construction 20.0%, trade 12.0%, manufacturing 8.6%, finance and real estate 2.6%, agriculture 1.9%, power and water 1.7%, mining and quarrying 1.4%; 70% of labor force was non-Kuwaiti

Organized labor: labor unions exist in oil industry and among government personnel

Government

Long-form name: State of Kuwait

Type: nominal constitutional monarchy

Capital: Kuwait

Administrative divisions: 4 governorates (muḥāfaẓat, singular—muḥāfaẓah); Al Aḥmadī, Al Jahrah, Al Kuwayt, Ḥawallī; note—there may be a new governorate of Farwaniyyah

Independence: 19 June 1961 (from UK)

Constitution: 16 November 1962 (some provisions suspended since 29 August 1962)

Legal system: civil law system with Islamic law significant in personal matters; has not accepted compulsory ICJ jurisdiction

National holiday: National Day, 25 February

Executive branch: amir, prime minister, deputy prime minister, Council of Ministers (cabinet)

Legislative branch: National Assembly (Majlis al 'Umma) dissolved 3 July 1986

Judicial branch: High Court of Appeal

Leaders:

Chief of State—Amir Shaykh Jabir al-Ahmad al-Jabir al-SABAH (since 31 December 1977);

Head of Government—Prime Minister and Crown Prince Sa'd al-'Abdallah al-Salim al-SABAH (since 8 February 1978); Deputy Prime Minister Salim al-Sabah al-Salim al-SABAH

Political parties and leaders: none

Suffrage: adult males who resided in Kuwait before 1920 and their male descendants at age 21; note—out of all citizens, only 8.3% are eligible to vote and only 3.5% actually vote

Kuwait (continued)

Elections:
National Assembly—dissolved 3 July 1986; new elections are scheduled for October 1992

Communists: insignificant

Other political or pressure groups: large (150,000) Palestinian community; several small, clandestine leftist and Shi'a fundamentalist groups are active; prodemocracy opposition

Member of: ABEDA, AfDB, AFESD, AL, AMF, BDEAC, CAEU, ESCWA, FAO, G-77, GATT, GCC, IAEA, IBRD, ICAO, ICC, IDA, IDB, IFAD, IFC, ILO, IMF, IMO, INMARSAT, INTELSAT, INTERPOL, IOC, ISO (correspondent), ITU, LORCS, NAM, OAPEC, OIC, OPEC, UN, UNCTAD, UNESCO, UNIDO, UPU, WFTU, WHO, WMO, WTO

Diplomatic representation: Ambassador Shaykh Sa'ud Nasir al-SABAH; Chancery at 2940 Tilden Street NW, Washington DC 20008; telephone (202) 966-0702; *US*—Ambassador Edward (Skip) GNEHM; Embassy at Bneid al-Gar (opposite the Hilton Hotel), Kuwait City (mailing address is P. O. Box 77 Safat, 13001 Safat, Kuwait City); telephone [965] 242-4151 through 4159

Flag: three equal horizontal bands of green (top), white, and red with a black trapezoid based on the hoist side

Economy

Overview: Up to the invasion by Iraq in August 1990, the oil sector had dominated the economy. Kuwait has the third-largest oil reserves in the world after Saudi Arabia and Iraq. Earnings from hydrocarbons generated over 90% of both export and government revenues and contributed about 40% to GDP. Most of the nonoil sector has traditionally been dependent upon oil-derived government revenues. Iraq's destruction of Kuwait's oil industry during the Gulf war has devastated the economy. Iraq destroyed or damaged more than 80% of Kuwait's 950 operating oil wells, as well as sabotaging key surface facilities. Western firefighters had brought about 140 of the 600 oil well fires and blowouts under control as of early June 1991. It could take two to three years to restore Kuwait's oil production to its prewar level of about 2.0 million barrels per day.

GDP: $19.8 billion, per capita $9,700; real growth rate 3.5% (1989)

Inflation rate (consumer prices): 3.3% (1989)

Unemployment rate: 0% (1989)

Budget: revenues $7.1 billion; expenditures $10.5 billion, including capital expenditures of $3.1 billion (FY88)

Exports: $11.5 billion (f.o.b., 1989); *commodities*—oil 90%; *partners*—Japan, Italy, FRG, US

Imports: $6.3 billion (f.o.b., 1989); *commodities*—food, construction materials, vehicles and parts, clothing; *partners*—Japan, US, FRG, UK

External debt: $7.2 billion (December 1989 est.)

Industrial production: growth rate 3% (1988); accounts for 52% of GDP

Electricity: 8,290,000 kW capacity; 10,000 million kWh produced, 5,000 kWh per capita (1989)

Industries: petroleum, petrochemicals, desalination, food processing, salt, construction

Agriculture: virtually none; dependent on imports for food; about 75% of potable water must be distilled or imported

Economic aid: donor—pledged $18.3 billion in bilateral aid to less developed countries (1979-89)

Currency: Kuwaiti dinar (plural—dinars); 1 Kuwaiti dinar (KD) = 1,000 fils

Exchange rates: Kuwaiti dinars (KD) per US$1—0.2915 (January 1990), 0.2937 (1989), 0.2790 (1988), 0.2786 (1987), 0.2919 (1986), 0.3007 (1985)

Fiscal year: 1 July-30 June

Communications

Highways: 3,000 km total; 2,500 km bituminous; 500 km earth, sand, light gravel

Pipelines: Ash Shuáybah, crude oil, 877 km; refined products, 40 km; natural gas, 165 km

Ports: Ash Shu'aybah, Ash Shuwaykh, Mīnā al Ahmadī

Merchant marine: 31 ships (1,000 GRT or over), totaling 1,332,159 GRT/2,099,303 DWT; includes 1 cargo, 4 livestock carrier, 20 petroleum, oils, and lubricants (POL) tanker, 5 liquefied gas, 1 bulk; note—all Kuwaiti ships greater than 1,000 GRT were outside Kuwaiti waters at the time of the Iraqi invasion; many of these ships transferred to the Liberian flag or to the flags of other Persian Gulf states; Kuwaiti tankers are currently managed from London and Kuwaiti cargo and container ships are managed from Dubai

Civil air: 19 major transport aircraft

Airports: 7 total, 4 usable; 4 with permanent-surface runways; none with runways over 3,659 m; 4 with runways 2,440-3,659 m; none with runways 1,220-2,439 m

Telecommunications: excellent international, adequate domestic facilities; 258,000 telephones; stations—3 AM, 2 FM, 3 TV; satellite earth stations—1 Indian Ocean INTELSAT, and 2 Atlantic Ocean INTELSAT; 1 INMARSAT, 1 ARABSAT; coaxial cable and radio relay to Iraq and Saudi Arabia

Defense Forces

Branches: Army, Navy, Air Force, National Police Force, National Guard

Manpower availability: males 15-49, 738,812; 441,611 fit for military service; 19,452 reach military age (18) annually

Defense expenditures: $1.1 billion, 4.8% of GDP (1990)

Laos

Geography

Total area: 236,800 km²; land area: 230,800 km²

Comparative area: slightly larger than Utah

Land boundaries: 5,083 km total; Burma 235 km, Cambodia 541 km, China 423 km, Thailand 1,754 km, Vietnam 2,130 km

Coastline: none—landlocked

Maritime claims: none—landlocked

Disputes: boundary dispute with Thailand

Climate: tropical monsoon; rainy season (May to November); dry season (December to April)

Terrain: mostly rugged mountains; some plains and plateaus

Natural resources: timber, hydropower, gypsum, tin, gold, gemstones

Land use: arable land 4%; permanent crops NEGL%; meadows and pastures 3%; forest and woodland 58%; other 35%; includes irrigated 1%

Environment: deforestation; soil erosion; subject to floods

Note: landlocked

People

Population: 4,113,223 (July 1991), growth rate 2.2% (1991)

Birth rate: 37 births/1,000 population (1991)

Death rate: 15 deaths/1,000 population (1991)

Net migration rate: 0 migrants/1,000 population (1991)

Infant mortality rate: 124 deaths/1,000 live births (1991)

Life expectancy at birth: 49 years male, 52 years female (1991)

Total fertility rate: 5.0 children born/woman (1991)

Nationality: noun—Lao (sing., Lao or Laotian); adjective—Lao or Laotian

Ethnic divisions: Lao 50%, Phoutheung (Kha) 15%, tribal Thai 20%, Meo, Hmong, Yao, and other 15%

Religion: Buddhist 85%, animist and other 15%

Language: Lao (official), French, and English

Literacy: 84% (male 92%, female 76%) age 15 to 45 having the ability to read and write (1985 est.)

Labor force: 1-1.5 million; 85-90% in agriculture (est.)

Organized labor: Lao Federation of Trade Unions is subordinate to the Communist party

Government

Long-form name: Lao People's Democratic Republic

Type: Communist state

Capital: Vientiane

Administrative divisions: 16 provinces (khouèng, singular and plural) and 1 municipality* (kampheng nakhon, singular and plural); Attapu, Bokeo, Bolikhamsai, Champasak, Houaphan, Khammouan, Louang Namtha, Louangphrabang, Oudômxai, Phôngsali, Saravan, Savannakhét, Sekong, Vientiane, Vientiane*, Xaignabouri, Xiangkhoang

Independence: 19 July 1949 (from France)

Constitution: draft constitution under discussion since 1976

Legal system: based on civil law system; has not accepted compulsory ICJ jurisdiction

National holiday: National Day (proclamation of the Lao People's Democratic Republic), 2 December (1975)

Executive branch: president, chairman and four vice chairmen of the Council of Ministers, Council of Ministers (cabinet)

Legislative branch: Supreme People's Assembly

Judicial branch: People's Supreme Court

Leaders:
Chief of State—Acting President PHOUMI VONGVICHIT (since 29 October 1986);
Head of Government—Chairman of the Council of Ministers General KAYSONE PHOMVIHAN (since 2 December 1975)

Political parties and leaders: Lao People's Revolutionary Party (LPRP), KAYSONE PHOMVIHAN, party chairman; includes Lao Patriotic Front and Alliance Committee of Patriotic Neutralist Forces; other parties moribund

Suffrage: universal at age 18

Elections:
Supreme People's Assembly—last held on 26 March 1989 (next to be held NA); results—percent of vote by party NA; seats—(79 total) number of seats by party NA

Other political or pressure groups: non-Communist political groups moribund; most leaders have fled the country

Member of: ACCT (associate), AsDB, CP, ESCAP, FAO, G-77, IBRD, ICAO, IDA, IFAD, ILO, IMF, INTERPOL, IOC, ITU, LORCS, NAM, PCA, UN, UNCTAD, UNESCO, UNIDO, UPU, WFTU, WHO, WMO, WTO

Diplomatic representation: Chargé d'Affaires LINTHONG PHETSAVAN; Chancery at 2222 S Street NW, Washington DC 20008; telephone (202) 332-6416 or 6417; *US*—Chargé d'Affaires Charles B. SALMON, Jr.; Embassy at Rue Bartholonie, Vientiane (mailing address is B. P. 114, Vientiane, or Box V, APO San Francisco 96346); telephone 2220, 2357, 2384

Flag: three horizontal bands of red (top), blue (double width), and red with a large white disk centered in the blue band

Economy

Overview: One of the world's poorest nations, Laos has had a Communist centrally planned economy with government ownership and control of productive enterprises of any size. Recently, however, the government has been decentralizing control and encouraging private enterprise. Laos is a landlocked country with a primitive infrastructure, that is, it has no railroads, a rudimentary road system, limited external and internal telecommunications, and electricity available in only a limited area. Subsistence agriculture is the main occupation, accounting for over 60% of GDP and providing about 85-90% of total employment. The predominant crop is rice. For the foreseeable future the economy will continue to depend for its survival on foreign aid from the IMF and other international sources; foreign aid from the USSR and Eastern Europe is being cut sharply.

GDP: $600 million, per capita $150; real growth rate 5% (1990 est.)

Inflation rate (consumer prices): 22% (1990 est.)

Unemployment rate: 21% (1989 est.)

Budget: revenues $83 million; expenditures $188.5 million, including capital expenditures of $94 million (1990 est.)

Exports: $72 million (f.o.b., 1990 est.); *commodities*—electricity, wood products, coffee, tin; *partners*—Thailand, Malaysia, Vietnam, USSR, US

Imports: $238 million (c.i.f., 1990 est.); *commodities*—food, fuel oil, consumer goods, manufactures; *partners*—Thailand, USSR, Japan, France, Vietnam

External debt: $1.1 billion (1990 est.)

Industrial production: growth rate 8% (1989 est.); accounts for about 20% of GDP

Electricity: 176,000 kW capacity; 1,100 million kWh produced, 270 kWh per capita (1990)

Industries: tin mining, timber, electric power, agricultural processing, construction

Agriculture: accounts for 60% of GDP and employs most of the work force; subsistence farming predominates; normally self-sufficient in non-drought years; principal

Laos (continued)

crops—rice (80% of cultivated land), sweet potatoes, vegetables, corn, coffee, sugarcane, cotton; livestock—buffaloes, hogs, cattle, chicken
Illicit drugs: illicit producer of cannabis and opium poppy for the international drug trade
Economic aid: US commitments, including Ex-Im (FY70-79), $276 million; Western (non-US) countries, ODA and OOF bilateral commitments (1970-88) $546 million; Communist countries (1970-89), $995 million
Currency: new kip (plural—kips); 1 new kip (NK) = 100 at
Exchange rates: new kips (NK) per US$1—695 (April 1991), 700 (September 1990), 576 (1989), 385 (1988), 200 (1987), 108 (1986), 95 (1985)
Fiscal year: 1 July-30 June

Communications

Highways: about 27,527 km total; 1,856 km bituminous or bituminous treated; 7,451 km gravel, crushed stone, or improved earth; 18,220 km unimproved earth and often impassable during rainy season mid-May to mid-September
Inland waterways: about 4,587 km, primarily Mekong and tributaries; 2,897 additional kilometers are sectionally navigable by craft drawing less than 0.5 m
Pipelines: 136 km, refined products
Ports: none
Airports: 65 total, 51 usable; 9 with permanent-surface runways; none with runways over 3,659 m; 2 with runways 2,440-3,659 m; 13 with runways 1,220-2,439 m
Telecommunications: service to general public considered poor; radio network provides generally erratic service to government users; 7,390 telephones (1986); stations—10 AM, no FM, 1 TV; 1 satellite earth station

---

Defense Forces

Branches: Lao People's Army (LPA; including naval, aviation, and militia elements), Air Force, National Police Department
Manpower availability: males 15-49, 991,864; 531,084 fit for military service; 45,548 reach military age (18) annually; conscription age NA
Defense expenditures: $NA, 3.8% of GDP (1987)

Lebanon

50 km

Tripoli
Al Hirmil
Jubayl
Ba'labakk
BEIRUT
Sidon
Jazzin
Tyre

Mediterranean Sea

Boundary representation is not necessarily authoritative.

Geography

Total area: 10,400 km²; land area: 10,230 km²
Comparative area: about 0.8 times the size of Connecticut
Land boundaries: 454 km total; Israel 79 km, Syria 375 km
Coastline: 225 km
Maritime claims:
Territorial sea: 12 nm
Disputes: separated from Israel by the 1949 Armistice Line; Israeli troops in southern Lebanon since June 1982; Syrian troops in northern Lebanon since October 1976
Climate: Mediterranean; mild to cool, wet winters with hot, dry summers
Terrain: narrow coastal plain; Al Biqā' (Bekaa Valley) separates Lebanon and Anti-Lebanon Mountains
Natural resources: limestone, iron ore, salt; water-surplus state in a water-deficit region
Land use: arable land 21%; permanent crops 9%; meadows and pastures 1%; forest and woodland 8%; other 61%; includes irrigated 7%
Environment: rugged terrain historically helped isolate, protect, and develop numerous factional groups based on religion, clan, ethnicity; deforestation; soil erosion; air and water pollution; desertification
Note: Nahr al Līṭānī only major river in Near East not crossing an international boundary

---

People

Population: 3,384,626 (July 1991), growth rate 1.4% (1991)
Birth rate: 28 births/1,000 population (1991)
Death rate: 7 deaths/1,000 population (1991)
Net migration rate: −7 migrants/1,000 population (1991)

Infant mortality rate: 48 deaths/1,000 live births (1991)
Life expectancy at birth: 66 years male, 71 years female (1991)
Total fertility rate: 3.6 children born/woman (1991)
Nationality: noun—Lebanese (sing., pl.); adjective—Lebanese
Ethnic divisions: Arab 95%, Armenian 4%, other 1%
Religion: Islam 75%, Christian 25%, Judaism NEGL%; 17 legally recognized sects—4 Orthodox Christian (Armenian Orthodox, Greek Orthodox, Nestorean, Syriac Orthodox), 7 Uniate Christian (Armenian Catholic, Caldean, Greek Catholic, Maronite, Protestant, Roman Catholic, Syrian Catholic), 5 Islam (Alawite or Nusayri, Druze, Isma'ilite, Shi'a, Sunni), and 1 Jewish
Language: Arabic and French (both official); Armenian, English
Literacy: 80% (male 88%, female 73%) age 15 and over can read and write (1990 est.)
Labor force: 650,000; industry, commerce, and services 79%, agriculture 11%, goverment 10% (1985)
Organized labor: 250,000 members (est.)

Government

Note: Between early 1975 and late 1976 Lebanon was torn by civil war between its Christians—then aided by Syrian troops—and its Muslims and their Palestinian allies. The cease-fire established in October 1976 between the domestic political groups generally held for about six years, despite occasional fighting. Syrian troops constituted as the Arab Deterrent Force by the Arab League have remained in Lebanon. Syria's move toward supporting the Lebanese Muslims and the Palestinians and Israel's growing support for Lebanese Christians brought the two sides into rough equilibrium, but no progress was made toward national reconciliation or political reforms—the original cause of the war.

Continuing Israeli concern about the Palestinian presence in Lebanon led to the Israeli invasion of Lebanon in June 1982. Israeli forces occupied all of the southern portion of the country and mounted a summer-long siege of Beirut, which resulted in the evacuation of the PLO from Beirut in September under the supervision of a multinational force (MNF) made up of US, French, and Italian troops.

Within days of the departure of the MNF, Lebanon's newly elected president, Bashir Gemayel, was assassinated. In the wake of his death, Christian militiamen massacred hundreds of Palestinian refugees in two Beirut camps. This prompted the return of the MNF to ease the security burden on Lebanon's weak Army and security forces. In late March 1984 the last MNF units withdrew.

Lebanese Parliamentarians met in Ta'if, Saudi Arabia, in late 1989 and concluded a national reconciliation pact that codified a new power-sharing formula, specifiying a Christian president but giving Muslims more authority. Rene Muawad was subsequently elected president on 4 November 1989, ending a 13-month period during which Lebanon had no president and rival Muslim and Christian governments. Muawad was assassinated 17 days later, on 22 November; on 24 November Ilyas Harawi was elected to succeed Muawad.

In October 1990, the chances for ending the 16 year old civil war and implementing Ta'if were markedly improved when Syrian and Lebanese forces ousted renegade Christian General Awn from his stronghold in East Beirut. Awn had defied the legitimate government and established a separate mini-state within East Beirut after being appointed acting Prime Minister by outgoing President Gemayel in 1988. Awn and his supporters feared Ta'if would diminish Christian power in Lebanon and increase the influence of Syria.

Since the removal of Awn, the Lebanese Government has reunited the capital city and implemented a phased plan to disarm the militias and gradually reestablish authority throughout Lebanon. The army has deployed from Beirut north along the coast road to Tripoli, southeast into the Shuf mountains, and south to the vicinity of Sidon. Many militiamen from Christian and Muslim groups have evacuated Beirut for their strongholds in the north, south, and east of the country. Some heavy weapons possessed by the militias have been turned over to the government, which has begun a plan to integrate some militiamen into the military and the internal security forces.

Lebanon and Syria signed a treaty of friendship and cooperation in May 1991. Lebanon continues to be partially occupied by Syrian troops, which are deployed in East and West Beirut, its southern suburbs, the Bekaa Valley, and throughout northern Lebanon.

Iran also maintains a small contingent of revolutionary guards in the Bekaa Valley and South Lebanon to support Lebanese Islamic fundamentalist groups.

Israel withdrew the bulk of its forces from the south in 1985, although it still retains troops in a 10-km-deep security zone north of its border with Lebanon. Israel arms and trains the Army of South Lebanon (ASL), which also occupies the security zone and is Israel's first line of defense against attacks on its northern border.

The following description is based on the present constitutional and customary practices of the Lebanese system.

Long-form name: Republic of Lebanon; note—may be changed to Lebanese Republic
Type: republic
Capital: Beirut
Administrative divisions: 5 governorates (muḥāfaẓat, singular—muḥāfaẓah); Al Biqā', Al Janūb, Ash Shamāl, Bayrūt, Jabal Lubnān
Independence: 22 November 1943 (from League of Nations mandate under French administration)
Constitution: 26 May 1926 (amended)
Legal system: mixture of Ottoman law, canon law, Napoleonic code, and civil law; no judicial review of legislative acts; has not accepted compulsory ICJ jurisdiction
National holiday: Independence Day, 22 November (1943)
Executive branch: president, prime minister, Cabinet; note—by custom, the president is a Maronite Christian, the prime minister is a Sunni Muslim, and the speaker of the legislature is a Shi'a Muslim
Legislative branch: unicameral National Assembly (Arabic—Majlis Alnuwab, French—Assemblée Nationale)
Judicial branch: four Courts of Cassation (three courts for civil and commercial cases and one court for criminal cases)
Leaders:
Chief of State—Ilyas HARAWI (since 24 November 1989);
Head of Government—Prime Minister 'Umar KARAMI (since 20 December 1990)
Political parties and leaders: political party activity is organized along largely sectarian lines; numerous political groupings exist, consisting of individual political figures and followers motivated by religious, clan, and economic considerations; most parties have well-armed militias, which are still involved in occasional clashes
Suffrage: compulsory for all males at age 21; authorized for women at age 21 with elementary education
Elections:
National Assembly—elections should be held every four years but security conditions have prevented elections since May 1972
Communists: the Lebanese Communist Party was legalized in 1970; members and sympathizers estimated at 2,000-3,000
Member of: ABEDA, ACCT, AFESD, AL, AMF, CCC, ESCWA, FAO, G-24, G-77, IAEA, IBRD, ICAO, ICC, ICFTU, IDA, IDB, IFAD, IFC, ILO, IMF, IMO, INTELSAT, INTERPOL, IOC, ITU, LORCS, NAM, OIC, PCA, UN, UNCTAD, UNESCO, UNHCR, UNIDO, UNRWA, UPU, WFTU, WHO, WIPO, WMO, WTO
Diplomatic representation: Ambassador Nassib S. LAHOUD; Chancery at 2560 28th Street NW, Washington DC 20008; telephone (202) 939-6300; there are Lebanese Consulates General in Detroit, New York, and Los Angeles;
US—Ambassador Ryan C. CROCKER; Embassy at Antelias, Beirut (mailing address is P. O. Box 70-840, Beirut, and FPO New York 09530); telephone [961] 417774 or 415802, 415803, 402200, 403300
Flag: three horizontal bands of red (top), white (double width), and red with a green and brown cedar tree centered in the white band

---

Economy

Overview: Since 1975 civil war has seriously damaged Lebanon's economic infrastructure, disrupted economic activity, and all but ended Lebanon's position as a Middle Eastern entrepôt and banking hub. Following October 1990, however, a tentative peace has enabled the central government to begin restoring control in Beirut, collect taxes, and regain access to key port and government facilities. The battered economy has also been propped up by a financially sound banking system and resilient small- and medium-scale manufacturers. Family remittances, foreign financial support to political factions, the narcotics trade, and international emergency aid are main sources of foreign exchange. Economic prospects for 1991 have brightened, particularly if the Syrian-backed government is able to maintain law and order and reestablish business confidence. Rebuilding war-ravaged Beirut is likely to provide a major stimulus to the Lebanese economy in 1991.
GDP: $3.3 billion, per capita $1,000; real growth rate −15% (1990 est.)
Inflation rate (consumer prices): 100% (1990 est.)
Unemployment rate: 35% (1990 est.)
Budget: revenues $120 million; expenditures $1.0 billion, including capital expenditures of $NA (1990 est.)
Exports: $1.0 billion (f.o.b., 1989 est.);
commodities—agricultural products, chemicals, textiles, precious and semiprecious metals and jewelry, metals and metal products;
partners—Saudi Arabia 16%, Switzerland 8%, Jordan 6%, Kuwait 6%, US 5%
Imports: $1.9 billion (c.i.f., 1989 est.);
commodities—NA;
partners—Italy 14%, France 12%, US 6%, Turkey 5%, Saudi Arabia 3%
External debt: $900 million (1990 est.)
Industrial production: growth rate NA%
Electricity: 1,381,000 kW capacity; 3,870 million kWh produced, 1,170 kWh per capita (1989)
Industries: banking, food processing, textiles, cement, oil refining, chemicals, jewelry, some metal fabricating

Lebanon *(continued)*

Agriculture: accounts for about one-third of GDP; principal products—citrus fruits, vegetables, potatoes, olives, tobacco, hemp (hashish), sheep, and goats; not self-sufficient in grain

Illicit drugs: illicit producer of opium poppy and cannabis for the international drug trade; opium poppy production in Al Biqa' is increasing; hashish production is shipped to Western Europe, Israel, and the Middle East

Economic aid: US commitments, including Ex-Im (FY70-88), $356 million; Western (non-US) countries, ODA and OOF bilateral commitments (1970-88), $608 million; OPEC bilateral aid (1979-89), $962 million; Communist countries (1970-89), $9 million

Currency: Lebanese pound (plural—pounds); 1 Lebanese pound (£L) = 100 piasters

Exchange rates: Lebanese pounds (£L) per US$1—974.22 (January 1991), 695.09 (1990), 496.69 (1989), 409.23 (1988), 224.60 (1987), 38.37 (1986), 16.42 (1985)

Fiscal year: calendar year

Communications

Railroads: 378 km total; 296 km 1.435-meter standard gauge, 82 km 1.050-meter gauge; all single track; system almost entirely inoperable

Highways: 7,370 km total; 6,270 km paved, 450 km gravel and crushed stone, 650 km improved earth

Pipelines: crude oil, 72 km (none in operation)

Ports: Beirut, Tripoli, Ra's Sil'ātā, Jūniyah, Sidon, Az Zahrānī, Tyre, Shikkā; northern ports are occupied by Syrian forces and southern ports are occupied or partially quarantined by Israeli forces

Merchant marine: 60 ships (1,000 GRT or over) totaling 257,220 GRT/379,691 DWT; includes 39 cargo, 1 refrigerated cargo, 2 vehicle carrier, 2 roll-on/roll-off cargo, 1 container, 8 livestock carrier, 1 petroleum, oils, and lubricants (POL) tanker, 1 chemical tanker, 1 specialized tanker, 3 bulk, 1 combination bulk

Civil air: 15 major transport aircraft

Airports: 9 total, 8 usable; 6 with permanent-surface runways; none with runways over 3,659 m; 3 with runways 2,440-3,659 m; 2 with runways 1,220-2,439 m; none under the direct control of the Lebanese Government

Telecommunications: rebuilding program disrupted; had fair system of radio relay, cable; 325,000 telephones; stations—5 AM, 3 FM, 15 TV; 1 inactive Indian Ocean INTELSAT satellite earth station; 3 submarine coaxial cables; radio relay to Jordan and Syria, inoperable

Defense Forces

Branches: Army (includes Navy and Air Force)

Manpower availability: males 15-49, 725,974; 449,912 fit for military service

Defense expenditures: $168 million, 7.3% of GDP (1991)

Lesotho

Geography

Total area: 30,350 km²; land area: 30,350 km²

Comparative area: slightly larger than Maryland

Land boundary: 909 km with South Africa

Coastline: none—landlocked

Maritime claims: none—landlocked

Climate: temperate; cool to cold, dry winters; hot, wet summers

Terrain: mostly highland with some plateaus, hills, and mountains

Natural resources: some diamonds and other minerals, water, agricultural and grazing land

Land use: arable land 10%; permanent crops 0%; meadows and pastures 66%; forest and woodland 0%; other 24%

Environment: population pressure forcing settlement in marginal areas results in overgrazing, severe soil erosion, soil exhaustion; desertification

Note: landlocked; surrounded by South Africa; Highlands Water Project will control, store, and redirect water to South Africa

People

Population: 1,801,174 (July 1991), growth rate 2.6% (1991)

Birth rate: 36 births/1,000 population (1991)

Death rate: 10 deaths/1,000 population (1991)

Net migration rate: 0 migrants/1,000 population (1991)

Infant mortality rate: 78 deaths/1,000 live births (1991)

Life expectancy at birth: 59 years male, 63 years female (1991)

Total fertility rate: 4.8 children born/woman (1991)

Nationality: noun—Mosotho (sing.), Basotho (pl.); adjective—Basotho

Ethnic divisions: Sotho 99.7%; Europeans 1,600, Asians 800

Religion: Christian 80%, rest indigenous beliefs

Language: Sesotho (southern Sotho) and English (official); also Zulu and Xhosa

Literacy: 59% (male 44%, female 68%) age 15 and over can read and write (1966)

Labor force: 689,000 economically active; 86.2% of resident population engaged in subsistence agriculture; roughly 60% of active male labor force works in South Africa

Organized labor: there are two trade union federations; the government favors formation of a single, umbrella trade union confederation

Government

Long-form name: Kingdom of Lesotho

Type: constitutional monarchy

Capital: Maseru

Administrative divisions: 10 districts; Berea, Butha-Buthe, Leribe, Mafeteng, Maseru, Mohales Hoek, Mokhotlong, Qachas Nek, Quthing, Thaba-Tseka

Independence: 4 October 1966 (from UK; formerly Basutoland)

Constitution: 4 October 1966, suspended January 1970

Legal system: based on English common law and Roman-Dutch law; judicial review of legislative acts in High Court and Court of Appeal; has not accepted compulsory ICJ jurisdiction

National holiday: Independence Day, 4 October (1966)

Executive branch: monarch, chairman of the Military Council, Military Council, Council of Ministers (cabinet)

Legislative branch: none—the bicameral Parliament was dissolved following the military coup in January 1986; note—a National Constituent Assembly convened in June 1990 to rewrite the constitution and debate issues of national importance, but it has no legislative authority

Judicial branch: High Court, Court of Appeal

Leaders:

Chief of State—King LETSIE III (since 12 November 1990 following dismissal of his father, exiled King MOSHOESHOE II, by Maj. Gen. LEKHANYA);

Head of Government—Chairman of the Military Council Col. Elias Phisoana RA-MAEMA (since 30 April 1991)

Political parties and leaders: Basotho National Party (BNP), Matete MAJARA (interim leader); Basutoland Congress Party (BCP), Ntsu MOKHEHLE; National Independent Party (NIP), A. C. MANYELI; Marematlou Freedom Party (MFP), S. H. MAPHELEBA; United Democratic Party, Charles MOFELI; Communist Party of Lesotho (CPL), Jacob KENYA

Suffrage: universal at age 21

Elections:

National Assembly—dissolved following the military coup in January 1986; military has pledged elections will take place in June 1992

Communists: small Lesotho Communist Party

Member of: ACP, AfDB, C, CCC, ECA, FAO, G-77, GATT, IBRD, ICAO, ICFTU, IDA, IFAD, IFC, ILO, IMF, INTERPOL, IOC, ITU, LORCS, NAM, OAU, SACU, SADCC, UN, UNCTAD, UNESCO, UNHCR, UNIDO, UPU, WCL, WHO, WIPO, WMO, WTO

Diplomatic representation: Ambassador W. T. VAN TONDER; Chancery at 2511 Massachusetts Avenue NW, Washington DC 20008; telephone (202) 797-5 534; *US*—Ambassador Leonard H.O. SPEARMAN, Jr.; Embassy at address NA, Maseru (mailing address is P. O. Box 333, Maseru 100); telephone [266] 312666

Flag: divided diagonally from the lower hoist side corner; the upper half is white bearing the brown silhouette of a large shield with crossed spear and club; the lower half is a diagonal blue band with a green triangle in the corner

Economy

Overview: Small, landlocked, and mountainous, Lesotho has no important natural resources other than water. Its economy is based on agriculture, light manufacturing, and remittances from laborers employed in South Africa ($153 million in 1989). The great majority of households gain their livelihoods from subsistence farming and migrant labor. Manufacturing depends largely on farm products to support the milling, canning, leather, and jute industries; other industries include textile, clothing, and light engineering. Industry's share of GDP rose from 6% in 1982 to 15% in 1989. Political and economic instability in South Africa raise uncertainties for Lesotho's economy, especially with respect to migrant worker remittances—over one-third of GDP.

GDP: $420 million, per capita $240; real growth rate 4.0% (1990 est.)

Inflation rate (consumer prices): 15% (1990 est.)

Unemployment rate: 23% (1988)

Budget: revenues $280 million; expenditures $288 million, including capital expenditures of $NA (FY92 est.)

Exports: $66 million (f.o.b., 1989); *commodities*—wool, mohair, wheat, cattle, peas, beans, corn, hides, skins, baskets; *partners*—South Africa 53%, EC 30%, North and South America 13% (1989)

Imports: $499 million (f.o.b., 1989); *commodities*—mainly corn, building materials, clothing, vehicles, machinery, medicines, petroleum, oil, and lubricants;

partners—South Africa 95%, EC 2% (1989)

External debt: $370 million (December 1990 est.)

Industrial production: growth rate 7.8% (1989 est.); accounts for 15% of GDP

Electricity: power supplied by South Africa

Industries: food, beverages, textiles, handicrafts, tourism

Agriculture: accounts for 18% of GDP and employs 60-70% of all households; exceedingly primitive, mostly subsistence farming and livestock; principal crops are corn, wheat, pulses, sorghum, barley

Economic aid: US commitments, including Ex-Im (FY70-89), $268 million; Western (non-US) countries, ODA and OOF bilateral commitments (1970-88), $754 million; OPEC bilateral aid (1979-89), $4 million; Communist countries (1970-89), $14 million

Currency: loti (plural—maloti); 1 loti (L) = 100 lisente

Exchange rates: maloti (M) per US$1— 2.5625 (January 1991), 2.5863 (1990), 2.6166 (1989), 2.2611 (1988), 2.0350 (1987), 2.2685 (1986), 2.1911 (1985); note—the Basotho loti is at par with the South African rand

Fiscal year: 1 April-31 March

Communications

Railroads: 1.6 km; owned, operated, and included in the statistics of South Africa

Highways: 5,167 km total; 508 km paved; 1,585 km crushed stone, gravel, or stabilized soil; 946 km improved earth, 2,128 km unimproved earth

Civil air: 2 major transport aircraft

Airports: 28 total, 28 usable; 3 with permanent surface runways; none with runways over 3,659 m; 1 with runways 2,440-3,659 m; 2 with runways 1,220-2,439 m

Telecommunications: rudimentary system consisting of a few land lines, a small radio relay system, and minor radiocommunication stations; 5,920 telephones; stations—2 AM, 2 FM, 1 TV; 1 Atlantic Ocean INTELSAT earth station

Defense Forces

Branches: Royal Lesotho Defense Force (RLDF; includes Army, Air Wing), Royal Lesotho Mounted Police

Manpower availability: males 15-49, 394,829; 212,967 fit for military service

Defense expenditures: $55 million, 8.6% of GDP (1990 est.)

Liberia

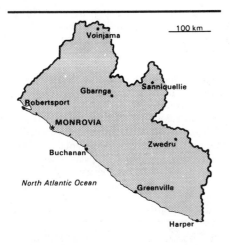

Geography

Total area: 111,370 km²; land area: 96,320 km²
Comparative area: slightly larger than Tennessee
Land boundaries: 1,585 km total; Guinea 563 km, Ivory Coast 716 km, Sierra Leone 306 km
Coastline: 579 km
Maritime claims:
Continental shelf: 200 m (depth) or to depth of exploitation;
Territorial sea: 200 nm
Climate: tropical; hot, humid; dry winters with hot days and cool to cold nights; wet, cloudy summers with frequent heavy showers
Terrain: mostly flat to rolling coastal plains rising to rolling plateau and low mountains in northeast
Natural resources: iron ore, timber, diamonds, gold
Land use: arable land 1%; permanent crops 3%; meadows and pastures 2%; forest and woodland 39%; other 55%; includes irrigated NEGL%
Environment: West Africa's largest tropical rain forest, subject to deforestation

People

Population: 2,730,446 (July 1991), growth rate 3.4% (1991)
Birth rate: 45 births/1,000 population (1991)
Death rate: 13 deaths/1,000 population (1991)
Net migration rate: 2 migrants/1,000 population (1991)
Infant mortality rate: 124 deaths/1,000 live births (1991)
Life expectancy at birth: 54 years male, 59 years female (1991)
Total fertility rate: 6.5 children born/woman (1991)
Nationality: noun—Liberian(s); adjective—Liberian

Ethnic divisions: indigenous African tribes, including Kpelle, Bassa, Gio, Kru, Grebo, Mano, Krahn, Gola, Gbandi, Loma, Kissi, Vai, and Bella 95%; descendants of repatriated slaves known as Americo-Liberians 5%
Religion: traditional 70%, Muslim 20%, Christian 10%
Language: English (official); more than 20 local languages of the Niger-Congo language group; English used by about 20%
Literacy: 40% (male 50%, female 29%) age 15 and over can read and write (1990 est.)
Labor force: 510,000, including 220,000 in the monetary economy; agriculture 70.5%, services 10.8%, industry and commerce 4.5%, other 14.2%; non-African foreigners hold about 95% of the top-level management and engineering jobs; 52% of population of working age
Organized labor: 2% of labor force

Government

Long-form name: Republic of Liberia
Type: republic
Capital: Monrovia
Administrative divisions: 13 counties; Bomi, Bong, Grand Bassa, Grand Cape Mount, Grand Jide, Grand Kru, Lofa, Margibi, Maryland, Montserrado, Nimba, Rivercess, Sino
Independence: 26 July 1847
Constitution: 6 January 1986
Legal system: dual system of statutory law based on Anglo-American common law for the modern sector and customary law based on unwritten tribal practices for indigenous sector
National holiday: Independence Day, 26 July (1847)
Executive branch: president, vice president, Cabinet
Legislative branch: bicameral National Assembly consists of an upper house or Senate and a lower house or House of Representatives
Judicial branch: People's Supreme Court
Leaders:
Chief of State and Head of Government—interim President Dr. Amos SAWYER (since 15 November 1990); interim Vice President Ronald DIGGS (since 15 November 1990); note—this is an interim government appointed by the Economic Community of West African States (ECOWAS) that will be replaced after elections are held under a West African-brokered peace plan; rival rebel factions led by Prince Y. JOHNSON and Charles TAYLOR are challenging the Sawyer government's legitimacy while observing a tenuous cease fire; the former president, Gen. Dr. Samuel Kanyon DOE, was ousted and killed on 9 September 1990 in a coup led by Prince Y. JOHNSON
Political parties and leaders: National Democratic Party of Liberia (NDPL), Augustus

CAINE, chairman; Liberian Action Party (LAP), Emmanuel KOROMAH, chairman; Unity Party (UP), Carlos SMITH, chairman; United People's Party (UPP), Gabriel Baccus MATTHEWS, chairman
Suffrage: universal at age 18
Elections:
President—last held on 15 October 1985 (next to be held NA); results—Gen. Dr. Samuel Kanyon DOE (NDPL) 50.9%, Jackson DOE (LAP) 26.4%, other 22.7%; note—President Doe was killed by rebel forces on 9 September 1990;
Senate—last held on 15 October 1985 (next to be held NA); results—percent of vote by party NA; seats—(26 total) NDPL 21, LAP 3, UP 1, LUP 1;
House of Representatives—last held on 15 October 1985 (next to be held 15 October 1991); results—percent of vote by party NA; seats—(64 total) NDPL 51, LAP 8, UP 3, LUP 2
Member of: ACP, AfDB, CCC, ECA, ECOWAS, FAO, G-77, IAEA, IBRD, ICAO, ICFTU, IDA, IFAD, IFC, ILO, IMF, IMO, INMARSAT, INTERPOL, IOC, ITU, LORCS, NAM, OAU, UN, UNCTAD, UNESCO, UPU, WCL, WHO, WIPO, WMO
Diplomatic representation: Ambassador Eugenia A. WORDSWORTH-STEVENSON; Chancery at 5201 16th Street NW, Washington DC 20011; telephone (202) 723-0437 through 0440; there is a Liberian Consulate General in New York;
US—Ambassador Peter J. de VOS; Embassy at 111 United Nations Drive, Monrovia (mailing address is P. O. Box 98, Monrovia, or APO New York 09155); telephone [231] 222991 through 222994
Flag: 11 equal horizontal stripes of red (top and bottom) alternating with white; there is a white five-pointed star on a blue square in the upper hoist-side corner; the design was based on the US flag

Economy

Overview: Civil war during 1990 destroyed much of Liberia's economy, especially the infrastructure in and around Monrovia. Expatriate businessmen fled the country, taking capital and expertise with them. Many will not return. Richly endowed with water, mineral resources, forests, and a climate favorable to agriculture, Liberia had been a producer and exporter of basic products, while local manufacturing, mainly foreign owned, had been small in scope. Political instability threatens prospects for economic reconstruction and repatriation of some 750,000 Liberian refugees who fled to neighboring countries.
GDP: $988 million, per capita $400; real growth rate 1.5% (1988)
Inflation rate (consumer prices): 12% (1989)

Unemployment rate: 43% urban (1988)
Budget: revenues $242.1 million; expenditures $435.4 million, including capital expenditures of $29.5 million (1989)
Exports: $505 million (f.o.b., 1989 est.); *commodities*—iron ore 61%, rubber 20%, timber 11%, coffee; *partners*—US, EC, Netherlands
Imports: $394 million (c.i.f., 1989 est.); *commodities*—rice, mineral fuels, chemicals, machinery, transportation equipment, other foodstuffs; *partners*—US, EC, Japan, China, Netherlands, ECOWAS
External debt: $1.6 billion (December 1990 est.)
Industrial production: growth rate 1.5% in manufacturing (1987); accounts for 22% of GDP
Electricity: 400,000 kW capacity; 730 million kWh produced, 290 kWh per capita (1989)
Industries: rubber processing, food processing, construction materials, furniture, palm oil processing, mining (iron ore, diamonds)
Agriculture: accounts for about 40% of GDP (including fishing and forestry); principal products—rubber, timber, coffee, cocoa, rice, cassava, palm oil, sugarcane, bananas, sheep, and goats; not self-sufficient in food, imports 25% of rice consumption
Economic aid: US commitments, including Ex-Im (FY70-89), $665 million; Western (non-US) countries, ODA and OOF bilateral commitments (1970-88), $853 million; OPEC bilateral aid (1979-89), $25 million; Communist countries (1970-89), $77 million
Currency: Liberian dollar (plural—dollars); 1 Liberian dollar (L$) = 100 cents
Exchange rates: Liberian dollars (L$) per US$1—1.00 (fixed rate since 1940); unofficial parallel exchange rate of L$2.5 = US$1, January 1989
Fiscal year: calendar year

Communications

Railroads: 480 km total; 328 km 1.435-meter standard gauge, 152 km 1.067-meter narrow gauge; all lines single track; rail systems owned and operated by foreign steel and financial interests in conjunction with Liberian Government
Highways: 10,087 km total; 603 km bituminous treated, 2,848 km all weather, 4,313 km dry weather; there are also 2,323 km of private, laterite-surfaced roads open to public use, owned by rubber and timber companies
Ports: Monrovia, Buchanan, Greenville, Harper (or Cape Palmas)
Merchant marine: 1,563 ships (1,000 GRT or over) totaling 53,053,254 DWT/94,597,871 DWT; includes 18 passenger, 1 short-sea passenger, 156 cargo, 47 refrigerated cargo, 15 roll-on/roll-off cargo, 67 vehicle carrier, 74 container, 5 barge carrier, 450 petroleum, oils, and lubricants (POL) tanker, 104 chemical, 60 combination ore/oil, 44 liquefied gas, 6 specialized tanker, 485 bulk, 1 multifunction large-load carrier, 30 combination bulk; note—a flag of convenience registry; all ships are foreign owned; the top four owning flags are US 19%, Japan 17%, Hong Kong 12%, and Norway 10%; China owns at least 28 ships, Bulgaria owns 3, and Poland owns 1
Civil air: 3 major transport aircraft
Airports: 75 total, 58 usable; 2 with permanent-surface runways; none with runways over 3,659 m; 1 with runways 2,440-3,659 m; 4 with runways 1,220-2,439 m
Telecommunications: telephone and telegraph service via radio relay network; main center is Monrovia; 8,500 telephones; stations—3 AM, 4 FM, 5 TV; 2 Atlantic Ocean INTELSAT earth stations

Defense Forces

Branches: Armed Forces of Liberia (includes Army, Navy, Air Force), Coast Guard, National Police Force
Manpower availability: males 15-49, 648,636; 346,349 fit for military service; no conscription
Defense expenditures: $NA, 2.4% of GDP (1987)

Libya

Geography

Total area: 1,759,540 km²; land area: 1,759,540 km²
Comparative area: slightly larger than Alaska
Land boundaries: 4,383 km total; Algeria 982 km, Chad 1,055 km, Egypt 1,150 km, Niger 354 km, Sudan 383 km, Tunisia 459 km
Coastline: 1,770 km
Maritime claims:
Territorial sea: 12 nm;
Gulf of Sidra closing line: 32° 30′ N
Disputes: claims and occupies the 100,000 km² Aozou Strip in northern Chad; maritime boundary dispute with Tunisia; Libya claims about 19,400 km² in northern Niger; Libya claims about 19,400 km² in southeastern Algeria
Climate: Mediterranean along coast; dry, extreme desert interior
Terrain: mostly barren, flat to undulating plains, plateaus, depressions
Natural resources: crude oil, natural gas, gypsum
Land use: arable land 1%; permanent crops 0%; meadows and pastures 8%; forest and woodland 0%; other 91%; includes irrigated NEGL%
Environment: hot, dry, dust-laden ghibli is a southern wind lasting one to four days in spring and fall; desertification; sparse natural surface-water resources
Note: the Great Manmade River Project, the largest water development scheme in the world, is being built to bring water from large aquifers under the Sahara to coastal cities

People

Population: 4,350,742 (July 1991), growth rate 3.0% (1991)
Birth rate: 36 births/1,000 population (1991)

Death rate: 6 deaths/1,000 population (1991)

Net migration rate: 0 migrants/1,000 population (1991)

Infant mortality rate: 62 deaths/1,000 live births (1991)

Life expectancy at birth: 66 years male, 71 years female (1991)

Total fertility rate: 5.1 children born/woman (1991)

Nationality: noun—Libyan(s); adjective—Libyan

Ethnic divisions: Berber and Arab 97%; some Greeks, Maltese, Italians, Egyptians, Pakistanis, Turks, Indians, and Tunisians

Religion: Sunni Muslim 97%

Language: Arabic; Italian and English widely understood in major cities

Literacy: 64% (male 75%, female 50%) age 15 and over can read and write (1990 est.)

Labor force: 1,000,000, includes about 280,000 resident foreigners; industry 31%, services 27%, government 24%, agriculture 18%

Organized labor: National Trade Unions' Federation, 275,000 members; General Union for Oil and Petrochemicals; Pan-Africa Federation of Petroleum Energy and Allied Workers

---

Government

Long-form name: Socialist People's Libyan Arab Jamahiriya

Type: Jamahiriya (a state of the masses); in theory, governed by the populace through local councils; in fact, a military dictatorship

Capital: Tripoli

Administrative divisions: 46 municipalities (baladīyat, singular—baladīyah); Ajdābiyā, Al Abyār, Al 'Azīzīyah, Al Baydā', Al Jufrah, Al Jumayl, Al Khums, Al Kufrah, Al Marj, Al Qarābūllī, Al Qubbah, Al 'Ujaylāt, Ash Shāṭi', Awbārī, Az Zahrā', Az Zāwiyah, Banghāzī, Banī Walīd, Bin Jawwād, Darnah, Ghadāmis, Gharyān, Ghāt, Jādū, Jālū, Janzūr, Masallātah, Miṣrātah, Mizdah, Murzuq, Nālūt, Qamīnis, Qaṣr Bin Ghashīr, Sabhā, Ṣabrātah, Shaḥḥāt, Ṣurmān, Surt, Tājūrā', Ṭarābulus, Tarhūnah, Ṭubruq, Tūkrah, Yafran, Zlīṭan, Zuwārah; note—the number of municipalities may have been reduced to 13 named Al Jabal al-Akhdar, Al Jabal al-Gharbi, Al Jabal al-Khums, Al Batnam, Al Kufrah, Al Marqab, Al Marzuq, Az Zāwiyah, Banghāzī, Khalij Surt, Sabhā, Tripoli, Wadi al-Hayat

Independence: 24 December 1951 (from Italy)

Constitution: 11 December 1969, amended 2 March 1977

Legal system: based on Italian civil law system and Islamic law; separate religious courts; no constitutional provision for judicial review of legislative acts; has not accepted compulsory ICJ jurisdiction

National holiday: Revolution Day, 1 September (1969)

Executive branch: revolutionary leader, chairman of the General People's Committee, General People's Committee (cabinet)

Legislative branch: unicameral General People's Congress

Judicial branch: Supreme Court

Leaders:
Chief of State—Revolutionary Leader Col. Mu'ammar Abu Minyar al-QADHAFI (since 1 September 1969);
Head of Government—Chairman of the General People's Committee (Premier) Abu Zayd 'Umar DURDA (since 7 October 1990)

Political parties and leaders: none

Suffrage: universal and compulsory at age 18

Elections: national elections are indirect through a hierarchy of revolutionary committees

Political parties: none

Communists: no organized party, negligible membership

Other political or pressure groups: various Arab nationalist movements and the Arab Socialist Resurrection (Ba'th) party with almost negligible memberships may be functioning clandestinely, as well as some Islamic elements

Member of: ABEDA, AfDB, AFESD, AL, AMF, AMU, CAEU, CCC, ECA, FAO, G-77, IAEA, IBRD, ICAO, IDA, IDB, IFAD, IFC, ILO, IMF, IMO, INTELSAT, INTERPOL, IOC, ITU, LORCS, NAM, OAPEC, OAU, OIC, OPEC, UN, UNCTAD, UNESCO, UNIDO, UPU, WHO, WIPO, WMO, WTO

Diplomatic representation: none

Flag: plain green; green is the traditional color of Islam (the state religion)

Economy

Overview: The socialist-oriented economy depends primarily upon revenues from the oil sector, which contributes practically all export earnings and about one-third of GNP. Since 1980, however, the sharp drop in oil prices and the resulting decline in export revenues have adversely affected economic development. In 1988 per capita GNP was the highest in Africa at $5,410, but it had been $2,000 higher in 1982. Severe cutbacks in imports over the past five years have led to shortages of basic goods and foodstuffs, although the reopening of the Libyan-Tunisian border in April 1988 and the Libyan-Egyptian border in December 1989 have somewhat eased shortages. Austerity budgets and a lack of trained technicians have undermined the government's ability to implement a number of planned infrastructure development projects. Windfall profits from the hike in

world oil prices in late 1990 improved the foreign payments position and may permit Tripoli to ease austerity measures. The non-oil industrial and construction sectors, which account for about 22% of GDP, have expanded from processing mostly agricultural products to include petrochemicals, iron, steel, and aluminum. Although agriculture accounts for less than 5% of GNP, it employs 18% of the labor force. Climatic conditions and poor soils severely limit farm output, requiring Libya to import about 75% of its food requirements.

GNP: $24 billion, per capita $5,860; real growth rate 3% (1989 est.)

Inflation rate (consumer prices): 20% (1988 est.)

Unemployment rate: 2% (1988 est.)

Budget: revenues $8.1 billion; expenditures $9.8 billion, including capital expenditures of $3.1 billion (1989 est.)

Exports: $6.1 billion (f.o.b., 1989 est.); *commodities*—petroleum, peanuts, hides; *partners*—Italy, USSR, FRG, Spain, France, Belgium/Luxembourg, Turkey

Imports: $6.2 billion (f.o.b., 1989 est.); *commodities*—machinery, transport equipment, food, manufactured goods; *partners*—Italy, USSR, FRG, UK, Japan

External debt: $3.5 billion, excluding military debt (December 1990 est.)

Industrial production: growth rate NA%; accounts for 43% of GDP (including oil)

Electricity: 4,705,000 kW capacity; 13,600 million kWh produced, 3,220 kWh per capita (1990)

Industries: petroleum, food processing, textiles, handicrafts, cement

Agriculture: 5% of GNP; cash crops—wheat, barley, olives, dates, citrus fruits, peanuts; 75% of food is imported

Economic aid: Western (non-US) countries, ODA and OOF bilateral commitments (1970-87), $242 million; no longer a recipient

Currency: Libyan dinar (plural—dinars); 1 Libyan dinar (LD) = 1,000 dirhams

Exchange rates: Libyan dinars (LD) per US$1—0.2669 (January 1991), 0.2699 (1990), 0.2922 (1989), 0.2853 (1988), 0.2706 (1987), 0.3139 (1986), 0.2961 (1985)

Fiscal year: calendar year

Communications

Highways: 32,500 km total; 24,000 km bituminous and bituminous treated, 8,500 km gravel, crushed stone and earth

Pipelines: crude oil 4,383 km; natural gas 1,947 km; refined products 443 km (includes 256 km liquid petroleum gas)

Ports: Tobruk, Tripoli, Banghazi, Misratah, Marsa el Brega

Merchant marine: 30 ships (1,000 GRT or over) totaling 807,539 GRT/1,452,847

Liechtenstein

DWT; includes 3 short-sea passenger, 11 cargo, 4 roll-on/roll-off cargo, 11 petroleum, oils, and lubricants (POL) tanker, 1 chemical tanker

Civil air: 59 major transport aircraft

Airports: 131 total, 123 usable; 53 with permanent-surface runways; 7 with runways over 3,659 m; 31 with runways 2,440-3,659 m; 44 with runways 1,220-2,439 m

Telecommunications: modern telecommunications system using radio relay, coaxial cable, tropospheric scatter, and domestic satellite stations; 370,000 telephones; stations—18 AM, 3 FM, 13 TV; satellite earth stations—1 Atlantic Ocean INTELSAT, 1 Indian Ocean INTELSAT, and 14 domestic; submarine cables to France and Italy; radio relay to Tunisia; tropospheric scatter to Greece; planned ARABSAT and Intersputnik satellite stations

Defense Forces

Branches: Armed Peoples of the Libyan Arab Jamahariya (includes Army, Navy, Air Force, Air Defense Command), National Police

Manpower availability: males 15-49, 1,023,335; 603,886 fit for military service; 52,059 reach military age (17) annually; conscription now being implemented

Defense expenditures: $NA, 11.1% of GNP (1987)

Geography

Total area: 160 km²; land area: 160 km²

Comparative area: about 0.9 times the size of Washington, DC

Land boundaries: 78 km total; Austria 37 km, Switzerland 41 km

Coastline: none—landlocked

Maritime claims: none—landlocked

Climate: continental; cold, cloudy winters with frequent snow or rain; cool to moderately warm, cloudy, humid summers

Terrain: mostly mountainous (Alps) with Rhine Valley in western third

Natural resources: hydroelectric potential

Land use: arable land 25%; permanent crops 0%; meadows and pastures 38%; forest and woodland 19%; other 18%

Environment: variety of microclimatic variations based on elevation

Note: landlocked

People

Population: 28,476 (July 1991), growth rate 0.6% (1991)

Birth rate: 13 births/1,000 population (1991)

Death rate: 7 deaths/1,000 population (1991)

Net migration rate: 0 migrants/1,000 population (1991)

Infant mortality rate: 5 deaths/1,000 live births (1991)

Life expectancy at birth: 73 years male, 81 years female (1991)

Total fertility rate: 1.5 children born/woman (1991)

Nationality: noun—Liechtensteiner(s); adjective—Liechtenstein

Ethnic divisions: Alemannic 95%, Italian and other 5%

Religion: Roman Catholic 87.3%, Protestant 8.3%, unknown 1.6%, other 2.8% (1988)

Language: German (official), Alemannic dialect

Literacy: 100% (male 100%, female 100%) age 10 and over can read and write (1981)

Labor force: 12,258; 5,078 foreign workers (mostly from Switzerland and Austria); industry, trade, and building 54.4%; services 41.6%; agriculture, fishing, forestry, and horticulture 4.0%

Organized labor: NA

Government

Long-form name: Principality of Liechtenstein

Type: hereditary constitutional monarchy

Capital: Vaduz

Administrative divisions: 11 communes (gemeinden, singular—gemeinde); Balzers, Eschen, Gamprin, Mauren, Planken, Ruggell, Schaan, Schellenberg, Triesen, Triesenberg, Vaduz

Independence: 23 January 1719, Imperial Principality of Liechtenstein established

Constitution: 5 October 1921

Legal system: local civil and penal codes; accepts compulsory ICJ jurisdiction, with reservations

National holiday: Saint Joseph's Day, 19 March

Executive branch: reigning prince, hereditary prince, head of government, deputy head of government

Legislative branch: unicameral Diet (Landtag)

Judicial branch: Supreme Court (Oberster Gerichtshof) for criminal cases and Superior Court (Obergericht) for civil cases

Leaders:
Chief of State—Prince HANS ADAM II (since 13 November 1989; assumed executive powers 26 August 1984); Heir Apparent Prince ALOIS von und zu Liechtenstein (born 11 June 1968);
Head of Government—Hans BRUNHART (since 26 April 1978); Deputy Head of Government Dr. Herbert WILLE (since 2 February 1986)

Political parties and leaders: Fatherland Union (VU), Dr. Otto HASLER; Progressive Citizens' Party (FBP), Emanuel VOGT; Free Electoral List (FW)

Suffrage: universal at age 18

Elections:
Diet—last held on 5 March 1989 (next to be held by March 1993); results—percent of vote by party NA; seats—(25 total) VU 13, FBP 12

Communists: none

Member of: CE, CSCE, EBRD, EFTA, IAEA, INTELSAT, INTERPOL, IOC, ITU, LORCS, UN, UNCTAD, UPU, WIPO

Diplomatic representation: in routine diplomatic matters, Liechtenstein is represented in the US by the Swiss Embassy;

Liechtenstein (continued)

US—the US has no diplomatic or consular mission in Liechtenstein, but the US Consul General at Zurich (Switzerland) has consular accreditation at Vaduz
Flag: two equal horizontal bands of blue (top) and red with a gold crown on the hoist side of the blue band

Economy

Overview: The prosperous economy is based primarily on small-scale light industry and tourism. Industry accounts for 54% of total employment, the service sector 42% (mostly based on tourism), and agriculture and forestry 4%. The sale of postage stamps to collectors is estimated at $10 million annually. Low business taxes (the maximum tax rate is 20%) and easy incorporation rules have induced about 25,000 holding or so-called letter box companies to establish nominal offices in Liechtenstein. Such companies, incorporated solely for tax purposes, provide 30% of state revenues. The economy is tied closely to that of Switzerland in a customs union, and incomes and living standards parallel those of the more prosperous Swiss groups.
GDP: $630 million, per capita $22,300; real growth rate NA% (1990 est.)
Inflation rate (consumer prices): 3.0% (1989 est.)
Unemployment rate: 0.1% (December 1986)
Budget: revenues $240 million; expenditures $197 million, including capital expenditures of NA (1988)
Exports: $1.28 billion (1988);
commodities—small specialty machinery, dental products, stamps, hardware, pottery;
partners—EC 40%, EFTA 22% (Switzerland 18%) (1988)
Imports: $NA;
commodities—machinery, metal goods, textiles, foodstuffs, motor vehicles;
partners—NA
External debt: $NA
Industrial production: growth rate NA%
Electricity: 23,000 kW capacity; 150 million kWh produced, 5,340 kWh per capita (1989)
Industries: electronics, metal manufacturing, textiles, ceramics, pharmaceuticals, food products, precision instruments, tourism
Agriculture: livestock, vegetables, corn, wheat, potatoes, grapes
Economic aid: none
Currency: Swiss franc, franken, or franco (plural—francs, franken, or franchi); 1 Swiss franc, franken, or franco (SwF) = 100 centimes, rappen, or centesimi
Exchange rates: Swiss francs, franken, or franchi (SwF) per US$1—1.2724 (January 1991), 1.3892 (1990), 1.6359 (1989), 1.4633 (1988), 1.4912 (1987), 1.7989 (1986), 2.4571 (1985)
Fiscal year: calendar year

Communications

Railroads: 18.5 km 1.435-meter standard gauge, electrified; owned, operated, and included in statistics of Austrian Federal Railways
Highways: 130.66 km main roads, 192.27 km byroads
Civil air: no transport aircraft
Airports: none
Telecommunications: automatic telephone system; 25,400 telephones; stations—no AM, no FM, no TV

Defense Forces

Branches: Police Department
Note: defense is responsibility of Switzerland

Luxembourg

Geography

Total area: 2,586 km²; land area: 2,586 km²
Comparative area: slightly smaller than Rhode Island
Land boundaries: 359 km total; Belgium 148 km, France 73 km, Germany 138 km
Coastline: none—landlocked
Maritime claims: none—landlocked
Climate: modified continental with mild winters, cool summers
Terrain: mostly gently rolling uplands with broad, shallow valleys; uplands to slightly mountainous in the north; steep slope down to Moselle floodplain in the southeast
Natural resources: iron ore (no longer exploited)
Land use: arable land 24%; permanent crops 1%; meadows and pastures 20%; forest and woodland 21%; other 34%
Environment: deforestation
Note: landlocked

People

Population: 388,017 (July 1991), growth rate 1.1% (1991)
Birth rate: 12 births/1,000 population (1991)
Death rate: 10 deaths/1,000 population (1991)
Net migration rate: 8 migrants/1,000 population (1991)
Infant mortality rate: 7 deaths/1,000 live births (1991)
Life expectancy at birth: 73 years male, 80 years female (1991)
Total fertility rate: 1.5 children born/woman (1991)
Nationality: noun—Luxembourger(s); adjective—Luxembourg
Ethnic divisions: Celtic base, with French and German blend; also guest and worker residents from Portugal, Italy, and European countries
Religion: Roman Catholic 97%, Protestant and Jewish 3%

Language: Luxembourgish, German, French; many also speak English
Literacy: 100% (male 100%, female 100%) age 15 and over can read and write (1980 est.)
Labor force: 169,600; one-third of labor force is foreign workers, mostly from Portugal, Italy, France, Belgium, and FRG; services 50%, industry 23.2%, government 14.4%, construction 9%, agriculture 3.4% (1987)
Organized labor: 100,000 (est.) members of four confederated trade unions

Government

Long-form name: Grand Duchy of Luxembourg
Type: constitutional monarchy
Capital: Luxembourg
Administrative divisions: 3 districts; Diekirch, Grevenmacher, Luxembourg
Independence: 1839
Constitution: 17 October 1868, occasional revisions
Legal system: based on civil law system; accepts compulsory ICJ jurisdiction
National holiday: National Day (public celebration of the Grand Duke's birthday), 23 June (1921)
Executive branch: grand duke, prime minister, vice prime minister, Council of Ministers (cabinet)
Legislative branch: unicameral Chamber of Deputies (Chambre des Députés); note—the Council of State (Conseil d'Etat) is an advisory body whose views are considered by the Chamber of Deputies
Judicial branch: Superior Court of Justice (Cour Supérieure de Justice)
Leaders:
Chief of State—Grand Duke JEAN (since 12 November 1964); Heir Apparent Prince HENRI (son of Grand Duke Jean, born 16 April 1955);
Head of Government—Prime Minister Jacques SANTER (since 21 July 1984); Vice Prime Minister Jacques F. POOS (since 21 July 1984)
Political parties and leaders: Christian Social Party (CSV), Jacques SANTER; Socialist Workers Party (LSAP), Jacques POOS; Liberal (DP), Colette FLESCH; Communist (KPL), André HOFFMANN; Green Alternative (GAP), Jean HUSS
Suffrage: universal and compulsory at age 18
Elections:
Chamber of Deputies—last held on 18 June 1989 (next to be held by June 1994); results—CSV 31.7%, LSAP 27.2%, DP 16.2%, Greens 8.4%, PAC 7.3%, KPL 5.1%, other 4.1%; seats—(60 total) CSV 22, LSAP 18, DP 11, Greens 4, PAC 4, KPL 1
Communists: 500 party members (1982)

Other political or pressure groups: group of steel industries representing iron and steel industry, Centrale Paysanne representing agricultural producers; Christian and Socialist labor unions; Federation of Industrialists; Artisans and Shopkeepers Federation
Member of: ACCT, Benelux, CCC, CE, COCOM, CSCE, EBRD, EC, ECE, EIB, EMS, FAO, GATT, IAEA, IBRD, ICAO, ICC, ICFTU, IDA, IEA, IFAD, IFC, ILO, IMF, INTELSAT, INTERPOL, IOC, IOM, ITU, LORCS, NATO, NEA, OECD, PCA, UN, UNCTAD, UNESCO, UNIDO, UPU, WCL, WEU, WHO, WIPO, WMO
Diplomatic representation: Ambassador André PHILIPPE; Chancery at 2200 Massachusetts Avenue NW, Washington DC 20008; telephone (202) 265-4171; there are Luxembourg Consulates General in New York and San Francisco;
US—Ambassador Edward M. ROWELL; Embassy at 22 Boulevard Emmanuel-Servais, 2535 Luxembourg City (mailing address is APO New York 09132); telephone [352] 460123
Flag: three equal horizontal bands of red (top), white, and light blue; similar to the flag of the Netherlands which uses a darker blue and is shorter; design was based on the flag of France

Economy

Overview: The stable economy features moderate growth, low inflation, and negligible unemployment. Agriculture is based on small but highly productive family-owned farms. The industrial sector, until recently dominated by steel, has become increasingly more diversified, particularly toward high-technology firms. During the past decade, growth in the financial sector has more than compensated for the decline in steel. Services, especially banking, account for a growing proportion of the economy. Luxembourg participates in an economic union with Belgium on trade and most financial matters and is also closely connected economically to the Netherlands.
GDP: $6.9 billion, per capita $18,000; real growth rate 2.5% (1990 est.)
Inflation rate (consumer prices): 3.5% (1990 est.)
Unemployment rate: 1.3% (1990 est.)
Budget: revenues $2.5 billion; expenditures $2.3 billion, including capital expenditures of NA (1988)
Exports: $5.4 billion (f.o.b., 1989); *commodities*—finished steel products, chemicals, rubber products, glass, aluminum, other industrial products; *partners*—EC 75%, US 5%
Imports: $6.2 billion (c.i.f., 1989 est.); *commodities*—minerals, metals, foodstuffs, quality consumer goods;

partners—Belgium 37%, FRG 31%, France 12%, US 2%
External debt: $131.6 million (1989 est.)
Industrial production: growth rate −1% (1990 est.); accounts for 25% of GDP
Electricity: 1,500,000 kW capacity; 1,163 million kWh produced, 3,170 kWh per capita (1989)
Industries: banking, iron and steel, food processing, chemicals, metal products, engineering, tires, glass, aluminum
Agriculture: accounts for less than 3% of GDP (including forestry); principal products—barley, oats, potatoes, wheat, fruits, wine grapes; cattle raising widespread
Economic aid: none
Currency: Luxembourg franc (plural—francs); 1 Luxembourg franc (LuxF) = 100 centimes
Exchange rates: Luxembourg francs (LuxF) per US$1—31.102 (January 1991), 33.418 (1990), 39.404 (1989), 36.768 (1988), 37.334 (1987), 44.672 (1986), 59.378 (1985); note—the Luxembourg franc is at par with the Belgian franc, which circulates freely in Luxembourg
Fiscal year: calendar year

Communications

Railroads: Luxembourg National Railways (CFL) operates 270 km 1.435-meter standard gauge; 162 km double track; 162 km electrified
Highways: 5,108 km total; 4,995 km paved, 57 km gravel, 56 km earth; about 80 km limited access divided highway
Inland waterways: 37 km; Moselle River
Pipelines: refined products, 48 km
Ports: Mertert (river port)
Merchant marine: 1 petroleum, oils, and lubricants (POL) tanker (1,000 GRT or over) totaling 1,731 GRT/2,460 DWT
Civil air: 13 major transport aircraft
Airports: 2 total, 2 usable; 1 with permanent-surface runways; 1 with runways over 3,659 m; 1 with runways less than 1,220 m
Telecommunications: adequate and efficient system, mainly buried cables; 230,000 telephones; stations—2 AM, 4 FM, 6 TV; 2 communication satellite earth stations operating in EUTELSAT and domestic systems

Defense Forces

Branches: Army, National Gendarmerie
Manpower availability: males 15-49, 100,476; 83,724 fit for military service; 2,297 reach military age (19) annually
Defense expenditures: $90 million, 1.2% of GDP (1990)

Macau

(overseas territory of Portugal)

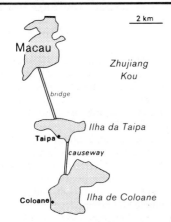

Geography

Total area: 16 km²; land area: 16 km²
Comparative area: about 0.1 times the size of Washington, DC
Land boundary: 0.34 km with China
Coastline: 40 km
Maritime claims: not known
Disputes: scheduled to become a Special Administrative Region of China in 1999
Climate: subtropical; marine with cool winters, warm summers
Terrain: generally flat
Natural resources: negligible
Land use: arable land 0%; permanent crops 0%; meadows and pastures 0%; forest and woodland 0%; other 100%
Environment: essentially urban; one causeway and one bridge connect the two islands to the peninsula on mainland
Note: 27 km west southwest of Hong Kong on the southeast coast of China

People

Population: 446,262 (July 1991), growth rate 1.0% (1991)
Birth rate: 15 births/1,000 population (1991)
Death rate: 5 deaths/1,000 population (1991)
Net migration rate: 0 migrants/1,000 population (1991)
Infant mortality rate: 7 deaths/1,000 live births (1991)
Life expectancy at birth: 75 years male, 79 years female (1991)
Total fertility rate: 2.1 children born/woman (1991)
Nationality: noun—Macanese (sing. and pl.); adjective—Macau
Ethnic divisions: Chinese 95%, Portuguese 3%, other 2%
Religion: Buddhist 45%, Roman Catholic 7%, Protestant 1%, none 45.8%, other 1.2% (1981)

Language: Portuguese (official); Cantonese is the language of commerce
Literacy: 90% (male 93%, female 86%) age 15 and over can read and write (1981)
Labor force: 180,000 (1986)
Organized labor: none

Government

Long-form name: none
Type: overseas territory of Portugal; scheduled to revert to China in 1999
Capital: Macau
Administrative divisions: 2 districts (concelhos, singular—concelho); Ilhas, Macau
Independence: none (territory of Portugal); Portugal signed an agreement with China on 13 April 1987 to return Macau to China on 20 December 1999; in the joint declaration, China promises to respect Macau's existing social and economic systems and lifestyle for 50 years after transition
Constitution: 17 February 1976, Organic Law of Macau
Legal system: Portuguese civil law system
National holiday: Day of Portugal, 10 June
Executive branch: president of Portugal, governor, Consultative Council (cabinet)
Legislative branch: Legislative Assembly
Judicial branch: Supreme Court
Leaders:
Chief of State—President (of Portugal) Mário Alberto SOARES (since 9 March 1986);
Head of Government—Governor Gen. Vasco Joachim Rocha VIEIRA (since 20 March 1991)
Political parties and leaders: Association to Defend the Interests of Macau; Macau Democratic Center; Group to Study the Development of Macau; Macau Independent Group
Suffrage: universal at age 18
Elections:
Legislative Assembly—last held on 9 November 1988 (next to be held November 1991); results—percent of vote by party NA; seats—(17 total; 6 elected by universal suffrage, 6 by indirect suffrage) number of seats by party NA
Other political or pressure groups: wealthy Macanese and Chinese representing local interests, wealthy pro-Communist merchants representing China's interests; in January 1967 the Macau Government acceded to Chinese demands that gave China veto power over administration
Member of: GATT, WTO (associate)
Diplomatic representation: as Chinese territory under Portuguese administration, Macanese interests in the US are represented by Portugal;
US—the US has no offices in Macau and US interests are monitored by the US Consulate General in Hong Kong
Flag: the flag of Portugal is used

Economy

Overview: The economy is based largely on tourism (including gambling), and textile and fireworks manufacturing. Efforts to diversify have spawned other small industries—toys, artificial flowers, and electronics. The tourist sector has accounted for roughly 25% of GDP, and the clothing industry has provided about two-thirds of export earnings. Macau depends on China for most of its food, fresh water, and energy imports. Japan and Hong Kong are the main suppliers of raw materials and capital goods.
GDP: $2.9 billion, per capita $6,560; real growth rate 6% (1990 est.)
Inflation rate (consumer prices): 9.5% (1989)
Unemployment rate: 2% (1989 est.)
Budget: revenues $305 million; expenditures $298 million, including capital expenditures of $NA (1989)
Exports: $1.7 billion (1989 est.);
commodities—textiles, clothing, toys;
partners—US 33%, Hong Kong 15%, FRG 12%, France 10% (1987)
Imports: $1.6 billion (1989 est.);
commodities—raw materials, foodstuffs, capital goods;
partners—Hong Kong 39%, China 21%, Japan 10% (1987)
External debt: $91 million (1985)
Industrial production: NA
Electricity: 203,000 kW capacity; 495 million kWh produced, 1,120 kWh per capita (1990)
Industries: clothing, textiles, toys, plastic products, furniture, tourism
Agriculture: rice, vegetables; food shortages—rice, vegetables, meat; depends mostly on imports for food requirements
Economic aid: none
Currency: pataca (plural—patacas); 1 pataca (P) = 100 avos
Exchange rates: patacas (P) per US$1—8.03 (1989), 8.044 (1988), 7.993 (1987), 8.029 (1986), 8.045 (1985); note—linked to the Hong Kong dollar at the rate of 1.03 patacas per Hong Kong dollar
Fiscal year: calendar year

Communications

Highways: 42 km paved
Ports: Macau
Civil air: no major transport aircraft
Airports: none useable, 1 under construction; 1 seaplane station
Telecommunications: fairly modern communication facilities maintained for domestic and international services; 52,000 telephones; stations—4 AM, 3 FM, no TV; 75,000 radio receivers (est.); international high-frequency radio communication facility; access to international communications

Madagascar

carriers provided via Hong Kong and China; 1 Indian Ocean INTELSAT earth station

Defense Forces

Manpower availability: males 15-49, 167,289; 93,142 fit for military service
Note: defense is responsibility of Portugal

Geography

Total area: 587,040 km²; land area: 581,540 km²
Comparative area: slightly less than twice the size of Arizona
Land boundaries: none
Coastline: 4,828 km
Maritime claims:
Exclusive economic zone: 200 nm;
Territorial sea: 12 nm
Disputes: claims Bassas da India, Europa Island, Glorioso Islands, Juan de Nova Island, and Tromelin Island (all administered by France)
Climate: tropical along coast, temperate inland, arid in south
Terrain: narrow coastal plain, high plateau and mountains in center
Natural resources: graphite, chromite, coal, bauxite, salt, quartz, tar sands, semiprecious stones, mica, fish
Land use: arable land 4%; permanent crops 1%; meadows and pastures 58%; forest and woodland 26%; other 11%; includes irrigated 2%
Environment: subject to periodic cyclones; deforestation; overgrazing; soil erosion; desertification
Note: world's fourth-largest island; strategic location along Mozambique Channel

People

Population: 12,185,318 (July 1991), growth rate 3.2% (1991)
Birth rate: 47 births/1,000 population (1991)
Death rate: 15 deaths/1,000 population (1991)
Net migration rate: 0 migrants/1,000 population (1991)
Infant mortality rate: 95 deaths/1,000 live births (1991)
Life expectancy at birth: 51 years male, 54 years female (1991)

Total fertility rate: 6.9 children born/woman (1991)
Nationality: noun—Malagasy (sing. and pl.); adjective—Malagasy
Ethnic divisions: basic split between highlanders of predominantly Malayo-Indonesian origin (Merina 1,643,000 and related Betsileo 760,000) on the one hand and coastal tribes, collectively termed the Côtiers, with mixed African, Malayo-Indonesian, and Arab ancestry (Betsimisaraka 941,000, Tsimihety 442,000, Antaisaka 415,000, Sakalava 375,000), on the other; there are also 11,000 European French, 5,000 Indians of French nationality, and 5,000 Creoles
Religion: indigenous beliefs 52%, Christian about 41%, Muslim 7%
Language: French and Malagasy (official)
Literacy: 80% (male 88%, female 73%) age 15 and over can read and write (1990 est.)
Labor force: 4,900,000; 90% nonsalaried family workers engaged in subsistence agriculture; 175,000 wage earners—agriculture 26%, domestic service 17%, industry 15%, commerce 14%, construction 11%, services 9%, transportation 6%, other 2%; 51% of population of working age (1985)
Organized labor: 4% of labor force

Government

Long-form name: Democratic Republic of Madagascar
Type: republic
Capital: Antananarivo
Administrative divisions: 6 provinces (plural—NA, singular—faritanin'); Antananarivo, Antsiranana, Fianarantsoa, Mahajanga, Toamasina, Toliara
Independence: 26 June 1960 (from France; formerly Malagasy Republic)
Constitution: 21 December 1975
Legal system: based on French civil law system and traditional Malagasy law; has not accepted compulsory ICJ jurisdiction
National holiday: Independence Day, 26 June (1960)
Executive branch: president, Supreme Council of the Revolution, prime minister, Council of Ministers
Legislative branch: unicameral Popular National Assembly (Assemblée Nationale Populaire)
Judicial branch: Supreme Court (Cour Suprême), High Constitutional Court (Haute Cour Constitutionnelle)
Leaders:
Chief of State—President Adm. Didier RATSIRAKA (since 15 June 1975);
Head of Government—Prime Minister Lt. Col. Victor RAMAHATRA (since 12 February 1988)
Political parties and leaders: a presidential decree issued early last year, legalized the existence of political parties outside of the

Ruling Front; some thirty political parties now exist in Madagascar, the most important of which remain the Advance Guard of the Malagasy Revolution (AREMA), Didier RATSIRAKA; Congress Party for Malagasy Independence (AKFM), RAKOTOVAO-ANDRIATIANA; Congress Party for Malagasy Independence-Revival (AKFM-R), Pastor Richard ANDRIAMANJATO; Movement for National Unity (VONJY), Dr. Marojama RAZANABAHINY; Malagasy Christian Democratic Union (UDECMA), Norbert ANDRIAMORA-SATA; Militants for the Establishment of a Proletarian Regime (MFM), Manandafy RAKOTONIRINA; National Movement for the Independence of Madagascar (MONIMA), Monja JAONA; Socialist Organization Monima (VSM, an offshoot of MONIMA), Tsihozony MAHARANGA
Suffrage: universal at age 18
Elections:
President—last held on 12 March 1989 (next to be held March 1996); results—Didier RATSIRAKA (AREMA) 62%, Manandafy RAKOTONIRINA (MFM/MFT) 20%, Dr. Jérôme Marojama RAZANABA-HINY (VONJY) 15%, Monja JAONA (MONIMA) 3%;
Popular National Assembly—last held on 28 May 1989 (next to be held May 1994); results—AREMA 88.2%, MFM 5.1%, AKFM 3.7%, VONJY 2.2%, other 0.8%; seats—(137 total) AREMA 120, MFM 7, AKFM 5, VONJY 4, MONIMA 1
Communists: Communist party of virtually no importance; small and vocal group of Communists has gained strong position in leadership of AKFM, the rank and file of which is non-Communist
Member of: ACP, AfDB, CCC, ECA, FAO, G-77, GATT, IAEA, IBRD, ICAO, ICC, IDA, IFAD, IFC, ILO, IMF, IMO, INTELSAT, INTERPOL, IOC, ITU, LORCS, NAM, OAU, UN, UNCTAD, UNESCO, UNHCR, UNIDO, UPU, WCL, WFTU, WIPO, WHO, WIPO, WMO, WTO
Diplomatic representation: Ambassador Pierrot Jocelyn RAJAONARIVELO; Chancery at 2374 Massachusetts Avenue NW, Washington DC 20008; telephone (202) 265-5525 or 5526; there is a Malagasy Consulate General in New York;
US—Ambassador Howard K. WALKER; Embassy at 14 and 16 Rue Rainitovo, Antsahavola, Antananarivo (mailing address is B. P. 620, Antananarivo); telephone 212-57, 209-56, 200-89, 207-18
Flag: two equal horizontal bands of red (top) and green with a vertical white band of the same width on hoist side

Economy

Overview: Madagascar is one of the poorest countries in the world. During the period 1980-85 it had a population growth of 3% a year and a −0.4% GDP growth rate. Agriculture, including fishing and forestry, is the mainstay of the economy, accounting for over 40% of GDP, employing about 80% of the labor force, and contributing to more than 70% of total export earnings. Industry is largely confined to the processing of agricultural products and textile manufacturing; in 1990 it accounted for only 16% of GDP and employed 3% of the labor force. In 1986 the government introduced a five-year development plan that stresses self-sufficiency in food (mainly rice) by 1990, increased production for exports, and reduced energy imports.
GDP: $2.4 billion, per capita $200; real growth rate 3.8% (1990 est.)
Inflation rate (consumer prices): 12% (1990)
Unemployment rate: NA%
Budget: revenues $390 million; expenditures $525 million, including capital expenditures of $240 million (1990 est.)
Exports: $290 million (f.o.b., 1990 est.); *commodities*—coffee 45%, vanilla 15%, cloves 11%, sugar, petroleum products; *partners*—France, Japan, Italy, FRG, US
Imports: $436 million (f.o.b., 1990 est.); *commodities*—intermediate manufactures 30%, capital goods 28%, petroleum 15%, consumer goods 14%, food 13%; *partners*—France, FRG, UK, other EC, US
External debt: $3.6 billion (1989)
Industrial production: growth rate 5.2% (1990 est.); accounts for 16% of GDP
Electricity: 119,000 kW capacity; 430 million kWh produced, 40 kWh per capita (1989)
Industries: agricultural processing (meat canneries, soap factories, breweries, tanneries, sugar refining plants), light consumer goods industries (textiles, glassware), cement, automobile assembly plant, paper, petroleum
Agriculture: accounts for 40% of GDP; cash crops—coffee, vanilla, sugarcane, cloves, cocoa; food crops—rice, cassava, beans, bananas, peanuts; cattle raising widespread; almost self-sufficient in rice
Illicit drugs: illicit producer of cannabis (cultivated and wild varieties) used mostly for domestic consumption
Economic aid: US commitments, including Ex-Im (FY70-89), $136 million; Western (non-US) countries, ODA and OOF bilateral commitments (1970-88), $2.9 billion; Communist countries (1970-89), $491 million
Currency: Malagasy franc (plural—francs); 1 Malagasy franc (FMG) = 100 centimes
Exchange rates: Malagasy francs (FMG) per US$1—1,454.6 (December 1990), 1,494.1 (1990), 1,603.4 (1989), 1,407.1 (1988), 1,069.2 (1987), 676.3 (1986), 662.5 (1985)
Fiscal year: calendar year

Communications

Railroads: 1,020 km 1.000-meter gauge
Highways: 40,000 km total; 4,694 km paved, 811 km crushed stone, gravel, or stabilized soil, 34,495 km improved and unimproved earth (est.)
Inland waterways: of local importance only; isolated streams and small portions of Canal des Pangalanes
Ports: Toamasina, Antsiranana, Mahajanga, Toliara
Merchant marine: 14 ships (1,000 GRT or over) totaling 59,416 GRT/82,869 DWT; includes 9 cargo, 2 roll-on/roll-off cargo, 1 petroleum, oils, and lubricants (POL) tanker, 1 chemical tanker, 1 liquefied gas
Civil air: 5 major transport aircraft
Airports: 148 total, 115 usable; 30 with permanent-surface runways; none with runways over 3,659 m; 3 with runways 2,440-3,659 m; 42 with runways 1,220-2,439 m
Telecommunications: above average system includes open-wire lines, coaxial cables, radio relay, and troposcatter links; submarine cable to Bahrain; satellite earth stations—1 Indian Ocean INTELSAT and 1 Atlantic Ocean INTELSAT; over 38,200 telephones; stations—14 AM, 1 FM, 7 (30 repeaters) TV

Defense Forces

Branches: Popular Armed Forces (includes Intervention Forces, Development Forces, Aeronaval Forces—includes Navy and Air Force), Gendarmerie, Presidential Security Regiment
Manpower availability: males 15-49, 2,637,866; 1,570,393 fit for military service; 119,882 reach military age (20) annually
Defense expenditures: $37 million, 2.2% of GDP (1989 est.)

Malawi

Lake Nyasa
Mzuzu
Chisamula Island
Likoma Island
LILONGWE
Zomba
Blantyre
200 km

Geography

Total area: 118,480 km²; land area: 94,080 km²
Comparative area: slightly larger than Pennsylvania
Land boundaries: 2,881 km total; Mozambique 1,569 km, Tanzania 475 km, Zambia 837 km
Coastline: none—landlocked
Maritime claims: none—landlocked
Disputes: dispute with Tanzania over the boundary in Lake Nyasa (Lake Malawi)
Climate: tropical; rainy season (November to May); dry season (May to November)
Terrain: narrow elongated plateau with rolling plains, rounded hills, some mountains
Natural resources: limestone; unexploited deposits of uranium, coal, and bauxite
Land use: arable land 25%; permanent crops NEGL%; meadows and pastures 20%; forest and woodland 50%; other 5%; includes irrigated NEGL%
Environment: deforestation
Note: landlocked

People

Population: 9,438,462 (July 1991), growth rate 1.8% (1991); note—900,000 Mozambican refugees in Malawi (1990 est.)
Birth rate: 52 births/1,000 population (1991)
Death rate: 18 deaths/1,000 population (1991)
Net migration rate: −17 migrants/1,000 population (1991)
Infant mortality rate: 136 deaths/1,000 live births (1991)
Life expectancy at birth: 48 years male, 51 years female (1991)
Total fertility rate: 7.6 children born/woman (1991)
Nationality: noun—Malawian(s); adjective—Malawian
Ethnic divisions: Chewa, Nyanja, Tumbuko, Yao, Lomwe, Sena, Tonga, Ngoni, Ngonde, Asian, European

Religion: Protestant 55%, Roman Catholic 20%, Muslim 20%; traditional indigenous beliefs are also practiced
Language: English and Chichewa (official); other languages important regionally
Literacy: 22% (male 34%, female 12%) age 15 and over can read and write (1966)
Labor force: 428,000 wage earners; agriculture 43%, manufacturing 16%, personal services 15%, commerce 9%, construction 7%, miscellaneous services 4%, other permanently employed 6% (1986)
Organized labor: small minority of wage earners are unionized

Government

Long-form name: Republic of Malawi
Type: one-party state
Capital: Lilongwe
Administrative divisions: 24 districts; Blantyre, Chikwawa, Chiradzulu, Chitipa, Dedza, Dowa, Karonga, Kasungu, Lilongwe, Machinga (Kasupe), Mangochi, Mchinji, Mulanje, Mwanza, Mzimba, Ncheu, Nkhata Bay, Nkhota Kota, Nsanje, Ntchisi, Rumphi, Salima, Thyolo, Zomba
Independence: 6 July 1964 (from UK; formerly Nyasaland)
Constitution: 6 July 1964; republished as amended January 1974
Legal system: based on English common law and customary law; judicial review of legislative acts in the Supreme Court of Appeal; has not accepted compulsory ICJ jurisdiction
National holiday: Independence Day, 6 July (1964)
Executive branch: president, Cabinet
Legislative branch: unicameral National Assembly
Judicial branch: High Court, Supreme Court of Appeal
Leaders:
Chief of State and Head of Government—President Dr. Hastings Kamuzu BANDA (since 6 July 1966; sworn in as President for Life 6 July 1971)
Political parties and leaders: only party—Malawi Congress Party (MCP), Maxwell PASHANE, administrative secretary; John TEMBO, treasurer general; top party position of secretary general vacant since 1983
Suffrage: universal at age 21
Elections:
President—President BANDA sworn in as President for Life on 6 July 1971;
National Assembly—last held 27-28 May 1987 (next to be held by May 1992); results—MCP is the only party; seats—(133 total, 112 elected) MCP 133
Communists: no Communist party
Member of: ACP, AfDB, C, CCC, ECA, FAO, G-77, GATT, IBRD, ICAO, ICFTU, IDA, IFAD, IFC, ILO, IMF, IMO, INTELSAT, INTERPOL, IOC, ISO (correspondent), ITU, LORCS, NAM, OAU, SADCC, UN, UNCTAD, UNESCO, UNIDO, UPU, WHO, WIPO, WMO, WTO
Diplomatic representation: Ambassador Robert B. MBAYA; Chancery at 2408 Massachusetts Avenue NW, Washington DC 20008; telephone (202) 797-1007;
US—Ambassador George A. TRAIL, III; Embassy in new capital city development area, address NA (mailing address is P. O. Box 30016, Lilongwe); telephone [265] 730-166
Flag: three equal horizontal bands of black (top), red, and green with a radiant, rising, red sun centered in the black band; similar to the flag of Afghanistan which is longer and has the national coat of arms superimposed on the hoist side of the black and red bands

Economy

Overview: A landlocked country, Malawi ranks among the world's least developed with a per capita GDP of $175. The economy is predominately agricultural and operates under a relatively free enterprise environment, with about 90% of the population living in rural areas. Agriculture accounts for 40% of GDP and 90% of export revenues. After two years of weak performance, economic growth improved significantly in 1988-90 as a result of good weather and a broadly based economic adjustment effort by the government. The economy depends on substantial inflows of economic assistance from the IMF, the World Bank, and individual donor nations. The closure of traditional trade routes through Mozambique continues to be a constraint on the economy.
GDP: $1.6 billion, per capita $175; growth rate 4.8% (1990 est.)
Inflation rate (consumer prices): 11.7% (1990)
Unemployment rate: NA%
Budget: revenues $398 million; expenditures $510 million, including capital expenditures of $154 million (FY91 est.)
Exports: $390 million (f.o.b., 1990 est.);
commodities—tobacco, tea, sugar, coffee, peanuts;
partners—US, UK, Zambia, South Africa, FRG
Imports: $560 million (c.i.f., 1990 est.);
commodities—food, petroleum, semimanufactures, consumer goods, transportation equipment;
partners—South Africa, Japan, US, UK, Zimbabwe
External debt: $1.4 billion (December 1990 est.)
Industrial production: growth rate 4.9% (1989 est.); accounts for about 18% of GDP (1988)

Malawi *(continued)*

Electricity: 181,000 kW capacity; 535 million kWh produced, 60 kWh per capita (1989)
Industries: agricultural processing (tea, tobacco, sugar), sawmilling, cement, consumer goods
Agriculture: accounts for 40% of GDP; cash crops—tobacco, sugarcane, cotton, tea, and corn; subsistence crops—potatoes, cassava, sorghum, pulses; livestock—cattle and goats
Economic aid: US commitments, including Ex-Im (FY70-89), $215 million; Western (non-US) countries, ODA and OOF bilateral commitments (1970-88), $2.0 billion
Currency: Malawian kwacha (plural—kwacha); 1 Malawian kwacha (MK) = 100 tambala
Exchange rates: Malawian kwacha (MK) per US$1—2.6300 (January 1991), 2.7289 (1990), 2.7595 (1989), 2.5613 (1988), 2.2087 (1987), 1.8611 (1986), 1.7191 (1985)
Fiscal year: 1 April-31 March

Communications

Railroads: 789 km 1.067-meter gauge
Highways: 13,135 km total; 2,364 km paved; 251 km crushed stone, gravel, or stabilized soil; 10,520 km earth and improved earth
Inland waterways: Lake Nyasa (Lake Malawi); Shire River, 144 km
Ports: Chipoka, Monkey Bay, Nkhata Bay, and Nkotakota—all on Lake Nyasa (Lake Malawi)
Civil air: 3 major transport aircraft
Airports: 48 total, 46 usable; 6 with permanent-surface runways; none with runways over 3,659 m; 1 with runways 2,440-3,659 m; 9 with runways 1,220-2,439 m
Telecommunications: fair system of openwire lines, radio relay links, and radio communication stations; 36,800 telephones; stations—8 AM, 4 FM, no TV; satellite earth stations—1 Indian Ocean INTELSAT and 1 Atlantic Ocean INTELSAT
Note: a majority of exports would normally go through Mozambique on the Beira or Nacala railroads, but now most go through South Africa because of insurgent activity and damage to rail lines

Defense Forces

Branches: Army (includes Air Wing and Naval Detachment), Police (includes paramilitary Mobile Force Unit), paramilitary Malawi Young Pioneers
Manpower availability: males 15-49, 1,960,082; 995,864 fit for military service
Defense expenditures: $22 million, 1.6% of GDP (1989 est.)

Malaysia

Geography

Total area: 329,750 km²; land area: 328,550 km²
Comparative area: slightly larger than New Mexico
Land boundaries: 2,669 km total; Brunei 381 km, Indonesia 1,782, Thailand 506 km
Coastline: 4,675 km total (2,068 km Peninsular Malaysia, 2,607 km East Malaysia)
Maritime claims:
Continental shelf: 200 m (depth) or to depth of exploitation, specified boundary in the South China Sea;
Exclusive fishing zone: 200 nm;
Exclusive economic zone: 200 nm;
Territorial sea: 12 nm
Disputes: involved in a complex dispute over the Spratly Islands with China, Philippines, Taiwan, and Vietnam; state of Sabah claimed by the Philippines; Brunei may wish to purchase the Malaysian salient that divides Brunei into two parts
Climate: tropical; annual southwest (April to October) and northeast (October to February) monsoons
Terrain: coastal plains rising to hills and mountains
Natural resources: tin, crude oil, timber, copper, iron ore, natural gas, bauxite
Land use: arable land 3%; permanent crops 10%; meadows and pastures NEGL%; forest and woodland 63%; other 24%; includes irrigated 1%
Environment: subject to flooding; air and water pollution
Note: strategic location along Strait of Malacca and southern South China Sea

People

Population: 17,981,698 (July 1991), growth rate 2.4% (1991)
Birth rate: 30 births/1,000 population (1991)
Death rate: 6 deaths/1,000 population (1991)

Net migration rate: 0 migrants/1,000 population (1991)
Infant mortality rate: 29 deaths/1,000 live births (1991)
Life expectancy at birth: 65 years male, 71 years female (1991)
Total fertility rate: 3.6 children born/woman (1991)
Nationality: noun—Malaysian(s); adjective—Malaysian
Ethnic divisions: Malay and other indigenous 59%, Chinese 32%, Indian 9%
Religion: Peninsular Malaysia—Malays nearly all Muslim, Chinese predominantly Buddhists, Indians predominantly Hindu; Sabah—Muslim 38%, Christian 17%, other 45%; Sarawak—tribal religion 35%, Buddhist and Confucianist 24%, Muslim 20%, Christian 16%, other 5%
Language: Peninsular Malaysia—Malay (official); English, Chinese dialects, Tamil; Sabah—English, Malay, numerous tribal dialects, Mandarin and Hakka dialects predominate among Chinese; Sarawak—English, Malay, Mandarin, numerous tribal languages
Literacy: 78% (male 86%, female 70%) age 15 and over can read and write (1990 est.)
Labor force: 6,800,000; agriculture 30.8%, manufacturing 17%, government 13.6%, construction 5.8%, finance 4.3%, business services, transport and communications 3.4%, mining 0.6%, other 24.5% (1989 est.)
Organized labor: 660,000, 10% of total labor force (1988)

Government

Long-form name: none
Type: Federation of Malaysia formed 9 July 1963; constitutional monarchy nominally headed by the paramount ruler (king) and a bicameral Parliament; Peninsular Malaysian states—hereditary rulers in all but Penang and Melaka, where governors are appointed by Malaysian Government; powers of state governments are limited by federal Constitution; Sabah—self-governing state, holds 20 seats in House of Representatives, with foreign affairs, defense, internal security, and other powers delegated to federal government; Sarawak—self-governing state within Malaysia, holds 27 seats in House of Representatives, with foreign affairs, defense, internal security, and other powers delegated to federal government
Capital: Kuala Lumpur
Administrative divisions: 13 states (negeri-negeri, singular—negeri) and 2 federal territories* (wilayah-wilayah persekutuan, singular—wilayah persekutuan); Johor, Kedah, Kelantan, Labuan*, Melaka, Negeri Sembilan, Pahang, Perak, Perlis, Pulau Pinang, Sabah, Sarawak, Selangor, Terengganu, Wilayah Persekutuan*
Independence: 31 August 1957 (from UK)

Constitution: 31 August 1957, amended 16 September 1963 when Federation of Malaya became Federation of Malaysia

Legal system: based on English common law; judicial review of legislative acts in the Supreme Court at request of supreme head of the federation; has not accepted compulsory ICJ jurisdiction

National holiday: National Day, 31 August (1957)

Executive branch: paramount ruler, deputy paramount ruler, prime minister, deputy prime minister, Cabinet

Legislative branch: bicameral Parliament (Parlimen) consists of an upper house or Senate (Dewan Negara) and a lower house or House of Representatives (Dewan Rakyat)

Judicial branch: Supreme Court

Leaders:
Chief of State—Paramount Ruler AZLAN Muhibbuddin Shah ibni Sultan Yusof Izzudin (since 26 April 1989); Deputy Paramount Ruler JA'AFAR ibni Abdul Rahman (since 26 April 1989);
Head of Government—Prime Minister Dr. MAHATHIR bin Mohamad (since 16 July 1981); Deputy Prime Minister Abdul GHAFAR Baba (since 7 May 1986)

Political parties and leaders: *Peninsular Malaysia*— National Front, a confederation of 13 political parties dominated by United Malays National Organization Baru (UMNO Baru), MAHATHIR bin Mohamad; Malaysian Chinese Association (MCA), LING Liong Sik; Gerakan Rakyat Malaysia, Datuk LIM Keng Yaik; Malaysian Indian Congress (MIC), Datuk S. Samy VELLU;
Sabah—Berjaya Party, Datuk Haji Mohammed NOOR Mansor; Bersatu Sabah (PBS), Joseph Pairin KITINGAN; United Sabah National Organizaton (USNO), Tun Datu Haji MUSTAPHA;
Sarawak—coalition Sarawak National Front composed of the Party Pesaka Bumiputra Bersatu (PBB), Datuk Patinggi Amar Haji Abdul TAIB Mahmud; Sarawak United People's Party (SUPP), Datuk Amar Stephen YONG Kuet Tze; Sarawak National Party (SNAP), Datuk James WONG Kim Min; Parti Bansa Dayak Sarawak (PBDS), Datuk Leo MOGGIE; major opposition parties are Democratic Action Party (DAP), LIM Kit Siang and Pan-Malaysian Islamic Party (PAS), Fadzil NOOR

Suffrage: universal at age 21

Elections:
House of Representatives—last held 21 October 1990 (next to be held by August 1995); results—National Front 52%, other 48%; seats—(180 total) National Front 127, DAP 20, PAS 7, independents 4, other 22; note—within the National Front, UMNO got 71 seats and MCA 18 seats

Communists: Peninsular Malaysia—about 1,000 armed insurgents on Thailand side of international boundary and about 200 full time inside Malaysia surrendered on 2 December 1989; about 50 Communist insurgents in Sarawak surrendered on 17 October 1990

Member of: APEC, AsDB, ASEAN, C, CCC, CP, ESCAP, FAO, G-77, GATT, IAEA, IBRD, ICAO, ICFTU, IDA, IDB, IFAD, IFC, ILO, IMF, IMO, INMARSAT, INTELSAT, INTERPOL, IOC, ISO, ITU, LORCS, NAM, OIC, UN, UNCTAD, UNESCO, UNIDO, UNIIMOG, UPU, WCL, WHO, WIPO, WMO

Diplomatic representation: Ambassador Abdul MAJID Mohamed; Chancery at 2401 Massachusetts Avenue NW, Washington DC 20008; telephone (202) 328-2700; there are Malaysian Consulates General in Los Angeles and New York;
US—Ambassador Paul M. CLEVELAND; Embassy at 376 Jalan Tun Razak, 50400 Kuala Lumpur (mailing address is P. O. Box No. 10035, 50700 Kuala Lumpur); telephone [60] (3) 248-9011

Flag: fourteen equal horizontal stripes of red (top) alternating with white (bottom); there is a blue rectangle in the upper hoist-side corner bearing a yellow crescent and a yellow fourteen-pointed star; the crescent and the star are traditional symbols of Islam; the design was based on the flag of the US

Economy

Overview: In 1988-90 booming exports helped Malaysia continue to recover from the severe 1985-86 recession. Real output grew by 8.8% in 1989 and 10% in 1990, helped by vigorous growth in manufacturing output, further increases in foreign direct investment, particularly from Japanese and Taiwanese firms facing higher costs at home, and increased oil production in 1990. Malaysia has become the world's third-largest producer of semiconductor devices (after the US and Japan) and the world's largest exporter of semiconductor devices. Inflation remained low as unemployment stood at 6% of the labor force and as the government followed prudent fiscal/monetary policies. The country is not self-sufficient in food, and some of the rural population subsists at the poverty level. Malaysia's high export dependence leaves it vulnerable to a recession in the OECD countries or a fall in world commodity prices.

GDP: $43.1 billion, per capita $2,460; real growth rate 10% (1990)

Inflation rate (consumer prices): 3.1% (1990 est.)

Unemployment rate: 6% (1990)

Budget: revenues $12.6 billion; expenditures $11.8 billion, including capital expenditures of $3.2 billion (1991 est.)

Exports: $28.9 billion (f.o.b., 1990 est.);
commodities—natural rubber, palm oil, tin, timber, petroleum, electronics, light manufactures;
partners—Singapore, US, Japan, EC

Imports: $26.5 billion (f.o.b., 1990 est.);
commodities—food, crude oil, consumer goods, intermediate goods, capital equipment, chemicals;
partners—Japan, US, Singapore, FRG, UK

External debt: $20.0 billion (1990)

Industrial production: growth rate 15.8% (1990 est.); accounts for 27% of GDP

Electricity: 5,600,000 kW capacity; 16,500 million kWh produced, 940 kWh per capita (1990)

Industries:
Peninsular Malaysia—rubber and oil palm processing and manufacturing, light manufacturing industry, electronics, tin mining and smelting, logging and processing timber;
Sabah—logging, petroleum production;
Sarawak—agriculture processing, petroleum production and refining, logging

Agriculture:
Peninsular Malaysia—natural rubber, palm oil, rice;
Sabah—mainly subsistence, but also rubber, timber, coconut, rice;
Sarawak—rubber, timber, pepper; there is a deficit of rice in all areas; fish catch of 608,000 metric tons in 1987

Illicit drugs: transit point for Golden Triangle heroin going to the US, Western Europe, and the Third World

Economic aid: US commitments, including Ex-Im (FY70-84), $170 million; Western (non-US) countries, ODA and OOF bilateral commitments (1970-88), $4.5 billion; OPEC bilateral aid (1979-89), $42 million

Currency: ringgit (plural—ringgits); 1 ringgit (M$) = 100 sen

Exchange rates: ringgits (M$) per US$1— 2.7151 (January 1991), 1.7048 (1990), 2.7088 (1989), 2.6188 (1988), 2.5196 (1987), 2.5814 (1986), 2.4830 (1985)

Fiscal year: calendar year

Communications

Railroads:
Peninsular Malaysia—1,665 km 1.04-meter gauge; 13 km double track, government owned;
Sabah—136 km 1.000-meter gauge

Highways:
Peninsular Malaysia—23,600 km (19,352 km hard surfaced, mostly bituminous-surface treatment, and 4,248 km unpaved);
Sabah—3,782 km;
Sarawak—1,644 km

Malaysia *(continued)*

Inland waterways:
Peninsular Malaysia—3,209 km;
Sabah—1,569 km;
Sarawak—2,518 km
Ports: Tanjong Kidurong, Kota Kinabalu, Kuching, Pasir Gudang, Penang, Port Kelang, Sandakan, Tawau
Merchant marine: 157 ships (1,000 GRT or over) totaling 1,530,756 GRT/2,246,358 DWT; includes 1 short-sea passenger, 65 cargo, 22 container, 2 vehicle carrier, 2 roll-on/roll-off cargo, 1 livestock carrier, 31 petroleum, oils, and lubricants (POL) tanker, 3 chemical tanker, 6 liquefied gas, 1 passenger-cargo, 23 bulk
Civil air: 53 major transport aircraft
Pipelines: crude oil, 1,307 km; natural gas, 379 km
Airports: 125 total, 119 usable; 32 with permanent-surface runways; 1 with runways over 3,659 m; 7 with runways 2,440-3,659 m; 18 with runways 1,220-2,439 m
Telecommunications: good intercity service provided to peninsular Malaysia mainly by microwave relay, adequate intercity radio relay network between Sabah and Sarawak via Brunei; international service good; good coverage by radio and television broadcasts; 994,860 telephones (1984); stations—28 AM, 3 FM, 33 TV; submarine cables extend to India and Sarawak; SEACOM submarine cable links to Hong Kong and Singapore; satellite earth stations—1 Indian Ocean INTELSAT and 1 Pacific Ocean INTELSAT, and 2 domestic

---

Defense Forces

Branches: Royal Malaysian Army, Royal Malaysian Navy, Royal Malaysian Air Force, Royal Malaysian Police Force, Marine Police, Sarawak Border Scouts
Manpower availability: males 15-49, 4,620,418; 2,815,910 fit for military service; 180,991 reach military age (21) annually
Defense expenditures: $1.7 billion, 3.9% of GDP (1990)

Maldives

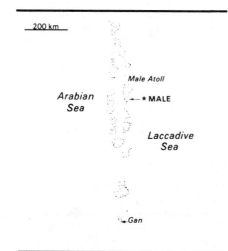

Geography

Total area: 300 km²; land area: 300 km²
Comparative area: slightly more than 1.5 times the size of Washington, DC
Land boundaries: none
Coastline: 644 km
Maritime claims:
Exclusive economic zone: 35-310 nm (defined by geographic coordinates; segment of zone coincides with maritime boundary with India);
Territorial sea: 12 nm
Climate: tropical; hot, humid; dry, northeast monsoon (November to March); rainy, southwest monsoon (June to August)
Terrain: flat with elevations only as high as 2.5 meters
Natural resources: fish
Land use: arable land 10%; permanent crops 0%; meadows and pastures 3%; forest and woodland 3%; other 84%
Environment: 1,200 coral islands grouped into 19 atolls
Note: archipelago of strategic location astride and along major sea lanes in Indian Ocean

---

People

Population: 226,200 (July 1991), growth rate 3.7% (1991)
Birth rate: 46 births/1,000 population (1991)
Death rate: 9 deaths/1,000 population (1991)
Net migration rate: 0 migrants/1,000 population (1991)
Infant mortality rate: 72 deaths/1,000 live births (1991)
Life expectancy at birth: 61 years male, '65 years female (1991)
Total fertility rate: 6.5 children born/woman (1991)
Nationality: noun—Maldivian(s); adjective—Maldivian

Ethnic divisions: admixtures of Sinhalese, Dravidian, Arab, and black
Religion: Sunni Muslim
Language: Divehi (dialect of Sinhala; script derived from Arabic); English spoken by most government officials
Literacy: 92% (male 92%, female 92%) age 15 and over can read and write (1985)
Labor force: 66,000 (est.); 25% engaged in fishing industry
Organized labor: none

Government

Long-form name: Republic of Maldives
Type: republic
Capital: Male
Administrative divisions: 19 district (atolls); Aliff, Baa, Daalu, Faafu, Gaafu Aliff, Gaafu Daalu, Haa Aliff, Haa Daalu, Kaafu, Laamu, Laviyani, Meemu, Naviyani, Noonu, Raa, Seenu, Shaviyani, Thaa, Waavu
Independence: 26 July 1965 (from UK)
Constitution: 4 June 1964
Legal system: based on Islamic law with admixtures of English common law primarily in commercial matters; has not accepted compulsory ICJ jurisdiction
National holiday: Independence Day, 26 July (1965)
Executive branch: president, Cabinet
Legislative branch: unicameral Citizens' Council (Majlis)
Judicial branch: High Court
Leaders:
Chief of State and Head of Government—President Maumoon Abdul GAYOOM (since 11 November 1978)
Political parties and leaders: no organized political parties; country governed by the Didi clan for the past eight centuries
Suffrage: universal at age 21
Elections:
President—last held 23 September 1988 (next to be held September 1994); results—President Maumoon Abdul GAYOOM reelected;
Citizens' Council—last held on 7 December 1989 (next to be held 7 December 1994); results—percent of vote NA; seats—(48 total, 40 elected)
Communists: negligible
Member of: AsDB, C, CP, ESCAP, FAO, G-77, GATT, IBRD, ICAO, IDA, IDB, IFAD, IFC, IMF, IMO, INTERPOL, IOC, ITU, NAM, OIC, SAARC, UN, UNCTAD, UNESCO, UNIDO, UPU, WHO, WMO, WTO
Diplomatic representation: Maldives does not maintain an embassy in the US, but does have a UN mission in New York; *US*—the US Ambassador to Sri Lanka is accredited to Maldives and makes periodic visits there; US Consular Agency, Midhath Hilmy, Male; telephone 2581

Flag: red with a large green rectangle in the center bearing a vertical white crescent; the closed side of the crescent is on the hoist side of the flag

Economy

Overview: The economy is based on fishing, tourism, and shipping. Agriculture is limited to the production of a few subsistence crops that provide only 10% of food requirements. Fishing is the largest industry, employing 25% of the work force and accounting for over 60% of exports; it is also an important source of government revenue. During the 1980s tourism has become one of the most important and highest growth sectors of the economy. In 1988 industry accounted for about 5% of GDP. Real GDP is officially estimated to have increased by about 10% annually during the period 1974-87, and GDP estimates for 1988 show a further growth of 9% on the strength of a record fish catch and an improved tourist season.

GDP: $136 million, per capita $670; real growth rate 9.2% (1988)

Inflation rate (consumer prices): 14% (1988 est.)

Unemployment rate: NEGL%

Budget: revenues $51 million; expenditures $50 million, including capital expenditures of $25 million (1988 est.)

Exports: $39.4 million (f.o.b., 1988); *commodities*—fish 57%, clothing 39%; *partners*—Thailand, Western Europe, Sri Lanka

Imports: $105.7 million (c.i.f., 1988); *commodities*—intermediate and capital goods 47%, consumer goods 42%, petroleum products 11%; *partners*—Japan, Western Europe, Thailand

External debt: $70 million (December 1989)

Industrial production: growth rate −5.0% (1988); accounts for 5% of GDP

Electricity: 5,000 kW capacity; 11 million kWh produced, 50 kWh per capita (1990)

Industries: fishing and fish processing, tourism, shipping, boat building, some coconut processing, garments, woven mats, coir (rope), handicrafts

Agriculture: accounts for almost 30% of GDP (including fishing); fishing more important than farming; limited production of coconuts, corn, sweet potatoes; most staple foods must be imported; fish catch of 63,000 tons (1988 est.)

Economic aid: US commitments, including Ex-Im (FY70-88), $28 million; Western (non-US) countries, ODA and OOF bilateral commitments (1970-88), $105 million; OPEC bilateral aid (1979-89), $14 million

Currency: rufiyaa (plural—rufiyaa); 1 rufiyaa (Rf) = 100 laaris

Exchange rates: rufiyaa (Rf) per US$1— 9.937 (January 1991), 9.509 (1990), 9.0408 (1989), 8.7846 (1988), 9.2230 (1987), 7.1507 (1986), 7.0981 (1985)

Fiscal year: calendar year

Communications

Highways: Male has 9.6 km of coral highways within the city

Ports: Male, Gan

Merchant marine: 17 ships (1,000 GRT or over) totaling 53,131 GRT/85,770 DWT; includes 14 cargo, 1 container, 1 petroleum, oils, and lubricants (POL) tanker, 1 bulk

Civil air: 1 major transport aircraft

Airports: 2 with permanent-surface runways 2,440-3,659 m

Telecommunications: minimal domestic and international facilities; 2,804 telephones; stations—2 AM, 1 FM, 1 TV; 1 Indian Ocean INTELSAT earth station

Defense Forces

Branches: National Security Service (paramilitary police force)

Manpower availability: males 15-49, 50,788; 28,378 fit for military service

Defense expenditures: $1.8 million, NA% of GDP (1984 est.)

Mali

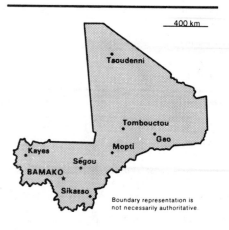

Boundary representation is not necessarily authoritative.

Geography

Total area: 1,240,000 km²; land area: 1,220,000 km²

Comparative area: slightly less than twice the size of Texas

Land boundaries: 7,243 km total; Algeria 1,376 km, Burkina 1,000 km, Guinea 858 km, Ivory Coast 532 km, Mauritania 2,237 km, Niger 821 km, Senegal 419 km

Coastline: none—landlocked

Maritime claims: none—landlocked

Disputes: the disputed international boundary between Burkina and Mali was submitted to the International Court of Justice (ICJ) in October 1983 and the ICJ issued its final ruling in December 1986, which both sides agreed to accept; Burkina and Mali are proceeding with boundary demarcation, including the tripoint with Niger

Climate: subtropical to arid; hot and dry February to June; rainy, humid, and mild June to November; cool and dry November to February

Terrain: mostly flat to rolling northern plains covered by sand; savanna in south, rugged hills in northeast

Natural resources: gold, phosphates, kaolin, salt, limestone, uranium; bauxite, iron ore, manganese, tin, and copper deposits are known but not exploited

Land use: arable land 2%; permanent crops NEGL%; meadows and pastures 25%; forest and woodland 7%; other 66%; includes irrigated NEGL%

Environment: hot, dust-laden harmattan haze common during dry seasons; desertification

Note: landlocked

People

Population: 8,338,542 (July 1991), growth rate 2.4% (1991)

Birth rate: 51 births/1,000 population (1991)

Mali (continued)

Death rate: 21 deaths/1,000 population (1991)

Net migration rate: −6 migrants/1,000 population (1991)

Infant mortality rate: 114 deaths/1,000 live births (1991)

Life expectancy at birth: 45 years male, 47 years female (1991)

Total fertility rate: 7.0 children born/woman (1991)

Nationality: noun—Malian(s); adjective—Malian

Ethnic divisions: Mande (Bambara, Malinke, Sarakole) 50%, Peul 17%, Voltaic 12%, Songhai 6%, Tuareg and Moor 5%, other 10%

Religion: Muslim 90%, indigenous beliefs 9%, Christian 1%

Language: French (official); Bambara spoken by about 80% of the population; numerous African languages

Literacy: 32% (male 41%, female 24%) age 15 and over can read and write (1990 est.)

Labor force: 2,666,000 (1986 est.); agriculture 80%, services 19%, industry and commerce 1% (1981); 50% of population of working age (1985)

Organized labor: National Union of Malian Workers (UNTM) is umbrella organization for over 13 national unions

Government

Long-form name: Republic of Mali

Type: republic; the single-party constitutional government was overthrown on 26 March 1991; the new ruling National Reconciliation Council has promised a multiparty democracy

Capital: Bamako

Administrative divisions: 7 regions (régions, singular—région); Gao, Kayes, Koulikoro, Mopti, Ségou, Sikasso, Tombouctou; note—there may be a new capital district of Bamako

Independence: 22 September 1960 (from France; formerly French Sudan)

Constitution: 2 June 1974, effective 19 June 1979; amended September 1981 and March 1985; suspended following the coup of 26 March 1991

Legal system: based on French civil law system and customary law; judicial review of legislative acts in Constitutional Section of Court of State; has not accepted compulsory ICJ jurisdiction

National holiday: Anniversary of the Proclamation of the Republic, 22 September (1960)

Executive branch: National Conciliation Council led by the military, following the coup of 26 March 1991

Legislative branch: unicameral National Assembly (Assemblé Nationale)

Judicial branch: Supreme Court (Cour Suprême)

Leaders:
Chief of State—following the military coup of 26 March 1991 President Gen. Moussa TRAORÉ was deposed and the National Reconciliation Council, led by Lt. Col. Amadou Toumani TOURE and Lt. Col. Kafougouna KONE, was installed;
Head of Government—Interim Premier Soumana SACKO (since 2 April 1991)

Political parties and leaders: formerly the only party, the Democratic Union of Malian People (UDPM), was disbanded after the coup of 26 March 1991, and the new regime legalized the formation of political parties on 5 April 1991; new political parties are—Union of Democratic Forces (UFD), Demba DIALLO; Union for Democracy and Development (UDD), Moussa Bala COULIBALY; Sudanese Union/African Democratic Rally (US-RDA), Mamadou Madeira KEITA; African Party for Solidarity and Justice (ADEMA), Alpha Oumar KONARE; Party for Democracy and Progress (PDP), Idrissa TRAORÉ; Democratic Party for Justice (PDJ), Abdul BA; Rally for Democracy and Progress (RDP), Almany SYLLA; Party for the Unity of Malian People (PUPM), Nock AGATTIA; Hisboulah al Islamiya, Hamidou DRAMERA; Union of Progressive Forces (UFP), Yacouba SIDIBE; National Congress of Democratic Initiative (CNID), Mountaga TALL; Assembly for Justice and Progress, Kady DRAME; other parties forming

Suffrage: universal at age 21

Elections:
President—last held on 9 June 1985 (next to be held June 1991); results—General Moussa TRAORÉ was reelected without opposition;
National Assembly—last held on 26 June 1988 (next to be held June 1991); results—UDPM is the only party; seats—(82 total) UDPM 82; note—following the military coup of 26 March 1991 President TRAORÉ was deposed and the UDPM was disbanded; the new ruling National Reconciliation Council, formed of 17 soldiers, has promised to institute a multiparty democracy and is expected to hold elections by December 1991

Communists: a few Communists and some sympathizers (no legal Communist party)

Member of: ACCT, ACP, AfDB, CCC, CEAO, ECA, ECOWAS, FAO, FZ, G-77, IAEA, IBRD, ICAO, IDA, IDB, IFAD, IFC, ILO, IMF, INTELSAT, INTERPOL, IOC, ITU, LORCS, NAM, OAU, OIC, UN, UNCTAD, UNESCO, UNIDO, UPU, WADB, WCL, WHO, WIPO, WMO, WTO

Diplomatic representation: Ambassador Mohamed Alhousseyni TOURE; Chancery at 2130 R Street NW, Washington DC 20008; telephone (202) 332-2249 or 939-8950;

US—Ambassador Herbert D. GELBER; Embassy at Rue Rochester NY and Rue Mohamed V., Bamako (mailing address is B. P. 34, Bamako); telephone [223] 223712

Flag: three equal vertical bands of green (hoist side), yellow, and red; uses the popular pan-African colors of Ethiopia

Economy

Overview: Mali is among the poorest countries in the world, with about 70% of its land area desert or semidesert. Economic activity is largely confined to the riverine area irrigated by the Niger. About 10% of the population live as nomads and some 80% of the labor force is engaged in agriculture and fishing. Industrial activity is concentrated on processing farm commodities.

GDP: $2.0 billion, per capita $250; real growth rate 9.9% (1989 est.)

Inflation rate (consumer prices): NA% (1987)

Unemployment rate: NA%

Budget: revenues $329 million; expenditures $519 million, including capital expenditures of $178 (1989 est.)

Exports: $285 million (f.o.b., 1989 est.); *commodities*—livestock, peanuts, dried fish, cotton, skins; *partners*—mostly franc zone and Western Europe

Imports: $513 million (f.o.b., 1989 est.); *commodities*—textiles, vehicles, petroleum products, machinery, sugar, cereals; *partners*—mostly franc zone and Western Europe

External debt: $2.2 billion (1989 est.)

Industrial production: growth rate 19.9% (1989 est.); accounts for 7% of GDP

Electricity: 253,000 kW capacity; 730 million kWh produced, 90 kWh per capita (1990)

Industries: small local consumer goods and processing, construction, phosphate, gold, fishing

Agriculture: accounts for 50% of GDP; most production based on small subsistence farms; cotton and livestock products account for over 70% of exports; other crops—millet, rice, corn, vegetables, peanuts; livestock—cattle, sheep, and goats

Economic aid: US commitments, including Ex-Im (FY70-89), $349 million; Western (non-US) countries, ODA and OOF bilateral commitments (1970-88), $2.65 billion; OPEC bilateral aid (1979-89), $92 million; Communist countries (1970-89), $190 million

Currency: Communauté Financière Africaine franc (plural—francs); 1 CFA franc (CFAF) = 100 centimes

Exchange rates: Communauté Financière Africaine francs (CFAF) per US$1—256.54 (January 1991), 272.26 (1990), 319.01

Malta

(1989), 297.85 (1988), 300.54 (1987),
346.30 (1986), 449.26 (1985)
Fiscal year: calendar year

Communications

Railroads: 642 km 1.000-meter gauge;
linked to Senegal's rail system through
Kayes
Highways: about 15,700 km total; 1,670 km
bituminous, 3,670 km gravel and improved
earth, 10,360 km unimproved earth
Inland waterways: 1,815 km navigable
Civil air: no major transport aircraft
Airports: 37 total, 29 usable; 8 with permanent-surface runways; none with runways
over 3,659 m; 6 with runways 2,440-3,659
m; 10 with runways 1,220-2,439 m
Telecommunications: domestic system poor
but improving; provides only minimal service with radio relay, wire, and radio communications stations; expansion of radio
relay in progress; 11,000 telephones; stations—2 AM, 2 FM, 2 TV; satellite earth
stations—1 Atlantic Ocean INTELSAT and
1 Indian Ocean INTELSAT

Defense Forces

Branches: Army, Air Force; paramilitary
Gendarmerie, Republican Guard, National
Guard, National Police
Manpower availability: males 15-49,
1,631,445; 940,954 fit for military service;
no conscription
Defense expenditures: $45 million, 2.4% of
GDP (1988)

Geography

Total area: 320 km²; land area: 320 km²
Comparative area: slightly less than twice
the size of Washington, DC
Land boundaries: none
Coastline: 140 km
Maritime claims:
Contiguous zone: 24 nm;
Continental shelf: 200 m (depth) or to depth
of exploitation;
Exclusive fishing zone: 25 nm;
Territorial sea: 12 nm
Climate: Mediterranean with mild, rainy
winters and hot, dry summers
Terrain: mostly low, rocky, flat to dissected
plains; many coastal cliffs
Natural resources: limestone, salt
Land use: arable land 38%; permanent crops
3%; meadows and pastures 0%; forest and
woodland 0%; other 59%; includes irrigated
3%
Environment: numerous bays provide good
harbors; fresh water very scarce—increasing
reliance on desalination
Note: strategic location in central Mediterranean, 93 km south of Sicily, 290 km north
of Libya

People

Population: 356,427 (July 1991), growth
rate 0.8% (1991)
Birth rate: 15 births/1,000 population
(1991)
Death rate: 8 deaths/1,000 population
(1991)
Net migration rate: 1 migrant/1,000 population (1991)
Infant mortality rate: 7 deaths/1,000 live
births (1991)
Life expectancy at birth: 74 years male, 79
years female (1991)
Total fertility rate: 2.0 children born/wo-
man (1991)

Nationality: noun—Maltese (sing. and pl.);
adjective—Maltese
Ethnic divisions: mixture of Arab, Sicilian,
Norman, Spanish, Italian, English
Religion: Roman Catholic 98%
Language: Maltese and English (official)
Literacy: 84% (male 86%, female 82%) age
15 and over can read and write (1985)
Labor force: 126,135; government (exclud-
ing job corps) 37%, services 26%, manufac-
turing 22%, training programs 9%, con-
struction 4%, agriculture 2% (1989)
Organized labor: about 40% of labor force

Government

Long-form name: Republic of Malta
Type: parliamentary democracy
Capital: Valletta
Administrative divisions: none (administra-
tion directly from Valletta)
Independence: 21 September 1964 (from
UK)
Constitution: 26 April 1974, effective 2 June
1974
Legal system: based on English common
law and Roman civil law; has accepted
compulsory ICJ jurisdiction, with
reservations
National holiday: Freedom Day, 31 March
Executive branch: president, prime minis-
ter, deputy prime minister, Cabinet
Legislative branch: unicameral House of
Representatives
Judicial branch: Constitutional Court and
Court of Appeal
Leaders:
Chief of State—President Vincent (Censu)
TABONE (since 4 April 1989);
Head of Government—Prime Minister Dr.
Edward (Eddie) FENECH ADAMI (since
12 May 1987); Deputy Prime Minister Dr.
Guido DE MARCO (since 14 May 1987)
Political parties and leaders: Nationalist
Party, Edward FENECH ADAMI; Malta
Labor Party, Karmenu MIFSUD BONNICI
Suffrage: universal at age 18
Elections:
House of Representatives—last held on 9
May 1987 (next to be held by May 1992);
results—NP 51.1%, MLP 48.9%; seats—
(usually 65 total, but additional seats are
given to the party with the largest popular
vote to ensure a legislative majority; current
total 69) MLP 34, NP 31 before popular
vote adjustment; MLP 34, NP 35 after
adjustment
Communists: fewer than 100 (est.)
Member of: C, CCC, CE, CSCE, EBRD,
ECE, FAO, G-77, GATT, IBRD, ICAO,
ICFTU, IFAD, ILO, IMF, IMO,
INTERPOL, IOC, ITU, NAM, PCA, UN,
UNCTAD, UNESCO, UNIDO, UPU,
WCL, WHO, WIPO, WMO, WTO

Malta (continued)

Diplomatic representation: Ambassador Salvatore J. STELLINI; Chancery at 2017 Connecticut Avenue NW, Washington DC 20008; telephone (202) 462-3611 or 3612; there is a Maltese Consulate General in New York;
US—Ambassador Sally J. NOVETZKE; Embassy at 2nd Floor, Development House, Saint Anne Street, Floriana, Valletta (mailing address is P. O. Box 535, Valletta); telephone [356] 240424, 240425, 243216, 243217, 243653, 223654
Flag: two equal vertical bands of white (hoist side) and red; in the upper hoist-side corner is a representation of the George Cross, edged in red

Economy

Overview: Significant resources are limestone, a favorable geographic location, and a productive labor force. Malta produces only about 20% of its food needs, has limited freshwater supplies, and has no domestic energy sources. Consequently, the economy is highly dependent on foreign trade and services. Manufacturing and tourism are the largest contributors to the economy. Manufacturing accounts for about 27% of GDP, with the electronics and textile industries major contributors. In 1989 inflation was held to a low 0.9%. Per capita GDP at $5,500 places Malta in the middle-income range of the world's nations.
GDP: $1.9 billion, per capita $5,500 (1988); real growth rate 6.4% (1989)
Inflation rate (consumer prices): 0.9% (1989)
Unemployment rate: 3.7% (1989)
Budget: revenues $1,020 million; expenditures $1,230 million, including capital expenditures of $380 million (1990 est.)
Exports: $866 million (f.o.b., 1989); *commodities*—clothing, textiles, footwear, ships;
partners—Italy 30%, FRG 22%, UK 11%
Imports: $1,328 million (f.o.b., 1989); *commodities*—food, petroleum, machinery and semimanufactured goods;
partners—Italy 30%, UK 16%, FRG 13%, US 4%
External debt: $90 million, medium and long-term (December 1987)
Industrial production: growth rate 19.2% (1989); accounts for 27% of GDP
Electricity: 328,000 kW capacity; 1,110 million kWh produced, 2,990 kWh per capita (1989)
Industries: tourism, electronics, ship repair yard, construction, food manufacturing, textiles, footwear, clothing, beverages, tobacco
Agriculture: accounts for 3% of GDP; overall, 20% self-sufficient; main products—potatoes, cauliflower, grapes, wheat, barley, tomatoes, citrus, cut flowers, green peppers, hogs, poultry, eggs; generally adequate supplies of vegetables, poultry, milk, pork products; seasonal or periodic shortages in grain, animal fodder, fruits, other basic foodstuffs
Economic aid: US commitments, including Ex-Im (FY70-81), $172 million; Western (non-US) countries, ODA and OOF bilateral commitments (1970-88), $333 million; OPEC bilateral aid (1979-89), $76 million; Communist countries (1970-88), $48 million
Currency: Maltese lira (plural—liri); 1 Maltese lira (LM) = 100 cents
Exchange rates: Maltese liri (LM) per US$1—0.3004 (January 1991), (1986), 0.4676 (1985)
Fiscal year: 1 April-31 March

Communications

Highways: 1,291 km total; 1,179 km paved (asphalt), 77 km crushed stone or gravel, 35 km improved and unimproved earth
Ports: Valletta, Marsaxlokk
Merchant marine: 415 ships (1,000 GRT or over) totaling 5,005,791 GRT/8,644,369 DWT; includes 3 passenger, 8 short-sea passenger, 160 cargo, 5 container, 2 passenger-cargo, 13 roll-on/roll-off cargo, 3 vehicle carrier, 1 barge carrier, 6 refrigerated cargo, 9 chemical tanker, 8 combination ore/oil, 2 specialized tanker, 1 liquefied gas, 79 petroleum, oils, and lubricants (POL) tanker, 104 bulk, 11 combination bulk; note—a flag of convenience registry; China owns 1 ship, USSR owns 7, Cuba owns 7, and Vietnam owns 1
Civil air: 7 major transport aircraft
Airports: 1 with permanent-surface runways 2,440-3,659 m
Telecommunications: modern automatic system centered in Valletta; 163,800 telephones; stations—9 AM, 4 FM, 2 TV; 1 submarine cable; 1 Atlantic Ocean INTELSAT earth station

Defense Forces

Branches: Armed Forces, Maltese Police Force
Manpower availability: males 15-49, 94,081; 75,222 fit for military service
Defense expenditures: $21.9 million, 1.3% of GDP (1989 est.)

Man, Isle of
(British crown dependency)

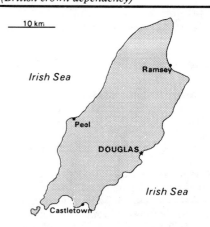

Geography

Total area: 588 km²; land area: 588 km²
Comparative area: slightly less than 3.5 times the size of Washington, DC
Land boundaries: none
Coastline: 113 km
Maritime claims:
Exclusive fishing zone: 200 nm;
Territorial sea: 3 nm
Climate: cool summers and mild winters; humid; overcast about half the time
Terrain: hills in north and south bisected by central valley
Natural resources: lead, iron ore
Land use: arable land NA%; permanent crops NA%; meadows and pastures NA%; forest and woodland NA%; other NA%; extensive arable land and forests
Environment: strong westerly winds prevail
Note: located in Irish Sea equidistant from England, Scotland, and Ireland

People

Population: 64,075 (July 1991), growth rate 0.1% (1991)
Birth rate: 11 births/1,000 population (1991)
Death rate: 14 deaths/1,000 population (1991)
Net migration rate: 4 migrants/1,000 population (1991)
Infant mortality rate: 9 deaths/1,000 live births (1991)
Life expectancy at birth: 72 years male, 78 years female (1991)
Total fertility rate: 1.8 children born/woman (1991)
Nationality: noun—Manxman, Manxwoman, adjective—Manx
Ethnic divisions: native Manx of Norse-Celtic descent; British
Religion: Anglican, Roman Catholic, Methodist, Baptist, Presbyterian, Society of Friends
Language: English, Manx Gaelic

Literacy: NA% (male NA%, female NA%) but compulsory education age 5 to 16
Labor force: 25,864 (1981)
Organized labor: 22 labor unions patterned along British lines

Government

Long-form name: none
Type: British crown dependency
Capital: Douglas
Administrative divisions: none (British crown dependency)
Independence: none (British crown dependency)
Constitution: 1961, Isle of Man Constitution Act
Legal system: English law and local statute
National holiday: Tynwald Day, 5 July
Executive branch: British monarch, lieutenant governor, prime minister, Executive Council (cabinet)
Legislative branch: bicameral Tynwald consists of an upper house or Legislative Council and a lower house or House of Keys
Judicial branch: High Court of Justice
Leaders:
Chief of State—Lord of Mann Queen ELIZABETH II (since 6 February 1952), represented by Lieutenant Governor Air Marshal Sir Laurence JONES (since NA 1990);
Head of Government—President of the Legislative Council Sir Charles KERRUISH (since NA 1990)
Political parties and leaders: there is no party system and members sit as independents
Suffrage: universal at age 21
Elections:
House of Keys—last held in 1986 (next to be held 1991); results—percent of vote NA; seats—(24 total) independents 24
Communists: probably none
Member of: none
Diplomatic representation: none (British crown dependency)
Flag: red with the Three Legs of Man emblem (*Trinacria*), in the center; the three legs are joined at the thigh and bent at the knee; in order to have the toes pointing clockwise on both sides of the flag, a two-sided emblem is used

Economy

Overview: Offshore banking, manufacturing, and tourism are key sectors of the economy. The government's policy of offering incentives to high-technology companies and financial institutions to locate on the island has paid off in expanding employment opportunities in high-income industries. As a result, agriculture and fishing, once the mainstays of the economy, have declined in their shares of GNP. Banking now contributes over 20% to GNP and manufacturing about 15%. Trade is mostly with the UK.
GNP: $490 million, per capita $7,573; real growth rate NA% (1988)
Inflation rate (consumer prices): NA%
Unemployment rate: 1.5% (1988)
Budget: revenues $130.4 million; expenditures $114.4 million, including capital expenditures of $18.1 million (FY85 est.)
Exports: $NA;
commodities—tweeds, herring, processed shellfish meat;
partners—UK
Imports: $NA;
commodities—timber, fertilizers, fish;
partners—UK
External debt: $NA
Industrial production: growth rate NA%
Electricity: 61,000 kW capacity; 190 million kWh produced, 2,930 kWh per capita (1989)
Industries: an important offshore financial center; financial services, light manufacturing, tourism
Agriculture: cereals and vegetables; cattle, sheep, pigs, poultry
Economic aid: NA
Currency: Manx pound (plural—pounds); 1 Manx pound (£M) = 100 pence
Exchange rates: Manx pounds (£M) per US$1—0.5171 (January 1991), 0.5603 (1990), 0.6099 (1989), 0.5614 (1988), 0.6102 (1987), 0.6817 (1986), 0.7714 (1985); the Manx pound is at par with the British pound
Fiscal year: 1 April-31 March

Communications

Railroads: 36 km electric track, 24 km steam track
Highways: 640 km motorable roads
Ports: Douglas, Ramsey, Peel
Merchant marine: 73 ships (1,000 GRT or over) totaling 1,634,471 GRT/2,906,039 DWT; includes 8 cargo, 6 container, 6 roll-on/roll-off cargo, 31 petroleum, oils, and lubricants (POL) tanker, 4 chemical tanker, 2 combination ore/oil, 3 liquefied gas, 13 bulk; note—a captive register of the United Kingdom, although not all ships on the register are British-owned
Airports: 2 total; 1 usable with permanent-surface runways 1,220-2,439 m
Telecommunications: 24,435 telephones; stations—1 AM, 4 FM, 4 TV

Defense Forces

Note: defense is the responsibility of the UK

Marshall Islands

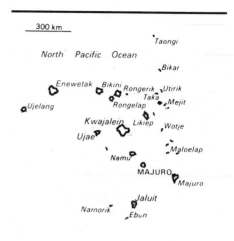

Geography

Total area: 181.3 km²; land area: 181.3 km²; includes the atolls of Bikini, Eniwetak, and Kwajalein
Comparative area: slightly larger than Washington, DC
Land boundaries: none
Coastline: 370.4 km
Maritime claims:
Contiguous zone: 24 nm;
Exclusive economic zone: 200 nm;
Territorial sea: 12 nm
Disputes: claims US territory of Wake Island
Climate: wet season May to November; hot and humid; islands border typhoon belt
Terrain: low coral limestone and sand islands
Natural resources: phosphate deposits, marine products, deep seabed minerals
Land use: arable land 0%; permanent crops 60%; meadows and pastures 0%; forest and woodland 0%; other 40%
Environment: occasionally subject to typhoons; two archipelagic island chains of 30 atolls and 1,152 islands
Note: located 3,825 km southwest of Honolulu in the North Pacific Ocean, about two-thirds of the way between Hawaii and Papua New Guinea; Bikini and Eniwetak are former US nuclear test sites; Kwajalein, the famous World War II battleground, is now used as a US missile test range

People

Population: 48,091 (July 1991), growth rate 3.9% (1991)
Birth rate: 47 births/1,000 population (1991)
Death rate: 8 deaths/1,000 population (1991)
Net migration rate: 0 migrants/1,000 population (1991)
Infant mortality rate: 53 deaths/1,000 live births (1991)

197

Marshall Islands (continued)

Life expectancy at birth: 61 years male, 64 years female (1991)
Total fertility rate: 7.1 children born/woman (1991)
Nationality: noun—Marshallese; adjective—Marshallese
Ethnic divisions: almost entirely Micronesian
Religion: predominantly Christian, mostly Protestant
Language: English universally spoken and is the official language; two major Marshallese dialects from Malayo-Polynesian family; Japanese
Literacy: 93% (male 100%, female 88%) age 15 and over can read and write (1980)
Labor force: 4,800 (1986)
Organized labor: none

Government

Long-form name: Republic of the Marshall Islands
Type: constitutional government in free association with the US; the Compact of Free Association entered into force 21 October 1986
Capital: Majuro
Administrative divisions: none
Independence: 21 October 1986 (from the US-administered UN trusteeship; formerly the Marshall Islands District of the Trust Territory of the Pacific Islands)
Constitution: 1 May 1979
Legal system: based on adapted Trust Territory laws, acts of the legislature, municipal, common, and customary laws
National holiday: Proclamation of the Republic of the Marshall Islands, 1 May (1979)
Executive branch: president, Cabinet
Legislative branch: unicameral Nitijela
Judicial branch: Supreme Court
Leaders:
Chief of State and Head of Government—President Amata KABUA (since 1979)
Political parties and leaders: no formal parties; President KABUA is chief political (and traditional) leader
Suffrage: universal at age 18
Elections:
President—last held NA November 1987 (next to be held November 1991); results—President Amata KABUA was reelected;
Parliament—last held NA November 1987 (next to be held November 1991); results—percent of vote NA; seats—(33 total)
Communists: none
Member of: ESCAP (associate), ICAO, SPC, SPF
Diplomatic representation: Ambassador Wilfred I. KENDALL; Chancery at 2433 Massachusetts Avenue, NW, Washington DC 20008; telephone (202) 234-5414;

US—Ambassador William BODDE, Jr.; Embassy at NA address (mailing address is P. O. Box 680, Majuro, Republic of the Marshall Islands 96960-4380); telephone 692-4011
Flag: blue with two stripes radiating from the lower hoist-side corner—orange (top) and white; there is a white star with four large rays and 20 small rays on the hoist side above the two stripes

Economy

Overview: Agriculture and tourism are the mainstays of the economy. Agricultural production is concentrated on small farms, and the most important commercial crops are coconuts, tomatoes, melons, and breadfruit. A few cattle ranches supply the domestic meat market. Small-scale industry is limited to handicrafts, fish processing, and copra. The tourist industry is the primary source of foreign exchange and employs about 10% of the labor force. The islands have few natural resources, and imports far exceed exports. In 1987 the US Government provided grants of $40 million out of the Marshallese budget of $55 million.
GDP: $63 million, per capita $1,500; real growth rate NA% (1989 est.)
Inflation rate (consumer prices): 5.6% (1981)
Unemployment rate: NA%
Budget: revenues $55 million; expenditures NA, including capital expenditures of NA (1987 est.)
Exports: $2.5 million (f.o.b., 1985);
commodities—copra, copra oil, agricultural products, handicrafts;
partners—NA
Imports: $29.2 million (c.i.f., 1985);
commodities—foodstuffs, beverages, building materials;
partners—NA
External debt: $NA
Industrial production: growth rate NA%
Electricity: 42,000 kW capacity; 80 million kWh produced, 1,840 kWh per capita (1990)
Industries: copra, fish, tourism; craft items from shell, wood, and pearl; offshore banking (embryonic)
Agriculture: coconuts, cacao, taro, breadfruit, fruits, copra; pigs, chickens
Economic aid: under the terms of the Compact of Free Association, the US is to provide approximately $40 million in aid annually
Currency: US currency is used
Exchange rates: US currency is used
Fiscal year: 1 October-30 September

Communications

Highways: macadam and concrete roads on major islands (Majuro, Kwajalein), otherwise stone-, coral-, or laterite-surfaced roads and tracks

Ports: Majuro
Merchant marine: 23 ships (1,000 GRT or over) totaling 1,654,871 GRT/3,236,549 DWT; includes 2 cargo, 3 container, 7 petroleum, oils, and lubricants (POL) tanker, 11 bulk carrier; note—a flag of convenience registry
Airports: 5 total, 5 usable; 4 with permanent-surface runways; 5 with runways 1,220-2,439 m
Telecommunications: telephone network—570 lines (Majuro) and 186 (Ebeye); telex services; islands interconnected by shortwave radio (used mostly for government purposes); stations—1 AM, 2 FM, 1 TV, 1 shortwave; 2 Pacific Ocean INTELSAT earth stations; US Government satellite communications system on Kwajalein

Defense Forces

Note: defense is the responsibility of the US

Martinique
(overseas department of France)

Geography

Total area: 1,100 km²; **land area:** 1,060 km²
Comparative area: slightly more than six times the size of Washington, DC
Land boundaries: none
Coastline: 290 km
Maritime claims:
Exclusive economic zone: 200 nm;
Territorial sea: 12 nm
Climate: tropical; moderated by trade winds; rainy season (June to October)
Terrain: mountainous with indented coastline; dormant volcano
Natural resources: coastal scenery and beaches, cultivable land
Land use: arable land 10%; permanent crops 8%; meadows and pastures 30%; forest and woodland 26%; other 26%; includes irrigated 5%
Environment: subject to hurricanes, flooding, and volcanic activity that result in an average of one major natural disaster every five years
Note: located 625 km southeast of Puerto Rico in the Caribbean Sea

People

Population: 345,180 (July 1991), growth rate 0.9% (1991)
Birth rate: 19 births/1,000 population (1991)
Death rate: 7 deaths/1,000 population (1991)
Net migration rate: −3 migrants/1,000 population (1991)
Infant mortality rate: 10 deaths/1,000 live births (1991)
Life expectancy at birth: 73 years male, 80 years female (1991)
Total fertility rate: 2.1 children born/woman (1991)
Nationality: noun—Martiniquais (sing. and pl.); adjective—Martiniquais

Ethnic divisions: African and African-Caucasian-Indian mixture 90%, Caucasian 5%, East Indian, Lebanese, Chinese less than 5%
Religion: Roman Catholic 95%, Hindu and pagan African 5%
Language: French, Creole patois
Literacy: 93% (male 92%, female 93%) age 15 and over can read and write (1982)
Labor force: 100,000; service industry 31.7%, construction and public works 29.4%, agriculture 13.1%, industry 7.3%, fisheries 2.2%, other 16.3%
Organized labor: 11% of labor force

Government

Long-form name: Department of Martinique
Type: overseas department of France
Capital: Fort-de-France
Administrative divisions: none (overseas department of France)
Independence: none (overseas department of France)
Constitution: 28 September 1958 (French Constitution)
Legal system: French legal system
National holiday: Taking of the Bastille, 14 July (1789)
Executive branch: government commissioner
Legislative branch: unicameral General Council and unicameral Regional Council
Judicial branch: Supreme Court
Leaders:
Chief of State—President François MITTERRAND (since 21 May 1981);
Head of Government—Government Commissioner Jean Claude ROURE (since 5 May 1989); President of the General Council Emile MAURICE (since NA 1988)
Political parties: Rally for the Republic (RPR), Stephen BAGO; Union of the Left composed of the Progressive Party of Martinique (PPM), Aimé CÉSAIRE; Socialist Federation of Martinique, Michael YOYO; and the Communist Party of Martinique (PCM), Armand NICOLAS; Union for French Democracy (UDF), Jean MARAN
Suffrage: universal at age 18
Elections:
General Council—last held on NA October 1988 (next to be held by March 1991); results—percent of vote by party NA; seats—(44 total) number of seats by party NA;
Regional Assembly—last held on 16 March 1986 (next to be held by March 1992); results—UDF/RPR coalition 49.8%, PPM/FSM/PCM coalition 41.3%, other 8.9%; seats—(41 total) PPM/FSM/PCM coalition 21, UDF/RPR coalition 20;
French Senate—last held 24 September 1989 (next to be held September 1992); results—percent of vote by party NA; seats—(2 total) UDF 1, PPM 1;

French National Assembly—last held on 5 and 12 June 1988 (next to be held June 1993); results—percent of vote by party NA; seats—(4 total) PPM 1, FSM 1, RPR 1, UDF 1
Communists: 1,000 (est.)
Other political or pressure groups: Proletarian Action Group (GAP); Alhed Marie-Jeanne Socialist Revolution Group (GRS), Martinique Independence Movement (MIM), Caribbean Revolutionary Alliance (ARC), Central Union for Martinique Workers (CSTM), Marc Pulvar; Frantz Fanon Circle; League of Workers and Peasants
Member of: FZ, WCL, WFTU
Diplomatic representation: as an overseas department of France, Martiniquais interests are represented in the US by France; *US*—Consul General Raymond G. ROBINSON; Consulate General at 14 Rue Blenac, Fort-de-France (mailing address is B. P. 561, Fort-de-France 97206); telephone [590] 63-13-03
Flag: the flag of France is used

Economy

Overview: The economy is based on sugarcane, bananas, tourism, and light industry. Agriculture accounts for about 12% of GDP and the small industrial sector for 10%. Sugar production has declined, with most of the sugarcane now used for the production of rum. Banana exports are increasing, going mostly to France. The bulk of meat, vegetable, and grain requirements must be imported, contributing to a chronic trade deficit that requires large annual transfers of aid from France. Tourism has become more important than agricultural exports as a source of foreign exchange. The majority of the work force is employed in the service sector and in administration. In 1986 per capita GDP was relatively high at $6,000. During 1986 the unemployment rate was 30% and was particularly severe among younger workers.
GDP: $2.0 billion, per capita $6,000; real growth rate NA% (1986)
Inflation rate (consumer prices): 2.9% (1989)
Unemployment rate: 30% (1986)
Budget: revenues $268 million; expenditures $268 million, including capital expenditures of $NA (1989 est.)
Exports: $196 million (f.o.b., 1988);
commodities—refined petroleum products, bananas, rum, pineapples;
partners—France 65%, Guadeloupe 24%, FRG (1987)
Imports: $1.3 billion (c.i.f., 1988);
commodities—petroleum products, foodstuffs, construction materials, vehicles, clothing and other consumer goods;
partners—France 65%, UK, Italy, FRG, Japan, US (1987)

Martinique *(continued)*

External debt: $NA
Industrial production: growth rate NA%
Electricity: 113,000 kW capacity; 564 million kWh produced, 1,660 kWh per capita (1990)
Industries: construction, rum, cement, oil refining, sugar, tourism
Agriculture: including fishing and forestry, accounts for about 12% of GDP; principal crops—pineapples, avocados, bananas, flowers, vegetables, and sugarcane for rum; dependent on imported food, particularly meat and vegetables
Economic aid: Western (non-US) countries, ODA and OOF bilateral commitments (1970-88), $9.9 billion
Currency: French franc (plural—francs); 1 French franc (F) = 100 centimes
Exchange rates: French francs (F) per US$1—5.1307 (January 1991), 5.4453 (1990), 6.3801 (1989), 5.9569 (1988), 6.0107 (1987), 6.9261 (1986), 8.9852 (1985)
Fiscal year: calendar year

Communications

Highways: 1,680 km total; 1,300 km paved, 380 km gravel and earth
Ports: Fort-de-France
Civil air: no major transport aircraft
Airports: 2 total; 2 usable; 1 with permanent-surface runways; 1 with runways 2,440-3,659 m; 1 with runways less than 2,439 m
Telecommunications: domestic facilities are adequate; 68,900 telephones; interisland radio relay links to Guadeloupe, Dominica, and Saint Lucia; stations—1 AM, 6 FM, 10 TV; 2 Atlantic Ocean INTELSAT earth stations

Defense Forces

Branches: French Forces, Gendarmerie
Manpower availability: males 15-49, 95,235; NA fit for military service
Note: defense is the responsibility of France

Mauritania

Geography

Total area: 1,030,700 km²; land area: 1,030,400 km²
Comparative area: slightly larger than three times the size of New Mexico
Land boundaries: 5,074 km total; Algeria 463 km, Mali 2,237 km, Senegal 813 km, Western Sahara 1,561 km
Coastline: 754 km
Maritime claims:
Continental shelf: edge of continental margin or 200 nm;
Exclusive economic zone: 200 nm;
Territorial sea: 12 nm
Disputes: boundary with Senegal
Climate: desert; constantly hot, dry, dusty
Terrain: mostly barren, flat plains of the Sahara; some central hills
Natural resources: iron ore, gypsum, fish, copper, phosphate
Land use: arable land 1%; permanent crops NEGL%; meadows and pastures 38%; forest and woodland 5%; other 56%; includes irrigated NEGL%
Environment: hot, dry, dust/sand-laden sirocco wind blows primarily in March and April; desertification; only perennial river is the Senegal

People

Population: 1,995,755 (July 1991), growth rate 3.1% (1991)
Birth rate: 49 births/1,000 population (1991)
Death rate: 18 deaths/1,000 population (1991)
Net migration rate: 0 migrants/1,000 population (1991)
Infant mortality rate: 94 deaths/1,000 live births (1991)
Life expectancy at birth: 44 years male, 50 years female (1991)
Total fertility rate: 7.2 children born/woman (1991)

Nationality: noun—Mauritanian(s); adjective—Mauritanian
Ethnic divisions: mixed Maur/black 40%, Maur 30%, black 30%
Religion: Muslim, nearly 100%
Language: Hasaniya Arabic (national); French (official); Toucouleur, Fula, Sarakole, Wolof
Literacy: 34% (male 47%, female 21%) age 10 and over can read and write (1990 est.)
Labor force: 465,000 (1981 est.); 45,000 wage earners (1980); agriculture 47%, services 29%, industry and commerce 14%, government 10%; 53% of population of working age (1985)
Organized labor: 30,000 members claimed by single union, Mauritanian Workers' Union

Government

Long-form name: Islamic Republic of Mauritania
Type: republic; military first seized power in bloodless coup 10 July 1978; a palace coup that took place on 12 December 1984 brought President Taya to power
Capital: Nouakchott
Administrative divisions: 12 regions (régions, singular—région); Adrar, Brakna, Dakhlet Nouadhibou, El 'Açâba, Gorgol, Guidimaka, Hodh ech Chargui, Hodh el Gharbi, Inchiri, Tagant, Tiris Zemmour, Trarza; note—there may be a new capital district of Nouakchott
Independence: 28 November 1960 (from France)
Constitution: 20 May 1961, abrogated after coup of 10 July 1978; provisional constitution published 17 December 1980 but abandoned in 1981; new constitutional charter published 27 February 1985
Legal system: based on Islamic law
National holiday: Independence Day, 28 November (1960)
Executive branch: president, Military Committee for National Salvation (CMSN), Council of Ministers (cabinet)
Legislative branch: unicameral National Assembly (Assemblée Nationale), dissolved after 10 July 1978 coup; legislative power resides with the CMSN
Judicial branch: Supreme Court (Cour Suprême)
Leaders:
Chief of State and Head of Government—President Col. Maaouya Ould Sid'Ahmed TAYA (since 12 December 1984)
Political parties and leaders: suspended
Suffrage: none
Elections: last presidential election August 1976; National Assembly dissolved 10 July 1978; no national elections are scheduled
Communists: no Communist party, but there is a scattering of Maoist sympathizers

Member of: ABEDA, ACCT (associate), ACP, AfDB, AFESD, AL, AMF, AMU, CAEU, CCC, CEAO, ECA, ECOWAS, FAO, G-77, GATT, IBRD, ICAO, IDA, IDB, IFAD, IFC, ILO, IMF, IMO, INTELSAT, INTERPOL, IOC, ITU, LORCS, NAM, OAU, OIC, UN, UNCTAD, UNESCO, UNIDO, UPU, WHO, WIPO, WMO, WTO

Diplomatic representation: Ambassador Abdellah OULD DADDAH; Chancery at 2129 Leroy Place NW, Washington DC 20008; telephone (202) 232-5700;
US—Ambassador William H. TWADDELL; Embassy at address NA, Nouakchott (mailing address is B. P. 222, Nouakchott); telephone [222] (2) 252-660 or 252-663

Flag: green with a yellow five-pointed star above a yellow, horizontal crescent; the closed side of the crescent is down; the crescent, star, and color green are traditional symbols of Islam

Economy

Overview: A majority of the population still depends on agriculture and livestock for a livelihood, even though most of the nomads and many subsistence farmers were forced into the cities by recurrent droughts in the 1970s and 1980s. Mauritania has extensive deposits of iron ore that account for almost 50% of total exports. The decline in world demand for this ore, however, has led to cutbacks in production. The nation's coastal waters are among the richest fishing areas in the world, but overexploitation by foreigners threatens this key source of revenue. The country's first deepwater port opened near Nouakchott in 1986. In recent years, the droughts, the conflict with Senegal, rising energy costs, and economic mismanagement have resulted in a substantial buildup of foreign debt. The government now has begun the second stage of an economic reform program in consultation with the World Bank, the IMF, and major donor countries.

GDP: $942 million, per capita $500; real growth rate 3.5% (1989 est.)

Inflation rate (consumer prices): 8.2% (1989 est.)

Unemployment rate: 21% (1989 est.)

Budget: revenues $280 million; expenditures $346 million, including capital expenditures of $61 million (1989 est.)

Exports: $519 million (f.o.b., 1989); *commodities*—iron ore, processed fish, small amounts of gum arabic and gypsum, unrecorded but numerically significant cattle exports to Senegal; *partners*—EC 57%, Japan 39%, Ivory Coast 2%

Imports: $567 million (c.i.f., 1989);

commodities—foodstuffs, consumer goods, petroleum products, capital goods; *partners*—EC 79%, Africa 5%, US 4%, Japan 2%

External debt: $2.3 billion (December 1989)

Industrial production: growth rate 4.4% (1988 est.); accounts for 10% of GDP

Electricity: 189,000 kW capacity; 136 million kWh produced, 70 kWh per capita (1989)

Industries: fishing, fish processing, mining of iron ore and gypsum

Agriculture: accounts for 29% of GDP (including fishing); largely subsistence farming and nomadic cattle and sheep herding except in Senegal river valley; crops—dates, millet, sorghum, root crops; fish products number-one export; large food deficit in years of drought

Economic aid: US commitments, including Ex-Im (FY70-89), $168 million; Western (non-US) countries, ODA and OOF bilateral commitments (1970-88), $1.2 billion; OPEC bilateral aid (1979-89), $490 million; Communist countries (1970-89), $277 million

Currency: ouguiya (plural—ouguiya); 1 ouguiya (UM) = 5 khoums

Exchange rates: ouguiya (UM) per US$1— 77.450 (January 1991), 80.609 (1990), 83.051 (1989), 75.261 (1988), 73.878 (1987), 74.375 (1986), 77.085 (1985)

Fiscal year: calendar year

Communications

Railroads: 670 km 1.435-meter standard gauge, single track, owned and operated by government mining company

Highways: 7,525 km total; 1,685 km paved; 1,040 km gravel, crushed stone, or otherwise improved; 4,800 km unimproved roads, trails, tracks

Inland waterways: mostly ferry traffic on the Senegal River

Ports: Nouadhibou, Nouakchott

Merchant marine: 1 cargo ship (1,000 GRT or over) totaling 1,290 GRT/1,840 DWT

Civil air: 2 major transport aircraft

Airports: 30 total, 29 usable; 9 with permanent-surface runways; none with runways over 3,659 m; 4 with runways 2,440-3,659 m; 17 with runways 1,220-2,439 m

Telecommunications: poor system of cable and open-wire lines, minor radio relay links, and radio communications stations; 5,200 telephones; stations—2 AM, no FM, 1 TV; satellite earth stations—1 Atlantic Ocean INTELSAT and 2 ARABSAT, with a third planned

Defense Forces

Branches: Army, Navy, Air Force, National Gendarmerie, National Guard, National Police, Presidential Guard, Nomad Security Guard

Manpower availability: males 15-49, 423,501; 206,733 fit for military service; conscription law not implemented

Defense expenditures: $37 million, 4.2% of GDP (1987)

Mauritius

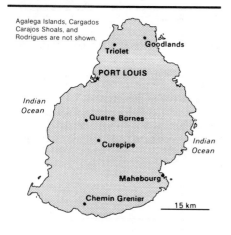

Agalega Islands, Cargados Carajos Shoals, and Rodrigues are not shown.

Triolet · · Goodlands

✈ PORT LOUIS

Indian
Ocean

· Quatre Bornes

Indian
Ocean

· Curepipe

Mahebourg ·

· Chemin Grenier

15 km

Geography

Total area: 1,860 km²; land area: 1,850 km²; includes Agalega Islands, Cargados Carajos Shoals (Saint Brandon), and Rodrigues
Comparative area: slightly less than 10.5 times the size of Washington, DC
Land boundaries: none
Coastline: 177 km
Maritime claims:
Continental shelf: edge of continental margin or 200 nm;
Exclusive economic zone: 200 nm;
Territorial sea: 12 nm
Disputes: claims Chagos Archipelago, which includes the island of Diego Garcia in UK-administered British Indian Ocean Territory; claims French-administered Tromelin Island
Climate: tropical modified by southeast trade winds; warm, dry winter (May to November); hot, wet, humid summer (November to May)
Terrain: small coastal plain rising to discontinuous mountains encircling central plateau
Natural resources: arable land, fish
Land use: arable land 54%; permanent crops 4%; meadows and pastures 4%; forest and woodland 31%; other 7%; includes irrigated 9%
Environment: subject to cyclones (November to April); almost completely surrounded by reefs
Note: located 900 km east of Madagascar in the Indian Ocean

People

Population: 1,081,000 (July 1991), growth rate 0.8% (1991)
Birth rate: 19 births/1,000 population (1991)
Death rate: 6 deaths/1,000 population (1991)
Net migration rate: −4 migrants/1,000 population (1991)

Infant mortality rate: 20 deaths/1,000 live births (1991)
Life expectancy at birth: 66 years male, 74 years female (1991)
Total fertility rate: 2.0 children born/woman (1991)
Nationality: noun—Mauritian(s); adjective—Mauritian
Ethnic divisions: Indo-Mauritian 68%, Creole 27%, Sino-Mauritian 3%, Franco-Mauritian 2%
Religion: Hindu 52%, Christian (Roman Catholic 26%, Protestant 2.3%) 28.3%, Muslim 16.6%, other 3.1%
Language: English (official), Creole, French, Hindi, Urdu, Hakka, Bojpoori
Literacy: 61% (male 72%, female 50%) age 13 and over can read and write (1962)
Labor force: 335,000; government services 29%, agriculture and fishing 27%, manufacturing 22%, other 22%; 43% of population of working age (1985)
Organized labor: 35% of labor force in more than 270 unions

Government

Long-form name: none
Type: parliamentary democracy
Capital: Port Louis
Administrative divisions: 9 districts and 3 dependencies*; Agalega Islands*, Black River, Cargados Carajos*, Flacq, Grand Port, Moka, Pamplemousses, Plaines Wilhems, Port Louis, Rivière du Rempart, Rodrigues*, Savanne
Independence: 12 March 1968 (from UK)
Constitution: 12 March 1968
Legal system: based on French civil law system with elements of English common law in certain areas
National holiday: Independence Day, 12 March (1968)
Executive branch: British monarch, governor general, prime minister, deputy prime minister, Council of Ministers (cabinet)
Legislative branch: unicameral Legislative Assembly
Judicial branch: Supreme Court
Leaders:
Chief of State—Queen ELIZABETH II (since 6 February 1952), represented by Governor General Sir Veerasamy RINGADOO (since 17 January 1986);
Head of Government—Prime Minister Sir Aneerood JUGNAUTH (since 12 June 1982); Deputy Prime Minister Prem NABABSING (since 26 September 1990) and Deputy Prime Minister Beergoonath GHURBURRUN (since 26 September 1990)
Political parties and leaders:
government coalition—Militant Socialist Movement (MSM), A. JUGNAUTH, and the Mauritian Militant Movement (MMM), Paul BERENGER;

opposition—Mauritian Labor Party (MLP), Sir Satcam BOOLELL; Socialist Workers Front, Sylvio MICHEL; Democratic Labor Movement, Anil BAICHOO; Mauritian Social Democratic Party (PMSD), G. DUVAL
Suffrage: universal at age 18
Elections:
Legislative Assembly—last held on 30 August 1987 (next to be held by 30 August 1992); results—percent of vote by party NA; seats—(70 total, 62 elected) MSM 24, MMM 21, MLP 10, PMSD 5, other 10
Communists: may be 2,000 sympathizers; several Communist organizations; Mauritius Lenin Youth Organization, Mauritius Women's Committee, Mauritius Communist Party, Mauritius People's Progressive Party, Mauritius Young Communist League, Mauritius Liberation Front, Chinese Middle School Friendly Association, Mauritius/USSR Friendship Society
Other political or pressure groups: various labor unions
Member of: ACCT, ACP, AfDB, C, CCC, ECA, FAO, G-77, GATT, IAEA, IBRD, ICAO, ICFTU, IDA, IFAD, IFC, ILO, IMF, IMO, INTELSAT, INTERPOL, IOC, ISO (correspondent), ITU, LORCS, NAM, OAU, PCA, UN, UNCTAD, UNESCO, UNIDO, UPU, WCL, WFTU, WHO, WIPO, WMO, WTO
Diplomatic representation: Ambassador Chitmansing JESSERAMSING; Chancery at Suite 134, 4301 Connecticut Avenue NW, Washington DC 20008; telephone (202) 244-1491 or 1492;
US—Ambassador Penne Percy KORTH; Embassy at 4th Floor, Rogers House, John Kennedy Street, Port Louis; telephone [230] 208-9763 through 208-9767
Flag: four equal horizontal bands of red (top), blue, yellow, and green

Economy

Overview: The economy is based on sugar, manufacturing (mainly textiles), and tourism. Sugarcane is grown on about 90% of the cultivated land area and accounts for 32% of export earnings. The government's development strategy is centered on industrialization (with a view to exports), agricultural diversification, and tourism. Economic performance in 1989 was impressive, with 5.0% real growth and low unemployment.
GDP: $2.1 billion, per capita $2,000; real growth rate 5.5% (FY89)
Inflation rate (consumer prices): 12.7% (1989)
Unemployment rate: 2.7% (1989 est.)
Budget: revenues $477 million; expenditures $540 million, including capital expenditures of $112 million (FY89)
Exports: $993 million (f.o.b., 1989);

commodities—textiles 44%, sugar 40%, light manufactures 10%;
partners—EC and US have preferential treatment, EC 77%, US 15%
Imports: $1.2 billion (f.o.b., 1989);
commodities—manufactured goods 50%, capital equipment 17%, foodstuffs 13%, petroleum products 8%, chemicals 7%;
partners—EC, US, South Africa, Japan
External debt: $670 million (December 1989)
Industrial production: growth rate 12.9% (FY87); accounts for 25% of GDP
Electricity: 233,000 kW capacity; 420 million kWh produced, 375 kWh per capita (1989)
Industries: food processing (largely sugar milling), textiles, wearing apparel, chemicals, metal products, transport equipment, nonelectrical machinery, tourism
Agriculture: accounts for 10% of GDP; about 90% of cultivated land in sugarcane; other products—tea, corn, potatoes, bananas, pulses, cattle, goats, fish; net food importer, especially rice and fish
Illicit drugs: illicit producer of cannabis for the international drug trade
Economic aid: US commitments, including Ex-Im (FY70-89), $76 million; Western (non-US) countries (1970-88), $628 million; Communist countries (1970-89), $54 million
Currency: Mauritian rupee (plural—rupees); 1 Mauritian rupee (MauR) = 100 cents
Exchange rates: Mauritian rupees (MauRs) per US$1—14.295 (January 1991), 14.839 (1990), 15.250 (1989), 13.438 (1988), 12.878 (1987), 13.466 (1986), 15.442 (1985)
Fiscal year: 1 July-30 June

Communications

Highways: 1,800 km total; 1,640 km paved, 160 km earth
Ports: Port Louis
Merchant marine: 9 ships (1,000 GRT or over) totaling 94,619 GRT/140,345 DWT; includes 2 passenger-cargo, 2 cargo, 1 container, 1 roll-on/roll-off cargo, 1 liquefied gas, 2 bulk
Civil air: 4 major transport aircraft
Airports: 5 total, 4 usable; 2 with permanent-surface runways; none with runways over 3,659 m; 1 with runways 2,440-3,659 m; 3 with runways 1,220-2,439 m
Telecommunications: small system with good service; new microwave link to Reunion; high-frequency radio links to several countries; 48,000 telephones; stations—2 AM, no FM, 4 TV; 1 Indian Ocean INTELSAT earth station

---

Defense Forces

Branches: paramilitary Special Mobile Force, Special Support Units, National Police Force, National Coast Guard
Manpower availability: males 15-49, 302,588; 155,176 fit for military service
Defense expenditures: $4 million, 0.2% of GDP (1988)

Mayotte
(territorial collectivity of France)

Geography

Total area: 375 km²; land area: 375 km²
Comparative area: slightly more than twice the size of Washington, DC
Land boundaries: none
Coastline: 185.2 km
Maritime claims:
Exclusive economic zone: 200 nm;
Territorial sea: 12 nm
Disputes: claimed by Comoros
Climate: tropical; marine; hot, humid, rainy season during northeastern monsoon (November to May); dry season is cooler (May to November)
Terrain: generally undulating with ancient volcanic peaks, deep ravines
Natural resources: negligible
Land use: arable land NA%; permanent crops NA%; meadows and pastures NA%; forest and woodland NA%; other NA%
Environment: subject to cyclones during rainy season
Note: part of Comoro Archipelago; located in the Mozambique Channel about halfway between Africa and Madagascar

---

People

Population: 75,027 (July 1991), growth rate 3.9% (1991)
Birth rate: 50 births/1,000 population (1991)
Death rate: 12 deaths/1,000 population (1991)
Net migration rate: 0 migrants/1,000 population (1991)
Infant mortality rate: 87 deaths/1,000 live births (1991)
Life expectancy at birth: 54 years male, 59 years female (1991)
Total fertility rate: 6.8 children born/woman (1991)
Nationality: noun—Mahorais (sing., pl.); adjective—Mahoran
Religion: Muslim 99%; remainder Christian, mostly Roman Catholic

Mayotte (continued)

Language: Mahorian (a Swahili dialect), French
Literacy: NA% (male NA%, female NA%)
Labor force: NA
Organized labor: NA

Government

Long-form name: Territorial Collectivity of Mayotte
Type: territorial collectivity of France
Capital: Dzaoudzi
Administrative divisions: none (territorial collectivity of France)
Independence: none (territorial collectivity of France)
Constitution: 28 September 1958 (French Constitution)
Legal system: French law
National holiday: Taking of the Bastille, 14 July (1789)
Executive branch: government commissioner
Legislative branch: unicameral General Council (Conseil Général)
Judicial branch: Supreme Court (Tribunal Supérieur d'Appel)
Leaders:
Chief of State—President François MITTERRAND (since 21 May 1981);
Head of Government—Prefect, Representative of the French Government Daniel LIMODIN (since NA 1990); President of the General Council Youssouf BAMANA (since NA 1976)
Political parties and leaders: Mahoran Popular Movement (MPM), Younoussa BAMANA; Party for the Mahoran Democratic Rally (PRDM), Daroueche MAOULIDA; Mahoran Rally for the Republic (RMPR), Mansour KAMARDINE; Union of the Center (UDC)
Suffrage: universal at age 18
Elections:
General Council—last held NA June 1988 (next to be held June 1993); results—percent of vote by party NA; seats—(17 total) MPM 9, RPR 6, other 2;
French Senate—last held on 24 September 1989 (next to be held September 1992); results—percent of vote by party NA; seats—(1 total) MPM 1;
French National Assembly—last held 5 and 12 June 1988 (next to be held June 1993); results—percent of vote by party NA; seats—(1 total) UDC 1
Communists: probably none
Member of: FZ
Diplomatic representation: as a territorial collectivity of France, Mahoran interests are represented in the US by France
Flag: the flag of France is used

Economy

Overview: Economic activity is based primarily on the agricultural sector, including fishing and livestock raising. Mayotte is not self-sufficient and must import a large portion of its food requirements, mainly from France. The economy and future development of the island is heavily dependent on French financial assistance.
GDP: $NA, per capita $NA; real growth rate NA%
Inflation rate (consumer prices): NA%
Unemployment rate: NA%
Budget: revenues NA; expenditures $37.3 million, including capital expenditures of NA (1985)
Exports: $4.0 million (f.o.b., 1984); *commodities*—ylang-ylang, vanilla; *partners*—France 79%, Comoros 10%, Reunion 9%
Imports: $21.8 million (f.o.b., 1984); *commodities*—building materials, transportation equipment, rice, clothing, flour; *partners*—France 57%, Kenya 16%, South Africa 11%, Pakistan 8%
External debt: $NA
Industrial production: growth rate NA%
Electricity: NA kW capacity; NA million kWh produced, NA kWh per capita
Industries: newly created lobster and shrimp industry
Agriculture: most important sector; provides all export earnings; crops—vanilla, ylang-ylang, coffee, copra; imports major share of food needs
Economic aid: Western (non-US) countries, ODA and OOF bilateral commitments (1970-87), $323.8 million
Currency: French franc (plural—francs); 1 French franc (F) = 100 centimes
Exchange rates: French francs (F) per US$1—5.1307 (January 1991), 5.4453 (1990), 6.3801 (1989), 5.9569 (1988), 6.0107 (1987), 6.9261 (1986), 8.9852 (1985)
Fiscal year: calendar year

Communications

Highways: 42 km total; 18 km bituminous
Civil air: no major transport aircraft
Airports: 1 with permanent-surface runway 1,220-2,439 m
Ports: Dzaoudzi
Telecommunications: small system administered by French Department of Posts and Telecommunications; includes radio relay and high-frequency radio communications for links with Comoros and international communications; 450 telephones; stations—1 AM, no FM, no TV

Defense Forces

Note: defense is the responsibility of France

Mexico

1000 km

Tijuana, Ciudad Juárez, Chihuahua, Monterrey, Matamoros, La Paz, Durango, Gulf of Mexico, Mérida, Guadalajara, MEXICO, Veracruz, Acapulco, Oaxaca, North Pacific Ocean

Geography

Total area: 1,972,550 km²; land area: 1,923,040 km²
Comparative area: slightly less than three times the size of Texas
Land boundaries: 4,538 km total; Belize 250 km, Guatemala 962 km, US 3,326 km
Coastline: 9,330 km
Maritime claims:
Contiguous zone: 24 nm;
Continental shelf: natural prolongation of continental margin or 200 nm;
Exclusive economic zone: 200 nm;
Territorial sea: 12 nm
Disputes: claims Clipperton Island (French possession)
Climate: varies from tropical to desert
Terrain: high, rugged mountains, low coastal plains, high plateaus, and desert
Natural resources: crude oil, silver, copper, gold, lead, zinc, natural gas, timber
Land use: arable land 12%; permanent crops 1%; meadows and pastures 39%; forest and woodland 24%; other 24%; includes irrigated 3%
Environment: subject to tsunamis along the Pacific coast and destructive earthquakes in the center and south; natural water resources scarce and polluted in north, inaccessible and poor quality in center and extreme southeast; deforestation; erosion widespread; desertification; serious air pollution in Mexico City and urban centers along US-Mexico border
Note: strategic location on southern border of US

People

Population: 90,007,304 (July 1991), growth rate 2.2% (1991)
Birth rate: 29 births/1,000 population (1991)
Death rate: 5 deaths/1,000 population (1991)

Net migration rate: −1 migrants/1,000 population (1991)

Infant mortality rate: 29 deaths/1,000 live births (1991)

Life expectancy at birth: 68 years male, 76 years female (1991)

Total fertility rate: 3.4 children born/woman (1991)

Nationality: noun—Mexican(s); adjective—Mexican

Ethnic divisions: mestizo (Indian-Spanish) 60%, Amerindian or predominantly Amerindian 30%, white or predominantly white 9%, other 1%

Religion: nominally Roman Catholic 97%, Protestant 3%

Language: Spanish

Literacy: 87% (male 90%, female 85%) age 15 and over can read and write (1985 est.)

Labor force: 26,100,000 (1988); services 31.4%, agriculture, forestry, hunting, and fishing 26%, commerce 13.9%, manufacturing 12.8%, construction 9.5%, transportation 4.8%, mining and quarrying 1.3%, electricity 0.3% (1986)

Organized labor: 35% of labor force

Government

Long-form name: United Mexican States

Type: federal republic operating under a centralized government

Capital: Mexico

Administrative divisions: 31 states (estados, singular—estado) and 1 federal district* (distrito federal); Aguascalientes, Baja California, Baja California Sur, Campeche, Chiapas, Chihuahua, Coahuila, Colima, Distrito Federal*, Durango, Guanajuato, Guerrero, Hidalgo, Jalisco, México, Michoacán, Morelos, Nayarit, Nuevo León, Oaxaca, Puebla, Querétaro, Quintana Roo, San Luis Potosí, Sinaloa, Sonora, Tabasco, Tamaulipas, Tlaxcala, Veracruz, Yucatán, Zacatecas

Independence: 16 September 1810 (from Spain)

Constitution: 5 February 1917

Legal system: mixture of US constitutional theory and civil law system; judicial review of legislative acts; accepts compulsory ICJ jurisdiction, with reservations

National holiday: Independence Day, 16 September (1810)

Executive branch: president, Cabinet

Legislative branch: bicameral National Congress (Congreso de la Unión) consists of an upper chamber or Senate (Cámara de Senadores) and a lower chamber or Chamber of Deputies (Cámara de Diputados)

Judicial branch: Supreme Court of Justice (Suprema Corte de Justicia)

Leaders:
Chief of State and Head of Government—President Carlos SALINAS de Gortari (since 1 December 1988)

Political parties and leaders: (recognized parties) Institutional Revolutionary Party (PRI), Luís Donaldo COLOSIO Murrieta; National Action Party (PAN), Luis ALVAREZ; Popular Socialist Party (PPS), Indalecio SAYAGO Herrera; Democratic Revolutionary Party (PRD), Cuauhtémoc CARDENAS Solórzano; Cardenist Front for the National Reconstruction Party (PFCRN), Rafael AGUILAR Talamantes; Authentic Party of the Mexican Revolution (PARM), Carlos Enrique CANTU Rosas

Suffrage: universal and compulsory (but not enforced) at age 18

Elections:
President—last held on 6 July 1988 (next to be held September 1994); results—Carlos SALINAS de Gortari (PRI) 50.74%, Cuauhtémoc CARDENAS Solórzano (FDN) 31.06%, Manuel CLOUTHIER (PAN) 16.81%; other 1.39%; note—several of the smaller parties ran a common candidate under a coalition called the National Democratic Front (FDN);
Senate—last held on 6 July 1988 (next to be held mid-year 1991); results—PRI 94%, FDN (now PRD) 6%; seats—(64 total) number of seats by party NA;
Chamber of Deputies—last held on 6 July 1988 (next to be held mid-year 1991); results—PRI 53%, PAN 20%, PFCRN 10%, PPS 6%, PARM 7%, PMS (now part of PRD) 4%; seats—(500 total) number of seats by party NA

Other political or pressure groups: Roman Catholic Church, Confederation of Mexican Workers (CTM), Confederation of Industrial Chambers (CONCAMIN), Confederation of National Chambers of Commerce (CONCANACO), National Peasant Confederation (CNC), UNE (no expansion), Revolutionary Workers Party (PRT), Mexican Democratic Party (PDM), Revolutionary Confederation of Workers and Peasants (CROC), Regional Confederation of Mexican Workers (CROM), Confederation of Employers of the Mexican Republic (COPARMEX), National Chamber of Transformation Industries (CANACINTRA), Business Coordination Council (CCE)

Member of: AG (observer), CCC, CDB, CG, EBRD, ECLAC, FAO, G-3, G-6, G-11, G-19, G-24, G-77, GATT, IADB, IAEA, IBRD, ICAO, ICC, ICFTU, IDA, IFAD, IFC, ILO, IMF, IMO, INTELSAT, INTERPOL, IOC, IOM (observer), ISO, ITU, LAES, LAIA, LORCS, NAM (observer), OAS, OPANAL, PCA, RG, UN, UNCTAD, UNESCO, UNIDO, UPU, WCL, WHO, WIPO, WMO, WTO

Diplomatic representation: Ambassador Gustavo PETRICIOLI Iturbide; Chancery at 1911 Pennsylvania Avenue NW, Washington DC 20006; telephone (202) 728-1600; there are Mexican Consulates General in Chicago, Dallas, Denver, El Paso, Houston, Los Angeles, New Orleans, New York, San Francisco, San Antonio, San Diego, and Consulates in Albuquerque, Atlanta, Austin, Boston, Brownsville (Texas), Calexico (California), Corpus Christi, Del Rio (Texas), Detroit, Douglas (Arizona), Eagle Pass (Texas), Fresno (California), Kansas City (Missouri), Laredo, McAllen (Texas), Miami, Nogales (Arizona), Oxnard (California), Philadelphia, Phoenix, Presidio (Texas), Sacramento, St. Louis, St. Paul (Minneapolis), Salt Lake City, San Bernardino, San Jose, San Juan (Puerto Rico), and Seattle; *US*—Ambassador John D. NEGROPONTE, Jr.; Embassy at Paseo de la Reforma 305, 06500 Mexico, D.F. (mailing address is P. O. Box 3087, Laredo, TX 78044-3087); telephone [52] (5) 211-0042; there are US Consulates General in Ciudad Juarez, Guadalajara, Monterrey, and Tijuana, and Consulates in Hermosillo, Matamoros, Mazatlan, Merida, and Nuevo Laredo

Flag: three equal vertical bands of green (hoist side), white, and red; the coat of arms (an eagle perched on a cactus with a snake is its beak) is centered in the white band

Economy

Overview: Mexico's economy is a mixture of state-owned industrial plants (notably oil), private manufacturing and services, and both large-scale and traditional agriculture. In the 1980s Mexico experienced severe economic difficulties: the nation accumulated large external debts as world petroleum prices fell; rapid population growth outstripped the domestic food supply; and inflation, unemployment, and pressures to emigrate became more acute. Growth in national output, however, appears to be recovering, rising from 1.4% in 1988 to 3.9% in 1990. The US is Mexico's major trading partner, accounting for two-thirds of its exports and imports. After petroleum, border assembly plants and tourism are the largest earners of foreign exchange. The government, in consultation with international economic agencies, is implementing programs to stabilize the economy and foster growth. In 1991 the government also plans to begin negotiations with the US and Canada on a free trade agreement.

GDP: $236 billion, per capita $2,680; real growth rate 3.9% (1990)

Inflation rate (consumer prices): 30% (1990)

Unemployment rate: 15-18% (1990 est.)

Budget: revenues $44.3 billion; expenditures $55.2 billion, including capital expenditures of $7.8 billion (1989)

Exports: $26.8 billion (f.o.b., 1990); *commodities*—crude oil, oil products, coffee, shrimp, engines, cotton; *partners*—US 66%, EC 16%, Japan 11%

Imports: $29.8 billion (c.i.f., 1990);

205

commodities—grain, metal manufactures, agricultural machinery, electrical equipment;
partners—US 62%, EC 18%, Japan 10%
External debt: $96.0 billion (1990)
Industrial production: growth rate 5.3% (1989); accounts for 27% of GDP
Electricity: 27,600,000 kW capacity; 108,976 million kWh produced, 1,240 kWh per capita (1990)
Industries: food and beverages, tobacco, chemicals, iron and steel, petroleum, mining, textiles, clothing, transportation equipment, tourism
Agriculture: accounts for 9% of GDP and over 25% of work force; large number of small farms at subsistence level; major food crops—corn, wheat, rice, beans; cash crops—cotton, coffee, fruit, tomatoes; fish catch of 1.4 million metric tons among top 20 nations (1987)
Illicit drugs: illicit cultivation of opium poppy and cannabis continues in spite of government eradication efforts; major link in chain of countries used to smuggle cocaine from South American dealers to US markets
Economic aid: US commitments, including Ex-Im (FY70-89), $3.1 billion; Western (non-US) countries, ODA and OOF bilateral commitments (1970-89), $7.1 billion; Communist countries (1970-89), $110 million
Currency: Mexican peso (plural—pesos); 1 Mexican peso (Mex$) = 100 centavos
Exchange rates: market rate of Mexican pesos (Mex$) per US$1—2,940.9 (January 1991), 2,812.6 (1990), 2,461.3 (1989), 2,273.1 (1988), 1,378.2 (1987), 611.8 (1986), 256.9 (1985)
Fiscal year: calendar year

Communications

Railroads: 20,680 km total; 19,950 km 1.435-meter standard gauge; 730 km 0.914-meter narrow gauge
Highways: 210,000 km total; 65,000 km paved, 30,000 km semipaved or cobblestone, 60,000 km rural roads (improved earth) or roads under construction, 55,000 km unimproved earth roads
Inland waterways: 2,900 km navigable rivers and coastal canals
Pipelines: crude oil, 28,200 km; refined products, 10,150 km; natural gas, 13,254 km; petrochemical, 1,400 km
Ports: Acapulco, Coatzacoalcos, Ensenada, Guaymas, Manzanillo, Mazatlan, Progreso, Puerto Vallarta, Salina Cruz, Tampico, Veracruz
Merchant marine: 64 ships (1,000 GRT or over) totaling 999,423 GRT/1,509,939 DWT; includes 4 short-sea passenger, 9 cargo, 2 refrigerated cargo, 2 roll-on/roll-off cargo, 31 petroleum, oils, and lubricants

(POL) tanker, 3 chemical tanker, 7 liquefied gas, 3 bulk, 3 combination bulk
Civil air: 174 major transport aircraft
Airports: 1,815 total, 1,537 usable; 195 with permanent-surface runways; 2 with runways over 3,659 m; 33 with runways 2,440-3,659 m; 276 with runways 1,220-2,439 m
Telecommunications: highly developed system with extensive radio relay links; connection into Central American Microwave System; 6.41 million telephones; stations—679 AM, no FM, 238 TV, 22 shortwave; 120 domestic satellite terminals; earth stations—4 Atlantic Ocean INTELSAT and 1 Pacific Ocean INTELSAT

Defense Forces

Branches: National Defense (includes Army and Air Force), Navy (includes Marines)
Manpower availability: males 15-49, 22,340,628; 16,360,596 fit for military service; 1,107,163 reach military age (18) annually
Defense expenditures: $1 billion, 0.6% of GDP (1988)

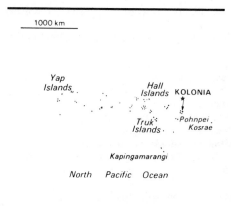

Geography

Total area: 702 km²; land area: 702 km²; includes Pohnpei, Truk, Yap, and Kosrae
Comparative area: slightly less than four times the size of Washington, DC
Land boundaries: none
Coastline: 6,112 km
Maritime claims:
Exclusive economic zone: 200 nm;
Territorial sea: 12 nm
Climate: tropical; heavy year-round rainfall, especially in the eastern islands; located on southern edge of the typhoon belt with occasional severe damage
Terrain: islands vary geologically from high mountainous islands to low, coral atolls; volcanic outcroppings on Pohnpei, Kosrae, and Truk
Natural resources: forests, marine products, deep-seabed minerals
Land use: arable land NA%; permanent crops NA%; meadows and pastures NA%; forest and woodland NA%; other NA%
Environment: subject to typhoons from June to December; four major island groups totaling 607 islands
Note: located 5,150 km west-southwest of Honolulu in the North Pacific Ocean, about three-quarters of the way between Hawaii and Indonesia

People

Population: 107,662 (July 1991), growth rate 2.5% (1991)
Birth rate: 34 births/1,000 population (1991)
Death rate: 5 deaths/1,000 population (1991)
Net migration rate: −4 migrants/1,000 population (1991)
Infant mortality rate: 26 deaths/1,000 live births (1991)
Life expectancy at birth: 68 years male, 73 years female (1991)
Total fertility rate: 5.0 children born/woman (1991)

Nationality: noun—Micronesian(s); adjective—Micronesian; Kosrae(s), Pohnpeian(s), Trukese, Yapese

Ethnic divisions: nine ethnic Micronesian and Polynesian groups

Religion: predominantly Christian, divided between Roman Catholic and Protestant; other churches include Assembly of God, Jehovah's Witnesses, Seventh-Day Adventist, Latter Day Saints, and the Bahá'í Faith

Language: English is the official and common language; most indigenous languages fall within the Austronesian language family, the exceptions are the Polynesian languages; major indigenous languages are Trukese, Pohnpeian, Yapese, and Kosrean

Literacy: 90% (male 90%, female 85%) age 15 and over can read and write (1980)

Labor force: NA; two-thirds are government employees; 45,000 people are between the ages of 15 and 65

Organized labor: NA

Government

Long-form name: Federated States of Micronesia (no short-form name)

Type: constitutional government in free association with the US; the Compact of Free Association entered into force 3 November 1986

Capital: Kolonia (on the island of Pohnpei); note—a new capital is being built about 10 km southwest in the Palikir valley

Administrative divisions: 4 states; Kosrae, Pohnpei, Chuuk, Yap

Independence: 3 November 1986 (from the US-administered UN Trusteeship; formerly the Kosrae, Pohnpei, Truk, and Yap districts of the Trust Territory of the Pacific Islands)

Constitution: 10 May 1979

Legal system: based on adapted Trust Territory laws, acts of the legislature, municipal, common, and customary laws

National holiday: Proclamation of the Federated States of Micronesia, 10 May (1979)

Executive branch: president, vice president, Cabinet

Legislative branch: unicameral Congress

Judicial branch: Supreme Court

Leaders:

Chief of State and Head of Government— President Bailey OLTER (since 11 May 1991); Vice President Jacob NENA (since 11 May 1991)

Political parties and leaders: no formal parties

Suffrage: universal at age 18

Elections:

President—last held 5 March 1991 (next to be held March 1994); results—Vice President Bailey OLTER elected president; *Congress*—last held on 5 March 1991 (next to be held March 1993); results—percent of vote NA; seats—(14 total)

Communists: none

Member of: ESCAP (associate), ICAO, SPC, SPF

Diplomatic representation: Ambassador Jesse B. MAREHALAU; Embassy at 706 G Street SE, Washington DC 20003; telephone (202) 544-2640;

US—Ambassador Aurelia BRAZEAL; Embassy at address NA, Kolonia (mailing address is P. O. Box 1286, Pohnpei, Federated States of Micronesia 96941); telephone 691-320-2187

Flag: light blue with four white five-pointed stars centered; the stars are arranged in a diamond pattern

Economy

Overview: Financial assistance from the US is the primary source of revenue, with the US pledged to spend $1 billion in the islands in the 1990s; also in December 1990 the US authorized the use of disaster relief funds for Micronesia because of damage from Typhoon Russ. In addition Micronesia earns about $4 million a year in fees from foreign commercial fishing concerns. Economic activity consists primarily of subsistence farming and fishing. The islands have few mineral deposits worth exploiting, except for high-grade phosphate. The potential for a tourist industry exists, but the remoteness of the location and a lack of adequate facilities hinder development.

GNP: $150 million, per capita $1,500; real growth rate NA% (1989 est.); note—GNP numbers reflect US spending

Inflation rate (consumer prices): NA%

Unemployment rate: 80% (1988)

Budget: revenues $110.8 million; expenditures NA, including capital expenditures of NA (1987 est.)

Exports: $1.6 million (f.o.b., 1983); *commodities*—copra; *partners*—NA

Imports: $48.9 million (c.i.f., 1983); *commodities*—NA; *partners*—NA

External debt: $NA

Industrial production: growth rate NA%

Electricity: 18,000 kW capacity; 40 million kWh produced, 380 kWh per capita (1990)

Industries: tourism, craft items from shell, wood, and pearl

Agriculture: mainly a subsistence economy; copra, black pepper; tropical fruits and vegetables, coconuts, cassava, sweet potatoes, pigs, chickens

Economic aid: under terms of the Compact of Free Association, the US will provide $1.3 billion in grant aid during the period 1986-2001

Currency: US currency is used

Exchange rates: US currency is used

Fiscal year: 1 October-30 September

Communications

Highways: 39 km of paved macadam and concrete roads on major islands, otherwise 187 km stone-, coral-, or laterite-surfaced roads

Ports: Colonia (Yap), Truk (Kosrae), Okat (Kosrae)

Airports: 11 total, 10 usable; 7 with permanent-surface runways; none with runways over 2,439 m; 6 with runways 1,220-2,439

Telecommunications: 16,000 radio receivers, 1,125 TV sets (est. 1987); telephone network—960 telephone lines at both Kolonia and Truk; islands interconnected by shortwave radio (used mostly for government purposes); stations—5 AM, 1 FM, 6 TV, 1 shortwave; 4 Pacific Ocean INTELSAT earth stations

Defense Forces

Note: defense is the responsibility of the US

Midway Islands
(territory of the US)

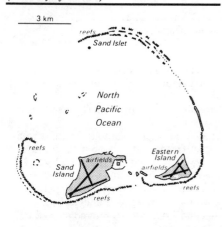

Geography

Total area: 5.2 km²; land area: 5.2 km²; includes Eastern Island and Sand Island
Comparative area: about nine times the size of The Mall in Washington, DC
Land boundaries: none
Coastline: 15 km
Maritime claims:
Contiguous zone: 12 nm;
Continental shelf: 200 m (depth);
Exclusive economic zone: 200 nm;
Territorial sea: 12 nm
Climate: tropical, but moderated by prevailing easterly winds
Terrain: low, nearly level
Natural resources: fish and wildlife
Land use: arable land 0%; permanent crops 0%; meadows and pastures 0%; forest and woodland 0%; other 100%
Environment: coral atoll
Note: located 2,350 km west-northwest of Honolulu at the western end of Hawaiian Islands group, about one-third of the way between Honolulu and Tokyo; closed to the public

People

Population: 453 US military personnel (1991)

Government

Long-form name: none
Type: unincorporated territory of the US administered by the US Navy, under command of the Barbers Point Naval Air Station in Hawaii and managed cooperatively by the US Navy and the Fish and Wildlife Service of the US Department of the Interior as part of the National Wildlife Refuge System
Diplomatic representation: none (territory of the US)
Flag: the US flag is used

Economy

Overview: The economy is based on providing support services for US naval operations located on the islands. All food and manufactured goods must be imported.
Electricity: supplied by US Military

Communications

Highways: 32 km total
Pipelines: 7.8 km
Ports: Sand Island
Airports: 3 total; 2 usable; 1 with permanent-surface runways; none with runways over 2,439 m; 2 with runways 1,220-2,439 m

Defense Forces

Note: defense is the responsibility of the US

Monaco

Geography

Total area: 1.9 km²; land area: 1.9 km²
Comparative area: about three times the size of The Mall in Washington, DC
Land boundary: 4.4 km with France
Coastline: 4.1 km
Maritime claims:
Territorial sea: 12 nm
Climate: Mediterranean with mild, wet winters and hot, dry summers
Terrain: hilly, rugged, rocky
Natural resources: none
Land use: arable land 0%; permanent crops 0%; meadows and pastures 0%; forest and woodland 0%; other 100%
Environment: almost entirely urban
Note: second-smallest independent state in world (after Vatican City)

People

Population: 29,712 (July 1991), growth rate 0.9% (1991)
Birth rate: 7 births/1,000 population (1991)
Death rate: 7 deaths/1,000 population (1991)
Net migration rate: 9 migrants/1,000 population (1991)
Infant mortality rate: 8 deaths/1,000 live births (1991)
Life expectancy at birth: 72 years male, 80 years female (1991)
Total fertility rate: 1.1 children born/woman (1991)
Nationality: noun—Monacan(s) or Monegasque(s); adjective—Monacan or Monegasque
Ethnic divisions: French 47%, Monegasque 16%, Italian 16%, other 21%
Religion: Roman Catholic 95%
Language: French (official), English, Italian, Monegasque
Literacy: NA% (male NA%, female NA%)
Labor force: NA
Organized labor: 4,000 members in 35 unions

Government

Long-form name: Principality of Monaco
Type: constitutional monarchy
Capital: Monaco
Administrative divisions: 4 quarters (quartiers, singular—quartier); Fontvieille, La Condamine, Monaco-Ville, Monte-Carlo
Independence: 1419, rule by the House of Grimaldi
Constitution: 17 December 1962
Legal system: based on French law; has not accepted compulsory ICJ jurisdiction
National holiday: National Day, 19 November
Executive branch: prince, minister of state, Council of Government (cabinet)
Legislative branch: National Council (Conseil National)
Judicial branch: Supreme Tribunal (Tribunal Suprême)
Leaders:
Chief of State—Prince RAINIER III (since November 1949); Heir Apparent Prince ALBERT Alexandre Louis Pierre (born 14 March 1958);
Head of Government Minister of State Jean AUSSEIL (since 10 September 1985)
Political parties and leaders: National and Democratic Union (UND), Democratic Union Movement (MUD), Monaco Action, Monegasque Socialist Party (PSM)
Suffrage: universal adult at age 25
Elections:
National Council—last held on 24 January 1988 (next to be held 24 January 1993); results—percent of vote by party NA; seats—(18 total) UND 18
Member of: ACCT, CSCE, ICAO, IMF (observer), IMO, INTELSAT, INTERPOL, IOC, ITU, LORCS, UN (observer), UNCTAD, UNESCO, UPU, WHO, WIPO
Diplomatic representation: Monaco maintains honorary consulates general in Boston, Chicago, Los Angeles, New Orleans, New York, and San Francisco, and honorary consulates in Dallas, Honolulu, Palm Beach, Philadelphia, and Washington;
US—no mission in Monaco, but the US Consul General in Marseille, France, is accredited to Monaco; Consul General R. Susan WOOD; Consulate General at 12 Boulevard Paul Peytral, 13286 Marseille Cedex (mailing address APO NY 09777); telephone [33] (91) 549-200
Flag: two equal horizontal bands of red (top) and white; similar to the flag of Indonesia which is longer and the flag of Poland which is white (top) and red

Economy

Overview: Monaco, situated on the French Mediterranean coast, is a popular resort, attracting tourists to its casino and pleasant climate. The Principality has successfully sought to diversify into services and small, high-value-added, non-polluting industries. The state has no income tax and low business taxes and thrives as a tax haven both for individuals who have established residence and for foreign companies that have set up businesses and offices. About 50% of Monaco's annual revenue comes from value-added taxes on hotels, banks, and the industrial sector; about 25% of revenue comes from tourism. Living standards are high, that is, roughly comparable to those in prosperous French metropolitan suburbs.
GDP: $324 million, per capita $11,000; real growth rate NA% (1990 est.)
Inflation rate (consumer prices): NA%
Unemployment rate: full employment (1989)
Budget: revenues $386 million; expenditures $426, including capital expenditures of $NA (1988 est.)
Exports: $NA; full customs integration with France, which collects and rebates Monacan trade duties; also participates in EC market system through customs union with France
Imports: $NA; full customs integration with France, which collects and rebates Monacan trade duties; also participates in EC market system through customs union with France
External debt: $NA
Industrial production: growth rate NA%
Electricity: 10,000 kW standby capacity (1988); power supplied by France
Industries: tourism, pharmaceuticals, precision instruments, glassmaking, printing, finance
Agriculture: NA
Economic aid: NA
Currency: French franc (plural—francs); 1 French franc (F) = 100 centimes
Exchange rates: French francs (F) per US$1—5.1307 (January 1991), 5.4453 (1990), 6.3801 (1989), 5.9569 (1988), 6.0107 (1987), 6.9261 (1986), 8.9852 (1985)
Fiscal year: calendar year

Communications

Railroads: 1.6 km 1.435-meter gauge
Highways: none; city streets
Ports: Monaco
Merchant marine: 1 petroleum, oils, and lubricants (POL) tanker (1,000 GRT or over) totaling 3,268 GRT/4,959 DWT
Civil air: no major transport aircraft
Airports: 1 usable airfield with permanent-surface runways
Telecommunications: served by the French communications system; automatic telephone system; 38,200 telephones; stations—3 AM, 4 FM, 5 TV; no communication satellite stations

Defense Forces

Note: defense is the responsibility of France

Mongolia

500 km

Geography

Total area: 1,565,000 km²; land area: 1,565,000 km²
Comparative area: slightly larger than Alaska
Land boundaries: 8,114 km total; China 4,673 km, USSR 3,441 km
Coastline: none—landlocked
Maritime claims: none—landlocked
Climate: desert; continental (large daily and seasonal temperature ranges)
Terrain: vast semidesert and desert plains; mountains in west and southwest; Gobi Desert in southeast
Natural resources: oil, coal, copper, molybdenum, tungsten, phosphates, tin, nickel, zinc, wolfram, fluorspar, gold
Land use: arable land 1%; permanent crops 0%; meadows and pastures 79%; forest and woodland 10%; other 10%; includes irrigated NEGL%
Environment: harsh and rugged
Note: landlocked; strategic location between China and Soviet Union

People

Population: 2,247,068 (July 1991), growth rate 2.7% (1991)
Birth rate: 34 births/1,000 population (1991)
Death rate: 8 deaths/1,000 population (1991)
Net migration rate: 0 migrants/1,000 population (1991)
Infant mortality rate: 48 deaths/1,000 live births (1991)
Life expectancy at birth: 63 years male, 67 years female (1991)
Total fertility rate: 4.6 children born/woman (1991)
Nationality: noun—Mongolian(s); adjective—Mongolian
Ethnic divisions: Mongol 90%, Kazakh 4%, Chinese 2%, Russian 2%, other 2%

Religion: predominantly Tibetan Buddhist, Muslim (about 4%), limited religious activity because of Communist regime
Language: Khalkha Mongol used by over 90% of population; minor languages include Turkic, Russian, and Chinese
Literacy: 90% (male NA%, female NA%) (1989 est.)
Labor force: NA, but primarily herding/agricultural; over half the adult population is in the labor force, including a large percentage of women; shortage of skilled labor
Organized labor: 425,000 members of the Central Council of Mongolian Trade Unions (CCMTU) controlled by the government (1984)

Government

Long-form name: Mongolian People's Republic; abbreviated MPR
Type: in transition from Communist state to republic
Capital: Ulaanbaatar
Administrative divisions: 18 provinces (aymguud, singular—aymag) and 3 municipalities* (hotuud, singular—hot); Arhangay, Bayanhongor, Bayan-Ölgiy, Bulgan, Darhan*, Dornod, Dornogovĭ, Dundgovĭ, Dzavhan, Erdenet*, Govĭ-Altay, Hentiy, Hovd, Hövsgöl, Ömnögovĭ, Övörhangay, Selenge, Sühbaatar, Töv, Ulaanbaatar*, Uvs
Independence: 13 March 1921 (from China; formerly Outer Mongolia)
Constitution: 6 July 1960
Legal system: blend of Russian, Chinese, and Turkish systems of law; no constitutional provision for judicial review of legislative acts; has not accepted compulsory ICJ jurisdiction
National holiday: People's Revolution Day, 11 July (1921)
Executive branch: chairman and deputy chairman of the Presidium of the People's Great Hural, premier, deputy premiers, Cabinet
Legislative branch: People's Great Hural, People's Small Hural
Judicial branch: Supreme Court
Leaders:
Chief of State—President Punsalmaagiyn OCHIRBAT (since 3 September 1990); Vice President Radnaasumbereliyn GONCHIGDORJ (since 7 September 1990);
Head of Government—Premier Dashiyn BYAMBASUREN (since 11 September 1990);
Political parties and leaders:
ruling party—Mongolian People's Revolutionary Party (MPRP), Budragchagiin DASH-YONDON, general secretary;
opposition—Social Democratic Party (SDP), Batbayar; Mongolian Democratic Association, Sanjasuren DZORIG, chief coordinator; Mongolian Party of National Progress, Ganbold;

other—Mongolian Democratic Party (MDP), Batuul; Free Labor Party, Maam; note—opposition parties were legalized in May 1990
Suffrage: universal at age 18
Elections:
President—last held 3 September 1990 (next to be held July 1994); results—Punsalmaagiyn OCHIRBAT elected by the People's Great Hural;
People's Great Hural—last held on 29 July 1990 (next to be held July 1994); results—MPRP 84.6, MDP 3.8%, PNP 1.4%, SDP 1%, independents 9.2%; seats—(430 total) MPRP 343;
People's Small Hural—last held on 29 July 1990 (next to be held July 1994); results—MPRP 62.3%, MDP 24.5%, SDP 7.5%, PNP 5.7%; seats—(50 total) MPRP 33
Communists: MPRP membership 90,000 (1990 est.)
Member of: AsDB, ESCAP, FAO, IAEA, IBEC, IBRD, ICAO, IIB, ILO, IMF, IOC, ISO, ITU, LORCS, NAM (guest), UN, UNCTAD, UNESCO, UNIDO, UPU, WFTU, WHO, WIPO, WMO, WTO
Diplomatic representation: Ambassador Gendengiyn NYAMDOO; Chancery, Tel. (202) 983-1962;
US—Ambassador Joseph E. LAKE; Deputy Chief of Mission Michael J. SENKO; Embassy at Ulaanbaatar, c/o American Embassy Beijing; Tel. 29095 and 29639
Flag: three equal, vertical bands of red (hoist side), blue, and red; centered on the hoist-side red band in yellow is a five-pointed star above the national emblem (*soyombo*—a columnar arrangement of abstract and geometric representations for fire, sun, moon, earth, water, and the yin-yang symbol)

Economy

Overview: Economic activity traditionally has been based on agriculture and the breeding of livestock—Mongolia has the highest number of livestock per person in the world. In recent years extensive mineral resources have been developed with Soviet support. The mining and processing of coal, copper, molybdenum, tin, tungsten, and gold account for a large part of industrial production. In early 1991 the Mongolian leadership was struggling with severe economic dislocations, mainly attributable to chaotic economic conditions in the USSR, by far Mongolia's leading trade and development partner. For example, the government doubled most prices in January 1991, and industrial production dropped 10% in the first quarter of 1991. Moscow almost certainly will be cutting aid in 1991.
GDP: $2.2 billion, per capita $1,000 (1990 est.); real growth rate NA%
Inflation rate (consumer prices): NA%

Unemployment rate: 10% (February 1991)
Budget: deficit of $240 million (1991 est.)
Exports: $784 million (f.o.b., 1988); *commodities*—livestock, animal products, wool, hides, fluorspar, nonferrous metals, minerals; *partners*—nearly all trade with Communist countries (about 80% with USSR)
Imports: $1.14 billion (f.o.b., 1988); *commodities*—machinery and equipment, fuels, food products, industrial consumer goods, chemicals, building materials, sugar, tea; *partners*—nearly all trade with Communist countries (about 80% with USSR)
External debt: $16.8 billion (yearend 1990); 98.6% with USSR
Industrial production: growth rate NA%
Electricity: 657,000 kW capacity; 2,950 million kWh produced, 1,380 kWh per capita (1990)
Industries: copper, processing of animal products, building materials, food and beverage, mining (particularly coal)
Agriculture: accounts for about 20% of GDP and provides livelihood for about 50% of the population; livestock raising predominates (sheep, goats, horses); crops—wheat, barley, potatoes, forage
Economic aid: about $300 million in trade credits and $34 million in grant aid from USSR and other CEMA countries, plus $7.4 million from UNDP (1990)
Currency: tughrik (plural—tughriks); 1 tughrik (Tug) = 100 mongos
Exchange rates: tughriks (Tug) per US$1—7.1 (1991), 5.63 (1990), 3.00 (1989)
Fiscal year: calendar year

Communications

Railroads: 1,750 km 1.524-meter broad gauge (1988)
Highways: 46,700 km total; 1,000 km hard surface; 45,700 km other surfaces (1988)
Inland waterways: 397 km of principal routes (1988)
Civil air: 25 major transport aircraft
Airports: 81 total, 31 usable; 11 with permanent-surface runways; fewer than 5 with runways over 3,659 m; fewer than 20 with runways 2,440-3,659 m; 12 with runways 1,220-2,439 m
Telecommunications: stations—12 AM, 1 FM, 1 TV (with 18 provincial relays); relay of Soviet TV; 120,000 TVs; 186,000 radios; at least 1 earth station

Defense Forces

Branches: Mongolian People's Army (includes Border Guards), Air Force
Manpower availability: males 15-49, 535,376; 349,548 fit for military service; 25,275 reach military age (18) annually
Defense expenditures: $NA, NA% of GDP

Montserrat
(dependent territory of the UK)

Geography

Total area: 100 km²; land area: 100 km²
Comparative area: about 0.6 times the size of Washington, DC
Land boundaries: none
Coastline: 40 km
Maritime claims:
Exclusive fishing zone: 200 nm;
Territorial sea: 3 nm
Climate: tropical; little daily or seasonal temperature variation
Terrain: volcanic islands, mostly mountainous, with small coastal lowland
Natural resources: negligible
Land use: arable land 20%; permanent crops 0%; meadows and pastures 10%; forest and woodland 40%; other 30%
Environment: subject to severe hurricanes from June to November
Note: located 400 km southeast of Puerto Rico in the Caribbean Sea

People

Population: 12,504 (July 1991), growth rate 1.0% (1991)
Birth rate: 16 births/1,000 population (1991)
Death rate: 10 deaths/1,000 population (1991)
Net migration rate: 4 migrants/1,000 population (1991)
Infant mortality rate: 9 deaths/1,000 live births (1991)
Life expectancy at birth: 74 years male, 80 years female (1991)
Total fertility rate: 2.2 children born/woman (1991)
Nationality: noun—Montserratian(s); adjective—Montserratian
Ethnic divisions: mostly black with a few Europeans
Religion: Anglican, Methodist, Roman Catholic, Pentecostal, Seventh-Day Adventist, other Christian denominations
Language: English

Literacy: 97% (male 97%, female 97%) age 15 and over having ever attended school (1970)
Labor force: 5,100; community, social, and personal services 40.5%, construction 13.5%, trade, restaurants, and hotels 12.3%, manufacturing 10.5%, agriculture, forestry, and fishing 8.8%, other 14.4% (1983 est.)
Organized labor: 30% of labor force, three trade unions with 1,500 members (1984 est.)

Government

Long-form name: none
Type: dependent territory of the UK
Capital: Plymouth
Administrative divisions: 3 parishes; Saint Anthony, Saint Georges, Saint Peter
Independence: none (dependent territory of the UK)
Constitution: 1 January 1960
Legal system: English common law and statute law
National holiday: Celebration of the Birthday of the Queen (second Saturday of June)
Executive branch: monarch, governor, Executive Council (cabinet), chief minister
Legislative branch: unicameral Legislative Council
Judicial branch: Supreme Court
Leaders:
Chief of State—Queen ELIZABETH II (since 6 February 1952), represented by Governor David TAYLOR (since NA 1990);
Head of Government—Chief Minister John A. OSBORNE (since NA 1978)
Political parties and leaders: People's Liberation Movement (PLM), John OSBORNE; Progressive Democratic Party (PDP), Howell BRAMBLE; United National Front (UNF), Dr. George IRISH; National Development Party (NDP), Bertrand OSBORNE
Suffrage: universal at age 18
Elections:
Legislative Council—last held on 25 August 1987 (next to be held NA 1992); results—percent of vote by party NA; seats—(11 total, 7 elected) PLM 4, NDP 2, PDP 1
Communists: probably none
Member of: CARICOM, CDB, ECLAC (associate), ICFTU, OECS, WCL
Diplomatic representation: none (dependent territory of the UK)
Flag: blue with the flag of the UK in the upper hoist-side quadrant and the Montserratian coat of arms centered in the outer half of the flag; the coat of arms features a woman standing beside a yellow harp with her arm around a black cross

Economy

Overview: The economy is small and open with economic activity centered on tourism

Montserrat (continued)

and construction. Tourism is the most important sector and accounted for 20% of GDP in 1986. Agriculture accounted for about 4% of GDP and industry 10%. The economy is heavily dependent on imports, making it vulnerable to fluctuations in world prices. Exports consist mainly of electronic parts sold to the US.
GDP: $54.2 million, per capita $4,500; real growth rate 12% (1988 est.)
Inflation rate (consumer prices): 3.6% (1988)
Unemployment rate: 3.0% (1987)
Budget: revenues $12.1 million; expenditures $14.3 million, including capital expenditures of $3.2 million (1988)
Exports: $2.3 million (f.o.b., 1988 est.); *commodities*—electronic parts, plastic bags, apparel, hot peppers, live plants, cattle; *partners*—NA
Imports: $30 million (c.i.f., 1988 est.); *commodities*—machinery and transportation equipment, foodstuffs, manufactured goods, fuels, lubricants, and related materials; *partners*—NA
External debt: $2.05 million (1987)
Industrial production: growth rate 8.1% (1986); accounts for 10% of GDP
Electricity: 5,270 kW capacity; 12.2 million kWh produced, 980 kWh per capita (1990)
Industries: tourism; light manufacturing—rum, textiles, electronic appliances
Agriculture: accounts for 4% of GDP; small-scale farming; food crops—tomatoes, onions, peppers; not self-sufficient in food, especially livestock products
Economic aid: Western (non-US) countries, ODA and OOF bilateral commitments (1970-88), $75 million
Currency: East Caribbean dollar (plural—dollars); 1 EC dollar (EC$) = 100 cents
Exchange rates: East Caribbean dollars (EC$) per US$1—2.70 (fixed rate since 1976)
Fiscal year: 1 April-31 March

Communications

Highways: 280 km total; about 200 km paved, 80 km gravel and earth
Ports: Plymouth
Airports: 1 with permanent-surface runway 1,036 m
Telecommunications: 3,000 telephones; stations—8 AM, 4 FM, 1 TV

Defense Forces

Branches: Police Force
Note: defense is the responsibility of the UK

Morocco

Geography

Total area: 446,550 km²; land area: 446,300 km²
Comparative area: slightly larger than California
Land boundaries: 2,002 km total; Algeria 1,559 km, Western Sahara 443 km
Coastline: 1,835 km
Maritime claims:
Contiguous zone: 24 nm;
Continental shelf: 200 m (depth) or to depth of exploitation;
Exclusive economic zone: 200 nm;
Territorial sea: 12 nm
Disputes: claims and administers Western Sahara, but sovereignty is unresolved; armed conflict in Western Sahara; Spain controls five places of sovereignty (plazas de soberanía) on and off the coast of Morocco—the coastal enclaves of Ceuta and Melilla, which Morocco contests, and the islands of Peñón de Alhucemas, Peñón de Vélez de la Gomera, and Islas Chafarinas
Climate: Mediterranean, becoming more extreme in the interior
Terrain: mostly mountains with rich coastal plains
Natural resources: phosphates, iron ore, manganese, lead, zinc, fish, salt
Land use: arable land 18%; permanent crops 1%; meadows and pastures 28%; forest and woodland 12%; other 41%; includes irrigated 1%
Environment: northern mountains geologically unstable and subject to earthquakes; desertification
Note: strategic location along Strait of Gibraltar

People

Population: 26,181,889 (July 1991), growth rate 2.1% (1991)
Birth rate: 30 births/1,000 population (1991)
Death rate: 8 deaths/1,000 population (1991)

Net migration rate: −1 migrant/1,000 population (1991)
Infant mortality rate: 76 deaths/1,000 live births (1991)
Life expectancy at birth: 63 years male, 66 years female (1991)
Total fertility rate: 3.8 children born/woman (1991)
Nationality: noun—Moroccan(s); adjective—Moroccan
Ethnic divisions: Arab-Berber 99.1%, non-Moroccan 0.7%, Jewish 0.2%
Religion: Muslim 98.7%, Christian 1.1%, Jewish 0.2%
Language: Arabic (official); several Berber dialects; French is language of business, government, diplomacy, and postprimary education
Literacy: 50% (male 61%, female 38%) age 15 and over can read and write (1990 est.)
Labor force: 7,400,000; agriculture 50%, services 26%, industry 15%, other 9% (1985)
Organized labor: about 5% of the labor force, mainly in the Union of Moroccan Workers (UMT) and the Democratic Confederation of Labor (CDT)

Government

Long-form name: Kingdom of Morocco
Type: constitutional monarchy
Capital: Rabat
Administrative divisions: 37 provinces (aqalim, singular—iqlim) and 5 municipalities* (wilāyat, singular—wilāyah); Agadir, Al Hoceīma, Azilal, Beni Mellal, Ben Slimane, Boulemane, Casablanca*, Chaouen, El Jadida, El Kelaa des Srarhna, Er Rachidia, Essaouira, Fès, Fès*, Figuig, Guelmim, Ifrane, Kenitra, Khemisset, Khenifra, Khouribga, Laâyoune, Larache, Marrakech, Marrakech*, Meknès, Meknès*, Nador, Ouarzazate, Oujda, Rabat-Salé*, Safi, Settat, Sidi Kacem, Tanger, Tan-Tan, Taounate, Taroudannt, Tata, Taza, Tétouan, Tiznit
Independence: 2 March 1956 (from France)
Constitution: 10 March 1972
Legal system: based on Islamic law and French and Spanish civil law system; judicial review of legislative acts in Constitutional Chamber of Supreme Court
National holiday: National Day (anniversary of King Hassan II's accession to the throne), 3 March (1961)
Executive branch: monarch, prime minister, Council of Ministers (cabinet)
Legislative branch: unicameral House of Representatives (Majlis Nawab)
Judicial branch: Supreme Court
Leaders:
Chief of State—King HASSAN II (since 3 March 1961);
Head of Government—Prime Minister Dr. Azzedine LARAKI (since 30 September 1986)

Political parties and leaders: Morocco has 15 political parties; the major ones are Istiqlal Party, M'Hamed BOUCETTA; Socialist Union of Popular Forces (USFP), Abderrahim BOUABID; Popular Movement (MP), Secretariat General; National Assembly of Independents (RNI), Ahmed OSMAN; National Democratic Party (PND), Mohamed Arsalane EL-JADIDI; Party for Progress and Socialism (PPS), Ali YATA; Constitutional Union (UC), Maati BOUABID

Suffrage: universal at age 21

Elections:
Chamber of Representatives—last held on 14 September 1984 (were scheduled for September 1990, but postponed until NA 1992); results—percent of vote by party NA; seats—(306 total, 206 elected) CU 83, RNI 61, MP 47, Istiqlal 41, USFP 36, PND 24, other 14

Communists: about 2,000

Member of: ABEDA, ACCT (associate), AfDB, AFESD, AL, AMF, AMU, CCC, EBRD, ECA, FAO, G-77, GATT, IAEA, IBRD, ICAO, ICC, IDA, IDB, IFAD, IFC, ILO, IMF, IMO, INTELSAT, INTERPOL, IOC, ISO, ITU, LORCS, OAS (observer), NAM, OIC, UN, UNCTAD, UNESCO, UNHCR, UNIDO, UPU, WHO, WIPO, WMO, WTO

Diplomatic representation: Ambassador Mohamed BELKHAYAT; Chancery at 1601 21st Street NW, Washington DC 20009; telephone (202) 462-7979; there is a Moroccan Consulate General in New York; *US*—Ambassador E. Michael USSERY; Embassy at 2 Avenue de Marrakech, Rabat (mailing address is P. O. Box 120, Rabat, or APO New York 09284); telephone [212] (7) 76-22-65; there are US Consulates General in Casablanca

Flag: red with a green pentacle (five-pointed, linear star) known as Solomon's seal in the center of the flag; green is the traditional color of Islam

---

Economy

Overview: The economy recovered moderately in 1990 because of the resolution of a trade dispute with India over phosphoric acid sales, a rebound in textile sales to the EC, and lower prices for food imports. In addition, a dramatic increase in worker remittances, increased Arab donor aid, and generous debt rescheduling agreements helped ease foreign payments pressures. On the down side, higher oil import costs fueled inflation. Servicing the $21 billion foreign debt, high unemployment, and Morocco's vulnerability to external forces remain severe problems for the 1990s.

GDP: $25.4 billion, per capita $990; real growth rate 2.5% (1990 est.)

Inflation rate (consumer prices): 6.6% (1990 est.)

Unemployment rate: 16% (1990 est.)

Budget: revenues $6.6 billion; expenditures $7.3 billion, including capital expenditures of $1.8 billion (1990 est.)

Exports: $4.0 billion (f.o.b., 1990 est.); *commodities*—food and beverages 30%, semiprocessed goods 23%, consumer goods 21%, phosphates 17%; *partners*—EC 58%, India 7%, Japan 5%, USSR 3%, US 2%

Imports: $5.9 billion (f.o.b., 1990 est.); *commodities*—capital goods 24%, semiprocessed goods 22%, raw materials 16%, fuel and lubricants 16%, food and beverages 13%, consumer goods 9%; *partners*—EC 53%, US 11%, Canada 4%, Iraq 3%, USSR 3%, Japan 2%

External debt: $21 billion (1990)

Industrial production: growth rate 4% (1989 est.); accounts for an estimated 20% of GDP

Electricity: 2,262,000 kW capacity; 8,140 million kWh produced, 320 kWh per capita (1990)

Industries: phosphate rock mining and processing, food processing, leather goods, textiles, construction, tourism

Agriculture: 50% of employment and 30% of export value; not self-sufficient in food; cereal farming and livestock raising predominate; barley, wheat, citrus fruit, wine, vegetables, olives; fishing catch of 491,000 metric tons in 1987

Illicit drugs: illicit producer of cannabis; trafficking on the increase for both domestic and international drug markets; shipments of cannabis mostly directed to Western Europe; occasional transit point for cocaine from South America destined for Western Europe.

Economic aid: US commitments, including Ex-Im (FY70-89), $1.3 billion; Western (non-US) countries, ODA and OOF bilateral commitments (1970-88), $7.0 billion; OPEC bilateral aid (1979-89), $4.8 billion; Communist countries (1970-89), $2.5 billion

Currency: Moroccan dirham (plural—dirhams); 1 Moroccan dirham (DH) = 100 centimes

Exchange rates: Moroccan dirhams (DH) per US$1—8.071 (January 1991), 8.242 (1990), 8.488 (1989), 8.209 (1988), 8.359 (1987), 9.104 (1986), 10.062 (1985)

Fiscal year: calendar year

Communications

Railroads: 1,893 km 1.435-meter standard gauge (246 km double track, 974 km electrified)

Highways: 59,198 km total; 27,740 km bituminous treated, 31,458 km gravel, crushed stone, improved earth, and unimproved earth

Pipelines: 362 km crude oil; 491 km (abandoned) refined products; 241 km natural gas

Ports: Agadir, Casablanca, El Jorf Lasfar, Kenitra, Mohammedia, Nador, Safi, Tangier; also Spanish-controlled Ceuta and Melilla

Merchant marine: 51 ships (1,000 GRT or over) totaling 315,169 GRT/487,490 DWT; includes 10 cargo, 2 container, 12 refrigerated cargo, 6 roll-on/roll-off cargo, 3 petroleum, oils, and lubricants (POL) tanker, 11 chemical tanker, 4 bulk, 3 short-sea passenger

Civil air: 23 major transport aircraft

Airports: 75 total, 67 usable; 26 with permanent-surface runways; 2 with runways over 3,659 m; 13 with runways 2,440-3,659 m; 27 with runways 1,220-2,439 m

Telecommunications: good system composed of wire lines, cables, and radio relay links; principal centers are Casablanca and Rabat, secondary centers are Fès, Marrakech, Oujda, Tangier, and Tétouan; 280,000 telephones; stations—14 AM, 6 FM, 47 TV; 5 submarine cables; satellite earth stations—2 Atlantic Ocean INTELSAT and 1 ARABSAT; radio relay to Gibraltar, Spain, and Western Sahara; coaxial cable to Algeria; microwave network linking Syria, Jordan, Egypt, Libya, Tunisia, Algeria and Morocco

---

Defense Forces

Branches: Royal Moroccan Army, Royal Moroccan Navy, Royal Moroccan Air Force, Royal Gendarmerie, Auxiliary Forces

Manpower availability: males 15-49, 6,437,152; 4,092,027 fit for military service; 299,535 reach military age (18) annually; limited conscription

Defense expenditures: $1.4 billion, 5.2% of GDP

Mozambique

Geography

Total area: 801,590 km²; land area: 784,090 km²

Comparative area: slightly less than twice the size of California

Land boundaries: 4,571 km total; Malawi 1,569 km, South Africa 491 km, Swaziland 105 km, Tanzania 756 km, Zambia 419 km, Zimbabwe 1,231 km

Coastline: 2,470 km

Maritime claims:

Exclusive economic zone: 200 nm;

Territorial sea: 12 nm

Climate: tropical to subtropical

Terrain: mostly coastal lowlands, uplands in center, high plateaus in northwest, mountains in west

Natural resources: coal, titanium

Land use: arable land 4%; permanent crops NEGL%; meadows and pastures 56%; forest and woodland 20%; other 20%; includes irrigated NEGL%

Environment: severe drought and floods occur in south; desertification

People

Population: 15,113,282 (July 1991), growth rate 4.6% (1991); note—900,000 Mozambican refugees in Malawi (1990 est.)

Birth rate: 46 births/1,000 population (1991)

Death rate: 17 deaths/1,000 population (1991)

Net migration rate: 17 migrants/1,000 population (1991)

Infant mortality rate: 134 deaths/1,000 live births (1991)

Life expectancy at birth: 46 years male, 49 years female (1991)

Total fertility rate: 6.4 children born/woman (1991)

Nationality: noun—Mozambican(s); adjective—Mozambican

Ethnic divisions: majority from indigenous tribal groups; Europeans about 10,000, Euro-Africans 35,000, Indians 15,000

Religion: indigenous beliefs 60%, Christian 30%, Muslim 10%

Language: Portuguese (official); many indigenous dialects

Literacy: 33% (male 45%, female 21%) age 15 and over can read and write (1990 est.)

Labor force: NA, but 90% engaged in agriculture

Organized labor: 225,000 workers belong to a single union, the Mozambique Workers' Organization (OTM)

Government

Long-form name: Republic of Mozambique

Type: republic

Capital: Maputo

Administrative divisions: 10 provinces (províncias, singular—província); Cabo Delgado, Gaza, Inhambane, Manica, Maputo, Nampula, Niassa, Sofala, Tete, Zambézia

Independence: 25 June 1975 (from Portugal)

Constitution: 30 November 1990

Legal system: based on Portuguese civil law system and customary law

National holiday: Independence Day, 25 June (1975)

Executive branch: president, prime minister, Cabinet

Legislative branch: unicameral Assembly of the Republic (Assembléia da República)

Judicial branch: People's Courts at all levels

Leaders:

Chief of State—President Joaquím Alberto CHISSANO (since 6 November 1986);

Head of Government—Prime Minister Mário da Graça MACHUNGO (since 17 July 1986)

Political parties and leaders: Front for the Liberation of Mozambique (FRELIMO)—formerly a Marxist organization with close ties to the USSR—was the only legal party before 30 November 1990 when the new Constitution went into effect establishing a multiparty system; note—the government has announced that multiparty elections will be held in 1991; parties such as the Liberal Democratic Party of Mozambique (PALMO), the Mozambique National Union (UNAMO), and the Mozambique National Movement (MONAMO) have already emerged

Suffrage: universal adult at age 18

Elections: electoral law—to be ratified in 1991—will provide for periodic, direct presidential and Assembly elections

Communists: about 200,000 FRELIMO members; note—FRELIMO no longer considers itself a Communist party

Member of: ACP, AfDB, CCC, ECA, FAO, FLS, G-77, IBRD, ICAO, IDA, IFAD, IFC, ILO, IMF, IMO, INTELSAT, INTERPOL, IOC, ITU, LORCS, NAM, OAU, SADCC, UN, UNCTAD, UNESCO, UNIDO, UPU, WHO, WMO

Diplomatic representation: Ambassador Hipolito PATRICIO; Chancery at Suite 570, 1990 M Street NW, Washington DC 20036; telephone (202) 293-7146;

US—Ambassador Townsend B. FRIEDMAN, Jr.; Embassy at Avenida Kenneth Kuanda, 193 Maputo (mailing address is P. O. Box 783, Maputo); telephone [258] (1) 49-27-97, 49-01-67, 49-03-50

Flag: three equal horizontal bands of green (top), black, and yellow with a red isosceles triangle based on the hoist side; the black band is edged in white; centered in the triangle is a yellow five-pointed star bearing a crossed rifle and hoe in black superimposed on an open white book

Economy

Overview: One of Africa's poorest countries, with a per capita GDP of little more than $100, Mozambique has failed to exploit the economic potential of its sizable agricultural, hydropower, and transportation resources. Indeed, national output, consumption, and investment declined throughout the first half of the 1980s because of internal disorders, lack of government administrative control, and a growing foreign debt. A sharp increase in foreign aid, attracted by an economic reform policy, has resulted in successive years of economic growth since 1985. Agricultural output, nevertheless, is at about only 75% of its 1981 level, and grain has to be imported. Industry operates at only 20-40% of capacity. The economy depends heavily on foreign assistance to keep afloat.

GDP: $1.6 billion, per capita $110; real growth rate 5.0% (1989 est.)

Inflation rate (consumer prices): 22.9% (1990 est.)

Unemployment rate: 50% (1989 est.)

Budget: revenues $186 million; expenditures $239 million, including capital expenditures of $208 million (1988 est.)

Exports: $90 million (f.o.b., 1989 est.);

commodities—shrimp 48%, cashews 21%, sugar 10%, copra 3%, citrus 3%;

partners—US, Western Europe, GDR, Japan

Imports: $764 million (c.i.f., 1989 est.), including aid;

commodities—food, clothing, farm equipment, petroleum;

partners—US, Western Europe, USSR

External debt: $5.1 billion (1990 est.)

Industrial production: growth rate 5% (1989 est.)

Electricity: 2,265,000 kW capacity; 1,740 million kWh produced, 120 kWh per capita (1989)

Industries: food, beverages, chemicals (fertilizer, soap, paints), petroleum products, textiles, nonmetallic mineral products (cement, glass, asbestos), tobacco

Namibia

Agriculture: accounts for 90% of the labor force, 50% of GDP, and about 90% of exports; cash crops—cotton, cashew nuts, sugarcane, tea, shrimp; other crops—cassava, corn, rice, tropical fruits; not self-sufficient in food
Economic aid: US commitments, including Ex-Im (FY70-89), $350 million; Western (non-US) countries, ODA and OOF bilateral commitments (1970-88), $3.8 billion; OPEC bilateral aid (1979-89), $37 million; Communist countries (1970-89), $890 million
Currency: metical (plural—meticais); 1 metical (Mt) = 100 centavos
Exchange rates: meticais (Mt) per US$1—1,700 (November 1990), 800.00 (1989), 528.60 (1988), 289.44 (1987), 40.43 (1986), 43.18 (1985)
Fiscal year: calendar year

Communications

Railroads: 3,288 km total; 3,140 km 1.067-meter gauge; 148 km 0.762-meter narrow gauge; Malawi-Nacala, Malawi-Beira, and Zimbabwe-Maputo lines are subject to closure because of insurgency
Highways: 26,498 km total; 4,593 km paved; 829 km gravel, crushed stone, stabilized soil; 21,076 km unimproved earth
Inland waterways: about 3,750 km of navigable routes
Pipelines: 306 km crude oil (not operating); 289 km refined products
Ports: Maputo, Beira, Nacala
Merchant marine: 5 cargo ships (1,000 GRT or over) totaling 7,806 GRT/12,873 DWT
Civil air: 5 major transport aircraft
Airports: 197 total, 145 usable; 27 with permanent-surface runways; 1 with runways over 3,659 m; 5 with runways 2,440-3,659 m; 27 with runways 1,220-2,439 m
Telecommunications: fair system of troposcatter, open-wire lines, and radio relay; 57,400 telephones; stations—15 AM, 3 FM, 1 TV; earth stations—1 Atlantic Ocean INTELSAT and 3 domestic

Defense Forces

Branches: Mozambique Armed Forces (including Army, Naval Command, Air Defense Forces, Border Guards), Militia
Manpower availability: males 15-49, 3,407,234; 1,957,123 fit for military service
Defense expenditures: $NA, 8.4% of GDP (1987)

Geography

Total area: 824,290 km²; land area: 823,290 km²
Comparative area: slightly more than half the size of Alaska
Land boundaries: 3,935 km total; Angola 1,376 km, Botswana 1,360 km, South Africa 966 km, Zambia 233 km
Coastline: 1,489 km
Maritime claims:
Exclusive fishing zone: 200 nm;
Territorial sea: 12 nm
Disputes: short section of boundary with Botswana is indefinite; quadripoint with Botswana, Zambia, and Zimbabwe is in disagreement; claim by Namibia to Walvis Bay and 12 offshore islands administered by South Africa
Climate: desert; hot, dry; rainfall sparse and erratic
Terrain: mostly high plateau; Namib Desert along coast; Kalahari Desert in east
Natural resources: diamonds, copper, uranium, gold, lead, tin, zinc, salt, vanadium, natural gas, fish; suspected deposits of oil, natural gas, coal, and iron ore
Land use: arable land 1%; permanent crops NEGL%; meadows and pastures 64%; forest and woodland 22%; other 13%; includes irrigated NEGL%
Environment: inhospitable with very limited natural water resources; desertification
Note: Walvis Bay area is an exclave of South Africa in Namibia

People

Population: 1,520,504 (July 1991), growth rate 3.6% (1991)
Birth rate: 45 births/1,000 population (1991)
Death rate: 10 deaths/1,000 population (1991)
Net migration rate: 0 migrants/1,000 population (1991)
Infant mortality rate: 69 deaths/1,000 live births (1991)

Life expectancy at birth: 58 years male, 63 years female (1991)
Total fertility rate: 6.6 children born/woman (1991)
Nationality: noun—Namibian(s); adjective—Namibian
Ethnic divisions: black 86%, white 6.6%, mixed 7.4%; about 50% of the population belong to the Ovambo tribe and 9% from the Kavangos tribe
Religion: predominantly Christian
Language: English is official language; Afrikaans is common language of most of population and about 60% of white population, German 32%, English 7%; several indigenous languages
Literacy: 38% (male 45%, female 31%) age 15 and over can read and write (1960)
Labor force: 500,000; agriculture 60%, industry and commerce 19%, services 8%, government 7%, mining 6% (1981 est.)
Organized labor: 20 trade unions representing about 90,000 workers

Government

Long-form name: Republic of Namibia
Type: republic
Capital: Windhoek
Administrative divisions: the former administrative structure of 26 districts has been abolished and 14 temporary regions are still in the process of being determined; note—the 26 districts were Bethanien, Boesmanland, Caprivi Oos, Damaraland, Gobabis, Grootfontein, Hereroland Oos, Hereroland Wes, Kaokoland, Karasburg, Karibib, Kavango, Keetmanshoop, Lüderitz, Maltahöhe, Mariental, Namaland, Okahandja, Omaruru, Otjiwarongo, Outjo, Owambo, Rehoboth, Swakopmund, Tsumeb, Windhoek
Independence: 21 March 1990 (from South African mandate)
Constitution: ratified 9 February 1990
Legal system: based on Roman-Dutch law and 1990 constitution
National holiday: Independence Day, 21 March 1990
Executive branch: president, Cabinet
Legislative branch: bicameral; House of Review (upper house, to be established with elections in 1992 by planned new regional authorities); National Assembly (lower house elected by universal suffrage)
Judicial branch: Supreme Court
Leaders:
Chief of State and Head of Government—President Sam NUJOMA (since 21 March 1990)
Political parties and leaders: South-West Africa People's Organization (SWAPO),

Namibia (continued)

Sam NUJOMA; Democratic Turnhalle Alliance (DTA), Dirk MUDGE; United Democratic Front (UDF), Justus GAROEB; Action Christian National (ACN), Kosie PRETORIUS; National Patriotic Front (NPF), Moses KATJIUONGUA; Federal Convention of Namibia (FCN), Hans DIERGAARDT; Namibia National Front (NNF), Vekuii RUKORO

Suffrage: universal at age 18
Elections:
President—last held 16 February 1990 (next to be held March 1995); Sam NUJOMA was elected president by the Constituent Assembly (now the National Assembly); *National Assembly*—last held on 7-11 November 1989 (next to be held by November 1994); results—percent of vote by party NA; seats—(72 total) SWAPO 41, DTA 21, UDF 4, ACN 3, NNF 1, FCN 1, NPF 1
Communists: no Communist party
Other political or pressure groups: NA
Member of: C, ECA (associate), FAO, FLS, IAEA, IBRD, ILO, IMF, ITU, NAM, OAU, SACU, SADCC, UN, UNCTAD, UNESCO, UNHCR, UNIDO, WCL, WFTU, WHO
Diplomatic representation: Ambassador Tuliameni KALOMOH; Chancery at 1413 K Street NW, 7th Floor, Washington, DC 20005 (mailing address is PO Box 34738, Washington DC 20043); telephone (202) 289-3871;
US—Ambassador Genta Hawkins HOLMES; Embassy at Ausplan Building, 14 Lossen St., Windhoek (mailing address is P. O. Box 9890, Windhoek 9000, Namibia); telephone [264] (61) 221-601, 222-675, 222-680
Flag: a large blue triangle with a yellow sunburst fills the upper left section, and an equal green triangle (solid) fills the lower right section; the triangles are separated by a red stripe which is contrasted by two narrow white edge borders

Economy

Overview: The economy is heavily dependent on the mining industry to extract and process minerals for export. Mining accounts for almost 30% of GDP. Namibia is the fourth-largest exporter of nonfuel minerals in Africa and the world's fifth-largest producer of uranium. Alluvial diamond deposits are among the richest in the world, making Namibia a primary source for gem-quality diamonds. Namibia also produces large quantities of lead, zinc, tin, silver, and tungsten, and it has substantial resources of coal. More than half the population depends on agriculture (largely subsistence agriculture) for its livelihood.
GNP: $1.8 billion, per capita $1,240; real growth rate −2.0% (1990 est.)

Inflation rate (consumer prices): 15.1% (1989)
Unemployment rate: over 30% (1990)
Budget: revenues $794.1 million; expenditures $999.6 million, including capital expenditures of $NA (FY91 est.)
Exports: $1,021 million (f.o.b., 1989); *commodities*—uranium, diamonds, zinc, copper, cattle, processed fish, karakul skins; *partners*—Switzerland, South Africa, FRG, Japan
Imports: $894 million (f.o.b., 1989); *commodities*—foodstuffs, petroleum products and fuel, machinery and equipment; *partners*—South Africa, FRG, US, Switzerland
External debt: about $27 million at independence; under a 1971 International Court of Justice (ICJ) ruling, Namibia may not be liable for debt incurred during its colonial period
Industrial production: growth rate NA%
Electricity: 486,000 kW capacity; 1,280 million kWh produced, 930 kWh per capita (1989)
Industries: meatpacking, fish processing, dairy products, mining (copper, lead, zinc, diamond, uranium)
Agriculture: mostly subsistence farming; livestock raising major source of cash income; crops—millet, sorghum, peanuts; fish catch potential of over 1 million metric tons not being fulfilled, 1987 catch reaching only 520,000 metric tons; not self-sufficient in food
Economic aid: Western (non-US) countries, ODA and OOF bilateral commitments (1970-87), $47.2 million
Currency: South African rand (plural—rand); 1 South African rand (R) = 100 cents
Exchange rates: South African rand (R) per US$1—2.625 (January 1991), 2.5863 (1990), 2.6166 (1989), 2.2611 (1988), 2.0350 (1987), 2.2685 (1986), 2.1911 (1985)
Fiscal year: 1 April-31 March

Communications

Railroads: 2,341 km 1.067-meter gauge, single track
Highways: 54,500 km; 4,079 km paved, 2,540 km gravel, 47,881 km earth roads and tracks
Ports: Luderitz; primary maritime outlet is Walvis Bay (South Africa)
Civil air: 2 major transport aircraft
Airports: 143 total, 123 usable; 21 with permanent-surface runways; 1 with runways over 3,659 m; 4 with runways 2,440-3,659 m; 67 with runways 1,220-2,439 m
Telecommunications: good urban, fair rural services; radio relay connects major towns, wires extend to other population centers; 62,800 telephones; stations—2 AM, 40 FM, 3 TV

Defense Forces

Branches: National Defense Force (Army), Police
Manpower availability: males 15-49, 309,978; 183,730 fit for military service
Defense expenditures: $NA, 4.9% of GNP (1986)

Nauru

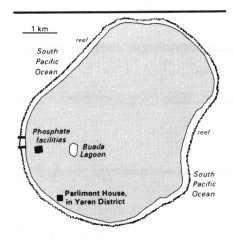

South Pacific Ocean

South Pacific Ocean

Phosphate facilities

Buada Lagoon

Parliment House, in Yaren District

reef

reef

1 km

Geography

Total area: 21 km²; land area: 21 km²
Comparative area: about 0.1 times the size of Washington, DC
Land boundaries: none
Coastline: 30 km
Maritime claims:
Exclusive fishing zone: 200 nm;
Territorial sea: 12 nm
Climate: tropical; monsoonal; rainy season (November to February)
Terrain: sandy beach rises to fertile ring around raised coral reefs with phosphate plateau in center
Natural resources: phosphates
Land use: arable land 0%; permanent crops 0%; meadows and pastures 0%; forest and woodland 0%; other 100%
Environment: only 53 km south of Equator
Note: Nauru is one of the three great phosphate rock islands in the Pacific Ocean—the others are Banaba (Ocean Island) in Kiribati and Makatea in French Polynesia

People

Population: 9,333 (July 1991), growth rate 1.4% (1991)
Birth rate: 19 births/1,000 population (1991)
Death rate: 5 deaths/1,000 population (1991)
Net migration rate: NEGL migrants/1,000 population (1991)
Infant mortality rate: 41 deaths/1,000 live births (1991)
Life expectancy at birth: 64 years male, 69 years female (1991)
Total fertility rate: 2.1 children born/woman (1991)
Nationality: noun—Nauruan(s); adjective—Nauruan
Ethnic divisions: Nauruan 58%, other Pacific Islander 26%, Chinese 8%, European 8%
Religion: Christian (two-thirds Protestant, one-third Roman Catholic)

Language: Nauruan, a distinct Pacific Island language (official); English widely understood, spoken, and used for most government and commercial purposes
Literacy: NA% (male NA%, female NA%)
Labor force: NA
Organized labor: NA

Government

Long-form name: Republic of Nauru
Type: republic
Capital: no capital city as such; government offices in Yaren District
Administrative divisions: 14 districts; Aiwo, Anabar, Anetan, Anibare, Baiti, Boe, Buada, Denigomodu, Ewa, Ijuw, Meneng, Nibok, Uaboe, Yaren
Independence: 31 January 1968 (from UN trusteeship under Australia, New Zealand, and UK); formerly Pleasant Island
Constitution: 29 January 1968
Legal system: own Acts of Parliament and British common law
National holiday: Independence Day, 31 January (1968)
Executive branch: president, Cabinet
Legislative branch: unicameral Parliament
Judicial branch: Supreme Court
Leaders:
Chief of State and Head of Government—President Bernard DOWIYOGO (since 12 December 1989)
Political parties and leaders: none
Suffrage: universal and compulsory at age 20
Elections:
President—last held 9 December 1989 (next to be held December 1992); results—Bernard DOWIYOGO elected by Parliament;
Parliament—last held on 9 December 1989 (next to be held December 1992); results—percent of vote NA; seats—(18 total) independents 18
Member of: C (special), ESCAP, ICAO, INTERPOL, ITU, SPC, SPF, UPU
Diplomatic representation: Ambassador-designate Theodore Conrad MOSES resident in Melbourne (Australia); there is a Nauruan Consulate in Agana (Guam); *US*—the US Ambassador to Australia is accredited to Nauru
Flag: blue with a narrow, horizontal, yellow stripe across the center and a large white 12-pointed star below the stripe on the hoist side; the star indicates the country's location in relation to the Equator (the yellow stripe) and the 12 points symbolize the 12 original tribes of Nauru

Economy

Overview: Revenues come from the export of phosphates, the reserves of which are expected to be exhausted by the year 2000. Phosphates have given Nauruans one of the

highest per capita incomes in the Third World—$10,000 annually. Few other resources exist so most necessities must be imported, including fresh water from Australia. The rehabilitation of mined land and the replacement of income from phosphates constitute serious long-term problems. Substantial investment in trust funds, out of phosphate income, will help cushion the transition.
GNP: over $90 million, per capita $10,000; real growth rate NA% (1989)
Inflation rate (consumer prices): NA%
Unemployment rate: 0%
Budget: revenues $69.7 million; expenditures $51.5 million, including capital expenditures of $NA (FY86 est.)
Exports: $93 million (f.o.b., 1984);
commodities—phosphates;
partners—Australia, NZ
Imports: $73 million (c.i.f., 1984);
commodities—food, fuel, manufactures, building materials, machinery;
partners—Australia, UK, NZ, Japan
External debt: $33.3 million
Industrial production: growth rate NA%
Electricity: 14,000 kW capacity; 50 million kWh produced, 5,430 kWh per capita (1990)
Industries: phosphate mining, financial services, coconuts
Agriculture: negligible; almost completely dependent on imports for food and water
Economic aid: Western (non-US) countries (1970-1988), $2 million
Currency: Australian dollar (plural—dollars); 1 Australian dollar ($A) = 100 cents
Exchange rates: Australian dollars ($A) per US$1—1.2834 (January 1991), 1.2799 (1990), 1.2618 (1989), 1.2752 (1988), 1.4267 (1987), 1.4905 (1986), 1.4269 (1985)
Fiscal year: 1 July-30 June

Communications

Railroads: 3.9 km; used to haul phosphates from the center of the island to processing facilities on the southwest coast
Highways: about 27 km total; 21 km paved, 6 km improved earth
Ports: Nauru
Merchant marine: 3 ships (1,000 GRT or over) totaling 31,261 GRT/39,838 DWT; includes 1 passenger-cargo, 2 bulk
Civil air: 3 major transport aircraft, one on order
Airports: 1 with permanent-surface runway 1,220-2,439 m
Telecommunications: adequate intraisland and international radio communications provided via Australian facilities; 1,600 telephones; 4,000 radios; stations—1 AM, no FM, no TV; 1 Pacific Ocean INTELSAT earth station

Nauru *(continued)*

Defense Forces

Branches: no regular armed forces; Police Force
Manpower availability: males 15-49, NA; NA fit for military service
Defense expenditures: no formal defense structure

Navassa Island
(territory of the US)

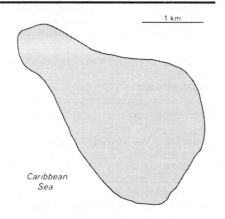

1 km

Caribbean
Sea

Geography

Total area: 5.2 km²; land area: 5.2 km²
Comparative area: about nine times the size of The Mall in Washington, DC
Land boundaries: none
Coastline: 8 km
Maritime claims:
Contiguous zone: 12 nm;
Continental shelf: 200 m (depth);
Exclusive economic zone: 200 nm;
Territorial sea: 12 nm
Disputes: claimed by Haiti
Climate: marine, tropical
Terrain: raised coral and limestone plateau, flat to undulating; ringed by vertical white cliffs (9 to 15 meters high)
Natural resources: guano
Land use: arable land 0%; permanent crops 0%; meadows and pastures 10%; forest and woodland 0%; other 90%
Environment: mostly exposed rock, but enough grassland to support goat herds; dense stands of fig-like trees, scattered cactus
Note: strategic location between Cuba, Haiti, and Jamaica in the Caribbean Sea; 160 km south of the US Naval Base at Guantánamo, Cuba

People

Population: uninhabited; transient Haitian fishermen and others camp on the island

Government

Long-form name: none (territory of the US)
Type: unincorporated territory of the US administered by the US Coast Guard

Economy

Overview: no economic activity

Communications

Ports: none; offshore anchorage only

Defense Forces

Note: defense is the responsibility of the US

Nepal

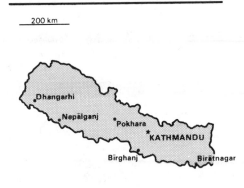

200 km

Geography

Total area: 140,800 km²; land area: 136,800 km²

Comparative area: slightly larger than Arkansas

Land boundaries: 2,926 km total; China 1,236 km, India 1,690 km

Coastline: none—landlocked

Maritime claims: none—landlocked

Climate: varies from cool summers and severe winters in north to subtropical summers and mild winter in south

Terrain: Terai or flat river plain of the Ganges in south, central hill region, rugged Himalayas in north

Natural resources: quartz, water, timber, hydroelectric potential, scenic beauty; small deposits of lignite, copper, cobalt, iron ore

Land use: arable land 17%; permanent crops NEGL%; meadows and pastures 13%; forest and woodland 33%; other 37%; includes irrigated 2%

Environment: contains eight of world's 10 highest peaks; deforestation; soil erosion; water pollution

Note: landlocked; strategic location between China and India

People

Population: 19,611,900 (July 1991), growth rate 2.4% (1991)

Birth rate: 39 births/1,000 population (1991)

Death rate: 15 deaths/1,000 population (1991)

Net migration rate: 0 migrants/1,000 population (1991)

Infant mortality rate: 98 deaths/1,000 live births (1991)

Life expectancy at birth: 51 years male, 50 years female (1991)

Total fertility rate: 5.5 children born/woman (1991)

Nationality: noun—Nepalese (sing. and pl.); adjective—Nepalese

Ethnic divisions: Newars, Indians, Tibetans, Gurungs, Magars, Tamangs, Bhotias, Rais, Limbus, Sherpas, as well as many smaller groups

Religion: only official Hindu state in world, although no sharp distinction between many Hindu (about 90% of population) and Buddhist groups (about 5% of population); Muslims 3%, other 2% (1981)

Language: Nepali (official); 20 languages divided into numerous dialects

Literacy: 26% (male 38%, female 13%) age 15 and over can read and write (1990 est.)

Labor force: 4,100,000; agriculture 93%, services 5%, industry 2%; severe lack of skilled labor

Organized labor: Teachers' Union and many other nonofficially recognized unions

Government

Long-form name: Kingdom of Nepal

Type: constitutional monarchy

Capital: Kathmandu

Administrative divisions: 14 zones (anchal, singular and plural); Bāgmatī, Bherī, Dhawalāgiri, Gandakī, Janakpur, Karnālī, Kosī, Lumbinī, Mahākālī, Mechī, Nārāyanī, Rāptī, Sagarmāthā, Setī

Independence: 1768, unified by Prithyi Narayan Shah

Constitution: 9 November 1990

Legal system: based on Hindu legal concepts and English common law; has not accepted compulsory ICJ jurisdiction

National holiday: Birthday of His Majesty the King, 28 December (1945)

Executive branch: monarch, prime minister, Council of Ministers

Legislative branch: bicameral Parliament consists of an upper house or National Council and a lower house or House of Representatives

Judicial branch: Supreme Court (Sarbochha Adalat)

Leaders:
Chief of State—King BIRENDRA Bir Bikram Shah Dev (since 31 January 1972, crowned King 24 February 1985); Heir Apparent Crown Prince DIPENDRA Bir Bikram Shah Dev, son of the King (born 21 June 1971);
Head of Government—Prime Minister Girija Prasad KOIRALA (since 29 May 1991)

Political parties and leaders:
ruling party—Nepali Congress Party (NCP), Girija Prasad KOIRALA, Ganesh Man SINGH, Krishna Prasad BHATTARAI;
center—the NDP has two factions: National Democratic Party/Chand (NDP/Chand), Lokinra Bahadur CHAND, and National Democratic Party/Thapa (NDP/Thapa), Surya Bahadur THAPA; Terai Rights Sadbhavana (Goodwill) Party, G. N. Naryan SINGH;
Communist—Communist Party of Nepal/United Marxist and Leninist

(CPN/UML), Man Mohan ADIKHARY; United People's Front (UPF), N. K. PRASAI; Rohit Party, N. M. BIJUKCHHE; Democratic Party, leader NA

Suffrage: universal at age 18

Elections:
House of Representatives—last held on 12 May 1991 (next to be held May 1996); results—NCP 38%, CPN/UML 28%, NDP/Chand 6%, UPF 5%, NDP/Thapa 5%, Terai Rights Sadbhavana Party 4%, Rohit 2%, CPN (Democratic) 1%, independent 4%, other 7%; seats—(205 total) NCP 110, CPN/UML 69, UPF 9, Terai Rights Sadbhavana Party 6, NDP/Chand 3, Rohit 2, CPN (Democratic) 2, NDP/Thapa 1, independent 3;
note—the new Constitution of 9 November 1990 gives Nepal a multiparty democracy system for the first time in 32 years

Communists: Communist Party of Nepal (CPN)

Other political or pressure groups: numerous small, left-leaning student groups in the capital; several small, radical Nepalese antimonarchist groups

Member of: AsDB, CCC, CP, ESCAP, FAO, G-77, IBRD, ICAO, IDA, IFAD, IFC, ILO, IMF, IMO, INTELSAT, INTERPOL, IOC, ITU, LORCS, NAM, SAARC, UN, UNCTAD, UNESCO, UNIDO, UNIFIL, UPU, WHO, WMO, WTO

Diplomatic representation: Ambassador Mohan Man SAINJU; Chancery at 2131 Leroy Place NW, Washington DC 20008; telephone (202) 667-4550; there is a Nepalese Consulate General in New York;
US—Ambassador Julia Chang BLOCH; Embassy at Pani Pokhari, Kathmandu; telephone [977] (1) 411179 or 412718, 411601, 411613, 413890

Flag: red with a blue border around the unique shape of two overlapping right triangles; the smaller, upper triangle bears a white stylized moon and the larger, lower triangle bears a white 12-pointed sun

Economy

Overview: Nepal is among the poorest and least developed countries in the world with a per capita income of less than $200. Real growth averaged 4% in the 1980s until FY89, when it plunged to 1.5% because of a trade/transit dispute with India. Though the impasse is over, political turmoil and inflated energy costs will probably constrain growth to under 4%. Agriculture is the mainstay of the economy, providing a livelihood for over 90% of the population and accounting for 60% of GDP. Industrial activity is limited, mainly involving the processing of agricultural produce (jute, sugarcane, tobacco, and grain). Production of textiles and carpets has expanded recently and accounted for 87% of foreign exchange earnings in FY89. Apart from agricultural

Nepal *(continued)*

land and forests, the only other exploitable natural resources are mica, hydropower, and tourism. Agricultural production in the late 1980s grew by about 5%, compared with a population growth of 2.6%. Forty percent or more of the population is undernourished partly because of poor distribution. Economic prospects for the 1990s are poor, with economic growth probably outpacing population growth only slightly.
GDP: $3.0 billion, per capita $160; real growth rate 2.1% (FY90)
Inflation rate (consumer prices): 10.0% (FY90 est.)
Unemployment rate: 5%; underemployment estimated at 25-40% (1987)
Budget: revenues $316.5 million; expenditures $618.5 million, including capital expenditures of $398 (FY91 est.)
Exports: $125 million (f.o.b., FY90), but does not include unrecorded border trade with India;
commodities—clothing, carpets, leather goods, grain;
partners—India 38%, US 23%, UK 6%, other Europe 9% (FY88)
Imports: $454.3illion (c.i.f., FY90 est.);
commodities—petroleum products 20%, fertilizer 11%, machinery 10%;
partners—India 36%, Japan 13%, Europe 4%, US 1% (FY88)
External debt: $2.5 billion (April 1990 est.)
Industrial production: growth rate 6% (FY90 est.); accounts for 7% of GDP
Electricity: 280,000 kW capacity; 540 million kWh produced, 30 kWh per capita (1990)
Industries: small rice, jute, sugar, and oilseed mills; cigarette, textiles, carpets, cement, brick; tourism
Agriculture: accounts for 60% of GDP and 90% of work force; farm products—rice, corn, wheat, sugarcane, root crops, milk, buffalo meat; not self-sufficient in food, particularly in drought years
Illicit drugs: illicit producer of cannabis for the domestic and international drug markets
Economic aid: US commitments, including Ex-Im (FY70-89), $304 million; Western (non-US) countries, ODA and OOF bilateral commitments (1980-88), $2.0 billion; OPEC bilateral aid (1979-89), $30 million; Communist countries (1970-89), $286 million
Currency: Nepalese rupee (plural—rupees); 1 Nepalese rupee (NR) = 100 paisa
Exchange rates: Nepalese rupees (NRs) per US$1—30.805 (January 1991), 29.370 (1990), 27.189 (1989), 23.289 (1988), 21.819 (1987), 21.230 (1986), 18.246 (1985)
Fiscal year: 16 July-15 July

Communications

Railroads: 52 km (1990), all 0.762-meter narrow gauge; all in Terai close to Indian border; 10 km from Raxaul to Birganj is government owned
Highways: 7,080 km total (1990); 2,898 km paved, 1,660 km gravel or crushed stone; also 2,522 km of seasonally motorable tracks
Civil air: 5 major and 11 minor transport aircraft
Airports: 37 total, 37 usable; 5 with permanent-surface runways; none with runways over 3,659 m; 1 with runways 2,440-3,659 m; 8 with runways 1,220-2,439 m
Telecommunications: poor telephone and telegraph service; fair radio communication and broadcast service; international radio communication service is poor; 50,000 telephones (1990); stations—88 AM, no FM, 1 TV; 1 Indian Ocean INTELSAT earth station

Defense Forces

Branches: Royal Nepalese Army, Royal Nepalese Army Air Service, Nepalese Police Force
Manpower availability: males 15-49, 4,669,421; 2,420,398 fit for military service; 233,404 reach military age (17) annually
Defense expenditures: $38 million, 2% of GDP (FY91)

Netherlands

Geography

Total area: 37,290 km²; land area: 33,940 km²
Comparative area: slightly less than twice the size of New Jersey
Land boundaries: 1,027 km total; Belgium 450 km, Germany 577 km
Coastline: 451 km
Maritime claims:
Continental shelf: not specific;
Territorial sea: 12 nm
Climate: temperate; marine; cool summers and mild winters
Terrain: mostly coastal lowland and reclaimed land (polders); some hills in southeast
Natural resources: natural gas, crude oil, fertile soil
Land use: arable land 25%; permanent crops 1%; meadows and pastures 34%; forest and woodland 9%; other 31%; includes irrigated 15%
Environment: 27% of the land area is below sea level and protected from the North Sea by dikes
Note: located at mouths of three major European rivers (Rhine, Maas or Meuse, Schelde)

People

Population: 15,022,393 (July 1991), growth rate 0.6% (1991)
Birth rate: 13 births/1,000 population (1991)
Death rate: 8 deaths/1,000 population (1991)
Net migration rate: 1 migrant/1,000 population (1991)
Infant mortality rate: 7 deaths/1,000 live births (1991)
Life expectancy at birth: 74 years male, 81 years female (1991)
Total fertility rate: 1.6 children born/woman (1991)

Nationality: noun—Dutchman(men), Dutchwoman(women); adjective—Dutch
Ethnic divisions: Dutch 96%, Moroccans, Turks, and other 4% (1988)
Religion: Roman Catholic 36%, Protestant 27%, other 6%, unaffiliated 31% (1988)
Language: Dutch
Literacy: 99% (male NA%, female NA%) age 15 and over can read and write (1979 est.)
Labor force: 5,300,000; services 50.1%, manufacturing and construction 28.2%, government 15.9%, agriculture 5.8% (1986)
Organized labor: 29% of labor force

Government

Long-form name: Kingdom of the Netherlands
Type: constitutional monarchy
Capital: Amsterdam, but government resides at The Hague
Administrative divisions: 12 provinces (provinciën, singular—provincie); Drenthe, Flevoland, Friesland, Gelderland, Groningen, Limburg, Noord-Brabant, Noord-Holland, Overijssel, Utrecht, Zeeland, Zuid-Holland
Dependent areas: Aruba, Netherlands Antilles
Independence: 1579 (from Spain)
Constitution: 17 February 1983
Legal system: civil law system incorporating French penal theory; judicial review in the Supreme Court of legislation of lower order rather than Acts of the States General; accepts compulsory ICJ jurisdiction, with reservations
National holiday: Queen's Day, 30 April (1938)
Executive branch: monarch, prime minister, vice prime minister, Cabinet, Cabinet of Ministers
Legislative branch: bicameral legislature (Staten Generaal) consists of an upper chamber or First Chamber (Eerste Kamer) and a lower chamber or Second Chamber (Tweede Kamer)
Judicial branch: Supreme Court (De Hoge Raad)
Leaders:
Chief of State—Queen BEATRIX Wilhelmina Armgard (since 30 April 1980); Heir Apparent WILLEM-ALEXANDER, Prince of Orange, son of Queen Beatrix (born 27 April 1967);
Head of Government—Prime Minister Ruud (Rudolph) F. M. LUBBERS (since 4 November 1982); Vice Prime Minister Wim KOK (since 2 November 1989)
Political parties and leaders: Christian Democratic Appeal (CDA), Willem van VELZEN; Labor (PvdA), Wim KOK; Liberal (VVD), Joris VOORHOEVE; Democrats '66 (D'66), Hans van MIERIO; Communist (CPN), Henk HOEKSTRA; a host of minor parties
Suffrage: universal at age 18

Elections:
First Chamber—last held on 9 June 1987 (next to be held 9 June 1991); results—elected by the country's 12 provincial councils; seats—(75 total) percent of seats by party NA;
Second Chamber—last held on 6 September 1989 (next to be held by September 1993); results—CDA 35.3%, PvdA 31.9%, VVD 14.6%, D'66 7.9%, other 10.3%; seats—(150 total) CDA 54, PvdA 49, VVD 22, D'66 12, other 13
Communists: about 6,000
Other political or pressure groups: large multinational firms; Federation of Netherlands Trade Union Movement (comprising Socialist and Catholic trade unions) and a Protestant trade union; Federation of Catholic and Protestant Employers Associations; the nondenominational Federation of Netherlands Enterprises; and IKV—Interchurch Peace Council
Member of: AfDB, AG (observer), AsDB, Benelux, BIS, CCC, CE, CERN, COCOM, CSCE, EBRD, EC, ECE, ECLAC, EIB, EMS, ESA, ESCAP, FAO, G-10, GATT, IADB, IAEA, IBRD, ICAO, ICC, ICFTU, IDA, IEA, IFAD, IFC, ILO, IMF, IMO, INMARSAT, INTELSAT, INTERPOL, IOC, IOM, ISO, ITU, LORCS, NATO, NEA, OAS (observer), OECD, PCA, UN, UNCTAD, UNESCO, UNHCR, UNIDO, UNTSO, UPU, WCL, WEU, WHO, WIPO, WMO, WTO
Diplomatic representation: Ambassador Johan Hendrick MEESMAN; Chancery at 4200 Linnean Avenue NW, Washington DC 20008; telephone (202) 244-5300; there are Dutch Consulates General in Chicago, Houston, Los Angeles, New York, and San Francisco;
US—Ambassador C. Howard WILKINS, Jr.; Embassy at Lange Voorhout 102, The Hague (mailing address APO New York 09159); telephone [31] (70) 362-4911; there is a US Consulate General in Amsterdam
Flag: three equal horizontal bands of red (top), white, and blue; similar to the flag of Luxembourg which uses a lighter blue and is longer

Economy

Overview: This highly developed and affluent economy is based on private enterprise. The government makes its presence felt, however, through many regulations, permit requirements, and welfare programs affecting most aspects of economic activity. The trade and financial services sector contributes over 50% of GDP. Industrial activity provides about 25% of GDP and is led by the food-processing, oil-refining, and metalworking industries. The highly mechanized agricultural sector employs only 5% of the labor force, but provides large surpluses for export and the domestic food-processing industry. An unemployment rate of 6.8% and a sizable budget deficit are currently the most serious economic problems.
GDP: $218.0 billion, per capita $14,600; real growth rate 3.1% (1990)
Inflation rate (consumer prices): 2.2% (1990 est.)
Unemployment rate: 6.8% (1990 est.)
Budget: revenues $68 billion; expenditures $76 billion, including capital expenditures of $7 billion (1990)
Exports: $107.8 billion (f.o.b., 1989); *commodities*—agricultural products, processed foods and tobacco, natural gas, chemicals, metal products, textiles, clothing; *partners*—EC 74.9% (FRG 28.3%, Belgium-Luxembourg 14.2%, France 10.7%, UK 10.2%), US 4.7% (1988)
Imports: $104.2 billion (c.i.f., 1989); *commodities*—raw materials and semifinished products, consumer goods, transportation equipment, crude oil, food products; *partners*—EC 63.8% (FRG 26.5%, Belgium-Luxembourg 23.1%, UK 8.1%), US 7.9% (1988)
External debt: none
Industrial production: growth rate 4.8% (1990 est.); accounts for 25% of GDP
Electricity: 22,216,000 kW capacity; 63,570 million kWh produced, 4,300 kWh per capita (1989)
Industries: agroindustries, metal and engineering products, electrical machinery and equipment, chemicals, petroleum, fishing, construction, microelectronics
Agriculture: accounts for 4% of GDP; animal production predominates; crops—grains, potatoes, sugar beets, fruits, vegetables; shortages of grain, fats, and oils
Economic aid: donor—ODA and OOF commitments (1970-89), $19.4 billion
Currency: Netherlands guilder, gulden, or florin (plural—guilders, gulden, or florins); 1 Netherlands guilder, gulden, or florin (f.) = 100 cents
Exchange rates: Netherlands guilders, gulden, or florins (f.) per US$1—1.7018 (January 1991), 1.8209 (1990), 2.1207 (1989), 1.9766 (1988), 2.0257 (1987), 2.4500 (1986), 3.3214 (1985)
Fiscal year: calendar year

Communications

Railroads: 3,037 km track (includes 1,871 km electrified and 1,800 km double track); 2,871 km 1.435-meter standard gauge operated by Netherlands Railways (NS); 166 km privately owned
Highways: 108,360 km total; 92,525 km paved (including 2,185 km of limited access, divided highways); 15,835 km gravel, crushed stone

Netherlands (continued)

Inland waterways: 6,340 km, of which 35% is usable by craft of 1,000 metric ton capacity or larger

Pipelines: 418 km crude oil; 965 km refined products; 10,230 km natural gas

Ports: maritime—Amsterdam, Delfzijl, Den Helder, Dordrecht, Eemshaven, Ijmuiden, Rotterdam, Scheveningen, Terneuzen, Vlissingen; inland—29 ports

Merchant marine: 344 ships (1,000 GRT or over) totaling 2,722,838 GRT/3,822,230 DWT; includes 2 short-sea passenger, 187 cargo, 32 refrigerated cargo, 23 container, 12 roll-on/roll-off cargo, 3 livestock carrier, 12 multifunction large-load carrier, 17 petroleum, oils, and lubricants (POL) tanker, 29 chemical tanker, 10 liquefied gas, 2 specialized tanker, 3 combination ore/oil, 9 bulk, 3 combination bulk; note—many Dutch-owned ships are also registered in the captive Netherlands Antilles register

Civil air: 98 major transport aircraft

Airports: 28 total, 28 usable; 18 with permanent-surface runways; none with runways over 3,659 m; 12 with runways 2,440-3,659 m; 3 with runways 1,220-2,439 m

Telecommunications: highly developed, well maintained, and integrated; extensive system of multiconductor cables, supplemented by radio relay links; 9,418,000 telephones; stations—6 AM, 20 (33 repeaters) FM, 22 (8 repeaters) TV, 5 submarine cables; communication satellite earth stations operating in INTELSAT (1 Indian Ocean and 2 Atlantic Ocean) and EUTELSAT systems

Defense Forces

Branches: Royal Netherlands Army, Royal Netherlands Navy (including Naval Air Service and Marine Corps), Royal Netherlands Air Force, Royal Constabulary

Manpower availability: males 15-49, 4,141,910; 3,658,056 fit for military service; 105,829 reach military age (20) annually

Defense expenditures: $6.8 billion, 2.7% of GDP (1990)

Netherlands Antilles
(part of the Dutch realm)

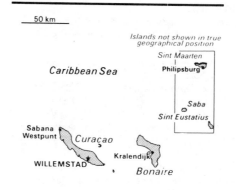

Geography

Total area: 960 km²; land area: 960 km²; includes Bonaire, Curaçao, Saba, Sint Eustatius, and Sint Maarten (Dutch part of the island of Saint Martin)

Comparative area: slightly less than 5.5 times the size of Washington, DC

Land boundaries: none

Coastline: 364 km

Maritime claims:

Exclusive fishing zone: 12 nm;

Territorial sea: 12 nm

Climate: tropical; modified by northeast trade winds

Terrain: generally hilly, volcanic interiors

Natural resources: phosphates (Curaçao only), salt (Bonaire only)

Land use: arable land 8%; permanent crops 0%; meadows and pastures 0%; forest and woodland 0%; other 92%

Environment: Curaçao and Bonaire are south of Caribbean hurricane belt, so rarely threatened; Sint Maarten, Saba, and Sint Eustatius are subject to hurricanes from July to October

Note: consists of two island groups—Curaçao and Bonaire are located off the coast of Venezuela, and Sint Maarten, Saba, and Sint Eustatius lie 800 km to the north

People

Population: 183,872 (July 1991), growth rate 0.2% (1991)

Birth rate: 18 births/1,000 population (1991)

Death rate: 5 deaths/1,000 population (1991)

Net migration rate: −10 migrants/1,000 population (1991)

Infant mortality rate: 8 deaths/1,000 live births (1991)

Life expectancy at birth: 74 years male, 79 years female (1991)

Total fertility rate: 2.0 children born/woman (1991)

Nationality: noun—Netherlands Antillean(s); adjective—Netherlands Antillean

Ethnic divisions: mixed African 85%; remainder Carib Indian, European, Latin, and Oriental

Religion: predominantly Roman Catholic; Protestant, Jewish, Seventh-Day Adventist

Language: Dutch (official); Papiamento, a Spanish-Portuguese-Dutch-English dialect predominates; English widely spoken; Spanish

Literacy: 94% (male 94%, female 93%) age 15 and over can read and write (1981)

Labor force: 89,000; government 65%, industry and commerce 28% (1983)

Organized labor: 60-70% of labor force

Government

Long-form name: none

Type: part of the Dutch realm—full autonomy in internal affairs granted in 1954

Capital: Willemstad

Administrative divisions: none (part of the Dutch realm)

Independence: none (part of the Dutch realm)

Constitution: 29 December 1954, Statute of the Realm of the Netherlands, as amended

Legal system: based on Dutch civil law system, with some English common law influence

National holiday: Queen's Day, 30 April (1938)

Executive branch: Dutch monarch, governor, prime minister, vice prime minister, Council of Ministers (cabinet)

Legislative branch: legislature (Staten)

Judicial branch: Joint High Court of Justice

Leaders:

Chief of State—Queen BEATRIX Wilhelmina Armgard (since 30 April 1980), represented by Governor General Jaime SALEH (since October 1989);

Head of Government—Prime Minister Maria LIBERIA-PETERS (since 17 May 1988, previously served from September 1984 to November 1985)

Political parties and leaders: political parties are indigenous to each island:

Curaçao—National People's Party (PNP), Maria LIBERIA-PETERS; New Antilles Movement (MAN), Domenico Felip MARTINA; Workers' Liberation Front (FOL), Wilson (Papa) GODETT; Socialist Independent (SI), George HUECK and Nelson MONTE; Democratic Party of Curaçao (DP), Augustín DÍAZ; Nos Patria, Chin BEHILIA;

Bonaire—Patriotic Union of Bonaire (UPB), C. V. Winklaar; Democratic Party of Bonaire (PDB), John Evert (Jopie) ABRAHAM; New Force, Rudy ELLIS;

Sint Maarten—Democratic Party of Sint Maarten (DP-St.M), Claude WATHEY; Patriotic Movement of Sint Maarten (SPM), Romeo PAPLOPHLET;
Sint Eustatius—Democratic Party of Sint Eustatius (DP-St.E), Albert K. Van PUTTEN; Windward Islands People's Movement (WIPM), Eric HENRIQUEZ;
Saba—Windward Islands People's Movement (WIPM Saba), Will JOHNSTON; Saba Democratic Labor Movement, Vernon HASSELL; Saba Unity Party, Carmen SIMMONDS
Suffrage: universal at age 18
Elections:
Staten—last held on 16 March 1990 (next to be held March 1994); results—percent of vote by party NA; seats—(22 total) PNP 7, FOL-SI-Curaçao 3, UPB 3, MAN 2, Democratic Party of Sint Maarten 2, Democratic Party of Curaçao 1, SPM-Sint Maarten 1, WIPM 1, Democratic Party of Sint Eustatius 1, Nos Patria-Curaçao 1; note—the government of Prime Minister Maria LIBERIA-PETERS is a coalition of several parties
Communists: small leftist groups
Member of: CARICOM (observer), ECLAC (associate), ICFTU, INTERPOL, IOC, UNESCO (associate), UPU, WCL, WMO, WTO (associate)
Diplomatic representation: as an autonomous part of the Netherlands, Netherlands Antillean interests in the US are represented by the Netherlands;
US—Consul General Sharon P. WILKINSON; Consulate General at Sint Anna Boulevard 19, Willemstad, Curaçao (mailing address P. O. Box 158, Willemstad, Curaçao); telephone [599] (9) 613066
Flag: white with a horizontal blue stripe in the center superimposed on a vertical red band also centered; five white five-pointed stars are arranged in an oval pattern in the center of the blue band; the five stars represent the five main islands of Bonaire, Curaçao, Saba, Sint Eustatius, and Sint Maarten

Economy

Overview: Tourism, petroleum refining, and offshore finance are the mainstays of the economy. The islands enjoy a high per capita income and a well-developed infrastructure compared with other countries in the region. Unlike many Latin American countries, the Netherlands Antilles has avoided large international debt. Almost all consumer and capital goods are imported, with the US being the major supplier.
GDP: $1.0 billion, per capita $5,500; real growth rate 3% (1988 est.)
Inflation rate (consumer prices): 3.9% (1989)
Unemployment rate: 20% (1988)
Budget: revenues $454 million; expenditures $525 million, including capital expenditures of $42 million (1989 est.)
Exports: $959 million (f.o.b., 1988);

commodities—petroleum products 98%;
partners—US 55%, UK 7%, Jamaica 5%
Imports: $935 million (c.i.f., 1988);
commodities—crude petroleum 64%, food, manufactures;
partners—Venezuela 52%, Nigeria 15%, US 12%
External debt: $701.2 million (December 1987)
Industrial production: growth rate NA%
Electricity: 125,000 kW capacity; 365 million kWh produced, 1,990 kWh per capita (1990)
Industries: tourism (Curaçao and Sint Maarten), petroleum refining (Curaçao), petroleum transshipment facilities (Curaçao and Bonaire), light manufacturing (Curaçao)
Agriculture: hampered by poor soils and scarcity of water; chief products—aloes, sorghum, peanuts, fresh vegetables, tropical fruit; not self-sufficient in food
Economic aid: Western (non-US) countries, ODA and OOF bilateral commitments (1970-88), $428 million
Currency: Netherlands Antillean guilder, gulden, or florin (plural—guilders, gulden, or florins); 1 Netherlands Antillean guilder, gulden, or florin (NAf.) = 100 cents
Exchange rates: Netherlands Antillean guilders, gulden, or florins (NAf.) per US$1—1.79 (fixed rate since 1989; 1.80 fixed rate 1971-88)
Fiscal year: calendar year

Communications

Highways: 950 km total; 300 km paved, 650 km gravel and earth
Ports: Willemstad, Philipsburg, Kralendijk
Merchant marine: 54 ships (1,000 GRT or over) totaling 431,958 GRT/441,056 DWT; includes 4 passenger, 19 cargo, 8 refrigerated cargo, 6 container, 6 roll-on/roll-off cargo, 7 multifunction large-load carrier, 1 chemical tanker, 1 liquefied gas, 2 bulk; note—all but a few are foreign owned, mostly in the Netherlands
Civil air: 5 major transport aircraft
Airports: 7 total, 7 usable; 7 with permanent-surface runways; none with runways over 3,659 m; 2 with runways 2,440-3,659 m; 2 with runways 1,220-2,439 m
Telecommunications: generally adequate facilities; extensive interisland radio relay links; stations—9 AM, 4 FM, 1 TV; 2 submarine cables; 2 Atlantic Ocean INTELSAT earth stations

Defense Forces

Branches: Royal Netherlands Navy, Marine Corps, Royal Netherlands Air Force, National Guard, Police Force
Manpower availability: males 15-49 49,249; 27,803 fit for military service; 1,634 reach military age (20) annually
Note: defense is responsibility of the Netherlands

New Caledonia
(overseas territory of France)

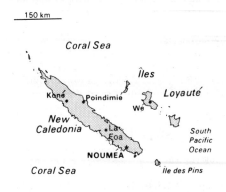

150 km

Islands of Huon and Chesterfield are not shown.

Geography

Total area: 19,060 km²; land area: 18,760 km²
Comparative area: slightly smaller than New Jersey
Land boundaries: none
Coastline: 2,254 km
Maritime claims:
Exclusive economic zone: 200 nm;
Territorial sea: 12 nm
Climate: tropical; modified by southeast trade winds; hot, humid
Terrain: coastal plains with interior mountains
Natural resources: nickel, chrome, iron, cobalt, manganese, silver, gold, lead, copper
Land use: arable land NEGL%; permanent crops NEGL%; meadows and pastures 14%; forest and woodland 51%; other 35%
Environment: typhoons most frequent from November to March
Note: located 1,750 km east of Australia in the South Pacific Ocean

People

Population: 171,559 (July 1991), growth rate 1.9% (1991)
Birth rate: 23 births/1,000 population (1991)
Death rate: 5 deaths/1,000 population (1991)
Net migration rate: 1 migrant/1,000 population (1991)
Infant mortality rate: 17 deaths/1,000 live births (1991)
Life expectancy at birth: 69 years male, 76 years female (1991)
Total fertility rate: 2.8 children born/woman (1991)
Nationality: noun—New Caledonian(s); adjective—New Caledonian
Ethnic divisions: Melanesian 42.5%, European 37.1%, Wallisian 8.4%, Polynesian 3.8%, Indonesian 3.6%, Vietnamese 1.6%, other 3.0%

New Caledonia *(continued)*

Religion: Roman Catholic 60%, Protestant 30%, other 10%
Language: French; 28 Melanesian-Polynesian dialects
Literacy: 91% (male 91%, female 90%) age 15 and over can read and write (1976)
Labor force: 50,469; foreign workers for plantations and mines from Wallis and Futuna, Vanuatu, and French Polynesia (1980 est.)
Organized labor: NA

Government

Long-form name: Territory of New Caledonia and Dependencies
Type: overseas territory of France since 1956
Capital: Nouméa
Administrative divisions: none (overseas territory of France); there are no first-order administrative divisions as defined by the US Government, but there are 3 provinces named Îles Loyauté, Nord, and Sud
Independence: none (overseas territory of France); note—a referendum on independence will be held in 1998, with a review of the issue in 1992
Constitution: 28 September 1958 (French Constitution)
Legal system: the 1988 Matignon Accords grant substantial autonomy to the islands; formerly under French law
National holiday: Taking of the Bastille, 14 July (1789)
Executive branch: high commissioner, Consultative Committee (cabinet)
Legislative branch: unicameral Territorial Assembly
Judicial branch: Court of Appeal
Leaders:
Chief of State—President François MITTERRAND (since 21 May 1981);
Head of Government High Commissioner and President of the Council of Government Bernard GRASSET (since 15 July 1988)
Political parties: white-dominated Rassemblement pour la Calédonie dans la République (RPCR), conservative, Jacques LAFLEUR—affiliated to France's Rassemblement pour la République (RPR); Melanesian proindependence Kanak Socialist National Liberation Front (FLNKS), Paul NÉAOUTYINE; Melanesian moderate Kanak Socialist Liberation (LKS), Nidoïsh NAISSELINE; National Front (FN), extreme right, Guy GEORGE; Caledonie Demain (CD), right-wing, Bernard MARANT; Union Océanienne (UO), conservative, Michel HEMA; Front Uni de Libération Kanak (FULK), proindependence, Yann CÉLÉNÉ
Suffrage: universal adult at age 18

Elections:
Territorial Assembly—last held 11 June 1989 (next to be held spring 1993); results—percent of vote by party—RPCR 44.5%, FLNKS 28.5%, FN 7%, CD 5%, UO 4%, other 11%; seats—(54 total) RPCR 27, FLNKS 19, FN 3, other 5; note—election boycotted by FULK;
French Senate—last held 24 September 1989 (next to be held September 1992); results—percent of vote by party NA; seats—(1 total) RPCR 1;
French National Assembly—last held 5 and 12 June 1988 (next to be held June 1993); results—percent of vote by party—RPR 83.5%, FN 13.5%, other 3%; seats—(2 total) RPCR 2
Communists: number unknown; Palita extreme left party; some politically active Communists deported during 1950s; small number of North Vietnamese
Member of: FZ, SPC, WFTU, WMO
Diplomatic representation: as an overseas territory of France, New Caledonian interests are represented in the US by France
Flag: the flag of France is used

Economy

Overview: New Caledonia has more than 25% of the world's known nickel resources. In recent years the economy has suffered because of depressed international demand for nickel, the principal source of export earnings. Only a negligible amount of the land is suitable for cultivation, and food accounts for about 25% of imports.
GNP: $973 million, per capita $5,790; real growth rate 2.4% (1990 est.)
Inflation rate (consumer prices): 4.1% (1989)
Unemployment rate: 16.0% (1989)
Budget: revenues $224.0 million; expenditures $211.0 million, including capital expenditures of NA (1985)
Exports: $344 million (f.o.b., 1989);
commodities—nickel metal 87%, nickel ore;
partners—France 52.3%, Japan 15.8%, US 6.4%
Imports: $389 million (c.i.f., 1989);
commodities—foods, fuels, minerals, machines, electrical equipment;
partners—France 44.0%, US 10%, Australia 9%
External debt: $NA
Industrial production: growth rate NA%
Electricity: 400,000 kW capacity; 2,200 million kWh produced, 12,790 kWh per capita (1990)
Industries: nickel mining
Agriculture: large areas devoted to cattle grazing; coffee, corn, wheat, vegetables; 60% self-sufficient in beef
Illicit drugs: illicit cannabis cultivation is becoming a principal source of income for some families

Economic aid: Western (non-US) countries, ODA and OOF bilateral commitments (1970-88), $3.9 billion
Currency: Comptoirs Français du Pacifique franc (plural—francs); 1 CFP franc (CFPF) = 100 centimes
Exchange rates: Comptoirs Français du Pacifique francs (CFPF) per US$1—93.28 (January 1991), 99.00 (1990), 115.99 (1989), 108.30 (1988), 109.27 (1987), 125.92 (1986), 163.35 (1985); note—linked at the rate of 18.18 to the French franc
Fiscal year: calendar year

Communications

Highways: 6,340 km total; only about 10% paved (1987)
Ports: Noumea, Nepoui, Poro, Thio
Civil air: 1 major transport aircraft
Airports: 29 total, 27 usable; 6 with permanent-surface runways; none with runways over 3,659 m; 1 with runways 2,440-3,659 m; 1 with runways 1,220-2,439 m
Telecommunications: 32,578 telephones (1987); stations—5 AM, 3 FM, 7 TV; 1 Pacific Ocean INTELSAT earth station

Defense Forces

Branches: Gendarmerie, Police Force
Manpower availability: males 15-49, 46,388; NA fit for military service
Note: defense is the responsibility of France

New Zealand

Geography

Total area: 268,680 km²; land area: 268,670 km²; includes Antipodes Islands, Auckland Islands, Bounty Islands, Campbell Island, Chatham Islands, and Kermadec Islands
Comparative area: about the size of Colorado
Land boundaries: none
Coastline: 15,134 km
Maritime claims:
Continental shelf: edge of continental margin or 200 nm;
Exclusive economic zone: 200 nm;
Territorial sea: 12 nm
Disputes: territorial claim in Antarctica (Ross Dependency)
Climate: temperate with sharp regional contrasts
Terrain: predominately mountainous with some large coastal plains
Natural resources: natural gas, iron ore, sand, coal, timber, hydropower, gold, limestone
Land use: arable land 2%; permanent crops 0%; meadows and pastures 53%; forest and woodland 38%; other 7%; includes irrigated 1%
Environment: earthquakes are common, though usually not severe

People

Population: 3,308,973 (July 1991), growth rate 0.4% (1991)
Birth rate: 15 births/1,000 population (1991)
Death rate: 8 deaths/1,000 population (1991)
Net migration rate: −3 migrants/1,000 population (1991)
Infant mortality rate: 10 deaths/1,000 live births (1991)
Life expectancy at birth: 72 years male, 79 years female (1991)
Total fertility rate: 1.9 children born/woman (1991)

Nationality: noun—New Zealander(s); adjective—New Zealand
Ethnic divisions: European 88%, Maori 8.9%, Pacific Islander 2.9%, other 0.2%
Religion: Anglican 24%, Presbyterian 18%, Roman Catholic 15%, Methodist 5%, Baptist 2%, other Protestant 3%, unspecified or none 9% (1986)
Language: English (official), Maori
Literacy: 99% (male NA%, female NA%) age 15 and over can read and write (1970)
Labor force: 1,591,900; services 67.4%, manufacturing 19.8%, primary production 9.3% (1987)
Organized labor: 681,000 members; 43% of labor force (1986)

Government

Long-form name: none; abbreviated NZ
Type: parliamentary democracy
Capital: Wellington
Administrative divisions: 93 counties, 9 districts*, and 3 town districts**; Akaroa, Amuri, Ashburton, Bay of Islands, Bruce, Buller, Chatham Islands, Cheviot, Clifton, Clutha, Cook, Dannevirke, Egmont, Eketahuna, Ellesmere, Eltham, Eyre, Featherston, Franklin, Golden Bay, Great Barrier Island, Grey, Hauraki Plains, Hawera*, Hawke's Bay, Heathcote, Hikurangi**, Hobson, Hokianga, Horowhenua, Hurunui, Hutt, Inangahua, Inglewood, Kaikoura, Kairanga, Kiwitea, Lake, Mackenzie, Malvern, Manaia**, Manawatu, Mangonui, Maniototo, Marlborough, Masterton, Matamata, Mount Herbert, Ohinemuri, Opotiki, Oroua, Otamatea, Otorohanga*, Oxford, Pahiatua, Paparua, Patea, Piako, Pohangina, Raglan, Rangiora*, Rangitikei, Rodney, Rotorua*, Runanga, Saint Kilda, Silverpeaks, Southland, Stewart Island, Stratford, Strathallan, Taranaki, Taumarunui, Taupo, Tauranga, Thames-Coromandel*, Tuapeka, Vincent, Waiapu, Waiheke, Waihemo, Waikato, Waikohu, Waimairi, Waimarino, Waimate, Waimate West, Waimea, Waipa, Waipawa*, Waipukurau*, Wairarapa South, Wairewa, Wairoa, Waitaki, Waitomo*, Waitotara, Wallace, Wanganui, Waverley**, Westland, Whakatane*, Whangarei, Whangaroa, Woodville
Dependent areas: Cook Islands, Niue, Tokelau
Independence: 26 September 1907 (from UK)
Constitution: no formal, written constitution; consists of various documents, including certain acts of the UK and New Zealand Parliaments; Constitution Act 1986 was to have come into force 1 January 1987, but has not been enacted
Legal system: based on English law, with special land legislation and land courts for Maoris; accepts compulsory ICJ jurisdiction, with reservations

National holiday: Waitangi Day (Treaty of Waitangi established British sovereignty), 6 February (1840)
Executive branch: British monarch, governor general, prime minister, deputy prime minister, Cabinet
Legislative branch: unicameral House of Representatives (commonly called Parliament)
Judicial branch: High Court, Court of Appeal
Leaders:
Chief of State—Queen ELIZABETH II (since 6 February 1952), represented by Governor General Dame Catherine TIZARD (since 12 December 1990);
Head of Government—Prime Minister James BOLGER (since 29 October 1990); Deputy Prime Minister Donald McKINNON (since 2 November 1990)
Political parties and leaders: National Party (NP; government), James BOLGER; New Zealand Labor Party (NZLP; opposition), Michael MOORE; New Labor Party (NLP), Jim ANDERTON; Democratic Party, Neil MORRISON; Green Party, no official leader; Socialist Unity Party (SUP; pro-Soviet), Kenneth DOUGLAS
Suffrage: universal at age 18
Elections:
House of Representatives—last held on 27 October 1990 (next to be held October 1993); results—NP 49%, LP 35%, Green Party 7%, New Labor 5%; seats—(97 total) NP 67, LP 29, NLP 1
Communists: SUP about 140, other groups, about 200
Member of: ANZUS (US suspended security obligations to NZ on 11 August 1986), APEC, AsDB, C, CCC, CP, EBRD, ESCAP, FAO, GATT, IAEA, IBRD, ICAO, ICFTU, IDA, IEA, IFAD, IFC, ILO, IMF, IMO, INMARSAT, INTELSAT, INTERPOL, IOC, IOM (observer), ISO, ITU, LORCS, OECD, PCA, SPC, SPF, UN, UNCTAD, UNESCO, UNIDO, UNIIMOG, UNTSO, UPU, WHO, WIPO, WMO
Diplomatic representation: Ambassador-designate Denis Bazely Gordon McLEAN; Chancery at 37 Observatory Circle NW, Washington DC 20008; telephone (202) 328-4800; there are New Zealand Consulates General in Los Angeles and New York;
US—Ambassador Della M. NEWMAN; Embassy at 29 Fitzherbert Terrace, Thorndon, Wellington (mailing address is P. O. Box 1190, Wellington, or FPO San Francisco 96690-0001); telephone [64] (4) 722-068; there is a US Consulate General in Auckland
Flag: blue with the flag of the UK in the upper hoist-side quadrant with four red five-pointed stars edged in white centered in the outer half of the flag; the stars represent the Southern Cross constellation

New Zealand (continued)

Economy

Overview: Since 1984 the government has been reorienting an agrarian economy dependent on a guaranteed British market to an open free market economy that can compete on the global scene. The government has hoped that dynamic growth would boost real incomes, reduce inflationary pressures, and permit the expansion of welfare benefits. The results have been mixed: inflation is down from double-digit levels but growth has been sluggish and unemployment, always a highly sensitive issue, has been at a record high 7.4%. In 1988 GDP fell by 1%, in 1989 grew by a moderate 2.4%, and was flat in 1990.
GDP: $40.2 billion, per capita $12,200; real growth rate 0.7% (1990)
Inflation rate (consumer prices): 6.5% (FY90)
Unemployment rate: 7.4% (March 1990)
Budget: revenues $17.6 billion; expenditures $18.3 billion, including capital expenditures of $NA (FY91 est.)
Exports: $8.8 billion (f.o.b., FY90);
commodities—wool, lamb, mutton, beef, fruit, fish, cheese, manufactures, chemicals, forestry products;
partners—EC 18.3%, Japan 17.9%, Australia 17.5%, US 13.5%, China 3.6%, South Korea 3.1%
Imports: $8.1 billion (f.o.b., FY90);
commodities—petroleum, consumer goods, motor vehicles, industrial equipment;
partners—Australia 19.7%, Japan 16.9%, EC 16.9%, US 15.3%, Taiwan 3.0%
External debt: $17.4 billion (1989)
Industrial production: growth rate 1.9% (1990); accounts for about 20% of GDP
Electricity: 7,800,000 kW capacity; 28,000 million kWh produced, 8,500 kWh per capita (1990)
Industries: food processing, wood and paper products, textiles, machinery, transportation equipment, banking and insurance, tourism, mining
Agriculture: accounts for about 9% of GNP and 10% of the work force; livestock predominates—wool, meat, dairy products all export earners; crops—wheat, barley, potatoes, pulses, fruits, and vegetables; surplus producer of farm products; fish catch reached a record 503,000 metric tons in 1988
Economic aid: donor—ODA and OOF commitments (1970-89), $526 million
Currency: New Zealand dollar (plural—dollars); 1 New Zealand dollar (NZ$) = 100 cents
Exchange rates: New Zealand dollars (NZ$) per US$1—1.6798 (January 1991), 1.6750 (1990), 1.6711 (1989), 1.5244 (1988), 1.6886 (1987), 1.9088 (1986), 2.0064 (1985)
Fiscal year: 1 July-30 June

Communications

Railroads: 4,716 km total; all 1.067-meter gauge; 274 km double track; 113 km electrified; over 99% government owned
Highways: 92,648 km total; 49,547 km paved, 43,101 km gravel or crushed stone
Inland waterways: 1,609 km; of little importance to transportation
Pipelines: 1,000 km natural gas; 160 km refined products; 150 km condensate
Ports: Auckland, Christchurch, Dunedin, Wellington, Tauranga
Merchant marine: 21 ships (1,000 GRT or over) totaling 204,269 GRT/281,375 DWT; includes 5 cargo, 1 container, 4 roll-on/roll-off cargo, 1 railcar carrier, 4 petroleum, oils, and lubricants (POL) tanker, 1 liquefied gas, 5 bulk
Civil air: about 40 major transport aircraft
Airports: 157 total, 157 usable; 33 with permanent-surface runways; none with runways over 3,659 m; 2 with runways 2,440-3,659 m; 46 with runways 1,220-2,439 m
Telecommunications: excellent international and domestic systems; 2,110,000 telephones; stations 64 AM, 2 FM, 14 TV; submarine cables extend to Australia and Fiji; 2 Pacific Ocean INTELSAT earth stations

Defense Forces

Branches: New Zealand Army, Royal New Zealand Navy, Royal New Zealand Air Force
Manpower availability: males 15-49, 874,443; 740,831 fit for military service; 28,814 reach military age (20) annually
Defense expenditures: $832 million, 1-2% of GDP (FY90)

Nicaragua

125 km

Geography

Total area: 129,494 km²; land area: 120,254 km²
Comparative area: slightly larger than New York State
Land boundaries: 1,231 km total; Costa Rica 309 km, Honduras 922 km
Coastline: 910 km
Maritime claims:
Contiguous zone: 25 nm security zone (status of claim uncertain);
Continental shelf: not specified;
Territorial sea: 200 nm
Disputes: territorial disputes with Colombia over the Archipelago de San Andrés y Providencia and Quita Sueño Bank; unresolved maritime boundary in Golfo de Fonseca
Climate: tropical in lowlands, cooler in highlands
Terrain: extensive Atlantic coastal plains rising to central interior mountains; narrow Pacific coastal plain interrupted by volcanoes
Natural resources: gold, silver, copper, tungsten, lead, zinc, timber, fish
Land use: arable land 9%; permanent crops 1%; meadows and pastures 43%; forest and woodland 35%; other 12%; including irrigated 1%
Environment: subject to destructive earthquakes, volcanoes, landslides, and occasional severe hurricanes; deforestation; soil erosion; water pollution

People

Population: 3,751,884 (July 1991), growth rate 2.8% (1991)
Birth rate: 37 births/1,000 population (1991)
Death rate: 7 deaths/1,000 population (1991)
Net migration rate: −1 migrant/1,000 population (1991)
Infant mortality rate: 60 deaths/1,000 live births (1991)

Life expectancy at birth: 60 years male, 65 years female (1991)

Total fertility rate: 4.7 children born/woman (1991)

Nationality: noun—Nicaraguan(s); adjective—Nicaraguan

Ethnic divisions: mestizo 69%, white 17%, black 9%, Indian 5%

Religion: Roman Catholic 95%, Protestant 5%

Language: Spanish (official); English- and Indian-speaking minorities on Atlantic coast

Literacy: 57% (male 57%, female 57%) age 15 and over can read and write (1971)

Labor force: 1,086,000; service 43%, agriculture 44%, industry 13% (1986)

Organized labor: 35% of labor force

Government

Long-form name: Republic of Nicaragua

Type: republic

Capital: Managua

Administrative divisions: 9 administrative regions encompassing 16 departments (departamentos, singular—departamento); Boaco, Carazo, Chinandega, Chontales, Estelí, Granada, Jinotega, León, Madriz, Managua, Masaya, Matagalpa, Nueva Segovia, Río San Juan, Rivas, Zelaya; note—Zelaya may have been replaced by 2 autonomous regions (regiónes autonomistas, singular—región autonomista) named North Atlantic Coast and South Atlantic Coast

Independence: 15 September 1821 (from Spain)

Constitution: January 1987

Legal system: civil law system; Supreme Court may review administrative acts

National holiday: Independence Day, 15 September (1821)

Executive branch: president, vice president, Cabinet

Legislative branch: National Assembly (Asamblea Nacional)

Judicial branch: Supreme Court (Corte Suprema) and municipal courts

Leaders:
Chief of State and Head of Government—President Violeta Barrios de CHAMORRO (since 25 April 1990); Vice President Virgilio GODOY (since 25 April 1990)

Political parties and leaders:
ruling coalition—National Opposition Union (UNO) is a 14-party alliance—National Conservative Party (PNC), Silviano MATAMOROS; Conservative Popular Alliance Party (PAPC), Myriam ARGUELLO; National Conservative Action Party (PANC), Hernaldo ZUNIGA; National Democratic Confidence Party (PDCN), Augustin JARQUIN; Independent Liberal Party (PLI), Wilfredo NAVARRO; Neo-Liberal Party (PALI), Andres ZUNIGA; Liberal Constitutionalist Party (PLC), Jose Ernesto

SOMARRIBA; National Action Party (PAN), Eduardo RIVAS; Nicaraguan Socialist Party (PSN), Gustavo TABLADA; Communist Party of Nicaragua (PCdeN), Eli ALTIMIRANO; Popular Social Christian Party (PPSC), Luis HUMBERTO; Nicaraguan Democratic Movement (MDN), Roberto URROZ; Social Democratic Party (PSD), Guillermo POTOY; Central American Integrationist Party (PIAC), Alejandro PEREZ;
opposition parties—Sandinista National Liberation Front (FSLN), Daniel ORTEGA; Central American Unionist Party (PUCA), Blanca ROJAS; Democratic Conservative Party of Nicaragua (PCDN), Jose BRENES; Liberal Party of National Unity (PLUIN), Eduardo CORONADO; Movement of Revolutionary Unity (MUR), Francisco SAMPER; Social Christian Party (PSC), Erick RAMIREZ; Revolutionary Workers' Party (PRT), Bonifacio MIRANDA; Social Conservative Party (PSOC), Fernando AGUERRO; Popular Action Movement—Marxist-Leninist (MAP-ML), Isidro TELLEZ; Popular Social Christian Party (PPSC), Mauricio DIAZ

Suffrage: universal at age 16

Elections:
President—last held on 25 February 1990 (next to be held February 1996); results—Violeta Barrios de CHAMORRO (UNO) 54.7%, Daniel ORTEGA Saavedra (FSLN) 40.8%, other 4.5%;
National Assembly—last held on 25 February 1990 (next to be held February 1996); results—UNO 53.9%, FSLN 40.8%, PSC 1.6%, MUR 1.0%; seats—(92 total) UNO 51, FSLN 39, PSC 1, MUR 1

Communists: 15,000-20,000

Other political or pressure groups: Permanent Congress of Workers (CPT), Confederation of Labor Unification (CUS), Autonomous Nicaraguan Workers' Central (CTN-A), Independent General Confederation of Workers (CTG-I), Communist Labor Action and Unity Central (CAUS), Nicaraguan Workers' Central (CST); Superior Council of Private Enterprise (COSEP) is an umbrella group of 11 different business groups, including the Chamber of Commerce, the Chamber of Industry, and the Nicaraguan Development Institute (INDE)

Member of: BCIE, CACM, ECLAC, FAO, G-77, GATT, IADB, IAEA, IBRD, ICAO, ICFTU, IDA, IFAD, IFC, ILO, IMF, IMO, INTELSAT, INTERPOL, IOC, IOM, ITU, LAES, LORCS, NAM, OAS, OPANAL, PCA, UN, UNCTAD, UNESCO, UNHCR, UNIDO, UPU, WCL, WFTU, WHO, WIPO, WMO

Diplomatic representation: Ambassador Ernesto PALAZIO; Chancery at 1627 New Hampshire Avenue NW, Washington DC 20009; telephone (202) 387-4371 or 4372;
US—Ambassador Harry W. SHLAUDEMAN; Embassy at Kilometer 4.5 Carretera Sur., Managua (mailing address is APO

Miami 34021); telephone [505] (2) 666010 or 666013, 666015 through 18, 666026, 666027, 666032 through 34

Flag: three equal horizontal bands of blue (top), white, and blue with the national coat of arms centered in the white band; the coat of arms features a triangle encircled by the words *REPUBLICA DE NICARAGUA* on the top and *AMERICA CENTRAL* on the bottom; similar to the flag of El Salvador which features a round emblem encircled by the words *REPUBLICA DE EL SALVADOR EN LA AMERICA CENTRAL* centered in the white band; also similar to the flag of Honduras, which has five blue stars arranged in an *X* pattern centered in the white band

Economy

Overview: Government control of the economy historically has been extensive, although the Chamorro government has pledged to reduce it. The financial system is directly controlled by the state, which also regulates wholesale purchasing, production, sales, foreign trade, and distribution of most goods. Over 50% of the agricultural and industrial firms are state owned. Sandinista economic policies and the war have produced a severe economic crisis. The foundation of the economy continues to be the export of agricultural commodities, largely coffee and cotton. Farm production fell by roughly 7% in 1989, the fifth successive year of decline. The agricultural sector employs 44% of the work force and accounts for 23% of GDP and 86% of export earnings. Industry, which employs 13% of the work force and contributes about 25% to GDP, showed a drop of 7% in 1989 and remains below pre-1979 levels. External debt is one of the highest in the world on a per capita basis. In 1990 the annual inflation rate was 11,800%, sharply up from 1,800% in 1989.

GDP: $1.7 billion, per capita $470; real growth rate −1.0% (1990 est.)

Inflation rate (consumer prices): 11,800% (1990)

Unemployment rate: 35% (1990)

Budget: revenues $244 million; expenditures $550 million, including capital expenditures of $73 million (1988)

Exports: $298 million (f.o.b., 1989);
commodities—coffee, cotton, sugar, bananas, seafood, meat, chemicals;
partners—OECD 75%, USSR and Eastern Europe 15%, other 10%

Imports: $710 million (c.i.f., 1989);
commodities—petroleum, food, chemicals, machinery, clothing;
partners—Latin America 30%, US 25%, EC 20%, USSR and Eastern Europe 10%, other 15% (1990 est.)

External debt: $9 billion (December 1990)

Nicaragua *(continued)*

Industrial production: growth rate –7% (1989); accounts for about 25% of GDP
Electricity: 415,000 kW capacity; 1,342 million kWh produced; 360 kWh per capita (1990)
Industries: food processing, chemicals, metal products, textiles, clothing, petroleum refining and distribution, beverages, footwear
Agriculture: accounts for 23% of GDP and 44% of work force; cash crops—coffee, bananas, sugarcane, cotton; food crops—rice, corn, cassava, citrus fruit, beans; variety of animal products—beef, veal, pork, poultry, dairy; normally self-sufficient in food
Economic aid: US commitments, including Ex-Im (FY70-89), $294 million; Western (non-US) countries, ODA and OOF bilateral commitments (1970-88), $1,186 million; Communist countries (1970-89), $3.5 billion
Currency: córdoba (plural—córdobas); 1 córdoba (C$) = 100 centavos
Exchange rates: córdobas (C$) per US$1—13,300,000 (January 1991), 15,655 (1989), 270 (1988), 102.60 (1987), 97.48 (1986), 38.90 (1985)
Fiscal year: calendar year

Communications

Railroads: 373 km 1.067-meter gauge, government owned; majority of system not operating; 3 km 1.435-meter gauge line at Puerto Cabezas (does not connect with mainline)
Highways: 25,930 km total; 4,000 km paved, 2,170 km gravel or crushed stone, 5,425 km earth or graded earth, 14,335 km unimproved; Pan-American highway 368.5 km
Inland waterways: 2,220 km, including 2 large lakes
Pipelines: crude oil, 56 km
Ports: Corinto, El Bluff, Puerto Cabezas, Puerto Sandino, Rama
Merchant marine: 2 cargo ships (1,000 GRT or over) totaling 2,161 GRT/2,500 DWT
Civil air: 12 major transport aircraft
Airports: 251 total, 162 usable; 10 with permanent-surface runways; none with runways over 3,659 m; 2 with runways 2,440-3,659 m; 12 with runways 1,220-2,439 m
Telecommunications: low-capacity radio relay and wire system being expanded; connection into Central American Microwave System; 60,000 telephones; stations—45 AM, no FM, 7 TV, 3 shortwave; earth stations—1 Intersputnik and 1 Atlantic Ocean INTELSAT

Defense Forces

Branches: Army, Navy, Air Force
Manpower availability: males 15-49, 845,961; 521,425 fit for military service; 44,222 reach military age (18) annually
Defense expenditures: $70 million, 3.8% of GDP (1991)

Niger

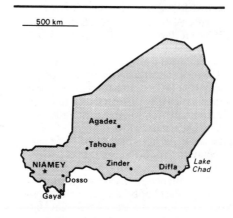

Geography

Total area: 1,267,000 km²; land area: 1,266,700 km²
Comparative area: slightly less than twice the size of Texas
Land boundaries: 5,697 km total; Algeria 956 km, Benin 266 km, Burkina 628 km, Chad 1,175 km, Libya 354 km, Mali 821 km, Nigeria 1,497 km
Coastline: none—landlocked
Maritime claims: none—landlocked
Disputes: Libya claims about 19,400 km² in northern Niger; demarcation of international boundaries in Lake Chad, the lack of which has led to border incidents in the past, is completed and awaiting ratification by Cameroon, Chad, Niger, and Nigeria; Burkina and Mali are proceeding with boundary demarcation, including the tripoint with Niger
Climate: desert; mostly hot, dry, dusty; tropical in extreme south
Terrain: predominately desert plains and sand dunes; flat to rolling plains in south; hills in north
Natural resources: uranium, coal, iron ore, tin, phosphates
Land use: arable land 3%; permanent crops 0%; meadows and pastures 7%; forest and woodland 2%; other 88%; includes irrigated NEGL%
Environment: recurrent drought and desertification severely affecting marginal agricultural activities; overgrazing; soil erosion
Note: landlocked

People

Population: 8,154,145 (July 1991), growth rate 3.4% (1991)
Birth rate: 50 births/1,000 population (1991)
Death rate: 16 deaths/1,000 population (1991)
Net migration rate: 0 migrants/1,000 population (1991)

Infant mortality rate: 129 deaths/1,000 live births (1991)
Life expectancy at birth: 49 years male, 53 years female (1991)
Total fertility rate: 7.0 children born/woman (1991)
Nationality: noun—Nigerien(s) adjective—Nigerien
Ethnic divisions: Hausa 56%; Djerma 22%; Fula 8.5%; Tuareg 8%; Beri Beri (Kanouri) 4.3%; Arab, Toubou, and Gourmantche 1.2%; about 4,000 French expatriates
Religion: Muslim 80%, remainder indigenous beliefs and Christians
Language: French (official); Hausa, Djerma
Literacy: 28% (male 40%, female 17%) age 15 and over can read and write (1990 est.)
Labor force: 2,500,000 wage earners (1982); agriculture 90%, industry and commerce 6%, government 4%; 51% of population of working age (1985)
Organized labor: negligible

Government

Long-form name: Republic of Niger
Type: republic; presidential system in which military officers hold key offices
Capital: Niamey
Administrative divisions: 7 departments (départements, singular—département); Agadez, Diffa, Dosso, Maradi, Niamey, Tahoua, Zinder
Independence: 3 August 1960 (from France)
Constitution: adopted NA December 1989 after 15 years of military rule
Legal system: based on French civil law system and customary law; has not accepted compulsory ICJ jurisdiction
National holidays: Republic Day, 18 December (1958)
Executive branch: president, prime minister, Council of Ministers (cabinet)
Legislative branch: National Assembly (Assemblée Nationale)
Judicial branch: State Court (Cour d'Etat), Court of Appeal (Cour d'Apel)
Leaders:
Chief of State—President Brig. Gen. Ali SAIBOU (since 14 November 1987);
Head of Government—Prime Minister Aliou MAHAMIDOU (since 2 March 1990)
Political parties and leaders: National Movement for the Development Society (MNSD), leader NA; other political parties now forming
Suffrage: universal adult at age 18
Elections:
President—last held December 1989 (next to be held NA 1996); results—President Ali SAIBOU was reelected without opposition;
National Assembly—last held 10 December 1989 (next to be held NA); results—MNSD was the only party; seats—(150 total) MNSD 150 (indirectly elected); note—Niger is to hold a national conference to

decide upon a transitional government and an agenda for multiparty elections
Communists: no Communist party; some sympathizers in outlawed Sawaba party
Member of: ACCT, ACP, AfDB, CCC, CEAO, ECA, ECOWAS, Entente, FAO, FZ, G-77, GATT, IAEA, IBRD, ICAO, IDA, IDB, IFAD, IFC, ILO, IMF, INTELSAT, INTERPOL, IOC, ITU, LORCS, NAM, OAU, OIC, UN, UNCTAD, UNESCO, UNIDO, UPU, WADB, WCL, WHO, WIPO, WMO, WTO
Diplomatic representation: Ambassador Moumouni Adamou DJERMAKOYE; Chancery at 2204 R Street NW, Washington DC 20008; telephone (202) 483-4224 through 4227;
US—Ambassador Carl C. CUNDIFF; Embassy at Avenue des Ambassades, Niamey (mailing address is B. P. 11201, Niamey); telephone [227] 72-26-61 through 64
Flag: three equal horizontal bands of orange (top), white, and green with a small orange disk (representing the sun) centered in the white band; similar to the flag of India which has a blue, spoked wheel centered in the white band

Economy

Overview: About 90% of the population is engaged in farming and stock rearing, activities which generate almost half the national income. The economy also depends heavily on exploitation of large uranium deposits. Uranium production grew rapidly in the mid-1970s, but tapered off in the early 1980s, when world prices declined. France is a major customer, while Germany, Japan, and Spain also make regular purchases. The depressed demand for uranium has contributed to an overall sluggishness in the economy, a severe trade imbalance, and a mounting external debt.
GDP: $2.0 billion, per capita $270; real growth rate −3.3% (1989 est.)
Inflation rate (consumer prices): −2.8% (1989)
Unemployment rate: NA%
Budget: revenues $220 million; expenditures $446 million, including capital expenditures of $190 million (FY89 est.)
Exports: $308 million (f.o.b., 1989 est.);
commodities—uranium 75%, livestock products, cowpeas, onions;
partners—France 65%, Nigeria 11%, Ivory Coast, Italy
Imports: $386 million (c.i.f., 1989 est.);
commodities—petroleum products, primary materials, machinery, vehicles and parts, electronic equipment, pharmaceuticals, chemical products, cereals, foodstuffs;
partners—France 32%, Ivory Coast 11%, Germany 5%, Italy 4%, Nigeria 4%
External debt: $1.8 billion (December 1990 est.)

Industrial production: growth rate 3.0% (1989 est.); accounts for 18% of GDP
Electricity: 102,000 kW capacity; 225 million kWh produced, 30 kWh per capita (1989)
Industries: cement, brick, textiles, food processing, chemicals, slaughterhouses, and a few other small light industries; uranium production began in 1971
Agriculture: accounts for roughly 40% of GDP and 90% of labor force; cash crops—cowpeas, cotton, peanuts; food crops—millet, sorghum, cassava, rice; livestock—cattle, sheep, goats; self-sufficient in food except in drought years
Economic aid: US commitments, including Ex-Im (FY70-89), $380 million; Western (non-US) countries, ODA and OOF bilateral commitments (1970-88), $3.0 billion; OPEC bilateral aid (1979-89), $504 million; Communist countries (1970-89), $61 million
Currency: Communauté Financière Africaine franc (plural—francs); 1 CFA franc (CFAF) = 100 centimes
Exchange rates: Communauté Financière Africaine francs (CFAF) per US$1—256.54 (January 1991), 272.26 (1990), 319.01 (1989), 297.85 (1988), 300.54 (1987), 346.30 (1986), 449.26 (1985)
Fiscal year: 1 October-30 September

Communications

Highways: 39,970 km total; 3,170 km bituminous, 10,330 km gravel and laterite, 3,470 km earthen, 23,000 km tracks
Inland waterways: Niger river is navigable 300 km from Niamey to Gaya on the Benin frontier from mid-December through March
Civil air: no major transport aircraft
Airports: 31 total, 29 usable; 7 with permanent-surface runways; none with runways over 3,659 m; 1 with runways 2,440-3,659 m; 12 with runways 1,220-2,439 m
Telecommunications: small system of wire, radiocommunications, and radio relay links concentrated in southwestern area; 11,900 telephones; stations—15 AM, 5 FM, 16 TV; satellite earth stations—1 Atlantic Ocean INTELSAT, 1 Indian Ocean INTELSAT, and 4 domestic

Defense Forces

Branches: Army, Air Force, paramilitary Gendarmerie, paramilitary Republican Guard, paramilitary Presidential Guard, paramilitary National Police
Manpower availability: males 15-49, 1,713,566; 923,634 fit for military service; 90,801 reach military age (18) annually
Defense expenditures: $20.6 million, 0.9% of GDP (1988)

Nigeria

Geography

Total area: 923,770 km²; land area: 910,770 km²
Comparative area: slightly more than twice the size of California
Land boundaries: 4,047 km total; Benin 773 km, Cameroon 1,690 km, Chad 87 km, Niger 1,497 km
Coastline: 853 km
Maritime claims:
Continental shelf: 200 m (depth) or to depth of exploitation;
Exclusive economic zone: 200 nm;
Territorial sea: 30 nm
Disputes: demarcation of international boundaries in Lake Chad, the lack of which has led to border incidents in the past, is completed and awaiting ratification by Cameroon, Chad, Niger, and Nigeria; Nigerian proposals to reopen maritime boundary negotiations and redemarcate the entire land boundary have been rejected by Cameroon
Climate: varies—equatorial in south, tropical in center, arid in north
Terrain: southern lowlands merge into central hills and plateaus; mountains in southeast, plains in north
Natural resources: crude oil, tin, columbite, iron ore, coal, limestone, lead, zinc, natural gas
Land use: arable land 31%; permanent crops 3%; meadows and pastures 23%; forest and woodland 15%; other 28%; includes irrigated NEGL%
Environment: recent droughts in north severely affecting marginal agricultural activities; desertification; soil degradation, rapid deforestation

People

Population: 122,470,574 (July 1991), growth rate 3.0% (1991)
Birth rate: 46 births/1,000 population (1991)

229

Nigeria (continued)

Death rate: 16 deaths/1,000 population (1991)

Net migration rate: NEGL migrants/1,000 population (1991)

Infant mortality rate: 118 deaths/1,000 live births (1991)

Life expectancy at birth: 48 years male, 50 years female (1991)

Total fertility rate: 6.5 children born/woman (1991)

Nationality: noun—Nigerian(s); adjective—Nigerian

Ethnic divisions: more than 250 tribal groups; Hausa and Fulani of the north, Yoruba of the southwest, and Ibos of the southeast make up 65% of the population; about 27,000 non-Africans

Religion: Muslim 50%, Christian 40%, indigenous beliefs 10%

Language: English (official); Hausa, Yoruba, Ibo, Fulani, and several other languages also widely used

Literacy: 51% (male 62%, female 40%) age 15 and over can read and write (1990 est.)

Labor force: 42,844,000; agriculture 54%, industry, commerce, and services 19%, government 15%; 49% of population of working age (1985)

Organized labor: 3,520,000 wage earners belong to 42 recognized trade unions, which come under a single national labor federation—the Nigerian Labor Congress (NLC)

Government

Long-form name: Federal Republic of Nigeria

Type: military government since 31 December 1983

Capital: Lagos; note—some government departments have relocated to the designated new capital in Abuja

Administrative divisions: 21 states and 1 territory*; Abuja Capital Territory*, Akwa Ibom, Anambra, Bauchi, Bendel, Benue, Borno, Cross River, Gongola, Imo, Kaduna, Kano, Katsina, Kwara, Lagos, Niger, Ogun, Ondo, Oyo, Plateau, Rivers, Sokoto

Independence: 1 October 1960 (from UK)

Constitution: 1 October 1979, amended 9 February 1984, revised 1989

Legal system: based on English common law, Islamic, and tribal law

National holiday: Independence Day, 1 October (1960)

Executive branch: president of the Armed Forces Ruling Council, Armed Forces Ruling Council, National Council of State, Council of Ministers (cabinet)

Legislative branch: National Assembly was dissolved after the military coup of 31 December 1983

Judicial branch: Supreme Court, Federal Court of Appeal

Leaders:
Chief of State and Head of Government—President and Commander in Chief of Armed Forces Gen. Ibrahim BABANGIDA (since 27 August 1985)

Political parties and leaders: two political parties established by the government in 1989—Social Democratic Party (SDP) and National Republican Convention (NRC)

Suffrage: universal at age 21

Elections:
President—scheduled for 1 October 1992; *National Assembly*—scheduled for early 1992

Communists: the pro-Communist underground consists of a small fraction of the Nigerian left; leftist leaders are prominent in the country's central labor organization but have little influence on the government

Member of: ACP, AfDB, C, CCC, ECA, ECOWAS, FAO, G-19, G-24, G-77, GATT, IAEA, IBRD, ICAO, ICC, IDA, IFAD, IFC, ILO, IMO, IMF, INMARSAT, INTELSAT, INTERPOL, IOC, ISO, ITU, LORCS, NAM, OAU, OIC, OPEC, PCA, UN, UNCTAD, UNESCO, UNHCR, UNIDO, UNIIMOG, UPU, WCL, WHO, WMO, WTO

Diplomatic representation: Ambassador Hamzat AHMADU; Chancery at 2201 M Street NW, Washington DC 20037; telephone (202) 822-1500; there are Nigerian Consulates General in Atlanta, New York and San Francisco;
US—Ambassador Lannon WALKER; Embassy at 2 Eleke Crescent, Victoria Island, Lagos (mailing address is P. O. Box 554, Lagos); telephone [234] (1) 610097; there is a US Consulate General in Kaduna

Flag: three equal vertical bands of green (hoist side), white, and green

Economy

Overview: Although Nigeria is Africa's leading oil-producing country, it remains poor with a $280 per capita GDP. In 1990, despite rising oil prices and a sharp drop in inflation, performance remained slack with continuing underutilization of industrial capacity and a second year of relatively weak agricultural performance. Agricultural production was up only 4.2% in 1990, still below the 1987 level. Industrial output showed a 7.2% increase, but remained below the 1985 level. Government efforts to reduce Nigeria's dependence on oil exports and to sustain noninflationary growth have fallen short due to inadequate new investment funds. Living standards continue to deteriorate from the higher level of the early 1980s oil boom.

GDP: $27.2 billion, per capita $230; real growth rate 2.7% (1990 est.)

Inflation rate (consumer prices): 16% (1990)

Unemployment rate: NA%

Budget: revenues $8.0 billion; expenditures $8.0 billion, including capital expenditures of $NA (1990 est.)

Exports: $13.0 billion (f.o.b., 1990 est.); *commodities*—oil 95%, cocoa, rubber; *partners*—EC 51%, US 32%

Imports: $9.5 billion (c.i.f., 1990 est.); *commodities*—consumer goods, capital equipment, chemicals, raw materials; *partners*—EC, US

External debt: $35 billion (December 1990 est.)

Industrial production: growth rate 7.2% (1990 est.); accounts for 23% of GDP, including petroleum

Electricity: 4,737,000 kW capacity; 11,270 million kWh produced, 100 kWh per capita (1989)

Industries: crude oil and mining—coal, tin, columbite; primary processing industries—palm oil, peanut, cotton, rubber, wood, hides and skins; manufacturing industries—textiles, cement, building materials, food products, footwear, chemical, printing, ceramics, steel

Agriculture: accounts for 28% of GNP and half of labor force; inefficient small-scale farming dominates; once a large net exporter of food and now an importer; cash crops—cocoa, peanuts, palm oil, rubber; food crops—corn, rice, sorghum, millet, cassava, yams; livestock—cattle, sheep, goats, pigs; fishing and forestry resources extensively exploited

Illicit drugs: illicit heroin and some cocaine trafficking; marijuana cultivation for domestic consumption and export; major transit country for heroin en route from Southwest Asia via Africa to Western Europe and the US; growing transit route for cocaine from South America via West Africa to Western Europe and the US

Economic aid: US commitments, including Ex-Im (FY70-89), $705 million; Western (non-US) countries, ODA and OOF bilateral commitments (1970-87), $2.5 billion; Communist countries (1970-89), $2.2 billion

Currency: naira (plural—naira); 1 naira (₦) = 100 kobo

Exchange rates: naira (₦) per US$1—8.707 (December 1990), 8.038 (1990), 7.3647 (1989), 4.5370 (1988), 4.0160 (1987), 1.7545 (1986), 0.8938 (1985)

Fiscal year: calendar year

Communications

Railroads: 3,505 km 1.067-meter gauge

Highways: 107,990 km total 30,019 km paved (mostly bituminous-surface treatment); 25,411 km laterite, gravel, crushed stone, improved earth; 52,560 km unimproved

Inland waterways: 8,575 km consisting of Niger and Benue Rivers and smaller rivers and creeks

Pipelines: 2,042 km crude oil; 500 km natural gas; 3,000 km refined products

Ports: Lagos, Port Harcourt, Calabar, Warri, Onne, Sapele

Merchant marine: 28 ships (1,000 GRT or over) totaling 420,658 GRT/668,951 DWT; includes 18 cargo, 1 refrigerated cargo, 1 roll-on/roll-off cargo, 6 petroleum, oils, and lubricants (POL) tanker, 1 chemical tanker, 1 bulk

Civil air: 76 major transport aircraft

Airports: 81 total, 68 usable; 32 with permanent-surface runways; 1 with runways over 3,659 m; 14 with runways 2,440-3,659 m; 21 with runways 1,220-2,439 m

Telecommunications: above-average system limited by poor maintenance; major expansion in progress; radio relay and cable routes; 155,000 telephones; stations—37 AM, 19 FM, 38 TV; 2 Atlantic Ocean INTELSAT, 1 Indian Ocean INTELSAT, domestic, with 19 stations; 1 coaxial submarine cable

---

Defense Forces

Branches: Army, Navy, Air Force, paramilitary Police Force

Manpower availability: males 15-49, 28,070,431; 16,040,870 fit for military service; 1,302,970 reach military age (18) annually

Defense expenditures: $300 million, 1% of GNP (1990 est.)

Niue
(free association with New Zealand)

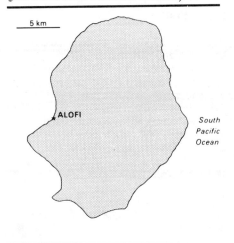

Geography

Total area: 260 km²; land area: 260 km²

Comparative area: slightly less than 1.5 times the size of Washington, DC

Land boundaries: none

Coastline: 64 km

Maritime claims:

Exclusive economic zone: 200 nm;
Territorial sea: 12 nm

Climate: tropical; modified by southeast trade winds

Terrain: steep limestone cliffs along coast, central plateau

Natural resources: fish, arable land

Land use: arable land 61%; permanent crops 4%; meadows and pastures 4%; forest and woodland 19%; other 12%

Environment: subject to typhoons

Note: one of world's largest coral islands; located about 460 km east of Tonga

---

People

Population: 1,908 (July 1991), growth rate −0.1% (1991)

Birth rate: NA births/1,000 population (1991)

Death rate: NA deaths/1,000 population (1991)

Net migration rate: NA migrants/1,000 population (1991)

Infant mortality rate: NA deaths/1,000 live births (1991)

Life expectancy at birth: NA years male, NA years female (1991)

Total fertility rate: NA children born/woman (1991)

Nationality: noun—Niuean(s); adjective—Niuean

Ethnic divisions: Polynesian, with some 200 Europeans, Samoans, and Tongans

Religion: Ekalesia Nieue (Niuean Church)—a Protestant church closely related to the London Missionary Society 75%, Mormon 10%, Roman Catholic, Jehovah's Witnesses, Seventh-Day Adventist 5%

Language: Polynesian tongue closely related to Tongan and Samoan; English

Literacy: NA% (male NA%, female NA%) but compulsory education age 5 to 14

Labor force: 1,000 (1981 est.); most work on family plantations; paid work exists only in government service, small industry, and the Niue Development Board

Organized labor: NA

Government

Long-form name: none

Type: self-governing territory in free association with New Zealand; Niue fully responsible for internal affairs; New Zealand retains responsibility for external affairs

Capital: Alofi

Administrative divisions: none

Independence: became a self-governing territory in free association with New Zealand on 19 October 1974

Constitution: 19 October 1974 (Niue Constitution Act)

Legal system: English common law

National holiday: Waitangi Day (Treaty of Waitangi established British sovereignty), 6 February (1840)

Executive branch: British monarch, premier, Cabinet

Legislative branch: Legislative Assembly

Judicial branch: Appeal Court of New Zealand, High Court

Leaders:

Chief of State—Queen ELIZABETH II (since 6 February 1952), represented by New Zealand Representative John SPRINGFORD (since 1974);

Head of Government—Premier Sir Robert R. REX (since NA October 1974)

Suffrage: universal adult at age 18

Political parties and leaders: Niue Island Party (NIP), Young VIVIAN

Elections:

Legislative Assembly—last held on 8 April 1990 (next to be held March 1993); results—percent of vote NA; seats—(20 total, 6 elected) independents 5, NIP 1

Member of: ESCAP (associate), SPC, SPF

Diplomatic representation: none (self-governing territory in free association with New Zealand)

Flag: yellow with the flag of the UK in the upper hoist-side quadrant; the flag of the UK bears five yellow five-pointed stars—a large one on a blue disk in the center and a smaller one on each arm of the bold red cross

---

Economy

Overview: The economy is heavily dependent on aid from New Zealand. Government expenditures regularly exceed revenues, with the shortfall made up by grants from New Zealand—the grants are used to

Niue *(continued)*

pay wages to public employees. The agricultural sector consists mainly of subsistence gardening, although some cash crops are grown for export. Industry consists primarily of small factories to process passion fruit, lime oil, honey, and coconut cream. The sale of postage stamps to foreign collectors is an important source of revenue. The island in recent years has suffered a serious loss of population because of migration of Niueans to New Zealand.

GNP: $2.1 million, per capita $1,000; real growth rate NA% (1989 est.)

Inflation rate (consumer prices): 9.6% (1984)

Unemployment rate: NA%

Budget: revenues $5.5 million; expenditures $6.3 million, including capital expenditures of $NA (FY85 est.)

Exports: $175,274 (f.o.b., 1985); *commodities*—canned coconut cream, copra, honey, passion fruit products, pawpaw, root crops, limes, footballs, stamps, handicrafts; *partners*—NZ 89%, Fiji, Cook Islands, Australia

Imports: $3.8 million (c.i.f., 1985); *commodities*—food, live animals, manufactured goods, machinery, fuels, lubricants, chemicals, drugs; *partners*—NZ 59%, Fiji 20%, Japan 13%, Western Samoa, Australia, US

External debt: $NA

Industrial production: growth rate NA%

Electricity: 1,500 kW capacity; 3 million kWh produced, 1,490 kWh per capita (1990)

Industries: tourist, handicrafts

Agriculture: copra, coconuts, passion fruit, honey, limes; subsistence crops—taro, yams, cassava (tapioca), sweet potatoes; pigs, poultry, beef cattle

Economic aid: Western (non-US) countries, ODA and OOF bilateral commitments (1970-88), $62 million

Currency: New Zealand dollar (plural—dollars); 1 New Zealand dollar (NZ$) = 100 cents

Exchange rates: New Zealand dollars (NZ$) per US$1—1.6798 (January 1991), 1.6750 (1990), 1.6711 (1989), 1.5244 (1988), 1.6886 (1987), 1.9088 (1986), 2.0064 (1985)

Fiscal year: 1 April-31 March

Communications

Highways: 123 km all-weather roads, 106 km access and plantation roads

Ports: none; offshore anchorage only

Airports: 1 with permanent-surface runway of 1,650 m

Telecommunications: single-line telephone system connects all villages on island; 383 telephones; 1,000 radio receivers (1987 est.); stations—1 AM, 1 FM, no TV

Defense Forces

Branches: Police Force

Note: defense is the responsibility of New Zealand

Norfolk Island
(territory of Australia)

Geography

Total area: 34.6 km²; land area: 34.6 km²

Comparative area: about 0.2 times the size of Washington, DC

Land boundaries: none

Coastline: 32 km

Maritime claims:

Exclusive fishing zone: 200 nm;

Territorial sea: 3 nm

Climate: subtropical, mild, little seasonal temperature variation

Terrain: volcanic formation with mostly rolling plains

Natural resources: fish

Land use: arable land 0%; permanent crops 0%; meadows and pastures 25%; forest and woodland 0%; other 75%

Environment: subject to typhoons (especially May to July)

Note: located 1,575 km east of Australia in the South Pacific Ocean

People

Population: 2,576 (July 1991), growth rate NEGL% (1991)

Birth rate: NA births/1,000 population (1991)

Death rate: NA deaths/1,000 population (1991)

Net migration rate: NA migrants/1,000 population (1991)

Infant mortality rate: NA deaths/1,000 live births (1991)

Life expectancy at birth: NA years male, NA years female (1991)

Total fertility rate: NA children born/woman (1991)

Nationality: noun—Norfolk Islander(s); adjective—Norfolk Islander(s)

Ethnic divisions: descendants of the Bounty mutiny; more recently, Australian and New Zealand settlers

Religion: Anglican 39%, Roman Catholic 11.7%, Uniting Church in Australia 16.4%,

Seventh-Day Adventist 4.4%, none 9.2%, unknown 16.9%, other 2.4% (1986)
Language: English (official) and Norfolk—a mixture of 18th century English and ancient Tahitian
Literacy: NA% (male NA%, female NA%)
Labor force: NA
Organized labor: NA

Government

Long-form name: Territory of Norfolk Island
Type: territory of Australia
Capital: Kingston (administrative center), Burnt Pine (commercial center)
Administrative divisions: none (territory of Australia)
Independence: none (territory of Australia)
Constitution: Norfolk Island Act of 1957
Legal system: wide legislative and executive responsibility under the Norfolk Island Act of 1979; Supreme Court
National holiday: Pitcairners Arrival Day Anniversary, 8 June (1856)
Executive branch: British monarch, governor general of Australia, administrator, Executive Council (cabinet)
Legislative branch: unicameral Legislative Assembly
Judicial branch: Supreme Court
Leaders:
Chief of State—Queen ELIZABETH II (since 6 February 1952), represented by Administrator H. B. MACDONALD (since NA 1989), who is appointed by the Governor General of Australia;
Head of Government—Assembly President and Chief Minister John Terence BROWN (since NA)
Political parties and leaders: NA
Suffrage: universal at age 18
Elections:
Legislative Assembly—last held 1989 (held every three years); results—percent of vote by party NA; seats—(9 total) percent of seats by party NA
Member of: none
Diplomatic representation: none (territory of Australia)
Flag: three vertical bands of green (hoist side), white, and green with a large green Norfolk Island pine tree centered in the slightly wider white band

Economy

Overview: The primary economic activity is tourism, which has brought a level of prosperity unusual among inhabitants of the Pacific Islands. The number of visitors has increased steadily over the years and reached 29,000 in FY89. Revenues from tourism have given the island a favorable balance of trade and helped the agricultural

sector to become self-sufficient in the production of beef, poultry, and eggs.
GDP: $NA, per capita $NA; real growth rate NA%
Inflation rate (consumer prices): NA%
Unemployment rate: NA%
Budget: revenues $NA; expenditures $4.2 million, including capital expenditures of $400,000 (FY89)
Exports: $1.7 million (f.o.b., FY86); *commodities*—postage stamps, seeds of the Norfolk Island pine and Kentia Palm, small quantities of avocados; *partners*—Australia, Pacific Islands, NZ, Asia, Europe
Imports: $15.6 million (c.i.f., FY86); *commodities*—NA; *partners*—Australia, Pacific Islands, NZ, Asia, Europe
External debt: NA
Industrial production: growth rate NA%
Electricity: 7,000 kW capacity; 8 million kWh produced, 3,160 kWh per capita (1990)
Industries: tourism
Agriculture: Norfolk Island pine seed, Kentia palm seed, cereals, vegetables, fruit, cattle, poultry
Economic aid: none
Currency: Australian dollar (plural—dollars); 1 Australian dollar ($A) = 100 cents
Exchange rates: Australian dollars ($A) per US$1—1.2834 (January 1991), 1.2799 (1990), 1.2618 (1989), 1.2752 (1988), 1.4267 (1987), 1.4905 (1986), 1.4269 (1985)
Fiscal year: 1 July-30 June

Communications

Highways: 80 km of roads, including 53 km of sealed roads; remainder are earth formed or coral surfaced
Ports: none; loading jetties at Kingston and Cascade
Airports: 1 with permanent-surface runways 1,220-2,439 m (Australian owned)
Telecommunications: 1,500 radio receivers (1982); radio link service with Sydney; 987 telephones (1983); stations—1 AM, no FM, no TV

Defense Forces

Note: defense is the responsibility of Australia

Northern Mariana Islands
(commonwealth associated with the US)

Geography

Total area: 477 km²; land area: 477 km²; includes Saipan, Rota, and Tinian
Comparative area: slightly more than 2.5 times the size of Washington, DC
Land boundaries: none
Coastline: 1,482 km
Maritime claims:
Contiguous zone: 12 nm;
Continental shelf: 200 m (depth);
Exclusive economic zone: 200 nm;
Territorial sea: 3 nm
Climate: tropical marine; moderated by northeast trade winds, little seasonal temperature variation; dry season December to July, rainy season July to October
Terrain: southern islands are limestone with level terraces and fringing coral reefs; northern islands are volcanic; highest elevation is 471 meters (Mt. Tagpochu on Saipan)
Natural resources: arable land, fish
Land use: arable land 1%; permanent crops NA%; meadows and pastures 19%; forest and woodland NA%; other NA%
Environment: Mt. Pagan is an active volcano (last erupted in October 1988); subject to typhoons during the rainy season
Note: strategic location 5,635 km west-southwest of Honolulu in the North Pacific Ocean, about three-quarters of the way between Hawaii and the Philippines

People

Population: 23,494 (July 1991), growth rate 3.4% (1991)
Birth rate: 43 births/1,000 population (1991)
Death rate: 6 deaths/1,000 population (1991)
Net migration rate: −3 migrants/1,000 population (1991)
Infant mortality rate: 17 deaths/1,000 live births (1991)
Life expectancy at birth: 65 years male, 70 years female (1991)

Northern Mariana
Islands *(continued)*

Total fertility rate: 5.8 children born/woman (1991)
Nationality: undetermined
Ethnic divisions: Chamorro majority; Carolinians and other Micronesians; Spanish, German, Japanese admixtures
Religion: Christian with a Roman Catholic majority, although traditional beliefs and taboos may still be found
Language: English, but Chamorro and Carolinian are also spoken in the home and taught in school
Literacy: 96% (male 97%, female 96%) age 15 and over can read and write (1980)
Labor force: 12,788 local; 18,799 foreign workers (1990 est.)
Organized labor: NA

Government

Long-form name: Commonwealth of the Northern Mariana Islands
Type: commonwealth associated with the US and administered by the Office of Territorial and International Affairs, US Department of the Interior
Capital: Saipan
Administrative divisions: none
Independence: none (commonwealth associated with the US)
Constitution: Covenant Agreement effective 3 November 1986
Legal system: NA
National holiday: Commonwealth Day, 8 January (1978)
Executive branch: governor, lieutenant governor
Legislative branch: bicameral Legislature consists of an upper house or Senate and a lower house or House of Representatives
Judicial branch: Supreme Court
Leaders:
Chief of State—President George BUSH (since 20 January 1989); Vice President Dan QUAYLE (since 20 January 1989);
Head of Government—Governor Lorenzo I. DeLeon GUERRERO (since NA 1990); Lieutenant Governor Benjamin T. MANGLONA (since NA 1990)
Political parties and leaders: Republican Party, Alonzo IGISOMAR; Democratic Party, Felicidad OGUMORO
Suffrage: universal at age 18; indigenous inhabitants are US citizens but do not vote in US presidential elections
Elections:
Governor—last held on NA November 1989 (next to be held November 1993); results—Lorenzo I. DeLeon GUERRERO, Republican Party, was elected governor;
Senate—last held on NA November 1989 (next to be held November 1991); results—percent of vote by party NA; seats—(9 total) number of seats by party NA;

House of Representatives—last held on NA November 1989 (next to be held November 1991); results—percent of vote by party NA; seats—(15 total) number of seats by party NA;
US House of Representatives—last held NA November 1989 (next to be held NA); results—percent of vote by party NA; seats—(1 total) party of nonvoting delegate NA
Member of: ESCAP (associate), SPC
Diplomatic representation: none
Flag: blue with a white five-pointed star superimposed on the gray silhouette of a latte stone (a traditional foundation stone used in building) in the center

Economy

Overview: The economy benefits substantially from financial assistance from the US. An agreement for the years 1986 to 1992 entitles the islands to $228 million for capital development, government operations, and special programs. Another major source of income is the tourist industry, which employs about 10% of the work force. The agricultural sector is made up of cattle ranches and small farms producing coconuts, breadfruit, tomatoes, and melons. Industry is small scale in nature—mostly handicrafts and fish processing.
GNP: $165 million, per capita $9,170; real growth rate NA% (1982)
Inflation rate (consumer prices): NA%
Unemployment rate: NA%
Budget: revenues $NA; expenditures $70.6 million, including capital expenditures of $NA (1987)
Exports: $153.9 million (1989);
commodities—manufactured goods, garments;
partners—NA
Imports: $313.7 million, a 43% increase over previous year (1989);
commodities—NA;
partners—NA
External debt: none
Industrial production: growth rate NA%
Electricity: 25,000 kW capacity; 35 million kWh produced, 1,540 kWh per capita (1990)
Industries: tourism, construction, light industry, handicrafts
Agriculture: coffee, coconuts, fruits, tobacco, cattle
Economic aid: none
Currency: US currency is used
Exchange rates: US currency is used
Fiscal year: 1 October-30 September

Communications

Highways: 300 km total (53 km primary, 55 km secondary, 192 km local)
Ports: Saipan, Rota, Tinian
Airports: 6 total, 4 usable; 3 with permanent-surface runways; none with runways over 3,659 m; 1 with runways 2,440-3,659 m; 2 with runways 1,220-2,439 m
Telecommunications: stations—2 AM, no FM, 1 TV; 2 Pacific Ocean INTELSAT earth stations

Defense Forces

Note: defense is the responsibility of the US

Norway

Geography

Total area: 324,220 km²; land area: 307,860 km²

Comparative area: slightly larger than New Mexico

Land boundaries: 2,544 km total; Finland 729 km, Sweden 1,619 km, USSR 196 km

Coastline: 21,925 km (3,419 km mainland; 2,413 km large islands; 16,093 km long fjords, numerous small islands, and minor indentations)

Maritime claims:

Contiguous zone: 10 nm;

Continental shelf: to depth of exploitation;

Exclusive economic zone: 200 nm;

Territorial sea: 4 nm

Disputes: maritime boundary dispute with USSR; territorial claim in Antarctica (Queen Maud Land); Denmark has challenged Norway's maritime claims beween Greenland and Jan Mayen

Climate: temperate along coast, modified by North Atlantic Current; colder interior; rainy year-round on west coast

Terrain: glaciated; mostly high plateaus and rugged mountains broken by fertile valleys; small, scattered plains; coastline deeply indented by fjords; arctic tundra in north

Natural resources: crude oil, copper, natural gas, pyrites, nickel, iron ore, zinc, lead, fish, timber, hydropower

Land use: arable land 3%; permanent crops 0%; meadows and pastures NEGL%; forest and woodland 27%; other 70%; includes irrigated NEGL%

Environment: air and water pollution; acid rain

Note: strategic location adjacent to sea lanes and air routes in North Atlantic; one of most rugged and longest coastlines in world; Norway and Turkey only NATO members having a land boundary with the USSR

People

Population: 4,273,442 (July 1991), growth rate 0.5% (1991)

Birth rate: 14 births/1,000 population (1991)

Death rate: 11 deaths/1,000 population (1991)

Net migration rate: 2 migrants/1,000 population (1991)

Infant mortality rate: 7 deaths/1,000 live births (1991)

Life expectancy at birth: 74 years male, 81 years female (1991)

Total fertility rate: 1.8 children born/woman (1991)

Nationality: noun—Norwegian(s); adjective—Norwegian

Ethnic divisions: Germanic (Nordic, Alpine, Baltic) and racial-cultural minority of 20,000 Lapps

Religion: Evangelical Lutheran (state church) 87.8%, other Protestant and Roman Catholic 3.8%, none 3.2%, unknown 5.2% (1980)

Language: Norwegian (official); small Lapp- and Finnish-speaking minorities

Literacy: 99% (male NA%, female NA%) age 15 and over can read and write (1976 est.)

Labor force: 2,167,000 (September 1990); services 34.7%, commerce 18%, mining and manufacturing 16.6%, banking and financial services 7.5%, transportation and communications 7.2%, construction 7.2%, agriculture, forestry, and fishing 6.4% (1989)

Organized labor: 66% of labor force (1985)

Government

Long-form name: Kingdom of Norway

Type: constitutional monarchy

Capital: Oslo

Administrative divisions: 19 provinces (fylker, singular—fylke); Akershus, Aust-Agder, Buskerud, Finnmark, Hedmark, Hordaland, Møre og Romsdal, Nordland, Nord-Trøndelag, Oppland, Oslo, Østfold, Rogaland, Sogn og Fjordane, Sør-Trøndelag, Telemark, Troms, Vest-Agder, Vestfold

Independence: 26 October 1905 (from Sweden)

Constitution: 17 May 1814, modified in 1884

Dependent areas: Bouvet Island, Jan Mayen, Svalbard

Legal system: mixture of customary law, civil law system, and common law traditions; Supreme Court renders advisory opinions to legislature when asked; accepts compulsory ICJ jurisdiction, with reservations

National holiday: Constitution Day, 17 May (1814)

Executive branch: monarch, prime minister, State Council (cabinet)

Legislative branch: unicameral Parliament (Stortinget) with an Upper Chamber (Lagting) and a Lower Chamber (Odelsting)

Judicial branch: Supreme Court (Hoiesterett)

Leaders:

Chief of State—King HARALD V (since 17 January 1991); Heir Apparent Crown Prince HAAKON MAGNUS (born 20 July 1973);

Head of Government—Prime Minister Gro Harlem BRUNDTLAND (since 3 November 1990)

Political parties and leaders: Labor, Gro Harlem BRUNDTLAND; Conservative, Kaci Kullmann FIVE; Center Party, Anne Enger LAHNSTEIN; Christian People's, Kjell Magne BONDEVIK; Socialist Left, Eric SOLHEIM; Norwegian Communist, Kåre Andre NILSEN; Progress, Carl I. HAGEN; Liberal, Arne FJORTOFT; Finnmark List, leader NA

Suffrage: universal at age 18

Elections:

Storting—last held on 11 September 1989 (next to be held 6 September 1993); results—Labor 34.3%, Conservative 22.2%, Progress 13.0%, Socialist Left 10.1%, Christian People's 8.5%, Center Party 6.6%, Finnmark List 0.3%, other 5%; seats—(165 total) Labor 63, Conservative 37, Progress 22, Socialist Left 17, Christian People's 14, Center Party 11, Finnmark List 1

Communists: 15,500 est.; 5,500 Norwegian Communist Party (NKP); 10,000 Workers Communist Party Marxist-Leninist (AKP-ML, pro-Chinese)

Member of: AfDB, AsDB, BIS, CCC, CE, CERN, COCOM, CSCE, EBRD, ECE, EFTA, ESA, FAO, GATT, IADB, IAEA, IBRD, ICAO, ICC, ICFTU, IDA, IEA, IFAD, IFC, ILO, IMF, IMO, INMARSAT, INTELSAT, INTERPOL, IOC, IOM, ISO, ITU, LORCS, NATO, NC, NEA, NIB, OECD, PCA, UN, UNAVEM, UNCTAD, UNESCO, UNHCR, UNIDO, UNIFIL, UNIIMOG, UNMOGIP, UNTSO, UPU, WHO, WIPO, WMO

Diplomatic representation: Ambassador Kjeld VIBE; Chancery at 2720 34th Street NW, Washington DC 20008; telephone (202) 333-6000; there are Norwegian Consulates General in Houston, Los Angeles, Minneapolis, New York, and San Francisco, and Consulates in Miami and New Orleans;

US—Ambassador Loret Miller RUPPE; Embassy at Drammensveien 18, 0244 Oslo 2 (mailing address is APO New York 09085); telephone [47] (2) 44-85-50

Flag: red with a blue cross outlined in white that extends to the edges of the flag; the vertical part of the cross is shifted to the hoist side in the style of the *Dannebrog* (Danish flag)

Economy

Overview: Norway is a prosperous capitalist nation with the resources to finance extensive welfare measures. Since 1975 exploitation of large crude oil and natural gas

Norway *(continued)*

reserves has helped maintain high growth; for the past five years growth has averaged 4.1%, the fourth-highest among OECD countries. Growth slackened in 1987-88 partially because of the sharp drop in world oil prices, but picked up again in 1989. The Brundtland government plans to push hard on environmental issues, as well as cutting unemployment, improving child care, upgrading major industries, and negotiating an EC–European Free Trade Association (EFTA) agreement on an Economic European Area.

GDP: $74.2 billion, per capita $17,400; real growth rate 3.1% (1990)

Inflation rate (consumer prices): 4.1% (1990)

Unemployment rate: 5.2% (1990, excluding people in job-training programs)

Budget: revenues $47.9 billion; expenditures $48.7 billion, including capital expenditures of $NA (1990)

Exports: $33.8 billion (f.o.b., 1990); *commodities*—petroleum and petroleum products 25%, natural gas 11%, fish 7%, aluminum 6%, ships 3.5%, pulp and paper; *partners*—EC 64.9%, Nordic countries 19.5%, developing countries 6.9%, US 6.2%, Japan 1.7% (1990)

Imports: $26.8 billion (c.i.f., 1990); *commodities*—machinery, fuels and lubricants, transportation equipment, chemicals, foodstuffs, clothing, ships; *partners*—EC 46.3%, Nordic countries 25.7%, developing countries 14.3%, US 8.1%, Japan 4.7% (1990)

External debt: $15 billion (December 1990)

Industrial production: growth rate 3.6% (1990)

Electricity: 26,735,000 kW capacity; 121,685 million kWh produced, 28,950 kWh per capita (1989)

Industries: petroleum and gas, food processing, shipbuilding, pulp and paper products, metals, chemicals, timber, mining, textiles, fishing

Agriculture: accounts for 2.8% of GNP and 6.4% of labor force; among world's top 10 fishing nations; livestock output exceeds value of crops; over half of food needs imported; fish catch of 1.76 million metric tons in 1989

Economic aid: donor—ODA and OOF commitments (1970-89), $4.4 billion

Currency: Norwegian krone (plural—kroner); 1 Norwegian krone (NKr) = 100 øre

Exchange rates: Norwegian kroner (NKr) per US$1—5.9060 (January 1991), 6.2597 (1990), 6.9045 (1989), 6.5170 (1988), 6.7375 (1987), 7.3947 (1986), 8.5972 (1985)

Fiscal year: calendar year

Communications

Railroads: 4,223 km 1.435-meter standard gauge; Norwegian State Railways (NSB) operates 4,219 km (2,450 km electrified and 96 km double track); 4 km other

Highways: 79,540 km total; 18,600 km concrete, bituminous, stone block; 19,980 km bituminous treated; 40,960 km gravel, crushed stone, and earth

Inland waterways: 1,577 km along west coast; 1.5-2.4 m draft vessels maximum

Pipelines: refined products, 53 km

Ports: Oslo, Bergen, Fredrikstad, Kristiansand, Stavanger, Trondheim

Merchant marine: 867 ships (1,000 GRT or over) totaling 23,270,845 GRT/41,199,182 DWT; includes 11 passenger, 23 short-sea passenger, 121 cargo, 3 passenger-cargo, 24 refrigerated cargo, 14 container, 50 roll-on/roll-off cargo, 18 vehicle carrier, 1 railcar carrier, 186 petroleum, oils, and lubricants (POL) tanker, 98 chemical tanker, 69 liquefied gas, 1 specialized tanker, 35 combination ore/oil, 204 bulk, 9 combination bulk; note—the government has created a captive register, the Norwegian International Ship Register (NIS), as a subset of the Norwegian register; ships on the NIS enjoy many benefits of flags of convenience and do not have to be crewed by Norwegians; the majority of ships (777) under the Norwegian flag are now registered with the NIS

Civil air: 76 major transport aircraft

Airports: 104 total, 103 usable; 64 with permanent-surface runways; none with runways over 3,659 m; 12 with runways 2,440-3,659 m; 16 with runways 1,220-2,439 m

Telecommunications: high-quality domestic and international telephone, telegraph, and telex services; 3,102,000 telephones; stations—8 AM, 46 (1,400 relays) FM, 55 (2,100 relays) TV; 4 coaxial submarine cables; communications satellite earth stations operating in the EUTELSAT, INTELSAT (1 Atlantic Ocean), MARISAT, and domestic systems

Defense Forces

Branches: Norwegian Army, Royal Norwegian Navy, Royal Norwegian Air Force, Home Guard

Manpower availability: males 15-49, 1,124,201; 942,158 fit for military service; 31,813 reach military age (20) annually

Defense expenditures: $3.3 billion, 3.3% of GDP (1990)

Oman

Geography

Total area: 212,460 km²; land area: 212,460 km²

Comparative area: slightly smaller than Kansas

Land boundaries: 1,374 km total; Saudi Arabia 676 km, UAE 410 km, Yemen 288 km

Coastline: 2,092 km

Maritime claims:
Continental shelf: to be defined;
Exclusive economic zone: 200 nm;
Territorial sea: 12 nm

Disputes: Administrative Line with Yemen; no defined boundary with most of UAE, Administrative Line in far north

Climate: dry desert; hot, humid along coast; hot, dry interior; strong southwest summer monsoon (May to September) in far south

Terrain: vast central desert plain, rugged mountains in north and south

Natural resources: crude oil, copper, asbestos, some marble, limestone, chromium, gypsum, natural gas

Land use: arable land NEGL%; permanent crops NEGL%; meadows and pastures 5%; forest and woodland 0%; other 95%; includes irrigated NEGL%

Environment: summer winds often raise large sandstorms and duststorms in interior; sparse natural freshwater resources

Note: strategic location with small foothold on Musandam Peninsula controlling Strait of Hormuz (17% of world's oil production transits this point going from Persian Gulf to Arabian Sea)

People

Population: 1,534,011 (July 1991), growth rate 3.5% (1991)

Birth rate: 41 births/1,000 population (1991)

Death rate: 6 deaths/1,000 population (1991)

Net migration rate: 0 migrants/1,000 population (1991)

Infant mortality rate: 40 deaths/1,000 live births (1991)
Life expectancy at birth: 65 years male, 68 years female (1991)
Total fertility rate: 6.7 children born/woman (1991)
Nationality: noun—Omani(s); adjective—Omani
Ethnic divisions: mostly Arab, with small Balochi, Zanzibari, and South Asian (Indian, Pakistani, Bangladeshi) groups
Religion: Ibadhi Muslim 75%; remainder Sunni Muslim, Shi'a Muslim, some Hindu
Language: Arabic (official); English, Balochi, Urdu, Indian dialects
Literacy: NA% (male NA%, female NA%)
Labor force: 430,000; agriculture (est.) 60%; 58% are non-Omani
Organized labor: trade unions are illegal

Government

Long-form name: Sultanate of Oman
Type: absolute monarchy; independent, with residual UK influence
Capital: Muscat
Administrative divisions: there are no first-order administrative divisions as defined by the US Government, but there are 7 planning regions (manāṭiq takhṭīṭīyah, singular—minṭaqah takhṭīṭīyah) that include 1 governorate* (muḥāfaẓah) and 50 districts (wilāyāt, singular—wilāyah);
al-Batinah—Awabi, Barka, Khabura, Liwa, Musanaa, Nakhl, Rustaq, Saham, Shinas, Sohar, Suwaiq, Wadi al-Maawil;
al-Dakhiliah—Adam, al-Hamra, Bahla, Bidbid, Haima, Izki, Manah, Nizwa, Sumail;
al-Dhahirah—al-Buraimi, Dhank, Ibri, Mhadha, Yanqul;
al-Janubiah—Dhalqut, Mirbat, Rokhyut, Sadah, Salalah, Shalim, Taqa, Thamrait;
al-Sharqiya—al Kamil and al-Wafi, al-Mudhaiby, al-Qabil, Bidiya, Dimaa and Tayin, Ibra, Jaalan Bani Bu Ali, Jaalan Bani Bu Hassan, Masirah, Sur, Wadi Bani Khalid;
Musandam—Daba al-Biya, Bukha, Khasab, Madha;
Muscat—Muscat*, Quriyat
Independence: 1650, expulsion of the Portuguese
Constitution: none
Legal system: based on English common law and Islamic law; ultimate appeal to the sultan; has not accepted compulsory ICJ jurisdiction
Executive branch: sultan, Cabinet
Legislative branch: State Consultative Assembly (advisory function only)
Judicial branch: none; traditional Islamic judges and a nascent civil court system
National holiday: National Day, 18 November

Leaders:
Chief of State and Head of Government—Sultan and Prime Minister QABOOS bin Sa'id Al Said (since 23 July 1970)
Political parties: none
Suffrage: none
Elections: none
Other political or pressure groups: outlawed Popular Front for the Liberation of Oman (PFLO), based in Yemen
Member of: ABEDA, AFESD, AL, AMF, ESCWA, FAO, G-77, GCC, IBRD, ICAO, IDA, IDB, IFAD, IFC, IMF, IMO, INMARSAT, INTELSAT, INTERPOL, IOC, ISO (correspondent), ITU, NAM, OIC, UN, UNCTAD, UNESCO, UNIDO, UPU, WFTU, WHO, WMO
Diplomatic representation: Ambassador Awadh Bader AL-SHANFARI; Chancery at 2342 Massachusetts Avenue NW, Washington DC 20008; telephone (202) 387-1980 through 1982;
US—Ambassador Richard W. BOEHM; Embassy at address NA, Muscat (mailing address is P. O. Box 50200 Madinat Qaboos, Muscat); telephone 698-989
Flag: three horizontal bands of white (top, double width), red, and green (double width) with a broad, vertical, red band on the hoist side; the national emblem (a *khanjar* dagger in its sheath superimposed on two crossed swords in scabbards) in white is centered at the top of the vertical band

Economy

Overview: Economic performance is closely tied to the fortunes of the oil industry. Petroleum accounts for nearly all export earnings, about 80% of government revenues, and roughly 40% of GDP. Oman has proved oil reserves of 4 billion barrels, equivalent to about 20 years' supply at the current rate of extraction. Although agriculture employs a majority of the population, urban centers depend on imported food.
GDP: $8.5 billion, per capita $6,400; real growth rate −3.0% (1987 est.)
Inflation rate (consumer prices): 1.3% (1989)
Unemployment rate: NA%
Budget: revenues $3.5 billion; expenditures $4.3 billion, including capital expenditures of $675 million (1989 est.)
Exports: $3.8 billion (f.o.b., 1989 est.);
commodities—petroleum, reexports, processed copper, dates, nuts, fish;
partners—Japan, South Korea, Taiwan
Imports: $2.4 billion (c.i.f., 1989 est.);
commodities—machinery, transportation equipment, manufactured goods, food, livestock, lubricants;
partners—UK, UAE, Japan, US
External debt: $3.1 billion (December 1989 est.)
Industrial production: growth rate 18.0% (1989 est.), including petroleum sector

Electricity: 1,136,000 kW capacity; 3,650 million kWh produced, 2,500 kWh per capita (1990)
Industries: crude oil production and refining, natural gas production, construction, cement, copper
Agriculture: accounts for 6% of GDP and 60% of the labor force (including fishing); less than 2% of land cultivated; largely subsistence farming (dates, limes, bananas, alfalfa, vegetables, camels, cattle); not self-sufficient in food; annual fish catch averages 100,000 metric tons
Economic aid: US commitments, including Ex-Im (FY70-89), $137 million; Western (non-US) countries, ODA and OOF bilateral commitments (1970-88), $122 million; OPEC bilateral aid (1979-89), $797 million
Currency: Omani rial (plural—rials); 1 Omani rial (RO) = 1,000 baiza
Exchange rates: Omani rials (RO) per US$1—0.3845 (fixed rate since 1986)
Fiscal year: calendar year

Communications

Highways: 22,800 km total; 3,800 km bituminous surface, 19,000 km motorable track
Pipelines: crude oil 1,300 km; natural gas 1,030 km
Ports: Mīnā' Qābūs, Mīnā' Raysūt
Merchant marine: 1 passenger ship (1,000 GRT or over) totaling 4,442 GRT/1,320 DWT
Civil air: 4 major transport aircraft
Airports: 122 total, 114 usable; 6 with permanent-surface runways; 1 with runways over 3,659 m; 8 with runways 2,440-3,659 m; 64 with runways 1,220-2,439 m
Telecommunications: fair system of open-wire, radio relay, and radio communications stations; 50,000 telephones; stations—3 AM, 3 FM, 11 TV; satellite earth stations—2 Indian Ocean INTELSAT, 1 ARABSAT, and 8 domestic

Defense Forces

Branches: Army, Navy, Air Force, Royal Oman Police
Manpower availability: males 15-49, 348,849; 197,870 fit for military service; 20,715 reach military age (14) annually
Defense expenditures: $1.0 billion, 12% of GDP (1991)

Pacific Islands, Trust Territory of the (Palau)

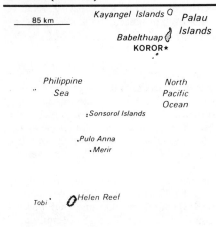

Geography

Total area: 458 km²; land area: 458 km²
Comparative area: slightly more than 2.5 times the size of Washington, DC
Land boundaries: none
Coastline: 1,519 km
Maritime claims:
Contiguous zone: 12 nm;
Continental shelf: 200 m (depth);
Exclusive fishing zone: 200 nm;
Territorial sea: 3 nm
Climate: wet season May to November; hot and humid
Terrain: islands vary geologically from the high mountainous main island of Babelthuap to low, coral islands usually fringed by large barrier reefs
Natural resources: forests, minerals (especially gold), marine products; deep-seabed minerals
Land use: arable land NA%; permanent crops NA%; meadows and pastures NA%; forest and woodland NA%; other NA%
Environment: subject to typhoons from June to December; archipelago of six island groups totaling over 200 islands in the Caroline chain
Note: important location 850 km southeast of the Philippines; includes World War II battleground of Peleliu and world-famous rock islands

People

Population: 14,411 (July 1991), growth rate 0.7% (1991)
Birth rate: 25 births/1,000 population (1991)
Death rate: 6 deaths/1,000 population (1991)
Net migration rate: −12 migrants/1,000 population (1991)
Infant mortality rate: 26 deaths/1,000 live births (1991)
Life expectancy at birth: 68 years male, 74 years female (1991)

Total fertility rate: 3.3 children born/woman (1991)
Nationality: noun—Palauan(s); adjective—Palauan
Ethnic divisions: Palauans are a composite of Polynesian, Malayan, and Melanesian races
Religion: predominantly Christian, mainly Roman Catholic
Language: Palauan is the official language, though English is commonplace; inhabitants of the isolated southwestern islands speak a dialect of Trukese
Literacy: 92% (male 93%, female 91%) age 15 and over can read and write (1980)
Labor force: NA
Organized labor: NA

Government

Long-form name: Trust Territory of the Pacific Islands (no short-form name); may change to Republic of Palau after independence; note—Belau, the native form of Palau, is sometimes used
Type: UN trusteeship administered by the US; constitutional government signed a Compact of Free Association with the US on 10 January 1986, after approval in a series of UN-observed plebiscites; until the UN trusteeship is terminated with entry into force of the Compact, Palau remains under US administration as the Palau District of the Trust Territory of the Pacific Islands
Capital: Koror; a new capital is being built about 20 km northeast in eastern Babelthuap
Administrative divisions: none
Independence: still part of the US-administered UN trusteeship (the last polity remaining under the trusteeship; the Republic of the Marshall Islands, Federated States of Micronesia, and Commonwealth of the Northern Marianas have left); administered by the Office of Territorial and International Affairs, US Department of Interior
Constitution: 11 January 1981
Legal system: based on Trust Territory laws, acts of the legislature, municipal, common, and customary laws
National holiday: Constitution Day, 9 July (1979)
Executive branch: US president, US vice president, national president, national vice president
Legislative branch: bicameral Parliament (Olbiil Era Kelulau or OEK) consists of an upper house or Senate and a lower house or House of Delegates
Judicial branch: Supreme Court
Leaders:
Chief of State—President George BUSH (since 20 January 1989); represented by the Assistant Secretary for Territorial Affairs, US Department of the Interior, Stella GUERRA (since NA July 1989);

Head of Government—President Ngiratkel ETPISON (since 2 November 1988)
Political parties: no formal parties
Suffrage: universal at age 18
Elections:
President—last held on 2 November 1988 (next to be held November 1992); Ngiratkel ETPISON 26.3%, Roman TMETUCHL 25.9%, Thomas REMENGESAU 19.5%, other 28.3%;
Senate—last held 2 November 1988 (next to be held November 1992); results—percent of vote NA; seats—(18 total);
House of Delegates—last held 2 November 1988 (next to be held November 1992); results—percent of vote NA; seats—(16 total)
Member of: ESCAP (associate), SPC, SPF (observer)
Diplomatic representation: none;
US—US Liaison Officer Lloyd MOSS; US Liaison Office at Top Side, Neeriyas, Koror (mailing address: P. O. Box 6028, Koror, Republic of Palau 96940); telephone 160-680-920 or 990
Flag: light blue with a large yellow disk (representing the moon) shifted slightly to the hoist side

Economy

Overview: The economy consists primarily of subsistence agriculture and fishing. Tourism provides some foreign exchange, although the remote location of Palau and a shortage of suitable facilities has hindered development. The government is the major employer of the work force, relying heavily on financial assistance from the US.
GDP: $31.6 million, per capita $2,260; real growth rate NA% (1986)
Inflation rate (consumer prices): NA%
Unemployment rate: 20% (1986)
Budget: revenues $6.0 million; expenditures NA, including capital expenditures of NA (1986)
Exports: $0.5 million (f.o.b., 1986);
commodities—NA;
partners—US, Japan
Imports: $27.2 million (c.i.f., 1986);
commodities—NA;
partners—US
External debt: $NA
Industrial production: growth rate NA%
Electricity: 16,000 kW capacity; 22 million kWh produced, 1,540 kWh per capita (1990)
Industries: tourism, craft items (shell, wood, pearl), some commercial fishing and agriculture
Agriculture: subsistence-level production of coconut, copra, cassava, sweet potatoes
Economic aid: US commitments, including Ex-Im (FY70-87), $2 billion; Western (non-US) countries, ODA and OOF bilateral commitments (1970-87), $62.6 million

Pacific Ocean

Currency: US currency is used
Exchange rates: US currency is used
Fiscal year: 1 October-30 September

Communications

Highways: 25.7 km paved macadam and concrete roads, otherwise stone-, coral-, or laterite-surfaced roads (1986)
Ports: Koror
Airports: 2 with permanent-surface runways 1,220-2,439 m
Telecommunications: stations—1 AM, 1 FM, 1 TV; 1 Pacific Ocean INTELSAT earth station

Defense Forces

Note: defense is the responsibility of the US and that will not change when the UN trusteeship terminates

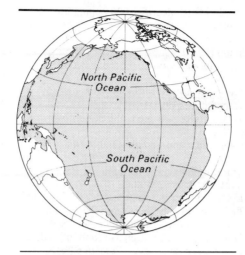

Geography

Total area: 165,384,000 km²; includes Arafura Sea, Banda Sea, Bellingshausen Sea, Bering Sea, Bering Strait, Coral Sea, East China Sea, Gulf of Alaska, Makassar Strait, Philippine Sea, Ross Sea, Sea of Japan, Sea of Okhotsk, South China Sea, Tasman Sea, and other tributary water bodies
Comparative area: slightly less than 18 times the size of the US; the largest ocean (followed by the Atlantic Ocean, Indian Ocean, and Arctic Ocean); covers about one-third of the global surface; larger than the total land area of the world
Coastline: 135,663 km
Climate: the western Pacific is monsoonal—a rainy season occurs during the summer months, when moisture-laden winds blow from the ocean over the land, and a dry season during the winter months, when dry winds blow from the Asian land mass back to the ocean
Terrain: surface in the northern Pacific dominated by a clockwise, warm water gyre (broad, circular system of currents) and in the southern Pacific by a counterclockwise, cool water gyre; sea ice occurs in the Bering Sea and Sea of Okhotsk during winter and reaches maximum northern extent from Antarctica in October; the ocean floor in the eastern Pacific is dominated by the East Pacific Rise, while the western Pacific is dissected by deep trenches; the world's greatest depth is 10,924 meters in the Marianas Trench
Natural resources: oil and gas fields, polymetallic nodules, sand and gravel aggregates, placer deposits, fish
Environment: endangered marine species include the dugong, sea lion, sea otter, seals, turtles, and whales; oil pollution in Philippine Sea and South China Sea; dotted with low coral islands and rugged volcanic islands in the southwestern Pacific Ocean; subject to tropical cyclones (typhoons) in southeast and east Asia from May to December (most frequent from July to October); tropical cyclones (hurricanes) may form south of Mexico and strike Central America and Mexico from June to October (most common in August and September); southern shipping lanes subject to icebergs from Antarctica; occasional El Niño phenomenon occurs off the coast of Peru when the trade winds slacken and the warm Equatorial Countercurrent moves south, which kills the plankton that is the primary food source for anchovies; consequently, the anchovies move to better feeding grounds, causing resident marine birds to starve by the thousands because of their lost food source
Note: the major choke points are the Bering Strait, Panama Canal, Luzon Strait, and the Singapore Strait; the Equator divides the Pacific Ocean into the North Pacific Ocean and the South Pacific Ocean; ships subject to superstructure icing in extreme north from October to May and in extreme south from May to October; persistent fog in the northern Pacific from June to December is a hazard to shipping; surrounded by a zone of violent volcanic and earthquake activity sometimes referred to as the Pacific Ring of Fire

Economy

Overview: The Pacific Ocean is a major contributor to the world economy and particularly to those nations its waters directly touch. It provides cheap sea transportation between East and West, extensive fishing grounds, offshore oil and gas fields, minerals, and sand and gravel for the construction industry. In 1985 over half (54%) of the world's total fish catch came from the Pacific Ocean, which is the only ocean where the fish catch has increased every year since 1978. Exploitation of offshore oil and gas reserves is playing an ever-increasing role in the energy supplies of Australia, New Zealand, China, US, and Peru. The high cost of recovering offshore oil and gas, combined with the wide swings in world prices for oil since 1985, has slowed but not stopped new drillings.
Industries: fishing, oil and gas production

Communications

Ports: Bangkok (Thailand), Hong Kong, Los Angeles (US), Manila (Philippines), Pusan (South Korea), San Francisco (US), Seattle (US), Shanghai (China), Singapore, Sydney (Australia), Vladivostok (USSR), Wellington (NZ), Yokohama (Japan)
Telecommunications: several submarine cables with network focused on Guam and Hawaii

239

Pakistan

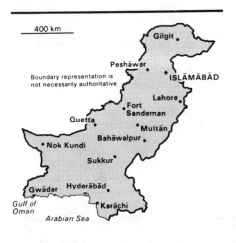

400 km

Boundary representation is not necessarily authoritative

Gilgit
Peshāwar
*ISLĀMĀBĀD
Lahore
Fort Sandeman
Quetta
Multān
Bahāwalpur
Nok Kundi
Sukkur
Gwādar
Hyderābād
Karāchi
Gulf of Oman
Arabian Sea

Geography

Total area: 803,940 km²; land area: 778,720 km²

Comparative area: slightly less than twice the size of California

Land boundaries: 6,774 km total; Afghanistan 2,430 km, China 523 km, India 2,912 km, Iran 909 km

Coastline: 1,046 km

Maritime claims:

Contiguous zone: 24 nm;

Continental shelf: edge of continental margin or 200 nm;

Exclusive economic zone: 200 nm;

Territorial sea: 12 nm

Disputes: boundary with India; Pashtun question with Afghanistan; Baloch question with Afghanistan and Iran; water sharing problems with upstream riparian India over the Indus

Climate: mostly hot, dry desert; temperate in northwest; arctic in north

Terrain: flat Indus plain in east; mountains in north and northwest; Balochistan plateau in west

Natural resources: land, extensive natural gas reserves, limited crude oil, poor quality coal, iron ore, copper, salt, limestone

Land use: arable land 26%; permanent crops NEGL%; meadows and pastures 6%; forest and woodland 4%; other 64%; includes irrigated 19%

Environment: frequent earthquakes, occasionally severe especially in north and west; flooding along the Indus after heavy rains (July and August); deforestation; soil erosion; desertification; water logging

Note: controls Khyber Pass and Malakand Pass, traditional invasion routes between Central Asia and the Indian Subcontinent

People

Population: 117,490,278 (July 1991), growth rate 2.5% (1991)

Birth rate: 43 births/1,000 population (1991)

Death rate: 13 deaths/1,000 population (1991)

Net migration rate: −5 migrants/1,000 population (1991)

Infant mortality rate: 109 deaths/1,000 live births (1991)

Life expectancy at birth: 56 years male, 57 years female (1991)

Total fertility rate: 6.6 children born/woman (1991)

Nationality: noun—Pakistani(s); adjective—Pakistani

Ethnic divisions: Punjabi, Sindhi, Pashtun (Pathan), Baloch, Muhajir (immigrants from India and their descendents)

Religion: Muslim 97% (Sunni 77%, Shi'a 20%), Christian, Hindu, and other 3%

Language: Urdu and English (both official); total spoken languages—Punjabi 64%, Sindhi 12%, Pashtu 8%, Urdu 7%, Balochi and other 9%; English is lingua franca of Pakistani elite and most government ministries, but official policies are promoting its gradual replacement by Urdu

Literacy: 35% (male 47%, female 21%) age 15 and over can read and write (1990 est.)

Labor force: 28,900,000; agriculture 54%, mining and manufacturing 13%, services 33%; extensive export of labor (1987 est.)

Organized labor: about 10% of industrial work force

Government

Long-form name: Islamic Republic of Pakistan

Type: parliamentary with strong executive, federal republic

Capital: Islāmābād

Administrative divisions: 4 provinces, 1 territory*, and 1 capital territory**; Balochistān, Federally Administered Tribal Areas*, Islāmābād Capital Territory**, North-West Frontier, Punjab, Sindh; note—the Pakistani-administered portion of the disputed Jammu and Kashmir region includes Azad Kashmir and the Northern Areas

Independence: 15 August 1947 (from UK; formerly West Pakistan)

Constitution: 10 April 1973, suspended 5 July 1977, restored with amendments, 30 December 1985

Legal system: based on English common law with provisions to accommodate Pakistan's stature as an Islamic state; accepts compulsory ICJ jurisdiction, with reservations

National holiday: Pakistan Day (proclamation of the republic), 23 March (1956)

Executive branch: president, prime minister, Cabinet

Legislative branch: bicameral Parliament (Mijlis-e-Shoora) consists of an upper house or Senate and a lower house or National Assembly

Judicial branch: Supreme Court, Federal Islamic (Shari'at) Court

Leaders:

Chief of State—President GHULAM ISHAQ Khan (since 13 December 1988);

Head of Government—Prime Minister Mian Nawaz SHARIF (since 6 November 1990);

Political parties and leaders: Islamic Democratic Alliance (Islami Jamuri Ittehad or IJI)—the Pakistan Muslim League (PML) led by Mohammed Khan JUNEJO is the main party in the IJI; Pakistan People's Party (PPP), Benazir BHUTTO; note—in September 1990 the PPP announced the formation of the People's Democratic Alliance (PDA), an electoral alliance including the following four parties—PPP, Solidarity Movement (Tehrik Istiqlal), Movement for the Implementation of Shi'a Jurisprudence (Tehrik-i-Nifaz Fiqh Jafariya or TNFJ), and the PML (Malik faction); Muhajir Qaumi Movement (MQM), Altaf HUSSAIN; Awami National Party (ANP), Khan Abdul Wali KHAN; Jamiat-ul-Ulema-i-Islam (JUI), Fazlur RAHMAN; Jamhoori Watan Party (JWP), Mohammad Akbar Khan BUGTI; Pakistan National Party (PNP), Mir Ghaus Bakhsh BIZENJO; Pakistan Khawa Milli Party (PKMP), leader NA; Assembly of Pakistani Clergy (Jamiat-ul-Ulema-e-Pakistan or JUP), Maulana Shah Ahmed NOORANI; Jamaat-i-Islami (JI), Qazi Hussain AHMED

Suffrage: universal at age 21

Elections:

President—last held on 12 December 1988 (next to be held December 1993); results—Ghulam Ishaq KHAN was elected by Parliament and the four provincial assemblies;

Senate—last held March 1991 (next to be held March 1994); results—elected by provincial assemblies; seats—(87 total) IJI 57, Tribal Area Representatives (nonparty) 8, PPP 5, ANP 5, JWP 4, MQM 3, PNP 2, PKMP 1, JUI 1, independent 1;

National Assembly—last held on 24 October 1990 (next to be held by October 1995); results—percent of vote by party NA; seats—(217 total) IJI 107, PDA 45, MQM 15, ANP 6, JUI 6, JWP 2, PNP 2, PKMP 1, independent 14, religious minorities 10, Tribal Area Representatives (nonparty) 8, vacant 1

Communists: the Communist party is officially banned but is allowed to operate openly

Other political or pressure groups: military remains dominant political force; ulema (clergy), industrialists, and small merchants also influential

Member of: AsDB, C, CCC, CP, ESCAP, FAO, G-19, G-24, G-77, GATT, IAEA, IBRD, ICAO, ICC, ICFTU, IDA, IDB, IFAD, IFC, ILO, IMF, IMO, INMARSAT, INTELSAT, INTERPOL, IOC, ISO, ITU, LORCS, NAM, OAS (observer), OIC, PCA, SAARC, UN, UNCTAD, UNESCO, UNHCR, UNIDO, UPU, WCL, WFTU, WHO, WIPO, WMO, WTO

Diplomatic representation: Ambassador Najmuddin SHAIKH; Chancery at 2315 Massachusetts Avenue NW, Washington DC 20008; telephone (202) 939-6200; there is a Pakistani Consulate General in New York;

US—Ambassador Robert B. OAKLEY; Embassy at Diplomatic Enclave, Ramna 5, Islāmābād (mailing address is P. O. Box 1048, Islāmābād or APO New York 09614); telephone [92] (51) 826161 through 79; there are US Consulates General in Karachi and Lahore, and a Consulate in Peshāwar

Flag: green with a vertical white band on the hoist side; a large white crescent and star are centered in the green field; the crescent, star, and color green are traditional symbols of Islam

---

Economy

Overview: Pakistan is a poor Third World country faced with the usual problems of rapidly increasing population, sizable government deficits, and heavy dependence on foreign aid. In addition, the economy must support a large military establishment and provide for the needs of 4 million Afghan refugees. A real economic growth rate averaging 5-6% in recent years has enabled the country to cope with these problems. Almost all agriculture and small-scale industry is in private hands, and the government seeks to privatize a portion of the large-scale industrial enterprises now publicly owned. In December 1988, Pakistan signed a three-year economic reform agreement with the IMF, which provides for a reduction in the government deficit and a liberalization of trade in return for further IMF financial support. Late in 1990, the IMF suspended assistance to Pakistan because the government failed to follow through on deficit reforms. Pakistan almost certainly will make little headway on raising living standards for its rapidly expanding population; at the current rate of growth, population would double in 29 years.

GNP: $43.3 billion, per capita $380; real growth rate 5.0% (FY90 est.)

Inflation rate (consumer prices): 9.8% (FY90 est.)

Unemployment rate: 10% (FY91 est.)

Budget: revenues $5.6 billion; expenditures $8.3 billion, including capital expenditures of $2.7 billion (FY91 est.)

Exports: $4.8 billion (f.o.b., FY90); *commodities*—rice, cotton, textiles, clothing; *partners*—EC 31%, Japan 11.6%, US 11.5% (FY89)

Imports: $6.5 billion (f.o.b., FY90); *commodities*—petroleum, petroleum products, machinery, transportation equipment, vegetable oils, animal fats, chemicals; *partners*—EC 26%, US 16%, Japan 14% (FY89)

External debt: $20.1 billion (1990 est.)

Industrial production: growth rate 7.5% (FY91 est.); accounts for almost 20% of GNP

Electricity: 7,575,000 kW capacity; 29,300 million kWh produced, 270 kWh per capita (1989)

Industries: textiles, food processing, beverages, petroleum products, construction materials, clothing, paper products, international finance, shrimp

Agriculture: 25% of GDP, over 50% of labor force; world's largest contiguous irrigation system; major crops—cotton, wheat, rice, sugarcane, fruits, and vegetables; livestock products—milk, beef, mutton, eggs; self-sufficient in food grain

Illicit drugs: illicit producer of opium poppy and cannabis for the international drug trade; government eradication efforts on poppy cultivation of limited success

Economic aid: (including Bangladesh before 1972) US commitments, including Ex-Im (FY70-89), $4.5 billion authorized (excluding what is now Bangladesh); Western (non-US) countries, ODA and OOF bilateral commitments (1980-88), $8.2 billion; OPEC bilateral aid (1979-89), $2.3 billion; Communist countries (1970-89), $3.2 billion

Currency: Pakistani rupee (plural—rupees); 1 Pakistani rupee (PRe) = 100 paisa

Exchange rates: Pakistani rupees (PRs) per US$1—22.072 (January 1991), 21.707 (1990), 20.541 (1989), 18.003 (1988), 17.399 (1987), 16.648 (1986), 15.928 (1985)

Fiscal year: 1 July-30 June

Communications

Railroads: 8,773 km total; 7,718 km broad gauge, 445 km meter gauge, and 610 km narrow gauge; 1,037 km broad-gauge double track; 286 km electrified; all government owned (1985)

Highways: 101,315 km total (1987); 40,155 km paved, 23,000 km gravel, 29,000 km improved earth, and 9,160 km unimproved earth or sand tracks (1985)

Pipelines: 250 km crude oil; 4,044 km natural gas; 885 km refined products (1987)

Ports: Gwadar, Karachi, Port Muhammad bin Qasim

Merchant marine: 29 ships (1,000 GRT or over) totaling 339,855 GRT/500,627 DWT; includes 4 passenger-cargo, 24 cargo, 1 petroleum, oils, and lubricants (POL) tanker

Civil air: 30 major transport aircraft

Airports: 115 total, 105 usable; 75 with permanent-surface runways; 1 with runways over 3,659 m; 31 with runways 2,440-3,659 m; 43 with runways 1,220-2,439 m

Telecommunications: good international radiocommunication service over microwave and INTELSAT satellite; domestic radio communications poor; broadcast service good; 813,000 telephones (1990); stations—19 AM, 8 FM, 29 TV; earth stations—1 Atlantic Ocean INTELSAT and 2 Indian Ocean INTELSAT

Defense Forces

Branches: Army, Navy, Air Force, Civil Armed Forces, National Guard

Manpower availability: males 15-49, 26,840,840; 16,466,334 fit for military service; 1,322,883 reach military age (17) annually

Defense expenditures: $2.9 billion, 6% of GNP (FY91)

Palmyra Atoll
(territory of the US)

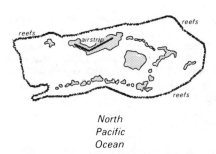

2 km

reefs
reefs
airstrip
reefs

North
Pacific
Ocean

Communications

Ports: none; offshore anchorage in West Lagoon
Airports: 1 with permanent-surface runway 1,220-2,439 m

Defense Forces

Note: defense is the responsibility of the US

Geography

Total area: 11.9 km²; land area: 11.9 km²
Comparative area: about 20 times the size of The Mall in Washington, DC
Land boundaries: none
Coastline: 14.5 km
Maritime claims:
Contiguous zone: 12 nm;
Continental shelf: 200 m (depth);
Exclusive economic zone: 200 nm;
Territorial sea: 12 nm
Climate: equatorial, hot, and very rainy
Terrain: low, with maximum elevations of about 2 meters
Natural resources: none
Land use: arable land 0%; permanent crops 0%; meadows and pastures 0%; forest and woodland 100%; other 0%
Environment: about 50 islets covered with dense vegetation, coconut trees, and balsa-like trees up to 30 meters tall
Note: located 1,600 km south-southwest of Honolulu in the North Pacific Ocean, almost halfway between Hawaii and American Samoa

People

Population: uninhabited

Government

Long-form name: none
Type: unincorporated territory of the US; privately owned, but administered by the Office of Territorial and International Affairs, US Department of the Interior

Economy

Overview: no economic activity

Panama

150 km

Caribbean Sea

Bocas del Toro
Colón
Panama Canal
PANAMA
David
Santiago
Gulf of Panama
La Palma
Chitré

North Pacific Ocean

Geography

Total area: 78,200 km²; land area: 75,990 km²
Comparative area: slightly smaller than South Carolina
Land boundaries: 555 km total; Colombia 225 km, Costa Rica 330 km
Coastline: 2,490 km
Maritime claims:
Territorial sea: 200 nm
Climate: tropical; hot, humid, cloudy; prolonged rainy season (May to January), short dry season (January to May)
Terrain: interior mostly steep, rugged mountains and dissected, upland plains; coastal areas largely plains and rolling hills
Natural resources: copper, mahogany forests, shrimp
Land use: arable land 6%; permanent crops 2%; meadows and pastures 15%; forest and woodland 54%; other 23%; includes irrigated NEGL%
Environment: dense tropical forest in east and northwest
Note: strategic location on eastern end of isthmus forming land bridge connecting North and South America; controls Panama Canal that links North Atlantic Ocean via Caribbean Sea with North Pacific Ocean

People

Population: 2,476,281 (July 1991), growth rate 2.1% (1991)
Birth rate: 26 births/1,000 population (1991)
Death rate: 5 deaths/1,000 population (1991)
Net migration rate: NEGL migrants/1,000 population (1991)
Infant mortality rate: 21 deaths/1,000 live births (1991)
Life expectancy at birth: 72 years male, 76 years female (1991)
Total fertility rate: 3.0 children born/woman (1991)

Nationality: noun—Panamanian(s); adjective—Panamanian

Ethnic divisions: mestizo (mixed Indian and European ancestry) 70%, West Indian 14%, white 10%, Indian 6%

Religion: Roman Catholic over 93%, Protestant 6%

Language: Spanish (official); English as native tongue 14%; many Panamanians bilingual

Literacy: 88% (male 88%, female 88%) age 15 and over can read and write (1990 est.)

Labor force: 770,472 (1987); government and community services 27.9%; agriculture, hunting, and fishing 26.2%; commerce, restaurants, and hotels 16%; manufacturing and mining 10.5%; construction 5.3%; transportation and communications 5.3%; finance, insurance, and real estate 4.2%; Canal Zone 2.4%; shortage of skilled labor, but an oversupply of unskilled labor

Organized labor: 17% of labor force (1986)

Government

Long-form name: Republic of Panama

Type: centralized republic

Capital: Panama

Administrative divisions: 9 provinces (provincias, singular—provincia) and 1 territory* (comarca); Bocas del Toro, Chiriquí, Coclé, Colón, Darién, Herrera, Los Santos, Panamá, San Blas*, Veraguas

Independence: 3 November 1903 (from Colombia; became independent from Spain 28 November 1821)

Constitution: 11 October 1972; major reforms adopted April 1983

Legal system: based on civil law system; judicial review of legislative acts in the Supreme Court of Justice; accepts compulsory ICJ jurisdiction, with reservations

National holiday: Independence Day, 3 November (1903)

Executive branch: president, two vice presidents, Cabinet

Legislative branch: unicameral Legislative Assembly (Asamblea Legislativa)

Judicial branch: Supreme Court of Justice (Corte Suprema de Justicia) currently being reorganized

Leaders:

Chief of State and Head of Government—President Guillermo ENDARA (since 20 December 1989, elected 7 May 1989); First Vice President Ricardo ARIAS Calderón (since 20 December 1989, elected 7 May 1989); Second Vice President Guillermo FORD (since 20 December 1989, elected 7 May 1989)

Political parties and leaders:

government alliance—Nationalist Republican Liberal Movement (MOLIRENA), Alfredo RAMIREZ; Authentic Liberal Party (PLA); Arnulfista Party (PA), Francisco ARTOLA;

opposition parties—Christian Democratic Party (PDC), Ricardo ARIAS Calderón; Democratic Revolutionary Party (PRD, ex-official government party), Gerardo GONZALEZ; Agrarian Labor Party (PALA), Carlos ELETA Almaran; Liberal Party (PL); People's Party (PdP, Soviet-oriented Communist party), Rubén DARIO Sousa Batista; Democratic Workers Party (PDT, leftist), Eduardo RIOS; National Action Party (PAN, rightist); Popular Action Party (PAPO), Carlos Iván ZUÑIGA; Socialist Workers Party (PST, leftist), José CAMBRA; Revolutionary Workers Party (PRT, leftist), Graciela DIXON

Suffrage: universal and compulsory at age 18

Elections:

President—last held on 7 May 1989, annulled but later upheld (next to be held May 1994); results—anti-NORIEGA coalition believed to have won about 75% of the total votes cast;

Legislative Assembly—last held on 27 January 1991 (next to be held May 1994); results—percent of vote by party NA; seats—(67 total) *progovernment parties*—PDC 28, MOLIRENA 16, PA 6, PLA 5; *opposition parties*—PRD 10, PALA 1, PL 1; note—the PDC went into opposition after President Guillermo ENDARA ousted the PDC from the coalition government in April 1991

Communists: People's Party (PdP), pro-Soviet mainline Communist party, did not obtain the necessary 3% of the total vote in the 1984 election to retain its legal status; about 3,000 members

Other political or pressure groups: National Council of Organized Workers (CONATO); National Council of Private Enterprise (CONEP); Panamanian Association of Business Executives (APEDE); National Civic Crusade; National Committee for the Right to Life

Member of: AG (associate), CG, ECLAC, FAO, G-77, IADB, IAEA, IBRD, ICAO, ICFTU, IDA, IFAD, IFC, ILO, IMF, IMO, INMARSAT, INTELSAT, INTERPOL, IOC, IOM, ITU, LAES, LAIA (observer), LORCS, NAM, OAS, OPANAL, PCA, UN, UNCTAD, UNESCO, UNIDO, UPU, WCL, WFTU, WHO, WIPO, WMO, WTO

Diplomatic representation: Ambassador Jaime FORD; Chancery at 2862 McGill Terrace NW, Washington DC 20008; telephone (202) 483-1407; the status of the Consulates General and Consulates has not yet been determined;

US—Ambassador Deane R. HINTON; Embassy at Avenida Balboa and Calle 38, Apartado 6959, Panama City 5 (mailing address is Box E, APO Miami 34002); telephone [507] 27-1777

Flag: divided into four, equal rectangles; the top quadrants are white with a blue five-pointed star in the center (hoist side) and plain red, the bottom quadrants are plain blue (hoist side) and white with a red five-pointed star in the center

Economy

Overview: GDP expanded by an estimated 5% in 1990, after contracting 1% in 1988 and 14% in 1989. Political stability prompted greater business confidence and consumer demand, leading to increased production by the agricultural, commercial, manufacturing, construction, and utilities sectors. The transportation sector and government services declined slightly due to slack early-1990 transits through the Panama Canal, lower oil pipeline flowthrough, and Panama City's budget cuts. Imports and exports posted gains during the year, and government revenues were up sharply over 1989's levels.

GDP: $4.8 billion, per capita $1,980; real growth rate 5% (1990 est.)

Inflation rate (consumer prices): 1.3% (1990 est.)

Unemployment rate: 20% (1990)

Budget: revenues $1.7 billion; expenditures $1.8 billion, including capital expenditures of $70 million (1990 est.)

Exports: $355 million (f.o.b., 1990 est.); *commodities*—bananas 27%, shrimp 21%, clothing 6%, coffee 4%, sugar 4%; *partners*—US 90%, Central America and Caribbean, EC (1989 est.)

Imports: $1,250 million (f.o.b., 1990); *commodities*—foodstuffs 13%, capital goods 12%, crude oil 12%, consumer goods, chemicals; *partners*—US 35%, Central America and Caribbean, EC, Mexico, Venezuela (1989 est.)

External debt: $5 billion (December 1990 est.)

Industrial production: growth rate 4.8% (1990 est.)

Electricity: 1,113,000 kW capacity; 3,264 million kWh produced, 1,350 kWh per capita (1990)

Industries: manufacturing and construction activities, petroleum refining, brewing, cement and other construction material, sugar mills, paper products

Agriculture: accounts for 12% of GDP (1990 est.), 25% of labor force (1989); crops—bananas, rice, corn, coffee, sugarcane; livestock; fishing; importer of food grain, vegetables, milk products

Economic aid: US commitments, including Ex-Im (FY70-89), $516 million; Western (non-US) countries, ODA and OOF bilateral commitments (1970-88), $575 million; Communist countries (1970-89), $4 million

Panama (continued)

Currency: balboa (plural—balboas); 1 balboa (B) = 100 centésimos
Exchange rates: balboas (B) per US$1—1.000 (fixed rate)
Fiscal year: calendar year

Communications

Railroads: 238 km total; 78 km 1.524-meter gauge, 160 km 0.914-meter gauge
Highways: 8,530 km total; 2,745 km paved, 3,270 km gravel or crushed stone, 2,515 km improved and unimproved earth
Inland waterways: 800 km navigable by shallow draft vessels; 82 km Panama Canal
Pipelines: crude oil, 130 km
Ports: Cristobal, Balboa, Puerto de La Bahía de Las Minas
Merchant marine: 2,932 ships (1,000 GRT or over) totaling 41,314,623 GRT/66,226,104 DWT; includes 22 passenger, 22 short-sea passenger, 5 passenger-cargo, 1,060 cargo, 188 refrigerated cargo, 165 container, 62 roll-on/roll-off cargo, 105 vehicle carrier, 8 livestock carrier, 5 multifunction large-load carrier, 301 petroleum, oils, and lubricants (POL) tanker, 175 chemical tanker, 27 combination ore/oil, 91 liquefied gas, 8 specialized tanker, 651 bulk, 37 combination bulk; note—all but 5 are foreign owned and operated; the top 4 foreign owners are Japan 36%, Greece 9%, Hong Kong 9%, and the US 8%; (China owns at least 127 ships, Vietnam 10, Yugoslavia 10, Cuba 5, Cyprus 3, and USSR 2)
Civil air: 16 major transport aircraft
Airports: 113 total, 101 usable; 41 with permanent-surface runways; none with runways over 3,659 m; 2 with runways 2,440-3,659 m; 15 with runways 1,220-2,439 m
Telecommunications: domestic and international facilities well developed; connection into Central American Microwave System; 2 Atlantic Ocean satellite antennas; 220,000 telephones; stations—91 AM, no FM, 23 TV; 1 coaxial submarine cable

Defense Forces

Branches: note—the Panamanian Defense Forces (PDF) ceased to exist as a military institution shortly after the United States invaded Panama on 20 December 1989; President Endara is attempting to restructure the forces into a civilian police service under the new name of Panamanian Public Forces (PPF); a Council of Public Security and National Defense under Menalco Solis in the office of the president coordinates the activities of the security forces; the Institutional Protection Service under Carlos Bares is attached to the presidency
Manpower availability: males 15-49, 644,895; 444,522 fit for military service; no conscription
Defense expenditures: $75.5 million, 1.5% of GDP (1990)

Papua New Guinea

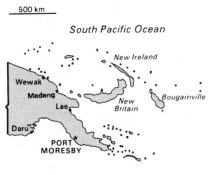

Geography

Total area: 461,690 km²; land area: 451,710 km²
Comparative area: slightly larger than California
Land boundary: 820 km with Indonesia
Coastline: 5,152 km
Maritime claims: (measured from claimed archipelagic baselines);
Continental shelf: 200 m (depth) or to depth of exploitation;
Exclusive economic zone: 200 nm;
Territorial sea: 12 nm
Climate: tropical; northwest monsoon (December to March), southeast monsoon (May to October); slight seasonal temperature variation
Terrain: mostly mountains with coastal lowlands and rolling foothills
Natural resources: gold, copper, silver, natural gas, timber, oil potential
Land use: arable land NEGL%; permanent crops 1%; meadows and pastures NEGL%; forest and woodland 71%; other 28%
Environment: one of world's largest swamps along southwest coast; some active volcanos; frequent earthquakes
Note: shares island of New Guinea with Indonesia

People

Population: 3,913,186 (July 1991), growth rate 2.3% (1991)
Birth rate: 34 births/1,000 population (1991)
Death rate: 11 deaths/1,000 population (1991)
Net migration rate: 0 migrants/1,000 population (1991)
Infant mortality rate: 66 deaths/1,000 live births (1991)
Life expectancy at birth: 55 years male, 56 years female (1991)
Total fertility rate: 4.9 children born/woman (1991)

Nationality: noun—Papua New Guinean(s); adjective—Papua New Guinean
Ethnic divisions: predominantly Melanesian and Papuan; some Negrito, Micronesian, and Polynesian
Religion: Roman Catholic 22%, Lutheran 16%, Presbyterian/Methodist/London Missionary Society 8%, Anglican 5%, Evangelical Alliance 4%, Seventh-Day Adventist 1%, other Protestant sects 10%; indigenous beliefs 34%
Language: 715 indigenous languages; English spoken by 1-2%, pidgin English widespread, Motu spoken in Papua region
Literacy: 52% (male 65%, female 38%) age 15 and over can read and write (1990 est.)
Labor force: 1,660,000; 732,806 in salaried employment; agriculture 54%, government 25%, industry and commerce 9%, services 8% (1980)
Organized labor: more than 50 trade unions, some with fewer than 20 members

Government

Long-form name: Independent State of Papua New Guinea
Type: parliamentary democracy
Capital: Port Moresby
Administrative divisions: 20 provinces; Central, Chimbu, Eastern Highlands, East New Britain, East Sepik, Enga, Gulf, Madang, Manus, Milne Bay, Morobe, National Capital, New Ireland, Northern, North Solomons, Sandaun, Southern Highlands, Western, Western Highlands, West New Britain
Independence: 16 September 1975 (from UN trusteeship under Australian administration)
Constitution: 16 September 1975
Legal system: based on English common law
National holiday: Independence Day, 16 September (1975)
Executive branch: British monarch, governor general, prime minister, deputy prime minister, National Executive Council (cabinet)
Legislative branch: unicameral National Parliament (sometimes referred to as the House of Assembly)
Judicial branch: Supreme Court
Leaders:
Chief of State—Queen Elizabeth II (since 6 February 1952), represented by Governor General Vincent ERI (since 18 January 1990);
Head of Government—Prime Minister Rabbie NAMALIU (since 4 July 1988); Deputy Prime Minister Ted DIRO (since 29 April 1990); note—Deputy Prime Minister Ted DIRO has the title only since he has been suspended pending trial for alleged corruption charges
Political parties: Papua New Guinea United Party (Pangu Party), Rabbie NAMALIU;

People's Progress Party (PPP), Sir Julius CHAN; United Party (UP), Paul TORATO; Papua Party (PP), Galeva KWARARA; National Party (NP), Paul PORA; Melanesian Alliance (MA), Fr. John MOMIS
Suffrage: universal at age 18
Elections:
National Parliament—last held 13 June-4 July 1987 (next to be held 4 July 1992); results—PP 14.7%, PDM 10.8%, PPP 6.1%, MA 5.6%, NP 5.1%, PAP 3.2%, independents 42.9%, other 11.6%; seats—(109 total) PP 26, PDM 17, NP 12, MA 7, PAP 6, PPP 5, independents 22, other 14
Communists: no significant strength
Member of: ACP, AsDB, ASEAN (observer), C, CP, ESCAP, FAO, G-77, IBRD, ICAO, ICFTU, IDA, IFAD, IFC, ILO, IMF, IMO, INTELSAT, INTERPOL, IOC, ISO, ITU, LORCS, NAM (observer), SPC, SPF, UN, UNCTAD, UNESCO, UNIDO, UPU, WHO, WMO
Diplomatic representation: Ambassador Margaret TAYLOR; Chancery at Suite 350, 1330 Connecticut Avenue NW, Washington DC 20036; telephone (202) 659-0856; *US*—Ambassador Robert W. FERRAND; Embassy at Armit Street, Port Moresby (mailing address is P. O. Box 1492, Port Moresby); telephone [675] 211-455 or 594, 654
Flag: divided diagonally from upper hoist-side corner; the upper triangle is red with a soaring yellow bird of paradise centered; the lower triangle is black with five white five-pointed stars of the Southern Cross constellation centered

---

Economy

Overview: Papua New Guinea is richly endowed with natural resources, but exploitation has been hampered by the rugged terrain and the high cost of developing an infrastructure. Agriculture provides a subsistence livelihood for 85% of the population. Mining of numerous deposits, including copper and gold, accounts for about 60% of export earnings. Budgetary support from Australia and development aid under World Bank auspices help sustain the economy.
GDP: $2.7 billion, per capita $725; real growth rate –3.0% (1989 est.)
Inflation rate (consumer prices): 4.5% (1989)
Unemployment rate: 5% (1988)
Budget: revenues $867 million; expenditures $873 million, including capital expenditures of $119 million (1990 est.)
Exports: $1.4 billion (f.o.b., 1989); *commodities*—gold, copper ore, coffee, cocoa, copra, palm oil, timber, lobster; *partners*—FRG, Japan, Australia, UK, Spain, US
Imports: $1.5 billion (c.i.f., 1989);

commodities—machinery and transport equipment, fuels, food, chemicals, consumer goods;
partners—Australia, Singapore, Japan, US, New Zealand, UK
External debt: $2.76 billion (December 1990)
Industrial production: growth rate NA%; accounts for 25% of GDP
Electricity: 397,000 kW capacity; 1,510 million kWh produced, 400 kWh per capita (1990)
Industries: copra crushing, oil palm processing, plywood processing, wood chip production, gold, silver, copper, construction, tourism
Agriculture: one-third of GDP; livelihood for 85% of population; fertile soils and favorable climate permits cultivating a wide variety of crops; cash crops—coffee, cocoa, coconuts, palm kernels; other products—tea, rubber, sweet potatoes, fruit, vegetables, poultry, pork; net importer of food for urban centers
Economic aid: US commitments, including Ex-Im (FY70-89), $40.6 million; Western (non-US) countries, ODA and OOF bilateral commitments (1970-88), $6.4 billion; OPEC bilateral aid (1979-89), $17 million
Currency: kina (plural—kina); 1 kina (K) = 100 toea
Exchange rates: kina (K) per US$1—1.0549 (January 1991), 1.0467 (1990), 1.1685 (1989), 1.1538 (1988), 1.1012 (1987), 1.0296 (1986), 1.0000 (1985)
Fiscal year: calendar year

Communications

Highways: 19,200 km total; 640 km paved, 10,960 km gravel, crushed stone, or stabilized-soil surface, 7,600 km unimproved earth
Inland waterways: 10,940 km
Ports: Anewa Bay, Lae, Madang, Port Moresby, Rabaul
Merchant marine: 9 ships (1,000 GRT or over) totaling 26,711 GRT/34,682 DWT; includes 5 cargo, 1 roll-on/roll-off cargo, 1 combination ore/oil, 2 bulk
Civil air: about 15 major transport aircraft
Airports: 567 total, 479 usable; 19 with permanent-surface runways; none with runways over 3,659 m; 1 with runways 2,440-3,659 m; 40 with runways 1,220-2,439 m
Telecommunications: services are adequate and being improved; facilities provide radiobroadcast, radiotelephone and telegraph, coastal radio, aeronautical radio, and international radiocommunication services; submarine cables extend to Australia and Guam; 51,700 telephones (1985); stations—31 AM, 2 FM, 2 TV (1987); 1 Pacific Ocean INTELSAT earth station

---

Defense Forces

Branches: Papua New Guinea Defense Force (including Army, Navy, Air Force)
Manpower availability: males 15-49, 983,175; 546,824 fit for military service
Defense expenditures: $42 million, 1.3% of GDP (1989 est.)

Paracel Islands

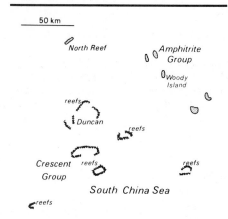

Geography

Total area: undetermined
Comparative area: undetermined
Land boundaries: none
Coastline: 518 km
Maritime claims: undetermined
Disputes: occupied by China, but claimed by Taiwan and Vietnam
Climate: tropical
Terrain: undetermined
Natural resources: none
Land use: arable land 0%; permanent crops 0%; meadows and pastures 0%; forest and woodland 0%; other 100%
Environment: subject to typhoons
Note: located 400 km east of Vietnam in the South China Sea about one-third of the way between Vietnam and the Philippines

People

Population: no permanent inhabitants

Government

Long-form name: none

Economy

Overview: no economic activity

Communications

Ports: small Chinese port facilities on Woody Island and Duncan Island currently under expansion
Airports: 1 on Woody Island

Defense Forces

Note: occupied by China

Paraguay

Boundary representation is not necessarily authoritative.

Geography

Total area: 406,750 km²; land area: 397,300 km²
Comparative area: slightly smaller than California
Land boundaries: 3,920 km total; Argentina 1,880 km, Bolivia 750 km, Brazil 1,290 km
Coastline: none—landlocked
Maritime claims: none—landlocked
Disputes: short section of the boundary with Brazil (just west of Guaíra Falls on the Rio Paraná) has not been determined
Climate: varies from temperate in east to semiarid in far west
Terrain: grassy plains and wooded hills east of Río Paraguay; Gran Chaco region west of Río Paraguay mostly low, marshy plain near the river, and dry forest and thorny scrub elsewhere
Natural resources: iron ore, manganese, limestone, hydropower, timber
Land use: arable land 20%; permanent crops 1%; meadows and pastures 39%; forest and woodland 35%; other 5%; includes irrigated NEGL%
Environment: local flooding in southeast (early September to June); poorly drained plains may become boggy (early October to June)
Note: landlocked; buffer between Argentina and Brazil

People

Population: 4,798,739 (July 1991), growth rate 2.9% (1991)
Birth rate: 35 births/1,000 population (1991)
Death rate: 6 deaths/1,000 population (1991)
Net migration rate: 0 migrants/1,000 population (1991)
Infant mortality rate: 47 deaths/1,000 live births (1991)
Life expectancy at birth: 67 years male, 72 years female (1991)

Total fertility rate: 4.7 children born/woman (1991)
Nationality: noun—Paraguayan(s); adjective—Paraguayan
Ethnic divisions: mestizo (Spanish and Indian) 95%, white and Indian 5%
Religion: Roman Catholic 90%; Mennonite and other Protestant denominations
Language: Spanish (official) and Guarani
Literacy: 90% (male 92%, female 88%) age 15 and over can read and write (1990 est.)
Labor force: 1,300,000; agriculture 44%, industry and commerce 34%, services 18%, government 4% (1986)
Organized labor: about 2% of labor force

Government

Long-form name: Republic of Paraguay
Type: republic
Capital: Asunción
Administrative divisions: 19 departments (departamentos, singular—departamento); Alto Paraguay, Alto Paraná, Amambay, Boquerón, Caaguazú, Caazapá, Canindeyú, Central, Chaco, Concepción, Cordillera, Guairá, Itapúa, Misiones, Ñeembucú, Nueva Asunción, Paraguarí, Presidente Hayes, San Pedro
Independence: 14 May 1811 (from Spain)
Constitution 25 August 1967
Legal system: based on Argentine codes, Roman law, and French codes; judicial review of legislative acts in Supreme Court of Justice; does not accept compulsory ICJ jurisdiction
National holiday: Independence Days, 14-15 May (1811)
Executive branch: president, Council of Ministers (cabinet), Council of State
Legislative branch: bicameral Congress (Congreso) consists of an upper chamber or Chamber of Senators (Cámara de Senadores) and a lower chamber or Chamber of Deputies (Cámara de Diputados)
Judicial branch: Supreme Court of Justice (Corte Suprema de Justicia)
Leaders:
Chief of State and Head of Government—President Gen. Andrés RODRÍGUEZ Pedotti (since 15 May 1989)
Political parties and leaders: Colorado Party, Luis María ARGAÑA, acting president; Authentic Radical Liberal Party (PLRA), Juan Manuel BENITEZ Florentin; Christian Democratic Party (PDC), Jorge Dario CRISTALDO; Febrerista Revolutionary Party (PRF), Euclides ACEVEDO; Popular Democratic Party (PDP), Hugo RICHER
Suffrage: universal and compulsory at age 18 and up to age 60
Elections:
President—last held 1 May 1989 (next to be held February 1993); results—Gen. RODRÍGUEZ 75.8%, Domingo LAINO 19.4%;

Chamber of Senators—last held 1 May 1989 (next to be held by May 1993); results—percent of vote by party NA; seats—(36 total) Colorado Party 24, PLRA 10, PLR 1, PRF 1;

Chamber of Deputies—last held on 1 May 1989 (next to be held by May 1994); results—percent of vote by party NA; seats—(72 total) Colorado Party 48, PLRA 19, PRF 2, PDC 1, PL 1, PLR 1

Communists: Oscar Creydt faction and Miguel Angel SOLER faction (both illegal); 3,000 to 4,000 (est.) party members and sympathizers in Paraguay, very few are hard core; party beginning to return from exile is small and deeply divided

Other political or pressure groups: Confederation of Workers (CUT); Roman Catholic Church

Member of: AG (observer), CCC, ECLAC, FAO, G-77, IADB, IAEA, IBRD, ICAO, IDA, IFAD, IFC, ILO, IMF, INTELSAT, INTERPOL, IOC, IOM, ITU, LAES, LAIA, LORCS, OAS, OPANAL, PCA, RG, UN, UNCTAD, UNESCO, UNIDO, UPU, WCL, WHO, WIPO, WMO

Diplomatic representation: Ambassador Marcos MARTINEZ MENDIETA; Chancery at 2400 Massachusetts Avenue NW, Washington DC 20008; telephone (202) 483-6960 through 6962; there are Paraguayan Consulates General in New Orleans and New York, and a Consulate in Houston; *US*—Ambassador Jon GLASSMAN; Embassy at 1776 Avenida Mariscal Lopez, Asunción (mailing address is C. P. 402, Asunción, or APO Miami 34036-0001); telephone [595] (21) 213-715

Flag: three equal, horizontal bands of red (top), white, and blue with an emblem centered in the white band; unusual flag in that the emblem is different on each side; the obverse (hoist side at the left) bears the national coat of arms (a yellow five-pointed star within a green wreath capped by the words *REPUBLICA DEL PARAGUAY*, all within two circles); the reverse (hoist side at the right) bears the seal of the treasury (a yellow lion below a red Cap of Liberty and the words *Paz y Justicia* (Peace and Justice) capped by the words *REPUBLICA DEL PARAGUAY*, all within two circles)

Economy

Overview: The economy is predominantly agricultural. Agriculture, including forestry, accounts for about 25% of GNP, employs about 45% of the labor force, and provides the bulk of exports. Paraguay has no known significant mineral or petroleum resources but does have a large hydropower potential. Since 1981 economic performance has declined compared with the boom period of 1976-81, when real GDP grew at an average annual rate of nearly 11%. During 1982-86

real GDP fell in three of five years, inflation jumped to an annual rate of 32%, and foreign debt rose. Factors responsible for the erratic behavior of the economy were the completion of the Itaipu hydroelectric dam, bad weather for crops, and weak international commodity prices for agricultural exports. In 1987 the economy experienced a minor recovery because of improved weather conditions and stronger international prices for key agricultural exports. The recovery continued through 1990, on the strength of bumper crops in 1988-89. The government, however, must follow through on promises of reforms needed to deal with escalating inflation, large fiscal deficits, growing debt arrearages, and falling reserves.

GDP: $4.6 billion, per capita $1,000; real growth rate 3.5% (1990 est.)

Inflation rate (consumer prices): 44% (1990 est.)

Unemployment rate: 12% (1989 est.)

Budget: revenues $1.2 billion; expenditures $1.2 billion, including capital expenditures of $487 million (1991)

Exports: $980 million (registered f.o.b., 1990 est.);
commodities—cotton, soybean, timber, vegetable oils, coffee, tung oil, meat products;
partners—EC 37%, Brazil 25%, Argentina 10%, Chile 6%, US 6%

Imports: $1.4 billion (registered c.i.f., 1990 est.);
commodities—capital goods 35%, consumer goods 20%, fuels and lubricants 19%, raw materials 16%, foodstuffs, beverages, and tobacco 10%;
partners—Brazil 30%, EC 20%, US 18%, Argentina 8%, Japan 7%

External debt: $1.7 billion (1989 est.)

Industrial production: growth rate 5.9% (1989 est.); accounts for 16% of GDP

Electricity: 5,169,000 kW capacity; 15,144 million kWh produced, 3,250 kWh per capita (1990)

Industries: meat packing, oilseed crushing, milling, brewing, textiles, other light consumer goods, cement, construction

Agriculture: accounts for 25% of GDP and 44% of labor force; cash crops—cotton, sugarcane; other crops—corn, wheat, tobacco, soybeans, cassava, fruits, and vegetables; animal products—beef, pork, eggs, milk; surplus producer of timber; self-sufficient in most foods

Illicit drugs: illicit producer of cannabis for the international drug trade; important transshipment point for Bolivian cocaine headed for the US and Europe

Economic aid: US commitments, including Ex-Im (FY70-89), $172 million; Western (non-US) countries, ODA and OOF bilateral commitments (1970-88), $1.05 billion

Currency: guaraní (plural—guaraníes); 1 guaraní (G) = 100 céntimos

Exchange rates: guaraníes (G) per US$1—1,204.5 (October 1989), 1,056.2 (1989), 550.00 (fixed rate 1986-February 1989), 339.17 (1986), 306.67 (1985)

Fiscal year: calendar year

Communications

Railroads: 970 km total; 440 km 1.435-meter standard gauge, 60 km 1.000-meter gauge, 470 km various narrow gauge (privately owned)

Highways: 21,960 km total; 1,788 km paved, 474 km gravel, and 19,698 km earth

Inland waterways: 3,100 km

Ports: Asuncion

Merchant marine: 14 ships (1,000 GRT or over) totaling 18,743 GRT/22,954 DWT; includes 12 cargo, 2 petroleum, oils, and lubricants (POL) tanker; note—1 naval cargo ship is sometimes used commercially

Civil air: 4 major transport aircraft

Airports: 851 total, 738 usable; 6 with permanent-surface runways; 1 with runways over 3,659 m; 2 with runways 2,440-3,659 m; 60 with runways 1,220-2,439 m

Telecommunications: principal center in Asunción; fair intercity microwave net; 78,300 telephones; stations—40 AM, no FM, 5 TV, 7 shortwave; 1 Atlantic Ocean INTELSAT earth station

Defense Forces

Branches: Army, Navy (including Naval Air and Marines), Air Force

Manpower availability: males 15-49, 1,130,690; 823,136 fit for military service; 51,415 reach military age (17) annually

Defense expenditures: $84 million, 1.4% of GDP (1988 est.)

Peru

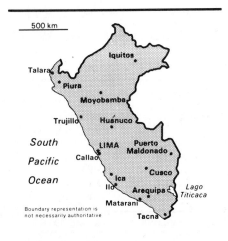

500 km

South Pacific Ocean

Boundary representation is not necessarily authoritative

Geography

Total area: 1,285,220 km²; land area: 1,280,000 km²
Comparative area: slightly smaller than Alaska
Land boundaries: 6,940 km total; Bolivia 900 km, Brazil 1,560 km, Chile 160 km, Colombia 2,900 km, Ecuador 1,420 km
Coastline: 2,414 km
Maritime claims:
Territorial sea: 200 nm
Disputes: two sections of the boundary with Ecuador are in dispute
Climate: varies from tropical in east to dry desert in west
Terrain: western coastal plain (costa), high and rugged Andes in center (sierra), eastern lowland jungle of Amazon Basin (selva)
Natural resources: copper, silver, gold, petroleum, timber, fish, iron ore, coal, phosphate, potash
Land use: arable land 3%; permanent crops NEGL%; meadows and pastures 21%; forest and woodland 55%; other 21%; includes irrigated 1%
Environment: subject to earthquakes, tsunamis, landslides, mild volcanic activity; deforestation; overgrazing; soil erosion; desertification; air pollution in Lima
Note: shares control of Lago Titicaca, world's highest navigable lake, with Bolivia

People

Population: 22,361,785 (July 1991), growth rate 2.0% (1991)
Birth rate: 28 births/1,000 population (1991)
Death rate: 8 deaths/1,000 population (1991)
Net migration rate: 0 migrants/1,000 population (1991)
Infant mortality rate: 66 deaths/1,000 live births (1991)
Life expectancy at birth: 62 years male, 67 years female (1991)

Total fertility rate: 3.5 children born/woman (1991)
Nationality: noun—Peruvian(s); adjective—Peruvian
Ethnic divisions: Indian 45%; mestizo (mixed Indian and European ancestry) 37%; white 15%; black, Japanese, Chinese, and other 3%
Religion: predominantly Roman Catholic
Language: Spanish and Quechua (both official), Aymara
Literacy: 85% (male 92%, female 29%) age 15 and over can read and write (1990 est.)
Labor force: 6,800,000 (1986); government and other services 44%, agriculture 37%, industry 19% (1988 est.)
Organized labor: about 40% of salaried workers (1983 est.)

Government

Long-form name: Republic of Peru
Type: republic
Capital: Lima
Administrative divisions: 24 departments (departamentos, singular—departamento) and 1 constitutional province* (provincia constitucional); Amazonas, Ancash, Apurímac, Arequipa, Ayacucho, Cajamarca, Callao*, Cusco, Huancavelica, Huánuco, Ica, Junín, La Libertad, Lambayeque, Lima, Loreto, Madre de Dios, Moquegua, Pasco, Piura, Puno, San Martín, Tacna, Tumbes, Ucayali; note—the 1979 Constitution and legislation enacted from 1987 to 1990 mandate the creation of regions (regiones, singular—región) intended to function eventually as autonomous economic and administrative entities; so far, 12 regions have been constituted from 23 existing departments—Amazonas (from Loreto), Andrés Avelino Cáceres (from Huánuco, Pasco, Junín), Arequipa (from Arequipa), Chavín (from Ancash), Grau (from Tumbes, Piura), Inca (from Cusco, Madre de Dios, Apurímac), La Libertad (from La Libertad), Los Libertadores-Huari (from Ica, Ayacucho, Huancavelica), Mariategui (from Moquegua, Tacna, Puno), Nor Oriental del Marañon (from Lambayeque, Cajamarca, Amazonas), San Martín (from San Martín), Ucayali (from Ucayali); formation of another region has been delayed by the reluctance of the constitutional province of Callao to merge with the department of Lima; because of inadequate funding from the central government, the regions have yet to assume their reponsibilities and at the moment co-exist with the departmental structure
Independence: 28 July 1821 (from Spain)
Constitution: 28 July 1980 (often referred to as the 1979 Constitution because the Constituent Assembly met in 1979, but the Constitution actually took effect the following year); reestablished civilian government

with a popularly elected president and bicameral legislature
Legal system: based on civil law system; has not accepted compulsory ICJ jurisdiction
National holiday: Independence Day, 28 July (1821)
Executive branch: president, two vice presidents, prime minister, Council of Ministers (cabinet)
Legislative branch: bicameral Congress (Congreso) consists of an upper chamber or Senate (Senado) and a lower chamber or Chamber of Deputies (Cámara de Diputados)
Judicial branch: Supreme Court of Justice (Corte Suprema de Justicia)
Leaders:
Chief of State—President Alberto FUJIMORI (since 28 July 1990); Vice President Maximo SAN ROMAN (since 28 July 1990); Vice President Carlos GARCIA (since 28 July 1990);
Head of Government—Prime Minister Carlos TORRES Y TORRES Lara (since 15 February 1991)
Political parties and leaders: Change 90 (Cambio 90), Alberto FUJIMORI; Democratic Front (FREDEMO), a loosely organized three-party coalition—Popular Christian Party (PPC), Luis BEDOYA Reyes; Popular Action Party (AP), Fernando BELAÚNDE Terry; and Liberty Movement; American Popular Revolutionary Alliance (APRA), Luis ALVA Castro; National Front of Workers and Peasants (FRENATRACA), Roger CÁCERES; United Left (IU), run by committee; Socialist Left (IS), Enrique BERNALES
Suffrage: universal at age 18
Elections:
President—last held on 10 June 1990 (next to be held April 1995); results—Alberto FUJIMORI 56.53%, Mario VARGAS Llosa 33.92%, other 9.55%;
Senate—last held on 8 April 1990 (next to be held April 1995); results—percent of vote by party NA; seats—(60 total) FREDEMO 20, APRA 16, Change 90 14, IU 6, IS 3, FRENATRACA 1;
Chamber of Deputies—last held 8 April 1990 (next to be held April 1995); results—percent of vote by party NA; seats—(180 total) FREDEMO 62, APRA 53, Change 90 32, IU 16, IS 4, FRENATRACA 3, other 10
Communists: Peruvian Communist Party-Unity (PCP-U), pro-Soviet, 2,000; other minor Communist parties
Other political or pressure groups:
leftist guerrilla groups—Shining Path, leader Abimael GUZMÁN; Túpac Amaru Revolutionary Movement, Nestor CERPA and Victor POLLAY
Member of: AG, CCC, ECLAC, FAO, G-11, G-19, G-24, G-77, GATT, IADB, IAEA, IBRD, ICAO, ICFTU, IDA, IFAD, IFC, ILO, IMF, IMO, INMARSAT, INTELSAT,

INTERPOL, IOC, IOM, ISO, ITU, LAES, LAIA, LORCS, NAM, OAS, OPANAL, PCA, RG, UN, UNCTAD, UNESCO, UNIDO, UNIIMOG, UPU, WCL, WFTU, WHO, WIPO, WMO, WTO
Diplomatic representation: Ambassador Roberto G. MACLEAN; Chancery at 1700 Massachusetts Avenue NW, Washington DC 20036; telephone (202) 833-9860 through 9869); Peruvian Consulates General are located in Chicago, Houston, Los Angeles, Miami, New York, Paterson (New Jersey), San Francisco, and San Juan (Puerto Rico);
US—Ambassador Anthony C.E. QUAINTON; Embassy at the corner of Avenida Inca Garcilaso de la Vega and Avenida Espana, Lima (mailing address is P. O. Box 1995, Lima 100, or APO Miami 34031); telephone [51] (14) 338-000
Flag: three equal, vertical bands of red (hoist side), white, and red with the coat of arms centered in the white band; the coat of arms features a shield bearing a llama, cinchona tree (the source of quinine), and a yellow cornucopia spilling out gold coins, all framed by a green wreath

Economy

Overview: The Peruvian economy is basically capitalistic, with a large dose of government welfare programs and government management of credit. In the 1980s the economy suffered from hyperinflation, declining per capita output, and mounting external debt. Peru was shut off from IMF and World Bank support in the mid-1980s because of its huge debt arrears. An austerity program implemented shortly after the Fujimori government took office in July 1990 contributed to a third consecutive yearly contraction of economic activity, but was able to generate a small recovery in the last quarter. After a burst of inflation as the program eliminated government price subsidies, monthly price increases eased to the single-digit level for the first time since mid-1988. Lima has restarted current payments to multilateral lenders and, although it faces $14 billion in arrears on its external debt, is working toward an accommodation with its creditors.
GDP: $19.3 billion, per capita $898; real growth rate −3.9% (1990 est.)
Inflation rate (consumer prices): 7,650% (1990)
Unemployment rate: 20.0%; underemployment estimated at 60% (1989)
Budget: revenues $1.3 billion; expenditures $2.1 billion, including capital expenditures of $NA (1990 est.)
Exports: $3.01 billion (f.o.b., 1990 est.); *commodities*—fishmeal, cotton, sugar, coffee, copper, iron ore, refined silver, lead, zinc, crude petroleum and byproducts;

partners—EC 22%, US 20%, Japan 11%, Latin America 8%, USSR 4%
Imports: $2.78 billion (f.o.b., 1990 est.); *commodities*—foodstuffs, machinery, transport equipment, iron and steel semimanufactures, chemicals, pharmaceuticals; *partners*—US 23%, Latin America 16%, EC 12%, Japan 7%, Switzerland 3%
External debt: $20.0 billion (December 1990)
Industrial production: growth rate −21% (1989); accounts for almost 25% of GDP
Electricity: 4,867,000 kW capacity; 15,540 million kWh produced, 710 kWh per capita (1990)
Industries: mining of metals, petroleum, fishing, textiles, clothing, food processing, cement, auto assembly, steel, shipbuilding, metal fabrication
Agriculture: accounts for 12% of GDP, 37% of labor force; commercial crops—coffee, cotton, sugarcane; other crops—rice, wheat, potatoes, plantains, coca; animal products—poultry, red meats, dairy, wool; not self-sufficient in grain or vegetable oil; fish catch of 4.6 million metric tons (1987), world's fifth-largest
Illicit drugs: world's largest coca leaf producer with about 121,000 hectares under cultivation; source of supply for most of the world's coca paste and cocaine base; about 85% of cultivation is for illicit production; most of cocaine base is shipped to Colombian drug dealers for processing into cocaine for the international drug market
Economic aid: US commitments, including Ex-Im (FY70-89), $1.7 billion; Western (non-US) countries, ODA and OOF bilateral commitments (1970-88), $3.95 billion; Communist countries (1970-89), $577 million
Currency: inti (plural—intis); 1 inti (I/) = 1,000 soles
Exchange rates: intis (I/) per US$1— 530,000 (January 1991), 187,886 (1990), 2,666 (1989), 128.83 (1988), 16.84 (1987), 13.95 (1986), 10.97 (1985)
Fiscal year: calendar year

Communications

Railroads: 1,884 km total; 1,584 km 1.435-meter standard gauge, 300 km 0.914-meter gauge
Highways: 56,645 km total; 6,030 km paved, 11,865 km gravel, 14,610 km improved earth, 24,140 km unimproved earth
Inland waterways: 8,600 km of navigable tributaries of Amazon system and 208 km Lago Titicaca
Pipelines: crude oil, 800 km; natural gas and natural gas liquids, 64 km
Ports: Callao, Ilo, Iquitos, Matarani, Talara
Merchant marine: 29 ships (1,000 GRT or over) totaling 321,541 GRT/516,859 DWT; includes 16 cargo, 1 refrigerated cargo,

1 roll-on/roll-off cargo, 3 petroleum, oils, and lubricants (POL) tanker, 8 bulk; note—in addition, 8 naval tankers and 1 naval cargo are sometimes used commercially
Civil air: 27 major transport aircraft
Airports: 222 total, 205 usable; 36 with permanent-surface runways; 2 with runways over 3,659 m; 24 with runways 2,440-3,659 m; 42 with runways 1,220-2,439 m
Telecommunications: fairly adequate for most requirements; nationwide radio relay system; 544,000 telephones; stations—273 AM, no FM, 140 TV, 144 shortwave; 2 Atlantic Ocean INTELSAT earth stations, 12 domestic antennas

Defense Forces

Branches: Army (Ejercito Peruano), Navy (Marina de Guerra del Peru), Air Force (Fuerza Aerea del Peru), Peruvian National Police
Manpower availability: males 15-49, 5,704,684; 3,859,123 fit for military service; 241,792 reach military age (20) annually
Defense expenditures: $430 million, 2.4% of GDP (1991)

Philippines

Geography

Total area: 300,000 km²; land area: 298,170 km²
Comparative area: slightly larger than Arizona
Land boundaries: none
Coastline: 36,289 km
Maritime claims: (measured from claimed archipelagic baselines);
Continental shelf: to depth of exploitation;
Exclusive economic zone: 200 nm;
Territorial sea: irregular polygon extending up to 100 nm from coastline as defined by 1898 treaty; since late 1970s has also claimed polygonal-shaped area in South China Sea up to 285 nm in breadth
Disputes: involved in a complex dispute over the Spratly Islands with China, Malaysia, Taiwan, and Vietnam; claims Malaysian state of Sabah
Climate: tropical marine; northeast monsoon (November to April); southwest monsoon (May to October)
Terrain: mostly mountains with narrow to extensive coastal lowlands
Natural resources: timber, crude oil, nickel, cobalt, silver, gold, salt, copper
Land use: arable land 26%; permanent crops 11%; meadows and pastures 4%; forest and woodland 40%; other 19%; includes irrigated 5%
Environment: astride typhoon belt, usually affected by 15 and struck by five to six cyclonic storms per year; subject to landslides, active volcanoes, destructive earthquakes, tsunami; deforestation; soil erosion; water pollution

People

Population: 65,758,788 (July 1991), growth rate 2.1% (1991)
Birth rate: 29 births/1,000 population (1991)
Death rate: 7 deaths/1,000 population (1991)

Net migration rate: -1 migrant/1,000 population (1991)
Infant mortality rate: 54 deaths/1,000 live births (1991)
Life expectancy at birth: 62 years male, 67 years female (1991)
Total fertility rate: 3.6 children born/woman (1991)
Nationality: noun—Filipino(s); adjective—Philippine
Ethnic divisions: Christian Malay 91.5%, Muslim Malay 4%, Chinese 1.5%, other 3%
Religion: Roman Catholic 83%, Protestant 9%, Muslim 5%, Buddhist and other 3%
Language: Pilipino (based on Tagalog) and English; both official
Literacy: 90% (male 90%, female 90%) age 15 and over can read and write (1990 est.)
Labor force: 24,120,000; agriculture 46%, industry and commerce 16%, services 18.5%, government 10%, other 9.5% (1989)
Organized labor: 3,945 registered unions; total membership 5.7 million (includes 2.8 million members of the National Congress of Farmers Organizations)

Government

Long-form name: Republic of the Philippines
Type: republic
Capital: Manila
Administrative divisions: 73 provinces and 61 chartered cities*; Abra, Agusan del Norte, Agusan del Sur, Aklan, Albay, Angeles*, Antique, Aurora, Bacolod*, Bago*, Baguio*, Bais*, Basilan, Basilan City*, Bataan, Batanes, Batangas, Batangas City*, Benguet, Bohol, Bukidnon, Bulacan, Butuan*, Cabanatuan*, Cadiz*, Cagayan, Cagayan de Oro*, Calbayog*, Caloocan*, Camarines Norte, Camarines Sur, Camiguin, Canlaon*, Capiz, Catanduanes, Cavite, Cavite City*, Cebu, Cebu City*, Cotabato*, Dagupan*, Danao*, Dapitan*, Davao City* Davao, Davao del Sur, Davao Oriental, Dipolog*, Dumaguete*, Eastern Samar, General Santos*, Gingoog*, Ifugao, Iligan*, Ilocos Norte, Ilocos Sur, Iloilo, Iloilo City*, Iriga*, Isabela, Kalinga-Apayao, La Carlota*, Laguna, Lanao del Norte, Lanao del Sur, Laoag*, Lapu-Lapu*, La Union, Legaspi*, Leyte, Lipa*, Lucena*, Maguindanao, Mandaue*, Manila*, Marawi*, Marinduque, Masbate, Mindoro Occidental, Mindoro Oriental, Misamis Occidental, Misamis Oriental, Mountain, Naga*, Negros Occidental, Negros Oriental, North Cotabato, Northern Samar, Nueva Ecija, Nueva Vizcaya, Olongapo*, Ormoc*, Oroquieta*, Ozamis*, Pagadian*, Palawan, Palayan*, Pampanga, Pangasinan, Pasay*, Puerto Princesa*, Quezon, Quezon City*, Quirino, Rizal, Romblon, Roxas*, Samar, San Carlos* (in Negros Occidental), San Carlos* (in Pangasinan), San Jose*, San Pablo*, Silay*,

Siquijor, Sorsogon, South Cotabato, Southern Leyte, Sultan Kudarat, Sulu, Surigao*, Surigao del Norte, Surigao del Sur, Tacloban*, Tagaytay*, Tagbilaran*, Tangub*, Tarlac, Tawitawi, Toledo*, Trece Martires*, Zambales, Zamboanga*, Zamboanga del Norte, Zamboanga del Sur
Independence: 4 July 1946 (from US)
Constitution: 2 February 1987, effective 11 February 1987
Legal system: based on Spanish and Anglo-American law; accepts compulsory ICJ jurisdiction, with reservations
National holiday: Independence Day (from Spain), 12 June (1898)
Executive branch: president, vice president, Cabinet
Legislative branch: bicameral Congress (Kongreso) consists of an upper house or Senate (Senado) and a lower house or House of Representatives (Kapulungan Ng Mga Kinatawan)
Judicial branch: Supreme Court
Leaders:
Chief of State and Head of Government—President Corazon C. AQUINO (since 25 February 1986); Vice President Salvador H. LAUREL (since 25 February 1986)
Political parties and leaders: PDP-Laban, Aquilino PIMENTEL; Struggle of Philippine Democrats (LDP), Neptali GONZALES; Nacionalista Party, Salvador LAUREL, Juan Ponce ENRILE; Liberal Party, Jovito SALONGA
Suffrage: universal at age 15
Elections:
President—last held 7 February 1986 (next election to be held May 1992); results—Corazon C. AQUINO elected, precipitating the fall of the MARCOS regime;
Senate—last held 11 May 1987 (next to be held May 1992); results—*pro-Aquino* LDP 63%, *liberal* LDP and PDP-Laban (Pimentel wing) 25%, *opposition* Nacionalista Party 4%, independent 8%; seats—(24 total) *pro-Aquino* LDP 15, *liberal* LDP-Laban (Pimentel wing) 6, *opposition* Nacionalista Party 1, independent 1;
House of Representatives—last held on 11 May 1987 (next to be held May 1992); results—*pro-Aquino* LDP 73%, *liberal* LDP and PDP-Laban (Pimentel wing) 10%, *opposition* Nacionalista Party 17%; seats—(250 total, 180 elected) number of seats by party NA
Communists: the Communist Party of the Philippines (CPP) controls about 18,000-23,000 full-time insurgents and is not recognized as a legal party; a second Communist party, the pro-Soviet Philippine Communist Party (PKP), has quasi-legal status
Member of: APEC, AsDB, ASEAN, CCC, CP, ESCAP, FAO, G-24, G-77, GATT, IAEA, IBRD, ICAO, ICFTU, IDA, IFAD, IFC, ILO, IMF, IMO, INMARSAT, INTELSAT, INTERPOL, IOC, IOM, ISO,

ITU, LORCS, NAM (observer), UN, UNC-TAD, UNESCO, UNIDO, UPU, WCL, WFTU, WHO, WIPO, WMO
Diplomatic representation: Ambassador Emmanuel PELAEZ; Chancery at 1617 Massachusetts Avenue NW, Washington DC 20036; telephone (202) 483-1414; there are Philippine Consulates General in Agana (Guam), Chicago, Honolulu, Houston, Los Angeles, New York, San Francisco, and Seattle;
US—Ambassador Nicholas PLATT; Embassy at 1201 Roxas Boulevard, Manila (mailing address is APO San Francisco 96528); telephone [63] (32) 211-101 through 3; there is a US Consulate in Cebu
Flag: two equal horizontal bands of blue (top) and red with a white equilateral triangle based on the hoist side; in the center of the triangle is a yellow sun with eight primary rays (each containing three individual rays) and in each corner of the triangle is a small yellow five-pointed star

Economy

Overview: The economy continues to recover from the political turmoil following the ouster of former President Marcos and several coup attempts. After two consecutive years of economic contraction (1984 and 1985), the economy has since 1986 had positive growth, although in 1990 the economy slowed considerably from 1989. The agricultural sector together with forestry and fishing, plays an important role in the economy, employing about 45% of the work force and providing almost 30% of GDP. The Philippines is the world's largest exporter of coconuts and coconut products. Manufacturing contributes about 25% of GDP. Major industries include food processing, chemicals, and textiles.
GNP: $45.2 billion, per capita $700; real growth rate 2.5% (1990 est.)
Inflation rate (consumer prices): 12.7% (1990 est.)
Unemployment rate: 9.3% (1990 est.)
Budget: $7.2 billion; expenditures $8.12 billion, including capital expenditures of $0.97 billion (1989 est.)
Exports: revenues $8.1 billion (f.o.b., 1990 est.);
commodities—electrical equipment 19%, textiles 16%, minerals and ores 11%, farm products 10%, coconut 10%, chemicals 5%, fish 5%, forest products 4%;
partners—US 36%, EC 19%, Japan 18%, ESCAP 9%, ASEAN 7%
Imports: $12.1 billion (c.i.f., 1990 est.);
commodities—raw materials 53%, capital goods 17%, petroleum products 17%;
partners—US 25%, Japan 17%, ESCAP 13%, EC 11%, ASEAN 10%, Middle East 10%

External debt: $28.4 billion (1990)
Industrial production: growth rate 1.9% (1990 est.); accounts for 30-35% of GNP
Electricity: 6,755,000 kW capacity; 28,000 million kWh produced, 420 kWh per capita (1990)
Industries: textiles, pharmaceuticals, chemicals, wood products, food processing, electronics assembly, petroleum refining, fishing
Agriculture: accounts for about one-third of GNP and 45% of labor force; major crops—rice, coconut, corn, sugarcane, bananas, pineapple, mango; animal products—pork, eggs, beef; net exporter of farm products; fish catch of 2 million metric tons annually
Illicit drugs: illicit producer of cannabis for the international drug trade; growers are producing more and better quality cannabis despite government eradication efforts
Economic aid: US commitments, including Ex-Im (FY70-89), $3.6 billion; Western (non-US) countries, ODA and OOF bilateral commitments (1970-88), $6.6 billion; OPEC bilateral aid (1979-89), $5 million; Communist countries (1975-89), $123 million
Currency: Philippine peso (plural—pesos); 1 Philippine peso (₱) = 100 centavos
Exchange rates: Philippine pesos (₱) per US$1—28.055 (January 1991), 24.311 (1990), 21.737 (1989), 21.095 (1988), 20.568 (1987), 20.386 (1986), 18.607 (1985)
Fiscal year: calendar year

Communications

Railroads: 378 km operable on Luzon, 34% government owned (1982)
Highways: 156,000 km total (1984); 29,000 km paved; 77,000 km gravel, crushed-stone, or stabilized-soil surface; 50,000 km unimproved earth
Inland waterways: 3,219 km; limited to shallow-draft (less than 1.5 m) vessels
Pipelines: refined products, 357 km
Ports: Cagayan de Oro, Cebu, Davao, Guimaras, Iloilo, Legaspi, Manila, Subic Bay
Merchant marine: 569 ships (1,000 GRT or over) totaling 8,429,829 GRT/15,171,692 DWT; includes 1 passenger, 9 short-sea passenger, 17 passenger-cargo, 163 cargo, 18 refrigerated cargo, 24 vehicle carrier, 8 livestock carrier, 10 roll-on/roll-off cargo, 8 container, 41 petroleum, oils, and lubricants (POL) tanker, 1 chemical tanker, 7 liquefied gas, 3 combination ore/oil, 252 bulk, 7 combination bulk; note—many Philippine flag ships are foreign owned and are on the register for the purpose of long-term bare-boat charter back to their original owners who are principally in Japan and Germany
Civil air: 53 major transport aircraft

Airports: 280 total, 235 usable; 71 with permanent-surface runways; none with runways over 3,659 m; 9 with runways 2,440-3,659 m; 50 with runways 1,220-2,439 m
Telecommunications: good international radio and submarine cable services; domestic and interisland service adequate; 872,900 telephones; stations—267 AM (including 6 US), 55 FM, 33 TV (including 4 US); submarine cables extended to Hong Kong, Guam, Singapore, Taiwan, and Japan; satellite earth stations—1 Indian Ocean INTELSAT, 2 Pacific Ocean INTELSAT, and 11 domestic

Defense Forces

Branches: Army, Navy (including Coast Guard), Marine Corps, Air Force, Constabulary
Manpower availability: males 15-49, 16,254,775; 11,491,155 fit for military service; 715,462 reach military age (20) annually
Defense expenditures: $1.1 billion, 2% of GNP (1990)

Pitcairn Islands
(dependent territory of the UK)

```
——— 100 km ———
```

`: Sandy`
`Oeno`
`° Henderson`
`Ducie`
`° ←→ ★ADAMSTOWN`
`Pitcairn`

South Pacific Ocean

Geography

Total area: 47 km²; land area: 47 km²
Comparative area: about 0.3 times the size of Washington, DC
Land boundaries: none
Coastline: 51 km
Maritime claims:
Exclusive fishing zone: 200 nm;
Territorial sea: 3 nm
Climate: tropical, hot, humid, modified by southeast trade winds; rainy season (November to March)
Terrain: rugged volcanic formation; rocky coastline with cliffs
Natural resources: miro trees (used for handicrafts), fish
Land use: arable land NA%; permanent crops NA%; meadows and pastures NA%; forest and woodland NA%; other NA%
Environment: subject to typhoons (especially November to March)
Note: located in the South Pacific Ocean about halfway between Peru and New Zealand

People

Population: 56 (July 1991), growth rate 0.0% (1991)
Birth rate: NA births/1,000 population (1991)
Death rate: NA deaths/1,000 population (1991)
Net migration rate: NA migrants/1,000 population (1991)
Infant mortality rate: NA deaths/1,000 live births (1991)
Life expectancy at birth: NA years male, NA years female (1991)
Total fertility rate: NA children born/woman (1991)
Nationality: noun—Pitcairn Islander(s); adjective—Pitcairn Islander
Ethnic divisions: descendants of Bounty mutineers
Religion: Seventh-Day Adventist 100%

Language: English (official); also a Tahitian/English dialect
Literacy: NA% (male NA%, female NA%)
Labor force: NA; no business community in the usual sense; some public works; subsistence farming and fishing
Organized labor: NA

Government

Long-form name: Pitcairn, Henderson, Ducie, and Oeno Islands
Type: dependent territory of the UK
Capital: Adamstown
Administrative divisions: none (dependent territory of the UK)
Independence: none (dependent territory of the UK)
Constitution: Local Government Ordinance of 1964
Legal system: local island by-laws
National holiday: Celebration of the Birthday of the Queen (second Saturday in June), 10 June 1989
Executive branch: British monarch, governor, island magistrate
Legislative branch: unicameral Island Council
Judicial branch: Island Court
Leaders:
Chief of State—Queen ELIZABETH II (since 6 February 1952), represented by the Governor and UK High Commissioner to New Zealand David Joseph MOSS (since NA 1990);
Head of Government—Island Magistrate and Chairman of the Island Council Brian YOUNG (since NA 1985)
Political parties and leaders: NA
Suffrage: universal at age 18 with three years residency
Elections:
Island Council—last held NA (next to be held NA); results—percent of vote by party NA; seats—(11 total, 5 elected) number of seats by party NA
Communists: none
Other political or pressure groups: NA
Member of: SPC
Diplomatic representation: none (dependent territory of the UK)
Flag: blue with the flag of the UK in the upper hoist-side quadrant and the Pitcairn Islander coat of arms centered on the outer half of the flag; the coat of arms is yellow, green, and light blue with a shield featuring a yellow anchor

Economy

Overview: The inhabitants exist on fishing and subsistence farming. The fertile soil of the valleys produces a wide variety of fruits and vegetables, including citrus, sugarcane, watermelons, bananas, yams, and beans.

Bartering is an important part of the economy. The major sources of revenue are the sale of postage stamps to collectors and the sale of handicrafts to passing ships.
GDP: $NA, per capita $NA; real growth rate NA%
Inflation rate (consumer prices): NA%
Unemployment rate: NA%
Budget: revenues $430,440; expenditures $429,983, including capital expenditures of $NA (FY87 est.)
Exports: $NA;
commodities—fruits, vegetables, curios;
partners—NA
Imports: $NA;
commodities—fuel oil, machinery, building materials, flour, sugar, other foodstuffs;
partners—NA
External debt: $NA
Industrial production: growth rate NA%
Electricity: 110 kW capacity; 0.30 million kWh produced, 5,360 kWh per capita (1990)
Industries: postage stamp sales, handicrafts
Agriculture: based on subsistence fishing and farming; wide variety of fruits and vegetables grown; must import grain products
Economic aid: none
Currency: New Zealand dollar (plural—dollars); 1 New Zealand dollar (NZ$) = 100 cents
Exchange rates: New Zealand dollars (NZ$) per US$1—1.6798 (January 1991), 1.6750 (1990), 1.6711 (1989), 1.5244 (1988), 1.6866 (1987), 1.9088 (1986), 2.0064 (1985)
Fiscal year: 1 April-31 March

Communications

Railroads: none
Highways: 6.4 km dirt roads
Ports: Bounty Bay
Airports: none
Telecommunications: 24 telephones; party line telephone service on the island; stations—1 AM, no FM, no TV; diesel generator provides electricity

Defense Forces

Note: defense is the responsibility of the UK

Poland

Baltic Sea

Boundary representation is not necessarily authoritative.

Geography

Total area: 312,680 km²; land area: 304,510 km²

Comparative area: slightly smaller than New Mexico

Land boundaries: 2,980 km total; Czechoslovakia 1,309 km, Germany 456 km, USSR 1,215 km

Coastline: 491 km

Maritime claims:

Territorial sea: 12 nm

Climate: temperate with cold, cloudy, moderately severe winters with frequent precipitation; mild summers with frequent showers and thundershowers

Terrain: mostly flat plain, mountains along southern border

Natural resources: coal, sulfur, copper, natural gas, silver, lead, salt

Land use: arable land 46%; permanent crops 1%; meadows and pastures 13%; forest and woodland 28%; other 12%; includes irrigated NEGL%

Environment: plain crossed by a few northflowing, meandering streams; severe air and water pollution in south

Note: historically, an area of conflict because of flat terrain and the lack of natural barriers on the North European Plain

People

Population: 37,799,638 (July 1991), growth rate 0.1% (1991)

Birth rate: 14 births/1,000 population (1991)

Death rate: 9 deaths/1,000 population (1991)

Net migration rate: −4 migrants/1,000 population (1991)

Infant mortality rate: 12 deaths/1,000 live births (1991)

Life expectancy at birth: 69 years male, 77 years female (1991)

Total fertility rate: 2.1 children born/woman (1991)

Nationality: noun—Pole(s); adjective—Polish

Ethnic divisions: Polish 97.6%, German 1.3%, Ukrainian 0.6%, Belorussian (Byelorussian) 0.5% (1990 est.)

Religion: Roman Catholic 95% (about 75% practicing), Russian Orthodox, Protestant, and other 5%

Language: Polish

Literacy: 98% (male 99%, female 98%) age 15 and over can read and write (1978)

Labor force: 17,104,000; industry and construction 36.1%; agriculture 27.3%; trade, transport, and communications 14.8%; government and other 21.8% (1989)

Organized labor: trade union pluralism

Government

Long-form name: Republic of Poland

Type: democratic state

Capital: Warsaw

Administrative divisions: 49 provinces (województwa, singular—województwo); Biała Podlaska, Białystok, Bielsko, Bydgoszcz, Chełm, Ciechanów, Częstochowa, Elbląg, Gdańsk, Gorzów, Jelenia Góra, Kalisz, Katowice, Kielce, Konin, Koszalin, Kraków, Krosno, Legnica, Leszno, Łódź, Łomża, Lublin, Nowy Sącz, Olsztyn, Opoie, Ostrołęka, Piła, Piotrków, Płock, Poznań, Przemyśl, Radom, Rzeszów, Siedlce, Sieradz, Skierniewice, Słupsk, Suwałki, Szczecin, Tarnobrzeg, Tarnów, Toruń, Wałbrzych, Warszawa, Włocławek, Wrocław, Zamość, Zielona Góra

Independence: 11 November 1918, independent republic proclaimed

Constitution: the Communist-imposed Constitution of 22 July 1952 will probably be replaced by a democratic Constitution in 1992

Legal system: mixture of Continental (Napoleonic) civil law and Communist legal theory; no judicial review of legislative acts; has not accepted compulsory ICJ jurisdiction

National holiday: Constitution Day, 3 May (1794)

Executive branch: president, prime minister, Council of Ministers (cabinet)

Legislative branch: bicameral National Assembly (Zgromadzenie Narodowe) consists of an upper house or Senate (Senat) and a lower house or Diet (Sejm)

Judicial branch: Supreme Court

Leaders:

Chief of State—President Lech WALESA (since 22 December 1990);

Head of Government—Prime Minister Jan Krzysztof BIELECKI (since 4 January 1991)

Political parties and leaders: *center-right agrarian parties*—Polish Peasant Party (PSL), Roman BARTOSZCZE, chairman; Polish Peasant Party-Solidarity, Gabriel JANOWSKI, chairman;

other center-right parties—Center Alliance, Jaroslaw KACZYNSKI, chairman; Christian National Union, Wieslaw CHRZANOWSKI, chairman; Christian Democratic Labor Party, Wladyslaw SILA-NOWICKI, chairman; Democratic Party, Jerzy JOZWIAK, chairman;

center-left parties—Polish Socialist Party, Jan Jozef LIPSKI, chairman; Democratic Union, Tadeusz MAZOWIECKI, chairman; ROAD, Wladyslaw FRASYNIUK and Zbigniew BUJAK, chairmen;

left-wing parties—Polish Socialist Party-Democratic Revolution, Piotr IKONOWICZ;

other—Social Democracy of the Republic of Poland (formerly the Communist party or Polish United Workers' Party/PZPR), Aleksander KWASNIEWSKI, chairman; Union of the Social Democracy of the Republic of Poland (breakaway faction of the PZPR), Tadeusz FISZBACH, chairman

Suffrage: universal at age 18

Elections:

President—first round held 25 November 1990, second round held 9 December 1990 (next to be held November 1995); results—second round Lech WALESA 74.7%, Stanislaw TYMINSKI 25.3%;

Senate—last held 4 and 18 June 1989 (next to be held late 1991); results—percent of vote by party NA; seats—(100 total) Solidarity 99, independent 1;

Diet—last held 4 and 18 June 1989 (next to be held late 1991); results—percent of vote by party NA; seats—(460 total) Communists 173, Solidarity 161, Polish Peasant Party 76, Democratic Party 27, Christian National Union 23; note—rules governing the election limited Solidarity's share of the vote to 35% of the seats; future elections, which will probably be held before late 1991, are to be freely contested

Communists: 70,000 members in the Communist successor parties (1990)

Other political or pressure groups: powerful Roman Catholic Church; Confederation for an Independent Poland (KPN), a nationalist group; Solidarity (trade union); All Poland Trade Union Alliance (OPZZ), populist program; Clubs of Catholic Intellectuals (KIKs); Freedom and Peace (WiP), a pacifist group; Independent Student Union (NZS)

Member of: BIS, CCC, CERN (observer, but scheduled to become a member 1 July 1991), CSCE, ECE, FAO, GATT, IAEA, IBEC, IBRD, ICAO, ICFTU, IDA, IIB, ILO, IMF, IMO, INMARSAT, IOC, ISO, ITU, LORCS, PCA, UN, UNCTAD, UNESCO, UNDOF, UNIDO, UNIIMOG, UPU, WCL, WFTU, WHO, WIPO, WMO, WTO

Diplomatic representation: Ambassador Kazimierz DZIEWANOWSKI; Chancery at 2640 16th Street NW, Washington DC

Poland (continued)

20009; telephone (202) 234-3800 through 3802; there are Polish Consulates General in Chicago, Los Angeles, and New York; *US*—Ambassador Thomas W. SIMONS, Jr.; Embassy at Aleje Ujazdowskie 29/31, Warsaw (mailing address is American Embassy Warsaw, c/o American Consulate General (WAW) or APO New York 09213-5010); telephone [48] (22) 283041 through 283049; there is a US Consulate General in Krakow and a Consulate in Poznan

Flag: two equal horizontal bands of white (top) and red—a crowned eagle is to be added; similar to the flags of Indonesia and Monaco which are red (top) and white

---

Economy

Overview: The economy, except for the agricultural sector, had followed the Soviet model of state ownership and control of productive assets. About 75% of agricultural production had come from the private sector and the rest from state farms. The economy has presented a picture of moderate but slowing growth against a background of underlying weaknesses in technology and worker motivation. GNP dropped by 2.0% in 1989 and by a further 8.9% in 1990. The inflation rate, after falling sharply from the 1982 peak of 100% to 22% in 1986, rose to a galloping rate of 640% in 1989 and dropped back to 250% in 1990. Shortages of consumer goods and some food items worsened in 1988-89. Agricultural products and coal are among the biggest hard currency earners, but manufactures are increasing in importance. Poland, with its hard currency debt of $48.5 billion, is severely limited in its ability to import much-needed hard currency goods. The sweeping political changes of 1989 disrupted normal economic channels and exacerbated shortages. In January 1990, the new Solidarity-led government adopted a cold turkey program for transforming Poland to a market economy. The government moved to eliminate subsidies, free prices, make the złoty convertible, and, in general, halt the hyperinflation. These financial measures were accompanied by plans to privatize the economy in stages. While inflation fell to an annual rate of 77.5% by November of 1990, the rise in unemployment and the drop in living standards have led to growing popular discontent and to a change of government in January 1991. The new government is continuing the previous government's economic program, while trying to speed privatization and to better cushion the populace from the dislocations associated with reform. Substantial outside aid will be needed if Poland is to make a successful transition in the 1990s.

GNP: $158.5 billion, per capita $4,200; real growth rate −8.9% (1990 est.)

Inflation rate (consumer prices): 250% (1990 est.)

Unemployment rate: 6.1% (end-December 1990)

Budget: revenues $20.9 billion; expenditures $23.4 billion, including capital expenditures of $2.8 billion (1989)

Exports: $12.9 billion (f.o.b., 1989); *commodities*—machinery and equipment 38%; fuels, minerals, and metals 21%; manufactured consumer goods 15%; agricultural and forestry products 4% (1989); *partners*—USSR 25%, FRG 14%, UK 6.5%, Czechoslovakia 5.5% (1989)

Imports: $12.8 billion (f.o.b., 1989); *commodities*—machinery and equipment 37%; fuels, minerals, and metals 31%; manufactured consumer goods 17%; agricultural and forestry products 5% (1989); *partners*—USSR 18%, FRG 16%, Austria 6%, Czechoslovakia 6% (1989)

External debt: $48.5 billion (January 1991)

Industrial production: growth rate −23% (State sector 1990 est.)

Electricity: 31,530,000 kW capacity; 136,300 million kWh produced, 3,610 kWh per capita (1990)

Industries: machine building, iron and steel, extractive industries, chemicals, shipbuilding, food processing, glass, beverages, textiles

Agriculture: accounts for 15% of GNP and 27% of labor force; 75% of output from private farms, 25% from state farms; productivity remains low by European standards; leading European producer of rye, rapeseed, and potatoes; wide variety of other crops and livestock; major exporter of pork products; normally self-sufficient in food

Economic aid: donor—bilateral aid to non-Communist less developed countries, $2.2 billion (1954-89)

Currency: złoty (plural—złotych); 1 złoty (Zł) = 100 groszy

Exchange rates: złotych (Zł) per US$1—11,100.00 (May 1991), 9,500 (1990), 1,439.18 (1989), 430.55 (1988), 265.08 (1987), 175.29 (1986), 147.14 (1985)

Fiscal year: calendar year

Communications

Railroads: 27,041 km total; 24,287 km 1.435-meter standard gauge, 397 km 1.520-meter broad gauge, 2,357 km narrow gauge; 8,987 km double track; 11,016 km electrified; government owned (1989)

Highways: 299,887 km total; 130,000 km improved hard surface (concrete, asphalt, stone block); 24,000 km unimproved hard surface (crushed stone, gravel); 100,000 km earth; 45,887 km other urban roads (1985)

Inland waterways: 3,997 km navigable rivers and canals (1989)

Pipelines: 4,500 km for natural gas; 1,986 km for crude oil; 360 km for refined products (1987)

Ports: Gdańsk, Gdynia, Szczecin, Świnoujście; principal inland ports are Gliwice on Kanał Gliwice, Wrocław on the Oder, and Warsaw on the Vistula

Merchant marine: 235 ships (1,000 GRT or over) totaling 2,957,600 GRT/4,163,820 DWT; includes 5 short-sea passenger, 92 cargo, 3 refrigerated cargo, 12 roll-on/roll-off cargo, 9 container, 3 petroleum, oils, and lubricants (POL) tanker, 4 chemical tanker, 107 bulk; Poland owns 1 ship (1,000 GRT or over) of 6,333 DWT operating under Liberian registry

Civil air: 48 major transport aircraft

Airports: 160 total, 160 usable; 85 with permanent-surface runways; 1 with runway over 3,659 m; 35 with runways 2,440-3,659 m; 65 with runways 1,220-2,439 m

Telecommunications: phone density is 10.5 phones per 100 residents (October 1990); 3.1 million subscribers; exchanges are 86% automatic (February 1990); stations—29 AM, 29 FM, 37 (5 Soviet relays) TV; 9.6 million TVs

---

Defense Forces

Branches: External Front Ground Forces, Navy, Air and Air Defense Forces, Internal Defense Forces (WOW), Territorial Defense Forces (JOT), Border Guards (WOP), Paramilitary Forces, Civil Defense (OC)

Manpower availability: males 15-49, 9,571,708; 7,543,565 fit for military service; 302,000 reach military age (19) annually

Defense expenditures: 22.3 trillion złotych, NA% of GDP (1991); note—conversion of defense expenditures into US dollars using the official administratively set exchange rate would produce misleading results

Portugal

125 km

North Atlantic Ocean

Braga
Porto
Covilhã
Coimbra
Portalegre
LISBON
Beja
Faro

Azores and Madeira Islands are not shown

Geography

Total area: 92,080 km²; land area: 91,640 km²; includes Azores and Madeira Islands
Comparative area: slightly smaller than Indiana
Land boundary: 1,214 km with Spain
Coastline: 1,793 km
Maritime claims:
Continental shelf: 200 m (depth) or to depth of exploitation;
Exclusive economic zone: 200 nm;
Territorial sea: 12 nm
Disputes: sovereignty over Timor Timur (East Timor Province) disputed with Indonesia
Climate: maritime temperate; cool and rainy in north, warmer and drier in south
Terrain: mountainous north of the Tagus, rolling plains in south
Natural resources: fish, forests (cork), tungsten, iron ore, uranium ore, marble
Land use: arable land 32%; permanent crops 6%; meadows and pastures 6%; forest and woodland 40%; other 16%; includes irrigated 7%
Environment: Azores subject to severe earthquakes
Note: Azores and Madeira Islands occupy strategic locations along western sea approaches to Strait of Gibraltar

People

Population: 10,387,617 (July 1991), growth rate 0.3% (1991)
Birth rate: 12 births/1,000 population (1991)
Death rate: 10 deaths/1,000 population (1991)
Net migration rate: 1 migrant/1,000 population (1991)
Infant mortality rate: 13 deaths/1,000 live births (1991)
Life expectancy at birth: 71 years male, 78 years female (1991)

Total fertility rate: 1.5 children born/woman (1991)
Nationality: noun—Portuguese (sing. and pl.); adjective—Portuguese
Ethnic divisions: homogeneous Mediterranean stock in mainland, Azores, Madeira Islands; citizens of black African descent who immigrated to mainland during decolonization number less than 100,000
Religion: Roman Catholic 97%, Protestant denominations 1%, other 2%
Language: Portuguese
Literacy: 85% (male 89%, female 82%) age 15 and over can read and write (1990 est.)
Labor force: 4,605,700; services 45%, industry 35%, agriculture 20% (1988)
Organized labor: about 55% of the labor force; the Communist-dominated General Confederation of Portuguese Workers—Intersindical (CGTP-IN) represents more than half of the unionized labor force; its main competition, the General Workers Union (UGT), is organized by the Socialists and Social Democrats and represents less than half of unionized labor

Government

Long-form name: Portuguese Republic
Type: republic
Capital: Lisbon
Administrative divisions: 18 districts (distritos, singular—distrito) and 2 autonomous regions* (regiões autónomas, singular—região autónoma); Aveiro, Açores (Azores)*, Beja, Braga, Bragança, Castelo Branco, Coimbra, Évora, Faro, Guarda, Leiria, Lisboa, Madeira*, Portalegre, Porto, Santarém, Setúbal, Viana do Castelo, Vila Real, Viseu
Dependent area: Macau (scheduled to become a Special Administrative Region of China in 1999)
Independence: 1140; independent republic proclaimed 5 October 1910
Constitution: 25 April 1976, revised 30 October 1982 and 1 June 1989
Legal system: civil law system; the Constitutional Tribunal reviews the constitutionality of legislation; accepts compulsory ICJ jurisdiction, with reservations
National holiday: Day of Portugal, 10 June
Executive branch: president, Council of State, prime minister, deputy prime minister, Council of Ministers (cabinet)
Legislative branch: unicameral Assembly of the Republic (Assembléia da República)
Judicial branch: Supreme Tribunal of Justice (Supremo Tribunal de Justiça)
Leaders:
Chief of State—President Dr. Mário Alberto Nobre Lopes SOARES (since 9 March 1986);
Head of Government—Prime Minister Aníbal CAVAÇO SILVA (since 6 November 1985)

Political parties and leaders: Social Democratic Party (PSD), Aníbal CAVAÇO Silva; Portuguese Socialist Party (PS), Jorge SAMPAIO; Party of Democratic Renewal (PRD), Hermínio MARTINHO; Portuguese Communist Party (PCP), Alvaro CUNHAL; Social Democratic Center (CDS), Diogo Freitas do AMARAL
Suffrage: universal at age 18
Elections:
President—last held 13 February 1991 (next to be held February 1996); results—Dr. Mário Lopes SOARES 70%, Basilio HORTA 14%, Carlos CARVALHAS 13%, Carlos MARQUES 3%;
Assembly of the Republic—last held 19 July 1987 (next to be held July 1991); results—Social Democrats 59.2%, Socialists 24.0%, Communists (in a front coalition) 12.4%, Democratic Renewal 2.8%, Center Democrats 1.6%; seats—(250 total) Social Democrats 148, Socialists 60, Communists (in a front coalition) 31, Democratic Renewal 7, Center Democrats 4
Communists: Portuguese Communist Party claims membership of 200,753 (December 1983)
Member of: AfDB, BIS, CCC, CE, CERN, COCOM, CSCE, EBRD, EC, ECE, ECLAC, EIB, FAO, GATT, IADB, IAEA, IBRD, ICAO, ICC, ICFTU, IEA, IFAD, IFC, ILO, IMF, IMO, INMARSAT, INTELSAT, INTERPOL, IOC, IOM, ISO, ITU, LAIA (observer), LORCS, NAM (guest), NATO, NEA, OAS (observer), OECD, PCA, UN, UNCTAD, UNESCO, UNIDO, UPU, WCL, WEU, WHO, WIPO, WMO, WTO
Diplomatic representation: Ambassador Joao Eduardo M. PEREIRA BASTOS; Chancery at 2125 Kalorama Road NW, Washington DC 20008; telephone (202) 328-8610; there are Portuguese Consulates General in Boston, New York, and San Francisco, and Consulates in Los Angeles, Newark (New Jersey), New Bedford (Massachusetts), and Providence (Rhode Island);
US—Ambassador Everett E. BRIGGS; Embassy at Avenida das Forcas Armadas, 1600 Lisbon (mailing address is APO New York 09678-0002); telephone [351] (1) 726-6600 or 6659, 8670, 8880; there is a US Consulate in Ponta Delgada (Azores)
Flag: two vertical bands of green (hoist side, two-fifths) and red (three-fifths) with the Portuguese coat of arms centered on the dividing line

Economy

Overview: During the past four years, the economy has made a sustained recovery from the severe recession of 1983-85. The economy grew by 14% during the 1987-89 period, largely because of strong domestic

Portugal (continued)

consumption and investment spending. Unemployment has declined for the third consecutive year, but inflation continues to be about three times the European Community average. The government is pushing economic restructuring and privatization measures in anticipation of the 1992 European Community timetable to form a single large market in Europe.
GDP: $57.8 billion, per capita $5,580; real growth rate 3.5% (1990)
Inflation rate (consumer prices): 13.4% (1990)
Unemployment rate: 5.5% (1990 est.)
Budget: revenues $21.6 billion; expenditures $23.8 billion, including capital expenditures of $6.9 billion (1990)
Exports: $16.3 billion (f.o.b., 1990); *commodities*—cotton textiles, cork and cork products, canned fish, wine, timber and timber products, resin, machinery, appliances; *partners*—EC 72%, other developed countries 13%, US 5%
Imports: $24.9 billion (c.i.f., 1990); *commodities*—petroleum, cotton, foodgrains, industrial machinery, iron and steel, chemicals; *partners*—EC 69%, other developed countries 11%, less developed countries 13%, US 4%
External debt: $18.4 billion (1990)
Industrial production: growth rate 4.9% (1989); accounts for 40% of GDP
Electricity: 6,729,000 kW capacity; 16,000 million kWh produced, 1,530 kWh per capita (1989)
Industries: textiles and footwear; wood pulp, paper, and cork; metalworking; oil refining; chemicals; fish canning; wine; tourism
Agriculture: accounts for 9% of GDP and 20% of labor force; small inefficient farms; imports more than half of food needs; major crops—grain, potatoes, olives, grapes; livestock sector—sheep, cattle, goats, poultry, meat, dairy products
Economic aid: US commitments, including Ex-Im (FY70-89), $1.8 billion; Western (non-US) countries, ODA and OOF bilateral commitments (1970-88), $1.13 billion
Currency: Portuguese escudo (plural—escudos); 1 Portuguese escudo (Esc) = 100 centavos
Exchange rates: Portuguese escudos (Esc) per US$1—134.46 (January 1991), 142.55 (1990), 157.46 (1989), 143.95 (1988), 140.88 (1987), 149.59 (1986), 170.39 (1985)
Fiscal year: calendar year

Communications

Railroads: 3,613 km total; state-owned Portuguese Railroad Co. (CP) operates 2,858 km 1.665-meter gauge (434 km electrified and 426 km double track), 755 km 1.000-meter gauge; 12 km (1.435-meter gauge) electrified, double track, privately owned
Highways: 73,661 km total; 61,599 km paved (bituminous, gravel, and crushed stone), including 140 km of limited-access divided highway; 7,962 km improved earth; 4,100 km unimproved earth (motorable tracks)
Inland waterways: 820 km navigable; relatively unimportant to national economy, used by shallow-draft craft limited to 300-metric-ton cargo capacity
Pipelines: crude oil, 11 km; refined products, 58 km
Ports: Leixões, Lisbon, Porto, Ponta Delgada (Azores), Velas (Azores), Setúbal, Sines
Merchant marine: 52 ships (1,000 GRT or over) totaling 684,350 GRT/1,190,454 DWT; includes 1 short-sea passenger, 20 cargo, 2 refrigerated cargo, 1 container, 1 roll-on/roll-off cargo, 12 petroleum, oils, and lubricants (POL) tanker, 2 chemical tanker, 2 liquefied gas, 10 bulk, 1 combination bulk; note—Portugal has created a captive register on Madeira (MAR) for Portuguese-owned ships that will have the taxation and crewing benefits of a flag of convenience; although only one ship currently is known to fly the Portuguese flag on the MAR register, it is likely that a majority of Portuguese flag ships will transfer to this subregister in a few years
Civil air: 29 major transport aircraft
Airports: 69 total, 63 usable; 36 with permanent-surface runways; 1 with runways over 3,659 m; 12 with runways 2,440-3,659 m; 7 with runways 1,220-2,439 m
Telecommunications: facilities are generally adequate; 2,690,000 telephones; stations—57 AM, 66 (22 relays) FM, 25 (23 relays) TV; 7 submarine cables; communication satellite ground stations operating in the INTELSAT (2 Atlantic Ocean and 1 Indian Ocean), EUTELSAT, and domestic systems (mainland and Azores)

Defense Forces

Branches: Army, Navy (including Marines), Air Force, National Republican Guard, Fiscal Guard, Public Security Police
Manpower availability: males 15-49, 2,621,116; 2,131,628 fit for military service; 88,718 reach military age (20) annually
Defense expenditures: $1.6 billion, 3% of GDP (1990)

Puerto Rico
(commonwealth associated with the US)

40 km

North   Atlantic   Ocean

Caribbean   Sea

Isla Desecheo and
Isla Mona are not shown.

Geography

Total area: 9,104 km²; land area: 8,959 km²
Comparative area: slightly less than three times the size of Rhode Island
Land boundaries: none
Coastline: 501 km
Maritime claims:
Contiguous zone: 12 nm;
Continental shelf: 200 m (depth);
Exclusive economic zone: 200 nm;
Territorial sea: 12 nm
Climate: tropical marine, mild, little seasonal temperature variation
Terrain: mostly mountains with coastal plain belt in north; mountains precipitous to sea on west coast
Natural resources: some copper and nickel; potential for onshore and offshore crude oil
Land use: arable land 8%; permanent crops 9%; meadows and pastures 41%; forest and woodland 20%; other 22%
Environment: many small rivers and high central mountains ensure land is well watered; south coast relatively dry; fertile coastal plain belt in north
Note: important location between the Dominican Republic and the Virgin Islands group along the Mona Passage—a key shipping lane to the Panama Canal; San Juan is one of the biggest and best natural harbors in the Caribbean

People

Population: 3,294,997 (July 1991), growth rate 0.1% (1991)
Birth rate: 19 births/1,000 population (1991)
Death rate: 8 deaths/1,000 population (1991)
Net migration rate: −10 migrants/1,000 population (1991)
Infant mortality rate: 16 deaths/1,000 live births (1991)
Life expectancy at birth: 69 years male, 76 years female (1991)

Total fertility rate: 2.1 children born/woman (1991)
Nationality: noun—Puerto Rican(s); adjective—Puerto Rican
Ethnic divisions: almost entirely Hispanic
Religion: Roman Catholic 85%, Protestant denominations and other 15%
Language: Spanish (official); English is widely understood
Literacy: 89% (male 90%, female 88%) age 15 and over can read and write (1980)
Labor force: 1,068,000; government 28%, manufacturing 15%, trade 14%, agriculture 3%, other 40% (1990)
Organized labor: 115,000 members in 4 unions; the largest is the General Confederation of Puerto Rican Workers with 35,000 members (1983)

Government

Long-form name: Commonwealth of Puerto Rico
Type: commonwealth associated with the US
Capital: San Juan
Administrative divisions: none (commonwealth associated with the US)
Independence: none (commonwealth associated with the US)
Constitution: ratified 3 March 1952; approved by US Congress 3 July 1952; effective 25 July 1952
National holiday: Constitution Day, 25 July (1952)
Legal system: based on Spanish civil code
Executive branch: US president, US vice president, governor
Legislative branch: bicameral Legislative Assembly consists of an upper house or Senate and a lower house or House of Representatives
Judicial branch: Supreme Court
Leaders:
Chief of State—President George BUSH (since 20 January 1989); Vice President Dan QUAYLE (since 20 January 1989);
Head of Government Governor Rafael HERNÁNDEZ Colón (since 2 January 1989)
Political parties and leaders: Popular Democratic Party (PPD), Rafael HERNÁNDEZ Colón; New Progressive Party (PNP), Carlos ROMERO Barceló; Puerto Rican Socialist Party (PSP), Juan MARI Bras and Carlos GALLISA; Puerto Rican Independence Party (PIP), Rubén BERRÍOS Martínez; Puerto Rican Communist Party (PCP), leader(s) unknown
Suffrage: universal at age 18; indigenous inhabitants are US citizens, but do not vote in US presidential elections
Elections:
Governor—last held 8 November 1988 (next to be held 3 November 1992); results—Rafael HERNÁNDEZ Colón (PPD)

48.7%, Baltasar CORRADA Del Rio (PNP) 45.8%, Rubén BERRIOS Martínez (PIP) 5.5%;
Senate—last held 8 November 1988 (next to be held 3 November 1992); results—percent of vote by party NA; seats—(27 total) PPD 18, PNP 8, PIP 1;
House of Representatives—last held 8 November 1988 (next to be held 3 November 1992); results—percent of vote by party NA; seats—(53 total) PPD 36, PNP 15, PIP 2;
US House of Representatives—last held 8 November 1988 (next to be held 3 November 1992); results—Puerto Rico elects one nonvoting representative
Other political or pressure groups: all have engaged in terrorist activities—Armed Forces for National Liberation (FALN), Volunteers of the Puerto Rican Revolution, Boricua Popular Army (also known as the Macheteros), Armed Forces of Popular Resistance
Member of: ECLAC, ICFTU, IOC, WCL, WFTU, WTO (associate)
Diplomatic representation: none (commonwealth associated with the US)
Flag: five equal horizontal bands of red (top and bottom) alternating with white; a blue isosceles triangle based on the hoist side bears a large white five-pointed star in the center; design based on the US flag

Economy

Overview: Puerto Rico has one of the most dynamic economies in the Caribbean region. Industry has surpassed agriculture as the primary sector of economic activity and income. Encouraged by duty-free access to the US and by tax incentives, US firms have invested heavily in Puerto Rico since the 1950s. Important new industries include pharmaceuticals, electronics, textiles, petrochemicals, and processed foods. Sugar production has lost out to dairy production and other livestock products as the main source of income in the agricultural sector. Tourism has traditionally been an important source of income for the island. The economy is slowly recovering from the disruptions caused by Hurricane Hugo in September 1989. The tourism infrastructure was especially hard hit.
GNP: $20.1 billion, per capita $6,100; real growth rate 3.6% (FY89)
Inflation rate (consumer prices): 6.3% (October 1989-90)
Unemployment rate: 14.9% (October 1990)
Budget: revenues $5.5 billion; expenditures $5.5 billion, including capital expenditures of $1.5 billion (FY89)
Exports: $16.4 billion (f.o.b., FY89);
commodities—pharmaceuticals, electronics, apparel, canned tuna, rum, beverage concentrates, medical equipment, instruments;

partners—US 87%
Imports: $14.0 billion (c.i.f., FY89);
commodities—chemicals, clothing, food, fish, petroleum products;
partners—US 60%
External debt: $NA
Industrial production: growth rate 1.6% (FY89)
Electricity: 4,149,000 kW capacity; 14,844 million kWh produced, 4,510 kWh per capita (1990)
Industries: manufacturing of pharmaceuticals, electronics, apparel, food products, instruments; tourism
Agriculture: accounts for 3% of labor force; crops—sugarcane, coffee, pineapples, plantains, bananas; livestock—cattle, chickens; imports a large share of food needs
Economic aid: none
Currency: US currency is used
Exchange rates: US currency is used
Fiscal year: 1 July-30 June

Communications

Railroads: 100 km rural narrow-gauge system for hauling sugarcane; no passenger railroads
Highways: 13,762 km paved
Ports: San Juan, Ponce, Mayaguez, Arecibo
Airports: 33 total; 23 usable; 19 with permanent-surface runways; none with runways over 3,659 m; 3 with runways 2,440-3,659 m; 4 with runways 1,220-2,439 m
Telecommunications: 900,000 or 99% of total households with TV; 1,067,787 telephones (1988); stations—50 AM, 63 FM, 9 TV (1990)

Defense Forces

Branches: paramilitary National Guard, Police Force
Manpower availability: males 15-49, 830,133; NA fit for military service
Note: defense is the responsibility of the US

Qatar

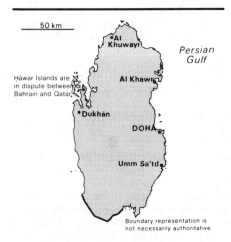

Boundary representation is not necessarily authoritative

Geography

Total area: 11,000 km²; land area: 11,000 km²
Comparative area: slightly smaller than Connecticut
Land boundaries: 60 km total; Saudi Arabia 40 km, UAE 20 km
Coastline: 563 km
Maritime claims:
Continental shelf: not specific;
Territorial sea: 3 nm
Disputes: boundary with UAE is in dispute; territorial dispute with Bahrain over the Ḥawār Islands
Climate: desert; hot, dry; humid and sultry in summer
Terrain: mostly flat and barren desert covered with loose sand and gravel
Natural resources: crude oil, natural gas, fish
Land use: arable land NEGL%; permanent crops 0%; meadows and pastures 5%; forest and woodland 0%; other 95%
Environment: haze, duststorms, sandstorms common; limited freshwater resources mean increasing dependence on large-scale desalination facilities
Note: strategic location in central Persian Gulf near major crude oil sources

People

Population: 518,478 (July 1991), growth rate 5.3% (1991)
Birth rate: 21 births/1,000 population (1991)
Death rate: 3 deaths/1,000 population (1991)
Net migration rate: 35 migrants/1,000 population (1991)
Infant mortality rate: 24 deaths/1,000 live births (1991)
Life expectancy at birth: 69 years male, 74 years female (1991)
Total fertility rate: 4.0 children born/woman (1991)

Nationality: noun—Qatari(s); adjective—Qatari
Ethnic divisions: Arab 40%, Pakistani 18%, Indian 18%, Iranian 10%, other 14%
Religion: Muslim 95%
Language: Arabic (official); English is commonly used as second language
Literacy: 76% (male 77%, female 72%) age 15 and over can read and write (1986)
Labor force: 104,000; 85% non-Qatari in private sector (1983)
Organized labor: trade unions are illegal

Government

Long-form name: State of Qatar
Type: traditional monarchy
Capital: Doha
Administrative divisions: none
Independence: 3 September 1971 (from UK)
Constitution: provisional constitution enacted 2 April 1970
Legal system: discretionary system of law controlled by the amir, although civil codes are being implemented; Islamic law is significant in personal matters
National holiday: Independence Day, 3 September (1971)
Executive branch: amir, Council of Ministers (cabinet)
Legislative branch: unicameral Advisory Council (Majlis al-Shura)
Judicial branch: Court of Appeal
Leaders:
Chief of State and Head of Government—Amir and Prime Minister Khalifa bin Hamad Al THANI (since 22 February 1972); Heir Apparent Hamad bin Khalifa AL THANI (appointed 31 May 1977; son of Amir)
Political parties and leaders: none
Suffrage: none
Elections:
Advisory Council—constitution calls for elections for part of this consultative body, but no elections have been held; seats—(30 total)
Member of: ABEDA, AFESD, AL, AMF, ESCWA, FAO, G-77, GCC, IAEA, IBRD, ICAO, IDB, IFAD, ILO, IMF, IMO, INMARSAT, INTELSAT, INTERPOL, IOC, ITU, LORCS, NAM, OAPEC, OIC, OPEC, UN, UNCTAD, UNESCO, UNIDO, UPU, WHO, WIPO, WMO
Diplomatic representation: Ambassador Hamad 'Abd al-'Aziz AL-KAWARI, Chancery at Suite 1180, 600 New Hampshire Avenue NW, Washington DC 20037; telephone (202) 338-0111;
US—Ambassador Mark G. HAMBLEY; Embassy at 149 Ali Bin Ahmed St., Farig Bin Omran (opposite the television station), Doha (mailing address is P. O. Box 2399, Doha); telephone [0974] 864701 through 864703
Flag: maroon with a broad white serrated band (nine white points) on the hoist side

Economy

Overview: Oil is the backbone of the economy and accounts for more than 85% of export earnings and roughly 75% of government revenues. Proved oil reserves of 3.3 billion barrels should ensure continued output at current levels for about 25 years. Oil has given Qatar a per capita GDP of about $12,500, among the highest in the world outside the OECD countries.
GDP: $6.6 billion, per capita $12,500 (1989 est.); real growth rate 5.0% (1988)
Inflation rate (consumer prices): 4.9% (1988 est.)
Unemployment rate: NA%
Budget: revenues $1.8 billion; expenditures $3.4 billion, including capital expenditures of $400 million (FY89 est.)
Exports: $2.6 billion (f.o.b., 1989 est.);
commodities—petroleum products 85%, steel, fertilizers;
partners—Japan, Italy, Thailand, Singapore
Imports: $1.4 billion (c.i.f., 1989 est.), excluding military equipment;
commodities—foodstuffs, beverages, animal and vegetable oils, chemicals, machinery and equipment;
partners—Japan, UK, US, Italy
External debt: $1.1 billion (December 1989 est.)
Industrial production: growth rate 0.6% (1987); accounts for 64% of GDP, including oil
Electricity: 1,514,000 kW capacity; 4,000 million kWh produced, 8,540 kWh per capita (1989)
Industries: crude oil production and refining, fertilizers, petrochemicals, steel, cement
Agriculture: farming and grazing on small scale, less than 2% of GDP; commercial fishing increasing in importance; most food imported
Economic aid: donor—pledged $2.7 billion in ODA to less developed countries (1979-88)
Currency: Qatari riyal (plural—riyals); 1 Qatari riyal (QR) = 100 dirhams
Exchange rates: Qatari riyals (QR) per US$1—3.6400 riyals (fixed rate)
Fiscal year: 1 April-31 March

Communications

Highways: 1,500 km total; 1,000 km bituminous, 500 km gravel or natural surface (est.)
Pipelines: crude oil, 235 km; natural gas, 400 km
Ports: Doha, Umm Sa'īd, Ḥālūl Island
Merchant marine: 20 ships (1,000 GRT or over) totaling 465,371 GRT/707,089 DWT; includes 12 cargo, 5 container, 3 petroleum, oils, and lubricants (POL) tanker

Civil air: 3 major transport aircraft
Airports: 4 total, 4 usable; 1 with permanent-surface runways; 1 with runways over 3,659 m; none with runways 2,440-3,659 m; 2 with runways 1,220-2,439 m
Telecommunications: modern system centered in Doha; 110,000 telephones; tropospheric scatter to Bahrain; radio relay to Saudi Arabia; submarine cable to Bahrain and UAE; stations—2 AM, 1 FM, 3 TV; earth stations—1 Atlantic Ocean INTELSAT, 1 Indian Ocean INTELSAT, 1 ARABSAT

Defense Forces

Branches: Army, Navy, Air Force, Police Department
Manpower availability: males 15-49, 235,516; 125,591 fit for military service; 4,243 reach military age (18) annually
Defense expenditures: $500 million, 8% of GDP (1989)

Reunion
(overseas department of France)

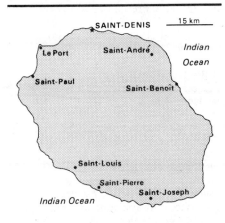

Geography

Total area: 2,510 km²; land area: 2,500 km²
Comparative area: slightly smaller than Rhode Island
Land boundaries: none
Coastline: 201 km
Maritime claims:
Exclusive economic zone: 200 nm;
Territorial sea: 12 nm
Climate: tropical, but moderates with elevation; cool and dry from May to November, hot and rainy from November to April
Terrain: mostly rugged and mountainous; fertile lowlands along coast
Natural resources: fish, arable land
Land use: arable land 20%; permanent crops 2%; meadows and pastures 4%; forest and woodland 35%; other 39%; includes irrigated 2%
Environment: periodic devastating cyclones
Note: located 750 km east of Madagascar in the Indian Ocean

People

Population: 607,086 (July 1991), growth rate 1.9% (1991)
Birth rate: 24 births/1,000 population (1991)
Death rate: 5 deaths/1,000 population (1991)
Net migration rate: 0 migrants/1,000 population (1991)
Infant mortality rate: 8 deaths/1,000 live births (1991)
Life expectancy at birth: 70 years male, 76 years female (1991)
Total fertility rate: 2.6 children born/woman (1991)
Nationality: noun—Reunionese (sing. and pl.); adjective—Reunionese
Ethnic divisions: most of the population is of intermixed French, African, Malagasy, Chinese, Pakistani, and Indian ancestry
Religion: Roman Catholic 94%

Language: French (official); Creole widely used
Literacy: 69% (male 67%, female 74%) age 15 and over can read and write (1982)
Labor force: NA; agriculture 30%, industry 21%, services 49% (1981); 63% of population of working age (1983)
Organized labor: General Confederation of Workers of Reunion (CGTR)

Government

Long-form name: Department of Reunion
Type: overseas department of France
Capital: Saint-Denis
Administrative divisions: none (overseas department of France)
Independence: none (overseas department of France)
Constitution: 28 September 1958 (French Constitution)
Legal system: French law
National holiday: Taking of the Bastille, 14 July (1789)
Executive branch: French president, commissioner of the Republic
Legislative branch: unicameral General Council, unicameral Regional Council
Judicial branch: Court of Appeals (Cour d'appel)
Leaders:
Chief of State—President François MITTERRAND (since 21 May 1981);
Head of Government—Commissioner of the Republic Daniel CONSTANTIN (since September 1989)
Political parties and leaders: Rally for the Republic (RPR), François MAS; Union for French Democracy (UDF), Gilbert GERARD; Communist Party of Reunion (PCR), Paul VERGÈS; France-Reunion Future (FRA), André THIEN AH KOON; Socialist Party (PS), Jean-Claude FRUTEAU; Social Democrats (CDS), other small parties
Suffrage: universal at age 18
Elections: *General Council*—last held March 1986 (next to be held 1992); results—percent of vote by party NA; seats—(36 total) number of seats by party NA;
Regional Council—last held 16 March 1986 (next to be held March 1991); results—RPR/UDF 36.8%, PCR 28.2%, FRA and other right wing 17.3%, PS 14.1%, other 3.6%; seats—(45 total) RPR/UDF 18, PCR 13, FRA and other right wing 8, PS 6;
French Senate—last held 24 September 1989 (next to be held September 1992); results—percent of vote by party NA; seats—(3 total) RPR-UDF 1, PS 1, independent 1;
French National Assembly—last held 5 and 12 June 1988 (next to be held June 1993); results—percent of vote by party NA; seats—(5 total) PCR 2, RPR 1, UDF-CDS 1, FRA 1

Reunion (continued)

Communists: Communist party small but has support among sugarcane cutters, the minuscule Popular Movement for the Liberation of Reunion (MPLR), and in the district of Le Port
Member of: FZ, WFTU
Diplomatic representation: as an overseas department of France, Reunionese interests are represented in the US by France
Flag: the flag of France is used

Economy

Overview: The economy has traditionally been based on agriculture. Sugarcane has been the primary crop for more than a century, and in some years it accounts for 85% of exports. The government has been pushing the development of a tourist industry to relieve high unemployment, which recently amounted to one-third of the labor force. The white and Indian communities are substantially better off than other segments of the population, adding to the social tensions generated by poverty and unemployment. The economic well-being of Reunion depends heavily on continued financial assistance from France.
GDP: $3.37 billion, per capita $6,000 (1987 est.); real growth rate 9% (1987 est.)
Inflation rate (consumer prices): 1.3% (1988)
Unemployment rate: 35% (February 1991)
Budget: revenues $358 million; expenditures $914 million, including capital expenditures of $NA (1986)
Exports: $166 million (f.o.b., 1988);
commodities—sugar 75%, rum and molasses 4%, perfume essences 4%, lobster 3%, vanilla and tea 1%;
partners—France, Mauritius, Bahrain, South Africa, Italy
Imports: $1.7 billion (c.i.f., 1988);
commodities—manufactured goods, food, beverages, tobacco, machinery and transportation equipment, raw materials, and petroleum products;
partners—France, Mauritius, Bahrain, South Africa, Italy
External debt: NA
Industrial production: growth rate NA%; about 25% of GDP
Electricity: 245,000 kW capacity; 546 million kWh produced, 965 kWh per capita (1989)
Industries: sugar, rum, cigarettes, several small shops producing handicraft items
Agriculture: accounts for 30% of labor force; dominant sector of economy; cash crops—sugarcane, vanilla, tobacco; food crops—tropical fruits, vegetables, corn; imports large share of food needs
Economic aid: Western (non-US) countries, ODA and OOF bilateral commitments (1970-88), $14.1 billion
Currency: French franc (plural—francs); 1 French franc (F) = 100 centimes

Exchange rates: French francs (F) per US$1—5.1307 (January 1991), 5.4453 (1990), 6.3801 (1989), 5.9569 (1988), 6.0107 (1987), 6.9261 (1986), 8.9852 (1985)
Fiscal year: calendar year

Communications

Highways: 2,800 km total; 2,200 km paved, 600 km gravel, crushed stone, or stabilized earth
Ports: Pointe des Galets
Civil air: 1 major transport aircraft
Airports: 2 total, 2 usable; 2 with permanent-surface runways; none with runways over 3,659 m; 1 with runways 2,440-3,659 m; 1 with runways 1,220-2,439 m
Telecommunications: adequate system for needs; modern open-wire line and radio relay network; principal center Saint-Denis; radiocommunication to Comoros, France, Madagascar; new radio relay route to Mauritius; 85,900 telephones; stations—3 AM, 13 FM, 1 (18 relays) TV; 1 Indian Ocean INTELSAT earth station

Defense Forces

Manpower availability: males 15-49, 162,017; 83,959 fit for military service; 5,979 reach military age (18) annually
Note: defense is the responsibility of France

Romania

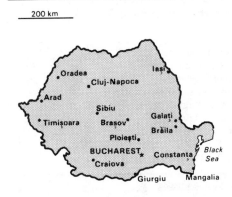

200 km

Geography

Total area: 237,500 km²; land area: 230,340 km²
Comparative area: slightly smaller than Oregon
Land boundaries: 2,904 km total; Bulgaria 608 km, Hungary 443 km, USSR 1,307 km, Yugoslavia 546 km
Coastline: 225 km
Maritime claims:
Continental shelf: 200 m (depth) or to depth of exploitation;
Exclusive economic zone: 200 nm;
Territorial sea: 12 nm
Climate: temperate; cold, cloudy winters with frequent snow and fog; sunny summers with frequent showers and thunderstorms
Terrain: central Transylvanian Basin is separated from the plain of Moldavia on the east by the Carpathian Mountains and separated from the Walachian Plain on the south by the Transylvanian Alps
Natural resources: crude oil (reserves being exhausted), timber, natural gas, coal, iron ore, salt
Land use: arable land 43%; permanent crops 3%; meadows and pastures 19%; forest and woodland 28%; other 7%; includes irrigated 11%
Environment: frequent earthquakes most severe in south and southwest; geologic structure and climate promote landslides, air pollution in south
Note: controls most easily traversable land route between the Balkans and western USSR

People

Population: 23,397,054 (July 1991), growth rate 0.5% (1991)
Birth rate: 16 births/1,000 population (1991)
Death rate: 10 deaths/1,000 population (1991)

Net migration rate: -1 migrant/1,000 population (1991)

Infant mortality rate: 18 deaths/1,000 live births (1991)

Life expectancy at birth: 69 years male, 75 years female (1991)

Total fertility rate: 2.1 children born/woman (1991)

Nationality: noun—Romanian(s); adjective—Romanian

Ethnic divisions: Romanian 89.1%; Hungarian 8.9%; German 0.4%; Ukrainian, Serb, Croat, Russian, Turk, and Gypsy 1.6%

Religion: Romanian Orthodox 70%, Roman Catholic 6%, Greek Catholic (Uniate) 3%, Protestant 6%, unaffiliated 15%

Language: Romanian, Hungarian, German

Literacy: 96% (male NA%, female NA%) age 15 and over can read and write (1970 est.)

Labor force: 10,690,000; industry 34%, agriculture 28%, other 38% (1987)

Organized labor: until December 1989, a single trade union system organized by the General Confederation of Romanian Trade Unions (UGSR) under control of the Communist Party; since Ceaușescu's overthrow, newly-created trade and professional trade unions are joining three umbrella organizations—Organization of Free Trade Unions, Fratia (Brotherhood), and the Alfa Cortel; many other trade unions have been formed

Government

Long-form name: none

Type: in transition from Communist state to republic

Capital: Bucharest

Administrative divisions: 40 counties (județe, singular—județ) and 1 municipality* (municipiu); Alba, Arad, Argeș, Bacău, Bihor, Bistrița-Năsăud, Botoșani, Brăila, Brașov, București*, Buzău, Călărași, Caraș-Severin, Cluj, Constanța, Covasna, Dîmbovița, Dolj, Galați, Gorj, Giurgiu, Harghita, Hunedoara, Ialomița, Iași, Maramureș, Mehedinți, Mureș, Neamț, Olt, Prahova, Sălaj, Satu Mare, Sibiu, Suceava, Teleorman, Timiș, Tulcea, Vaslui, Vîlcea, Vrancea

Independence: 1881 (from Turkey); republic proclaimed 30 December 1947

Constitution: 21 August 1965; new constitution being drafted

Legal system: former mixture of civil law system and Communist legal theory that increasingly reflected Romanian traditions is being revised

National holiday: National Day of Romania, 1 December (1990)

Executive branch: president, vice president, prime minister, Council of Ministers (cabinet)

Legislative branch: bicameral Parliament consists of an upper house or Senate (Senat) and a lower house or House of Deputies (Adunarea Deputaților)

Judicial branch: Supreme Court of Justice

Leaders:

Chief of State—President Ion ILIESCU (since 20 June 1990, previously President of Provisional Council of National Unity since 23 December 1989);

Head of Government—Prime Minister of Council of Ministers Petre ROMAN (since 23 December 1989)

Political parties and leaders: National Salvation Front (FSN), Ion STOICA; Magyar Democratic Union (UDMR), Geza DOMOKOS; National Liberal Party (PNL), Radu CAMPEANU; National Peasants' Christian and Democratic Party (PNTCD), Corneliu COPOSU; Ecology Movement (MER), leader NA; Romanian National Unity Party (AUR), Radu CEONTEA; there are now more than 100 other parties; note—although the Communist Party has ceased to exist, a small proto-Communist party, the Socialist Labor Party, has been formed

Suffrage: universal at age 18

Elections:

President—last held 20 May 1990 (next to be held NA 1992); results—Ion ILIESCU 85%, Radu CAMPEANU 10.5%, Ion RATIU 3.8%;

Senate—last held 20 May 1990 (next to be held NA 1992); results—FSN 67%, other 33%; seats—(118 total) FSN 92, UDMR 12, PNL 9, AUR 2, PNTCD 1, MER 1, other 1;

House of Deputies—last held 20 May 1990 (next to be held NA 1992); results—FSN 66%, UDMR 7%, PNL 6%, MER 2%, PNTCD 2%, AUR 2%, other 15%; seats—(387 total) FSN 263, UDMR 29, PNL 29, PNTCD 12, MER 12, AUR 9, other 33

Communists: 3,400,000 (November 1984); Communist Party has ceased to exist

Member of: BIS, CCC, CSCE, ECE, FAO, G-9, G-77, GATT, IAEA, IBEC, IBRD, ICAO, IFAD, IFC, IIB, ILO, IMF, IMO, INTERPOL, IOC, ITU, LORCS, NAM (guest), PCA, UN, UNCTAD, UNESCO, UNIDO, UPU, WFTU, WHO, WIPO, WMO, WTO

Diplomatic representation: Ambassador Virgil CONSTANTINESCU; Chancery at 1607 23rd Street NW, Washington DC 20008; telephone (202) 232-4747;

US—Ambassador Alan GREEN, Jr.; Embassy at Strada Tudor Arghezi 7-9, Bucharest (mailing address is APO New York 09213); telephone [40] (0) 10-40-40

Flag: three equal vertical bands of blue (hoist side), yellow, and red; the national coat of arms that used to be centered in the yellow band, has been removed; now similar to the flags of Andorra and Chad

Economy

Overview: Industry, which accounts for one-third of the labor force and generates over half the GNP, suffers from an aging capital plant and persistent shortages of energy. The year 1990 witnessed about a 20% drop in industrial production because of energy and input shortages and labor unrest. In recent years the agricultural sector has had to contend with drought, mismanagement, and shortages of inputs. A drought in 1990 contributed to a lackluster harvest, a problem compounded by corruption and a poor distribution system. The new government is slowly loosening the tight central controls of Ceaușescu's command economy. It has instituted moderate land reforms, with close to one-half of cropland now in private hands, and it has allowed changes in prices for private agricultural output. Also, the new regime is permitting the establishment of private enterprises, largely in services, handicrafts, and small-scale industry. New laws providing for the privatization of large state firms have been passed. However, most of the early privatization will involve converting state firms into joint-stock companies. The selling of shares to the public has not yet been worked out. Furthermore, the government has halted the old policy of diverting food from domestic consumption to hard currency export markets. So far, the government does not seem willing to adopt a thoroughgoing market system, that is, there is great caution in decontrolling prices because of public opposition. The government has sharply raised price ceilings instead of lifting them entirely.

GNP: $69.9 billion, per capita $3,000; real growth rate -10.8% (1990 est.)

Inflation rate (consumer prices): 50% (1990 est.)

Unemployment rate: NA%

Budget: revenues $28.4 billion; expenditures $28.4 billion, including capital expenditures of $12.3 billion (1989)

Exports: $9.2 billion (f.o.b., 1990 est.); *commodities*—machinery and equipment 34.7%, fuels, minerals and metals 24.7%, manufactured consumer goods 16.9%, agricultural materials and forestry products 11.9%, other 11.6% (1986); *partners*—USSR 27%, Eastern Europe 23%, EC 15%, US 5%, China 4% (1987)

Imports: $10.9 billion (f.o.b., 1990 est.); *commodities*—fuels, minerals, and metals 51.0%, machinery and equipment 26.7%, agricultural and forestry products 11.0%, manufactured consumer goods 4.2% (1986); *partners*—Communist countries 60%, non-Communist countries 40% (1987)

External debt: $400 million (mid-1990)

Industrial production: growth rate -20% (1990 est.)

Romania *(continued)*

Electricity: 22,700,000 kW capacity; 64,200 million kWh produced, 2,760 kWh per capita (1990)
Industries: mining, timber, construction materials, metallurgy, chemicals, machine building, food processing, petroleum
Agriculture: accounts for 15% of GNP and 28% of labor force; major wheat and corn producer; other products—sugar beets, sunflower seed, potatoes, milk, eggs, meat, grapes
Economic aid: donor—$4.4 billion in bilateral aid to non-Communist less developed countries (1956-89)
Currency: leu (plural—lei); 1 leu (L) = 100 bani
Exchange rates: lei (L) per US$1—60.00 (June 1991), 22.432 (1990), 14.922 (1989), 14.277 (1988), 14.557 (1987), 16.153 (1986), 17.141 (1985)
Fiscal year: calendar year

Communications

Railroads: 11,275 km total; 10,860 km 1.435-meter standard gauge, 370 km narrow gauge, 45 km broad gauge; 3,411 km electrified, 3,060 km double track; government owned (1987)
Highways: 72,799 km total; 15,762 km concrete, asphalt, stone block; 20,208 km asphalt treated; 27,729 km gravel, crushed stone, and other paved surfaces; 9,100 km unpaved roads (1985)
Inland waterways: 1,724 km (1984)
Pipelines: 2,800 km crude oil; 1,429 km refined products; 6,400 km natural gas
Ports: Constanta, Galati, Braila, Mangalia; inland ports are Giurgiu, Drobeta-Turnu Severin, Orsova
Merchant marine: 294 ships (1,000 GRT or over) totaling 3,767,465 GRT/5,893,700 DWT; includes 1 passenger-cargo, 191 cargo, 2 container, 1 rail-car carrier, 11 roll-on/roll-off cargo, 2 livestock carrier, 15 petroleum, oils, and lubricants (POL) tanker, 69 bulk, 2 combination ore/oil
Civil air: 59 major transport aircraft
Airports: 165 total, 165 usable; 25 with permanent-surface runways; 15 with runways 2,440-3,659 m; 15 with runways 1,220-2,439 m
Telecommunications: about 2.3 million telephone customers; 89% of phone network is automatic; present phone density is 9.85 per 100 residents; roughly 3,300 villages with no service (February 1990); stations—39 AM, 29 FM, 39 TV (1990)

Defense Forces

Branches: French—Army, Navy, Air Force, Gendarmerie
Manpower availability: males 15-49, 5,801,986; 4,912,789 fit for military service; 192,996 reach military age (20) annually
Defense expenditures: 15 billion lei (unofficial), NA% of GDP (1991); note—conversion of defense expenditures into US dollars using the official administratively set exchange rate would produce misleading results

Rwanda

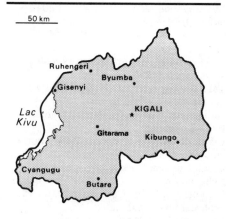

Geography

Total area: 26,340 km²; land area: 24,950 km²
Comparative area: slightly smaller than Maryland
Land boundaries: 893 km total; Burundi 290 km, Tanzania 217 km, Uganda 169 km, Zaire 217 km
Coastline: none—landlocked
Maritime claims: none—landlocked
Climate: temperate; two rainy seasons (February to April, November to January); mild in mountains with frost and snow possible
Terrain: mostly grassy uplands and hills; mountains in west
Natural resources: gold, cassiterite (tin ore), wolframite (tungsten ore), natural gas, hydropower
Land use: arable land 29%; permanent crops 11%; meadows and pastures 18%; forest and woodland 10%; other 32%; includes irrigated NEGL%
Environment: deforestation; overgrazing; soil exhaustion; soil erosion; periodic droughts
Note: landlocked

People

Population: 7,902,644 (July 1991), growth rate 3.8% (1991)
Birth rate: 52 births/1,000 population (1991)
Death rate: 15 deaths/1,000 population (1991)
Net migration rate: 0 migrants/1,000 population (1991)
Infant mortality rate: 110 deaths/1,000 live births (1991)
Life expectancy at birth: 51 years male, 54 years female (1991)
Total fertility rate: 8.4 children born/woman (1991)
Nationality: noun and adjective—Rwandan(s)
Ethnic divisions: Hutu 90%, Tutsi 9%, Twa (Pygmoid) 1%

Religion: Roman Catholic 65%, Protestant 9%, Muslim 1%, indigenous beliefs and other 25%

Language: Kinyarwanda, French (official); Kiswahili used in commercial centers

Literacy: 50% (male 64%, female 37%) age 15 and over can read and write (1990 est.)

Labor force: 3,600,000; agriculture 93%, government and services 5%, industry and commerce 2%; 49% of population of working age (1985)

Organized labor: NA

Government

Long-form name: Republic of Rwanda

Type: republic; presidential system in which military leaders hold key offices; on 31 December 1990, the government announced a National Political Charter to serve as a basis for transition to a presidential/parliamentary political system; the charter will be voted upon in a national referendum to be held June 1991

Capital: Kigali

Administrative divisions: 10 prefectures (préfectures, singular—préfecture in French; plural—NA, singular—prefegitura in Kinyarwanda); Butare, Byumba, Cyangugu, Gikongoro, Gisenyi, Gitarama, Kibungo, Kibuye, Rigali, Ruhengeri

Constitution: 17 December 1978

Independence: 1 July 1962 (from UN trusteeship under Belgian administration)

Legal system: based on German and Belgian civil law systems and customary law; judicial review of legislative acts in the Supreme Court; has not accepted compulsory ICJ jurisdiction

National holiday: Independence Day, 1 July (1962)

Executive branch: president, Council of Ministers (cabinet)

Legislative branch: unicameral National Development Council (Conseil National de Développement)

Judicial branch: Constitutional Court (consists of the Court of Cassation and the Council of State in joint session)

Leaders:
Chief of State and Head of Government—President Maj. Gen. Juvénal HABYARIMANA (since 5 July 1973)

Political parties and leaders: only party—National Revolutionary Movement for Development (MRND), Maj. Gen. Juvénal HABYARIMANA; note—the MRND is officially a development movement, not a party

Suffrage: universal adult, exact age NA

Elections:
President—last held 19 December 1988 (next to be held December 1993); results—President Maj. Gen. Juvénal HABYARIMANA reelected;

National Development Council—last held 19 December 1988 (next to be held December 1993); results—MRND is the only party; seats—(70 total); MRND 70

Communists: no Communist party

Member of: ACCT, ACP, AfDB, ECA, CCC, CEEAC, CEPGL, FAO, G-77, GATT, IBRD, ICAO, IDA, IFAD, IFC, ILO, IMF, INTELSAT, INTERPOL, IOC, ITU, LORCS, NAM, OAU, UN, UNCTAD, UNESCO, UNIDO, UPU, WCL, WHO, WIPO, WMO, WTO

Diplomatic representation: Ambassador Aloys UWIMANA; Chancery at 1714 New Hampshire Avenue NW, Washington DC 20009; telephone (202) 232-2882;
US—Ambassador Robert A. FLATEN; Embassy at Boulevard de la Revolution, Kigali (mailing address is B. P. 28, Kigali); telephone [250] 75601 through 75603 or 72126 through 72128

Flag: three equal vertical bands of red (hoist side), yellow, and green with a large black letter *R* centered in the yellow band; uses the popular pan-African colors of Ethiopia; similar to the flag of Guinea, which has a plain yellow band

Economy

Overview: Almost 50% of GDP comes from the agricultural sector; coffee and tea make up 80-90% of total exports. The amount of fertile land is limited, however, and deforestation and soil erosion have created problems. The industrial sector in Rwanda is small, contributing only 16% to GDP. Manufacturing focuses mainly on the processing of agricultural products. The Rwandan economy remains dependent on coffee exports and foreign aid, with no relief in sight. Weak international prices since 1986 have caused the economy to contract and per capita GDP to decline. A structural adjustment program with the World Bank began in October 1990. An outbreak of insurgency, also in October, has dampened any prospects for economic improvement.

GDP: $2.2 billion, per capita $300; real growth rate −2.2% (1989 est.)

Inflation rate (consumer prices): 1% (1989)

Unemployment rate: NA%

Budget: revenues $391 million; expenditures $491 million, including capital expenditures of $225 million (1989 est.)

Exports: $117 million (f.o.b., 1989 est.);
commodities—coffee 85%, tea, tin, cassiterite, wolframite, pyrethrum;
partners—FRG, Belgium, Italy, Uganda, UK, France, US

Imports: $293 million (f.o.b., 1989 est.);
commodities—textiles, foodstuffs, machines and equipment, capital goods, steel, petroleum products, cement and construction material;

partners—US, Belgium, FRG, Kenya, Japan

External debt: $689 million (December 1990 est.)

Industrial production: growth rate 1.2% (1988); accounts for 16% of GDP

Electricity: 26,000 kW capacity; 112 million kWh produced, 15 kWh per capita (1989)

Industries: mining of cassiterite (tin ore) and wolframite (tungsten ore), tin, cement, agricultural processing, small-scale beverage production, soap, furniture, shoes, plastic goods, textiles, cigarettes

Agriculture: accounts for almost 50% of GDP and about 90% of the labor force; cash crops—coffee, tea, pyrethrum (insecticide made from chrysanthemums); main food crops—bananas, beans, sorghum, potatoes; stock raising; self-sufficiency declining; country imports foodstuffs as farm production fails to keep up with a 3.8% annual growth in population

Economic aid: US commitments, including Ex-Im (FY70-89), $128 million; Western (non-US) countries, ODA and OOF bilateral commitments (1970-88), $1.8 billion; OPEC bilateral aid (1979-89), $45 million; Communist countries (1970-89), $58 million

Currency: Rwandan franc (plural—francs); 1 Rwandan franc (RF) = 100 centimes

Exchange rates: Rwandan francs (RF) per US$1—120.00 (December 1990), 82.60 (1990), 79.98 (1989), 76.45 (1988), 79.67 (1987), 87.64 (1986), 101.26 (1985)

Fiscal year: calendar year

Communications

Highways: 4,885 km total; 460 km paved, 1,725 km gravel and/or improved earth, 2,700 km unimproved

Inland waterways: Lac Kivu navigable by shallow-draft barges and native craft

Civil air: 1 major transport aircraft

Airports: 8 total, 8 usable; 3 with permanent-surface runways; none with runways over 3,659 m; 1 with runways 2,440-3,659 m; 2 with runways 1,220-2,439 m

Telecommunications: fair system with low-capacity radio relay system centered on Kigali; 6,600 telephones; stations—2 AM, 5 FM, no TV; earth stations—1 Indian Ocean INTELSAT and 1 SYMPHONIE

Defense Forces

Branches: Army, Gendarmerie

Manpower availability: males 15-49, 1,651,224; 842,480 fit for military service; no conscription

Defense expenditures: $37 million, 1.6% of GDP (1988 est.)

Saint Helena
(dependent territory of the UK)

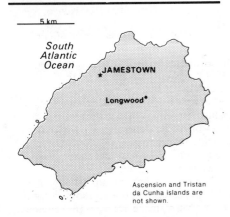

South Atlantic Ocean

5 km

JAMESTOWN

Longwood*

Ascension and Tristan da Cunha islands are not shown.

Geography

Total area: 410 km²; land area: 410 km²; includes Ascension, Gough Island, Inaccessible Island, Nightingale Island, and Tristan da Cunha
Comparative area: slightly more than 2.3 times the size of Washington, DC
Land boundaries: none
Coastline: 60 km
Maritime claims:
Exclusive fishing zone: 200 nm;
Territorial sea: 12 nm
Climate: tropical; marine; mild, tempered by trade winds
Terrain: rugged, volcanic; small scattered plateaus and plains
Natural resources: fish; Ascension is a breeding ground for sea turtles and sooty terns; no minerals
Land use: arable land 7%; permanent crops 0%; meadows and pastures 7%; forest and woodland 3%; other 83%
Environment: very few perennial streams
Note: located 1,920 km west of Angola, about two-thirds of the way between South America and Africa; Napoleon Bonaparte's place of exile and burial; the remains were taken to Paris in 1840

People

Population: 6,695 (July 1991), growth rate 0.6% (1991)
Birth rate: 13 births/1,000 population (1991)
Death rate: 8 deaths/1,000 population (1991)
Net migration rate: NEGl migrants/1,000 population (1991)
Infant mortality rate: 46 deaths/1,000 live births (1991)
Life expectancy at birth: 70 years male, 75 years female (1991)
Total fertility rate: 1.4 children born/woman (1991)

Nationality: noun—Saint Helenian(s); adjective—Saint Helenian
Ethnic divisions: NA
Religion: Anglican majority; also Baptist, Seventh-Day Adventist, and Roman Catholic
Language: English
Literacy: 98% (male 97%, female 98%) age 15 and over can read and write (1987)
Labor force: NA
Organized labor: Saint Helena General Workers' Union, 472 members; crafts 17%, professional and technical 10%, service 10%, management and clerical 9%, farming and fishing 9%, transport 6%, sales 5%, and other 34%

Government

Long-form name: none
Type: dependent territory of the UK
Capital: Jamestown
Administrative divisions: 2 dependencies and 1 administrative area*; Ascension*, Saint Helena, Tristan da Cunha
Independence: none (dependent territory of the UK)
Constitution: 1 January 1967
Legal system: NA
National holiday: Celebration of the Birthday of the Queen (second Saturday in June), 10 June 1989
Executive branch: British monarch, governor, Executive Council (cabinet)
Legislative branch: unicameral Legislative Council
Judicial branch: Supreme Court
Leaders:
Chief of State—Queen ELIZABETH II (since 6 February 1952);
Head of Government—Governor and Commander in Chief Robert F. STIMSON (since 1987)
Political parties and leaders: Saint Helena Labor Party, G. A. O. THORNTON; Saint Helena Progressive Party, leader unknown; note—both political parties inactive since 1976
Suffrage: NA
Elections:
Legislative Council—last held October 1984 (next to be held NA); results—percent of vote by party NA; seats—(15 total, 12 elected) number of seats by party NA
Communists: probably none
Member of: ICFTU
Diplomatic representation: none (dependent territory of the UK)
Flag: blue with the flag of the UK in the upper hoist-side quadrant and the Saint Helenian shield centered on the outer half of the flag; the shield features a rocky coastline and three-masted sailing ship

Economy

Overview: The economy depends primarily on financial assistance from the UK. The local population earns some income from fishing, the rearing of livestock, and sales of handicrafts. Because there are few jobs, a large proportion of the work force has left to seek employment overseas.
GDP: $NA, per capita $NA; real growth rate NA%
Inflation rate (consumer prices): -1.1% (1986)
Unemployment rate: NA%
Budget: revenues $3.2 million; expenditures $2.9 million, including capital expenditures of NA (1984)
Exports: $23.9 thousand (f.o.b., 1984);
commodities—fish (frozen and salt-dried skipjack, tuna), handicrafts;
partners—South Africa, UK
Imports: $2.4 million (c.i.f., 1984);
commodities—food, beverages, tobacco, fuel oils, animal feed, building materials, motor vehicles and parts, machinery and parts;
partners—UK, South Africa
External debt: $NA
Industrial production: growth rate NA%
Electricity: 9,800 kW capacity; 10 million kWh produced, 1,390 kWh per capita (1989)
Industries: crafts (furniture, lacework, fancy woodwork), fish
Agriculture: maize, potatoes, vegetables; timber production being developed; crawfishing on Tristan da Cunha
Economic aid: Western (non-US) countries, ODA and OOF bilateral commitments (1970-88), $184 million
Currency: Saint Helenian pound (plural—pounds); 1 Saint Helenian pound (£S) = 100 pence
Exchange rates: Saint Helenian pounds (£S) per US$1—0.5171 (January 1991), 0.5603 (1990), 0.6099 (1989), 0.5614 (1988), 0.6102 (1987), 0.6817 (1986), 0.7714 (1985); note—the Saint Helenian pound is at par with the British pound
Fiscal year: 1 April-31 March

Communications

Highways: 87 km bitumen-sealed roads, 20 km earth roads on Saint Helena; 80 km bitumen-sealed on Ascension; 2.7 km bitumen-sealed on Tristan da Cunha
Ports: Jamestown (Saint Helena), Georgetown (Ascension)
Merchant marine: 1 passenger-cargo ship totaling 6,767 GRT/5,600 DWT
Airports: 1 with permanent-surface runway 2,440-3,659 m on Ascension

Saint Kitts and Nevis

Telecommunications: 1,500 radio receivers; stations—1 AM, no FM, no TV; 550 telephones in automatic network; HF radio links to Ascension, then into worldwide submarine cable and satellite networks; major coaxial cable relay point between South Africa, Portugal, and UK at Ascension; 2 Atlantic Ocean INTELSAT earth stations

Defense Forces

Note: defense is the responsibility of the UK

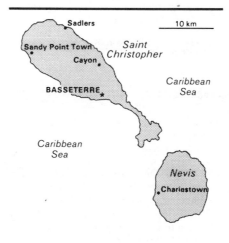

Geography

Total area: 269 km²; land area: 269 km²
Comparative area: slightly more than 1.5 times the size of Washington, DC
Land boundaries: none
Coastline: 135 km
Maritime claims:
Contiguous zone: 24 nm;
Exclusive economic zone: 200 nm;
Territorial sea: 12 nm
Climate: subtropical tempered by constant sea breezes; little seasonal temperature variation; rainy season (May to November)
Terrain: volcanic with mountainous interiors
Natural resources: negligible
Land use: arable land 22%; permanent crops 17%; meadows and pastures 3%; forest and woodland 17%; other 41%
Environment: subject to hurricanes (July to October)
Note: located 320 km east-southeast of Puerto Rico

People

Population: 40,293 (July 1991), growth rate 0.4% (1991)
Birth rate: 24 births/1,000 population (1991)
Death rate: 10 deaths/1,000 population (1991)
Net migration rate: −10 migrants/1,000 population (1991)
Infant mortality rate: 39 deaths/1,000 live births (1991)
Life expectancy at birth: 64 years male, 71 years female (1991)
Total fertility rate: 2.6 children born/woman (1991)
Ethnic divisions: mainly of black African descent
Nationality: noun—Kittsian(s), Nevisian(s); adjective—Kittsian, Nevisian
Religion: Anglican, other Protestant sects, Roman Catholic
Language: English

Literacy: 98% (male 98%, female 98%) age 15 and over having ever attended school (1970)
Labor force: 20,000 (1981)
Organized labor: 6,700

Government

Long-form name: Federation of Saint Kitts and Nevis
Type: constitutional monarchy
Capital: Basseterre
Administrative divisions: 14 parishs; Christ Church Nichola Town, Saint Anne Sandy Point, Saint George Basseterre, Saint George Gingerland, Saint James Windward, Saint John Capisterre, Saint John Figtree, Saint Mary Cayon, Saint Paul Capisterre, Saint Paul Charlestown, Saint Peter Basseterre, Saint Thomas Lowland, Saint Thomas Middle Island, Trinity Palmetto Point
Independence: 19 September 1983 (from UK)
Constitution: 19 September 1983
Legal system: based on English common law
National holiday: Independence Day, 19 September (1983)
Executive branch: British monarch, governor general, prime minister, deputy prime minister, Cabinet
Legislative branch: unicameral National Assembly
Judicial branch: Eastern Caribbean Supreme Court
Leaders:
Chief of State—Queen ELIZABETH II (since 6 February 1952), represented by Governor General Sir Clement Athelston ARRINDELL (since 19 September 1983, previously Governor General of the Associated State since NA November 1981);
Head of Government—Prime Minister Dr. Kennedy Alphonse SIMMONDS (since 19 September 1983, previously Premier of the Associated State since NA February 1980); Deputy Prime Minister Michael Oliver POWELL (since NA)
Political parties and leaders: People's Action Movement (PAM), Kennedy SIMMONDS; Saint Kitts and Nevis Labor Party (SKNLP), Lee MOORE; Nevis Reformation Party (NRP), Simeon DANIEL; Concerned Citizens Movement (CCM), Vance AMORY
Suffrage: universal adult at age NA
Elections:
House of Assembly—last held 21 March 1989 (next to be held by 21 March 1994); seats—(14 total, 11 elected) PAM 6, SKNLP 2, NRP 2, CCM 1
Communists: none known
Member of: ACP, C, CARICOM, CDB, ECLAC, FAO, IBRD, ICFTU, IDA, IFAD, IMF, INTERPOL, OAS, OECS, UN, UNCTAD, UNESCO, UNIDO, UPU, WCL, WHO

Saint Kitts and Nevis *(continued)*

Diplomatic representation: Minister-Counselor (Deputy Chief of Mission), Chargé d'Affaires ad interim Erstein M. EDWARDS; Chancery at Suite 540, 2501 M Street NW, Washington DC 20037; telephone (202) 833-3550;
US—none
Flag: divided diagonally from the lower hoist side by a broad black band bearing two white five-pointed stars; the black band is edged in yellow; the upper triangle is green, the lower triangle is red

---

Economy

Overview: The economy has historically depended on the growing and processing of sugarcane and on remittances from overseas workers. In recent years, tourism and export-oriented manufacturing have assumed larger roles.
GDP: $97.5 million, per capita $2,400; real growth rate 4.6% (1988)
Inflation rate (consumer prices): 5% (1989)
Unemployment rate: 15% (1989)
Budget: revenues $38.1 million; expenditures $68.1 million, including capital expenditures of $31.5 million (1991)
Exports: $32.8 million (f.o.b., 1989);
commodities—sugar, clothing, electronics, postage stamps;
partners—US 53%, UK 22%, Trinidad and Tobago 5%, OECS 5% (1988)
Imports: $89.6 million (f.o.b., 1989);
commodities—foodstuffs, intermediate manufactures, machinery, fuels;
partners—US 36%, UK 17%, Trinidad and Tobago 6%, Canada 3%, Japan 3%, OECS 4% (1988)
External debt: $26.4 million (1988)
Industrial production: growth rate 11.8% (1988 est.); accounts for 17% of GDP
Electricity: 15,800 kW capacity; 45 million kWh produced, 1,120 kWh per capita (1990)
Industries: sugar processing, tourism, cotton, salt, copra, clothing, footwear, beverages
Agriculture: accounts for 10% of GDP; cash crop—sugarcane; subsistence crops—rice, yams, vegetables, bananas; fishing potential not fully exploited; most food imported
Economic aid: US commitments, including Ex-Im (FY85-88), $10.7 million; Western (non-US) countries, ODA and OOF bilateral commitments (1970-88), $57 million
Currency: East Caribbean dollar (plural—dollars); 1 EC dollar (EC$) = 100 cents
Exchange rates: East Caribbean dollars (EC$) per US$1—2.70 (fixed rate since 1976)
Fiscal year: calendar year

Communications

Railroads: 58 km 0.760-meter narrow gauge on Saint Kitts for sugarcane
Highways: 300 km total; 125 km paved, 125 km otherwise improved, 50 km unimproved earth
Ports: Basseterre (Saint Kitts), Charlestown (Nevis)
Civil air: no major transport aircraft
Airports: 2 total, 2 usable; 2 with permanent-surface runways; none with runways over 3,659 m; 1 with runways 2,440-3,659 m; none with runways 1,220-2,439 m
Telecommunications: good interisland VHF/UHF/SHF radio connections and international link via Antigua and Barbuda and Saint Martin; 2,400 telephones; stations—2 AM, no FM, 4 TV

Defense Forces

Branches: Royal Saint Kitts and Nevis Police Force, Coast Guard
Manpower availability: NA
Defense expenditures: $NA, NA% of GDP

Saint Lucia

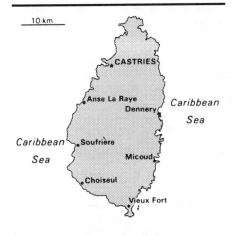

Geography

Total area: 620 km²; land area: 610 km²
Comparative area: slightly less than 3.5 times the size of Washington, DC
Land boundaries: none
Coastline: 158 km
Maritime claims:
Contiguous zone: 24 nm;
Exclusive economic zone: 200 nm;
Territorial sea: 12 nm
Climate: tropical, moderated by northeast trade winds; dry season from January to April, rainy season from May to August
Terrain: volcanic and mountainous with some broad, fertile valleys
Natural resources: forests, sandy beaches, minerals (pumice), mineral springs, geothermal potential
Land use: arable land 8%; permanent crops 20%; meadows and pastures 5%; forest and woodland 13%; other 54%; includes irrigated 2%
Environment: subject to hurricanes and volcanic activity; deforestation; soil erosion
Note: located 700 km southeast of Puerto Rico

People

Population: 153,075 (July 1991), growth rate 2.2% (1991)
Birth rate: 31 births/1,000 population (1991)
Death rate: 5 deaths/1,000 population (1991)
Net migration rate: −4 migrants/1,000 population (1991)
Infant mortality rate: 18 deaths/1,000 live births (1991)
Life expectancy at birth: 69 years male, 74 years female (1991)
Total fertility rate: 3.5 children born/woman (1991)
Nationality: noun—Saint Lucian(s); adjective—Saint Lucian

Ethnic divisions: African descent 90.3%, mixed 5.5%, East Indian 3.2%, Caucasian 0.8%

Religion: Roman Catholic 90%, Protestant 7%, Anglican 3%

Language: English (official), French patois

Literacy: 67% (male 65%, female 69%) age 15 and over having ever attended school (1980)

Labor force: 43,800; agriculture 43.4%, services 38.9%, industry and commerce 17.7% (1983 est.)

Organized labor: 20% of labor force

Government

Long-form name: none

Type: parliamentary democracy

Capital: Castries

Administrative divisions: 11 quarters; Anse-la-Raye, Castries, Choiseul, Dauphin, Dennery, Gros-Islet, Laborie, Micoud, Praslin, Soufrière, Vieux-Fort

Independence: 22 February 1979 (from UK)

Constitution: 22 February 1979

Legal system: based on English common law

National holiday: Independence Day, 22 February (1979)

Executive branch: British monarch, governor general, prime minister, Cabinet

Legislative branch: bicameral Parliament consists of an upper house or Senate and a lower house or House of Assembly

Judicial branch: Eastern Caribbean Supreme Court

Leaders:
Chief of State—Queen ELIZABETH II (since 6 February 1952), represented by Acting Governor General Sir Stanislaus Anthony JAMES (since 10 October 1988);
Head of Government—Prime Minister John George Melvin COMPTON (since 3 May 1982)

Political parties and leaders: United Workers' Party (UWP), John COMPTON; Saint Lucia Labor Party (SLP), Julian HUNTE; Progressive Labor Party (PLP), George ODLUM

Suffrage: universal at age 18

Elections:
House of Assembly—last held 6 April 1987 (next to be held by April 1992); results—percent of vote by party NA; seats—(17 total) UWP 10, SLP 7

Communists: negligible

Member of: ACCT (associate), ACP, C, CARICOM, CDB, ECLAC, FAO, G-77, IBRD, ICAO, ICFTU, IDA, IFAD, IFC, ILO, IMF, IMO, INTERPOL, LORCS, NAM, OAS, OECS, UN, UNCTAD, UNESCO, UNIDO, UPU, WCL, WHO, WMO

Diplomatic representation: Ambassador Dr. Joseph Edsel EDMUNDS; Chancery at Suite 309, 2100 M Street NW, Washington DC 30037; telephone (202) 463-7378 or 7379; there is a Saint Lucian Consulate General in New York;
US—none

Flag: blue with a gold isosceles triangle below a black arrowhead; the upper edges of the arrowhead have a white border

Economy

Overview: Since 1983 the economy has shown an impressive average annual growth rate of almost 5% because of strong agricultural and tourist sectors. Saint Lucia also possesses an expanding industrial base supported by foreign investment in manufacturing and other activities, such as in data processing. The economy, however, remains vulnerable because the important agricultural sector is dominated by banana production. Saint Lucia is subject to periodic droughts and/or tropical storms, and its protected market agreement with the UK for bananas may end in 1992.

GDP: $273 million, per capita $1,830; real growth rate 4.0% (1989)

Inflation rate (consumer prices): 4.4% (1989)

Unemployment rate: 16.0% (1988)

Budget: revenues $131 million; expenditures $149 million, including capital expenditures of $71 million (FY90 est.)

Exports: $111.9 million (f.o.b., 1989); *commodities*—bananas 54%, clothing 17%, cocoa, vegetables, fruits, coconut oil; *partners*—UK 51%, CARICOM 20%, US 19%, other 10%

Imports: $265.9 million (c.i.f., 1989); *commodities*—manufactured goods 23%, machinery and transportation equipment 27%, food and live animals 18%, chemicals 10%, fuels 6%; *partners*—US 35%, CARICOM 16%, UK 15%, Japan 7%, Canada 4%, other 23%

External debt: $54.5 million (1989)

Industrial production: growth rate 3.5% (1990 est.); accounts for 7% of GDP

Electricity: 32,500 kW capacity; 112 million kWh produced, 730 kWh per capita (1990)

Industries: clothing, assembly of electronic components, beverages, corrugated boxes, tourism, lime processing, coconut processing

Agriculture: accounts for 16% of GDP and 43% of labor force; crops—bananas, coconuts, vegetables, citrus fruit, root crops, cocoa; imports food for the tourist industry

Economic aid: Western (non-US) countries, ODA and OOF bilateral commitments (1970-88), $118 million

Currency: East Caribbean dollar (plural—dollars); 1 EC dollar (EC$) = 100 cents

Exchange rates: East Caribbean dollars (EC$) per US$1—2.70 (fixed rate since 1976)

Fiscal Year: 1 April-31 March

Communications

Highways: 760 km total; 500 km paved; 260 km otherwise improved

Ports: Castries

Civil air: 2 major transport aircraft

Airports: 2 total, 2 usable; 2 with permanent-surface runways; none with runways over 3,659 m; 1 with runways 2,440-3,659 m; 1 with runways 1,220-2,439

Telecommunications: fully automatic telephone system; 9,500 telephones; direct radio relay link with Martinique and Saint Vincent and the Grenadines; interisland troposcatter link to Barbados; stations—4 AM, 1 FM, 1 TV (cable)

Defense Forces

Branches: Royal Saint Lucia Police Force, Coast Guard

Manpower availability: males 15-49, 38,050; NA fit for military service

Defense expenditures: $NA, NA% of GDP

Saint Pierre and Miquelon
(territorial collectivity of France)

Geography

Total area: 242 km²; land area: 242 km²; includes eight small islands in the Saint Pierre and the Miquelon groups
Comparative area: slightly less than 1.5 times the size of Washington, DC
Land boundaries: none
Coastline: 120 km
Maritime claims:
Exclusive economic zone: 200 nm;
Territorial sea: 12 nm
Disputes: focus of maritime boundary dispute between Canada and France
Climate: cold and wet, with much mist and fog; spring and autumn are windy
Terrain: mostly barren rock
Natural resources: fish, deepwater ports
Land use: arable land 13%; permanent crops 0%; meadows and pastures 0%; forest and woodland 4%; other 83%
Environment: vegetation scanty
Note: located 25 km south of Newfoundland, Canada, in the North Atlantic Ocean

People

Population: 6,356 (July 1991), growth rate 0.4% (1991)
Birth rate: 17 births/1,000 population (1991)
Death rate: 7 deaths/1,000 population (1991)
Net migration rate: −6 migrants/1,000 population (1991)
Infant mortality rate: 9 deaths/1,000 live births (1991)
Life expectancy at birth: 72 years male, 79 years female (1991)
Total fertility rate: 2.2 children born/woman (1991)
Nationality: noun—Frenchman(men), Frenchwoman(women); adjective—French
Ethnic divisions: originally Basques and Bretons (French fishermen)
Religion: Roman Catholic 98%

Language: French
Literacy: 99% (male 99%, female 99%) age 15 and over can read and write (1982)
Labor force: 2,850 (1988)
Organized labor: Workers' Force trade union

Government

Long-form name: Territorial Collectivity of Saint Pierre and Miquelon
Type: territorial collectivity of France
Capital: Saint-Pierre
Administrative divisions: none (territorial collectivity of France)
Independence: none (territorial collectivity of France); note—has been under French control since 1763
Constitution: 28 September 1958 (French Constitution)
Legal system: French law
National holiday: National Day, 14 July (Taking of the Bastille)
Executive branch: commissioner of the Republic
Legislative branch: unicameral General Council
Judicial branch: Superior Tribunal of Appeals (Tribunal Supérieur d'Appel)
Leaders:
Chief of State—President François MITTERRAND (since 21 May 1981);
Head of Government—Commissioner of the Republic Jean-Pierre MARQUIE (since February 1989); President of the General Council Marc PLANTEGENEST (since NA)
Political parties and leaders: Socialist Party (PS); Union for French Democracy (UDF/CDS), Gerard GRIGNON
Suffrage: universal at age 18
Elections:
General Council—last held September-October 1988 (next to be held September 1994); results—percent of vote by party NA; seats—(19 total) Socialist and other left-wing parties 13, UDF and right-wing parties 6;
French President—last held 8 May 1988 (next to be held May 1995); results—(second ballot) Jacques CHIRAC 56%, François MITTERRAND 44%;
French Senate—last held 24 September 1989 (next to be held September 1992); results—percent of vote by party NA; seats—(1 total) PS 1;
French National Assembly—last held 5 and 12 June 1988 (next to be held June 1993); results—percent of vote by party NA; seats—(1 total) UDF/CDS 1
Member of: FZ, WFTU
Diplomatic representation: as a territorial collectivity of France, local interests are represented in the US by France
Flag: the flag of France is used

Economy

Overview: The inhabitants have traditionally earned their livelihood by fishing and by servicing fishing fleets operating off the coast of Newfoundland. The economy has been declining, however, because the number of ships stopping at Saint Pierre has dropped steadily over the years. In March 1989, an agreement between France and Canada set fish quotas for Saint Pierre's trawlers fishing in Canadian and Canadian-claimed waters for three years. The agreement settles a longstanding dispute that had virtually brought fish exports to a halt. The islands are heavily subsidized by France. Imports come primarily from Canada and France.
GDP: $50 million, per capita $7,900; real growth rate NA% (1990 est.)
Inflation rate (consumer prices): NA%
Unemployment rate: 8.3% (1988)
Budget: revenues $18.3 million; expenditures $18.3 million, including capital expenditures of $5.5 million (1989)
Exports: $24.1 million (f.o.b., 1988);
commodities—fish and fish products, fox and mink pelts;
partners—US 58%, France 17%, UK 11%, Canada, Portugal
Imports: $61.6 million (c.i.f., 1988);
commodities—meat, clothing, fuel, electrical equipment, machinery, building materials;
partners—Canada, France, US, Netherlands, UK
External debt: $NA
Industrial production: growth rate NA%
Electricity: 10,000 kW capacity; 25 million kWh produced, 3,970 kWh per capita (1989)
Industries: fish processing and supply base for fishing fleets; tourism
Agriculture: vegetables, cattle, sheep and pigs for local consumption; fish catch, 20,500 metric tons (1989)
Economic aid: Western (non-US) countries, ODA and OOF bilateral commitments (1970-88), $493 million
Currency: French franc (plural—francs); 1 French franc (F) = 100 centimes
Exchange rates: French francs (F) per US$1—5.1307 (January 1991), 5.4453 (1990), 6.3801 (1989), 5.9569 (1988), 6.0107 (1987), 6.9261 (1986), 8.9852 (1985)
Fiscal year: calendar year

Communications

Highways: 120 km total; 60 km paved (1985)
Ports: Saint Pierre
Civil air: no major transport aircraft

Saint Vincent and the Grenadines

Airports: 2 total, 2 usable; 2 with permanent-surface runways, none with runways over 2,439 m; 1 with runway 1,220-2,439 m
Telecommunications: 3,601 telephones; stations—1 AM, 3 FM, no TV; radiotelecommunication with most countries in the world; 1 earth station in French domestic system

Defense Forces

Note: defense is the responsibility of France

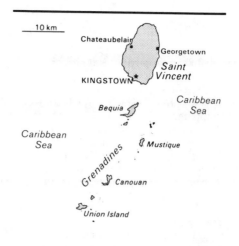

Geography

Total area: 340 km²; land area: 340 km²
Comparative area: slightly less than twice the size of Washington, DC
Land boundaries: none
Coastline: 84 km
Maritime claims:
Contiguous zone: 24 nm;
Exclusive economic zone: 200 nm;
Territorial sea: 12 nm
Climate: tropical; little seasonal temperature variation; rainy season (May to November)
Terrain: volcanic, mountainous; Soufrière volcano on the island of Saint Vincent
Natural resources: negligible
Land use: arable land 38%; permanent crops 12%; meadows and pastures 6%; forest and woodland 41%; other 3%; includes irrigated 3%
Environment: subject to hurricanes; Soufrière volcano is a constant threat
Note: some islands of the Grenadines group are administered by Grenada

People

Population: 114,221 (July 1991), growth rate 1.4% (1991)
Birth rate: 27 births/1,000 population (1991)
Death rate: 6 deaths/1,000 population (1991)
Net migration rate: −7 migrants/1,000 population (1991)
Infant mortality rate: 31 deaths/1,000 live births (1991)
Life expectancy at birth: 68 years male, 72 years female (1991)
Total fertility rate: 2.8 children born/woman (1991)
Nationality: noun—Saint Vincentian(s) or Vincentian(s); adjectives—Saint Vincentian or Vincentian
Ethnic divisions: mainly of black African descent; remainder mixed, with some white, East Indian, Carib Indian

Religion: Anglican, Methodist, Roman Catholic, Seventh-Day Adventist
Language: English, some French patois
Literacy: 96% (male 96%, female 96%) age 15 and over having ever attended school (1970)
Labor force: 67,000 (1984 est.)
Organized labor: 10% of labor force

Government

Long-form name: none
Type: constitutional monarchy
Capital: Kingstown
Administrative divisions: 6 parishes; Charlotte, Grenadines, Saint Andrew, Saint David, Saint George, Saint Patrick
Independence: 27 October 1979 (from UK)
Constitution: 27 October 1979
Legal system: based on English common law
National holiday: Independence Day, 27 October (1979)
Executive branch: British monarch, governor general, prime minister, Cabinet
Legislative branch: unicameral House of Assembly
Judicial branch: Eastern Caribbean Supreme Court
Leaders:
Chief of State—Queen ELIZABETH II (since 6 February 1952), represented by Governor General David JACK (since 29 Septermber 1989);
Head of Government—Prime Minister James F. MITCHELL (since 30 July 1984)
Political parties and leaders: New Democratic Party (NDP), James (Son) MITCHELL; Saint Vincent Labor Party (SVLP), Vincent BEACH; United People's Movement (UPM), Adrian SAUNDERS; Movement for National Unity (MNU), Ralph GONSALVES; National Reform Party (NRP), Joel MIGUEL
Suffrage: universal at age 18
Elections:
House of Assembly—last held 16 May 1989 (next to be held July 1994); results—percent of vote by party NA; seats—(21 total; 15 elected representatives and 6 appointed senators) NDP 15
Member of: ACP, C, CARICOM, CDB, ECLAC, FAO, G-77, IBRD, ICAO, ICFTU, IDA, IFAD, IMF, IMO, INTERPOL, IOC, ITU, LORCS, OAS, OECS, UN, UNCTAD, UNESCO, UNIDO, UPU, WCL, WFTU, WHO
Diplomatic representation: none
Flag: three vertical bands of blue (hoist side), gold (double width), and green; the gold band bears three green diamonds arranged in a *V* pattern

Saint Vincent and the Grenadines

(continued)

Economy

Overview: Agriculture, dominated by banana production, is the most important sector of the economy. The services sector, based mostly on a growing tourist industry, is also important. The economy continues to have a high unemployment rate of 30% because of an overdependence on the weather-plagued banana crop as a major export earner. Government progress toward diversifying into new industries has been relatively unsuccessful.

GDP: $146 million, per capita $1,315; real growth rate 5.9% (1989 est.)

Inflation rate (consumer prices): 2.6% (1989)

Unemployment rate: 30% (1989 est.)

Budget: revenues $62 million; expenditures $67 million, including capital expenditures of $21 million (FY90 est.)

Exports: $74.6 million (f.o.b., 1989); *commodities*—bananas 45%, eddoes and dasheen (taro), sweet potatoes, spices, light manufactures; *partners*—UK 43%, CARICOM 37%, US 15%

Imports: $127.5 million (c.i.f., 1989); *commodities*—foodstuffs, machinery and equipment, chemicals and fertilizers, minerals and fuels; *partners*—US 42%, CARICOM 19%, UK 15%

External debt: $42.2 million (FY89)

Industrial production: growth rate 0% (1989); accounts for 14% of GDP

Electricity: 16,600 kW capacity; 64 million kWh produced, 570 kWh per capita (1990)

Industries: food processing (sugar, flour), cement, furniture, clothing, starch, sheet metal, beverage

Agriculture: accounts for 15% of GDP and 60% of labor force; provides bulk of exports; products—bananas, coconuts, sweet potatoes, spices; small numbers of cattle, sheep, hogs, goats; small fish catch used locally

Economic aid: US commitments, including Ex-Im (FY70-87), $11 million; Western (non-US) countries, ODA and OOF bilateral commitments (1970-88), $76 million

Currency: East Caribbean dollar (plural—dollars); 1 EC dollar (EC$) = 100 cents

Exchange rates: East Caribbean dollars (EC$) per US$1—2.70 (fixed rate since 1976)

Fiscal year: calendar year (as of January 1991); previously 1 July-30 June

Communications

Highways: about 1,000 km total; 300 km paved; 400 km improved; 300 km unimproved

Ports: Kingstown

Merchant marine: 242 ships (1,000 GRT or over) totaling 1,855,061 GRT/2,919,872 DWT; includes 1 passenger, 2 passenger-cargo, 132 cargo, 11 container, 15 roll-on/roll-off cargo, 9 refrigerated cargo, 13 petroleum, oils, and lubricants (POL) tanker, 4 chemical tanker, 4 liquefied gas, 44 bulk, 6 combination bulk, 1 vehicle carrier; note—China owns 3 ships; a flag of convenience registry

Civil air: no major transport aircraft

Airports: 6 total, 6 usable; 4 with permanent-surface runways; none with runways over 2,439 m; 1 with runways 1,220-2,439 m

Telecommunications: islandwide fully automatic telephone system; 6,500 telephones; VHF/UHF interisland links to Barbados and the Grenadines; new SHF links to Grenada and Saint Lucia; stations—2 AM, no FM, 1 TV (cable)

Defense Forces

Branches: Royal Saint Vincent and the Grenadines Police Force, Coast Guard

Manpower availability: males 15-49, 28,339; NA fit for military service

Defense expenditures: $NA, NA% of GDP

San Marino

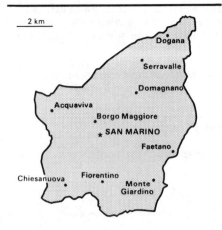

Geography

Total area: 60 km²; land area: 60 km²

Comparative area: about 0.3 times the size of Washington, DC

Land boundary: 39 km with Italy

Coastline: none—landlocked

Maritime claims: none—landlocked

Climate: Mediterranean; mild to cool winters; warm, sunny summers

Terrain: rugged mountains

Natural resources: building stones

Land use: arable land 17%; permanent crops 0%; meadows and pastures 0%; forest and woodland 0%; other 83%

Environment: dominated by the Appenines

Note: landlocked; world's smallest republic; enclave of Italy

People

Population: 23,264 (July 1991), growth rate 0.6% (1991)

Birth rate: 8 births/1,000 population (1991)

Death rate: 7 deaths/1,000 population (1991)

Net migration rate: 5 migrants/1,000 population (1991)

Infant mortality rate: 8 deaths/1,000 live births (1991)

Life expectancy at birth: 74 years male, 79 years female (1991)

Total fertility rate: 1.3 children born/woman (1991)

Nationality: noun—Sanmarinese (sing. and pl.); adjective—Sanmarinese

Ethnic divisions: Sanmarinese, Italian

Religion: Roman Catholic

Language: Italian

Literacy: 96% (male 96%, female 95%) age 14 and over can read and write (1976)

Labor force: about 4,300

Organized labor: Democratic Federation of Sanmarinese Workers (affiliated with

ICFTU) has about 1,800 members; Communist-dominated General Federation of Labor, 1,400 members

Government

Long-form name: Republic of San Marino
Type: republic
Capital: San Marino
Administrative divisions: 9 municipalities (castelli, singular—castello); Acquaviva, Borgo Maggiore, Chiesanuova, Domagnano, Faetano, Fiorentino, Monte Giardino, San Marino, Serravalle
Independence: 301 AD (by tradition)
Constitution: 8 October 1600; electoral law of 1926 serves some of the functions of a constitution
Legal system: based on civil law system with Italian law influences; has not accepted compulsory ICJ jurisdiction
National holiday: Anniversary of the Foundation of the Republic, 3 September
Executive branch: two captains regent, Congress of State (cabinet); real executive power is wielded by the secretary of state for foreign affairs and the secretary of state for internal affairs
Legislative branch: unicameral Great and General Council (Consiglio Grande e Generale)
Judicial branch: Council of Twelve (Consiglio dei XII)
Leaders:
Co-Chiefs of State—Captain Regent Aldamiro BARTOLINI and Captain Regent Ottaviano ROSSI (since 1 April 1990);
Head of Government—Prime Minister Gabriele GATTI (since July 1986)
Political parties and leaders: Christian Democratic Party (DCS), Gabriele GATTI; San Marino Democratic Progressive Party (PPDS) formerly San Marino Communist Party (PCS), Gilberto GHIOTTI; San Marino Socialist Party (PSS), Remy GIACOMINI; Democratic Movement (MD), Emilio Della BALDA; San Marino Social Democratic Party (PSDS), Augusto CASALI; San Marino Republican Party (PRS), Cristoforo BUSCARINI
Suffrage: universal at age 18
Elections:
Grand and General Council—last held 29 May 1988 (next to be held by May 1993); results—percent of vote by party NA; seats—(60 total) DCS 27, PCS 18, PSU 8, PSS 7
Communists: about 300 members
Other political parties or pressure groups: political parties influenced by policies of their counterparts in Italy
Member of: CE, CSCE, ICAO, ICFTU, ILO, IMF (observer), IOC, IOM (observer), ITU, LORCS, NAM (guest), UN (observer), UNCTAD, UNESCO, UPU, WHO, WTO

Diplomatic representation: San Marino maintains honorary Consulates General in Washington and New York, and an honorary Consulate in Detroit;
US—no mission in San Marino, but the Consul General in Florence (Italy) is accredited to San Marino; Consulate General at Lungarno Amerigo Vespucci, 38, 50123 Firenze, Italy (mailing address is APO New York 09019-0007); telephone [39] (55) 239-8276 through 8279 and 217-605
Flag: two equal horizontal bands of white (top) and light blue with the national coat of arms superimposed in the center; the coat of arms has a shield (featuring three towers on three peaks) flanked by a wreath, below a crown and above a scroll bearing the word *LIBERTAS* (Liberty)

Economy

Overview: More than 2 million tourists visit each year, contributing about 60% to GDP. The sale of postage stamps to foreign collectors is another important income producer. The manufacturing sector employs nearly 40% of the labor force and agriculture less than 4%. The per capita level of output and standard of living are comparable to northern Italy.
GDP: $393 million, per capita $17,000; real growth rate 2% (1990 est.)
Inflation rate (consumer prices): 6% (1990)
Unemployment rate: 6.5% (1985)
Budget: revenues $99.2 million; expenditures $NA, including capital expenditures of $NA (1983)
Exports: trade data are included with the statistics for Italy; commodity trade consists primarily of exchanging building stone, lime, wood, chestnuts, wheat, wine, baked goods, hides, and ceramics for a wide variety of consumer manufactures
Imports: see **Exports**
External debt: $NA
Industrial production: growth rate NA%
Electricity: supplied by Italy
Industries: wine, olive oil, cement, leather, textile, tourist
Agriculture: employs less than 4% of labor force; products—wheat, grapes, corn, olives, meat, cheese, hides; small numbers of cattle, pigs, horses; depends on Italy for food imports
Economic aid: NA
Currency: Italian lira (plural—lire); 1 Italian lira (Lit) = 100 centesimi; also mints its own coins
Exchange rates: Italian lire (Lit) per US$1—1,134.4 (January 1991), 1,198.1 (1990), 1,372.1 (1989), 1,301.6 (1988), 1,296.1 (1987), 1,490.8 (1986), 1,909.4 (1985)
Fiscal year: calendar year

Communications

Highways: 104 km
Telecommunications: automatic telephone system; 11,700 telephones; stations—no AM, 20 FM, no TV; radio relay and cable links into Italian networks; no communication satellite facilities

Defense Forces

Branches: public security or police force of less than 50 people
Manpower availability: all fit men ages 16-60 constitute a militia that can serve as an army
Defense expenditures: $NA, NA% of GDP

Sao Tome and Principe

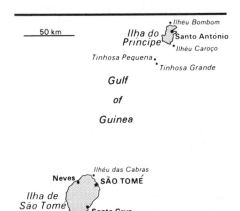

Geography

Total area: 960 km²; land area: 960 km²
Comparative area: slightly less than 5.5 times the size of Washington, DC
Land boundaries: none
Coastline: 209 km
Maritime claims: (measured from claimed archipelagic baselines);
Exclusive economic zone: 200 nm;
Territorial sea: 12 nm
Climate: tropical; hot, humid; one rainy season (October to May)
Terrain: volcanic, mountainous
Natural resources: fish
Land use: arable land 1%; permanent crops 20%; meadows and pastures 1%; forest and woodland 75%; other 3%
Environment: deforestation; soil erosion
Note: located south of Nigeria and west of Gabon near the Equator in the North Atlantic Ocean

People

Population: 128,499 (July 1991), growth rate 3.0% (1991)
Birth rate: 38 births/1,000 population (1991)
Death rate: 8 deaths/1,000 population (1991)
Net migration rate: 0 migrants/1,000 population (1991)
Infant mortality rate: 60 deaths/1,000 live births (1991)
Life expectancy at birth: 64 years male, 68 years female (1991)
Total fertility rate: 5.3 children born/woman (1991)
Nationality: noun—Sao Tomean(s); adjective—Sao Tomean
Ethnic divisions: mestiço, angolares (descendents of Angolan slaves), forros (descendents of freed slaves), servicais (contract laborers from Angola, Mozambique, and Cape Verde), tongas (children of servicais born on the islands), and Europeans (primarily Portuguese)

Religion: Roman Catholic, Evangelical Protestant, Seventh-Day Adventist
Language: Portuguese (official)
Literacy: 57% (male 73%, female 42%) age 15 and over can read and write (1981)
Labor force: 21,096 (1981); most of population engaged in subsistence agriculture and fishing; labor shortages on plantations and of skilled workers; 56% of population of working age (1983)
Organized labor: NA

Government

Long-form name: Democratic Republic of Sao Tome and Principe
Type: republic
Capital: São Tomé
Administrative divisions: 2 districts (concelhos, singular—concelho); Príncipe, São Tomé
Independence: 12 July 1975 (from Portugal)
Constitution: 5 November 1975, approved 15 December 1982
Legal system: based on Portuguese law system and customary law; has not accepted compulsory ICJ jurisdiction
National holiday: Independence Day, 12 July (1975)
Executive branch: president, prime minister, Council of Ministers (cabinet)
Legislative branch: unicameral People's National Assembly (Assembléia Popular Nacional)
Judicial branch: Supreme Court
Leaders:
Chief of State—President Miguel TROVOADA (since 4 April 1991);
Head of Government—Prime Minister Daniel Lima Dos Santos DAIO (since 21 January 1991)
Political parties and leaders: Party for Democratic Convergence-Reflection Group (PCD-GR), Prime Minister Daniel Lima Dos Santos DAIO, secretary general; Movement for the Liberation of Sao Tome and Principe (MLSTP), Carlos da GRAÇIA; Christian Democratic Front (FDC), Alphonse Dos SANTOS; Democratic Opposition Coalition (CODO), leader NA; other small parties
Suffrage: universal at age 18
Elections:
President—last held 3 March 1991 (next to be held March 1996); results—Miguel TROVOADA was elected without opposition in Sao Tome's first multiparty presidential election;
National People's Assembly—last held 20 January 1991 (next to be held January 1996); results—PCD-GR 54.4%, MLSTP 30.5%, CODO 5.2%, FDC 1.5%, other 8.3%; seats—(55 total) PCD-GR 33, MLSTP 21, CODO 1; note—this was the first National Assembly multiparty election in Sao Tome

Member of: ACP, AfDB, CEEAC, ECA, FAO, G-77, IBRD, ICAO, IDA, IFAD, ILO, IMF, INTERPOL, ITU, LORCS, NAM, OAU, UN, UNCTAD, UNESCO, UNIDO, UPU, WHO, WMO, WTO
Diplomatic representation: Ambassador Joaquim Rafael BRANCO; Chancery (temporary) at 801 Second Avenue, Suite 1504, New York, NY 10017; telephone (212) 697-4211;
US—Ambassador Keith L. WAUCHOPE in Gabon is accredited to Sao Tome and Principe on a nonresident basis and makes periodic visits to the islands
Flag: three horizontal bands of green (top), yellow (double width), and green with two black five-pointed stars placed side by side in the center of the yellow band and a red isosceles triangle based on the hoist side; uses the popular pan-African colors of Ethiopia

Economy

Overview: The economy has remained dependent on cocoa since the country gained independence nearly 15 years ago. Since then, however, cocoa production has gradually deteriorated because of drought and mismanagement, so that by 1987 output had fallen to less than 50% of its former levels. As a result, a shortage of cocoa for export has created a serious balance-of-payments problem. Production of less important crops, such as coffee, copra, and palm kernels, has also declined. The value of imports generally exceeds that of exports by a ratio of 4 to 1. The emphasis on cocoa production at the expense of other food crops has meant that Sao Tome has to import 90% of food needs. It also has to import all fuels and most manufactured goods. Over the years, Sao Tome has been unable to service its external debt, which amounts to roughly 80% of export earnings. Considerable potential exists for development of a tourist industry, and the government has taken steps to expand facilities in recent years. The government also implemented a Five-Year Plan covering 1986-90 to restructure the economy and reschedule external debt service payments in cooperation with the International Development Association and Western lenders.
GDP: $46.0 million, per capita $380; real growth rate 1.5% (1989)
Inflation rate (consumer prices): 36% (1989 est.)
Unemployment rate: NA%
Budget: revenues $10.2 million; expenditures $36.8 million, including capital expenditures of $22.5 million (1989)
Exports: $5.9 million (f.o.b., 1989 est.);
commodities—cocoa 85%, copra, coffee, palm oil;
partners—FRG, GDR, Netherlands, China

Saudi Arabia

Imports: $26.8 million (f.o.b., 1989 est.); *commodities*—machinery and electrical equipment 54%, food products 23%, other 23%;
partners—Portugal, GDR, Angola, China
External debt: $110 million (1990 est.)
Industrial production: growth rate 7.1% (1986)
Electricity: 5,000 kW capacity; 12 million kWh produced, 100 kWh per capita (1990)
Industries: light construction, shirts, soap, beer, fisheries, shrimp processing
Agriculture: dominant sector of economy, primary source of exports; cash crops—cocoa (85%), coconuts, palm kernels, coffee; food products—bananas, papaya, beans, poultry, fish; not self-sufficient in food grain and meat
Economic aid: US commitments, including Ex-Im (FY70-89), $8 million; Western (non-US) countries, ODA and OOF bilateral commitments (1970-87), $59 million
Currency: dobra (plural—dobras); 1 dobra (Db) = 100 céntimos
Exchange rates: dobras (Db) per US$1—122.48 (December 1988), 72.827 (1987), 36.993 (1986), 41.195 (1985)
Fiscal year: calendar year

Communications

Highways: 300 km (two-thirds are paved); roads on Príncipe are mostly unpaved and in need of repair
Ports: São Tomé, Santo António
Civil air: 8 major transport aircraft
Airports: 2 total, 2 usable; 2 with permanent-surface runways 1,220-2,439 m
Telecommunications: minimal system; 2,200 telephones; stations—1 AM, 2 FM, no TV; 1 Atlantic Ocean INTELSAT earth station

Defense Forces

Branches: Army, Navy, National Police
Manpower availability: males 15-49, 28,984; 15,287 fit for military service
Defense expenditures: $NA, 1.6% of GDP (1980)

Boundary representation is not necessarily authoritative

Geography

Total area: 2,149,690 km²; land area: 2,149,690 km²
Comparative area: slightly less than one-fourth the size of US
Land boundaries: 4,410 km total; Iraq 488 km, Iraq-Saudi Arabia Neutral Zone 198 km, Jordan 742 km, Kuwait 222 km, Oman 676 km, Qatar 40 km, UAE 586 km, Yemen 1,458 km
Coastline: 2,510 km
Maritime claims:
Contiguous zone: 18 nm;
Continental shelf: not specific;
Territorial sea: 12 nm
Disputes: no defined boundaries with Yemen and UAE; shares Neutral Zone with Iraq—in December 1981, Iraq and Saudi Arabia signed a boundary agreement that divides the zone between them, but the agreement must be ratified before it becomes effective; Kuwaiti ownership of Qārūh and Umm al Marādim Islands is disputed by Saudi Arabia
Climate: harsh, dry desert with great extremes of temperature
Terrain: mostly uninhabited, sandy desert
Natural resources: crude oil, natural gas, iron ore, gold, copper
Land use: arable land 1%; permanent crops NEGL%; meadows and pastures 39%; forest and woodland 1%; other 59%; includes irrigated NEGL%
Environment: no perennial rivers or permanent water bodies; developing extensive coastal seawater desalination facilities; desertification
Note: extensive coastlines on Persian Gulf and Red Sea provide great leverage on shipping (especially crude oil) through Persian Gulf and Suez Canal

People

Population: 17,869,558 (July 1991), growth rate 4.2% (1991); note—the population figure is based on growth since the last official Saudi census of 1974 that reported a total of 7 million persons and included foreign workers; estimates from other sources may be 15-30% lower
Birth rate: 37 births/1,000 population (1991)
Death rate: 6 deaths/1,000 population (1991)
Net migration rate: 12 migrants/1,000 population (1991)
Infant mortality rate: 69 deaths/1,000 live births (1991)
Life expectancy at birth: 65 years male, 68 years female (1991)
Total fertility rate: 6.7 children born/woman (1991)
Nationality: noun—Saudi(s); adjective—Saudi or Saudi Arabian
Ethnic divisions: Arab 90%, Afro-Asian 10%
Religion: Muslim 100%
Language: Arabic
Literacy: 62% (male 73%, female 48%) age 15 and over can read and write (1990 est.)
Labor force: 4,200,000; about 60% are foreign workers; government 34%, industry and oil 28%, services 22%, and agriculture 16%
Organized labor: trade unions are illegal

Government

Long-form name: Kingdom of Saudi Arabia
Type: monarchy
Capital: Riyadh
Administrative divisions: 14 emirates (imārāt, singular—imārah); Al Bāḥah, Al Ḥudūd ash Shamālīyah, Al Jawf, Al Madīnah, Al Qaṣīm, Al Qurayyāt, Ar Riyāḍ, Ash Sharqīyah, 'Asīr, Ḥā'il, Jīzān, Makkah, Najrān, Tabūk
Independence: 23 September 1932 (unification)
Constitution: none; governed according to Shari'a (Islamic law)
Legal system: based on Islamic law, several secular codes have been introduced; commercial disputes handled by special committees; has not accepted compulsory ICJ jurisdiction
National holiday: Unification of the Kingdom, 23 September (1932)
Executive branch: monarch and prime minister, crown prince and deputy prime minister, Council of Ministers
Legislative branch: none
Judicial branch: Supreme Council of Justice
Leaders:
Chief of State and Head of Government—King and Prime Minister FAHD bin 'Abd al-'Aziz Al Sa'ud (since 13 June 1982); Crown Prince and Deputy Prime Minister 'ABDALLAH bin 'Abd al-'Aziz Al Sa'ud (half-brother to the King, appointed heir to the throne 13 June 1982)
Suffrage: none
Elections: none

Saudi Arabia *(continued)*

Communists: negligible
Member of: ABEDA, AfDB, AFESD, AL, AMF, CCC, ESCWA, FAO, G-19, G-77, GCC, IAEA, IBRD, ICAO, ICC, IDA, IDB, IFAD, IFC, ILO, IMF, IMO, INMARSAT, INTELSAT, INTERPOL, IOC, ISO, ITU, LORCS, NAM, OAPEC, OAS (observer), OIC, OPEC, UN, UNCTAD, UNESCO, UNIDO, UPU, WFTU, WHO, WIPO, WMO
Diplomatic representation: Ambassador BANDAR Bin Sultan; Chancery at 601 New Hampshire Avenue NW, Washington DC 20037; telephone (202) 342-3800; there are Saudi Arabian Consulates General in Houston, Los Angeles, and New York; *US*—Ambassador Charles W. FREEMAN, Jr.; Embassy at Collector Road M, Diplomatic Quarter, Riyadh (mailing address is P. O. Box 9041, Riyadh 11143, or APO New York 09038); telephone [966] (1) 488-3800; there are US Consulates General in Dhahran and Jiddah (Jeddah)
Flag: green with large white Arabic script (that may be translated as There is no God but God; Muhammad is the Messenger of God) above a white horizontal saber (the tip points to the hoist side); green is the traditional color of Islam

Economy

Overview: The petroleum sector accounts for roughly 70% of budget revenues, 33% of GDP, and almost all export earnings. Saudi Arabia has the largest reserves of petroleum in the world, ranks as the largest exporter of petroleum, plays a leading role in OPEC, and invests substantial amounts abroad.
GDP: $79 billion, per capita $4,800; real growth rate 0.5% (1989 est.)
Inflation rate (consumer prices): 0% (1990 est.)
Unemployment rate: 0% (1989 est.)
Budget: revenues $31.5 billion; expenditures $38.2 billion, including capital expenditures of $6.9 billion (1990)
Exports: $28.3 billion (f.o.b., 1989 est.); *commodities*—petroleum and petroleum products 85%; *partners*—US 22%, Japan 20%, Singapore 7%, France 5%
Imports: $19.2 billion (f.o.b., 1989 est.); *commodities*—manufactured goods, transportation equipment, construction materials, processed food products; *partners*—UK 17%, US 15%, Japan 12%, FRG 6%
External debt: $18.9 billion (December 1989 est.)
Industrial production: growth rate −1.1% (1989 est.); accounts for 37% of GDP, including petroleum
Electricity: 25,205,000 kW capacity; 50,500 million kWh produced, 2,950 kWh per capita (1990)

Industries: crude oil production, petroleum refining, basic petrochemicals, cement, small steel-rolling mill, construction, fertilizer, plastic
Agriculture: accounts for about 10% of GDP, 16% of labor force; fastest growing economic sector; subsidized by government; products—wheat, barley, tomatoes, melons, dates, citrus fruit, mutton, chickens, eggs, milk; approaching self-sufficiency in food
Economic aid: donor—pledged $64.7 billion in bilateral aid (1979-89)
Currency: Saudi riyal (plural—riyals); 1 Saudi riyal (SR) = 100 halalas
Exchange rates: Saudi riyals (SR) per US$1—3.7450 (fixed rate since late 1986), 3.7033 (1986), 3.6221 (1985)
Fiscal year: calendar year

Communications

Railroads: 886 km 1.435-meter standard gauge
Highways: 74,000 km total; 35,000 km bituminous, 39,000 km gravel and improved earth
Pipelines: 6,400 km crude oil; 150 km refined products; 2,200 km natural gas, includes 1,600 km of natural gas liquids
Ports: Jiddah, Ad Dammām, Ras Tanura, Jīzān, Al Jubayl, Yanbu' al Baḥr, Yanbu' al Sinaiyah
Merchant marine: 84 ships (1,000 GRT or over) totaling 1,492,174 GRT/2,436,635 DWT; includes 1 passenger, 6 short-sea passenger, 14 cargo, 12 roll-on/roll-off cargo, 3 container, 6 refrigerated cargo, 5 livestock carrier, 26 petroleum, oils, and lubricants (POL) tanker, 8 chemical tanker, 1 liquefied gas, 1 specialized tanker, 1 bulk
Civil air: 182 major transport aircraft available
Airports: 207 total, 188 usable; 69 with permanent-surface runways; 13 with runways over 3,659 m; 38 with runways 2,440-3,659 m; 103 with runways 1,220-2,439 m
Telecommunications: good system with extensive microwave and coaxial cable systems; 1,624,000 telephones; stations—21 AM, 16 FM, 97 TV; radio relay to Bahrain, Jordan, Kuwait, Qatar, UAE, Yemen, and Sudan; coaxial cable to Kuwait; submarine cable to Djibouti and Egypt; earth stations—3 Atlantic Ocean INTELSAT, 2 Indian Ocean INTELSAT, 1 ARABSAT, 1 INMARSAT, 1 ARABSAT

Defense Forces

Branches: Army, Navy, Air Force, Air Defense Force, National Guard, Coast Guard, Frontier Force, Special Security Force, Public Security Force
Manpower availability: males 15-49, 6,663,217; 3,724,610 fit for military service; 165,167 reach military age (17) annually
Defense expenditures: $13.9 billion, 16.9% of GDP (1990 est.)

Senegal

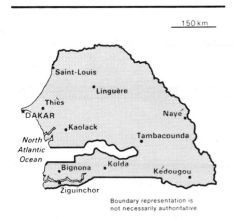

Boundary representation is not necessarily authoritative

Geography

Total area: 196,190 km²; land area: 192,000 km²

Comparative area: slightly smaller than South Dakota

Land boundaries: 2,640 km total; The Gambia 740 km, Guinea 330 km, Guinea-Bissau 338 km, Mali 419 km, Mauritania 813 km

Coastline: 531 km

Maritime claims:

Contiguous zone: 24 nm;

Continental shelf: edge of continental margin or 200 nm;

Exclusive fishing zone: 200 nm;

Territorial sea: 12 nm

Disputes: short section of the boundary with The Gambia is indefinite; the International Court of Justice (ICJ) rendered its decision on the Guinea-Bissau/Senegal maritime boundary in favor of Senegal—that decision has been rejected by Guinea-Bissau; boundary with Mauritania

Climate: tropical; hot, humid; rainy season (December to April) has strong southeast winds; dry season (May to November) dominated by hot, dry harmattan wind

Terrain: generally low, rolling, plains rising to foothills in southeast

Natural resources: fish, phosphates, iron ore

Land use: arable land 27%; permanent crops 0%; meadows and pastures 30%; forest and woodland 31%; other 12%; includes irrigated 1%

Environment: lowlands seasonally flooded; deforestation; overgrazing; soil erosion; desertification

Note: The Gambia is almost an enclave

People

Population: 7,952,657 (July 1991), growth rate 3.1% (1991)

Birth rate: 44 births/1,000 population (1991)

Death rate: 13 deaths/1,000 population (1991)

Net migration rate: 0 migrants/1,000 population (1991)

Infant mortality rate: 86 deaths/1,000 live births (1991)

Life expectancy at birth: 54 years male, 56 years female (1991)

Total fertility rate: 6.2 children born/woman (1991)

Nationality: noun—Senegalese (sing. and pl.); adjective—Senegalese

Ethnic divisions: Wolof 36%, Fulani 17%, Serer 17%, Toucouleur 9%, Diola 9%, Mandingo 9%, European and Lebanese 1%, other 2%

Religion: Muslim 92%, indigenous beliefs 6%, Christian 2% (mostly Roman Catholic)

Language: French (official); Wolof, Pulaar, Diola, Mandingo

Literacy: 38% (male 52%, female 25%) age 15 and over can read and write (1990 est.)

Labor force: 2,509,000; 77% subsistence agricultural workers; 175,000 wage earners—private sector 40%, government and parapublic 60%; 52% of population of working age (1985)

Organized labor: majority of wage-labor force represented by unions; however, dues-paying membership very limited; major confederation is National Confederation of Senegalese Labor (CNTS), an affiliate of governing party

Government

Long-form name: Republic of Senegal

Type: republic under multiparty democratic rule

Capital: Dakar

Administrative divisions: 10 regions (régions, singular—région); Dakar, Diourbel, Fatick, Kaolack, Kolda, Louga, Saint-Louis, Tambacounda, Thiès, Ziguinchor

Independence: 4 April 1960 (from France); The Gambia and Senegal signed an agreement on 12 December 1981 (effective 1 February 1982) that called for the creation of a loose confederation to be known as Senegambia, but the agreement was dissolved on 30 September 1989

Constitution: 3 March 1963, last revised in 1984

Legal system: based on French civil law system; judicial review of legislative acts in Supreme Court, which also audits the government's accounting office; has not accepted compulsory ICJ jurisdiction

National holiday: Independence Day, 4 April (1960)

Executive branch: president, prime minister, Council of Ministers (cabinet)

Legislative branch: unicameral National Assembly (Assemblée Nationale)

Judicial branch: Supreme Court (Cour Suprême)

Leaders:

Chief of State—President Abdou DIOUF (since 1 January 1981);

Head of Government—Prime Minister Habib THIAM (since 7 April 1991)

Political parties and leaders: Socialist Party (PS), President Abdou DIOUF; Senegalese Democratic Party (PDS), Abdoulaye WADE; 13 other small uninfluential parties

Suffrage: universal at age 21

Elections:

President—last held 28 February 1988 (next to be held February 1993); results—Abdou DIOUF (PS) 73%, Abdoulaye WADE (PDS) 26%, other 1%;

National Assembly—last held 28 February 1988 (next to be held February 1993); results—PS 71%, PDS 25%, other 4%; seats—(120 total) PS 103, PDS 17

Communists: small number of Communists and sympathizers

Other political or pressure groups: students, teachers, labor, Muslim Brotherhoods

Member of: ACCT, ACP, AfDB, CCC, CEAO, ECA, ECOWAS, FAO, FZ, G-77, GATT, IAEA, IBRD, ICAO, ICC, IDA, IDB, IFAD, IFC, ILO, IMF, IMO, INTELSAT, INTERPOL, IOC, ISO (correspondent), ITU, LORCS, NAM, OAU, OIC, PCA, UN, UNCTAD, UNESCO, UNIDO, UNIIMOG, UPU, WADB, WCL, WFTU, WHO, WIPO, WMO, WTO

Diplomatic representation: Ambassador Ibra Deguene KA; Chancery at 2112 Wyoming Avenue NW, Washington DC 20008; telephone (202) 234-0540 or 0541;

US—Ambassador George E. MOOSE; Embassy on Avenue Jean XXIII at the corner of Avenue Kleber, Dakar (mailing address is B. P. 49, Dakar); telephone [221] 23-42-96 or 23-34-24

Flag: three equal vertical bands of green (hoist side), yellow, and red with a small green five-pointed star centered in the yellow band; uses the popular pan-African colors of Ethiopia

Economy

Overview: The agricultural sector accounts for about 20% of GDP and provides employment for about 75% of the labor force. About 40% of the total cultivated land is used to grow peanuts, an important export crop. The principal economic resource is fishing, which brought in about $200 million or about 25% of total foreign exchange earnings in 1987. Mining is dominated by the extraction of phosphate, but production has faltered because of reduced worldwide demand for fertilizers in recent years. Over the past 10 years tourism has become increasingly important to the economy.

GDP: $4.6 billion, per capita $615; real growth rate 0.6% (1989 est.)

Senegal (continued)

Inflation rate (consumer prices): 0.4% (1989 est.)
Unemployment rate: 3.5% (1987)
Budget: revenues $921 million; expenditures $1,024 million; including capital expenditures of $14 million (FY89 est.)
Exports: $801 million (f.o.b., 1989 est.); *commodities*—manufactures 30%, fish products 27%, peanuts 11%, petroleum products 11%, phosphates 10%; *partners*—US, France, other EC, Ivory Coast, India
Imports: $1.0 billion (c.i.f., 1989 est.); *commodities*—semimanufactures 30%, food 27%, durable consumer goods 17%, petroleum 12%, capital goods 14%; *partners*—US, France, other EC, Nigeria, Algeria, China, Japan
External debt: $4.1 billion (1989)
Industrial production: growth rate 4.7% (1989); accounts for 17% of GDP
Electricity: 210,000 kW capacity; 760 million kWh produced, 100 kWh per capita (1989)
Industries: fishing, agricultural processing, phosphate mining, petroleum refining, building materials
Agriculture: including fishing, accounts for 20% of GDP and more than 75% of labor force; major products—peanuts (cash crop), millet, corn, sorghum, rice, cotton, tomatoes, green vegetables; estimated two-thirds self-sufficient in food; fish catch of 299,000 metric tons in 1987
Economic aid: US commitments, including Ex-Im (FY70-89), $551 million; Western (non-US) countries, ODA and OOF bilateral commitments (1970-88), $4.8 billion; OPEC bilateral aid (1979-89), $589 million; Communist countries (1970-89), $295 million
Currency: Communauté Financière Africaine franc (plural—francs); 1 CFA franc (CFAF) = 100 centimes
Exchange rates: Communauté Financière Africaine francs (CFAF) per US$1—256.54 (January 1991), 272.26 (1990), 319.01 (1989), 297.85 (1988), 300.54 (1987), 346.30 (1986), 449.26 (1985)
Fiscal year: 1 July-30 June

Communications

Railroads: 1,034 km 1.000-meter gauge; all single track except 70 km double track Dakar to Thies
Highways: 14,000 km total; 3,770 km paved, 10,230 km laterite or improved earth
Inland waterways: 900 km total; 785 km on the Sénégal, 115 km on the Saloum
Ports: Dakar, Kaolack
Merchant marine: 3 ships (1,000 GRT and over) totaling 9,263 GRT/15,167 DWT; includes 2 cargo, 1 bulk
Civil air: 2 major transport aircraft

Airports: 25 total, 20 usable; 10 with permanent-surface runways; none with runways over 3,659 m; 1 with runways 2,440-3,659 m; 15 with runways 1,220-2,439 m
Telecommunications: above-average urban system, using radio relay and cable; 40,200 telephones; stations—8 AM, no FM, 1 TV; 3 submarine cables; 1 Atlantic Ocean INTELSAT earth station

Defense Forces

Branches: Army, Navy, Air Force, paramilitary Gendarmerie; Sûreté Nationale
Manpower availability: males 15-49, 1,749,540; 913,806 fit for military service; 91,607 reach military age (18) annually
Defense expenditures: $100 million, 2% of GDP (1989 est.)

Seychelles

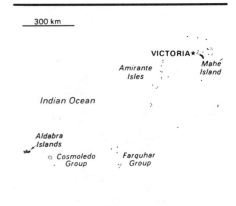

Geography

Total area: 455 km²; land area: 455 km²
Comparative area: slightly more than 2.5 times the size of Washington, DC
Land boundaries: none
Coastline: 491 km
Maritime claims:
Continental shelf: edge of continental margin or 200 nm;
Exclusive economic zone: 200 nm;
Territorial sea: 12 nm
Disputes: claims Tromelin Island
Climate: tropical marine; humid; cooler season during southeast monsoon (late May to September); warmer season during northwest monsoon (March to May)
Terrain: Mahé Group is granitic, narrow coastal strip, rocky, hilly; others are coral, flat, elevated reefs
Natural resources: fish, copra, cinnamon trees
Land use: arable land 4%; permanent crops 18%; meadows and pastures 0%; forest and woodland 18%; other 60%
Environment: lies outside the cyclone belt, so severe storms are rare; short droughts possible; no fresh water, catchments collect rain; 40 granitic and about 50 coralline islands
Note: located north-northeast of Madagascar in the Indian Ocean

People

Population: 68,932 (July 1991), growth rate 0.9% (1991)
Birth rate: 23 births/1,000 population (1991)
Death rate: 7 deaths/1,000 population (1991)
Net migration rate: −8 migrants/1,000 population (1991)
Infant mortality rate: 15 deaths/1,000 live births (1991)
Life expectancy at birth: 65 years male, 75 years female (1991)

Total fertility rate: 2.5 children born/woman (1991)
Nationality: noun—Seychellois (sing. and pl.); adjective—Seychelles
Ethnic divisions: Seychellois (mixture of Asians, Africans, Europeans)
Religion: Roman Catholic 90%, Anglican 8%, other 2%
Language: English and French (official); Creole
Literacy: 58% (male 56%, female 60%) age 15 and over can read and write (1971)
Labor force: 27,700; industry and commerce 31%, services 21%, government 20%, agriculture, forestry, and fishing 12%, other 16% (1985); 57% of population of working age (1983)
Organized labor: three major trade unions

Government

Long-form name: Republic of Seychelles
Type: republic
Capital: Victoria
Administrative divisions: 23 administrative districts; Anse aux Pins, Anse Boileau, Anse Étoile, Anse Louis, Anse Royale, Baie Lazare, Baie Sainte Anne, Beau Vallon, Bel Air, Bel Ombre, Cascade, Glacis, Grand' Anse (on Mahé Island), Grand' Anse (on Praslin Island), La Digue, La Rivière Anglaise, Mont Buxton, Mont Fleuri, Plaisance, Pointe La Rue, Port Glaud, Saint Louis, Takamaka
Independence: 29 June 1976 (from UK)
Constitution: 5 June 1979
Legal system: based on English common law, French civil law, and customary law
National holiday: Liberation Day (anniversary of coup), 5 June (1977)
Executive branch: president, Council of Ministers
Legislative branch: unicameral People's Assembly (Assemblée du Peuple)
Judicial branch: Court of Appeal, Supreme Court
Leaders:
Chief of State and Head of Government—President France Albert RENÉ (since 5 June 1977)
Political parties and leaders: only party—Seychelles People's Progressive Front (SPPF), France Albert RENÉ
Suffrage: universal at age 17
Elections:
President—last held 9-11 June 1989 (next to be held June 1994); results—President France Albert RENÉ reelected without opposition;
National Assembly—last held 5 December 1987 (next to be held December 1992); results—SPPF is the only party; seats—(25 total, 23 elected) SPPF 23
Communists: negligible, although some Cabinet ministers espouse pro-Soviet line

Other political or pressure groups: trade unions, Roman Catholic Church
Member of: ACCT, ACP, AfDB, C, ECA, FAO, G-77, IBRD, ICAO, ICFTU, IFAD, IFC, ILO, IMF, IMO, INTERPOL, IOC, NAM, OAU, UN, UNCTAD, UNESCO, UNIDO, UPU, WCL, WHO, WMO
Diplomatic representation: Second Secretary, Chargé d'Affaires ad interim Marc R. MARENGO; Chancery (temporary) at 820 Second Avenue, Suite 201, New York, NY 10017; telephone (212) 687-9766;
US—Ambassador James B. MORAN; Embassy at 4th Floor, Victoria House, Victoria (mailing address is Box 148, Victoria, and Victoria House, Box 251, Victoria, Mahe, Seychelles, or APO New York 09030-0006); telephone (248) 25256
Flag: three horizontal bands of red (top), white (wavy), and green; the white band is the thinnest, the red band is the thickest

---

Economy

Overview: In this small, open, tropical island economy, the tourist industry employs about 30% of the labor force and provides the main source of hard currency earnings. In recent years the government has encouraged foreign investment in order to upgrade hotels and other services. At the same time, the government has moved to reduce the high dependence on tourism by promoting the development of farming, fishing, and small-scale manufacturing.
GDP: $283 million, per capita $4,100; real growth rate 7.0% (1989)
Inflation rate (consumer prices): 1.5% (1989)
Unemployment rate: 9% (1987)
Budget: revenues $170 million; expenditures $173 million, including capital expenditures of $NA (1989)
Exports: $31 million (f.o.b., 1989 est.);
commodities—fish, copra, cinnamon bark, petroleum products (reexports);
partners—France 63%, Pakistan 12%, Reunion 10%, UK 7% (1987)
Imports: $164 million (f.o.b., 1989 est.);
commodities—manufactured goods, food, tobacco, beverages, machinery and transportation equipment, petroleum products;
partners—UK 20%, France 14%, South Africa 13%, PDRY 13%, Singapore 8%, Japan 6% (1987)
External debt: $171 million (1990 est.)
Industrial production: growth rate 7% (1987); accounts for 10% of GDP
Electricity: 25,000 kW capacity; 67 million kWh produced, 960 kWh per capita (1989)
Industries: tourism, processing of coconut and vanilla, fishing, coir rope factory, boat building, printing, furniture, beverage
Agriculture: accounts for 7% of GDP, mostly subsistence farming; cash crops—coconuts, cinnamon, vanilla; other products—sweet potatoes, cassava, bananas; broiler

chickens; large share of food needs imported; expansion of tuna fishing under way
Economic aid: US commitments, including Ex-Im (FY78-89), $26 million; Western (non-US) countries, ODA and OOF bilateral commitments (1978-88), $310 million; OPEC bilateral aid (1979-89), $5 million; Communist countries (1970-89), $60 million
Currency: Seychelles rupee (plural—rupees); 1 Seychelles rupee (SRe) = 100 cents
Exchange rates: Seychelles rupees (SR) per US$1—5.0878 (January 1991), 5.3369 (1990), 5.6457 (1989), 5.3836 (1988), 5.6000 (1987), 6.1768 (1986), 7.1343 (1985)
Fiscal year: calendar year

Communications

Highways: 260 km total; 160 km bituminous, 100 km crushed stone or earth
Ports: Victoria
Merchant marine: 1 refrigerated cargo (1,000 GRT or over) totaling 1,827 GRT/2,170 DWT
Civil air: 3 major transport aircraft
Airports: 14 total, 14 usable; 8 with permanent-surface runways; none with runways over 3,659 m; 1 with runways 2,440-3,659 m; none with runways 1,220-2,439 m
Telecommunications: direct radio communications with adjacent islands and African coastal countries; 13,000 telephones; stations—2 AM, no FM, 1 TV; 1 Indian Ocean INTELSAT earth station; USAF tracking station

---

Defense Forces

Branches: Army, Navy, Air Force, Presidential Protection Unit, Police Force, Militia
Manpower availability: males 15-49, 17,399; 8,933 fit for military service
Defense expenditures: $12 million, 6% of GDP (1990 est.)

Sierra Leone

Geography

Total area: 71,740 km²; land area: 71,620 km²

Comparative area: slightly smaller than South Carolina

Land boundaries: 958 km total; Guinea 652 km, Liberia 306 km

Coastline: 402 km

Maritime claims:

Territorial sea: 200 nm

Climate: tropical; hot, humid; summer rainy season (May to December); winter dry season (December to April)

Terrain: coastal belt of mangrove swamps, wooded hill country, upland plateau, mountains in east

Natural resources: diamonds, titanium ore, bauxite, iron ore, gold, chromite

Land use: arable land 25%; permanent crops 2%; meadows and pastures 31%; forest and woodland 29%; other 13%; includes irrigated NEGL%

Environment: extensive mangrove swamps hinder access to sea; deforestation; soil degradation

People

Population: 4,274,543 (July 1991), growth rate 2.6% (1991)

Birth rate: 46 births/1,000 population (1991)

Death rate: 20 deaths/1,000 population (1991)

Net migration rate: 0 migrants/1,000 population (1991)

Infant mortality rate: 151 deaths/1,000 live births (1991)

Life expectancy at birth: 42 years male, 48 years female (1991)

Total fertility rate: 6.1 children born/woman (1991)

Nationality: noun—Sierra Leonean(s); adjective—Sierra Leonean

Ethnic divisions: native African 99% (Temne 30%, Mende 30%); Creole, European, Lebanese, and Asian 1%; 13 tribes

Religion: Muslim 30%, indigenous beliefs 30%, Christian 10%, other or none 30%

Language: English (official); regular use limited to literate minority; principal vernaculars are Mende in south and Temne in north; Krio is the language of the resettled ex-slave population of the Freetown area and is lingua franca

Literacy: 21% (male 31%, female 11%) age 15 and over can read and write English, Mende, Temne, or Arabic (1990 est.)

Labor force: 1,369,000 (est.); agriculture 65%, industry 19%, services 16% (1981); only about 65,000 earn wages (1985); 55% of population of working age

Organized labor: 35% of wage earners

Government

Long-form name: Republic of Sierra Leone

Type: republic under presidential regime

Capital: Freetown

Administrative divisions: 4 provinces; Eastern, Northern, Southern, Western

Independence: 27 April 1961 (from UK)

Constitution: 14 June 1978

Legal system: based on English law and customary laws indigenous to local tribes; has not accepted compulsory ICJ jurisdiction

National holiday: Republic Day, 27 April (1961)

Executive branch: president, two vice presidents, Cabinet

Legislative branch: unicameral House of Representatives

Judicial branch: Supreme Court

Leaders:

Chief of State and Head of Government—President Gen. Joseph Saidu MOMOH (since 28 November 1985); First Vice President Abu Bakar KAMARA (since 4 April 1987); Second Vice President Salia JUSU-SHERIFF (since 4 April 1987)

Political parties and leaders: only party—All People's Congress (APC), Gen. Joseph Saidu MOMOH; note—constitutional referendum to adopt a multiparty system is scheduled for June 1991

Suffrage: universal at age 18

Elections:

President—last held 1 October 1985 (next to be held October 1992); results—Gen. Joseph Saidu MOMOH was elected without opposition;

House of Representatives—last held 30 May 1986 (next to be held February 1992); results—APC is the only party; seats—(127 total, 105 elected) APC 105

Communists: no party, although there are a few Communists and a slightly larger number of sympathizers

Member of: ACP, AfDB, C, CCC, ECA, ECOWAS, FAO, G-77, GATT, IAEA, IBRD, ICAO, ICFTU, IDA, IDB, IFAD, IFC, ILO, IMF, IMO, INTERPOL, IOC, ITU, LORCS, NAM, OAU, OIC, UN, UNCTAD, UNESCO, UNIDO, UPU, WCL, WHO, WIPO, WMO, WTO

Diplomatic representation: Ambassador George CAREW; Chancery at 1701 19th Street NW, Washington DC 20009; telephone (202) 939-9261;

US—Ambassador Johnny YOUNG; Embassy at the corner of Walpole and Siaka Stevens Street, Freetown; telephone [232] (22) 26481

Flag: three equal horizontal bands of light green (top), white, and light blue

Economy

Overview: The economic and social infrastructure is not well developed. Subsistence agriculture dominates the economy, generating about one-third of GDP and employing about two-thirds of the working population. Manufacturing accounts for less than 10% of GDP, consisting mainly of the processing of raw materials and of light manufacturing for the domestic market. Diamond mining provides an important source of hard currency. The economy suffers from high unemployment, rising inflation, large trade deficits, and a growing dependency on foreign assistance. The government in 1990 was attempting to get the budget deficit under control and, in general, to bring economic policy in line with the recommendations of the IMF and the World Bank.

GDP: $1,302 million, per capita $325; real growth rate 1.8% (FY89)

Inflation rate (consumer prices): over 100% (1990)

Unemployment rate: NA%

Budget: revenues $134 million; expenditures $187 million, including capital expenditures of $32 million (FY91 est.)

Exports: $138 million (f.o.b., 1989);

commodities—rutile 50%, bauxite 17%, cocoa 11%, diamonds 3%, coffee 3%;

partners—US, UK, Belgium, FRG, other Western Europe

Imports: $183 million (c.i.f., 1989);

commodities—capital goods 40%, food 32%, petroleum 12%, consumer goods 7%, light industrial goods;

partners—US, EC, Japan, China, Nigeria

External debt: $632 million (1990 est.)

Industrial production: growth rate −19% (FY88 est.); accounts for 8% of GDP

Electricity: 83,000 kW capacity; 180 million kWh produced, 45 kWh per capita (1989)

Industries: mining (diamonds, bauxite, rutile), small-scale manufacturing (beverages, textiles, cigarettes, footwear), petroleum refinery

Agriculture: accounts for over 30% of GDP and two-thirds of the labor force; largely subsistence farming; cash crops—coffee, cocoa, palm kernels; harvests of food staple

Singapore

rice meets 80% of domestic needs; annual fish catch averages 53,000 metric tons
Economic aid: US commitments, including Ex-Im (FY70-89), $161 million; Western (non-US) countries, ODA and OOF bilateral commitments (1970-87), $698 million; OPEC bilateral aid (1979-89), $18 million; Communist countries (1970-89), $101 million
Currency: leone (plural—leones); 1 leone (Le) = 100 cents
Exchange rates: leones per US$1—196.0784 (January 1991), 144.9275 (1990), 58.1395 (1989), 31.2500 (1988), 30.7692 (1987), 8.3963 (1986), 4.7304 (1985)
Fiscal year: 1 July-30 June

Communications

Railroads: 84 km 1.067-meter narrow-gauge mineral line is used on a limited basis because the mine at Marampa is closed
Highways: 7,400 km total; 1,150 km bituminous, 490 km laterite (some gravel), remainder improved earth
Inland waterways: 800 km; 600 km navigable year round
Ports: Freetown, Pepel
Civil air: no major transport aircraft
Airports: 12 total, 8 usable; 5 with permanent-surface runways; none with runways over 3,659 m; 1 with runways 2,440-3,659 m; 3 with runways 1,220-2,439 m
Telecommunications: marginal telephone and telegraph service; national microwave radio relay system unserviceable at present; 23,650 telephones; stations—1 AM, 1 FM, 1 TV; 1 Atlantic Ocean INTELSAT earth station

Defense Forces

Branches: Army, Navy, Police
Manpower availability: males 15-49, 939,214; 453,877 fit for military service; no conscription
Defense expenditures: $6 million, 0.7% of GDP (1988 est.)

Geography

Total area: 632.6 km²; land area: 622.6 km²
Comparative area: slightly less than 3.5 times the size of Washington, DC
Land boundaries: none
Coastline: 193 km
Maritime claims:
Exclusive fishing zone: not specific;
Territorial sea: 3 nm
Climate: tropical; hot, humid, rainy; no pronounced rainy or dry seasons; thunderstorms occur on 40% of all days (67% of days in April)
Terrain: lowland; gently undulating central plateau contains water catchment area and nature preserve
Natural resources: fish, deepwater ports
Land use: arable land 4%; permanent crops 7%; meadows and pastures 0%; forest and woodland 5%; other 84%
Environment: mostly urban and industrialized
Note: focal point for Southeast Asian sea routes

People

Population: 2,756,330 (July 1991), growth rate 1.3% (1991)
Birth rate: 18 births/1,000 population (1991)
Death rate: 5 deaths/1,000 population (1991)
Net migration rate: 0 migrants/1,000 population (1991)
Infant mortality rate: 8 deaths/1,000 live births (1991)
Life expectancy at birth: 72 years male, 77 years female (1991)
Total fertility rate: 2.0 children born/woman (1991)
Nationality: noun—Singaporean(s), adjective—Singapore
Ethnic divisions: Chinese 76.4%, Malay 14.9%, Indian 6.4%, other 2.3%
Religion: majority of Chinese are Buddhists or atheists; Malays are nearly all Muslim (minorities include Christians, Hindus, Sikhs, Taoists, Confucianists)
Language: Chinese, Malay, Tamil, and English (all official); Malay (national)
Literacy: 88% (male 93%, female 84%) age 15 and over can read and write (1990 est.)
Labor force: 1,280,000; financial, business, and other services 35.3%, manufacturing 29.0%, commerce 22.8%, construction 6.6%, other 6.3% (1989)
Organized labor: 210,000; 16.1% of labor force (1989)

Government

Long-form name: Republic of Singapore
Type: republic within Commonwealth
Capital: Singapore
Administrative divisions: none
Independence: 9 August 1965 (from Malaysia)
Constitution: 3 June 1959, amended 1965; based on preindependence State of Singapore Constitution
Legal system: based on English common law; has not accepted compulsory ICJ jurisdiction
National holiday: National Day, 9 August (1965)
Executive branch: president, prime minister, two deputy prime ministers, Cabinet
Legislative branch: unicameral Parliament
Judicial branch: Supreme Court
Leaders:
Chief of State—President WEE Kim Wee (since 3 September 1985);
Head of Government—Prime Minister GOH Chok Tong (since 28 November 1990); Deputy Prime Minister LEE Hsien Loong (since 28 November 1990); Deputy Prime Minister ONG Teng Cheong (since 2 January 1985)
Political parties and leaders:
government—People's Action Party (PAP), LEE Kuan Yew, secretary general;
opposition—Workers' Party (WP), J. B. JEYARETNAM; Singapore Democratic Party (SDP), CHIAM See Tong; National Solidarity Party (NSP), SOON Kia Seng; United People's Front (UPF), Harbans SINGH; Barisan Sosialis (BS, Socialist Front), leader NA
Suffrage: universal and compulsory at age 20
Elections:
President—last held 31 August 1989 (next to be held August 1993); results—President WEE Kim Wee was reelected by Parliament without opposition;
Parliament—last held 3 September 1988 (next to be held NA September 1993); results—PAP 61.8%, WP 18.4%, SDP 11.5%, NSP 3.7%, UPF 1.3%, other 3.3%; seats—(81 total) PAP 80, SDP 1; note—BS has 1 nonvoting seat

Singapore (continued)

Communists: 200-500; Barisan Sosialis infiltrated by Communists; note—Communist party illegal
Member of: APEC, AsDB, ASEAN, C, CCC, CP, ESCAP, G-77, GATT, IAEA, IBRD, ICAO, ICC, ICFTU, IFC, ILO, IMF, IMO, INMARSAT, INTELSAT, INTERPOL, IOC, ISO, ITU, LORCS, NAM, UN, UNCTAD, UPU, WHO, WMO
Diplomatic representation: Ambassador S. R. NATHAN; Chancery at 1824 R Street NW, Washington DC 20009; telephone (202) 667-7555;
US—Ambassador Robert D. ORR; Embassy at 30 Hill Street, Singapore 0617 (mailing address is FPO San Francisco 96699); telephone [65] 338-0251
Flag: two equal horizontal bands of red (top) and white; near the hoist side of the red band, there is a vertical, white crescent (closed portion is toward the hoist side) partially enclosing five white five-pointed stars arranged in a circle

Economy

Overview: Singapore has an open entrepreneurial economy with strong service and manufacturing sectors and excellent international trading links derived from its entrepôt history. During the 1970s and early 1980s, the economy expanded rapidly, achieving an average annual growth rate of 9%. Per capita GDP is among the highest in Asia. In 1985 the economy registered its first drop in 20 years and achieved less than a 2% increase in 1986. Recovery was strong based on rising demand for Singapore's products in OECD countries and improved competitiveness of domestic manufactures. The economy grew 8.3% in 1990. Singapore's position as a major oil refining and services center helped it weather the Persian Gulf crisis.
GDP: $34.6 billion, per capita $12,700; real growth rate 8.3% (1990)
Inflation rate (consumer prices): 3.4% (1990)
Unemployment rate: 1.7% (1990)
Budget: revenues $8.0 billion; expenditures $7.2 billion, including capital expenditures of $2.4 billion (FY90 est.)
Exports: $52.5 billion (f.o.b., 1990); *commodities*—includes transshipments to Malaysia—petroleum products, rubber, electronics, manufactured goods; *partners*—US 21%, EC 14%, Malaysia 13%, Japan 9%
Imports: $60.6 billion (c.i.f., 1990); *commodities*—includes transshipments from Malaysia—capital equipment, petroleum, chemicals, manufactured goods, foodstuffs; *partners*—Japan 20%, US 16%, Malaysia 14%, EC 13%
External debt: $3.9 billion (1990)

Industrial production: growth rate 9% (1990 est.); accounts for 29% of GDP (1989)
Electricity: 4,000,000 kW capacity; 14,400 million kWh produced, 5,300 kWh per capita (1990)
Industries: petroleum refining, electronics, oil drilling equipment, rubber processing and rubber products, processed food and beverages, ship repair, entrepôt trade, financial services, biotechnology
Agriculture: occupies a position of minor importance in the economy; self-sufficient in poultry and eggs; must import much of other food; major crops—rubber, copra, fruit, vegetables
Economic aid: US commitments, including Ex-Im (FY70-83), $590 million; Western (non-US) countries, ODA and OOF bilateral commitments (1970-87), $882 million
Currency: Singapore dollar (plural—dollars); 1 Singapore dollar (S$) = 100 cents
Exchange rates: Singapore dollars per US$1—1.7454 (January 1991), 1.8125 (1990), 1.9503 (1989), 2.0124 (1988), 2.1060 (1987), 2.1774 (1986), 2.2002 (1985)
Fiscal year: 1 April-31 March

Communications

Railroads: 38 km of 1.000-meter gauge
Highways: 2,597 km total (1984)
Ports: Singapore
Merchant marine: 435 ships (1,000 GRT or over) totaling 8,259,085 GRT/13,553,438 DWT; includes 1 passenger-cargo, 121 cargo, 66 container, 6 roll-on/roll-off cargo, 11 refrigerated cargo, 18 vehicle carrier, 1 livestock carrier, 118 petroleum, oils, and lubricants (POL) tanker, 5 chemical tanker, 3 combination ore/oil, 1 specialized tanker, 7 liquefied gas, 75 bulk, 2 combination bulk; note—many Singapore flag ships are foreign owned
Civil air: 38 major transport aircraft (est.)
Airports: 9 total, 9 usable; 9 with permanent-surface runways; 2 with runways over 3,659 m; 4 with runways 2,440-3,659 m; 2 with runways 1,220-2,439 m
Telecommunications: good domestic facilities; good international service; good radio and television broadcast coverage; 1,110,000 telephones; stations—13 AM, 4 FM, 2 TV; submarine cables extend to Malaysia (Sabah and peninsular Malaysia), Indonesia, and the Philippines; satellite earth stations—1 Indian Ocean INTELSAT and 1 Pacific Ocean INTELSAT

Defense Forces

Branches: Army, Navy, Air Force, People's Defense Force, Police Force
Manpower availability: males 15-49, 842,721; 625,546 fit for military service
Defense expenditures: $1.7 billion, 4% of GDP (1990 est.)

Solomon Islands

Geography

Total area: 28,450 km²; land area: 27,540 km²
Comparative area: slightly larger than Maryland
Land boundaries: none
Coastline: 5,313 km
Maritime claims: (measured from claimed archipelagic baselines):
Exclusive economic zone: 200 nm;
Territorial sea: 12 nm
Climate: tropical monsoon; few extremes of temperature and weather
Terrain: mostly rugged mountains with some low coral atolls
Natural resources: fish, forests, gold, bauxite, phosphates
Land use: arable land 1%; permanent crops 1%; meadows and pastures 1%; forest and woodland 93%; other 4%
Environment: subject to typhoons, which are rarely destructive; geologically active region with frequent earth tremors
Note: located just east of Papua New Guinea in the South Pacific Ocean

People

Population: 347,115 (July 1991), growth rate 3.5% (1991)
Birth rate: 40 births/1,000 population (1991)
Death rate: 5 deaths/1,000 population (1991)
Net migration rate: 0 migrants/1,000 population (1991)
Infant mortality rate: 39 deaths/1,000 live births (1991)
Life expectancy at birth: 67 years male, 72 years female (1991)
Total fertility rate: 6.2 children born/woman (1991)
Nationality: noun—Solomon Islander(s); adjective—Solomon Islander
Ethnic divisions: Melanesian 93.0%, Polynesian 4.0%, Micronesian 1.5%, European 0.8%, Chinese 0.3%, other 0.4%

Religion: almost all at least nominally Christian; Anglican 34%, Roman Catholic 19%, Baptist 17%, United (Methodist/Presbyterian) 11%, Seventh-Day Adventist 10%, other Protestant 5%
Language: 120 indigenous languages; Melanesian pidgin in much of the country is lingua franca; English spoken by 1-2% of population
Literacy: NA% (male NA%, female NA%)
Labor force: 23,448 economically active; agriculture, forestry, and fishing 32.4%; services 25%; construction, manufacturing, and mining 7.0%; commerce, transport, and finance 4.7% (1984)
Organized labor: NA, but most of the cash-economy workers have trade union representation

Government

Long-form name: none
Type: independent parliamentary state within Commonwealth
Capital: Honiara
Administrative divisions: 7 provinces and 1 town*; Central, Guadalcanal, Honiara*, Isabel, Makira, Malaita, Temotu, Western
Independence: 7 July 1978 (from UK; formerly British Solomon Islands)
Constitution: 7 July 1978
Legal system: common law
National holiday: Independence Day, 7 July (1978)
Executive branch: British monarch, governor general, prime minister, Cabinet
Legislative branch: unicameral National Parliament
Judicial branch: High Court
Leaders:
Chief of State—Queen ELIZABETH II (since 6 February 1952), represented by Governor General George LEPPING (since 27 June 1989, previously acted as governor general since 7 July 1988);
Head of Government—Prime Minister Solomon MAMALONI (since 28 March 1989); Deputy Prime Minister Sir Baddeley DEVESI (since NA October 1990)
Political parties and leaders: People's Alliance Party (PAP); United Party (UP), Sir Peter KENILOREA; Solomon Islands Liberal Party (SILP), Bartholemew ULUFA-'ALU; Nationalist Front for Progress (NFP), Andrew NORI; Labor Party (LP), Joses TUHANUKU
Suffrage: universal at age 21
Elections:
National Parliament—last held 22 February 1989 (next to be held February 1993); results—percent of vote by party NA; seats—(38 total) PAP 13, UP 6, NFP 4, SILP 4, LP 2, independents 9
Member of: ACP, AsDB, C, ESCAP, FAO, G-77, IBRD, ICAO, IDA, IFAD, IFC, ILO, IMF, IMO, IOC, ITU, SPC, SPF, UN, UNCTAD, UPU, WFTU, WHO, WMO

Diplomatic representation: Ambassador (vacant) resides in Honiara (Solomon Islands); *US*—the ambassador in Papua New Guinea is accredited to the Solomon Islands; Embassy at Mud Alley, Honiara (mailing address is American Embassy, P. O. Box 561, Honiara); telephone (677) 23890
Flag: divided diagonally by a thin yellow stripe from the lower hoist-side corner; the upper triangle (hoist side) is blue with five white five-pointed stars arranged in an *X* pattern; the lower triangle is green

Economy

Overview: About 90% of the population depend on subsistence agriculture, fishing, and forestry for at least part of their livelihood. Agriculture, fishing, and forestry contribute about 75% to GDP, with the fishing and forestry sectors being important export earners. The service sector contributes about 25% to GDP. Most manufactured goods and petroleum products must be imported. The islands are rich in undeveloped mineral resources such as lead, zinc, nickel, and gold. The economy suffered from a severe cyclone in mid-1986 that caused widespread damage to the infrastructure.
GDP: $156 million, per capita $500 (1988); real growth rate 5.0% (1989 est.)
Inflation rate (consumer prices): 14.9% (1989)
Unemployment rate: NA%
Budget: revenues $44 million; expenditures $45 million, including capital expenditures of $22 million (1989 est.)
Exports: $75 million (f.o.b., 1989); *commodities*—fish 46%, timber 31%, copra 5%, palm oil 5%; *partners*—Japan 51%, UK 12%, Thailand 9%, Netherlands 8%, Australia 2%, US 2% (1985)
Imports: $117 million (f.o.b., 1988); *commodities*—plant and machinery 30%, fuel 19%, food 16%; *partners*—Japan 36%, US 23%, Singapore 9%, UK 9%, NZ 9%, Australia 4%, Hong Kong 4%, China 3% (1985)
External debt: $128 million (1988 est.)
Industrial production: growth rate 0% (1987); accounts for 5% of GDP
Electricity: 21,000 kW capacity; 39 million kWh produced, 115 kWh per capita (1990)
Industries: copra, fish (tuna)
Agriculture: including fishing and forestry, accounts for about 75% of GDP; mostly subsistence farming; cash crops—cocoa, beans, coconuts, palm kernels, timber; other products—rice, potatoes, vegetables, fruit, cattle, pigs; not self-sufficient in food grains; 90% of the total fish catch of 44,500 metric tons was exported (1988)
Economic aid: Western (non-US) countries, ODA and OOF bilateral commitments (1985), $16.1 million

Currency: Solomon Islands dollar (plural—dollars); 1 Solomon Islands dollar (SI$) = 100 cents
Exchange rates: Solomon Islands dollars (SI$) per US$1—2.5934 (January 1991), 2.5288 (1990), 2.2932 (1989), 2.0825 (1988), 2.0033 (1987), 1.7415 (1986), 1.4808 (1985)
Fiscal year: calendar year

Communications

Highways: about 2,100 km total (1982); 30 km sealed, 290 km gravel, 980 km earth, 800 private logging and plantation roads of varied construction
Ports: Honiara, Ringi Cove
Civil air: no major transport aircraft
Airports: 31 total, 29 usable; 2 with permanent-surface runways; none with runways over 2,439 m; 2 with runways 1,220-2,439 m
Telecommunications: 3,000 telephones; stations—4 AM, no FM, no TV; 1 Pacific Ocean INTELSAT earth station

Defense Forces

Branches: Police Force
Manpower availability: males 15-49, 77, 169; NA fit for military service
Defense expenditures: $NA, NA% of GDP

Somalia

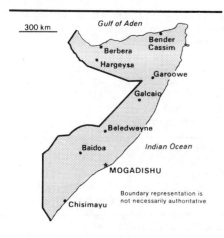

300 km

Gulf of Aden

Bender Cassim

Berbera

Hargeysa

Garoowe

Galcaio

Beledweyne

Baidoa

Indian Ocean

MOGADISHU

Chisimayu

Boundary representation is not necessarily authoritative

Geography

Total area: 637,660 km²; land area: 627,340 km²

Comparative area: slightly smaller than Texas

Land boundaries: 2,340 km total; Djibouti 58 km, Ethiopia 1,600 km, Kenya 682 km

Coastline: 3,025 km

Maritime claims:

Territorial sea: 200 nm

Disputes: southern half of boundary with Ethiopia is a Provisional Administrative Line; territorial dispute with Ethiopia over the Ogaden; possible claims to Djibouti and parts of Ethiopia and Kenya based on unification of ethnic Somalis

Climate: desert; northeast monsoon (December to February), cooler southwest monsoon (May to October); irregular rainfall; hot, humid periods (tangambili) between monsoons

Terrain: mostly flat to undulating plateau rising to hills in north

Natural resources: uranium, and largely unexploited reserves of iron ore, tin, gypsum, bauxite, copper, salt

Land use: arable land 2%; permanent crops NEGL%; meadows and pastures 46%; forest and woodland 14%; other 38%; includes irrigated 3%

Environment: recurring droughts; frequent dust storms over eastern plains in summer; deforestation; overgrazing; soil erosion; desertification

Note: strategic location on Horn of Africa along southern approaches to Bab el Mandeb and route through Red Sea and Suez Canal

People

Population: 6,709,161 (July 1991), growth rate 3.3% (1991)

Birth rate: 46 births/1,000 population (1991)

Death rate: 13 deaths/1,000 population (1991)

Net migration rate: 0 migrants/1,000 population (1991)

Infant mortality rate: 116 deaths/1,000 live births (1991)

Life expectancy at birth: 56 years male, 56 years female (1991)

Total fertility rate: 7.2 children born/woman (1991)

Nationality: noun—Somali(s); adjective—Somali

Ethnic divisions: Somali 85%, rest mainly Bantu; Arabs 30,000, Europeans 3,000, Asians 800

Religion: almost entirely Sunni Muslim

Language: Somali (official); Arabic, Italian, English

Literacy: 24% (male 36%, female 14%) age 15 and over can read and write (1990 est.)

Labor force: 2,200,000; very few are skilled laborers; pastoral nomad 70%, agriculture, government, trading, fishing, handicrafts, and other 30%; 53% of population of working age (1985)

Organized labor: General Federation of Somali Trade Unions is controlled by the government

Government

Long-form name: Somali Democratic Republic

Type: republic

Capital: Mogadishu

Administrative divisions: 16 regions (plural—NA, singular—gobolka); Bakool, Banaadir, Bari, Bay, Galguduud, Gedo, Hiiraan, Jubbada Dhexe, Jubbada Hoose, Mudug, Nugaal, Sanaag, Shabeellaha Dhexe, Shabeellaha Hoose, Togdheer, Woqooyi Galbeed

Independence: 1 July 1960 (from a merger of British Somaliland, which became independent from the UK on 26 June 1960, and Italian Somaliland, which became independent from the Italian-administered UN trusteeship on 1 July 1960, to form the Somali Republic)

Constitution: 25 August 1979, presidential approval 23 September 1979

National holiday: Anniversary of the Revolution, 21 October (1969)

Executive branch: president, two vice presidents, prime minister, Council of Ministers (cabinet)

Legislative branch: unicameral People's Assembly (Golaha Shacbiga)

Judicial branch: Supreme Court

Leaders:

Chief of State—Interim President ALI Mahdi Mohamed (since 27 January 1991);

Head of Government—Prime Minister OMAR Arteh Ghalib (since 27 January 1991); Deputy Prime Minister MOHAMED Abshir Mussa (since 27 January 1991)

Political parties and leaders: the United Somali Congress (USC) ousted the former regime on 27 January 1991; note—formerly the only party was the Somali Revolutionary Socialist Party (SRSP), headed by former President and Commander in Chief of the Army Maj. Gen. Mohamed Siad BARRE

Suffrage: universal at age 18

Elections:

President—last held 23 December 1986 (next to be held NA); results—President Siad was reelected without opposition;

People's Assembly—last held 31 December 1984 (next to be held NA); results—SRSP was the only party; seats—(177 total, 171 elected) SRSP 171; note—the United Somali Congress (USC) ousted the regime of Maj. Gen. Mohamed SIAD Barre on 27 January 1991; the provisional government has promised that a democratically elected government will be established

Communists: probably some Communist sympathizers in the government hierarchy

Member of: ACP, AfDB, AFESD, AL, AMF, CAEU, ECA, FAO, G-77, IBRD, ICAO, IDA, IDB, IFAD, IFC, IGADD, ILO, IMF, IMO, INTELSAT, INTERPOL, IOC, IOM (observer), ITU, LORCS, NAM, OAU, OIC, UN, UNCTAD, UNESCO, UNHCR, UNIDO, UPU, WHO, WIPO, WMO

Diplomatic representation: Ambassador ABDIKARIM Ali Omar; Chancery at Suite 710, 600 New Hampshire Avenue NW, Washington DC 20037; telephone (202) 342-1575; there is a Somali Consulate General in New York;

US—Ambassador James K. BISHOP; Embassy at K-7, AFGOI Road, Mogadishu (mailing address is P. O. Box 574, Mogadishu); telephone [252] (01) 39971; note—US Embassy evacuated and closed indefinitely in January 1991

Flag: light blue with a large white five-pointed star in the center; design based on the flag of the UN (Italian Somaliland was a UN trust territory)

Economy

Overview: One of the world's poorest and least developed countries, Somalia has few resources. Agriculture is the most important sector of the economy, with the livestock sector accounting for about 40% of GDP and about 65% of export earnings. Nomads and seminomads who are dependent upon livestock for their livelihoods make up more than half of the population. Crop production generates only 10% of GDP and employs about 20% of the work force. The main export crop is bananas; sugar, sorghum, and corn are grown for the domestic market. The small industrial sector is based on the processing of agricultural products and accounts for less than 10% of GDP. Serious economic problems facing the nation are the external debt of $1.9 billion and double-digit inflation.

GDP: $1.7 billion, per capita $210; real growth rate −1.4% (1988)

Inflation rate (consumer prices): 81.7% (1988 est.)

Unemployment rate: NA%

Budget: revenues $190 million; expenditures $195 million, including capital expenditures of $111 million (1989 est.)

Exports: $58.0 million (f.o.b., 1988); *commodities*—livestock, hides, skins, bananas, fish; *partners*—US 0.5%, Saudi Arabia, Italy, FRG (1986)

Imports: $354.0 million (c.i.f., 1988); *commodities*—textiles, petroleum products, foodstuffs, construction materials; *partners*—US 13%, Italy, FRG, Kenya, UK, Saudi Arabia (1986)

External debt: $1.9 billion (1989)

Industrial production: growth rate −5.0% (1988); accounts for 5% of GDP

Electricity: 72,000 kW capacity; 60 million kWh produced, 7 kWh per capita (1990)

Industries: a few small industries, including sugar refining, textiles, petroleum refining

Agriculture: dominant sector, led by livestock raising (cattle, sheep, goats); crops—bananas, sorghum, corn, mangoes, sugarcane; not self-sufficient in food; fishing potential largely unexploited

Economic aid: US commitments, including Ex-Im (FY70-89), $639 million; Western (non-US) countries, ODA and OOF bilateral commitments (1970-87), $3.2 billion; OPEC bilateral aid (1979-89), $1.1 billion; Communist countries (1970-89), $336 million

Currency: Somali shilling (plural—shillings); 1 Somali shilling (So.Sh.) = 100 centesimi

Exchange rates: Somali shillings (So. Sh.) per US$1—3,800.00 (December 1990), 490.7 (1989), 170.45 (1988), 105.18 (1987), 72.00 (1986), 39.49 (1985)

Fiscal year: calendar year

Communications

Highways: 15,215 km total; including 2,335 km bituminous surface, 2,880 km gravel, and 10,000 km improved earth or stabilized soil (1983)

Pipelines: 15 km crude oil

Ports: Mogadishu, Berbera, Chisimayu

Merchant marine: 3 ships (1,000 GRT or over) totaling 6,913 GRT/9,457 DWT; includes 2 cargo, 1 refrigerated cargo

Civil air: 2 major transport aircraft

Airports: 61 total, 46 usable; 8 with permanent-surface runways; 2 with runways over 3,659 m; 5 with runways 2,440-3,659 m; 22 with runways 1,220-2,439 m

Telecommunications: minimal telephone and telegraph service; radio relay and troposcatter system centered on Mogadishu connects a few towns; 6,000 telephones; stations—2 AM, no FM, 1 TV; 1 Indian Ocean INTELSAT earth station; scheduled to receive an ARABSAT station

Defense Forces

Branches: Somali National Army (including Navy, Air Force, and Air Defense Force), National Police Force, National Security Service

Manpower availability: males 15-49, 1,601,690; 902,732 fit for military service

Defense expenditures: $NA, NA% of GDP

South Africa

Geography

Total area: 1,221,040 km²; land area: 1,221,040 km²; includes Walvis Bay, Marion Island, and Prince Edward Island

Comparative area: slightly less than twice the size of Texas

Land boundaries: 4,973 km total; Botswana 1,840 km, Lesotho 909 km, Mozambique 491 km, Namibia 1,078 km, Swaziland 430 km, Zimbabwe 225 km

Coastline: 2,881 km

Maritime claims:
Continental shelf: 200 m (depth) or to depth of exploitation;
Exclusive fishing zone: 200 nm;
Territorial sea: 12 nm

Disputes: claim by Namibia to Walvis Bay exclave and 12 offshore islands administered by South Africa

Climate: mostly semiarid; subtropical along coast; sunny days, cool nights

Terrain: vast interior plateau rimmed by rugged hills and narrow coastal plain

Natural resources: gold, chromium, antimony, coal, iron ore, manganese, nickel, phosphates, tin, uranium, gem diamonds, platinum, copper, vanadium, salt, natural gas

Land use: arable land 10%; permanent crops 1%; meadows and pastures 65%; forest and woodland 3%; other 21%; includes irrigated 1%

Environment: lack of important arterial rivers or lakes requires extensive water conservation and control measures

Note: Walvis Bay is an exclave of South Africa in Namibia; South Africa completely surrounds Lesotho and almost completely surrounds Swaziland

People

Population: 40,600,518 (July 1991), growth rate 2.7% (1991); includes the 10 so-called homelands, which are not recognized by the US;

South Africa (continued)

four independent homelands—Bophuthatswana 2,419,515, growth rate 2.83%; Ciskei 1,056,552, growth rate 2.96%; Transkei 4,553,994, growth rate 4.16%; Venda 691,273, growth rate 3.83%;

six other homelands—Gazankulu 772,532, growth rate 3.98%; Kangwane 576,573, growth rate 3.62%; KwaNdebele 360,582, growth rate 3.38%; KwaZulu 5,546,082, growth rate 3.60%; Lebowa 2,812,630, growth rate 3.91%; QwaQwa 277,957, growth rate 3.60%

Birth rate: 34 births/1,000 population (1991)

Death rate: 8 deaths/1,000 population (1991)

Net migration rate: NEGL migrants/1,000 population (1991)

Infant mortality rate: 51 deaths/1,000 live births (1991)

Life expectancy at birth: 61 years male, 67 years female (1991)

Total fertility rate: 4.4 children born/woman (1991)

Nationality: noun—South African(s); adjective—South African

Ethnic divisions: black 75.2%, white 13.6%, Colored 8.6%, Indian 2.6%

Religion: most whites and Coloreds and about 60% of blacks are Christian; about 60% of Indians are Hindu; Muslim 20%

Language: Afrikaans, English (both official); many vernacular languages, including Zulu, Xhosa, North and South Sotho, Tswana

Literacy: 76% (male 78%, female 75%) age 15 and over can read and write (1980)

Labor force: 11,000,000 economically active (1989); services 34%, agriculture 30%, industry and commerce 29%, mining 7% (1985)

Organized labor: about 17% of total labor force is unionized; African unions represent 15% of black labor force

---

Government

Long-form name: Republic of South Africa; abbreviated RSA

Type: republic

Capital: administrative, Pretoria; legislative, Cape Town; judicial, Bloemfontein

Administrative divisions: 4 provinces; Cape, Natal, Orange Free State, Transvaal; there are 10 homelands not recognized by the US—4 independent (Bophuthatswana, Ciskei, Transkei, Venda) and 6 other (Gazankulu, Kangwane, KwaNdebele, KwaZulu, Lebowa, QwaQwa)

Independence: 31 May 1910 (from UK)

Constitution: 3 September 1984

Legal system: based on Roman-Dutch law and English common law; accepts compulsory ICJ jurisdiction, with reservations

National holiday: Republic Day, 31 May (1910)

Executive branch: state president, Executive Council (cabinet), Ministers' Councils (from the three houses of Parliament)

Legislative branch: tricameral Parliament (Parlement) consists of the House of Assembly (Volksraad; whites), House of Representatives (Raad van Verteenwoordigers; Coloreds), and House of Delegates (Raad van Afgevaardigdes; Indians)

Judicial branch: Supreme Court

Leaders:

Chief of State and Head of Government—State President Frederik W. DE KLERK (since 13 September 1989)

Political parties and leaders: *white political parties and leaders*—National Party (NP), Frederik W. DE KLERK (majority party); Conservative Party (CP), Dr. Andries P. TREURNICHT (official opposition party); Herstigte National Party (HNP), Jaap MARAIS; Democratic Party (DP), Zach DE BEER;

Colored political parties and leaders—Labor Party (LP), Allan HENDRICKSE (majority party); Democratic Reform Party (DRP), Carter EBRAHIM; United Democratic Party (UDP), Jac RABIE; Freedom Party;

Indian political parties and leaders—Solidarity, J. N. REDDY (majority party); National People's Party (NPP), Amichand RAJBANSI; Merit People's Party

Suffrage: universal at age 18, but voting rights are racially based

Elections:

House of Assembly (whites)—last held 6 September 1989 (next to be held by March 1995); results—NP 58%, CP 23%, DP 19%; seats—(178 total, 166 elected) NP 103, CP 41, DP 34;

House of Representatives (Coloreds)—last held 6 September 1989 (next to be held by September 1994); results—percent of vote by party NA; seats—(85 total, 80 elected) LP 69, DRP 5, UDP 3, Freedom Party 1, independents 2;

House of Delegates (Indians)—last held 6 September 1989 (next to be held by September 1994); results—percent of vote by party NA; seats—(45 total, 40 elected) Solidarity 16, NPP 9, Merit People's Party 3, United Party 2, Democratic Party 2, People's Party 1, National Federal Party 1, independents 6

Communists: small Communist party legalized in 1990 after 30-year ban, Daniel TLOOME, chairman and Joe SLOVO, general secretary

Other political or pressure groups: African National Congress (ANC), Nelson Mandela, president; Pan-Africanist Congress (PAC), Clarence MAKWETU

Member of: BIS, CCC, ECA, GATT, IAEA, IBRD, ICAO, ICC, IDA, IFC, IMF, INTELSAT, ISO, ITU, LORCS, SACU, UN, UNCTAD, WFTU, WHO, WIPO, WMO (suspended)

Diplomatic representation: Ambassador Harry SCHWARZ; Chancery at 3051 Massachusetts Avenue NW, Washington DC 20008; telephone (202) 232-4400; there are South African Consulates General in Beverly Hills (California), Chicago, Houston, and New York;

US—Ambassador William L. SWING; Embassy at Thibault House, 225 Pretorius Street, Pretoria; telephone [27] (12) 28-4266; there are US Consulates General in Cape Town, Durban, and Johannesburg

Flag: actually four flags in one—three miniature flags reproduced in the center of the white band of the former flag of the Netherlands which has three equal horizontal bands of orange (top), white, and blue; the miniature flags are a vertically hanging flag of the old Orange Free State with a horizontal flag of the UK adjoining on the hoist side and a horizontal flag of the old Transvaal Republic adjoining on the other side

---

Economy

Overview: Many of the white one-seventh of the South African population enjoy incomes, material comforts, and health and educational standards equal to those of Western Europe. In contrast, most of the remaining population suffers from the poverty patterns of the Third World, including unemployment, lack of job skills, and barriers to movement into higher-paying fields. Inputs and outputs thus do not move smoothly into the most productive employments, and the effectiveness of the market is further lowered by international constraints on dealings with South Africa. The main strength of the economy lies in its rich mineral resources, which provide two-thirds of exports. Average growth of less than 2% in output in recent years falls far short of the 5-6% level needed to cut into the high unemployment rate.

GDP: $101.7 billion, per capita $2,600; real growth rate −0.9% (1990)

Inflation rate (consumer prices): 14.4% (1990)

Unemployment rate: 22% (1989); blacks 25-30%, up to 50% in homelands (1988 est.)

Budget: revenues $28.9 billion; expenditures $32.8 billion, including capital expenditures of $1.1 billion (FY92 est.)

Exports: $23.4 billion (f.o.b., 1990); *commodities*—gold 39%, minerals and metals 33%, food 5%, chemicals 3%; *partners*—Italy, Japan, US, FRG, UK, other EC, Hong Kong

Imports: $17 billion (c.i.f., 1990); *commodities*—machinery 32%, transport equipment 15%, chemicals 11%, oil, textiles, scientific instruments, base metals; *partners*—FRG, Japan, UK, US, Italy

External debt: $19.5 billion (July 1990)

Industrial production: growth rate NA%; accounts for about 45% of GDP

Electricity: 34,941,000 kW capacity; 158,000 million kWh produced, 4,100 kWh per capita (1989)

Industries: mining (world's largest producer of platinum, gold, chromium), automobile assembly, metalworking, machinery, textile, iron and steel, chemical, fertilizer, foodstuffs

Agriculture: accounts for about 5% of GDP and 30% of labor force; diversified agriculture, with emphasis on livestock; products—cattle, poultry, sheep, wool, milk, beef, corn, wheat; sugarcane, fruits, vegetables; self-sufficient in food

Economic aid: NA

Currency: rand (plural—rand); 1 rand (R) = 100 cents

Exchange rates: rand (R) per US$1—2.5625 (January 1991), 2.5863 (1990), 2.6166 (1989), 2.2611 (1988), 2.0350 (1987), 2.2685 (1986), 2.1911 (1985)

Fiscal year: 1 April-31 March

Communications

Railroads: 20,638 km route distance total; 35,079 km of 1.067-meter gauge trackage (counts double and multiple tracking as single track); 314 km of 610 mm gauge

Highways: 188,309 km total; 54,013 km paved, 134,296 km crushed stone, gravel, or improved earth

Pipelines: 931 km crude oil; 1,748 km refined products; 322 km natural gas

Ports: Durban, Cape Town, Port Elizabeth, Richard's Bay, Saldanha, Mosselbaai, Walvis Bay

Merchant marine: 7 ships (1,000 GRT or over) totaling 229,245 GRT/218,929 DWT; includes 6 container, 1 vehicle carrier

Civil air: 81 major transport aircraft

Airports: 917 total, 765 usable; 130 with permanent-surface runways; 5 with runways over 3,659 m; 10 with runways 2,440-3,659 m; 224 with runways 1,220-2,439 m

Telecommunications: the system is the best developed, most modern, and has the highest capacity in Africa; it consists of carrier-equipped open-wire lines, coaxial cables, radio relay links, fiber optic cable, and radiocommunication stations; key centers are Bloemfontein, Cape Town, Durban, Johannesburg, Port Elizabeth, and Pretoria; 4,500,000 telephones; stations—14 AM, 286 FM, 67 TV; 1 submarine cable; earth stations—1 Indian Ocean INTELSAT and 2 Atlantic Ocean INTELSAT

Defense Forces

Branches: Army, Navy, Air Force, Medical Services

Manpower availability: males 15-49, 9,797,349; 5,980,786 fit for military service; 426,615 reach military age (18) annually; obligation for service in Citizen Force or Commandos begins at 18; volunteers for service in permanent force must be 17; national service obligation is one year; figures include the so-called homelands not recognized by the US

Defense expenditures: $3.67 billion, 11% of GDP (FY92)

South Georgia and the South Sandwich Islands
(dependent territory of the UK)

Geography

Total area: 4,066 km²; land area: 4,066 km²; includes Shag and Clerke Rocks

Comparative area: slightly larger than Rhode Island

Land boundaries: none

Coastline: undetermined

Maritime claims:

Territorial sea: 12 nm

Disputes: administered by the UK, claimed by Argentina

Climate: variable, with mostly westerly winds throughout the year, interspersed with periods of calm; nearly all precipitation falls as snow

Terrain: most of the islands, rising steeply from the sea, are rugged and mountainous; South Georgia is largely barren and has steep, glacier-covered mountains; the South Sandwich Islands are of volcanic origin with some active volcanoes

Natural resources: fish

Land use: arable land 0%; permanent crops 0%; meadows and pastures 0%; forest and woodland 0%; other 100%; largely covered by permanent ice and snow with some sparse vegetation consisting of grass, moss, and lichen

Environment: reindeer, introduced early in this century, live on South Georgia; weather conditions generally make it difficult to approach the South Sandwich Islands; the South Sandwich Islands are subject to active volcanism

Note: the north coast of South Georgia has several large bays, which provide good anchorage

People

Population: no permanent population; there is a small military garrison on South Georgia and the British Antarctic Survey has a biological station on Bird Island; the South Sandwich islands are uninhabited

285

South Georgia and the South Sandwich Islands *(continued)*

Government

Long-form name: South Georgia and the South Sandwich Islands (no short-form name)
Type: dependent territory of the UK
Capital: Grytviken on South Georgia is the garrison town
Administrative divisions: none (dependent territory of the UK)
Independence: none (dependent territory of the UK)
Constitution: 3 October 1985
Legal system: English common law
National holiday: Liberation Day, 14 June (1982)
Executive branch: British monarch, commissioner
Legislative branch: none
Judicial branch: none
Leaders:
Chief of State—Queen ELIZABETH II (since 6 February 1952), represented by Commissioner William Hugh FULLERTON (since 1988; resident at Stanley, Falkland Islands)

Economy

Overview: Some fishing takes place in adjacent waters. There is a potential source of income from harvesting fin fish and krill. The islands receive income from postage stamps produced in the UK.
Budget: revenues $291,777; expenditures $451,011, including capital expenditures of $NA (FY88 est.)
Electricity: 900 kW capacity; 2 million kWh produced, NA kWh per capita (1990)

Communications

Highways: NA
Ports: Grytviken Harbour on South Georgia
Airports: 5 total, 5 usable; 2 with permanent-surface runways; 1 with runway 2,440-3,659 m
Telecommunications: coastal radio station at Grytviken; no broadcast stations

Defense Forces

Note: defense is the responsibility of the UK

Soviet Union

2000 km

The United States Government has not recognized the incorporation of Estonia, Latvia, and Lithuania into the Soviet Union. Other boundary representation is not necessarily authoritative.

Geography

Total area: 22,402,200 km²; land area: 22,272,000 km²
Comparative area: slightly less than 2.5 times the size of US
Land boundaries: 19,933 km total; Afghanistan 2,384 km, Czechoslovakia 98 km, China 7,520 km, Finland 1,313 km, Hungary 135 km, Iran 1,690 km, North Korea 17 km, Mongolia 3,441 km, Norway 196 km, Poland 1,215 km, Romania 1,307 km, Turkey 617 km
Coastline: 42,777 km
Maritime claims:
Continental shelf: 200 m (depth) or to depth of exploitation;
Exclusive economic zone: 200 nm;
Territorial sea: 12 nm
Disputes: bilateral negotiations are under way to resolve disputed sections of the boundary with China; US Government has not recognized the incorporation of Estonia, Latvia, and Lithuania into the Soviet Union; Etorofu, Kunashiri, and Shikotan Islands and the Habomai island group occupied by Soviet Union since 1945, claimed by Japan; maritime dispute with Norway over portion of Barents Sea; has made no territorial claim in Antarctica (but has reserved the right to do so) and does not recognize the claims of any other nation; Kurdish question among Iran, Iraq, Syria, Turkey, and the USSR
Climate: mostly temperate to arctic continental; winters vary from cool along Black Sea to frigid in Siberia; summers vary from hot in southern deserts to cool along Arctic coast
Terrain: broad plain with low hills west of Urals; vast coniferous forest and tundra in Siberia, deserts in Central Asia, mountains in south
Natural resources: self-sufficient in oil, natural gas, coal, and strategic minerals (except bauxite, alumina, tantalum, tin, tungsten, fluorspar, and molybdenum), timber, gold, manganese, lead, zinc, nickel, mercury, potash, phosphates; note—the USSR is the world's largest producer of oil and natural gas, third in coal
Land use: arable land 10%; permanent crops NEGL%; meadows and pastures 17%; forest and woodland 41%; other 32%; includes irrigated 1%
Environment: despite size and diversity, small percentage of land is arable and much is too far north; some of most fertile land is water deficient or has insufficient growing season; many better climates have poor soils; hot, dry, desiccating sukhovey wind affects south; desertification; continuous permafrost over much of Siberia is a major impediment to development
Note: largest country in world, but unfavorably located in relation to major sea lanes of world

People

Population: 293,047,571 (July 1991), growth rate 0.7% (1991)
Birth rate: 17 births/1,000 population (1991)
Death rate: 10 deaths/1,000 population (1991)
Net migration rate: 0 migrants/1,000 population (1991)
Infant mortality rate: 23 deaths/1,000 live births (1991)
Life expectancy at birth: 65 years male, 74 years female (1991)
Total fertility rate: 2.4 children born/woman (1991)
Nationality: noun—Soviet(s); adjective—Soviet
Ethnic divisions: Russian 50.78%, Ukrainian 15.45%, Uzbek 5.84%, Belorussian (Byelorussian) 3.51%, Kazakh 2.85%, Azeri 2.38%, Armenian 1.62%, Tajik 1.48%, Georgian 1.39%, Moldovan 1.17%, Lithuanian 1.07%, Turkmen 0.95%, Kirghiz 0.89%, Latvian 0.51%, Estonian 0.36%, other 9.75%
Religion: Russian Orthodox 20%, Muslim 10%, Protestant, Georgian Orthodox, Armenian Orthodox, and Roman Catholic 7%, Jewish less than 1%, atheist 60% (est.)
Language: Russian (official); more than 200 languages and dialects (at least 18 with more than 1 million speakers); Slavic group 75%, other Indo-European 8%, Altaic 12%, Uralian 3%, Caucasian 2%
Literacy: 98% (male 99%, female 97%) age 15 and over can read and write (1989)
Labor force: 152,300,000 civilians; industry and other nonagricultural fields 80%, agriculture 20%; shortage of skilled labor (1989)
Organized labor: the vast majority of workers are union members; official unions are organized within the General Confederation of Trade Unions (GCTU) and still operate within general guidelines set up by

the CPSU and Soviet Government; a large number of independent trade unions have been formed since President Gorbachev came to power; most are locally or regionally based and represent workers from one enterprise or a group of enterprises; there are a few independent unions that claim a nationwide following, the most prominent of which is Independent Miners Trade Union set up by the country's coal miners

Government

Long-form name: Union of Soviet Socialist Republics; abbreviated USSR
Type: in transition to multiparty federal system
Capital: Moscow
Administrative divisions: 1 soviet federative socialist republic* (sovetskaya federativnaya sotsialstcheskaya respublika) and 14 soviet socialist republics (sovetskiye sotsialisticheskiye respubliki, singular—sovetskaya sotsialisticheskaya respublika); Armenian Soviet Socialist Republic, Azerbaijan Soviet Socialist Republic, Belorussian (Byelorussian) Soviet Socialist Republic, Estonian Soviet Socialist Republic, Georgian Soviet Socialist Republic, Kazakh Soviet Socialist Republic, Kirghiz Soviet Socialist Republic, Latvian Soviet Socialist Republic, Lithuanian Soviet Socialist Republic, Russian Soviet Federative Socialist Republic*, Soviet Socialist Republic of Moldova, Tajik Soviet Socialist Republic, Turkmen Soviet Socialist Republic, Ukrainian Soviet Socialist Republic, Uzbek Soviet Socialist Republic; note—Russian Soviet Federative Socialist Republic is often abbreviated RSFSR and Soviet Socialist Republic is often abbreviated SSR; the parliaments in Armenia, Azerbaijan, Estonia, Georgia, Latvia, and Lithuania have removed the words Soviet Socialist from the names of their republics, but the central government has not recognized those changes; the parliament in Kirghiziya changed the name Kirghiz Soviet Socialist Republic to Republic of Kyrgyzstan, but the central government has not recognized that change
Independence: 30 December 1922 (Union of Soviet Socialist Republics established)
Constitution: 7 October 1977
Legal system: civil law system as modified by Communist legal theory; no judicial review of legislative acts; has not accepted compulsory ICJ jurisdiction
National holiday: Great October Socialist Revolution, 7-8 November (1917)
Executive branch: president
Legislative branch: the Congress of People's Deputies (S'ezd Narodnykh Deputatov) is the supreme organ of USSR state power and selects the bicameral Supreme Soviet (Verkhovnyi Sovyet) which consists of two coequal houses—Soviet of the Union (Soviet Soiuza) and Soviet of Nationalities (Soviet Natsional'nostei)
Judicial branch: Supreme Court of the USSR
Leaders:
Chief of State—President Mikhail Sergeyevich GORBACHEV (since 14 March 1990; General Secretary of the Central Committee of the Communist Party since 11 March 1985); Vice President Gennadiy Ivanovich YANAYEV (since 27 December 1990);
Head of Government—Prime Minister Valentin Sergeyevich PAVLOV (since 14 January 1991); First Deputy Prime Minister Vitaliy Khusseynovich DOGUZHIYEV (since 14 January 1991); First Deputy Prime Minister Vladimir Makarovich VELICHKO (since 14 January 1991); First Deputy Prime Minister Vladimir Ivanovich SHCHERBAKOV (since 16 May 1991); Deputy Prime Minister Nikolay Pavlovich LAVEROV (since 14 January 1991); Deputy Prime Minister Yuriy Dmitriyevich MASLYUKOV (since 14 January 1991); Deputy Prime Minister Lev Dmitriyevich RYABEV (since 14 January 1991); Deputy Prime Minister Fedor Petrovich SEN'KO (since 28 February 1991); Deputy Prime Minister Bikhodzhal Fatkhidinovna RAKHIMOVA (since 16 May 1991)
Political parties and leaders: nascent multiparty system—dominant party is the Communist Party of the Soviet Union (CPSU), President Mikhail Sergeyevich GORBACHEV, general secretary of the Central Committee of the CPSU
Suffrage: universal at age 18
Elections:
President—last held 14 March 1990 (next to be held NA 1995); results—Mikhail Sergeyevich GORBACHEV was elected by the Congress of People's Deputies;
Congress of People's Deputies—last held 17 December 1990 (next to be held NA); results—NA; seats—(2,250 total) CPSU NA, non-CPSU NA;
USSR Supreme Soviet—consists of the Council of the Union and the Council of Nationalities and holds two sessions annually;
Council of the Union—last held Spring 1991 (next to be held Fall 1991); results—NA; seats—(271 total) CPSU NA, non-CPSU NA;
Council of Nationalities—last held Spring 1991 (next to be held Fall 1991); results—NA; seats—(271 total) CPSU NA, non-CPSU NA
Communists: about 19 million party members, with membership declining; at least 800,000 party members resigned in the first nine months of 1990
Other political or pressure groups: Komsomol, trade unions, and other organizations that facilitate Communist control; regional popular fronts, informal organizations, and nascent parties with varying attitudes toward the Communist Party establishment
Member of: CSCE, ECE, ESCAP, IAEA, IBEC, ICAO, ICFTU, IIB, ILO, IMO, INMARSAT, INTERPOL, IOC, ISO, ITU, LORCS, PCA, UN, UNCTAD, UNESCO, UNIDO, UN Security Council, UN Trusteeship Council, UNTSO, UPU, WFTU, WHO, WIPO, WMO, WTO
Diplomatic representation: Ambassador-nominee Viktor KOMPLEKTOV; Chancery at 1125 16th Street NW, Washington DC 20036; telephone (202) 628-7551 or 8548; there is a Soviet Consulate General in San Francisco;
US—Ambassador Robert S. STRAUSS; Embassy at Ulitsa Chaykovskogo 19/21/23, Moscow (mailing address is APO New York 09862); telephone [7] (095) 252-2450 through 59; there is a US Consulate General in Leningrad
Flag: red with the yellow silhouette of a crossed hammer and sickle below a yellow-edged five-pointed red star in the upper hoist-side corner

Economy

Overview: The first six years of *perestroyka* (economic and political restructuring) have undermined the institutions and processes of the Soviet command economy without replacing them with efficiently functioning markets. The initial reforms have featured greater authority for enterprise managers over prices, wages, product mix, investment, sources of supply, and customers. But in the absence of effective market discipline, the result has been the disappearance of low-price goods, excessive wage increases, an even larger volume of unfinished construction projects, and, in general, continued economic stagnation. The Gorbachev regime has made at least four serious errors in economic policy in these six years: the unpopular and short-lived antialcohol campaign; the initial cutback in imports of consumer goods; the failure to act decisively at the beginning for the privatization of agriculture; and the buildup of a massive overhang of unspent rubles in the hands of households and enterprises. The regime has vacillated among a series of ambitious economic policy prescriptions put forth by leading economists and political leaders. The plans vary from proposals for (a) quick marketization of the economy; (b) gradual marketization; (c) a period of retrenchment to ensure a stable base for future marketization; and (d) a return to disciplined central planning and allocation. The economy, caught between two systems, is suffering from even greater mismatches between what is being produced and what would serve the best interests of enterprises and households. Meanwhile, the seething nationality problems have been dislocating regional patterns of economic specialization and pose a further major threat to growth prospects over the next few years. Official Soviet statistics report GNP fell by 2% in 1990, but the actual decline was substantially greater. Whatever the numerical decline, it does not capture the increasing disjointures in the economy evidenced by emptier shelves, longer lines, increased barter, and widespread strikes.

GNP: approximately $2,660 billion, per capita $9,130; real growth rate −2.4% to −5.0% (1990 est. based on a reconstruciton of offical Soviet statistics); note—because of the continued unraveling of Soviet economic and statistical controls, the estimate is subject to even greater uncertainties than in earlier years; the dollar estimates most likely overstate Soviet GNP to some extent because of an incomplete allowance for the poor quality, narrow assortment, and low performance characteristics of Soviet goods and services; the −2.4% growth figure is based on the application of CIA's usual estimating methods whereas the −5.0% figure is corrected for measurement problems that worsened sharply in 1990

Inflation rate (consumer prices): 14% (1990 est.)

Unemployment rate: official Soviet statistics imply an unemployment rate of 1 to 2 percent in 1990; USSR's first official unemployment estimate, however, is acknowledged to be rough

Budget: revenues 422 billion rubles; expenditures 510 billion rubles, including capital expenditures of 53 billion rubles (1990 est.)

Exports: $109.3 billion (f.o.b., 1989); *commodities*—petroleum and petroleum products, natural gas, metals, wood, agricultural products, and a wide variety of manufactured goods (primarily capital goods and arms); *partners*—Eastern Europe 46%, EC 16%, Cuba 6%, US, Afghanistan (1989)

Imports: $114.7 billion (c.i.f., 1989); *commodities*—grain and other agricultural products, machinery and equipment, steel products (including large-diameter pipe), consumer manufactures; *partners*—Eastern Europe 50%, EC 13%, Cuba, China, US (1989)

External debt: $55 billion (1990)

Industrial production: growth rate −2.4% (1990 est.)

Electricity: 350,000,000 kW capacity; 1,740,000 million kWh produced, 5,920 kWh per capita (1990)

Industries: diversified, highly developed capital goods and defense industries; comparatively less developed consumer goods industries

Agriculture: accounts for roughly 20% of GNP and labor force; production based on large collective and state farms; inefficiently managed; wide range of temperate crops and livestock produced; world's third-largest grain producer after the US and China; shortages of grain, oilseeds, and meat; world's leading producer of sawnwood and roundwood; annual fish catch among the world's largest

Illicit drugs: illegal producer of cannabis and opium poppy, mostly for domestic consumption; government has begun eradication program to control cultivation; used as a transshipment country for illicit drugs to Western Europe

Economic aid: donor—extended to non-Communist less developed countries (1954-89), $49.6 billion; extended to other Communist countries (1954-89), $154 billion

Currency: ruble (plural—rubles); 1 ruble (R) = 100 kopeks

Exchange rates: rubles (R) per US$1— 0.580 (1990), 0.629 (1989), 0.629 (1988), 0.633 (1987), 0.704 (1986), 0.838 (1985); note—as of 1 April 1991 the official exchange rate remained administratively set; it should not be used indiscriminately to convert domestic rubles to dollars; in November 1990 the USSR introduced a commercial exchange rate of 1.8 rubles to the dollar used for accounting purposes within the USSR and which was still in force on 1 April 1991; on 1 April 1991 the USSR introduced a new foreign-currency market for foreign companies and individuals; the rate will be fixed twice a week based on supply and demand; as of 4 April 1991 the rate was 27.6 rubles to the dollar; Soviet citizens traveling abroad are restricted to buying $200 a year at prevailing rates

Fiscal year: calendar year

Communications

Railroads: 147,400 km total; 53,900 km electrified; does not include industrial lines (1989)

Highways: 1,757,000 km total; 1,310,600 km hard-surfaced (asphalt, concrete, stone block, asphalt treated, gravel, crushed stone); 446,400 km earth (1989)

Inland waterways: 123,700 km navigable, exclusive of Caspian Sea (1989)

Pipelines: 82,000 km crude oil and refined products; 206,500 km natural gas (1987)

Ports: Leningrad, Riga, Tallinn, Kaliningrad, Liepaja, Ventspils, Murmansk, Arkhangel'sk, Odessa, Novorossiysk, Il'ichevsk, Nikolayev, Sevastopol', Vladivostok, Nakhodka; inland ports are Astrakhan', Baku, Nizhniy Novgorod (Gor'kiy), Kazan', Khabarovsk, Krasnoyarsk, Kuybyshev, Moscow, Rostov, Volgograd, Kiev

Merchant marine: 1,565 ships (1,000 GRT or over) totaling 15,243,228 GRT/20,874,488 DWT; includes 52 passenger, 898 cargo, 52 container, 11 barge

carrier, 4 roll-on/float off cargo, 5 railcar carrier, 114 roll-on/roll-off cargo, 230 petroleum, oils, and lubricants (POL) tanker, 5 liquefied gas, 17 combination ore/oil, 4 specialized liquid carrier, 13 chemical tanker, 160 bulk; note—594 merchant ships are based in Black Sea, 366 in Baltic Sea, 398 in Soviet Far East, and 207 in Barents Sea and White Sea; the Soviet Union has been transferring merchant ships to a variety of flags of convenience; at the beginning of 1991 the USSR had 64 ships under foreign flags (Cyprus 52, Malta 7, Panama 2, Vanuatu 2, and Honduras 1)

Civil air: 4,000 major transport aircraft

Airports: 7,192 total, 4,607 usable; 1,163 with permanent-surface runways; 33 with runways over 3,659 m; 491 with runways 2,440-3,659 m; 661 with runways 1,220-2,439 m

Telecommunications: 37 million telephone subscribers; phone density of 37 per 100 households; urban phone density is 9.2 phones per 100 residents; rural phone density is 2.9 per 100 residents (June 1990); automatic telephone dialing with 70 countries and between 25 Soviet cities (April 1989); stations—457 AM, 131 FM, over 900 TV; 90 million TV's (December 1990)

Defense Forces

Branches: Ground Forces, Navy, Air Forces, Air Defense Forces, Strategic Rocket Forces, Command and General Support, Security Forces

Manpower availability: males 15-49, 70,058,651; 55,931,817 fit for military service; 2,265,935 reach military age (18) annually (down somewhat from 2,500,000 a decade ago); approximately 35-40% receive deferments for health, education, or other reasons

Defense expenditures: 63.9 billion rubles, NA% of GDP

Spain

Bay of Biscay
300 km
La Coruña • Bilbao
León • Zaragoza
• Valladolid • Barcelona
Salamanca
MADRID • Balearic Sea
Valencia
Córdoba • Alicante □ Balearic Islands
Sevilla • Málaga
North Atlantic Ocean
Strait of Gibraltar
Mediterranean Sea
Canary Islands, Ceuta, and Melilla are not shown.

Geography

Total area: 504,750 km²; land area: 499,400 km²; includes Balearic Islands, Canary Islands, and five places of sovereignty (plazas de soberanía) on and off the coast of Morocco—Ceuta, Mellila, Islas Chafarinas, Peñón de Alhucemas, and Peñón de Vélez de la Gomera
Comparative area: slightly more than twice the size of Oregon
Land boundaries: 1,903.2 km total; Andorra 65 km, France 623 km, Gibraltar 1.2 km, Portugal 1,214 km
Coastline: 4,964 km
Maritime claims:
Exclusive economic zone: 200 nm;
Territorial sea: 12 nm
Disputes: Gibraltar question with UK; Spain controls five places of sovereignty (plazas de soberanía) on and off the coast of Morocco—the coastal enclaves of Ceuta and Melilla which Morocco contests as well as the islands of Peñón de Alhucemas, Peñón de Vélez de la Gomera, and Islas Chafarinas
Climate: temperate; clear, hot summers in interior, more moderate and cloudy along coast; cloudy, cold winters in interior, partly cloudy and cool along coast
Terrain: large, flat to dissected plateau surrounded by rugged hills; Pyrenees in north
Natural resources: coal, lignite, iron ore, uranium, mercury, pyrites, fluorspar, gypsum, zinc, lead, tungsten, copper, kaolin, potash, hydropower
Land use: arable land 31%; permanent crops 10%; meadows and pastures 21%; forest and woodland 31%; other 7%; includes irrigated 6%
Environment: deforestation; air pollution
Note: strategic location along approaches to Strait of Gibraltar

People

Population: 39,384,516 (July 1991), growth rate 0.3% (1991)

Birth rate: 11 births/1,000 population (1991)
Death rate: 8 deaths/1,000 population (1991)
Net migration rate: 0 migrants/1,000 population (1991)
Infant mortality rate: 6 deaths/1,000 live births (1991)
Life expectancy at birth: 75 years male, 82 years female (1991)
Total fertility rate: 1.5 children born/woman (1991)
Nationality: noun—Spaniard(s); adjective—Spanish
Ethnic divisions: composite of Mediterranean and Nordic types
Religion: Roman Catholic 99%, other sects 1%
Language: Castilian Spanish; second languages include Catalan 17%, Galician 7%, Basque 2%
Literacy: 95% (male 97%, female 93%) age 15 and over can read and write (1990 est.)
Labor force: 14,621,000; services 53%, industry 24%, agriculture 14%, constrction 9% (1988)
Organized labor: less 10% of labor force (1988)

Government

Long-form name: Kingdom of Spain
Type: parliamentary monarchy
Capital: Madrid
Administrative divisions: 17 autonomous communities (comunidades autónomas, singular—comunidad autónoma); Andalucía, Aragón, Asturias, Canarias, Cantabria, Castilla-La Mancha, Castilla y León, Cataluña, Comunidad Valenciana, Extremadura, Galicia, Islas Baleares, La Rioja, Madrid, Murcia, Navarra, Pais Vasco; note—there are five places of sovereignty on and off the coast of Morocco (Ceuta, Mellila, Islas Chafarinas, Peñón de Alhucemas, and Peñón de Vélez de la Gomera) with administrative status unknown
Independence: 1492 (expulsion of the Moors and unification)
Constitution: 6 December 1978, effective 29 December 1978
Legal system: civil law system, with regional applications; does not accept compulsory ICJ jurisdiction
National holiday: National Day, 12 October
Executive branch: monarch, president of the government (prime minister), deputy prime minister, Council of Ministers (cabinet), Council of State
Legislative branch: bicameral The General Courts or National Assembly (Las Cortes Generales) consists of an upper house or Senate (Senado) and a lower house or Congress of Deputies (Congreso de los Diputados)

Judicial branch: Supreme Court (Tribunal Supremo)
Leaders:
Chief of State—King JUAN CARLOS I (since 22 November 1975);
Head of Government—Prime Minister Felipe GONZÁLEZ Márquez (since 2 December 1982); Deputy Prime Minister Narcis SERRA (since 13 March 1991)
Political parties and leaders: principal national parties, from right to left—Popular Party (PP), José Maria AZNAR; Popular Democratic Party (PDP), Luis DE GRANDES; Social Democratic Center (CDS), Adolfo SUÁREZ González; Spanish Socialist Workers Party (PSOE), Felipe GONZÁLEZ Márquez; Socialist Democracy Party (DS), Ricardo Garcia DAMBORENEA; Spanish Communist Party (PCE), Julio ANGUITA; chief regional parties— Convergence and Unity (CiU), Jordi PUJOL Saley, in Catalonia; Basque Nationalist Party (PNV), Xabier ARZALLUS; Basque Solidarity (EA), Carlos GARAICOETXEA Urizza; Basque Popular Unity (HB), Jon IDIGORAS; Basque Left (EE), Kepa AULESTIA; Andalusian Party (PA), Pedro PACHECO; Independent Canary Group (AIC); Aragon Regional Party (PAR); Valencian Union (UV)
Suffrage: universal at age 18
Elections:
Senate—last held 29 October 1989 (next to be held October 1993); results—NA; seats (208) PSOE 106, PP 79, CiU 10, PNV 4, HB 3, AIC 1, other 5;
Congress of Deputies—last held 29 October 1989 (next to be held October 1993); results—PSOE 39.6%, PP 25.8%, CDS 9%, Communist-led coalition (IU) 9%, CiU 5%, Basque Nationalist Party 1.2%, HB 1%, Andalusian Party 1%, other 8.4%; seats—(350 total) PSOE 175, PP 106, CiU 18, IU 17, CDS 14, PNV 5, HB 4, other 11
Communists: PCE membership declined from a possible high of 160,000 in 1977 to roughly 60,000 in 1987; the party gained almost 1 million voters and 10 deputies in the 1989 election; voters came mostly from the disgruntled socialist left; remaining strength is in labor, where it dominates the Workers Commissions trade union (one of the country's two major labor centrals), which claims a membership of about 1 million; experienced a modest recovery in 1986 national election, nearly doubling the share of the vote it received in 1982
Other political or pressure groups: on the extreme left, the Basque Fatherland and Liberty (ETA) and the First of October Antifascist Resistance Group (GRAPO) use terrorism to oppose the government; free labor unions (authorized in April 1977) include the Communist-dominated Workers Commissions (CCOO); the Socialist General Union of Workers (UGT), and the

Spain (continued)

smaller independent Workers Syndical Union (USO); the Catholic Church; business and landowning interests; Opus Dei; university students

Member of: AG (observer), AsDB, BIS, CCC, CE, CERN, CSCE, EBRD, EC, ECE, ECLAC, EIB, ESA, FAO, G-8, GATT, IADB, IAEA, IBRD, ICAO, ICC, ICFTU, IDA, IEA, IFAD, IFC, ILO, IMF, IMO, INMARSAT, INTELSAT, INTERPOL, IOC, IOM (observer), ISO, ITU, LAIA (observer), LORCS, NAM (guest), NATO, NEA, OAS (observer), OECD, PCA, UN, UNAVEM, UNCTAD, UNESCO, UNIDO, UPU, WCL, WEU, WHO, WIPO, WMO, WTO

Diplomatic representation: Ambassador Jaime de OJEDA; Chancery at 2700 15th Street NW, Washington DC 20009; telephone (202) 265-0190 or 0191; there are Spanish Consulates General in Boston, Chicago, Houston, Los Angeles, Miami, New Orleans, New York, San Francisco, and San Juan (Puerto Rico);
US—Ambassador Joseph ZAPPALA; Embassy at Serrano 75, 28006 Madrid (mailing address is APO New York 09285); telephone [34] (1) 577-4000; there is a US Consulate General in Barcelona and a Consulate in Bilbao

Flag: three horizontal bands of red (top), yellow (double width), and red with the national coat of arms on the hoist side of the yellow band; the coat of arms includes the royal seal framed by the Pillars of Hercules which are the two promontories (Gibraltar and Ceuta) on either side of the eastern end of the Strait of Gibraltar

Economy

Overview: This Western capitalistic economy has done well since Spain joined the EC in 1986. With annual increases in real GNP averaging about 5% in the 1987-90 period, Spain has been the fastest growing member of the EC. Increased investment—both domestic and foreign—has been the most important factor pushing the economic expansion. Inflation moderated to 4.8% in 1988, but an overheated economy caused inflation to reach almost 7% in 1989-90. Another economic problem facing Spain is an unemployment rate of 16.3%, the highest in Europe.

GDP: $435.9 billion, per capita $11,100; real growth rate 3.7% (1990)

Inflation rate (consumer prices): 6.7% (1990)

Unemployment rate: 16.3% (1990)

Budget: revenues $100.1 billion; expenditures $111.6 billion, including capital expenditures of $NA (1990)

Exports: $55.6 billion (f.o.b., 1990); *commodities*—foodstuffs, live animals, wood, footwear, machinery, chemicals; *partners*—EC 67.8%, US 6.5%, other developed countries 9%

Imports: $87.7 billion (c.i.f., 1990); *commodities*—petroleum, footwear, machinery, chemicals, grain, soybeans, coffee, tobacco, iron and steel, timber, cotton, transport equipment;
partners—EC 59.7%, US 8.5%, other developed countries 11.5%, Middle East 3.4%

External debt: $37 billion (1990 est.)

Industrial production: growth rate 3.5% (1990 est.)

Electricity: 46,589,000 kW capacity; 141,000 million kWh produced, 3,590 kWh per capita (1990)

Industries: textiles and apparel (including footwear), food and beverages, metals and metal manufactures, chemicals, shipbuilding, automobiles, machine tools

Agriculture: accounts for 5% of GNP and 14% of labor force; major products—grain, vegetables, olives, wine grapes, sugar beets, citrus fruit, beef, pork, poultry, dairy; largely self-sufficient in food; fish catch of 1.4 million metric tons is among top 20 nations

Economic aid: US commitments, including Ex-Im (FY70-87), $1.9 billion; Western (non-US) countries, ODA and OOF bilateral commitments (1970-79), $545.0 million; not currently a recipient

Currency: peseta (plural—pesetas); 1 peseta (Pta) = 100 céntimos

Exchange rates: pesetas (Ptas) per US$1—95.20 (January 1991), 101.93 (1990), 118.38 (1989), 116.49 (1988), 123.48 (1987), 140.05 (1986), 170.04 (1985)

Fiscal year: calendar year

Communications

Railroads: 15,430 km total; Spanish National Railways (RENFE) operates 12,691 km 1.668-meter gauge, 6,184 km electrified, and 2,295 km double track; FEVE (government-owned narrow-gauge railways) operates 1,821 km of predominantly 1.000-meter gauge and 441 km electrified; privately owned railways operate 918 km of predominantly 1.000-meter gauge, 512 km electrified, and 56 km double track

Highways: 150,839 km total; 82,513 km national (includes 2,433 km limited-access divided highway, 63,042 km bituminous treated, 17,038 km intermediate bituminous, concrete, or stone block) and 68,326 km provincial or local roads (bituminous treated, intermediate bituminous, or stone block)

Inland waterways: 1,045 km, but of minor economic importance

Pipelines: 265 km crude oil; 1,794 km refined products; 1,666 km natural gas

Ports: Algeciras, Alicante, Almería, Barcelona, Bilbao, Cádiz, Cartagena, Castellón de la Plana, Ceuta, El Ferrol del Caudillo, Puerto de Gijón, Huelva, La Coruña, Las Palmas (Canary Islands), Mahón, Málaga, Melilla, Rota, Santa Cruz de Tenerife, Sagunto, Tarragona, Valencia, Vigo, and 175 minor ports

Merchant marine: 304 ships (1,000 GRT or over) totaling 3,367,529 GRT/5,984,306 DWT; includes 2 passenger, 9 short-sea passenger, 105 cargo, 17 refrigerated cargo, 14 container, 29 roll-on/roll-off cargo, 4 vehicle carrier, 50 petroleum, oils, and lubricants (POL) tanker, 14 chemical tanker, 7 liquefied gas, 1 combination ore/oil, 4 specialized tanker, 48 bulk

Civil air: 172 major transport aircraft

Airports: 104 total, 98 usable; 61 with permanent-surface runways; 4 with runways over 3,659 m; 22 with runways 2,440-3,659 m; 25 with runways 1,220-2,439 m

Telecommunications: generally adequate, modern facilities; 15,350,464 telephones; stations—206 AM, 411 (134 relays) FM, 143 (1,297 relays) TV; 17 coaxial submarine cables; communications satellite earth stations operating in INTELSAT (5 Atlantic Ocean, 1 Indian Ocean), MARISAT, and ENTELSAT systems

Defense Forces

Branches: Army, Navy, Air Force, Marines, Civil Guard

Manpower availability: males 15-49, 10,134,256; 8,222,987 fit for military service; 339,749 reach military age (20) annually

Defense expenditures: $8.6 billion, 2% of GDP (1990)

Spratly Islands

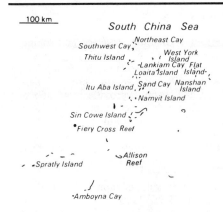

Sri Lanka

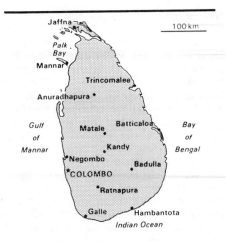

Communications

Airports: 3 total, 2 usable; none with runways over 2,439 m; 1 with runways 1,220-2,439 m
Ports: no natural harbors

Defense Forces

Note: approximately 50 small islands or reefs are occupied by China, Malaysia, the Philippines, Taiwan, and Vietnam

Geography

Total area: less than 5 km²; land area: less than 5 km²; includes 100 or so islets, coral reefs, and sea mounts scattered over the South China Sea
Comparative area: undetermined
Land boundaries: none
Coastline: 926 km
Maritime claims: undetermined
Disputes: China, Malaysia, the Philippines, Taiwan, and Vietnam claim all or part of the Spratly Islands
Climate: tropical
Terrain: flat
Natural resources: fish, guano; oil and natural gas potential
Land use: arable land 0%; permanent crops 0%; meadows and pastures 0%; forest and woodland 0%; other 100%
Environment: subject to typhoons; includes numerous small islands, atolls, shoals, and coral reefs
Note: strategically located near several primary shipping lanes in the central South China Sea; serious navigational hazard

People

Population: no permanent inhabitants; garrisons

Government

Long-form name: none

Economy

Overview: Economic activity is limited to commercial fishing and phosphate mining. Geological surveys carried out several years ago suggest that substantial reserves of oil and natural gas may lie beneath the islands; commercial exploitation has yet to be developed.
Industries: some guano mining

Geography

Total area: 65,610 km²; land area: 64,740 km²
Comparative area: slightly larger than West Virginia
Land boundaries: none
Coastline: 1,340 km
Maritime claims:
Contiguous zone: 24 nm;
Continental shelf: edge of continental margin or 200 nm;
Exclusive economic zone: 200 nm;
Territorial sea: 12 nm
Climate: tropical; monsoonal; northeast monsoon (December to March); southwest monsoon (June to October)
Terrain: mostly low, flat to rolling plain; mountains in south-central interior
Natural resources: limestone, graphite, mineral sands, gems, phosphates, clay
Land use: arable land 16%; permanent crops 17%; meadows and pastures 7%; forest and woodland 37%; other 23%; includes irrigated 8%
Environment: occasional cyclones, tornados; deforestation; soil erosion
Note: only 29 km from India across the Palk Strait; near major Indian Ocean sea lanes

People

Population: 17,423,736 (July 1991), growth rate 1.2% (1991)
Birth rate: 20 births/1,000 population (1991)
Death rate: 6 deaths/1,000 population (1991)
Net migration rate: −2 migrants/1,000 population (1991)
Infant mortality rate: 21 deaths/1,000 live births (1991)
Life expectancy at birth: 69 years male, 74 years female (1991)
Total fertility rate: 2.3 children born/woman (1991)

Sri Lanka (continued)

Nationality: noun—Sri Lankan(s); adjective—Sri Lankan
Ethnic divisions: Sinhalese 74%; Tamil 18%; Moor 7%; Burgher, Malay, and Veddha 1%
Religion: Buddhist 69%, Hindu 15%, Christian 8%, Muslim 8%
Language: Sinhala (official); Sinhala and Tamil listed as national languages; Sinhala spoken by about 74% of population, Tamil spoken by about 18%; English commonly used in government and spoken by about 10% of the population
Literacy: 86% (male 91%, female 81%) age 15 and over can read and write (1981)
Labor force: 6,600,000; agriculture 45.9%, mining and manufacturing 13.3%, trade and transport 12.4%, services and other 28.4% (1985 est.)
Organized labor: about 33% of labor force, over 50% of which are employed on tea, rubber, and coconut estates

Government

Long-form name: Democratic Socialist Republic of Sri Lanka
Type: republic
Capital: Colombo
Administrative divisions: 24 districts; Amparai, Anuradhapura, Badulla, Batticaloa, Colombo, Galle, Gampaha, Hambantota, Jaffna, Kalutara, Kandy, Kegalla, Kurunegala, Mannar, Matale, Matara, Moneragala, Mullaittivu, Nuwara Eliya, Polonnaruwa, Puttalam, Ratnapura, Trincomalee, Vavuniya; note—the administrative structure may now include 8 provinces (Central, North Central, North Eastern, North Western, Sabaragamuwa, Southern, Uva, and Western) and 25 districts (with Kilinochchi added to the existing districts)
Independence: 4 February 1948 (from UK; formerly Ceylon)
Constitution: 31 August 1978
Legal system: a highly complex mixture of English common law, Roman-Dutch, Muslim, and customary law; has not accepted compulsory ICJ jurisdiction
National holiday: Independence and National Day, 4 February (1948)
Executive branch: president, prime minister, Cabinet
Legislative branch: unicameral Parliament
Judicial branch: Supreme Court
Leaders:
Chief of State—President Ranasinghe PREMADASA (since 2 January 1989);
Head of Government—Prime Minister Dingiri Banda WIJETUNGE (since 6 March 1989)
Political parties and leaders: United National Party (UNP), Ranasinghe PREMADASA; Sri Lanka Freedom Party (SLFP), Sirimavo BANDARANAIKE; Sri Lanka Muslim Congress (SLMC), M. H. M. ASHRAFF; All Ceylon Tamil Congress (ACTC),

Kumar PONNAMBALAM; People's United Front (MEP, or Mahajana Eksath Peramuna), Dinesh GUNAWARDENE; Eelam Democratic Front (EDF), Edward Sebastian PILLAI; Tamil United Liberation Front (TULF), leader (vacant); Eelam Revolutionary Organization of Students (EROS), Velupillai BALAKUMARAN; New Socialist Party (NSSP, or Nava Sama Samaja Party), Vasudeva NANAYAKKARA; Lanka Socialist Party/Trotskyite (LSSP, or Lanka Sama Samaja Party), Colin R. de SILVA; Sri Lanka People's Party (SLMP, or Sri Lanka Mahajana Party), Chandrika Bandaranaike KUMARANATUNGA; Communist Party/Moscow (CP/M), K. P. SILVA; Communist Party/Beijing (CP/B), N. SHANMUGATHASAN; note—the United Socialist Alliance (USA) includes the NSSP, LSSP, SLMP, CP/M, and CP/B
Suffrage: universal at age 18
Elections:
President—last held 19 December 1988 (next to be held December 1994); results—Ranasinghe PREMADASA (UNP) 50%, Sirimavo BANDARANAIKE (SLFP) 45%, other 5%;
Parliament—last held 15 February 1989 (next to be held by February 1995); results—UNP 51%, SLFP 32%, SLMC 4%, TULF 3%, USA 3%, EROS 3%, MEP 1%, other 3%; seats—(225 total) UNP 125, SLFP 67, other 33
Other political or pressure groups: Liberation Tigers of Tamil Eelam (LTTE) and other smaller Tamil separatist groups; Janatha Vimukthi Peramuna (JVP or People's Liberation Front); Buddhist clergy; Sinhalese Buddhist lay groups; labor unions
Member of: AsDB, C, CCC, CP, ESCAP, FAO, G-24, G-77, GATT, IAEA, IBRD, ICAO, ICC, ICFTU, IDA, IFAD, IFC, ILO, IMF, IMO, INMARSAT, INTELSAT, INTERPOL, IOC, ISO, ITU, LORCS, NAM, PCA, SAARC, UN, UNCTAD, UNESCO, UNIDO, UPU, WCL, WFTU, WHO, WIPO, WMO, WTO
Diplomatic representation: Ambassador W. Susanta De ALWIS; Chancery at 2148 Wyoming Avenue NW, Washington DC 20008; telephone (202) 483-4025 through 4028; there is a Sri Lankan Consulate in New York; *US*—Ambassador Marion V. CREEKMORE, Jr.; Embassy at 210 Galle Road, Colombo 3 (mailing address is P. O. Box 106, Colombo); telephone [94] (1) 448007
Flag: yellow with two panels; the smaller hoist-side panel has two equal vertical bands of green (hoist side) and orange; the other panel is a large dark red rectangle with a yellow lion holding a sword and there is a yellow bo leaf in each corner; the yellow field appears as a border that goes around the entire flag and extends between the two panels

Economy

Overview: Agriculture, forestry, and fishing dominate the economy, employing about 45% of the labor force and accounting for 26% of GDP. The plantation crops of tea, rubber, and coconuts provide about 35% of export earnings. The economy has been plagued by high rates of unemployment since the late 1970s. Economic growth, which has been depressed by ethnic unrest, accelerated in 1990 as domestic conditions began to improve.
GDP: $6.6 billion, per capita $380; real growth rate 4.5% (1990 est.)
Inflation rate (consumer prices): 23% (1990)
Unemployment rate: 20% (1990 est.)
Budget: revenues $1.7 billion; expenditures $2.2 billion, including capital expenditures of $0.5 billion (1990)
Exports: $1.6 billion (f.o.b., 1989); *commodities*—tea, textiles and garments, petroleum products, coconut, rubber, agricultural products, gems and jewelry, marine products; *partners*—US 26%, FRG, Japan, UK, Belgium, Taiwan, Hong Kong, China
Imports: $2.2 billion (c.i.f., 1989); *commodities*—food and beverages, textiles and textile materials, petroleum, machinery and equipment; *partners*—Japan, Saudi Arabia, US 5.6%, India, Singapore, FRG, UK, Iran
External debt: $5.6 billion (1989)
Industrial production: growth rate 6% (1989 est.); accounts for 18% of GDP
Electricity: 1,300,000 kW capacity; 4,200 million kWh produced, 240 kWh per capita (1990)
Industries: processing of rubber, tea, coconuts, and other agricultural commodities; cement, petroleum refining, textiles, tobacco, clothing
Agriculture: accounts for 26% of GDP and nearly half of labor force; most important staple crop is paddy rice; other field crops—sugarcane, grains, pulses, oilseeds, roots, spices; cash crops—tea, rubber, coconuts; animal products—milk, eggs, hides, meat; not self-sufficient in rice production
Economic aid: US commitments, including Ex-Im (FY70-89), $1.0 billion; Western (non-US) countries, ODA and OOF bilateral commitments (1980-88), $4.9 billion; OPEC bilateral aid (1979-89), $169 million; Communist countries (1970-89), $369 million
Currency: Sri Lankan rupee (plural—rupees); 1 Sri Lankan rupee (SLRe) = 100 cents
Exchange rates: Sri Lankan rupees (SLRs) per US$1—40.272 (January 1991), 40.063 (1990), 36.047 (1989), 31.807 (1988), 29.445 (1987), 28.017 (1986), 27.163 (1985)
Fiscal year: calendar year

Sudan

Communications

Railroads: 1,948 km total (1989); all 1.868-meter broad gauge; 102 km double track; no electrification; government owned
Highways: 75,263 km total (1988); 27,637 km paved (mostly bituminous treated), 32,887 km crushed stone or gravel, 14,739 km improved earth or unimproved earth; several thousand km of mostly unmotorable tracks (1988 est.)
Inland waterways: 430 km; navigable by shallow-draft craft
Pipelines: crude and refined products, 62 km (1987)
Ports: Colombo, Trincomalee
Merchant marine: 34 ships (1,000 GRT or over) totaling 364,466 GRT/551,686 DWT; includes 18 cargo, 6 refrigerated cargo, 5 container, 2 petroleum, oils, and lubricants (POL) tanker, 3 bulk
Civil air: 8 major transport (including 1 leased)
Airports: 14 total, 13 usable; 12 with permanent-surface runways; none with runways over 3,659 m; 1 with runways 2,440-3,659 m; 7 with runways 1,220-2,439 m
Telecommunications: good international service; 114,000 telephones (1982); stations—12 AM, 5 FM, 5 TV; submarine cables extend to Indonesia and Djibouti; 2 Indian Ocean INTELSAT earth stations

Defense Forces

Branches: Army, Navy, Air Force, Police Force
Manpower availability: males 15-49, 4,636,767; 3,625,289 fit for military service; 178,010 reach military age (18) annually
Defense expenditures: $300 million, 5% of GDP (1991)

Geography

Total area: 2,505,810 km²; land area: 2,376,000 km²
Comparative area: slightly more than one quarter the size of US
Land boundaries: 7,697 km total; Central African Republic 1,165 km, Chad 1,360 km, Egypt 1,273 km, Ethiopia 2,221 km, Kenya 232 km, Libya 383 km, Uganda 435 km, Zaire 628 km
Coastline: 853 km
Maritime claims:
Contiguous zone: 18 nm;
Continental shelf: 200 m (depth) or to depth of exploitation;
Territorial sea: 12 nm
Disputes: administrative boundary with Kenya does not coincide with international boundary; administrative boundary with Egypt does not coincide with international boundary
Climate: tropical in south; arid desert in north; rainy season (April to October)
Terrain: generally flat, featureless plain; mountains in east and west
Natural resources: small reserves of crude oil, iron ore, copper, chromium ore, zinc, tungsten, mica, silver, crude oil
Land use: arable land 5%; permanent crops NEGL%; meadows and pastures 24%; forest and woodland 20%; other 51%; includes irrigated 1%
Environment: dominated by the Nile and its tributaries; dust storms; desertification
Note: largest country in Africa

People

Population: 27,220,088 (July 1991), growth rate 3.0% (1991)
Birth rate: 44 births/1,000 population (1991)
Death rate: 13 deaths/1,000 population (1991)
Net migration rate: −1 migrants/1,000 population (1991)

Infant mortality rate: 85 deaths/1,000 live births (1991)
Life expectancy at birth: 52 years male, 54 years female (1991)
Total fertility rate: 6.4 children born/woman (1991)
Nationality: noun—Sudanese (sing. and pl.); adjective—Sudanese
Ethnic divisions: black 52%, Arab 39%, Beja 6%, foreigners 2%, other 1%
Religion: Sunni Muslim (in north) 70%, indigenous beliefs 20%, Christian (mostly in south and Khartoum) 5%
Language: Arabic (official), Nubian, Ta Bedawie, diverse dialects of Nilotic, Nilo-Hamitic, and Sudanic languages, English; program of Arabization in process
Literacy: 27% (male 43%, female 12%) age 15 and over can read and write (1990 est.)
Labor force: 6,500,000; agriculture 80%, industry and commerce 10%, government 6%; labor shortages for almost all categories of skilled employment (1983 est.); 52% of population of working age (1985)
Organized labor: trade unions suspended following 30 June 1989 coup; now in process of being legalized anew

Government

Long-form name: Republic of the Sudan
Type: military; civilian government suspended and martial law imposed after 30 June 1989 coup
Capital: Khartoum
Administrative divisions: 9 states (wilāyāt, singular—wilāyat or wilāyah*); A'ālī an Nīl, Al Wusṭá*, Al Istiwā'īyah*, Al Kharṭūm, Ash Shamālīyah*, Ash Sharqīyah*, Baḥr al Ghazāl, Dārfūr, Kurdufān
Independence: 1 January 1956 (from Egypt and UK; formerly Anglo-Egyptian Sudan)
Constitution: 12 April 1973, suspended following coup of 6 April 1985; interim constitution of 10 October 1985 suspended following coup of 30 June 1989
Legal system: based on English common law and Islamic law; as of 20 January 1991, the Revolutionary Command Council imposed Islamic law in the six northern states of Al Wusṭá, Al Kharṭūm, Ash Shamālīyah, Ash Sharqīyah, Dārfūr, and Kurdufān; the council is still studying criminal provisions under Islamic law; Islamic law will apply to all residents of the six northern states regardless of their religion; some separate religious courts; accepts compulsory ICJ jurisdiction, with reservations
National holiday: Independence Day, 1 January (1956)
Executive branch: executive and legislative authority vested in a 13-member Revolutionary Command Council (RCC); chairman of the RCC acts as prime minister; in July 1989 RCC appointed a predominately

civilian 22-member cabinet to function as advisers

Legislative branch: none

Judicial branch: Supreme Court, Special Revolutionary Courts

Leaders:
Chief of State and Head of Government—Revolutionary Command Council Chairman and Prime Minister Lt. Gen. Umar Hasan Ahmad al-BASHIR (since 30 June 1989); Deputy Chairman of the Command Council and Deputy Prime Minister Maj. Gen. al-Zubayr Muhammad SALIH Ahmed (since 9 July 1989)

Political parties and leaders: none; banned following 30 June 1989 coup

Suffrage: none

Elections: none

Member of: ABEDA, ACP, AfDB, AFESD, AL, AMF, CAEU, CCC, ECA, FAO, G-77, IAEA, IBRD, ICAO, IDA, IDB, IFAD, IFC, IGADD, ILO, IMF, IMO, INTELSAT, INTERPOL, IOC, ISO, ITU, LORCS, NAM, OAU, OIC, PCA, UN, UNCTAD, UNESCO, UNHCR, UNIDO, UPU, WFTU, WHO, WIPO, WMO, WTO

Diplomatic representation: Ambassador 'Abdallah Ahmad 'ABDALLAH; Chancery at 2210 Massachusetts Avenue NW, Washington DC 20008; telephone (202) 338-8565 through 8570; there is a Sudanese Consulate General in New York;
US—Ambassador James R. CHEEK; Embassy at Shar'ia Ali Abdul Latif, Khartoum (mailing address is P. O. Box 699, Khartoum, or APO New York 09668); telephone 74700 or 74611

Flag: three equal horizontal bands of red (top), white, and black with a green isosceles triangle based on the hoist side

Economy

Overview: Sudan, one of the world's poorest countries, is buffeted by civil war, chronic political instability, adverse weather, and counterproductive economic policies. The economy is dominated by governmental entities that account for more than 70% of new investment. The private sector's main areas of activity are agriculture and trading, with most private industrial investment predating 1980. The economy's base is agriculture, which employs 80% of the work force. Industry mainly processes agricultural items. Sluggish economic performance over the past decade, attributable largely to declining annual rainfall, has reduced levels of per capita income and consumption. A high foreign debt and huge arrearages continue to cause difficulties. In 1990 the International Monetary Fund took the unusual step of declaring Sudan noncooperative on account of its nonpayment of arrearages to the Fund.

GDP: $8.5 billion, per capita $330; real growth rate −7% (FY90 est.)

Inflation rate (consumer prices): 60% (FY90 est.)

Unemployment rate: NA

Budget: revenues $514 million; expenditures $1.3 billion, including capital expenditures of $183 million (FY89 est.)

Exports: $465 million (f.o.b., FY90 est.); *commodities*—cotton 52%, sesame, gum arabic, peanuts; *partners*—Western Europe 46%, Saudi Arabia 14%, Eastern Europe 9%, Japan 9%, US 3% (FY88)

Imports: $1.0 billion (c.i.f., FY90 est.); *commodities*—petroleum products 28%, manufactured goods, machinery and equipment, medicines and chemicals; *partners*—Western Europe 32%, Africa and Asia 15%, US 13%, Eastern Europe 3% (FY88)

External debt: $12.3 billion (December 1990 est.)

Industrial production: growth rate 0.7% (FY89); accounts for 11% of GDP

Electricity: 606,000 kW capacity; 900 million kWh produced, 37 kWh per capita (1989)

Industries: cotton ginning, textiles, cement, edible oils, sugar, soap distilling, shoes, petroleum refining

Agriculture: accounts for 35% of GNP and 80% of labor force; water shortages; two-thirds of land area suitable for raising crops and livestock; major products—cotton, oil-seeds, sorghum, millet, wheat, gum arabic, sheep; marginally self-sufficient in most foods

Economic aid: US commitments, including Ex-Im (FY70-89), $1.5 billion; Western (non-US) countries, ODA and OOF bilateral commitments (1970-88), $4.8 billion; OPEC bilateral aid (1979-89), $3.1 billion; Communist countries (1970-89), $588 million

Currency: Sudanese pound (plural—pounds); 1 Sudanese pound (£Sd) = 100 piasters

Exchange rates: official rate—Sudanese pounds (£Sd) per US$1—4.5004 (fixed rate since 1987), 2.8121 (1987), 2.5000 (1986), 2.2883 (1985); note—commercial exchange rate 12.2 (May 1990)

Fiscal year: 1 July-30 June

Communications

Railroads: 5,500 km total; 4,784 km 1.067-meter gauge, 716 km 1.6096-meter-gauge plantation line

Highways: 20,000 km total; 1,600 km bituminous treated, 3,700 km gravel, 2,301 km improved earth, 12,399 km unimproved earth and track

Inland waterways: 5,310 km navigable

Pipelines: refined products, 815 km

Ports: Port Sudan, Suakin

Merchant marine: 5 ships (1,000 GRT or over) totaling 42,277 GRT/59,588 DWT; includes 3 cargo, 2 roll-on/roll-off cargo

Civil air: 14 major transport aircraft

Airports: 78 total, 66 usable; 8 with permanent-surface runways; none with runways over 3,659 m; 4 with runways 2,440-3,659 m; 30 with runways 1,220-2,439 m

Telecommunications: large, well-equipped system by African standards, but barely adequate and poorly maintained; consists of radio relay, cables, radio communications, and troposcatter; domestic satellite system with 14 stations; 73,400 telephones; stations—4 AM, 1 FM, 2 TV; earth stations—1 Atlantic Ocean INTELSAT and 1 ARABSAT

Defense Forces

Branches: Army, Navy, Air Force, Air Defense Force

Manpower availability: males 15-49, 6,176,917; 3,792,635 fit for military service; 306,695 reach military age (18) annually

Defense expenditures: $610 million, 7.2% of GDP (1989 est)

Suriname

Geography

Total area: 163,270 km²; land area: 161,470 km²

Comparative area: slightly larger than Georgia

Land boundaries: 1,707 km total; Brazil 597 km, French Guiana 510 km, Guyana 600 km

Coastline: 386 km

Maritime claims:

Exclusive economic zone: 200 nm;

Territorial sea: 12 nm

Disputes: claims area in French Guiana between Litani Rivier and Rivière Marouini (both headwaters of the Lawa); claims area in Guyana between New (Upper Courantyne) and Courantyne/Kutari Rivers (all headwaters of the Courantyne)

Climate: tropical; moderated by trade winds

Terrain: mostly rolling hills; narrow coastal plain with swamps

Natural resources: timber, hydropower potential, fish, shrimp, bauxite, iron ore, and small amounts of nickel, copper, platinum, gold

Land use: arable land NEGL%; permanent crops NEGL%; meadows and pastures NEGL%; forest and woodland 97%; other 3%; includes irrigated NEGL%

Environment: mostly tropical rain forest

People

Population: 402,385 (July 1991), growth rate 1.4% (1991)

Birth rate: 26 births/1,000 population (1991)

Death rate: 6 deaths/1,000 population (1991)

Net migration rate: −6 migrants/1,000 population (1991)

Infant mortality rate: 39 deaths/1,000 live births (1991)

Life expectancy at birth: 66 years male, 71 years female (1991)

Total fertility rate: 2.9 children born/woman (1991)

Nationality: noun—Surinamer(s); adjective—Surinamese

Ethnic divisions: Hindustani (East Indian) 37.0%, Creole (black and mixed) 31.0%, Javanese 15.3%, Bush black 10.3%, Amerindian 2.6%, Chinese 1.7%, Europeans 1.0%, other 1.1%

Religion: Hindu 27.4%, Muslim 19.6%, Roman Catholic 22.8%, Protestant (predominantly Moravian) 25.2%, indigenous beliefs about 5%

Language: Dutch (official); English widely spoken; Sranan Tongo (Surinamese, sometimes called Taki-Taki) is native language of Creoles and much of the younger population and is lingua franca among others; also Hindi Suriname Hindustani (a variant of Bhoqpuri) and Javanese

Literacy: 95% (male 95%, female 95%) age 15 and over can read and write (1990 est.)

Labor force: 104,000 (1984)

Organized labor: 49,000 members of labor force

Government

Long-form name: Republic of Suriname

Type: republic

Capital: Paramaribo

Administrative divisions: 10 districts (distrikten, singular—distrikt); Brokopondo, Commewijne, Coronie, Marowijne, Nickerie, Para, Paramaribo, Saramacca, Sipaliwini, Wanica

Independence: 25 November 1975 (from Netherlands; formerly Netherlands Guiana or Dutch Guiana)

Constitution: ratified 30 September 1987

Legal system: NA

National holiday: Independence Day, 25 November (1975)

Executive branch: president, vice president and prime minister, Cabinet of Ministers, Council of State; note—commander in chief of the National Army maintains significant power

Legislative branch: unicameral National Assembly (Assemblée Nationale)

Judicial branch: Supreme Court

Leaders:

Chief of State and Head of Government—Interim President Johannes Samuel Petrus KRAAG (since 29 December 1990, following 24 December 1990 military coup); Interim Vice President and Prime Minister Jules Albert WIJDENBOSCH (since 29 December 1990 following 24 December 1990 military coup)

Political parties and leaders:

promilitary—New Democratic Party (NDP), Jules Albert WIJDENBOSCH, Frank PLAYFAIR;

leftists (all small groups)—Democratic Alternative '91 (DA '91), Gerard BRUNINGS, a coalition of five parties formed in January

1991—Alternative Forum, Gerard BRUNINGS, Winston JESSURUN; Reformed Progressive Party (HPP), Panalall PARMISSER; Party for Brotherhood and Unity in Politics (BEP), Caprino ALLENDY; Pendawalima, Marsha JAMIN; and Independent Progressive Group, Karam RAMSUNDERSINGH; Revolutionary People's Party (RVP), Michael NAARENDORP; Progressive Workers and Farmers (PALU), Iwan KROLIS;

traditional ethnic-based parties—The New Front (NF), Henck ARRON, a coalition formed of four parties following the 24 December 1990 military coup—Progressive Reform Party (VHP), Jaggernath LACHMON; National Party of Suriname (NPS), Henck ARRON; Indonesian Peasants Party (KTPI), Willy SOEMITA; and Suriname Labor Party (SLP), Frank DERBY

Suffrage: universal at age 18

Elections:

National Assembly—last held 25 May 1991 (next to be held May 1996); results—percent of vote NA; seats—(51 total) NF 30, NDP 12, DA '91 9

Member of: ACP, CARICOM (observer), ECLAC, FAO, GATT, G-77, IADB, IBRD, ICAO, ICFTU, IFAD, ILO, IMF, IMO, INTERPOL, IOC, ITU, LAES, LORCS, NAM, OAS, OPANAL, UN, UNCTAD, UNESCO, UNIDO, UPU, WCL, WHO, WIPO, WMO

Diplomatic representation: Ambassador Willem A. UDENHOUT; Chancery at Suite 108, 4301 Connecticut Avenue NW, Washington DC 20008; telephone (202) 244-7488 or 7490 through 7492; there is a Surinamese Consulate General in Miami; *US*—Ambassador John (Jack) P. LEONARD; Embassy at Dr. Sophie Redmonstraat 129, Paramaribo (mailing address is P. O. Box 1821, Paramaribo); telephone [597] 72900, 77881, or 76459

Flag: five horizontal bands of green (top, double width), white, red (quadruple width), white, and green (double width); there is a large yellow five-pointed star centered in the red band

Economy

Overview: The economy is dominated by the bauxite industry, which accounts for about 70% of export earnings and 40% of tax revenues. The economy has been in trouble since the Dutch ended development aid in 1982. A drop in world bauxite prices that started in the late 1970s and continued until late 1986, was followed by the outbreak of a guerrilla insurgency in the interior. The guerrillas targeted the economic infrastructure, crippling the important bauxite sector and shutting down other export industries. These problems have created high inflation, high unemployment,

Suriname *(continued)*

widespread black market activity, and a bad climate for foreign investment. A small gain in economic growth of 2.0% was registered in 1989 due to reduced guerrilla activity and improved international markets for bauxite.
GDP: $1.35 billion, per capita $3,400; real growth rate 2.0% (1989 est.)
Inflation rate (consumer prices): 50% (1989 est.)
Unemployment rate: 33% (1990)
Budget: revenues $466 million; expenditures $716 million, including capital expenditures of $123 million (1989 est.)
Exports: $425 million (f.o.b., 1988 est.); *commodities*—alumina, bauxite, aluminum, rice, wood and wood products, shrimp and fish, bananas; *partners*—Norway 33%, Netherlands 20%, US 15%, FRG 9%, Brazil 5%, UK 5%, Japan 3%, other 10%
Imports: $370 million (f.o.b., 1988 est.); *commodities*—capital equipment, petroleum, foodstuffs, cotton, consumer goods; *partners*—US 37%, Netherlands 15%, Netherlands Antilles 11%, Trinidad and Tobago 9%, Brazil 5%, UK 3%, other 20%
External debt: $138 million (1990 est.)
Industrial production: growth rate 16.4% (1988 est.); accounts for 22% of GDP
Electricity: 458,000 kW capacity; 2,018 million kWh produced, 5,090 kWh per capita (1990)
Industries: bauxite mining, alumina and aluminum production, lumbering, food processing, fishing
Agriculture: accounts for 11% of both GDP and labor force; paddy rice planted on 85% of arable land and represents 60% of total farm output; other products—bananas, palm kernels, coconuts, plantains, peanuts, beef, chicken; shrimp and forestry products of increasing importance; self-sufficient in most foods
Economic aid: US commitments, including Ex-Im (FY70-83), $2.5 million; Western (non-US) countries, ODA and OOF bilateral commitments (1970-87), $1.45 billion
Currency: Surinamese guilder, gulden, or florin (plural—guilders, gulden, or florins); 1 Surinamese guilder, gulden, or florin (Sf.) = 100 cents
Exchange rates: Surinamese guilders, gulden, or florins (Sf.) per US$1—1.7850 (fixed rate)
Fiscal year: calendar year

Communications

Railroads: 166 km total; 86 km 1.000-meter gauge, government owned, and 80 km 1.435-meter standard gauge; all single track
Highways: 8,300 km total; 500 km paved; 5,400 km bauxite gravel, crushed stone, or improved earth; 2,400 km sand or clay

Inland waterways: 1,200 km; most important means of transport; oceangoing vessels with drafts ranging from 4.2 m to 7 m can navigate many of the principal waterways
Ports: Paramaribo, Moengo
Merchant marine: 3 ships (1,000 GRT or over) totaling 6,472 GRT/8,914 DWT; includes 2 cargo, 1 container
Civil air: 2 major transport aircraft
Airports: 46 total, 42 usable; 6 with permanent-surface runways; none with runways over 3,659 m; 1 with runways 2,440-3,659 m; 1 with runways 1,220-2,439 m
Telecommunications: international facilities good; domestic radio relay system; 27,500 telephones; stations—5 AM, 14 FM, 6 TV, 1 shortwave; 2 Atlantic Ocean INTELSAT earth stations

Defense Forces

Branches: National Army (including Navy which is company-size, small Air Force element), Civil Police
Manpower availability: males 15-49, 107,544; 64,146 fit for military service
Defense expenditures: $91 million, 7.2% of GDP (1990 est.)

Svalbard
(territory of Norway)

Geography

Total area: 62,049 km²; land area: 62,049 km²; includes Spitsbergen and Bjørnøya (Bear Island)
Comparative area: slightly smaller than West Virginia
Land boundaries: none
Coastline: 3,587 km
Maritime claims:
Exclusive fishing zone: 200 nm unilaterally claimed by Norway, not recognized by USSR;
Territorial sea: 4 nm
Disputes: focus of maritime boundary dispute between Norway and USSR
Climate: arctic, tempered by warm North Atlantic Current; cool summers, cold winters; North Atlantic Current flows along west and north coasts of Spitsbergen, keeping water open and navigable most of the year
Terrain: wild, rugged mountains; much of high land ice covered; west coast clear of ice about half the year; fjords along west and north coasts
Natural resources: coal, copper, iron ore, phosphate, zinc, wildlife, fish
Land use: arable land 0%; permanent crops 0%; meadows and pastures 0%; forest and woodland 0%; other 100%; there are no trees and the only bushes are crowberry and cloudberry
Environment: great calving glaciers descend to the sea
Note: located 445 km north of Norway where the Arctic Ocean, Barents Sea, Greenland Sea, and Norwegian Sea meet

People

Population: 3,942 (July 1991), growth rate NA% (1991); about one-third of the population resides in the Norwegian areas (Longyearbyen and Svea on Vestspitsbergen) and two-thirds in the Soviet areas (Barentsburg and Pyramiden on Vestspitsbergen); about 9 persons live at the Polish research station

Birth rate: NA births/1,000 population (1991)

Death rate: NA deaths/1,000 population (1991)

Net migration rate: NA migrants/1,000 population (1991)

Infant mortality rate: NA deaths/1,000 live births (1991)

Life expectancy at birth: NA years male, NA years female (1991)

Total fertility rate: NA children born/woman (1991)

Ethnic divisions: Russian 64%, Norwegian 35%, other 1% (1981)

Language: Russian, Norwegian

Literacy: NA% (male NA%, female NA%)

Labor force: NA

Organized labor: none

Government

Long-form name: none

Type: territory of Norway administered by the Ministry of Industry, Oslo, through a governor (sysselmann) residing in Longyearbyen, Spitsbergen; by treaty (9 February 1920) sovereignty was given to Norway

Capital: Longyearbyen

Leaders:
Chief of State—King HARALD V (since 17 January 1991);
Head of Government—Governor Leif ELDRING (since NA)

Member of: none

Flag: the flag of Norway is used

Economy

Overview: Coal mining is the major economic activity on Svalbard. By treaty (9 February 1920), the nationals of the treaty powers have equal rights to exploit mineral deposits, subject to Norwegian regulation. Although US, UK, Dutch, and Swedish coal companies have mined in the past, the only companies still mining are Norwegian and Soviet. Each company mines about half a million tons of coal annually. The settlements on Svalbard are essentially company towns. The Norwegian state-owned coal company employs nearly 60% of the Norwegian population on the island, runs many of the local services, and provides most of the local infrastructure. There is also some trapping of seal, polar bear, fox, and walrus.

Budget: revenues $13.3 million, expenditures $13.3 million, including capital expenditures of $NA (1990)

Electricity: 21,000 kW capacity; 45 million kWh produced, 11,420 kWh per capita (1989)

Currency: Norwegian krone (plural—kroner); 1 Norwegian krone (NKr) = 100 øre

Exchange rates: Norwegian kroner (NKr) per US$1—5.9060 (January 1991), 6.2597 (1990), 6.9045 (1989), 6.5170 (1988), 6.7375 (1987), 7.3947 (1986), 8.5972 (1985)

Communications

Ports: limited facilities—Ny-Alesund, Advent Bay

Airports: 4 total, 4 usable; 1 with permanent-surface runways; none with runways over 2,439 m; 1 with runways 1,220-2,439 m

Telecommunications: 5 meteorological/radio stations; stations—1 AM, 1 (2 relays) FM, 1 TV

Defense Forces

Note: demilitarized by treaty (9 February 1920)

Swaziland

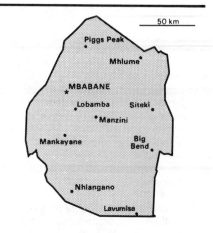

Geography

Total area: 17,360 km²; land area: 17,200 km²

Comparative area: slightly smaller than New Jersey

Land boundaries: 535 km total; Mozambique 105 km, South Africa 430 km

Coastline: none—landlocked

Maritime claims: none—landlocked

Climate: varies from tropical to near temperate

Terrain: mostly mountains and hills; some moderately sloping plains

Natural resources: asbestos, coal, clay, tin, hydropower, forests, and small gold and diamond deposits

Land use: arable land 8%; permanent crops NEGL%; meadows and pastures 67%; forest and woodland 6%; other 19%; includes irrigated 2%

Environment: overgrazing; soil degradation; soil erosion

Note: landlocked; almost completely surrounded by South Africa

People

Population: 859,336 (July 1991), growth rate 2.7% (1991)

Birth rate: 44 births/1,000 population (1991)

Death rate: 12 deaths/1,000 population (1991)

Net migration rate: −5 migrants/1,000 population (1991)

Infant mortality rate: 101 deaths/1,000 live births (1991)

Life expectancy at birth: 51 years male, 59 years female (1991)

Total fertility rate: 6.2 children born/woman (1991)

Nationality: noun—Swazi(s); adjective—Swazi

Ethnic divisions: African 97%, European 3%

Religion: Christian 60%, indigenous beliefs 40%

Swaziland (continued)

Language: English and siSwati (official); government business conducted in English
Literacy: 55% (male 57%, female 54%) age 15 and over can read and write (1976)
Labor force: 195,000; over 60,000 engaged in subsistence agriculture; about 92,000 wage earners (many only intermittently), with agriculture and forestry 36%, community and social services 20%, manufacturing 14%, construction 9%, other 21%; 24,000-29,000 employed in South Africa (1987)
Organized labor: about 10% of wage earners

Government

Long-form name: Kingdom of Swaziland
Type: monarchy; independent member of Commonwealth
Capital: Mbabane (administrative); Lobamba (legislative)
Administrative divisions: 4 districts; Hhohho, Lubombo, Manzini, Shiselweni
Independence: 6 September 1968 (from UK)
Constitution: none; constitution of 6 September 1968 was suspended on 12 April 1973; a new constitution was promulgated 13 October 1978, but has not been formally presented to the people
Legal system: based on South African Roman-Dutch law in statutory courts, Swazi traditional law and custom in traditional courts; has not accepted compulsory ICJ jurisdiction
National holiday: Somhlolo (Independence) Day, 6 September (1968)
Executive branch: monarch, prime minister, Cabinet
Legislative branch: bicameral Parliament is advisory and consists of an upper house or Senate and a lower house or House of Assembly
Judicial branch: High Court, Court of Appeal
Leaders:
Chief of State—King MSWATI III (since 25 April 1986);
Head of Government—Prime Minister Obed DLAMINI (since 12 July 1989)
Political parties: none; banned by the Constitution promulgated on 13 October 1978
Suffrage: none
Elections: no direct elections
Communists: no Communist party
Member of: ACP, AfDB, C, CCC, ECA, FAO, G-77, IBRD, ICAO, ICFTU, IDA, IFAD, IFC, ILO, IMF, INTELSAT, INTERPOL, IOC, ITU, LORCS, NAM, OAU, PCA, SACU, SADCC, UN, UNCTAD, UNESCO, UNIDO, UPU, WHO, WIPO, WMO
Diplomatic representation: Ambassador Absalom Vusani MAMBA; Chancery at 4301 Connecticut Avenue NW, Washington DC 20008; telephone (202) 362-6683;
US—Ambassador Stephen H. ROGERS; Embassy at Central Bank Building, Warner Street, Mbabane (mailing address is P. O. Box 199, Mbabane); telephone [268] 46441 through 5
Flag: three horizontal bands of blue (top), red (triple width), and blue; the red band is edged in yellow; centered in the red band is a large black and white shield covering two spears and a staff decorated with feather tassels, all placed horizontally

Economy

Overview: The economy is based on subsistence agriculture, which occupies much of the labor force and contributes about 23% to GDP. Manufacturing, which includes a number of agroprocessing factories, accounts for another 26% of GDP. Mining has declined in importance in recent years; high-grade iron ore deposits were depleted in 1978, and health concerns cut world demand for asbestos. Exports of sugar and forestry products are the main earners of hard currency. Surrounded by South Africa, except for a short border with Mozambique, Swaziland is heavily dependent on South Africa, from which it receives 92% of its imports and to which it sends about 40% of its exports.
GNP: $563 million, per capita $670; real growth rate 5.0% (1990 est.)
Inflation rate (consumer prices): 13% (1990)
Unemployment rate: NA%
Budget: revenues $322.9 million; expenditures $325.5 million, including capital expenditures of $NA (FY92 est.)
Exports: $543 million (f.o.b., 1990);
commodities—soft drink concentrates, sugar, wood pulp, citrus, canned fruit;
partners—South Africa 40% (est.), EC, Canada
Imports: $651 million (f.o.b., 1990);
commodities—motor vehicles, machinery, transport equipment, petroleum products, foodstuffs, chemicals;
partners—South Africa 92% (est.), Japan, Belgium, UK
External debt: $290 million (1990)
Industrial production: growth rate NA; accounts for 26% of GDP (1989)
Electricity: 50,000 kW capacity; 130 million kWh produced, 170 kWh per capita (1989)
Industries: mining (coal and asbestos), wood pulp, sugar
Agriculture: accounts for 23% of GDP and over 60% of labor force; mostly subsistence agriculture; cash crops—sugarcane, citrus fruit, cotton, pineapples; other crops and livestock—corn, sorghum, peanuts, cattle, goats, sheep; not self-sufficient in grain
Economic aid: US commitments, including Ex-Im (FY70-89), $142 million; Western (non-US) countries, ODA and OOF bilateral commitments (1970-88), $488 million
Currency: lilangeni (plural—emalangeni); 1 lilangeni (E) = 100 cents

Exchange rates: emalangeni (E) per US$1—2.5625 (January 1991), 2.5863 (1990), 2.6166 (1989), 2.2611 (1988), 2.0350 (1987), 2.2685 (1986), 2.1911 (1985); note—the Swazi emalangeni is at par with the South African rand
Fiscal year: 1 April-31 March

Communications

Railroads: 297 km plus 71 km disused, 1.067-meter gauge, single track
Highways: 2,853 km total; 510 km paved, 1,230 km crushed stone, gravel, or stabilized soil, and 1,113 km improved earth
Civil air: 1 major transport aircraft
Airports: 23 total, 22 usable; 1 with permanent-surfaced runways; none with runways over 3,659 m; 1 with runways 2,440-3,659 m; 1 with runways 1,220-2,439 m
Telecommunications: system consists of carrier-equipped open-wire lines and low-capacity radio relay links; 15,400 telephones; stations—6 AM, 6 FM, 10 TV; 1 Atlantic Ocean INTELSAT earth station

Defense Forces

Branches: Umbutfo Swaziland Defense Force, Royal Swaziland Police Force
Manpower availability: males 15-49, 185,562; 107,254 fit for military service
Defense expenditures: $8 million, 1.3% of GDP (1988)

Sweden

Geography

Total area: 449,964 km²; land area: 410,928 km²

Comparative area: slightly smaller than California

Land boundaries: 2,205 km total; Finland 586 km, Norway 1,619 km

Coastline: 3,218 km

Maritime claims:
Continental shelf: 200 m (depth) or to depth of exploitation;
Exclusive fishing zone: 200 nm;
Territorial sea: 12 nm

Climate: temperate in south with cold, cloudy winters and cool, partly cloudy summers; subarctic in north

Terrain: mostly flat or gently rolling lowlands; mountains in west

Natural resources: zinc, iron ore, lead, copper, silver, timber, uranium, hydropower potential

Land use: arable land 7%; permanent crops 0%; meadows and pastures 2%; forest and woodland 64%; other 27%; includes irrigated NEGL%

Environment: water pollution; acid rain

Note: strategic location along Danish Straits linking Baltic and North Seas

People

Population: 8,564,317 (July 1991), growth rate 0.4% (1991)

Birth rate: 13 births/1,000 population (1991)

Death rate: 11 deaths/1,000 population (1991)

Net migration rate: 3 migrants/1,000 population (1991)

Infant mortality rate: 6 deaths/1,000 live births (1991)

Life expectancy at birth: 75 years male, 81 years female (1991)

Total fertility rate: 1.9 children born/woman (1991)

Nationality: noun—Swede(s); adjective—Swedish

Ethnic divisions: homogeneous white population; small Lappish minority; foreign born or first-generation immigrants (Finns, Yugoslavs, Danes, Norwegians, Greeks, Turks) about 12%

Religion: Evangelical Lutheran 94%, Roman Catholic 1.5%, Pentecostal 1%, other 3.5% (1987)

Language: Swedish, small Lapp- and Finnish-speaking minorities; immigrants speak native languages

Literacy: 99% (male NA%, female NA%) age 15 and over can read and write (1979 est.)

Labor force: 4,572,000 (October 1990); government services 37.4%, mining, manufacturing, electricity, and water service 23.1%, private services 22.2%, transportation and communications 7%, construction 6.3%, agriculture, forestry, fishing, and hunting 3.8%, other 0.2% (1988)

Organized labor: 80% of labor force (1990 est.)

Government

Long-form name: Kingdom of Sweden

Type: constitutional monarchy

Capital: Stockholm

Administrative divisions: 24 provinces (län, singular and plural); Älvsborgs Län, Blekinge Län, Gävleborgs Län, Göteborgs och Bohus Län, Gotlands Län, Hallands Län, Jämtlands Län, Jönköpings Län, Kalmar Län, Kopparbergs Län, Kristianstads Län, Kronobergs Län, Malmöhus Län, Norrbottens Län, Örebro Län, Östergötlands Län, Skaraborgs Län, Södermanlands Län, Stockholms Län, Uppsala Län, Värmlands Län, Västerbottens Län, Västernorrlands Län, Västmanlands Län

Independence: 6 June 1809, constitutional monarchy established

Constitution: 1 January 1975

Legal system: civil law system influenced by customary law; accepts compulsory ICJ jurisdiction, with reservations

National holiday: Day of the Swedish Flag, 6 June

Executive branch: monarch, prime minister, Cabinet

Legislative branch: unicameral Parliament (Riksdag)

Judicial branch: Supreme Court (Högsta Domstolen)

Leaders:
Chief of State—King CARL XVI Gustaf (since 19 September 1973); Heir Apparent Princess VICTORIA Ingrid Alice Désirée, daughter of the King (born 14 July 1977);
Head of Government—Prime Minister Ingvar CARLSSON (since 12 March 1986); Deputy Prime Minister Odd ENGSTRÖM (since 27 February 1990)

Political parties and leaders: Moderate (conservative), Carl BILDT; Center, Olof JOHANSSON; Liberal People's Party, Bengt WESTERBERG; Social Democratic, Ingvar CARLSSON; Left Party (VP), Lars WERNER; Swedish Communist Party (SKP), Rune PETTERSSON; Communist Workers' Party, Rolf HAGEL; Christian Democratic Party, Alf SVENSSON; Green Party, no formal leader

Suffrage: universal at age 18

Elections:
Riksdag—last held 18 September 1988 (next to be held September 1991); results—Social Democratic 43.2%, Moderate (conservative) 18.3%, Liberal People's Party 12.2%, Center 11.3%, Left Party 5.9%, Green Party 5.5%, Christian Democrats 3.0%; seats—(349 total) Social Democratic 156, Moderate (conservative) 66, Liberal People's Party 44, Center 42, Left Party 21, Green Party 20

Communists: VP and SKP; VP, formerly the Left Party-Communists, is reported to have roughly 17,800 members and attracted 5.8% of the vote in the 1988 election; VP dropped the Communist label in 1990, but maintains a Marxist ideology

Member of: AfDB, AG (observer) AsDB, BIS, CCC, CE, CERN, CSCE, EBRD, ECE, EFTA, ESA, FAO, G-6, G-8, G-9, G-10, GATT, IADB, IAEA, IBRD, ICAO, ICC, ICFTU, IDA, IEA, IFAD, IFC, ILO, IMF, IMO, INMARSAT, INTERPOL, INTELSAT, IOC, IOM (observer), ISO, ITU, LORCS, NAM (guest), NC, NEA, NIB, OECD, PCA, UN, UNCTAD, UNESCO, UNFICYP, UNHCR, UNIDO, UNIFIL, UNIIMOG, UNMOGIP, UNTSO, UPU, WHO, WIPO, WMO

Diplomatic representation: Ambassador Anders THUNBORG; Chancery at Suite 1200, 600 New Hampshire Avenue NW, Washington DC 20037; telephone (202) 944-5600; there are Swedish Consulates General in Chicago, Los Angeles, Minneapolis, and New York;
US—Ambassador Charles E. REDMAN; Embassy at Strandvagen 101, S-115 89 Stockholm; telephone [46] (8) 783-5300

Flag: blue with a yellow cross that extends to the edges of the flag; the vertical part of the cross is shifted to the hoist side in the style of the *Dannebrog* (Danish flag)

Economy

Overview: Aided by a long period of peace and neutrality during World War I through World War II, Sweden has achieved an enviable standard of living under a mixed system of high-tech capitalism and extensive welfare benefits. It has essentially full employment, a modern distribution system, excellent internal and external communications, and a skilled labor force. Timber, hydropower, and iron ore constitute the resource base of an economy that is heavily

Sweden *(continued)*

oriented toward foreign trade. Privately owned firms account for about 90% of industrial output, of which the engineering sector accounts for 50% of output and exports. For some observers, the Swedish model has succeeded in making economic efficiency and social egalitarianism complementary, rather than competitive, goals. Others argue that the Swedish model is on the verge of collapsing by pointing to the serious economic problems Sweden faces in 1991: high inflation and absenteeism, growing unemployment and deficits, and declining international competitiveness. In 1990, to improve the economy, the government approved a mandate for Sweden to seek EC membership and an austerity and privatization package and implemented a major tax reform. These reforms may succeed in turning the economy around in 1992.
GDP: $137.8 billion, per capita $16,200; real growth rate 0.3% (1990)
Inflation rate (consumer prices): 10.9% (1990)
Unemployment rate: 1.6% (1990)
Budget: revenues $60.1 billion; expenditures $56.7 billion, including capital expenditures of $NA (FY89)
Exports: $57.5 billion (f.o.b., 1990); *commodities*—machinery, motor vehicles, paper products, pulp and wood, iron and steel products, chemicals, petroleum and petroleum products; *partners*—EC 54.4%, (FRG 14.2%, UK 10.1%, Denmark 6.6%), US 8.6%, Norway 8.2%
Imports: $54.7 billion (c.i.f., 1990); *commodities*—machinery, petroleum and petroleum products, chemicals, motor vehicles, foodstuffs, iron and steel, clothing; *partners*—EC 55.3%, US 8.4%
External debt: $14.1 billion (December 1990)
Industrial production: growth rate −2.0% (1990)
Electricity: 39,716,000 kW capacity; 142,000 million kWh produced, 16,700 kWh per capita (1990)
Industries: iron and steel, precision equipment (bearings, radio and telephone parts, armaments), wood pulp and paper products, processed foods, motor vehicles
Agriculture: animal husbandry predominates, with milk and dairy products accounting for 37% of farm income; main crops—grains, sugar beets, potatoes; 100% self-sufficient in grains and potatoes, 85% self-sufficient in sugar beets
Economic aid: donor—ODA and OOF commitments (1970-89), $10.3 billion
Currency: Swedish krona (plural—kronor); 1 Swedish krona (SKr) = 100 öre
Exchange rates: Swedish kronor (SKr) per US$1—5.6402 (January 1991), 5.9188 (1990), 6.4469 (1989), 6.1272 (1988), 6.3404 (1987), 7.1236 (1986), 8.6039 (1985)
Fiscal year: 1 July-30 June

Communications

Railroads: 12,000 km total; Swedish State Railways (SJ)—10,819 km 1.435-meter standard gauge, 6,955 km electrified and 1,152 km double track; 182 km 0.891-meter gauge; 117 km rail ferry service; privately owned railways—511 km 1.435-meter standard gauge (332 km electrified); 371 km 0.891-meter gauge (all electrified)
Highways: 97,400 km (51,899 km paved, 20,659 km gravel, 24,842 km unimproved earth)
Inland waterways: 2,052 km navigable for small steamers and barges
Pipelines: 84 km natural gas
Ports: Gävle, Göteborg, Halmstad, Helsingborg, Kalmar, Malmö, Stockholm; numerous secondary and minor ports
Merchant marine: 182 ships (1,000 GRT or over) totaling 2,226,923 GRT/2,879,057 DWT; includes 9 short-sea passenger, 29 cargo, 3 container, 45 roll-on/roll-off cargo, 11 vehicle carrier, 2 railcar carrier, 28 petroleum, oils, and lubricants (POL) tanker, 27 chemical tanker, 6 specialized tanker, 1 liquefied gas, 8 combination ore/oil, 12 bulk, 1 combination bulk
Civil air: 115 major transports
Airports: 256 total, 254 usable; 137 with permanent-surface runways; none with runways over 3,659 m; 10 with runways 2,440-3,659 m; 92 with runways 1,220-2,439 m
Telecommunications: excellent domestic and international facilities; 8,200,000 telephones; stations—4 AM, 56 (321 relays) FM, 111 (925 relays) TV; 5 submarine coaxial cables; communication satellite earth stations operating in the INTELSAT (1 Atlantic Ocean) and EUTELSAT systems

Defense Forces

Branches: Swedish Army, Royal Swedish Navy, Royal Swedish Air Force
Manpower availability: males 15-49, 2,136,227; 1,865,645 fit for military service; 55,198 reach military age (19) annually
Defense expenditures: $4.9 billion, 2.5% of GDP (FY90)

Switzerland

Geography

Total area: 41,290 km²; land area: 39,770 km²
Comparative area: slightly more than twice the size of New Jersey
Land boundaries: 1,852 km total; Austria 164 km, France 573 km, Italy 740 km, Liechtenstein 41 km, Germany 334 km
Coastline: none—landlocked
Maritime claims: none—landlocked
Climate: temperate, but varies with altitude; cold, cloudy, rainy/snowy winters; cool to warm, cloudy, humid summers with occasional showers
Terrain: mostly mountains (Alps in south, Jura in northwest) with a central plateau of rolling hills, plains, and large lakes
Natural resources: hydropower potential, timber, salt
Land use: arable land 10%; permanent crops 1%; meadows and pastures 40%; forest and woodland 26%; other 23%; includes irrigated 1%
Environment: dominated by Alps
Note: landlocked; crossroads of northern and southern Europe

People

Population: 6,783,961 (July 1991), growth rate 0.6% (1991)
Birth rate: 12 births/1,000 population (1991)
Death rate: 9 deaths/1,000 population (1991)
Net migration rate: 3 migrants/1,000 population (1991)
Infant mortality rate: 5 deaths/1,000 live births (1991)
Life expectancy at birth: 75 years male, 83 years female (1991)
Total fertility rate: 1.6 children born/woman (1991)
Nationality: noun—Swiss (sing. & pl.); adjective—Swiss
Ethnic divisions: total population—German 65%, French 18%, Italian 10%, Romansch

1%, other 6%; Swiss nationals—German 74%, French 20%, Italian 4%, Romansch 1%, other 1%

Religion: Roman Catholic 47.6%, Protestant 44.3%, other 8.1% (1980)

Language: total population—German 65%, French 18%, Italian 12%, Romansch 1%, other 4%; Swiss nationals—German 74%, French 20%, Italian 4%, Romansch 1%, other 1%

Literacy: 99% (male NA%, female NA%) age 15 and over can read and write (1980 est.)

Labor force: 3,310,000; 904,095 foreign workers, mostly Italian; services 50%, industry and crafts 33%, government 10%, agriculture and forestry 6%, other 1% (1989)

Organized labor: 20% of labor force

Government

Long-form name: Swiss Confederation

Type: federal republic

Capital: Bern

Administrative divisions: 26 cantons (cantons, singular—canton in French; cantoni, singular—cantone in Italian; kantone, singular—kanton in German); Aargau, Ausser-Rhoden, Basel-Landschaft, Basel-Stadt, Bern, Fribourg, Genève, Glarus, Graubünden, Inner-Rhoden, Jura, Luzern, Neuchâtel, Nidwalden, Obwalden, Sankt Gallen, Schaffhausen, Schwyz, Solothurn, Thurgau, Ticino, Uri, Valais, Vaud, Zug, Zürich

Independence: 1 August 1291

Constitution: 29 May 1874

Legal system: civil law system influenced by customary law; judicial review of legislative acts, except with respect to federal decrees of general obligatory character; accepts compulsory ICJ jurisdiction, with reservations

National holiday: Anniversary of the Founding of the Swiss Confederation, 1 August (1291)

Executive branch: president, vice president, Federal Council (German—Bundesrat, French—Conseil Fédéral, Italian—Consiglio Federale)

Legislative branch: bicameral Federal Assembly (German—Bundesversammlung, French—Assemblée Fédérale, Italian—Assemblea Federale) consists of an upper council or Council of States (German—Ständerat, French—Conseil des Etats, Italian—Consiglio degli Stati) and a lower council or National Council (German—Nationalrat, French—Conseil National, Italian—Consiglio Nazionale)

Judicial branch: Federal Supreme Court

Leaders:

Chief of State and Head of Government—President Flavio COTTI (1991 calendar year; presidency rotates annually); Vice President René FELBER (term runs concurrently with that of president)

Political parties and leaders: Social Democratic Party (SPS), Helmut HUBACHER, chairman; Radical Democratic Party (FDP), Bruno HUNZIKER, president; Christian Democratic People's Party (CVP), Eva SEGMÜLLER-WEBER, chairman; Swiss People's Party (SVP), Hans UHLMANN, president; Workers' Party (PdA), Jean SPIELMANN, general secretary; National Action Party (NA), Rudolph KELLER, chairman; Independents' Party (LdU), Dr. Franz JAEGER, president; Republican Party (RP), Franz BAUMGARTNER, president; Liberal Party (LPS), Gilbert COUTAU, president; Evangelical People's Party (EVP), Max DÜNKI, president; Progressive Organizations of Switzerland (POCH), Georg DEGEN, secretary; Green Party (GP), Peter SCHMID, president; Unitary Socialist Party (PSU), Dario ROBBIANI, president

Suffrage: universal at age 20

Elections:

Council of States—last held throughout 1987 (next to be held NA); results—percent of vote by party NA; seats—(46 total) CVP 19, FDP 14, SPS 5, SVP 4, other 4;

National Council—last held 18 October 1987 (next to be held October 1991); results—FDP 22.9%, CVP 20.0%, SPS 18.4%, SVP 11.0%, GP 4.8%, other 22.9%; seats—(200 total) FDP 51, CVP 42, SPS 41, SVP 25, GP 9, other 32

Communists: 4,500 members (est.)

Member of: AfDB, AG (observer), AsDB, BIS, CCC, CE, CERN, CSCE, EBRD, ECE, EFTA, ESA, FAO, G-8, G-10, GATT, IADB, IAEA, ICAO, ICC, ICFTU, IEA, IFAD, ILO, IMF (observer), IMO, INMARSAT, INTELSAT, INTERPOL, IOC, IOM, ISO, ITU, LORCS, NAM (guest), NEA, OAS (observer), OECD, PCA, UN (observer), UNCTAD, UNESCO, UNHCR, UNIDO, UPU, WCL, WHO, WIPO, WMO, WTO

Diplomatic representation: Ambassador Edouard BRUNNER; Chancery at 2900 Cathedral Avenue NW, Washington DC 20008; telephone (202) 745-7900; there are Swiss Consulates General in Atlanta, Chicago, Houston, Los Angeles, New York, and San Francisco;

US—Ambassador Joseph B. GILDENHORN; Embassy at Jubilaeumstrasse 93, 3005 Bern; telephone [41] (31) 437-011; there is a Branch Office of the Embassy in Geneva and a Consulate General in Zurich

Flag: red square with a bold, equilateral white cross in the center that does not extend to the edges of the flag

Economy

Overview: Switzerland's economic success is matched in few, if any, other nations. Per capita output, general living standards, education and science, health care, and diet are unsurpassed in Europe. Inflation remains low because of sound government policy and harmonious labor-management relations. Unemployment is negligible, a marked contrast to the larger economies of Western Europe. This economic stability helps promote the important banking and tourist sectors. Since World War II, Switzerland's economy has adjusted smoothly to the great changes in output and trade patterns in Europe and presumably can adjust to the challenges of the 1990s, in particular, the further economic integration of Western Europe and the amazingly rapid changes in East European political/economic prospects.

GDP: $126 billion, per capita $18,700; real growth rate 2.6% (1990)

Inflation rate (consumer prices): 5.3% (1990)

Unemployment rate: 0.5% (1990)

Budget: revenues $24.0 billion; expenditures $23.8 billion, including capital expenditures of $NA (1990)

Exports: $63.4 billion (f.o.b., 1990); *commodities*—machinery and equipment, precision instruments, metal products, foodstuffs, textiles and clothing; *partners*—Western Europe 64% (EC 56%, other 8%), US 9%, Japan 4%

Imports: $70.5 billion (c.i.f., 1990); *commodities*—agricultural products, machinery and transportation equipment, chemicals, textiles, construction materials; *partners*—Western Europe 78% (EC 71%, other 7%), US 6%

External debt: $NA

Industrial production: growth rate 2.1% (1990)

Electricity: 17,710,000 kW capacity; 59,070 million kWh produced, 8,930 kWh per capita (1989)

Industries: machinery, chemicals, watches, textiles, precision instruments

Agriculture: dairy farming predominates; less than 50% self-sufficient; food shortages—fish, refined sugar, fats and oils (other than butter), grains, eggs, fruits, vegetables, meat

Economic aid: donor—ODA and OOF commitments (1970-89), $3.5 billion

Currency: Swiss franc, franken, or franco (plural—francs, franken, or franchi); 1 Swiss franc, franken, or franco (SwF) = 100 centimes, rappen, or centesimi

Exchange rates: Swiss francs, franken, or franchi (SwF) per US$1—1.2724 (January 1991), 1.3892 (1990), 1.6359 (1989), 1.4633 (1988), 1.4912 (1987), 1.7989 (1986), 2.4571 (1985)

Fiscal year: calendar year

Communications

Railroads: 5,174 km total; 2,971 km are government owned and 2,203 km are nongovernment owned; the government

301

Switzerland (continued)

network consists of 2,897 km 1.435-meter standard gauge and 74 km 1.000-meter narrow gauge track; 1,432 km double track, 99% electrified; the nongovernment network consists of 710 km 1.435-meter standard gauge, 1,418 km 1.000-meter gauge, and 75 km 0.790-meter gauge track, 100% electrified

Highways: 62,145 km total (all paved), of which 18,620 km are canton and 1,057 km are national highways (740 km autobahn); 42,468 km are communal roads

Pipelines: 314 km crude oil; 1,506 km natural gas

Inland waterways: 65 km; Rhine (Basel to Rheinfelden, Schaffhausen to Bodensee); 12 navigable lakes

Ports: Basel (river port)

Merchant marine: 20 ships (1,000 GRT or over) totaling 258,678 GRT/441,555 DWT; includes 6 cargo, 2 roll-on/roll-off cargo, 3 chemical tanker, 2 specialized tanker, 7 bulk

Civil air: 89 major transport aircraft

Airports: 67 total, 65 usable; 42 with permanent-surface runways; 2 with runways over 3,659 m; 6 with runways 2,440-3,659 m; 17 with runways 1,220-2,439 m

Telecommunications: excellent domestic, international, and broadcast services; 5,890,000 telephones; stations—6 AM, 36 (400 relays) FM, 145 (1,250 relays) TV; communications satellite earth stations operating in the INTELSAT (4 Atlantic Ocean and 1 Indian Ocean) and EUTELSAT systems

Defense Forces

Branches: Army, Air Force, Frontier Guards, Fortification Guards

Manpower availability: males 15-49, 1,802,005; 1,549,347 fit for military service; 42,619 reach military age (20) annually

Defense expenditures: $4.6 billion, 2% of GDP (1990)

Syria

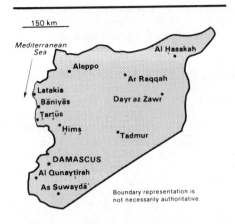

150 km

Mediterranean Sea

Al Hasakah

Aleppo

Ar Raqqah

Latakia

Bāniyās

Dayr az Zawr

Ṭarṭūs

Ḥimṣ

Tadmur

DAMASCUS

Al Qunaytirah

As Suwaydā

Boundary representation is not necessarily authoritative

Geography

Total area: 185,180 km²; land area: 184,050 km² (including 1,295 km² of Israeli-occupied territory)

Comparative area: slightly larger than North Dakota

Land boundaries: 2,253 km total; Iraq 605 km, Israel 76 km, Jordan 375 km, Lebanon 375 km, Turkey 822 km

Coastline: 193 km

Maritime claims:

Contiguous zone: 6 nm beyond territorial sea limit;

Territorial sea: 35 nm

Disputes: separated from Israel by the 1949 Armistice Line; Golan Heights is Israeli occupied; Hatay question with Turkey; periodic disputes with Iraq over Euphrates water rights; ongoing dispute over water development plans by Turkey for the Tigris and Euphrates Rivers; Kurdish question among Iran, Iraq, Syria, Turkey, and the USSR

Climate: mostly desert; hot, dry, sunny summers (June to August) and mild, rainy winters (December to February) along coast

Terrain: primarily semiarid and desert plateau; narrow coastal plain; mountains in west

Natural resources: crude oil, phosphates, chrome and manganese ores, asphalt, iron ore, rock salt, marble, gypsum

Land use: arable land 28%; permanent crops 3%; meadows and pastures 46%; forest and woodland 3%; other 20%; includes irrigated 3%

Environment: deforestation; overgrazing; soil erosion; desertification

Note: there are 38 Jewish settlements in the Israeli-occupied Golan Heights

People

Population: 12,965,996 (July 1991), growth rate 3.8% (1991); in addition, there are at least 12,000 Druze and 13,000 Jewish settlers in the Israeli-occupied Golan Heights (1990 est.)

Birth rate: 43 births/1,000 population (1991)

Death rate: 5 deaths/1,000 population (1991)

Net migration rate: 0 migrants/1,000 population (1991)

Infant mortality rate: 37 deaths/1,000 live births (1991)

Life expectancy at birth: 68 years male, 71 years female (1991)

Total fertility rate: 6.7 children born/woman (1991)

Nationality: noun—Syrian(s); adjective—Syrian

Ethnic divisions: Arab 90.3%; Kurds, Armenians, and other 9.7%

Religion: Sunni Muslim 74%, Alawite, Druze, and other Muslim sects 16%, Christian (various sects) 10%, tiny Jewish communities in Damascus, Al Qamishli, and Aleppo

Language: Arabic (official), Kurdish, Armenian, Aramaic, Circassian; French widely understood

Literacy: 64% (male 78%, female 51%) age 15 and over can read and write (1990 est.)

Labor force: 2,400,000; miscellaneous and government services 36%, agriculture 32%, industry and construction 32%; majority unskilled; shortage of skilled labor (1984)

Organized labor: 5% of labor force

Government

Long-form name: Syrian Arab Republic

Type: republic; under leftwing military regime since March 1963

Capital: Damascus

Administrative divisions: 14 provinces (muḥāfaẓat, singular—muḥāfaẓah); Al Ḥasakah, Al Lādhiqīyah, Al Qunayṭirah, Ar Raqqah, As Suwaydā', Dar'ā, Dayr az Zawr, Dimashq, Ḥalab, Ḥamāh, Ḥimṣ, Idlib, Rif Dimashq, Ṭarṭūs

Independence: 17 April 1946 (from League of Nations mandate under French administration); formerly United Arab Republic

Constitution: 13 March 1973

Legal system: based on Islamic law and civil law system; special religious courts; has not accepted compulsory ICJ jurisdiction

National holiday: National Day, 17 April (1946)

Executive branch: president, three vice presidents, prime minister, three deputy prime ministers, Council of Ministers (cabinet)

Legislative branch: unicameral People's Council (Majlis al-Chaab)

Judicial branch: Supreme Constitutional Court, High Judicial Council, Court of Cassation, State Security Courts

Leaders:

Chief of State—President Hafiz al-ASAD (since 22 February 1971); Vice Presidents 'Abd al-Halim KHADDAM, Rif'at al-ASAD, and Muhammad Zuhayr MASHARIQA (since 11 March 1984);

Head of Government—Prime Minister Mahmud ZU'BI (since 1 November 1987); Deputy Prime Minister Lt. Gen. Mustafa TALAS (since 11 March 1984); Deputy Prime Minister Salim YASIN (since NA December 1981); Deputy Prime Minister Mahmud QADDUR (since NA May 1985)
Political parties and leaders: ruling party is the Arab Socialist Resurrectionist (Ba'th) Party; the Progressive National Front is dominated by Ba'thists but includes independents and members of the Syrian Arab Socialist Party (ASP), Arab Socialist Union (ASU), Syrian Communist Party (SCP), Arab Socialist Unionist Movement, and Democratic Socialist Union Party
Suffrage: universal at age 18
Elections:
President—last held 10-11 February 1985 (next to be held February 1992); results—President Hafiz al-ASAD was reelected without opposition;
People's Council—last held 22-23 May 1990 (next to be held May 1994); results—Ba'th 53.6%, ASU 3.2%, SCP 3.2%, Arab Socialist Unionist Movement 2.8%, ASP 2%, Democratic Socialist Union Party 1.6%, independents 33.6%; seats—(250 total) Ba'th 134, ASU 8, SCP 8, Arab Socialist Unionist Movement 7, ASP 5, Democratic Socialist Union Party 4, independents 84; the People's Council was expanded to 250 seats total prior to the May 1990 election
Communists: mostly sympathizers, numbering about 5,000
Other political or pressure groups: non-Ba'th parties have little effective political influence; Communist party ineffective; greatest threat to Asad regime lies in factionalism in the military; conservative religious leaders; Muslim Brotherhood
Member of: ABEDA, AFESD, AL, AMF, CAEU, CCC, ESCWA, FAO, G-24, G-77, IAEA, IBRD, ICAO, ICC, IDA, IDB, IFAD, IFC, ILO, IMF, IMO, INTELSAT, INTERPOL, IOC, ISO, ITU, LORCS, NAM, OAPEC, OIC, UN, UNCTAD, UNESCO, UNIDO, UNRWA, UPU, WFTU, WHO, WMO, WTO
Diplomatic representation: Ambassador Walid MOUALEM; Chancery at 2215 Wyoming Avenue NW, Washington DC 20008; telephone (202) 232-6313;
US—Ambassador Edward P. DJEREJIAN; Embassy at Abu Rumaneh, Al Mansur Street No.2, Damascus (mailing address is P. O. Box 29, Damascus); telephone [963] (11) 333052 or 332557, 330416, 332814, 332315, 714108, 337178, 333232, 334352
Flag: three equal horizontal bands of red (top), white, and black with two small green five-pointed stars in a horizontal line centered in the white band; similar to the flag of Yemen which has a plain white band and of Iraq which has three green stars (plus an

Arabic inscription) in a horizontal line centered in the white band; also similar to the flag of Egypt which has a symbolic eagle centered in the white band

Economy

Overview: Syria's rigidly structured Ba'thist economy turned out slightly more goods in 1990 than in 1983, when the population was 20% smaller. Economic difficulties are attributable, in part, to severe drought in several recent years, costly but unsuccessful attempts to match Israel's military strength, a falloff in Arab aid, and insufficient foreign exchange earnings to buy needed inputs for industry and agriculture. Socialist policy, embodied in a thicket of bureaucratic regulations, in many instances has driven away or pushed underground the mercantile and entrepreneurial spirit for which Syrian businessmen have long been famous. Two bright spots: a sizable number of villagers have benefited from land redistribution, electrification, and other rural development programs; and a recent find of light crude oil has enabled Syria to cut oil imports. A long-term concern is the additional drain of upstream Euphrates water by Turkey when its vast dam and irrigation projects are completed toward the end of the 1990s. Output in 1990 rebounded from the very bad year of 1989, as agricultural production and oil revenues increased substantially.
GDP: $20.0 billion, per capita $1,600; real growth rate 12% (1990 est.)
Inflation rate (consumer prices): 50% (1990 est.)
Unemployment rate: NA%
Budget: revenues $4.8 billion; expenditures $5.5 billion, including capital expenditures of $2.1 billion (1990 est.)
Exports: $2.3 billion (f.o.b., 1990 est.);
commodities—petroleum 40%, textiles 30%, farm products 13%, phosphates (1989);
partners—USSR and Eastern Europe 42%, EC 31%, Arab countries 17%, US/Canada 2% (1989)
Imports: $2.5 billion (f.o.b., 1990 est.);
commodities—foodstuffs and beverages 21%, metal and metal products 16%, machinery 14%, textiles, petroleum (1989);
partners—EC 42%, USSR and Eastern Europe 13%, other Europe 13%, US/Canada 8%, Arab countries 6% (1989)
External debt: $5.2 billion in hard currency (1990 est.)
Industrial production: growth rate 17% (1990 est.); accounts for 19% of GDP
Electricity: 2,867,000 kW capacity; 6,000 million kWh produced, 500 kWh per capita (1989)
Industries: textiles, food processing, beverages, tobacco, phosphate rock mining, petroleum

Agriculture: accounts for 27% of GDP and one-third of labor force; all major crops (wheat, barley, cotton, lentils, chickpeas) grown mainly on rainfed land causing wide swings in production; animal products—beef, lamb, eggs, poultry, milk; not self-sufficient in grain or livestock products
Economic aid: US commitments, including Ex-Im (FY70-81), $538 million; Western (non-US) ODA and OOF bilateral commitments (1970-88), $1.2 billion; OPEC bilateral aid (1979-89), $12.3 billion; Communist countries (1970-89), $3.3 billion
Currency: Syrian pound (plural—pounds); 1 Syrian pound (£S) = 100 piasters
Exchange rates: Syrian pounds (£S) per US$1—11.2250 (fixed rate since 1987), 3.9250 (fixed rate 1976-87)
Fiscal year: calendar year

Communications

Railroads: 2,241 km total; 1,930 km standard gauge, 311 km 1.050-meter narrow gauge; note—the Tartus-Latakia line is nearly complete
Highways: 27,000 km total; 21,000 km paved, 3,000 km gravel or crushed stone, 3,000 km improved earth
Inland waterways: 672 km; of little economic importance
Pipelines: 1,304 km crude oil; 515 km refined products
Ports: Tartus, Latakia, Baniyas
Merchant marine: 22 ships (1,000 GRT or over) totaling 61,951 GRT/86,552 DWT; includes 18 cargo, 2 roll-on/roll-off cargo, 1 vehicle carrier, 1 bulk
Civil air: 35 major transport aircraft
Airports: 99 total, 96 usable; 24 with permanent-surface runways; none with runways over 3,659 m; 21 with runways 2,440-3,659 m; 4 with runways 1,220-2,439 m
Telecommunications: fair system currently undergoing significant improvement; 512,600 telephones; stations—9 AM, 1 FM, 40 TV; satellite earth stations—1 Indian Ocean INTELSAT earth station, with 1 Intersputnik station under construction; 1 submarine cable; coaxial cable and radio relay to Iraq, Jordan, Turkey, and Lebanon (inactive)

Defense Forces

Branches: Syrian Arab Army, Syrian Arab Navy, Syrian Arab Air Force, Syrian Arab Air Defense Forces, Police and Security Force
Manpower availability: males 15-49, 2,825,214; 1,584,887 fit for military service; 149,105 reach military age (19) annually
Defense expenditures: $1.6 billion, 10.9% of GDP (1988 est.)

Tanzania

Geography

Total area: 945,090 km²; land area: 886,040 km²; includes the islands of Mafia, Pemba, and Zanzibar
Comparative area: slightly larger than twice the size of California
Land boundaries: 3,402 km total; Burundi 451 km, Kenya 769 km, Malawi 475 km, Mozambique 756 km, Rwanda 217 km, Uganda 396 km, Zambia 338 km
Coastline: 1,424 km
Maritime claims:
Exclusive economic zone: 200 nm;
Territorial sea: 12 nm
Disputes: boundary dispute with Malawi in Lake Nyasa; Tanzania-Zaire-Zambia tripoint in Lake Tanganyika may no longer be indefinite since it is reported that the indefinite section of the Zaire-Zambia boundary has been settled
Climate: varies from tropical along coast to temperate in highlands
Terrain: plains along coast; central plateau; highlands in north, south
Natural resources: hydropower potential, tin, phosphates, iron ore, coal, diamonds, gemstones, gold, natural gas, nickel
Land use: arable land 5%; permanent crops 1%; meadows and pastures 40%; forest and woodland 47%; other 7%; includes irrigated NEGL%
Environment: lack of water and tsetse fly limit agriculture; recent droughts affected marginal agriculture; Kilimanjaro is highest point in Africa

People

Population: 26,869,175 (July 1991), growth rate 3.4% (1991)
Birth rate: 50 births/1,000 population (1991)
Death rate: 15 deaths/1,000 population (1991)
Net migration rate: −1 migrants/1,000 population (1991)
Infant mortality rate: 105 deaths/1,000 live births (1991)

Life expectancy at birth: 50 years male, 55 years female (1991)
Total fertility rate: 7.0 children born/woman (1991)
Nationality: noun—Tanzanian(s); adjective—Tanzanian
Ethnic divisions: mainland—native African consisting of well over 100 tribes 99%; Asian, European, and Arab 1%
Religion:
mainland—Christian 33%, Muslim 33%, indigenous beliefs 33%;
Zanzibar—almost all Muslim
Language: Swahili and English (official); English primary language of commerce, administration, and higher education; Swahili widely understood and generally used for communication between ethnic groups; first language of most people is one of the local languages; primary education is generally in Swahili
Literacy: 46% (male 62%, female 31%) age 15 and over can read and write (1978)
Labor force: 732,200 wage earners; 90% agriculture, 10% industry and commerce (1986 est.)
Organized labor: 15% of labor force

Government

Long-form name: United Republic of Tanzania
Type: republic
Capital: Dar es Salaam; some government offices have been transferred to Dodoma, which is planned as the new national capital in the 1990s
Administrative divisions: 25 regions; Arusha, Dar es Salaam, Dodoma, Iringa, Kigoma, Kilimanjaro, Lindi, Mara, Mbeya, Morogoro, Mtwara, Mwanza, Pemba North, Pemba South, Pwani, Rukwa, Ruvuma, Shinyanga, Singida, Tabora, Tanga, Zanzibar Central/South, Zanzibar North, Zanzibar Urban/West, Ziwa Magharibi
Independence: Tanganyika became independent 9 December 1961 (from UN trusteeship under British administration); Zanzibar became independent 19 December 1963 (from UK); Tanganyika united with Zanzibar 26 April 1964 to form the United Republic of Tanganyika and Zanzibar; renamed United Republic of Tanzania 29 October 1964
Constitution: 15 March 1984 (Zanzibar has its own Constitution but remains subject to provisions of the union Constitution)
Legal system: based on English common law; judicial review of legislative acts limited to matters of interpretation; has not accepted compulsory ICJ jurisdiction
National holiday: Union Day, 26 April (1964)
Executive branch: president, first vice president and prime minister of the union, second vice president and president of Zanzibar, Cabinet

Legislative branch: unicameral National Assembly (Bunge)
Judicial branch: Court of Appeal, High Court
Leaders:
Chief of State—President Ali Hassan MWINYI (since 5 November 1985); First Vice President John MALECELA (since 9 November 1990); Second Vice President Salmin AMOUR (since 9 November 1990); *Head of Government*—Prime Minister John MALECELA (since 9 November 1990)
Political parties and leaders: only party—Chama Cha MAPINDUZI (CCM or Revolutionary Party), Ali Hassan MWINYI, party chairman
Suffrage: universal at age 18
Elections:
President—last held 28 October 1990 (next to be held October 1995); results—Ali Hassan MWINYI was elected without opposition;
National Assembly—last held 28 October 1990 (next to be held October 1995); results—CCM is the only party; seats—(241 total, 168 elected) CCM 168
Communists: no Communist party; a few Communist sympathizers
Member of: ACP, AfDB, C, CCC, EADB, ECA, FAO, FLS, G-6, G-77, GATT, IAEA, IBRD, ICAO, IDA, IFAD, IFC, ILO, IMF, IMO, INTELSAT, INTERPOL, IOC, ISO, ITU, LORCS, NAM, OAU, SADCC, UN, UNCTAD, UNESCO, UNHCR, UNIDO, UPU, WCL, WHO, WIPO, WMO, WTO
Diplomatic representation: Ambassador-designate Charles Musama NYIRABU; Chancery at 2139 R Street NW, Washington DC 20008; telephone (202) 939-6125; *US*—Ambassador Edmund DE JARNETTE; Embassy at 36 Laibon Road (off Bagamoyo Road), Dar es Salaam (mailing address is P. O. Box 9123, Dar es Salaam); telephone [255] (51) 37501 through 37504
Flag: divided diagonally by a yellow-edged black band from the lower hoist-side corner; the upper triangle (hoist side) is green and the lower triangle is blue

Economy

Overview: Tanzania is one of the poorest countries in the world. The economy is heavily dependent on agriculture, which accounts for about 47% of GDP, provides 85% of exports, and employs 90% of the work force. Industry accounts for 8% of GDP and is mainly limited to processing agricultural products and light consumer goods. The economic recovery program announced in mid-1986 has generated notable increases in agricultural production and financial support for the program by bilateral donors. The World Bank and the International Monetary Fund have increased the availability of imports and provided funds to rehabilitate Tanzania's deteriorated economic infrastructure.

GDP: $5.92 billion, per capita $240; real growth rate 4.3% (FY89 est.)

Inflation rate (consumer prices): 31.2 (1989)

Unemployment rate: NA%

Budget: revenues $495 million; expenditures $631 million, including capital expenditures of $118 million (FY90)

Exports: $380 million (f.o.b., 1989); *commodities*—coffee, cotton, sisal, tea, cashew nuts, meat, tobacco, diamonds, coconut products, pyrethrum, cloves (Zanzibar); *partners*—FRG, UK, Japan, Netherlands, Kenya, Hong Kong, US

Imports: $1.2 billion (c.i.f., 1989); *commodities*—manufactured goods, machinery and transportation equipment, cotton piece goods, crude oil, foodstuffs; *partners*—FRG, UK, US, Japan, Italy, Denmark

External debt: $5.8 billion (December 1990 est.)

Industrial production: growth rate 4.2% (1988); accounts for 8% of GDP

Electricity: 401,000 kW capacity; 895 million kWh produced, 35 kWh per capita (1989)

Industries: primarily agricultural processing (sugar, beer, cigarettes, sisal twine), diamond mine, oil refinery, shoes, cement, textiles, wood products, fertilizer

Agriculture: accounts for over 40% of GDP; topography and climatic conditions limit cultivated crops to only 5% of land area; cash crops—coffee, sisal, tea, cotton, pyrethrum (insecticide made from chrysanthemums), cashews, tobacco, cloves (Zanzibar); food crops—corn, wheat, cassava, bananas, fruits, and vegetables; small numbers of cattle, sheep, and goats; not self-sufficient in food grain production

Economic aid: US commitments, including Ex-Im (FY70-89), $400 million; Western (non-US) countries, ODA and OOF bilateral commitments (1970-88), $9.2 billion; OPEC bilateral aid (1979-89), $44 million; Communist countries (1970-89), $614 million

Currency: Tanzanian shilling (plural—shillings); 1 Tanzanian shilling (TSh) = 100 cents

Exchange rates: Tanzanian shillings (TSh) per US$1—196.60 (January 1991), 195.06 (1990), 143.377 (1989), 99.292 (1988), 64.260 (1987), 32.698 (1986), 17.472 (1985)

Fiscal year: 1 July-30 June

Communications

Railroads: 3,555 km total; 960 km 1.067-meter gauge; 2,595 km 1.000-meter gauge, 6.4 km double track, 962 km Tazara Railroad 1.067-meter gauge; 115 km 1.000-meter gauge planned by end of decade

Highways: total 81,900 km, 3,600 km paved; 5,600 km gravel or crushed stone; remainder improved and unimproved earth

Pipelines: 982 km crude oil

Inland waterways: Lake Tanganyika, Lake Victoria, Lake Nyasa

Ports: Dar es Salaam, Mtwara, Tanga, and Zanzibar are ocean ports; Mwanza on Lake Victoria and Kigoma on Lake Tanganyika are inland ports

Merchant marine: 7 ships (1,000 GRT or over) totaling 20,784 GRT/25,860 DWT; includes 2 passenger-cargo, 3 cargo, 1 roll-on/roll-off cargo, 1 petroleum, oils, and lubricants (POL) tanker

Civil air: 6 major transport aircraft

Airports: 105 total, 93 usable; 12 with permanent-surface runways; none with runways over 3,659 m; 3 with runways 2,440-3,659 m; 44 with runways 1,220-2,439 m

Telecommunications: fair system of open wire, radio relay, and troposcatter; 103,800 telephones; stations—12 AM, 4 FM, 2 TV; 1 Indian Ocean INTELSAT earth station

Defense Forces

Branches: Tanzanian People's Defense Force (TPDF; including Army, Navy, and Air Force); paramilitary Police Field Force Unit; Militia

Manpower availability: males 15-49, 5,545,022; 3,200,744 fit for military service

Defense expenditures: $111 million, 3.9% of GDP (1988)

Thailand

Geography

Total area: 514,000 km²; land area: 511,770 km²

Comparative area: slightly more than twice the size of Wyoming

Land boundaries: 4,863 km total; Burma 1,800 km, Cambodia 803 km, Laos 1,754 km, Malaysia 506 km

Coastline: 3,219 km

Maritime claims:

Exclusive economic zone: 200 nm;

Territorial sea: 12 nm

Disputes: boundary dispute with Laos; unresolved maritime boundary with Vietnam

Climate: tropical; rainy, warm, cloudy southwest monsoon (mid-May to September); dry, cool northeast monsoon (November to mid-March); southern isthmus always hot and humid

Terrain: central plain; eastern plateau (Khorat); mountains elsewhere

Natural resources: tin, rubber, natural gas, tungsten, tantalum, timber, lead, fish, gypsum, lignite, fluorite

Land use: arable land 34%; permanent crops 4%; meadows and pastures 1%; forest and woodland 30%; other 31%; includes irrigated 7%

Environment: air and water pollution; land subsidence in Bangkok area

Note: controls only land route from Asia to Malaysia and Singapore

People

Population: 56,814,069 (July 1991), growth rate 1.4% (1991)

Birth rate: 20 births/1,000 population (1991)

Death rate: 6 deaths/1,000 population (1991)

Net migration rate: 0 migrants/1,000 population (1991)

Infant mortality rate: 37 deaths/1,000 live births (1991)

Life expectancy at birth: 66 years male, 71 years female (1991)

Thailand (continued)

Total fertility rate: 2.2 children born/woman (1991)
Nationality: noun—Thai (sing. and pl.); adjective—Thai
Ethnic divisions: Thai 75%, Chinese 14%, other 11%
Religion: Buddhism 95%, Muslim 3.8%, Christianity 0.5%, Hinduism 0.1%, other 0.5% (1991)
Language: Thai; English is the secondary language of the elite; ethnic and regional dialects
Literacy: 93% (male 96%, female 90%) age 15 and over can read and write (1990 est.)
Labor force: 30,870,000; agriculture 62%, industry 13%, commerce 11%, services (including government) 14% (1989 est.)
Organized labor: 309,000 union members (1989)

Government

Long-form name: Kingdom of Thailand; under martial law since military takeover 23 February 1991
Type: constitutional monarchy; under martial law since military coup of 23 February 1991
Capital: Bangkok
Administrative divisions: 73 provinces (changwat, singular and plural); Ang Thong, Buriram, Chachoengsao, Chai Nat, Chaiyaphum, Chanthaburi, Chiang Mai, Chiang Rai, Chon Buri, Chumphon, Kalasin, Kamphaeng Phet, Kanchanaburi, Khon Kaen, Krabi, Krung Thep Mahanakhon, Lampang, Lamphun, Loei, Lop Buri, Mae Hong Son, Maha Sarakham, Nakhon Nayok, Nakhon Pathom, Nakhon Phanom, Nakhon Ratchasima, Nakhon Sawan, Nakhon Si Thammarat, Nan, Narathiwat, Nong Khai, Nonthaburi, Pathum Thani, Pattani, Phangnga, Phatthalung, Phayao, Phetchabun, Phetchaburi, Phichit, Phitsanulok, Phra Nakhon Si Ayutthaya, Phrae, Phuket, Prachin Buri, Prachuap Khiri Khan, Ranong, Ratchaburi, Rayong, Roi Et, Sakon Nakhon, Samut Prakan, Samut Sakhon, Samut Songkhram, Sara Buri, Satun, Sing Buri, Sisaket, Songkhla, Sukhothai, Suphan Buri, Surat Thani, Surin, Tak, Trang, Trat, Ubon Ratchathani, Udon Thani, Uthai Thani, Uttaradit, Yala, Yasothon
Independence: 1238 (traditional founding date); never colonized
Constitution: 22 December 1978; interim constitution promulgated by National Peace-Keeping Council on 1 March 1991
Legal system: based on civil law system, with influences of common law; has not accepted compulsory ICJ jurisdiction; martial law in effect since 23 February 1991 military coup
National holiday: Birthday of His Majesty the King, 5 December (1927)
Executive branch: monarch, interim prime minister, three interim deputy prime ministers, interim Council of Ministers (cabinet),

Privy Council; following the military coup of 23 February 1991 a National Peace-Keeping Council was set up
Legislative branch: bicameral National Assembly (Rathasatha) consists of an upper house or Senate (Vuthisatha) and a lower house or House of Representatives (Saphaphoothan-Rajsadhorn); following the military coup of 23 February 1991 the National Assembly was dissolved and a new interim National Legislative Assembly has been formed until elections are held in April 1992
Judicial branch: Supreme Court (Sarndika)
Leaders:
Chief of State—King PHUMIPHON ADUNLAYADET (since 9 June 1946); Heir Apparent Crown Prince WACHIRALONGKON (born 28 July 1952);
Head of Government—Interim Prime Minister ANAN Panyarachun (since 4 March 1991); Interim Deputy Prime Minister SANO Unakun (since 6 March 1991); Interim Deputy Prime Minister Police Gen. PHAO Sarasin (since 6 March 1991); Interim Deputy Prime Minister MICHAI Ruchupan (since 6 March 1991);
National Peace-Keeping Council (ruling junta)—Chairman Gen. SUNTHON Khongsomphong; Vice Chairman Gen. SUCHINDA Khraprayun; Vice Chairman Adm. PRAPHAT Kritsanachan; Vice Chairman Air Chief Mar. KASET Rotchananin; Vice Chairman Police Gen. SAWAT Amonwiwat
Political parties and leaders: under martial law political parties are prohibited from meeting; leaders of several parties have resigned and other parties are fragmenting; it is unclear which of the following parties functioning at the time of the military coup will still be in existence by the time new elections are held;
Thai Nation Party (TNP); Solidarity Party; Thai Citizens Party (TCP); People's Party (Ratsadon); Thai People's Party; Social Action Party (SAP); Democrat Party (DP); Mass Party; Force of Truth Party (Phalang Dharma); People's Party (Prachachon); New Aspiration Party; United Democracy Party; Liberal Party; Social Democratic Force
Suffrage: universal at age 21
Elections:
House of Representatives—last held 24 July 1988 (next to be held by April 1992 for a new National Legislative Assembly according to the National Peace-Keeping Council); results—TNP 27%, SAP 15%, DP 13%, TCP 9%, other 36%; seats—(357 total) TNP 96, Solidarity 62, SAP 53, DP 48, TCP 31, People's Party (Ratsadon) 21, Thai People's Party (Prachachon) 17, Force of Truth Party (Phalang Dharma) 15, United Democracy Party 5, Mass Party 5, Liberal 3, Social Democratic Force 1; note—the House of

Representatives was dissolved 23 February 1991; the new interim National Legislative Assembly has 292 seats with 148 of the seats held by active and retired military officers
Communists: illegal Communist party has 500 to 1,000 members; armed Communist insurgents throughout Thailand total 300 to 500 (est.)
Member of: APEC, AsDB, ASEAN, CCC, CP, ESCAP, FAO, G-77, GATT, IAEA, IBRD, ICAO, ICC, ICFTU, IDA, IFAD, IFC, ILO, IMF, IMO, INTELSAT, INTERPOL, IOC, IOM, ISO, ITU, LORCS, PCA, UN, UNCTAD, UNESCO, UNHCR, UNIDO, UPU, WCL, WHO, WIPO, WMO
Diplomatic representation: Ambassador-designate PHIRAPHONG Kasemsi; Embassy at 2300 Kalorama Road NW, Washington DC 20008; telephone (202) 483-7200; there are Thai Consulates General in Chicago, Los Angeles, and New York; *US*—Ambassador Daniel A. O'DONAHUE; Embassy at 95 Wireless Road, Bangkok (mailing address is APO San Francisco 96346); telephone [66] (2) 252-504019; there is a US Consulate General in Chiang Mai and Consulates in Songkhla and Udorn
Flag: five horizontal bands of red (top), white, blue (double width), white, and red

---

Economy

Overview: Thailand, one of the more advanced developing countries in Asia, enjoyed a year of 9% growth in 1990, although down from the double-digit rates of 1987-89. The increasingly sophisticated manufacturing sector benefited from export-oriented investment, but the agricultural sector contracted 2%, primarily because of weaker demand in Thailand's major overseas markets for commodities such as rice. The trade deficit almost doubled in 1990, to $9 billion, but earnings from tourism ($4.7 billion), remittances, and net capital inflows helped keep the balance of payments in surplus. The government has followed fairly sound fiscal and monetary policies, aided by increased tax receipts from the fast-moving economy. In 1990 the government approved new projects—especially for telecommunications and roads—needed to refurbish the country's now overtaxed infrastructure. Although growth in 1991 will slow further, Thailand's economic outlook remains good, assuming the continuation of prudent government policies in the wake of the 23 February 1991 military coup.
GNP: $79 billion, per capita $1,400; real growth rate 10% (1990 est.)
Inflation rate (consumer prices): 8% (1990 est.)
Unemployment rate: 4.9% (1990 est.)

Budget: revenues $15.2 billion; expenditures $15.2 billion, including capital expenditures of $4.1 billion (FY91)

Exports: $23.0 billion (f.o.b., 1990 est.); *commodities*—light manufactures 66%, fishery products 12%, rice 8%, tapioca 8%, manufactured gas, corn, tin; *partners*—US 22%, Japan 17%, Singapore 7%, Netherlands, FRG, Hong Kong, UK, Malaysia, China (1989)

Imports: $32.0 billion (c.i.f., 1990 est.); *commodities*—machinery and parts 23%, petroleum products 13%, chemicals 11%, iron and steel, electrical appliances; *partners*—Japan 30%, US 11%, Singapore 8%, FRG 5%, Taiwan, South Korea, China, Malaysia, UK (1989)

External debt: $26.9 billion (end 1990 est.)

Industrial production: growth rate 14% (1990 est.); accounts for almost 27% of GDP

Electricity: 7,270,000 kW capacity; 29,000 million kWh produced, 530 kWh per capita (1990)

Industries: tourism is the largest source of foreign exchange; textiles and garments, agricultural processing, beverages, tobacco, cement, other light manufacturing, such as jewelry; electric appliances and components, integrated circuits, furniture, plastics; world's second-largest tungsten producer and third-largest tin producer

Agriculture: accounts for 15% of GNP and 62% of labor force; leading producer and exporter of rice and cassava (tapioca); other crops—rubber, corn, sugarcane, coconuts, soybeans; except for wheat, self-sufficient in food; fish catch of 2.8 million tons (1989)

Illicit drugs: a minor producer, major illicit trafficker of heroin, particularly from Burma and Laos, and cannabis for the international drug market; eradication efforts have reduced the area of cannabis cultivation and shifted some production to neighboring countries; opium poppy cultivation has been affected by eradication efforts

Economic aid: US commitments, including Ex-Im (FY70-89), $870 million; Western (non-US) countries, ODA and OOF bilateral commitments (1970-88), $8.1 billion; OPEC bilateral aid (1979-89), $19 million

Currency: baht (plural—baht); 1 baht (B) = 100 satang

Exchange rates: baht (B) per US$1—25.224 (January 1991), 25.585 (1990), 25.702 (1989), 25.294 (1988), 25.723 (1987), 26.299 (1986), 27.159 (1985)

Fiscal year: 1 October-30 September

Communications

Railroads: 3,940 km 1.000-meter gauge, 99 km double track

Highways: 44,534 km total; 28,016 km paved, 5,132 km earth surface, 11,386 km under development

Inland waterways: 3,999 km principal waterways; 3,701 km with navigable depths of 0.9 m or more throughout the year; numerous minor waterways navigable by shallow-draft native craft

Pipelines: natural gas, 350 km; refined products, 67 km

Ports: Bangkok, Pattani, Phuket, Sattahip, Si Racha

Merchant marine: 136 ships (1,000 GRT or over) totaling 521,565 GRT/791,570 DWT; includes 2 short-sea passenger, 79 cargo, 9 container, 29 petroleum, oils, and lubricants (POL) tanker, 9 liquefied gas, 1 chemical tanker, 3 bulk, 3 refrigerated cargo, 1 combination bulk

Civil air: 41 (plus 2 leased) major transport aircraft

Airports: 127 total, 103 usable; 56 with permanent-surface runways; 1 with runways over 3,659 m; 12 with runways 2,440-3,659 m; 28 with runways 1,220-2,439 m

Telecommunications: service to general public inadequate; bulk of service to government activities provided by multichannel cable and radio relay network; 739,500 telephones (1987); stations—over 200 AM, 100 FM, and 11 TV in government-controlled networks; satellite earth stations—1 Indian Ocean INTELSAT and 1 Pacific Ocean INTELSAT; domestic satellite system being developed

Defense Forces

Branches: Royal Thai Army, Royal Thai Navy (including Royal Thai Marine Corps), Royal Thai Air Force, Paramilitary Forces

Manpower availability: males 15-49, 16,028,159; 9,778,003 fit for military service; 604,483 reach military age (18) annually

Defense expenditures: $2.4 billion, 3% of GNP (1990 est.)

Togo

Geography

Total area: 56,790 km²; land area: 54,390 km²

Comparative area: slightly smaller than West Virginia

Land boundaries: 1,647 km total; Benin 644 km, Burkina 126 km, Ghana 877 km

Coastline: 56 km

Maritime claims:
Exclusive economic zone: 200 nm;
Territorial sea: 30 nm

Climate: tropical; hot, humid in south; semiarid in north

Terrain: gently rolling savanna in north; central hills; southern plateau; low coastal plain with extensive lagoons and marshes

Natural resources: phosphates, limestone, marble

Land use: arable land 25%; permanent crops 1%; meadows and pastures 4%; forest and woodland 28%; other 42%; includes irrigated NEGL%

Environment: hot, dry harmattan wind can reduce visibility in north during winter; recent droughts affecting agriculture; deforestation

People

Population: 3,810,616 (July 1991), growth rate 3.6% (1991)

Birth rate: 49 births/1,000 population (1991)

Death rate: 13 deaths/1,000 population (1991)

Net migration rate: 0 migrants/1,000 population (1991)

Infant mortality rate: 110 deaths/1,000 live births (1991)

Life expectancy at birth: 54 years male, 58 years female (1991)

Total fertility rate: 7.1 children born/woman (1991)

Nationality: noun—Togolese (sing. and pl.); adjective—Togolese

Togo *(continued)*

Ethnic divisions: 37 tribes; largest and most important are Ewe, Mina, and Kabyè; under 1% European and Syrian-Lebanese
Religion: indigenous beliefs about 70%, Christian 20%, Muslim 10%
Language: French, both official and language of commerce; major African languages are Ewe and Mina in the south and Dagomba and Kabyè in the north
Literacy: 43% (male 56%, female 31%) age 15 and over can read and write (1990 est.)
Labor force: NA; agriculture 78%, industry 22%; about 88,600 wage earners, evenly divided between public and private sectors; 50% of population of working age (1985)
Organized labor: one national union, the National Federation of Togolese Workers

Government

Long-form name: Republic of Togo
Type: republic; one-party presidential regime
Capital: Lomé
Administrative divisions: 21 circumscriptions (circonscriptions, singular—circonscription); Amlamé (Amou), Aného (Lacs), Atakpamé (Ogou), Badou (Wawa), Bafilo (Assoli), Bassar (Bassari), Dapaong (Tône), Kanté (Kéran), Klouto (Kloto), Kpagouda (Binah), Lama-Kara (Kozah), Lomé (Golfe), Mango (Oti), Niamtougou (Doufelgou), Notsé (Haho), Sotouboua, Tabligbo (Yoto), Tchamba, Tchaoudjo, Tsévié (Zio), Vogan (Vo); note—the 21 units may now be called prefectures (préfectures, singular—préfecture) and reported name changes for individual units are included in parentheses
Independence: 27 April 1960 (from UN trusteeship under French administration, formerly French Togo)
Constitution: 30 December 1979, effective 13 January 1980
Legal system: French-based court system
National holiday: Liberation Day (anniversary of coup), 13 January (1967)
Executive branch: president, Council of Ministers (cabinet)
Legislative branch: unicameral National Assembly (Assemblée Nationale)
Judicial branch: Court of Appeal (Cour d'Appel), Supreme Court (Cour Suprême)
Leaders:
Chief of State and Head of Government— President Gen. Gnassingbé EYADÉMA (since 14 April 1967)
Political parties and leaders: Rally of the Togolese People (RPT) led by President EYADÉMA was the only party until the formation of multiple parties was legalized 12 April 1991; more than 10 parties formed as of mid-May, though none yet legally registered; a National Conference to determine transition regime is scheduled for 10-20 June 1991
Suffrage: universal adult at age NA

Elections:
President—last held 21 December 1986 (next to be held December 1993); results— Gen. EYADÉMA was reelected without opposition;
National Assembly—last held 4 March 1990 (next to be held March 1995); results—RPT was the only party; seats—(77 total) RPT 77
Communists: no Communist party
Member of: ACCT, ACP, AfDB, CEAO (observer), ECA, ECOWAS, Entente, FAO, FZ, G-77, GATT, IBRD, ICAO, ICC, IDA, IFAD, IFC, ILO, IMF, IMO, INTELSAT, INTERPOL, IOC, ITU, LORCS, NAM, OAU, UN, UNCTAD, UNESCO, UNIDO, UPU, WADB, WCL, WHO, WIPO, WMO, WTO
Diplomatic representation: Ambassador Ellom-Kodjo SCHUPPIUS; Chancery at 2208 Massachusetts Avenue NW, Washington DC 20008; telephone (202) 234-4212 or 4213;
US—Ambassador Harmon E. KIRBY; Embassy at Rue Pelletier Caventou and Rue Vauban, Lomé (mailing address is B. P. 852, Lomé); telephone [228] 21-29-91 through 94 and 21-77-17
Flag: five equal horizontal bands of green (top and bottom) alternating with yellow; there is a white five-pointed star on a red square in the upper hoist-side corner; uses the popular pan-African colors of Ethiopia

Economy

Overview: The economy is heavily dependent on subsistence agriculture, which accounts for about 35% of GDP and provides employment for 78% of the labor force. Primary agricultural exports are cocoa, coffee, and cotton, which together account for about 30% of total export earnings. Togo is self-sufficient in basic foodstuffs when harvests are normal. In the industrial sector phosphate mining is by far the most important activity, with phosphate exports accounting for about 40% of total foreign exchange earnings. Togo serves as a regional commercial and trade center. The government actively encourages foreign investment.
GDP: $1.4 billion, per capita $395; real growth rate 3.6% (1989 est.)
Inflation rate (consumer prices): −1.2% (1989)
Unemployment rate: 2.0% (1987)
Budget: revenues $330 million; expenditures $363 million, including capital expenditures of $101 million (1990 est.)
Exports: $331 million (f.o.b., 1989 est.);
commodities—phosphates, cocoa, coffee, cotton, manufactures, palm kernels;
partners—EC 70%, Africa 9%, US 2%, other 19% (1985)
Imports: $344 million (f.o.b., 1989);

commodities—food, fuels, durable consumer goods, other intermediate goods, capital goods;
partners—EC 61%, US 6%, Africa 4%, Japan 4%, other 25% (1989)
External debt: $1.3 billion (1990 est.)
Industrial production: growth rate 4.9% (1987 est.); 6% of GDP
Electricity: 179,000 kW capacity; 209 million kWh produced, 60 kWh per capita (1990)
Industries: phosphate mining, agricultural processing, cement, handicrafts, textiles, beverages
Agriculture: cash crops—coffee, cocoa, cotton; food crops—yams, cassava, corn, beans, rice, millet, sorghum; livestock production not significant; annual fish catch, 10,000-14,000 tons
Economic aid: US commitments, including Ex-Im (FY70-89), $132 million; Western (non-US) countries, ODA and OOF bilateral commitments (1970-88), $1.8 billion; OPEC bilateral aid (1979-89), $35 million; Communist countries (1970-89), $51 million
Currency: Communauté Financière Africaine franc (plural—francs); 1 CFA franc (CFAF) = 100 centimes
Exchange rates: Communauté Financière Africaine francs (CFAF) per US$1—256.54 (January 1991), 272.26 (1990), 319.01 (1989), 297.85 (1988), 300.54 (1987), 346.30 (1986), 449.26 (1985)
Fiscal year: calendar year

Communications

Railroads: 515 km 1.000-meter gauge, single track
Highways: 6,462 km total; 1,762 km paved; 4,700 km unimproved roads
Inland waterways: none
Ports: Lomé, Kpeme (phosphate port)
Merchant marine: 7 ships (1,000 GRT or over) totaling 38,906 GRT/70,483 DWT; includes 4 roll-on/roll-off cargo, 3 multifunction large-load carrier
Civil air: 3 major transport aircraft
Airports: 9 total, 9 usable; 2 with permanent-surface runways; none with runways over 3,659 m; 2 with runways 2,440-3,659 m none with runways 1,220-2,439 m
Telecommunications: fair system based on network of open-wire lines supplemented by radio relay routes; 12,000 telephones; stations—2 AM, no FM, 3 (2 relays) TV; earth stations—1 Atlantic Ocean INTELSAT and 1 SYMPHONIE

Defense Forces

Branches: Army, Navy, Air Force, paramilitary Gendarmerie
Manpower availability: males 15-49, 799,597; 420,092 fit for military service; no conscription
Defense expenditures: $44 million, 3.7% of GDP (1987)

Tokelau
(territory of New Zealand)

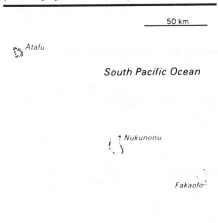

50 km

Atafu

South Pacific Ocean

Nukunonu

Fakaofo

Geography

Total area: 10 km²; land area: 10 km²
Comparative area: about 17 times the size of The Mall in Washington, DC
Land boundaries: none
Coastline: 101 km
Maritime claims:
Exclusive economic zone: 200 nm;
Territorial sea: 12 nm
Climate: tropical; moderated by trade winds (April to November)
Terrain: coral atolls enclosing large lagoons
Natural resources: negligible
Land use: arable land 0%; permanent crops 0%; meadows and pastures 0%; forest and woodland 0%; other 100%
Environment: lies in Pacific typhoon belt
Note: located 3,750 km southwest of Honolulu in the South Pacific Ocean, about halfway between Hawaii and New Zealand

People

Population: 1,700 (July 1991), growth rate 0.0% (1991)
Birth rate: NA births/1,000 population (1991)
Death rate: NA deaths/1,000 population (1991)
Net migration rate: NA migrants/1,000 population (1991)
Infant mortality rate: NA deaths/1,000 live births (1991)
Life expectancy at birth: NA years male, NA years female (1991)
Total fertility rate: NA children born/woman (1991)
Nationality: noun—Tokelauan(s); adjective—Tokelauan
Ethnic divisions: all Polynesian, with cultural ties to Western Samoa
Religion: Congregational Christian Church 70%, Roman Catholic 28%, other 2%; on Atafu, all Congregational Christian Church of Samoa; on Nukunonu, all Roman Catholic; on Fakaofo, both denominations, with the Congregational Christian Church predominant

Language: Tokelauan (a Polynesian language) and English
Literacy: NA% (male NA%, female NA%)
Labor force: NA
Organized labor: NA

Government

Long-form name: none
Type: territory of New Zealand
Capital: none, each atoll has its own administrative center
Administrative divisions: none (territory of New Zealand)
Independence: none (territory of New Zealand)
Constitution: administered under the Tokelau Islands Act of 1948, as amended in 1970
Legal system: British and local statutes
National holiday: Waitangi Day (Treaty of Waitangi established British sovereignty over New Zealand), 6 February (1840)
Executive branch: administrator (appointed by the Minister of Foreign Affairs in New Zealand), official secretary
Legislative branch: Council of Elders (Taupulega) on each atoll
Judicial branch: High Court in Niue, Supreme Court in New Zealand
Leaders:
Chief of State—Queen ELIZABETH II (since 6 February 1952);
Head of Government—Administrator Neil WALTER; Official Secretary M. NORRISH, Office of Tokelau Affairs
Suffrage: NA
Elections: NA
Communists: probably none
Member of: SPC
Diplomatic representation: none (territory of New Zealand)
Flag: the flag of New Zealand is used

Economy

Overview: Tokelau's small size, isolation, and lack of resources greatly restrain economic development and confine agriculture to the subsistence level. The people must rely on aid from New Zealand to maintain public services, annual aid being substantially greater than GDP. The principal sources of revenue come from sales of copra, postage stamps, souvenir coins, and handicrafts. Money is also remitted to families from relatives in New Zealand.
GDP: $1.4 million, per capita $800; real growth rate NA% (1988 est.)
Inflation rate (consumer prices): NA%
Unemployment rate: NA%
Budget: revenues $430,830; expenditures $2.8 million, including capital expenditures of $37,300 (FY87)
Exports: $98,000 (f.o.b., 1983);
commodities—stamps, copra, handicrafts;

partners—NZ
Imports: $323,400 (c.i.f., 1983);
commodities—foodstuffs, building materials, fuel;
partners—NZ
External debt: none
Industrial production: growth rate NA%
Electricity: 200 kW capacity; 300,000 kWh produced, 180 kWh per capita (1990)
Industries: small-scale enterprises for copra production, wood work, plaited craft goods; stamps, coins; fishing
Agriculture: coconuts, copra; basic subsistence crops—breadfruit, papaya, bananas; pigs, poultry, goats
Economic aid: Western (non-US) countries, ODA and OOF bilateral commitments (1970-88), $24 million
Currency: New Zealand dollar (plural—dollars); 1 New Zealand dollar (NZ$) = 100 cents
Exchange rates: New Zealand dollars (NZ$) per US$1—1.6798 (January 1991), 1.6750 (1990), 1.6711 (1989), 1.5244 (1988), 1.6886 (1987), 1.9088 (1986), 2.0064 (1985)
Fiscal year: 1 April-31 March

Communications

Ports: none; offshore anchorage only
Airports: none; lagoon landings by amphibious aircraft from Western Samoa
Telecommunications: telephone service between islands and to Western Samoa

Defense Forces

Note: defense is the responsibility of New Zealand

Tonga

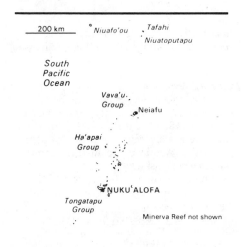

Geography

Total area: 748 km²; land area: 718 km²
Comparative area: slightly more than four times the size of Washington, DC
Land boundaries: none
Coastline: 419 km
Maritime claims:
Continental shelf: no specific limits;
Exclusive economic zone: 200 nm;
Territorial sea: 12 nm
Climate: tropical; modified by trade winds; warm season (December to May), cool season (May to December)
Terrain: most islands have limestone base formed from uplifted coral formation; others have limestone overlying volcanic base
Natural resources: fish, fertile soil
Land use: arable land 25%; permanent crops 55%; meadows and pastures 6%; forest and woodland 12%; other 2%
Environment: archipelago of 170 islands (36 inhabited); subject to cyclones (October to April); deforestation
Note: located about 2,250 km north-northwest of New Zealand, about two-thirds of the way between Hawaii and New Zealand

People

Population: 102,272 (July 1991), growth rate 0.9% (1991)
Birth rate: 26 births/1,000 population (1991)
Death rate: 7 deaths/1,000 population (1991)
Net migration rate: −10 migrants/1,000 population (1991)
Infant mortality rate: 23 deaths/1,000 live births (1991)
Life expectancy at birth: 65 years male, 70 years female (1991)
Total fertility rate: 3.8 children born/woman (1991)
Nationality: noun—Tongan(s); adjective—Tongan
Ethnic divisions: Polynesian; about 300 Europeans

Religion: Christian; Free Wesleyan Church claims over 30,000 adherents
Language: Tongan, English
Literacy: 100% (male 100%, female 100%) age 15 and over can read and write a simple message in Tongan or English (1976)
Labor force: NA; 70% agriculture; 600 engaged in mining
Organized labor: none

Government

Long-form name: Kingdom of Tonga
Type: hereditary constitutional monarchy
Capital: Nuku'alofa
Administrative divisions: three island groups; Ha'apai, Tongatapu, Vava'u
Independence: 4 June 1970 (from UK; formerly Friendly Islands)
Constitution: 4 November 1875, revised 1 January 1967
Legal system: based on English law
National holiday: Emancipation Day, 4 June (1970)
Executive branch: monarch, prime minister, deputy prime minister, Council of Ministers (cabinet), Privy Council
Legislative branch: unicameral Legislative Assembly (Fale Alea)
Judicial branch: Supreme Court
Leaders:
Chief of State—King Taufa'ahau TUPOU IV (since 16 December 1965);
Head of Government—Prime Minister Prince Fatafehi TU'IPELEHAKE (since 16 December 1965)
Political parties and leaders: Democratic Reform Movement, 'Akolisi POHIVA
Suffrage: all literate, tax-paying males and all literate females over 21
Elections:
Legislative Assembly—last held 14-15 February 1990 (next to be held NA February 1993); results—percent of vote NA; seats—(29 total, 9 elected) 6 proreform, 3 traditionalist
Communists: none known
Member of: ACP, AsDB, C, ESCAP, FAO, G-77, IBRD, ICAO, IDA, IFAD, IFC, IMF, INTERPOL, IOC, ITU, LORCS, SPC, SPF, UNCTAD, UNESCO, UNIDO, UPU, WHO
Diplomatic representation: Ambassador Siosaia a'Ulupekotofa TUITA resides in London;
US—the US has no offices in Tonga; the Ambassador to Fiji is accredited to Tonga and makes periodic visits
Flag: red with a bold red cross on a white rectangle in the upper hoist-side corner

Economy

Overview: The economy's base is agriculture, which employs about 70% of the labor

force and contributes 50% to GDP. Coconuts, bananas, and vanilla beans are the main crops and make up two-thirds of exports. The country must import a high proportion of its food, mainly from New Zealand. The manufacturing sector accounts for only 11% of GDP. Tourism is the primary source of hard currency earnings, but the island remains dependent on sizable external aid and remittances to sustain its trade deficit.
GDP: $86 million, per capita $850; real growth rate 3.6% (FY89 est.)
Inflation rate (consumer prices): 4.5% (FY89)
Unemployment rate: NA%
Budget: revenues $30.6 million; expenditures $48.9 million, including capital expenditures of $22.5 million (FY89 est.)
Exports: $9.6 million (f.o.b., FY90 est.);
commodities—coconut oil, desiccated coconut, copra, bananas, taro, vanilla beans, fruits, vegetables, fish;
partners—NZ 54%, Australia 30%, US 8%, Fiji 5% (FY87)
Imports: $59.9 million (c.i.f., FY90 est.);
commodities—food products, beverages and tobacco, fuels, machinery and transport equipment, chemicals, building materials;
partners—NZ 39%, Australia 25%, Japan 9%, US 6%, EC 5% (FY87)
External debt: $42.0 million (FY89)
Industrial production: growth rate 15% (FY86); accounts for 11% of GDP
Electricity: 6,000 kW capacity; 8 million kWh produced, 80 kWh per capita (1990)
Industries: tourism, fishing
Agriculture: dominated by coconut, copra, and banana production; vanilla beans, cocoa, coffee, ginger, black pepper
Economic aid: US commitments, including Ex-Im (FY70-89), $16 million; Western (non-US) countries, ODA and OOF bilateral commitments (1970-88), $240 million
Currency: pa'anga (plural—pa'anga); 1 pa'anga (T$) = 100 seniti
Exchange rates: pa'anga (T$) per US$1—1.2832 (January 1991), 1.2809 (1990), 1.2637 (1989), 1.2799 (1988), 1.4282 (1987), 1.4960 (1986), 1.4319 (1985)
Fiscal year: 1 July-30 June

Communications

Highways: 198 km sealed road (Tongatapu); 74 km (Vava'u); 94 km unsealed roads usable only in dry weather
Ports: Nukualofa, Neiafu, Pangai
Merchant marine: 6 ships (1,000 GRT or over) totaling 35,857 GRT/480,726 DWT; includes 2 cargo, 1 roll-on/roll-off cargo, 2 container, 1 liquefied gas
Civil air: no major transport aircraft
Airports: 6 total, 6 usable; 1 with permanent-surface runways; none with runways

Trinidad and Tobago

over 3,659 m; 1 with runways 2,440-3,659; 1 with runways 1,220-2,439 m
Telecommunications: 3,529 telephones; 66,000 radios; no TV sets; stations—1 AM, no FM, no TV; 1 Pacific Ocean INTELSAT earth station

Defense Forces

Branches: Land Force, Maritime Division, Royal Tongan Marines, Royal Tongan Guard, Police
Manpower availability: NA
Defense expenditures: $NA, NA% of GDP

Geography

Total area: 5,130 km²; land area: 5,130 km²
Comparative area: slightly smaller than Delaware
Land boundaries: none
Coastline: 362 km
Maritime claims:
Continental shelf: outer edge of continental margin or 200 nm;
Exclusive economic zone: 200 nm;
Territorial sea: 12 nm
Climate: tropical; rainy season (June to December)
Terrain: mostly plains with some hills and low mountains
Natural resources: crude oil, natural gas, asphalt
Land use: arable land 14%; permanent crops 17%; meadows and pastures 2%; forest and woodland 44%; other 23%; includes irrigated 4%
Environment: outside usual path of hurricanes and other tropical storms
Note: located 11 km from Venezuela

People

Population: 1,285,297 (July 1991), growth rate 1.1% (1991)
Birth rate: 21 births/1,000 population (1991)
Death rate: 6 deaths/1,000 population (1991)
Net migration rate: −4 migrants/1,000 population (1991)
Infant mortality rate: 18 deaths/1,000 live births (1991)
Life expectancy at birth: 68 years male, 73 years female (1991)
Total fertility rate: 2.4 children born/woman (1991)
Nationality: noun—Trinidadian(s), Tobagonian(s); adjective—Trinidadian, Tobagonian
Ethnic divisions: black 43%, East Indian 40%, mixed 14%, white 1%, Chinese 1%, other 1%

Religion: Roman Catholic 32.2%, Hindu 24.3%, Anglican 14.4%, other Protestant 14%, Muslim 6%, none or unknown 9.1%
Language: English (official), Hindi, French, Spanish
Literacy: 95% (male 97%, female 93%) age 15 and over can read and write (1980)
Labor force: 463,900; construction and utilities 18.1%; manufacturing, mining, and quarrying 14.8%; agriculture 10.9%; other 56.2% (1985 est.)
Organized labor: 22% of labor force (1988)

Government

Long-form name: Republic of Trinidad and Tobago
Type: parliamentary democracy
Capital: Port-of-Spain
Administrative divisions: 8 counties, 3 municipalities*, and 1 ward**; Arima*, Caroni, Mayaro, Nariva, Port-of-Spain*, Saint Andrew, Saint David, Saint George, Saint Patrick, San Fernando*, Tobago**, Victoria
Independence: 31 August 1962 (from UK)
Constitution: 31 August 1976
Legal system: based on English common law; judicial review of legislative acts in the Supreme Court; has not accepted compulsory ICJ jurisdiction
National holiday: Independence Day, 31 August (1962)
Executive branch: president, prime minister, Cabinet
Legislative branch: bicameral Parliament consists of an upper house or Senate and a lower house or House of Representatives
Judicial branch: Court of Appeal, Supreme Court
Leaders:
Chief of State—President Noor Mohammed HASSANALI (since 18 March 1987);
Head of Government—Prime Minister Arthur Napoleon Raymond ROBINSON (since 18 December 1986)
Political parties and leaders: National Alliance for Reconstruction (NAR), A. N. R. ROBINSON; People's National Movement (PNM), Patrick MANNING; United National Congress (UNC), Basdeo PANDAY; Movement for Social Transformation (MOTION), David ABDULLAH
Suffrage: universal at age 18
Elections:
House of Representatives—last held 15 December 1986 (next to be held by December 1991); results—NAR 66%, PNM 32%, other 2%; seats—(36 total) NAR 33, PNM 3; note—in 1989 six members were expelled from the NAR and formed the UNC, while retaining their parliamentary seats; as a result seats held are NAR 27, UNC 6, PNM 3
Communists: Communist Party of Trinidad and Tobago; Trinidad and Tobago Peace Council, James MILLETTE

Trinidad and Tobago *(continued)*

Other political pressure groups: National Joint Action Committee (NJAC), radical antigovernment black-identity organization; Trinidad and Tobago Peace Council, leftist organization affiliated with the World Peace Council; Trinidad and Tobago Chamber of Industry and Commerce; Trinidad and Tobago Labor Congress, moderate labor federation; Council of Progressive Trade Unions, radical labor federation
Member of: ACP, C, CARICOM, CCC, CDB, ECLAC, FAO, G-24, G-77, GATT, IADB, IBRD, ICAO, ICFTU, IDA, IFAD, IFC, ILO, IMF, IMO, INTELSAT, INTERPOL, IOC, ISO, ITU, LAES, LORCS, NAM, OAS, OPANAL, UN, UNCTAD, UNESCO, UNIDO, UPU, WFTU, WHO, WIPO, WMO
Diplomatic representation: Ambassador Angus Albert KHAN; Chancery at 1708 Massachusetts Avenue NW, Washington DC 20036; telephone (202) 467-6490; Trinidad and Tobago has a Consulate General in New York;
US—Ambassador Charles A. GARGANO; Embassy at 15 Queen's Park West, Port-of-Spain (mailing address is P. O. Box 752, Port-of-Spain); telephone (809) 622-6372 through 6376, 6176
Flag: red with a white-edged black diagonal band from the upper hoist side

---

Economy

Overview: Trinidad and Tobago's petroleum-based economy began to emerge from a lengthy depression in 1990. The economy fell sharply through most of the 1980s, largely because of the decline in oil prices. This sector accounts for 80% of export earnings and more than 25% of GDP. The government, in response to the oil revenue loss, pursued a series of austerity measures that pushed the unemployment rate as high as 22% in 1988. The economy showed signs of recovery in 1990, however, helped along by rising oil prices. Agriculture employs only about 11% of the labor force and produces about 3% of GDP. Since this sector is small, it has been unable to absorb the large numbers of the unemployed. The government currently seeks to diversify its export base.
GDP: $4.05 billion, per capita $3,363; real growth rate −3.7% (1989)
Inflation rate (consumer prices): 11.4% (1989)
Unemployment rate: 20% (1990)
Budget: revenues $1.5 billion; expenditures $1.7 billion, including capital expenditures of $NA (1991 est.)
Exports: $1.7 billion (f.o.b., 1990 est.); *commodities*—includes reexports—petroleum and petroleum products 82%, steel products 9%, fertilizer, sugar, cocoa, coffee, citrus (1988);

partners—US 53%, CARICOM 16%, EC 10%, Latin America 3% (1989)
Imports: $1.3 billion (c.i.f., 1990 est.); *commodities*—raw materials and intermediate goods 47%, capital goods 26%, consumer goods 26% (1988);
partners—US 51%, Latin America 10%, UK 8%, Canada 5%, CARICOM 6% (1989)
External debt: $2.5 billion (1989)
Industrial production: growth rate 5.2%, excluding oil refining (1986); accounts for 30% of GDP, including petroleum
Electricity: 1,176,000 kW capacity; 3,468 million kWh produced, 2,730 kWh per capita (1990)
Industries: petroleum, chemicals, tourism, food processing, cement, beverage, cotton textiles
Agriculture: highly subsidized sector; major crops—cocoa and sugarcane; sugarcane acreage is being shifted into rice, citrus, coffee, vegetables; poultry sector most important source of animal protein; must import large share of food needs
Economic aid: US commitments, including Ex-Im (FY70-89), $373 million; Western (non-US) countries, ODA and OOF bilateral commitments (1970-88), $443 million
Currency: Trinidad and Tobago dollar (plural—dollars); 1 Trinidad and Tobago dollar (TT$) = 100 cents
Exchange rates: Trinidad and Tobago dollars (TT$) per US$1—4.2500 (January 1991), 4.2500 (1990), 4.2500 (1989), 3.8438 (1988), 3.6000 (1987), 3.6000 (1986), 2.4500 (1985)
Fiscal year: calendar year

Communications

Railroads: minimal agricultural system near San Fernando
Highways: 8,000 km total; 4,000 km paved, 1,000 km improved earth, 3,000 km unimproved earth
Pipelines: 1,032 km crude oil; 19 km refined products; 904 km natural gas
Ports: Port-of-Spain, Point Lisas, Pointe-a-Pierre
Civil air: 14 major transport aircraft
Airports: 6 total, 5 usable; 3 with permanent-surface runways; none with runways over 3,659 m; 2 with runways 2,440-3,659 m; 2 with runways 1,220-2,439 m
Telecommunications: excellent international service via tropospheric scatter links to Barbados and Guyana; good local service; 109,000 telephones; stations—2 AM, 4 FM, 5 TV; 1 Atlantic Ocean INTELSAT earth station

---

Defense Forces

Branches: Trinidad and Tobago Defense Force (Army), Coast Guard, Air Wing, Trinidad and Tobago Police Service
Manpower availability: males 15-49, 339,260; 245,086 fit for military service
Defense expenditures: $59 million, 1.6% of GDP (1989 est.)

Tromelin Island

(French possession)

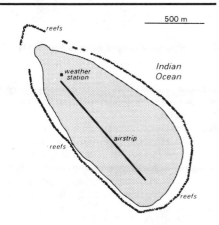

Geography

Total area: 1 km²; land area: 1 km²
Comparative area: about 1.7 times the size of The Mall in Washington, DC
Land boundaries: none
Coastline: 3.7 km
Maritime claims:
Contiguous zone: 12 nm;
Continental shelf: 200 m (depth) or to depth of exploitation;
Exclusive economic zone: 200 nm;
Territorial sea: 12 nm
Disputes: claimed by Madagascar, Mauritius, and Seychelles
Climate: tropical
Terrain: sandy
Natural resources: fish
Land use: arable land 0%; permanent crops 0%; meadows and pastures 0%; forest and woodland 0%; other—scattered bushes 100%
Environment: wildlife sanctuary
Note: located 350 km east of Madagascar and 600 km north of Reunion in the Indian Ocean; climatologically important location for forecasting cyclones

People

Population: uninhabited

Government

Long-form name: none
Type: French possession administered by Commissioner of the Republic Daniel CONSTANTIN, resident in Reunion

Economy

Overview: no economic activity

Communications

Airports: 1 with runway less than 1,220 m
Ports: none; offshore anchorage only
Telecommunications: important meteorological station

Defense Forces

Note: defense is the responsibility of France

Tunisia

Geography

Total area: 163,610 km²; land area: 155,360 km²
Comparative area: slightly larger than Georgia
Land boundaries: 1,424 km total; Algeria 965 km, Libya 459 km
Coastline: 1,148 km
Maritime claims:
Territorial sea: 12 nm
Disputes: maritime boundary dispute with Libya
Climate: temperate in north with mild, rainy winters and hot, dry summers; desert in south
Terrain: mountains in north; hot, dry central plain; semiarid south merges into the Sahara
Natural resources: crude oil, phosphates, iron ore, lead, zinc, salt
Land use: arable land 20%; permanent crops 10%; meadows and pastures 19%; forest and woodland 4%; other 47%; includes irrigated 1%
Environment: deforestation; overgrazing; soil erosion; desertification
Note: strategic location in central Mediterranean; only 144 km from Italy across the Strait of Sicily; borders Libya on east

People

Population: 8,276,096 (July 1991), growth rate 2.1% (1991)
Birth rate: 26 births/1,000 population (1991)
Death rate: 5 deaths/1,000 population (1991)
Net migration rate: 0 migrants/1,000 population (1991)
Infant mortality rate: 38 deaths/1,000 live births (1991)
Life expectancy at birth: 70 years male, 74 years female (1991)
Total fertility rate: 3.3 children born/woman (1991)

Tunisia (continued)

Nationality: noun—Tunisian(s); adjective—Tunisian

Ethnic divisions: Arab 98%, European 1%, Jewish less than 1%

Religion: Muslim 98%, Christian 1%, Jewish less than 1%

Language: Arabic (official); Arabic and French (commerce)

Literacy: 65% (male 74%, female 56%) age 15 and over can read and write (1990 est.)

Labor force: 2,250,000; agriculture 32%; shortage of skilled labor

Organized labor: about 360,000 members claimed, roughly 20% of labor force; General Union of Tunisian Workers (UGTT), quasi-independent of Constitutional Democratic Party

Government

Long-form name: Republic of Tunisia; note—may be changed to Tunisian Republic

Type: republic

Capital: Tunis

Administrative divisions: 23 governorates (wilāyat, singular—wilāyah); Al Kāf, Al Mahdīyah, Al Munastīr, Al Qaṣrayn, Al Qayrawān, Aryānah, Bājah, Banzart, Bin 'Arūs, Jundūbah, Madanīn, Nābul, Qābis, Qafṣah, Qibilī, Ṣafāqis, Sīdī Bū Zayd, Silyānah, Sūsah, Taṭāwīn, Tawzar, Tūnis, Zaghwān

Independence: 20 March 1956 (from France)

Constitution: 1 June 1959

Legal system: based on French civil law system and Islamic law; some judicial review of legislative acts in the Supreme Court in joint session

National holiday: National Day, 20 March (1956)

Executive branch: president, prime minister, Cabinet

Legislative branch: unicameral Chamber of Deputies (Majlis al-Nuwaab)

Judicial branch: Court of Cassation (Cour de Cassation)

Leaders:
Chief of State—President Gen. Zine el Abidine BEN ALI (since 7 November 1987);
Head of Government—Prime Minister Hamed KAROUI (since 26 September 1989)

Political parties and leaders: Constitutional Democratic Rally Party (RCD), President BEN ALI (official ruling party); Movement of Democratic Socialists (MDS), Ahmed Mestiri; five other political parties are legal, including the Communist Party

Suffrage: universal at age 20

Elections:
President—last held 2 April 1989 (next to be held April 1994); results—Gen. Zine el Abidine BEN ALI was reelected without opposition;

Chamber of Deputies—last held 2 April 1989 (next to be held April 1994); results—RCD 80.7%, independents/Islamists 13.7%, MDS 3.2%, other 2.4%; seats—(141 total) RCD 141

Communists: a small number of nominal Communists, mostly students

Member of: ABEDA, ACCT, AfDB, AFESD, AL, AMF, AMU, CCC, ECA, FAO, G-77, GATT, IAEA, IBRD, ICAO, ICC, ICFTU, IDA, IDB, IFAD, IFC, ILO, IMF, IMO, INMARSAT, INTELSAT, INTERPOL, IOC, ISO, ITU, LORCS, NAM, OAU, OIC, UN, UNCTAD, UNESCO, UNHCR, UNIDO, UPU, WHO, WIPO, WMO, WTO

Diplomatic representation: Ambassador-designate Habib LAZREG; Chancery at 1515 Massachusetts Avenue NW, Washington DC 20005; telephone (202) 862-1850; *US*—Ambassador Robert H. PELLETREAU, Jr.; Embassy at 144 Avenue de la Liberte, 1002 Tunis-Belvedere; telephone [216] (1) 782-566

Flag: red with a white disk in the center bearing a red crescent nearly encircling a red five-pointed star; the crescent and star are traditional symbols of Islam

Economy

Overview: The economy depends primarily on petroleum, phosphates, tourism, and exports of light manufactures for continued growth. Following two years of drought-induced economic decline, the economy made a strong recovery in 1990 as a result of a bountiful harvest, continued export growth, and higher domestic investment. Continued high inflation and unemployment have eroded popular support for the government, however, and forced Tunis to slow the pace of economic reform. Nonetheless, the government appears committed to implementing its IMF-supported structural adjustment program and to servicing its foreign debt.

GDP: $10 billion, per capita $1,235; real growth rate 6.5% (1990 est.)

Inflation rate (consumer prices): 7.4% (1989)

Unemployment rate: 15.4% (1989)

Budget: revenues $3.8 billion; expenditures $4.9 billion, including capital expenditures of $970 million (1991 est.)

Exports: $3.3 billion (f.o.b., 1990 est.); *commodities*—hydrocarbons, agricultural products, phosphates and chemicals; *partners*—EC 73%, Middle East 9%, US 1%, Turkey, USSR

Imports: $4.8 billion (f.o.b., 1990 est.); *commodities*—industrial goods and equipment 57%, hydrocarbons 13%, food 12%, consumer goods; *partners*—EC 68%, US 7%, Canada, Japan, USSR, China, Saudi Arabia, Algeria

External debt: $7.4 billion (December 1990 est.)

Industrial production: growth rate 5% (1989); accounts for 38% of GDP, including petroleum

Electricity: 1,493,000 kW capacity; 4,210 million kWh produced, 530 kWh per capita (1989)

Industries: petroleum, mining (particularly phosphate and iron ore), textiles, footwear, food, beverages

Agriculture: accounts for 16% of GDP and one-third of labor force; output subject to severe fluctuations because of frequent droughts; export crops—olives, dates, oranges, almonds; other products—grain, sugar beets, wine grapes, poultry, beef, dairy; not self-sufficient in food; fish catch of 99,200 metric tons (1987)

Economic aid: US commitments, including Ex-Im (FY70-89), $730 million; Western (non-US) countries, ODA and OOF bilateral commitments (1970-88), $4.9 billion; OPEC bilateral aid (1979-89), $684 million; Communist countries (1970-89), $410 million

Currency: Tunisian dinar (plural—dinars); 1 Tunisian dinar (TD) = 1,000 millimes

Exchange rates: Tunisian dinars (TD) per US$1—0.8408 (January 1991), 0.8783 (1990), 0.9493 (1989), 0.8578 (1988), 0.8287 (1987), 0.7940 (1986), 0.8345 (1985)

Fiscal year: calendar year

Communications

Railroads: 2,154 km total; 465 km 1.435-meter standard gauge; 1,689 km 1.000-meter gauge

Highways: 17,700 km total; 9,100 km bituminous; 8,600 km improved and unimproved earth

Pipelines: 797 km crude oil; 86 km refined products; 742 km natural gas

Ports: Bizerte, Gabes, Sfax, Sousse, Tunis, La Goulette, Zarzis

Merchant marine: 21 ships (1,000 GRT or over) totaling 160,172 GRT/218,970 DWT; includes 1 short-sea passenger, 4 cargo, 2 roll-on/roll-off cargo, 2 petroleum, oils, and lubricants (POL) tanker, 6 chemical tanker, 1 liquefied gas, 5 bulk

Civil air: 13 major transport aircraft

Airports: 29 total, 28 usable; 14 with permanent-surface runways; none with runways over 3,659 m; 7 with runways 2,440-3,659 m; 7 with runways 1,220-2,439 m

Telecommunications: the system is above the African average; facilities consist of open-wire lines, multiconductor cable, and radio relay; key centers are Ṣafāqis, Sūsah, Bizerte, and Tunis; 233,000 telephones; stations—18 AM, 4 FM, 14 TV; 4 submarine cables; earth stations—1 Atlantic Ocean INTELSAT and 1 ARABSAT with back-up control station; coaxial cable to Algeria; radio relay to Algeria, Libya, and Italy

Turkey

Defense Forces

Branches: Army, Navy, Air Force, paramilitary forces
Manpower availability: males 15-49, 2,052,191; 1,180,614 fit for military service; 90,218 reach military age (20) annually
Defense expenditures: $315 million, 2.6% of GDP (1990 est.)

400 km

Black Sea

İstanbul · Samsun
ANKARA · Sivas · Trabzon
Bursa · Kayseri · Erzurum
İzmir · Konya · Diyarbakır · Van
Antalya · Adana

Mediterranean
Sea

Geography

Total area: 780,580 km²; land area: 770,760 km²
Comparative area: slightly larger than Texas
Land boundaries: 2,715 km total; Bulgaria 240 km, Greece 206 km, Iran 499 km, Iraq 331 km, Syria 822 km, USSR 617 km
Coastline: 7,200 km
Maritime claims:
Exclusive economic zone: in Black Sea only—to the maritime boundary agreed upon with the USSR;
Territorial sea: 6 nm in the Aegean Sea, 12 nm in Black Sea and Mediterranean Sea
Disputes: complex maritime and air (but not territorial) disputes with Greece in Aegean Sea; Cyprus question; Hatay question with Syria; ongoing dispute with downstream riparians (Syria and Iraq) over water development plans for the Tigris and Euphrates rivers; Kurdish question among Iran, Iraq, Syria, Turkey, and the USSR
Climate: temperate; hot, dry summers with mild, wet winters; harsher in interior
Terrain: mostly mountains; narrow coastal plain; high central plateau (Anatolia)
Natural resources: antimony, coal, chromium, mercury, copper, borate, sulphur, iron ore
Land use: arable land 30%; permanent crops 4%; meadows and pastures 12%; forest and woodland 26%; other 28%; includes irrigated 3%
Environment: subject to severe earthquakes, especially along major river valleys in west; air pollution; desertification
Note: strategic location controlling the Turkish straits (Bosporus, Sea of Marmara, Dardanelles) that link Black and Aegean Seas; Turkey and Norway only NATO members having a land boundary with the USSR

People

Population: 58,580,993 (July 1991), growth rate 2.2% (1991)

Birth rate: 28 births/1,000 population (1991)
Death rate: 6 deaths/1,000 population (1991)
Net migration rate: 0 migrants/1,000 population (1991)
Infant mortality rate: 54 deaths/1,000 live births (1991)
Life expectancy at birth: 68 years male, 72 years female (1991)
Total fertility rate: 3.6 children born/woman (1991)
Nationality: noun—Turk(s); adjective—Turkish
Ethnic divisions: Turkish 80%, Kurdish 17%, other 3% (est.)
Religion: Muslim (mostly Sunni) 99.8%, other (Christian and Jews) 0.2%
Language: Turkish (official), Kurdish, Arabic
Literacy: 81% (male 90%, female 71%) age 15 and over can read and write (1990 est.)
Labor force: 18,800,000; agriculture 56%, services 30%, industry 14%; about 1,000,000 Turks work abroad (1987)
Organized labor: 10-15% of labor force

Government

Long-form name: Republic of Turkey
Type: republican parliamentary democracy
Capital: Ankara
Administrative divisions: 73 provinces (iller, singular—il); Adana, Adıyaman, Afyon, Ağrı, Aksaray, Amasya, Ankara, Antalya, Artvin, Aydın, Balıkesir, Batman, Bayburt, Bilecik, Bingöl, Bitlis, Bolu, Burdur, Bursa, Çanakkale, Çankiri, Çorum, Denizli, Diyarbakır, Edirne, Elazığ, Erzincan, Erzurum, Eskişehir, Gaziantep, Giresun, Gümüşhane, Hakkâri, Hatay, İçel, Isparta, İstanbul, İzmir, Kahraman Maraş, Karaman, Kars, Kastamonu, Kayseri, Kirikkale, Kırklareli, Kırşehir, Kocaeli, Konya, Kütahya, Malatya, Manisa, Mardin, Muğla, Muş, Nevşehir, Niğde, Ordu, Rize, Sakarya, Samsun, Siirt, Sinop, Sirnak, Sivas, Tekirdağ, Tokat, Trabzon, Tunceli, Urfa, Uşak, Van, Yozgat, Zonguldak
Independence: 29 October 1923 (successor state to the Ottoman Empire)
Constitution: 7 November 1982
Legal system: derived from various continental legal systems; accepts compulsory ICJ jurisdiction, with reservations
National holiday: Anniversary of the Declaration of the Republic, 29 October (1923)
Executive branch: president, Presidential Council, prime minister, deputy prime minister, Cabinet
Legislative branch: unicameral Grand National Assembly (Büyük Millet Meclisi)
Judicial branch: Court of Cassation
Leaders:
Chief of State—President Turgut ÖZAL (since 9 November 1989);

Turkey (continued)

Head of Government—Prime Minister Mesut YILMAZ (since 30 June 1991); Deputy Prime Minister Ekrem PAKDAMIRLI (since 30 June 1991)

Political parties and leaders: Motherland Party (ANAP), Mesut YILMAZ; Social Democratic People's Party (SHP), Erdal İNÖNÜ; Correct Way Party (DYP), Süleyman DEMİREL; People's Labor Party (HEP), Fehmi ISIKLAR; Socialist Unity Party (SBP), leader NA; Democratic Center Party (DMP), Bedrettin DALAN; Great Anatolia Party (BAP), leader NA; Democratic Left Party (DSP), Bülent ECEVIT; Refah Party (RP), Necmettin ERBAKAN; Democratic Center Party (DSP), Bedrettin DALAN; Grand National Party (GNP), leader NA

Suffrage: universal at age 21

Elections:
Grand National Assembly—last held 29 November 1987 (next to be held November 1992); results—ANAP 36%, SHP 25%, DYP 19%, other 20%; seats—(450 total) ANAP 275, SHP 82, DYP 60, HEP 9, SBP 4, DMP 2, BAP 1, independent 6, vacant 11

Communists: strength and support negligible

Member of: AsDB, BIS, CCC, CE, CERN (observer), COCOM, CSCE, EBRD, ECE, FAO, GATT, IAEA, IBRD, ICAO, ICC, ICFTU, IDA, IDB, IEA, IFAD, IFC, ILO, IMF, IMO, INTELSAT, INTERPOL, IOC, IOM (observer), ISO, ITU, LORCS, NATO, NEA, OECD, OIC, PCA, UN, UNCTAD, UNESCO, UNHCR, UNIDO, UNIIMOG, UNRWA, UPU, WHO, WIPO, WMO, WTO

Diplomatic representation: Ambassador Nuzhet KANDEMIR; Chancery at 1606 23rd Street NW, Washington DC 20008; telephone (202) 387-3200; there are Turkish Consulates General in Chicago, Houston, Los Angeles, and New York;
US—Ambassador Morton ABRAMOWITZ; Embassy at 110 Ataturk Boulevard, Ankara (mailing address is APO New York 09257-0006); telephone [90] (4) 126 54 70; there are US Consulates General in İstanbul and İzmir, and a Consulate in Adana

Flag: red with a vertical white crescent (the closed portion is toward the hoist side) and white five-pointed star centered just outside the crescent opening

Economy

Overview: The economic reforms that Turkey launched in 1980 continue to bring an impressive stream of benefits. The economy has grown steadily since the early 1980s, with real growth in per capita GDP increasing more than 6% annually. Agriculture remains the most important economic sector, employing about 55% of the labor force, accounting for almost 20% of GDP, and contributing about 20% to exports. Impressive growth in recent years has not solved all of the economic problems facing Turkey. Inflation and interest rates remain high, and a large budget deficit will continue to provide difficulties for a country undergoing a substantial transformation from a centrally controlled to a free market economy. The government has launched a multi-million-dollar development program in the southeastern region, which includes the building of a dozen dams on the Tigris and Euphrates rivers to generate electric power and irrigate large tracts of farmland. The planned tapping of huge additional quantities of Euphrates water has raised serious concern in the downstream riparian nations of Syria and Iraq.

GDP: $178.0 billion, per capita $3,100; real growth rate 7.6% (1990)

Inflation rate (consumer prices): 60.3% (1990)

Unemployment rate: 10.4% (1990 est.)

Budget: revenues $27.6 billion; expenditures $34.4 billion, including capital expenditures of $6.6 billion (1991)

Exports: $11.8 billion (f.o.b., 1989); *commodities*—industrial products 78%, crops and livestock products 20%; *partners*—FRG 18%, Italy 8%, Iraq 8%, US 8%, UK 5%, France 4%

Imports: $16.0 billion (f.o.b., 1989); *commodities*—crude oil, machinery, transport equipment, metals, pharmaceuticals, dyes, plastics, rubber, mineral fuels, fertilizers, chemicals; *partners*—FRG 15%, US 11%, Iraq 10%, Italy 7%, France 6%, UK 5%

External debt: $42.8 billion (June 1990)

Industrial production: growth rate 5.9% (1989 est.); accounts for 32% of GDP

Electricity: 14,315,000 kW capacity; 41,000 million kWh produced, 720 kWh per capita (1990)

Industries: textiles, food processing, mining (coal, chromite, copper, boron minerals), steel, petroleum, construction, lumber, paper

Agriculture: accounts for 20% of GDP and employs majority of population; products—tobacco, cotton, grain, olives, sugar beets, pulses, citrus fruit, variety of animal products; self-sufficient in food most years

Illicit drugs: one of the world's major suppliers of licit opiate products; government maintains strict controls over areas of opium poppy cultivation and output of poppy straw concentrate

Economic aid: US commitments, including Ex-Im (FY70-89), $2.3 billion; Western (non-US) countries, ODA and OOF bilateral commitments (1970-87), $8.6 billion; OPEC bilateral aid (1979-89), $665 million; Communist countries (1970-89), $4.5 billion

Currency: Turkish lira (plural—liras); 1 Turkish lira (TL) = 100 kuruş

Exchange rates: Turkish liras (TL) per US$1—2,873.9 (December 1990), 2,608.6 (1990), 2,121.7 (1989), 1,422.3 (1988), 857.2 (1987), 674.5 (1986), 522.0 (1985)

Fiscal year: calendar year

Communications

Railroads: 8,401 km 1.435-meter standard gauge; 479 km electrified

Highways: 49,615 km total; 26,915 km bituminous; 16,500 km gravel or crushed stone; 4,000 km improved earth; 2,200 km unimproved earth (1985)

Inland waterways: about 1,200 km

Pipelines: 1,738 km crude oil; 2,321 km refined products; 708 km natural gas

Ports: İskenderun, İstanbul, Mersin, İzmir

Merchant marine: 340 ships (1,000 GRT or over) totaling 3,583,720 GRT/6,220,642 DWT; includes 8 short-sea passenger, 1 passenger-cargo, 190 cargo, 1 container, 4 roll-on/roll-off cargo, 3 refrigerated cargo, 1 livestock carrier, 37 petroleum, oils, and lubricants (POL) tanker, 9 chemical tanker, 2 liquefied gas, 7 combination ore/oil, 1 specialized tanker, 72 bulk, 4 combination bulk

Civil air: 39 major transport aircraft (1990)

Airports: 115 total, 109 usable; 64 with permanent-surface runways; 3 with runways over 3,659 m; 30 with runways 2,440-3,659 m; 26 with runways 1,220-2,439 m

Telecommunications: fair domestic and international systems; trunk radio relay network; 3,400,000 telephones; stations—15 AM; 45 (60 repeaters) FM; 67 (504 repeaters) TV; satellite communications ground stations operating in the INTELSAT (2 Atlantic Ocean) and EUTELSAT systems; 1 submarine telephone cable

Defense Forces

Branches: Land Forces, Navy (including Naval Air and Naval Infantry), Air Force, Coast Guard, Gendarmerie

Manpower availability: males 15-49, 14,861,358; 9,083,559 fit for military service; 606,871 reach military age (20) annually

Defense expenditures: $5.6 billion, 5% of GDP (1990)

Turks and Caicos Islands
(dependent territory of the UK)

Geography

Total area: 430 km²; land area: 430 km²
Comparative area: slightly less than 2.5 times the size of Washington, DC
Land boundaries: none
Coastline: 389 km
Maritime claims:
Exclusive fishing zone: 200 nm;
Territorial sea: 12 nm
Climate: tropical; marine; moderated by trade winds; sunny and relatively dry
Terrain: low, flat limestone; extensive marshes and mangrove swamps
Natural resources: spiny lobster, conch
Land use: arable land 2%; permanent crops 0%; meadows and pastures; 0%; forest and woodland 0%; other 98%
Environment: 30 islands (eight inhabited); subject to frequent hurricanes
Note: located 190 km north of the Dominican Republic in the North Atlantic Ocean

People

Population: 9,983 (July 1991), growth rate 2.2% (1991)
Birth rate: 25 births/1,000 population (1991)
Death rate: 5 deaths/1,000 population (1991)
Net migration rate: 2 migrants/1,000 population (1991)
Infant mortality rate: 14 deaths/1,000 live births (1991)
Life expectancy at birth: 72 years male, 78 years female (1991)
Total fertility rate: 3.8 children born/woman (1991)
Nationality: no noun or adjectival forms
Ethnic divisions: majority of African descent
Religion: Baptist 41.2%, Methodist 18.9%, Anglican 18.3%, Seventh-Day Adventist 1.7%, other 19.9% (1980)
Language: English (official)
Literacy: 98% (male 99%, female 98%) age 15 and over having ever attended school (1970)

Labor force: NA; majority engaged in fishing and tourist industries; some subsistence agriculture
Organized labor: Saint George's Industrial Trade Union

Government

Long-form name: none
Type: dependent territory of the UK
Capital: Grand Turk (Cockburn Town)
Administrative divisions: none (dependent territory of the UK)
Independence: none (dependent territory of the UK)
Constitution: introduced 30 August 1976, suspended in 1986, and a Constitutional Commission is currently reviewing its contents
Legal system: based on laws of England and Wales with a small number adopted from Jamaica and The Bahamas
National holiday: Constitution Day, 30 August (1976)
Executive branch: British monarch, governor, Executive Council
Legislative branch: unicameral Legislative Council
Judicial branch: Supreme Court
Leaders:
Chief of State—Queen ELIZABETH II (since 6 February 1953), represented by Governor Michael J. BRADLEY (since 1987);
Head of Government—Chief Minister Oswald O. SKIPPINGS (since 3 March 1988)
Political parties and leaders: People's Democratic Movement (PDM), Oswald SKIPPINGS; Progressive National Party (PNP), Dan MALCOLM and Norman SAUNDERS; National Democratic Alliance (NDA), Ariel MISSICK
Suffrage: universal at age 18
Elections:
Legislative Council—last held on 3 March 1988 (next to be held NA); results—PDM 60%, PNP 30%, other 10%; seats—(20 total, 13 elected) PDM 11, PNP 2
Communists: none
Member of: CDB
Diplomatic representation: as a dependent territory of the UK, the interests of the Turks and Caicos Islands are represented in the US by the UK;
US—none
Flag: blue with the flag of the UK in the upper hoist-side quadrant and the colonial shield centered on the outer half of the flag; the shield is yellow and contains a conch shell, lobster, and cactus

Economy

Overview: The economy is based on fishing, tourism, and offshore banking. Subsistence farming—corn and beans—exists only on the Caicos Islands, so that most foods, as well as nonfood products, must be imported.
GDP: $44.9 million, per capita $5,000; real growth rate NA% (1986)
Inflation rate (consumer prices): NA%
Unemployment rate: 12% (1989)
Budget: revenues $12.4 million; expenditures $15.8 million, including capital expenditures of $2.6 million (FY87)
Exports: $2.9 million (f.o.b., FY84); *commodities*—lobster, dried and fresh conch, conch shells; *partners*—US, UK
Imports: $26.3 million (c.i.f., FY84); *commodities*—foodstuffs, drink, tobacco, clothing; *partners*—US, UK
External debt: $NA
Industrial production: growth rate NA%
Electricity: 9,050 kW capacity; 11.1 million kWh produced, 1,140 kWh per capita (1990)
Industries: fishing, tourism, offshore financial services
Agriculture: subsistence farming prevails, based on corn and beans; fishing more important than farming; not self-sufficient in food
Economic aid: Western (non-US) countries, ODA and OOF bilateral commitments (1970-88), $100 million
Currency: US currency is used
Exchange rates: US currency is used
Fiscal year: calendar year

Communications

Highways: 121 km, including 24 km tarmac
Ports: Grand Turk, Salt Cay, Providenciales, Cockburn Harbour
Civil air: Air Turks and Caicos (passenger service) and Turks Air Ltd. (cargo service)
Airports: 7 total, 7 usable; 4 with permanent-surface runways; none with runways over 2,439 m; 4 with runways 1,220-2,439 m
Telecommunications: fair cable and radio services; 1,446 telephones; stations—3 AM, no FM, several TV; 2 submarine cables; 1 Atlantic Ocean INTELSAT earth station

Defense Forces

Note: defense is the responsibility of the UK

Tuvalu

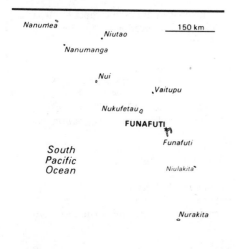

South Pacific Ocean

Geography

Total area: 26 km²; land area: 26 km²
Comparative area: about 0.1 times the size of Washington, DC
Land boundaries: none
Coastline: 24 km
Maritime claims:
Exclusive economic zone: 200 nm;
Territorial sea: 12 nm
Climate: tropical; moderated by easterly trade winds (March to November); westerly gales and heavy rain (November to March)
Terrain: very low-lying and narrow coral atolls
Natural resources: fish
Land use: arable land 0%; permanent crops 0%; meadows and pastures 0%; forest and woodland 0%; other 100%
Environment: severe tropical storms are rare
Note: located 3,000 km east of Papua New Guinea in the South Pacific Ocean

People

Population: 9,317 (July 1991), growth rate 1.9% (1991)
Birth rate: 29 births/1,000 population (1991)
Death rate: 10 deaths/1,000 population (1991)
Net migration rate: 0 migrants/1,000 population (1991)
Infant mortality rate: 33 deaths/1,000 live births (1991)
Life expectancy at birth: 61 years male, 63 years female (1991)
Total fertility rate: 3.1 children born/woman (1991)
Nationality: noun—Tuvaluans(s); adjective—Tuvaluan
Ethnic divisions: 96% Polynesian
Religion: Church of Tuvalu (Congregationalist) 97%, Seventh-Day Adventist 1.4%, Baha'i 1%, other 0.06%
Language: Tuvaluan, English
Literacy: NA% (male NA%, female NA%)
Labor force: NA
Organized labor: none

Government

Long-form name: none
Type: democracy
Capital: Funafuti
Administrative divisions: none
Independence: 1 October 1978 (from UK; formerly Ellice Islands)
Constitution: 1 October 1978
National holiday: Independence Day, 1 October (1978)
Executive branch: British monarch, governor general, prime minister, deputy prime minister, Cabinet
Legislative branch: unicameral Parliament (Palamene)
Judicial branch: High Court
Leaders:
Chief of State—Queen ELIZABETH II (since 6 February 1952), represented by Governor General Tupua LEUPENA (since 1 March 1986);
Head of Government—Prime Minister Bikenibeu PAENIU (since 16 October 1989); Deputy Prime Minister Dr. Alesana SELUKA (since October 1989)
Political parties and leaders: none
Suffrage: universal at age 18
Elections:
Parliament—last held 28 September 1989 (next to be held by September 1993); results—percent of vote NA; seats—(12 total)
Member of: ACP, C (special), ESCAP, SPC, SPF, UPU
Diplomatic representation: Ambassador (vacant);
US—none
Flag: light blue with the flag of the UK in the upper hoist-side quadrant; the outer half of the flag represents a map of the country with nine yellow five-pointed stars symbolizing the nine islands

Economy

Overview: Tuvalu consists of a scattered group of nine coral atolls with poor soil. The country has no known mineral resources and few exports. Subsistence farming and fishing are the primary economic activities. The islands are too small and too remote for development of a tourist industry. Government revenues largely come from the sale of stamps and coins and worker remittances. Substantial income is received annually from an international trust fund established in 1987 by Australia, New Zealand, and the UK and supported also by Japan and South Korea.
GNP: $4.6 million, per capita $530; real growth rate NA% (1989 est.)
Inflation rate (consumer prices): 3.9% (1984)
Unemployment rate: NA%
Budget: revenues $4.3 million; expenditures $4.3 million, including capital expenditures of $NA (1989)

Exports: $1.0 million (f.o.b., 1983 est.);
commodities—copra;
partners—Fiji, Australia, NZ
Imports: $2.8 million (c.i.f., 1983 est.);
commodities—food, animals, mineral fuels, machinery, manufactured goods;
partners—Fiji, Australia, NZ
External debt: $NA
Industrial production: growth rate NA
Electricity: 2,600 kW capacity; 3 million kWh produced, 330 kWh per capita (1990)
Industries: fishing, tourism, copra
Agriculture: coconuts, copra
Economic aid: US commitments, including Ex-Im (FY70-87), $1 million; Western (non-US) countries, ODA and OOF bilateral commitments (1970-87), $96 million
Currency: Tuvaluan dollar and Australian dollar (plural—dollars); 1 Tuvaluan dollar ($T) or 1 Australian dollar ($A) = 100 cents
Exchange rates: Tuvaluan dollars ($T) or Australian dollars ($A) per US$1—1.2834 (January 1991), 1.2799 (1990), 1.2618 (1989), 1.2752 (1988), 1.4267 (1987), 1.4905 (1986), 1.4269 (1985)
Fiscal year: NA

Communications

Highways: 8 km gravel
Ports: Funafuti, Nukufetau
Merchant marine: 1 passenger-cargo (1,000 GRT or over) totaling 1,043 GRT/450 DWT
Civil air: no major transport aircraft
Airports: 1 with runway 1,220-2,439 m
Telecommunications: stations—1 AM, no FM, no TV; 300 radiotelephones; 4,000 radios; 108 telephones

Defense Forces

Branches: Police Force
Manpower availability: NA
Defense expenditures: $NA, NA% of GDP

Uganda

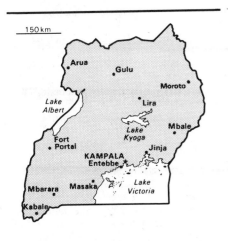

Geography

Total area: 236,040 km²; land area: 199,710 km²

Comparative area: slightly smaller than Oregon

Land boundaries: 2,698 km total; Kenya 933 km, Rwanda 169 km, Sudan 435 km, Tanzania 396 km, Zaire 765 km

Coastline: none—landlocked

Maritime claims: none—landlocked

Climate: tropical; generally rainy with two dry seasons (December to February, June to August); semiarid in northeast

Terrain: mostly plateau with rim of mountains

Natural resources: copper, cobalt, limestone, salt

Land use: arable land 23%; permanent crops 9%; meadows and pastures 25%; forest and woodland 30%; other 13%; includes irrigated NEGL%

Environment: straddles Equator; deforestation; overgrazing; soil erosion

Note: landlocked

People

Population: 18,690,070 (July 1991), growth rate 3.7% (1991)

Birth rate: 51 births/1,000 population (1991)

Death rate: 15 deaths/1,000 population (1991)

Net migration rate: 0 migrants/1,000 population (1991)

Infant mortality rate: 94 deaths/1,000 live births (1991)

Life expectancy at birth: 50 years male, 52 years female (1991)

Total fertility rate: 7.3 children born/woman (1991)

Nationality: noun—Ugandan(s); adjective—Ugandan

Ethnic divisions: African 99%, European, Asian, Arab 1%

Religion: Roman Catholic 33%, Protestant 33%, Muslim 16%, rest indigenous beliefs

Language: English (official); Luganda and Swahili widely used; other Bantu and Nilotic languages

Literacy: 48% (male 62%, female 35%) age 15 and over can read and write (1990 est.)

Labor force: 4,500,000 (est.); subsistence agriculture 94%, wage earners (est.) 6%; 50% of population of working age (1983)

Organized labor: 125,000 union members

Government

Long-form name: Republic of Uganda

Type: republic

Capital: Kampala

Administrative divisions: 10 provinces; Busoga, Central, Eastern, Karamoja, Nile, North Buganda, Northern, South Buganda, Southern, Western

Independence: 9 October 1962 (from UK)

Constitution: 8 September 1967, in process of constitutional revision

Legal system: government plans to restore system based on English common law and customary law and reinstitute a normal judicial system; accepts compulsory ICJ jurisdiction, with reservations

National holiday: Independence Day, 9 October (1962)

Executive branch: president, prime minister, three deputy prime ministers, Cabinet

Legislative branch: unicameral National Resistance Council

Judicial branch: Court of Appeal, High Court

Leaders:
Chief of State—President Lt. Gen. Yoweri Kaguta MUSEVENI (since 29 January 1986); Vice President Samson Babi Mululu KISEKKA (since NA January 1991);
Head of Government—Prime Minister George Cosmas ADYEBO (since NA January 1991)

Political parties and leaders: only party—National Resistance Movement (NRM); note—the Uganda Patriotic Movement (UPM), Ugandan People's Congress (UPC), Democratic Party (DP), and Conservative Party (CP) are all proscribed from conducting public political activities

Suffrage: universal at age 18

Elections:
National Resistance Council—last held 11-28 February 1989 (next to be held after January 1995); results—NRM is the only party; seats—(278 total, 210 indirectly elected) 210 members elected without party affiliation

Other political parties or pressure groups: Uganda People's Front (UPF), Uganda People's Christian Democratic Army (UPCDA), Ruwenzori Movement

Communists: possibly a few sympathizers

Member of: ACP, AfDB, C, CCC, EADB, ECA, FAO, G-77, GATT, IAEA, IBRD, ICAO, ICFTU, IDA, IDB, IFAD, IFC, IGADD, ILO, IMF, INTELSAT, INTERPOL, IOC, ITU, LORCS, NAM, OAU, OIC, PCA, UN, UNCTAD, UNESCO, UNHCR, UNIDO, UPU, WHO, WIPO, WMO, WTO

Diplomatic representation: Ambassador Stephen Kapimpina KATENTA-APULI; 5909 16th Street NW, Washington DC 20011; telephone (202) 726-7100 through 7102;
US—Ambassador James CARSON; Embassy at Parliament Avenue, Kampala (mailing address is P. O. Box 7007, Kampala); telephone [256] (41) 259792, 259793, 259795

Flag: six equal horizonal bands of black (top), yellow, red, black, yellow, and red; a white disk is superimposed at the center and depicts a red-crested crane (the national symbol) facing the staff side

Economy

Overview: Uganda has substantial natural resources, including fertile soils, regular rainfall, and sizable mineral deposits of copper and cobalt. The economy has been devastated by much political instability, mismanagement, and civil war since independence in 1962, keeping Uganda poor with a per capita income of about $300. (GDP remains below the levels of the early 1970s, as does industrial production.) Agriculture is the most important sector of the economy, employing over 80% of the work force. Coffee is the major export crop and accounts for the bulk of export revenues. Since 1986 the government has acted to rehabilitate and stabilize the economy by undertaking currency reform, raising producer prices on export crops, increasing petroleum prices, and improving civil service wages. The policy changes are especially aimed at dampening inflation, which was running at over 300% in 1987, and boosting production and export earnings.

GDP: $4.9 billion, per capita $290 (1988); real growth rate 6.1% (1989 est.)

Inflation rate (consumer prices): 30% (FY90)

Unemployment rate: NA%

Budget: revenues $365 million; expenditures $545 million, including capital expenditures of $165 million (FY89 est.)

Exports: $273 million (f.o.b., 1989);
commodities—coffee 97%, cotton, tea;
partners—US 25%, UK 18%, France 11%, Spain 10%

Imports: $652 million (c.i.f., 1989);
commodities—petroleum products, machinery, cotton piece goods, metals, transportation equipment, food;
partners—Kenya 25%, UK 14%, Italy 13%

External debt: $1.9 billion (1990 est.)

Industrial production: growth rate 15.0% (1989 est.); accounts for 5% of GDP

Uganda (continued)

Electricity: 173,000 kW capacity; 312 million kWh produced, 18 kWh per capita (1989)

Industries: sugar, brewing, tobacco, cotton textiles, cement

Agriculture: accounts for 57% of GDP and 83% of labor force; cash crops—coffee, tea, cotton, tobacco; food crops—cassava, potatoes, corn, millet, pulses; livestock products—beef, goat meat, milk, poultry; self-sufficient in food

Economic aid: US commitments, including Ex-Im (1970-89), $145 million; Western (non-US) countries, ODA and OOF bilateral commitments (1970-88), $1.2 billion; OPEC bilateral aid (1979-89), $60 million; Communist countries (1970-89), $169 million

Currency: Ugandan shilling (plural—shillings); 1 Ugandan shilling (USh) = 100 cents

Exchange rates: Ugandan shillings (USh) per US$1—563.18 (January 1991), 428.85 (1990), 223.09 (1989), 106.14 (1988), 42.84 (1987), 14.00 (1986), 6.72 (1985)

Fiscal year: 1 July-30 June

Communications

Railroads: 1,300 km, 1.000-meter-gauge single track

Highways: 26,200 km total; 1,970 km paved; 5,849 km crushed stone, gravel, and laterite; remainder earth roads and tracks

Inland waterways: Lake Victoria, Lake Albert, Lake Kyoga, Lake George, Lake Edward; Victoria Nile, Albert Nile; principal inland water ports are at Jinja and Port Bell, both on Lake Victoria

Merchant marine: 1 roll-on/roll-off cargo (1,000 GRT or over) totaling 1,697 GRT

Civil air: 4 major transport aircraft

Airports: 37 total, 28 usable; 5 with permanent-surface runways; 1 with runways over 3,659 m; 3 with runways 2,440-3,659 m; 10 with runways 1,220-2,439 m

Telecommunications: fair system with radio relay and radio communications stations; 61,600 telephones; stations—10 AM, no FM, 9 TV; satellite communications ground stations—1 Atlantic Ocean INTELSAT and 1 Indian Ocean INTELSAT

Defense Forces

Branches: Army, Navy, Air Force

Manpower availability: males 15-49, about 3,980,637; about 2,162,241 fit for military service

Defense expenditures: $68 million, 1.5% of GDP (1988)

United Arab Emirates

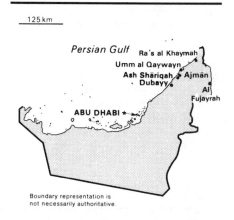

Boundary representation is not necessarily authoritative.

Geography

Total area: 83,600 km²; land area: 83,600 km²

Comparative area: slightly smaller than Maine

Land boundaries: 1,016 km total; Oman 410 km, Saudi Arabia 586 km, Qatar 20 km

Coastline: 1,448 km

Maritime claims:

Continental shelf: defined by bilateral boundaries or equidistant line

Exclusive economic zone: 200 nm;

Territorial sea: 3 nm (assumed), 12 nm for Ash Shāriqah (Sharjah)

Disputes: boundary with Qatar is in dispute; no defined boundary with Saudi Arabia; no defined boundary with most of Oman, but Administrative Line in far north; claims three islands in the Persian Gulf occupied by Iran (Jazīreh-ye Abū Mūsá or Abū Mūsá, Jazīreh-ye Tonb-e Bozorg or Greater Tunb, and Jazīreh-ye Tonb-e Kūchek or Lesser Tunb)

Climate: desert; cooler in eastern mountains

Terrain: flat, barren coastal plain merging into rolling sand dunes of vast desert wasteland; mountains in east

Natural resources: crude oil and natural gas

Land use: arable land NEGL%; permanent crops NEGL%; meadows and pastures 2%; forest and woodland NEGL%; other 98%; includes irrigated NEGL%

Environment: frequent dust and sand storms; lack of natural freshwater resources being overcome by desalination plants; desertification

Note: strategic location along southern approaches to Strait of Hormuz, a vital transit point for world crude oil

---

People

Population: 2,389,759 (July 1991), growth rate 5.7% (1991)

Birth rate: 30 births/1,000 population (1991)

Death rate: 3 deaths/1,000 population (1991)

Net migration rate: 30 migrants/1,000 population (1991)

Infant mortality rate: 23 deaths/1,000 live births (1991)

Life expectancy at birth: 69 years male, 74 years female (1991)

Total fertility rate: 4.9 children born/woman (1991)

Nationality: noun—Emirian(s), adjective—Emirian

Ethnic divisions: Emirian 19%, other Arab 23%, South Asian (fluctuating) 50%, other expatriates (includes Westerners and East Asians) 8%; less than 20% of the population are UAE citizens (1982)

Religion: Muslim 96% (Shi'a 16%); Christian, Hindu, and other 4%

Language: Arabic (official); Persian and English widely spoken in major cities; Hindi, Urdu

Literacy: 68% (male 70%, female 63%) age 10 and over but definition of literacy not available (1980)

Labor force: 580,000 (1986 est.); industry and commerce 85%, agriculture 5%, services 5%, government 5%; 80% of labor force is foreign

Organized labor: trade unions are illegal

Government

Long-form name: United Arab Emirates (no short-form name); abbreviated UAE

Type: federation with specified powers delegated to the UAE central government and other powers reserved to member emirates

Capital: Abu Dhabi

Administrative divisions: 7 emirates (imārāt, singular—imārah); Abū Ẓaby (Abu Dhabi), 'Ajmān, Al Fujayrah, Ash Shāriqah, Dubayy, Ra's al Khaymah, Umm al Qaywayn

Independence: 2 December 1971 (from UK; formerly Trucial States)

Constitution: 2 December 1971 (provisional)

Legal system: secular codes are being introduced by the UAE Government and in several member shaykhdoms; Islamic law remains influential

National holiday: National Day, 2 December (1971)

Executive branch: president, vice president, Supreme Council of Rulers, prime minister, Council of Ministers

Legislative branch: unicameral Federal National Council (Majlis Watani Itihad)

Judicial branch: Union Supreme Court

Leaders:

Chief of State—President Shaykh Zayid bin Sultan Al NUHAYYAN, (since 2 December 1971), ruler of Abu Dhabi; Vice President Shaykh Maktum bin Rashid al-MAKTUM (since 8 October 1990), ruler of Dubayy;

Head of Government—Prime Minister Shaykh Maktum bin Rashid al-MAKTUM (since 8 October 1990), ruler of Dubayy; Deputy Prime Minister Sultan bin Zayid Al NUHAYYAN (since 20 November 1990)
Political parties and leaders: none
Suffrage: none
Elections: none
Communists: NA
Other political or pressure groups: a few small clandestine groups are active
Member of: ABEDA, AFESD, AL, AMF, CAEU, CCC, ESCWA, FAO, G-77, GCC, IAEA, IBRD, ICAO, IDA, IDB, IFAD, IFC, ILO, IMF, IMO, INMARSAT, INTELSAT, INTERPOL, IOC, ISO (correspondent), ITU, LORCS, NAM, OAPEC, OIC, OPEC, UN, UNCTAD, UNESCO, UNIDO, UPU, WHO, WIPO, WMO, WTO
Diplomatic representation: Ambassador Abdullah bin Zayid Al NUHAYYAN; Chancery at Suite 740, 600 New Hampshire Avenue NW, Washington DC 20037; telephone (202) 338-6500;
US—Ambassador Edward S. WALKER, Jr.; Embassy at Al-Sudan Street, Abu Dhabi (mailing address is P. O. Box 4009, Abu Dhabi); telephone [971] (2) 336691; there is a US Consulate General in Dubayy (Dubai)
Flag: three equal horizontal bands of green (top), white, and black with a thicker vertical red band on the hoist side

---

Economy

Overview: The UAE has an open economy with one of the world's highest incomes per capita outside the OECD nations. This wealth is based on oil and gas, and the fortunes of the economy fluctuate with the prices of those commodities. Since 1973, when petroleum prices shot up, the UAE has undergone a profound transformation from an impoverished region of small desert principalities to a modern state with a high standard of living. At present levels of production, crude oil reserves should last for over 100 years.
GDP: $27.3 billion, per capita $12,100; real growth rate 10% (1989 est.)
Inflation rate (consumer prices): 3–4% (1989 est.)
Unemployment rate: NEGL (1988)
Budget: revenues $3.8 billion; expenditures $3.7 billion, including capital expenditures of $NA (1989 est.)
Exports: $15.0 billion (f.o.b., 1989 est.);
commodities—crude oil 65%, natural gas, reexports, dried fish, dates;
partners—US, EC, Japan
Imports: $9.0 billion (f.o.b., 1989 est.);
commodities—food, consumer and capital goods;
partners—EC, Japan, US
External debt: $11.0 billion (December 1989 est.)

Industrial production: growth rate −9.3% (1986)
Electricity: 5,773,000 kW capacity; 15,400 million kWh produced, 6,830 kWh per capita (1990)
Industries: petroleum, fishing, petrochemicals, construction materials, some boat building, handicrafts, pearling
Agriculture: accounts for 2% of GNP and 5% of labor force; cash crop—dates; food products—vegetables, watermelons, poultry, eggs, dairy, fish; only 25% self-sufficient in food
Economic aid: donor—pledged $9.1 billion in bilateral aid to less developed countries (1979-89)
Currency: Emirian dirham (plural—dirhams); 1 Emirian dirham (Dh) = 100 fils
Exchange rates: Emirian dirhams (Dh) per US$1—3.6710 (fixed rate)
Fiscal year: calendar year

Communications

Highways: 2,000 km total; 1,800 km bituminous, 200 km gravel and graded earth
Pipelines: 830 km crude oil; 870 km natural gas, including natural gas liquids
Ports: Al Fujayrah, Khawr Fakkan, Mīnā' Jabal 'Alī, Mīnā' Khālid, Mīnā' Rāshid, Mīnā' Ṣaqr, Mīnā' Zāyid
Merchant marine: 57 ships (1,000 GRT or over) totaling 925,424 GRT/1,543,716 DWT; includes 22 cargo, 8 container, 2 roll-on/roll-off cargo, 20 petroleum, oils, and lubricants (POL) tanker, 5 bulk
Civil air: 8 major transport aircraft
Airports: 38 total, 35 usable; 20 with permanent-surface runways; 7 with runways over 3,659 m; 5 with runways 2,440-3,659 m; 5 with runways 1,220-2,439 m
Telecommunications: adequate system of radio relay and coaxial cable; key centers are Abu Dhabi and Dubayy; 386,600 telephones; stations—8 AM, 3 FM, 12 TV; satellite communications ground stations—1 Atlantic Ocean INTELSAT, 2 Indian Ocean INTELSAT and 1 ARABSAT; submarine cables to Qatar, Bahrain, India, and Pakistan; tropospheric scatter to Bahrain; radio relay to Saudi Arabia

---

Defense Forces

Branches: Army, Navy, Air Force, Federal Police Force
Manpower availability: males 15-49, 940,130; 516,218 fit for military service
Defense expenditures: $1.59 billion, 6.8% of GDP (1988)

United Kingdom

Geography

Total area: 244,820 km^2; land area: 241,590 km^2; includes Rockall and Shetland Islands
Comparative area: slightly smaller than Oregon
Land boundary: Ireland 360 km
Coastline: 12,429 km
Maritime claims:
Continental shelf: as defined in continental shelf orders or in accordance with agreed upon boundaries;
Exclusive fishing zone: 200 nm;
Territorial sea: 12 nm
Disputes: Northern Ireland question with Ireland; Gibraltar question with Spain; Argentina claims Falkland Islands (Islas Malvinas); Argentina claims South Georgia and the South Sandwich Islands; Mauritius claims island of Diego Garcia in British Indian Ocean Territory; Rockall continental shelf dispute involving Denmark, Iceland, and Ireland (Ireland and the UK have signed a boundary agreement in the Rockall area); territorial claim in Antarctica (British Antarctic Territory)
Climate: temperate; moderated by prevailing southwest winds over the North Atlantic Current; more than half of the days are overcast
Terrain: mostly rugged hills and low mountains; level to rolling plains in east and southeast
Natural resources: coal, crude oil, natural gas, tin, limestone, iron ore, salt, clay, chalk, gypsum, lead, silica
Land use: arable land 29%; permanent crops NEGL%; meadows and pastures 48%; forest and woodland 9%; other 14%; includes irrigated 1%
Environment: pollution control measures improving air, water quality; because of heavily indented coastline, no location is more than 125 km from tidal waters
Note: lies near vital North Atlantic sea lanes; only 35 km from France and now being linked by tunnel under the English Channel

United Kingdom (continued)

People

Population: 57,515,307 (July 1991), growth rate 0.3% (1991)

Birth rate: 14 births/1,000 population (1991)

Death rate: 11 deaths/1,000 population (1991)

Net migration rate: 0 migrants/1,000 population (1991)

Infant mortality rate: 7 deaths/1,000 live births (1991)

Life expectancy at birth: 73 years male, 79 years female (1991)

Total fertility rate: 1.8 children born/woman (1991)

Nationality: noun—Briton(s), British (collective pl.); adjective—British

Ethnic divisions: English 81.5%, Scottish 9.6%, Irish 2.4%, Welsh 1.9%, Ulster 1.8%, West Indian, Indian, Pakistani, and other 2.8%

Religion: Anglican 27.0 million, Roman Catholic 5.3 million, Presbyterian 2.0 million, Methodist 760,000, Jewish 410,000

Language: English, Welsh (about 26% of population of Wales), Scottish form of Gaelic (about 60,000 in Scotland)

Literacy: 99% (male NA%, female NA%) age 15 and over can read and write (1978 est.)

Labor force: 28,966,000; services 60.6%, manufacturing and construction 27.2%, government 8.9%, energy 2.1%, agriculture 1.2% (June 1990)

Organized labor: 35.7% of labor force (1989)

Government

Long-form name: United Kingdom of Great Britain and Northern Ireland; abbreviated UK

Type: constitutional monarchy

Capital: London

Administrative divisions: 47 counties, 7 metropolitan counties, 26 districts, 9 regions, and 3 islands areas;

England—39 counties, 7 metropolitan counties*; Avon, Bedford, Berkshire, Buckingham, Cambridge, Cheshire, Cleveland, Cornwall, Cumbria, Derby, Devon, Dorset, Durham, East Sussex, Essex, Gloucester, Greater London*, Greater Manchester*, Hampshire, Hereford and Worcester, Hertford, Humberside, Isle of Wight, Kent, Lancashire, Leicester, Lincoln, Merseyside*, Norfolk, Northampton, Northumberland, North Yorkshire, Nottingham, Oxford, Shropshire, Somerset, South Yorkshire*, Stafford, Suffolk, Surrey, Tyne and Wear*, Warwick, West Midlands*, West Sussex, West Yorkshire*, Wiltshire;

Northern Ireland—26 districts; Antrim, Ards, Armagh, Ballymena, Ballymoney, Banbridge, Belfast, Carrickfergus, Castlereagh, Coleraine, Cookstown, Craigavon, Down, Dungannon, Fermanagh, Larne, Limavady, Lisburn, Londonderry, Magherafelt, Moyle, Newry and Mourne, Newtownabbey, North Down, Omagh, Strabane;

Scotland—9 regions, 3 islands areas*; Borders, Central, Dumfries and Galloway, Fife, Grampian, Highland, Lothian, Orkney*, Shetland*, Strathclyde, Tayside, Western Isles*;

Wales—8 counties; Clwyd, Dyfed, Gwent, Gwynedd, Mid Glamorgan, Powys, South Glamorgan, West Glamorgan

Independence: 1 January 1801, United Kingdom established

Constitution: unwritten; partly statutes, partly common law and practice

Dependent areas: Anguilla, Bermuda, British Indian Ocean Territory, British Virgin Islands, Cayman Islands, Falkland Islands, Gibraltar, Guernsey, Hong Kong (scheduled to become a Special Administrative Region of China in 1997), Jersey, Isle of Man, Montserrat, Pitcairn Islands, Saint Helena, South Georgia and the South Sandwich Islands, Turks and Caicos Islands

Legal system: common law tradition with early Roman and modern continental influences; no judicial review of Acts of Parliament; accepts compulsory ICJ jurisdiction, with reservations

National holiday: Celebration of the Birthday of the Queen (second Saturday in June), 10 June 1989

Executive branch: monarch, prime minister, Cabinet

Legislative branch: bicameral Parliament consists of an upper house or House of Lords and a lower house or House of Commons

Judicial branch: House of Lords

Leaders:
Chief of State—Queen ELIZABETH II (since 6 February 1952); Heir Apparent Prince CHARLES (son of the Queen, born 14 November 1948);

Head of Government—Prime Minister John MAJOR (since 28 November 1990); Deputy Prime Minister (vacant);

Political parties and leaders: Conservative and Unionist Party, John MAJOR; Labor Party, Neil KINNOCK; Social and Liberal Democratic Party (SLDP; formed from the merger of the Liberal Party and the Social Democratic Party), Jeremy (Paddy) ASHDOWN; Scottish National Party, Alex SALMOND; Welsh National Party (Plaid Cymru), Dafydd THOMAS; Ulster Unionist Party (Northern Ireland), James MOLYNEAUX; Democratic Unionist Party (Northern Ireland), Rev. Ian PAISLEY; Ulster Popular Unionist Party (Northern Ireland), James KILFEDDER; Social Democratic and Labor Party (SDLP, Northern Ireland), John HUME; Sinn Fein (Northern Ireland), Gerry ADAMS; Alliance Party (Northern Ireland), John ALDERDICE; Communist Party, Nina TEMPLE

Suffrage: universal at age 18

Elections:
House of Commons—last held 11 June 1987 (next to be held by June 1992); results—Conservative 43%, Labor 32%, Liberal/Social Democratic 23%, other 2%; seats—(650 total) Conservative 376, Labor 228, Liberal/Social Democratic 22, Ulster Unionist (Northern Ireland) 9, Scottish National 4, Welsh National 3, Democratic Unionist (Northern Ireland) 3, Social Democratic and Labor (Northern Ireland) 3, Ulster Popular Unionist (Northern Ireland) 1, Sinn Fein (Northern Ireland) 1; note—the Liberal Party and the Social Democratic Party merged to become the Social and Liberal Democratic Party in 1988

Communists: 15,961

Other political or pressure groups: Trades Union Congress, Confederation of British Industry, National Farmers' Union, Campaign for Nuclear Disarmament

Member of: AfDB, AG (observer), AsDB, BIS, C, CCC, CDB, CE, CERN, COCOM, CP, CSCE, EBRD, EC, ECA (associate), ECE, ECLAC, EIB, ESCAP, ESA, FAO, G-5, G-7, G-10, GATT, IADB, IAEA, IBRD, ICAO, ICC, ICFTU, IDA, IEA, IFAD, IFC, ILO, IMF, IMO, INMARSAT, INTELSAT, INTERPOL, IOC, IOM (observer), ISO, ITU, LORCS, NATO, NEA, OECD, PCA, SPC, UN, UNCTAD, UNFICYP, UNHCR, UNIDO, UNRWA, UN Security Council, UN Trusteeship Council, UPU, WCL, WEU, WHO, WIPO, WMO

Diplomatic representation: Ambassador Sir Antony ACLAND; Chancery at 3100 Massachusetts Avenue NW, Washington DC 20008; telephone (202) 462-1340; there are British Consulates General in Atlanta, Boston, Chicago, Cleveland, Houston, Los Angeles, New York, and San Francisco, and Consulates in Dallas, Miami, and Seattle; *US*—Ambassador Raymond SEITZ; Embassy at 24/31 Grosvenor Square, London, W.1A1AE, (mailing address is FPO New York 09509); telephone [44] (71) 499-9000; there are US Consulates General in Belfast and Edinburgh

Flag: blue with the red cross of Saint George (patron saint of England) edged in white superimposed on the diagonal red cross of Saint Patrick (patron saint of Ireland) which is superimposed on the diagonal white cross of Saint Andrew (patron saint of Scotland); known as the Union Flag or Union Jack; the design and colors (especially the Blue Ensign) have been the basis for a number of other flags including dependencies, Commonwealth countries, and others

Economy

Overview: The UK is one of the world's great trading powers and financial centers, and its economy ranks among the four largest in Europe. The economy is essentially capitalistic with a generous admixture of social welfare programs and government ownership. Over the last decade the Thatcher government halted the expansion of welfare measures and promoted extensive reprivatization of the government economic sector. Agriculture is intensive, highly mechanized, and efficient by European standards, producing about 60% of food needs with only 1% of the labor force. Industry is a mixture of public and private enterprises, employing about 27% of the work force and generating 22% of GDP. The UK is an energy-rich nation with large coal, natural gas, and oil reserves; primary energy production accounts for 12% of GDP, one of the highest shares of any industrial nation. In mid-1990 the economy fell into recession after eight years of strong economic expansion, which had raised national output by one quarter. Britain's inflation rate, which has been consistently well above those of her major trading partners, is expected to decline in 1991. Between 1986 and 1990 unemployment fell from 11% to about 6%, but it is now rising rapidly because of the economic slowdown. As a major trading nation, the UK will continue to be greatly affected by world boom or recession, swings in the international oil market, productivity trends in domestic industry, and the terms on which the economic integration of Europe proceeds.

GDP: $858.3 billion, per capita $15,000; real growth rate 0.8% (1990)
Inflation rate (consumer prices): 9.3% (1990)
Unemployment rate: 5.7% (1990)
Budget: revenues $385.0 billion; expenditures $385.5 billion, including capital expenditures of $35.0 billion (FY91 est.)
Exports: $188.9 billion (f.o.b., 1990); *commodities*—manufactured goods, machinery, fuels, chemicals, semifinished goods, transport equipment; *partners*—EC 50.7% (FRG 11.9%, France 10.2%, Netherlands 7.0%), US 13.1%
Imports: $222 billion (c.i.f., 1990); *commodities*—manufactured goods, machinery, semifinished goods, foodstuffs, consumer goods; *partners*—EC 52.6% (FRG 16.6%, France 8.9%, Netherlands 7.9%), US 10.8%
External debt: $10.5 billion (1990)
Industrial production: growth rate 0% (1990)
Electricity: 98,000,000 kW capacity; 316,500 million kWh produced, 5,520 kWh per capita (1990)
Industries: machinery and transportation equipment, metals, food processing, paper and paper products, textiles, chemicals, clothing, other consumer goods, motor vehicles, aircraft, shipbuilding, petroleum, coal

Agriculture: accounts for only 1.5% of GNP and 1% of labor force; highly mechanized and efficient farms; wide variety of crops and livestock products produced; about 60% self-sufficient in food and feed needs; fish catch of 665,000 metric tons (1987)
Economic aid: donor—ODA and OOF commitments (1970-89), $21.0 billion
Currency: British pound or pound sterling (plural—pounds); 1 British pound (£) = 100 pence
Exchange rates: British pounds (£) per US$1—0.5171 (January 1991), 0.5603 (1990), 0.6099 (1989), 0.5614 (1988), 0.6102 (1987), 0.6817 (1986), 0.7714 (1985)
Fiscal year: 1 April-31 March

Communications

Railroads: Great Britain—16,629 km total; British Railways (BR) operates 16,629 km 1.435-meter standard gauge (4,205 km electrified and 12,591 km double or multiple track); several additional small standard-gauge and narrow-gauge lines are privately owned and operated; Northern Ireland Railways (NIR) operates 332 km 1.600-meter gauge, 190 km double track
Highways: UK, 362,982 km total; Great Britain, 339,483 km paved (including 2,573 km limited-access divided highway); Northern Ireland, 23,499 km (22,907 paved, 592 km gravel)
Inland waterways: 2,291 total; British Waterways Board, 606 km; Port Authorities, 706 km; other, 979 km
Pipelines: 933 km crude oil, almost all insignificant; 2,993 km refined products; 12,800 km natural gas
Ports: London, Liverpool, Felixstowe, Tees and Hartlepool, Dover, Sullom Voe, Southampton
Merchant marine: 251 ships (1,000 GRT or over) totaling 4,643,056 GRT/6,214,450 DWT; includes 7 passenger, 21 short-sea passenger, 39 cargo, 34 container, 22 roll-on/roll-off cargo, 10 refrigerated cargo, 1 vehicle carrier, 1 railcar carrier, 74 petroleum, oils, and lubricants (POL) tanker, 4 chemical tanker, 9 liquefied gas, 1 combination ore/oil, 1 specialized tanker, 25 bulk, 2 combination bulk
Civil air: 618 major transport aircraft
Airports: 520 total, 388 usable; 252 with permanent-surface runways; 1 with runways over 3,659 m; 37 with runways 2,440-3,659 m; 133 with runways 1,220-2,439 m
Telecommunications: modern, efficient domestic and international system; 30,200,000 telephones; excellent country-wide broadcast systems; stations—223 AM, 165 (401 relays) FM, 207 (3,210 relays) TV; 40 coaxial submarine cables; satellite communication ground stations operating in

INTELSAT (7 Atlantic Ocean and 3 Indian Ocean), MARISAT, and EUTELSAT systems

Defense Forces

Branches: Army, Royal Navy (including Royal Marines), Royal Air Force
Manpower availability: males 15-49, 14,475,433; 12,167,324 fit for military service; no conscription
Defense expenditures: $41 billion, 4.8% of GDP (FY90)

United States

Geography

Total area: 9,372,610 km²; land area: 9,166,600 km²; includes only the 50 states and District of Colombia

Comparative area: about four-tenths the size of USSR; about one-third the size of Africa; about one-half the size of South America (or slightly larger than Brazil); slightly smaller than China; about two and one-half times the size of Western Europe

Land boundaries: 12,248 km total; Canada 8,893 km (including 2,477 km with Alaska), Mexico 3,326 km, Cuba (US naval base at Guantánamo) 29 km

Coastline: 19,924 km

Maritime claims:
Contiguous zone: 12 nm;
Continental shelf: not specified;
Exclusive economic zone: 200 nm;
Territorial sea: 12 nm

Disputes: maritime boundary disputes with Canada; US Naval Base at Guantánamo is leased from Cuba and only mutual agreement or US abandonment of the area can terminate the lease; Haiti claims Navassa Island; US has made no territorial claim in Antarctica (but has reserved the right to do so) and does not recognize the claims of any other nation; Marshall Islands claims Wake Island

Climate: mostly temperate, but varies from tropical (Hawaii) to arctic (Alaska); arid to semiarid in west with occasional warm, dry chinook wind

Terrain: vast central plain, mountains in west, hills and low mountains in east; rugged mountains and broad river valleys in Alaska; rugged, volcanic topography in Hawaii

Natural resources: coal, copper, lead, molybdenum, phosphates, uranium, bauxite, gold, iron, mercury, nickel, potash, silver, tungsten, zinc, crude oil, natural gas, timber

Land use: arable land 20%; permanent crops NEGL%; meadows and pastures 26%; forest and woodland 29%; other 25%; includes irrigated 2%

Environment: pollution control measures improving air and water quality; acid rain; agricultural fertilizer and pesticide pollution; management of sparse natural water resources in west; desertification; tsunamis, volcanoes, and earthquake activity around Pacific Basin; continuous permafrost in northern Alaska is a major impediment to development

Note: world's fourth-largest country (after USSR, Canada, and China)

People

Population: 252,502,000 (July 1991), growth rate 0.8% (1991)

Birth rate: 15 births/1,000 population (1991)

Death rate: 9 deaths/1,000 population (1991)

Net migration rate: 2 migrants/1,000 population (1991)

Infant mortality rate: 10 deaths/1,000 live births (1991)

Life expectancy at birth: 72 years male, 79 years female (1991)

Total fertility rate: 1.8 children born/woman (1991)

Nationality: noun—American(s); adjective—American

Ethnic divisions: white 85%, black 12%, other 3% (1985)

Religion: Protestant 61% (Baptist 21%, Methodist 12%, Lutheran 8%, Presbyterian 4%, Episcopalian 3%, other Protestant 13%), Roman Catholic 25%, Jewish 2%, other 5%, none 7%

Language: predominantly English; sizable Spanish-speaking minority

Literacy: 97% (male 97%, female 97%) age 15 and over having completed 5 or more years of schooling (1980)

Labor force: 126,424,000 (includes armed forces and unemployed); civilian labor force 124,787,000 (1990)

Organized labor: 16,729,000 members; 16.1% of total wage and salary employment which was 103,905,000 (1990)

Government

Long-form name: United States of America; abbreviated US or USA

Type: federal republic; strong democratic tradition

Capital: Washington, DC

Administrative divisions: 50 states and 1 district*; Alabama, Alaska, Arizona, Arkansas, California, Colorado, Connecticut, Delaware, District of Columbia*, Florida, Georgia, Hawaii, Idaho, Illinois, Indiana, Iowa, Kansas, Kentucky, Louisiana, Maine, Maryland, Massachusetts, Michigan, Minnesota, Mississippi, Missouri, Montana, Nebraska, Nevada, New Hampshire, New Jersey, New Mexico, New York, North Carolina, North Dakota, Ohio, Oklahoma, Oregon, Pennsylvania, Rhode Island, South Carolina, South Dakota, Tennessee, Texas, Utah, Vermont, Virginia, Washington, West Virginia, Wisconsin, Wyoming

Independence: 4 July 1776 (from England)

Constitution: 17 September 1787, effective 4 June 1789

Dependent areas: American Samoa, Baker Island, Guam, Howland Island; Jarvis Island, Johnston Atoll, Kingman Reef, Midway Islands, Navassa Island, Northern Mariana Islands, Palmyra Atoll, Puerto Rico, Virgin Islands, Wake Island. Since 18 July 1947, the US has administered the Trust Territory of the Pacific Islands, but recently entered into a new political relationship with three of the four political units. The Northern Mariana Islands is a Commonwealth associated with the US (effective 3 November 1986). Palau concluded a Compact of Free Association with the US that was approved by the US Congress but to date the Compact process has not been completed in Palau, which continues to be administered by the US as the Trust Territory of the Pacific Islands. The Federated States of Micronesia signed a Compact of Free Association with the US (effective 3 November 1986). The Republic of the Marshall Islands signed a Compact of Free Association with the US (effective 21 October 1986).

Legal system: based on English common law; judicial review of legislative acts; accepts compulsory ICJ jurisdiction, with reservations

National holiday: Independence Day, 4 July (1776)

Executive branch: president, vice president, Cabinet

Legislative branch: bicameral Congress consists of an upper house or Senate and a lower house or House of Representatives

Judicial branch: Supreme Court

Leaders:
Chief of State and Head of Government— President George BUSH (since 20 January 1989); Vice President Dan QUAYLE (since 20 January 1989)

Political parties and leaders: Republican Party, Clayton YEUTTER, national committee chairman; Jeanie AUSTIN, co-chairman; Democratic Party, Ronald H. BROWN, national committee chairman; several other groups or parties of minor political significance

Suffrage: universal at age 18

Elections:
*President—*last held 8 November 1988 (next to be held 3 November 1992); results—George BUSH (Republican Party) 53.37%, Michael DUKAKIS (Democratic Party) 45.67%, other 0.96%;

Senate—last held 6 November 1990 (next to be held 3 November 1992); results—Democratic Party 51%, Republican Party 47%, other 2%; seats—(100 total) Democratic Party 56, Republican Party 44; *House of Representatives*—last held 6 November 1990 (next to be held 3 November 1992); results—Democratic Party 52%, Republican Party 44%, other 4%; seats—(435 total) Democratic Party 267, Republican Party 167, Socialist 1

Communists: Communist Party (claimed 15,000-20,000 members), Gus HALL, general secretary; Socialist Workers Party (claimed 1,800 members), Jack BARNES, national secretary

Member of: AfDB, AG (observer), ANZUS, APEC, AsDB, BIS, CCC, COCOM, CP, CSCE, EBRD, ECE, ECLAC, FAO, ES-CAP, G-2, G-5, G-7, G-8, G-10, GATT, IADB, IAEA, IBRD, ICAO, ICC, ICFTU, IDA, IEA, IFAD, IFC, ILO, IMF, IMO, INMARSAT, INTELSAT, INTERPOL, IOC, IOM, ISO, ITU, LORCS, NATO, NEA, OAS, OECD, PCA, SPC, UN, UNCTAD, UNHCR, UNIDO, UNRWA, UN Security Council, UN Trusteeship Council, UNTSO, UPU, WCL, WHO, WIPO, WMO, WTO

Diplomatic representation: US Representative to the UN, Ambassador Thomas R. PICKERING; Mission at 799 United Nations Plaza, New York, NY 10017; telephone (212) 415-4444 (afternoon hours)

Flag: thirteen equal horizontal stripes of red (top and bottom) alternating with white; there is a blue rectangle in the upper hoist-side corner bearing 50 small white five-pointed stars arranged in nine offset horizontal rows of six stars (top and bottom) alternating with rows of five stars; the 50 stars represent the 50 states, the 13 stripes represent the 13 original colonies; known as Old Glory; the design and colors have been the basis for a number of other flags including Chile, Liberia, Malaysia, and Puerto Rico

Economy

Overview: The US has the most powerful, diverse, and technologically advanced economy in the world, with a per capita GNP of $21,800, the largest among major industrial nations. In 1989 the economy enjoyed its seventh successive year of substantial growth, the longest in peacetime history. The expansion featured moderation in wage and consumer price increases and a steady reduction in unemployment to 5.2% of the labor force. In 1990, however, growth slowed to 1% because of a combination of factors, such as the worldwide increase in interest rates, Iraq's invasion of Kuwait in August, the subsequent spurt in oil prices,

and a general decline in business and consumer confidence. Ongoing problems for the 1990s include inadequate investment in education and other economic infrastructure, rapidly rising medical costs, and sizable budget and trade deficits.

GNP: $5,465 billion, per capita $21,800; real growth rate 1.0% (1990)

Inflation rate (consumer prices): 5.4% (1990)

Unemployment rate: 5.5% (1990)

Budget: revenues $1,106 billion; expenditures $1,272 billion, including capital expenditures of $NA (FY90 est.)

Exports: $393.9 billion (f.o.b., 1990); *commodities*—capital goods, automobiles, industrial supplies and raw materials, consumer goods, agricultural products; *partners*—Western Europe 27.3%, Canada 22.1%, Japan 12.1% (1989)

Imports: $516.2 billion (c.i.f., 1990); *commodities*—crude and partly refined petroleum, machinery, automobiles, consumer goods, industrial raw materials, food and beverages; *partners*—Western Europe 21.5%, Japan 19.7%, Canada 18.8% (1989)

External debt: $581 billion (December 1989)

Industrial production: growth rate 1.0% (1990)

Electricity: 776,550,000 kW capacity; 3,020,000 million kWh produced, 12,080 kWh per capita (1990)

Industries: leading industrial power in the world, highly diversified; petroleum, steel, motor vehicles, aerospace, telecommunications, chemicals, electronics, food processing, consumer goods, fishing, lumber, mining

Agriculture: accounts for 2% of GNP and 2.8% of labor force; favorable climate and soils support a wide variety of crops and livestock production; world's second-largest producer and number-one exporter of grain; surplus food producer; fish catch of 5.0 million metric tons (1988)

Illicit drugs: illicit producer of cannabis for domestic consumption with 1987 production estimated at 3,500 metric tons or about 25% of the available marijuana; ongoing eradication program aimed at small plots and greenhouses has not reduced production

Economic aid: donor—commitments, including ODA and OOF, (FY80-89), $115.7 billion

Currency: United States dollar (plural—dollars); 1 United States dollar (US$) = 100 cents

Exchange rates: *British pounds* (£) per US$—0.5171 (January 1991), 0.5603 (1990), 0.6099 (1989), 0.5614 (1988), 0.6102 (1987), 0.6817 (1986), 0.7714 (1985); *Canadian dollars* (Can$) per US$—1.1559 (January 1991), 1.1668 (1990), 1.1840

(1989), 1.2307 (1988), 1.3260 (1987), 1.3895 (1986), 1.3655 (1985); *French francs* (F) per US$—5.1307 (January 1991), 5.4453 (1990), 6.3801 (1989), 5.9569 (1988), 6.0107 (1987), 6.9261 (1986), 8.9852 (1985); *Italian lire* (Lit) per US$—1,134.4 (January 1991), 1,198.1 (1990), 1.372.1 (1989), 1,301.6 (1988), 1,296.1 (1987), 1,490.8 (1986), 1,909.4 (1985); *Japanese yen* (¥) per US$—133.88 (January 1991), 144.79 (1990), 137.96 (1989), 128.15 (1988), 144.64 (1987), 168.52 (1986), 238.54 (1985); *German deutsche marks* (DM) per US$—1.5100 (January 1991), 1.6157 (1990), 1.8800 (1989), 1.7562 (1988), 1.7974 (1987), 2.1715 (1986), 2.9440 (1985)

Fiscal year: 1 October-30 September

Communications

Railroads: 270,312 km

Highways: 6,365,590 km, including 88,641 km expressways

Inland waterways: 41,009 km of navigable inland channels, exclusive of the Great Lakes (est.)

Pipelines: 275,800 km petroleum, 305,300 km natural gas (1985)

Ports: Anchorage, Baltimore, Beaumont, Boston, Charleston, Cleveland, Duluth, Freeport, Galveston, Hampton Roads, Honolulu, Houston, Jacksonville, Long Beach, Los Angeles, Milwaukee, Mobile, New Orleans, New York, Philadelphia, Portland (Oregon), Richmond (California), San Francisco, Savannah, Seattle, Tampa, Wilmington

Merchant marine: 404 ships (1,000 GRT or over) totaling NA GRT/NA DWT); includes 3 passenger-cargo, 44 cargo, 23 bulk, 180 tanker, 13 tanker tug-barge, 11 liquefied gas, 130 intermodal; in addition there are 231 government-owned vessels

Civil air: 3,297 commercial multiengine transport aircraft, including 2,989 jet, 231 turboprop, 77 piston (1985)

Airports: 14,177 total, 12,417 usable; 4,820 with permanent surface-runways; 63 with runways over 3,659 m; 325 with runways 2,440-3,659 m; 2,524 with runways 1,220-2,439 m

Telecommunications: 182,558,000 telephones; stations—4,892 AM, 5,200 FM (including 3,915 commercial and 1,285 public broadcasting), 7,296 TV (including 796 commercial, 300 public broadcasting, and 6,200 commercial cable); 495,000,000 radio receivers (1982); 150,000,000 TV sets (1982); satellite communications ground stations—45 Atlantic Ocean INTELSAT and 16 Pacific Ocean INTELSAT

United States *(continued)*

Defense Forces

Branches: Department of the Army, Department of the Navy (including Marine Corps), Department of the Air Force
Manpower availability: males 15-49, 66, 458,000; NA fit for military service
Defense expenditures: $312.9 billion, 5.7% of GNP (1990)

Uruguay

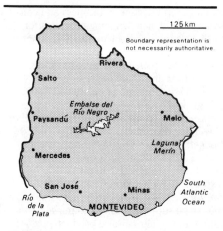

Geography

Total area: 176,220 km²; land area: 173,620 km²
Comparative area: slightly smaller than Washington State
Land boundaries: 1,564 km total; Argentina 579 km, Brazil 985 km
Coastline: 660 km
Maritime claims:
Continental shelf: 200 m (depth) or to depth of exploitation;
Territorial sea: 200 nm (overflight and navigation permitted beyond 12 nm)
Disputes: short section of boundary with Argentina is in dispute; two short sections of the boundary with Brazil are in dispute (Arroyo de la Invernada area of the Rio Quarai and the islands at the confluence of the Rio Quarai and the Uruguay)
Climate: warm temperate; freezing temperatures almost unknown
Terrain: mostly rolling plains and low hills; fertile coastal lowland
Natural resources: soil, hydropower potential, minor minerals
Land use: arable land 8%; permanent crops NEGL%; meadows and pastures 78%; forest and woodland 4%; other 10%; includes irrigated 1%
Environment: subject to seasonally high winds, droughts, floods

People

Population: 3,121,101 (July 1990), growth rate 0.6% (1991)
Birth rate: 17 births/1,000 population (1991)
Death rate: 10 deaths/1,000 population (1991)
Net migration rate: −1 migrants/1,000 population (1991)
Infant mortality rate: 22 deaths/1,000 live births (1991)
Life expectancy at birth: 69 years male, 76 years female (1991)
Total fertility rate: 2.4 children born/woman (1991)

Nationality: noun—Uruguayan(s); adjective—Uruguayan
Ethnic divisions: white 88%, mestizo 8%, black 4%
Religion: Roman Catholic (less than half adult population attends church regularly) 66%, Protestant 2%, Jewish 2%, nonprofessing or other 30%
Language: Spanish
Literacy: 96% (male 97%, female 96%) age 15 and over can read and write (1990 est.)
Labor force: 1,300,000; government 25%, manufacturing 19%, agriculture 11%, commerce 12%, utilities, construction, transport, and communications 12%, other services 21% (1988 est.)
Organized labor: Interunion Workers' Assembly/National Workers' Confederation (PIT/CNT) Labor Federation

Government

Long-form name: Oriental Republic of Uruguay
Type: republic
Capital: Montevideo
Administrative divisions: 19 departments (departamentos, singular—departamento); Artigas, Canelones, Cerro Largo, Colonia, Durazno, Flores, Florida, Lavalleja, Maldonado, Montevideo, Paysandú, Río Negro, Rivera, Rocha, Salto, San José, Soriano, Tacuarembó, Treinta y Tres
Independence: 25 August 1828 (from Brazil)
Constitution: 27 November 1966, effective February 1967, suspended 27 June 1973, new constitution rejected by referendum 30 November 1980
Legal system: based on Spanish civil law system; accepts compulsory ICJ jurisdiction
National holiday: Independence Day, 25 August (1828)
Executive branch: president, vice president, Council of Ministers (cabinet)
Legislative branch: bicameral General Assembly (Asamblea General) consists of an upper chamber or Chamber of Senators (Cámara de Senadores) and a lower chamber or Chamber of Representatives (Cámera de Representantes)
Judicial branch: Supreme Court
Leaders:
Chief of State and Head of Government—President Luis Alberto LACALLE (since 1 March 1990); Vice President Gonzalo AGUIRRE (since 1 March 1990)
Political parties and leaders: National (Blanco) Party, Luis Alberto LACALLE Herrera; Colorado Party, Jorge BATLLE Ibáñez; Broad Front Coalition, Líber SEREGNI Mosquera—includes Communist Party led by Jaime PEREZ and National Liberation Movement (MLN) or Tupamaros led by Eleuterio FERNANDEZ Huidobro; New Space Coalition consists of the Party of the Government of the People (PGP), Hugo

BATALLA; Christian Democratic Party (PDC), Héctor LESCANO; and Civic Union, Humberto CÌGANDA
Suffrage: universal and compulsory at age 18
Elections:
President—last held 26 November 1989 (next to be held November 1994); results—Luis Alberto LACALLE Herrera (Blanco) 37%, Jorge BATLLE Ibáñez (Colorado) 29%, Líber SEREGNI Mosquera (Broad Front) 20%;
Chamber of Senators—last held 26 November 1989 (next to be held November 1994); results—Blanco 40%, Colorado 30%, Broad Front 23% New Space 7%; seats—(30 total) Blanco 12, Colorado 9, Broad Front 7, New Space 2;
Chamber of Representatives—last held NA November 1989 (next to be held November 1994); results—Blanco 39%, Colorado 30%, Broad Front 22%, New Space 8%, other 1%; seats—(99 total) number of seats by party NA
Communists: 50,000
Member of: AG (observer), CCC, ECLAC, FAO, G-11, G-77, GATT, IADB, IAEA, IBRD, ICAO, ICC, IFAD, IFC, ILO, IMF, IMO, INTELSAT, INTERPOL, IOC, IOM, ISO (correspondent), ITU, LAES, LAIA, LORCS, NAM (observer), OAS, OPANAL, PCA, RG, UN, UNCTAD, UNESCO, UNIDO, UNIIMOG, UNMOGIP, UPU, WCL, WHO, WIPO, WMO, WTO
Diplomatic representation: Ambassador Eduardo MACGILLICUDDEY; Chancery at 1918 F Street NW, Washington DC 20006; telephone (202) 331-1313 through 1316; there are Uruguayan Consulates General in Los Angeles, Miami, and New York, and a Consulate in New Orleans;
US—Ambassador Richard C. BROWN; Embassy at Lauro Muller 1776, Montevideo (mailing address is APO Miami 34035); telephone [598] (2) 23-60-61
Flag: nine equal horizontal stripes of white (top and bottom) alternating with blue; there is a white square in the upper hoist-side corner with a yellow sun bearing a human face known as the Sun of May and 16 rays alternately triangular and wavy

---

Economy

Overview: The economy is slowly recovering from the deep recession of the early 1980s. In 1988 real GDP grew by only 0.5% and in 1989 by 1.5%. The recovery was led by growth in the agriculture and fishing sectors, agriculture alone contributing 20% to GDP, employing about 11% of the labor force, and generating a large proportion of export earnings. Raising livestock, particularly cattle and sheep, is the major agricultural activity. In 1990, despite healthy exports and an improved current account, domestic growth remained weak because of government concentration on the external sector, adverse weather conditions, and prolonged strikes. Bringing down high inflation, reducing a large fiscal deficit, and avoiding frequent strikes remain major economic problems for the government.
GDP: $9.2 billion, per capita $2,970; real growth rate 1% (1990 est.)
Inflation rate (consumer prices): 129% (1990)
Unemployment rate: 8.8% (1990 est.)
Budget: revenues $1.2 billion; expenditures $1.4 billion, including capital expenditures of $165 million (1988)
Exports: $1.7 billion (f.o.b., 1990); *commodities*—hides and leather goods 17%, beef 10%, wool 9%, fish 7%, rice 4%; *partners*—Brazil 17%, US 15%, FRG 10%, Argentina 10% (1987)
Imports: $1.28 billion (f.o.b., 1990); *commodities*—fuels and lubricants 15%, metals, machinery, transportation equipment, industrial chemicals; *partners*—Brazil 24%, Argentina 14%, US 8%, FRG 8% (1987)
External debt: $4.2 billion (1990 est.)
Industrial production: growth rate −2.1% (1989 est.)
Electricity: 1,950,000 kW capacity; 5,274 million kWh produced, 1,740 kWh per capita (1990)
Industries: meat processing, wool and hides, sugar, textiles, footwear, leather apparel, tires, cement, fishing, petroleum refining, wine
Agriculture: large areas devoted to extensive livestock grazing; wheat, rice, corn, sorghum; self-sufficient in most basic foodstuffs
Economic aid: US commitments, including Ex-Im (FY70-88), $105 million; Western (non-US) countries, ODA and OOF bilateral commitments (1970-88), $293 million; Communist countries (1970-89), $69 million
Currency: new Uruguayan peso (plural—pesos); 1 new Uruguayan peso (N$Ur) = 100 centésimos
Exchange rates: new Uruguayan pesos (N$Ur) per US$1—1,626.4 (January 1991), 1,171.0 (1990), 605.5 (1989), 359.44 (1988), 226.67 (1987), 151.99 (1986), 101.43 (1985)
Fiscal year: calendar year

Communications

Railroads: 3,000 km, all 1.435-meter standard gauge and government owned
Highways: 49,900 km total; 6,700 km paved, 3,000 km gravel, 40,200 km earth
Inland waterways: 1,600 km; used by coastal and shallow-draft river craft
Ports: Montevideo, Punta del Este
Merchant marine: 4 ships (1,000 GRT or over) totaling 65,212 GRT/116,613 DWT; includes 2 cargo, 1 container, 1 petroleum, oils, and lubricants (POL) tanker
Civil air: 14 major transport aircraft
Airports: 91 total, 86 usable; 16 with permanent-surface runways; none with runways over 3,659 m; 2 with runways 2,440-3,659 m; 17 with runways 1,220-2,439 m
Telecommunications: most modern facilities concentrated in Montevideo; new nationwide radio relay network; 337,000 telephones; stations—99 AM, no FM, 26 TV, 9 shortwave; 2 Atlantic Ocean INTELSAT earth stations

---

Defense Forces

Branches: Army, Navy (including Naval Air Arm and Marines), Air Force, Coast Guard, Grenadier Guards, Police
Manpower availability: males 15-49, 735,971; 597,302 fit for military service; no conscription
Defense expenditures: $168 million, 2.2% of GDP (1988)

Vanuatu

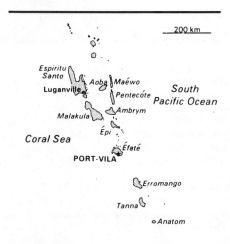

Geography

Total area: 14,760 km²; land area: 14,760 km²; includes more than 80 islands
Comparative area: slightly larger than Connecticut
Land boundary: none
Coastline: 2,528 km
Maritime claims: (measured from claimed archipelagic baselines);
Contiguous zone: 24 nm;
Continental shelf: edge of continental margin or 200 nm;
Exclusive economic zone: 200 nm;
Territorial sea: 12 nm
Climate: tropical; moderated by southeast trade winds
Terrain: mostly mountains of volcanic origin; narrow coastal plains
Natural resources: manganese, hardwood forests, fish
Land use: arable land 1%; permanent crops 5%; meadows and pastures 2%; forest and woodland 1%; other 91%
Environment: subject to tropical cyclones or typhoons (January to April); volcanism causes minor earthquakes
Note: located 5,750 km southwest of Honolulu in the South Pacific Ocean about three-quarters of the way between Hawaii and Australia

People

Population: 170,319 (July 1991), growth rate 3.1% (1991)
Birth rate: 36 births/1,000 population (1991)
Death rate: 5 deaths/1,000 population (1991)
Net migration rate: 0 migrants/1,000 population (1991)
Infant mortality rate: 36 deaths/1,000 live births (1991)
Life expectancy at birth: 67 years male, 72 years female (1991)
Total fertility rate: 5.4 children born/woman (1991)

Nationality: noun—Ni-Vanuatu (singular and plural); adjective—Ni-Vanuatu
Ethnic divisions: indigenous Melanesian 94%, French 4%, remainder Vietnamese, Chinese, and various Pacific Islanders
Religion: Presbyterian 36.7%, Anglican 15%, Catholic 15%, indigenous beliefs 7.6%, Seventh-Day Adventist 6.2%, Church of Christ 3.8%, other 15.7%
Language: English and French (official); pidgin (known as Bislama or Bichelama)
Literacy: 53% (male 57%, female 48%) age 15 and over can read and write (1979)
Labor force: NA
Organized labor: 7 registered trade unions—largest include Oil and Gas Workers' Union, Vanuatu Airline Workers' Union

Government

Long-form name: Republic of Vanuatu
Type: republic
Capital: Port-Vila
Administrative divisions: 11 island councils; Ambrym, Aoba/Maéwo, Banks/Torres, Éfaté, Épi, Malakula, Paama, Pentecôte, Santo/Malo, Shepherd, Taféa
Independence: 30 July 1980 (from France and UK; formerly New Hebrides)
Constitution: 30 July 1980
Legal system: unified system being created from former dual French and British systems
National holiday: Independence Day, 30 July (1980)
Executive branch: president, prime minister, Council of Ministers (cabinet)
Legislative branch: unicameral Parliament; note—the National Council of Chiefs advises on matters of custom and land
Judicial branch: Supreme Court
Leaders:
Chief of State—President Frederick TIMA-KATA (since 30 January 1989);
Head of Government—Prime Minister Father Walter Hadye LINI (since 30 July 1980); Deputy Prime Minister (vacant)
Political parties and leaders: National Party (Vanua'aku Pati), Walter LINI; Union of Moderate Parties, Maxine CARLOT; Melanesian Progressive Party, Barak SOPE
Suffrage: universal at age 18
Elections:
Parliament—last held 30 November 1987 (next to be held by November 1991); bye-lections were held in December 1988 to fill vacancies resulting from the expulsion of opposition members for boycotting sessions; results—percent of vote by party NA; seats—(46 total) National Party 26, Union of Moderate Parties 19, independent 1
Member of: ACCT, ACP, AsDB, C, ESCAP, FAO, G-77, IBRD, ICAO, ICFTU, IDA, IFC, IMF, IMO, IOC, ITU, NAM, SPC, SPF, UN, UNCTAD, UNIDO, UPU, WFTU, WHO, WMO

Diplomatic representation: Vanuatu does not have a mission in Washington; *US*—the ambassador in Papua New Guinea is accredited to Vanuatu
Flag: two equal horizontal bands of red (top) and green (bottom) with a black isosceles triangle (based on the hoist side) all separated by a black-edged yellow stripe in the shape of a horizontal Y (the two points of the Y face the hoist side and enclose the triangle); centered in the triangle is a boar's tusk encircling two crossed *namele* leaves, all in yellow

Economy

Overview: The economy is based primarily on subsistence farming that provides a living for about 80% of the population. Fishing and tourism are the other mainstays of the economy. Mineral deposits are negligible; the country has no known petroleum deposits. A small light industry sector caters to the local market. Tax revenues come mainly from import duties.
GDP: $137 million, per capita $860; real growth rate 4.3% (1989 est.)
Inflation rate (consumer prices): 7.8% (1989 est.)
Unemployment rate: NA%
Budget: revenues $90.0 million; expenditures $103.0 million, including capital expenditures of $45.0 million (1989 est.)
Exports: $14.5 million (f.o.b., 1989 est.);
commodities—copra 59%, cocoa 11%, meat 9%, fish 8%, timber 4%;
partners—Netherlands 34%, France 27%, Japan 17%, Belgium 4%, New Caledonia 3%, Singapore 2% (1987)
Imports: $58.4 million (f.o.b., 1989 est.);
commodities—machines and vehicles 25%, food and beverages 23%, basic manufactures 18%, raw materials and fuels 11%, chemicals 6%;
partners—Australia 36%, Japan 13%, NZ 10%, France 8%, Fiji 5% (1987)
External debt: $30 million (1990 est.)
Industrial production: growth rate NA%
Electricity: 17,000 kW capacity; 30 million kWh produced, 180 kWh per capita (1990)
Industries: food and fish freezing, forestry processing, meat canning
Agriculture: export crops—copra, cocoa, coffee, and fish; subsistence crops—copra, taro, yams, coconuts, fruits, and vegetables
Economic aid: Western (non-US) countries, ODA and OOF bilateral commitments (1970-88), $565 million
Currency: vatu (plural—vatu); 1 vatu (VT) = 100 centimes
Exchange rates: vatu (VT) per US$1— 109.62 (January 1991), 116.57 (1990), 116.04 (1989), 104.43 (1988), 109.85 (1987), 106.08 (1986), 106.03 (1985)
Fiscal year: calendar year

Vatican City

Communications

Railroads: none
Highways: 1,027 km total; at least 240 km sealed or all-weather roads
Ports: Port-Vila, Luganville, Palikoulo, Santu
Merchant marine: 129 ships (1,000 GRT or over) totaling 2,242,850 GRT/3,447,671 DWT; includes 33 cargo, 13 refrigerated cargo, 8 container, 11 vehicle carrier, 1 livestock carrier, 5 petroleum, oils, and lubricants (POL) tanker, 1 chemical tanker, 1 liquefied gas, 55 bulk, 1 combination bulk; note—a flag of convenience registry; the USSR has 2 ships under the Vanuatu flag
Civil air: no major transport aircraft
Airports: 32 total, 28 usable; 2 with permanent-surface runways; none with runways over 3,659 m; 1 with runways 2,440-3,659 m; 1 with runways 1,220-2,439 m
Telecommunications: stations—2 AM, no FM, no TV; 3,000 telephones; satellite communications ground stations—1 Pacific Ocean INTELSAT

Defense Forces

Branches: no military forces; Vanuatu Police Force, paramilitary force
Manpower availability: males 15-49, 41, 183; NA fit for military service
Defense expenditures: $NA, NA% of GDP

250 meters

Vatican Museums

Saint Peter's Basilica

Saint Peter's Square

Geography

Total area: 0.438 km²; land area: 0.438 km²
Comparative area: about 0.7 times the size of The Mall in Washington, DC
Land boundary: 3.2 km with Italy
Coastline: none—landlocked
Maritime claims: none—landlocked
Climate: temperate; mild, rainy winters (September to mid-May) with hot, dry summers (May to September)
Terrain: low hill
Natural resources: none
Land use: arable land 0%; permanent crops 0%; meadows and pastures 0%; forest and woodland 0%; other 100%
Environment: urban
Note: landlocked; enclave of Rome, Italy; world's smallest state; outside the Vatican City, 13 buildings in Rome and Castel Gandolfo (the pope's summer residence) enjoy extraterritorial rights

People

Population: 778 (July 1991), growth rate NEGL% (1991)
Nationality: no noun or adjectival forms
Ethnic divisions: primarily Italians but also Swiss and other nationalities
Religion: Roman Catholic
Language: Italian, Latin, and various other languages
Literacy: 100% (male NA%, female NA%)
Labor force: high dignitaries, priests, nuns, guards, and 3,000 lay workers who live outside the Vatican
Organized labor: Association of Vatican Lay Workers, 1,800 members (1987)

Government

Long-form name: State of the Vatican City; note—the Vatican City is the physical seat of the Holy See, which is the central government of the Roman Catholic Church
Type: monarchical-sacerdotal state

Capital: Vatican City
Independence: 11 February 1929 (from Italy)
Constitution: Apostolic Constitution of 1967 (effective 1 March 1968)
National holiday: Installation Day of the Pope (John Paul II), 22 October (1978); note—Pope John Paul II was elected on 16 October 1978
Executive branch: pope
Legislative branch: unicameral Pontifical Commission
Judicial branch: none; normally handled by Italy
Leaders:
Chief of State—Pope JOHN PAUL II (Karol WOJTYŁA; since 16 October 1978);
Head of Government—Secretary of State Archbishop Angelo SODANO
Political parties and leaders: none
Suffrage: limited to cardinals less than 80 years old
Elections:
Pope—last held 16 October 1978 (next to be held after the death of the current pope); results—Karol WOJTYŁA was elected for life by the College of Cardinals
Communists: NA
Other political or pressure groups: none (exclusive of influence exercised by church officers)
Member of: CSCE, IAEA, ICFTU, IMF (observer), INTELSAT, IOM (observer), ITU, OAS (observer), UN (observer), UNCTAD, UNHCR, UPU, WIPO, WTO (observer)
Diplomatic representation: Apostolic Pro-Nuncio Archbishop Agostino CACCIAVILLAN; 3339 Massachusetts Avenue NW, Washington DC 20008; telephone (202) 333-7121;
US—Ambassador Thomas P. MELADY; Embassy at Villino Pacelli, Via Aurelia 294, 00165 Rome (mailing address is APO New York 09794); telephone [396] 639-0558
Flag: two vertical bands of yellow (hoist side) and white with the crossed keys of Saint Peter and the papal tiara centered in the white band

Economy

Overview: This unique, noncommercial economy is supported financially by contributions (known as Peter's Pence) from Roman Catholics throughout the world, the sale of postage stamps, tourist mementos, fees for admission to museums, and the sale of publications. The incomes and living standards of lay workers are comparable to, or somewhat better than, those of counterparts who work in the city of Rome.
Budget: revenues $76.6 million; expenditures $168 million, including capital expenditures of $NA (1991)

Vatican City (continued)

Electricity: 5,000 kW standby capacity (1990); power supplied by Italy
Industries: printing and production of a small amount of mosaics and staff uniforms; worldwide banking and financial activities
Currency: Vatican lira (plural—lire); 1 Vatican lira (VLit) = 100 centesimi
Exchange rates: Vatican lire (VLit) per US$1—1,134.4 (January 1991), 1,198.1 (1990), 1,372.1 (1989), 1,301.6 (1988), 1,296.1 (1987), 1,490.8 (1986), 1,909.4 (1985); note—the Vatican lira is at par with the Italian lira which circulates freely
Fiscal year: calendar year

Communications

Railroads: 850 m, 750 mm gauge (links with Italian network near the Rome station of Saint Peter's)
Highways: none; all city streets
Telecommunications: stations—3 AM, 4 FM, no TV; 2,000-line automatic telephone exchange; no communications satellite systems

Defense Forces

Note: defense is the responsibility of Italy; Swiss Papal Guards are posted at entrances to the Vatican City

Venezuela

Caribbean Sea
Maracaibo
CARACAS
Cumaná
Ciudad Guayana
San Cristóbal
San Fernando
Puerto Ayacucho
400 km
Boundary representation is not necessarily authoritative.

Geography

Total area: 912,050 km²; land area: 882,050 km²
Comparative area: slightly more than twice the size of California
Land boundaries: 4,993 km total; Brazil 2,200 km, Colombia 2,050 km, Guyana 743 km
Coastline: 2,800 km
Maritime claims:
Contiguous zone: 15 nm;
Continental shelf: 200 m (depth) or to depth of exploitation;
Exclusive economic zone: 200 nm;
Territorial sea: 12 nm
Disputes: claims all of Guyana west of the Essequibo river; maritime boundary dispute with Colombia in the Gulf of Venezuela
Climate: tropical; hot, humid; more moderate in highlands
Terrain: Andes mountains and Maracaibo lowlands in northwest; central plains (llanos); Guyana highlands in southeast
Natural resources: crude oil, natural gas, iron ore, gold, bauxite, other minerals, hydropower, diamonds
Land use: arable land 3%; permanent crops 1%; meadows and pastures 20%; forest and woodland 39%; other 37%; includes irrigated NEGL%
Environment: subject to floods, rockslides, mudslides; periodic droughts; increasing industrial pollution in Caracas and Maracaibo
Note: on major sea and air routes linking North and South America

People

Population: 20,189,361 (July 1991), growth rate 2.4% (1991)
Birth rate: 28 births/1,000 population (1991)
Death rate: 4 deaths/1,000 population (1991)

Net migration rate: 1 migrant/1,000 population (1991)
Infant mortality rate: 26 deaths/1,000 live births (1991)
Life expectancy at birth: 71 years male, 78 years female (1991)
Total fertility rate: 3.4 children born/woman (1991)
Nationality: noun—Venezuelan(s); adjective—Venezuelan
Ethnic divisions: mestizo 67%, white 21%, black 10%, Indian 2%
Religion: nominally Roman Catholic 96%, Protestant 2%
Language: Spanish (official); Indian dialects spoken by about 200,000 Amerindians in the remote interior
Literacy: 88% (male 87%, female 90%) age 15 and over can read and write (1981 est.)
Labor force: 5,800,000; services 56%, industry 28%, agriculture 16% (1985)
Organized labor: 32% of labor force

Government

Long-form name: Republic of Venezuela
Type: republic
Capital: Caracas
Administrative divisions: 20 states (estados, singular—estado), 2 territories* (territorios, singular—territorio), 1 federal district** (distrito federal), and 1 federal dependence*** (dependencia federal); Amazonas*, Anzoátegui, Apure, Aragua, Barinas, Bolívar, Carabobo, Cojedes, Delta Amacuro*, Dependencias Federales***, Distrito Federal**, Falcón, Guárico, Lara, Mérida, Miranda, Monagas, Nueva Esparta, Portuguesa, Sucre, Táchira, Trujillo, Yaracuy, Zulia; note—the federal dependence consists of 11 federally controlled island groups with a total of 72 individual islands
Independence: 5 July 1811 (from Spain)
Constitution: 23 January 1961
Legal system: based on Napoleonic code; judicial review of legislative acts in Cassation Court only; has not accepted compulsory ICJ jurisdiction
National holiday: Independence Day, 5 July (1811)
Executive branch: president, Council of Ministers (cabinet)
Legislative branch: bicameral Congress of the Republic (Congreso de la Republica) consists of an upper chamber or Senate (Senado) and a lower chamber or Chamber of Deputies (Cámara de Diputados)
Judicial branch: Supreme Court of Justice (Corte Suprema de Justica)
Leaders:
Chief of State and Head of Government—President Carlos Andrés PÉREZ (since 2 February 1989)
Political parties and leaders: Social Christian Party (COPEI), Eduardo FERNÁNDEZ, secretary general; Democratic Action

(AD), Gonzalo BARRIOS, president, and Humberto CELLI, secretary general; Movement Toward Socialism (MAS), Argelia LAYA, president, and Freddy MUÑOZ, secretary general

Suffrage: universal and compulsory at age 18, though poorly enforced

Elections:
President—last held 4 December 1988 (next to be held December 1993); results—Carlos Andrés PÉREZ (AD) 54.6%, Eduardo FERNÁNDEZ (COPEI) 41.7%, other 3.7%;
Senate—last held 4 December 1988 (next to be held December 1993); results—percent of vote by party NA; seats—(49 total) AD 23, COPEI 22, other 4; note—3 former presidents (1 from AD, 2 from COPEI) hold lifetime senate seats;
Chamber of Deputies—last held 4 December 1988 (next to be held December 1993); results—AD 43.7%, COPEI 31.4%, MAS 10.3%, other 14.6%; seats—(201 total) AD 97, COPEI 67, MAS 18, other 19

Communists: 10,000 members (est.)

Other political or pressure groups: FEDECAMARAS, a conservative business group; Venezuelan Confederation of Workers, the Democratic Action-dominated labor organization

Member of: AG, CDB, CG, ECLAC, FAO, G-3, G-11, G-19, G-24, G-77, GATT, IADB, IAEA, IBRD, ICAO, ICC, ICFTU, IFAD, IFC, ILO, IMF, IMO, INTELSAT, INTERPOL, IOC, IOM, ISO, ITU, LAES, LAIA, LORCS, NAM, OAS, OPANAL, OPEC, PCA, RG, UN, UNCTAD, UNESCO, UNHCR, UNIDO, UPU, WFTU, WHO, WIPO, WMO, WTO

Diplomatic representation: Ambassador Simón Alberto CONSALVI Bottaro; Chancery at 2445 Massachusetts Avenue NW, Washington DC 20008; telephone (202) 797-3800; there are Venezuelan Consulates General in Baltimore, Boston, Chicago, Houston, Miami, New Orleans, New York, Philadelphia, San Francisco, and San Juan (Puerto Rico);
US—Ambassador Michael Martin SKOL; Embassy at Avenida Francisco de Miranda and Avenida Principal de la Floresta, Caracas (mailing address is P. O. Box 62291, Caracas 1060-A, or APO Miami 34037); telephone [58] (2) 285-3111 or 2222; there is a US Consulate in Maracaibo

Flag: three equal horizontal bands of yellow (top), blue, and red with the coat of arms on the hoist side of the yellow band and an arc of seven white five-pointed stars centered in the blue band

Economy

Overview: Petroleum is the cornerstone of the economy and accounted for 21% of GDP, 60% of central government revenues, and 81% of export earnings in 1989. President Pérez introduced an economic readjustment program when he assumed office in February 1989. Lower tariffs and price supports, a free market exchange rate, and market-linked interest rates have thrown the economy into confusion, causing about an 8% decline in GDP in 1989, but the economy recovered part way in 1990.

GDP: $42.4 billion, per capita $2,150; real growth rate 4.4% (1990 est.)

Inflation rate (consumer prices): 40.7% (1990)

Unemployment rate: 10.4% (1990)

Budget: revenues $8.4 billion; expenditures $8.6 billion, including capital expenditures of $5.9 billion (1989)

Exports: $12.1 billion (f.o.b., 1989 est.); *commodities*—petroleum 81%, bauxite and aluminum, iron ore, agricultural products, basic manufactures; *partners*—US 50.7%, Europe 13.7%, Japan 4.0% (1989)

Imports: $8.7 billion (f.o.b., 1989); *commodities*—foodstuffs, chemicals, manufactures, machinery and transport equipment; *partners*—US 44%, FRG 8.0%, Japan 4%, Italy 7%, Canada 2% (1989)

External debt: $33.2 billion (1990)

Industrial production: growth rate −11% (1989 est.); accounts for one-fourth of GDP, including petroleum

Electricity: 19,733,000 kW capacity; 54,660 million kWh produced, 2,780 kWh per capita (1990)

Industries: petroleum, iron-ore mining, construction materials, food processing, textiles, steel, aluminum, motor vehicle assembly

Agriculture: accounts for 6% of GDP and 16% of labor force; products—corn, sorghum, sugarcane, rice, bananas, vegetables, coffee, beef, pork, milk, eggs, fish; not self-sufficient in food other than meat

Illicit drugs: illicit producer of cannabis and coca leaf for the international drug trade on a small scale; however, large quantities of cocaine do transit the country

Economic aid: US commitments, including Ex-Im (FY70-86), $488 million; Communist countries (1970-89), $10 million

Currency: bolívar (plural—bolívares); 1 bolívar (Bs) = 100 céntimos

Exchange rates: bolívares (Bs) per US$1—51.331 (January 1991), 46.900 (1990), 34.6815 (1989), 14.5000 (fixed rate 1987-88), 8.0833 (1986), 7.5000 (1985)

Fiscal year: calendar year

Communications

Railroads: 542 km total; 363 km 1.435-meter standard gauge all single track, government owned; 179 km 1.435-meter gauge, privately owned

Highways: 77,785 km total; 22,780 km paved, 24,720 km gravel, 14,450 km earth roads, and 15,835 km unimproved earth

Inland waterways: 7,100 km; Río Orinoco and Lago de Maracaibo accept oceangoing vessels

Pipelines: 6,370 km crude oil; 480 km refined products; 4,010 km natural gas

Ports: Amuay Bay, Bajo Grande, El Tablazo, La Guaira, Puerto Cabello, Puerto Ordaz

Merchant marine: 58 ships (1,000 GRT or over) totaling 811,650 GRT/1,294,077 DWT; includes 1 short-sea passenger, 1 passenger cargo, 22 cargo, 1 container, 2 roll-on/roll-off cargo, 17 petroleum, oils, and lubricants (POL) tanker, 1 chemical tanker, 2 liquefied gas, 9 bulk, 1 vehicle carrier, 1 combination bulk

Civil air: 58 major transport aircraft

Airports: 296 total, 277 usable; 137 with permanent-surface runways; none with runways over 3,659 m; 13 with runways 2,440-3,659 m; 88 with runways 1,220-2,439 m

Telecommunications: modern and expanding; 1,440,000 telephones; stations—181 AM, no FM, 59 TV, 26 shortwave; 3 submarine coaxial cables; satellite communications ground stations—1 Atlantic Ocean INTELSAT and 3 domestic

Defense Forces

Branches: Ground Forces (Army), Naval Forces (including Navy, Marines, Coast Guard), Air Forces, Armed Forces of Cooperation (National Guard)

Manpower availability: males 15-49, 5,220,183; 3,782,548 fit for military service; 216,132 reach military age (18) annually

Defense expenditures: $1.9 billion, 4.3% of GDP (1991)

Vietnam

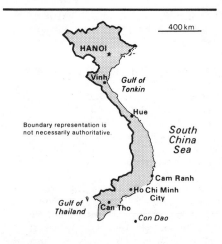

400 km

HANOI
Vinh
Gulf of
Tonkin
Hue
South
China
Sea
Cam Ranh
Ho Chi Minh
City
Gulf of
Thailand
Can Tho
Con Dao

Boundary representation is
not necessarily authoritative.

Geography

Total area: 329,560 km²; land area: 325,360
Comparative area: slightly larger than New Mexico
Land boundaries: 3,818 km total; Cambodia 982 km, China 1,281 km, Laos 1,555 km
Coastline: 3,444 km (excluding islands)
Maritime claims:
Contiguous zone: 24 nm;
Continental shelf: edge of continental margin or 200 nm;
Exclusive economic zone: 200 nm;
Territorial sea: 12 nm
Disputes: offshore islands and three sections of the boundary with Cambodia are in dispute; maritime boundary with Cambodia not defined; occupied Cambodia on 25 December 1978; sporadic border clashes with China; involved in a complex dispute over the Spratly Islands with China, Malaysia, Philippines, and Taiwan; unresolved maritime boundary with Thailand; maritime boundary dispute with China in the Gulf of Tonkin; Paracel Islands occupied by China but claimed by Vietnam and Taiwan; unresolved maritime boundary with Thailand
Climate: tropical in south; monsoonal in north with hot, rainy season (mid-May to mid-September) and warm, dry season (mid-October to mid-March)
Terrain: low, flat delta in south and north; central highlands; hilly, mountainous in far north and northwest
Natural resources: phosphates, coal, manganese, bauxite, chromate, offshore oil deposits, forests
Land use: arable land 22%; permanent crops 2%; meadows and pastures 1%; forest and woodland 40%; other 35%; includes irrigated 5%
Environment: occasional typhoons (May to January) with extensive flooding

People

Population: 67,568,033 (July 1991), growth rate 2.1% (1991)

Birth rate: 29 births/1,000 population (1991)
Death rate: 8 deaths/1,000 population (1991)
Net migration rate: -1 migrant/1,000 population (1991)
Infant mortality rate: 48 deaths/1,000 live births (1991)
Life expectancy at birth: 63 years male, 67 years female (1991)
Total fertility rate: 3.7 children born/woman (1991)
Nationality: noun—Vietnamese (sing. and pl.); adjective—Vietnamese
Ethnic divisions: predominantly Vietnamese 85-90%; Chinese 3%; ethnic minorities include Muong, Thai, Meo, Khmer, Man, Cham; other mountain tribes
Religion: Buddhist, Confucian, Taoist, Roman Catholic, indigenous beliefs, Islamic, Protestant
Language: Vietnamese (official), French, Chinese, English, Khmer, tribal languages (Mon-Khmer and Malayo-Polynesian)
Literacy: 88% (male 92%, female 84%) age 15 and over can read and write (1990 est.)
Labor force: 32.7 million; agricultural 65%, industrial and service 35% (1990 est.)
Organized labor: reportedly over 90% of wage and salary earners are members of the Vietnam Federation of Trade Unions (VFTU)

Government

Long-form name: Socialist Republic of Vietnam; abbreviated SRV
Type: Communist state
Capital: Hanoi
Administrative divisions: 41 provinces (tinh, singular and plural), 3 municipalities* (thành phô, singular and plural); An Giang, Bac Thai, Ben Tre, Binh Dinh, Cao Bang, Cuu Long, Dak Lak, Dong Nai, Dong Thap, Gia Lai-Kon Tum, Ha Bac, Hai Hung, Hai Phong*, Ha Nam Ninh, Ha Noi*, Ha Son Binh, Ha Tuyen, Hau Giang, Hoang Lien Son, Ho Chi Minh*, Khanh Hoa, Kien Giang, Lai Chau, Lam Dong, Lang Son, Long An, Minh Hai, Nghe Tinh, Phu Yen, Quang Binh, Quang Nam-Da Nang, Quang Ngai, Quang Ninh, Quang Tri, Song Be, Son La, Tay Ninh, Thai Binh, Thanh Hoa, Thua Thien, Thuan Hai, Tien Giang, Vinh Phu, Vung Tau-Con Dao; note—diacritical marks are not included
Independence: 2 September 1945 (from France)
Constitution: 18 December 1980
Legal system: based on Communist legal theory and French civil law system
National holiday: Independence Day, 2 September (1945)
Executive branch: chairman of the Council of State, Council of State, chairman of the Council of Ministers, Council of Ministers

Legislative branch: unicameral National Assembly (Quoc-Hoi)
Judicial branch: Supreme People's Court
Leaders:
Chief of State—Chairman of the Council of State Vo Chi CONG (since 18 June 1987);
Head of Government—Chairman of the Council of Ministers (Premier) Do MUOI (since 22 June 1988)
Political parties and leaders: only party—Vietnam Communist Party (VCP), Nguyen Van LINH
Suffrage: universal at age 18
Elections:
National Assembly—last held 19 April 1987 (next to be held April 1992); results—VCP is the only party; seats—(496 total) VCP or VCP-approved 496
Communists: nearly 2 million
Member of: ACCT, AsDB, ESCAP, FAO, G-77, IAEA, IBEC, IBRD, ICAO, IDA, IFAD, IFC, IIB, IMF, IMO, INTELSAT, IOC, ISO, ITU, LORCS, NAM, UN, UNCTAD, UNESCO, UNIDO, UPU, WCL, WFTU, WHO, WIPO, WMO, WTO
Diplomatic representation: none
Flag: red with a large yellow five-pointed star in the center

Economy

Overview: This is a centrally planned, developing economy with extensive government ownership and control of productive facilities. The economy is primarily agricultural; the sector employs about 65% of the labor force and accounts for almost half of GNP. Rice is the staple crop; substantial amounts of maize, sorghum, cassava, and sweet potatoes are also grown. The government permits sale of surplus grain on the open market. Most of the mineral resources are located in the north, including coal, which is an important export item. Oil was discovered off the southern coast in 1986 with production reaching 54,000 b/d in 1990 and expected to increase in the years ahead. Following the end of the war in 1975, heavy-handed government measures undermined efforts at an efficient merger of the agricultural resources of the south and the industrial resources of the north. The economy remains heavily dependent on foreign aid and has received assistance from Communist countries, Sweden, and UN agencies. Inflation, although down from recent triple-digit levels, is still a major weakness and is showing signs of accelerating upwards again. Per capita output is among the world's lowest. Since late 1986 the government has sponsored a broad reform program that seeks to turn more economic activity over to the private sector.
GNP: $15.2 billion, per capita $230; real growth rate 2.4% (1990 est.)

Inflation rate (consumer prices): 65% (1990 est.)
Unemployment rate: 33% (1990 est.)
Budget: revenues $892 million; expenditures $1.3 billion, including capital expenditures of $344 million (1990 est.)
Exports: $2.3 billion (f.o.b., 1990 est.); *commodities*—agricultural and handicraft products, coal, minerals, crude petroleum, ores, seafood; *partners*—USSR, Eastern Europe, Japan, Singapore
Imports: $2.6 billion (c.i.f., 1990 est.); *commodities*—petroleum products, steel products, railroad equipment, chemicals, medicines, raw cotton, fertilizer, grain; *partners*—USSR, Eastern Europe, Japan, Singapore
External debt: $16.8 billion (1990 est.)
Industrial production: growth rate 10% (1989); accounts for 30% of GNP
Electricity: 2,740,000 kW capacity; 7,500 million kWh produced, 110 kWh per capita (1990)
Industries: food processing, textiles, machine building, mining, cement, chemical fertilizer, glass, tires, oil, fishing
Agriculture: accounts for half of GNP; paddy rice, corn, potatoes make up 50% of farm output; commercial crops (rubber, soybeans, coffee, tea, bananas) and animal products other 50%; since 1989 self-sufficient in food staple rice; fish catch of 943,100 metric tons (1989 est.)
Economic aid: US commitments, including Ex-Im (FY70-74), $3.1 billion; Western (non-US) countries, ODA and OOF bilateral commitments (1970-88), $2.8 billion; OPEC bilateral aid (1979-89), $61 million; Communist countries (1970-89), $12.0 billion
Currency: new dong (plural—new dong); 1 new dong (D) = 100 xu
Exchange rates: new dong (D) per US$1—7,530 (May 1991), 7,280 (December 1990), 3,996 (March 1990), 2,047 (1988), 225 (1987), 18 (1986), 12 (1985); note—1985-89 figures are end of year
Fiscal year: calendar year

Communications

Railroads: 3,059 km total; 2,454 1.000-meter gauge, 151 km 1.435-meter standard gauge, 230 km dual gauge (three rails), and 224 km not restored to service
Highways: about 85,000 km total; 9,400 km bituminous, 48,700 km gravel or improved earth, 26,900 km unimproved earth
Pipelines: 150 km, refined products
Inland waterways: about 17,702 km navigable; more than 5,149 km navigable at all times by vessels up to 1.8 meter draft
Ports: Da Nang, Haiphong, Ho Chi Minh City

Merchant marine: 87 ships (1,000 GRT or over) totaling 364,596 GRT/539,174 DWT; includes 2 short-sea passenger, 69 cargo, 4 refrigerated cargo, 1 roll-on/roll-off cargo, 1 vehicle carrier, 8 petroleum, oils, and lubricants (POL) tanker, 2 bulk; note—Vietnam owns 11 cargo ships (1,000 GRT or over) totaling 106,759 DWT under the registry of Panama and Malta
Civil air: controlled by military
Airports: 100 total, 100 usable; 50 with permanent-surface runways; 10 with runways 2,440-3,659 m; 20 with runways 1,220-2,439 m
Telecommunications: 35,000 telephones in Ho Chi Minh City (1984); stations—16 AM, 1 FM, 2 TV; 2,300,000 TV sets; 6,000,000 radio receivers; at least 2 satellite earth stations, including 1 Indian Ocean INTELSAT

Defense Forces

Branches: Army, Navy (including Marines and Naval Infantry), Air Force
Manpower availability: males 15-49, 16,260,120; 10,377,105 fit for military service; 809,617 reach military age (17) annually
Defense expenditures: $NA, 19.4% of GNP (1986 est.)

Virgin Islands
(territory of the US)

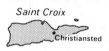

Geography

Total area: 352 km²; land area: 349 km²
Comparative area: slightly less than twice the size of Washington, DC
Land boundaries: none
Coastline: 188 km
Maritime claims:
Contiguous zone: 12 nm;
Continental shelf: 200 m (depth);
Exclusive economic zone: 200 nm;
Territorial sea: 12 nm
Climate: subtropical, tempered by easterly tradewinds, relatively low humidity, little seasonal temperature variation; rainy season May to November
Terrain: mostly hilly to rugged and mountainous with little level land
Natural resources: sun, sand, sea, surf
Land use: arable land 15%; permanent crops 6%; meadows and pastures 26%; forest and woodland 6%; other 47%
Environment: rarely affected by hurricanes; subject to frequent severe droughts, floods, earthquakes; lack of natural freshwater resources
Note: important location 1,770 km southeast of Miami and 65 km east of Puerto Rico, along the Anegada Passage—a key shipping lane for the Panama Canal; Saint Thomas has one of the best natural, deepwater harbors in the Caribbean

People

Population: 99,404 (July 1991), growth rate 0.7% (1991)
Birth rate: 22 births/1,000 population (1991)
Death rate: 5 deaths/1,000 population (1991)
Net migration rate: −10 migrants/1,000 population (1991)
Infant mortality rate: 19 deaths/1,000 live births (1991)
Life expectancy at birth: 70 years male, 76 years female (1991)

Virgin Islands *(continued)*

Total fertility rate: 2.7 children born/woman (1991)
Nationality: noun—Virgin Islander(s); adjective—Virgin Islander
Ethnic divisions: West Indian (45% born in the Virgin Islands and 29% born elsewhere in the West Indies) 74%, US mainland 13%, Puerto Rican 5%, other 8%; black 80%, white 15%, other 5%; Hispanic origin 14%
Religion: Baptist 42%, Roman Catholic 34%, Episcopalian 17%, other 7%
Language: English (official), but Spanish and Creole are widely spoken
Literacy: NA% (male NA%, female NA%)
Labor force: 45,500 (1988)
Organized labor: 90% of the government labor force

Government

Long-form name: Virgin Islands of the United States
Type: organized, unincorporated territory of the US administered by the Office of Territorial and International Affairs, US Department of the Interior
Capital: Charlotte Amalie
Administrative divisions: none (territory of the US)
Independence: none (territory of the US)
Constitution: Revised Organic Act of 22 July 1954 serves as the constitution
Legal system: based on US
National holiday: Transfer Day (from Denmark to US), 31 March (1917)
Executive branch: US president, governor, lieutenant governor
Legislative branch: unicameral Senate
Judicial branch: US District Court handles civil matters over $50,000, felonies (persons 15 years of age and over), and federal cases; Territorial Court handles civil matters up to $50,000 small claims, juvenile, domestic, misdemeanors, and traffic cases
Leaders:
Chief of State and Head of Government—President George BUSH (since 20 January 1989), represented by Governor Alexander A. FARRELLY (since 5 January 1987); Lieutenant Governor Derek HODGE (since 5 January 1987)
Political parties and leaders: Democratic Party, Marilyn STAPLETON; Independent Citizens' Movement (ICM), Virdin BROWN; Republican Party, Charlotte-Poole DAVIS
Suffrage: universal at age 18; indigenous inhabitants are US citizens, but do not vote in US presidential elections
Elections:
Governor—last held NA 1986 (next to be held NA 1990); results—Alexander FARRELLY (Democratic Party) defeated Adelbert BRYAN (ICM);

Senate—last held 6 November 1990 (next to be held 3 November 1992); results—percent of vote by party NA; seats—(15 total) number of seats by party NA;
US House of Representatives—last held 6 November 1990 (next to be held 3 November 1992); results—the Virgin Islands elects one nonvoting representative
Member of: ECLAC (associate), IOC
Diplomatic representation: none (territory of the US)
Flag: white with a modified US coat of arms in the center between the large blue initials *V* and *I*; the coat of arms shows an eagle holding an olive branch in one talon and three arrows in the other with a superimposed shield of vertical red and white stripes below a blue panel

Economy

Overview: Tourism is the primary economic activity, accounting for more than 70% of GDP and 70% of employment. The manufacturing sector consists of textile, electronics, pharmaceutical, and watch assembly plants. The agricultural sector is small, most food being imported. International business and financial services are a small but growing component of the economy. The world's largest petroleum refinery is at Saint Croix.
GDP: $1.0 billion, per capita $9,000; real growth rate NA% (1985)
Inflation rate (consumer prices): NA%
Unemployment rate: 2.0% (1990)
Budget: revenues $470 million; expenditures $322 million, including capital expenditures of $NA (FY90)
Exports: $2.2 billion (f.o.b., 1988); *commodities*—refined petroleum products; *partners*—US, Puerto Rico
Imports: $3.7 billion (c.i.f., 1988); *commodities*—crude oil, foodstuffs, consumer goods, building materials; *partners*—US, Puerto Rico
External debt: $NA
Industrial production: growth rate 12%
Electricity: 358,000 kW capacity; 532 million kWh produced, 5,360 kWh per capita (1990)
Industries: tourism, petroleum refining, watch assembly, rum distilling, construction, pharmaceuticals, textiles, electronics
Agriculture: truck gardens, food crops (small scale), fruit, sorghum, Senepol cattle
Economic aid: Western (non-US) countries, ODA and OOF bilateral commitments (1970-88), $34.5 million
Currency: US currency is used
Exchange rates: US currency is used
Fiscal year: 1 October-30 September

Communications

Highways: 856 km total
Ports: Saint Croix—Christiansted, Frederiksted; Saint Thomas—Long Bay, Crown Bay, Red Hook; Saint John—Cruz Bay
Airports: 2 total, 2 usable; 2 with permanent-surface runways 1,220-2,439 m; international airports on Saint Thomas and Saint Croix
Telecommunications: 44,280 telephones; stations—4 AM, 6 FM, 3 TV; modern system using fiber-optic cable, submarine cable, microwave radio, and satellite facilities; 90,000 radios; 56,000 TVs

Defense Forces

Note: defense is the responsibility of the US

Wake Island
(territory of the US)

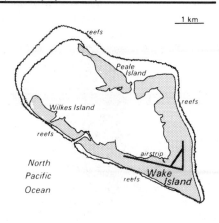

Geography

Total area: 6.5 km²; land area: 6.5 km²
Comparative area: about 11 times the size of The Mall in Washington, DC
Land boundaries: none
Coastline: 19.3 km
Maritime claims:
Contiguous zone: 12 nm;
Continental shelf: 200 m (depth);
Exclusive economic zone: 200 nm;
Territorial sea: 12 nm
Disputes: claimed by the Republic of the Marshall Islands
Climate: tropical
Terrain: atoll of three coral islands built up on an underwater volcano; central lagoon is former crater, islands are part of the rim; average elevation less than four meters
Natural resources: none
Land use: arable land 0%; permanent crops 0%; meadows and pastures 0%; forest and woodland 0%; other 100%
Environment: subject to occasional typhoons
Note: strategic location 3,700 km west of Honolulu in the North Pacific Ocean, about two-thirds of the way between Hawaii and the Northern Mariana Islands; emergency landing location for transpacific flights

People

Population: 195 (January 1990); no indigenous inhabitants; 302 temporary population
Note: population peaked about 1970 with over 1,600 persons during the Vietnam conflict

Government

Long-form name: none
Type: unincorporated territory of the US administered by the US Air Force (under an agreement with the US Department of Interior) since 24 June 1972
Flag: the US flag is used

Economy

Overview: Economic activity is limited to providing services to US military personnel and contractors located on the island. All food and manufactured goods must be imported.
Electricity: supplied by US military

Communications

Ports: none; because of the reefs, there are only two offshore anchorages for large ships
Airports: 1 with permanent-surface runways 2,440 to 3,659 m
Telecommunications: underwater cables to Guam and through Midway to Honolulu; AFRTS radio and television service provided by satellite; stations—1 AM, no FM, no TV
Note: formerly an important commercial aviation base, now used only by US military and some commercial cargo planes

Defense Forces

Note: defense is the responsibility of the US

Wallis and Futuna
(overseas territory of France)

Geography

Total area: 274 km²; land area: 274 km²; includes Île Uvéa (Wallis Island), Île Futuna (Futuna Island), Île Alofi, and 20 islets
Comparative area: slightly larger than Washington, DC
Land boundaries: none
Coastline: 129 km
Maritime claims:
Exclusive economic zone: 200 nm;
Territorial sea: 12 nm
Climate: tropical; hot, rainy season (November to April); cool, dry season (May to October)
Terrain: volcanic origin; low hills
Natural resources: negligible
Land use: arable land 5%; permanent crops 20%; meadows and pastures 0%; forest and woodland 0%; other 75%
Environment: both island groups have fringing reefs
Note: located 4,600 km southwest of Honolulu in the South Pacific Ocean about two-thirds of the way from Hawaii to New Zealand

People

Population: 16,590 (July 1991), growth rate 3.0% (1991)
Birth rate: 28 births/1,000 population (1991)
Death rate: 6 deaths/1,000 population (1991)
Net migration rate: 8 migrants/1,000 population (1991)
Infant mortality rate: 30 deaths/1,000 population (1991)
Life expectancy at birth: 70 years male, 71 years female (1991)
Total fertility rate: 3.7 children born/woman (1991)
Nationality: noun—Wallisian(s), Futunan(s), or Wallis and Futuna Islanders; adjective—Wallisian, Futunan, or Wallis and Futuna Islander

Wallis and Futuna (continued)

Ethnic divisions: almost entirely Polynesian
Religion: largely Roman Catholic
Language: French, Wallisian (indigenous Polynesian language)
Literacy: 50% (male 50%, female 51%) at all ages can read and write (1969)
Labor force: NA
Organized labor: NA

Government

Long-form name: Territory of the Wallis and Futuna Islands
Type: overseas territory of France
Capital: Mata-Utu (on Île Uvéa)
Administrative divisions: none (overseas territory of France)
Independence: none (overseas territory of France)
Constitution: 28 September 1958 (French Constitution)
Legal system: French
National holiday: Taking of the Bastille, 14 July (1789)
Executive branch: French president, high administrator; note—there are three traditional kings with limited powers
Legislative branch: unicameral Territorial Assembly (Assemblée Territoriale)
Judicial branch: none; justice generally administered under French law by the chief administrator, but the three traditional kings administer customary law and there is a magistrate in Mata-Utu
Leaders:
Chief of State—President François MITTERRAND (since 21 May 1981);
Head of Government—Chief Administrator Roger DUMEC (since 15 July 1988)
Political parties and leaders: Rally for the Republic (RPR); Union Populaire Locale (UPL); Union Pour la Démocratie Française (UDF); Lua kae tahi (Giscardians); Mouvement des Radicaux de Gauche (MRG)
Suffrage: universal adult at age 18
Elections:
Territorial Assembly—last held 15 March 1987 (next to be held March 1992); results—percent of vote by party NA; seats—(20 total) RPR 7, UPL 6, UDF and Lua kae tahi 7;
French Senate—last held NA September 1989 (next to be held by September 1992); results—percent of vote by party NA; seats—(1 total) RPR 1;
French National Assembly—last held 12 June 1988 (next to be held by September 1992); results—percent of vote by party NA; seats—(1 total) MRG 1
Member of: FZ, SPC
Diplomatic representation: as an overseas territory of France, local interests are represented in the US by France
Flag: the flag of France is used

Economy

Overview: The economy is limited to traditional subsistence agriculture, with about 80% of the labor force earning its livelihood from agriculture (coconuts and vegetables), livestock (mostly pigs), and fishing. About 4% of the population is employed in government. Revenues come from French Government subsidies, licensing of fishing rights to Japan and South Korea, import taxes, and remittances from expatriate workers in New Caledonia. Wallis and Futuna imports food, fuel, clothing, machinery, and transport equipment, but its exports are negligible, consisting of copra and handicrafts.
GDP: $7.5 million, per capita $470; real growth rate NA% (1990 est.)
Inflation rate (consumer prices): NA%
Unemployment rate: NA%
Budget: revenues $2.7 million; expenditures $2.7 million, including capital expenditures of $NA (1983)
Exports: negligible;
commodities—copra, handicrafts;
partners—NA
Imports: $6.9 million (c.i.f., 1983);
commodities—foodstuffs, manufactured goods, transportation equipment, fuel;
partners—France, Australia, New Zealand
External debt: $NA
Industrial production: growth rate NA%
Electricity: 1,200 kW capacity; 1 million kWh produced, 70 kWh per capita (1990)
Industries: copra, handicrafts, fishing, lumber
Agriculture: dominated by coconut production, with subsistence crops of yams, taro, bananas, and herds of pigs and goats
Economic aid: Western (non-US) countries, ODA and OOF bilateral commitments (1970-88), $118 million
Currency: Comptoirs Français du Pacifique franc (plural—francs); 1 CFP franc (CFPF) = 100 centimes
Exchange rates: Comptoirs Français du Pacifique francs (CFPF) per US$1—93.28 (January 1991), 99.0 (1990), 115.99 (1989), 108.30 (1988), 109.27 (1987), 125.92 (1986), 163.35 (1985); note—linked at the rate of 18.18 to the French franc
Fiscal year: NA

Communications

Highways: 100 km on Île Uvéa, 16 km sealed; 20 km earth surface on Île Futuna
Inland waterways: none
Ports: Mata-Utu, Leava
Airports: 2 total; 2 usable; 1 with permanent-surface runways; none with runways over 2,439 m; 1 with runways 1,220-2,439 m
Telecommunications: 225 telephones; stations—1 AM, no FM, no TV

Defense Forces

Note: defense is the responsibility of France

West Bank

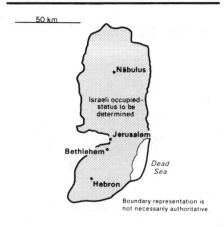

50 km

Nâbulus

Israeli occupied-status to be determined

Jerusalem

Bethlehem

Hebron

Dead Sea

Boundary representation is not necessarily authoritative.

Note: The war between Israel and the Arab states in June 1967 ended with Israel in control of the West Bank and the Gaza Strip, the Sinai, and the Golan Heights. As stated in the 1978 Camp David Accords and reaffirmed by President Reagan's 1 September 1982 peace initiative, the final status of the West Bank and the Gaza Strip, their relationship with their neighbors, and a peace treaty between Israel and Jordan are to be negotiated among the concerned parties. Camp David further specifies that these negotiations will resolve the respective boundaries. Pending the completion of this process, it is US policy that the final status of the West Bank and the Gaza Strip has yet to be determined. In the view of the US, the term West Bank describes all of the area west of the Jordan River under Jordanian administration before the 1967 Arab-Israeli war. However, with respect to negotiations envisaged in the framework agreement, it is US policy that a distinction must be made between Jerusalem and the rest of the West Bank because of the city's special status and circumstances. Therefore, a negotiated solution for the final status of Jerusalem could be different in character from that of the rest of the West Bank.

Geography

Total area: 5,860 km²; land area: 5,640 km²; includes West Bank, East Jerusalem, Latrun Salient, Jerusalem No Man's Land, and the northwest quarter of the Dead Sea, but excludes Mt. Scopus
Comparative area: slightly larger than Delaware
Land boundaries: 404 km total; Israel 307 km, Jordan 97 km;
Coastline: none—landlocked
Maritime claims: none—landlocked
Disputes: Israeli occupied with status to be determined
Climate: temperate, temperature and precipitation vary with altitude, warm to hot summers, cool to mild winters
Terrain: mostly rugged dissected upland, some vegetation in west, but barren in east

Natural resources: negligible

Land use: arable land 27%, permanent crops 0%, meadows and pastures 32%, forest and woodland 1%, other 40%

Environment: highlands are main recharge area for Israel's coastal aquifers

Note: landlocked; there are 175 Jewish settlements in the West Bank and 14 Israeli-built Jewish neighborhoods in East Jerusalem

People

Population: 1,086,081 (July 1991), growth rate 2.6% (1991); in addition, there are 90,000 Jewish settlers in the West Bank and 120,000 in East Jerusalem (1990 est.)

Birth rate: 37 births/1,000 population (1991)

Death rate: 6 deaths/1,000 population (1991)

Net migration rate: −4 migrants/1,000 population (1991)

Infant mortality rate: 47 deaths/1,000 live births (1991)

Life expectancy at birth: 65 years male, 69 years female (1991)

Total fertility rate: 4.9 children born/woman (1991)

Nationality: NA

Ethnic divisions: Palestinian Arab and other 88%, Jewish 12%

Religion: Muslim (predominantly Sunni) 80%, Jewish 12%, Christian and other 8%

Language: Arabic, Israeli settlers speak Hebrew, English widely understood

Literacy: NA% (male NA%, female NA%)

Labor force: NA; excluding Israeli Jewish settlers—small industry, commerce, and business 29.8%, construction 24.2%, agriculture 22.4%, service and other 23.6% (1984)

Organized labor: NA

Government

Long-form name: none

Note: The West Bank is currently governed by Israeli military authorities and Israeli civil administration. It is US policy that the final status of the West Bank will be determined by negotiations among the concerned parties. These negotiations will determine how the area is to be governed.

Economy

Overview: Economic progress in the West Bank has been hampered by Israeli military occupation and the effects of the Palestinian uprising. Industries using advanced technology or requiring sizable financial resources have been discouraged by a lack of financial resources and Israeli policy. Capital investment has largely gone into residential housing, not into productive assets that could compete with Israeli industry. A major share of GNP is derived from remittances of workers employed in Israel and neighboring Gulf states but remittances from the Gulf dropped dramatically in the wake of Iraq's invasion of Kuwait in August 1990. Israeli reprisals against Palestinian unrest in the West Bank since 1987 have pushed unemployment up and lowered living standards. The Persian Gulf crisis of 1990-91 also dealt a blow to the economy. Many Palestinians returned from the Gulf, exacerbating unemployment. Export revenues have plunged because of the loss of export markets in Jordan and the Gulf.

GNP: $1.0 billion, per capita $1,000; real growth rate −15% (1988 est.)

Inflation rate (consumer prices): NA%

Unemployment rate: 40% (1990 est.)

Budget: revenues $47.4 million; expenditures $45.7 million, including capital expenditures of NA (FY86)

Exports: $150 million (f.o.b., 1988 est.); *commodities*—NA; *partners*—Jordan, Israel

Imports: $410 million (c.i.f., 1988 est.); *commodities*—NA; *partners*—Jordan, Israel

External debt: $NA

Industrial production: growth rate NA%

Electricity: power supplied by Israel

Industries: generally small family businesses that produce cement, textiles, soap, olive-wood carvings, and mother-of-pearl souvenirs; the Israelis have established some small-scale modern industries in the settlements and industrial centers

Agriculture: olives, citrus and other fruits, vegetables, beef, and dairy products

Economic aid: none

Currency: new Israeli shekel (plural—shekels) and Jordanian dinar (plural—dinars); 1 new Israeli shekel (NIS) = 100 new agorot and 1 Jordanian dinar (JD) = 1,000 fils

Exchange rates: new Israeli shekels (NIS) per US$1—2.35 (May 1991), 2.0161 (1990), 1.9164 (1989), 1.5989 (1988), 1.5946 (1987), 1.4878 (1986), 1.1788 (1985); Jordanian dinars (JD) per US$1—0.6670 (January 1991), 0.6636 (1990), 0.5704 (1989), 0.3709 (1988), 0.3387 (1987), 0.3499 (1986), 0.3940 (1985)

Fiscal year: previously 1 April-31 March; FY91 will be 1 April-31 December and starting 1 January 1992 the fiscal year will conform to the calendar year

Communications

Highways: small indigenous road network, Israelis developing east-west axial highways

Airports: 2 total, 2 usable; 2 with permanent-surface runways; none with runways over 2,439 m; 1 with runways 1,220-2,439 m

Telecommunications: open-wire telephone system currently being upgraded; stations—no AM, no FM, no TV

Defense Forces

Branches: NA

Manpower availability: males 15-49, 257,740; NA fit for military service

Defense expenditures: $NA, NA% of GDP

Western Sahara

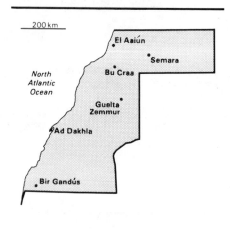

Geography

Total area: 266,000 km²; land area: 266,000 km²

Comparative area: slightly smaller than Colorado

Land boundaries: 2,046 km total; Algeria 42 km, Mauritania 1,561 km, Morocco 443 km

Coastline: 1,110 km

Maritime claims: contingent upon resolution of sovereignty issue

Disputes: claimed and administered by Morocco, but sovereignty is unresolved and guerrilla fighting continues in the area

Climate: hot, dry desert; rain is rare; cold offshore currents produce fog and heavy dew

Terrain: mostly low, flat desert with large areas of rocky or sandy surfaces rising to small mountains in south and northeast

Natural resources: phosphates, iron ore

Land use: arable land NEGL%; permanent crops 0%; meadows and pastures 19%; forest and woodland 0%; other 81%

Environment: hot, dry, dust/sand-laden sirocco wind can occur during winter and spring; widespread harmattan haze exists 60% of time, often severely restricting visibility; sparse water and arable land

People

Population: 196,737 (July 1991), growth rate 2.6% (1991)

Birth rate: 48 births/1,000 population (1991)

Death rate: 23 deaths/1,000 population (1991)

Net migration rate: 1 migrant/1,000 population (1991)

Infant mortality rate: 177 deaths/1,000 live births (1991)

Life expectancy at birth: 39 years male, 41 years female (1991)

Total fertility rate: 7.3 children born/woman (1991)

Nationality: noun—Saharan(s), Moroccan(s); adjective—Saharan, Moroccan

Ethnic divisions: Arab and Berber

Religion: Muslim

Language: Hassaniya Arabic, Moroccan Arabic

Literacy: NA% (male NA%, female NA%)

Labor force: 12,000; 50% animal husbandry and subsistence farming

Organized labor: NA

Government

Long-form name: none

Type: legal status of territory and question of sovereignty unresolved; territory contested by Morocco and Polisario Front (Popular Front for the Liberation of the Saguia el Hamra and Rio de Oro), which in February 1976 formally proclaimed a government in exile of the Sahrawi Arab Democratic Republic (SADR); territory partitioned between Morocco and Mauritania in April 1976, with Morocco acquiring northern two-thirds; Mauritania, under pressure from Polisario guerrillas, abandoned all claims to its portion in August 1979; Morocco moved to occupy that sector shortly thereafter and has since asserted administrative control; the Polisario's government in exile was seated as an OAU member in 1984; guerrilla activities continue sporadically.

Capital: none

Administrative divisions: none (under de facto control of Morocco)

Leaders: none

Member of: none

Diplomatic representation: none

Economy

Overview: Western Sahara, a territory poor in natural resources and having little rainfall, has a per capita GDP of just a few hundred dollars. Fishing and phosphate mining are the principal industries and sources of income. Most of the food for the urban population must be imported. All trade and other economic activities are controlled by the Moroccan Government.

GDP: $NA, per capita $NA; real growth rate NA%

Inflation rate (consumer prices): NA%

Unemployment rate: NA%

Budget: revenues $NA; expenditures $NA, including capital expenditures of $NA

Exports: $8 million (f.o.b., 1982 est.); *commodities*—phosphates 62%; *partners*—Morocco claims and administers Western Sahara, so trade partners are included in overall Moroccan accounts

Imports: $30 million (c.i.f., 1982 est.); *commodities*—fuel for fishing fleet, foodstuffs; *partners*—Morocco claims and administers Western Sahara, so trade partners are included in overall Moroccan accounts

External debt: $NA

Industrial production: growth rate NA%

Electricity: 60,000 kW capacity; 79 million kWh produced, 425 kWh per capita (1989)

Industries: phosphate, fishing, handicrafts

Agriculture: limited largely to subsistence agriculture; some barley is grown in non-drought years; fruit and vegetables are grown in the few oases; food imports are essential; camels, sheep, and goats are kept by the nomadic natives; cash economy exists largely for the garrison forces

Economic aid: NA

Currency: Moroccan dirham (plural—dirhams); 1 Moroccan dirham (DH) = 100 centimes

Exchange rates: Moroccan dirhams (DH) per US$1—8.071 (January 1991), 8.242 (1990), 8.488 (1989), 8.209 (1988), 8.359 (1987), 9.104 (1986), 10.062 (1985)

Fiscal year: NA

Communications

Highways: 6,100 km total; 1,350 km surfaced, 4,750 km improved and unimproved earth roads and tracks

Ports: El Aaiun, Ad Dakhla

Airports: 16 total, 14 usable; 3 with permanent-surface runways; none with runways over 3,659 m; 3 with runways 2,440-3,659 m; 6 with runways 1,220-2,439 m

Telecommunications: sparse and limited system; tied into Morocco's system by radio relay, tropospheric scatter, and 2 Atlantic Ocean INTELSAT earth stations linked to Rabat, Morocco; 2,000 telephones; stations—2 AM, no FM, 2 TV

Defense Forces

Branches: NA

Manpower availability: NA

Defense expenditures: $NA, NA% of GDP

Western Samoa

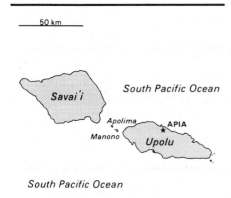

50 km

Savai'i

South Pacific Ocean

Apolima
APIA
Manono
Upolu

South Pacific Ocean

Geography

Total area: 2,860 km²; land area: 2,850 km²
Comparative area: slightly smaller than Rhode Island
Land boundaries: none
Coastline: 403 km
Maritime claims:
Exclusive economic zone: 200 nm;
Territorial sea: 12 nm
Climate: tropical; rainy season (October to March), dry season (May to October)
Terrain: narrow coastal plain with volcanic, rocky, rugged mountains in interior
Natural resources: hardwood forests, fish
Land use: arable land 19%; permanent crops 24%; meadows and pastures NEGL%; forest and woodland 47%; other 10%
Environment: subject to occasional typhoons; active volcanism
Note: located 4,300 km southwest of Honolulu in the South Pacific Ocean about halfway between Hawaii and New Zealand

People

Population: 190,346 (July 1991), growth rate 2.3% (1991)
Birth rate: 34 births/1,000 population (1991)
Death rate: 6 deaths/1,000 population (1991)
Net migration rate: −4 migrants/1,000 population (1991)
Infant mortality rate: 47 deaths/1,000 live births (1991)
Life expectancy at birth: 64 years male, 69 years female (1991)
Total fertility rate: 4.5 children born/woman (1991)
Nationality: noun—Western Samoan(s); adjective—Western Samoan
Ethnic divisions: Samoan; Euronesians (persons of European and Polynesian blood) about 7%, Europeans 0.4%
Religion: Christian 99.7% (about half of population associated with the London

Missionary Society; includes Congregational, Roman Catholic, Methodist, Latter Day Saints, Seventh-Day Adventist)
Language: Samoan (Polynesian), English
Literacy: 97% (male 97%, female 97%) age 15 and over can read and write (1971)
Labor force: 38,000; 22,000 employed in agriculture (1987 est.)
Organized labor: Public Service Association (PSA)

Government

Long-form name: Independent State of Western Samoa
Type: constitutional monarchy under native chief
Capital: Apia
Administrative divisions: 11 districts; A'ana, Aiga-i-le-Tai, Atua, Fa'asaleleaga, Gaga'emauga, Gagaifomauga, Palauli, Satupa'itea, Tuamasaga, Va'a-o-Fonoti, Vaisigano
Independence: 1 January 1962 (from UN trusteeship administered by New Zealand)
Constitution: 1 January 1962
Legal system: based on English common law and local customs; judicial review of legislative acts with respect to fundamental rights of the citizen; has not accepted compulsory ICJ jurisdiction
National holiday: National Day, 1 June
Executive branch: monarch, Executive Council, prime minister, Cabinet
Legislative branch: unicameral Legislative Assembly (Fono)
Judicial branch: Supreme Court, Court of Appeal
Leaders:
Chief of State—Susuga Malietoa TANUMAFILI II (Co-Chief of State from 1 January 1962 until becoming sole Chief of State on 5 April 1963);
Head of Government—Prime Minister TOFILAU Eti Alesana (since 7 April 1988)
Political parties and leaders: Human Rights Protection Party (HRPP), TOFILAU Eti, chairman; Samoan National Development Party (SNDP), VA'AI Kolone, chairman
Suffrage: universal adult at age NA, but only matai (head of family) are able to run for the Legislative Assembly
Elections:
Legislative Assembly—last held NA February 1991 (next to be held by February 1994); results—percent of vote by party NA; seats—(47 total) HRPP 30, SNDP 14, independent 3
Member of: ACP, AsDB, C, ESCAP, FAO, G-77, IBRD, ICFTU, IDA, IFAD, IFC, IMF, IOC, ITU, LORCS, SPC, SPF, UN, UNCTAD, UNESCO, UPU, WHO
Diplomatic representation: Ambassador Fili (Felix) Tuaopepe WENDT; Chancery (temporary) at the Western Samoan Mission to the UN, 820 2nd Avenue, New York, NY 10017 (212) 599-6196;

US—the ambassador to New Zealand, Della Newman, is accredited to Western Samoa (mailing address is P.O. Box 3430, Apia); telephone (685) 21-631
Flag: red with a blue rectangle in the upper hoist-side quadrant bearing five white five-pointed stars representing the Southern Cross constellation

Economy

Overview: Agriculture employs more than half of the labor force, contributes 50% to GDP, and furnishes 90% of exports. The bulk of export earnings comes from the sale of coconut oil and copra. The economy depends on emigrant remittances and foreign aid to support a level of imports about five times export earnings. Tourism has become the most important growth industry, and construction of the first international hotel is under way.
GDP: $115 million, per capita $620; real growth rate −4.5% (1990 est.)
Inflation rate (consumer prices): 17% (1990 est.)
Unemployment rate: NA%; shortage of skilled labor
Budget: revenues $70 million; expenditures $73 million, including capital expenditures of $41 million (1990)
Exports: $9.4 million (f.o.b., 1990 est.);
commodities—coconut oil and cream 54%, taro 12%, copra 9%, cocoa 3%;
partners—NZ 28%, EC 23%, American Samoa 23%, Australia 11%, US 6% (1990)
Imports: $87 million (c.i.f., 1990 est.);
commodities—intermediate goods 58%, food 17%, capital goods 12%;
partners—New Zealand 31%, Australia 20%, Japan 15%, Fiji 15%, US 5%, EC 4% (1987)
External debt: $83 million (December 1990 est.)
Industrial production: growth rate −4.3% (1990 est.); accounts for 14% of GDP
Electricity: 29,000 kW capacity; 45 million kWh produced, 240 kWh per capita (1990)
Industries: timber, tourism, food processing, fishing
Agriculture: accounts for 50% of GDP; coconuts, fruit (including bananas, taro, yams)
Economic aid: US commitments, including Ex-Im (FY70-89), $18 million; Western (non-US) countries, ODA and OOF bilateral commitments (1970-88), $291 million; OPEC bilateral aid (1979-89), $4 million
Currency: tala (plural—tala); 1 tala (WS$) = 100 sene
Exchange rates: tala (WS$) per US$1—2.3170 (January 1991), 2.3095 (1990), 2.2686 (1989), 2.0790 (1988), 2.1204 (1987), 2.2351 (1986), 2.2437 (1985)
Fiscal year: calendar year

Western Samoa (continued)

Communications

Highways: 2,042 km total; 375 km sealed; remainder mostly gravel, crushed stone, or earth
Ports: Apia
Merchant marine: 3 ships (1,000 GRT or over) totaling 24,930 GRT/34,135 DWT; includes 2 container, 1 roll-on/roll-off cargo
Civil air: 3 major transport aircraft
Airports: 3 total, 3 usable; 1 with permanent-surface runways; none with runways over 3,659 m; 1 with runways 2,440-3,659 m; none with runways 1,220-2,439 m
Telecommunications: 7,500 telephones; 70,000 radios; stations—1 AM, no FM, no TV; 1 Pacific Ocean INTELSAT station

Defense Forces

Branches: Department of Police and Prisons
Manpower availability: males 15-49, 49, 119; NA fit for military service
Defense expenditures: $NA, NA% of GDP

World

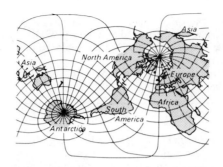

Geography

Total area: 510,072,000 km²; 361,132,000 km² (70.8%) is water and 148,940,000 km² (29.2%) is land
Comparative area: land area about 16 times the size of the US
Land boundaries: 442,000 km
Coastline: 359,000 km
Maritime claims:
Contiguous zone: generally 24 nm, but varies from 4 nm to 25 nm;
Continental shelf: generally 200 nm, but some are 200 meters in depth;
Exclusive fishing zone: most are 200 nm, but varies from 3 nm to 200 nm;
Exclusive economic zone: 200 nm; only the Maldives varies from 35-310 nm;
Territorial sea: generally 12 nm, but varies from 3 nm to 50 nm;
note—32 nations and miscellaneous areas are landlocked and include Afghanistan, Andorra, Austria, Bhutan, Bolivia, Botswana, Burkina, Burundi, Central African Republic, Chad, Czechoslovakia, Hungary, Iraq-Saudi Arabia Neutral Zone, Laos, Lesotho, Liechtenstein, Luxembourg, Malawi, Mali, Mongolia, Nepal, Niger, Paraguay, Rwanda, San Marino, Swaziland, Switzerland, Uganda, Vatican City, West Bank, Zambia, Zimbabwe
Disputes: major international land boundary disputes—Argentina-Uruguay, Bangladesh-India, Brazil-Paraguay, Brazil-Uruguay, Cambodia-Vietnam, Chad-Libya, China-India, China-USSR, Ecuador-Peru, Egypt-Sudan, El Salvador-Honduras, Ethiopia-Somalia, French Guiana-Suriname, Guyana-Suriname, Guyana-Venezuela, Israel-Jordan, Israel-Syria, North Korea-South Korea, Oman-UAE, Oman-Yemen, Qatar-UAE, Saudi Arabia-Yemen
Climate: two large areas of polar climates separated by two rather narrow temperate zones from a wide equatorial band of tropical to subtropical climates

Terrain: highest elevation is Mt. Everest at 8,848 meters and lowest depression is the Dead Sea at 392 meters below sea level; greatest ocean depth is the Marianas Trench at 10,924 meters
Natural resources: the oceans represent the last major frontier for the discovery and development of natural resources
Land use: arable land 10%; permanent crops 1%; meadows and pastures 24%; forest and woodland 31%; other 34%; includes irrigated 1.6%
Environment: large areas subject to severe weather (tropical cyclones), natural disasters (earthquakes, landslides, tsunamis, volcanic eruptions), overpopulation, industrial disasters, pollution (air, water, acid rain, toxic substances), loss of vegetation (overgrazing, deforestation, desertification), loss of wildlife resources, soil degradation, soil depletion, erosion

People

Population: 5,419,643,132 (July 1991), growth rate 1.7% (1991)
Birth rate: 26 births/1,000 population (1991)
Death rate: 9 deaths/1,000 population (1991)
Infant mortality rate: 66 deaths/1,000 live births (1991)
Life expectancy at birth: 61 years male, 65 years female (1991)
Total fertility rate: 3.3 children born/woman (1991)
Literacy: 74% (male 81%, female 67%) age 15 and over can read and write (1990 est.)
Labor force: 2.2 billion (1991)
Organized labor: NA

Government

Administrative divisions: 170 sovereign nations plus 72 dependent, other, and miscellaneous areas
Legal system: varies among each of the entities; 162 are parties to the United Nations International Court of Justice (ICJ) or World Court
Diplomatic representation: there are 159 members of the UN

Economy

Overview: In 1990 the world economy grew at an estimated 1.0%, considerably lower than the estimated 3.0% for 1989 and the 3.4% for 1988. The technologically advanced areas—North America, Japan, and Western Europe—together account for 67% of the gross world product (GWP) of $20.9 trillion; these developed areas grew in the aggregate at 2.3% in 1990. In contrast, output in the USSR and Eastern Europe fell an average of 5.2%; these countries account for

Yemen

15% of GWP. Experience in the developing countries continued mixed, with the newly industrializing economies generally maintaining their rapid growth, and many others struggling with debt, rampant inflation, and inadequate investment. This third group contributed 18% of GWP and grew on average 2.3% in 1990; output in this group is probably understated because of lack of data and the method of calculation used. The year 1990 witnessed continued political and economic upheavals in the USSR and Eastern Europe, which are in between systems, lacking both the rough discipline of the command economy and the institutions of the market economy. As for prospects in the 1990s, the addition of nearly 100 million people a year to an already overcrowded globe will exacerbate the problems of pollution, desertification, underemployment, epidemics, and famine.

GWP (gross world product): $20.9 trillion, per capita $3,930; real growth rate 1.0% (1990 est.)

Inflation rate (consumer prices): developed countries 5%; developing countries 100%, with wide variations (1990 est.)

Unemployment rate: NA%

Exports: $3.33 trillion (f.o.b., 1990 est.); *commodities*—the whole range of industrial and agricultural goods and services; *partners*—in value, 74% of exports from industrial countries

Imports: $3.45 trillion (c.i.f., 1990 est.); *commodities*—the whole range of industrial and agricultural goods and services; *partners*—in value, about 75% of imports by the industrial countries

External debt: $1.0 trillion for less developed countries (1990 est.)

Industrial production: growth rate 3% (1990 est.)

Electricity: 2,864,000,000 kW capacity; 11,450,000 million kWh produced, 2,150 kWh per capita (1990)

Industries: chemicals, energy, machinery, electronics, metals, mining, textiles, food processing

Agriculture: cereals (wheat, maize, rice), sugar, livestock products, tropical crops, fruit, vegetables, fish

Economic aid: NA

Communications

Ports: Mina al Ahmadi (Kuwait), Chiba, Houston, Kawasaki, Kobe, Marseille, New Orleans, New York, Rotterdam, Yokohama

Defense Forces

Branches: ground, maritime, and air forces at all levels of technology

Manpower availability: males 15-49, 1,412, 502,000; NA fit for military service

Defense expenditures: $1.1 trillion, 5.3% of GWP (1990 est.)

Geography

Total area: 527,970 km²; land area: 527,970 km²; includes Perim, Socotra, the former Yemen Arab Republic (YAR or North Yemen), and the former People's Democratic Republic of Yemen (PDRY or South Yemen)

Comparative area: slightly larger than twice the size of Wyoming

Land boundaries: 1,746 km total; Oman 288 km, Saudi Arabia 1,458 km

Coastline: 1,906 km

Maritime claims:

Contiguous zone: North—18 nm; South—24 nm;

Continental shelf: North—200 meters (depth); South—edge of continental margin or 200 nm;

Exclusive economic zone: North—no claim; South 200 nm;

Territorial sea: 12 nm

Disputes: undefined section of boundary with Saudi Arabia; Administrative Line with Oman

Climate: desert; hot and humid along west coast; temperate in western mountains; extraordinarily hot, dry, harsh desert in east

Terrain: narrow coastal plain backed by flat-topped hills and rugged mountains; dissected upland desert plains in center slope into the desert interior of the Arabian Peninsula

Natural resources: crude oil, fish, rock salt, marble; small deposits of coal, gold, lead, nickel, and copper; fertile soil in west

Land use: arable land 6%; permanent crops NEGL%; meadows and pastures 30%; forest and woodland 7%; other 57%; includes irrigated NEGL%

Environment: subject to sand and dust storms in summer; scarcity of natural freshwater resources; overgrazing; soil erosion; desertification

Note: controls Bab el Mandeb, the strait linking the Red Sea and the Gulf of Aden, one of world's most active shipping lanes

People

Population: 10,062,633 (July 1991), growth rate 3.2% (1991)

Birth rate: 51 births/1,000 population (1991)

Death rate: 16 deaths/1,000 population (1991)

Net migration rate: −3 migrants/1,000 population (1991)

Infant mortality rate: 121 deaths/1,000 live births (1991)

Life expectancy at birth: 49 years male, 51 years female (1991)

Total fertility rate: 7.4 children born/woman (1991)

Nationality: noun—Yemeni(s); adjective—Yemeni

Ethnic divisions: North—Arab 90%, Afro-Arab (mixed) 10%; South—almost all Arabs; a few Indians, Somalis, and Europeans

Religion: North—Muslim 100% (Sunni and Shi'a); South—Sunni Muslim, some Christian and Hindu

Language: Arabic

Literacy: 38% (male 53%, female 26%) age 15 and over can read and write (1990 est.)

Labor force: North—NA number of workers with agriculture and herding 70%, and expatriate laborers 30% (est.); South—477,000 with agriculture 45.2%, services 21.2%, construction 13.4%, industry 10.6%, commerce and other 9.6% (1983)

Organized labor: North—NA; South—348,200 and the General Confederation of Workers of the People's Democratic Republic of Yemen had 35,000 members

Government

Long-form name: Republic of Yemen

Type: republic

Capital: Sanaa

Administrative divisions: 17 governorates (muḥāfaẓat, singular—muḥāfaẓah); Abyan, 'Adan, Al Bayḍā', Al Ḥudaydah, Al Jawf, Al Mahrah, Al Maḥwīt, Dhamār, Ḥaḍramawt, Ḥajjah, Ibb, Laḥij, Ma'rib, Ṣa'dah, Şan'ā', Shabwah, Ta'izz

Independence: Republic of Yemen was established on 22 May 1990 with the merger of the Yemen Arab Republic [Yemen (Sanaa) or North Yemen] and the Marxist-dominated People's Democratic Republic of Yemen [Yemen (Aden) or South Yemen]; previously North Yemen had become independent on NA November 1918 (from the Ottoman Empire) and South Yemen had become independent on 30 November 1967 (from the UK); the union is to be solidified during a 30-month transition period, which coincides with the remainder of the five-year terms of both legislatures

Constitution: 16 April 1991

Yemen (continued)

Legal system: based on Islamic law, Turkish law, English common law, and local customary law; does not accept compulsory ICJ jurisdiction

National holiday: Proclamation of the Republic, 22 May (1990)

Executive branch: five-member Presidential Council (president, vice president, two members from northern Yemen and one member from southern Yemen), prime minister

Legislative branch: unicameral House of Representatives; note—northern Yemen's Consultative Assembly (Majlis Chura) and southern Yemen's Supreme People's Council (Majlis al-Sha'b al-A'la) will combine to form the basis for the new unicameral House of Representatives

Judicial branch: North—State Security Court; South—Federal High Court

Leaders:
Chief of State and Head of Government President 'Ali 'Abdallah SALIH (since 22 May 1990, the former president of North Yemen); Vice President Ali Salim al-BIDH (since 22 May 1990, secretary general of the Yemeni Socialist Party); Presidential Council Member Salim Salih MUHAMMED (southern Yemen); Presidential Council Member Kadi Abdul-Karim al-ARASHI (northern Yemen); Presidential Council Member Abdul-Aziz ABDUL-GHANI (northern Yemen); Prime Minister Haydar Abu Bakr al-'ATTAS (since 22 May 1990, former president of South Yemen)

Political parties and leaders: General People's Congress, 'Ali 'Abdallah SALIH; Yemeni Socialist Party (YSP; formerly South Yemen's ruling party—a coalition of National Front, Ba'th, and Communist Parties), Ali Salim al-BIDH

Suffrage: universal at age 18

Elections:
House of Representatives—last held NA (next to be held 26-27 May, 12 June, and 24 July 1991); results—percent of vote NA; seats—(301); number of seats by party NA; note—the 301 members of the new House of Representatives will come from North Yemen's Consultative Assembly (159 members), South Yemen's Supreme People's Council (111 members), and appointments by the New Presidential Council (31 members)

Communists: small number in North, greater but unknown number in South

Other political or pressure groups: conservative tribal groups, Muslim Brotherhood, leftist factions—pro-Iraqi Ba'thists, Nasirists, National Democratic Front (NDF)

Member of: ACC, AFESD, AL, AMF, CAEU, ESCWA, FAO, G-77, IBRD, ICAO, IDA, IDB, IFAD, IFC, ILO, IMF, IMO, INTELSAT, INTERPOL, IOC, ITU, LORCS, NAM, OIC, UN, UNCTAD, UNESCO, UNIDO, UPU, WFTU, WHO, WIPO, WMO, WTO

Diplomatic representation: Ambassador Muhsin Ahmad al-AYNI; Chancery at Suite 840, 600 New Hampshire Avenue NW, Washington DC 20037; telephone (202) 965-4760 or 4761; there is a Yemeni Consulate General in Detroit and a Consulate in San Francisco;
US—Ambassador Charles F. DUNBAR; Embassy at Dhahr Himyar Zone, Sheraton Hotel District, Sanaa (mailing address is P. O. Box 22347 Sanaa, Republic of Yemen or Sanaa—Department of State, Washington, D. C. 20521-6330); telephone [967] (2) 238-842 through 238-852

Flag: three equal horizontal bands of red (top), white, and black; similar to the flag of Syria which has two green stars and of Iraq which has three green stars (plus an Arabic inscription) in a horizontal line centered in the white band; also similar to the flag of Egypt which has a symbolic eagle centered in the white band

---

Economy

Overview: Whereas the northern city Sanaa is the political capital of a united Yemen, the southern city Aden, with its refinery and port facilities, is the economic and commercial capital. Future economic development depends heavily on Western-assisted development of promising oil resources. South Yemen's willingness to merge stemmed partly from the steady decline in Soviet economic support.
North—The low level of domestic industry and agriculture have made northern Yemen dependent on imports for virtually all of its essential needs. Large trade deficits have been made up for by remittances from Yemenis working abroad and foreign aid. Once self-sufficient in food production, northern Yemen has been a major importer. Land once used for export crops—cotton, fruit, and vegetables—has been turned over to growing qat, a mildly narcotic shrub chewed by Yemenis that has no significant export market. Oil export revenues started flowing in late 1987 and boosted 1988 earnings by about $800 million.
South—This has been one of the poorest Arab countries, with a per capita GNP of about $500. A shortage of natural resources, a widely dispersed population, and an arid climate have made economic development difficult. The economy has grown at an average annual rate of only 2-3% since the mid-1970s. The economy had been organized along socialist lines, dominated by the public sector. Economic growth has been constrained by a lack of incentives, partly stemming from centralized control over production decisions, investment allocation, and import choices.

GDP: $5.3 billion, per capita $545; real growth rate NA% (1990 est.)

Inflation rate (consumer prices):
North—16.9% (1988);
South—0% (1989)

Unemployment rate:
North—13% (1986);
South—NA%

Budget:
North—revenues $1.4 billion; expenditures $2.2 billion, including capital expenditures of $590 million (1988 est.);
South—revenues and grants $435 million; expenditures $1.0 billion, including capital expenditure of $460 million (1988 est.)

Exports:
North—$606 million (f.o.b., 1989);
commodities—crude oil, cotton, coffee, hides, vegetables;
partners—FRG 29%, US 26%, Netherlands 12%;
South—$113.8 million (f.o.b., 1989 est.);
commodities—cotton, hides, skins, dried and salted fish;
partners—Japan, North Yemen, Italy

Imports:
North—$1.3 billion (f.o.b., 1988);
commodities—textiles and other manufactured consumer goods, petroleum products, sugar, grain, flour, other foodstuffs, and cement;
partners—Saudi Arabia 12%, France 6%, US 5%, Australia 5% (1985);
South—$553.9 million (f.o.b., 1989 est.);
commodities—grain, consumer goods, crude oil, machinery, chemicals;
partners—USSR, UK, Ethiopia

External debt: $5.75 billion (December 1989 est.)

Industrial production:
North—growth rate 2% in manufacturing (1988);
South—growth rate NA% in manufacturing

Electricity: 670,000 kW capacity; 1,100 million kWh produced, 110 kWh per capita (1990)

Industries: crude oil production and petroleum refining; small-scale production of cotton textiles and leather goods; food processing; handicrafts; fishing; small aluminum products factory; cement

Agriculture:
North—accounted for 26% of GDP and 70% of labor force; farm products—grain, fruits, vegetables, qat (mildly narcotic shrub), coffee, cotton, dairy, poultry, meat, goat meat; not self-sufficient in grain;
South—accounted for 17% of GNP and 45% of labor force; products—grain, qat (mildly narcotic shrub), coffee, fish, livestock; fish and honey major exports; most food imported

Economic aid: US commitments, including Ex-Im (FY70-89), $389 million; Western (non-US) countries, ODA and OOF bilateral commitments (1970-88), $1.9 billion;

Yugoslavia

OPEC bilateral aid (1979-89), $3.2 billion; Communist countries (1970-89), $2.4 billion

Currency:
North Yemeni riyal (plural—riyals); 1 North Yemeni riyal (YR) = 100 fils; South Yemeni dinar (plural—dinars); 1 South Yemeni dinar (YD) = 1,000 fils

Exchange rates:
North Yemeni riyals (YR) per US$1— 9.7600 (January 1990), 9.7600 (1989), 9.7717 (1988), 10.3417 (1987), 9.6392 (1986), 7.3633 (1985); South Yemeni dinars (YD) per US$1— 0.3454 (fixed rate)

Fiscal year: calendar year

Communications

Highways: 15,500 km; 4,000 km bituminous, 11,500 km natural surface (est.)

Pipelines: crude oil, 424 km; refined products, 32 km

Ports: Aden, Al Hudaydah, Al Khalf, Mocha, Nishtūn, Ra's Kathib, Ṣalīf

Merchant marine: 3 ships (1,000 GRT or over) totaling 4,309 GRT/6,568 DWT; includes 2 cargo, 1 petroleum, oils, and lubricants (POL) tanker

Civil air: 15 major transport aircraft

Airports: 49 total, 40 usable; 10 with permanent-surface runways; none with runways over 3,659 m; 20 with runways 2,440-3,659 m; 12 with runways 1,220-2,439 m

Telecommunications: the North has a poor but improving system with new radio relay and cable networks, while the South has a small system of open-wire, radio relay, multiconductor cable, and radio communications stations; 65,000 telephones (est.); stations—4 AM, no FM, 22 TV; satellite earth stations—2 Indian Ocean INTELSAT, 1 Atlantic Ocean INTELSAT, 1 Intersputnik, 2 ARABSAT; radio relay to Saudi Arabia, and Djibouti

Defense Forces

Branches: Army, Navy, Air Force, Police

Manpower availability: males 15-49, 1,906,887; 1,084,122 fit for military service; 134,158 reach military age (14) annually

Defense expenditures: $1.06 billion, 20% of GDP (1990)

Geography

Total area: 255,800 km²; land area: 255,400 km²

Comparative area: slightly larger than Wyoming

Land boundaries: 2,961 km total; Albania 486 km, Austria 311 km, Bulgaria 539 km, Greece 246 km, Hungary 631 km, Italy 202 km, Romania 546 km

Coastline: 3,935 km (including 2,414 km offshore islands)

Maritime claims:
Continental shelf: 200 m (depth) or to depth of exploitation;
Territorial sea: 12 nm

Disputes: Kosovo question with Albania; Macedonia question with Bulgaria and Greece

Climate: temperate; hot, relatively dry summers with mild, rainy winters along coast; warm summer with cold winters inland

Terrain: mostly mountains with large areas of karst topography; plain in north

Natural resources: coal, copper, bauxite, timber, iron ore, antimony, chromium, lead, zinc, asbestos, mercury, crude oil, natural gas, nickel, uranium

Land use: arable land 28%; permanent crops 3%; meadows and pastures 25%; forest and woodland 36%; other 8%; includes irrigated 1%

Environment: subject to frequent and destructive earthquakes

Note: controls the most important land routes from central and western Europe to Aegean Sea and Turkish straits

People

Population: 23,976,040 (July 1991), growth rate 0.6% (1991)

Birth rate: 14 births/1,000 population (1991)

Death rate: 9 deaths/1,000 population (1991)

Net migration rate: 0 migrants/1,000 population (1991)

Infant mortality rate: 21 deaths/1,000 live births (1991)

Life expectancy at birth: 70 years male, 76 years female (1991)

Total fertility rate: 1.9 children born/woman (1991)

Nationality: noun—Yugoslav(s); adjective—Yugoslav

Ethnic divisions: Serb 36.3%, Croat 19.7%, Muslim 8.9%, Slovene 7.8%, Albanian 7.7%, Macedonian 5.9%, Yugoslav 5.4%, Montenegrin 2.5%, Hungarian 1.9%, other 3.9% (1981 census)

Religion: Eastern Orthodox 50%, Roman Catholic 30%, Muslim 9%, Protestant 1%, other 10%

Language: Serbo-Croatian, Slovene, Macedonian (all official); Albanian, Hungarian

Literacy: 90% (male 96%, female 84%) age 15 and over can read and write (1981)

Labor force: 9,600,000; agriculture 22%, mining and manufacturing 27%; about 5% of labor force are guest workers in Western Europe (1986)

Organized labor: badly fractured labor movement, with no unified national labor federation; several republics have competing union federations within their borders

Government

Long-form name: Socialist Federal Republic of Yugoslavia; abbreviated SFRY

Type: federal republic in form; four of six republics have non-Communist governments

Capital: Belgrade

Administrative divisions: 6 republics (republike, singular—republika); Bosna i Hercegovina (Bosnia and Hercegovina), Crna Gora (Montenegro), Hrvatska (Croatia), Makedonija (Macedonia), Slovenija (Slovenia), Srbija (Serbia); note—there are two nominally autonomous provinces (autonomne pokajine, singular—autonomna pokajina) within Srbija—Kosovo and Vojvodina

Independence: 1 December 1918; independent monarchy established from the Kingdoms of Serbia and Montenegro, parts of the Turkish Empire, and the Austro-Hungarian Empire; SFRY proclaimed 29 November 1945

Constitution: 21 February 1974, amendments to the Constitution have passed the Federal Assembly and are being considered at the republic level

Legal system: mixture of civil law system and Communist legal theory; has not accepted compulsory ICJ jurisdiction; a new legal code is being formulated

National holiday: Proclamation of the Socialist Federal Republic of Yugoslavia, 29 November (1945)

Executive branch: president of the Presidency, vice president of the Presidency, Presidency, president of the Federal Executive

Council, two vice presidents of the Federal Executive Council, Federal Executive Council

Legislative branch: bicameral Federal (Skupština) consists of an upper chamber or Chamber of Republics and Provinces (Vece Republika i Pokrajina) and a lower chamber or Federal Chamber

Judicial branch: Federal Court (Savezna Sud), Constitutional Court

Leaders:

Chief of State—President of the Presidency Stjepan MESIC from Hrvatska (Croatia), one-year term expires 15 May 1992; Vice President of the Presidency Branko KOSTIC from Crna Gora (Montenegro), one-year term expires 15 May 1992; note—the offices of president and vice president rotate annually among members of the Presidency with the current vice president assuming the presidency and a new vice president selected from area which has gone the longest without filling the position (the current sequence is Hrvatska, Crna Gora, Vojvodina, Kosovo, Makedonija, Bosna i Hercegovina, Slovenija, and Srbija);

Head of Government—President of the Federal Executive Council Ante MARKOVIĆ (since 16 March 1989); Vice President of the Federal Executive Council Aleksandar MITROVIĆ (since 16 March 1989); Vice President of the Federal Executive Council Živko PREGL (since 16 March 1989)

Political parties and leaders: there are over 100 political parties operating, some only in one republic and others country-wide

Suffrage: at age 16 if employed, universal at age 18

Elections: direct federal elections may never be held because of inter-republic differences over Yugoslavia's future structure

Other political or pressure groups: there are no national political groups; all significant groups are found within the republics

Member of: AfDB, AG (observer), BIS, CCC, CERN (observer), CSCE, ECE, FAO, G-9, G-19, G-24, G-77, GATT, IADB, IAEA, IBRD, ICAO, ICC, IDA, IFAD, IFC, ILO, IMF, IMO, INTELSAT, INTERPOL, IOC, IOM (observer), ISO, ITU, LORCS, NAM, OECD (special), PCA, UN, UNAVEM, UNCTAD, UNESCO, UNHCR, UNIDO, UNIIMOG, UPU, WHO, WIPO, WMO, WTO

Diplomatic representation: Ambassador Dzevad MUJEZINOVIĆ; Chancery at 2410 California Street NW, Washington DC 20008; telephone (202) 462-6566; there are Yugoslav Consulates General in Chicago, Cleveland, New York, Pittsburgh, and San Francisco;

US—Ambassador Warren ZIMMERMAN; mailing address Box 5070, Belgrade or APO New York 09213-5070; telephone [38] (11) 645-655; there is a US Consulate General in Zagreb

Flag: three equal horizontal bands of blue (top), white, and red with a large red five-pointed star edged in yellow superimposed in the center over all three bands

Economy

Overview: For 20 years Communist Yugoslavia had been trying to replace the Stalinist command economy with a decentralized semimarket system that features worker self-management councils in all large plants. This hybrid system neared collapse in late 1989 when inflation soared. The government applied shock therapy in 1990 under an IMF standby program that provides tight control over monetary expansion, a freeze on wages, the pegging of the dinar to the deutsche mark, and a partial price freeze on energy, transportation, and communal services. This program brought hyperinflation to a halt and encouraged a rise in foreign investment. Since June 1990, however, inflation has rebounded and threatens to rise further in 1991. Estimated annual inflation for 1990 is 164%. Other huge problems remain: rising unemployment, the low quality of industrial output, and striking differences in income between the poorer southern regions and the comparatively well-off northern areas. Even so, political issues far outweigh economic problems in importance.

GNP: $120.1 billion, per capita $5,040; real growth rate −6.3% (1990 est.)

Inflation rate (consumer prices): 164% (1990)

Unemployment rate: 16% (1990)

Budget: revenues $6.4 billion; expenditures $6.4 billion, including capital expenditures of $NA (1990)

Exports: $13.3 billion (f.o.b., 1990 est.); *commodities*—raw materials and semimanufactures 50%, consumer goods 31%, capital goods and equipment 19%; *partners*—EC 53%, USSR and Eastern Europe 27%, less developed countries 12.9%, US 4.8%, other 2.3%

Imports: $17.6 billion (c.i.f., 1990 est.); *commodities*—raw materials and semimanufactures 79%, capital goods and equipment 15%, consumer goods 6%; *partners*—EC 53.5%, USSR and Eastern Europe 22.8%, less developed countries 15.4%, US 4.6%, other 3.7%

External debt: $18.0 billion, medium and long term (December 1990)

Industrial production: growth rate −10.9% (1990)

Electricity: 21,000,000 kW capacity; 83,400 million kWh produced, 3,500 kWh per capita (1990)

Industries: metallurgy, machinery and equipment, petroleum, chemicals, textiles, wood processing, food processing, pulp and paper, motor vehicles, building materials

Agriculture: diversified, with many small private holdings and large combines; main crops—corn, wheat, tobacco, sugar beets, sunflowers; occasionally a net exporter of corn, tobacco, foodstuffs, live animals

Economic aid: donor—about $3.5 billion in bilateral aid to non-Communist less developed countries (1966-89)

Currency: Yugoslav dinar (plural—dinars); 1 Yugoslav dinar (YD) = 100 paras; note—on 1 January 1990, Yugoslavia began issuing a new currency with 1 new dinar equal to 10,000 YD

Exchange rates: Yugoslav dinars (YD) per US$1—13.605 (January 1991), 11.318 (1990), 2.876 (1989), 0.252 (1988), 0.074 (1987), 0.038 (1986), 0.027 (1985); note—as of January 1991 the new dinar is linked to the German deutsche mark at the rate of 9 new dinars per 1 deustche mark

Fiscal year: calendar year

Communications

Railroads: 9,349 km total; (all 1.435-meter standard gauge) including 931 km double track, 3,760 km electrified (1988)

Highways: 122,062 km total; 73,527 km asphalt, concrete, stone block; 33,663 km macadam, asphalt treated, gravel, crushed stone; 14,872 km earth (1988)

Inland waterways: 2,600 km (1982)

Pipelines: 1,373 km crude oil; 2,900 km natural gas; 150 km refined products

Ports: Rijeka, Split, Koper, Bar, Ploce; inland port is Belgrade

Merchant marine: 277 ships (1,000 GRT or over) totaling 3,780,095 GRT/6,031,359 DWT; includes 3 passenger, 4 short-sea passenger, 133 cargo, 5 refrigerated cargo, 19 container, 10 roll-on/roll-off cargo, 3 multifunction large-load carrier, 9 petroleum, oils, and lubricants (POL) tanker, 3 chemical tanker, 2 combination ore/oil, 75 bulk, 11 combination bulk; note—Yugoslavia owns 13 ships (1,000 GRT or over) totaling 253,400 GRT/429,613 DWT under the registry of Liberia, Panama, and Cyprus

Civil air: 57 major transport aircraft

Airports: 179 total, 179 usable; 54 with permanent-surface runways; none with runways over 3,659 m; 23 with runways 2,440-3,659 m; 20 with runways 1,220-2,439 m

Telecommunications: 1.6 million telephones (97% automatic)—7,500 public telephone booths; stations—85 AM, 69 FM, 103 TV; 4.65 million radios; 4.1 million TVs (1990); 92% of country receives No. 1 television program (1990)

Defense Forces

Branches: Yugoslav People's Army—Ground Forces, Naval Forces, Air and Air Defense Forces, Frontier Guard, Territorial Defense Force, Civil Defense

Zaire

Manpower availability: males 15-49, 6,176,693; 5,001,024 fit for military service; 189,886 reach military age (19) annually

Defense expenditures: 70.85 billion dinars, 4-6% of GDP (1991 est.); note—conversion of defense expenditures into US dollars using the official administratively set exchange rate would produce misleading results

500 km

Boundary representation is not necessarily authoritative.

Geography

Total area: 2,345,410 km²; land area: 2,267,600 km²

Comparative area: slightly more than one-quarter the size of US

Land boundaries: 10,271 km total; Angola 2,511 km, Burundi 233 km, Central African Republic 1,577 km, Congo 2,410 km, Rwanda 217 km, Sudan 628 km, Uganda 765 km, Zambia 1,930 km

Coastline: 37 km

Maritime claims:

Territorial sea: 12 nm

Disputes: Tanzania-Zaire-Zambia tripoint in Lake Tanganyika may no longer be indefinite since it is reported that the indefinite section of the Zaire-Zambia boundary has been settled; long section with Congo along the Congo River is indefinite (no division of the river or its islands has been made)

Climate: tropical; hot and humid in equatorial river basin; cooler and drier in southern highlands; cooler and wetter in eastern highlands; north of Equator—wet season April to October, dry season December to February; south of Equator—wet season November to March, dry season April to October

Terrain: vast central basin is a low-lying plateau; mountains in east

Natural resources: cobalt, copper, cadmium, crude oil, industrial and gem diamonds, gold, silver, zinc, manganese, tin, germanium, uranium, radium, bauxite, iron ore, coal, hydropower potential

Land use: arable land 3%; permanent crops NEGL%; meadows and pastures 4%; forest and woodland 78%; other 15%; includes irrigated NEGL%

Environment: dense tropical rainforest in central river basin and eastern highlands; periodic droughts in south

Note: straddles Equator; very narrow strip of land is only outlet to South Atlantic Ocean

People

Population: 37,832,407 (July 1991), growth rate 3.3% (1991)

Birth rate: 46 births/1,000 population (1991)

Death rate: 13 deaths/1,000 population (1991)

Net migration rate: 0 migrants/1,000 population (1991)

Infant mortality rate: 99 deaths/1,000 live births (1991)

Life expectancy at birth: 52 years male, 56 years female (1991)

Total fertility rate: 6.2 children born/woman (1991)

Nationality: noun—Zairian(s); adjective—Zairian

Ethnic divisions: over 200 African ethnic groups, the majority are Bantu; four largest tribes—Mongo, Luba, Kongo (all Bantu), and the Mangbetu-Azande (Hamitic) make up about 45% of the population

Religion: Roman Catholic 50%, Protestant 20%, Kimbanguist 10%, Muslim 10%, other syncretic sects and traditional beliefs 10%

Language: French (official), Lingala, Swahili, Kingwana, Kikongo, Tshiluba

Literacy: 72% (male 84%, female 61%) age 15 and over can read and write (1990 est.)

Labor force: 15,000,000; agriculture 75%, industry 13%, services 12%; wage earners 13% (1981); population of working age 51% (1985)

Organized labor: National Union of Zairian Workers (UNTZA) was the only officially recognized trade union until April 1990; other unions are now in process of seeking official recognition

Government

Long-form name: Republic of Zaire

Type: republic with a strong presidential system

Capital: Kinshasa

Administrative divisions: 10 regions (régions, singular—région) and 1 town* (ville); Bandundu, Bas-Zaïre, Équateur, Haut-Zaïre, Kasai-Occidental, Kasai-Oriental, Kinshasa*, Maniema, Nord-Kivu, Shaba, Sud-Kivu

Independence: 30 June 1960 (from Belgium; formerly Belgian Congo, then Congo/Leopoldville, then Congo/Kinshasa)

Constitution: 24 June 1967, amended August 1974, revised 15 February 1978; amended 1990; new constitution to be promulgated in 1991

Legal system: based on Belgian civil law system and tribal law; has not accepted compulsory ICJ jurisdiction

National holiday: Anniversary of the Regime (Second Republic), 24 November (1965)

Executive branch: president, prime minister, Executive Council (cabinet)
Legislative branch: unicameral Legislative Council (Conseil Législatif)
Judicial branch: Supreme Court (Cour Suprême)
Leaders:
Chief of State—President Marshal MOBUTU Sese Seko Kuku Ngbendu wa Za Banga (since 24 November 1965);
Head of Government—Prime Minister MULUMBA Lukoji (since 15 March 1991)
Political parties and leaders: sole legal party until January 1991—Popular Movement of the Revolution (MPR); other parties include Democratic Social Christian Party (PDSC), Union for Democracy and Social Progress (UDPS), Union of Federalists and Independent Republicans (UFERI), and Congolese National Movement-Lumumba (MNC-L)
Suffrage: universal and compulsory at age 18
Elections:
President—last held 29 July 1984 (next to be held before December 1991); results—President MOBUTU was reelected without opposition;
Legislative Council—last held 6 September 1987 (next to be held in 1991, probably on a multiparty basis); results—MPR was the only party; seats—(210 total) MPR 210; note—MPR still holds majority of seats but some deputies have joined other parties
Communists: no Communist party
Member of: ACCT, ACP, AfDB, APC, CCC, CEEAC, CEPGL, CIPEC, ECA, FAO, G-19, G-24, G-77, GATT, IAEA, IBRD, ICAO, ICC, IDA, IFAD, IFC, ILO, IMF, IMO, INTELSAT, INTERPOL, IOC, ITU, LORCS, NAM, OAU, PCA, UN, UNCTAD, UNESCO, UNHCR, UNIDO, UPU, WCL, WHO, WIPO, WMO, WTO
Diplomatic representation: Ambassador TATANENE Manata; Chancery at 1800 New Hampshire Avenue NW, Washington DC 20009; telephone (202) 234-7690 or 7691; *US*—Ambassador Melissa F. WELLS; Embassy at 310 Avenue des Aviateurs, Kinshasa (mailing address is APO New York 09662); telephone [243] (12) 21532; there is a US Consulate General in Lubumbashi
Flag: light green with a yellow disk in the center bearing a black arm holding a red flaming torch; the flames of the torch are blowing away from the hoist side; uses the popular pan-African colors of Ethiopia

Economy

Overview: In 1990, in spite of large mineral resources and one of the most developed and diversified economies in Sub-Saharan Africa, Zaire had a GDP per capita of only about $200, one of the lowest on the continent. The country's chronic economic problems worsened in 1990, with copper production down 20% to a 20-year low, inflation near 250% compared with 100% in 1987-89, and IMF and most World Bank support suspended until the institution of agreed-on changes. Agriculture, a key sector of the economy, employs 75% of the population but generates under 25% of GDP. The main potential for economic development has been the extractive industries. Mining and mineral processing account for about one-third of GDP and two-thirds of total export earnings. Zaire is the world's largest producer of diamonds.
GDP: $6.6 billion, per capita $180; real growth rate −2% (1990 est.)
Inflation rate (consumer prices): 242% (1990)
Unemployment rate: NA%
Budget: revenues $685 million; expenditures $1.1 billion, does not include capital expenditures mostly financed by donors (1990)
Exports: $2.2 billion (f.o.b., 1989 est.);
commodities—copper 37%, coffee 24%, diamonds 12%, cobalt, crude oil;
partners—US, Belgium, France, FRG, Italy, UK, Japan, South Africa
Imports: $2.1 billion (f.o.b., 1989 est.);
commodities—consumer goods, foodstuffs, mining and other machinery, transport equipment, fuels;
partners—South Africa, US, Belgium, France, FRG, Italy, Japan, UK
External debt: $7.9 billion (December 1990 est.)
Industrial production: growth rate −3.1%; accounts for 30% of GDP (1988)
Electricity: 2,575,000 kW capacity; 5,550 million kWh produced, 150 kWh per capita (1990)
Industries: mining, mineral processing, consumer products (including textiles, footwear, and cigarettes), processed foods and beverages, cement, diamonds
Agriculture: cash crops—coffee, palm oil, rubber, quinine; food crops—cassava, bananas, root crops, corn
Illicit drugs: illicit producer of cannabis, mostly for domestic consumption
Economic aid: US commitments, including Ex-Im (FY70-89), $1.1 billion; Western (non-US) countries, ODA and OOF bilateral commitments (1970-88), $6.4 billion; OPEC bilateral aid (1979-89), $35 million; Communist countries (1970-89), $263 million
Currency: zaïre (plural—zaïre); 1 zaïre (Z) = 100 makuta
Exchange rates: zaïre (Z) per US$1— 2,113.55 (January 1991), 718.58 (1990), 381.445 (1989), 187.070 (1988), 112.403 (1987), 59.625 (1986), 49.873 (1985)
Fiscal year: calendar year

Communications

Railroads: 5,254 km total; 3,968 km 1.067-meter gauge (851 km electrified); 125 km 1.000-meter gauge; 136 km 0.615-meter gauge; 1,025 km 0.600-meter gauge
Highways: 146,500 km total; 2,550 km bituminous, 46,450 km gravel and improved earth; remainder unimproved earth
Inland waterways: 15,000 km including the Congo, its tributaries, and unconnected lakes
Pipelines: refined products 390 km
Ports: Matadi, Boma, Banana
Merchant marine: 4 ships (1,000 GRT or over) totaling 41,802 GRT/60,496 DWT; includes 1 passenger cargo, 3 cargo
Civil air: 38 major transport aircraft
Airports: 308 total, 255 usable; 24 with permanent-surface runways; 1 with runways over 3,659 m; 6 with runways 2,440-3,659 m; 71 with runways 1,220-2,439 m
Telecommunications: barely adequate wire and radio relay service; 31,200 telephones; stations—10 AM, 4 FM, 18 TV; satellite earth stations—1 Atlantic Ocean INTELSAT, 14 domestic

Defense Forces

Branches: Army, Navy, Air Force, paramilitary National Gendarmerie, paramilitary Civil Guard
Manpower availability: males 15-49, 8,240,412; 4,192,991 fit for military service
Defense expenditures: $49 million, 0.8% of GDP (1988)

Zambia

Boundary representation is not necessarily authoritative.

Geography

Total area: 752,610 km²; land area: 740,720 km²
Comparative area: slightly larger than Texas
Land boundaries: 5,664 km total; Angola 1,110 km, Malawi 837 km, Mozambique 419 km, Namibia 233 km, Tanzania 338 km, Zaire 1,930 km, Zimbabwe 797 km
Coastline: none—landlocked
Maritime claims: none—landlocked
Disputes: quadripoint with Botswana, Namibia, and Zimbabwe is in disagreement; Tanzania-Zaire-Zambia tripoint in Lake Tanganyika may no longer be indefinite since it is reported that the indefinite section of the Zaire-Zambia boundary has been settled
Climate: tropical; modified by altitude; rainy season (October to April)
Terrain: mostly high plateau with some hills and mountains
Natural resources: copper, cobalt, zinc, lead, coal, emeralds, gold, silver, uranium, hydropower potential
Land use: arable land 7%; permanent crops NEGL%; meadows and pastures 47%; forest and woodland 27%; other 19%; includes irrigated NEGL%
Environment: deforestation; soil erosion; desertification
Note: landlocked

People

Population: 8,445,724 (July 1991), growth rate 3.5% (1991)
Birth rate: 49 births/1,000 population (1991)
Death rate: 12 deaths/1,000 population (1991)
Net migration rate: −2 migrants/1,000 population (1991)
Infant mortality rate: 79 deaths/1,000 live births (1991)
Life expectancy at birth: 55 years male, 58 years female (1991)
Total fertility rate: 6.9 children born/woman (1991)
Nationality: noun—Zambian(s); adjective—Zambian
Ethnic divisions: African 98.7%, European 1.1%, other 0.2%
Religion: Christian 50-75%, Muslim and Hindu, remainder indigenous beliefs 1%
Language: English (official); about 70 indigenous languages
Literacy: 73% (male 81%, female 65%) age 15 and over can read and write (1990 est.)
Labor force: 2,455,000; 85% agriculture; 6% mining, manufacturing, and construction; 9% transport and services
Organized labor: about 238,000 wage earners are unionized

Government

Long-form name: Republic of Zambia
Type: multiparty system; on 17 December 1990, President Kenneth KAUNDA signed into law the constitutional amendment that officially reintroduced the multiparty system in Zambia and ending 17 years of one-party rule
Capital: Lusaka
Administrative divisions: 9 provinces; Central, Copperbelt, Eastern, Luapula, Lusaka, Northern, North-Western, Southern, Western
Independence: 24 October 1964 (from UK; formerly Northern Rhodesia)
Constitution: 25 August 1973
Legal system: based on English common law and customary law; judicial review of legislative acts in an ad hoc constitutional council; has not accepted compulsory ICJ jurisdiction
National holiday: Independence Day, 24 October (1964)
Executive branch: president, prime minister, Cabinet
Legislative branch: unicameral National Assembly
Judicial branch: Supreme Court
Leaders:
Chief of State—President Dr. Kenneth David KAUNDA (since 24 October 1964);
Head of Government—Prime Minister Gen. Malimba MASHEKE (since 15 March 1989)
Political parties and leaders: United National Independence Party (UNIP), Kenneth KAUNDA; Movement for Multiparty Democracy (MMD), Frederick CHILUBA; National Democratic Alliance (NADA), leader NA; Democratic Party, leader NA
Suffrage: universal at age 18
Elections:
President—last held 26 October 1988 (next to be held mid-1991); results—President Kenneth KAUNDA was reelected without opposition;
National Assembly—last held 26 October 1988 (next to be held mid-1991); results—UNIP was the only party; seats—(136 total, 125 elected) UNIP 125
Communists: no Communist party
Member of: ACP, AfDB, C, CCC, ECA, FAO, FLS, G-19, G-77, GATT, IAEA, IBRD, ICAO, IDA, IFAD, IFC, ILO, IMF, INTELSAT, INTERPOL, IOC, ITU, LORCS, NAM, OAU, SADCC, UN, UNCTAD, UNESCO, UNIDO, UNIIMOG, UPU, WCL, WHO, WIPO, WMO, WTO
Diplomatic representation: Ambassador Paul J. F. LUSAKA; Chancery at 2419 Massachusetts Avenue NW, Washington DC 20008; telephone (202) 265-9717 through 9721;
US—Ambassador Gordon L. STREET; Embassy at corner of Independence Avenue and United Nations Avenue, Lusaka (mailing address is P. O. Box 31617, Lusaka); telephone [2601] 228-595, 228-596, 228-598, 228-601, 228-602, 228-603, 251-419
Flag: green with a panel of three vertical bands of red (hoist side), black, and orange below a soaring orange eagle, on the outer edge of the flag

Economy

Overview: The economy has been in decline for more than a decade with falling imports and growing foreign debt. Economic difficulties stem from a sustained drop in copper production and ineffective economic policies. In 1990 real GDP stood only slightly higher than that of 10 years before, while an annual population growth of more than 3% has brought a decline in per capita GDP of 25% during the same period. A high inflation rate has also added to Zambia's economic woes in recent years.
GDP: $4.7 billion, per capita $580; real growth rate −2% (1990)
Inflation rate (consumer prices): 80% (1990)
Unemployment rate: NA%
Budget: revenues $1.5 billion; expenditures $1.5 billion, including capital expenditures of $300 million (1991 est.)
Exports: $1.1 million (f.o.b., 1990);
commodities—copper, zinc, cobalt, lead, tobacco;
partners—EC, Japan, South Africa, US
Imports: $1.1 million (c.i.f., 1990);
commodities—machinery, transportation equipment, foodstuffs, fuels, manufactures;
partners—EC, Japan, South Africa, US
External debt: $7.2 billion (December 1990)
Industrial production: growth rate 2.9% (1990); accounts for one-third of GDP
Electricity: 1,900,000 kW capacity; 8,245 million kWh produced, 1,050 kWh per capita (1989)
Industries: copper mining and processing, transport, construction, foodstuffs, beverages, chemicals, textiles, and fertilizer

Zambia *(continued)*

Agriculture: accounts for 15% of GDP and 85% of labor force; crops—corn (food staple), sorghum, rice, peanuts, sunflower, tobacco, cotton, sugarcane, cassava; cattle, goats, beef, eggs; marginally self-sufficient in corn

Economic aid: US commitments, including Ex-Im (1970-89), $484 million; Western (non-US) countries, ODA and OOF bilateral commitments (1970-88), $4.5 billion; OPEC bilateral aid (1979-89), $60 million; Communist countries (1970-89), $533 million

Currency: Zambian kwacha (plural—kwacha); 1 Zambian kwacha (ZK) = 100 ngwee

Exchange rates: Zambian kwacha (ZK) per US$1—43.2900 (January 1991), 28.9855 (1990), 12.9032 (1989), 8.2237 (1988), 8.8889 (1987), 7.3046 (1986), 2.7137 (1985)

Fiscal year: calendar year

Communications

Railroads: 1,266 km, all 1.067-meter gauge; 13 km double track

Highways: 36,370 km total; 6,500 km paved, 7,000 km crushed stone, gravel, or stabilized soil; 22,870 km improved and unimproved earth

Inland waterways: 2,250 km, including Zambezi and Luapula Rivers, Lake Tanganyika

Pipelines: 1,724 km crude oil

Ports: Mpulungu (lake port)

Civil air: 6 major transport aircraft

Airports: 121 total, 106 usable; 13 with permanent-surface runways; 1 with runways over 3,659 m; 4 with runways 2,440-3,659 m; 23 with runways 1,220-2,439 m

Telecommunications: facilities are among the best in Sub-Saharan Africa; high-capacity radio relay connects most larger towns and cities; 71,700 telephones; stations—11 AM, 3 FM, 9 TV; satellite earth stations—1 Indian Ocean INTELSAT and 1 Atlantic Ocean INTELSAT

Defense Forces

Branches: Army, Air Force, Police, paramilitary

Manpower availability: males 15-49, 1,755,585; 920,878 fit for military service

Defense expenditures: $NA, NA% of GDP

Zimbabwe

Geography

Total area: 390,580 km²; land area: 386,670 km²

Comparative area: slightly larger than Montana

Land boundaries: 3,066 km total; Botswana 813 km, Mozambique 1,231 km, South Africa 225 km, Zambia 797 km

Coastline: none—landlocked

Maritime claims: none—landlocked

Disputes: quadripoint with Botswana, Namibia, and Zambia is in disagreement

Climate: tropical; moderated by altitude; rainy season (November to March)

Terrain: mostly high plateau with higher central plateau (high veld); mountains in east

Natural resources: coal, chromium ore, asbestos, gold, nickel, copper, iron ore, vanadium, lithium, tin, platinum group metals

Land use: arable land 7%; permanent crops NEGL%; meadows and pastures 12%; forest and woodland 62%; other 19%; includes irrigated NEGL%

Environment: recurring droughts; floods and severe storms are rare; deforestation; soil erosion; air and water pollution

Note: landlocked

People

Population: 10,720,459 (July 1991), growth rate 2.9% (1991)

Birth rate: 41 births/1,000 population (1991)

Death rate: 8 deaths/1,000 population (1991)

Net migration rate: −3 migrants/1,000 population (1991)

Infant mortality rate: 61 deaths/1,000 live births (1991)

Life expectancy at birth: 60 years male, 64 years female (1991)

Total fertility rate: 5.6 children born/woman (1991)

Nationality: noun—Zimbabwean(s); adjective—Zimbabwean

Ethnic divisions: African 98% (Shona 71%, Ndebele 16%, other 11%); white 1%, mixed and Asian 1%

Religion: syncretic (part Christian, part indigenous beliefs) 50%, Christian 25%, indigenous beliefs 24%, a few Muslim

Language: English (official); Shona, Sindebele

Literacy: 67% (male 74%, female 60%) age 15 and over can read and write (1990 est.)

Labor force: 3,100,000; agriculture 74%, transport and services 16%, mining, manufacturing, construction 10% (1987)

Organized labor: 17% of wage and salary earners have union membership

Government

Long-form name: Republic of Zimbabwe

Type: parliamentary democracy

Capital: Harare

Administrative divisions: 8 provinces; Manicaland, Mashonaland Central, Mashonaland East, Mashonaland West, Masvingo (Victoria), Matabeleland North, Matabeleland South, Midlands

Independence: 18 April 1980 (from UK; formerly Southern Rhodesia)

Constitution: 21 December 1979

Legal system: mixture of Roman-Dutch and English common law

National holiday: Independence Day, 18 April (1980)

Executive branch: executive president, 2 vice presidents, Cabinet

Legislative branch: unicameral Parliament

Judicial branch: Supreme Court

Leaders:
Chief of State and Head of Government—Executive President Robert Gabriel MUGABE (since 31 December 1987); Co-Vice President Simon Vengai MUZENDA (since 31 December 1987); Co-Vice President Joshua M. NKOMO (since 6 August 1990)

Political parties and leaders: Zimbabwe African National Union-Patriotic Front (ZANU-PF), Robert MUGABE; Zimbabwe African National Union-Sithole (ZANU-S), Ndabaningi SITHOLE; Zimbabwe Unity Movement (ZUM), Edgar TEKERE

Suffrage: universal at age 18

Elections:
Executive President—last held 28-30 March 1990 (next to be held NA March 1995); results—Robert MUGABE 78.3%; Edgar TEKERE 21.7%;
Parliament—last held 28-30 March 1990 (next to be held NA March 1995); results—percent of vote by party NA; seats—(150 total, 120 elected) ZANU 117, ZUM 2, ZANU-S 1

Communists: no Communist party

Member of: ACP, AfDB, C, CCC, ECA, FAO, FLS, G-77, GATT, IAEA, IBRD, ICAO, IDA, IFAD, IFC, ILO, IMF, INTELSAT, INTERPOL, IOC, IOM (observer), ITU, LORCS, NAM, OAU, PCA, SADCC, UN, UNCTAD, UNESCO, UNIDO, UPU, WCL, WHO, WIPO, WMO, WTO

Diplomatic representation: Counselor (Political Affairs), Head of Chancery, Ambassador Stanislaus Garikai CHIGWEDERE; Chancery at 2852 McGill Terrace NW, Washington DC 20008; telephone (202) 332-7100;

US—Ambassador (vacant); Embassy at 172 Herbert Chitapo Avenue, Harare (mailing address is P. O. Box 3340, Harare); telephone [263] (4) 794-521

Flag: seven equal horizontal bands of green, yellow, red, black, red, yellow, and green with a white equilateral triangle edged in black based on the hoist side; a yellow Zimbabwe bird is superimposed on a red five-pointed star in the center of the triangle

Economy

Overview: Agriculture employs three-fourths of the labor force and supplies almost 40% of exports. The manufacturing sector, based on agriculture and mining, produces a variety of goods and contributes 35% to GDP. Mining accounts for only 5% of both GDP and employment, but supplies of minerals and metals account for about 40% of exports. Wide year-to-year fluctuations in agricultural production over the past six years have resulted in an uneven growth rate, one that on average matched the 3% annual increase in population.
GDP: $5.6 billion, per capita $540; real growth rate 4.2% (1990 est.)
Inflation rate (consumer prices): 13% (1989)
Unemployment rate: at least 20% (1990 est.)
Budget: revenues $2.7 billion; expenditures $3.3 billion, including capital expenditures of $330 million (FY91)
Exports: $1.7 billion (f.o.b., 1989); *commodities*—agricultural 35% (tobacco 20%, other 15%), manufactures 20%, gold 10%, ferrochrome 10%, cotton 5%; *partners*—Europe 55% (EC 40%, Netherlands 5%, other 10%), Africa 20% (South Africa 10%, other 10%), US 5%
Imports: $1.4 billion (c.i.f., 1989); *commodities*—machinery and transportation equipment 37%, other manufactures 22%, chemicals 16%, fuels 15%; *partners*—EC 31%, Africa 29% (South Africa 21%, other 8%), US 8%, Japan 4%
External debt: $2.96 billion (December 1989 est.)
Industrial production: growth rate 4.7% (1988 est.); accounts for 35% of GDP
Electricity: 2,036,000 kW capacity; 5,460 million kWh produced, 540 kWh per capita (1989)
Industries: mining, steel, clothing and footwear, chemicals, foodstuffs, fertilizer, beverage, transportation equipment, wood products

Agriculture: accounts for about 15% of GDP and employs 74% of population; 40% of land area divided into 4,500 large commercial farms and 42% in communal lands; crops—corn (food staple), cotton, tobacco, wheat, coffee, sugarcane, peanuts; livestock—cattle, sheep, goats, pigs; self-sufficient in food
Economic aid: US commitments, including Ex-Im (FY80-89), $389 million; Western (non-US) countries, ODA and OOF bilateral commitments (1970-88), $2.3 billion; OPEC bilateral aid (1979-89), $36 million; Communist countries (1970-89), $134 million
Currency: Zimbabwean dollar (plural—dollars); 1 Zimbabwean dollar (Z$) = 100 cents
Exchange rates: Zimbabwean dollars (Z$) per US$1—2.6724 (January 1991), 2.4480 (1990), 2.1133 (1989), 1.8018 (1988), 1.6611 (1987), 1.6650 (1986), 1.6119 (1985)
Fiscal year: 1 July-30 June

Communications

Railroads: 2,745 km 1.067-meter gauge; 42 km double track; 355 km electrified
Highways: 85,237 km total; 15,800 km paved, 39,090 km crushed stone, gravel, stabilized soil: 23,097 km improved earth; 7,250 km unimproved earth
Inland waterways: Lake Kariba is a potential line of communication
Pipelines: 8 km, refined products
Civil air: 12 major transport aircraft
Airports: 499 total, 415 usable; 23 with permanent-surface runways; 2 with runways over 3,659 m; 3 with runways 2,440-3,659 m; 35 with runways 1,220-2,439 m
Telecommunications: system was once one of the best in Africa, but now suffers from poor maintenance; consists of radio relay links, open-wire lines, and radio communications stations; 247,000 telephones; stations—8 AM, 18 FM, 8 TV; 1 Atlantic Ocean INTELSAT earth station

Defense Forces

Branches: Zimbabwe National Army, Air Force of Zimbabwe, Police Support Unit, Paramilitary Police, People's Militia
Manpower availability: males 15-49, 2,263,724; 1,399,354 fit for military service
Defense expenditures: $412.4 million, NA% of GDP (FY91 est.)

Taiwan

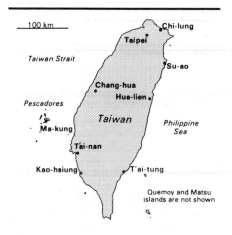

Geography

Total area: 35,980 km²; land area: 32,260 km²; includes the Pescadores, Matsu, and Quemoy
Comparative area: slightly less than three times the size of Connecticut
Land boundaries: none
Coastline: 1,448 km
Maritime claims:
Exclusive economic zone: 200 nm;
Territorial sea: 12 nm
Disputes: involved in complex dispute over the Spratly Islands with China, Malaysia, Philippines, and Vietnam; Paracel Islands occupied by China, but claimed by Vietnam and Taiwan; Japanese-administered Senkaku-shotō (Senkaku Islands/Diaoyu Tai) claimed by China and Taiwan
Climate: tropical; marine; rainy season during southwest monsoon (June to August); cloudiness is persistent and extensive all year
Terrain: eastern two-thirds mostly rugged mountains; flat to gently rolling plains in west
Natural resources: small deposits of coal, natural gas, limestone, marble, and asbestos
Land use: arable land 24%; permanent crops 1%; meadows and pastures 5%; forest and woodland 55%; other 15%; irrigated 14%
Environment: subject to earthquakes and typhoons

People

Population: 20,658,702 (July 1991), growth rate 1.1% (1991)
Birth rate: 16 births/1,000 population (1991)
Death rate: 5 deaths/1,000 population (1991)
Net migration rate: NEGL migrants/1,000 population (1991)
Infant mortality rate: 6 deaths/1,000 live births (19901
Life expectancy at birth: 72 years male, 78 years female (1991)

Total fertility rate: 1.8 children born/woman (1991)
Nationality: noun—Chinese (sing., pl.); adjective—Chinese
Ethnic divisions: Taiwanese 84%, mainland Chinese 14%, aborigine 2%
Religion: mixture of Buddhist, Confucian, and Taoist 93%, Christian 4.5%, other 2.5%
Language: Mandarin Chinese (official); Taiwanese and Hakka dialects also used
Literacy: 91.2% (male NA%, female NA%) age 15 and over can read and write (1990)
Labor force: 7,900,000; industry and commerce 53%, services 22%, agriculture 15.6%, civil administration 7% (1989)
Organized labor: 1,300,000 or about 18.4% (government controlled) (1983)

Administration

Long-form name: none
Type: one-party presidential regime; opposition political parties legalized in March, 1989
Capital: Taipei
Administrative divisions: the authorities in Taipei claim to be the government of all China; in keeping with that claim, the central administrative divisions include 2 provinces (sheng, singular and plural) and 2 municipalities* (shih, singular and plural)—Fu-chien (some 20 offshore islands of Fujian Province including Quemoy and Matsu), Kao-hsiung*, T'ai-pei*, and Taiwan (the island of Taiwan and the Pescadores islands); the more commonly referenced administrative divisions are those of Taiwan Province—16 counties (hsien, singular and plural), 5 municipalities* (shih, singular and plural), and 2 special municipalities** (chuan-shih, singular and plural); Chang-hua, Chia-i, Chia-i*, Chi-lung*, Hsin-chu, Hsin-chu*, Hua-lien, I-lan, Kao-hsiung, Kao-hsiung**, Miao-li, Nan-t'ou, P'eng-hu, P'ing-tung, T'ai-chung, T'ai-chung*, T'ai-nan, T'ai-nan*, T'ai-pei, T'ai-pei**, T'ai-tung, T'ao-yüan, and Yün-lin; the provincial capital is at Chung-hsing-hsin-ts'un; note—Taiwan uses the Wade-Giles system for romanization
Constitution: 25 December 1947, presently undergoing revision
Legal system: based on civil law system; accepts compulsory ICJ jurisdiction, with reservations
National holiday: National Day (Anniversary of the Revolution), 10 October (1911)
Executive branch: president, vice president, premier of the Executive Yüan, vice premier of the Executive Yüan, Executive Yüan
Legislative branch: unicameral Legislative Yüan
Judicial branch: Judicial Yüan
Leaders:
Chief of State—President LI Teng-hui (since 13 January 1988); Vice President LI Yuan-zu (since 20 May 1990);

Head of Government—Premier (President of the Executive Yüan) HAO Po-ts'un (since 2 May 1990); Vice Premier (Vice President of the Executive Yüan) SHIH Ch'i-yang (since NA July 1988)
Political parties and leaders: Kuomintang (Nationalist Party), LI Teng-hui, chairman; Democratic Socialist Party and Young China Party controlled by Kuomintang; Democratic Progressive Party (DPP); Labor Party; 27 other minor parties
Suffrage: universal at age 20
Elections:
President—last held 21 March 1990 (next to be held March 1996); results—President LI Teng-hui was reelected by the National Assembly;
Vice President—last held 21 March 1990 (next to be held March 1996); results—LI Yuan-zu was elected by the National Assembly;
Legislative Yüan—last held 2 December 1989 (next to be held December 1992); results—KMT 65%, DPP 33%, independents 2%; seats—(304 total, 102 elected) KMT 78, DPP 21, independents 3;
National Assembly:—originally elected in November 1947 (last supplementary election in December 1986; Assembly will be completely reelected in December 1991)
Member of: expelled from UN General Assembly and Security Council on 25 October 1971 and withdrew on same date from other charter-designated subsidiary organs; expelled from IMF/World Bank group April/May 1980; seeking to join GATT; attempting to retain membership in INTELSAT; suspended from IAEA in 1972, but still allows IAEA controls over extensive atomic development; AsDB, ICC, ICFTU, IOC
Diplomatic representation: none; unofficial commercial and cultural relations with the people of the US are maintained through a private instrumentality, the Coordination Council for North American Affairs (CCNAA) with headquarters in Taipei and field offices in Washington and 10 other US cities with all addresses and telephone numbers NA;
US—unofficial commercial and cultural relations with the people of Taiwan are maintained through a private institution, the American Institute in Taiwan (AIT), which has offices in Taipei at #7 Lane 134, telephone [886] (2) 709-2000, and in Kao-hsiung at #2 Chung Cheng 3d Road, telephone [886] (7) 224-0154 through 0157, and the American Trade Center at Room 3207 International Trade Building, Taipei World Trade Center, 333 Keelung Road Section 1, Taipei 10548, telephone [886] (2) 720-1550
Flag: red with a dark blue rectangle in the upper hoist-side corner bearing a white sun with 12 triangular rays

Economy

Overview: Taiwan has a dynamic capitalist economy with considerable government guidance of investment and foreign trade and partial government ownership of some large banks and industrial firms. Real growth in GNP has averaged about 9% a year during the past three decades. Export growth has been even faster and has provided the impetus for industrialization. Agriculture contributes about 4% to GNP, down from 35% in 1952. Taiwan currently ranks as number 13 among major trading countries. Traditional labor-intensive industries are steadily being replaced with more capital- and technology-intensive industries.
GNP: $150.8 billion, per capita $7,380; real growth rate 5.2% (1990)
Inflation rate (consumer prices): 4.4% (1990)
Unemployment rate: 1.7% (1990)
Budget: revenues $30.3 billion; expenditures $30.1 billion, including capital expenditures of $NA (FY91 est.)
Exports: $67.2 billion (f.o.b., 1990);
commodities—textiles 15.6%, electrical machinery 18.2%, general machinery and equipment 14.8%, basic metals and metal products 7.8%, foodstuffs 1.7%, plywood and wood products 1.6% (1989);
partners—US 36.2%, Japan 13.7% (1989)
Imports: $54.7 billion (c.i.f., 1990);
commodities—machinery and equipment 15.3%, crude oil 5%, chemical and chemical products 11.1%, basic metals 13.0%, foodstuffs 2.2% (1989);
partners—Japan 31%, US 23%, FRG 5% (1989)
External debt: $1.1 billion (December 1990 est.)
Industrial production: growth rate 4.7% (1990 est.)
Electricity: 17,000,000 kW capacity; 68,000 million kWh produced, 3,310 kWh per capita (1990)
Industries: electronics, textiles, chemicals, clothing, food processing, plywood, sugar milling, cement, shipbuilding, petroleum
Agriculture: accounts for 4% of GNP and 16% of labor force (includes part-time farmers); heavily subsidized sector; major crops—vegetables, rice, fruit, tea; livestock—hogs, poultry, beef, milk, cattle; not self-sufficient in wheat, soybeans, corn; fish catch increasing, 1.4 million metric tons (1988)
Economic aid: US, including Ex-Im (FY46-82), $4.6 billion; Western (non-US) countries, ODA and OOF bilateral commitments (1970-88), $445 million
Currency: New Taiwan dollar (plural—dollars); 1 New Taiwan dollar (NT$) = 100 cents

Exchange rates: New Taiwan dollars per US$1—27.2 (January 1991), 27.243 (November 1990), 26.407 (1989), 28.589 (1988), 31.845 (1987), 37.838 (1986), 39.849 (1985)
Fiscal year: 1 July-30 June

Communications

Railroads: about 4,600 km total track with 1,075 km common carrier lines and 3,525 km industrial lines; common carrier lines consist of the 1.067-meter gauge 708 km West Line and the 367 km East Line; a 98.25 km South Link Line connection is under construction; common carrier lines owned by the government and operated by the Railway Administration under Ministry of Communications; industrial lines owned and operated by government enterprises
Highways: 20,041 km total; 17,095 km bituminous or concrete, 2,371 km crushed stone or gravel, 575 km graded earth
Pipelines: 615 km refined products, 97 km natural gas
Ports: Kao-hsiung, Chi-lung (Keelung), Hua-lien, Su-ao, T'ai-tung
Merchant marine: 226 ships (1,000 GRT or over) totaling 6,557,167 GRT/9,153,646 DWT; includes 1 short-sea passenger, 52 cargo, 17 refrigerated cargo, 75 container, 15 petroleum, oils, and lubricants (POL) tanker, 3 combination ore/oil, 1 specialized tanker, 62 bulk
Airports: 38 total, 37 usable; 33 with permanent-surface runways; 3 with runways over 3,659 m; 16 with runways 2,440-3,659 m; 8 with runways 1,220-2,439 m
Telecommunications: best developed system in Asia outside of Japan; 7,800,000 telephones; extensive microwave transmission links on east and west coasts; stations—91 AM, 23 FM, 15 TV (13 relays); 8,620,000 radios; 6,386,000 TVs (5,680,000 color, 706,000 monochrome); earth stations—1 Pacific Ocean INTELSAT and 1 Indian Ocean INTELSAT; submarine cable links to Japan (Okinawa), the Philippines, Guam, Singapore, Hong Kong, Indonesia, Australia, Middle East, and Western Europe

---

Defense Forces

Branches: Army, Navy (including Marines), Air Force, Taiwan Garrison Command, Ministry of National Defense
Manpower availability: males 15-49, 5,874,345; 4,577,294 fit for military service; about 187,807 currently reach military age (19) annually
Defense expenditures: $9.10 billion, 4.5% of GDP (FY91)

Appendix A:

The United Nations System

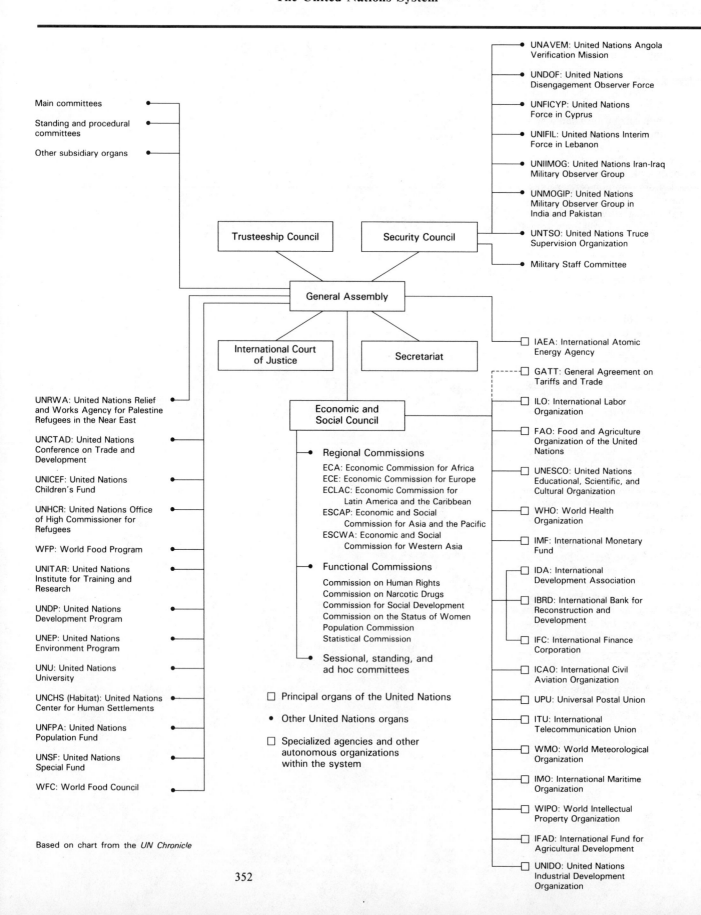

Main committees

Standing and procedural committees

Other subsidiary organs

Trusteeship Council

Security Council

UNAVEM: United Nations Angola Verification Mission

UNDOF: United Nations Disengagement Observer Force

UNFICYP: United Nations Force in Cyprus

UNIFIL: United Nations Interim Force in Lebanon

UNIIMOG: United Nations Iran-Iraq Military Observer Group

UNMOGIP: United Nations Military Observer Group in India and Pakistan

UNTSO: United Nations Truce Supervision Organization

Military Staff Committee

General Assembly

International Court of Justice

Secretariat

IAEA: International Atomic Energy Agency

GATT: General Agreement on Tariffs and Trade

ILO: International Labor Organization

Economic and Social Council

FAO: Food and Agriculture Organization of the United Nations

UNRWA: United Nations Relief and Works Agency for Palestine Refugees in the Near East

UNCTAD: United Nations Conference on Trade and Development

UNICEF: United Nations Children's Fund

UNHCR: United Nations Office of High Commissioner for Refugees

WFP: World Food Program

UNITAR: United Nations Institute for Training and Research

UNDP: United Nations Development Program

UNEP: United Nations Environment Program

UNU: United Nations University

UNCHS (Habitat): United Nations Center for Human Settlements

UNFPA: United Nations Population Fund

UNSF: United Nations Special Fund

WFC: World Food Council

● Regional Commissions

ECA: Economic Commission for Africa
ECE: Economic Commission for Europe
ECLAC: Economic Commission for Latin America and the Caribbean
ESCAP: Economic and Social Commission for Asia and the Pacific
ESCWA: Economic and Social Commission for Western Asia

● Functional Commissions

Commission on Human Rights
Commission on Narcotic Drugs
Commission for Social Development
Commission on the Status of Women
Population Commission
Statistical Commission

● Sessional, standing, and ad hoc committees

□ Principal organs of the United Nations

● Other United Nations organs

□ Specialized agencies and other autonomous organizations within the system

UNESCO: United Nations Educational, Scientific, and Cultural Organization

WHO: World Health Organization

IMF: International Monetary Fund

IDA: International Development Association

IBRD: International Bank for Reconstruction and Development

IFC: International Finance Corporation

ICAO: International Civil Aviation Organization

UPU: Universal Postal Union

ITU: International Telecommunication Union

WMO: World Meteorological Organization

IMO: International Maritime Organization

WIPO: World Intellectual Property Organization

IFAD: International Fund for Agricultural Development

UNIDO: United Nations Industrial Development Organization

Based on chart from the *UN Chronicle*

Appendix B:

International Organization and Group Abbreviations

A	ABEDA	Arab Bank for Economic Development in Africa
	ACC	Arab Cooperation Council
	ACCT	Agency for Cultural and Technical Cooperation
	ACP	African, Caribbean, and Pacific Countries
	AfDB	African Development Bank
	AFESD	Arab Fund for Economic and Social Development
	AG	Andean Group
	AL	Arab League
	ALADI	Asociación Latinoamericana de Integración; see Latin American Integration Association (LAIA)
	AMF	Arab Monetary Fund
	AMU	Arab Maghreb Union
	ANZUS	Australia-New Zealand-United States Security Treaty
	APEC	Asia Pacific Economic Cooperation
	AsDB	Asian Development Bank
	ASEAN	Association of Southeast Asian Nations
B	BAD	Banque Africaine de Développement; see African Development Bank (AfDB)
	BADEA	Banque Arabe de Développement Economique en Afrique; see Arab Bank for Economic Development in Africa (ABEDA)
	BCIE	Banco Centroamericano de Integración Económico; see Central American Bank for Economic Integration (BCIE)
	BDEAC	Banque de Développment des États de l'Afrique Centrale; see Central African States Development Bank (BDEAC)
	Benelux	Benelux Economic Union
	BID	Banco Interamericano de Desarvollo; see Inter-American Development Bank (IADB)
	BIS	Bank for International Settlements
	BOAD	Banque Ouest-Africaine de Développement; see West African Development Bank (WADB)
C	C	Commonwealth
	CACM	Central American Common Market
	CAEU	Council of Arab Economic Unity
	CARICOM	Caribbean Community and Common Market
	CCC	Customs Cooperation Council
	CDB	Caribbean Development Bank
	CE	Council of Europe
	CEAO	Communauté Economique de l'Afrique de l'Ouest; see West African Economic Community (CEAO)
	CEEAC	Communauté Economique des États de l'Afrique Centrale; see Economic Community of Central African States (CEEAC)
	CEMA	Council for Mutual Economic Assistance; also known as CMEA or Comecon; abolished 1 January 1991
	CEPGL	Communauté Economique des Pays des Grands Lacs; see Economic Community of the Great Lakes Countries (CEPGL)
	CERN	Conseil Européen pour la Recherche Nucléaire; see European Organization for Nuclear Research (CERN)
	CG	Contadora Group
	CMEA	Council for Mutual Economic Assistance (CEMA); also known as Comecon; abolished 1 January 1991

		COCOM	Coordinating Committee on Export Controls
		Comecon	Council for Mutual Economic Assistance (CEMA); also known as CMEA; abolished 1 January 1991
		CP	Colombo Plan
		CSCE	Conference on Security and Cooperation in Europe
	D	DC	developed country
	E	EADB	East African Development Bank
		EBRD	European Bank for Reconstruction and Development
		EC	European Community
		ECA	Economic Commission for Africa
		ECAFE	Economic Commission for Asia and the Far East; see Economic and Social Commission for Asia and the Pacific (ESCAP)
		ECE	Economic Commission for Europe
		ECLA	Economic Commission for Latin America; see Economic Commission for Latin America and the Caribbean (ECLAC)
		ECLAC	Economic Commission for Latin America and the Caribbean
		ECOSOC	Economic and Social Council
		ECOWAS	Economic Community of West African States
		ECWA	Economic Commission for Western Asia; see Economic and Social Commission for Western Asia (ESCWA)
		EFTA	European Free Trade Association
		EIB	European Investment Bank
		Entente	Council of the Entente
		ESA	European Space Agency
		ESCAP	Economic and Social Commission for Asia and the Pacific
		ESCWA	Economic and Social Commission for Western Asia
	F	FAO	Food and Agriculture Organization
		FLS	Front Line States
		FZ	Franc Zone
	G	G-2	Group of 2
		G-3	Group of 3
		G-5	Group of 5
		G-6	Group of 6 (not to be confused with the Big Six)
		G-7	Group of 7
		G-8	Group of 8
		G-9	Group of 9
		G-10	Group of 10
		G-11	Group of 11
		G-19	Group of 19
		G-24	Group of 24
		G-30	Group of 30
		G-33	Group of 33
		G-77	Group of 77
		GATT	General Agreement on Tariffs and Trade
		GCC	Gulf Cooperation Council

H	Habitat	see United Nations Center for Human Settlements (UNCHS)
I	IADB	Inter-American Development Bank
	IAEA	International Atomic Energy Agency
	IBEC	International Bank for Economic Cooperation
	IBRD	International Bank for Reconstruction and Development
	ICAO	International Civil Aviation Organization
	ICC	International Chamber of Commerce
	ICEM	Intergovernmental Committee for European Migration; see International Organization for Migration (IOM)
	ICFTU	International Confederation of Free Trade Unions
	ICJ	International Court of Justice
	ICM	Intergovernmental Committee for Migration; see International Organization for Migration (IOM)
	ICRC	International Committee of the Red Cross
	IDA	International Development Association
	IDB	Islamic Development Bank
	IEA	International Energy Agency
	IFAD	International Fund for Agricultural Development
	IFC	International Finance Corporation
	IGADD	Inter-Governmental Authority on Drought and Development
	IIB	International Investment Bank
	ILO	International Labor Organization
	IMCO	Intergovernmental Maritime Consultative Organization; see International Maritime Organization (IMO)
	IMF	International Monetary Fund
	IMO	International Maritime Organization
	INMARSAT	International Maritime Satellite Organization
	INTELSAT	International Telecommunications Satellite Organization
	INTERPOL	International Criminal Police Organization
	IOC	International Olympic Committee
	IOM	International Organization for Migration
	ISO	International Organization for Standardization
	ITU	International Telecommunication Union
L	LAES	Latin American Economic System
	LAIA	Latin American Integration Association
	LAS	League of Arab States; see Arab League (AL)
	LDC	less developed country
	LLDC	least developed country
	LORCS	League of Red Cross and Red Crescent Societies
N	NAM	Nonaligned Movement
	NATO	North Atlantic Treaty Organization
	NC	Nordic Council
	NEA	Nuclear Energy Agency
	NIB	Nordic Investment Bank
	NIC	newly industrializing country; see newly industrializing economy (NIE)
	NIE	newly industrializing economy

O	OAPEC	Organization of Arab Petroleum Exporting Countries
	OAS	Organization of American States
	OAU	Organization of African Unity
	OECD	Organization for Economic Cooperation and Development
	OECS	Organization of Eastern Caribbean States
	OIC	Organization of the Islamic Conference
	OPANAL	Agency for the Prohibition of Nuclear Weapons in Latin America and the Caribbean
	OPEC	Organization of Petroleum Exporting Countries
P	PCA	Permanent Court of Arbitration
R	RG	Rio Group
S	SAARC	South Asian Association for Regional Cooperation
	SACU	Southern African Customs Union
	SADCC	Southern African Development Coordination Conference
	SELA	Sistema Económico Latinoamericana; see Latin American Economic System (LAES)
	SPC	South Pacific Commission
	SPF	South Pacific Forum
U	UDEAC	Union Douanière et Economique de l'Afrique Centrale; see Central African Customs and Economic Union (UDEAC)
	UN	United Nations
	UNAVEM	United Nations Angola Verification Mission
	UNCHS	United Nations Center for Human Settlements (also known as Habitat)
	UNCTAD	United Nations Conference on Trade and Development
	UNDOF	United Nations Disengagement Observer Force
	UNDP	United Nations Development Program
	UNEP	United Nations Environment Program
	UNESCO	United Nations Educational, Scientific, and Cultural Organization
	UNFICYP	United Nations Force in Cyprus
	UNFPA	United Nations Fund for Population Activities; see UN Population Fund (UNFPA)
	UNHCR	United Nations Office of the High Commissioner for Refugees
	UNICEF	United Nations International Children's Emergency Fund; see United Nations Children's Fund (UNICEF)
	UNIDO	United Nations Industrial Development Organization
	UNIFIL	United Nations Interim Force in Lebanon
	UNIIMOG	United Nations Iran-Iraq Military Observer Group
	UNMOGIP	United Nations Military Observer Group in India and Pakistan
	UNRWA	United Nations Relief and Works Agency for Palestine Refugees in the Near East
	UNTSO	United Nations Truce Supervision Organization
	UPU	Universal Postal Union
	USSR/EE	USSR/Eastern Europe
W	WADB	West African Development Bank
	WCL	World Confederation of Labor
	WEU	Western European Union
	WFC	World Food Council

WFP	World Food Program
WFTU	World Federation of Trade Unions
WHO	World Health Organization
WIPO	World Intellectual Property Organization
WMO	World Meteorological Organization
WP	Warsaw Pact (members met 1 July 1991 to dissolve the alliance)
WTO	World Tourism Organization

note: not all international organizations and groups have abbreviations

Appendix C:

International Organizations and Groups

advanced developing countries	another term for those less developed countries (LDCs) with particularly rapid industrial development; see newly industrializing economies (NIEs)
African, Caribbean, and Pacific Countries (ACP) *established*—1 April 1976 *aim*—members have a preferential economic and aid relationship with the EC;	*members*—(66) Angola, Antigua and Barbuda, The Bahamas, Barbados, Belize, Benin, Botswana, Burkina, Burundi, Cameroon, Cape Verde, Central African Republic, Chad, Comoros, Congo, Djibouti, Dominica, Equatorial Guinea, Ethiopia, Fiji, Gabon, The Gambia, Ghana, Grenada, Guinea, Guinea-Bissau, Guyana, Ivory Coast, Jamaica, Kenya, Kiribati, Lesotho, Liberia, Madagascar, Malawi, Mali, Mauritania, Mauritius, Mozambique, Niger, Nigeria, Papua New Guinea, Rwanda, Saint Kitts and Nevis, Saint Lucia, Saint Vincent and the Grenadines, Sao Tome and Principe, Senegal, Seychelles, Sierra Leone, Solomon Islands, Somalia, Sudan, Suriname, Swaziland, Tanzania, Togo, Tonga, Trinidad and Tobago, Tuvalu, Uganda, Vanuatu, Western Samoa, Zaire, Zambia, Zimbabwe
African Development Bank (AfDB), also known as Banque Africaine de Développement (BAD) *established*—4 August 1963; *aim*—to promote economic and social development;	*regional members*—(50) Algeria, Angola, Benin, Botswana, Burkina, Burundi, Cameroon, Cape Verde, Central African Republic, Chad, Comoros, Congo, Djibouti, Egypt, Equatorial Guinea, Ethiopia, Gabon, The Gambia, Ghana, Guinea, Guinea-Bissau, Ivory Coast, Kenya, Lesotho, Liberia, Libya, Madagascar, Malawi, Mali, Mauritania, Mauritius, Morocco, Mozambique, Niger, Nigeria, Rwanda, Sao Tome and Principe, Senegal, Seychelles, Sierra Leone, Somalia, Sudan, Swaziland, Tanzania, Togo, Tunisia, Uganda, Zaire, Zambia, Zimbabwe; *nonregional members*—(25) Argentina, Australia, Austria, Belgium, Brazil, Canada, China, Denmark, Finland, France, Germany, India, Italy, Japan, South Korea, Kuwait, Netherlands, Norway, Portugal, Saudi Arabia, Sweden, Switzerland, UK, US, Yugoslavia
Agence de Coopération Culturelle et Technique (ACCT)	see Agency for Cultural and Technical Cooperation (ACCT)
Agency for Cultural and Technical Cooperation (ACCT)—acronym from Agence de Coopération Culturelle et Technique; *established*—21 March 1970; *aim*—to promote cultural and technical cooperation among French-speaking countries;	*members*—(30) Belgium, Benin, Burkina, Burundi, Canada, Central African Republic, Chad, Comoros, Congo, Djibouti, Dominica, France, Gabon, Guinea, Haiti, Ivory Coast, Lebanon, Luxembourg, Mali, Mauritius, Monaco, Niger, Rwanda, Senegal, Seychelles, Togo, Tunisia, Vanuatu, Vietnam, Zaire; *associate members*—(7) Cameroon, Egypt, Guinea-Bissau, Laos, Mauritania, Morocco, Saint Lucia; *participating governments*—(2) New Brunswick (Canada), Quebec (Canada)
Agency for the Prohibition of Nuclear Weapons in Latin America and the Caribbean (OPANAL)—acronym from Organismo para la Proscripción de las Armas Nucleares en la América Latina y el Caribe (OPANAL); *established*—14 February 1967; *aim*—to encourage the peaceful uses of atomic energy and prohibit nuclear weapons;	*members*—(25) Antigua and Barbuda, The Bahamas, Barbados, Bolivia, Brazil, Chile, Colombia, Costa Rica, Dominican Republic, Ecuador, El Salvador, Grenada, Guatemala, Haiti, Honduras, Jamaica, Mexico, Nicaragua, Panama, Paraguay, Peru, Suriname, Trinidad and Tobago, Uruguay, Venezuela; *observer*—(1) Cuba
Andean Group (AG) *established*—26 May 1969, effective 16 October 1969; *aim*—to promote harmonious development through economic integration;	*members*—(5) Bolivia, Colombia, Ecuador, Peru, Venezuela; *associate member*—(1) Panama; *observers*—(26) Argentina, Australia, Austria, Belgium, Brazil, Canada, Costa Rica, Denmark, Egypt, Finland, France, Germany, India, Israel, Italy, Japan, Mexico, Netherlands, Paraguay, Spain, Sweden, Switzerland, UK, US, Uruguay, Yugoslavia

Arab Bank for Economic Development in Africa (ABEDA), also known as Banque Arabe de Développement Economique en Afrique (BADEA);	*members*—(17 plus the Palestine Liberation Organization) Algeria, Bahrain, Egypt, Iraq, Jordan, Kuwait, Lebanon, Libya, Mauritania, Morocco, Oman, Qatar, Saudi Arabia, Sudan, Syria, Tunisia, UAE, Palestine Liberation Organization; note—these are all the members of the Arab League except Djibouti, Somalia, and Yemen
established—18 February 1974, effective 16 September 1974;	
aim—to promote economic development;	
Arab Cooperation Council (ACC)	*members*—(4) Egypt, Iraq, Jordan, Yemen
established—16 February 1989;	
aim—to promote economic cooperation and integration, possibly leading to an Arab Common Market;	
Arab Fund for Economic and Social Development (AFESD)	*members*—(20 plus the Palestine Liberation Organization) Algeria, Bahrain, Djibouti, Egypt (suspended from 1979 to 1988), Iraq, Jordan, Kuwait, Lebanon, Libya, Mauritania, Morocco, Oman, Qatar, Saudi Arabia, Somalia, Sudan, Syria, Tunisia, UAE, Yemen, Palestine Liberation Organization
established—16 May 1968;	
aim—to promote economic and social development;	
Arab League (AL), also known as League of Arab States (LAS);	*members*—(20 plus the Palestine Liberation Organization) Algeria, Bahrain, Djibouti, Egypt, Iraq, Jordan, Kuwait, Lebanon, Libya, Mauritania, Morocco, Oman, Qatar, Saudi Arabia, Somalia, Sudan, Syria, Tunisia, UAE, Yemen, Palestine Liberation Organization
established—22 March 1945;	
aim—to promote economic, social, political, and military cooperation;	
Arab Maghreb Union (AMU)	*members*—(5) Algeria, Libya, Mauritania, Morocco, Tunisia
established—17 February 1989;	
aim—to promote cooperation and integration among the Arab states of northern Africa;	
Arab Monetary Fund (AMF)	*members*—(19 plus the Palestine Liberation Organization) Algeria, Bahrain, Egypt, Iraq, Jordan, Kuwait, Lebanon, Libya, Mauritania, Morocco, Oman, Qatar, Saudi Arabia, Somalia, Sudan, Syria, Tunisia, UAE, Yemen, Palestine Liberation Organization
established—27 April 1976, effective 2 February 1977;	
aim—to promote Arab cooperation, development, and integration in monetary and economic affairs;	
Asia Pacific Economic Cooperation (APEC)	*members*—(12) all ASEAN members (Brunei, Indonesia, Malaysia, Philippines, Singapore, Thailand) plus Australia, Canada, Japan, South Korea, NZ, US
established—NA November 1989;	
aim—to promote trade and investment in the Pacific basin;	

Asian Development Bank (AsDB) *established*—19 December 1966; *aim*—to promote regional economic cooperation;	*regional members*—(34) Afghanistan, Australia, Bangladesh, Bhutan, Burma, Cambodia, China, Cook Islands, Fiji, Hong Kong, India, Indonesia, Japan, Kiribati, South Korea, Laos, Malaysia, Maldives, Mongolia, Nepal, NZ, Pakistan, Papua New Guinea, Philippines, Singapore, Solomon Islands, Sri Lanka, Taiwan, Thailand, Tonga, Turkey, Vanuatu, Vietnam, Western Samoa; *nonregional members*—(15) Austria, Belgium, Canada, Denmark, Finland, France, Germany, Italy, Netherlands, Norway, Spain, Sweden, Switzerland, UK, US
Asociación Latinoamericana de Integración (ALADI)	see Latin American Integration Association (LAIA)
Association of Southeast Asian Nations (ASEAN) *established*—9 August 1967; *aim*—regional economic, social, and cultural cooperation among the non-Communist countries of Southeast Asia;	*members*—(6) Brunei, Indonesia, Malaysia, Philippines, Singapore, Thailand; *observer*—(1) Papua New Guinea
Australia-New Zealand-United States Security Treaty (ANZUS) *established*—1 September 1951, effective 29 April 1952; *aim*—trilateral mutual security agreement, although the US suspended security obligations to NZ on 11 August 1986;	*members*—(3) Australia, NZ, US
Banco Centroamericano de Integración Económico (BCIE)	see Central American Bank for Economic Integration (BCIE)
Banco Interamericano de Desarvollo (BID)	see Inter-American Development Bank (IADB)
Bank for International Settlements (BIS) *established*—20 January 1930, effective 17 March 1930; *aim*—to promote cooperation among central banks in international financial settlements;	*members*—(29) Australia, Austria, Belgium, Bulgaria, Canada, Czechoslovakia, Denmark, Finland, France, Germany, Greece, Hungary, Iceland, Ireland, Italy, Japan, Netherlands, Norway, Poland, Portugal, Romania, South Africa, Spain, Sweden, Switzerland, Turkey, UK, US, Yugoslavia
Banque Africaine de Développement (BAD)	see African Development Bank (AfDB)
Banque Arabe de Développement Economique en Afrique (BADEA)	see Arab Bank for Economic Development in Africa (ABEDA)
Banque de Développement des États de l'Afrique Centrale (BDEAC)	see Central African States Development Bank (BDEAC)
Banque Ouest-Africaine de Développement (BOAD)	see West African Development Bank (WADB)
Benelux Economic Union (Benelux)—acronym from Belgium, Netherlands, and Luxembourg; *established*—3 February 1958, effective 1 November 1960; *aim*—to develop closer economic cooperation and integration;	*members*—(3) Belgium, Luxembourg, Netherlands

Big Seven—membership is the same as the Group of 7;

established—NA;

aim—to discuss and coordinate major economic policies;

members—(7) Big Six (Canada, France, Germany, Italy, Japan, UK) plus the US

Big Six—not to be confused with the Group of 6;

established—NA;

aim—economic cooperation;

members—(6) Canada, France, Germany, Italy, Japan, UK

Caribbean Community and Common Market (CARICOM)

established—4 July 1973, effective 1 August 1973;

aim—to promote economic integration and development, especially among the less developed countries;

members—(13) Antigua and Barbuda, The Bahamas, Barbados, Belize, Dominica, Grenada, Guyana, Jamaica, Montserrat, Saint Kitts and Nevis, Saint Lucia, Saint Vincent and the Grenadines, Trinidad and Tobago;

observers—(7) Anguilla, Bermuda, British Virgin Islands, Dominican Republic, Haiti, Netherlands Antilles, Suriname

Caribbean Development Bank (CDB)

established—18 October 1969, effective 26 January 1970;

aim—to promote economic development and cooperation;

regional members—(20) Anguilla, Antigua and Barbuda, The Bahamas, Barbados, Belize, British Virgin Islands, Cayman Islands, Colombia, Dominica, Grenada, Guyana, Jamaica, Mexico, Montserrat, Saint Kitts and Nevis, Saint Lucia, Saint Vincent and the Grenadines, Trinidad and Tobago, Turks and Caicos Islands, Venezuela;

nonregional members—(3) Canada, France, UK

Cartagena Group

see Group of 11

Central African Customs and Economic Union (UDEAC)—acronym from Union Douanière et Economique de l'Afrique Centrale;

established—8 December 1964, effective 1 January 1966;

aim—to promote the establishment of a Central African Common Market;

members—(6) Cameroon, Central African Republic, Chad, Congo, Equatorial Guinea, Gabon

Central African States Development Bank (BDEAC)—acronym from Banque de Développement des États de l'Afrique Centrale;

established—3 December 1975;

aim—to provide loans for economic development;

members—(9) Cameroon, Central African Republic, Chad, Congo, Equatorial Guinea, France, Gabon, Germany, Kuwait

Central American Bank for Economic Integration (BCIE)—acronym from Banco Centroamericano de Integración Económico; *established*—13 December 1960; *aim*—to promote economic integration and development;	*members*—(5) Costa Rica, El Salvador, Guatemala, Honduras, Nicaragua
Central American Common Market (CACM) *established*—13 December 1960, effective 3 June 1961; *aim*—to promote establishment of a Central American Common Market;	*members*—(5) Costa Rica, El Salvador, Guatemala, Honduras, Nicaragua
centrally planned economies	a term applied mainly to the traditionally Communist states that looked to the USSR for leadership; many are now evolving toward more democratic and market-oriented systems; also known formerly as the Second World or as the Communist countries; through the 1980s, this group included Albania, Bulgaria, Cambodia, China, Cuba, Czechoslovakia, GDR, Hungary, North Korea, Laos, Mongolia, Poland, Romania, USSR, Vietnam, Yugoslavia
Colombo Plan (CP) *established*—1 July 1951; *aim*—to promote economic and social development in Asia and the Pacific;	*members*—(26) Afghanistan, Australia, Bangladesh, Bhutan, Burma, Cambodia, Canada, Fiji, India, Indonesia, Iran, Japan, South Korea, Laos, Malaysia, Maldives, Nepal, NZ, Pakistan, Papua New Guinea, Philippines, Singapore, Sri Lanka, Thailand, UK, US
Commission for Social Development *established*—21 June 1946 as the Social Commission, renamed 29 July 1966; *aim*—ECOSOC organization dealing with social development programs;	*members*—(32) selected on a rotating basis from all regions
Commission on Human Rights *established*—18 February 1946; *aim*—ECOSOC organization dealing with human rights;	*members*—(43) selected on a rotating basis from all regions
Commission on Narcotic Drugs *established*—16 February 1946; *aim*—ECOSOC organization dealing with illicit drugs;	*members*—(40) selected on a rotating basis from all regions with emphasis on producing and processing countries
Commission on the Status of Women *established*—21 June 1946; *aim*—ECOSOC organization dealing with women's rights;	*members*—(32) selected on a rotating basis from all regions

Commonwealth (C) *established*—31 December 1931; *aim*—voluntary association that evolved from the British Empire and that seeks to foster multinational cooperation and assistance;	*members*—(48) Antigua and Barbuda, Australia, The Bahamas, Bangladesh, Barbados, Belize, Botswana, Brunei, Canada, Cyprus, Dominica, The Gambia, Ghana, Grenada, Guyana, India, Jamaica, Kenya, Kiribati, Lesotho, Malawi, Malaysia, Maldives, Malta, Mauritius, Namibia, NZ, Nigeria, Pakistan, Papua New Guinea, Saint Kitts and Nevis, Saint Lucia, Saint Vincent and the Grenadines, Seychelles, Sierra Leone, Singapore, Solomon Islands, Sri Lanka, Swaziland, Tanzania, Tonga, Trinidad and Tobago, Uganda, UK, Vanuatu, Western Samoa, Zambia, Zimbabwe; *special members*—(2) Nauru, Tuvalu
Communauté Economique de l'Afrique de l'Ouest (CEAO)	see West African Economic Community (CEAO)
Communauté Economique des États de l'Afrique Centrale (CEEAC)	see Economic Community of Central African States (CEEAC)
Communauté Economique des Pays des Grands Lacs (CEPGL)	see Economic Community of the Great Lakes Countries (CEPGL)
Communist countries	traditionally the Marxist-Leninist states with authoritarian governments and command economies based on the Soviet model; see centrally planned economies
Conference on Security and Cooperation in Europe (CSCE) *established*—NA November 1972; *aim*—discusses issues of mutual concern and reviews implementation of the Helsinki Agreement;	*members*—(35) Andorra, Austria, Belgium, Bulgaria, Canada, Cyprus, Czechoslovakia, Denmark, Finland, France, Germany, Greece, Hungary, Iceland, Ireland, Italy, Liechtenstein, Luxembourg, Malta, Monaco, Netherlands, Norway, Poland, Portugal, Romania, San Marino, Spain, Sweden, Switzerland, Turkey, UK, US, USSR, Vatican City, Yugoslavia
Conseil Européen pour la Recherche Nucléaire (CERN)	see European Organization for Nuclear Research (CERN)
Contadora Group (CG)	Contadora Group was established 5 January 1983 (on the Panamanian island of Contadora) to reduce tensions and conflicts in Central America but evolved into the Rio Group (RG); members included Colombia, Mexico, Panama, Venezuela
Cooperation Council for the Arab States of the Gulf	see Gulf Cooperation Council (GCC)
Coordinating Committee on Export Controls (COCOM) *established*—NA 1949; *aim*—compiles strategic embargo list of goods not to be sold by the West to Eastern bloc countries;	*members*—(15) Belgium, Canada, Denmark, France, Germany, Greece, Italy, Japan, Luxembourg, Netherlands, Norway, Portugal, Turkey, UK, US
Council for Mutual Economic Assistance (CEMA)	Council for Mutual Economic Assistance, also known as CMEA or Comecon, was established 25 January 1949 to promote the development of socialist economies and was abolished 1 January 1991; members included Afghanistan (observer), Albania (had not participated since 1961 break with USSR), Angola (observer), Bulgaria, Cuba, Czechoslovakia, Ethiopia (observer), GDR, Hungary, Laos (observer), Mongolia, Mozambique (observer), Nicaragua (observer), Poland, Romania, USSR, Vietnam, Yemen (observer), Yugoslavia (associate)
Council of Arab Economic Unity (CAEU) *established*—3 June 1957, effective 30 May 1964; *aim*—to promote economic integration among Arab nations;	*members*—(11) Egypt, Iraq, Jordan, Kuwait, Libya, Mauritania, Somalia, Sudan, Syria, UAE, Yemen

Council of Europe (CE) *established*—5 May 1949, effective 3 August 1949; *aim*—to promote increased unity and quality of life in Europe;	*members*—(24) Austria, Belgium, Cyprus, Denmark, Finland, France, Germany, Greece, Hungary, Iceland, Ireland, Italy, Liechtenstein, Luxembourg, Malta, Netherlands, Norway, Portugal, San Marino, Spain, Sweden, Switzerland, Turkey, UK
Council of the Entente (Entente) *established*—29 May 1959; *aim*—to promote economic, social, and political coordination;	*members*—(5) Benin, Burkina, Ivory Coast, Niger, Togo
Customs Cooperation Council (CCC) *established*—15 December 1950; *aim*—to promote international cooperation in customs matters;	*members*—(104) Algeria, Argentina, Australia, Austria, The Bahamas, Bangladesh, Belgium, Botswana, Brazil, Bulgaria, Burkina, Burundi, Cameroon, Canada, Central African Republic, Chile, China, Congo, Cuba, Cyprus, Czechoslovakia, Denmark, Egypt, Ethiopia, Finland, France, Gabon, The Gambia, Germany, Ghana, Greece, Guatemala, Guyana, Haiti, Hong Kong, Hungary, Iceland, India, Indonesia, Iran, Ireland, Israel, Italy, Ivory Coast, Jamaica, Japan, Jordan, Kenya, South Korea, Lebanon, Lesotho, Liberia, Libya, Luxembourg, Madagascar, Malawi, Malaysia, Mali, Malta, Mauritania, Mauritius, Mexico, Morocco, Mozambique, Nepal, Netherlands, NZ, Niger, Nigeria, Norway, Pakistan, Paraguay, Peru, Philippines, Poland, Portugal, Romania, Rwanda, Saudi Arabia, Senegal, Sierra Leone, Singapore, South Africa, Spain, Sri Lanka, Sudan, Swaziland, Sweden, Switzerland, Syria, Tanzania, Thailand, Trinidad and Tobago, Tunisia, Turkey, Uganda, UAE, UK, US, Uruguay, Yugoslavia, Zaire, Zambia, Zimbabwe
developed countries (DCs)	the top group in the comprehensive but mutually exclusive hierarchy of developed countries (DCs), USSR/Eastern Europe (USSR/EE), and less developed countries (LDCs); includes the market-oriented economies of the mainly democratic nations in the Organization for Economic Cooperation and Development (OECD), Bermuda, Israel, South Africa, and the European ministates; also known as the First World, high-income countries, the North, industrial countries; generally have a per capita GNP/GDP in excess of $10,000 although some OECD countries and South Africa have figures well under $10,000 and three of the excluded OPEC countries have figures of $10,000 or more; *the 34 DCs are* Andorra, Australia, Austria, Belgium, Bermuda, Canada, Denmark, Faroe Islands, Finland, France, Germany, Greece, Iceland, Ireland, Israel, Italy, Japan, Liechtenstein, Luxembourg, Malta, Monaco, Netherlands, NZ, Norway, Portugal, San Marino, South Africa, Spain, Sweden, Switzerland, Turkey, UK, US, Vatican City
developing countries	an imprecise term for the less developed countries with growing economies; see less developed countries (LDCs)
East African Development Bank (EADB) *established*—6 June 1967, effective 1 December 1967; *aim*—to promote economic development;	*members*—(3) Kenya, Tanzania, Uganda
Economic and Social Commission for Asia and the Pacific (ESCAP) *established*—28 March 1947 as Economic Commission for Asia and the Far East (ECAFE); *aim*—to promote economic development as a regional commission for the UN's ECOSOC;	*members*—(38) Afghanistan, Australia, Bangladesh, Bhutan, Brunei, Burma, Cambodia, China, Fiji, France, India, Indonesia, Iran, Japan, South Korea, Laos, Malaysia, Maldives, Mongolia, Nauru, Nepal, Netherlands, NZ, Pakistan, Papua New Guinea, Philippines, Singapore, Solomon Islands, Sri Lanka, Thailand, Tonga, Tuvalu, UK, US, USSR, Vanuatu, Vietnam, Western Samoa; *associate members*—(9) Cook Islands, Guam, Hong Kong, Kiribati, Marshall Islands, Federated States of Micronesia, Niue, Northern Mariana Islands, Trust Territory of the Pacific Islands (Palau)

Economic and Social Commission for Western Asia (ESCWA)	*members*—(12) Bahrain, Egypt, Iraq, Jordan, Kuwait, Lebanon, Oman, Qatar, Saudi Arabia, Syria, UAE, Yemen
established—9 August 1973 as Economic Commission for Western Asia (ECWA);	
aim—to promote economic development as a regional commission for the UN's ECOSOC;	
Economic and Social Council (ECOSOC)	*members*—(54) selected on a rotating basis from all regions
established—26 June 1945, effective 24 October 1945;	
aim—to coordinate the economic and social work of the UN; includes five regional commissions (see Economic Commission for Africa, Economic Commission for Europe, Economic Commission for Latin America and the Caribbean, Economic and Social Commission for Asia and the Pacific, Economic and Social Commission for Western Asia) and six functional commissions (see Commission for Social Development, Commission on Human Rights, Commission on Narcotic Drugs, Commission on the Status of Women, Population Commission, and Statistical Commission);	
Economic Commission for Africa (ECA)	*members*—(51) Algeria, Angola, Benin, Botswana, Burkina, Burundi, Cameroon, Cape Verde, Central African Republic, Chad, Comoros, Congo, Djibouti, Egypt, Equatorial Guinea, Ethiopia, Gabon, The Gambia, Ghana, Guinea, Guinea-Bissau, Ivory Coast, Kenya, Lesotho, Liberia, Libya, Madagascar, Malawi, Mali, Mauritania, Mauritius, Morocco, Mozambique, Niger, Nigeria, Rwanda, Sao Tome and Principe, Senegal, Seychelles, Sierra Leone, Somalia, South Africa, Sudan, Swaziland, Tanzania, Togo, Tunisia, Uganda, Zaire, Zambia, Zimbabwe;
established—29 April 1958;	
aim—to promote economic development as a regional commission of the UN's ECOSOC;	
	associate members—(3) France, Namibia, UK
Economic Commission for Asia and the Far East (ECAFE)	see Economic and Social Commission for Asia and the Pacific (ESCAP)
Economic Commission for Europe (ECE)	*members*—(33) Albania, Austria, Belgium, Bulgaria, Byelorussian Soviet Socialist Republic, Canada, Cyprus, Czechoslovakia, Denmark, Finland, France, Germany, Greece, Hungary, Iceland, Ireland, Italy, Luxembourg, Malta, Netherlands, Norway, Poland, Portugal, Romania, Spain, Sweden, Switzerland, Turkey, UK, Ukrainian Soviet Socialist Republic, US, USSR, Yugoslavia
established—28 March 1947;	
aim—to promote economic development as a regional commission of the UN's ECOSOC;	
Economic Commission for Latin America (ECLA)	see Economic Commission for Latin America and the Caribbean (ECLAC)
Economic Commission for Latin America and the Caribbean (ECLAC)	*members*—(41) Antigua and Barbuda, Argentina, The Bahamas, Barbados, Belize, Bolivia, Brazil, Canada, Chile, Colombia, Costa Rica, Cuba, Dominica, Dominican Republic, Ecuador, El Salvador, France, Grenada, Guatemala, Guyana, Haiti, Honduras, Jamaica, Mexico, Netherlands, Nicaragua, Panama, Paraguay, Peru, Portugal, Puerto Rico, Saint Kitts and Nevis, Saint Lucia, Saint Vincent and the Grenadines, Spain, Suriname, Trinidad and Tobago, UK, US, Uruguay, Venezuela;
established—25 February 1948 as Economic Commission for Latin America (ECLA);	
aim—to promote economic development as a regional commission of the UN's ECOSOC;	*associate members*—(5) Aruba, British Virgin Islands, Montserrat, Netherlands Antilles, Virgin Islands

Economic Commission for Western Asia (ECWA)	see Economic and Social Commission for Western Asia (ESCWA)
Economic Community of Central African States (CEEAC)—acronym from Communauté Economique des États de l'Afrique Centrale; *established*—18 October 1983; *aim*—to promote regional economic cooperation and establish a Central African Common Market;	*members*—(10) Burundi, Cameroon, Central African Republic, Chad, Congo, Equatorial Guinea, Gabon, Rwanda, Sao Tome and Principe, Zaire; *observer*—(1) Angola
Economic Community of the Great Lakes Countries (CEPGL)—acronym from Communauté Economique des Pays des Grands Lacs; *established*—26 September 1976; *aim*—to promote regional economic cooperation and integration;	*members*—(3) Burundi, Rwanda, Zaire
Economic Community of West African States (ECOWAS) *established*—28 May 1975; *aim*—to promote regional economic cooperation;	*members*—(16) Benin, Burkina, Cape Verde, The Gambia, Ghana, Guinea, Guinea-Bissau, Ivory Coast, Liberia, Mali, Mauritania, Niger, Nigeria, Senegal, Sierra Leone, Togo
European Bank for Reconstruction and Development (EBRD) *established*—15 April 1991; *aim*—to facilitate the transition of seven centrally planned economies in Europe (Bulgaria, Czechoslovakia, Hungary, Poland, Romania, USSR, and Yugoslavia) to market economies by committing 60% of its loans to privatization;	*members*—(34) Australia, Austria, Belgium, Canada, Cyprus, Denmark, European Community (EC), Egypt, European Investment Bank (EIB), Finland, France, Germany, Greece, Iceland, Ireland, Israel, Italy, Japan, South Korea, Liechtenstein, Luxembourg, Malta, Mexico, Morocco, Netherlands, NZ, Norway, Portugal, Spain, Sweden, Switzerland, Turkey, UK, US; note—includes all 12 members of the EC as individual countries and the EC itself as an institution
European Community (EC) *established*—8 April 1965, effective 1 July 1967; *aim*—a fusing of the European Atomic Energy Community (Euratom), the European Coal and Steel Community (ESC), and the European Economic Community (EEC or Common Market); the EC plans to establish a completely integrated common market in 1992 and an eventual federation of Europe;	*members*—(12) Belgium, Denmark, France, Germany, Greece, Ireland, Italy, Luxembourg, Netherlands, Portugal, Spain, UK

European Free Trade Association (EFTA)	*members*—(7) Austria, Finland, Iceland, Liechtenstein, Norway, Sweden, Switzerland
established—4 January 1960, effective 3 May 1960;	
aim—to promote expansion of free trade;	
European Investment Bank (EIB)	*members*—(12) Belgium, Denmark, Frane, Germany, Greece, Ireland, Italy, Luxembourg, Netherlands, Portugal, Spain, UK
established—25 March 1957, effective 1 January 1958;	
aim—to promote economic development of the EC;	
European Organization for Nuclear Research (CERN)—acronym retained from the predecessor organization Conseil Européen pour la Recherche Nucléaire;	*members*—(14) Austria, Belgium, Denmark, France, Germany, Greece, Italy, Netherlands, Norway, Portugal, Spain, Sweden, Switzerland, UK;
	observers—(3) Poland (scheduled to become a member 1 July 1991), Turkey, Yugoslavia
established—1 July 1953, effective 29 September 1954;	
aim—to foster nuclear research for peaceful purposes only;	
European Space Agency (ESA)	*members*—(13) Austria, Belgium, Denmark, France, Germany, Ireland, Italy, Netherlands, Norway, Spain, Sweden, Switzerland, UK;
established—31 July 1973, effective 1 May 1975;	*associate member*—(1) Finland
aim—to promote peaceful cooperation in space research and technology;	
First World	another term for countries with advanced, industrialized economies; see developed countries (DCs)
Food and Agriculture Organization (FAO)	*members*—(157) all UN members except Brunei, Byelorussian Soviet Socialist Republic, Liechtenstein, Singapore, South Africa, Ukrainian Soviet Socialist Republic, USSR; other members are Cook Islands, North Korea, South Korea, Switzerland, Tonga
established—16 October 1945;	
aim—UN specialized agency to raise living standards and increase availability of agricultural products;	
Four Dragons	the four small Asian less developed countries (LDCs) that have experienced unusually rapid economic growth; also known as the Four Tigers; this group includes Hong Kong, South Korea, Singapore, Taiwan
Four Tigers	another term for the Four Dragons; see Four Dragons
Franc Zone (FZ)	*members*—(15) Benin, Burkina, Cameroon, Central African Republic, Chad, Comoros, Congo, Equatorial Guinea, France, Gabon, Ivory Coast, Mali, Niger, Senegal, Togo; note—France includes metropolitan France, the four overseas departments of France (French Guiana, Guadeloupe, Martinique, Reunion), the two territorial collectivities of France (Mayotte, Saint Pierre and Miquelon), and the three overseas territories of France (French Polynesia, New Caledonia, Wallis and Futuna)
established—NA;	
aim—monetary union among countries whose currencies are linked to the French franc;	

Front Line States (FLS)

established—NA;

aim—to achieve black majority rule in South Africa;

members—(7) Angola, Botswana, Mozambique, Namibia, Tanzania, Zambia, Zimbabwe

---

General Agreement on Tariffs and Trade (GATT)

established—30 October 1947, effective 1 January 1948;

aim—to promote the expansion of international trade on a nondiscriminatory basis;

members—(101) Antigua and Barbuda, Argentina, Australia, Austria, Bangladesh, Barbados, Belgium, Belize, Benin, Bolivia, Botswana, Brazil, Burkina, Burma, Burundi, Cameroon, Canada, Central African Republic, Chad, Chile, Colombia, Congo, Costa Rica, Cuba, Cyprus, Czechoslovakia, Denmark, Dominican Republic, Egypt, Finland, France, Gabon, The Gambia, Germany, Ghana, Greece, Guyana, Haiti, Hong Kong, Hungary, Iceland, India, Indonesia, Ireland, Israel, Italy, Ivory Coast, Jamaica, Japan, Kenya, South Korea, Kuwait, Lesotho, Luxembourg, Macau, Madagascar, Malawi, Malaysia, Maldives, Malta, Mauritania, Mauritius, Mexico, Morocco, Netherlands, NZ, Nicaragua, Niger, Nigeria, Norway, Pakistan, Peru, Philippines, Poland, Portugal, Romania, Rwanda, Senegal, Sierra Leone, Singapore, South Africa, Spain, Sri Lanka, Suriname, Sweden, Switzerland, Tanzania, Thailand, Togo, Trinidad and Tobago, Tunisia, Turkey, Uganda, UK, US, Uruguay, Venezuela, Yugoslavia, Zaire, Zambia, Zimbabwe

---

Group of 2 (G-2)

established—informal term that came into use about 1986;

aim—bilateral economic cooperation between the two most powerful economic giants;

members—(2) Japan, US

Group of 3 (G-3)

established—NA October 1990;

aim—mechanism for policy coordination;

members—(3) Colombia, Mexico, Venezuela

Group of 5 (G-5)

established—22 September 1985;

aim—the five major non-Communist economic powers;

members—(5) France, Germany, Japan, UK, US

Group of 6 (G-6)—not to be confused with the Big Six;

established—22 May 1984;

aim—seeks to achieve nuclear disarmament;

members—(6) Argentina, Greece, India, Mexico, Sweden, Tanzania

---

Group of 7 (G-7)—membership is the same as the Big Seven;

established—22 September 1985;

aim—the seven major non-Communist economic powers;

members—(7) Group of 5 (France, Germany, Japan, UK, US) plus Canada and Italy

Group of 8 (G-8)

established—NA October 1975;

aim—the developed countries (DCs) that participated in the Conference on International Economic Cooperation (CIEC), held in several sessions between NA December 1975 and 3 June 1977;

members—(8) Australia, Canada, EC (as one member), Japan, Spain, Sweden, Switzerland, US

Group of 9 (G-9)

established—NA;

aim—informal group that meets occasionally on matters of mutual interest;

members—(9) Austria, Belgium, Bulgaria, Denmark, Finland, Hungary, Romania, Sweden, Yugoslavia

Group of 10 (G-10), also known as the Paris Club;

established—NA October 1962;

aim—wealthiest members of the IMF who provide most of the money to be loaned and act as the informal steering committee; name persists in spite of the addition of Switzerland on NA April 1984;

members—(11) Belgium, Canada, France, Germany, Italy, Japan, Netherlands, Sweden, Switzerland, UK, US

Group of 11 (G-11), also known as the Cartagena Group;

established—22 June 1984, in Cartagena, Colombia;

aim—forum for largest debtor nations in Latin America;

members—(11) Argentina, Bolivia, Brazil, Chile, Colombia, Dominican Republic, Ecuador, Mexico, Peru, Uruguay, Venezuela

Group of 19 (G-19)

established—NA October 1975;

aim—the less developed countries (LDCs) that participated in the Conference on International Economic Cooperation (CIEC) held in several sessions between NA December 1975 and 3 June 1977;

members—(19) Algeria, Argentina, Brazil, Cameroon, Egypt, India, Indonesia, Iran, Iraq, Jamaica, Mexico, Nigeria, Pakistan, Peru, Saudi Arabia, Venezuela, Yugoslavia, Zaire, Zambia

Group of 24 (G-24)

established—NA January 1972;

aim—to promote the interests of developing countries in Africa, Asia, and Latin America within the IMF;

members—(24) Algeria, Argentina, Brazil, Colombia, Egypt, Ethiopia, Gabon, Ghana, Guatemala, India, Iran, Ivory Coast, Lebanon, Mexico, Nigeria, Pakistan, Peru, Philippines, Sri Lanka, Syria, Trinidad and Tobago, Venezuela, Yugoslavia, Zaire

Group of 30 (G-30)	*members*—(30) informal group of 30 leading international bankers, economists, financial experts, and businessmen organized by Johannes Witteveen (former managing director of the IMF)
established—NA 1979;	
aim—to discuss and propose solutions to the world's economic problems;	
Group of 33 (G-33)	*members*—(33) leading economists from 13 countries
established—NA 1987;	
aim—to promote solutions to international economic problems;	
Group of 77 (G-77) *established*—NA October 1967; *aim*—to promote economic cooperation among developing countries; name persists in spite of increased membership;	*members*—(123 plus the Palestine Liberation Organization) Afghanistan, Algeria, Angola, Antigua and Barbuda, Argentina, The Bahamas, Bahrain, Bangladesh, Barbados, Belize, Benin, Bhutan, Bolivia, Botswana, Brazil, Burkina, Burma, Burundi, Cambodia, Cameroon, Cape Verde, Central African Republic, Chad, Chile, Colombia, Comoros, Congo, Costa Rica, Cuba, Cyprus, Djibouti, Dominica, Dominican Republic, Ecuador, Egypt, El Salvador, Equatorial Guinea, Ethiopia, Fiji, Gabon, The Gambia, Ghana, Grenada, Guatemala, Guinea, Guinea-Bissau, Guyana, Haiti, Honduras, India, Indonesia, Iran, Iraq, Ivory Coast, Jamaica, Jordan, Kenya, North Korea, South Korea, Kuwait, Laos, Lebanon, Lesotho, Liberia, Libya, Madagascar, Malawi, Malaysia, Maldives, Mali, Malta, Mauritania, Mauritius, Mexico, Morocco, Mozambique, Nepal, Nicaragua, Niger, Nigeria, Oman, Pakistan, Panama, Papua New Guinea, Paraguay, Peru, Philippines, Qatar, Romania, Rwanda, Saint Lucia, Saint Vincent and the Grenadines, Sao Tome and Principe, Saudi Arabia, Senegal, Seychelles, Sierra Leone, Singapore, Solomon Islands, Somalia, Sri Lanka, Sudan, Suriname, Swaziland, Syria, Tanzania, Thailand, Togo, Tonga, Trinidad and Tobago, Tunisia, Uganda, UAE, Uruguay, Vanuatu, Venezuela, Vietnam, Western Samoa, Yemen, Yugoslavia, Zaire, Zambia, Zimbabwe, Palestine Liberation Organization
Gulf Cooperation Council (GCC), also known as the Cooperation Council for the Arab States of the Gulf; *established*—25-26 May 1981; *aim*—to promote regional cooperation in economic, social, political, and military affairs;	*members*—(6) Bahrain, Kuwait, Oman, Qatar, Saudi Arabia, UAE
Habitat	see United Nations Center for Human Settlements (UNCHS)
high-income countries	another term for the industrialized countries with high per capita GNPs/GDPs; see developed countries (DCs)
industrial countries	another term for the developed countries; see developed countries (DCs)
Inter-American Development Bank (IADB), also known as Banco Interamericano de Desarrollo (BID); *established*—8 April 1959; effective 30 December 1959; *aim*—to promote economic and social development in Latin America;	*members*—(44) Argentina, Austria, The Bahamas, Barbados, Belgium, Bolivia, Brazil, Canada, Chile, Colombia, Costa Rica, Denmark, Dominican Republic, Ecuador, El Salvador, Finland, France, Germany, Guatemala, Guyana, Haiti, Honduras, Israel, Italy, Jamaica, Japan, Mexico, Netherlands, Nicaragua, Norway, Panama, Paraguay, Peru, Portugal, Spain, Suriname, Sweden, Switzerland, Trinidad and Tobago, UK, US, Uruguay, Venezuela, Yugoslavia

Inter-Governmental Authority on Drought and Development (IGADD)

established—NA January 1986;

aim—to promote cooperation on drought-related matters;

members—(6) Djibouti, Ethiopia, Kenya, Somalia, Sudan, Uganda

---

International Atomic Energy Agency (IAEA)

established—26 October 1956, effective 29 July 1957;

aim—to promote peaceful uses of atomic energy;

members—(111) Afghanistan, Albania, Algeria, Argentina, Australia, Austria, Bangladesh, Belgium, Bolivia, Brazil, Bulgaria, Burma, Byelorussian Soviet Socialist Republic, Cambodia, Cameroon, Canada, Chile, China, Colombia, Costa Rica, Cuba, Cyprus, Czechoslovakia, Denmark, Dominican Republic, Ecuador, Egypt, El Salvador, Ethiopia, Finland, France, Gabon, Germany, Ghana, Greece, Guatemala, Haiti, Hungary, Iceland, India, Indonesia, Iran, Iraq, Ireland, Israel, Italy, Ivory Coast, Jamaica, Japan, Jordan, Kenya, North Korea, South Korea, Kuwait, Lebanon, Liberia, Libya, Liechtenstein, Luxembourg, Madagascar, Malaysia, Mali, Mauritius, Mexico, Mongolia, Morocco, Namibia, Netherlands, NZ, Nicaragua, Niger, Nigeria, Norway, Pakistan, Panama, Paraguay, Peru, Philippines, Poland, Portugal, Qatar, Romania, Saudi Arabia, Senegal, Sierra Leone, Singapore, South Africa, Spain, Sri Lanka, Sudan, Sweden, Switzerland, Syria, Tanzania, Thailand, Tunisia, Turkey, Uganda, Ukrainian Soviet Socialist Republic, UAE, UK, US, USSR, Uruguay, Vatican City, Venezuela, Vietnam, Yugoslavia, Zaire, Zambia, Zimbabwe

---

International Bank for Economic Cooperation (IBEC)

established—22 October 1963;

aim—to promote economic cooperation and development;

members—(9) Bulgaria, Cuba, Czechoslovakia, Hungary, Mongolia, Poland, Romania, USSR, Vietnam

---

International Bank for Reconstruction and Development (IBRD), also known as the World Bank;

established—22 July 1944, effective 27 December 1945;

aim—UN specialized agency that initially promoted economic rebuilding after World War II and now provides economic development loans;

members—(152) all UN members except Albania, Angola, Brunei, Bulgaria, Byelorussian Soviet Socialist Republic, Cuba, Czechoslovakia, Liechtenstein, Ukrainian Soviet Socialist Republic, USSR; other members are Kiribati, South Korea, Tonga

---

International Chamber of Commerce (ICC)

established—NA 1919;

aim—to promote free trade, private enterprise, and represent business interests at national and international levels;

members—(60 national councils) Argentina, Australia, Austria, Belgium, Brazil, Burkina, Cameroon, Canada, Colombia, Cyprus, Denmark, Ecuador, Egypt, Finland, France, Gabon, Germany, Greece, Iceland, India, Indonesia, Iran, Ireland, Israel, Italy, Ivory Coast, Japan, Jordan, South Korea, Kuwait, Lebanon, Luxembourg, Madagascar, Mexico, Morocco, Netherlands, Nigeria, Norway, Pakistan, Portugal, Saudi Arabia, Senegal, Singapore, South Africa, Spain, Sri Lanka, Sweden, Switzerland, Syria, Taiwan, Thailand, Togo, Tunisia, Turkey, UK, US, Uruguay, Venezuela, Yugoslavia, Zaire

---

International Civil Aviation Organization (ICAO)

established—7 December 1944, effective 4 April 1947;

aim—UN specialized agency to promote international cooperation in civil aviation;

members—(161) all UN members except Albania, Belize, Byelorussian Soviet Socialist Republic, Dominica, Liechtenstein, Namibia, Saint Kitts and Nevis, Ukrainian Soviet Socialist Republic, Western Samoa; other members are Cook Islands, Kiribati, North Korea, South Korea, Marshall Islands, Federated States of Micronesia, Monaco, Nauru, San Marino, Switzerland, Tonga

International Committee of the Red Cross (ICRC)	members—(25 individuals) all Swiss nationals
established—NA 1863; aim—to provide humanitarian aid in wartime;	
International Confederation of Free Trade Unions (ICFTU) established—NA December 1949; aim—to promote the trade union movement;	members—(142 national organizations in the following 95 areas) Antigua and Barbuda, Argentina, Australia, Austria, The Bahamas, Bangladesh, Barbados, Belgium, Bermuda, Botswana, Brazil, Burkina, Canada, Central African Republic, Chad, Chile, Colombia, Costa Rica, Cyprus, Denmark, Dominica, Dominican Republic, Ecuador, El Salvador, Falkland Islands, Fiji, Finland, France, The Gambia, Germany, Greece, Grenada, Guatemala, Guyana, Honduras, Hong Kong, Iceland, India, Indonesia, Israel, Italy, Jamaica, Japan, Kiribati, South Korea, Lebanon, Lesotho, Liberia, Luxembourg, Malawi, Malaysia, Malta, Mauritius, Mexico, Montserrat, Netherlands, Netherlands Antilles, NZ, Nicaragua, Norway, Pakistan, Panama, Papua New Guinea, Peru, Philippines, Poland, Portugal, Puerto Rico, Saint Helena, Saint Kitts and Nevis, Saint Lucia, Saint Vincent and the Grenadines, San Marino, Seychelles, Sierra Leone, Singapore, Spain, Sri Lanka, Suriname, Swaziland, Sweden, Switzerland, Taiwan, Thailand, Trinidad and Tobago, Tunisia, Turkey, Uganda, UK, US, USSR, Vanuatu, Vatican City, Venezuela, Western Samoa
International Court of Justice (ICJ), also known as the World Court; established—26 June 1945, effective 24 October 1945; aim—primary judicial organ of the UN;	members—(15 judges) elected by the General Assembly and Security Council to represent all principal legal systems
International Criminal Police Organization (INTERPOL) established—13 June 1956; aim—to promote international cooperation between criminal police authorities;	members—(151) Algeria, Andorra, Angola, Antigua and Barbuda, Argentina, Aruba, Australia, Austria, The Bahamas, Bahrain, Bangladesh, Barbados, Belgium, Belize, Benin, Bolivia, Botswana, Brazil, Brunei, Burkina, Burma, Burundi, Cambodia, Cameroon, Canada, Cape Verde, Central African Republic, Chad, Chile, China, Colombia, Congo, Costa Rica, Cuba, Cyprus, Denmark, Djibouti, Dominica, Dominican Republic, Ecuador, Egypt, Equatorial Guinea, Ethiopia, Fiji, Finland, France, Gabon, The Gambia, Germany, Ghana, Greece, Grenada, Guatemala, Guinea, Guyana, Haiti, Honduras, Hungary, Iceland, India, Indonesia, Iran, Iraq, Ireland, Israel, Italy, Ivory Coast, Jamaica, Japan, Jordan, Kenya, Kiribati, South Korea, Kuwait, Laos, Lebanon, Lesotho, Liberia, Libya, Liechtenstein, Luxembourg, Madagascar, Malawi, Malaysia, Maldives, Mali, Malta, Mauritania, Mauritius, Mexico, Monaco, Morocco, Mozambique, Nauru, Nepal, Netherlands, Netherlands Antilles, NZ, Nicaragua, Niger, Nigeria, Northern Ireland, Norway, Oman, Pakistan, Panama, Papua New Guinea, Paraguay, Peru, Philippines, Portugal, Qatar, Romania, Rwanda, Saint Kitts and Nevis, Saint Lucia, Saint Vincent and the Grenadines, Sao Tome and Principe, Saudi Arabia, Senegal, Seychelles, Sierra Leone, Singapore, Somalia, Spain, Sri Lanka, Sudan, Suriname, Swaziland, Sweden, Switzerland, Syria, Tanzania, Thailand, Togo, Tonga, Trinidad and Tobago, Tunisia, Turkey, Uganda, UAE, UK, US, USSR, Uruguay, Venezuela, Yemen, Yugoslavia, Zaire, Zambia, Zimbabwe
International Development Association (IDA) established—26 January 1960, effective 24 September 1960; aim—UN specialized agency and IBRD affiliate that provides economic loans for low income countries;	members—(136); Part I—(22 more economically advanced countries) Australia, Austria, Belgium, Canada, Denmark, Finland, France, Germany, Iceland, Ireland, Italy, Japan, Kuwait, Luxembourg, Netherlands, NZ, Norway, South Africa, Sweden, UAE, UK, US; Part II—(114 less developed nations) Afghanistan, Algeria, Argentina, Bangladesh, Belize, Benin, Bhutan, Bolivia, Botswana, Brazil, Burkina, Burma, Burundi, Cambodia, Cameroon, Cape Verde, Central African Republic, Chad, Chile, China, Colombia, Comoros, Congo, Costa Rica, Cyprus, Djibouti, Dominica, Dominican Republic, Ecuador, Egypt, El Salvador, Equatorial Guinea, Ethiopia, Fiji, Gabon, The Gambia, Ghana, Greece, Grenada, Guatemala, Guinea, Guinea-Bissau, Guyana, Haiti, Honduras, Hungary, India, Indonesia, Iran, Iraq, Israel, Ivory Coast, Jordan, Kenya, Kiribati, South Korea, Laos, Lebanon, Lesotho, Liberia, Libya, Madagascar, Malawi, Malaysia, Maldives, Mali, Mauritania, Mauritius, Mexico, Morocco, Mozambique, Nepal, Nicaragua, Niger, Nigeria, Oman, Pakistan, Panama, Papua New Guinea, Paraguay, Peru, Philippines, Poland, Rwanda, Saint Kitts and Nevis, Saint Lucia, Saint Vincent and the Grenadines, Sao Tome and Principe, Saudi Arabia, Senegal, Sierra Leone, Solomon Islands, Somalia, Spain, Sri Lanka, Sudan, Swaziland, Syria, Tanzania, Thailand, Togo, Tonga, Trinidad and Tobago, Tunisia, Turkey, Uganda, Vanuatu, Vietnam, Western Samoa, Yemen, Yugoslavia, Zaire, Zambia, Zimbabwe

International Energy Agency (IEA) *established*—15 November 1974; *aim*—established by the OECD to promote cooperation on energy matters, especially emergency oil sharing and relations between oil consumers and oil producers;	*members*—(21) Australia, Austria, Belgium, Canada, Denmark, Germany, Greece, Ireland, Italy, Japan, Luxembourg, Netherlands, NZ, Norway, Portugal, Spain, Sweden, Switzerland, Turkey, UK, US
International Finance Corporation (IFC) *established*—25 May 1955, effective 20 July 1956; *aim*—UN specialized agency and IBRD affiliate that helps private enterprise sector in economic development;	*members*—(133) Afghanistan, Antigua and Barbuda, Argentina, Australia, Austria, The Bahamas, Bangladesh, Barbados, Belgium, Belize, Benin, Bolivia, Botswana, Brazil, Burkina, Burma, Burundi, Cameroon, Canada, Chile, China, Colombia, Congo, Costa Rica, Cyprus, Denmark, Djibouti, Dominica, Dominican Republic, Ecuador, Egypt, El Salvador, Ethiopia, Fiji, Finland, France, Gabon, The Gambia, Germany, Ghana, Greece, Grenada, Guatemala, Guinea, Guinea-Bissau, Guyana, Haiti, Honduras, Hungary, Iceland, India, Indonesia, Iran, Iraq, Ireland, Israel, Italy, Ivory Coast, Jamaica, Japan, Jordan, Kenya, Kiribati, South Korea, Kuwait, Lebanon, Lesotho, Liberia, Libya, Luxembourg, Madagascar, Malawi, Malaysia, Maldives, Mali, Mauritania, Mauritius, Mexico, Morocco, Mozambique, Nepal, Netherlands, NZ, Nicaragua, Niger, Nigeria, Norway, Oman, Pakistan, Panama, Papua New Guinea, Paraguay, Peru, Philippines, Portugal, Romania, Rwanda, Saint Lucia, Saudi Arabia, Senegal, Seychelles, Sierra Leone, Singapore, Solomon Islands, Somalia, South Africa, Spain, Sri Lanka, Sudan, Swaziland, Sweden, Syria, Tanzania, Thailand, Togo, Tonga, Trinidad and Tobago, Tunisia, Turkey, Uganda, UAE, UK, US, Uruguay, Vanuatu, Venezuela, Vietnam, Western Samoa, Yemen, Yugoslavia, Zaire, Zambia, Zimbabwe
International Fund for Agricultural Development (IFAD) *established*—NA November 1974; *aim*—UN specialized agency that promotes agricultural development;	*members*—(144); Category I—(21 industrialized aid contributors) Australia, Austria, Belgium, Canada, Denmark, Finland, France, Germany, Greece, Ireland, Italy, Japan, Luxembourg, Netherlands, NZ, Norway, Spain, Sweden, Switzerland, UK, US; Category II—(12 petroleum-exporting aid contributors) Algeria, Gabon, Indonesia, Iran, Iraq, Kuwait, Libya, Nigeria, Qatar, Saudi Arabia, UAE, Venezuela; Category III—(111 aid recipients) Afghanistan, Angola, Antigua and Barbuda, Argentina, Bangladesh, Barbados, Belize, Benin, Bhutan, Bolivia, Botswana, Brazil, Burkina, Burma, Burundi, Cameroon, Cape Verde, Central African Republic, Chad, Chile, China, Colombia, Comoros, Congo, Costa Rica, Cuba, Cyprus, Djibouti, Dominica, Dominican Republic, Ecuador, Egypt, El Salvador, Equatorial Guinea, Ethiopia, Fiji, The Gambia, Ghana, Grenada, Guatemala, Guinea, Guinea-Bissau, Guyana, Haiti, Honduras, India, Israel, Ivory Coast, Jamaica, Jordan, Kenya, North Korea, South Korea, Laos, Lebanon, Lesotho, Liberia, Madagascar, Malawi, Malaysia, Maldives, Mali, Malta, Mauritania, Mauritius, Mexico, Morocco, Mozambique, Nepal, Nicaragua, Niger, Oman, Pakistan, Panama, Papua New Guinea, Paraguay, Peru, Philippines, Portugal, Romania, Rwanda, Saint Kitts and Nevis, Saint Lucia, Saint Vincent and the Grenadines, Sao Tome and Principe, Senegal, Seychelles, Sierra Leone, Solomon Islands, Somalia, Sri Lanka, Sudan, Suriname, Swaziland, Syria, Tanzania, Thailand, Togo, Tonga, Trinidad and Tobago, Tunisia, Turkey, Uganda, Uruguay, Vietnam, Western Samoa, Yemen, Yugoslavia, Zaire, Zambia, Zimbabwe
International Investment Bank (IIB) *established*—7 July 1970; *aim*—to promote economic development;	*members*—(9) Bulgaria, Cuba, Czechoslovakia, Hungary, Mongolia, Poland, Romania, USSR, Vietnam
International Labor Organization (ILO) *established*—11 April 1919 (affiliated with the UN 14 December 1946); *aim*—UN specialized agency concerned with world labor issues;	*members*—(148) all UN members except Albania, Bhutan, Brunei, The Gambia, Liechtenstein, Maldives, Oman, Saint Kitts and Nevis, Saint Vincent and the Grenadines, South Africa, Vanuatu, Vietnam, Western Samoa; other members are San Marino, Switzerland

International Maritime Organization (IMO)—name changed from Intergovernmental Maritime Consultative Organization (IMCO) on 22 May 1982;

established—17 March 1958;

aim—UN specialized agency concerned with world maritime affairs;

members—(132) Algeria, Angola, Antigua and Barbuda, Argentina, Australia, Austria, The Bahamas, Bahrain, Bangladesh, Barbados, Belgium, Benin, Bolivia, Brazil, Brunei, Bulgaria, Burma, Cambodia, Cameroon, Canada, Cape Verde, Chile, China, Colombia, Congo, Costa Rica, Cuba, Cyprus, Czechoslovakia, Denmark, Djibouti, Dominica, Dominican Republic, Ecuador, Egypt, El Salvador, Equatorial Guinea, Ethiopia, Fiji, Finland, France, Gabon, The Gambia, Germany, Ghana, Greece, Guatemala, Guinea, Guinea-Bissau, Guyana, Haiti, Honduras, Hungary, Iceland, India, Indonesia, Iran, Iraq, Ireland, Israel, Italy, Ivory Coast, Jamaica, Japan, Jordan, Kenya, North Korea, South Korea, Kuwait, Lebanon, Liberia, Libya, Madagascar, Malawi, Malaysia, Maldives, Malta, Mauritania, Mauritius, Mexico, Monaco, Morocco, Mozambique, Nepal, Netherlands, NZ, Nicaragua, Nigeria, Norway, Oman, Pakistan, Panama, Papua New Guinea, Peru, Philippines, Poland, Portugal, Qatar, Romania, Saint Lucia, Saint Vincent and the Grenadines, Saudi Arabia, Senegal, Seychelles, Sierra Leone, Singapore, Solomon Islands, Somalia, Spain, Sri Lanka, Sudan, Suriname, Sweden, Switzerland, Syria, Tanzania, Thailand, Togo, Trinidad and Tobago, Tunisia, Turkey, UAE, UK, US, USSR, Uruguay, Vanuatu, Venezuela, Vietnam, Yemen, Yugoslavia, Zaire;

associate member—(1) Hong Kong

International Maritime Satellite Organization (INMARSAT)

established—3 September 1976, effective 26 July 1979;

aim—to provide worldwide communications for maritime and other applications;

members—(55) Algeria, Argentina, Australia, Bahrain, Belgium, Brazil, Bulgaria, Byelorussian Soviet Socialist Republic, Canada, Chile, China, Colombia, Czechoslovakia, Denmark, Egypt, Finland, France, Gabon, Germany, Greece, India, Indonesia, Iran, Iraq, Israel, Italy, Japan, South Korea, Kuwait, Liberia, Malaysia, Netherlands, NZ, Nigeria, Norway, Oman, Pakistan, Panama, Peru, Philippines, Poland, Portugal, Qatar, Saudi Arabia, Singapore, Spain, Sri Lanka, Sweden, Switzerland, Tunisia, Ukrainian Soviet Socialist Republic, UAE, UK, US, USSR

International Monetary Fund (IMF)

established—22 July 1944, effective 27 December 1945;

aim—UN specialized agency concerned with world monetary stability and economic development;

members—(154) all UN members except Albania, Brunei, Bulgaria, Byelorussian Soviet Socialist Republic, Cuba, Liechtenstein, Ukrainian Soviet Socialist Republic, USSR; other members are Kiribati, South Korea, Tonga

International Olympic Committee (IOC)

established—23 June 1894;

aim—to promote the Olympic ideals and administer the Olympic games;

1992 Winter Olympics in Albertville, France (8-23 February);

1992 Summer Olympics in Barcelona, Spain (25 July-9 August);

1994 Winter Olympics in Lillehammer, Norway (12-27 February);

1996 Summer Olympics in Atlanta, United States (20 July-4 August):

1998 Winter Olympics in Nagano, Japan (date NA);

members—(165) Afghanistan, Albania, Algeria, American Samoa, Andorra, Angola, Antigua and Barbuda, Argentina, Aruba, Australia, Austria, The Bahamas, Bahrain, Bangladesh, Barbados, Belgium, Belize, Benin, Bermuda, Bhutan, Bolivia, Botswana, Brazil, British Virgin Islands, Brunei, Bulgaria, Burkina, Burma, Cameroon, Canada, Cayman Islands, Central African Republic, Chad, Chile, China, Colombia, Congo, Cook Islands, Costa Rica, Cuba, Cyprus, Czechoslovakia, Denmark, Djibouti, Dominican Republic, Ecuador, Egypt, El Salvador, Equatorial Guinea, Ethiopia, Fiji, Finland, France, Gabon, The Gambia, Germany, Ghana, Greece, Grenada, Guam, Guatemala, Guinea, Guyana, Haiti, Honduras, Hong Kong, Hungary, Iceland, India, Indonesia, Iran, Iraq, Ireland, Israel, Italy, Ivory Coast, Jamaica, Japan, Jordan, Kenya, North Korea, South Korea, Kuwait, Laos, Lebanon, Lesotho, Liberia, Libya, Liechtenstein, Luxembourg, Madagascar, Malawi, Malaysia, Maldives, Mali, Malta, Mauritania, Mauritius, Mexico, Monaco, Mongolia, Morocco, Mozambique, Nepal, Netherlands, Netherlands Antilles, NZ, Nicaragua, Niger, Nigeria, Norway, Oman, Pakistan, Panama, Papua New Guinea, Paraguay, Peru, Philippines, Poland, Portugal, Puerto Rico, Qatar, Romania, Rwanda, Saint Vincent and the Grenadines, San Marino, Saudi Arabia, Senegal, Seychelles, Sierra Leone, Singapore, Solomon Islands, Somalia, Spain, Sri Lanka, Sudan, Suriname, Swaziland, Sweden, Switzerland, Syria, Taiwan, Tanzania, Thailand, Togo, Tonga, Trinidad and Tobago, Tunisia, Turkey, Uganda, UAE, UK, US, USSR, Uruguay, Vanuatu, Venezuela, Vietnam, Virgin Islands, Western Samoa, Yemen, Yugoslavia, Zaire, Zambia, Zimbabwe

International Organization for Migration (IOM)—established as Provisional Intergovernmental Committee for the Movement of Migrants from Europe; renamed Intergovernmental Committee for European Migration (ICEM) on 15 November 1952; renamed Intergovernmental Committee for Migration (ICM) on NA November 1980; current name adopted 14 November 1989;

established—5 December 1951;

aim—to facilitate orderly international emigration and immigration;

members—(35) Argentina, Australia, Austria, Belgium, Bolivia, Chile, Colombia, Costa Rica, Cyprus, Denmark, Dominican Republic, Ecuador, El Salvador, Germany, Greece, Guatemala, Honduras, Israel, Italy, Kenya, South Korea, Luxembourg, Netherlands, Nicaragua, Norway, Panama, Paraguay, Peru, Philippines, Portugal, Switzerland, Thailand, US, Uruguay, Venezuela;

observers—(22) Belize, Brazil, Canada, Cape Verde, Egypt, Finland, France, Ghana, Guinea-Bissau, Japan, Mexico, NZ, San Marino, Somalia, Sovereign Military Order of Malta, Spain, Sweden, Turkey, UK, Vatican City, Yugoslavia, Zimbabwe

---

International Organization for Standardization (ISO)

established—NA February 1947;

aim—to promote the development of international standards;

members—(72 national standards organizations) Albania, Algeria, Argentina, Australia, Austria, Bangladesh, Belgium, Brazil, Bulgaria, Canada, Chile, China, Colombia, Cuba, Cyprus, Czechoslovakia, Denmark, Egypt, Ethiopia, Finland, France, Germany, Ghana, Greece, Hungary, India, Indonesia, Iran, Iraq, Ireland, Israel, Italy, Ivory Coast, Jamaica, Japan, Kenya, North Korea, South Korea, Malaysia, Mexico, Mongolia, Morocco, Netherlands, NZ, Nigeria, Norway, Pakistan, Papua New Guinea, Peru, Philippines, Poland, Portugal, Saudi Arabia, Singapore, South Africa, Spain, Sri Lanka, Sudan, Sweden, Switzerland, Syria, Tanzania, Thailand, Trinidad and Tobago, Tunisia, Turkey, UK, US, USSR, Venezuela, Vietnam, Yugoslavia;

correspondent members—(14) Bahrain, Barbados, Brunei, Guinea, Hong Kong, Iceland, Jordan, Kuwait, Malawi, Mauritius, Oman, Senegal, UAE, Uruguay

---

International Red Cross and Red Crescent Movement

established—NA 1928;

aim—to promote worldwide humanitarian aid through the International Committee of the Red Cross (ICRC) in wartime, and League of Red Cross and Red Crescent Societies (LORCS) in peacetime;

members—(9) 2 representatives from ICRC, 2 from LORCS, and 5 from national societies elected by the international conference of the International Red Cross and Red Crescent Movement

---

International Telecommunication Union (ITU)

established—9 December 1932, effective 1 January 1934, affiliated with the UN 15 November 1947;

aim—UN specialized agency concerned with world telecommunications;

members—(164) all UN members except Dominica, Saint Kitts and Nevis, Saint Lucia, Seychelles; other members are Kiribati, North Korea, South Korea, Monaco, Nauru, San Marino, Switzerland, Tonga, Vatican City

---

International Telecommunications Satellite Organization (INTELSAT)

established—20 August 1971, effective 12 February 1973;

aim—to develop and operate a global commercial telecommunications satellite system;

members—(118) Afghanistan, Algeria, Angola, Argentina, Australia, Austria, The Bahamas, Bangladesh, Barbados, Belgium, Benin, Bolivia, Brazil, Burkina, Cameroon, Canada, Central African Republic, Chad, Chile, China, Colombia, Congo, Costa Rica, Cyprus, Denmark, Dominican Republic, Ecuador, Egypt, El Salvador, Ethiopia, Fiji, Finland, France, Gabon, Germany, Ghana, Greece, Guatemala, Guinea, Haiti, Honduras, Iceland, India, Indonesia, Iran, Iraq, Ireland, Israel, Italy, Ivory Coast, Jamaica, Japan, Jordan, Kenya, South Korea, Kuwait, Lebanon, Libya, Liechtenstein, Luxembourg, Madagascar, Malawi, Malaysia, Mali, Mauritania, Mauritius, Mexico, Monaco, Morocco, Mozambique, Nepal, Netherlands, NZ, Nicaragua, Niger, Nigeria, Norway, Oman, Pakistan, Panama, Papua New Guinea, Paraguay, Peru, Philippines, Portugal, Qatar, Rwanda, Saudi Arabia, Senegal, Singapore, Somalia, South Africa, Spain, Sri Lanka, Sudan, Swaziland, Sweden, Switzerland, Syria, Tanzania, Thailand, Togo, Trinidad and Tobago, Tunisia, Turkey, Uganda, UAE, UK, US, Uruguay, Vatican City, Venezuela, Vietnam, Yemen, Yugoslavia, Zaire, Zambia, Zimbabwe

Islamic Development Bank (IDB) *established*—15 December 1973; *aim*—to promote Islamic economic aid and social development;	*members*—(43 plus the Palestine Liberation Organization) Afghanistan, Algeria, Bahrain, Bangladesh, Benin, Brunei, Burkina, Cameroon, Chad, Comoros, Djibouti, Egypt, Gabon, The Gambia, Guinea, Guinea-Bissau, Indonesia, Iran, Iraq, Jordan, Kuwait, Lebanon, Libya, Malaysia, Maldives, Mali, Mauritania, Morocco, Niger, Oman, Pakistan, Qatar, Saudi Arabia, Senegal, Sierra Leone, Somalia, Sudan, Syria, Tunisia, Turkey, Uganda, UAE, Yemen, Palestine Liberation Organization
Latin American Economic System (LAES), also known as Sistema Económico Latinoamericana (SELA); *established*—17 October 1975; *aim*—to promote economic and social development through regional cooperation;	*members*—(26) Argentina, Barbados, Bolivia, Brazil, Chile, Colombia, Costa Rica, Cuba, Dominican Republic, Ecuador, El Salvador, Grenada, Guatemala, Guyana, Haiti, Honduras, Jamaica, Mexico, Nicaragua, Panama, Paraguay, Peru, Suriname, Trinidad and Tobago, Uruguay, Venezuela
Latin American Integration Association (LAIA), also known as Asociación Latinoamericana de Integración (ALADI); *established*—12 August 1980, effective 18 March 1981; *aim*—to promote freer regional trade;	*members*—(11) Argentina, Bolivia, Brazil, Chile, Colombia, Ecuador, Mexico, Paraguay, Peru, Uruguay, Venezuela; *observers*—(13) Andean Group, Costa Rica, Cuba, Dominican Republic, Guatemala, Honduras, Inter-American Development Bank, Organization of American States, Panama, Portugal, Spain, UN Development Program, Economic Commission for Latin America and the Caribbean
League of Arab States (LAS)	see Arab League (AL)
League of Red Cross and Red Crescent Societies (LORCS) *established*—5 May 1919; *aim*—to provide humanitarian aid in peacetime;	*members*—(147) Afghanistan, Albania, Algeria, Angola, Argentina, Australia, Austria, The Bahamas, Bahrain, Bangladesh, Barbados, Belgium, Belize, Benin, Bolivia, Botswana, Brazil, Bulgaria, Burkina, Burma, Burundi, Cambodia, Cameroon, Canada, Cape Verde, Central African Republic, Chad, Chile, China, Colombia, Congo, Costa Rica, Cuba, Czechoslovakia, Denmark, Djibouti, Dominica, Dominican Republic, Ecuador, Egypt, El Salvador, Ethiopia, Fiji, Finland, France, The Gambia, Germany, Ghana, Greece, Grenada, Guatemala, Guinea, Guinea-Bissau, Guyana, Haiti, Honduras, Hungary, Iceland, India, Indonesia, Iran, Iraq, Ireland, Italy, Ivory Coast, Jamaica, Japan, Jordan, Kenya, North Korea, South Korea, Kuwait, Laos, Lebanon, Lesotho, Liberia, Libya, Liechtenstein, Luxembourg, Madagascar, Malawi, Malaysia, Mali, Mauritania, Mauritius, Mexico, Monaco, Mongolia, Morocco, Mozambique, Nepal, Netherlands, NZ, Nicaragua, Niger, Nigeria, Norway, Pakistan, Panama, Papua New Guinea, Paraguay, Peru, Philippines, Poland, Portugal, Qatar, Romania, Rwanda, Saint Lucia, Saint Vincent and the Grenadines, San Marino, Sao Tome and Principe, Saudi Arabia, Senegal, Sierra Leone, Singapore, Somalia, South Africa, Spain, Sri Lanka, Sudan, Suriname, Swaziland, Sweden, Switzerland, Syria, Tanzania, Thailand, Togo, Tonga, Trinidad and Tobago, Tunisia, Turkey, Uganda, UAE, UK, US, USSR, Uruguay, Venezuela, Vietnam, Western Samoa, Yemen, Yugoslavia, Zaire, Zambia, Zimbabwe; *associate members*—(2) Equatorial Guinea, Gabon
least developed countries (LLDCs)	that subgroup of the less developed countries (LDCs) initially identified by the UN General Assembly in 1971 as having no significant economic growth, per capita GNPs/GDPs normally less than $500, and low literacy rates; also known as the undeveloped countries; *the 41 LLDCs are* Afghanistan, Bangladesh, Benin, Bhutan, Botswana, Burkina, Burma, Burundi, Cape Verde, Central African Republic, Chad, Comoros, Djibouti, Equatorial Guinea, Ethiopia, The Gambia, Guinea, Guinea-Bissau, Haiti, Kiribati, Laos, Lesotho, Malawi, Maldives, Mali, Mauritania, Mozambique, Nepal, Niger, Rwanda, Sao Tome and Principe, Sierra Leone, Somalia, Sudan, Tanzania, Togo, Tuvalu, Uganda, Vanuatu, Western Samoa, Yemen

less developed countries (LDCs)	the bottom group in the comprehensive but mutually exclusive hierarchy of developed countries (DCs), USSR/Eastern Europe (USSR/EE), and less developed countries (LDCs); mainly countries with low levels of output, living standards, and technology; per capita GNPs/GDPs are generally below $5,000 and often less than $1,000; includes the advanced developing countries, developing countries, Four Dragons (Four Tigers), least developed countries (LLDCs), low-income countries, middle-income countries, newly industrializing economies (NIEs), the South, Third World, underdeveloped countries, undeveloped countries;
	the 173 LDCs are Afghanistan, Algeria, American Samoa, Angola, Anguilla, Antigua and Barbuda, Argentina, Aruba, The Bahamas, Bahrain, Bangladesh, Barbados, Belize, Benin, Bhutan, Bolivia, Botswana, Brazil, British Virgin Islands, Brunei, Burkina, Burma, Burundi, Cambodia, Cameroon, Cape Verde, Cayman Islands, Central African Republic, Chad, Chile, China, Christmas Island, Cocos Islands, Colombia, Comoros, Congo, Cook Islands, Costa Rica, Cuba, Cyprus, Czechoslovakia, Djibouti, Dominica, Dominican Republic, Ecuador, Egypt, El Salvador, Equatorial Guinea, Ethiopia, Falkland Islands, Fiji, French Guiana, French Polynesia, Gabon, The Gambia, Gaza Strip, Ghana, Gibraltar, Greenland, Grenada, Guadeloupe, Guam, Guatemala, Guernsey, Guinea, Guinea-Bissau, Guyana, Haiti, Honduras, Hong Kong, India, Indonesia, Iran, Iraq, Ivory Coast, Jamaica, Jersey, Jordan, Kenya, Kiribati, North Korea, South Korea, Kuwait, Laos, Lebanon, Lesotho, Liberia, Libya, Macau, Madagascar, Malawi, Malaysia, Maldives, Mali, Isle of Man, Marshall Islands, Martinique, Mauritania, Mauritius, Mayotte, Mexico, Federated States of Micronesia, Mongolia, Montserrat, Morocco, Mozambique, Namibia, Nauru, Nepal, Netherlands Antilles, New Caledonia, Nicaragua, Niger, Nigeria, Niue, Norfolk Island, Northern Mariana Islands, Oman, Trust Territory of the Pacific Islands (Palau), Pakistan, Panama, Papua New Guinea, Paraguay, Peru, Philippines, Pitcairn Islands, Puerto Rico, Qatar, Reunion, Rwanda, Saint Helena, Saint Kitts and Nevis, Saint Lucia, Saint Pierre and Miquelon, Saint Vincent and the Grenadines, Sao Tome and Principe, Saudi Arabia, Senegal, Seychelles, Sierra Leone, Singapore, Solomon Islands, Somalia, Sri Lanka, Sudan, Suriname, Swaziland, Syria, Taiwan, Tanzania, Thailand, Togo, Tokelau, Tonga, Trinidad and Tobago, Tunisia, Turks and Caicos Islands, Tuvalu, UAE, Uganda, Uruguay, Vanuatu, Venezuela, Vietnam, Virgin Islands, Wallis and Futuna, West Bank, Western Sahara, Western Samoa, Yemen, Zaire, Zambia, Zimbabwe
low-income countries	another term for the less developed countries with below-average per capita GNPs/GDPs; see less developed countries (LDCs)
middle-income countries	another term for the less developed countries with above-average per capita GNPs/GDPs; see less develped countries (LDCs)
newly industrializing countries (NICs)	former term for the newly industrializing economies; see newly industrializing economies (NIEs)
newly industrializing economies (NIEs)	that subgroup of the less developed countries (LDCs) that has experienced particularly rapid industrialization of their economies; formerly known as the newly industrializing countries (NICs); also known as advanced developing countries; usually includes the Four Dragons (Hong Kong, South Korea, Singapore, Taiwan) plus Brazil and Mexico
Nonaligned Movement (NAM) *established*—1-6 September 1961; *aim*—political and military cooperation apart from the traditional East or West blocs;	*members*—(101 plus the Palestine Liberation Organization) Afghanistan, Algeria, Angola, Argentina, The Bahamas, Bahrain, Bangladesh, Barbados, Belize, Benin, Bhutan, Bolivia, Botswana, Burkina, Burundi, Cambodia, Cameroon, Cape Verde, Central African Republic, Chad, Colombia, Comoros, Congo, Cuba, Cyprus, Djibouti, Ecuador, Egypt, Equatorial Guinea, Ethiopia, Gabon, The Gambia, Ghana, Grenada, Guinea, Guinea-Bissau, Guyana, India, Indonesia, Iran, Iraq, Ivory Coast, Jamaica, Jordan, Kenya, North Korea, Kuwait, Laos, Lebanon, Lesotho, Liberia, Libya, Madagascar, Malawi, Malaysia, Maldives, Mali, Malta, Mauritania, Mauritius, Morocco, Mozambique, Namibia, Nepal, Nicaragua, Niger, Nigeria, Oman, Pakistan, Panama, Peru, Qatar, Rwanda, Saint Lucia, Sao Tome and Principe, Saudi Arabia, Senegal, Seychelles, Sierra Leone, Singapore, Somalia, Sri Lanka, Sudan, Suriname, Swaziland, Syria, Tanzania, Togo, Trinidad and Tobago, Tunisia, Uganda, UAE, Vanuatu, Venezuela, Vietnam, Yemen, Yugoslavia, Zaire, Zambia, Zimbabwe, Palestine Liberation Organization; *observers*—(9) Antigua and Barbuda, Brazil, Costa Rica, Dominica, El Salvador, Mexico, Papua New Guinea, Philippines, Uruguay; *guests*—(12) Australia, Austria, Dominican Republic, Finland, Greece, Mongolia, Portugal, Romania, San Marino, Spain, Sweden, Switzerland

Nordic Council (NC) *established*—16 March 1952, effective 12 February 1953; *aim*—to promote regional economic, cultural, and environmental cooperation;	*members*—(5) Denmark, Finland, Iceland, Norway, Sweden; note—Denmark includes Faroe Islands and Greenland
Nordic Investment Bank (NIB) *established*—4 December 1975, effective 1 June 1976; *aim*—to promote economic cooperation and development;	*members*—(5) Denmark, Finland, Iceland, Norway, Sweden
North	a popular term for the rich industrialized countries generally located in the northern portion of the Northern Hemisphere; the counterpart of the South; see developed countries (DCs)
North Atlantic Treaty Organization (NATO) *established*—17 September 1949; *aim*—mutual defense and cooperation in other areas;	*members*—(16) Belgium, Canada, Denmark, France, Germany, Greece, Iceland, Italy, Luxembourg, Netherlands, Norway, Portugal, Spain, Turkey, UK, US
Nuclear Energy Agency (NEA) *established*—NA 1958; *aim*—associated with OECD, seeks to promote the peaceful uses of nuclear energy;	*members*—(23) Australia, Austria, Belgium, Canada, Denmark, Finland, France, Germany, Greece, Iceland, Ireland, Italy, Japan, Luxembourg, Netherlands, Norway, Portugal, Spain, Sweden, Switzerland, Turkey, UK, US
Organismo para la Proscripción de las Armas Nucleares en la América Latina y el Caribe (OPANAL)	see Agency for the Prohibition of Nuclear Weapons in Latin America and the Caribbean (OPANAL)
Organization for Economic Cooperation and Development (OECD) *established*—14 December 1960, effective 30 September 1961; *aim*—to promote economic cooperation and development;	*members*—(24) Australia, Austria, Belgium, Canada, Denmark, Finland, France, Germany, Greece, Iceland, Ireland, Italy, Japan, Luxembourg, Netherlands, NZ, Norway, Portugal, Spain, Sweden, Switzerland, Turkey, UK, US; *special member*—(1) Yugoslavia
Organization of African Unity (OAU) *established*—25 May 1963; *aim*—to promote unity and cooperation among African states;	*members*—(51) Algeria, Angola, Benin, Botswana, Burkina, Burundi, Cameroon, Cape Verde, Central African Republic, Chad, Comoros, Congo, Djibouti, Egypt, Equatorial Guinea, Ethiopia, Gabon, The Gambia, Ghana, Guinea, Guinea-Bissau, Ivory Coast, Kenya, Lesotho, Liberia, Libya, Madagascar, Malawi, Mali, Mauritania, Mauritius, Mozambique, Namibia, Niger, Nigeria, Rwanda, Sahrawi Arab Democratic Republic, Sao Tome and Principe, Senegal, Seychelles, Sierra Leone, Somalia, Sudan, Swaziland, Tanzania, Togo, Tunisia, Uganda, Zaire, Zambia, Zimbabwe
Organization of American States (OAS) *established*—30 April 1948, effective 13 December 1951; *aim*—to promote peace and security as well as economic and social development;	*members*—(35) Antigua and Barbuda, Argentina, The Bahamas, Barbados, Belize, Bolivia, Brazil, Canada, Chile, Colombia, Costa Rica, Cuba (excluded from formal participation since 1962), Dominica, Dominican Republic, Ecuador, El Salvador, Grenada, Guatemala, Guyana, Haiti, Honduras, Jamaica, Mexico, Nicaragua, Panama, Paraguay, Peru, Saint Kitts and Nevis, Saint Lucia, Saint Vincent and the Grenadines, Suriname, Trinidad and Tobago, US, Uruguay, Venezuela; *observers*—(22) Algeria, Austria, Belgium, Cyprus, EC, Egypt, Equatorial Guinea, Finland, France, Germany, Greece, Israel, Italy, Japan, Morocco, Netherlands, Pakistan, Portugal, Saudi Arabia, Spain, Switzerland, Vatican City

Organization of Arab Petroleum Exporting Countries (OAPEC)	*members*—(10) Algeria, Bahrain, Egypt, Iraq, Kuwait, Libya, Qatar, Saudi Arabia, Syria, UAE
established—9 January 1968;	
aim—to promote cooperation in the petroleum industry;	
Organization of Eastern Caribbean States (OECS)	*members*—(7) Antigua and Barbuda, Dominica, Grenada, Montserrat, Saint Kitts and Nevis, Saint Lucia, Saint Vincent and the Grenadines;
established—18 June 1981, effective 4 July 1981;	*associate member*—(1) British Virgin Islands
aim—to promote political, economic, and defense cooperation;	
Organization of Petroleum Exporting Countries (OPEC)	*members*—(13) Algeria, Ecuador, Gabon, Indonesia, Iran, Iraq, Kuwait, Libya, Nigeria, Qatar, Saudi Arabia, UAE, Venezuela
established—14 September 1960;	
aim—to coordinate petroleum policies;	
Organization of the Islamic Conference (OIC)	*members*—(44 plus the Palestine Liberation Organization) Afghanistan, Algeria, Bahrain, Bangladesh, Benin, Brunei, Burkina, Cameroon, Chad, Comoros, Djibouti, Egypt, Gabon, The Gambia, Guinea, Guinea-Bissau, Indonesia, Iran, Iraq, Jordan, Kuwait, Lebanon, Libya, Malaysia, Maldives, Mali, Mauritania, Morocco, Niger, Nigeria, Oman, Pakistan, Qatar, Saudi Arabia, Senegal, Sierra Leone, Somalia, Sudan, Syria, Tunisia, Turkey, Uganda, UAE, Yemen, Palestine Liberation Organization; note—Afghanistan was suspended in January 1980, but in March 1989 the self-proclaimed Afghan Interim Government based in Pakistan was given membership;
established—22-25 September 1969;	
aim—to promote Islamic solidarity and cooperation in economic, social, cultural, and political affairs;	
	observer—(1) Turkish-Cypriot administered area of Cyprus
Paris Club	see Group of 10
Permanent Court of Arbitration (PCA)	*members*—(75) Argentina, Australia, Austria, Belgium, Bolivia, Brazil, Bulgaria, Burkina, Byelorussian Soviet Socialist Republic, Cambodia, Cameroon, Canada, Chile, China, Colombia, Cuba, Czechoslovakia, Denmark, Dominican Republic, Ecuador, Egypt, El Salvador, Fiji, Finland, France, Germany, Greece, Guatemala, Haiti, Honduras, Hungary, Iceland, India, Iran, Iraq, Israel, Italy, Japan, Laos, Lebanon, Luxembourg, Malta, Mauritius, Mexico, Netherlands, NZ, Nicaragua, Nigeria, Norway, Pakistan, Panama, Paraguay, Peru, Poland, Portugal, Romania, Senegal, Spain, Sri Lanka, Sudan, Swaziland, Sweden, Switzerland, Thailand, Turkey, Uganda, Ukrainian Soviet Socialist Republic, UK, US, USSR, Uruguay, Venezuela, Yugoslavia, Zaire, Zimbabwe
established—NA 1899;	
aim—to facilitate the settlement of international disputes;	
Population Commission	*members*—(27) selected on a rotating basis from all regions
established—3 October 1946;	
aim—ECOSOC organization dealing with population matters;	
Rio Group (RG)	*members*—(11) Argentina, Bolivia, Brazil, Chile, Colombia, Ecuador, Mexico, Paraguay, Peru, Uruguay, Venezuela; note—Panama was expelled in 1988
established—NA 1988;	
aim—a consultation mechanism on regional Latin American issues;	
Second World	another term for the traditionally Marxist-Leninist states with authoritarian governments and command economies based on the Soviet model; see centrally planned economies

socialist countries	in general, countries in which the government owns and plans the use of the major factors of production; note—the term is sometimes used incorrectly as a synonym for Communist countries
South	a popular term for the poorer, less industrialized countries generally located south of the developed countries; the counterpart of the North; see less developed countries (LDCs)
South Asian Association for Regional Cooperation (SAARC) *established*—8 December 1985; *aim*—to promote economic, social, and cultural cooperation;	*members*—(7) Bangladesh, Bhutan, India, Maldives, Nepal, Pakistan, Sri Lanka
South Pacific Commission (SPC) *established*—6 February 1947, effective 29 July 1948; *aim*—to promote regional cooperation in economic and social matters;	*members*—(27) American Samoa, Australia, Cook Islands, Fiji, France, French Polynesia, Guam, Kiribati, Marshall Islands, Federated States of Micronesia, Nauru, New Caledonia, NZ, Niue, Northern Mariana Islands, Trust Territory of the Pacific Islands (Palau), Papua New Guinea, Pitcairn Islands, Solomon Islands, Tokelau, Tonga, Tuvalu, UK, US, Vanuatu, Wallis and Futuna, Western Samoa
South Pacific Forum (SPF) *established*—5 August 1971; *aim*—to promote regional cooperation in political matters;	*members*—(15) Australia, Cook Islands, Fiji, Kiribati, Marshall Islands, Federated States of Micronesia, Nauru, NZ, Niue, Papua New Guinea, Solomon Islands, Tonga, Tuvalu, Vanuatu, Western Samoa; *observer*—(1) Trust Territory of the Pacific Islands (Palau)
Southern African Customs Union (SACU) *established*—11 December 1969; *aim*—to promote free trade and cooperation in customs matters;	*members*—(9) Bophuthatswana, Botswana, Ciskei, Lesotho, Namibia, South Africa, Swaziland, Transkei, Venda
Southern African Development Coordination Conference (SADCC) *established*—1 April 1980; *aim*—to promote regional economic development and reduce dependence on South Africa;	*members*—(10) Angola, Botswana, Lesotho, Malawi, Mozambique, Namibia, Swaziland, Tanzania, Zambia, Zimbabwe
Statistical Commission *established*—21 June 1946; *aim*—ECOSOC organization dealing with development and standardization of national statistics;	*members*—(24) selected on a rotating basis from all regions
Third World	another term for the less developed countries; see less developed countries (LDCs)
underdeveloped countries	refers to those less developed countries with the potential for above-average economic growth; see less developed countries (LDCs)
undeveloped countries	refers to those extremely poor less developed countries (LDCs) with little prospect for economic growth; see least developed countries (LLDCs)
Union Douanière et Economique de l'Afrique Centrale (UDEAC)	see Central African Customs and Economic Union (UDEAC)

United Nations (UN)

established—26 June 1945, effective 24 October 1945;

aim—to maintain international peace and security as well as promote cooperation involving economic, social, cultural and humanitarian problems;

members—(159) Afghanistan, Albania, Algeria, Angola, Antigua and Barbuda, Argentina, Australia, Austria, The Bahamas, Bahrain, Bangladesh, Barbados, Belgium, Belize, Benin, Bhutan, Bolivia, Botswana, Brazil, Brunei, Bulgaria, Burkina, Burma, Burundi, Byelorussian Soviet Socialist Republic, Cambodia, Cameroon, Canada, Cape Verde, Central African Republic, Chad, Chile, China, Colombia, Comoros, Congo, Costa Rica, Cuba, Cyprus, Czechoslovakia, Denmark, Djibouti, Dominica, Dominican Republic, Ecuador, Egypt, El Salvador, Equatorial Guinea, Ethiopia, Fiji, Finland, France, Gabon, The Gambia, Germany, Ghana, Greece, Grenada, Guatemala, Guinea, Guinea-Bissau, Guyana, Haiti, Honduras, Hungary, Iceland, India, Indonesia, Iran, Iraq, Ireland, Israel, Italy, Ivory Coast, Jamaica, Japan, Jordan, Kenya, Kuwait, Laos, Lebanon, Lesotho, Liberia, Libya, Liechtenstein, Luxembourg, Madagascar, Malawi, Malaysia, Maldives, Mali, Malta, Mauritania, Mauritius, Mexico, Mongolia, Morocco, Mozambique, Namibia, Nepal, Netherlands, NZ, Nicaragua, Niger, Nigeria, Norway, Oman, Pakistan, Panama, Papua New Guinea, Paraguay, Peru, Philippines, Poland, Portugal, Qatar, Romania, Rwanda, Saint Kitts and Nevis, Saint Lucia, Saint Vincent and the Grenadines, Sao Tome and Principe, Saudi Arabia, Senegal, Seychelles, Sierra Leone, Singapore, Solomon Islands, Somalia, South Africa, Spain, Sri Lanka, Sudan, Suriname, Swaziland, Sweden, Syria, Tanzania, Thailand, Togo, Trinidad and Tobago, Tunisia, Turkey, Uganda, Ukrainian Soviet Socialist Republic, UAE, UK, US, USSR, Uruguay, Vanuatu, Venezuela, Vietnam, Western Samoa, Yemen, Yugoslavia, Zaire, Zambia, Zimbabwe; note—all UN members are represented in the General Assembly;

observers—(6) North Korea, South Korea, Monaco, San Marino, Switzerland, Vatican City

---

United Nations Angola Verification Mission (UNAVEM)

established—20 December 1988;

aim—established by the UN Security Council to verify the withdrawal of Cuban troops from Angola;

members—(10) Algeria, Argentina, Brazil, Congo, Czechoslovakia, India, Jordan, Norway, Spain, Yugoslavia

---

United Nations Center for Human Settlements (UNCHS or Habitat)

established—12 October 1978;

aim—to assist in solving human settlement problems;

members—(58) selected on a rotating basis from all regions

United Nations Children's Fund (UNICEF)—acronym retained from the predecessor organization UN International Children's Emergency Fund;

established—11 December 1946;

aim—to help establish child health and welfare services;

members—(41) selected on a rotating basis from all regions

United Nations Conference on Trade and Development (UNCTAD)

established—30 December 1964;

aim—to promote international trade;

members—(166) all UN members plus North Korea, South Korea, Monaco, San Marino, Switzerland, Tonga, Vatican City

United Nations Development Program (UNDP)

established—22 November 1965;

aim—to provide technical assistance to stimulate economic and social development;

members—(48) selected on a rotating basis from all regions

United Nations Disengagement Observer Force (UNDOF)

established—31 May 1974;

aim—established by the UN Security Council to observe the 1973 Arab-Israeli ceasefire;

members—(4) Austria, Canada, Finland, Poland

United Nations Educational, Scientific, and Cultural Organization (UNESCO)

established—16 November 1945, effective 4 November 1946;

aim—to promote cooperation in education, science, and culture;

members—(159) all UN members except Brunei, Liechtenstein, Singapore, Solomon Islands, South Africa, UK, US, Vanuatu; other members are Cook Islands, Kiribati, North Korea, South Korea, Monaco, San Marino, Switzerland, Tonga;

associate members—(3) Aruba, British Virgin Islands, Netherlands Antilles

---

United Nations Environment Program (UNEP)

established—15 December 1972;

aim—to promote international cooperation on all environmental matters;

members—(58) selected on a rotating basis from all regions

United Nations Force in Cyprus (UNFICYP)

established—4 March 1964;

aim—established by the UN Security Council to serve as a peacekeeping force beween Greek Cypriots and Turkish Cypriots in Cyprus;

members—(8) Australia, Austria, Canada, Denmark, Finland, Ireland, Sweden, UK

United Nations General Assembly

established—26 June 1945, effective 24 October 1945;

aim—primary deliberative organ in the UN;

members—(159) all UN members are represented in the General Assembly

---

United Nations Industrial Development Organization (UNIDO)

established—17 November 1966, effective 1 January 1967;

aim—UN specialized agency that promotes industrial development especially among the members;

members—(150) all UN members except Antigua and Barbuda, Australia, Brunei, Cambodia, Chad, Djibouti, Iceland, Liberia, Liechtenstein, Singapore, Solomon Islands, South Africa, Western Samoa; other members are North Korea, South Korea, Switzerland, Tonga

United Nations Interim Force in Lebanon (UNIFIL)	*members*—(9) Fiji, Finland, France, Ghana, Ireland, Italy, Nepal, Norway, Sweden
established—19 March 1978;	
aim—established by the UN Security Council to confirm the withdrawal of Israeli forces, restore peace, and reestablish Lebanese authority in southern Lebanon;	
United Nations Iran-Iraq Military Observer Group (UNIIMOG)	*members*—(26) Argentina, Australia, Austria, Bangladesh, Canada, Denmark, Finland, Ghana, Hungary, India, Indonesia, Ireland, Italy, Kenya, Malaysia, NZ, Nigeria, Norway, Peru, Poland, Senegal, Sweden, Turkey, Uruguay, Yugoslavia, Zambia
established—9 August 1988;	
aim—established by the UN Security Council to observe the 1988 Iran-Iraq ceasefire;	
United Nations Military Observer Group in India and Pakistan (UNMOGIP)	*members*—(8) Belgium, Chile, Denmark, Finland, Italy, Norway, Sweden, Uruguay
established—13 August 1948;	
aim—established by the UN Security Council to observe the 1949 India-Pakistan ceasefire;	
United Nations Office of the High Commissioner for Refugees (UNHCR)	*members*—(43) Algeria, Argentina, Australia, Austria, Belgium, Brazil, Canada, China, Colombia, Denmark, Finland, France, Germany, Greece, Iran, Israel, Italy, Japan, Lebanon, Lesotho, Madagascar, Morocco, Namibia, Netherlands, Nicaragua, Nigeria, Norway, Pakistan, Somalia, Sudan, Sweden, Switzerland, Tanzania, Thailand, Tunisia, Turkey, Uganda, UK, US, Vatican City, Venezuela, Yugoslavia, Zaire
established—3 December 1949, effective 1 January 1951;	
aim—to try to ensure the humanitarian treatment of refugees and find permanent solutions to refugee problems;	
United Nations Population Fund (UNFPA)—acronym retained from predecessor organization UN Fund for Population Activities;	*members*—(48) selected on a rotating basis from all regions
established—NA July 1967;	
aim—to promote assistance in dealing with population problems;	
United Nations Relief and Works Agency for Palestine Refugees in the Near East (UNRWA)	*members*—(10) Belgium, Egypt, France, Japan, Jordan, Lebanon, Syria, Turkey, UK, US
established—8 December 1949;	
aim—to provide assistance to Palestinian refugees;	
United Nations Secretariat	*members*—Secretary General appointed for a five-year term by the General Assembly on the recommendation of the Security Council
established—26 June 1945, effective 24 October 1945;	
aim—primary administrative organ of the UN;	

United Nations Security Council	*permanent members*—(5) China, France, UK, US, USSR;
established—26 June 1945, effective 24 October 1945;	*nonpermanent members*—(10) elected for two year terms by the UN General Assembly; Austria (1991-92), Belgium (1991-92), Cuba (1990-91), Ecuador (1991-92), India (1991-92), Ivory Coast (1990-91), Romania (1990-91), Yemen (1990-91), Zaire (1990-91), Zimbabwe (1991-92)
aim—to maintain international peace and security;	
United Nations Truce Supervision Organization (UNTSO)	*members*—(16) Argentina, Australia, Austria, Canada, Chile, Denmark, Finland, France, Ireland, Italy, Netherlands, NZ, Norway, Sweden, US, USSR
established—NA May 1948;	
aim—initially established by the UN Security Council to supervise the 1948 Arab-Israeli ceasefire and subsequently extended to work in the Sinai, Lebanon, Jordan, Afghanistan, and Pakistan;	
United Nations Trusteeship Council	*members*—(5) China, France, UK, US, USSR
established—26 June 1945, effective 24 October 1945;	
aim—to supervise the administration of the UN trust territories; only one of the original 11 trusteeships remains—the Trust Territory of the Pacific Islands (Palau);	
Universal Postal Union (UPU)	*members*—(168) all UN members except Antigua and Barbuda, Namibia, South Africa; other members are Kiribati, North Korea, South Korea, Monaco, Nauru, Netherlands Antilles, San Marino, Switzerland, Tonga, Tuvalu, UK Overseas Territories, Vatican City
established—9 October 1874, affiliated with the UN 15 November 1947, effective 1 July 1948;	
aim—UN specialized agency that promotes international postal cooperation;	
USSR/Eastern Europe (USSR/EE)	the middle group in the comprehensive but mutually exclusive hierarchy of developed countries (DCs), USSR/Eastern Europe (USSR/EE), and less developed countries (LDCs); these countries are in political and economic transition; this group includes Albania, Bulgaria, Czechoslovakia, Hungary, Poland, Romania, USSR, Yugoslavia
Warsaw Pact (WP)	was established 14 May 1955 to promote mutual defense; members met on 1 July 1991 to dissolve the alliance; member states—Bulgaria, Czechoslovakia, Hungary, Poland, Romania, USSR—are now in the process of ratifying this agreement
West African Development Bank (WADB), also known as Banque Ouest-Africaine de Développement (BOAD);	*members*—(7) Benin, Burkina, Ivory Coast, Mali, Niger, Senegal, Togo
established—14 November 1973;	
aim—to promote economic development and integration;	
West African Economic Community (CEAO)—acronym from Communauté Economique de l'Afrique de l'Ouest;	*members*—(7) Benin, Burkina, Ivory Coast, Mali, Mauritania, Niger, Senegal;
	observers—(2) Guinea, Togo
established—3 June 1972;	
aim—to promote regional economic development;	

Western European Union (WEU)	*members*—(9) Belgium, France, Germany, Italy, Luxembourg, Netherlands, Portugal, Spain, UK
established—23 October 1954, effective 6 May 1955; *aim*—mutual defense and progressive political unification;	
World Bank	see International Bank for Reconstruction and Development (IBRD)
World Confederation of Labor (WCL) *established*—19 June 1920 as the International Federation of Christian Trade Unions (IFCTU), renamed 4 October 1968; *aim*—to promote the trade union movement;	*members*—(93 national organizations) Algeria, Angola, Antigua and Barbuda, Argentina, Aruba, Austria, Bangladesh, Belgium, Belize, Benin, Bolivia, Botswana, Brazil, Burkina, Cameroon, Canada, Cape Verde, Central African Republic, Chad, Chile, Colombia, Costa Rica, Cuba, Cyprus, Dominica, Dominican Republic, Ecuador, El Salvador, France, French Guiana, Gabon, The Gambia, Ghana, Grenada, Guadaloupe, Guatemala, Guinea, Guyana, Haiti, Honduras, Hong Kong, Indonesia, Italy, Ivory Coast, Jamaica, Kenya, Lesotho, Liberia, Liechtenstein, Luxembourg, Madagascar, Malaysia, Mali, Malta, Martinique, Mauritius, Mexico, Montserrat, Namibia, Netherlands, Netherlands Antilles, Nicaragua, Niger, Nigeria, Pakistan, Panama, Paraguay, Peru, Philippines, Poland, Portugal, Puerto Rico, Rwanda, Saint Kitts and Nevis, Saint Lucia, Saint Vincent and the Grenadines, Senegal, Seychelles, Sierra Leone, Spain, Sri Lanka, Suriname, Switzerland, Tanzania, Thailand, Togo, UK, US, Uruguay, Vietnam, Zaire, Zambia, Zimbabwe
World Court	see International Court of Justice (ICJ)
World Federation of Trade Unions (WFTU) *established*—NA 1945; *aim*—to promote the trade union movement;	*members*—(74 plus the Palestine Liberation Organization) Afghanistan, Albania, Angola, Argentina, Austria, Bahrain, Bangladesh, Benin, Bolivia, Bulgaria, Burkina, Cambodia, China, Congo, Costa Rica, Cuba, Cyprus, Czechoslovakia, Dominican Republic, Ecuador, El Salvador, Ethiopia, France, French Guiana, The Gambia, Germany, Guadaloupe, Guatemala, Guinea-Bissau, Guyana, Haiti, Honduras, Hungary, India, Indonesia, Iran, Iraq, Jamaica, Jordan, North Korea, Kuwait, Laos, Lebanon, Madagascar, Martinique, Mauritius, Mongolia, Namibia, New Caledonia, Nicaragua, Oman, Pakistan, Panama, Peru, Philippines, Poland, Puerto Rico, Reunion, Romania, Saint Pierre and Miquelon, Saint Vincent and the Grenadines, Saudi Arabia, Senegal, Solomon Islands, South Africa, Sri Lanka, Sudan, Syria, Trinidad and Tobago, USSR, Vanuatu, Venezuela, Vietnam, Yemen, Palestine Liberation Organization
World Food Council (WFC) *established*—17 December 1974; *aim*—ECOSOC organization that studies world food problems and recommends solutions;	*members*—(36) selected on a rotating basis from all regions
World Food Program (WFP) *established*—24 November 1961; *aim*—ECOSOC organization that provides food aid to assist in development or disaster relief;	*members*—(30) selected on a rotating basis from all regions
World Health Organization (WHO) *established*—22 July 1946, effective 7 April 1948; *aim*—UN specialized agency concerned with health matters;	*members*—(165) all UN members except Belize, Liechtenstein; other members are Cook Islands, Kiribati, North Korea, South Korea, Monaco, San Marino, Switzerland, Tonga

World Intellectual Property Organization (WIPO)

established—14 July 1967, effective 26 April 1970;

aim—UN specialized agency concerned with the protection of literary, artistic, and scientific works;

members—(124) Algeria, Angola, Argentina, Australia, Austria, The Bahamas, Bangladesh, Barbados, Belgium, Benin, Brazil, Bulgaria, Burkina, Burundi, Byelorussian Soviet Socialist Republic, Cameroon, Canada, Central African Republic, Chad, Chile, China, Colombia, Congo, Costa Rica, Cuba, Cyprus, Czechoslovakia, Denmark, Ecuador, Egypt, El Salvador, Fiji, Finland, France, Gabon, The Gambia, Germany, Ghana, Greece, Guatemala, Guinea, Guinea-Bissau, Haiti, Honduras, Hungary, Iceland, India, Indonesia, Iraq, Ireland, Israel, Italy, Ivory Coast, Jamaica, Japan, Jordan, Kenya, North Korea, South Korea, Lebanon, Lesotho, Liberia, Libya, Liechtenstein, Luxembourg, Madagascar, Malawi, Malaysia, Mali, Malta, Mauritania, Mauritius, Mexico, Monaco, Mongolia, Morocco, Netherlands, NZ, Nicaragua, Niger, Norway, Pakistan, Panama, Paraguay, Peru, Philippines, Poland, Portugal, Qatar, Romania, Rwanda, Saudi Arabia, Senegal, Sierra Leone, Somalia, South Africa, Spain, Sri Lanka, Sudan, Suriname, Swaziland, Sweden, Switzerland, Tanzania, Thailand, Togo, Trinidad and Tobago, Tunisia, Turkey, Uganda, Ukrainian Soviet Socialist Republic, UAE, UK, US, USSR, Uruguay, Vatican City, Venezuela, Vietnam, Yemen, Yugoslavia, Zaire, Zambia, Zimbabwe

World Meteorological Organization (WMO)

established—11 October 1947, effective 4 April 1951;

aim—specialized UN agency concerned with meteorological cooperation;

members—(159) all UN members except Bhutan, Equatorial Guinea, Grenada, Liechtenstein, Namibia, Saint Kitts and Nevis, Saint Vincent and the Grenadines, Western Samoa; South Africa is included although WMO membership is suspended; other members are British Caribbean Territories, French Polynesia, Hong Kong, North Korea, South Korea, Netherlands Antilles, New Caledonia, Switzerland

World Tourism Organization (WTO)

established—2 January 1975;

aim—promote tourism as a means of contributing to economic development, international understanding, and peace;

members—(104) Afghanistan, Algeria, Angola, Argentina, Australia, Austria, Bangladesh, Belgium, Benin, Bolivia, Brazil, Bulgaria, Burkina, Burundi, Cambodia, Cameroon, Canada, Chad, Chile, China, Colombia, Congo, Cuba, Cyprus, Czechoslovakia, Dominican Republic, Ecuador, Egypt, Ethiopia, Finland, France, Gabon, The Gambia, Germany, Ghana, Greece, Grenada, Guinea, Haiti, Hungary, India, Indonesia, Iran, Iraq, Israel, Italy, Ivory Coast, Jamaica, Japan, Jordan, Kenya, North Korea, South Korea, Kuwait, Laos, Lebanon, Lesotho, Libya, Madagascar, Malawi, Maldives, Mali, Malta, Mauritania, Mauritius, Mexico, Mongolia, Morocco, Nepal, Netherlands, Niger, Nigeria, Pakistan, Panama, Peru, Poland, Portugal, Romania, Rwanda, San Marino, Sao Tome and Principe, Senegal, Sierra Leone, Spain, Sri Lanka, Sudan, Switzerland, Syria, Tanzania, Togo, Tunisia, Turkey, Uganda, UAE, US, USSR, Uruguay, Venezuela, Vietnam, Yemen, Yugoslavia, Zaire, Zambia, Zimbabwe;

associate members—(4) Aruba, Macau, Netherlands Antilles, Puerto Rico;

permanent observer—(1) Vatican City

Appendix D:

Weights and Measures

Mathematical Power	Name
10^{18} or 1,000,000,000,000,000,000	one quintillion
10^{15} or 1,000,000,000,000,000	one quadrillion
10^{12} or 1,000,000,000,000	one trillion
10^{9} or 1,000,000,000	one billion
10^{6} or 1,000,000	one million
10^{3} or 1,000	one thousand
10^{2} or 100	one hundred
10^{1} or 10	ten
10^{0} or 1	one
10^{-1} or 0.1	one tenth
10^{-2} or 0.01	one hundredth
10^{-3} or 0.001	one thousandth
10^{-6} or 0.000 001	one millionth
10^{-9} or 0.000 000 001	one billionth
10^{-12} or 0.000 000 000 001	one trillionth
10^{-15} or 0.000 000 000 000 001	one quadrillionth
10^{-18} or 0.000 000 000 000 000 001	one quintillionth

Metric Interrelationships

Conversions from a multiple or submultiple to the basic units of meters, liters, or grams can be done using the table. For example, to convert from kilometers to meters, multiply by 1,000 (9.26 kilometers equals 9,260 meters) or to convert from meters to kilometers, multiply by 0.001 (9,260 meters equals 9.26 kilometers)

Prefix	Symbol	Length, weight, capacity	Area	Volume
exa	E	10^{18}	10^{36}	10^{54}
peta	P	10^{15}	10^{30}	10^{45}
tera	T	10^{12}	10^{24}	10^{36}
giga	G	10^{9}	10^{18}	10^{27}
mega	M	10^{6}	10^{12}	10^{18}
hectokilo	hk	10^{5}	10^{10}	10^{15}
myria	ma	10^{4}	10^{8}	10^{12}
kilo	k	10^{3}	10^{6}	10^{9}
hecto	h	10^{2}	10^{4}	10^{6}
deka	da	10^{1}	10^{2}	10^{3}
basic unit	—	1 meter, 1 gram, 1 liter	1 meter^2	1 meter^3
deci	d	10^{-1}	10^{-2}	10^{-3}
centi	c	10^{-2}	10^{-4}	10^{-6}
milli	m	10^{-3}	10^{-6}	10^{-9}
decimilli	dm	10^{-4}	10^{-8}	10^{-12}
centimilli	cm	10^{-5}	10^{-10}	10^{-15}
micro	u	10^{-6}	10^{-12}	10^{-18}
nano	n	10^{-9}	10^{-18}	10^{-27}
pico	p	10^{-12}	10^{-24}	10^{-36}
femto	f	10^{-15}	10^{-30}	10^{-45}
atto	a	10^{-18}	10^{-36}	10^{-54}

Equivalents

Unit	Metric Equivalent	US Equivalent
acre	0.404 685 64 hectares	43,560 feet^2
acre	4,046.856 4 meters^2	4,840 yards^2
acre	0.004 046 856 4 kilometers^2	0.001 562 5 miles^2, statute
are	100 meters^2	119.599 yards^2
barrel (petroleum, US)	158.987 29 liters	42 gallons
(proof spirits, US)	151.416 47 liters	40 gallons
(beer, US)	117.347 77 liters	31 gallons
bushel	35.239 07 liters	4 pecks
cable	219.456 meters	120 fathoms
chain (surveyor's)	20.116 8 meters	66 feet
cord (wood)	3.624 556 meters^3	128 feet^3
cup	0.236 588 2 liters	8 ounces, liquid
degrees, celsius	(water boils at 100°C, freezes at 0°C)	multiply by 1.8 and add 32 to obtain °F
degrees, fahrenheit	subtract 32 and divide by 1.8 to obtain °C	(water boils at 212°F, freezes at 32°F)
dram, avoirdupois	1.771 845 2 grams	0.062 5 ounces, avoirdupois
dram, troy	3.887 934 6 grams	0.125 ounces, troy
dram, liquid (US)	3.696 69 milliliters	0.125 ounces, liquid
fathom	1.828 8 meters	6 feet
foot	30.48 centimeters	12 inches
foot	0.304 8 meters	0.333 333 3 yards
foot	0.000 304 8 kilometers	0.000 189 39 miles, statute
foot^2	929.030 4 centimeters^2	144 inches^2
foot^2	0.092 903 04 meters^2	0.111 111 1 yards^2
foot^3	28.316 846 592 liters	7.480 519 gallons
foot^3	0.028 316 847 meters^3	1,728 inches^3
furlong	201.168 meters	220 yards
gallon, liquid (US)	3.785 411 784 liters	4 quarts, liquid
gill (US)	118.294 118 milliliters	4 ounces, liquid
grain	64.798 91 milligrams	0.002 285 71 ounces, avdp.
gram	1,000 milligrams	0.035 273 96 ounces, avdp.
hand (height of horse)	10.16 centimeters	4 inches
hectare	10,000 meters^2	2.471 053 8 acres
hundredweight, long	50.802 345 kilograms	112 pounds, avoirdupois
hundredweight, short	45.359 237 kilograms	100 pounds, avoirdupois
inch	2.54 centimeters	0.083 333 33 feet
inch^2	6.451 6 centimeters^2	0.006 944 44 feet^2
inch^3	16.387 064 centimeters^3	0.000 578 7 feet^3
inch^3	16.387 064 milliliters	0.029 761 6 pints, dry
inch^3	16.387 064 milliliters	0.034 632 0 pints, liquid
kilogram	0.001 tons, metric	2.204 623 pounds, avdp.
kilometer	1,000 meters	0.621 371 19 miles, statute
kilometer^2	100 hectares	247.105 38 acres
kilometer^2	1,000,000 meters^2	0.386 102 16 miles^2, statute
knot (1 nautical mi/hr)	1.852 kilometers/hour	1.151 statute miles/hour
league, nautical	5.559 552 kilometers	3 miles, nautical
league, statute	4.828.032 kilometers	3 miles, statute

Unit	Metric Equivalent	US Equivalent
link (surveyor's)	20.116 8 centimeters	7.92 inches
liter	0.001 meters^3	61.023 74 inches^3
liter	0.1 dekaliter	0.908 083 quarts, dry
liter	1,000 milliliters	1.056 688 quarts, liquid
meter	100 centimeters	1.093 613 yards
meter^2	10,000 centimeters^2	1.195 990 yards^2
meter^3 1,000 liters	1.307 951 yards^3	
micron	0.000 001 meter	0.000 039 4 inches
mil	0.025 4 millimeters	0.001 inch
mile, nautical	1.852 kilometers	1.150 779 4 miles, statute
mile^2, nautical	3.429 904 kilometers^2	1.325 miles^2, statute
mile, statute	1.609 344 kilometers	5,280 feet or 8 furlongs
mile^2, statute	258.998 811 hectares	640 acres or 1 section
mile^2, statute	2.589 988 11 kilometers^2	0.755 miles^2, nautical
minim (US)	0.061 611 52 milliliters	0.002 083 33 ounces, liquid
ounce, avoirdupois	28.349 523 125 grams	437.5 grains
ounce, liquid (US)	29.573 53 milliliters	0.062 5 pints, liquid
ounce, troy	31.103 476 8 grams	480 grains
pace 76.2 centimeters	30 inches	
peck	8.809 767 5 liters	8 quarts, dry
pennyweight	1.555 173 84 grams	24 grains
pint, dry (US)	0.550 610 47 liters	0.5 quarts, dry
pint, liquid (US)	0.473 176 473 liters	0.5 quarts, liquid
point (typographical)	0.351 459 8 millimeters	0.013 837 inches
pound, avoirdupois	453.592 37 grams	16 ounces, avourdupois
pound, troy	373.241 721 6 grams	12 ounces, troy
quart, dry (US)	1.101 221 liters	2 pints, dry
quart, liquid (US)	0.946 352 946 liters	2 pints, liquid
quintal	100 kilograms	220.462 26 pounds, avdp.
rod	5.029 2 meters	5.5 yards
scruple	1.295 978 2 grams	20 grains
section (US)	2.589 988 1 kilometers^2	1 mile^2, statute or 640 acres
span	22.86 centimeters	9 inches
stere	1 meter^3	1.307 95 yards^3
tablespoon	14.786 76 milliliters	3 teaspoons
teaspoon	4.928 922 milliliters	0.333 333 tablespoons
ton, long or deadweight	1,016.046 909 kilograms	2,240 pounds, avoirdupois
ton, metric	1,000 kilograms	2,204.623 pounds, avoirdupois
ton, metric	1,000 kilograms	32,150.75 ounces, troy
ton, register	2.831 684 7 meters^3	100 feet^3
ton, short	907.184 74 kilograms	2,000 pounds, avoirdupois
township (US)	93.239 572 kilometers^2	36 miles^2, statute
yard	0.914 4 meters	3 feet
yard^2	0.836 127 36 meters^2	9 feet^2
yard^3	0.764 554 86 meters^3	27 feet^3
yard^3	764.554 857 984 liters	201.974 gallons

Appendix E:

Cross-Reference List of Geographic Names

This list indicates where various names including all United States Foreign Service Posts, alternate names, former names, and political or geographical portions of larger entities can be found in *The World Factbook*. Spellings are not necessarily those approved by the United States Board on Geographic Names (BGN). Alternate names are included in parentheses; additional information is included in brackets.

Name	Entry in *The World Factbook*
A	
Abidjan [US Embassy]	Ivory Coast
Abu Dhabi [US Embassy]	United Arab Emirates
Acapulco [US Consular Agency]	Mexico
Accra [US Embassy]	Ghana
Adana [US Consulate]	Turkey
Addis Ababa [US Embassy]	Ethiopia
Adelaide [US Consular Agency]	Australia
Adélie Land (Terre Adélie) [claimed by France]	Antarctica
Aden	Yemen
Aden, Gulf of	Indian Ocean
Admiralty Islands	Papua New Guinea
Adriatic Sea	Atlantic Ocean
Aegean Islands	Greece
Aegean Sea	Atlantic Ocean
Afars and Issas, French Territory of the (F.T.A.I.)	Djibouti
Agalega Islands	Mauritius
Aland Islands	Finland
Alaska	United States
Alaska, Gulf of	Pacific Ocean
Aldabra Islands	Seychelles
Alderney	Guernsey
Aleutian Islands	United States
Alexander Island	Antarctica
Alexandria [US Consulate General]	Egypt
Algiers [US Embassy]	Algeria
Alhucemas, Peñón de	Spain
Alphonse Island	Seychelles
Amami Strait	Pacific Ocean
Amindivi Islands	India
Amirante Isles	Seychelles
Amman [US Embassy]	Jordan
Amsterdam [US Consulate General]	Netherlands
Amsterdam Island (Île Amsterdam)	French Southern and Antarctic Lands
Amundsen Sea	Pacific Ocean
Amur	China; Soviet Union
Andaman Islands	India
Andaman Sea	Indian Ocean
Anegada Passage	Atlantic Ocean
Anglo-Egyptian Sudan	Sudan
Anjouan	Comoros
Ankara [US Embassy]	Turkey
Annobón	Equatorial Guinea
Antananarivo [US Embassy]	Madagascar
Antipodes Islands	New Zealand
Antwerp [US Consulate General]	Belgium
Aozou Strip [claimed by Libya]	Chad
Aqaba, Gulf of	Indian Ocean
Arabian Sea	Indian Ocean
Arafura Sea	Pacific Ocean
Argun	China; Soviet Union
Ascension Island	Saint Helena
Assumption Island	Seychelles
Asuncion [US Embassy]	Paraguay
Asuncion Island	Northern Mariana Islands

Name	Entry in *The World Factbook*
Atacama	Chile
Athens [US Embassy]	Greece
Attu	United States
Auckland [US Consulate General]	New Zealand
Auckland Islands	New Zealand
Australes Îles (Îles Tubuai)	French Polynesia
Axel Heiberg Island	Canada
Azores	Portugal
Azov, Sea of	Atlantic Ocean

B

Name	Entry in *The World Factbook*
Bab el Mandeb	Indian Ocean
Babuyan Channel	Pacific Ocean
Babuyan Islands	Philippines
Baffin Bay	Arctic Ocean
Baffin Island	Canada
Baghdad [US Embassy]	Iraq
Balabac Strait	Pacific Ocean
Balearic Islands	Spain
Balearic Sea (Iberian Sea)	Atlantic Ocean
Bali [US Consular Agency]	Indonesia
Bali Sea	Indian Ocean
Balintang Channel	Pacific Ocean
Balintang Islands	Philippines
Balleny Islands	Antarctica
Balochistān	Pakistan
Baltic Sea	Atlantic Ocean
Bamako [US Embassy]	Mali
Banaba (Ocean Island)	Kiribati
Bandar Seri Begawan [US Embassy]	Brunei
Banda Sea	Pacific Ocean
Bangkok [US Embassy]	Thailand
Bangui [US Embassy]	Central African Republic
Banjul [US Embassy]	Gambia, The
Banks Island	Canada
Banks Islands (Îles Banks)	Vanuatu
Barcelona [US Consulate General]	Spain
Barents Sea	Arctic Ocean
Barranquilla [US Consulate]	Colombia
Bashi Channel	Pacific Ocean
Basilan Strait	Pacific Ocean
Bass Strait	Indian Ocean
Batan Islands	Philippines
Bavaria (Bayern)	Germany
Beagle Channel	Atlantic Ocean
Bear Island (Bjørnøya)	Svalbard
Beaufort Sea	Arctic Ocean
Bechuanaland	Botswana
Beijing [US Embassy]	China
Beirut [US Embassy]	Lebanon
Belau	Pacific Islands, Trust Territory of the (Palau)
Belem [US Consular Agency]	Brazil
Belep Islands (Îles Belep)	New Caledonia
Belfast [US Consulate General]	United Kingdom
Belgian Congo	Zaire
Belgrade [US Embassy]	Yugoslavia
Belize City [US Embassy]	Belize
Belle Isle, Strait of	Atlantic Ocean
Bellinghausen Sea	Pacific Ocean
Belmopan	Belize
Bengal, Bay of	Indian Ocean
Bering Sea	Pacific Ocean
Bering Strait	Pacific Ocean

Name	Entry in *The World Factbook*
Berkner Island	Antarctica
Berlin [Branch Office]	Germany
Berlin, East	Germany
Berlin, West	Germany
Bern [US Embassy]	Switzerland
Bessarabia	Romania; Soviet Union
Bijagós, Arquipélago dos	Guinea-Bissau
Bikini Atoll	Marshall Islands
Bilbao [US Consulate]	Spain
Bioko	Equatorial Guinea
Biscay, Bay of	Atlantic Ocean
Bishop Rock	United Kingdom
Bismarck Archipelago	Papua New Guinea
Bismarck Sea	Pacific Ocean
Bissau [US Embassy]	Guinea-Bissau
Bjørnøya (Bear Island)	Svalbard
Black Rock	Falkland Islands (Islas Malvinas)
Black Sea	Atlantic Ocean
Boa Vista	Cape Verde
Bogotá [US Embassy]	Colombia
Bombay [US Consulate General]	India
Bonaire	Netherlands Antilles
Bonifacio, Strait of	Atlantic Ocean
Bonin Islands	Japan
Bonn [US Embassy]	Germany
Bophuthatswana	South Africa
Bora-Bora	French Polynesia
Bordeaux [US Consulate General]	France
Borneo	Brunei; Indonesia; Malaysia
Bornholm	Denmark
Bosporus	Atlantic Ocean
Bothnia, Gulf of	Atlantic Ocean
Bougainville Island	Papua New Guinea
Bougainville Strait	Pacific Ocean
Bounty Islands	New Zealand
Brasilia [US Embassy]	Brazil
Brazzaville [US Embassy]	Congo
Bridgetown [US Embassy]	Barbados
Brisbane [US Consulate]	Australia
British East Africa	Kenya
British Guiana	Guyana
British Honduras	Belize
British Solomon Islands	Solomon Islands
British Somaliland	Somalia
Brussels [US Embassy, US Mission to European Communities, US Mission to the North Atlantic Treaty Organization (USNATO)]	Belgium
Bucharest [US Embassy]	Romania
Budapest [US Embassy]	Hungary
Buenos Aires [US Embassy]	Argentina
Bujumbura [US Embassy]	Burundi

C

Name	Entry in *The World Factbook*
Cabinda	Angola
Cabot Strait	Atlantic Ocean
Caicos Islands	Turks and Caicos Islands
Cairo [US Embassy]	Egypt
Calcutta [US Consulate General]	India
Calgary [US Consulate General]	Canada
California, Gulf of	Pacific Ocean
Campbell Island	New Zealand
Canal Zone	Panama
Canary Islands	Spain

Name	Entry in *The World Factbook*
Canberra [US Embassy]	Australia
Cancun [US Consular Agency]	Mexico
Canton (Guangzhou)	China
Canton Island	Kiribati
Cape Town [US Consulate General]	South Africa
Caracas [US Embassy]	Venezuela
Cargados Carajos Shoals	Mauritius
Caroline Islands	Micronesia, Federated States of; Pacific Islands, Trust Territory of the
Caribbean Sea	Atlantic Ocean
Carpentaria, Gulf of	Pacific Ocean
Casablanca [US Consulate General]	Morocco
Cato Island	Australia
Cebu [US Consulate]	Philippines
Celebes	Indonesia
Celebes Sea	Pacific Ocean
Celtic Sea	Atlantic Ocean
Central African Empire	Central African Republic
Ceuta	Spain
Ceylon	Sri Lanka
Chafarinas, Islas	Spain
Chagos Archipelago (Oil Islands)	British Indian Ocean Territory
Channel Islands	Guernsey; Jersey
Chatham Islands	New Zealand
Cheju-do	Korea, South
Cheju Strait	Pacific Ocean
Chengdu [US Consulate General]	China
Chesterfield Islands (Îles Chesterfield)	New Caledonia
Chiang Mai [US Consulate General]	Thailand
Chihli, Gulf of (Bo Hai)	Pacific Ocean
China, People's Republic of	China
China, Republic of	Taiwan
Choiseul	Solomon Islands
Christchurch [US Consular Agency]	New Zealand
Christmas Island [Indian Ocean]	Australia
Christmas Island [Pacific Ocean] (Kiritimati)	Kiribati
Chukchi Sea	Arctic Ocean
Ciskei	South Africa
Ciudad Juarez [US Consulate General]	Mexico
Cochabamba [US Consular Agency]	Bolivia
Coco, Isla del	Costa Rica
Cocos Islands	Cocos (Keeling) Islands
Colombo [US Embassy]	Sri Lanka
Colon [US Consular Agency]	Panama
Colón, Archipiélago de (Galapagos Islands)	Ecuador
Commander Islands (Komandorskiye Ostrova)	Soviet Union
Conakry [US Embassy]	Guinea
Congo (Brazzaville)	Congo
Congo (Kinshasa)	Zaire
Congo (Leopoldville)	Zaire
Con Son Islands	Vietnam
Cook Strait	Pacific Ocean
Copenhagen [US Embassy]	Denmark
Coral Sea	Pacific Ocean
Corn Islands (Islas del Maíz)	Nicaragua
Corsica	France
Cosmoledo Group	Seychelles
Côte d'Ivoire	Ivory Coast
Cotonou [US Embassy]	Benin
Crete	Greece
Crooked Island Passage	Atlantic Ocean
Crozet Islands (Îles Crozet)	French Southern and Antarctic Lands

Name	Entry in *The World Factbook*
Curaçao [US Consulate General]	Netherlands Antilles
Cusco [US Consular Agency]	Peru

D

Name	Entry in *The World Factbook*
Dahomey	Benin
Daitō Islands	Japan
Dakar [US Embassy]	Senegal
Daman (Damão)	India
Damascus [US Embassy]	Syria
Danger Atoll	Cook Islands
Danish Straits	Atlantic Ocean
Danzig (Gdańsk)	Poland
Dao Bach Long Vi	Vietnam
Dardanelles	Atlantic Ocean
Dar es Salaam [US Embassy]	Tanzania
Davis Strait	Atlantic Ocean
Deception Island	Antarctica
Denmark Strait	Atlantic Ocean
D'Entrecasteaux Islands	Papua New Guinea
Devon Island	Canada
Dhahran [US Consulate General]	Saudi Arabia
Dhaka [US Embassy]	Bangladesh
Diego Garcia	British Indian Ocean Territory
Diego Ramírez	Chile
Diomede Islands [Little Diomede]	Soviet Union [Big Diomede]; United States
Diu	India
Djibouti [US Embassy]	Djibouti
Dodecanese	Greece
Doha [US Embassy]	Qatar
Douala [US Consulate General]	Cameroon
Dover, Strait of	Atlantic Ocean
Drake Passage	Atlantic Ocean
Dubai [US Consulate General]	United Arab Emirates
Dublin [US Embassy]	Ireland
Durango [US Consular Agency]	Mexico
Durban [US Consulate General]	South Africa
Dusseldorf [US Consulate General]	Germany
Dutch East Indies	Indonesia
Dutch Guiana	Suriname

E

Name	Entry in *The World Factbook*
East China Sea	Pacific Ocean
Easter Island (Isla de Pascua)	Chile
Eastern Channel (East Korea Strait or Tsushima Strait)	Pacific Ocean
East Germany (German Democratic Republic)	Germany
East Korea Strait (Eastern Channel or Tsushima Strait)	Pacific Ocean
East Pakistan	Bangladesh
East Siberian Sea	Arctic Ocean
East Timor (Portuguese Timor)	Indonesia
Edinburgh [US Consulate General]	United Kingdom
Elba	Italy
Ellef Ringnes Island	Canada
Ellesmere Island	Canada
Ellice Islands	Tuvalu
Elobey, Islas de	Equatorial Guinea
Enderbury Island	Kiribati
Enewetak Atoll (Eniwetok Atoll)	Marshall Islands
England	United Kingdom
English Channel	Atlantic Ocean
Eniwetok Atoll	Marshall Islands
Epirus, Northern	Albania; Greece
Eritrea	Ethiopia
Essequibo [claimed by Venezuela]	Guyana
Estonia	Soviet Union [de facto]
Etorofu	Soviet Union [de facto]

	Name	Entry in *The World Factbook*
F	Farquhar Group	Seychelles
	Fernando de Noronha	Brazil
	Fernando Po (Bioko)	Equatorial Guinea
	Finland, Gulf of	Atlantic Ocean
	Florence [US Consulate General]	Italy
	Florida, Straits of	Atlantic Ocean
	Formosa	Taiwan
	Formosa Strait (Taiwan Strait)	Pacific Ocean
	Fort-de-France [US Consulate General]	Martinique
	Frankfurt am Main [US Consulate General]	Germany
	Franz Josef Land	Soviet Union
	Freetown [US Embassy]	Sierra Leone
	French Cameroon	Cameroon
	French Indochina	Cambodia; Laos; Vietnam
	French Guinea	Guinea
	French Sudan	Mali
	French Territory of the Afars and Issas (F.T.A.I.)	Djibouti
	French Togo	Togo
	Friendly Islands	Tonga
	Fukuoka [US Consulate]	Japan
	Funchal [US Consular Agency]	Portugal
	Fundy, Bay of	Atlantic Ocean
	Futuna Islands (Hoorn Islands)	Wallis and Futuna
G	Gaborone [US Embassy]	Botswana
	Galapagos Islands (Archipiélago de Colón)	Ecuador
	Galleons Passage	Atlantic Ocean
	Gambier Islands (Îles Gambier)	French Polynesia
	Gaspar Strait	Indian Ocean
	Geneva [Branch Office of the US Embassy, US Mission to European Office of the UN and Other International Organizations]	Switzerland
	Genoa [US Consulate General]	Italy
	George Town [US Consular Agency]	Cayman Islands
	Georgetown [US Embassy]	Guyana
	German Democratic Republic (East Germany)	Germany
	Germany, Federal Republic of (West Germany)	Germany
	Gibraltar, Strait of	Atlantic Ocean
	Gilbert Islands	Kiribati
	Goa	India
	Gold Coast	Ghana
	Golan Heights	Syria
	Good Hope, Cape of	South Africa
	Goteborg [US Consulate General]	Sweden
	Gotland	Sweden
	Gough Island	Saint Helena
	Grand Banks	Atlantic Ocean
	Grand Cayman	Cayman Islands
	Grand Turk [US Consular Agency]	Turks and Caicos Islands
	Great Australian Bight	Indian Ocean
	Great Belt (Store Baelt)	Atlantic Ocean
	Great Britain	United Kingdom
	Great Channel	Indian Ocean
	Greater Sunda Islands	Brunei; Indonesia; Malaysia
	Green Islands	Papua New Guinea
	Greenland Sea	Arctic Ocean
	Grenadines, Northern	Saint Vincent and the Grenadines
	Grenadines, Southern	Grenada
	Guadalajara [US Consulate General]	Mexico
	Guadalcanal	Solomon Islands
	Guadalupe, Isla de	Mexico
	Guangzhou [US Consulate General]	China

Name	Entry in *The World Factbook*
Guantanamo [US Naval Base]	Cuba
Guatemala [US Embassy]	Guatemala
Gubal, Strait of	Indian Ocean
Guinea, Gulf of	Atlantic Ocean
Guayaquil [US Consulate General]	Ecuador

H

Name	Entry in *The World Factbook*
Ha'apai Group	Tonga
Habomai Islands	Soviet Union [de facto]
Hague, The [US Embassy]	Netherlands
Haifa [US Consular Agency]	Israel
Hainan Dao	China
Halifax [US Consulate General]	Canada
Halmahera	Indonesia
Hamburg [US Consulate General]	Germany
Hamilton [US Consulate General]	Bermuda
Hanoi	Vietnam
Harare [US Embassy]	Zimbabwe
Hatay	Turkey
Havana [US post not maintained, representation by US Interests Section (USINT) of the Swiss Embassy]	Cuba
Hawaii	United States
Heard Island	Heard Island and McDonald Islands
Helsinki [US Embassy]	Finland
Hermosillo [US Consulate]	Mexico
Hispaniola	Dominican Republic; Haiti
Hokkaido	Japan
Holy See, The	Vatican City
Hong Kong [US Consulate General]	Hong Kong
Honiara [US Consulate]	Solomon Islands
Honshu	Japan
Hormuz, Strait of	Indian Ocean
Horn, Cape (Cabo de Hornos)	Chile
Horne, Îles de	Wallis and Futuna
Horn of Africa	Ethiopia; Somalia
Hudson Bay	Arctic Ocean
Hudson Strait	Arctic Ocean

I

Name	Entry in *The World Factbook*
Inaccessible Island	Saint Helena
Indochina	Cambodia; Laos; Vietnam
Inner Mongolia (Nei Mongol)	China
Ionian Islands	Greece
Ionian Sea	Atlantic Ocean
Irian Jaya	Indonesia
Irish Sea	Atlantic Ocean
Islamabad [US Embassy]	Pakistan
Islas Malvinas	Falkland Islands (Islas Malvinas)
Istanbul [US Consulate General]	Turkey
Italian Somaliland	Somalia
Iwo Jima	Japan
Izmir [US Consulate General]	Turkey

J

Name	Entry in *The World Factbook*
Jakarta [US Embassy]	Indonesia
Japan, Sea of	Pacific Ocean
Java	Indonesia
Java Sea	Indian Ocean
Jeddah [US Consulate General]	Saudi Arabia
Jerusalem [US Consulate General]	Israel; West Bank
Johannesburg [US Consulate General]	South Africa
Juan de Fuca, Strait of	Pacific Ocean
Juan Fernández, Isla de	Chile
Juventud, Isla de la (Isle of Youth)	Cuba

K

Name	Entry in *The World Factbook*
Kabul [US Embassy now closed]	Afghanistan
Kaduna [US Consulate General]	Nigeria
Kalimantan	Indonesia

Name	Entry in *The World Factbook*
Kamchatka Peninsula (Poluostrov Kamchatka)	Soviet Union
Kampala [US Embassy]	Uganda
Kampuchea	Cambodia
Karachi [US Consulate General]	Pakistan
Kara Sea	Arctic Ocean
Karimata Strait	Indian Ocean
Kathmandu [US Embassy]	Nepal
Kattegat	Atlantic Ocean
Kauai Channel	Pacific Ocean
Keeling Islands	Cocos (Keeling) Islands
Kerguelen, Îles	French Southern and Antarctic Lands
Kermadec Islands	New Zealand
Khabarovsk	Soviet Union
Khartoum [US Embassy]	Sudan
Khmer Republic	Cambodia
Kiel Canal (Nord-Ostsee Kanal)	Atlantic Ocean
Khuriya Muriya Islands (Kuria Muria Islands)	Oman
Khyber Pass	Pakistan
Kigali [US Embassy]	Rwanda
Kingston [US Embassy]	Jamaica
Kinshasa [US Embassy]	Zaire
Kiritimati (Christmas Island)	Kiribati
Kithira Strait	Atlantic Ocean
Kodiak Island	United States
Kola Peninsula (Kol'skiy Poluostrov)	Soviet Union
Kolonia [US Special Office]	Micronesia, Federated States of
Korea Bay	Pacific Ocean
Korea, Democratic People's Republic of	Korea, North
Korea, Republic of	Korea, South
Korea Strait	Pacific Ocean
Koror [US Special Office]	Pacific Islands, Trust Territory of
Kosovo	Yugoslavia
Kowloon	Hong Kong
Krakow [US Consulate]	Poland
Kuala Lumpur [US Embassy]	Malaysia
Kunashiri (Kunashir)	Soviet Union [de facto]
Kuril Islands	Soviet Union [de facto]
Kuwait [US Embassy]	Kuwait
Kwajalein Atoll	Marshall Islands
Kyushu	Japan

L

Name	Entry in *The World Factbook*
Labrador	Canada
Laccadive Islands	India
Laccadive Sea	Indian Ocean
La Coruna [US Consular Agency]	Spain
Lagos [US Embassy]	Nigeria
Lahore [US Consulate General]	Pakistan
Lakshadweep	India
La Paz [US Embassy]	Bolivia
La Perouse Strait	Pacific Ocean
Laptev Sea	Arctic Ocean
Las Palmas [US Consular Agency]	Spain
Latvia	Soviet Union [de facto]
Lau Group	Fiji
Leningrad [US Consulate General]	Soviet Union
Lesser Sunda Islands	Indonesia
Leyte	Philippines
Liancourt Rocks [claimed by Japan]	Korea, South
Libreville [US Embassy]	Gabon
Ligurian Sea	Atlantic Ocean
Lilongwe [US Embassy]	Malawi
Lima [US Embassy]	Peru

Name	Entry in *The World Factbook*
Lincoln Sea	Arctic Ocean
Line Islands	Kiribati; Palmyra Atoll
Lisbon [US Embassy]	Portugal
Lithuania	Soviet Union [de facto]
Lombok Strait	Indian Ocean
Lome [US Embassy]	Togo
London [US Embassy]	United Kingdom
Lord Howe Island	Australia
Louisiade Archipelago	Papua New Guinea
Loyalty Islands (Îles Loyauté)	New Caledonia
Lubumbashi [US Consulate General]	Zaire
Lusaka [US Embassy]	Zambia
Luxembourg [US Embassy]	Luxembourg
Luzon	Philippines
Luzon Strait	Pacific Ocean
Lyon [US Consulate General]	France

M

Name	Entry in *The World Factbook*
Macao	Macau
Macedonia	Bulgaria; Greece; Yugoslavia
Macquarie Island	Australia
Madeira Islands	Portugal
Madras [US Consulate General]	India
Madrid [US Embassy]	Spain
Magellan, Strait of	Atlantic Ocean
Mahé Island	Seychelles
Maíz, Islas del (Corn Islands)	Nicaragua
Majorca (Mallorca)	Spain
Majuro [US Special Office]	Marshall Islands
Makassar Strait	Pacific Ocean
Malabo [US Embassy]	Equatorial Guinea
Malacca, Strait of	Indian Ocean
Malaga [US Consular Agency]	Spain
Malagasy Republic	Madagascar
Male [US post not maintained, representation from Colombo, Sri Lanka]	Maldives
Mallorca (Majorca)	Spain
Malpelo, Isla de	Colombia
Malta Channel	Atlantic Ocean
Malvinas, Islas	Falkland Islands (Islas Malvinas)
Managua [US Embassy]	Nicaragua
Manama [US Embassy]	Bahrain
Manaus [US Consular Agency]	Brazil
Manchukuo	China
Manchuria	China
Manila [US Embassy]	Philippines
Manipa Strait	Pacific Ocean
Mannar, Gulf of	Indian Ocean
Manua Islands	American Samoa
Maputo [US Embassy]	Mozambique
Maracaibo [US Consulate]	Venezuela
Marcus Island (Minami-tori-shima)	Japan
Mariana Islands	Guam; Northern Mariana Islands
Marion Island	South Africa
Marmara, Sea of	Atlantic Ocean
Marquesas Islands (Îles Marquises)	French Polynesia
Marseille [US Consulate General]	France
Martin Vaz, Ilhas	Brazil
Más a Tierra (Robinson Crusoe Island)	Chile
Mascarene Islands	Mauritius; Reunion
Maseru [US Embassy]	Lesotho
Matamoros [US Consulate]	Mexico
Mazatlan [US Consulate]	Mexico

Name	Entry in *The World Factbook*
Mbabane [US Embassy]	Swaziland
McDonald Islands	Heard Island and McDonald Islands
Medan [US Consulate]	Indonesia
Mediterranean Sea	Atlantic Ocean
Melbourne [US Consulate General]	Australia
Melilla	Spain
Merida [US Consulate]	Mexico
Messina, Strait of	Atlantic Ocean
Mexico [US Embassy]	Mexico
Mexico, Gulf of	Atlantic Ocean
Milan [US Consulate General]	Italy
Minami-tori-shima	Japan
Mindanao	Philippines
Mindoro Strait	Pacific Ocean
Minicoy Island	India
Mogadishu [US Embassy]	Somalia
Mombasa [US Consulate]	Kenya
Mona Passage	Atlantic Ocean
Monrovia [US Embassy]	Liberia
Montego Bay [US Consular Agency]	Jamaica
Monterrey [US Consulate General]	Mexico
Montevideo [US Embassy]	Uruguay
Montreal [US Consulate General, US Mission to the International Civil Aviation Organization (ICAO)]	Canada
Moravian Gate	Czechoslovakia
Moroni [US Embassy]	Comoros
Mortlock Islands	Micronesia, Federated States of
Moscow [US Embassy]	Soviet Union
Mozambique Channel	Indian Ocean
Mulege [US Consular Agency]	Mexico
Munich [US Consulate General]	Germany
Musandam Peninsula	Oman; United Arab Emirates
Muscat [US Embassy]	Oman
Muscat and Oman	Oman
Myanma, Myanmar	Burma

	Name	Entry in *The World Factbook*
N	Naha [US Consulate General]	Japan
	Nairobi [US Embassy]	Kenya
	Nampo-shoto	Japan
	Naples [US Consulate General]	Italy
	Nassau [US Embassy]	Bahamas, The
	Natuna Besar Islands	Indonesia
	N'Djamena [US Embassy]	Chad
	Netherlands East Indies	Indonesia
	Netherlands Guiana	Suriname
	Nevis	Saint Kitts and Nevis
	New Delhi [US Embassy]	India
	Newfoundland	Canada
	New Guinea	Indonesia; Papua New Guinea
	New Hebrides	Vanuatu
	New Siberian Islands	Soviet Union
	New Territories	Hong Kong
	New York, New York [US Mission to the United Nations (USUN)]	United States
	Niamey [US Embassy]	Niger
	Nice [US Consular Agency]	France
	Nicobar Islands	India
	Nicosia [US Embassy]	Cyprus
	Nightingale Island	Saint Helena
	North Atlantic Ocean	Atlantic Ocean
	North Channel	Atlantic Ocean
	Northeast Providence Channel	Atlantic Ocean

Name	Entry in *The World Factbook*
Northern Epirus	Albania; Greece
Northern Grenadines	Saint Vincent and the Grenadines
Northern Ireland	United Kingdom
Northern Rhodesia	Zambia
North Island	New Zealand
North Korea	Korea, North
North Pacific Ocean	Pacific Ocean
North Sea	Atlantic Ocean
North Vietnam	Vietnam
Northwest Passages	Arctic Ocean
North Yemen (Yemen Arab Republic)	Yemen
Norwegian Sea	Atlantic Ocean
Nouakchott [US Embassy]	Mauritania
Novaya Zemlya	Soviet Union
Nuevo Laredo [US Consulate]	Mexico
Nyasaland	Malawi

O

Name	Entry in *The World Factbook*
Oahu	United States
Oaxaca [US Consular Agency]	Mexico
Ocean Island (Banaba)	Kiribati
Ocean Island (Kure Island)	United States
Ogaden	Ethiopia; Somalia
Oil Islands (Chagos Archipelago)	British Indian Ocean Territory
Okhotsk, Sea of	Pacific Ocean
Okinawa	Japan
Oman, Gulf of	Indian Ocean
Ombai Strait	Pacific Ocean
Oporto [US Consulate]	Portugal
Oran [US Consulate]	Algeria
Øresund (The Sound)	Atlantic Ocean
Orkney Islands	United Kingdom
Osaka-Kobe [US Consulate General]	Japan
Oslo [US Embassy]	Norway
Otranto, Strait of	Atlantic Ocean
Ottawa [US Embassy]	Canada
Ouagadougou [US Embassy]	Burkina
Outer Mongolia	Mongolia

P

Name	Entry in *The World Factbook*
Pagan	Northern Mariana Islands
Palau	Pacific Islands, Trust Territory of the
Palawan	Philippines
Palermo [US Consulate General]	Italy
Palk Strait	Indian Ocean
Palma de Mallorca [US Consular Agency]	Spain
Pamirs	China; Soviet Union
Panama [US Embassy]	Panama
Panama Canal	Panama
Panama, Gulf of	Pacific Ocean
Paramaribo [US Embassy]	Suriname
Parece Vela	Japan
Paris [US Embassy, US Mission to the Organization for Economic Cooperation and Development (OECD), US Observer Mission at the UN Educational, Scientific, and Cultural Organization (UNESCO)]	France
Pascua, Isla de (Easter Island)	Chile
Passion, Île de la	Clipperton Island
Pashtunistan	Afghanistan; Pakistan
Peking (Beijing)	China
Pemba Island	Tanzania
Pentland Firth	Atlantic Ocean
Perim	Yemen
Perouse Strait, La	Pacific Ocean
Persian Gulf	Indian Ocean

Name	Entry in *The World Factbook*
Perth [US Consulate]	Australia
Pescadores	Taiwan
Peshawar [US Consulate]	Pakistan
Peter I Island	Antarctica
Philip Island	Norfolk Island
Philippine Sea	Pacific Ocean
Phoenix Islands	Kiribati
Pines, Isle of (Isla de la Juventud)	Cuba
Piura [US Consular Agency]	Peru
Pleasant Island	Nauru
Ponape (Pohnpei)	Micronesia
Ponta Delgada [US Consulate]	Portugal
Port-au-Prince [US Embassy]	Haiti
Port Louis [US Embassy]	Mauritius
Port Moresby [US Embassy]	Papua New Guinea
Porto Alegre [US Consulate]	Brazil
Port-of-Spain [US Embassy]	Trinidad and Tobago
Port Said [US Consular Agency]	Egypt
Portuguese Guinea	Guinea-Bissau
Portuguese Timor (East Timor)	Indonesia
Poznan [US Consulate]	Poland
Prague [US Embassy]	Czechoslovakia
Praia [US Embassy]	Cape Verde
Pretoria [US Embassy]	South Africa
Pribilof Islands	United States
Prince Edward Island	Canada
Prince Edward Islands	South Africa
Prince Patrick Island	Canada
Principe	Sao Tome and Principe
Puerto Plata [US Consular Agency]	Dominican Republic
Puerto Vallarta [US Consular Agency]	Mexico
Pusan [US Consulate]	South Korea
P'yŏngyang	Korea North
Q Quebec [US Consulate General]	Canada
Queen Charlotte Islands	Canada
Queen Elizabeth Islands	Canada
Queen Maud Land [claimed by Norway]	Antarctica
Quito [US Embassy]	Ecuador
R Rabat [US Embassy]	Morocco
Ralik Chain	Marshall Islands
Rangoon [US Embassy]	Burma
Ratak Chain	Marshall Islands
Recife [US Consulate]	Brazil
Redonda	Antigua and Barbuda
Red Sea	Indian Ocean
Revillagigedo Island	United States
Revillagigedo Islands	Mexico
Reykjavik [US Embassy]	Iceland
Rhodes	Greece
Rhodesia	Zimbabwe
Rhodesia, Northern	Zambia
Rhodesia, Southern	Zimbabwe
Rio de Janeiro [US Consulate General]	Brazil
Río de Oro	Western Sahara
Río Muni	Equatorial Guinea
Riyadh [US Embassy]	Saudi Arabia
Robinson Crusoe Island (Más a Tierra)	Chile
Rocas, Atol das	Brazil
Rockall [disputed]	United Kingdom
Rodrigues	Mauritius

Name	Entry in *The World Factbook*
Rome [US Embassy, US Mission to the UN Agencies for Food and Agriculture (FODAG)]	Italy
Roncador Cay	Colombia
Roosevelt Island	Antarctica
Ross Dependency [claimed by New Zealand]	Antarctica
Ross Island	Antarctica
Ross Sea	Antarctica
Rota	Northern Mariana Islands
Rotuma	Fiji
Ryukyu Islands	Japan

S

Name	Entry in *The World Factbook*
Saba	Netherlands Antilles
Sabah	Malaysia
Sable Island	Canada
Sahel	Burkina; Cape Verde; Chad; The Gambia; Guinea-Bissau; Mali; Mauritania; Niger; Senegal
Saigon (Ho Chi Minh City)	Vietnam
Saint Brandon	Mauritius
Saint Christopher and Nevis	Saint Kitts and Nevis
Saint George's [US Embassy]	Grenada
Saint George's Channel	Atlantic Ocean
Saint John's [US Embassy]	Antigua and Barbuda
Saint Lawrence, Gulf of	Atlantic Ocean
Saint Lawrence Island	United States
Saint Lawrence Seaway	Atlantic Ocean
Saint Martin	Guadeloupe
Saint Martin (Sint Maarten)	Netherlands Antilles
Saint Paul Island	Canada
Saint Paul Island	United States
Saint Paul Island (Île Saint-Paul)	French Southern and Antarctic Lands
Saint Peter and Saint Paul Rocks (Penedos de São Pedro é São Paulo)	Brazil
Saint Vincent Passage	Atlantic Ocean
Saipan	Northern Mariana Islands
Sakhalin Island (Ostrov Sakhalin)	Soviet Union
Sala y Gómez, Isla	Chile
Salisbury (Harare)	Zimbabwe
Salvador de Bahia [US Consular Agency]	Brazil
Salzburg [US Consulate General]	Austria
Sanaa [US Embassy]	Yemen
San Ambrosio	Chile
San Andrés y Providencia, Archipiélago	Colombia
San Bernardino Strait	Pacific Ocean
San Félix, Isla	Chile
San Jose [US Embassy]	Costa Rica
San Luis Potosi [US Consular Agency]	Mexico
San Miguel Allende [US Consular Agency]	Mexico
San Salvador [US Embassy]	El Salvador
Santa Cruz [US Consular Agency]	Bolivia
Santa Cruz Islands	Solomon Islands
Santiago [US Embassy]	Chile
Santo Domingo [US Embassy]	Dominican Republic
Sao Luis [US Consular Agency]	Brazil
Sao Paulo [US Consulate General]	Brazil
São Pedro e São Paulo, Penedos de	Brazil
Sapporo [US Consulate General]	Japan
Sapudi Strait	Indian Ocean
Sarawak	Malaysia
Sardinia	Italy
Sargasso Sea	Atlantic Ocean
Sark	Guernsey
Scotia Sea	Atlantic Ocean

Name	Entry in *The World Factbook*
Scotland	United Kingdom
Scott Island	Antarctica
Senyavin Islands	Micronesia, Federated States of
Seoul [US Embassy]	Korea, South
Serrana Bank	Colombia
Serranilla Bank	Colombia
Severnaya Zemlya (Northland)	Soviet Union
Seville [US Consular Agency]	Spain
Shag Island	Heard Island and McDonald Islands
Shag Rocks	Falkland Islands (Islas Malvinas)
Shanghai [US Consulate General]	China
Shenyang [US Consulate General]	China
Shetland Islands	United Kingdom
Shikoku	Japan
Shikotan (Shikotan-tō)	Japan
Siam	Thailand
Sibutu Passage	Pacific Ocean
Sicily	Italy
Sicily, Strait of	Atlantic Ocean
Sikkim	India
Sinai	Egypt
Singapore [US Embassy]	Singapore
Singapore Strait	Pacific Ocean
Sinkiang (Xinjiang)	China
Sint Eustatius	Netherlands Antilles
Sint Maarten (Saint Martin)	Netherlands Antilles
Skagerrak	Atlantic Ocean
Slovakia	Czechoslovakia
Society Islands (Îles de la Société)	French Polynesia
Socotra	Yemen
Sofia [US Embassy]	Bulgaria
Solomon Islands, northern	Papua New Guinea
Solomon Islands, southern	Solomon Islands
Soloman Sea	Pacific Ocean
Songkhla [US Consulate]	Thailand
Sound, The (Øresund)	Atlantic Ocean
South Atlantic Ocean	Atlantic Ocean
South China Sea	Pacific Ocean
Southern Grenadines	Grenada
Southern Rhodesia	Zimbabwe
South Georgia Sandwich Islands	South Georgia and the South
South Island	New Zealand
South Korea	Korea, South
South Orkney Islands	Antarctica
South Pacific Ocean	Pacific Ocean
South Sandwich Islands	South Georgia and the South Sandwich Islands
South Shetland Islands	Antarctica
South Tyrol	Italy
South Vietnam	Vietnam
South-West Africa	Namibia
South Yemen (People's Democratic Republic of Yemen)	Yemen
Spanish Guinea	Equatorial Guinea
Spanish Sahara	Western Sahara
Spitsbergen	Svalbard
Stockholm [US Embassy]	Sweden
Strasbourg [US Consulate General]	France
Stuttgart [US Consulate General]	Germany
Suez, Gulf of	Indian Ocean
Sulu Archipelago	Philippines
Sulu Sea	Pacific Ocean
Sumatra	Indonesia
Sumba	Indonesia

Name	Entry in *The World Factbook*
Sunda Islands (Soenda Isles)	Indonesia; Malaysia
Sunda Strait	Indian Ocean
Surabaya [US Consulate]	Indonesia
Surigao Strait	Pacific Ocean
Surinam	Suriname
Suva [US Embassy]	Fiji
Swains Island	American Samoa
Swan Islands	Honduras
Sydney [US Consulate General]	Australia

T

Name	Entry in *The World Factbook*
Tahiti	French Polynesia
Taipei	Taiwan
Taiwan Strait	Pacific Ocean
Tampico [US Consular Agency]	Mexico
Tanganyika	Tanzania
Tangier [US Consulate General]	Morocco
Tarawa	Kiribati
Tartar Strait	Pacific Ocean
Tasmania	Australia
Tasman Sea	Pacific Ocean
Taymyr Peninsula (Poluostrov Taymyra)	Soviet Union
Tegucigalpa [US Embassy]	Honduras
Tehran [US post not maintained, representation by Swiss Embassy]	Iran
Tel Aviv [US Embassy]	Israel
Terre Adélie (Adélie Land) [claimed by France]	Antarctica
Thailand, Gulf of	Pacific Ocean
Thessaloniki [US Consulate General]	Greece
Thurston Island	Antarctica
Tibet (Xizang)	China
Tierra del Fuego	Argentina; Chile
Tijuana [US Consulate General]	Mexico
Timor	Indonesia
Timor Sea	Indian Ocean
Tinian	Northern Mariana Islands
Tiran, Strait of	Indian Ocean
Tobago	Trinidad and Tobago
Tokyo [US Embassy]	Japan
Tonkin, Gulf of	Pacific Ocean
Toronto [US Consulate General]	Canada
Torres Strait	Pacific Ocean
Trans-Jordan	Jordan
Transkei	South Africa
Transylvania	Romania
Trieste [US Consular Agency]	Italy
Trindade, Ilha de	Brazil
Tripoli [US post not maintained, representation by Belgian Embassy]	Libya
Tristan da Cunha Group	Saint Helena
Trobriand Islands	Papua New Guinea
Trucial States	United Arab Emirates
Truk Islands	Micronesia
Tsugaru Strait	Pacific Ocean
Tuamotu Islands (Îles Tuamotu)	French Polynesia
Tubuai Islands (Îles Tubuai)	French Polynesia
Tunis [US Embassy]	Tunisia
Turin [US Consulate]	Italy
Turkish Straits	Atlantic Ocean
Turks Island Passage	Atlantic Ocean
Tyrol, South	Italy
Tyrrhenian Sea	Atlantic Ocean

	Name	Entry in *The World Factbook*
U	Udorn [US Consulate]	Thailand
	Ulaanbaatar	Mongolia
	Ullŭng-do	Korea, South
	Unimak Pass [strait]	Pacific Ocean
	United Arab Republic	Egypt; Syria
	Upper Volta	Burkina
V	Vaduz [US post not maintained, representation from Zürich, Switzerland]	Liechtenstein
	Vākhān Corridor (Wākhān)	Afghanistan
	Valencia [US Consular Agency]	Spain
	Valletta [US Embassy]	Malta
	Vancouver [US Consulate General]	Canada
	Vancouver Island	Canada
	Van Diemen Strait	Pacific Ocean
	Vatican City [US Embassy]	Vatican City
	Vélez de la Gomera, Peñón de Spain Venda	South Africa
	Veracruz [US Consular Agency]	Mexico
	Verde Island Passage	Pacific Ocean
	Victoria [US Embassy]	Seychelles
	Vienna [US Embassy, US Mission to International Organizations in Vienna (UNVIE)]	Austria
	Vientiane [US Embassy]	Laos
	Volcano Islands	Japan
	Vostok Island	Kiribati
	Vrangelya, Ostrov (Wrangel Island)	Soviet Union
W	Wakhan Corridor (now Vākhān Corridor)	Afghanistan
	Wales	United Kingdom
	Walvis Bay	South Africa
	Warsaw [US Embassy]	Poland
	Washington, DC [The Permanent Mission of the USA to the Organization of American States (OAS)]	United States
	Weddell Sea	Atlantic Ocean
	Wellington [US Embassy]	New Zealand
	Western Channel (West Korea Strait)	Pacific Ocean
	West Germany (Federal Republic of Germany)	Germany
	West Korea Strait (Western Channel)	Pacific Ocean
	West Pakistan	Pakistan
	Wetar Strait	Pacific Ocean
	White Sea	Arctic Ocean
	Windhoek	Namibia
	Windward Passage	Atlantic Ocean
	Winnipeg [US Consular Agency]	Canada
	Wrangel Island (Ostrov Vrangelya) Soviet Union	
Y	Yaounde [US Embassy]	Cameroon
	Yap Islands	Micronesia
	Yellow Sea	Pacific Ocean
	Yemen (Aden) [People's Democratic Republic of Yemen]	Yemen
	Yemen Arab Republic	Yemen
	Yemen, North [Yemen Arab Republic]	Yemen
	Yemen (Sanaa) [Yemen Arab Republic]	Yemen
	Yemen, People's Democratic Republic of	Yemen
	Yemen, South [People's Democratic Republic of Yemen]	Yemen
	Youth, Isle of (Isla de la Juventud)	Cuba
	Yucatan Channel	Atlantic Ocean
Z	Zagreb [US Consulate General]	Yugoslavia
	Zanzibar	Tanzania
	Zurich [US Consulate General]	Switzerland

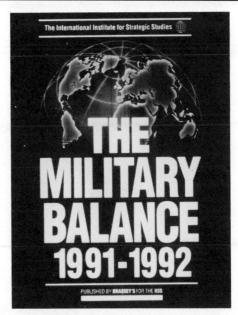
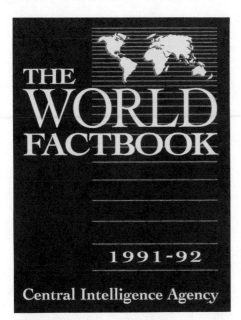
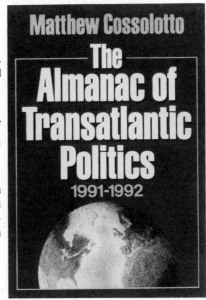

ESSENTIAL REFERENCE SOURCES FROM BRASSEY'S

☐ Absolutely! Please enter my order today. (This form may be photocopied.)

QUANTITY   PRICE

THE WORLD FACTBOOK: 1991-92 by Central Intelligence Agency

1. ___   0-02-8810133-3/Hardcover Only/$28.00   ___

Never before readily available to the general public, this is the U.S. governments' highly acclaimed source of important unclassifed data on every country from Afghanistan to Zimbabwe.

THE ALMANAC OF TRANSATLANTIC POLITICS by Matthew Cossolotto

2. ___   0-08-035978-7/Hardcover/$45.00   ___
3. ___   0-08-035979-5/Softcover/$32.00   ___

A wealth of information about political and economic life on both sides of the Atlantic. Contains photographs and biographical sketches of leading political figures, membership lists for parliamentary bodies, highlights of recent election campaigns, and much more.

INTERNATIONAL MILITARY & DEFENSE ENCYCLOPEDIA, Trevor N. Dupuy, Ed.

4. ___   0-02-881011-2/Hardcover Only/$995.00 before 12/31/92   ___
                           $1,250.00 after 12/31/92

Six illustrated, meticulously indexed volumes provide one comprehensive, reliable reference source for military and defense information from around the world.

THE MILITARY BALANCE: 1991-1992 by the International Institute for Strategic Studies

5. ___   0-08-041324-2/Hardcover Only/$67.95   ___

This annual survey presents the type, number, and deployment of the armed forces of the world together with information about each one's population, GNP and defense expenditures.

_____   SUBTOTAL _____
                                        Please add state/local tax _____
                          Shipping/Handling ($2.50 per book) _____
                                                                TOTAL _____

Payment enclosed: ☐ Personal Check   ☐ Money Order
Please charge my: ☐ American Express   ☐ MasterCard   ☐ Visa

Credit Card Number: _____   Expires: _____

Signature: _____   Date: _____

SHIP TO: BILL TO: (*Credit Card Customers Only*)

_____   _____
_____   _____
_____   _____
_____   _____

                                                           Prices subject to change

---

MAIL ORDERS TO:
Macmillan Distribution Center/ Attn: Brassey's Book Orders
100 Front Street/Box 500/Riverside, NJ/08075-7500
OR CALL TOLL-FREE 1-800-257-5755
OR FAX TOLL-FREE 1-800-562-1272

FC# 2038